Financial Accounting

Financial Accounting

Jane L. Reimers

Rollins College
Crummer Graduate School of Business

Pearson Education International

Library of Congress Cataloging-in-Publication Data
Reimers, Jane L.
    Financial accounting / Jane L. Reimers.
        p. cm.
    Includes index.
    ISBN 0-13-149201-2
    1. Accounting. 2. Financial statements. I. Title.
HF5635.R35 2007
657—dc22

2005054601

Executive Editor: Steve Sartori
Editorial Director: Jeff Shelstad
Director, Market Development:
    Annie Todd
Market Development Manager:
    Kathleen McLellan
Senior Development Editor: Lena
    Buonanno
Director of Development: Steve
    Deitmer
Assistant Editor: Joanna Doxey
**Media Product Development
    Manager:** Nancy Welcher
Executive Marketing Manager: John
    Wannemacher
Marketing Assistant: Tina Panagiotou
**Associate Director, Production
    Editorial:** Judy Leale
Production Editor: Michael Reynolds
Permissions Supervisor: Charles
    Morris
Manufacturing Buyer: Diane Peirano
Creative Director: Maria Lange

Designer: Steve Frim
Cover Design/Illustration: Maria
    Lange
Illustrator (Interior): Argosy
Director, Image Resource Center:
    Melinda Reo
Manager, Rights and Permissions:
    Zina Arabia
Manager, Visual Research: Beth
    Brenzel
**Manager, Cover Visual Research &
    Permissions:** Karen Sanatar
Image Permission Coordinator:
    Craig A. Jones
Photo Researcher: Abbey Reip
Manager, Print Production: Christy
    Mahon
Formatter: Suzanne Duda
**Composition/Full-Service Project
    Management:** GGS Book Services
Printer/Binder: Courier/Kendallville
Typeface: 10.5/11.5 ITC Century
    Book

Credits and acknowledgments borrowed from other sources and reproduced, with permission, in this textbook appear on appropriate page within text (or on page C1).

Pearson Education LTD.
Pearson Education Singapore, Pte. Ltd
Pearson Education, Canada, Ltd
Pearson Education–Japan

Pearson Education Australia PTY, Limited
Pearson Education North Asia Ltd
Pearson Educación de Mexico, S.A. de C.V.
Pearson Education Malaysia, Pte. Ltd

10 9 8 7 6 5 4 3 2 1
ISBN 0-13-149201-2

For my son

brief contents

chapter 2

Preparing Financial Statements and Analyzing Business Transactions   42

You make the call: Can Southwest get a loan?   43

Objectives, Assumptions, and Qualities of Financial Reporting   44

Financial reporting   45
Qualities of accounting information   45
Assumptions and principles underlying financial reporting   46
Materiality and conservatism in financial reporting   48

A Closer Look at the Balance Sheet   48

Current and non-current assets   49
Current and non-current liabilities   50
Shareholders' equity   51

A Closer Look at the Income Statement   52

Recognizing revenue and expenses   52
Earnings per share—a number you've heard about   53

Accounting in the News: Ethics
Your Bonus Is on the Line. What Would You Do?   54

A Closer Look at the Statement of Changes in Shareholders' Equity   54

A Closer Look at the Statement of Cash Flows   55

*End-of-chapter resource materials repeat in all chapters

chapter 3

The Accounting Information System and the Accounting Cycle   98

chapter 4

Accrual Accounting Concepts and the Accounting Cycle   154

chapter 5

Accounting for Merchandising Operations   224

chapter 6

Reporting and Analyzing Inventory   276

chapter **7**

Cash, Accounts Receivable, and Bad Debts Expense   328

chapter 8

Reporting and Interpreting Long-Term Operational Assets   380

chapter **9**

Reporting and Understanding Liabilities   440

Reporting and Understanding Shareholders' Equity   512

You make the call: How does a Papa John's shareholder earn a return on an
investment in the company's stock?   513

chapter

Preparing and Analyzing the Statement of Cash Flows   558

You make the call: Does The Home Depot's statement of cash flows indicate that the company is in good financial shape?   559

chapter 12

Using Financial Statement Analysis to Evaluate Firm Performance   618

You make the call: Should you invest in Wal-Mart or Target?   619

---

chapter 13

Quality of Earnings and Corporate Governance   670

You make the call: WorldCom's $11 billion fraud—how did everyone miss the signs?   671

Why Are Earnings Important?   672

Accounting in the News: Ethics
Hardee's Focus: Ethics not Earnings   673

The Quality of Earnings   673

From Jane Reimers
(and her best friend Muzby):

Professor of Accounting at Rollins College, Crummer Graduate School of Business

"How accounting is driving change in business"

Until the accounting scandals rocked the business world in the early 2000s, there had been little motivation to change how we accounting professors taught introductory financial accounting. We focused on the basic principles and practices that resulted in the kinds of financial statements that have existed for decades. But then accounting hit the headlines.

The fall of Enron and Andersen along with the current struggles to implement the Sarbanes-Oxley Act of 2002 have changed both accounting and business. That's why I wrote this book—to integrate current business events with accounting information just as they are inextricably linked in the world. No longer does a professor have to defend the importance of accounting. A simple review of the headlines in *The Wall Street Journal, BusinessWeek,* and even most hometown papers, confirms accounting's crucial role in the functioning of our capital markets.

To motivate students in any major—from sports management and fashion design to finance and accounting—to understand something about accounting and business, we must engage them in current business events. We have an opportunity to integrate risk and control and ethics to provide real meaning to the basic accounting we teach. For example, using current events to explain why investors and managers care about earnings will enliven the fundamental accounting principles we teach.

Accounting educators sense the tremendous teaching challenges and opportunities that we face: Today's business environment has changed and so have the needs of our students. In our business curriculum, we need to teach more about corporate governance and how our students, as future business leaders, will be responsible for maintaining corporate integrity and investor confidence. Corporate governance is a part of financial reporting, and it easily fits into the discussion of the uses of financial statements. Using this relationship, my goal is to offer students a more engaging and complete picture of accounting in today's business world. Take a look.

My Teaching Background...

I have taught introductory financial accounting for over 20 years. After earning my Ph.D. from the University of Michigan, I spent 4 years at Duke, 14 years at Florida State, and the past 3 years at Rollins College in Winter Park, Florida. My students have been traditional and nontraditional, and they have been accounting and other business majors, economics majors, fashion design majors, and more. I have lectured in auditoriums, taught in small- and medium-sized classrooms, and coordinated an online course for hundreds of students. With an undergraduate degree in education and graduate degrees in accounting and with my teaching experience, I have written a book for this exact time in the history of accounting education. I hope both students and instructors come away with the enthusiasm and respect I have for accounting.

Jane L. Reimers

www.prenhall.com/reimers

HOW ACCOUNTING IS CHANGING BUSINESS

This book has a traditional organization and covers core accounting concepts, as you will see on the pages that follow. I have blended three special features into this traditional presentation based on my teaching experiences, current events, and extensive market feedback.

Getting Started: What's Your Business IQ?

I received feedback from hundreds of accounting professors during the development of this book, and I learned that many of them face a common and substantial challenge on the first day of class: Some students lack basic business knowledge and vocabulary. I address this challenge in "Getting Started: What's Your Business IQ?" "Getting Started" introduces basic business terminology and concepts. Students take a short quiz—called "Test Your Business IQ"—to assess their business knowledge and vocabulary and then check their answers in the context of current events and businesses they recognize. I feature several exciting businesses, such as Google, Starbucks, and Wal-Mart, that students are familiar with and may want to work for some day. Each subsequent chapter includes an additional "Business IQ" quiz so that students continue to build their business knowledge and vocabulary throughout the class. As students progress through each chapter, they will deepen their understanding that *business* and *accounting* are inseparable.

Getting Started:

Business IQ

What's Your Business IQ?

Do you use a debit or credit card? Then, you may know what it's like to keep a record of your purchases and to make sure that you have enough funds to cover those purchases. Whether you want to buy a new pair of jeans, buy a music CD, or go away for spring break, you'll need to review your statements to help make your decision. Businesses make decisions the same way: They keep track of their spending and make decisions based on the money they have, the money they expect to receive, and the money they might be able to raise. A **business** is an organization that provides goods and services to customers. A business, however, has more complicated paperwork to track than just a debit card or credit card statement. Whether a business is large or small, it needs accountants to track all the money coming in and going out—otherwise, it won't be in business long!

Regardless of your major or future career, basic business knowledge can help you succeed. If you become a manager, you'll need to know how many people you can hire, what salary you can pay them, what you can afford to buy, and how much to charge customers. If you join a marketing department at a company, you'll need to know how much you can spend on an advertising campaign. To answer these types of questions, you'll need some basic accounting knowledge. **Accounting** is the process of gathering, organizing, and summarizing financial information about a firm's activities. Because accounting looks at the entire firm, every firm can reap major benefits from a strong knowledge of how accounting works.

Even if you have no intention of working for a business, accounting can help you. Nonprofit organizations and government agencies must also track expenditures and work within budgets. Making sure that the numbers add up is a key function in almost every group, from the smallest start-up

Have You Increased Your Business IQ?

Answer these questions to find out.

1. According to accountants, useful information should be
   a. Relevant
   b. Brief
   c. Easy to understand
   d. Thorough
2. A classified balance sheet provides
   a. A direct match between each asset and its source of financing
   b. A separate subtotal for current assets and current liabilities
   c. Dates of capital contributions
   d. Amount of dividends paid

Here is what reviewers have said about "Getting Started":

The coverage of basic vocabulary and concepts of business will help bring the more naïve students (which many are) to a better starting point so that they can relate more easily to the accounting presented. I find it to be very much on-target and expect it will be very helpful to students.

Sue Gunckel, *Albuquerque Technical Vocational Institute*

I agree most strongly that [the Prologue will] allow instructors to be more ambitious/flexible in terms of what is covered early in the course, and at what pace. It always catches me off guard when a student does not know what I think is a basic business term.

Julie Burkey, *Goldey-Beacom College*

I really like this prologue. We make many assumptions about how "current" we think our students are about business topics and I have found they are not that informed. It is great for them to learn terms right in the beginning so we all start on the same page. Those students who are already familiar with these concepts, and there will be some, can skip this portion. Or, if all students are tested early on this material, those students who are informed will start out with a strong confidence boost.

Sue Minke, *Indiana University-Purdue University–Ft. Wayne*

BUSINESS RISK, CONTROL, AND ETHICS

Set within the traditional accounting sequence of chapters, I cover business risk, control, and ethics in *each* chapter. For example, in Chapter 2, I cover the risks of inaccurate financial records and how to control those risks. In Chapter 4, I cover controls that help a firm reduce the risk of failing to record a transaction. With the current environment in accounting and the implementation of the Sarbanes-Oxley Act, this integrated coverage helps students see and appreciate how risk, control, and ethics are crucial in every aspect of business and financial reporting. The integrated coverage also helps students understand that corporate governance is the responsibility of all employees of a company—not just the managers and accountants. Students who take this first course have diverse majors—most will not continue on as accounting majors—and it's important that nonaccounting majors, especially those majoring in business, have exposure to these topics in this course as they are unlikely to get it in other classes.

Here is a reviewer comment about this risk and control coverage:

> Discussion of controls throughout the text in areas where they are most pertinent is an excellent idea. Most texts discuss them completely in one chapter and usually with cash. The examples are excellent—especially the one about receiving a free purchase if the clerk does not provide a receipt . . .
>
> Richard Moellenberndt, *Washburn University*

Chapter 13, "Quality of Earnings and Corporate Governance"

Chapter 13, "Quality of Earnings and Corporate Governance," is the capstone chapter that shows students how accounting fraud happens, how the Sarbanes-Oxley Act has enacted regulations to improve corporate governance, and how to measure the quality of a firm's corporate governance. The chapter also summarizes the accounting scandals that came to light in the early 2000s and the results of several high-profile trials of top executives at companies such as Tyco and WorldCom. Although many professors who reviewed the book's table of contents told me they might not have time to cover Chapter 13, they decided after reading the chapter that they would make time for this material.

Here is how reviewers describe Chapter 13:

> I would encourage any instructor to consider including a unit similar to the coverage in Chapter 13 . . .
>
> James Benedum, *Milwaukee Area Technical College*

I am very impressed by this chapter. The extensive discussion of the recent accounting scandals brings to the classroom contemporary issues, which are rarely covered in introductory accounting texts. My current text has no equivalent chapter, so I find this a refreshing improvement . . .

Yaw Mensah, *Rutgers University, New Brunswick*

This is an ideal "Capstone" chapter for any Financial Accounting course . . .

Diana DeWald, *Manatee Community College*

SPECIAL FEATURES

I love it!

Nancy Snow, *University of Toledo*

As you can see from the table of contents, this book is very traditionally organized. Within that traditional organization, however, there are several elements our many reviewers and focus group participants consider unique and useful to the teaching and study of accounting:

		Assets		=	Liabilities		+	Shareholders' Equity		
								Contributed Capital	+	Retained Earnings		
	Cash	Accounts Receivable	Equipment	Accounts Payable	Notes Payable		Revenues	Expenses	Dividends
1.	+2,000						+2,000			
2.	+4,000				+4,000					
3.	−1,400								−1,400	
4.	−5,000		+5,000							
5.	+6,000							+6,000		
6.	−20									−20
	5,580	+	5,000	=	4,000	+	2,000	+	4,580	

■ Income Statement   ■ Statement of Changes in Shareholders' Equity   ■ Balance Sheet   ■ Statement of Cash Flows

I think the color model is great! My students would find it easy to understand. It draws their attention to a specific statement and the parts of that statement. What a good idea.

Pam Legner, *College of DuPage*

Color-coded accounting equation:
I use the model shown here to present the accounting equation and the financial statements.

Rather than extending the financial statement model to more columns, I want to show how three of the statements (income statement, statement of changes in shareholders' equity, and statement of cash flows) tie to—and provide details about—the balance sheet.

Each financial statement has a unique color. Students will see these colors throughout the chapters when we present a financial statement. Students can use the color-coded accounting equation worksheet to help prepare financial statements in homework assignments and exams. Please refer to the book's inside cover for details about the color-coded equation.

COVERAGE AND ORGANIZATION

My coverage of the accountant's role in today's business is woven into a book that has a traditional organization of chapters and thorough coverage of core topics including debits and credits, the accounting equation, the accounting cycle, and the statement of cash flows. The organization and topic sequence, including appendices, has been very carefully constructed based on my own teaching experience and detailed feedback from over 200 reviewers and focus group participants. As a result, I'm quite confident that the organization is logical and reflects the preferences of the great majority of accounting instructors.

The key items to note about this organization are:

1. The accounting equation is introduced in the first two chapters so that students are comfortable with transactions and financial statements before they learn debits and credits in Chapter 3.

2. The chapter sequence generally matches the balance sheet organization, except for the chapter on inventory cost flows (Chapter 6). That chapter is directly after the merchandising chapter (Chapter 5) to give students a complete picture of inventory rather than a less effective piecemeal approach.

3. The statement of cash flows is integrated throughout the book in a very intuitive, rather than procedural, way. Comprehensive coverage of the preparation of the statement of cash flows appears in Chapter 11. This gives students an opportunity to understand the content of a statement of cash flows even if he or she never learns the procedures to prepare one.

4. As noted earlier, each chapter concludes with a "Business Risk, Control, and Ethics" section that reinforces the importance of accounting information and how all employees play a role in controlling business risks.

A summary of the key points of each chapter follows.

Chapter	What Students Learn . . .	What Professors Have Said About This Chapter . . .
Getting Started What's Your Business IQ?	Foundational business terms in the context of real-world businesses. Sarbanes-Oxley Act.	This prologue covers material that I often find necessary to explain in class. It would make lectures go more smoothly if all students had that information. I believe that all students would benefit from this, even those with extensive background. *Pamela Stuerke, University of Rhode Island*
Chapter 1: The Link Between Business and Accounting	Accounting information includes four basic financial statements and accompanying notes.	The whole balance sheet is explained very well. Love the boxes and especially love the explanation of the date. I have never seen that in an accounting text! *Sue Minke, Indiana-Purdue at Ft. Wayne*
Chapter 2: Preparing Financial Statements and Analyzing Business Transactions	The accounting equation shows how business transactions affect the financial statements.	Transaction analysis: . . . These precise analysis explanations are wonderful. This is the thought process that I take my students through when teaching, and this is great detail. *Mary Hollars, Vincennes University*
Chapter 3: The Accounting Information System and the Accounting Cycle Appendix: Using T-accounts to Analyze Problems	Debits and credits are a clever way to keep track of business transactions.	The explanation of debit and credit is very good. It is one of the best I have seen. Students have particular difficulty grasping this concept *Timothy Baker, California State University–Fresno*

Chapter 4: Accrual Accounting Concepts and the Accounting Cycle	Accruals and deferrals demonstrate the difference between cash-basis accounting and accrual-basis accounting. Generally Accepted Accounting Principles are accrual-based.	This is really good! (Action before dollars or dollars before action). It's so short but absolutely on target and easy for students to understand. This is a good chapter. It is well-organized and does a good job of explaining and illustrating the different situations that result in adjusting entries. *Wendy Duffy, Illinois State University*
Chapter 5: Accounting for Merchandising Operations Appendix: Recording Transactions Using Periodic Inventory	Merchandising firms have special terminology and accounts. Perpetual and periodic inventory systems are introduced, focusing on perpetual record keeping. The journal entries for a periodic record-keeping system are shown in an appendix.	The single greatest strength is the inclusion of the operating cycle in the material. This explanation of the process is the best I have read at an introductory level. The inclusion of risks and controls add a depth that is missing in the other texts I have used or reviewed. This puts the process in perspective for students. I loved it. *Sherri Anderson, Sonoma State University*
Chapter 6: Reporting and Analyzing Inventory Appendix A: Perpetual Inventory Systems Appendix B: Inventory Errors Appendix C: Gross Profit Method of Estimating Ending Inventory	A firm's inventory cost flow assumption—like LIFO or FIFO—is an important accounting choice and affects both the balance sheet and the income statement. Because students need to learn concepts rather than detailed record keeping for inventory, the chapter focuses on the periodic method, with the perpetual inventory details in an appendix. The switch from the focus on perpetual in Chapter 5 to a focus on periodic is done to keep the bookkeeping complications to a minimum. In both chapters, the focus is on the concepts rather than the bookkeeping.	The chapter presentation would appeal to a traditional preparer-basis approach faculty member or a user-basis faculty member such as myself. The presentation is written in a manner which permits this selection of the material. *Noel McKeon, Florida Community College* The author does a great job explaining the concepts of inventory and uses clear examples to demonstrate the concepts. *Sandy Cereola, James Madison University*
Chapter 7: Cash, Accounts Receivable, and Bad Debts Expense	Cash and accounts receivable are two of a firm's most important assets. Cash, in particular, must be carefully controlled because it can be easy to steal.	Excellent on the bank reconciliation. It flows exactly as I teach. It is much better than the current text. *Timothy Baker, California State University–Fresno* This is likely the best analysis of how to perform a bank reconciliation that I have ever seen. *Hank Adler, Chapman University*
Chapter 8: Reporting and Interpreting Long-Term Operational Assets Appendix: Depreciation and Taxes	Firms have a large variety of fixed assets—building, machinery, factories, trademarks, patents, and more. The cost of an asset that lasts longer than a year must be allocated to the accounting periods in which the asset is used.	This chapter is well-organized and clear. Everything I would want to see in this chapter is here. Chapter 8 earns an A from me. *Wendy Duffy, Illinois State University* Real-world financial statements: They are outstanding and very helpful. I think students would find them very useful. *Joanie Sompayrac, University of Tennessee–Chattanooga*
Chapter 9: Reporting and Understanding Liabilities Appendix A: Time Value of Money and Present Values Appendix B: Calculating the Proceeds from a Bond Issued at a Premium or a Discount	Almost all firms use someone else's money to help them run their operations. The borrowed money can be short-term, such as making purchases on account (using credit), or long-term, such as mortgages, loans, and bonds.	Great discussion of financial leverage. This is a difficult topic for students to grasp. It is presented clearly and understandably. *Timothy Baker, California State University–Fresno* The author's writing style is almost conversational. I think this is a tremendous strength in discussing concepts that are foreign to many beginning accounting students. *Theresa Guiterrez, University of Northern Colorado*

Chapter 10: Reporting and Understanding Shareholders' Equity	The owners' share of the firm is called equity. Building equity for the owners is one of the primary goals of a business.	This is a great chapter.... I particularly like Exhibit 10.2 and how it visually depicts shares authorized, issued, and outstanding. In addition, I like the coverage given to preferred stock dividends. What a great way to end this chapter by talking about the ramifications of SOX! *Treba Marsh, Stephen F. Austin University*
Chapter 11: Preparing and Analyzing the Statement of Cash Flows	The statement of cash flows explains the change in cash from one year to the next and shows all cash inflows and all cash outflows.	The coverage of the cash flow statement is handled extremely well in this chapter. The author does a great job of outlining and explaining both the direct and indirect method and her examples back up her methodology. *Sandy Cereola, James Madison University* This chapter on the cash flow statement is one of the best written that I have encountered. Reimers has captured the direct and indirect methods in a unique presentation. *Diana DeWald, Manatee Community College*
Chapter 12: Using Financial Statement Analysis to Evaluate Firm Performance **Appendix A:** Comprehensive Income **Appendix B:** Investments in Securities	Analyze accounting information in each of the financial statements.	The section on understanding ratios is excellent. Many students do not realize this basic information about ratio analysis. You present it in a clear and understandable way. *Timothy Baker, California State University–Fresno* In my past experience, I have had to restrict the amount of coverage of the investments topic. The concise coverage in this chapter provides the right balance for instructors interested in a much more limited coverage, while providing the option for other instructors to cover the topic in much more detail. *Yaw Mensha, Rutgers University–New Brunswick*
Chapter 13: Quality of Earnings and Corporate Governance	The quality of the information in financial statements depends on decisions made by the firm's management. How a corporation governs itself can affect the quality of earnings and the quality of all information provided by the firm.	It is a great summary that pulls together the discussions from previous chapters. It is easy to read with just enough detail to make it worth reading, but not enough to be overly confusing for the average introductory accounting student. *Janice Klimek, Central Missouri State*
2005 Annual Report: Wal-Mart **10-K:** Target	How to use information in an annual report and a 10-K to make decisions.	

Integration of Statement of Cash Flows

The statement of cash flows is briefly and intuitively discussed in Chapters 1, 2, 4, 7 and 8, before full coverage in Chapter 11. Reviewers were convinced, after seeing how the coverage was integrated throughout, that this intuitive presentation would be an asset for their students. Understanding the statement of cash flows has become more important as the questions about the quality of earnings have increased during the past several years. Some managers and analysts believe it is the most important financial statement. Even though it is one of the most difficult statements to prepare in practice, it is one of the easiest statements to understand intuitively. This integrated coverage of the cash flow statement will make students comfortable with the meaning of the statement beginning early in the course.

Here is how a reviewer described the integration of statement of cash flows:

> Integration of statement of cash flows in every chapter is a wonderful advantage.
>
> Dori Danko, *Grand Valley State University*

You Make the Call

"You Make the Call" opens each chapter, provides background information about the focus company, and asks students to answer questions related to that company. In Chapter 1, for example, the focus company is Apple Computer. I return to this company throughout the chapter in both the narrative and exhibits to explain and illustrate concepts. As students read through the chapter, they will gradually build their understanding of the focus company along with the concepts of the chapter and be able to answer the questions from the opener on their own. The "You Make the Call" section that concludes the chapter explains the answers to the questions so that students can confirm their understanding of the concept addressed in the feature. Here is the "You Make the Call" that opens Chapter 1:

Apple Computer

YOU make the call:

Who owns Apple Computer, Inc.?

Apple Computer took the music world by storm in 2001 with the introduction of the iPod. Here's what *BusinessWeek* had to say: "Just as the Mac revolutionized the computer industry, Apple is once again in the business of changing the world. This time, it's the world of music. Its diminutive iPod . . . is the most radical change in how people listen to music since SONY Corp. introduced the Walkman in 1979."

How did Apple start out? Steve Wozniak was an engineer who worked as a calculator technician at Hewlett-Packard in the 1970s. Steve Jobs, pictured here, persuaded Wozniak to quit Hewlett-Packard and start a company.

YOU make the call:

Who owns Apple Computer, Inc.?

We started this chapter with a question about who owns Apple Computer. When Apple began, there were just two owners. In 1977, partners Steve Jobs and Steve Wozniak formally incorporated their business. Then, the two owners made the stock available to selected employees and friends, so there were several "owners" but none owned as much of Apple Computer as the two original partners. Then, on December 12, 1980, the company offered its stock for sale on the NASDAQ Stock Exchange. That day, everyone who purchased shares in Apple Computer became an owner of the company. Today, a little more than 60% of the stock of Apple Computer, Inc. is held by large investors (pension plans and investment companies); less than 2% is held by insider investors who work for the company. Perhaps, you and I hold a share or two and are among the owners of Apple Computer, Inc.

Accounting in the NEWS

Google This: "Copyright Law"

Google can search an astonishing 8 billion Web pages. That's not much compared with the knowledge stored in the world's libraries. It's little wonder, then, that many scholars and readers were thrilled when Google (GOOG) announced in December 2004 that it planned to scan the complete texts of millions of books from major libraries around the globe and make them searchable online.

Google's library project would make digital versions of whatever libraries hand over—including copyrighted books—regardless of whether authors or publishers agree. Already, five major libraries—Harvard, Stanford, Oxford, Michigan, and the New York Public Library—are sending books for Google to digitize. The goal is to gather as much of the world's knowledge as

possible and make it accessible on Google. For public domain books, users will be able to see full text. For copyrighted books, viewing will be "only a few sentences," says Google. When Google gets up to speed, its scanning machines will be able to process 5,000 books a day. At the time this book is going to press, Google has postponed its plan. It has given publishers until November 2005 to opt out of the program. In late 2005, a group of major book publishers announced the filing of a lawsuit against Google over its plans to digitally copy and distribute copyrighted works without permission of the copyright owners. The suit is being coordinated and funded by the Association of American Publishers (AAP). See if you can get the latest news on Google's plan.

Do you think Google's project violates the current copyright laws? Many attorneys believe it does, and you can be sure that authors and publishers are concerned about the protection of their books. What does copyright law have to do with accounting?

Imagine having millions of volumes of books in one vast index that you can access from your computer. Is this a good idea, or is Google freeloading on the work of authors and publishers?

Q How many web pages can Google search?

A 8 billion

Source: Burt Helm and Hardy Green, "Google This: Copyright Law," *Business Week Online—News and Commentary*, June 5, 2005. Reprinted from the June 5, 2005 issue of *BusinessWeek Online—News Commentary*. Copyright © 2005 by The McGraw-Hill Companies. Reprinted by permission. "Publishers Sue Google Over Plans to Digitize Books," Association of American Publishers, Inc., October 19, 2005.

Accounting in the News

Reading the newspaper and other periodicals is an important part of understanding the current business climate. In each chapter, one or more "Accounting in the News" features present a stimulating and provocative news story about one of the following areas:

1. financial statement analysis
2. international business
3. technology
4. risk and control
5. ethics

These current events should spark students' interest, and this feature will emphasize how accounting affects business. These stories should also stir up some interesting class discussion. Sources of this feature include the *Wall Street Journal*, *New York Times*, and *FORTUNE*.

The MP3 Store: Continuing Case

This student-friendly continuing case begins in Chapter 1, at the end of the chapter, with The MP3 Store's first month of business. Each successive chapter will show the next month of business. This case serves two functions:

1. It helps students to see how the financial statements for one period relate to the prior and the subsequent months' statements and
2. It helps students build and improve their Excel skills. See page 95 for an example

Can You Do It?

This self-test feature provides students with an opportunity to test and apply their understanding of a section before moving on. The feature includes the questions and the answers on the same page so that students can check their progress. See page 102 for an example.

In Other Words . . .

This margin feature presents synonymous terms that students are likely to see in the newspaper and in practice. For example, in Chapter 2, I alert students that *non-current* assets are also known as *long-term* assets. See page 50 for an example

Let's Take a Test Drive

This major section appears in each chapter and summarizes its key concepts. The goal of this summary section is to use the focus company that is introduced in the chapter opener and integrated throughout the chapter to review the concepts and mechanics of the chapter. Students test their knowledge by completing problems and seeing the solution.

The section includes three categories:

1. *Real-World Problem* Presents a problem that could potentially face the focus company.
2. *Concepts* Reviews the concepts of the chapter and how they relate to the real-world problem.
3. *Mechanics* Presents a problem and step-by-step solution that helps students practice the mechanics of accounting.

See page 69 for an example.

PRACTICE...PRACTICE...PRACTICE

As we all know, practice is essential to developing any skill. This is definitely true in learning accounting skills. Each chapter ends with a wide array of summary and practice materials, as I'll explain later in this preface, that were developed to appeal to a variety of teaching and learning styles. For example, multiple-choice questions help students assess their comprehension of concepts and simple computations; short exercises provide more challenging practice opportunities than the multiple choice; and problem sets provide the most comprehensive practice opportunities. Instructors in small- or medium-size classrooms can use the group exercises to encourage students to work in teams to solve an accounting problem. The problems and exercises are annotated with both a learning objective and a description so that instructors can easily select which problems and exercises to assign based on the goals of the class. An Excel icon marks those problems and exercises that can be completed using Excel. Complete solutions for all questions, problems, and exercises appear in the Solutions Manual. Here are the end-of-chapter features:

Problem Set A

LO 1, 2, 3, 4 **P3-1A. Record journal entries; post to T-accounts; and prepare a trial balance.**
Sharp Electronics Repair Service, Inc., was started on July 1. The following selected events and transactions took place during July.

1. Stockholders contributed $125,000 cash to the business in exchange for common stock.
2. Purchased equipment costing $70,000 by signing a long-term note.
3. Purchased advertising in local newspaper for $3,000 cash.
4. Purchased supplies for $42,000 on account.
5. Paid salaries of $2,500 to employees.
6. Paid $1,000 for a one-year insurance policy.
7. Paid $600 cash dividends.
8. Earned service revenues of $38,500 on account.
9. Paid $25,000 on accounts payable.

Required

a. Prepare journal entries for the given transactions.
b. Set up T-accounts and post the journal entries to the accounts.
c. Prepare Sharp's trial balance at July 31.

LO 1, 2, 3, 4 **P3-2A. Record** ...
prepare a trial ...
The following transac...
for Shelby Dog Groo...
first year of busines...

1. Formed the busi...
   investors in exch...
2. Purchased groom...
3. Paid operating e...
4. Earned service r...
5. Paid utilities exp...
6. Paid employees...
7. Paid vendors $1...
8. Collected $25,00...
9. The Shelby Dog...
   paying a dividen...

Problem Set B

Your professor may ask you to complete selected "Group B" exercises and problems using Prentice Hall Grade Assist (**PHGA**). PHGA is an online tool that can help you master the chapter's topics by providing multiple variations of exercises and problems. You can rework these exercises and problems—each time with new data—as many times as you need, with immediate feedback and grading.

LO 1, 2, 3, 4 **P3-1B. Record journal entries, post to T-accounts, and prepare a trial balance.**
Flexsteel Cleaning Corporation was started on March 1. The following events and transactions took place during March.

1. Stockholders contributed $345,600 cash to the business in exchange for common stock.
2. Purchased land costing $170,000 with $70,000 cash and a long-term note for $100,000.
3. Paid for advertising for March on Google's web site, $1,500 cash.
4. Purchased supplies for $62,000 on account.
5. Paid salaries of $5,500 to employees for work done.
6. Paid $1,000 for insurance for future use.
7. Paid $2,000 cash dividends.
8. Earned service revenues of $120,350 on account.
9. Paid $60,000 on accounts payable.

Required

a. Prepare journal entries for the given transactions.
b. Set up T-accounts and post the journal entries to the accounts.
c. Prepare Flexsteel Cleaning Corporation's trial balance at March 31.

LO 1, 2, 3, 4 **P3-2B. Record journal entries, post to T-accounts, and prepare a trial balance and financial statements.**
The following transactions occurred during the fiscal year ended September 30, 2005, for Toy Box Learning Center, a children's tutoring service. This was the firm's first year of business.

1. Formed the business as a corporation, issuing $100,000 in common stock to local investors.
2. Purchased supplies for $35,000 on account.
3. Paid rent expense for the year in the amount of $6,000.
4. Paid insurance expense for the year in the amount of $750.

Have You Increased Your Business IQ? Boxes: Help students assess their overall business knowledge and vocabulary.

Questions: Assess comprehension of basic concepts.

Multiple Choice: Test comprehension of key terms and the student's ability to handle simple computations.

Short Exercises: Test and reinforce understanding of the mechanics of the chapter.

Exercises, Sets A and B: Provide more in-depth exercises than the short exercises that test and reinforce understanding of the mechanics of the chapter.

Problems, Sets A and B: Provide problems to solve in class and to assign as homework.

Prentice Hall Grade Assist (PHGA): Provides multiple variables of Exercise Set B and Problem Set B to complete online. Students can rework these exercises and problems—each time with new data—as many times as they need, with immediate feedback and grading.

Financial Statement Analysis Problems: Apply the chapter's concepts to financial statements from real-world companies such as Amazon.com, Tootsie Roll, and Bed Bath & Beyond.

Select problems ask students to analyze the *Wal-Mart* annual report or the *Target* 10-K statement that appear in the back of the book

Critical Thinking Problems: Promote and teach creative thinking beyond the mechanics so students have a chance to apply what they've learned in class to the diverse business situations they may face in the workforce. These problems are divided into three categories: Risk and Control, Ethics, and Group.

Internet Exercises: Encourage students to research information from specific company Web sites.

TEACHING AND LEARNING SUPPORT

Financial Accounting is accompanied by a comprehensive print and online supplement package for instructor and student.

At-a-Glance Supplements Grid

	Instructor's Manual	Test Bank	Instructor Solutions Manual	Solution Acetates	Interactive Excel Solutions	PowerPoint Lectures	Prentice Hall Grade Assist	Companion Web Site
Print	✓	✓	✓					
Online	✓	✓	✓	✓	✓	✓	✓	✓
Instructor's CD-ROM	✓	✓	✓		✓	✓		

Print Supplements for the Instructor

Solutions Manual

This manual contains solutions to all end-of-chapter questions, multiple-choice questions, short exercises, Exercise Sets A and B, Problem Sets A and B, Financial Statement Analysis Problems, Critical Thinking Problems, and Internet Exercises. Solutions were prepared by Jane Reimers and Lynn Stallworth of South East Louisiana State University. The solutions manual is available in three formats: (1) Excel, (2) Word, and (3) print. Select solutions are also available in acetate form. You can access the solutions in Excel and Word formats by visiting the Instructor's Resource Center on the Prentice Hall catalog site at www.prenhall.com/reimers or on the Instructor's CD. You will need a Pearson Educator username and password to retrieve materials from the catalog site.

The accuracy checkers did a particularly painstaking and thorough job of helping proof the end-of-chapter problems and solutions, exhibits, equations, and features of the book in page proof stage. I am grateful for their time and commitment to the book:

Bob Bauman, *Allan Hancock Joint Community College*
Patricia Doherty, *Boston University*
Carolyn Streuly
Cathy Xanthaky Larson, *Middlesex Community College*
James Emig, *Villanova University*

Test Bank

The Test Bank includes over 2,000 questions (about 150 questions per chapter) of the following types:

✓ Multiple Choice
✓ Matching
✓ True/False
✓ Computational Problems
✓ Essay

In addition to testing key terms and concepts and computational skills, the test bank also provides questions for use in testing students' understanding of content presented in two special features of the main book: "Accounting in the News" and "Business Risk, Control, and Ethics."

A unique feature of the Test Bank is its application of Bloom's Taxonomy, which was developed by psychologists, teachers, and test experts. Each chapter begins with a matrix displaying learning objectives vertically and Bloom's classifications horizontally, creating cells in which test questions are categorized and slotted. This arrangement greatly facilitates test construction and allows for emphasis by specific learning goals and level of difficulty. Professors have the option of testing students' comprehension at three levels: knowledge, understanding, and application

✓ Questions in the *Knowledge* category focus on the meaning of key terms and the correct use of the terms. They involve straightforward recall of information in the text.
✓ Questions in the *Understanding* category require students to explain concepts and principles. These questions require some analysis on the student's part.
✓ Questions in the *Application* category require students to apply principles to solve a problem. These questions usually entail more complex analysis than those in the first two categories.

Each Test Bank question is also classified by learning objective and by level of difficulty (Easy, Moderate, Difficult).

Use the TestGen software to electronically generate tests. See the "Technology Supplements" section on the pages that follow for more on TestGen software.

The Test Bank was prepared by Joanie Sompayrac of the University of Tennessee at Chattanooga and Sandra Cereola of James Madison University. Carolyn Streuly accuracy-checked the test bank, and Barbara Croteau of University of California at Santa Rosa and Rita Kingery-Cook of University of Delaware provided feedback on content and features.

Instructor's Manual

The Instructor's Manual includes the following teaching support resources per each chapter:

- ✓ Chapter overview and learning objectives.
- ✓ Suggested priority of chapter topics.
- ✓ Assignment grid.
- ✓ Teaching tips on how to integrate PowerPoint presentations, student companion Web site resources, and accounting cycle tutorial.
- ✓ Teaching tips on how to integrate special features in the book such as the "Accounting in the News" boxes and the "Business Risk, Control, and Ethics" coverage.

The Instructor's Manual was prepared by Angela Sandberg of Jacksonville State University. The Instructor's Manual is also available to instructors online at www.prenhall.com/reimers and on the Instructor's Resource CD-ROM.

Solution Acetates

Solutions to select end-of-chapter exercises and problems are available in acetate form for classroom presentation in class.

Print Supplements for the Student

Working Papers

Provides students with a "blank slate" Excel grid in which students can complete the solutions to the end-of-chapter questions and problems.

Study Guide

The student Study Guide is a comprehensive review of financial accounting and is a powerful tool when used to prepare for class and for exams.

Each chapter includes:

✓ Brief summary of the chapter
✓ Self-test questions:

  Matching (definition)
  Mutiple Choice
  Fill-in-the-Blank
  True or False
  Exercises
  Critical Thinking Exercises (Essay)
  Demonstration Problem
  Solutions

The Study Guide was prepared by Lawrence Logan of University of Massachusetts at Dartmouth.

Technology Supplements for the Instructor

The following technology supplements are research based and have been designed to provide maximum utility and ease of use.

PowerPoint Lecture Presentation

These instructor PowerPoints summarize and reinforce key text material. They also capture classroom attention with *original* problems and solved step-by-step exercises. There are approximately 35 slides per chapter. The PowerPoint Presentation was prepared by Rick Newmark of University of Northern Colorado. They are included in the Instructor's CD-ROM and also may be downloaded from www.prenhall.com/reimers.

TestGen

This test-generating program permits instructors to edit, add, or delete questions from the test banks; edit or create tests; analyze test results; and organize a database of tests and student results. This new software provides many options for organizing and displaying tests, along with a search-and-sort feature.

Interactive Excel Solutions

Solutions to select end-of-chapter exercises and problems are available in interactive Excel format so that instructors can present material in a dynamic, step-by-step sequence in class. This supplement is available to both the instructor and the student. The interactive Excel solutions were prepared by Kathleen O'Donnell of State University of New York, Onondaga Community College.

Instructor's Resource Center Online at www.prenhall.com/reimers or on CD

The password-protected site and resource CD contains the following electronic files:

- ✓ PowerPoint Lecture Notes
- ✓ Test Bank
- ✓ Solutions Manual
- ✓ Instructor's Manual
- ✓ Spreadsheet Template Solutions
- ✓ Interactive Excel Solutions
- ✓ TestGen
- ✓ Test banks formatted for use with WebCT, Blackboard, and Course Compass

Technology Supplements for the Student

Prentice Hall Grade Assist (PHGA)

An online homework and assessment system that allows the instructor to create assignments for student practice, homework, or quizzes. Most of the items in Problem Set B and Exercise Set B are provided in an algorithmic format so that each student gets a slightly different problem with a different answer/solution. This feature allows students multiple attempts at each exercise and solution, with immediate feedback, for practice and improved competency. Prentice Hall Grade Assist grades the results, which can be exported to an Excel worksheet.

Reimers Web Site

The book's Web site—www.prenhall.com/reimers—contains the following:

- ✓ Self-study quizzes—interactive study guide for each chapter.
- ✓ Spreadsheet templates that students can use to complete homework assignments for each chapter.
- ✓ An accounting cycle tutorial.

OneKey in Blackboard, WebCT, and Course Compass

Prentice Hall's OneKey course is all instructors and students need for anytime online access to interactive materials that enhance this text. Premium Resources that are hosted on OneKey include: Prentice Hall Grade Assist and Research Navigator.

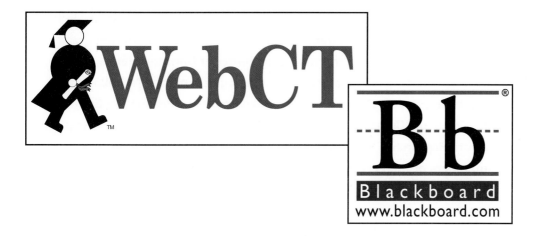

A WORD OF THANKS...

This book would not have been possible without the commitment and dedication of the Prentice Hall team. Without the contributions of Developmental Editor Lean Buonanno, this book would not have made it to successful completion. Lena, you are one of the finest, most talented, professional, hard-working people I have ever had the pleasure to work with. Thanks also to the hard work of dozens of people behind the scenes: Steve Deitmer, Director of Development; Joanna Doxey, Assistant Editor; Jeff Shelstad, Editorial Director; Annie Todd, Director of Market Development; Glenn Turner and Meg Turner of Burrston House; John Wannemacher, Executive Marketing Manager; Kathleen McLellan, Marketing Development Manager; Mike Reynolds, Production Editor; Maria Lange, Creative Director; Steve Frim, Designer; and Abby Reip, Photo Researcher. I also thank Bill Larkin and Beth Toland, former members of the Prentice Hall team, for making significant contributions to the early phases of the book's development and providing unwavering support.

Thanks also to Tina Carpenter, Ann DeCapite, Chris Evans, Greg Gerard, and John Salter for their inspiration and significant contributions to the book. Special thanks to my friends Jule Gassenheimer, Charles Brandon, Ralph Drtina, and to my other colleagues in the Crummer Graduate School of Business, Rollins College, who have provided support and encouragement. The exceedingly high quality of the school, staff, colleagues, and students makes this the best job I have ever had.

I wish to express my gratitude to the many people who reviewed the manuscript, the names of whom are provided elsewhere in this preface. Your comments and suggestions were invaluable. I learned so much from all of you. To those colleagues who braved the Chicago weather in January to spend a weekend talking about my book, thank you all very much. Your contributions helped shape this book, and I know you will see your influence in many places.

Finally, special thanks to my family and friends who provided love, understanding, and perspective during the past two years. I am especially indebted to my son for his insights, advice, and encouragement.

THE ROAD TO REIMERS
COVER TO COVER, COAST TO COAST...

REVIEWERS

Through three drafts of the manuscript, I received guidance and insights at several critical junctures from many trusted reviewers who provided clear-cut recommendations on how to improve and refine the content, presentation, and organization. Their contributions influenced every page of this text.

FOCUS GROUPS

I had the good fortune to meet many of my fellow accounting professors at focus groups conducted in Boston, Chicago, and Orlando, and to benefit from the feedback generated by those I couldn't attend that the publisher sponsored in San Francisco, Los Angeles, and Austin. The 50 plus instructors who attended the six sessions discussed the course and their teaching needs and what should be included in a text and supplements to successfully meet those needs. My thanks go to each of these instructors for their time and valuable advice.

Reviewers & Affiliations

1.	Todd DeZoort	University of Alabama
2.	Karen Oxner	Hendrix College
3.	Stephanie Farewell	University of Arkansas, Little Rock
4.	Larry Tartaglino	Cabrillo College
5.	James Macklin	California State University, Northridge
6.	Kim Tan	California State University, Stanislaus
7.	Jim Patten	California State University, Bakersfield
8.	Ashok Natarajan	California State Polytechnic University, Pomona
9.	Micah Frankel	California State University, East Bay
10	Marianne James	California State University, Los Angeles
11.	Tim Baker	California State University, Fresno
12.	Ephram Smith	California State University, Fullerton
13.	Betty Chavis	California State University, Fullerton
14.	Cheryl Furbee	Cabrillo College
15.	Lynn Stallworth	Southeastern Louisiana University
16.	Hank Adler	Chapman University
17.	Virginia Smith	St. Mary's College of California
18.	David Bojarsky	California State University, Long Beach
19.	Ken Fowler	San Jose State University
20.	Kurt Hull	California State University, Los Angeles
21.	David Angelovich	Napa Valley College
22.	Robert Kiddoo	California State University, Northridge
23.	Robert Miller	California State University, Fullerton
24.	Nasrollah Ahadiat	California State Polytechnic University, Pomona
25.	Thomas Dalton	University of San Diego
26.	David Weiner	University of San Francisco
27.	Terry Lease	Sonoma State University
28.	Rosemary Nurre	College of San Mateo
29.	Mark Judd	University of San Diego
30.	Gun-Ho Joh	San Diego State University
31.	Rada Brooks	University of California, Berkeley
32.	Gina Lord	Santa Rosa Junior College
33.	Sherri Anderson	Sonoma State University
34.	Janice Carr	California Polytechnic State University, San Luis Obispo
35.	Helen Brubeck	San Jose State University
36.	Jeanne Miller	Cypress College
37.	Barbara Croteau	Santa Rosa Junior College
38.	Hassan Hefzi	California State Polytechnic University, Pomona
39.	Khalid Nainar	McMaster University
40.	Steve Fortin	McGill University
41.	Richard Newmark	University of Northern Colorado
42.	Theresa Guiterrez	University of Northern Colorado
43.	Bruce Bradford	Fairfield University
44.	Robin Tarpley	George Washington University

THE ROAD TO REIMERS
COVER TO COVER, COAST TO COAST...

45.	Harvey Iglarsh	Georgetown University
46.	Julie Burkey	Goldey Beacom College
47.	Rita Kingery-Cook	University of Delaware
48.	Bill Urquhart	Florida Atlantic University
49.	Diana Dewald	Manatee Community College
50.	Noel McKeon	Florida Community College, Jacksonville
51.	Hubert Gill	University of North Florida
52.	William Stephens	University of South Florida
53.	Jane Wiese	Valencia Community College
54.	Delano Berry	Florida International University
55.	Gregory Yost	University of West Florida
56.	Toni Clegg	Palm Beach Community College
57.	Progyan Basu	University of Georgia
58.	Linda Mullins	Georgia Perimeter College, Lawrenceville
59.	Dana R. Hermanson	Kennesaw State University
60.	Ernest Cappazzoci	Kennesaw State University
61.	Lynne Bible	Berry College
62.	Thomas Kam	Hawaii Pacific University
63.	Franklin Plewa	Idaho State University
64.	Ken Hart	Brigham Young University, Idaho
65.	Kevin Packard	Brigham Young University, Idaho
66.	G. Adna Ames	Brigham Young University, Idaho
67.	Shondra Johnson	Illinois State University
68.	Wendy Duffy	Illinois State University
69.	Sherry Helmuth	Elgin Community College
70.	Pam Legner	College of Dupage
71.	George Heyman	Oakton Community College
72.	George Krull	Bradley University
73.	Deborah Pavelka	Roosevelt University
74.	Brian Leventhal	University of Illinois, Chicago
75.	Brian McGuire	University of Southern Indiana
76.	Mehmet Kocakulah	University of Southern Indiana
77.	Sue Minke	Indiana University/Purdue University at Fort Wayne
78.	Cindy Van Oosterum	Ivy Tech State College, South Bend
79.	Juan Rivera	University of Notre Dame
80.	Mary Hollars	Vincennes University
81.	Lisa Nash	Vincennes University
82.	Jack Hatcher	Purdue University
83.	George Durler	Emporia State University
84.	Richard Moellenberndt	Washburn University
85.	Arlen Honts	Friends University
86.	Harold Little	Western Kentucky University
87.	Tim Nygaard	Madisonville Community College
88.	Debbie Wright	Madisonville Community College
89.	Scott Meisel	Morehead State University
90.	Robert Braun	Southeastern Louisiana University
91.	Tommy Phillips	Louisiana Tech University
92.	Cathy Larson	Middlesex Community College
93.	Elliott Levy	Bentley College
94.	Tracy Noga	Bentley College
95.	Tom Hogan	University of Massachusetts, Boston
96.	Kiran Verma	University of Massachusetts, Boston
97.	Mindy Nikkin	Simmons College
98.	Tom Whalen	Suffolk University
99.	Patricia Bancroft	Bridgewater State College
100.	Kathleen Sevigny	Bridgewater State College
101.	Larry Logan	University of Massachusetts, Dartmouth
102.	Doug Larson	Salem State College
103.	Walter Kearney	Northeastern University, School of Professional and Continuing Studies
104.	Sherry Mirbod	Montgomery College
105.	Dori Danko	Grand Valley State University
106.	Stan Linquist	Grand Valley State University
107.	Rita Grant	Grand Valley State University
108.	Philip Kintzele	Central Michigan University
109.	Barbara Ross	Eastern Michigan University
110.	Abo Habib	Minnesota State University
111.	Candice Heino	Anoka Ramsey Community College
112.	Joel Strong	St. Cloud State University
113.	Sandra Byrd	Southwest Missouri State University, Springfield
114.	Gail Hoover	Rockhurst University
115.	Laverne Thomas-Vertrees	St. Louis Community College, Meramec
116.	Anne Wessely	St. Louis Community College, Meramec
117.	Janice Klimek	Central Missouri State University
118.	Jack Elfrink	Central Missouri State University
119.	Cecil Hill	Jackson State University
120.	Roberta Humphrey	University of Mississippi
121.	Terri Herron	University of Montana
122.	Susan Swanger	Western Carolina University
123.	Kathryn Yarbrough	University of North Carolina, Charlotte
124.	Amanda Roach	Coastal Carolina Community College
125.	Mike Dodge	Coastal Carolina Community College
126.	Mark S. Beasley	North Carolina State University
127.	Susan Eldridge	University of Nebraska, Omaha
128.	Ron Flinn	Creighton University
129.	Vasant Raval	Creighton University
130.	Sungsoo Kim	Rutgers University, Camden
131.	Ramish Narasimhan	Montclair State University
132.	Florence McGovern	Bergen County Community College
133.	Gerald Miller	College of New Jersey
134.	Ping Zhou	Baruch College
135.	Shifei Chang	Rowan University
136.	Evelyn McDowell	Rider University
137.	Chiaho Chang	Montclair State University
138.	Yaw Mensah	Rutgers University, New Brunswick
139.	Charles Birnberg	Bergen County Community College
140.	Sue Gunkel	Albuquerque Technical Vocational Institute Community College

141.	Martin Epstein	Albuquerque Technical Vocational Institute Community College
142.	Dawn Addington	Albuquerque Technical Vocational Institute Community College
143.	Ann Brooks	University of New Mexico, Albuquerque
144.	Norman Coulter	University of New Mexico, Albuquerque
145.	Jeanne Yamamura	University of Nevada, Reno
146.	Warren Schlesinger	Ithaca College
147.	Don Raux	Siena College
148.	Randy Elder	Syracuse University
149.	Mo Onsi	Syracuse University
150.	Sal Marino	Westchester Community College, The State University of New York
151.	John Strefeler	Mount Union College
152.	Dave Albrecht	Bowling Green State University
153.	Dennis O'Reilly	Xavier University
154.	Joyce Allen	Xavier University
155.	Maggie Houston	Wright State University
156.	Elsa Parsegian	Youngstown State University
157.	Nancy Snow	University of Toledo
158.	Phil Fink	University of Toledo
159.	Sheen Liu	Youngstown State University
160.	Bambi Hora	University of Central Oklahoma
161.	John Wilguess	Oklahoma State University
162.	Carol Brown	Oregon State University
163.	Monica Banyi	Oregon State University
164.	Bruce Darling	Lane Community College
165.	James Emig	Villanova University
166.	Christian Wurst	Temple University
167.	Charles Fazzi	St. Vincent College
168.	Corolyn Clark	Saint Joseph's University
169.	Bob Derstine	Villanova University
170.	Tara Shawver	King's College
171.	Pamela Stuerke	University of Rhode Island
172.	Allan Graham	University of Rhode Island
173.	Ann Kelley	Providence College

174.	Allen Winters	Clemson University
175.	Angela Letourneau	Winthrop University
176.	Joanie Sompayrac	University of Tennessee, Chattanooga
177.	James Lukawitz	University of Memphis
178.	Andrew Morgret	University of Memphis
179.	Annie McGowan	Texas A&M University, College Station
180.	Virginia Fullwood	Texas A&M University, Commerce
181.	Shawn Miller	Cy-Fair College
182.	Barbara Scofield	University of Dallas
183.	Michael Tydlaska	Mountain View College
184.	Barbara Merino	University of North Texas, Denton
185.	Sue Cullers	Tarleton State University, Stephenville
186.	Gerald Lobo	University of Houston
187.	Robert Ricketts	Texas Tech University, Lubbock
188.	Thomas Young	Tomball College
189.	Dawn Kelley	Texas Tech University, Lubbock
190.	Treba Marsh	Stephen F. Austin State University
191.	Cindy Vest	Tarrant County Community College
192.	Gary Bridges	University of Texas, San Antonio
193.	Pam San Miguel	University of Texas, San Antonio
194.	Sandra Solomon	University of Texas, Tyler
195.	Dean Wallace	Collin County Community College
196.	Ben Beam	Utah Valley State College
197.	David Durkee	Weber State University
198.	Sandra Cereola	James Madison University
199.	Felix Amenkhiennan	Radford University
200.	Paul Clikeman	University of Richmond
201.	Than Butt	Champlain College
202.	Bob Holtfreter	Central Washington University
203.	Dan Law	Gonzaga University
204.	James Benedum	Milwaukee Area Technical College
205.	Chris Luchs	Marshall University
206.	Anonymous	
207.	Anonymous	

STUDENT FOCUS GROUPS

In my efforts to produce the best possible book I could, I also knew that we shouldn't limit our formal research and input to instructors. In addition to class-testing, we engaged a group of 12 highly opinionated students from various schools in the Philadelphia area who had just taken the financial accounting course. They provided valuable feedback regarding everything from what information they'd like in a Prologue to what types of companies they find most interesting as examples. My thanks goes to these students as well as the instructors who selected them: Corolyn Clark of Saint Joseph's University, Bob Derstine of Villanova University, and Christian E. Wurst, Jr. of Temple University.

208.	Laura Gowdy	St. Joseph's University
209.	Erin Larsen	St. Joseph's University
210.	Thomas Rosenthal	St. Joseph's University
211.	Thomas Viscuso	St. Joseph's University
212.	Cristina Ackas	Temple University
213.	William Lepone	Temple University

214.	Sean McGann	Temple University
215.	Theresa Meyer	Temple University
216.	Megan Evans	Villanova University
217.	Kurt Kolakauskas	Villanova University
218.	Angela Lazzaruolo	Villanova University
219.	Justin Winig	Villanova University

REAL-WORLD COMPANIES FEATURED

This book includes financial statements from companies across the country. Many companies provided us with their logos to include next to their statements.

220.	Apple Computer, Inc.	Sunnyvale, CA	237.	Land O'Lakes, Inc.	San Jose, CA
221.	Southwest Airlines Co.	Dallas, TX	238.	Tweeter Home Entertainment Group	Canton, MA
222.	Cisco Systems, Inc.	San Jose, CA	239.	The Kroger Co.	Cincinnati, OH
223.	Bed Bath & Beyond	Union, NJ	240.	AT&T	New York City, NY
224.	Target Corporation	Minneapolis, MN	241.	Ethan Allen	Danbury, CT
225.	Best Buy	Richfield, MN	242.	Pixar	Emeryville, CA
226.	Hershey Foods Corporation	Hershey, PA	243.	Winnebago Industries, Inc.	Forest City, IL
227.	Staples, Inc.	Framingham, MA	244.	Sears, Roebuck and Co.	Hoffman Estates, IL
228.	Dell Inc.	Round Rock, TX	245.	The Sherwin-Williams Company	Cleveland, OH
229.	Papa John's Pizza	Louisville, KY	246.	May Department Stores	New York City, NY
230.	The Home Depot	Atlanta, GA	247.	The Limited, Inc.	Columbus, OH
231.	Wal-Mart	Bentonville, AR	248.	Gap Inc.	San Bruno, CA
232.	WorldCom	Ashburn, VA	249.	Johnson & Johnson	New Brunswick, NJ
233.	The Home Depot	Atlanta, GA	250.	Tiffany & Co.	New York City, NY
234.	La-Z-Boy Incorporated	Monroe, MI	251.	General Mills, Inc.	Golden Valley, MN
235.	Time Warner Inc.	New York City, NY	252.	J & J Snack Foods Corp.	Pennsauken, NJ
236.	Barnes & Noble, Inc.	New York City, NY			

Financial Accounting

Business IQ

What's Your Business IQ?

Do you use a debit or credit card? Then, you may know what it's like to keep a record of your purchases and to make sure that you have enough funds to cover those purchases. Whether you want to buy a new pair of jeans, buy a music CD, or go away for spring break, you'll need to review your finances to help make your decision. Businesses make decisions the same way: They keep track of their spending and make decisions based on the money they have, the money they expect to receive, and the money they might be able to raise. A **business** is an organization that provides goods and services to customers. A business, however, has more complicated paperwork to track than just a debit card or credit card statement. Whether a business is large or small, it needs accountants to track all the money coming in and going out—otherwise, it won't be in business long!

Regardless of your major or future career, basic business knowledge can help you succeed. If you become a manager, you'll need to know how many people you can hire, what salary you can pay them, what you can afford to buy, and how much to charge customers. If you join a marketing department at a company, you'll need to know how much you can spend on an advertising campaign. To answer these types of questions, you'll need some basic accounting knowledge. **Accounting** is the process of gathering, organizing, and summarizing financial information about a firm's activities. Because accounting looks at the entire firm, every firm can reap major benefits from a strong knowledge of how accounting works.

Even if you have no intention of working for a business, accounting can help you. Nonprofit organizations and government agencies must also track expenditures and work within budgets. Making sure that the numbers add up is a key function in almost every group, from the smallest start-up company to the largest governments in the world.

Before diving into accounting terms and procedures, let's find out if you already understand businesses and the terms we use to talk about them. Test your business IQ by answering the following questions. Select only one answer for each question. Then, use the instructions that follow to calculate your business IQ.

1. How does a business measure its financial success?
a. Its costs are decreasing
b. Its revenues are increasing
c. Its profits are increasing
d. It's gaining new customers

2. Which of these types of organizations is not normally called a business?
a. A manufacturing organization
b. A service organization
c. A merchandising organization
d. A nonprofit organization

3. How are the legal forms of businesses defined?
a. By geographic location
b. By number of employees
c. By number of owners
d. By number of separate offices the business owns.

4. What is the stock market?
a. It's where shares of a corporation's stock are bought and sold to the investing public
b. It's a company in London where people can buy and sell stock in any company
c. It's a type of bank where you go to buy shares of stock
d. It's the fund where Social Security payments are kept

5. What does it mean for a business to "go public"?
a. It's when a company becomes a corporation
b. It's the day a store opens its doors to the public
c. It's when a company starts trading its stock on the stock market.
d. It's when a business tells the truth about its financial status.

6. What does *CFO* mean?
a. It's a company's tax status
b. Central Finance Operations
c. Chief Financial Officer
d. Chief Executive Officer

7. How often do businesses normally report their finances each year?
a. Either 5 or 6, depending on the type of company

b. 4
c. 3
d. 12

8. What is GAAP?
a. The accounting guidelines that firms use to prepare their financial reports
b. A new clothing store created by the people at the GAP
c. The difference between a firm's revenues and expenses
d. The gap between a company's available cash and the cash needed to run the business

9. What is accounting fraud?
a. It's when top executives borrow money from the company
b. It's when employees steal office equipment or supplies for personal use
c. It's when top executives make up numbers to make a company look more profitable than it is
d. It's a division of the U.S. government that monitors company behavior

10. What is corporate governance?
a. A special department in each business that ensures that employees are following the company's rules
b. A special department in the government that oversees business activities
c. The way a corporation manages the complex relationships between and among management shareholders, board of directors, and others who have a stake in the corporation
d. The rules and regulations the Securities and Exchange Commission follows

At the end of each chapter, you'll be able to test your improving knowledge of how businesses work in a feature entitled "Have You Increased Your Business IQ?" By the end of the course, you'll understand how to gather, read, and interpret accounting information.

FIGURE OUT YOUR BUSINESS IQ >>>

[Answers: 1. c, 2. d, 3. c, 4. a, 5. c, 6. c, 7. b, 8. a, 9. c, 10. c]

Give yourself two points for every correct answer. Use the chart below to learn what your score means and what you should do next.

If your score is ...	that means ...	so, you should ...
0–4	you're in the range of most students taking their first accounting course. This book will help you build your business IQ.	read the rest of this chapter with great care. As you read later chapters, be sure to take the "Have You Increased Your Business IQ" quiz at the end of the chapter.
6–8	you have a very good foundation from which to build your knowledge of how businesses gather and use accounting information.	learn all of the accounting you can. It's a well-known fact that accounting is the language of business, and you certainly want to be able to speak the language.
10	accounting can be your best friend on your way to working at a business or starting your own business.	read the *Financial Times*, *BusinessWeek*, and the *Wall Street Journal*. You're on your way to the top!

Let's review the correct answers from the Business IQ test you just took.

QUESTION 1: How Does a Business Measure Its Financial Success?

People who start businesses and operate businesses are most often driven by the desire to make a profit.

Revenues are the amounts the firm earns for providing goods or services to its customers. **Expenses** are costs incurred to generate that revenue—money going out in order to create money coming in. **Profit** is the difference between revenues and expenses for a specific period of time. If the expenses total more than the revenues, the "negative profit" is called a **loss**. If a business has increasing revenues, that is a good sign, but revenues don't tell the whole story—the company's expenses may be increasing faster than its revenues. Similarly, decreasing costs and gaining new customers are good, but the financial health of a company is determined by its profits. Only when profits are positive is a business doing well. >>>

QUESTION 2: Which of These Types of Organizations Is Not Normally Considered a Business?

There are three general types of businesses: service, manufacturing, and merchandising. Generally, a nonprofit organization is not considered a business because the main purpose of a business is to make a profit.

Although most businesses can be classified as one of these three types of organization, many large businesses are a combination of two or more.

If you surf the Internet, you probably use a search engine like Google. Google gives people an easy-to-use search engine and provides businesses a place to advertise. Who created Google? Two Stanford University graduates and entrepreneurs—Larry Page and Sergey Brin—founded Google in 1998. An **entrepreneur** is someone who is inventive and willing to take financial risks to start a business.

A service business: Businesses that provide Internet services, legal representation, or house cleaning services are called service businesses. In the United States, the service sector accounts for 72 percent of the economy's output. ∨∨∨

On August 19, 2004, executives at Google had a nice problem to solve: What would they do with the $2 billion in cash they raised at their initial public offering? The money came from investors. By investing in a firm, you become part owner of that firm. Google stock sold for a low of $95 and a high of $104.06 in August 2004. By November 2005, Google's stock soared to $400 a share.

(Sources: Karen Talley, "Google Rises After Big Stock Sale; Dana Skids on a Profit Warning," Dow Jones Newswires, September 16, 2005, p. C4; Paul R. La Monica, "Google Jumps in Rocky Debut," CNN.com, August 20, 2004; and Vauhini Vara, "Technology Shares Slip, But Google Passes $200," Wall Street Journal, January 13, 2005.)

A manufacturing business: Businesses that produce tangible goods like cars and furniture are manufacturing businesses. If a business makes the items it sells, it's a manufacturing company. General Motors (GM) is a classic example of a manufacturing company. GM is also in the service industry because you can purchase a car that has GM's OnStar service. If you have an emergency or are lost or need some travel advice, you can press a button in your car and talk to a GM service representative who will help you out.

GM is the world's largest automaker. The company has manufacturing operations in 32 countries and sells vehicles in 200 countries. In 2004, GM sold nearly 9 million cars and trucks globally. To attract customers in June and July 2005, GM created the "Employee Discount for Everyone" program, which offered consumers the same steep discounts from manufacturer's suggested retail prices that its employees get.
(Source: www.gm.com)

A merchandising business: Businesses that purchase products from other businesses and resell those products to customers are called merchandising businesses. Starbucks and Wal-Mart are two examples of merchandising businesses that you probably know.

Starbucks is the world's largest chain of coffee shops with over 7,500 stores worldwide, including the United States, Canada, France, Japan, and China. In 2005, the company announced plans to open about 1,800 stores in 2006, including about 1,300 in the United States. More than 25 million people visit a Starbucks each day.

(Source: Steven Gray, "Starbucks Posts, 29% Rise in Net on Pricier Drinks," Wall Street Journal, *July 28, 2005, p. B3)*

Wal-Mart is the world's largest retailer, with $285.2 billion in sales in the fiscal year ended January 31, 2005. The company employs 1.6 million people worldwide. Wal-Mart is the leading seller of groceries in the United States, with a 19 percent share of the market. Wal-Mart is also becoming the leading seller of toys, CDs, and many other product categories in the United States. In June 2005, the company had over $20 billion in sales.

(Source: Wal-mart.com, September 1, 2005; and Forbes.com, July 7, 2005)

QUESTION 3: How Are the Legal Forms of Businesses Defined?

Businesses differ based on how many people own them. The legal form of the business is generally defined by whether a business has one owner, a small set of partners, or a broader set of shareholders. There are three main forms of ownership:

Sole Proprietorships: One Owner

If one individual owns a business, like an artist who sells paintings, it is a **sole proprietorship**. A new business often starts as a sole proprietorship because it is the easiest and least expensive type of business to start.

17

Partnerships: Two or More Owners

A business **partnership** is owned by two or more people. Common examples of partnerships are law firms and accounting firms.

Corporations: Many Owners

A **corporation** is a legal organization with the right to own property and enter into contracts. Most corporations—like Wal-Mart—have many shareholders, although there is no minimum number of owners required. Wal-Mart, for example, has some 333,000 shareholders ranging from members of the public, who might own only a few shares of the company, to the descendants of founder Sam Walton, who together own over a billion shares in the giant retailer.

(Source: DSN Retailing Today, *July 11, 2005)*

QUESTION 4: What Is the Stock Market?

Anyone can become a part-owner of a corporation if the corporation is publicly traded on a stock market.

If you purchase **stock** in a company, it means that you own part of that company. For example, in 2004, Google offered ownership—stock—to the public. Investors purchased shares of Google for a total of $2 billion. These investors are called **shareholders** and are considered owners of the firm. The **stock market** is where people buy and sell stock of public corporations. Two of the largest stock markets are the New York Stock Exchange (pictured) and the American Stock Exchange. Overseas, the Tokyo Stock Exchange is the main stock market of Japan, and the London Stock Exchange is the main stock market in the United Kingdom.

QUESTION 5: What Does It Mean for a Business to "Go Public"?

When a company "goes public," that means a company starts trading its stock on the stock market. On one hand, going public can help a company raise millions or billions of dollars to enable it to invest in new activities or to expand. On the other hand, going public involves obeying a tough set of regulations that help ensure that the company faithfully reports its activities to prospective shareholders. Here we see Warner Music Group, with guitarist Jimmy Page of Led Zepplin, going public on May 11, 2005. Warner is the only stand-alone music company to be publicly traded in the United States.

QUESTION 6: What Does *CFO* Mean?

CFO stands for Chief Financial Officer. The CFO ensures that the accounting information for his or her company is accurate and shared with shareholders and government agencies such as the Internal Revenue Service.

QUESTION 7: How Often Do Businesses Report Their Finances Each Year?

Before answering question 7, let's explore what it means to "report" finances. Let's say you purchased stock in Google in 2004. As a new owner, you want to know whether Google is making a profit or losing money, so that you can decide what to do with your original investment and whether or not to purchase more stock in the company. You're not the only one interested in Google's finances. Government agencies such as the Internal Revenue Service (IRS) and the **Securities and Exchange Commission** (SEC) want to know the company's profits as well. The IRS levies taxes on companies based on their profits and other financial activities. The SEC regulates the stock markets and sets rules for publicly traded corporations. To protect shareholders, the SEC requires publicly traded corporations to have a board of directors, a group of people who are responsible for deciding if any of the firm's profits should be distributed to the shareholders, overseeing corporate affairs, reviewing the corporation's long-term plans, and hiring the firm's management. In August 2005, Christopher Cox, shown above, was sworn in as Securities and Exchange Commission chairman.

A company reports its finances to the public and government quarterly: once every three months. **19**

stock market and expect their money to grow over the years. What happens, however, when businesspeople commit **accounting fraud**—deliberately falsifying financial information to make their company look more profitable than it really is? Employees, shareholders, and the entire economy suffer serious financial losses. Did you know that over 25,000 accredited accountants, auditors, attorneys, and criminologists are Certified Fraud Examiners (CFEs)? CFEs go beyond the traditional audit function to help their clients implement fraud prevention and detection measures. Specifically, CFEs address risks that could lead to fraud. Their role is to help businesses understand where they are vulnerable. CFEs like to tailor audits to evaluate fraud risk factors, such as poor communication of ethical standards, large amounts of cash on hand, and inadequate internal controls. You'll learn more about internal risk and control in each chapter.

(Source: www.startheregoplaces.com/cpastoday/cpasspeak/cpasspeak.asp)

QUESTION 8: What Is GAAP?

GAAP is short for Generally Accepted Accounting Principles. These are the accounting guidelines that firms use to prepare the financial reports that go to shareholders and the government. The GAAP guidelines help companies determine how to record all the complex financial activities in which they engage. Standards, such as GAAP, mean the shareholders can understand financial reports because those financial reports follow standardized formats and definitions.

QUESTION 9: What Is Accounting Fraud?

We all buy products from various businesses such as Starbucks, Wal-Mart, and Amazon.com, and most of us rely on businesses for jobs. Many people also invest money in companies through the

QUESTION 10: What Is Corporate Governance?

Corporate governance is the way a firm governs itself. It is the way a firm manages the relationships between and among the (1) board of directors, (2) firm management, (3) shareholders, (4) employees, and (5) any others with a stake in the company. After scandals such as Enron and WorldCom, investors lost confidence in the stock market. The new emphasis on corporate governance aims to restore that confidence. Without confidence in a corporation and its financial reports, potential shareholders will withhold their investments in that firm. Without shareholder investment, firms

often lack the money they need to help finance growth and new business ventures. You'll learn more about corporate governance in Chapter 13, "Quality of Earnings and Corporate Governance."

In 2002, Congress passed the **Sarbanes-Oxley Act (SOX)** to help restore the public's confidence in the running and financial reporting of corporations.

There is no reason your business IQ cannot go up and up and up! As you study the 13 chapters of this textbook, think about the financial information that firms provide their bankers, investors, shareholders, and managers. Test your business IQ at the end of each chapter. You will be surprised at how much you will be able to learn about business and how your knowledge of accounting will help you in your future career in business or elsewhere.

Ethics Matter...

I magine that you graduate and gain an entry-level position with one of the largest companies in America. You work your way up to a manager's position and enjoy a comfortable salary and live in a nice place. One day you discover that top managers are creating fake reports about the financial security of the company and are treating themselves to high salaries and bonuses. What do you do?

This is not a fictional story. Sherron Watkins was a vice president at Enron, an energy company that was the seventh largest company in the United States based on revenue. Watkins discovered that executives were hiding millions of dollars in debt and had led employees and investors to believe the company was profitable when it was actually in financial trouble. As an accountant, Watkins had the skill to read *and evaluate* the company's financial records. She also had the ethics and strength—her nickname is "Buzzsaw"—to write a memo in August 2001 to then CEO, Kenneth Lay, pointing out the company "could implode in a wave of accounting scandals."

Enron filed for bankruptcy in December 2001, and thousands of employees lost their jobs. In 2002, Watkins testified before the U.S. Congress and Senate. In 2004, Andrew Fastow, the former CFO, was sentenced to 10 years in prison after pleading guilty to securities and wire fraud. Lay is scheduled to go on trial for fraud in 2006.

(Source: Mimi Swartz and Sherron Watkins, Power Failure *(New York: Doubleday, 2004); and Frank Pellegrini, "Person of the Week: 'Enron Whistleblower' Sherron Watkins For Putting It in Writing and Marking the Investigative Trail,"* TIME*, January 18, 2002)*

Senator Paul Sarbanes of Maryland, now retired (on the right), and Congressman Michael Oxley of Ohio developed the Sarbanes-Oxley Act (SOX), a sweeping corporate accountability bill signed into law by President Bush on July 30, 2002.

Sherron Watkins testified before the U.S. Congress and Senate at the beginning of 2002 and was selected as one of three "People of the Year 2002" by *TIME* magazine.

Enron Corporation executives hid the company's poor financial performance. The company filed for bankruptcy in 2001, and it cost thousands of people their jobs and made the stock of the company worthless. To add insult to injury, Enron executives were paid $680 million in the year prior to the firm's bankruptcy.

CEO Bernard Ebbers was sentenced to 25 years in prison in July 2005 for his role in an $11 billion accounting scandal. Ebbers agreed to pay $5 million and forfeit nearly everything he owns to settle a civil lawsuit brought by investors who lost billions of dollars in WorldCom's collapse. Another settlement calls for Ebbers to turn over his assets to a trust that eventually will sell them off for an expected $25 million to $40 million.

A former basketball coach and milkman, Bernie Ebbers became the talk of Wall Street in the late 1990s when his company, WorldCom, became the nation's second-largest long-distance company. It wasn't long before the tide turned. In 2002, the company laid off about 17,000 employees and filed for bankruptcy protection after disclosing it had overstated revenues by $3.8 *billion*. What happened? Accounting fraud was at the heart of the company's failure. Betty Vinson, a manager in WorldCom's accounting department, provided federal prosecutors with information that helped them convict several WorldCom executives of fraud. In 2005, a jury convicted Ebbers of falsely boosting the company's profits. Investors lost billions of dollars because they thought WorldCom was a profitable company. Employees lost their jobs and retirement plans. Ebbers is now serving a 25-year sentence in a federal prison for his role in an $11 billion fraud—the largest in U.S. history.

(Source: Dionne Searcy, Shawn Young, and Kara Scannell, "Ebbers Is Sentenced to 25 Years for $11 Billion WorldCom Fraud," Wall Street Journal, *July 14, 2005, p. A1)*

To say that investors were defrauded and retirees lost money in the accounting scandals is only part of the story. The Securities and Exchange Commission, a governmental agency created by congress to regulate the securities markets and protect investors, has set up so-called Fair Funds in dozens of cases, ranging from a $750 million settlement with WorldCom, now MCI, to a $25 million settlement with Lucent Technologies. Time Warner agreed to pay $300 million to settle alleged accounting improprieties, and the banks accused of aiding fraud at Enron are contributing more than $400 million.

In an effort to restore investor confidence and improve financial reporting, Congress passed the Sarbanes-Oxley Act in 2002—known in business circles as SOX. The act was written and sponsored by Senator Paul Sarbanes of Maryland, now retired, and Mike Oxley of Ohio. SOX holds top managers personally accountable for the information in the financial statements. This act also requires that outside auditors attest to management's report on internal controls, and it imposes penalties including jail time and fines for fraud. SOX gives employees, auditors, boards of directors, and managers both rights and responsibilities to help ensure that companies are operating in a lawful and ethical manner. You'll be reading about SOX throughout this course.

(Source: Deborah Solomon, "For Wronged Investors, It's Payback Time: The SEC Begins Doling Out Funds from Settlement Pools, But the Wait Can Be Long," Wall Street Journal, July 7, 2005, D1.)

Are you an accounting major, or are you considering this major?

According to both AccountingWeb.com and the Job Outlook 2005 survey, accounting is now the number one major on college campuses. Many companies need auditors who can help them comply with SOX. "Sarbanes-Oxley is the accounting full-employment act," said Ron Kucic, director of the school of accounting at Denver University's Daniels College of Business. And demand for more accounting work isn't just at publicly traded companies, to which SOX applies, but also at private companies, which are coming under pressure from lenders, investors, and others to meet SOX standards.

[Sources: Tom Locke, "Accounting Students in High Demand," Denver Business Journal, September 17, 2004; and http://ceae.aicpa.org/Accounting+is+Number +1.htm.]

Yes, accounting scandals have been making headlines in recent years, but the American economic system remains strong. It has faced its problems head-on and worked out solutions. As Representative Michael Oxley, coauthor of SOX, writes on his Web site: "No economic system in the history of the world could withstand the body blows we have taken in the past few years—9/11, the corporate scandals, the bursting of the tech bubble—and emerge stronger for it." As you will see throughout this course, accounting information plays a key role in running American business and keeping the American economy moving in the right direction.

Financial Accounting

chapter

The Link Between Business and Accounting

Here's where you've been . . .

- **You assessed your knowledge of basic business terminology and learned about the Sarbanes-Oxley Act of 2002.**

Here's where you're going . . .

- **You'll learn why accounting is vital to business and how to recognize the four basic financial statements.**

CHAPTER 1

YOU make the call:

Who owns Apple Computer, Inc.?

Apple Computer took the music world by storm in 2001 with the introduction of the iPod. Here's what *BusinessWeek* had to say: "Just as the Mac revolutionized the computer industry, Apple is once again in the business of changing the world. This time, it's the world of music. Its diminutive iPod . . . is the most radical change in how people listen to music since SONY Corp. introduced the Walkman in 1979."

How did Apple start out? Steve Wozniak was an engineer who worked as a calculator technician at Hewlett-Packard in the 1970s. Steve Jobs, pictured here, persuaded Wozniak to quit Hewlett-Packard and start a company. The company started in Jobs's garage

as a partnership between the two friends, and it was formally incorporated on July 3, 1977.

On December 12, 1980, Apple Computer, Inc., went public, which means the company began selling its shares of stock to the public. The price started at $22 per share and was trading at $29 by the end of the day.

Who owned Apple Computer, Inc., in 1977? Who owns Apple Computer, Inc. today? At the end of the chapter, the *You make the call* feature will show you how to use what you learned in this chapter to answer these questions.

Source: Peter Burrows, "Show Time!" *BusinessWeek*, February 2, 2004, p. 58.

Learning Objectives

When you are finished studying this chapter, you should be able to:

1. Define accounting and explain why accounting information is important.
2. Identify the users of accounting information, and explain how financial accounting standards are determined.
3. Explain the contents of the four basic financial statements.
4. Explain financial statement analysis and the use of ratio analysis.
5. Recognize the risks associated with being in business and how to control those risks.

LEARNING OBJECTIVE 1
Define accounting and explain why accounting information is important.

Transaction: A business activity such as buying or selling a good or service that results in an economic exchange with another business or individual.

Study Tip

A transaction is the basis for recording the financial events that affect a business.

Accounting: The process of identifying, measuring, and communicating financial business information to various users.

What Is Accounting and Why Is It Important to Business?

If you picked up a newspaper lately, you probably saw a story about accounting in the headlines. In July 2005, Bernard Ebbers, the former head of telecommunications giant WorldCom was sentenced to a 25-year prison sentence for an $11 billion accounting fraud at the company—the largest accounting fraud in U.S. history. Ken Lay, the former head of energy-giant Enron, is scheduled to go on trial in 2006. In 2001, the bankruptcy of Enron, an energy-production corporation, wiped out millions of dollars of employees' pension funds. As Enron's external auditor, accounting firm Arthur Andersen (known simply as Andersen) was involved in the scandal. External auditors are accountants hired by a firm to examine its financial records. The Enron scandal proved to be the demise of the well-known accounting firm. The executives of Enron did not fully disclose the company's debt to investors, and the executives of WorldCom recorded **transactions**—business activities—in the company's accounting records in a way that hid expenses and made the company look more profitable than it was. Both companies filed for bankruptcy protection, and their investors and employees lost billions of dollars.

The bold key terms and definitions that you see in the narrative and also in the margin are essential accounting concepts that also appear in the glossary in the back of the book. Read these terms and definitions and the study tips in the margin to learn the language of accounting and prepare for your exams.

Reading and interpreting the accounting stories in the news will help you understand today's business environment. Although accounting is often called the "language of business," accounting is more than that. Accounting is how every company keeps score—Are we making enough money? Are we spending too much money? Managers use accounting information to make business decisions such as how many goods to produce and at what price to sell those goods. Formally, **accounting** is the process of identifying, measuring, and communicating financial business information to various users. Accounting is one of the most important sources of information for people who wish to invest in businesses. So it is important for business people and investors to understand what they see in a firm's reported accounting information.

Keep in mind that only the bad accounting news makes news headlines. Of the thousands of businesses that operate in the world, the vast majority operate responsibly and report financial information as accurately as possible.

As you learn about accounting, you'll understand what happens when companies like Xerox, Tyco, HealthSouth, and Adelphia get caught "cooking the books." Read *Accounting in the News* for a preview.

In each chapter, you will find one or more *Accounting in the News* features that present a relevant news story from newspapers and journals such as *The Wall Street Journal*, *The New York Times*, and *Fortune Magazine*.

Accounting in the NEWS

Ethics

Cooking the Books at HealthSouth Corporation

In July 2005, former HealthSouth chief executive officer (CEO) Richard Scrushy was found innocent of any criminal wrongdoing in the $2.7 billion accounting fraud at his former company. The jury did not believe that he helped the company "cook the books." Cooking the books means falsifying accounting information to make a company's financial performance look better than it actually is. As you learn about accounting records—the books—you'll see how a firm's accounting records should be kept and you'll see how a firm can cook the books. Even though the CEO of HealthSouth was found not guilty of financial statement fraud, other employees at the company pled guilty and are serving prison terms. Here's how HealthSouth's employees cooked the books.

The company's business divisions around the country would send their accounting information—legitimate amounts—to the corporate offices in Birmingham. There, finance department employees would add to the information to improve the company's reported income. According to the testimony of an accountant who reviewed the records after the fraud was discovered, "They just made up the numbers."

As you study the topics in this book, you'll learn about ways to prevent that from happening!

Thinking Critically

Do you think employees who "cook the books" at healthcare companies should face stiffer penalties than employees who do that at companies that manufacture furniture or computers? Why or why not?

In 2005, some employees of HealthSouth Corporation pled guilty to financial statement fraud. Headquartered in Birmingham, Alabama, HealthSouth is one of the nation's largest healthcare service providers.

Q How did HealthSouth "cook the books"?

A They simply made up the numbers they wanted to report.

Source: Dan Morse and Evelina Shmukler, "Witness Details How Books Were Cooked at HealthSouth," *Wall Street Journal Online,* January 28, 2005.

Before you can understand how and why some companies cook the books, you have to learn about "the books"—a company's accounting records. But even before that, you have to understand what business is all about.

What does a business do?

How does a business get started and, once started, how does it succeed? Generally, a business is formed to provide goods or services for the purpose of making money for its owners. If you want to start a business, your first step is to obtain financial resources—and that means money. One of the most famous start-up companies is Apple Computer, Inc. This internationally known computer company started with $1,300, which Steve Jobs and Steve Wozniak obtained from the sale of some personal items. In Jobs's garage, they put together one of the earliest personal computers and sold it for $666. Today, Apple Computer, Inc. has made a name in the MP3 market with its iPod. The nearby photo shows the iPod Special U2 Edition, which features the laser-engraved signatures of each member of the Irish band.

From the smallest local store to the internationally known Apple Computer, this is what all businesses have in common: They provide us with goods and services. A business may start from scratch and create its products, or it may take products made by others and sell those products to the final consumer.

Here are examples of products or services that companies provide:

- Apple Computer: a computer and iPod that you can purchase.
- Amazon.com: the convenience to shop online from your apartment or home.
- Best Buy: a variety of electronic products.

In the first quarter of 2005, Apple Computer sold over 4.5 million iPods. Here is the iPod Special U2 Edition, released in October 2004 in conjunction with a new U2 CD.

In Other Words:
A business is also called a *company* or a *firm.*

A firm that creates or adds value to earn money for its owners is called a *for-profit* firm. In contrast, a firm that provides goods or services for the sole purpose of helping people instead of making a profit is called a *not-for-profit organization*. A not-for-profit organization, such as the St. Jude Children's Hospital or the Salvation Army, is more likely than a firm to be called an organization or agency. Even though it's called not-for-profit, this type of organization doesn't mind making a profit. What's different is that a not-for-profit organization uses any profit to provide more goods and services to the people it serves rather than distributing profits to its owners. Both for-profit organizations and not-for-profit organizations provide value. Throughout this book, we will be dealing primarily with for-profit organizations—businesses.

Accounting information needed to operate a firm

As a firm carries out its activities—acquiring what it needs to create products and services, selling those products, and collecting the payment for those sales—accountants record information about these activities in the firm's information system. Whether computerized or not, an accounting system is a firm's fundamental information system. Without the financial information that accountants gather, a firm's manager could not make day-to-day decisions. Consider some examples of the kinds of information accountants record:

> **Inventory:** Goods purchased by a firm to be sold to its customers or used to make products to be sold to its customers.

1. The amount of money the firm receives from its investors and from creditors.
2. Purchases of equipment, materials, and services the firm needs to operate.
3. Purchases of **inventory**—goods to be sold to customers.
4. Sales and the collection for those sales.

> **Profit:** The difference between revenue and the costs of earning that revenue.

This is all accounting information. Both insiders—the owners and the firm's employees—and outsiders—the creditors, governmental agencies, and potential investors—use the information.

A business must successfully plan, implement, and evaluate its activities. If a business does these three things well, it will survive. If a business does these things very well, it will make a profit. So far, we have used the term *profit* in a very general way—to make money. Now let's get very specific. **Profit** is the difference between the **revenue**, the amount a business earns for the products it sells or the services it provides, and the cost of selling those products or providing those services. When a firm evaluates new projects, it will estimate the amount of revenue it plans to earn and the costs of earning that revenue. The firm wants to be sure the project will earn a profit.

Study Tip

The term *profit* can apply to a specific project, department, product line, or even a business. Profit does not necessarily pertain to a specific period of time.

The "Can you do it?" feature gives you a chance to test and apply your understanding of a section before moving on. If you don't get the correct answers, review the preceding pages.

> **Revenue:** The amount a business earns for the goods it sells or the services it provides.

Can **YOU** do it?

1. What is accounting?
2. Define profit.

Answers (1) Accounting is the process of identifying, measuring, and communicating financial information to people who need it to make decisions. (2) Profit is the difference between revenue—what a department, project, or firm earns—and costs of earning the revenue.

Using Financial Reports to Make Decisions

LEARNING OBJECTIVE 2
Identify the users of accounting information and explain how financial accounting standards are determined.

Now that you know what a business does, we are ready to discuss the specific type of information that business transactions generate and how people use this information.

To start their new firm, the founders of Apple Computer had many decisions to make. First, how would they finance the business? What organizational form should the business take? How many computers should they make? From which companies should they buy the components? How much should they charge for their computers? How much should they pay for a magazine advertisement?

The sequence of business activities of getting cash, using cash to purchase inputs, changing those inputs into products or services, providing the product or service to customers, and eventually getting cash back is called an **operating cycle**. An operating cycle for Apple Computer is shown in Exhibit 1.1.

Operating cycle: The sequence of business activities starting with getting cash, using cash to purchase inputs, changing those inputs into products or services, and providing the product or service to customers, eventually getting cash back.

After Apple completes one operating cycle, it has more decisions to make: Should it make more iPods and go through the operating cycle again? If so, should it buy more components than it bought the first time and from the same

Exhibit 1.1

The Operating Cycle

An operating cycle for Apple starts with cash. Then Apple makes the iPods for its inventory. Then, Apple sells the iPods. Finally, Apple collects cash from its customers. The company has come full circle—cash to more cash.

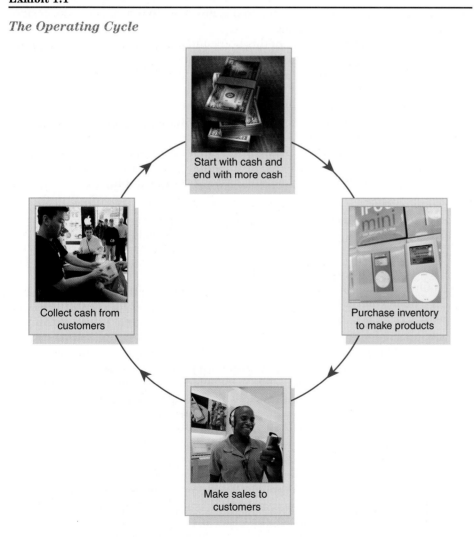

Start with cash and end with more cash

Purchase inventory to make products

Make sales to customers

Collect cash from customers

supplier? Accountants at Apple can help managers answer these questions by providing the following information:

- The revenue from sales during the accounting period. An *accounting period* is any length of time that a company uses to evaluate its performance. It can be a month, a quarter (three months), or a year.
- The costs Apple Computer incurred so those sales could be made.
- The components Apple has left at the end of the period.

Apple also needs information on the reliability of different suppliers and the quality of their merchandise to decide what supplier to use. However, most managers want to see the accounting information before making this decision. If the numbers aren't good, there is no reason to waste any time researching the reliability of suppliers.

Internal and external financial statement users

Accounting information is used by people both internal and external to the company. The most prominent internal users of accounting information are the managers of a firm. Managers plan, implement, and evaluate the operation of the firm. To perform these functions effectively, managers must have information about what the firm has done, what it is currently doing, and what it should be doing. *Management accounting* is the area of accounting that is specifically concerned with internal information and is not governed by any common standards or regulations for reporting.

Financial accounting, the topic of this book and course, is the area of accounting that is specifically concerned with communicating accounting information to external users. A firm provides this information in the form of *financial statements*, which are reports about the financial condition and performance of the firm. Specific standards and guidelines that you will study in this book and course govern the preparation of the financial statements. Although financial accounting provides information to users external to the firm, we have seen that managers also need this information to make decisions.

The following *external users* need information about a firm: the government, creditors, potential investors, vendors, customers, and employees.

- *Government:* A state's department of revenue needs information to calculate the sales tax due from the company. The Internal Revenue Service (IRS) requires firms to submit information about their income and expenses.
- *Creditors:* Banks, and other institutions, lend money to firms. A bank requires information about a company's financial performance to determine whether or not the company will be able to repay the loan.
- *Potential investors:* Would you like to own stock in Apple Computer? If yes, you are a potential investor. Suppose the founders of Apple Computer want to find additional owners for the business. That means they want people to invest money in the business in return for a portion of ownership in the company. A potential owner—like you—wants reliable information about the business before investing. The Securities and Exchange Commission (SEC), a government agency that you will learn about in the next section, requires that companies whose stock is publicly traded provide potential investors with information that is accurate and reliable. That means the information in the firms' financial statements must be audited. Audited information has been examined by professional accountants, called **certified public accountants (CPAs)**. Although CPAs often prepare tax returns and do bookkeeping, these functions can be performed by other individuals. An H&R Block employee who is not a CPA can prepare your tax return, and a bookkeeper who is not a CPA can keep a firm's books. But only a CPA can

Certified public accountant (CPA): Someone who has met specific education and exam requirements that are set up by the states to make sure only individuals with the appropriate accounting knowledge and other qualifications can perform financial statement audits of corporations.

perform an audit of a firm's financial statements. We'll talk more about auditing when we evaluate the financial statements of real companies.

- *Vendors, customers, and employees:* These groups need useful information about the company's financial condition to decide whether to work for, or do business with, the company.

Who sets the guidelines for financial reporting?

With all of these people using financial accounting information, it is important for firms to use similar reporting guidelines when preparing their financial statements. That way, all external users will know how to read and analyze the information. The financial statements are based on a broad set of guidelines called **generally accepted accounting principles (GAAP)**.

Who is responsible for establishing these guidelines? Exhibit 1.2 shows the hierarchy of groups involved in setting auditing and accounting standards. The responsibility starts with Congress. Congress established the **Securities and Exchange Commission (SEC)** by passing the Securities Acts of 1933 and 1934. These acts were a response to the stock market crash of 1929, which preceded the Great Depression. The SEC was given authority to monitor the activities and financial reporting of corporations that sell shares of ownership on the major stock exchanges.

Generally accepted accounting principles (GAAP): A broad set of accounting guidelines that a firm must follow when preparing its financial statements.

Securities and Exchange Commission (SEC): A governmental agency created by Congress to regulate the stock market and establish and enforce reporting standards for publicly traded corporations.

Exhibit 1.2

Who Sets the Guidelines for Financial Reporting?

Securities and Exchange Commission (SEC)

The United States Congress established the Securities and Exchange Commission (SEC). The SEC delegated the responsibility of establishing accounting and auditing standards to two groups: the Financial Accounting Standards Board (FASB) to set accounting standards and the Public Company Accounting Oversight Board (PCAOB) to set auditing standards.

Public Company Accounting Oversight Board (PCAOB)

In response to the 2001–2002 discovery of accounting scandals, the SEC created the PCAOB to oversee the auditing profession and the audit of public companies.

Financial Accounting Standards Board (FASB)

The SEC has delegated much of the standards-setting responsibility to the FASB. The SEC retains and sometimes exercises the right to set accounting standards.

Financial Accounting Standards Board (FASB): A group of professional business people, accountants, and accounting scholars in the private sector (not government employees) who are responsible for setting current accounting standards.

Public Company Accounting Oversight Board (PCAOB): A private-sector, non-profit corporation created to oversee the auditors of public companies.

The SEC has delegated much of the responsibility for setting financial standards to an independent group called the **Financial Accounting Standards Board (FASB)**. This is a group of professional business people, accountants, and accounting scholars in the private sector, that is, non-governmental employees, who are responsible for setting current accounting standards. Accounting standards dictate the way businesses report their activities, so businesses are very interested in what the FASB does. As a result of the 2001–2002 exposure of numerous scandals in accounting, a new independent board was established to oversee the auditing profession and auditing standards: the **Public Company Accounting Oversight Board (PCAOB)**. According to the official PCAOB web site (www.pcaobus.org), the PCAOB is a "private-sector, non-profit corporation created to oversee the auditors of public companies in order to protect the interests of investors and further the public interest in the preparation of informative, fair, and independent audit reports."

Can **YOU** do it?

1. Who sets accounting standards?
2. What is a CPA?

Answers (1) The Securities and Exchange Commission (SEC) and the Financial Accounting Standards Board (FASB) set most of the accounting standards. (2) A CPA (certified public accountant) is an accountant who has the credentials to perform financial statement audits.

LEARNING OBJECTIVE 3

Explain the contents of the four basic financial statements.

The Basic Financial Statements and the Accounting Equation

Now that you have learned who uses financial information and why, it's time to dig a little deeper into the specifics of the information. There are four financial statements plus accompanying notes that a company uses to report its past performance and its financial condition:

1. balance sheet
2. income statement
3. statement of changes in owners' equity[1]
4. statement of cash flows
5. notes to the financial statements

Monetary unit assumption: An assumption that only information that can be expressed in monetary units (dollars in the United States) will be included in the financial statements.

Only information that can be expressed in monetary units, dollars in the United States, is included in the financial statements. This is called the **monetary unit assumption**. As you learn about the items reported on each financial statement, you'll see that this assumption will help you determine what is and what is not included on the financial statements.

Notes to the financial statements: Information that describes the company's major accounting policies and provides other disclosures to help external users better understand the financial statements.

A company's set of financial statements includes the four basic statements—balance sheet, income statement, statement of changes in owners' equity, and the statement of cash flows—as well as an important section called **notes to the financial statements**. These notes, sometimes referred to as *footnotes*, are an integral part of the set of financial statements. The notes describe the company's major accounting policies and provide other disclosures to help external users better understand the financial statements. As you learn about the four

[1]When a firm has only one owner, the statement refers to *owner's* equity. When a firm has more than one owner, the statement refers to *owners'* equity. This book will generally use the plural form when the number of owners is unclear.

statements, remember that you will be able to find additional information about each in the notes.

Balance sheet

A **balance sheet** describes the financial position of a company at a specific point in time. The balance sheet is a snapshot that captures the items of value the business possesses at a particular time—assets—and how the company has financed those assets—with debt or contributions from owners. **Assets** are economic resources owned by a firm. Assets are the result of the firm's past transactions, but they offer potential future benefits because the firm can use them to generate revenue.

A balance sheet has three categories:

- assets
- liabilities
- owners' equity

The following relationship, called the **accounting equation**, is the basis for the balance sheet:

Assets	=	Liabilities	+	Owners' Equity
Assets	=	Claims		
		Of creditors		Of owners

Remember that a transaction is the most basic business activity. A transaction results from an exchange between the firm and an outside party. Each transaction that takes place in a business can be recorded in the accounting equation. When an asset is obtained, it belongs to either the firm's creditors or to the firm's owners. Creditors are people or companies to whom a firm owes money. For example, if you have a car loan, the bank that loaned you the money is your creditor. Creditors have a claim to any assets they provided. They will want the asset or its equivalent back at a specific point in time. Owners have a claim to any assets they provided, but they will not necessarily get them back at a particular time. Every transaction changes the accounting equation, yet the accounting equation must stay in *balance*. In Chapter 2, you'll learn how business transactions are organized and combined to produce the four basic financial statements. For now, we'll look at the form and content of each statement.

Notice the special feature in the margin called "In Other Words." Read this information to learn about synonymous terms that you are likely to read in the newspaper and hear about in class.

Exhibit 1.3 shows a condensed balance sheet for Apple Computer. You won't understand all of the items on this financial statement yet, but you will be able to identify some specific characteristics of the statement as you progress through the chapter. Refer to this exhibit as you read about the information contained in a balance sheet.

Apple's assets, listed in Exhibit 1.3, include Cash, Short-Term Investments, *Accounts Receivable*—amounts a firm is owed by its customers, and *Property, Plant and Equipment*—assets that a firm will use over several years. Items like these are called *accounts*. An account is a device used for keeping a record of all events that affect that particular item. For example, all amounts that customers owe the firm are kept together in the recordkeeping device—an account—called *Accounts Receivable*. Asset is a broader term that describes certain types of accounts such as those Apple has listed here.

As you can see in the accounting equation, for every asset the firm has, someone has the right—the claim—to that asset. There is a claim on every asset in a business. As you just read, there are two groups who might have claims to a company's assets: creditors and owners.

Balance sheet: One of the four basic financial statements that shows the financial position of the firm at a specific point in time.

Assets: Economic resources owned by a business as a result of past transactions that will be used in the future to generate benefits for the business.

Accounting equation: Assets = Liabilities + Owners' Equity

In Other Words: The balance sheet is also called the *statement of financial position*.

In Other Words: The accounting equation is sometimes referred to as the *balance sheet equation*.

A balance sheet shows a company's assets, liabilities, and owners' equity at a specific point in time.

Exhibit 1.3

Condensed Balance Sheet for Apple Computer

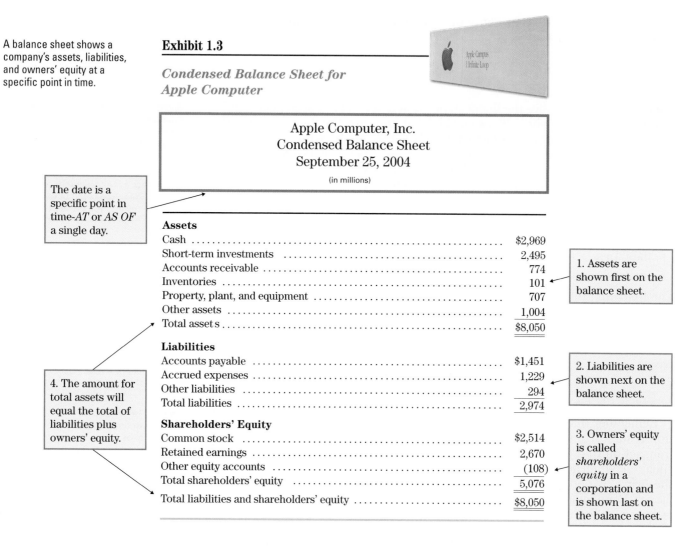

> The date is a specific point in time-*AT* or *AS OF* a single day.

> 4. The amount for total assets will equal the total of liabilities plus owners' equity.

Apple Computer, Inc.
Condensed Balance Sheet
September 25, 2004

(in millions)

Assets

Cash	$2,969
Short-term investments	2,495
Accounts receivable	774
Inventories	101
Property, plant, and equipment	707
Other assets	1,004
Total assets	$8,050

> 1. Assets are shown first on the balance sheet.

Liabilities

Accounts payable	$1,451
Accrued expenses	1,229
Other liabilities	294
Total liabilities	2,974

> 2. Liabilities are shown next on the balance sheet.

Shareholders' Equity

Common stock	$2,514
Retained earnings	2,670
Other equity accounts	(108)
Total shareholders' equity	5,076
Total liabilities and shareholders' equity	$8,050

> 3. Owners' equity is called *shareholders' equity* in a corporation and is shown last on the balance sheet.

Liabilities: Amounts the business owes to creditors; the company's debts.

Study Tip

The word *payable* denotes a liability account.

Owners' equity: Claims of the owner to the firm's assets.

Shareholders' equity (stockholders' equity): Owners' equity of a corporation.

Contributed capital: Equity resulting from the contributions of owners, also known as Paid-in capital.

The claims of creditors are called *liabilities*. **Liabilities** are amounts the business owes to creditors, those who have loaned money to the company and have not yet been fully repaid. Liabilities are the company s debts. For example, the amount of a loan, like a loan Apple might get from the local bank, is a liability, often called a *note payable*. *Accounts Payable*—amounts a firm owes to its suppliers—is Apple's largest liability. The word *payable* always denotes a liability. Like assets, the term *liability* describes a group of accounts. Liability accounts include Accounts Payable, Salaries Payable, and Loans Payable.

The claims of the owners to the firm's assets are called **owners' equity**. Apple has $5,076 million in shareholders' equity. Those are the owners' claims to the firm's assets. For corporations, owners are called shareholders, so owners' equity of a corporation is known as **shareholders' equity**, or **stockholders' equity**.

There are two ways for the owners to increase their claims to the assets of the business. One is by making contributions, and the other is by *earning* the increase. Contributions from owners are called **contributed capital**. The most common type of contributed capital is **common stock**. That's why owners are often called *stockholders*—because they own stock in the company. Stock represents a share of ownership in the firm resulting from the contributions of owners. On the balance sheet, the amount for common stock is part of owners' contributions. You'll learn more about common stock in Chapter 10. When a firm is successful, the equity that results from doing business and is kept in the company rather than paid out to stockholders is called **retained earnings**. You'll see the difference between contributed capital and retained earnings more clearly each time you prepare a balance sheet.

Can **YOU** do it?

1. List the two parts of shareholders' equity.
2. Give the basis for the balance sheet.

Answers (1) Contributed capital and retained earnings (2) The accounting equation: Assets = Liabilities + Owners' Equity

Common stock: A share of ownership in a corporation; the amount owners paid to get the stock is part of contributed capital on the balance sheet.

Retained earnings: Equity that results from doing business and is kept in the company rather than paid out to stockholders.

Income statement

The most well-known financial statement is the *income statement*. The **income statement** is the financial statement that describes the performance of a company during a specific period of time, called an *accounting period*. The income statement shows all the revenues—the amount earned from sales or services—a company earns during an accounting period minus all the costs incurred to earn that revenue. The costs incurred to earn revenue for a specific period of time are called **expenses**. The specific period is often a year. A business year, which may or may not coincide with a calendar year, is called a *fiscal year*.

Recall, the balance sheet gives the amount of assets, the amount of liabilities, and the amount of shareholders' equity of a business at a specific date. In contrast, the income statement describes the activity of a company during an accounting period, which could be any amount of time for which the company wants to report its performance. The accounting period is usually a month, a quarter, or a year. Look at the income statement for Apple Computer in Exhibit 1.4. The first number on the 2004 income statement shows the amount of sales the company made during the year ended September 25, 2004—$8,279 million (that's $8,279,000,000). The expenses shown are for the same period. A firm's

Study Tip

Owners' investments in a firm are contributions from the firm's point of view. These amounts are investments from a shareholders' point of view. When you are learning accounting, always remember to take the *firm's* point of view.

Income statement: The financial statement that describes the financial performance of a company during an accounting period.

Expenses: Costs incurred to earn revenue during an accounting period.

An income statement shows revenue and expenses for a certain period of time. Here the time period is the year ended on September 25, 2004.

Exhibit 1.4

Income Statement for Apple Computer

Apple Computer, Inc.
Condensed Income Statement
For the year ended September 25, 2004
(in millions)

The income statement covers a *period* of time.

A firm's revenue from its sales or services is shown first.

Net sales	$8,279
Operating expenses	
Cost of goods sold	6,020
Research and development	489
Selling, general, and administrative	1,421
Other expenses	73
Net income	$ 276

Expenses follow the revenue, usually with more categories.

Net income is often called the "bottom line."

Net income: The difference between revenues and expenses when revenues exceed expenses for a specific period of time.

In Other Words:
Net income is also known as *net earnings.*

profit for a specific period of time is called **net income**. Apple has broken its revenues and expenses into different categories, and you'll learn more about them as you progress through the book. For now, it's enough to know that the income statement has all the firm's revenues and all the firm's expenses for an accounting period.

Notice two important things about the income statement. First, an income statement covers a period of time. For Apple Computer, it is the fiscal year ended September 25, 2004. Apple's fiscal year ends the last Saturday in September. Second, money contributed by the owners or borrowed from creditors is not shown on the income statement. These sources of funds are not revenue.

The difference between the balance sheet and the income statement

You should get a better idea of the difference between the balance sheet and the income statement by thinking about your own personal finances. If you were asked to prepare a personal balance sheet, you would list all your assets, such as your cash on hand and the cost of your car, clothes, computer, and CD collection. Then, you would list all the people to whom you owe money and how much money you owe to each. This list might include credit card companies and a bank for a car loan. All these assets and liabilities are measured in dollars. You must record a specific date for your balance sheet. For example, if you were listing your assets and liabilities on the last day of 2007, your balance sheet date would be December 31, 2007. Remember the accounting equation:

In Other Words:
The income statement is also called the *statement of earnings*, the *statement of operations*, and the *profit and loss statement* (*P&L*).

Assets = Liabilities + Owners' Equity

If you subtract the amount of your liabilities—what you owe to others—from your assets, the difference is your equity or your net worth in terms of the original cost of the assets. In other words, any increase in the value of your assets since you purchased them will not be reflected in this total. This is the approach accountants use to prepare a balance sheet for a company. Owners' equity is sometimes called the *residual*, which means it is the amount left over after the claims of creditors are deducted from a company's assets. Another way to put this is that your equity is equal to your net assets—the assets remaining after the claims of creditors are subtracted. Exhibit 1.5 shows the types of items that would make up your personal balance sheet.

You have assets—computer, clothes, motorcycle, or car. The amount of money you owe creditors is their claim to your assets. What's left over is your equity. Remember that every item on the balance sheet is given in monetary units—dollars in the United States.

Exhibit 1.5

Your Personal Balance Sheet

Assets		=	Liabilities		+	Owners' Equity
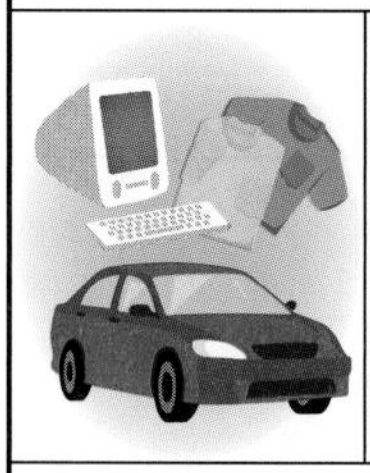	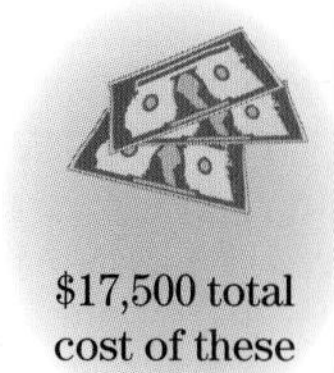 $17,500 total cost of these goods		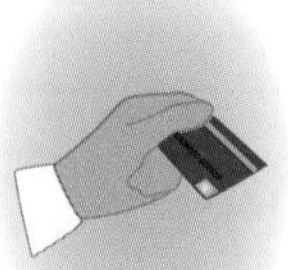	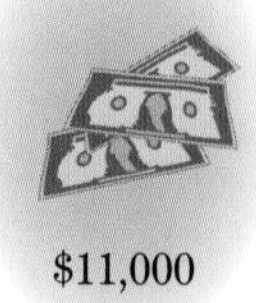 $11,000		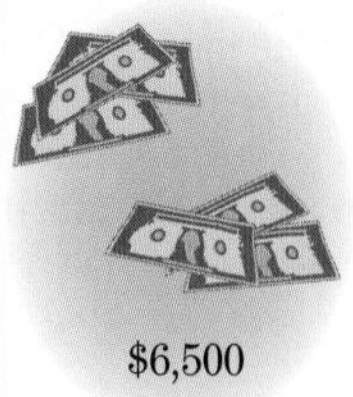 $6,500
These are your assets—items of value.			This is what you owe to creditors.			What's left over is your claim to the assets. It's your net worth—or equity.
Total assets = $17,500			Total liabilities and owner's equity = $17,500			

Compare your balance sheet to an income statement. If you constructed a personal income statement, it would cover a period of time. For example, what was your net income during the year 2007? You'd list all income you earned during the year and then subtract all your expenses during the same year. The difference would be your net income for the year. There's no equation to balance. The income statement lists sources of income and subtracts the related expenses, leaving a difference—positive, you hope—called *net income*. If the subtraction of expenses from revenues results in a negative number, that amount is called a **net loss**.

> **Net loss:** The negative amount that results when expenses are greater than revenues.

> **In Other Words:** A slang expression for net loss is "in the red." That's because accountants used to record a loss with red ink to make it stand out in the accounting records.

 Can **YOU** do it **?**

> Describe the difference in the time periods captured by the income statement and the balance sheet.
>
> *Answer* The income statement covers a period of time, and the balance sheet is at a specific moment in time.

> **Study Tip**
>
> Dividends are not an expense and are not shown on the income statement. They are considered a distribution of earnings.

Statement of changes in shareholders' equity

As its name suggests, the statement of changes in shareholders' equity shows the changes that have taken place in shareholders' equity during a period. For a corporation, the statement is usually called the *statement of changes in shareholders' equity*, because the owners are known as shareholders. The statement starts with the amount of contributed capital on a given balance sheet date and summarizes the additions and subtractions from that amount during a specific period.

The second part of the statement starts with the beginning balance in Retained Earnings and then shows the additions and the deductions made to Retained Earnings during the year. Net income is the most common addition. **Dividends**, which are distributions of the firm's earnings to its shareholders, are the most common deduction. The amount of contributed capital and the balance in Retained Earnings are then added to show the total amount of shareholders' equity at the end of the accounting period.

The change in the amount of retained earnings is only a part of the statement of changes in shareholders' equity, but it is the part that concerns us most in this course. So, you may be asked to prepare only a **statement of retained earnings**. This is a short statement that starts with the amount in Retained Earnings at the beginning of the period, adds net income for the period (or subtracts net loss), deducts dividends, and then shows the ending balance in Retained Earnings. Exhibit 1.6 shows a condensed version of the statement of retained earnings for Apple Computer, Inc.

When a company prepares its annual financial statements, there are several more items that will be included in the statement of changes in shareholders' equity. Because many of the items included on the statement are somewhat advanced, we'll save the details for Chapter 10. For now, think about the statement in the two parts described here: contributed capital and retained earnings.

> **Dividends:** Distributions of a firm's earnings to its shareholders.

> **In Other Words:** The statement of changes in shareholders' equity is often simply called the statement of owners' equity.

> **Statement of retained earnings:** The part of the statement of changes in shareholders' equity that shows how the balance in Retained Earnings changed during the year.

Statement of cash flows

The **statement of cash flows** helps managers form a complete picture of the financial position of a company. The statement is a summary of all the cash that has come into a business—its cash receipts—and all the cash that has gone out of the business—its cash payments—during an accounting period. In other words, the statement of cash flows shows all the cash inflows and all the cash outflows for a

> **Statement of cash flows:** The financial statement that summarizes all the cash that has come into a business—its cash receipts—and all the cash that has gone out of the business—its cash payments—during an accounting period.

The statement of retained earnings is just a part of the statement of changes in shareholders' equity. It shows how the balance in Retained Earnings changed from the beginning-of-the-year balance to the end-of-the-year balance.

Exhibit 1.6

Statement of Retained Earnings for Apple Computer, Inc.

Apple Computer, Inc.
Statement of Retained Earnings
For the year ended September 25, 2004
(in millions)

Retained earnings, September 27, 2003	$2,394
Add net income	276
Deduct dividends	—
Retained earnings, September 25, 2004	$2,670

fiscal period. The statement of cash flows is *not* the same as the income statement for two reasons: (1) accountants measure revenue as the amount the company has earned during the period, even if it is not equal to the amount of cash actually collected; and (2) accountants measure expenses as the costs incurred to generate those revenues, even if they are not the same as the amounts actually paid in cash. The income statement captures the economic effects of transactions, while the statement of cash flows captures the inflows and outflows of cash. For example, if you buy a couple of DVDs at Target and use a Target charge account to pay for your purchase, Target will count that as revenue even though you will not pay them the cash until sometime in the future.

Cash is important to the success of any firm, and it is the statement of cash flows that gives a complete picture of the firm's cash transactions for the period. Exhibit 1.7 shows an abbreviated cash flow statement for Apple Computer, Inc.

You'll see that the statement of cash flows is divided into three sections:

1. cash from operating activities
2. cash from investing activities
3. cash from financing activities

Operating activities: Those cash transactions that pertain to the day-to-day, general running of the business.

The first type of cash flows is from operating activities. **Operating activities** are transactions that pertain to the day-to-day, general running of the business. All of the cash collected from customers and all of the cash paid for operating expenses are included in *cash generated by operating activities.*

Investing activities: Cash transactions related to the purchase and sale of assets that last longer than a year.

The second type of cash flows is from investing activities. **Investing activities** are cash transactions related to the purchase and sale of assets that normally last longer than a year. If Apple Computer decided to purchase, for cash, a building to store its inventory, that purchase would be an investing activity—not an operating activity—because Apple Computer is not in the business of buying and selling buildings. Notice that Apple Computer had a net cash outflow from investing activities during the fiscal year ended in 2004. In 2004, the company spent more cash on the purchase of long-term assets than it received from the sale of long-term assets.

Financing activities: Cash transactions involving a company's long-term creditors or owners—the firm's sources of capital.

The third type of cash flows is from financing activities. **Financing activities** are transactions involving a company's long-term creditors or its owners—the firm's sources of funding. These two sources for financing a business, usually in the

Exhibit 1.7

*From the Statement of Cash Flows
for Apple Computer*

The statement of cash flows is divided into three sections, based on the type of cash flow: (1) cash from operating activities, (2) cash from investing activities, and (3) cash from financing activities.

Apple Computer, Inc.
Summary of the Statement of Cash Flows
For the year ended September 25, 2004
(in millions)

The statement of cash flows is for a period of time, here the fiscal year.

There are three types of cash flows: operating, investing, and financing.

Cash generated by operating activities	$ 934
Cash generated (used for) investing activities	(1,488)
Cash generated by financing activities	127
Increase (decrease) in cash	(427)
Cash at the beginning of the year	3,396
Cash at the end of the year	$2,969

The beginning cash balance is added to the year's net cash flow to give the ending cash balance.

form of cash, are contributions from owners and loans from creditors. Financing outflows include repayment of the principal of loans to creditors and distributions to owners. Both the contributed capital from the owner and the proceeds from the bank loan are financing cash flows. Although the details are not shown in Exhibit 1.7, Apple Computer generated cash from issuing new common stock. Exhibit 1.8 shows the three types of cash flows.

You should begin to see the relationships among the four financial statements. In Chapter 2, we'll discuss each statement in more detail. For now, let's take a brief look at how the financial statements are related.

Study Tip

Any interest paid or received is classified as an operating cash flow.

Exhibit 1.8

Examples of Apple Computer's Cash Flows

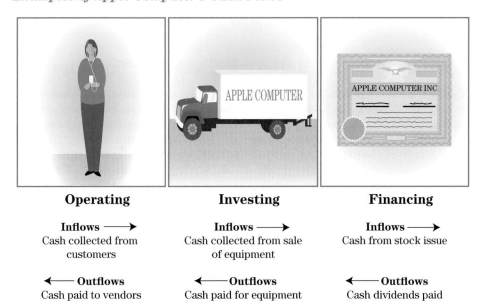

Operating	**Investing**	**Financing**
Inflows ⟶	Inflows ⟶	Inflows ⟶
Cash collected from customers	Cash collected from sale of equipment	Cash from stock issue
⟵ Outflows	⟵ Outflows	⟵ Outflows
Cash paid to vendors	Cash paid for equipment	Cash dividends paid

1. Why is it necessary for a firm to have both an income statement and a statement of cash flows?

2. Explain how the two statements are different.

Answers (1) Revenues and expenses are not necessarily cash transactions. To get a complete picture of a firm's financial position, we need to know both the economic activity, reported on the income statement, and the cash activity, reported on the statement of cash flows. (2) The income statement includes only revenues and expenses for the period, even if the cash was received or paid at a different time. The statement of cash flows includes all cash inflows and outflows for the period. It includes the cash collected and disbursed for operations, and it also includes cash flows from investing and financing activities (which are never included on the income statement).

The relationships among the financial statements

A company engages in transactions during the year. Apple Computer, for example, purchases computer chips, pays employee salaries, pays for magazine advertisements, and receives payment from the sale of its iPods and computers. At its fiscal year-end, the company will take the following steps:

Study Tip

The four financial statements are prepared in the following order: income statement first, statement of changes in shareholders' equity second, balance sheet third, and statement of cash flows last. Keeping that sequence in mind will help you see the relationships among the statements.

1. *Prepare an income statement* showing all of its revenues minus all of its expenses, resulting in net income or net loss.

2. *Prepare a statement of changes in shareholders' equity.* In the retained earnings portion of the statement, the net income from the income statement in Step 1 will be added to the previous year's Retained Earnings balance to bring the balance up-to-date. Dividends, which are not shown on the income statement, are subtracted from Retained Earnings.

3. *Prepare a balance sheet.* The balances at year end in Contributed Capital and Retained Earnings from the statement of shareholders' equity in Step 2 are used in the shareholders' equity section of the balance sheet to get the balance sheet to balance.

4. *Prepare a statement of cash flows* showing how the Cash balance on the balance sheet, from Step 3, changed during the year. All of the year's cash transactions are shown, and the statement shows how the prior year's Cash balance combined with the current year's cash transactions results in the Cash balance you see on the year-end balance sheet.

Exhibit 1.9 shows how Apple's financial statements fit together.

Reporting to the Securities and Exchange Commission

Publicly traded corporations sell their stock in the public stock exchanges like the New York Stock Exchange (NYSE). These corporations must prepare the four basic financial statements and extensive accompanying notes every year and submit them to the Securities and Exchange Commission (SEC). The SEC makes these statements and notes available to the public on its web site (www.sec.gov).

10-K: A comprehensive summary of a company's performance firms are required to submit to the SEC within 60 days of the end of the company's fiscal year.

One of the most important filings a company must make to the SEC is the **10-K**. Part of a 10-K is a company's audited financial statements, without the sales pitch and story found in its glossy annual report. Compare Wal-Mart's annual report to Target's 10-K, both in the back of the book, to see some of the differences. The 10-K also includes information you won't find in most annual reports, like insider stock holdings and brief biographies of the management team. The report must be filed within 60 days after the end of the company's fiscal year.

Exhibit 1.9

Relationships Among the Financial Statements

1. The income statement is prepared first by taking total revenue and subtracting all expenses for an accounting period.

Apple Computer, Inc.
Income Statement
For the year ended September 25, 2004
(in millions)

Net sales.	$8,279
Operating expenses	
Cost of goods sold	6,020
Research and development	489
Selling, general, and administrative.	1,421
Other expenses	73
Net income	$ 276

2. Net income is used to calculate the ending balance in Retained Earnings.

Apple Computer, Inc.
Statement of Retained Earnings
For the year ended September 25, 2004
(in millions)

Retained earnings, September 27, 2003.	$2,394
Add net income.	276
Deduct dividends	—
Retained earnings, September 25, 2004.	$2,670

Apple Computer, Inc.
Condensed Balance Sheet
At September 25, 2004
(in millions)

Assets	
Cash	$2,969
Short-term investments	2,495
Accounts receivable	774
Inventories.	101
Property, plant, and equipment	707
Other assets.	1,004
Total assets	$8,050
Liabilities	
Accounts payable.	$1,451
Accrued expenses	1,229
Other liabilities.	294
Total liabilities	2,974
Common stock	2,514
Retained earnings.	2,670
Other equity accounts.	(108)
Total shareholders' equity	5,076
Total liabilities and shareholders' equity	$8,050

Apple Computer, Inc.
Summary of the Statement of Cash Flows
For the year ended September 25, 2004
(in millions)

Cash at the beginning of the year.	$3,396
Cash generated by operating activities	934
Cash generated by (used for) investing activities	(1,488)
Cash generated by financing activities	127
Increase (decrease) in cash.	(427)
Cash at the end of the year	$2,969

4. The Statement of Cash Flows gives the details of how the company ended up with this amount of cash on its year—end balance sheet.

3. The balance in Retained Earnings is used in the Shareholders' Equity section of the Balance Sheet, which is the 3rd statement to be prepared.

Financial Statement Analysis

Both internal and external financial statement users analyze the information on financial statements, and they often make comparisons between periods of time and between companies in their analysis. A **ratio** is an expression of a mathematical relationship between one quantity and another. For example, a manager may want to measure the relationship between sales revenue and operating expenses. If operating expenses were 60% of revenue in Year 1 and

LEARNING OBJECTIVE 4

Explain financial statement analysis and the use of ratio analysis.

Ratio: An expression of a mathematical relationship between one quantity and another.

Accounting in the NEWS

Financial Statement Analysis

What Does a Financial Analyst Do?

Before buying or selling stock in a company, a potential investor should evaluate that company's past financial performance and the company's future goals for creating new or improved products or expanding into new markets. Many investors rely on financial analysts to provide this information. According to the 2004–05 *Occupational Outlook Handbook* of the Bureau of Labor Statistics, financial analysts and personal financial advisors held 298,000 jobs in 2002. Financial analysts often have degrees in accounting, and the outlook for jobs in this area is excellent.

According to the Bureau of Labor Statistics, faster-than-average employment growth for financial analysts and personal financial advisors is expected through 2012.

Financial analysts face keen competition for jobs, especially at top securities firms such as Merrill Lynch, where pay can be six figures. Perhaps you should consider majoring in accounting! These accounting specialists gather financial information, analyze it, and make recommendations to their clients. They read company financial statements, meet with company officials, assess trends in the industry, and keep abreast of new regulations that may affect the industry.

Q. What are some important sources of information for financial analysts?

A Sources include a firm's financial statements, industry data, and officials from the firm.

According to Princetonreview.com, financial analyst candidates must be able to meet and interact with clients, handle a heavy work load, prioritize and complete work under strict deadlines, work as part of a team, and work with computer spreadsheet and other programs.

Source: "Financial Analysts and Personal Financial Advisors," *Occupational Outlook Handbook*, 2004–05 Edition, May 17, 2004, www.bls.gov/oco.

70% of revenue in Year 2, the manager would be concerned. A ratio comparing the two quantities can be computed for several periods, and the trend will provide information managers can use to evaluate operations. When users of financial statements compute ratios to analyze a firm's past performance and forecast its future performance, it is called **ratio analysis**. In each chapter, you will learn about ratios that are commonly used to evaluate and compare companies. Learning these ratios will help you interpret financial statements. Analysts compare the amounts on a single financial statement, as well as the amounts on different firms' financial statements.

Managers, investors, and other financial statement users analyze the information in financial statements. However, there are actually accountants who analyze financial statements as a career. Read *Accounting in the News* for information about what a financial analyst does. Perhaps this is an accounting career you'd like to consider.

> **Ratio analysis:** Using ratios to analyze a firm's past performance and forecast its future performance.

LEARNING OBJECTIVE 5

Recognize the risks associated with being in business and how to control those risks.

Business risk, control, & ethics

You will see a business risk, control, and ethics section in every chapter. It is important for you to read this material because it will help you see the relationship between business and accounting. Both errors and fraud can be reduced by understanding the risks associated with a particular business activity and knowing what controls can reduce the risks. As a current or future manager, this is important knowledge for you to have.

By now, you know what a business does and how it communicates financial information. Maybe you'd like to have your own business. Starting a business is more than having a good idea and obtaining financing. These steps are a good beginning, but they must be followed with sound business planning for acquiring goods and services and selling the company's products or services. Part of that planning is identifying the risks involved.

What is a risk?

A risk may be generally defined as anything that exposes us to potential injury or loss. In business, risks can turn into significant financial losses, scandals, or total company failure. There are hundreds of risks that any business faces. Here are a few examples:

- the risk of product failure that might result in the death of consumers
- the risk that an employee or customer will steal assets from the company
- the risk that poor-quality inventory will be purchased and sold

Before we discuss the details of the business activities in the chapters to follow, think about the risks of being in business and how people who want to start a business can minimize the risks. Read the ***Accounting in the News*** feature to learn about the risks that face small businesses and how they can minimize those risks.

Why do people take risks? Every risk brings a potential reward. An entrepreneur like Steve Jobs put his money and his reputation at risk to start Apple Computer. Why? For the potential of developing a successful business. To deal with the risks and increase the chances to reap the rewards, a firm must establish and maintain control over its operations, assets, and information system. A *control* is an activity performed to minimize or eliminate a risk. Controls inside a company are called *internal controls*. Controls are not simply designed to minimize risks by preventing errors but to prevent fraud as well. In the Firestone tire case, the firm suffered from more than the risk of a faulty product. There were accusations of unethical conduct by the firm's managers in an effort to

Bridgestone/Firestone, Inc., testified before the Senate Commerce Committee in 2002 about the recall of an estimated 6.5 million tires. Here, Congressman Fred Upton of Michigan displays a Firestone tire with a tread separation that came off a friend's Ford Explorer. Faulty Firestone tires were blamed for 148 deaths, mostly involving Ford Motor Company's Explorer Sport-utility vehicles.

Accounting in the NEWS

Risk and Control

What Creates the Most Risk for a Small Business?

Have you ever thought about starting your own business? If you have, it's important that you recognize the risks involved. Did you know that *80 percent* of all new small businesses fail in their first five years? According to the Bureau of Labor Statistics, most small business failures occur in the first two years. You can minimize the risk of failure by knowing the reasons businesses fail. According to Michael Gerber, CEO of an international small business consulting firm, these are the top three:

1. *Lack of management systems.* Too often people start a business

without a way to evaluate what is and what is not working. It's all about information.

2. *Lack of vision and purpose by the principals.* Successful entrepreneurs have a purpose or goal, and the business is the way to achieve it.

3. *Lack of financial planning and review.* Do your accounting homework. Understand the difference between generating income and building equity.

There are plenty of resources to help you start your business. Go to www.sba.gov for the Small Business Administration's resources and lots of excellent links to help you start your business.

Q Name the top three reasons why small businesses fail.

A Lack of management systems, lack of vision and purpose, and lack of financial planning and review.

Why do 80 percent of small businesses fail?

Sources: "Business Failure Rates Higher in the First Two Years," *Small Business Trends,* July 7, 2005, http://www.smallbusinesses.blogspot.com/; "Why a Large Number of Small Businesses Fail," *Home Office Computing,* May, 1994, p. 16.

hide problems with the faulty tires. Controls are designed to minimize risks, but nothing can substitute for firm values and ethics.

As we study the variety of business transactions a company engages in, we'll look at how managers can control the risks involved in each transaction.

Ethics in financial reporting and the Sarbanes-Oxley Act of 2002

One of the biggest risks of being in business is losing investor confidence. This is true for a small business owner and for the world's largest corporation. Publicly traded firms can lose more than customers. If investors don't want to buy a company's stock, the stock price will plummet. This will make it difficult for a company to raise the money it might need to expand or develop new products or technologies. To minimize this risk, a business must avoid fraud at all costs and adhere to the highest ethical standards. The scandals that came to light in the early 2000s stunned the financial world and seriously reduced investor confidence, and that hurt all businesses. These scandals included Enron, WorldCom, Tyco, ImClone, Adelphia, Rite Aid, and Krispy Kreme. The scandals have raised serious questions about accounting practices of these companies and the financial reporting practices of all companies.

Sarbanes-Oxley (SOX) Act of 2002: A law passed by Congress that sets new regulations for the ways corporations govern themselves, including requirements to make a corporation's internal controls more effective and procedures for increasing the understandability of financial reporting.

In response to the financial reporting scandals uncovered in 2001 and 2002, the United States Congress passed a new law—the **Sarbanes-Oxley (SOX) Act of 2002**—to address, among others, the problems with financial reporting. Sarbanes-Oxley set new regulations for the ways corporations govern themselves (formally called *corporate governance*), including requirements to make a corporation's internal controls more effective and procedures to increase the transparency of financial reporting. This new law brings serious, sweeping changes to corporate governance. We'll learn more about corporate governance and the difficulties of implementing the SOX Act in Chapter 13.

The demand for auditing

When reading about the business scandals, perhaps you've seen the question, "Where were the auditors?" Auditors are certified public accountants (CPAs) whose job it is to examine a company's financial statements and attest to the fair presentation of the financial position and financial performance of the company. That examination is called an **audit**. For a well-functioning economy, investors must have confidence in the information they receive about the companies that raise money in the marketplace. This need creates a demand for auditing. The SEC requires an annual, independent audit for every publicly traded company. Private companies may also need an audit—for the owners or possible investors.

Audit: An examination of a company's financial statements by certified public accountants to provide evidence that the financial position and the financial performance of the company are fairly stated.

The Enron debacle resulted in the demise of one of the oldest and most respected auditing firms in the world, Andersen. Not only was Andersen accused of failing to perform an adequate audit of Enron's financial statements, the firm was also accused of shredding documents in an effort to conceal its actions. Many people wondered where the auditors were while Enron was violating its own company policy and violating GAAP to keep debt off of its balance sheet. Although this scandal and others that followed have created questions about both accounting standards and auditing procedures, the demand for auditing is stronger than ever.

Accompanying every public company's annual financial statements is an audit opinion. Exhibit 1.10 shows the audit opinion from the most recent financial statements of Apple Computer, Inc. Read the audit opinion shown in the exhibit and think about whether or not it increases your confidence in the reliability of the financial statements.

Every public company is required to have an annual audit. The audit report will accompany the annual financial statements in the annual report and the 10-K. The language is very precise because the SEC and auditing firms want investors to know that there is no guarantee that the statements are error-free.

Exhibit 1.10

Report of the Independent Auditors for Apple Computer, Inc.

REPORT OF INDEPENDENT REGISTERED PUBLIC ACCOUNTING FIRM

The Board of Directors and Shareholders
Apple Computer, Inc.:

> *Consolidated* means that financial information from any companies owned or controlled by Apple have been included in Apple's financial statements.

We have audited the accompanying consolidated balance sheets of Apple Computer, Inc. and subsidiaries as of September 25, 2004 and September 27, 2003, and the related consolidated statements of operations, shareholders' equity, and cash flows for each of the years in the three-year period ended September 25, 2004. These consolidated financial statements are the responsibility of the Company's management. Our responsibility is to express an opinion on these consolidated financial statements based on our audits.

> What do you think *reasonable assurance* means?

We conducted our audits in accordance with the standards of the Public Company Accounting Oversight Board (United States). Those standards require that we plan and perform the audit to obtain reasonable assurance about whether the financial statements are free of material misstatement. An audit includes examining, on a test basis, evidence supporting the amounts and disclosures in the consolidated financial statements. An audit also includes assessing the accounting principles used and significant estimates made by management, as well as evaluating the overall financial statement presentation. We believe that our audits provide a reasonable basis for our opinion.

> What does it mean for the statements to *present fairly*?

In our opinion, the consolidated financial statements referred to above present fairly, in all material respects, the financial position of Apple Computer, Inc. and subsidiaries as of September 25, 2004 and September 27, 2003, and the results of their operations and their cash flows for each of the years in the three-year period ended September 25, 2004, in conformity with U.S. generally accepted accounting principles.

As discussed in Note 1 to the consolidated financial statements, the Company changed its method of accounting for asset retirement obligations and for financial instruments with characteristics of both liabilities and equity in 2003 and changed its method of accounting for goodwill in 2002.

KPMG LLP
Mountain View, California
October 12, 2004

YOU make the call:

Who owns Apple Computer, Inc.?

We started this chapter with a question about who owns Apple Computer. When Apple began, there were just two owners. In 1977, partners Steve Jobs and Steve Wozniak formally incorporated their business. Then, the two owners made the stock available to selected employees and friends, so there were several "owners" but none owned as much of Apple Computer as the two original partners. Then, on December 12, 1980, the company offered its stock for sale on the NASDAQ Stock Exchange. That day, everyone who purchased shares in Apple Computer became an owner of the company. Today, a little more than 60% of the stock of Apple Computer, Inc. is held by large investors (pension plans and investment companies); less than 2% is held by insider investors who work for the company. Perhaps, you and I hold a share or two and are among the owners of Apple Computer, Inc.

Let's Take a Test Drive

The final section of each chapter summarizes the chapter's key concepts and gives you an opportunity to test your understanding. These sections will help you make sure you understand what you have learned before moving on to the next chapter.

Real-World Problem:
Apple Computer

Steve Jobs and Steve Wozniak had a creative idea to design a product that millions of people would want. It took more than a great idea, however, to make Apple Computer what it is today. Today Apple Computer, Inc., is a FORTUNE 500 company (#301 in 2004), with revenues of $8,279 million and profits of $276 million. One of its best-known products is the iPod, a digital music player. In the first three months of its 2005 fiscal year, Apple shipped over four and a half million iPods. That's a 525% increase from the same quarter of 2004.

Concepts

Apple Computer began when Jobs and Wozniak acquired financing to start the company. The firm used the financing to lease office space, buy computer parts, and pay skilled employees. Information about these business activities—acquiring financing, leasing property, purchasing parts, and hiring labor—is presented in four major financial statements and the accompanying notes. After being in business for a period of time, Apple provided these financial statements to people external to the firm: investors, creditors, employees, and customers.

The Mechanics

Suppose the following transactions occurred during Apple Computer, Inc.'s first month of business (after the company incorporated but had not offered the stock to the public). (All transactions are fictitious.):

1. Steve Jobs and Steve Wozniak together contributed $50,000 from their former partnership to start Apple Computer, Inc. In return, the corporation issued 100 shares of common stock to each of them.
2. The company paid $20,000 cash for parts for new computers that it planned to make during the next few months.
3. The company rented office space for the month for $350 cash.
4. The company hired and paid employees for work done during the month for a total of $1,500.
5. The company sold computers for $40,000 cash. (These computers were made from the parts the company purchased in number 2 above.)
6. The company paid $400 in dividends to its shareholders.
7. On the last day of the month, the company purchased $12,000 worth of office furniture and equipment on credit. (Apple signed a 60-day note—borrowed the money—from the furniture and equipment company.)

Instructions

1. For each transaction, tell whether the related accounting information will affect the income statement, the balance sheet, or both.
2. For each transaction, tell whether it is an operating, investing, or financing activity.
3. For each transaction, identify an asset or a liability that is affected by the transaction, and tell whether it is an increase or a decrease to the asset or liability you named.

Solution

Transaction	Is the balance sheet or income statement affected?	Which cash flow activity?	Which asset or liability is affected?
1. Steve Jobs and Steve Wozniak together contributed $50,000 cash to start Apple Computer, Inc. In return, the corporation issued 100 shares of common stock to each of them.	Balance sheet	Financing	Asset: Cash—increased
2. The company paid $20,000 cash for parts for new computers that it planned to make during the next few months.	Balance sheet	Operating	Assets: Inventory—increased; Cash—decreased
3. The company rented office space for the month for $350 cash.	Balance sheet and income statement	Operating	Asset: Cash—decreased
4. The company hired and paid employees for work done during the month for a total of $1,500.	Balance sheet and income statement	Operating	Asset: Cash—decreased
5. The company sold computers for $40,000 cash. (These computers were made from the parts the company purchased in #2 above.)	Balance sheet and income statement	Operating	Asset: Cash—increased; Inventory—decreased
6. The company paid $400 in dividends to its shareholders.	Balance sheet	Financing	Asset: Cash—decreased
7. On the last day of the month, the company purchased $12,000 worth of office furniture and equipment on credit. (Apple signed a 60-day note with the furniture and equipment company.)	Balance sheet	Investing	Assets: Equipment and furniture—increased; Liability: Notes Payable—increased

Rapid Review

"Rapid Review" summarizes the key points of the chapter and ties those points back to the learning objectives that opened the chapter. Read this section before you move on to the next chapter.

1. **Define accounting and explain why accounting information is important.** Accounting is the process of identifying, measuring, and communicating financial business information to various users. Accounting information captures and summarizes a firm's financial transactions and provides information about revenues and expenses to people who use this information to make decisions.

2. **Identify the users of accounting information, and explain how financial accounting standards are determined.** Business owners and managers, creditors, potential investors, customers, employees, vendors, and governmental agencies all use accounting information to evaluate a firm's financial condition and performance. The financial statements are based on a set of guidelines called *generally accepted accounting principles (GAAP)*. Congress has given the authority for setting accounting standards to the SEC. The SEC shares the task with the FASB, an independent standards-setting body.

3. **Explain the contents of the four basic financial statements.** There are four basic financial statements: the income statement, the balance sheet, the statement of changes in owners' equity, and the statement of cash flows. The accompanying notes are also a part of the firm's financial statements.
   - The *income statement* shows a firm's performance for a period of time. It consists of Revenues and Expenses, and the difference is Net Income.

- The *statement of changes in owners' equity* shows the changes in Owners' Equity—both Contributed Capital and Retained Earnings—for a period of time.
- The *balance sheet* presents the financial position of the firm at a specific point in time. The *accounting equation*, Assets = Liabilities + Owners' Equity, is the basis of the balance sheet.
- The *statement of cash flows* presents all the cash inflows and outflows for a period of time. It accounts for the difference between the balances in Cash on the balance sheets at the end of two consecutive accounting periods.

4. **Explain financial statement analysis and the use of ratio analysis.** *Financial statement analysis* is the process of analyzing the information in the four financial statements and the accompanying notes to evaluate a company's past performance and predict its future performance. The most common tool for this analysis is the use of ratios. *Ratios* are comparisons of various financial statement amounts that are used to evaluate companies of different sizes and types.

5. **Recognize the risks associated with being in business and how to control those risks.** Being in business presents risk to its owners. The most common reason businesses fail are (1) lack of management systems, (2) lack of vision and purpose by the owners, and (3) lack of financial planning and review. In this course, we'll focus on the third reason. The Sarbanes-Oxley Act of 2002 was passed in an effort to reduce misleading financial reporting.

Key Terms

10-K, p. 18
Accounting, p. 4
Accounting equation, p. 11
Assets, p. 11
Audit, p. 22
Balance sheet, p. 11
Certified public accountant (CPA) , p. 8
Common stock, p. 12
Contributed capital, p. 12
Dividends, p. 15
Expenses, p. 13
Financial Accounting Standards Board (FASB), p. 10
Financing activities, p. 16
Generally accepted accounting principles (GAAP), p. 9

Income statement, p. 13
Inventory, p. 6
Investing activities, p. 16
Liabilities, p. 12
Monetary unit assumption, p. 10
Net income, p. 14
Net loss, p. 15
Notes to the financial statements, p. 10
Operating activities, p. 16
Operating cycle, p. 7
Owners' equity, p. 12
Profit, p. 6
Public Company Accounting Oversight Board (PCAOB), p. 10
Ratio, p. 19
Ratio analysis, p. 20

Retained earnings, p. 13
Revenue, p. 6
Sarbanes-Oxley Act (SOX), p. 22
Securities and Exchange Commission (SEC), p. 9
Shareholders' equity (Stockholders' equity), p. 12
Statement of cash flows, p. 15
Statement of retained earnings, p. 15
Transaction, p. 4

Have You Increased Your Business IQ?

Answer these questions to find out.

1. A financial statement audit is
   a. An internal review of the firm's financial risks
   b. An independent review of the firm's financial statements
   c. A report to the SEC also known as a 10-K
   d. A report on the firm's sources and uses of cash
2. The balance sheet is
   a. A financial statement that reports a firm's performance over a period of time
   b. A financial statement that reports the firm's inflows and outflows of cash
   c. A financial statement that shows how shareholders' equity has changed during a period of time
   d. A financial statement that shows a firm's financial position at a point in time

3. The Securities and Exchange Commission is
   a. A governmental agency responsible for financial reporting of publicly traded firms
   b. An elected body that sets accounting standards
   c. A group of financial experts that set the rules for the way firms spend their excess cash
   d. A congressional committee charged with overseeing the accounting profession
4. A CPA is an accountant who
   a. Prepares tax returns
   b. Helps firms with their accounting
   c. Is certified to be an auditor
   d. Any or all of the above
5. The purpose of the Sarbanes-Oxley Act of 2002 is to
   a. Prevent all corporate fraud
   b. Punish firms like Enron and WorldCom for their misleading financial statements
   c. Make financial reporting more understandable and dependable
   d. Make sure accountants are fully employed for years to come

Now, check your answers.

1. b   2. d   3. a   4. d   5. c

- If you answered all 5 questions correctly, you've increased your business IQ by studying this chapter. It doesn't mean you've mastered all of the accounting concepts in the chapter. It simply means that you understand some of the general business concepts presented in this chapter.
- If you answered 2 to 4 questions correctly, you've made some progress but your business IQ has plenty of room to grow. You might want to skim over the chapter again.
- If you answered 0 or 1 question correctly, you can do more to improve your business IQ. Better study the chapter again.

Questions

1. Define accounting.
2. What is the purpose of a business?
3. Do all businesses share the goal of making a profit? Explain your answer.
4. Does a not-for-profit organization need to generate a profit? Explain your answer.
5. Identify some of the people who need business information. Why do they need business information?
6. Name the four basic financial statements.
7. Describe the information that each of the four basic financial statements provides.
8. What is contributed capital? Why is it important to a business?
9. What are generally accepted accounting principles (GAAP)?
10. What group of people is responsible for establishing GAAP?
11. What makes the income statement different from the statement of cash flows?
12. What are some of the risks associated with being in business?
13. Describe the purpose of the Sarbanes-Oxley Act.
14. What is financial statement analysis? Who conducts financial statement analysis and for what purpose?

Multiple Choice

1. The accounting equation says that the dollar amount of assets must equal
   a. The dollar amount of equity
   b. The dollar amount of cash
   c. The dollar amount of liabilities plus the dollar amount of equity
   d. Can never be greater than the dollar amount of equity
2. Which financial statement is based on the accounting equation?
   a. The income statement
   b. The balance sheet
   c. The statement of changes in shareholders' equity
   d. The statement of cash flows
3. The Puppy Store acquires 50 doggie beds from a supplier for $500 in cash. For the statement of cash flows, what type of transaction is this?
   a. Financing
   b. Investing
   c. Operating
   d. Sales

4. The two parts of owners' equity are
   a. Assets and liabilities
   b. Net income and common stock
   c. Contributed capital and retained earnings
   d. Revenues and expenses
5. Tom started a business by investing $5,000 of his own money. Then, the business borrowed $3,000 from Tom's uncle. How much equity does the new business have?
   a. $8,000
   b. $5,000
   c. $3,000
   d. $2,000
6. A company borrowed $5,000 cash from the National Bank. As a result of this transaction
   a. Assets would decrease by $5,000
   b. Liabilities would increase by $5,000
   c. Equity would increase by $5,000
   d. Revenue would increase by $5,000
7. When a company pays workers in cash, how is the cash outflow classified on the statement of cash flows?
   a. Cash from investing activities
   b. Cash from input activities
   c. Cash from financing activities
   d. Cash from operating activities
8. During its first year of business, West Company earned service revenue of $2,000 cash. What financial statement(s) will reflect this transaction?
   a. Balance sheet (cash)
   b. Income statement (revenue)
   c. Statement of cash flows (operating cash flow)
   d. All of the above
9. During the first year of business, Deto Company paid $3,000 cash dividends to its two shareholders. On which financial statement will the $3,000 explicitly appear?
   a. The income statement
   b. The statement of cash flows
   c. The balance sheet
   d. All of the above statements
10. The balance sheet of United Studios at December 31 showed assets of $30,000 and owners' equity of $20,000. What were the liabilities at December 31?
    a. $10,000
    b. $20,000
    c. $30,000
    d. $50,000

Short Exercises

LO 1

SE1-1. Importance of accounting.

What does a business do, and why is accounting information needed to support those activities?

LO 2

SE1-2. Identify users of accounting information.

Describe possible ways each of the following would use accounting information to evaluate a firm's financial performance:

a. Bank loan officer.
b. Potential investor
c. Financial analyst
d. Potential supplier
e. SEC

LO 2

SE1-3. Accounting rules.

Match the following groups with the correct description.

Group	Description
SEC	Has the ultimate authority for setting accounting standards.
FASB	Governmental agency assigned responsibility for accounting standards for publicly traded companies.
Congress	Established by the Sarbanes-Oxley Act to police auditors.
PCAOB	Private sector group that establishes most accounting rules.

LO 3

SE1-4. Classify financial statement items.

Classify each item listed according to the balance sheet headings of assets, liabilities, or owners' equity.

a. Cash
b. Contributions from owners
c. Inventory
d. Land and buildings
e. Notes payable
f. Retained earnings

SE1-5. Calculate missing amount.   LO 3
Given the following items and amounts on ABC Company's December 31, 2007 balance sheet, how much cash did ABC have on hand on December 31, 2007?

Cash	?
Inventory	$100
Equipment	$400
Liabilities	$450
Owners' equity	$650

SE1-6. Calculate missing amount.   LO 3
Given the following items on Tif Company's December 31, 2006 balance sheet, how much did the company owe its creditors on December 31, 2006?

Cash	$ 1,725	Liabilities	?
Inventory	223		
Equipment	10,647	Contributed capital	$9,300
Other assets	8,235	Retained earnings	5,000
Total	$20,830		

SE1-7. Calculate missing amount.   LO 3
For each of the following, calculate the missing amount:

a. Revenues $560; Expenses $350; Net Income = _____
b. Net Income $500; Expenses $475; Revenues = _____
c. Expenses $600; Revenues $940; Net Income = _____
d. Revenues $1,240; Net Income $670; Expenses = _____
e. Net Income $6,450; Expenses $2,500; Revenues = _____

SE1-8. Calculate owners' equity.   LO 3
Donkey Doughnut Company shows $125,000 worth of assets on its December 31, 2006 balance sheet. If the company's total liabilities are $35,750, what is the amount of owners' equity?

SE1-9. Calculate owners' equity.   LO 3
Logan Enterprises has $50,000 in cash, $10,000 in inventory, $20,000 balance due to creditors, and $15,000 balance due from customers. What is the amount of owners' equity?

SE1-10. Calculate owners' equity.   LO 3
Given the amounts for the balance sheet on December 31, 2007, how much owners' equity did College Bookstore have on December 31, 2007?

Cash	$200
Inventory	$500
Other Assets	$300
Accounts Payable	$100
Notes Payable	$ 50
Salaries Payable	$100
Owners' Equity	?

SE1-11. Calculate retained earnings.   LO 3
After its first year of business, Holt's Computer Repair, Inc., had $6,000 in assets, $3,000 in liabilities, and $1,000 in contributed capital. What is the amount of retained earnings at the end of the corporation's first year of business?

SE1-12. Calculate retained earnings.   LO 3
Lester's Music Store had a Retained Earnings balance of $1,000 on December 31, 2006. For the year ended December 31, 2007, sales were $12,500 and expenses were $6,500. Cash dividends of $2,000 were distributed on December 31, 2007. What was the amount of retained earnings on December 31, 2007?

SE1-13. Calculate net income (loss).   LO 3
Sue King started a business with $10,000 of personal savings and $5,000 from the bank. The company earned $6,000 cash from services provided. The rent expense is $450 monthly. The company also paid employees $4,000 during the month. Did Sue's new business make a profit during the first month of business? If so, how much?

SE1-14. Identify and classify financial statement items.   LO 3
Hold Me produces carrying cases for the Apple iPod. The items given below were shown on Hold Me's financial statements presented in the company's 2005 annual

report. For each item, give the type of financial statement item (asset, liability, owners' equity, revenue, expense) and the financial statement on which it appears.

    a. Interest Expense
    b. Accounts Receivable
    c. Equipment
    d. Paid-in Capital
    e. Sales Revenue

LO 5   **SE1-15. Identify business risks.**

Give three risks of being in business and what can be done to minimize those risks.

Exercise Set A

LO 1, 2, 3   **E1-1A. Analyze a balance sheet.**

Use the balance sheet for Pet Specialty Supplies, Inc., at December 31, 2005 to answer the following questions:

Balance Sheet
Pet Specialty Supplies, Inc.
At December 31, 2005

Assets		Liabilities and Owners' Equity	
Cash	$ 3,000	Accounts Payable	$ 1,500
Short-term Investments	30	Notes Payable (van)	12,500
Accounts Receivable	465		
Inventory	725	Paid-in capital	2,000
Prepaid Insurance	500	Retained Earnings	4,020
Prepaid Rent	300		
Mobile Grooming Van (net)	15,000		
	$20,020		$20,020

    a. List the assets the company had on December 31, 2005. Who had claim to these assets?
    b. List the liabilities the company had on December 31, 2005.
    c. Who are the potential users of this financial information?

LO 3   **E1-2A. Identify business activities.**

For each of the following transactions of Charlie's Hot Dogs, tell whether it is an operating, investing, or financing activity on the statement of cash flows. (Assume all transactions are for cash.)

    a. Charlie's Hot Dogs was started with a contribution from Charlie of $2,000 and a loan of $1,000 from the bank.
    b. Charlie's Hot Dogs purchased $1,000 worth of hot dogs and buns (his inventory) for cash.
    c. Charlie's Hot Dogs hired a friend with a steamer to cook the hot dogs and deliver a portion of them ready to sell to him at noon each day. For this service, Charlie's Hot Dogs paid $30 each day for a total of five days.
    d. Charlie's Hot Dogs sold all of his hot dog and bun inventory for total cash revenues of $4,000.
    e. Charlie's Hot Dogs paid the city a $25 fee, due monthly, for his license.
    f. Charlie's Hot Dogs repaid $200 of the bank loan along with $10 of interest for the first month.

LO 3   **E1-3A. Analyze effect on shareholders' equity.**

For each of the following transactions of the Hard Rock Candy Corporation, tell whether it (1) increases, (2) decreases, or (3) has no effect on shareholders' equity. Consider both shareholders' equity components—contributed capital and retained earnings.

    a. Two friends get together, each contributing $5,000 to start the Hard Rock Candy Corporation.
    b. Hard Rock purchases equipment for $1,000 cash.
    c. Hard Rock purchases $6,000 worth of supplies for cash.
    d. Hard Rock pays expenses of $2,000 for electricity and phone for the month.
    e. Hard Rock makes cash sales to customers of $4,500 during the month.

f. Hard Rock pays employees $300 for hours worked during the month.
g. Hard Rock declares and distributes $500 of dividends to each of its owners at the end of the month.

E1-4A. Identify cash flows.   LO 3
For each of the transactions in E1-3A, tell whether it is an operating, investing, or financing cash flow.

E1-5A. Identify income statement transactions.   LO 3
Tell whether or not each of the following transactions of Joe's Auto Repair will be reflected on the income statement. For each transaction that does affect income, tell whether it increases or decreases net income.

a. Joe's issues checks for the salaries of its employees.
b. Joe's purchases a building.
c. Joe's earns revenue from providing services to customers.
d. Joe's borrows money from a local bank, signing a five-year note payable.
e. Joe's pays dividends to its shareholders.

E1-6A. Identify balance sheet transactions.   LO 3
Which of the following transactions will affect assets, liabilities, or both? For each item that does affect one or both of these balance sheet accounts, tell whether it is an increase or decrease.

a. A company repays a loan plus interest.
b. A company receives cash from customers.
c. A company issues new stock for cash.
d. A company pays dividends to its shareholders.

E1-7A. Identify business activities.   LO 3
Assume each of the following transactions of Pony D Riding Stables is a cash transaction. Tell how each cash flow would be classified on the statement of cash flows: (1) operating, (2) investing, or (3) financing.

a. Dedee makes a contribution of $100,000 from her personal funds to start the Pony D Riding Stables.
b. The company purchases three horses and some equipment for $35,000 in cash.
c. The company purchases $6,000 worth of advertising time on the local radio station for cash.
d. The company pays rent of $10,000 for barn and pasture space as well as use of 50 acres of land for riding trails.
e. The company pays several people to clean stables at a cost of $500 for the month.
f. The first customers pay Pony D Riding Stables $3,000 for six months' worth of riding lessons.

E1-8A. Identify business activities.   LO 3
For each of the following transactions of Blue Box Corporation, tell whether it is an operating activity, an investing activity, or a financing activity.

a. Blue Box received $10,000 in sales revenues.
b. Blue Box paid $30,000 cash for a new piece of equipment.
c. Blue Box paid $2,500 of a $5,000 notes payable to creditors.
d. Blue Box paid $1,500 for rent expense.
e. Blue Box's owner provided $8,000 in additional financing.
f. Blue Box distributed $2,000 in dividends.

E1-9A. Analyze effect of business transactions on assets.   LO 3
For each of the following transactions of Front End Fashions, Inc. determine if there is an increase, decrease, or no effect on assets.

a. Front End Fashions sold inventory that cost $15,000 for $25,000 cash.
b. Front End Fashions purchased land for $20,500 and financed the purchase at the bank.
c. Front End Fashions paid monthly rent of $1,200.
d. Front End Fashions paid its associates wages of $4,500.
e. Front End Fashions paid $1,000 toward the bank loan; $900 of the payment was principal and $100 was interest.
f. Front End Fashions purchased $450 of office supplies for cash.
g. Front End Fashions collected $12,000 from customers on account.
h. Front End Fashions purchased equipment for $10,000 cash.

LO 3 **E1-10A. Analyze effect of business transactions on net income.**

For each of the following transactions of Fun Movie Productions, Inc., determine if there is an increase, decrease, or no effect on net income.

a. Fun Movie earned $10,000 in service revenue.
b. Fun Movie recorded operating expenses of $3,000.
c. Fun Movie paid monthly rent of $1,500.
d. Fun Movie paid employees $2,500 for work done.
e. Fun Movie purchased land for $7,500.
f. Fun Movie invested $4,000 in another company.
g. Fun Movie paid $1,000 in cash dividends.

LO 3 **E1-11A. Calculate missing amounts.**

Fill in the amounts for X, Y, and Z in the following table. (The company started business on January 1, 2006.)

	Dec. 31, 2006	Dec. 31, 2007
Assets	$1,000	$2,500
Liabilities	X	1,000
Contributed Capital	300	300
Retained Earnings	Y	Z
Revenue	300	2,500
Expenses	100	1,500

LO 3 **E1-12A. Identify and classify financial statement items.**

More Company sells a variety of products. The following items were shown on More's financial statements presented in the company's 2007 annual report. Whenever possible, classify each item below as an asset, liability, owners' equity, revenue, or expense. If the item is not one of these but is a subtotal or total on a financial statement, indicate on which financial statement it will appear. (*Hint:* some items will appear on more than one financial statement.)

a. Interest Revenue
b. Accounts Payable
c. Land
d. Cash
e. Common Stock
f. Retained Earnings
g. Rent Expense
h. Total Stockholders' Equity
i. Total Assets
j. Net Income
k. Operating Expenses
l. Total Operating Expenses
m. Net Cash Generated by Operating Activities

LO 4 **E1-13A. Explain purpose of financial statement analysis.**

Every time Apple Computer issues its annual financial statements, financial analysts prepare extensive ratio analysis on each statement and on those of Apple's competitors. What is financial statement analysis? What is ratio analysis?

LO 5 **E1-14A. Identify business risks.**

Name four possible risks Steve Jobs and Steve Wozniak might have considered as they started their business, Apple Computer, Inc.

Exercise Set B

> Your professor may ask you to complete selected "Group B" exercises and problems using Prentice Hall Grade Assist (**PHGA**). PHGA is an online tool that can help you master the chapter's topics by providing multiple variations of exercises and problems. You can rework these exercises and problems—each time with new data—as many times as you need, with immediate feedback and grading.

LO 1, 2, 3 **E1-1B. Analyze a balance sheet.**

Use the balance sheet for Rainy Day Umbrellas & Raincoats, Inc., at June 30, 2007 to answer the following questions:

a. List the assets the company had on June 30, 2007. Who had claim to these assets?
b. List the liabilities the company had on June 30, 2007.
c. Who are the potential users of this financial information?

Exercise Set B   33

Balance Sheet
Rainy Day Umbrellas & Raincoats, Inc.
At June 30, 2007

Assets		Liabilities and Owners' Equity	
Cash	$ 4,500	Accounts Payable	$ 2,500
Short-term Investments	350	Notes Payable (equipment)	10,250
Accounts Receivable	385		
Inventory	250	Paid-in Capital	3,450
Prepaid Insurance	200	Retained Earnings	2,485
Prepaid Rent	500		
Equipment (net)	12,500		
	$18,685		$18,685

E1-2B. Identify business activities.   LO 3

For each of the following transactions of Mick & June's Coffee Shop, tell whether it is an operating, investing, or financing activity for the statement of cash flows. (Assume all transactions are for cash.)

a. Mick & June's was started with a contribution from Mick and June of $25,000 and a loan of $10,000 from the bank.
b. Mick & June's purchased $2,500 worth of coffee supplies (inventory) for cash.
c. Mick & June's hired one employee to help wait on customers. For his service, Mick & June's paid $50 each day for a total of five days.
d. Mick & June's sold enough cups of coffee to generate cash revenues of $4,000 the first month.
e. Due to high demand, Mick & June's purchased a new espresso machine for $14,500.
f. Mick & June's repaid $150 of the bank loan along with $15 of interest for the first month.

E1-3B. Analyze effect on owners' equity.   LO 3

For each of the following transactions of It's About Time Moving Co., tell whether it (1) increases, (2) decreases, or (3) has no effect on owners' equity. Consider both owners' equity components—contributed capital and retained earnings.

a. Two friends get together, each contributing $27,500 to start the It's About Time Moving Co.
b. It's About Time purchases two moving trucks for $40,000 cash.
c. It's About Time purchases $4,500 worth of supplies for cash.
d. It's About Time pays expenses of $1,000 for gas and auto insurance.
e. It's About Time earns service revenue from customers of $6,250 during the month.
f. It's About Time pays employees $375 for hours worked during the month.
g. It's About Time declares and distributes $225 dividends to each of its owners at the end of the month.

E1-4B. Identify cash flows.   LO 3

For each of the transactions in E1-3B, tell whether it is an operating, investing, or financing cash flow.

E1-5B. Identify income statement transactions.   LO 3

Tell whether or not each of the following cash transactions of John's Plumbing Solutions will be reflected on the income statement. For each that does affect income, tell whether it increases or decreases net income.

a. John's issues checks for the salaries of its employees.
b. John's purchases a truck.
c. John's earns revenue from providing services to customers.
d. John's borrows money from a family friend, signing a two-year note payable.
e. John's pays dividends to its shareholders.

E1-6B. Identify balance sheet transactions.   LO 3

Which of the following transactions will affect assets, liabilities, or both? For each item that does affect these balance sheets accounts, tell whether it is an increase or decrease.

a. A company buys a new car with cash.
b. A company pays off its Accounts Payable.
c. A company collects some of its Accounts Receivable.
d. A company pays remaining principal owed on a loan from the bank.

LO 3   **E1-7B. Identify business activities.**

Assume each transaction below of Cookie Dough & More Ice Cream Co. is a cash transaction. Tell how each cash flow would be classified on the statement of cash flows: (1) operating, (2) investing, or (3) financing.

   a. William makes a contribution of $75,000 to start the Cookie Dough & More Ice Cream Co. from his personal funds.

   b. The company purchases a building and some equipment for $45,000 in cash.

   c. The company purchases $5,500 worth of advertising time on a local television station for cash.

   d. The company pays electricity and insurance expenses of $1,500 for the month.

   e. The company pays several people to help make ice cream at a cost of $350 for the month.

   f. The company collects $2,500 for ice cream and catering services for National Bank's grand opening.

LO 3   **E1-8B. Identify business activities.**

For each of the following transactions of More Where That Came From Consultants, Inc., tell whether it is an operating activity, an investing activity, or a financing activity.

   a. The firm received $15,000 for services performed.

   b. The firm paid $125,000 cash for a new building.

   c. The firm paid $2,500 of a $5,000 notes payable to creditors.

   d. The firm paid $1,500 for salaries expense.

   e. The firm's owners provided $6,750 in additional financing.

   f. The firm distributed $2,250 in dividends.

LO 3   **E1-9B. Analyze effect of business transactions on assets.**

For each of the following transactions of Office Supplies Galore, Inc., determine if there is an increase, decrease, or no effect on the assets.

   a. Office Supplies Galore sold inventory that cost $8,500 for $15,000 cash.

   b. Office Supplies Galore purchased equipment for $120,500 by signing a 20-year note.

   c. Office Supplies Galore paid monthly utility and insurance expense of $1,150.

   d. The sales associate's wages were paid in the amount of $3,200.

   e. Office Supplies Galore paid $3,000 toward the 20-year note; $2,700 of the payment was principal and $300 was interest.

   f. Office Supplies Galore purchased $15,000 of inventory on account.

   g. Office Supplies Galore collected $18,500 from customers on account.

   h. Office Supplies Galore purchased new computers for $18,000 cash.

LO 3   **E1-10B. Analyze effect of business transactions on net income.**

For each of the following transactions of Pastas of Italy, Inc., determine if there is an increase, decrease, or no effect on net income

   a. Pastas of Italy earned $18,750 in revenues from its customers.

   b. Pastas of Italy had operating expenses of $2,500.

   c. Pastas of Italy paid monthly insurance expense of $1,875.

   d. Pastas of Italy paid $1,500 for special advertisements made.

   e. Pastas of Italy purchased a truck for $18,750.

   f. Pastas of Italy paid $1,500 in cash dividends.

   g. Pastas of Italy invested $10,500 in another company.

LO 3   **E1-11B. Calculate missing amounts.**

Fill in the amounts for X, Y, and Z in the table shown. (The company started business on July 1, 2008.)

	June 30 2009	June 30 2010
Assets	$2,000	$4,250
Liabilities	X	2,500
Contributed Capital	500	700
Retained Earnings	Y	Z
Revenue	800	7,200
Expenses	250	6,700

E1-12B. Identify and classify financial statement items.

DEF Photography, Inc., specializes in family photography. The following items were shown on DEF's financial statements presented in the company's 2010 annual report.

Whenever possible, classify each item as an asset, liability, owners' equity, revenue, or expense. If the item is not one of these but is a subtotal or total on a financial statement, simply indicate on which financial statement it will appear. (*Hint:* Some items will appear on more than one financial statement.)

LO 3

a. Sales Revenue
b. Notes Payable
c. Equipment
d. Accounts Receivable
e. Common Stock
f. Retained Earnings
g. Interest Expense

h. Total Stockholders' Equity
i. Total Liabilities
j. Net Loss
k. Salaries Expense
l. Total Assets
m. Net Cash Generated by Investing Activities

E1-13B. Explain purpose of financial statement analysis.

LO 4

Every time Dell Computer issues its annual financial statements, financial analysts prepare extensive ratio analysis on each statement and on those of Dell's competitors. What is financial statement analysis? What is ratio analysis?

E1-14B. Identify business risks.

LO 5

Name four possible risks Michael Dell might have considered as he started his business, Dell Computer, Inc.

Problem Set A

P1-1A. Analyze business transactions and the effect on the financial statements.

LO 2, 3

The following transactions apply to Small's Appliance Service Company during May 2007.

1. The owner started the business by depositing $5,000 in a business checking account on May 1.
2. The company provided services to clients and received $3,500 in cash.
3. The company borrowed $1,200 from the bank for the business.
4. The company paid $1,000 of salaries expense.
5. The company purchased a new computer for $3,000 cash to use to keep track of its customers.
6. The company made a distribution of $1,500 to the owner.

Required

a. Study each of the transactions. Consider what is happening to assets in each case. What are the total assets of the company at the end of May 2007? (You may want to use the accounting equation to help you.)
b. Consider what is happening to liabilities in each transaction. What are the total liabilities of the company at the end of May 2007?
c. Classify each transaction as operating, investing, or financing.
d. What was net income for May?
e. Based on the data provided, who might find the information on Small's Appliance Service Company's financial statements useful?

P1-2A. Analyze business transactions and the effect on the financial statements.

LO 3

Mitch Johnson is the owner of Wolverine Company. The following events are for Wolverine Company for the year 2008, the first year of operations. All transactions are cash.

1. Mitch contributed $15,000 to start the business Wolverine Company.
2. Creditors loaned Wolverine Company $7,000.
3. Wolverine Company provided services to its customers and received $7,500.
4. Wolverine Company paid expenses amounting to $6,000.
5. Wolverine Company paid dividends of $1,000 to its shareholders.

Required

For each transaction listed, indicate whether the balance sheet or income statement is affected by the transaction and then explain how they are affected. For example, the first transaction affects the balance sheet by increasing Cash and increasing owners' equity.

a. What is net income for the year ended December 31, 2008?
b. What is the balance in the Cash account at December 31, 2008?

LO 3   **P1-3A. Analyze business transactions and the effect on the financial statements.**

The following business transactions occurred during Gator's Antiques, Inc., first month of business.

1. Philip Gator began his antique business by depositing $15,000 into the business checking account.
2. Gator's provided services to customers for $25,000 cash.
3. Gator's paid travel expenses in the amount of $700.
4. Gator's Antiques borrowed $1,000 from the bank for operating capital.
5. Gator's purchased office supplies for $150 cash.
6. During the month, Gator's paid $3,500 for operating expenses.
7. Gator's paid the monthly rent on the retail space in the amount of $500.
8. Gator's paid employees $1,200.
9. Gator's paid dividends of $100 to the owner, Philip Gator.
10. Gator's purchased equipment costing $7,500 by signing a note payable with the bank.

Required

For each transaction (items 1–10), do the following:

a. Identify whether it is an operating, investing, or financing transaction.
b. Determine whether there is an increase, decrease, or no effect on the assets of the business.
c. Determine whether there is an increase, decrease, or no effect on net income.
d. Indicate which financial statements each item affects: the income statement (IS), the balance sheet (BS), the statement of changes in owner's equity (OE), or the statement of cash flows (CF). (*Hint:* Some will affect more than one statement.)

LO 3   **P1-4A. Analyze business transactions and the effect on the financial statements.**

Using transactions 1–10 in P1-3A, answer the following questions.

Required

a. What is the cash balance at the end of Gator's first month of business?
b. Does Gator's Antiques have any liabilities? If so, how much?
c. Which assets will appear on the balance sheet at the end of Gator's first month of business?
d. Did Gator's Antiques generate net income or net loss for its first month of business? How much?

Problem Set B

Your professor may ask you to complete selected "Group B" exercises and problems using Prentice Hall Grade Assist (**PHGA**). PHGA is an online tool that can help you master the chapter's topics by providing multiple variations of exercises and problems. You can rework these exercises and problems—each time with new data—as many times as you need, with immediate feedback and grading.

LO 3   **P1-1B. Analyze business transactions and the effect on the financial statements.**

The following transactions apply to Jordan's Car Detailing Service Company during April 2006.

1. Jordan (the owner) started his own business by depositing $6,500 in a business checking account on April 1.
2. Jordan and his assistant, Mark, provided services to customers and received $9,500.
3. Jordan's paid Mark $1,500 for April's salary.
4. Jordan's borrowed $1,600 from the local bank for the business.
5. Jordan's bought a wet/dry vacuum for $8,000 cash.
6. Jordan's made a distribution of $2,500 to the owner.

Required

a. What are the total assets of the company at the end of April 2006?
b. What are the total liabilities of the company at the end of April 2006?
c. Classify each transaction as operating, investing, or financing.

d. What was net income for April?

e. Based on the data provided, who might find the information on Jordan's Car Detailing Service financial statements useful?

P1-2B. Analyze business transactions and the effect on the financial statements.   LO 3

The following events are for Southeast Sandblasting Company, for the year 2006, the first year of operations.

1. A group of friends began the company with a total investment of $54,000.
2. Southeast Sandblasting Company rented sandblasting equipment for a year and paid cash of $30,000.
3. Southeast Sandblasting Company provided sandblasting services to the local community college and received $60,000.
4. Southeast Sandblasting Company paid operating expenses amounting to $25,000.
5. Southeast Sandblasting Company borrowed $15,000 from a local bank.
6. Southeast Sandblasting Company paid dividends of $5,000 to shareholders.

Required

a. For each transaction listed, indicate whether the balance sheet or income statement is affected by the transaction and then explain how it is affected. For example, the first transaction affects the balance sheet by increasing Cash and increasing owners' equity.

b. What is net income for the year ended December 31, 2006?

c. What is the balance in the Cash account at December 31, 2006?

P1-3B. Analyze business transactions and the effect on the financial statements.   LO 3

The following business transactions occurred during the first month of business for Dolphin's Dinghies, Inc. Unless otherwise stated, the transaction was for cash.

1. Douglas Dolphin began his dinghy business by depositing $40,000 into the business checking account.
2. Dolphin's Dinghies paid expenses in the amount of $250.
3. Dolphin's Dinghies borrowed $5,000 from the bank for operating capital.
4. Dolphin's Dinghies purchased $350 of office supplies (for future use).
5. During the month, Dolphin's repaired customers' dinghies for $8,900 cash.
6. Dolphin's Dinghies paid the monthly rent on the retail space in the amount of $1,200.
7. Dolphin's Dinghies paid the staff $3,000.
8. Dolphin's Dinghies paid other operating expenses during the month of $1,500.
9. Dolphin's Dinghies purchased equipment costing $17,000 by signing a note payable with the bank.
10. Dolphin's Dinghies paid a dividend of $175 to the owner, Douglas Dolphin.

Required

For each transaction (items 1–10), do the following:

a. Identify whether it is an operating, investing, or financing transaction.
b. Determine whether there is an increase, decrease, or no effect on the assets of the business.
c. Determine whether there is an increase, decrease, or no effect on net income.
d. Indicate which financial statement item would be affected by each transaction: the income statement (IS), the balance sheet (BS), the statement of changes in owners' equity (OE), or the statement of cash flows (CF). (*Hint:* Some will affect more than one statement.)

P1-4B. Analyze business transactions and the effect on the financial statements.   LO 3

Using transactions 1–10 in P1-3B, answer the following questions.

Required

a. What is the Cash balance at the end of Dolphin's first month of business?
b. Does Dolphin's Dinghies have any liabilities? If so, how much?
c. Which assets will appear on the balance sheet at the end of Dolphin's first month of business?
d. Did Dolphin's Dinghies generate net income or net loss for its first month of business? How much?

Financial Statement Analysis

LO 3   **FSA1-1.** Use Apple Computer, Inc.'s balance sheets given here to answer the following questions.

		Apple Computer, Inc. **Condensed Balance Sheets** (in millions)		
	At		9/25/04	9/27/03
Current assets:				
Cash and cash equivalents			$2,969	$3,396
Short-term investments			2,495	1,170
Accounts receivable (net)............................			774	766
Inventories			101	56
Other current assets			716	499
Total current assets			7,055	5,887
Property, plant, and equipment (net)			707	669
Goodwill			80	85
Other assets			208	174
Total assets			$8,050	$6,815
Current liabilities:				
Accounts payable			$1,451	$1,154
Accrued expenses			1,229	899
Current debt			—	304
Total current liabilities			2,680	2,357
Other non-current liabilities			294	235
Total liabilities...................................			2,974	2,592
Common stock			2,514	1,926
Retained earnings.................................			2,670	2,394
Other equity accounts			(108)	(97)
Total shareholders' equity			5,076	4,223
Total liabilities and shareholders' equity			$8,050	$6,815

Required

a. What date marks the end of Apple's most recent fiscal year?
b. Did Apple earn a net income or net loss during the most recent year? How can you tell?
c. Did the owners of Apple make any capital contributions during the most recent year (or did Apple get some new owners)?
d. Did Apple buy or sell any major equipment during the most recent year? How can you tell?
e. On the last day of the most recent fiscal year, did Apple have any debts? If so, what was the total amount?

LO 3   **FSA1-2.** Information from the statement of cash flows for Apple Computer, Inc., for the year ended September 25, 2004, is shown on the following page. Use it to answer the following questions.

Required

a. Did Apple purchase any equipment during the year?
b. What was Apple's Net Income (loss) during the year?
c. If you were to examine Apple's balance sheet at September 25, 2004, what amount would be shown for Cash and Cash Equivalents?
d. Was cash generated from operations or used by operations? By what amount?
e. Did Apple receive any new contributions from owners during the year? How can you tell?
f. What was the primary source of cash for Apple for the year ended September 25, 2004? What does this say to you about Apple's operations for this year?

Apple Computer, Inc.
Adapted Statement of Cash Flows
For the year ended September 25, 2004
(in millions)

Cash and cash equivalents, beginning of the year	$3,396
Operating Activities:	
Net income (loss)	276
Adjustments to reconcile net income to cash	
generated by operating activities:	658
Cash generated by operating activities	934
Investing Activities:	
Purchase of short-term investments	(3,270)
Proceeds from maturities of	
short-term investments	1,141
Proceeds from sales of short-term investments	801
Proceeds from sale of non-current investments	5
Purchase of property, plant, and equipment	(176)
Other...	11
Cash generated by (used for) investing activities	(1,488)
Financing Activities:	
Payment of long-term debt	(300)
Proceeds from issuance of common stock	427
Cash generated by (used for) financing activities	127
Increase (decrease) in cash and cash equivalents ..	(427)
Cash and cash equivalents, end of the year	$2,969

FSA1-3. Use the 10-K report from Target, Inc., in Appendix B at the back of the book to answer these questions.

LO 2, 3, 5

Required

a. Suppose you inherited $10,000 when your great-uncle passed away and you want to invest in a promising company. Would you invest in Target? What information in the 10-K report would be useful in your decision? Be specific. Is there any information that is not provided in the 10-K report that you would want to have before making your decision?

b. What is your opinion of the information in the 10-K report? For example, do you think it is accurate? Useful? Interesting? Informative? Why or why not?

Critical Thinking Problems

Risk and Control
Being in business is risky. Imagine that you are starting a business. What type of business would you start? What are the most significant risks you face with your business? What controls would you put into effect to minimize those risks?

Group Problem
Look at the four basic financial statements for Wal-Mart in Appendix A at the back of the book. Find the Total Assets, Liabilities, and Shareholders' Equity for the two most recent years. As a group, discuss the change in the company's financial position without looking at the income statement. Jot down your opinions. Then, study the income statement for the most recent year. Do the results support your opinions about the balance sheet changes? What information do these statements provide for your analysis? What additional information would be useful? After answering these questions as a group, look at the notes to the financial statements. Do the notes help answer any of your questions?

Then, make a list of 10–12 questions you have about the financial statements. Try to answer them and discuss why you would like answers to these questions. Save the list so you can check to see how many of the questions you are able to answer at the end of the course.

Ethics

Does your school have an honor code? If it does, it very likely addresses the issue of cheating on assignments or exams. Have you ever cheated on an exam? Have you ever "borrowed" a friend's assignment and used it to help you complete yours? Have you ever been a witness to a violation of the honor code by your peers? Compare Target's code of ethics (go to Corporate Governance—Business Conduct Guide—found at www.targetcorp.com/targetcorp_group/investor-relations/investor-relations.jhtml) to your school's honor code. How are they similar in purpose and scope? How are they different? If you compare your behavior to that of some of the executives of Enron, WorldCom, or Tyco, how do you stack up?

Internet Exercise: The Walt Disney Company

The Walt Disney Company is a diversified worldwide entertainment company with interests in ABC TV, ESPN, film production, theme parks, publishing, a cruise line, Infoseek, and the NHL Mighty Ducks. By using the Disney web site you can explore vacation options and get Disney's latest financial information. Please go to the Disney web site at http://corporate.disney.go.com/investors/ to complete the following exercises.

IE1-1. What is the Walt Disney Company key objective?
   Go to Financial Information and click on the most recent annual report.

   a. What are the key businesses of the Walt Disney Company? Identify whether you think the primary business activity is manufacturing, merchandising, or service for each key business segment.
   b. Use the Site Map to find Financial Highlights. Identify the amount of Total Revenues and Operating Income for the most recent year. On which financial statement will you find these amounts reported?
   c. Use the Site Map to find Financial Review. What key business segment earns the greatest proportion of revenues? Identify the proportion of revenues earned by each key business segment, listing them in the order of greatest proportion to least proportion. Does this order surprise you? Explain why or why not.

   Please note: Internet web sites are constantly being updated. Therefore, if the information is not found where indicated, please explore the annual report further to find the information.

Additional Study Materials

Visit www.prenhall.com/reimers for self-study quizzes and spreadsheet templates to use to complete homework assignments.

CONTINUING CASE STUDY

Building your Excel skills with The MP3 Store

January is the first month of business for The MP3 Store. The new owners will spend the first two months getting the business ready to open. The estimated opening date is March 1. During the firm's first month, January 2006, The MP3 Store engaged in the following transactions:

January 1 The MP3 Store was started with contributions from three college classmates. They decided to form a corporation and issue stock to the owners in return for $10,000 from each, for a total of $30,000 of contributed capital.

January 5 Paid $3,600 for six-months' rent in advance for a small store on Easy Street. A year's lease will begin March 1. Record this payment as an asset called Prepaid Rent (something with future value to the firm).

January 15 Purchased office supplies for $500 cash. Again, record the purchase as an asset, Supplies.

January 20 Issued additional stock for $10,000 to another friend who decided he wanted to get in on the business.

Instructions

1. Open a new Excel worksheet.
2. Input the appropriate three-line balance sheet heading beginning in Cell A1 and ending in Cell A3. Don't worry about position now. You will center your headings at the end of the problem. If you want to change the way the date line appears, select **Format, Cells, Number, Date** to choose the desired format.
3. Input Assets in Cell A5; Liabilities and Shareholders' Equity in Cell D5. Make the headings bold by selecting the cells containing the text and clicking the **Bold** **B** button. Resize Column D so that the heading fits in the column.

   (*Hint:* There are different ways you can resize a column. One option is to hold down your left mouse button and drag when you see the arrow depicted here:

Drag to resize		
A	**B**	⟷**C**
1		
2		
3		

   You may also resize columns by double-clicking your left mouse button when you see the arrow just depicted. Double-clicking will automatically resize your column based on the longest line.)
4. Beginning in Cell A6 and ending in Cell A9, input your titles—Cash, Prepaid Rent, Supplies, Total Assets. Highlight Cells A6–A8 and click the **Increase Indent** button to indent the account names.

   (*Hint:* To highlight cells, click on the first cell to be highlighted, press and hold the Shift key, and then use the appropriate arrow key(s) to select the other cells.)
5. Input the dollar amounts for Prepaid Rent and Supplies in Cells B7 and B8. Highlight the cells and format your numbers by selecting **Format, Cells** and **Number** from the menu. Choose the currency format with Symbol: None and Negative numbers: (1,234).
6. Input a formula to calculate the cash balance (Cell B6).

   (*Hint:* Input the dollar amounts of cash contributed by the owners and use cell references to subtract the dollar amount of the items purchased with cash. =30000+10000-B7-B8)
7. Use the **AutoSum** **Σ** button to calculate Total Assets in Cell B9.
8. Format Cell B6 using the same method detailed in Step 5. Select "$" as the symbol. Format Cell B9 by selecting **Edit, Repeat Format Cells** from the menu or by clicking Ctrl V. Select **Format, Cells** and **Border** from the menu to appropriately border Cell B9.
9. Beginning in Cells D6 and E6, input the appropriate titles and dollar amounts to complete the Liabilities and Equity section of your balance sheet. Compute the Total Liabilities and Equity by copying Cell B9 to Cell E9.

   (*Hint:* There are several ways you can copy Cell B9. One option is click Ctrl C. Another is to click the **Copy** button. A third option is to select **Edit, Copy** from the menu. To paste the formula and borders into Cell E9 you may click Ctrl V, use the **Paste** button, or select **Edit, Paste** from the menu. A final option for pasting the function is simply to hit the Enter key. You may use any of the options to copy and any of them to paste the copied cell.)
10. Complete your balance sheet by centering your heading across columns A–E. Highlight the cells to be centered and click the **Merge and Center** button. Each row must be centered separately.
11. Print your file and save it to disk by clicking the **Save** button. Name your file MP31.

chapter 2

Preparing Financial Statements and Analyzing Business Transactions

Here's where you've been . . .

- You learned that a business provides goods and services to make a profit.

- You learned that managers, shareholders, creditors, and the government monitor the profitability of a business by reviewing the four basic financial statements—the income statement, the statement of changes in shareholders' equity, the balance sheet, and the statement of cash flows.

Here's where you're going . . .

- You'll learn more about the type of information contained in the four basic financial statements.

- You'll learn how to analyze transactions using the accounting equation and how to use those transactions to prepare the four basic financial statements.

YOU make the call:

Can Southwest get a loan?

The airline industry is very competitive with many airlines competing for your business, such as Continental, U.S. Air, American, and Southwest Airlines. But now bargain-fare airlines, like Jet Blue and Song, and airline websites, like Travelocity.com and Expedia.com make it easier to find the lowest fares. With all this competition, it's not surprising that many airlines need loans from banks to maintain and improve planes and services.

Suppose Southwest Airlines wants to start a new airline for commuter flights, but the company does not have the cash it needs for this expansion. Southwest is planning to borrow the money from a local bank. A new accounting clerk at Southwest decides that the most recent income statement will provide all the information the bank needs to approve a loan. Do you think an income statement will provide enough information to satisfy the bank? *You make the call.*

Learning Objectives

When you are finished studying this chapter, you should be able to:

1. Explain the objectives, assumptions, and qualities of financial reporting.
2. Identify the parts of the balance sheet and describe their characteristics.
3. Identify the parts of the income statement and describe their characteristics.
4. Identify the parts of the statement of changes in shareholders' equity and describe their characteristics.
5. Identify the parts of the statement of cash flows and describe their characteristics.
6. Explain the purpose of the notes to the financial statements.
7. Analyze business transactions using the accounting equation and prepare the four basic financial statements.
8. Compute and explain the current ratio.
9. Identify the risks of inaccurate financial records and how to control those risks.

LEARNING OBJECTIVE 1

Explain the objectives, assumptions, and qualities of financial reporting.

Objectives, Assumptions, and Qualities of Financial Reporting

Anyone who owns stock in Southwest Airlines will want to know if the company is profitable. A quick look at the income statement for Southwest Airlines in Exhibit 2.1 will show you that the company had a net income of $313 million for the fiscal year ended December 31, 2004. Recall that the difference between all of the company's revenues and all of its expenses is *net income*. Why does the Securities and Exchange Commission (SEC) require Southwest to prepare this statement and the others you've learned about in Chapter 1?

Southwest's total revenue was greater than its total expenses by $313 million for the year ended December 31, 2004. That's net income for the year. It was not quite as good a year as the previous one. Can you see what changed from 2003 to 2004?

Exhibit 2.1

Southwest Airlines Condensed Income Statements

<table>
<tr><td colspan="3" align="center">Southwest Airlines
Condensed Income Statements
(in millions)</td></tr>
</table>

(For the year ended)	31-Dec-04	31-Dec-03
Total operating revenue	$6,530	$5,937
Total operating expenses	5,976	5,454
Operating income (loss)	554	483
Other income and (expenses)	(65)	225
Income before income taxes	489	708
Provision for income taxes	176	266
Net income	$313	$442
Earnings per share basic	$ 0.40	$ 0.56
Earnings per share diluted	$ 0.38	$ 0.54

Study Tip

A year in the life of a business is called a fiscal year, and a firm can select any 12-month period for its fiscal year.

Financial reporting

As you learned in Chapter 1, the SEC requires that a publicly traded company periodically provide financial information to its shareholders so that they can evaluate the firm's past performance and predict the firm's future performance. Privately-held firms—regardless of their size—also prepare financial information for owners, creditors, and potential investors. Preparing and presenting financial information is generally known as *financial reporting*. The financial information reported includes:

- The four financial statements—the income statement, the statement of changes in shareholders' equity, the balance sheet, and the statement of cash flows
- The notes to the financial statements

The information contained in the financial statements is based on a firm's transactions. As you learned in Chapter 1, transactions are the economic exchanges between a firm and outside entities. These exchanges are analyzed and recorded in the accounting records and are eventually summarized and condensed into the financial statements. The resulting information included in the financial statements is intended to be useful to owners, potential investors, creditors, analysts, and others as they evaluate the past performance, future potential, and financial position of the firm. For example, managers analyze the financial statements to identify specific areas where the company isn't doing well, and the information allows them to make appropriate changes. A potential investor may use the financial statements when trying to decide whether or not the company is a good investment.

To understand a firm's financial statements, you'll need to become familiar with the assumptions accountants make and the principles they must follow when preparing financial statements. Then, you'll learn how to analyze the business transactions that make up the financial statements.

Qualities of accounting information

As you learned in Chapter 1, the Financial Accounting Standards Board (FASB) is the primary U.S. accounting standards-setting body. When setting accounting standards for *generally accepted accounting principles* (GAAP), the FASB has the overall goal of making sure accounting information helps investors and potential investors make decisions about the firm. *Usefulness* is the most important characteristic of accounting information. That means the information influences decisions. Because external parties cannot examine the company's day-to-day accounting records, the financial statements are an important source of information to investors and other external parties. What makes information useful? According to the FASB, the information must be relevant, reliable, comparable, and consistent.

Study Tip

GAAP includes the various methods, guidelines, practices, and other procedures that have evolved over time in response to changes in the business environment.

Relevant For information to be **relevant**, it needs to be significant enough to influence business decisions. The information should help confirm or correct the users' expectations. No matter how significant the information is, however, it must be timely to be relevant. For example, the price of fuel is extremely important information to Southwest, and a manager needs this information to make decisions about ticket prices. However, if the firm reports fuel prices only monthly, the information won't be timely enough to be relevant. To be relevant information must be useful in predicting the future. Currently, the SEC requires firms to submit their financial information within 60 days of the end of the firm's fiscal year.

Relevant: Describes information that is important and timely, with the potential to influence decisions.

Reliable When information is **reliable**, you can depend on it and can verify its accuracy. The information is completely independent of the person reporting it. To be reliable, the information in the financial statements must be a faithful

Reliable: Describes information that is verifiable and a faithful representation of a firm's financial performance.

representation of what it intends to convey. For example, Adolph Coors Brewing Company reported $5.82 billion dollars in sales for the year ended December 26, 2004. This amount must be true and verifiable; otherwise, the information could be misleading to investors. As you learned in Chapter 1, it's part of the auditors' job to make sure Coors has the documentation to confirm the accuracy of its sales amount. Anyone who examines Coors' sales records should come up with the same amount.

Comparability: Describes information that can be compared across firms because they use the same accounting principles.

Comparable In addition to being relevant and reliable, useful information possesses **comparability**. This characteristic means investors will be able to compare corresponding financial information between two similar companies—how one company's net income compares with another company's net income. In putting together financial statements, accountants must allow for meaningful comparisons. Because there are often alternative ways to account for the same transaction within GAAP, companies must disclose the methods they select. This disclosure allows educated investors to adjust the reported amounts to make them comparable. For example, Sears may account for its inventories by averaging the cost of its purchases, while Wal-Mart may use a method that assumes the first items purchased are the first items sold. As a requirement of GAAP, Sears and Wal-Mart will disclose these choices in the notes to their financial statements so that investors can compare the inventory information of the companies.

Consistency: The use of the same accounting methods from period to period.

Consistent To be useful, accounting information must be consistent. **Consistency** is the characteristic that makes it possible to track a company's result from one year to the next. Only if we use the same accounting methods from period to period are we able to make meaningful comparisons. For example, net sales for Callaway Golf Company for 2004 were $934 million, and net sales for 2003 were $814 million. Only when these two numbers are based on the same set of accounting methods can investors determine why sales increased between the year ended December 31, 2003 and the year ended December 31, 2004. If the increase was caused partly or solely by the change in the way the company measured sales, then investors would be misled about the company's actual performance. Financial statement users want to rely on the firm's consistent application of accounting standards.

Exhibit 2.2 summarizes the desired qualitative[1] characteristics information must have to be considered useful by the Financial Accounting Standards Board.

Assumptions and principles underlying financial reporting

Financial information pertains to only the firm, not to any other parties such as the firm's owners. This distinction between the financial information of the firm and the financial information of other firms or people is called the **separate entity assumption**. It means that the financial statements of a business do not include any information about the finances of individual owners or other companies.

Separate entity assumption: Assumption that the financial statements of a business do not include any personal financial information about owners or any other entity.

Let's look at the income statement, which summarizes a company's revenues and expenses. Recall that you learned about the *monetary unit assumption* in Chapter 1. This assumption means that the items on the financial statements are expressed in amounts of money. As you can see from Southwest's income statement in Exhibit 2.1, the company earned a net income for each of the last two years. The operating revenue for the year ended December 31, 2004

In Other Words: The separate entity assumption is also called the economic entity assumption.

[1]This is the expression that the FASB uses for characteristics that are non-quantitative. They are the qualities that accounting information should possess.

Exhibit 2.2

Qualitative Characteristics of Accounting Information

Chief Executive Officer   Chief Financial Officer

Company A   Company B

2005   2006

Relevance:
Information that will provide a basis for forecasts of future firm performance by the CEO and CFO, among others. What's ahead for this company?

Reliability:
Information that is neutral and verifiable. Is the information independent of the specific person who prepared it?

Comparability:
Different companies use the same set of accounting rules. Does the information allow meaningful comparisons of two different companies?

Consistency:
A company uses the same rules from year to year. Does the information allow meaningful comparisons of a company's performance at different points in time?

amounted to $6.53 billion. This is the total amount the company earned for providing goods and services during the year. The operating expenses were $5.976 billion. This amount was the cost to Southwest of providing services to its customers. Southwest also had other miscellaneous revenue and expenses, including income taxes. Southwest Airlines had a net income of $313 million. This information pertains to Southwest's performance. Suppose you heard that one of the major shareholders of Southwest purchased a new yacht. No part of that transaction would be part of Southwest's financial reports because of the separate-entity assumption.

At a minimum, firms prepare new financial statements every year. For internal use, financial statements are prepared more frequently. The SEC requires publicly traded firms like Southwest to prepare a new set of financial statements each quarter, which will enable users to compare the company's performance from one quarter (every three months) to the next. Accountants divide the life of a business into time periods so they can prepare reports about the company's performance during those time periods. This creation of time periods is called the **time-period assumption**. Although most companies report financial information every three months, only the annual financial information is audited. Most companies, like Southwest Airlines, use the calendar year as the fiscal year.

Assets are recorded at their original cost to the company. This is known as the **historical-cost principle**. That's because the cost of an asset is a reliable amount—it is unbiased and verifiable.

Accountants assume a company will continue to remain in business for the foreseeable future, unless they have clear evidence it will either close or go bankrupt. This is called the **going-concern assumption**. With this assumption, financial statement values are meaningful, representing the future value of the assets and future obligations of the liabilities. Would the bank loan money to Southwest if it was not going to continue operating in the foreseeable future? If the firm expects to liquidate, the values on the financial statements lose their meaning. If a company is not a going concern, the values on the financial statements would need to be liquidation values to be useful.

Time-period assumption: The assumption that the life of a business can be divided into meaningful time periods for financial reporting.

Historical-cost principle: Measuring assets at their cost at the time of the purchase.

Going-concern assumption: The assumption that a company will continue operating in the foreseeable future.

Materiality and conservatism in financial reporting

As you have read about the four financial statements and the notes to the statements, you have learned about the qualities of financial information and the assumptions and principles that provide the foundation of financial reporting. Without these assumptions and principles, managers, investors, and analysts could not rely on the information to make decisions.

To complete the foundation for financial reporting and to enable you to gain a full understanding of the information contained in the financial statements, you'll need to know about two constraints that apply to the preparation of the statements. A *constraint* in financial accounting is a limit or control imposed by GAAP. There are two constraints: materiality and conservatism.

Materiality refers to the size or significance of an item or transaction on the company's overall financial performance or financial position. An item is material if it is large enough to influence investor decisions. For example, the cost of fuel, the amounts paid to employees, and the cost of buying or leasing airplanes are all material items for Southwest. An item is considered immaterial if it is too small to influence investors. GAAP doesn't apply to immaterial items. For example, suppose Southwest Airlines made an error and failed to record the revenue from your $350 ticket purchase last spring. Because Southwest's total revenue was over $6 billion, the company would not have to correct this single error. The item is considered immaterial.

Conservatism refers to the choices accountants make when preparing the financial statements. When there is any question about how to account for a transaction, the accountant should select the treatment that will be least likely to overstate income or overstate assets. Accountants believe it is better to understate income or assets than it is to overstate either. Remember that conservatism this does not mean that assets or income should be intentionally understated. For example, Southwest's December 31, 2004 balance sheet shows total property and equipment of over $8 billion. GAAP requires Southwest to evaluate these assets to make sure they are not overstated with respect to their future revenue-generating potential.

LEARNING OBJECTIVE 2

Identify the parts of the balance sheet and describe their characteristics.

A Closer Look at the Balance Sheet

In the previous section, you learned about the assumptions and qualities of financial accounting. In this section, you'll see how an accountant uses those assumptions and qualities to prepare one of the four basic financial statements—the balance sheet. As you learn the details of the financial statements, see how the items included and the way they are valued achieve the goals of providing useful information; that is, relevant, reliable, consistent, and comparable information. First, we'll discuss the three components of the balance sheet:

1. Assets, current and long term
2. Liabilities, current and long term
3. Equity, contributed capital and retained earnings

Current and non-current assets

Exhibit 2.3 shows a condensed balance sheet at December 31, 2004 for Southwest Airlines. The company's assets, listed first on the company's balance sheet, are the company's economic resources at a specific point in time—the balance sheet date. We discussed assets in Chapter 1, but now we are going to examine them closely. According to GAAP[2] an asset has three essential characteristics: (1) it has a probable future benefit that involves a capacity to contribute directly or indirectly to future net cash inflows, (2) a particular entity can obtain the benefit and control others' access to the asset, and (3) the transaction that resulted in the entity's right to the benefit of the asset has already occurred.

Exhibit 2.3

Southwest Airlines Condensed Balance Sheet

Southwest's assets, also referred to as economic resources, were $11,337 million in 2004. Southwest's creditors had claim to $5,813 million of those assets, and Southwest's shareholders had claim to the remaining $5,524 million.

> Southwest Airlines
> Condensed Balance Sheet
> At December 31, 2004
> (in millions)

These will be used to repair planes that will, in turn, produce revenue for the company.

Assets

Current assets		
Cash	$ 1,305	
Accounts receivable	248	
Parts and supplies	137	
Prepaid expenses and other current assets	482	
Total current assets		$ 2,172
Flight and ground equipment	8,041	
Other non-current assets	1,124	
Total non-current assets		9,165
Total assets		$11,337

Current assets are those that will be used in the next 12 months.

Liabilities

Current liabilities		
Accounts payable	$ 420	
Current maturities of long-term debt	146	
Accrued liabilities	1,047	
Air traffic liability	529	
Total current liabilities		$ 2,142
Non-current liabilities		
Long-term debt	1,700	
Other non-current liabilities	1,971	
Total non-current liabilities		3,671
Total liabilities		5,813

Currrent liabilities are those that will be paid off in the next 12 months.

Stockholders' equity

Common stock		790
Other contributed capital		299
Retained earnings		4,089
Other equity		346
		5,524
Total liabilities and stockholders' equity		$11,337

Together, Common stock and Other contributed capital equal the total amount contributed by the shareholders.

[2]This information can be found in FASB's *Statement of Financial Accounting Concepts No. 6.*

Let's look at some examples from Southwest's balance sheet, shown in Exhibit 2.3. Accounts Receivable is one of the first assets listed. The amounts customers owe Southwest will produce cash inflows for the firm, are controlled by the firm, and are the result of past transactions. That's a perfect fit with GAAP's definition of an asset. The next asset shown is Parts and Supplies, which is the cost of the items Southwest needs to repair and maintain its planes. These parts contribute to cash inflows—they help keep the planes flying, which brings cash into the company. Southwest controls parts and supplies and will receive the benefits from them. Parts and supplies were recorded when they were purchased, a past transaction. Again, this asset fits GAAP's definition of an asset. The next asset, Prepaid expenses and other current assets, are goods and services the firm has purchased in advance. Included are items like insurance, rent, and supplies that have not been used.

Assets are listed on the balance sheet in order of *liquidity*, which is a measure of how easily an asset can be converted into cash. For example, Accounts Receivable is listed before Parts and Supplies because the amounts in Accounts Receivable are expected to be converted to cash very quickly. The Parts and Supplies, however, are part of a more complicated conversion to cash. The parts are used on planes that provide the source of Southwest's revenue. There isn't a direct route from Parts and Supplies to cash, but Southwest plans to use those parts and supplies in the next year to help the company generate revenue.

Current assets are assets the company plans to turn into cash or use to earn revenue in the next fiscal year. Both Accounts Receivable and Parts and Supplies are examples of current assets. If Southwest had any investments that it planned to keep no longer than a year, they would be included as current assets.

The assets that will not be used up within 12 months are called *non-current assets*. The airplanes Southwest owns are examples of non-current assets. Each plane will be used for much longer than a year to help Southwest earn revenue. Other non-current assets include any investments the firm has made that it intends to keep longer than a year. Look again at Exhibit 2.3, which shows Southwest's balance sheet. Note how the asset section shows both current and non-current assets. Balance sheets separate current and non-current assets so the financial statements users can see which assets are most liquid. Current assets are more liquid than non-current assets and are therefore available for immediate use. The non-current assets will provide benefits for the firm over a longer period of time—more than a year.

We've talked about the asset component of the balance sheet. Next, we'll talk about the liability component.

Current and non-current liabilities

Exhibit 2.3 shows that Southwest Airlines had $5.813 billion in liabilities. As you will recall from Chapter 1, liabilities are amounts that the business owes to its creditors—the claims of creditors. These claims exist because the creditors gave something to the firm, and they want it or its equivalent returned to them. Usually, claims will be paid to creditors in cash. Liabilities, like assets, are the result of past transactions or events. For example, when a company purchases inventory on credit, the transaction creates a liability called Accounts Payable. This liability is the amount a company owes its suppliers. Recall that the word payable indicates a liability. Once incurred, a liability continues as an obligation of the company until the company pays it.

Liabilities, like assets, can be current or non-current. If an obligation will be settled with a current asset, it's called a **current liability**. Typically, a company pays off a current liability within one year. A company pays off *non-current liabilities* over a period longer than one year. Just as most balance sheets show the current assets with a subtotal before showing the non-current assets, most show the current liabilities with a subtotal before showing the non-current liabilities.

Current assets: The assets the company plans to turn into cash or use to generate revenue in the next fiscal year.

In Other Words: Non-current assets are also known as long-term assets.

Study Tip

Liquidity is a measure of how easily an asset can be converted to cash. Notice that assets are listed on the balance sheet in order of liquidity. Almost all balance sheets start with Cash as the first asset.

Current liabilities: Obligations the company will settle with current assets.

In Other Words: Non-current liabilities are also known as long-term liabilities.

Grouping similar items together results in a format called a **classified balance sheet**. Look again at the balance sheet for Southwest shown in Exhibit 2.3. It is a classified balance sheet because it has two classifications of assets and liabilities—current and non-current.

Sometimes, a company will pay an additional amount for the right to delay payment of a liability. This amount is called **interest**. Interest is the cost of using someone else's money. You pay interest when you carry a balance on your credit card from one month to the next. Southwest's balance sheet shows long-term debt of $1.700 billion, which it does not plan to repay in the next year. Therefore, the company will have to pay interest to the creditor along with the principal amount of the debt—the actual amount borrowed. Any portion that the firm will pay in the next year will be shown as a current liability.

> **Classified balance sheet:** A balance sheet that shows a subtotal for many items including current assets and current liabilities.

> **Interest:** The cost of using someone else's money for some period of time.

Can **YOU** do it?

1. Explain the difference between current and non-current assets.
2. Explain the difference between current and non-current liabilities.
3. Describe the characteristics of a classified balance sheet.

Answers (1) Current assets are those assets that a company will use to help produce revenue in the coming year. Non-current assets are those assets that a company will use for longer than a year. (2) Current liabilities are debts the company plans to repay in the next year. Non-current liabilities are debts the company repays over a period longer than one year. (3) A classified balance sheet groups like items together, with a subtotal for current assets and a subtotal for current liabilities.

Shareholders' equity

We've looked at two key components of a company's balance sheet: assets and liabilities. We now look at the third component: equity. As you learned in Chapter 1, equity is the owners' claims to the assets of the company. There are two ways owners can create equity in a company. The first way is through Contributed Capital, which means owners are making capital contributions. Usually, the capital owners give the firm is cash, but it could be another asset, such as land or equipment. In return for their capital contributions, owners receive shares of stock in the firm.

The second, and preferred way to create equity in a business, is to make a profit. Equity is created when the firm increases assets, and the owners have a claim to those assets. When Southwest sells a ticket and the ticket is used, the revenue from that sale increases assets, which increases the shareholders' equity in the company. When Southwest pays its pilots, the expense decreases assets and consequently reduces shareholders' equity. As you learned in Chapter 1, this type of shareholders' equity is called Retained Earnings. It's the part of shareholders' equity that represents the net income earned less any dividends paid to owners over the life of a firm.

In corporations, the two types of equity are separated on the balance sheet. In the shareholders' equity section of a corporation, you'll see both Contributed Capital and Retained Earnings. When a corporation issues stock to its owners, the contributed capital is reported as Common Stock. In a sole proprietorship or partnership, both types of equity—contributed and earned—are together called Capital. Separating these amounts for corporations provides information for potential investors about how much the owners have actually invested in the corporation.

Look at the shareholders' equity section of Southwest's balance sheet in Exhibit 2.3. The contributed capital accounts are Common Stock and Other Contributed Capital. Owners had contributed $790 + $299 (in millions), or $1,089 to Southwest as of December 31, 2004. Compare Contributed Capital to the firm's Retained Earnings of $4,089. Retained Earnings represents the increase in assets from doing business to which the owners have the claim. Southwest has earned quite a bit of equity for the owners.

Can **YOU** do it**?**

1. Define Retained Earnings.
2. Define Contributed Capital.

Answers (1) Retained Earnings is the equity the company has earned, less any distributions made to owners, over the life of the firm. (2) Contributed Capital consists of contributions the owners have made to the firm.

LEARNING OBJECTIVE 3

Identify the parts of the income statement and describe their characteristics.

A Closer Look at the Income Statement

Now that we have covered the balance sheet, we are ready to analyze the income statement. Refer to Exhibit 2.1 on page 44, the Income Statement for Southwest Airlines, as you read about the income statement.

Recognizing revenue and expenses

The income statement is a summary of the firm's activities for a period of time. Recall that revenues are the amounts earned by the firm, and expenses are the costs incurred to earn those revenues. The income statement lists all revenues and all expenses for the accounting period. When should revenue be included on an income statement? According to GAAP, revenue should be included when it is earned and its collection is reasonably assured. This timing is called the **revenue-recognition principle**. Recognizing revenue means including it on the income statement for the period—the month, the quarter, or the year. When Southwest provides a plane ride for a customer in exchange for a ticket, Southwest has earned the revenue. In Southwest's case, the firm collects the revenue in advance of earning it. When a customer purchases a ticket, no revenue will be shown on the income statement because the airline hasn't earned it yet. The time to recognize revenue is when an exchange actually takes place, or when the earnings process is complete. For example, when the plane has landed and the customer arrives at a destination, there is no doubt the transaction is complete. Often, revenue recognition coincides with the cash payment. However, the cash can be exchanged either before or after the service is rendered.

Revenue-recognition principle: The principle that revenue should be recognized when it is earned and its collection is reasonably assured.

Study Tip

Remember that dividends are not an expense. Dividends are a distribution of earnings and will appear on only the statement of changes in shareholders' equity in the retained earnings portion of the statement.

What about expenses? The timing of expense recognition depends on when the revenue that results from that expense is recognized. The **matching principle** is the basis for the income statement. According to the matching principle, expenses are included on the same income statement as the revenue they helped to generate. Operating, sales, and administrative expenses are all included on the income statement.

Matching principle: Expenses are recognized—shown on the income statement—in the same period as the revenue they helped generate.

Study Tip

If a cost has been incurred but the purchased item or service has not been consumed, it is classified as an asset until it is used.

Does the customer actually have to pay the company in cash before a sale can be counted as revenue? No. When a sale is made on credit, the seller will record revenue even though the buyer hasn't paid for the purchase at that time. Similarly, a cost incurred in the generation of revenue does not have to be paid to be included as an expense on the income statement. In calculating the revenue and expenses for an income statement, accountants do not follow the cash. Instead, they use the time when the goods are delivered, or the services rendered, as the signal to record the revenue.

Accountants use the expressions *virtually complete* and *economic substance* to describe the same idea—that a transaction does not have to be technically complete for a firm to recognize the resulting revenue. When the firm has done what is needed to earn the revenue and has earned the right to payment, the revenue is recognized. When a company sells a product, delivers the goods, and receives the customer's promise to pay, the transaction is considered virtually complete. Cash may come before the transaction is complete or it may come afterward.

Accrual-basis accounting refers to recognizing revenues when the economic substance of the transaction is complete and recognizing expenses when they have been incurred to earn the related revenue. The exchange of cash is not used to measure income and expenses for the income statement.

For some firms, it is difficult to know when to recognize revenue because there is so much disagreement among accountants about revenue recognition. They agree that revenue should be recognized—put on the income statement—when the revenue has actually been earned and the transaction is virtually complete, but they often can't agree exactly when that has happened. For example, think about when a company like Coca-Cola should recognize revenue. Here's how the sales process goes. First, a customer—like Wal-Mart—places an order with Coca-Cola. Then, Coca-Cola delivers the order to Wal-Mart. Next, the company sends an invoice to Wal-Mart. Finally, Wal-Mart pays for the product. This presents a number of different possibilities for the timing of revenue recognition: when Wal-Mart places the order, when Coca-Cola delivers the order, or when Wal-Mart pays for the order. In this example, Coca-Cola recognizes the revenue when the goods are delivered because Coca-Cola has completed everything it is required to do to earn the revenue and has the right to receive payment.

Can **YOU** do it?

1. Explain accrual-basis accounting.
2. Describe why revenue recognition is a problem.
3. Explain the matching principle.

Answers (1) Transactions are recorded in the period they are completed, no matter when the cash is exchanged. Revenue is recognized when earned, and expenses are matched to the revenues they helped generate. (2) Companies want to recognize revenue as soon as possible to improve their earnings. The emphasis that the market places on earnings motivates managers to recognize revenue as soon as possible. (3) Expenses go on the same income statement as the revenue they help generate.

Earnings per share—a number you've heard about

At the bottom of the income statement, you'll see an important amount called **earnings per share (EPS)**. EPS is determined by dividing net income for an accounting period by the weighted average number of outstanding shares of common stock.[3] EPS is a number that analysts and investors watch carefully. When you read about a company announcing its earnings, you are reading about EPS.

Managers are concerned about EPS because they know analysts use that number to draw conclusions about the company's financial performance. An increase or decrease in a company's EPS will affect its stock price. In a later chapter, we'll look at the calculation of EPS. For now, it's enough for you to realize that the numbers on the income statement are extremely important to managers for many reasons, one of which is because they are used to compute

---

[3]Technically, EPS is (Net Income − Preferred Dividends) divided by the weighted average number of common shares outstanding. Preferred dividends will be discussed in Chapter 10.

Accounting in the NEWS

Your Bonus Is on the Line. What Would You Do?

Managers and investors closely watch a company's earnings per share (EPS). Ira Zar, a former CFO (chief financial officer) of Computer Associates, pleaded guilty to fraud and obstruction charges. In his plea, Zar revealed that in 2000, he and two other senior executives conspired to keep the company's books open to record additional sales from the first quarter of 2000 into the quarter ended December 31, 1999, to meet Wall Street's expectations for that quarter. Prosecutors say that Computer Associates "backdated" more than $1 *billion* in sales in 2000. This means the company was recognizing revenue too early.

In 1998, three top executives of Computer Associates—CEO Sanjay Kumar, founder Charles Wang, and executive Richard Artzt, received bonuses totaling $1.1 billion, one of the largest amounts ever given to American executives.

These bonuses were tied to the performance of the company's stock. The executives later returned a portion of the bonus money to settle shareholder lawsuits. In September 2004, Sanjay Kumar was charged with securities fraud, conspiracy, and obstruction of justice in connection with the accounting scandal.

Now, put these two ideas together—stock price and executive bonuses. When a manager's bonus is tied to the performance of the company's stock, what sort of message does that send to the managers?

Thinking Critically

If you were a manager whose bonus depended on your company's stock performance, how far would you go to meet Wall Street's expectations? Would you count a sale made on January 3 or 4 in the previous December's sales? How about sales made in February or March?

Q What was the motivation of the top executives of Computer Associates to falsify earnings?

A The executives received huge bonuses for meeting specific stock price goals.

If managers receive bonuses based on how their company's stock performs, they may be tempted to manipulate earnings. Top executives at Computer Associates did just that—and got caught. The executives returned their bonuses and were charged with fraud and conspiracy.

EPS. Look back at Southwest's income statement in Exhibit 2.1 on page 44. You'll find EPS near the bottom of the income statement. Read more about the importance of earnings per share in *Accounting in the News*.

A Closer Look at the Statement of Changes in Shareholders' Equity

The statement of changes in shareholders' equity, often called simply the statement of shareholders' equity, describes the change in the shareholders' equity accounts—contributed capital accounts and Retained Earnings account—from the beginning of the fiscal year to the year-end balance sheet date. The first part of the statement shows the change in contributed capital, and the second part shows the change in Retained Earnings.

The first part of the statement starts with the beginning balance in Contributed Capital. Then, it shows any additions, which would be the result of new contributions from owners[4] during the year. Deductions from Contributed Capital are rare, and we won't see any in this text or this course. So the beginning balance and the additions add up to the ending balance in Contributed

---

[4]Usually, new contributions come from issuing new stock.

Exhibit 2.4

From Southwest Airlines' Statement of Retained Earnings

southwest.com

> From Southwest Airlines'
> Statement of Retained Earnings
> For the Year Ended December 31, 2004
>
> (in millions)
>
> | | |
> |---|---:|
> | Retained Earnings, 1/01/04 | $3,883 |
> | Net income | 313 |
> | Dividends | (14) |
> | Other adjustments (for employee stock plans)** | (93) |
> | Retained Earnings, 12/31/04 | $4,089 |
>
> **This is an advanced topic and will not be covered in this book.

In general, the ending balance in Retained Earnings is equal to beginning Retained Earnings plus net income minus dividends. Even though real financial statements often have a slightly more complicated computation, like the adjustment for employee stock plans in this one from Southwest's financial statements, we will deal with only the general case in introductory accounting.

Capital. The second part of the statement starts with the beginning balance in Retained Earnings. Net income is shown as an addition to Retained Earnings, and any dividends paid are shown as a deduction from Retained Earnings. Remember that Retained Earnings is increased because assets have increased from the activities of the firm, and the owner has the claim to those assets. The beginning balance plus net income minus dividends results in the ending balance in Retained Earnings. Exhibit 2.4 shows a statement of retained earnings—the second part of the statement of changes in shareholders' equity—from Southwest's 2004 financial statements.

A Closer Look at the Statement of Cash Flows

LEARNING OBJECTIVE 5

Identify the parts of the statement of cash flows and describe their characteristics.

We've analyzed the balance sheet, the income statement, and the statement of changes in shareholders' equity. Let's now turn our attention to the statement of cash flows. Thousands of companies go bankrupt each year because they fail to plan their cash flows effectively. The main reason for small business failure is that owners underestimate how much money they are going to need.[5] A secondary reason is poor cash flow planning. In other words, businesses fail because they don't have enough money, and they don't plan effective cash flows with the money they do have. When the time comes to pay their bills, they don't have enough cash on hand. Even though the focus of financial reporting is to prepare financial statements for shareholders and investors, the information about cash flows is equally useful to managers of a company.

As you learned in Chapter 1, GAAP requires a company to prepare a statement of cash flows to show all the cash the company has received and all the cash the company has disbursed during the accounting period. The statement of cash flows explains the details of the change in the cash balance during the accounting period. The change can be either a net increase or decrease in cash. As you also learned in Chapter 1, the statement of cash flow includes three sections that relate to the three business activities:

---

[5]From Jeff Wuorio, "10 Reasons Why Businesses Fail," May 7, 2004, www.bcentral.com/articles/wuorio/150.asp.

The types of cash flows for the statement of cash flows should be familiar to you. You learned about these in Chapter 1.

Exhibit 2.5

Types of Cash Flows

	Operating Activities	Investing Activities	Financing Activities
Cash inflows...	From customers who purchase products. From interest or dividend income earned from bank deposits.	From sale of property and equipment.	From issuing long-term debt. From issuing stock.
Cash outflows...	To suppliers for the purchase of inventory. To employees in the form of salaries.	To purchase plant and equipment. To purchase investments in other firms.	To repay long-term debt principal. To pay dividends to owners.

operating, investing, and financing. As a quick refresher, look at Exhibit 2.5 at the top of this page, which gives common examples of cash flows from all three cash flow activities.

Next, look at the condensed statement of cash flows from Southwest's 2004 financial statements in Exhibit 2.6. You'll see each of the three sections we've discussed.

Notice that the last number on the statement of cash flows is the same as the cash balance on the December 31, 2004, balance sheet shown in Exhibit 2.3 on page 49.

Exhibit 2.6

From Southwest's Statement of Cash Flows

southwest.com

Southwest Airlines
Condensed Statement of Cash Flows
For the year ended December 31, 2004
(in millions)

Net cash provided by operating activities	$1,157
Net cash used in investing activities	(1,850)
Net cash provided by financing activities	133
Net increase (decrease) in cash	(560)
Cash at the beginning of the year	1,865
Cash balance at December 31, 2004	$1,305

Can **YOU** do it?

1. Describe the statement of cash flows. Give an example of a cash inflow and a cash outflow in each category.
2. Explain why the statement of cash flows is necessary and useful to a company.
3. Explain the focus of financial reporting.

Answers (1) The statement of cash flows shows all of the cash receipts and all of the cash disbursements for the accounting period. The statement explains the change in cash during the period. Collection of cash from customers is an example of a cash inflow from operating activities; payment for inventory is an example of a cash outflow. Cash received from selling equipment is a cash inflow from investing activities; cash payment for land is a cash outflow. Cash received from the bank as a loan is a cash inflow from financing activities; cash dividends paid to shareholders is a cash outflow. (2) Having enough cash on hand to pay suppliers is crucial to the success of a business. The statement of cash flows helps a company understand its cash position. (3) The focus of financial reporting is earnings. The stock market analysts and investors pay more attention to earnings than any other single number.

Notes to the Financial Statements

LEARNING OBJECTIVE 6

Explain the purpose of the notes to the financial statements.

On the bottom of most printed financial statements you'll see small print that reads something like, "See accompanying notes." Every set of financial statements is followed by many pages of notes to satisfy GAAP requirements that companies provide information about any circumstances or events that would make a difference to the users of the statements. This principle is called the **full-disclosure principle**. Without the information provided in the notes, the financial statements would be almost useless. The notes describe the accounting methods the company has chosen from among the alternatives allowed by GAAP, and they also provide details that explain the numbers found on the statements. For example, Ford Motor Company's balance sheet will have the dollar amount of inventory, but the details of the *types* of inventory will not be shown on the statement. Instead, those details will be disclosed in the notes.

Full-disclosure principle: The principle that requires companies to disclose any circumstances and events that would make a difference to the users of the statements.

Exhibit 2.7 shows part of note 1 from Southwest's financial statements. The note describes the accounting choices the firm has made. In Southwest's 10-K, the financial statements take up 5 pages and the notes that follow take up 17 pages.

Exhibit 2.7

Notes to the Financial Statements

southwest.com

The notes to the financial statements always begin with a summary of the firm's significant accounting policies.

NOTES TO CONSOLIDATED FINANCIAL STATEMENTS
DECEMBER 31, 2004

1. SUMMARY OF SIGNIFICANT ACCOUNTING POLICIES

BASIS OF PRESENTATION Southwest Airlines Co. (Southwest) is a major domestic airline that provides point-to-point, low-fare service. The Consolidated Financial Statements include the accounts of Southwest and its wholly owned subsidiaries (the Company). All significant intercompany balances and transactions have been eliminated. The preparation of financial statements in conformity with accounting principles generally accepted in the United States (GAAP) requires management to make estimates and assumptions that affect the amounts reported in the financial statements and accompanying notes. Actual results could differ from these estimates.

LEARNING OBJECTIVE 7

Analyze business transactions using
the accounting equation and prepare
the four basic financial statements.

Business Transactions and Financial Statements

Now that we have discussed the basic financial statements, you should understand what information each of the four statements provides and the qualities
the information should have. Next, you'll learn how to analyze business transactions and use them to prepare the four financial statements.

Analyzing transactions

In the normal course of business, an accountant must record hundreds, or
sometimes thousands, of transactions in the accounting system. Let's look
carefully at the transactions for starting a company. Exhibit 2.8 shows six
transactions for Clint's Consulting Company.

Before you can record a transaction, you have to understand what the transaction is all about. First, identify any assets, liabilities, or equity amounts that are
affected by the transaction and any possible revenue or expense amounts.
Remember the five basic categories of accounts are: (1) assets, (2) liabilities, (3)
equity, (4) revenue, and (5) expense. Next, figure out which specific account will
be increased or decreased. For example, the transaction of a cash sale will affect
assets and revenue. Which asset? Cash. Which revenue? Sales. Then, determine
the dollar amount involved in the transaction. Exhibit 2.9 shows the typical
accounts you will see when you analyze transactions. To summarize, here are the
steps you need to follow to analyze a transaction:

1. Determine which of the following types of accounts are affected by the
   transaction: asset, liability, equity, revenue, expense.
2. Identify whether the account increases or decreases.
3. Determine the amount.
4. Show the effect of the transaction in the accounting equation.

Let's analyze each of the transactions shown in Exhibit 2.8.

Transaction 1: The company receives a contribution of $2,000 in exchange for
ownership in the company. The shareholders' contributions take the form of
common stock in a corporation. Referring to the four steps just presented, analyze the transaction. Remember that every business transaction keeps the
accounting equation in balance.

1. Assets and equity are affected.
2. Specifically, Cash and Common Stock are affected.

Exhibit 2.8

Transactions for Clint's Consulting Company

	Transactions during January
1.	Clint and some friends contribute $2,000 to start the business.
2.	Clint's Consulting, Inc., borrows $4,000 from a local bank to begin the business, which is to be repaid in six months
3.	Clint's pays $1,400 cash for operating expenses.
4.	Clint's acquires office equipment for $5,000 cash.
5.	Clint's earns $6,000 for service revenue, all paid in cash by clients.
6.	The company pays $20 interest to the bank at the end of January.

Exhibit 2.9

Typical Accounts Used in Transaction Analysis

Assets	Liabilities	Shareholders' Equity	Revenues	Expenses
Cash	Accounts Payable	Common Stock	Sales Revenue	Cost of Goods Sold
Accounts Receivable	Salaries Payable	Additional Paid-in Capital	Service Revenue	Operating Expenses
Inventory	Utilities Payable	Retained Earnings	Interest Revenue	Salary Expense
Supplies	Notes Payable			Selling and Administrative Expenses
Prepaid items (rent, insurance)				Marketing Expenses
Property, Plant, and Equipment (PP&E)				Interest Expense

3. Both are increased by $2,000.

4. This is how transaction 1 affects the accounting equation:

Accounting Equation				
Assets	**=**	**Liabilities**	**+**	**Shareholders' Equity**
				Contributed Capital + **Retained Earnings**
Cash				Common Stock
2,000				2,000

Transaction 2: Clint's Consulting Company borrows $4,000 from a local bank. The loan will be repaid in six months.

1. Assets and liabilities are affected.

2. Cash is increased and Notes Payable is increased.

3. The amount is $4,000.

4. This is how transaction 2 affects the accounting equation:

Accounting Equation				
Assets	**=**	**Liabilities**	**+**	**Shareholders' Equity**
				Contributed Capital + **Retained Earnings**
Cash		Notes Payable		
4,000		4,000		

Transaction 3: The firm spends $1,400 cash for operating expenses.

1. Assets and expenses are affected.

2. The Cash account is decreased, and the Operating Expenses account is increased. Expenses decrease Retained Earnings, so the increase in

Operating Expenses is shown in the accounting equation as a decrease in the Retained Earnings column.

3. The amount is $1,400.

4. This is how transaction 3 affects the accounting equation:

Accounting Equation							
Assets	**=**	**Liabilities**	**+**		**Shareholders' Equity**		
				Contributed Capital	**+**	**Retained Earnings**	
Cash						Operating Expenses	
–1,400						–1,400	

Transaction 4: Clint's Consulting acquires office equipment at a cost of $5,000 for cash. This transaction increases the asset Equipment by $5,000 and decreases the asset Cash by $5,000.

Accounting Equation							
Assets	**=**	**Liabilities**	**+**		**Shareholders' Equity**		
				Contributed Capital	**+**	**Retained Earnings**	
Cash	Equipment						
–5,000	5,000						

Transaction 5: Clint's earned $6,000 for service revenue, all paid in cash by clients. This transaction increases the asset Cash by $6,000 and increases Service Revenue (and consequently Retained Earnings) by $6,000.

Accounting Equation							
Assets	**=**	**Liabilities**	**+**		**Shareholders' Equity**		
				Contributed Capital	**+**	**Retained Earnings**	
Cash						Service Revenue	
6,000						6,000	

Transaction 6: Clint's Consulting paid $20 interest to the bank. The asset Cash is decreased by $20, and the expense Interest Expense is increased by $20, which decreases Retained Earnings.

Accounting Equation							
Assets	**=**	**Liabilities**	**+**		**Shareholders' Equity**		
				Contributed Capital	**+**	**Retained Earnings**	
Cash						Interest Expense	
–20						–20	

Finding the financial statements on the accounting equation worksheet

The information for the four basic financial statements—the income statement, the statement of changes in shareholders' equity, the balance sheet, and the statement of cash flows—can all be found on the accounting equation worksheet. Exhibit 2.10 shows all of the transactions for Clint's Consulting in an accounting equation worksheet. Each financial statement has a unique color. You will see these colors throughout the chapters identifying the different financial statements:

Study Tip

The accounting equation worksheet is not exactly the same as the balance sheet. The balance sheet is a condensed summary of the transactions.

- Red identifies an income statement. The transactions that affect the income statement will have an amount shown in the red section on the accounting equation worksheet.

- Yellow identifies the statement of shareholders' equity. The transactions that affect shareholders' equity will have an amount in the yellow section. Notice that net income is embedded in the yellow section. That's because net income will be part of the statement of changes in shareholders' equity.

- Blue identifies the balance sheet. Only the summary of the transactions—the ending balances in each account—will be shown on the balance sheet.

- Green identifies the statement of cash flows. The cash inflows and outflows are all found in the cash column of the accounting equation worksheet. These are explained in the statement of cash flows.

Use the color-coded accounting equation worksheet in Exhibit 2.10 to help you prepare financial statements in your homework assignments.

Exhibit 2.10

Accounting Equation Worksheet for Clint's Consulting

	Assets				= Liabilities		+ Shareholders' Equity				
							Contributed Capital	+ Retained Earnings			
	Cash	Accounts Receivable	Equipment	Accounts Payable	Notes Payable			Revenues	Expenses	Dividends
1.	+2,000						+2,000				
2.	+4,000				+4,000						
3.	−1,400									−1,400	
4.	−5,000		+5,000								
5.	+6,000								+6,000		
6.	−20										−20
	5,580	+	5,000	=	4,000	+	2,000	+	4,580		

■ Income Statement   ■ Statement of Changes in Shareholders' Equity   ■ Balance Sheet   ■ Statement of Cash Flows

All of a firm's transactions can be shown in the accounting equation worksheet. The *income statement,* indicated by the red box, provides the details of revenues earned and expenses incurred. The transactions are then condensed into one number—Net income—which becomes part of the *statement of changes in shareholders' equity,* indicated by the yellow box. Then, the information from the statement of changes in shareholders' equity is summarized as part of the *balance sheet,* shown in blue. All of the transactions have, either directly or indirectly, affected the balance sheet. The *statement of cash flows,* indicated by the green box, will provide the details of how a company got its cash and how it spent its cash during the accounting period.

Suppose a company provides services for $500 cash. Show how this transaction affects the accounting equation.

Solution:

Assets	=	Liabilities	+	Contributed Capital	+	Retained Earnings
500 Cash						500 Service Revenue

Study Tip

Revenues and expenses are shown under the Retained Earnings column of the worksheet because they eventually get added to (revenue) and subtracted from (expenses) Retained Earnings. However, revenue and expense accounts are *not* considered Retained Earnings accounts. They are considered income statement accounts.

Statement of retained earnings: The portion of the statement of changes in shareholders' equity that describes the changes to Retained Earnings—increased by Net income and decreased by Dividends.

The income statement shows the revenues and expenses for an accounting period.

Preparing an income statement, statement of changes in shareholders' equity, and balance sheet

You can prepare the financial statements for Clint's Consulting Company from the accounting equation worksheet in Exhibit 2.10. The income statement is always prepared first. The heading of an income statement indicates the period covered by the statement. Here, the time period is the month of January. Exhibit 2.11 shows the income statement for Clint's for the month.

What is *not* included on the income statement is as important as what *is* included. Neither the owners' contributions nor amounts borrowed from creditors are included in the income statement, because this statement includes only items from operations. Look back at Exhibit 2.10. You'll see that the income statement contains the information shown in red. Also, note that dividends are not included on the income statement.

The second statement the accountant prepares is the statement of changes in shareholders' equity. The income statement was prepared first because net income is needed to update Retained Earnings. The information shown in red in Exhibit 2.10 can now be summarized by one number, Net income, which will be shown as an addition to Retained Earnings on the statement of changes in shareholders' equity. Recall that the statement of changes in shareholders' equity has two parts: changes in Contributed Capital and changes in Retained Earnings. When only the changes in Retained Earnings are shown, the statement is called a **statement of retained earnings**.[6] Exhibit 2.12 shows the full statement of changes in shareholders' equity for the month of January.

Exhibit 2.11

Income Statement

Clint's Consulting Company
Income Statement
For the month of January

Service revenue		$6,000
Expenses:		
Operating expenses	$1,400	
Interest expense	20	1,420
Net income		$4,580

[6]In actual financial statements, the statement of retained earnings is rarely shown separately. It is shown alone only when the changes in equity are restricted to changes in Retained Earnings.

Exhibit 2.12

Statement of Changes in Shareholders' Equity

> The beginning balances are zero here because it is the firm's first year of business. The ending balances for January will be the beginning balances for February.

Clint's Consulting Company
Statement of Changes in Shareholders' Equity
For the month of January

Contributed Capital:
Beginning balance .... $ ——
Contributions during the month 2,000
Ending balance 2,000

Retained Earnings:
Beginning balance .... $ ——
Net income 4,580
Dividends .... ——
Ending balance 4,580
Total shareholders' equity $6,580

Study Tip

Retained Earnings will equal net income only in the first year of a firm's operation and as long as no dividends are paid. After the first year, the Retained Earnings balance will equal all of the net income the firm has earned since its inception minus all dividends paid since its inception.

The third statement is the balance sheet, shown in Exhibit 2.13. When we prepared the income statement, we collapsed the red area in Exhibit 2.10 to one number, and then we used that number in the Retained Earnings part of the statement of changes in shareholders' equity. For the balance sheet, we collapse the yellow area into two numbers—contributed capital and retained earnings. The remaining balance sheet numbers are the totals from each column in the worksheet.

Exhibit 2.13

Balance Sheet

> The amounts for Contributed Capital and Retained Earnings come from the statement of changes in shareholders' equity. Notice that in this case, Retained Earnings equals net income. That is true only because it is Clint's first month of business, and the company did not pay dividends. Remember that Retained Earnings equals all of the net incomes a company has earned since its inception minus all dividends paid out during the life of the company.

Clint's Consulting Company
Balance Sheet
At January 31

Assets
Current assets
Cash .... $ 5,580
Non-current assets
Equipment 5,000
    Total assets $10,580

Liabilities and Shareholders' equity
Current liabilities
Notes payable .... $ 4,000
Shareholders' equity
Contributed capital 2,000
Retained earnings 4,580
    Total liabilities and shareholders' equity $10,580

Exhibit 2.14

Cash Transactions for Clint's Consulting

Cash $
(1) +2,000
(2) +4,000
(3) −1,400
(4) −5,000
(5) +6,000
(6)   −20

Preparing a statement of cash flows

Before we leave Clint's Consulting Company, we need to prepare the final statement—the statement of cash flows. Exhibit 2.14 shows all of the cash transaction amounts from the worksheet in Exhibit 2.10. Each must be included on the statement.

Transaction 1: Cash contribution received from owner. This is a financing activity for $2,000. All cash exchanged between a company and its owners is classified as cash from financing activities.

Transaction 2: Cash proceeds from bank loan. This is a financing activity for $4,000. When a company receives cash by borrowing money, the cash flow is a financing cash flow. Conversely, when a company repays the loan principal, the cash outflow is a financing cash flow. All interest payments, however, are classified as operating cash flows.

Transaction 3: Cash paid for operating expenses. This is an operating cash flow of $1,400. A company classifies the cash it spends in the normal course of its business activities as cash flow from operations.

Transaction 4: Cash paid for equipment. This is an investing cash flow of $5,000. When a company spends cash on an asset that will last for more than a year, the cash flow is considered an investing cash outflow. When a company such as Southwest Airlines purchases a Boeing 737, the cash flow is an investing cash flow.

Transaction 5: Provided services to customers for cash. This is an operating cash flow of $6,000. All cash amounts collected from customers are operating cash flows.

Transaction 6: Paid interest on the note payable. This is an operating cash flow of $20. Although you may think interest has more to do with financing than with operations, the FASB decided that interest is a cost of doing business that should be included in the firm's operating cash flows. Both interest revenue collected and interest expense disbursed are considered cash flows from operations.

As you know by now, the statement of cash flows shows all of the cash inflows and outflows for the period. The net amount will be the difference between the beginning-of-the-period cash balance and the end-of-the-period cash balance. Because these transactions are the first for a startup company, the beginning cash balance for Clint's is zero. Look at the balance sheet in Exhibit 2.13 to see that the ending cash balance is $5,580. In Exhibit 2.15, you can see how a statement of cash flows for the period shows exactly what caused the change in cash during that period.

The relationship among the financial statements

It is easy to see the relationship among the statements by looking at all four of them together, as shown in Exhibit 2.16. Remember, you prepare the statements in this order: (1) income statement, (2) statement of changes in shareholders' equity, (3) balance sheet, and (4) statement of cash flows. Follow the arrows in Exhibit 2.16 to see why this order is necessary. Notice that net income is used to calculate Retained Earnings. Then, Retained Earnings is used on the balance sheet.

LEARNING OBJECTIVE 8

Compute and explain the current ratio.

Financial Statement Analysis: The Current Ratio

Every business must pay its bills. Suppliers, in particular, want to evaluate a company's ability to meet its current obligations. Simply looking at how much cash a company has does not provide enough information. As you learned in

Exhibit 2.15

Statement of Cash Flows for Clint's Consulting

This statement of cash flows shows all of the cash inflows and outflows for the period. The net increase in cash equals the ending cash balance (on the balance sheet) because this is Clint's first month of business, and the firm started with no cash.

Clint's Consulting Company
Statement of Cash Flows
For the month of January

Cash from operating activities		
Cash collected from customers	$6,000	
Cash paid for operating expenses	(1,400)	
Cash paid for interest	(20)	
Total cash from operating activities		$4,580
Cash from investing activities		
Cash for equipment		(5,000)
Cash from financing activities		
Cash proceeds from loans	$4,000	
Cash contributions from owners	2,000	6,000
Net increase in cash		5,580
Beginning cash balance		—
Ending cash balance		$5,580

Chapter 1, a financial ratio is a comparison of different amounts on the financial statements. Several ratios measure the short-term liquidity of a company. The most common is the **current ratio**, which accountants compute by dividing the total amount of current assets by the total amount of current liabilities:

Current ratio: A liquidity ratio that measures a firm's ability to meet its short-term obligations.

$$\text{Current ratio} = \frac{\text{Current assets}}{\text{Current liabilities}}$$

The ratio gives information about a company's ability to fund its current operations in the short run.

Using the current ratio, investors can compare the liquidity of one company to that of other companies of different types and sizes. Recall that liquidity is a measure of how easily a company can turn its current assets into cash to pay its debts as they come due. This information would be important to a supplier considering extending credit to a company. The current ratio also provides information about the liquidity of a single company over time.

Look at the balance sheet for Southwest Airlines in Exhibit 2.3 on page 49. The current ratio for the fiscal year ended December 31, 2004 is:

$2,172$ million $\div$ $2,142$ million $= 1.01$

The current assets for the year ended December 31, 2003 totaled $2,313 million, and the current liabilities for the same period were $1,723. So the current ratio for the fiscal year ended December 31, 2003 is:

$2,313$ million $\div$ $1,723$ million $= 1.34$

Another way to think about the current ratio is to say that Southwest Airlines has $1.34 of current assets with which to pay off each $1.00 of its current liabilities.

Can you see why companies often strive to have a current ratio of 1 or greater? That would mean a firm has enough current assets to pay off its current

Exhibit 2.16

The Relationships Among the Statements

Clint's Consulting Company
Income Statement
For the month of January

Service revenue		$ 6,000
Expenses:		
Operating expenses	$ 1,400	
Interest expense	20	1,420
Net income		$ 4,580

Clint's Consulting Company
Statement of Changes in
Shareholders' Equity
For the month of January

Contributed Capital	
Beginning balance	$ —
Contributions during the month	2,000
Ending balance	2,000
Retained Earnings	
Beginning balance	$ —
Net income	4,580
Dividends	—
Ending balance	4,580
Total shareholders' equity	$ 6,580

Clint's Consulting Company
Balance Sheet
At January 31

Assets	
Current assets	
Cash	$ 5,580
Non-current assets	
Equipment	5,000
Total assets	$10,580
Liabilities and shareholders' equity	
Current liabilities	
Notes payable	4,000
Owner's equity	
Contributed capital	2,000
Retained earnings	4,580
Total liabilities and shareholders' equity	$10,580

Clint's Consulting Company
Statement of Cash Flows
For the month of January

Cash from operating activities	
Cash collected from customers	$ 6,000
Cash paid for operating expenses	(1,400)
Cash paid for interest	(20)
Cash from operating activities	$ 4,580
Cash from investing activities	
Cash for equipment	(5,000)
Cash from financing activities	
Cash proceeds from loans	4,000
Cash contributions from owners	2,000
Cash from financing activities	6,000
Net increase in cash	5,580
Beginning cash balance	0
Ending cash balance	$ 5,580

---

liabilities. When using ratio analysis, it is often interesting to compare a firm's ratios to those of a competitor in the same industry. Delta Airlines, for example, had a current ratio of 0.74 at December 31, 2003. Delta has been in serious financial trouble, and the current ratio less than 1 might be confirmation of this. In September 2005 Delta Airlines filed for bankruptcy protection. This means the firm will have a chance to reorganize and will not have to pay all of its debts.

The reduction in Southwest's current ratio from 2003 to 2004 indicates a reduction in the company's liquidity. Looking at the current ratio for two consecutive years gives some information about Southwest Airlines, but you would need much more information to reach any conclusions. As you learn more about financial statements, you'll learn additional ratios and several ways to analyze a company's financial statements.

You might be surprised to know that some firms actually try to keep their current ratio *below* 1. If a firm generates a great deal of cash, it may know that it will generate sufficient cash to pay its current liabilities as they come due. Darden Restaurants, owners of Olive Garden, Red Lobster, and Smokey Bones, had a current ratio of 0.51 for its fiscal year ended May 30, 2004. Here's what Darden's management had to say about the current ratio in the firm's annual report:

> Cash flows generated from operating activities provide us with a significant source of liquidity. Since substantially all our sales are for cash and cash equivalents, and accounts payable are generally due in 5 to 30 days, we are able to carry current liabilities in excess of current assets.

Business risk, control, & ethics

LEARNING OBJECTIVE 9

Identify the risks of inaccurate financial records and how to control those risks.

Now that we've discussed the general characteristics of accounting information and the information shown on the four basic financial statements, let's take a look at how companies make sure the information in those statements is complete, accurate, and reliable.

Inaccurate or incomplete information can put the company at risk. For example, when Xerox was investigated by the SEC for accounting errors, the firm had to lower its revenue for the period from 1997 to 2001. The restatement reduced pre-tax income for the period by $1.4 billion, and the stock price dropped 13%. A drop in its stock price hurts a company's ability to borrow money and decreases the value of the owners' investment in the firm. In addition, mistakes in a firm's financial statements can cost the firm millions of dollars in fines by the Securities and Exchange Commission (SEC).

An SEC investigation of Xerox led to that company having to restate its revenue for 1999–2001. The restatement caused the company's stock to drop by 13%. Headquartered in Stamford, Connecticut, Xerox employs 58,100 people worldwide. The company's revenues for 2004 were $15.7 billion.

Controls to ensure accuracy and completeness

Recall from Chapter 1 that internal controls are company policies and procedures designed to reduce risk. Specifically, internal controls are designed to protect the assets of a firm and to ensure the accuracy and reliability of the accounting records. Accountants are especially interested in the specific controls designed to ensure that financial statements are both accurate and complete. Internal controls are designed to protect the accounting system from both unintentional errors and fraud.

Sometimes it is difficult to determine if improper accounting is the result of errors or fraud. For example, in March of 2004, the SEC filed charges against Computron for improperly recording more than $9 million in revenue on its financial statements. Also, in 2004, the SEC investigated the Mexican unit of Xerox Corporation for improperly recording revenue. Xerox officials in Mexico didn't accurately report receivables—officials overstated how much customers owed them—and improperly classified sales, leases, and rentals, violating GAAP. The causes for this improper accounting were (1) a failure of the Mexican executives to adhere to Xerox's corporate policies and procedures, and (2) inadequate internal controls. These accounting failures point out that a company needs internal controls to make sure accounting information is accurate and complete. As you learned in Chapter 1, controls are policies and procedures a company uses to minimize those risks. Read about managing risk in *Accounting in the News*.

Exhibit 2.17 summarizes three types of controls a company can use to minimize the risk of errors in the accounting system: preventive controls, detective controls, and corrective controls.

Accounting in the NEWS

Risk and Control

How the Sarbanes-Oxley Act Will Help Companies Manage Risks

Investors want to be sure the information on a company's financial statements is accurate. To make sure all legitimate transactions are accurately recorded, a company must have internal controls to protect its accounting system. Controls are procedures and policies to help the company achieve these objectives. For example, most companies have a procedure for reimbursing employees for business expenses. The procedures are designed to make sure only legitimate expenses are reimbursed. The Sarbanes-Oxley Act (SOX) requires public companies to include a separate report on the effectiveness of their internal controls with the annual report they submit to the Securities and Exchange Commission

(SEC). In addition, the company's external auditors will evaluate and report on management's risk assessment. Information about the effectiveness of a company's internal controls will be available to all financial statement users—investors, creditors, competitors, and customers. How do you think this requirement will affect companies? A 2004 survey of approximately 270 board directors from U.S. companies reported annual Sarbanes-Oxley compliance costs of $16 million on average. Another study conducted at the same time reported that 44% of the senior executives questioned admitted their firms do not have a clear view of their total compliance spending. Putting a dollar figure on how much Sarbanes-Oxley has cost corporate America is extremely difficult. Often-cited estimates range from $1.6 million to $4.4 million per company each year.

Q Who has to report on a firm's internal controls?

A Both management and the external auditors must report on a firm's internal controls.

The Sarbanes-Oxley Act gives investors more confidence that the numbers that appear in annual reports are accurate.

Source: AMR Research Document #16794, December 8, 2003, www.amrreserach.com. Reprinted by permission of AMR Research. "The High Costs of Sarbox Compliance," by Stephen Taub. CFO.com, November 24, 2004. Carl Bialik, "How Much is it Really Costing to Comply with Sarbanes-Oxley?" *Wall Street Journal*, June 16, 2005

A company's accounting information system consists of three major types of controls: ones that prevent errors, ones that detect errors, and ones that correct errors.

Exhibit 2.17

Types of Internal Controls

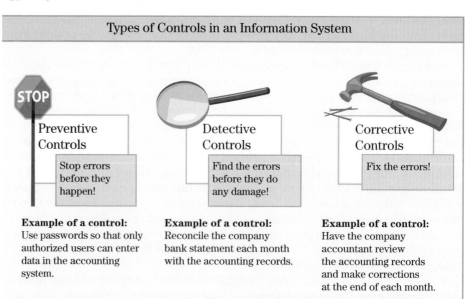

Types of Controls in an Information System

Preventive Controls	Detective Controls	Corrective Controls
Stop errors before they happen!	Find the errors before they do any damage!	Fix the errors!
Example of a control: Use passwords so that only authorized users can enter data in the accounting system.	**Example of a control:** Reconcile the company bank statement each month with the accounting records.	**Example of a control:** Have the company accountant review the accounting records and make corrections at the end of each month.

Preventive Controls These types of controls help prevent errors in an accounting system. When you order something from Amazon.com, the company gives you more than one chance to review and confirm your order. The computer program is designed to automatically insert the price of each item you order. These are controls that Amazon has put in place to help prevent errors from entering its accounting system.

Detective Controls Detective controls are those that help a company find errors. For example, at the end of every work day, a cashier at Target will count the money, ATM receipts, and credit card receipts in his or her drawer and compare the total to the total sales entered in the computer. This control will help Target find errors in its sales and receipts. Once the errors are found, they must be corrected.

Corrective Controls Corrective controls are those that correct any errors that have been discovered. Target has a policy for handling cash shortages—perhaps the cashier must make up any shortage. Frequently, corrective controls are policies and procedures a company has in place for handling any errors that are detected.

As you learn more about accounting, you will see examples of preventive, detective, and corrective controls. Keep in mind that to be effective, a system of internal control must rely on the people who perform the duties assigned to them. An internal control system is only as effective as the people who execute it. Human error, collusion—two or more people working together to circumvent a policy or procedure—and changing conditions can all weaken a system of internal control.

YOU make the call:

Can Southwest Airlines Get a Loan?

We started this chapter with a question about Southwest Airlines getting a loan from the bank. A new clerk thought an income statement was enough information. Now that you've studied all of the financial statements, do you think the information on the income statement will be sufficient for the bank? The answer is no. The income statement will simply tell the bank how the company has performed during the past year. It doesn't provide any information about the firm's ability to pay its bills. A bank would also want to see a balance sheet and a statement of cash flows. One financial statement doesn't tell the whole story about any company.

Let's Take a Test Drive

Real-World Problem:
Southwest Airlines

Southwest Airlines earned over $6 billion in revenue during 2004. At the end of 2004, Southwest was operating 2,800 flights every day. Each year the airline flies more than 65 million passengers to 60 airports. That means there were thousands of transactions between Southwest and its customers, investors, creditors, and employees. To keep track of all of these transactions and to assure the preparation of useful financial statements, Southwest must have an extensive accounting information system. Every quarter, Southwest will prepare the financial statements you studied in this chapter.

Concepts

Southwest will prepare the four basic financial statements and extensive notes to communicate its financial position and the year's performance at the end of its fiscal year. The goal of accounting standards is to ensure that the information is *relevant*, *reliable*, *comparable*, and *consistent*. All of these qualities should make the information useful to investors, analysts, creditors, and others who use it.

The accounting standards, known as Generally Accepted Accounting Principles (GAAP), are based on several assumptions:

- *Time-period assumption:* Southwest's financial statements will apply to a specific, finite period of time.
- *Separate-entity assumption:* The information in Southwest's financial statements will pertain to only the company, not any unrelated companies or any of the owners.
- *Monetary-unit assumption:* Only items that can be measured in dollars are included in Southwest's financial statements.
- *Going-concern assumption:* The statements will be prepared with the assumption that Southwest is an ongoing business for the foreseeable future.

Southwest's accounting system will record revenues and expenses using *accrual-basis accounting*. That is, it will

1. Record transactions at their historical cost.
2. Recognize revenue, which means including it on the income statement, in the period it is earned.
3. Match expenses to the revenues they help generate.

The financial statements will include an extensive set of accompanying notes because GAAP requires *full disclosure* of any information that would make a difference to investors.

All of the standards and guidelines of GAAP are applied with two constraints. If an item is too small to have any significance, it is called immaterial and does not have to conform to the standards. As you can imagine, *materiality* is a highly debatable issue in many circumstances. The other constraint is *conservatism*. Accounting makes sure assets and revenues are not overstated. When there is a legitimate doubt about how to apply an accounting standard, the one that minimizes assets and net income should be chosen.

The Mechanics

Although Southwest Airlines has a very sophisticated system for recording business transactions, we will use the accounting equation worksheet to record, organize, and summarize a small number of typical transactions. Then, we'll use the information to prepare the four financial statements. Suppose Southwest Airlines decided to start a new airline for short flights and to keep separate accounting records and financial statements for this new company. The new company will be called SW2. During its first year of business, suppose SW2 engaged in the following transactions (in millions of dollars):

1. Issued SW2 stock (received contributions from owners) in the amount of $250.
2. Borrowed $850 from a local bank with a 6-year note.
3. Purchased new flight equipment for $650 cash.
4. Paid $25 for operating expenses.
5. Purchased new ground equipment for cash of $300.
6. Collected $800 from customers for flights taken.
7. Paid salaries to employees of $480.
8. Purchased spare parts and supplies for $20 on account. They have not been used but will be in the next year.
9. Paid dividends to new shareholders of $5.

Instructions

1. Set up an accounting equation worksheet like the one in Exhibit 2.10 and record each transaction on the worksheet. (Ignore interest and depreciation expense.)
2. Prepare the four basic financial statements from the worksheet.

Solution

	Assets					=	Liabilities	+	Shareholders' Equity			
									Contributed Capital	+	Retained Earnings	
	Cash	Equipment	Parts and Supplies	Accounts Payable	Notes Payable				Common Stock	Revenues	Expenses	Dividends
1.	+250								+250			
2.	+850				+850							
3.	−650	+650										
4.	−25										−25	
5.	−300	+300										
6.	+800									+800		
7.	−480										−480	
8.			+20	+20								
9.	−5											−5
	440	+ 950	+ 20	= 20	+ 850			+	250	+ 800	−505	−5

Check: Assets = $1,410   Liabilities + SH Equity = $1,410

■ Income Statement   ■ Statement of Changes in Shareholders' Equity   ■ Balance Sheet   ■ Statement of Cash Flows

From the accounting equation worksheet, you can prepare the financial statements. Start with the income statement. The red square indicates the revenues and expenses. In this case, it is a very condensed income statement. That is, the company would have many types of revenue accounts and many more expense accounts in its internal recordkeeping:

The next statement you prepare is the Statement of Changes in Shareholders' Equity. Notice how net income is used in this statement:

SW2 Airlines
Income Statement
For the year ended June 30
(in millions)

Revenue	$800
Expenses	505
Net income	$295

SW2 Airlines
Statement of Changes in Shareholders' Equity
For the year ended June 30
(in millions)

Contributed Capital	
Beginning balance	$ —
Common stock issued	250
Ending balance	250
Retained Earnings	
Beginning balance	$ —
Net income	295
Dividends	(5)
Ending balance	290
Total shareholders' equity	$540

These amounts will go to the equity section of the balance sheet.

The balance sheet is prepared next. Notice that revenues, expenses, and dividends are *not* shown on the balance sheet. Those amounts have been folded into the Retained Earnings balance.

SW2 Airlines
Balance Sheet
At June 30

> The change in cash from the beginning of the year (0 in this example) to the amount on the year-end balance sheet of $440 will be explained by the statement of cash flows.

Assets

Cash	$ 440
Parts and supplies	20
Equipment	950
Total assets.	$1,410

Liabilities and shareholders' equity

Liabilities

> These amounts came from the statement of changes in shareholders' equity.

Accounts payable	$ 20
Note payable	850
Shareholders' equity	
Contributed capital	250
Retained earnings	290
Total liabilities and shareholders' equity	$1,410

Finally, you prepare the statement of cash flows. To do this, go down the list of transactions in the cash column of the worksheet and identify each as cash from operating activities, cash from investing activities, or cash from financing activities.

- All cash collected from customers and all cash paid for the expenses to run the day-to-day operations of the firm are cash flows from operations. For SW2, these are (4) cash paid for operating expenses, (6) cash collected from customers, and (7) cash paid to employees for salaries.

- All cash paid for equipment (assets that last longer than a year) are cash flows from investing activities. For SW2, these are (3) purchase of flight equipment and (5) purchase of ground equipment.

- All cash used to finance the business—from owners and long-term creditors—are cash flows from financing activities. For SW2, these are (1) issue of stock, (2) receipt of proceeds from loan, and (9) payment of dividends to shareholders.

Notice that transaction (8), purchase of parts and supplies on account, does not affect the statement of cash flows. Why not? No cash is involved in the transaction. When the cash is paid in the next year, it will be an operating cash flow.

SW2
Statement of Cash Flows
For the Year Ended June 30
(in millions)

Cash from operating activities		
Cash collected from customers	$800	
Cash paid for operating expenses	(25)	
Cash paid to employees	(480)	$295
Cash from investing activities		
Cash paid for flight equipment	650	
Cash paid for ground equipment	300	(950)
Cash from financing activities		
Contributions from owners	250	
Cash proceeds from loan	850	
Cash paid for dividends	(5)	1,095
Increase in cash		440
Add beginning cash		0
Ending cash balance		$440

> This is the cash balance found on the balance sheet.

Rapid Review

1. **Explain the objectives, assumptions, and qualities of financial reporting.** The objective of financial reporting is to provide useful information to investors, analysts, creditors, and other interested parties. To make the financial statements useful, the people who use them need to understand the standards and the choices used in their construction. These standards are called *Generally Accepted Accounting Principles (GAAP)*. The financial statements are subject to the assumptions, principles, and constraints shown in Exhibit 2.18.

2. **Identify the parts of the balance sheet and describe their characteristics.** The basic elements of the balance sheet are:

   a. *Assets*—probable future benefits as the result of past transactions

   b. *Liabilities*—debts or obligations as the result of past transactions

   c. *Shareholders' equity*—claims of the owners provided by their contributions or by earnings of the company.

3. **Identify the parts of the income statement and describe their characteristics.** The basic elements of the income statement are:

   a. *Revenues*—amounts earned by a firm for providing goods and services

   b. *Expenses*—the costs of earning the period's revenues

   c. *Net income*—a company's earnings for the period, equal to revenues minus expenses

4. **Identify the parts of the statement of changes in shareholders' equity and describe their characteristics.**

Exhibit 2.18

Assumptions, Principles, and Constraints of Financial Reporting

Assumptions:	Time-period assumption	The life of a business can be divided into artificial time periods for financial reporting.
	Separate-entity assumption	Financial statements of a firm contain financial information about only that firm.
	Monetary-unit assumption (Chapter 1)	Only items that can be measured in monetary units are included in the financial statements.
	Going-concern assumption	A company will remain in business for the foreseeable future.
Principles:	Historical-cost principle	Assets are recorded at cost.
	Revenue-recognition principle	Revenue is recognized when it is earned and collection is reasonably assured.
	Matching principle	Expenses are recognized in the same period as the revenue they helped generate.
	Full-disclosure principle	A company should provide information about any circumstances and events that would make a difference to the users of the financial statements.
Constraints:	Materiality	Materiality refers to the size or significance of an item or transaction on the company's financial statements. Only material items must conform to GAAP.
	Conservatism	When there is any question about how to account for a transaction, the accountant should select the treatment that will be least likely to overstate income or overstate assets.

a. *Changes in Contributed Capital*—beginning amount plus any new contributions made during the year to arrive at the ending balance

b. *Changes in Retained Earnings*—beginning amount plus net income minus dividends to arrive at the ending balance

5. **Identify the parts of the statement of cash flows and describe their characteristics.** The basic elements of the statement of cash flows are:

a. *Cash from operations*—cash flows from the normal operations of the firm

b. *Cash from investing activities*—cash flows from the purchase and sales of productive assets of the firm and investments in other firms

c. *Cash from financing activities*—cash flows from owners and from long-term creditors that fund the firm

6. **Explain the purpose of the notes to the financial statements.** In addition to the four basic financial statements, a company provides a set of notes that contain important details about the numbers in the statements and other information needed to evaluate the company's

performance and financial position. The notes are an important part of the financial statements.

7. **Analyze business transactions using the accounting equation and prepare the four basic financial statements.** Every transaction a business records for its financial statements can be put on an accounting equation worksheet. The equation stays in balance with every transaction. The information from the transactions is arranged in such a way that the four financial statements can be extracted from the worksheet.

8. **Compute and explain the current ratio.** The most common ratio used to measure a company's short-term liquidity is the *current ratio*. The current ratio measures a company's ability to meet its short-term obligations.

$$\text{Current ratio} = \frac{\text{Current assets}}{\text{Current liabilities}}$$

9. **Identify the risks of inaccurate financial records and how to control those risks.** One way to think about controls in an accounting system is in terms of preventive controls, detective controls, and corrective controls needed to ensure complete and accurate financial records.

Key Terms

Accrual-basis accounting, p. 53

Classified balance sheet, p. 51

Comparability, p. 46

Consistency, p. 46

Current assets, p. 50

Current liabilities, p. 50

Current ratio, p. 65

Earnings per share (EPS), p. 53

Full-disclosure principle, p. 57

Going-concern assumption, p. 47

Historical-cost principle, p. 47

Interest, p. 51

Matching principle, p. 52

Relevant, p. 45

Reliable, p. 45

Revenue-recognition principle, p. 52

Separate entity assumption, p. 46

Statement of retained earnings, p. 62

Time-period assumption, p. 47

Have You Increased Your Business IQ?

Answer these questions to find out.

1. According to accountants, useful information should be
   a. Relevant
   b. Brief
   c. Easy to understand
   d. Thorough

2. A classified balance sheet provides
   a. A direct match between each asset and its source of financing
   b. A separate subtotal for current assets and current liabilities
   c. Dates of capital contributions
   d. Amount of dividends paid
3. The revenue-recognition principle requires which of the following before revenue is included on the income statement?
   a. All cash must be collected
   b. All related expenses must have been paid for
   c. Revenue must be earned even though payment may not have been collected
   d. Partial payment must be collected
4. Earnings per share is
   a. A CPA with special training.
   b. Net income divided by sales
   c. Stock price at a firm's fiscal year-end
   d. Net income divided by the weighted average number of shares outstanding
5. A statement of retained earnings is
   a. A part of the statement of changes in shareholders' equity
   b. A summary of what has happened in the firm's contributed capital accounts during the period
   c. Prepared after the statement of cash flows so that cash dividends can be properly calculated
   d. The statement considered most important by financial analysts

Now, check your answers.

1. a   2. b   3. c   4. d   5. a

- If you answered all five questions correctly, you've increased your business IQ by studying this chapter. It doesn't mean you've mastered all of the accounting concepts in the chapter. It simply means that you understand some of the general business concepts presented in this chapter.
- If you answered 2 to 4 questions correctly, you've made some progress, but your business IQ has plenty of room to grow. You might want to skim over the chapter again.
- If you answered 0 or 1 question correctly, you can do more to improve your business IQ. Better study the chapter again.

Questions

1. What is the primary quality that managers and external users want in financial information?
2. Name the four characteristics that help make accounting information useful.
3. What is the FASB? What does it do?
4. What is the separate entity assumption?
5. Explain materiality and give an example of both a material and an immaterial item.
6. What is the matching principle? To which category of accounts does this principle relate?
7. Explain the importance of the full-disclosure principle.
8. What is a current asset? What is a current liability?
9. What are the differences between Accounts Receivable and Accounts Payable?
10. What are the two ways that equity is generated in a business?
11. What are some common names for shareholders' equity?
12. Explain accrual-basis accounting.
13. What is the revenue-recognition principle? To which category of accounts does this principle relate?
14. Is revenue always recognized when cash is collected? Explain your answer.
15. What does the balance sheet report about a firm? Name the types of accounts that appear on the balance sheet.
16. What does the income statement report about a firm? Name the types of accounts that appear on the income statement.
17. What is the purpose of the statement of cash flows? How are the cash flows categorized? What is the significance of classifying cash flows into these categories?

18. Explain the relationship among the four financial statements.
19. Give an example of each of the following controls: preventive, detective, and corrective.
20. Define the current ratio and explain what it measures.

Multiple Choice

Use the following information to answer the first two questions.

A firm started the year with $100,000 cash. Here are some of the transactions that took place during the year. The firm:

1) Purchased equipment for $50,000 cash.
2) Issued stock for $250,000 cash.
3) Purchased inventory for $85,000 cash.
4) Provided services to customers for $50,000 on account.
5) Paid cash dividends of $40,000 to shareholders.
6) Sold equipment for $10,000.

1. On the statement of cash flows for the year, what amount would be shown as cash from investing activities?
   a. $50,000 inflow
   b. $50,000 outflow
   c. $40,000 outflow
   d. $210,000 inflow

2. On the statement of cash flows for the year, what amount would be shown as cash from financing activities?
   a. $250,000 inflow
   b. $210,000 inflow
   c. $285,000 inflow
   d. $50,000 outflow

3. IFR Company earned $30,000 revenue and had net income of $8,350 for the year. Dividends of $1,000 were paid to shareholders. How much were IFR's expenses for the year?
   a. $21,650
   b. $22,650
   c. $29,000
   d. $9,350

4. Home Health Care started the year with a balance in Retained Earnings of $74,500. During the year, the firm had net income of $15,400 and paid its shareholders dividends of $2,000. What was the balance in Retained Earnings at the end of the year?
   a. $72,500
   b. $74,500
   c. $87,900
   d. $89,900

Use the following information to answer the next three questions.

Jimmy's Tire Company was started on May 1 with a contribution of $10,000 from Jimmy in exchange for common stock. The company then borrowed

$30,000 from a local bank. With some of the cash, the company rented a building and paid May's rent of $500. The company also purchased equipment for cash of $7,000. Jimmy spent the entire month getting the shop ready to open, and the company paid him a salary of $1,000 for his work. No other transactions occurred during May, the firm's first month of business.

5. What was the company's cash balance at the end of the first month?
   a. $31,500
   b. $24,500
   c. $40,000
   d. $33,000

6. What was the company's net income (loss) for the month?
   a. $31,500
   b. $21,500
   c. $(8,500)
   d. $(1,500)

7. What were total assets at the end of the first month?
   a. $40,000
   b. $38,500
   c. $31,500
   d. $24,500

Use the following information for the next three questions.

Hantuck Company had the following accounts and balances at the end of the year:

Cash	$2,060
Accounts payable	875
Inventory	1,200
Property and equipment	9,500
Accounts receivable	950
Salaries payable	200
Long-term notes payable	3,500
Short-term notes payable	1,500

8. Suppose the accounts listed comprise all of the firm's asset and liability accounts. How much equity do the owners of the firm have?
   a. $13,710
   b. $7,635
   c. $9,385
   d. $2,060

9. What is the firm's current ratio?
   a. 1.81
   b. 0.61
   c. 0.56
   d. 1.63

10. Suppose the firm pays its accounts payable of $875. Both Cash and Accounts Payable are reduced by $875. How does this payment change the current ratio?

a. The ratio will remain unchanged.
b. The ratio will increase.
c. The ratio will decrease.
d. Cannot be determined from the given information.

Short Exercises

SE2-1. Identify financial statement items. LO 2, 3

For each of the following, tell whether it is an income statement item or a balance sheet item.

Revenue   Equity   Expenses
Assets   Liabilities

SE2-2. Identify financial statement items. LO 2, 3, 4, 5

For each of the following items, give the financial statement on which it would appear. (*Hint:* some items will appear on more than one financial statement.)

Cash   Contributed capital
Sales revenue   Accounts receivable
Cost of goods sold   Cash from operations
Equipment   Retained earnings
Long-term debt   Net income

SE2-3. Identify accounting principles and constraints. LO 1

Give the accounting principle, assumption, constraint, or quality that is most applicable to each of the following:

a. All items purchased (except inventory) for less than $25 are expensed as incurred—even if they will last longer than a year.
b. Personal transactions of the owner are kept separately from business transactions.
c. The company uses the same inventory method from period to period.

SE2-4. Identify accounting principles and constraints. LO 1

Give the accounting principle, assumption, constraint, or information quality that is most applicable to each of the following:

a. Equipment is recorded as an asset and expensed over the periods in which it is used.
b. The company prepares financial statements regularly.
c. When insurance is purchased in advance, it is recorded as an asset.
d. Assets like inventory are valued in dollars, not units, for the financial statements.

SE2-5. Identify accounting principles and constraints. LO 1

For each of the following, give the accounting principle that is best described:

a. Cargill Company reports revenue when it is earned instead of when the cash is collected.
b. The land on the Meyer Company balance sheet is valued at what it cost, even though it is worth much more.
c. C&S Corporation recognizes depreciation expense for a computer over five years, the period in which the computer is used to help generate revenue for the business.
d. The president of Swift Company thought that it would help the company's balance sheet to include as an asset some land he and his wife personally own. The accountant rejected the idea.

SE2-6. Revenue recognition. LO 3

Which of the following transactions would result in recognizing revenue for the current year? All transactions occurred in the current year.

a. Collected cash in advance for services to be rendered next year.
b. Provided services to customers on account.
c. Collected cash from customers for services rendered during the current year.
d. Signed a contract to provide future services for the firm's largest client.
e. Received cash contributions from a new stock issue.
f. Paid employees for work done this year.

LO 3

SE2-7. Prepare an income statement.

Use these items to prepare an income statement for Upstart Company for the year ending June 30, 2007.

Service revenue	$800
Other operating expenses	$75
Salary expenses	$150
Rent expense	$200

LO 2

SE2-8. Prepare the current asset section of the balance sheet.

The Upstart Company has the following account balances at June 30, 2007:

Cash	$20,670
Supplies	$1,600
Accounts receivable	$12,000
Equipment	$10,600
Other current assets	$5,500

Prepare the asset section of the balance sheet. Be sure to list the accounts in order of liquidity.

LO 5

SE2-9. Calculate increase (decrease) in cash.

Use these items to calculate the net increase or decrease in cash during the period.

Cash from investing activities	($5,000)
Cash from operating activities	$24,500
Cash from financing activities	$3,500

LO 5

SE2-10. Analyze and classify cash flows.

Indicate whether each of the following transactions result in an increase or decrease in Babyland's cash account and classify each as an operating, investing, or financing cash flow.

a. Babyland purchased $5,000 of baby cribs for cash.
b. The company sold a building, allowing the buyer to give them a short-term note for $25,000.
c. Babyland issued stock to investors for $5,000 cash.

LO 2

SE2-11. Identify balance sheet items.

For each item that follows, tell whether it is an asset, a liability, or a shareholders' equity item.

a. Prepaid insurance
b. Accounts receivable
c. Contributed capital
d. Notes payable
e. Cash
f. Equipment
g. Accounts payable
h. Supplies
i. Inventory

LO 2

SE2-12. Classify accounts.

For each of the following items, tell whether it is a current liability or a non-current liability.

a. Accounts payable
b. Note payable (due in three years)
c. Salaries payable
d. Note payable (due in three months)

LO 2

SE2-13. Classify accounts.

For each of the following items, tell whether it is a current asset or a non-current asset.

a. Furniture and fixtures
b. Cash
c. Short-term investments
d. Property and equipment
e. Supplies
f. Prepaid insurance
g. Accounts receivable

SE2-14. Classify cash flows.   LO 5

For each transaction, classify the cash flow as (1) operating, (2) investing, or (3) financing for the statement of cash flows.

a. A company pays $5,000 cash for a new piece of equipment.
b. A company issues a note payable and receives cash in the amount of $3,000.
c. A company pays $250 for utility expenses.

SE2-15. Analyze notes to the financial statements.   LO 6

Some financial statement analysts believe the notes to the financial statements are the most important part of the financial statements. Write a paragraph to support that opinion.

SE2-16. Analyze business transactions and effects on the accounting equation.   LO 7

Somerset Corporation had the following business transactions during the year:

a. The owners contributed a total of $5,000 to the corporation.
b. Somerset purchased equipment costing $2,500 by signing a note at First National Bank to be repaid in one year.
c. Somerset provided services to customers totaling $6,000 cash.
d. Somerset paid the corporation's operating expenses of $1,500.
e. At the end of the year, Somerset paid $25 interest on the note.

Use the accounting equation worksheet to show the effect of each business transaction for Somerset.

SE2-17. Relationships among financial statements.   LO 7

For each of the following, compute the missing amount.

Assets	Liabilities	Contributed Capital	Retained Earnings
$10,000	$3,500	$6,000	a.
b.	$23,500	$75,000	$30,000
$23,600	c.	$10,000	$11,000
$96,000	$20,000	d.	$45,000

SE2-18. Identify risks and controls.   LO 9

For each of the controls given below, tell whether it is primarily a preventive control, a detective control, or a corrective control.

a. Retro Clothing, Inc., has an online purchase system that automatically inserts the total price of each item a customer orders.
b. The teller double checks the account number on the loan payment before applying payment.
c. External auditors are hired to audit the year-end financial statements.

SE2-19. Calculate and explain the current ratio.   LO 8

Given the following information, compute the current ratio for the two years shown. Explain the trend in the ratio for both years and what you think it means.

From balance sheet at	12/31/2005	12/31/2006
Current assets	$150,000	$180,000
Current liabilities	$100,000	$175,000

Exercise Set A

E2-1A. Prepare an income statement.   LO 3

Use the following to prepare an income statement for Crenshaw Consultants, Inc., for the year ended December 31, 2010.

Service revenues	$54,000
Rent expense	1,000
Salary expense	6,000
Other operating expenses	24,000
Administrative expenses	8,500

LO 2, 3, 4, 5   **E2-2A. Identify financial statement items.**

For each of the following items, give the financial statement(s) on which it would appear:

Cash	Accounts receivable
Accounts payable	Buildings and equipment
Revenue	Insurance expense
Cash from investing activities	Operating expenses
Land	Cash from financing activities
Common Stock	

LO 2   **E2-3A. Prepare the asset section of a classified balance sheet.**

The following accounts and their respective balances were taken from the March 1, 2006, asset section of the Bargain Buy, Inc. balance sheet. (Dollars are in millions.) Use the information to prepare the asset section of a classified balance sheet. Be sure to list the current assets in order of their liquidity.

Merchandise inventory	$2,046	Other current assets	$96
Land and buildings	1,081	Cash and cash equivalents	312
Furniture and equipment	208	Other non-current assets	595
Notes receivable (short-term)	55	Accounts receivable	701

LO 2   **E2-4A. Prepare the asset section of a classified balance sheet.**

Use the following information (in thousands of dollars) from the December 28, 2006, balance sheet of Domino's, Inc., to prepare the asset section of a classified balance sheet.

Property, plant, and equipment	$127,067	Accounts receivable	$64,571
Other current assets	56,099	Cash and cash equivalents	42,726
Inventories	19,480	Other non-current assets	139

LO 2   **E2-5A. Prepare a classified balance sheet.**

The following items were taken from the December 31, 2007 financial statements of Edge Instruments, Inc. (All dollars are in millions.) Prepare a classified balance sheet as of December 31, 2007.

Property and equipment	$4,776	Accounts payable	1,560
Common stock	1,980	Other non-current liabilities	1,200
Long-term investments	3,218	Retained earnings	10,348
Short-term investments	1,689	Other current assets	554
Cash	1,240	Other non-current assets	2,487
Accounts receivable	1,200	Current portion of long-term debt	340
Inventories	1,134	Long-term debt	870

LO 2, 3, 4, 5   **E2-6A. Classify financial statement items.**

The following accounts and balances were taken from the financial statements of Quality Products, Inc. For each item, identify the financial statement(s) on which the item would appear. Then, identify each balance sheet item as an asset, a liability, or a shareholders' equity account.

Equipment	$231,300
Accounts receivable	52,300
Cash	57,890
Short-term notes payable	23,200
Cash from investing activities	89,300
Land	45,200
Common stock	100,000
Retained earnings	75,000
Cash from financing activities	45,980
Accounts payable	32,100
Long-term mortgage payable	54,000
Interest payable	2,500
Cash from operating activities	34,350

LO 2   **E2-7A. Identify financial statement items.**

The items shown below were taken from the financial statements of the Giant Corporation at June 30, 2006. Identify each item as an asset, a liability, or a shareholders' equity account.

Salaries payable	$3,607
Equipment	14,280
Accounts payable	3,660
Long-term note payable	2,000
Common stock	15,000
Cash	35,879
Accounts receivable	14,250
Interest receivable	1,000
Retained earnings	25,200

E2-8A. Analyze business transactions and prepare financial statements.   LO 2, 3, 4, 5, 7

LaTasha opened a children's daycare center as a corporation called 4-Kids. From the 2008 transactions listed below, prepare the income statement, the statement of cash flows, statement of changes in shareholders' equity, and balance sheet for the year ended December 31, 2008.

a. The business was started with LaTasha's contribution of $5,000 on January 1, 2008. The owner's contributions take the form of common stock in the corporation.
b. On January 1, the company borrowed $10,000 from First Bank for 36 months. Interest expense owed at the end of the year is $800.
c. The company purchased $8,000 of furniture and equipment for cash.
d. The company provided services for $10,000 cash.
e. Operating expenses paid in cash totaled $7,500.

E2-9A. Analyze business transactions and classify cash flows.   LO 5, 7

Show each transaction in the accounting equation. Then, classify each cash flow as operating, investing, or financing.

a. Everest, Inc., received cash contributions from owners in the amount of $15,000.
b. Everest purchased $4,000 worth of equipment for cash.
c. Everest purchased supplies for $500 cash, to be used at a later date.
d. Everest borrowed $3,000 by issuing a note to the local bank.

E2-10A. Analyze business transactions and effects on the accounting equation.   LO 7

The following transactions took place during Networking Solutions' first year of business. Show each transaction in the accounting equation.

a. Networking Solutions received a $20,000 investment from the owner.
b. The company purchased $8,000 of new office furniture on account.
c. The company paid $2,000 for computers for cash.
d. The company paid $3,000 for next year's rent. (*Hint:* Future value for the firm.)
e. The company paid $4,000 of the amount owed for the furniture.
f. The company declared and distributed $1,000 of dividends.

E2-11A. Analyze business transactions and prepare a balance sheet.   LO 7

The Brain Trust Consulting Company began business in January 2006. The following transactions took place during the first month of business. Prepare an income statement for the month of January and a balance sheet at January 31.

a. Owners invested $50,000 in exchange for stock.
b. Paid rent of $1,250 for January.
c. Paid $10,000 for operating expenses.
d. Provided services to customers for $25,000 on account.
e. At the end of the month, the company purchased computer equipment for $16,000 cash.

E2-12A. Classify cash flows.   LO 5

Refer to the transactions in E2-11A. For each transaction that involves cash, identify the section of the statement of cash flows in which the item would appear.

E2-13A. Analyze business transactions.   LO 7

The following transactions pertain to a start-up company called Nuts and Bolts. Record each transaction in the accounting equation.

a. On February 1, the company was started with owners' contributions of $5,000 in exchange for common stock.
b. On February 2, Nuts and Bolts purchased supplies for $3,000.

c. On February 4, the company secured a bank loan for $10,000.

d. On February 8, the company purchased $4,600 worth of inventory.

e. On February 12, the company paid $500 for an insurance policy to begin on March 1. (*Hint:* Future value to the firm.)

LO 5

E2-14A. **Classify cash flows.**

Give the section of the statement of cash flows in which each of the following would appear (operating, investing, or financing).

Additions to property and equipment	$(725)
Net proceeds from issuance of long-term debt	18
Issuance of common stock	40
Supplies	(225)
Long-term debt payments	(13)

LO 1, 6

E2-15A. **Analyze notes to the financial statements and accounting principles.**

The first note to a company's financial statements describes significant accounting policies. Look at the notes to the statements for Target, Inc. in Appendix B at the back of the book. Find three examples that demonstrate one of the assumptions, principles, or constraints discussed in the chapter. What do you find that supports the main objective of accounting information?

LO 8

E2-16A. **Calculate and explain the current ratio.**

The following data were taken from the 2006 and 2005 financial statements of Henry's Furniture. (All dollars in thousands.) Calculate the current ratio for each year. What happened to the company's liquidity during the year?

	2006	2005
Current assets	256,485	265,960
Total assets	433,202	406,974
Current liabilities	104,196	101,929
Total liabilities	180,466	182,093
Total shareholders' equity	252,736	224,881

LO 9

E2-17A. **Risks and controls.**

Give two or three examples of controls that you believe would minimize the risk of errors in the accounting records of Target, Inc.

Exercise Set B

Your professor may ask you to complete selected "Group B" exercises and problems using Prentice Hall Grade Assist (**PHGA**). PHGA is an online tool that can help you master the chapter's topics by providing multiple variations of exercises and problems. You can rework these exercises and problems—each time with new data—as many times as you need, with immediate feedback and grading.

LO 3

E2-1B. **Prepare an income statement.**

Use the following to prepare an income statement for Michael & Trina's Dazzling Landscape Service, Inc., for the year ended December 31, 2009.

Service revenue	$22,500
Rent expense	1,500
Salary expense	1,225
Other operating expenses	9,850
Insurance expense	2,500

LO 2, 3, 4, 5

E2-2B. **Identify financial statement items.**

For each item, give the financial statement on which it would appear.

Computer	Interest receivable
Notes payable	Accounts payable
Service revenue	Travel expense
Cash from operating activities	Administrative expenses
Equipment	Cash from investing activities

E2-3B. Prepare the asset section of a classified balance sheet.   LO 2

The following accounts and their respective balances were taken from the April 30, 2007 asset section of the Quality Angel Fish Corporation balance sheet. (Dollars are in millions.) Use the information to prepare the asset section of a classified balance sheet. Be sure to list the current assets in order of their liquidity.

Inventory	$2,150	Other current assets	$115
Property, plant, & equipment	85,100	Cash and cash equivalents	345
Computer	1,225	Other non-current assets	650
Loan receivable (short-term)	35	Accounts receivable	750

E2-4B. Prepare the asset section of a classified balance sheet.   LO 2

Use the following information (in thousands of dollars) from the December 28, 2006 balance sheet of John's Gourmet Pizzas, Inc., to prepare the asset section of a classified balance sheet.

Land and building	$153,025	Accounts receivable	$15,500
Other non-current assets	150	Cash and cash equivalents	15,800
Pizza ingredients inventory	18,500	Other current assets	45,500

E2-5B. Prepare a classified balance sheet.   LO 2

The following items were taken from the June 30, 2008 financial statements of End Music Supply, Inc. (All dollars are in thousands.) Prepare a classified balance sheet as of June 30, 2008.

Land and building	$5,800	Accounts payable	1,073
Common stock	2,104	Other non-current liabilities	1,311
Long-term investments	2,200	Retained earnings	10,450
Short-term investments	1,370	Other current assets	656
Cash	1,300	Other non-current assets	2,300
Accounts receivable	1,140	Current portion of long-term debt	203
Inventories	1,195	Long-term debt	820

E2-6B. Classify financial statement items.   LO 2, 3, 4, 5

The following accounts and balances were taken from the financial statements of Brand Names at a Discount, Inc. For each, identify the financial statement(s) on which the item would appear. Then, for each balance sheet item, tell whether it is an asset, a liability, or a shareholders' equity account.

Van	$50,500
Interest receivable	32,500
Cash	78,000
Short-term loan payable	15,875
Cash from operating activities	28,000
Building	31,853
Common stock	75,000
Retained earnings	100,000
Cash from investing activities	40,000
Interest payable	650
Long-term mortgage payable	85,000
Salaries payable	1,315
Cash from financing activities	10,000

E2-7B. Identify financial statement items.   LO 2

The items shown below were taken from the financial statements of the Juicy Bubble Gum Company at December 31, 2007. For each item shown, tell whether it is an asset, a liability, or a shareholders' equity account.

Accounts payable	$1,385
Computer	2,525
Interest payable	3,521
Long-term note payable	1,875
Common stock	3,815
Short-term loan receivable	10,375
Interest receivable	1,520
Retained earnings	16,785

LO 2, 3, 4, 5, 7   **E2-8B. Analyze business transactions and prepare financial statements.**

Janice and Susan opened a cleaning service as a corporation called Cleaning Plus. From the 2009 transactions listed below prepare the income statement, the statement of cash flows, statement of changes in shareholders' equity, and the balance sheet for the year ended December 31, 2009.

    a. The business was started with Janice and Susan's contribution of $2,500 each on January 1, 2009, in return for common stock.

    b. On January 1, the company borrowed $17,500 from Hometown Bank for 48 months. Interest expense owed at the end of the year is $675.

    c. The company purchased a company van for $15,000 with cash.

    d. The company provided cleaning services for $21,850 cash.

    e. Operating expenses paid in cash totaled $1,500.

LO 5, 7   **E2-9B. Analyze business transactions and classify cash flows.**

Show each transaction below in the accounting equation. Then, classify each cash flow as operating, investing, or financing.

    a. FYI Company received cash contributions from owners in the amount of $18,800.

    b. FYI purchased a $2,500 computer with cash.

    c. FYI purchased office supplies for $375 cash, to be used at a later date.

    d. FYI borrowed $5,000 by issuing a long-term note to the local bank.

LO 7   **E2-10B. Analyze business transactions and effects on the accounting equation.**

The following transactions took place during the first year of business of Solving Your Credit Problems, Inc. Show each transaction in the accounting equation.

    a. Solving received a $125,000 contribution from the owner.

    b. The company purchased property, plant, and equipment for $250,000 by signing a mortgage with Lending Center Mortgage Company.

    c. Solving paid $3,500 for operating equipment with cash.

    d. The company paid $2,500 for next year's insurance (*Hint:* future value).

    e. The company paid $10,500 of the amount owed for the property, plant, and equipment.

LO 2, 7   **E2-11B. Analyze business transactions and prepare a balance sheet.**

The Here-For-You Cable Company began business in July 2008. Record the following transactions that took place during the first month in the accounting equation. Then, prepare a statement of changes in shareholders' equity and an income statement for the month of July and a balance sheet at July 31.

    a. Here-for-You Cable Company owners contributed invested $75,000 in exchange for common stock.

    b. Here paid general operating expenses of $8,275 for July.

    c. Here paid $5,000 for rent and utility expenses.

    d. Here provided cable services to customers for $18,750 on account.

    e. At the end of the month, Here purchased new satellite equipment for $16,875 in cash.

LO 5   **E2-12B. Classify cash flows.**

Refer to the transactions in E2-11B. For each transaction that involves cash, identify the section of the statement of cash flows in which the item would appear.

LO 7   **E2-13B. Analyze business transactions.**

The following transactions pertain to a startup company called Hammer and Nails. Record each transaction in the accounting equation.

    a. On May 1, the company was started with owners' contributions of $7,325 in exchange for common stock.

    b. On May 3, Hammer and Nails purchased advertising for $1,875.

    c. On May 15, the company secured a bank loan for $12,750.

    d. On May 25, the company purchased $3,250 worth of supplies on account.

    e. On May 28, Hammer and Nails paid $750 for an insurance policy to begin on July 1 (*Hint:* future value).

E2-14B. Classify cash flows.   LO 5

Indicate the section of the statement of cash flows in which each of the following would appear (operating, investing, or financing).

Additions to building	$(25,000)
Net proceeds (cash collected) from issuance of long-term debt	150,000
Issuance of common stock	65,000
Operating expenses	(13,275)
Long-term debt payments	(1,500)

E2-15B. Analyze notes to the financial statements and accounting principles.   LO 1, 6

The first note to a company's financial statements describes significant accounting policies. Look at the notes to the statements for Wal-Mart. Find three examples that demonstrate one of the assumptions, principles, or constraints discussed in the chapter. What do you find that supports the main objective of accounting information?

E2-16B. Calculate and explain the current ratio.   LO 8

The following data were taken from the 2007 and 2006 financial statements of Jenny's Quality Furniture, Inc. (All dollars in thousands.) Calculate the current ratio for each year. What happened to the company's liquidity during the year?

	2007	2006
Current assets	230,875	256,294
Total assets	421,850	394,872
Current liabilities	110,850	107,895
Total liabilities	165,432	167,670
Total shareholders' equity	220,750	195,500

E2-17B. Risks and controls.   LO 9

Give two or three examples of controls that you believe would minimize the risk of errors in the accounting records of Wal-Mart, Inc.

Problem Set A

P2-1A. Prepare an income statement.   LO 3

The following were taken from Dell Computer Corporation's income statement for the year ended January 31, 2003 (in millions of dollars).

Provision for income taxes (tax expense)	$ 905
Research and development expenses	455
Cost of goods sold expense*	29,055
Selling and administrative expenses	3,050
Investment and other income	183
Sales revenue	$35,404

*This is a special expense that we will discuss in Chapter 5.

Required

a. Prepare an income statement for the year ended January 31, 2003.
b. Suppose the company paid dividends of $200 (in millions) during the year. How would that affect net income? Why?

P2-2A. Prepare a classified balance sheet and calculate the current ratio.   LO 2, 9

The following were taken from Gateway's 2002 balance sheet. (Dollars in thousands.)

Property, plant, and equipment	$481,011
Other current liabilities	240,315
Short-term investments (*Hint:* future value)	601,118
Accounts receivable	197,817
Contributed capital	739,139
Other long-term liabilities	127,118
Other current assets	602,073
Salaries payable	395,422

Delivery vans	23,292
Other non-current assets	49,732
Cash and cash equivalents	465,603
Accrued liabilities	421,425
Inventory	88,761
Accounts payable	278,609
Retained earnings	307,379

Required

a. Prepare a classified balance sheet.

b. Calculate the current ratio and explain what it measures.

LO 2. 8   **P2-3A. Prepare a classified balance sheet and calculate the current ratio.**

The following items are taken from the September 28, 2003, balance sheet of Starbucks. (Dollars in thousands.)

Common stock	$959,103
Other non-current assets	140,399
Short-term investments (*Hint:* future value)	149,104
Other current assets	116,626
Long-term debt	4,354
Cash and cash equivalents	200,907
Other current liabilities	439,719
Retained earnings	1,069,683
Accounts payable	168,984
Other long-term liabilities	34,262
Accounts receivable	114,448
Property and equipment	1,384,902
Inventories	342,944
Long-term investments (*Hint:* future value)	280,416
Additional paid-in (contributed) capital	53,641

Required

a. Prepare a classified balance sheet for Starbucks at September 28, 2003.

b. Calculate the current ratio and explain what it indicates.

LO 2. 8   **P2-4A. Prepare a classified balance sheet and calculate the current ratio.**

The following items are taken from the December 31, 2009, financial statements of Sedona, Inc. (Dollars in thousands.)

Prepaid insurance	$1,800
Equipment	31,000
Accounts payable	5,200
Cash	4,300
Accounts receivable	7,500
Salaries payable	3,000
Common stock	5,900
Retained earnings	C
Long-term debt	5,000

Required

a. Determine the amount of retained earnings (in thousands) that will appear on Sedona's year-end balance sheet.

b. Prepare a classified balance sheet at December 31, 2009.

c. Calculate the current ratio.

LO 5. 7   **P2-5A. Analyze business transactions and prepare a balance sheet and statement of cash flows.**

GiGi opened a shop called Just Apples to sell her famous applesauce. The following transactions occurred during her first week of business as she prepared to open her shop.

1. GiGi started the business as a corporation with $25,000 on July 1, 2008.
2. On July 5, the company purchased $9,000 worth of apples for cash.
3. On July 6, the company also purchased $4,000 worth of jars, lids, and labels for cash.
4. On July 7, Just Apples paid its only employee $500 for one week's work.
5. On July 7, the company borrowed $10,000 from Local Bank. The loan was for two months.

Required

a. Record each transaction in an accounting equation worksheet.
b. Prepare a balance sheet at July 7, 2008.
c. Prepare a statement of cash flows for the week ended July 7, 2008.

P2-6A. Analyze business transactions and prepare a balance sheet and statement of cash flows.

LO 2, 5, 7

The accounting records for Sonny's Snowboard Company contained the following balances at December 31, 2006:

Assets		Liabilities and Equity	
Cash	$40,000	Accounts payable	$17,000
Accounts receivable	16,500	Common stock	45,000
Land	20,000	Retained earnings	14,500
Total assets	$76,500	Total liabilities and shareholders' equity	$76,500

The following transactions occurred during Sonny's 2007 fiscal year:

1. The company acquired an additional $20,000 from the owners by issuing common stock.
2. Sonny's purchased a computer for $17,000 cash.
3. The company borrowed $10,000 by issuing a three-year note.
4. The company paid $1,200 in cash to rent office space for the year.
5. The company declared and distributed $5,000 cash dividends to the owners.
6. The company purchased land for $8,000 cash.
7. Cash payments on accounts payable amounted to $6,000.
8. Sonny's purchased $1,300 of supplies on account for future use.

Required

a. Record each of these in an accounting equation worksheet. (Be sure to put the beginning balances at the top of the worksheet.)
b. Prepare a balance sheet at December 31, 2007.
c. Prepare a statement of cash flows for the year ended December 31, 2007.

P2-7A. Analyze transactions from the accounting equation; prepare the four financial statements; and calculate the current ratio.

LO 3, 5, 7, 8

The following accounting equation worksheet shows the transactions for Blairstone Consulting & Advising, Inc., for the first month of business, April 2009.

	Assets			=	Liabilities		+	Shareholders' Equity	
	Cash	Accounts receivable	Supplies		Accounts payable	Notes payable (5-year)		Contributed Capital	Retained Earnings
1	$3,000							$3,000 Common stock	
2	50,000					50,000			
3			5,000		5,000				
4		2,500							2,500 Revenue
5	10,000								10,000 Revenue
6	(8,000)		8,000						
7	1,200	(1,200)							
8	(3,400)				(3,400)				
9	(3,100)								(3,100) Expense
10	(500)								(500) Dividends

Required

a. Analyze each transaction in the accounting equation worksheet and describe the underlying exchange that resulted in each entry.
b. Has the company been profitable this month? Explain.
c. Prepare an income statement for the month ended April 30, 2009.
d. Prepare a statement of shareholders' equity for the month ended April 30, 2009.
e. Prepare a statement of cash flows for the month ended April 30, 2009.
f. Prepare a balance sheet at April 30, 2009.
g. Calculate the current ratio for the month of April. What does this ratio measure?

LO 2, 3, 4, 5, 7 **P2-8A. Analyze business transactions and prepare the financial statements.**

The following cash transactions took place during March 2007, the first month of business for Circus Cruise Corporation.

1. J. B. Cruise started a business, Circus Cruise Corporation, by contributing $6,000.
2. The company earned $900 in cash revenue.
3. Expenses amounted to $650 and were paid in cash.
4. The company paid dividends of $25.
5. On March 31, the company borrowed $3,000 from the local bank by signing a three-year note.

Required

a. Show how each transaction affects the accounting equation.
b. Prepare the four basic financial statements for the month of March.

LO 2, 8 **P2-9A. Identify errors; prepare a classified balance sheet; and calculate the current ratio.**

An inexperienced accountant has put together the following balance sheet for Wings and Things, Inc. The balances shown are at June 30, 2011.

Assets		**Liabilities and Shareholders' Equity**	
Current assets:		Current liabilities:	
Cash	$ 27,000	Inventory	$ 2,000
Accounts receivable	6,000	Interest receivable	5,000
Land	30,000	Salaries payable	8,000
Supplies	5,000	Intangible assets	39,000
Operating expenses	2,000	Accounts payable	3,000
Total current assets	70,000	Total current liabilities	57,000
Salaries payable	46,000	Shareholder's equity	
Buildings	36,000	Retained earnings	40,000
Equipment	13,000	Common stock	62,000
Intangible assets	6,000	Short-term note payable	10,000
Total non-current assets	101,000	Total shareholders' equity	112,000
Total assets	**$171,000**	Total liabilities and equity	**$169,000**

Required

a. Identify the errors in the balance sheet presented above.
b. Using good form, prepare a corrected, classified balance sheet.
c. Calculate the current ratio for the corrected amounts from the balance sheet prepared in b.
d. Explain why it is important to properly follow GAAP when preparing financial statements.

Problem Set B

Your professor may ask you to complete selected "Group B" exercises and problems using Prentice Hall Grade Assist (**PHGA**). PHGA is an online tool that can help you master the chapter's topics by providing multiple variations of exercises and problems. You can rework these exercises and problems—each time with new data—as many times as you need, with immediate feedback and grading.

LO 3 **P2-1B. Prepare an income statement.**

The following were taken from Pier 1 Imports' income statement for the year ended March 1, 2005. (Dollars in thousands.)

Provision for income taxes (tax expense)	$75,988
Interest and investment income	3,047
Cost of goods sold expense*	1,001,462
Selling and administrative expenses	502,319
Other expenses	46,432
Net sales	1,754,867
Interest expense	2,327

*This is a special expense that we will discuss in Chapter 5.

Required

a. Prepare an income statement.
b. Suppose the company gave a $300 (in thousands) dividend to its shareholders. How would that affect the income statement? Why?

P2-2B. Prepare a classified balance sheet and calculate the current ratio.   LO 2, 8

The following have been adapted from Pepsico's balance sheet at December 27, 2003. (Dollars in millions.)

Accounts payable and other current liabilities	$5,213
Accounts and notes receivable	2,830
Other current assets	687
Income taxes, payable	611
Property, plant, and equipment	7,828
Cash and cash equivalents	820
Short-term obligations	591
Retained earnings	15,961
Short-term investments (Hint: future value)	1,181
Long-term debt obligations	1,702
Other long-term liabilities	693
Other non-current assets	5,186
Contributed capital	556
Inventories	1,412
Delivery trucks	5,383

Required

a. Prepare a classified balance sheet.
b. Calculate the current ratio and explain what it measures.

P2-3B. Prepare a classified balance sheet and calculate the current ratio.   LO 2, 8

The following items were taken from the January 30, 2003 balance sheet of Albertsons, Inc. (Dollars in millions.)

Retained earnings	$4,793
Accounts payable	2,009
Cash and cash equivalents	162
Short-term investments	90
Accounts receivable	647
Long-term debt	4,950
Supplies	2,973
Salaries payable	599
Contributed capital	494
Other current assets	486
Other long-term liabilities	1,616
Land and buildings	9,029
Other long-term assets	1,914
Other current liabilities	840

Required

a. Prepare a classified balance sheet for Albertson's as of January 30, 2003.
b. Calculate the current ratio and explain what it indicates.

P2-4B. Prepare a classified balance sheet and calculate the current ratio.   LO 2, 4, 8

These items were taken from the December 31, 2007 financial statements of Harris, Inc. (Dollars in millions.)

Contributed capital	$20,000
Other current assets	45,800
Long-term debt	51,000
Accounts receivable	30,700
Cash	78,500
Accounts payable	84,500

Salaries payable	21,350
Buildings and equipment	8,000
Retained earnings	?
Intangible assets	40,000
Long-term investments	34,850

Required

a. Determine the amount of retained earnings (in millions) that will appear on Harris's year-end balance sheet.
b. Prepare a classified balance sheet at December 31, 2007.
c. Calculate the current ratio.

LO 2, 5, 7   **P2-5B. Analyze business transactions and prepare a balance sheet and statement of cash flows.**
The following information is a partial list of transactions from Mills Hobby Shop's first week of business. The company was started as a corporation on March 1, 2006.

1. On March 1, 2006, Mills Hobby Shop, Inc., was started with $10,000 from its owner, Marc Mills.
2. On March 1, Mills Hobby Shop paid $6,000 cash for a short-term investment.
3. On March 2, the company purchased on account $10,000 of merchandise to sell.
4. On March 5, the company purchased some new display shelves for $2,000 cash.
5. On March 7, Mills signed a three-month note for $10,000 at 12% from City National Bank.

Required

a. Record each transaction in an accounting equation worksheet.
b. Prepare a balance sheet at March 7, 2006.
c. Prepare a statement of cash flows for the week ended March 7, 2006.

LO 2, 5, 7   **P2-6B. Analyze business transactions and prepare a balance sheet and statement of cash flows.**
The accounting records for Beta Company contained the following balances as of December 31, 2005.

Assets		Liabilities and Shareholders' Equity	
Cash	$50,000	Accounts payable	$17,500
Accounts receivable	26,500	Contributed capital	48,600
Land	14,100	Retained earnings	24,500
	$90,600		$90,600

The following accounting events apply to Beta's 2006 fiscal year:

1. Beta purchased a computer for $20,000 cash.
2. Beta purchased $1,900 of supplies on account for future use. Beta used Accounts Payable to record the obligation.
3. The company distributed $2,000 cash to the owners.
4. The company purchased land that cost $15,000 in cash.
5. Cash payments on accounts payable amounted to $16,000.
6. On December 31, the company borrowed $30,000 by issuing a two-year note.

Required

a. Record each of these in an accounting equation worksheet. (Be sure to put the beginning balances at the top of the worksheet.)
b. Prepare a balance sheet at December 31, 2006.
c. Prepare a statement of cash flows for the year ended December 31, 2006.

LO 2, 3, 4, 5, 7   **P2-7B. Analyze business transactions and prepare the financial statements.**
The following cash transactions took place during July 2008, the first month of business for Michael's Spa, a corporation.

1. Michael London and Matt Bryan started Michael's Spa by contributing $12,000 cash each.
2. The company earned $3,100 cash in massage revenue.
3. The company paid employees $985 cash.
4. Miscellaneous expenses amounted to $650 cash.

5. The company paid cash dividends of $500.
6. On July 31, the company borrowed $8,000 from the local bank, to be repaid at the end of June 2010.

Required

a. Show how each transaction affects the accounting equation.
b. Prepare the four basic financial statements for the month of July.

P2-8B. Analyze transactions using the accounting equation; prepare the four financial statements; and calculate the current ratio.   LO 2, 3, 4, 5, 7, 8

The following accounting equation worksheet shows the transactions for Jackie Knight's Furniture Repairs, a corporation, for November 2007, the first month of business.

		Assets		=	Liabilities	+		Shareholders' Equity	
	Cash	Accounts receivable	Supplies		Accounts payable	Notes payable (3-year)	Contributed Capital		Retained Earnings
1	$5,000						$5,000 Common stock		
2	20,000					20,000			
3	−5,000								−5,000 operating expenses
4	1,500								1,500 Service revenue
5		10,000							10,000 Service revenue
6			4,000		4,000				
7	6,000	−6,000							
8	−1,400				−1,400				
9	−2,100								−2,100 Salary expense
10	−200								−200 Dividends

Required

a. Analyze each transaction in the accounting equation worksheet and describe the underlying exchange that resulted in each entry.
b. Has the company been profitable this month? Explain.
c. Prepare an income statement for the month ended November 30, 2007.
d. Prepare a statement of changes in shareholders' equity for the month ended November 30, 2007.
e. Prepare a balance sheet at November 30, 2007.
f. Prepare a statement of cash flows for the month ended November 30, 2007.
g. Calculate the current ratio for the month of November. What does this ratio measure?

P2-9B. Identify errors; prepare a classified balance sheet; and calculate the current ratio.   LO 2, 8

An inexperienced accountant has put together a balance sheet for Art Objects, Inc. The balances shown are at September 30, 2006.

Assets		Liabilities and Equity	
Current assets:		Current liabilities:	
Inventory	$ 30,000	Accounts receivable	$ 2,000
Cash	6,000	Other long-term assets	5,000
Land	28,000	Salaries payable	8,000
Other current assets	5,000	Intangible assets	35,000
Interest receivable	2,000	Accounts payable	4,000
Total current assets	71,000	Total current liabilities	54,000
Accounts payable	42,000	Shareholders' equity	
Buildings	36,000	Retained earnings	52,000
Equipment	18,000	Common stock	47,000
Miscellaneous long-term assets	6,000	Short-term note payable	20,000
Total non-current assets	102,000	Total shareholders' equity	119,000
Total assets	$173,000	Total liabilities and equity	$173,000

Required

a. Identify the errors in the balance sheet presented above.
b. Using good form, prepare a corrected, classified balance sheet.
c. Calculate the current ratio using the corrected amounts from the balance sheet prepared in b.
d. Explain why it is important to properly follow GAAP when preparing financial statements.

Financial Statement Analysis

LO 2, 8   **FSA2-1.** The balance sheets for Tootsie Roll Industries, Inc., are shown below.

Tootsie Roll Balance Sheets (in thousands)		

	31-Dec-02	31-Dec-03
Assets		
Cash	$105,507	$ 84,084
Investments	40,737	86,961
Receivables	22,686	18,131
Inventory	43,645	46,086
Other current assets	12,373	8,443
Total current assets	224,948	243,705
Property, plant, & equipment	128,869	129,163
Other non-current assets	292,263	292,429
Total assets	$646,080	$665,297
Liabilities		
Accounts payable	12,505	11,947
Dividends payable	3,579	3,589
Accrued liabilities	35,825	38,834
Income taxes payable	11,187	8,517
Total current liabilities	63,096	62,887
Non-current liabilities	56,244	65,829
Total liabilities	119,340	128,716
Contributed capital	391,079	393,496
Retained earnings	148,705	156,786
Other shareholders' equity accounts	(13,044)	(13,701)
	526,740	536,581
Total liabilities and shareholders' equity	$646,080	$665,297

Required

a. What were the total current assets at December 31, 2002? 2003?
b. How are the assets ordered on the balance sheet?
c. What were the total current liabilities at December 31, 2002? 2003?
d. Calculate the current ratio for each year. What information do these numbers provide?

FSA2-2. Selected information from the balance sheets for Wal-Mart and Sears are presented below. Although some accounts are not listed, all of the current assets and current liabilities are given.

LO 2. 8

(dollars in millions)	Sears at January 3, 2004	Wal-Mart at January 31, 2004
Cash	$ 9,057	5,199
Accounts receivable	2,689	1,254
Inventory	5,335	26,612
Other current assets	1,115	1,356
Property, plant, and equipment	6,788	55,201
Accounts payable	3,106	19,332
Other accrued liabilities (short term)	10,653	18,086
Long-term debt	4,218	17,102
Total shareholders' equity	6,401	43,623

Required

a. For each company provide the following values at the end of the given fiscal year.
   1. Current assets
   2. Current liabilities
   3. Current ratio
b. Based on your answers above, discuss the relative liquidity of the two companies.

FSA2-3. A condensed statement of cash flows for Apple Computer for the year ended September 28, 2002, is shown below. Use the financial statement to answer the following questions.

LO 5

Apple Computer, Inc.
Adapted from the Statement of Cash Flows
For the year ended September 28, 2002
(in millions)

Cash and cash equivalents, beginning of the year	$2,310
Cash generated by operating activities	89
Investing cash flows:	
Purchase of short-term investments	(4,144)
Proceeds from maturities of short-term investments	2,846
Proceeds from sales of short-term investments	1,254
Purchase of property, plant, and equipment	(174)
Proceeds from sales of equity investments	25
Cash used for business acquisitions	(52)
Other	(7)
Cash generated by (used for) investing activities	(252)
Financing cash flows:	
Proceeds from issuance of common stock	105
Cash generated by (used for) financing activities	105
Increase (decrease) in cash and cash equivalents	(58)
Cash and cash equivalents, end of the year	$2,252

Required

a. Did Apple purchase any equipment during the year?
b. If you were to examine Apple's balance sheet at September 28, 2002, what amount would be shown for cash and cash equivalents?
c. Was cash generated from operations or used by operations? In what amount?
d. Did Apple receive any new contributions from owners during the year? How can you tell?

Critical Thinking Problems

Risk and Controls
Look at the information in the Wal-Mart annual report in Appendix A in addition to the financial statements. What kinds of risks does Wal-Mart face? Use the information in the annual report and your own experience to answer this question.

Ethics
Ken Jones wants to start a small business and has asked his uncle to loan him $10,000. He has prepared a business plan and some financial statements that indicate the business could be very profitable. Ken is afraid his uncle will want some ownership in the company for his investment, but Ken doesn't want to share what he believes will be a hugely successful company. What are the ethical issues Ken must face as he prepares to present his business plan to his uncle? Do you think he should try to emphasize the risks of ownership to his uncle to convince him it would be preferable to be a creditor? Why or why not?

Group Assignment
Look at the four basic financial statements for Southwest Airlines shown in the chapter: income statement—Exhibit 2.1, balance sheet—Exhibit 2.3, statement of retained earnings—Exhibit 2.4, and statement of cash flows—Exhibit 2.6. Work together to find numbers that show the links between the various financial statements. Then, write a brief explanation of how the statements relate to each other.

Internet Exercise: Hoover's and Pfizer

Hoover's Online, The Business Network offers information about companies, industries, people, and related news items. For researching a company, this Web site is a good place to start gathering basic information http://www.hoovers.com.

IE2-1. Use the Find A Specific Company search feature by typing in Pfizer. Then, select Pfizer, Inc. from the list produced.
  a. What type of company is Pfizer?
  b. List three products manufactured by Pfizer.
  c. List three of Pfizer's top competitors.

IE2-2. Scroll down until you find Financials on the right menu bar. Use the financial statements listed there to answer these questions:
  a. For the most recent year, list the amounts reported for revenue, cost of goods sold, and total net income. Does the amount reported for revenue represent cash received from customers during the year? If not, what does it represent? What does the amount reported for cost of goods sold represent? Is Pfizer a profitable company? How can you tell?
  b. For the most recent year list the amounts reported for total assets, total liabilities, and total (owner's) equity. Does the accounting equation hold true? Are assets primarily financed with liabilities or equities?
  c. Does Pfizer use accrual based or cash based accounting? How can you tell?

Additional Study Materials

Visit www.prenhall.com/reimers for self-study quizzes and spreadsheet templates to use to complete homework assignments.

CONTINUING CASE STUDY

Building your Excel skills with The MP3 Store

In this exercise, the information provided in the MP3 case will be used to create an Excel worksheet and financial statements. During February the owners of The MP3 Store are preparing to open for business. They have been informed that the store they rented won't be ready until April, so the owners have decided to start advertising and begin repairing MP3 players while waiting for the retail store to open. During the second month in business, The MP3 Store engaged in the following transactions:

February 3   Paid the printer $400 for brochures and distributed them during February.

February 20   Purchased a one-year liability insurance policy. Coverage will start when the store opens. (Record as a current asset called Prepaid Insurance.)

February 28   During the month, the owners repaired a total of 75 MP3 players and collected a total of $3,600 from customers for the repairs. The cost of the parts to make the MP3 repairs was $1,200. The parts were purchased for $1,000 in cash and $200 on account.

Instructions

1. Open a new Excel worksheet.
2. Create the following bold column headings beginning in Cell A1 and ending in Column I: **Date, Description, Cash +, Other Assets =** (*two column heading*), **Liabilities +** (*two column heading*), **Contributed Capital +, Retained Earnings**. Adjust the column widths as needed.
3. Center your two-column headings across both columns by highlighting both cells and clicking the **Merge and Center** button. Highlight all your headings and click the **Center** button to center all column headings.
4. Select Cell H1 and choose **Format, Column, Width** from the menu bar. Set the width to 12. Wrap the Contributed Capital text by selecting Cell H1, choosing **Format, Cells, Alignment** from the menu bar and clicking on the **Wrap Text** box. Repeat with Retained Earnings text.
5. Underline your heading by selecting **Format, Cells, Border**.
6. Input the beginning balances from the end of January. List the other assets (Prepaid Rent and Supplies) separately with the dollar amounts in Column D and the titles in Column E. Adjust the width of the Description column so that Beginning Balances appear in Cell B2.
7. Input the February 3 transaction as follows: Type Advertising in Cell B4. Input the formula –400 in Cell C4. Copy the contents of C4 to cell I4 using the **Copy** and **Paste** function discussed in Chapter 1.

8. Repeat Step 7 for the rest of the February transactions. Adjust column widths and wrap text as appropriate. Format your numbers by selecting **Format, Cells**, and **Number**. Highlight the cells to be formatted and choose the Accounting format with no symbol or decimal places. *Hints:* (1) Input the cost of the insurance policy in the "Other Assets" column and then use a formula to input the deduction to cash (=D5 * –1). (2) The transaction for Cost of Repairs has three inputs—Cash, Accounts Payable, and Retained Earnings. Input the Cash and Accounts Payable amounts and use a formula to calculate the deduction from Retained Earnings.
9. Total the cash column by highlighting the numbers in the column and clicking the **Auto Sum** Σ button. Copy the total cash formula to the other columns as appropriate. Format totals as needed using the Accounting format and the $. Select **Format, Cells**, and **Border** to underline the last transaction and double underline the totals.
10. Save your file to disk by clicking the **Save** button. Name your file MP32.
11. Prepare an income statement, statement of changes in shareholders' equity, and balance sheet for the month of February. Use the techniques you learned in this lesson and in Chapter 1 to set up your statements. To facilitate spacing set up your statements as follows. DO NOT START UNTIL YOU READ THE TIPS AND TRICKS LISTED UNDER THE

SET-UP. To facilitate spacing, set up your statements as follows:

Income Statement: Statement headings in Columns A10–A12; titles beginning in Cell A14 and dollar amounts and totals in Columns C and D as appropriate.

Statement of Changes in Shareholders' Equity: Statement headings in Columns H10–H12; titles beginning in Cell H14 and dollar amounts and totals in Column J.

Balance Sheet: Statement headings in Columns A21–A23; titles beginning in Cells A25 and E25 and dollar amounts and totals in Columns C and G.

Tips and Tricks

- Excel is very user-friendly and does not require you to input the same information (number or title) more than once. Use what you have already done in the transaction analysis to fill in your statements. For example: The first line of your income statement should be Repair Revenue. If you set your transaction file up like the solution, the Repair Revenue transaction is recorded in Row 6 with the words *Repair Revenue* in Cell B6 and the dollar amount of the revenue in Cell I6. Instead of retyping or recalculating the information, simply click on cell A14 and input =B6. Click on cell D14 and input =I6. Use this process every time you are repeating information that is already in the worksheet. Use your preferred **Copy** and **Paste** technique to copy and change the statement headings.

- **AutoSum** Σ will not work for every sum that you need in your statements. The plus sign may be used to add two or more cells that are not next to each other. For example, if the ending balance of Contributed Capital is in Cell J17 and the ending balance of Retained Earnings is in Cell J22, then Total Shareholders' Equity is = J17+J22. You may either type the formula in the total cell or input the = or + sign and then click on the cells that you are adding together (= <Click> J17 + <Click> J22).

12. If you have followed all the instructions, you should be able to print your worksheet on one page if you use the landscape mode. Select **File, Print Preview** from the menu bar. Click the **Setup** button, choose **Landscape** and **Fit to 1 page(s) wide by 1 tall**.

13. Save your file to disk by clicking the **Save** 💾 button and exit Excel.

chapter 3

The Accounting Information System and the Accounting Cycle

Here's where you've been . . .

- **You learned about the characteristics of accounting information.**

- **You learned about the four financial statements.**

- **You learned the accounting equation and how it is used.**

- **You learned how to prepare the financial statements.**

Here's where you're going . . .

- **You'll learn about the general ledger system.**

- **You'll learn about the accounting cycle.**

- **You'll learn how to make journal entries.**

YOU make the call:

Should Cisco allow its salespeople to enter their transactions directly into the firm's accounting system?

Imagine your life without the Internet: You couldn't e-mail your friends, shop online, or do research for a term paper. Just a few decades ago, no one had heard of the Internet.

Now, the majority of us use the Internet daily. Cisco Systems, Inc., is the worldwide leader in creating networking products for the Internet. According to the company, its vision is to change the way people work, live, play, and learn.

Suppose that one of Cisco's new accounting clerks wants to contribute to this climate of change by changing the way the company's accounting department records sales transactions. She suggests that all salespeople record their sales transactions directly into the firm's accounting system rather than submit them to her department for processing. That will give her more time for financial statement analysis.

What are the pros and cons of allowing the salespeople to input their own transactions? How do you think the CFO will react to the suggestion? *You make the call.*

Learning Objectives

When you are finished studying this chapter, you should be able to:

1. Explain the general ledger system and use debits and credits to record balance sheet transactions.
2. Use debits and credits to record income statement transactions.
3. Explain the first three steps in the accounting cycle and the purpose of each step.
4. Post journal entries to the general ledger and prepare a trial balance.
5. Compute and explain working capital and the quick ratio.
6. Recognize the risks and controls associated with using a traditional accounting system.

LEARNING OBJECTIVE 1

Explain the general ledger system and use debits and credits to record balance sheet transactions.

Keeping Track of Business Transactions

Now that you understand the information that each of the four financial statements provides, the qualitative characteristics the information should have, and how to analyze routine business transactions, you are ready to learn how accountants organize and summarize transactions.

The recording process

For several centuries, accountants have used a system called the general ledger system to track business transactions, organize them, and summarize them for the financial statements. A general ledger system is simply a method of keeping accounting records. One unique characteristic of this system has always been its exclusivity—accounting information is kept separate from the information gathered by marketing, production, sales, and human resources. However, the development of computers and software that can manage large amounts of information has led many companies to use a single, integrated information system. Instead of keeping data separately in their own record-keeping system, accountants are increasingly getting information from the company's overall information system. Read more about these information systems in *Accounting in the News*.

Although new technology has made it possible for firms to use sophisticated information systems, there are two reasons to learn about the traditional general ledger accounting system. First, many small and medium-size companies use a traditional general ledger system (usually in computerized form). Second, new integrated information systems are designed to produce the financial records in the same format as those produced by a general ledger system. That is, the general ledger system underlies both manual and computerized accounting systems. We will use the general ledger system, which can be a manual system, to demonstrate how transactions are recorded, classified, and summarized for the financial statements.

Study Tip

Keep in mind that no matter how simple or how sophisticated a company's information system, a company designs its accounting system to produce the information that GAAP requires for the financial statements.

How transactions increase and decrease balance sheet accounts—debits and credits

You have learned that transactions increase or decrease assets, liabilities, and shareholders' equity; and we have used the accounting equation to analyze these effects. However, this is not an efficient way for a firm with thousands of

Accounting in the NEWS

Technology

ERP Software Captures the Data

The most common name for company-wide, integrated information systems is Enterprise Resource Planning (ERP) systems, and they are changing the way businesses manage, process, and use information. ERP systems are computer-based software programs designed to process an organization's transactions and integrate information for planning, production, financial reporting, and customer service. Companies like General Motors, IBM, and Wal-Mart, universities like Florida State, Emory, Northeastern, and Cornell, and a majority of companies with annual revenues exceeding $1 billion have implemented ERP systems.

ERP systems vary from company to company, depending on the company's needs. There are a few key features that all ERP systems share:

- ERP packaged software, designed for business environments, is available in either a traditional or Web-based format. Packaged software is software that is commercially available—for purchase or lease—from a software vendor, as opposed to being developed in-house.
  - An ERP system is composed of modules relating to specific functions. There are modules for:

Accounting, including financial, managerial, and international accounting.

Logistics, including materials requirement planning, production, distribution, sales management, and customer management.

Human resources, including payroll, benefits, and compensation management.

- All the modules work together with a common database. This creates an enterprise-wide system instead of separate, independent systems for each function of the business.

Business intelligence (BI) software takes ERP systems to a new level of data integration and analysis. The positive outlook for BI software may be due, in part, to developments in accounting. According to *BusinessWeek*, new regulations, like the required internal control reporting under the Sarbanes-Oxley Act, will increase the demand for more "intelligent" systems.

Q What types of information does an ERP system collect for a firm?

Enterprise Resource Planning systems allows employees in various parts of a company to share data about transactions with customers. This sharing of information speeds up decision making and helps improve customer service.

A Information about the firm's transactions for all of the business functions—human resources, accounting, production, marketing, and operations.

transactions to keep track of its accounting information. In the fifteenth century, Paccioli, a monk who is often called the father of accounting, wrote about a system that uses the direction of the effect that a transaction has on an account to help keep track of a firm's transactions. To show how the system works, we'll use a diagram called a **T-account**. A T-account represents the place you will keep track of additions and subtractions from an account as you learn about the general ledger system. Transactions that increase an account go on one side of the T-account. Transactions that decrease an account go on the other side of the T-account.

The increase side of a particular T-account is determined by the side of the accounting equation on which the account is located. Exhibit 3.1 shows how debits and credits work in the accounting equation.The following list shows you how transactions are recorded in T-accounts:

- Asset accounts—like Cash, Accounts Receivable, and Inventory—have the increase side on the left side of their T-accounts because those accounts are on the left side of the accounting equation.

- Liability accounts—like Accounts Payable and Notes Payable—have the increase side on the right side of their T-accounts because those accounts are on the right side of the accounting equation.

> **T-account:** A diagram resembling the letter T that represents the place you will keep track of additions and subtractions from an account as you learn about the general ledger system.

The terms *debit* and *credit* simply refer to a side—left or right—of an account. Whether a debit is an increase or decrease depends on which type of account you are referring to. A debit increases an asset, but a debit decreases a liability or shareholders' equity account. Similarly, a credit decreases an asset, but a credit increases a liability or equity account.

Exhibit 3.1

Accounting Equation with Debits and Credits

Assets		=	Liabilities		+	Shareholders' Equity			
+	−		−	+		**Contributed Capital**		**Retained Earnings**	
Debit (DR) side	Credit (CR) side		Dr	Cr		−	+	−	+
						Dr	Cr	Dr	Cr

Debit (abbreviated as DR): The left side of an account.

Credit (abbreviated as CR): The right side of an account.

Study Tip

There is nothing bad or good about a debit or a credit. The way we use the word *credit* in everyday language is not the way accountants use it. Getting *credit* for something like the accounting course you are taking is a good thing, but a credit in accounting is neither bad nor good. It's just the right side of an account.

- Equity accounts—like Common Stock and Retained Earnings—have the increase side on the right side of their T-accounts because those accounts are on the right side of the accounting equation.

- **Debit** means the left side of an account. **Credit** means the right side of an account. Numbers we put on the left side of the account are called *debits*, and numbers we put on the right side are called *credits*. *Crediting* an account means we are entering a number on the right side of the account. *Debiting* an account means we are entering a number on the left side of the account.

When we want to add an amount to the Cash balance, we will put the number of that amount on the left side of the T-account for cash—so that's a debit.[1] When we pay cash and want to subtract the amount paid from the cash account, we will put the number of that amount on the right side—so that's a credit. The increase side of an account is called its normal balance. The *normal balance* in the cash account is a debit. Because we put the amount of cash we receive on the debit side and the amount of cash we pay out on the credit side, it makes sense that our Cash account will normally have a debit

Can YOU do it?

Indicate whether each of the following accounts normally has a debit (DR) or credit (CR) balance and what type of account it is. The first one is done for you as a guide.

Account title	Asset	Liability	Shareholders' Equity
Accounts Payable		CR	
Accounts Receivable			
Cash			
Furniture and Fixtures			
Capital Stock			
Retained Earnings			
Land			
Building			

Answer Accounts Receivable, Cash, Furniture and Fixtures, Land, and Building are all assets and have a normal debit (DR) balance. Capital Stock and Retained Earnings are Shareholders' Equity accounts and have a normal credit (CR) balance.

[1]When you receive cash, you probably think about crediting your account. That is actually the bank's point of view with your account. When the bank receives cash, it will debit its own Cash account and will credit an Account Payable with your name on it. So when you make a deposit, the bank credits your account. That is, the bank puts a number on the right side of your account. Sometimes it's easier to simply forget any preconceived meaning you have for the words *debit* and *credit*.

balance. It's not normal to spend more cash than you have. If you did that with your bank account, you wouldn't be getting any money from the ATM for the weekend!

In accounting, we record debits and credits to accounts as a way to increase and decrease the total balance of the account. Debiting and crediting accounts have the same effect as adding and subtracting numbers to an account, as we did in Chapter 2. In a firm's accounting records, errors due to incorrectly putting a debit or a credit in an account are never erased. The errors are left in place, and the accounting clerk fixes them by adding additional debits or credits to correct the previous errors. That way the firm always has a record of everything that happens to an account—even the mistakes! (However, in an accounting class it's a good idea for you to use a pencil for your homework so you *can* erase and correct errors you make.)

Journals and the general ledger

Keeping track of financial information with a traditional record-keeping system that uses debits and credits is called *bookkeeping*. A firm records transactions in chronological order in a book or a computer file called a **journal**. The record of a transaction using debits and credits is called a **journal entry**. Most companies use more than one journal because each department may need its own journal if transactions occur at the same time in different locations. For simplicity, we'll use only one journal for all of the transactions we record.

Exhibit 3.2 shows a typical journal entry. The transaction is the receipt of cash for money the firm has borrowed. The transaction increases assets, Cash, and increases liabilities, Notes Payable. Notice the following:

Journal: A record in which transactions are initially recorded in chronological order.

Journal entry: The record of a transaction using debits and credits.

- A journal entry will have a date or some other form of reference to make it easy to trace. (We won't always have a date with our examples, but a real company always has the date of a transaction.)

- Debits are written first, and credits are written below the debits and indented—both the account names and the amounts.

- Debits are in the left column and the credits are in the right column. Remember that debit means left and credit means right.

- The dollar amount of debits equals the dollar amount of credits. This is always true, just like the two sides of the accounting equation are equal when we use the accounting equation to show the effects of a transaction.

- A journal entry always includes a brief explanation of the transaction.

Because a company may have thousands of transactions during an accounting period, it would be difficult, if not impossible, to try to gather and use the information from a chronological record such as the journal. To be useful, the information needs to be reorganized so that transactions that involve the same resources are grouped together. For example, when all transactions that

Exhibit 3.2

An Example of a Journal Entry

Date or Reference	Transaction	Debit	Credit
June 1	Cash	165,000	
	Notes Payable		165,000
	To record the receipt of cash from a loan		

General ledger: The primary record of a company's financial information. The general ledger contains all of the accounts maintained by the company—asset, liability, shareholders' equity, revenue, and expense accounts.

Posting: The process of transferring the amounts from the journal to the general ledger.

Study Tip

A firm usually does not post individual journal entries like we will do as we learn the general ledger system. A firm commonly posts totals from a number of transactions.

Study Tip

In accounting, when we say the balance in a specific account is, for example, $100, we do not mean there is cash in the account (like your checking account). The balance in an account is a dollar amount that has been recorded for that asset, liability, shareholders' equity, revenue, or expense account. Only the balance in the Cash account is cash.

Chart of accounts: A list of all of the accounts in a firm's accounting records along with account numbers to assist in maintaining accurate accounting records.

involve cash are grouped together, the company's Cash balance can be easily determined. Regrouping the journal entries into accounts makes it possible for managers to see the amounts of the company's assets and liabilities. The transactions from the journal, or journals, are copied to another book (or computerized file) called the **general ledger** using a process called **posting** the transactions to the general ledger. The posting process involves reorganizing the transactions from the journal entries. Posting is done daily, weekly, or monthly, depending on the size of the company.

The general ledger is the primary record of a company's financial information and is organized by accounts. Recall that an account is the basic classification unit of accounting information. An account is the record used to accumulate the monetary amount for each asset, liability, equity, revenue, and expense. You can think of each item on the balance sheet and each item on the income statement as an account and each account as a page in the general ledger. On the page for a particular account, a company will record all the additions to, and deductions from, that account. For example, one account in the general ledger is Cash. On the Cash page(s) in the general ledger, you find every cash collection and every cash disbursement made by the company. To make it easy to find the amount of cash on hand, the Cash account has a running balance. That means a new balance is calculated after every entry. A company's cash account is like your record of your bank account. You subtract money when you use your debit card, and you add money when you make a deposit. The resulting total, which remains in your bank account, is your running balance. If you keep a running balance, it is easy to find out how much cash you have in your account. Have you discovered what happens when you don't keep your bank balance current?

Accounts in the general ledger include Cash, Accounts Receivable, Inventory, Prepaid Insurance, Equipment, Accounts Payable, Notes Payable, Contributed Capital, Retained Earnings, Sales Revenue, and Operating Expenses. How many accounts does a company have? Every company is different, and the number of accounts depends on the detail the company wants in its financial records. For example, one company could have an account called Utilities Expenses in which many different utility-related expenses could be accumulated. Another company might prefer to have a separate account for each type of utility expense—a separate page in the general ledger for Electricity Expense, Gas Expense, and Water Expense. The number of accounts is determined by the amount of detail a company wants to be able to retrieve from its records. If a company such as Lands' End uses very few office supplies, it would be a waste of time and space to keep a separate account for those expenses. Instead, office supplies could be recorded in a more general account like Operating Expenses. A company such as BB&T (Branch Banking and Trust) that uses many office supplies would definitely want to keep a separate account for those expenses.

All of a company's accounts can be found on the company's **chart of accounts**. A chart of accounts is a list of the company's accounts with corresponding account numbers to assist in maintaining accurate accounting records. Exhibit 3.3 shows a simple chart of accounts. Most companies have many accounts, and they combine the similar ones for the financial statement accounts. When we look at the financial statements, we can't really tell how many individual accounts a company has in its general ledger because many smaller accounts may be combined into one account to create a financial statement account.

In Exhibit 3.3, the first three groups of accounts are balance sheet accounts. The last two are income statement accounts. When you look at Cisco Systems' income statements, shown in Exhibit 3.4 on page 106, imagine all of the transactions that were recorded to produce over $22 billion in total net sales. Remember that all of the information on the income statement pertains to a fiscal year. Cisco's accounting system undoubtedly has hundreds of different accounts.

Exhibit 3.3

An Example of a Chart of Accounts

A chart of accounts is a company's list of all accounts in its general ledger. There are five types of accounts: Asset, Liability, Shareholders' Equity, Revenue, and Expense.

Chart of Accounts

Account number	Account name
[101]	Cash in checking
[102]	Cash in savings
[104]	Payroll account
[114]	Accounts Receivable
[120]	Supplies
[130]	Prepaid Insurance
[140]	Office Equipment
[200]	Notes Payable
[201]	Accounts Payable
[210]	Salaries Payable—administrative
[211]	Salaries Payable—sales staff
[220]	Interest Payable—loans
[221]	Interest Payable—bonds
[230]	Notes Payable
[231]	Bonds Payable
[300]	Contributed Capital
[320]	Retained Earnings
[500]	Service Revenue
[510]	Sales Revenue
[600]	Supplies Expense
[610]	Insurance Expense
[613]	Rent Expense
[619]	Utilities Expense

This first group of accounts is a list of ASSET accounts.

This second group is a list of LIABILITY accounts.

These are SHAREHOLDERS' EQUITY accounts.

These are REVENUE accounts.

These are EXPENSE accounts.

Can **YOU** do it?

Explain the difference between a journal and the general ledger.

Answer A journal is a book (or electronic record) where transactions are recorded chronologically using journal entries. A journal is sometimes called the book of original entry. A company usually has many journals. The general ledger is a record of transactions organized by account. A company has only one general ledger. The transactions from the journal are reorganized when they are posted to the general ledger.

Recording Income Statement Transactions

LEARNING OBJECTIVE 2

Use debits and credits to record income statement transactions.

So far you've learned how debits and credits work with balance sheet accounts. Now let's turn to the income statement accounts, beginning with revenue accounts.

Recording revenue

You learned in Chapter 1 that Retained Earnings is an account that contains all of the profits earned by a company less all distributions to owners. As an equity account, the Retained Earnings balance increases with credits and decreases with debits. Because revenues increase Retained Earnings, revenue accounts also increase with credits, just like Retained Earnings. In the general ledger system, revenue accounts keep track of all the revenue a company earns during an accounting period. The amounts are not actually recorded in

To produce its income statement(s), Cisco Systems must record and organize thousands of transactions. A general ledger accounting system would be one way to do that. In practice, Cisco Systems actually uses a much more sophisticated record-keeping system. No matter what system the company uses to record its accounting information, the income statement(s) would be the same. Even though there are accounts you are not yet familiar with on this statement, you should understand the basic ideas of the income statement.

Exhibit 3.4

Cisco Systems Income Statements

Cisco Systems, Inc.
Income Statements
For Fiscal Years 2003 and 2004
(in millions)

For the years ended	July 26, 2003	July 31, 2004
Net Sales		
Product	$15,565	$18,550
Service	3,313	3,495
Total net sales	18,878	22,045
Cost of Sales		
Product	4,594	5,766
Service	1,051	1,153
Total cost of sales	5,645	6,919
Gross Margin	13,233	15,126
Operating Expenses:		
Research and development	3,135	3,080
Sales and marketing (including advertising)	4,116	4,445
General and administrative	702	804
Payroll taxes on stock options exercises	–	16
Amortization of deferred stock option compensation	–	244
Amortization of purchased intangible assets	394	242
In-process research and development	4	3
Total operating expenses	8,351	8,834
Operating Income (Loss)	4,882	6,292
Interest income	660	512
Other income (loss), net	(529)	188
Interest and other income (loss), net	131	700
Income (Loss) Before Provision for Income Taxes	5,013	6,992
Provision for income taxes	1,435	2,024
Income before cumulative effect of an accounting change		4,968
*Cumulative effect of accounting change, net of tax		(567)
Net Income (Loss)	$ 3,578	$ 4,401

*As of May 2006, the cumulative effect of a change in accounting principle will no longer be shown on the income statement. It will be recorded directly to Retained Earnings.

the Retained Earnings account during the period. Instead, a company records all of the revenue it earns in temporary accounts called revenue accounts. Examples of revenue accounts are Sales Revenue, Service Revenue, and Interest Revenue. On the income statement for Cisco Systems, there are two revenue accounts related to the sales of products and services. These revenue accounts appear first on the income statement. Interest Income has its own total, shown after a subtotal for Operating Income.

When Cisco Systems provides $1,000 worth of services for cash, the company will make this journal entry:

Transaction	Debit	Credit
Cash	1,000	
Service Revenue		1,000
To record Service Revenue earned and collected		

Exhibit 3.5

Expanded Accounting Equation with Debits and Credits

Accounting Equation									

Assets = **Liabilities** + **Shareholders' Equity**

Assets		=	Liabilities		+	Shareholders' Equity			
+	−		−	+		**Contributed Capital**		**Retained Earnings**	
Debit (DR) side	Credit (CR) side		Dr	Cr		− | +		− | +	
						Dr | Cr		Dr | Cr	

Revenues		**Expenses**		**Dividends**	
−	+	+	−	+	−
Dr	Cr	Dr	Cr	Dr	Cr

Revenues have the same debit/credit rules as Retained Earnings. That's because when Revenues go up, Retained Earnings goes up. Expenses and Dividends are just the opposite. Expenses and Dividends have the opposite debit/credit rules as Retained Earnings because increases in Expenses and Dividends reduce Retained Earnings.

Cash, an asset, is increased with a debit. Service Revenue, a revenue account, is increased with a credit. Notice, too, that debits of $1,000 equal credits of $1,000.

Exhibit 3.5, above, shows the debit and credit rules for the expanded accounting equation.

Recording expenses

What about expenses? Again, think about Retained Earnings. Because it is an equity account, Retained Earnings decreases with debits. Because expenses decrease Retained Earnings, expense accounts are increased with debits. That is, when a company records an expense, the accountant records the expense on the debit side of the expense account. When an accountant says that a particular transaction "increases" an expense, it simply means that an expense has been incurred and added to the company's list of expenses to be reported on the period's income statement. Expenses are recorded in temporary expense accounts during an accounting period, not in the Retained Earnings account. Examples of expense accounts are *Operating Expenses, Selling Expenses, Salary Expense*, and *Interest Expense*. Cisco Systems has two major categories of expenses on its income statement: *Cost of Sales* for both products and services and *Operating Expenses*. A third category of expenses is *Income Tax Expense*, often called *Provision for Income Taxes*, and always appears near the end of the income statement.

When Cisco Systems pays $1,200 for operating expenses, the company will make this journal entry:

Study Tip

Don't confuse what accountants mean by "increasing an expense" with the everyday expression that you might use. "Increase your expenses" simply means an expense has already been incurred and added to the list of expenses.

Transaction	Debit	Credit
Operating Expenses	1,200	
Cash		1,200
To record cash payment for operating expenses		

Operating Expenses, an expense account, is increased with a debit. Cash, an asset account, is decreased with a credit. Notice that debits of $1,200 equal credits of $1,200.

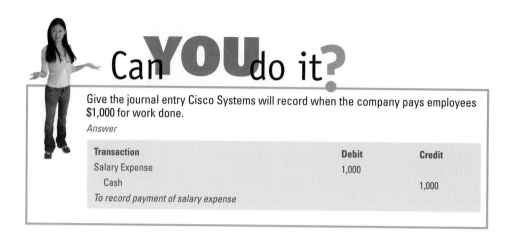

Can **YOU** do it?

Give the journal entry Cisco Systems will record when the company pays employees $1,000 for work done.

Answer

Transaction	Debit	Credit
Salary Expense	1,000	
Cash		1,000
To record payment of salary expense		

LEARNING OBJECTIVE 3

Explain the first three steps in the accounting cycle and the purpose of each step.

Accounting cycle: The steps an accountant follows to analyze and record business transactions, prepare the financial statements, and get ready for the next accounting period.

These are the steps in the accounting cycle. You'll learn how to execute steps 1–3 in this chapter.

The Accounting Cycle

The **accounting cycle** refers to the steps an accountant must follow to analyze and record business transactions, prepare financial statements, and get ready for the next accounting period. The cycle is a timeline for an accounting period that shows what an accounting information system must accomplish from the beginning of one accounting period to its very end. Exhibit 3.6 shows the 8 steps of the accounting cycle. In this chapter, we'll concentrate on steps 1, 2, and 3. In the next chapter, we'll cover steps 4–8 to complete the accounting cycle.

The steps in the accounting cycle are as follows:

1. Analyze and record transactions in the journal.
2. Post the journal entries to the general ledger.

Exhibit 3.6

The Accounting Cycle

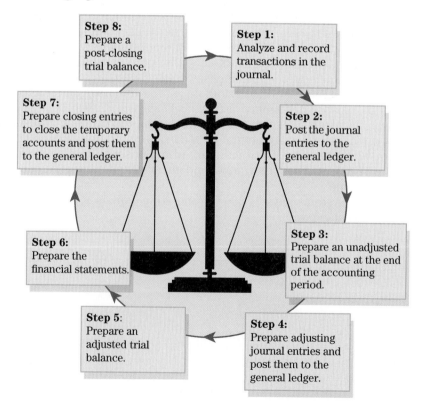

Step 8: Prepare a post-closing trial balance.

Step 1: Analyze and record transactions in the journal.

Step 2: Post the journal entries to the general ledger.

Step 3: Prepare an unadjusted trial balance at the end of the accounting period.

Step 4: Prepare adjusting journal entries and post them to the general ledger.

Step 5: Prepare an adjusted trial balance.

Step 6: Prepare the financial statements.

Step 7: Prepare closing entries to close the temporary accounts and post them to the general ledger.

3. Prepare an unadjusted trial balance at the end of the accounting period.

4. Prepare adjusting journal entries and post them to the general ledger.

5. Prepare an adjusted trial balance.

6. Prepare the financial statements.

7. Prepare closing entries to close the temporary accounts and post them to the general ledger.

8. Prepare a post-closing trial balance.

Step 1: Analyze and Record the Transactions in the Journal
Accountants need a complete record of transactions to prepare the financial statements. They analyze the transactions to determine what happened and why. Changes in assets show the changes in the firm's resources, and the corresponding changes in liability or equity accounts explain what happened. For example, stock is issued for cash. The increase in the asset, Cash, is explained by the increase in Contributed Capital. The asset increased because of shareholders' contributions.

Analyzing the transaction is one of the most difficult parts in the accounting cycle. Which accounts are affected by a transaction? Think about the accounting equation to determine if the transaction affects assets, liabilities, and/or equity. Remember that revenues are amounts *earned*, even if the cash hasn't been collected. Expenses are costs that have been incurred to earn the revenue. When a firm purchases a computer or truck, should it be recorded as an asset (future value) or an expense (consumed to generate revenue)? Think about these questions as you analyze a transaction.

Then, the accountant must decide the specific accounts to use. Recall the simple chart of accounts in Exhibit 3.3. These are just some of the accounts a company may have. Look at the examples in the chapter to help you find the appropriate accounts to use.

Step 2: Post the Journal Entries to the General Ledger The journal entries are reorganized as they are posted to the general ledger. No matter how many journals a company has, all the journal entries will feed into only one general ledger. *Posting* refers to this process of reorganizing the information from the transactions into the accounts affected by the transactions.

Step 3: Prepare an Unadjusted Trial Balance Recall that debits and credits are tools to keep the basic accounting equation in balance with every journal entry. Because debits and credits are equal with every transaction, the general ledger should always be in balance. A **trial balance** is a list of all a company's accounts, each with its debit or credit balance, prepared to make sure the accounting records are in balance. Before computers, preparing a trial balance was an important step in catching any posting errors. That's the function it will serve for us, too. A trial balance also provides a useful summary of the general ledger at any point in time.

Recording and Posting Transactions and Preparing an Unadjusted Trial Balance

An accountant must record hundreds, or sometimes thousands, of business transactions in the accounting system. In this section, we'll see how a company called Quality Web Designs keeps track of its many transactions.

Recording a series of transactions

Let's look at some transactions for starting a company. Exhibit 3.7 shows the transactions for Quality Web Designs, a company started on June 1, 2007, by an ambitious college student majoring in computer science.

Study Tip

Having a trial balance that balances does not mean the accounting records are error-free. It only means the debits entered are equal to the credits entered in the records. Both debit and credit amounts and the accounts could be wrong.

Trial balance: A list of all of the accounts in the general ledger with their respective debit or credit balances at a given point in time. The trial balance ensures that debits = credits in the accounting records.

LEARNING OBJECTIVE 4

Post journal entries to the general ledger and prepare a trial balance.

Exhibit 3.7

Transactions for Quality Web Designs

	Date	Transaction
1	June 1	Received $50,000 cash from its shareholders in exchange for common stock.
2	June 2	Paid $1,500 cash for operating expenses for June.
3	June 5	Paid $1,200 for a year's worth of insurance, with the policy starting on July 1. The insurance will be recorded as an asset, Prepaid Insurance, because it has not been used. The June 30 balance sheet will show $1,200 as an asset—something of future value to the firm.
4	June 10	Performed services for clients on account, $3,000.
5	June 14	Received a bill from AOL for $50 for Internet service for June. Bill will be paid in July.
6	June 18	Paid cash of $645 for operating expenses, of which $100 was for advertising.
7	June 24	Received cash of $1,000 from customers billed on June 10.
8	June 30	Purchased a printer for $600 by signing a note payable due on December 31.

Study Tip

In accounting, we use the expression "on account" to describe selling or buying something using credit rather than cash. We use a different expression for what we commonly think of as buying or selling using credit because the word "credit" has many meanings, and accountants use it most often to mean the right side of an account.

Transaction 1: The first transaction is a financing activity: The firm receives a contribution of $50,000 in exchange for ownership in the company. The owners' contributions take the form of common stock in a corporation. As we learned in the first chapter, every business transaction keeps the accounting equation in balance. Here's how we record this transaction in the accounting equation, as we did in Chapter 2.

Accounting Equation					
Assets	**=**	**Liabilities**	**+**	**Shareholders' Equity**	
				Contributed Capital	**+** **Retained Earnings**
Cash				Common Stock	
50,000				50,000	

However, instead of using the accounting equation, accountants use journal entries to record transactions. The general ledger's system of debits and credits will have the dollar amount of debits equal to the dollar amount of credits in every journal entry. Here is the journal entry for transaction 1:

Date	Transaction	Debit	Credit
6/1/07	Cash	50,000	
	Common Stock		50,000
	To record shareholders' contributions in exchange for common stock		

The Cash account is increased by $50,000. Cash is an asset, on the left side of the accounting equation, so the accountant will debit the Cash account for $50,000. Common Stock, a shareholders' equity account, is increased because that explains where the cash came from. Shareholders' equity is on the right side of the accounting equation, so the accountant will credit a contributed capital account, here Common Stock, for $50,000. Notice that in this case two accounts are increased—one with a debit and one with a credit. In some transactions, both accounts are increased. In other transactions, one account may be increased and one account may be decreased, or two accounts may be decreased. There is no requirement for a journal entry to have both an increase and a decrease, but the dollar amount of debits must equal the dollar amount of credits.

Transaction 2: The company pays $1,500 for operating expenses.

Accounting Equation					
Assets	**=**	**Liabilities**	**+**	**Shareholders' Equity**	
				Contributed Capital +	**Retained Earnings**
Cash					Operating Expenses
−1,500					−1,500

Assets are decreased, and the shareholders' claims have been reduced. The accounting equation is in balance with a $1,500 reduction in Cash and a $1,500 reduction in Retained Earnings, shown as an addition to Operating Expenses. Because the expense is recorded in an expense account, rather than in the actual Retained Earnings account, the journal entry actually increases an expense account.

Date	Transaction	Debit	Credit
6/2/07	Operating Expenses	1,500	
	Cash		1,500
	To record the payment of current expenses		

Transaction 3: The company pays $1,200 for an insurance policy that begins July 1.

Accounting Equation					
Assets	**=**	**Liabilities** +		**Shareholders' Equity**	
				Contributed Capital +	**Retained Earnings**
Cash	Prepaid Insurance				
−1,200	1,200				

Because the insurance is not being used until July 1, Quality Web Designs will record the insurance as an asset—Prepaid Insurance. This is an asset that represents the value of the insurance that the company has not yet used.

Date	Transaction	Debit	Credit
6/5/07	Prepaid Insurance	1,200	
	Cash		1,200
	To record the payment for future insurance		

Transaction 4: The company provides services to customers on account for $3,000. The cash won't be collected until next month.

Accounting Equation						
Assets	=	Liabilities	+	Shareholders' Equity		
				Contributed Capital	+	Retained Earnings
Accounts Receivable						Service Revenue
3,000						3,000

The journal entry is recorded with a debit to Accounts Receivable and a credit to Service Revenue.

Date	Transaction	Debit	Credit
6/10/07	Accounts Receivable	3,000	
	Service Revenue		3,000
	To record service revenue that has been earned on account		

Notice that this transaction increases an asset account—Accounts Receivable—and increases a revenue account—Service Revenue.

Transaction 5: The company receives a bill from AOL for providing Internet service for June but will not be paid until July. The company will record an expense—which decreases Retained Earnings—and an increase in a liability, Other Payables.

Accounting Equation						
Assets	=	Liabilities	+	Shareholders' Equity		
				Contributed Capital	+	Retained Earnings
		Other Payables				Operating Expenses
		50				−50

Date	Transaction	Debit	Credit
6/14/07	Operating Expenses	50	
	Other Payables		50
	To record Internet expense		

Transaction 6: The company pays $645 for miscellaneous operating expenses, including $100 for advertising. Advertising costs are recorded as expenses, not assets, per GAAP. So we can group all of these expenses together. Notice that, as usual, the expenses are shown in the Retained Earnings column as a reduction. The amount is actually recorded in an expense account, with the balance increased by $645. The negative sign denotes how the transaction affects Retained Earnings.

Accounting Equation

Assets	=	Liabilities	+	Shareholders' Equity		
				Contributed Capital	+	Retained Earnings
Cash						Operating Expenses
−645						−645

The journal entry is a debit to the expense account and a credit to reduce Cash.

Date	Transaction	Debit	Credit
6/18/07	Operating Expenses	645	
	Cash		645
	To record payment for operating expenses		

Transaction 7: The company receives cash of $1,000 from customers billed in Transaction 4.

Accounting Equation

Assets		=	Liabilities	+	Shareholders' Equity		
					Contributed Capital	+	Retained Earnings
Cash	Accounts Receivable						
1,000	−1,000						

The journal entry is a debit to Cash because Cash is increased, and a credit to reduce Accounts Receivable. Notice that no revenue is recognized because it was already recognized in transaction 4. The transaction of receiving the cash simply exchanges one asset—Accounts Receivable—for another—Cash.

Date	Transaction	Debit	Credit
6/24/07	Cash	1,000	
	Accounts Receivable		1,000
	To record collection on accounts receivable		

Transaction 8: The company purchases a printer for $600 and signs a note due on December 31. Assets are increased and liabilities are increased.

Accounting Equation

Assets	=	Liabilities	+	Shareholders' Equity		
				Contributed Capital	+	Retained Earnings
Equipment		Notes Payable				
600		600				

The journal entry is a debit to Equipment and a credit to Notes Payable. This journal entry increases both accounts.

Date	Transaction	Debit	Credit
6/30/07	Equipment	600	
	Notes Payable		600
	To record purchase of equipment with a short-term note		

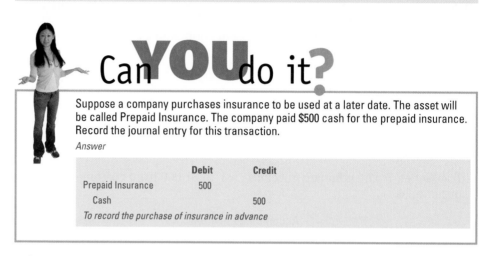

Can **YOU** do it?

Suppose a company purchases insurance to be used at a later date. The asset will be called Prepaid Insurance. The company paid $500 cash for the prepaid insurance. Record the journal entry for this transaction.

Answer

	Debit	Credit
Prepaid Insurance	500	
Cash		500
To record the purchase of insurance in advance		

Posting transactions to the general ledger

A company must post each of the journal entries to its general ledger. How often this is done depends on the number of journal entries a company normally makes. Some computerized systems post every journal entry automatically when it is entered into the system. Other systems require a specific instruction to post the entries.

The accounts for Quality Web Designs all begin with a zero balance because this is the firm's first year of business. Each journal entry is recorded and posted to the general ledger. After all the journal entries are posted, it is easy to calculate the balance in any account. Exhibit 3.8 shows the journal entries and the T-accounts. The arrows in the exhibit show you how the journal entries are posted to the T-accounts, our representation of the general ledger.

Preparing a trial balance

Before accounting software like QuickBooks or Peachtree was developed, accountants used a trial balance—a list of all of the firm's accounts with their balances—to make sure that, at any point in time, debits equal credits in the accounting records. Although it is rare to manually create a trial balance today, it is important to know what a trial balance is because most accounting software automatically creates one for accountants to use. Exhibit 3.9(a) on page 116 shows an unadjusted trial balance for Quality Web Designs. It's called an *unadjusted* trial balance because we have not reviewed the accounts for adjustments that might be needed to ensure that the financial statements are accurate. We'll learn about adjusting journal entries in Chapter 4.

While a trial balance can tell us if debits and credits are equal in our accounting records, it will not ensure that there are no errors in our records. In a journal entry, we could debit Inventory by mistake instead of Accounts Receivable when we receive a customer's payment. The trial balance would still balance, but the amounts in Accounts Receivable and Inventory would be wrong. We could also make a journal entry for $4,000 when it should have been for $40,000. If both the debit and the credit were $4,000, the journal entry would

Exhibit 3.8

Journal Entries and T-Accounts for Quality Web Design

General Journal

Date	Transaction	Debit	Credit
1. June 1	Cash	50,000	
	Common Stock		50,000
	To record shareholders' contributions in exchange for common stock		
2. June 2	Operating Expenses	1,500	
	Cash		1,500
	To record the payment of current expenses		
3. June 5	Prepaid Insurance	1,200	
	Cash		1,200
	To record the payment for future insurance		
4. June 10	Accounts Receivable	3,000	
	Service Revenue		3,000
	To record service revenue that has been earned on account		
5. June 14	Operating Expenses	50	
	Other Payables		50
	To record Internet expenses		
6. June 18	Operating Expenses	645	
	Cash		645
	To record payment for operating expenses		
7. June 24	Cash	1,000	
	Accounts Receivable		1,000
	To record collection on AR		
8. June 30	Equipment	600	
	Notes Payable (short term)		600
	To record purchase of equipment with a short-term note		

Assets   =   Liabilities + Shareholders' Equity

Cash (Asset)

(1)	50,000	1,500	(2)
(7)	1,000	1,200	(3)
		645	(6)
	47,655		

Accounts Receivable (Asset)

(4)	3,000	1,000	(7)
	2,000		

Prepaid Insurance (Asset)

(3)	1,200	
	1,200	

Office Equipment (Asset)

(8)	600	
	600	

Other Payables (Liability)

	50 (5)
	50

Notes Payable (Liability)

	600 (8)
	600

Common Stock (Shareholders' Equity)

	50,000 (1)
	50,000

Service Revenue (Revenue)

	3,000 (4)
	3,000

Operating Expenses (Expenses)

(2)	1,500	
(5)	50	
(6)	645	
	2,195	

balance but be incorrect. The trial balance would still be in balance if we left out a journal entry completely. A trial balance that actually balances does not assure us that there are no errors, but a trial balance that does *not* balance assures us that there definitely is at least one error.

Preparing an income statement and a balance sheet

Until we discuss adjusting entries in the next chapter, we'll skip accounting cycle steps 4 and 5, and go directly to preparing the financial statements. In actual accounting systems, the steps related to adjusting the accounts must be completed before the statements are prepared. An accountant can use a trial balance to prepare the statements. Exhibit 3.9(a) shows the trial balance for Quality Web Designs. You can see that the total of the debit column equals the total of the credit column.

Let's start by preparing an income statement for the month of June for Quality Web Designs. Can you pick out the revenue and expense accounts for the income statement? They are: Service Revenue and Operating Expenses. These accounts make the simple income statement, shown in Exhibit 3.9(b).

As you look at the trial balance to get ready to prepare the balance sheet, you may notice that there is no Retained Earnings account listed. Because this is the first year of operations, Quality Web Designs has no Retained Earnings yet. Remember that Retained Earnings is the sum of all the net incomes a company has earned in its life reduced by any net losses and by the total amount of dividends paid to shareholders. After we calculate the month's net income, we will need that amount in Retained Earnings to make the balance sheet actually balance. Exhibit 3.9(c) shows a statement of retained earnings, and (d) shows the balance sheet for Quality Web Designs. Both statements' titles show the company name, the statement name, and a reference to the period covered

Exhibit 3.9

Trial Balance, Income Statement, Statement of Retained Earnings, and Balance Sheet for Quality Web Designs

(a) Trial Balance

Account	Debit	Credit
Cash	$47,655	
Accounts receivable	2,000	
Prepaid insurance	1,200	
Equipment	600	
Other payables		$ 50
Notes payable		600
Common stock		50,000
Service revenue		3,000
Operating expenses	2,195	
	$53,650	$53,650

(b) Income Statement

Quality Web Designs
Income Statement
For the month ended June 30

Service revenue	$ 3,000
Operating expenses	2,195
Net income	$ 805

(c) Statement of Retained Earnings

Quality Web Designs
Statement of Retained Earnings
For the month ended June 30

Beginning Retained Earnings	$ 0
Add Net income	805
Deduct Dividends	0
Ending Retained Earnings	$ 805

(d) Balance Sheet

Quality Web Designs
Balance Sheet
At June 30

Assets

Cash	$47,655
Accounts receivable	2,000
Prepaid insurance	1,200
Total current assets	50,855
Office equipment	600
Total assets	$51,455

Liabilities and Shareholders' Equity

Other payables	$ 50
Notes payable	600
Total current liabilities	650
Common stock	50,000
Retained earnings	805
Total liabilities and shareholders' equity	$51,455

(a) A trial balance is a list of all the company's accounts and their respective debit and credit balances. (b) The income statement can be prepared from the accounts in the lower part of the trial balance. (c) Statement of retained earnings is part of the statement of changes in shareholders' equity. It shows how Retained Earnings changed during the month. In this case, the balance went from 0 to $805. (d) An accountant can use a trial balance to prepare the balance sheet. Here you can see that the trial balance and balance sheet are very similar.

(statement of retained earnings) or the date of the statement (balance sheet). On the balance sheet, the assets are listed first and the liabilities and shareholders' equity are listed below the assets. (Some balance sheets show the assets side-by-side with the liabilities and equity sections.) The amounts can be easily traced to the trial balance. Compare the trial balance to the balance sheet so you can see exactly how the amounts are formally reported.

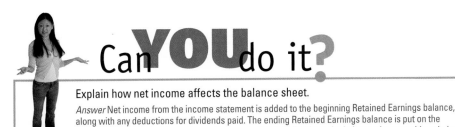

Can **YOU** do it?

Explain how net income affects the balance sheet.

Answer Net income from the income statement is added to the beginning Retained Earnings balance, along with any deductions for dividends paid. The ending Retained Earnings balance is put on the balance sheet. Without including net income in Retained Earnings, the balance sheet would not balance.

Financial Statement Analysis

LEARNING OBJECTIVE 5

Compute and explain working capital and the quick ratio.

You've learned how to analyze transactions and record them in the general ledger system. You've also learned how to prepare the financial statements from the information in the general ledger system. Preparing the financial statements is an important step toward understanding what the numbers mean. Only when you know how the numbers for the financial statements have been calculated are you ready to analyze the statements and assess the financial performance of a firm.

Working capital

In Chapter 2, you learned about the current ratio and how it provides information about the company's liquidity and ability to meet its short-term obligations. **Working capital** is another measure used to evaluate liquidity. Working capital is defined as *current assets minus current liabilities*. The current ratio gives a relative measure of a company's ability to finance its operations, and the amount of working capital gives an absolute measure. Look at the information from the balance sheet of La-Z-Boy in Exhibit 3.10.

Working capital: Current assets minus current liabilities.

The working capital at April 26, 2003, was $464,907,000.

Current assets	–	Current liabilities	=	Working capital
$679,494,000	–	$214,587,000	=	$464,907,000

Calculate the working capital at April 27, 2004. If you subtract the current liabilities from the current assets, you should get $370,353,000. Current assets have decreased for La-Z-Boy during the year, between the two balance sheet dates, from $679,494,000 to $653,674,000 . During the same time, current liabilities have increased from $214,587,000 to $283,321,000. These two changes add up to a significant decrease in working capital. Any company considering doing business with La-Z-Boy might compute working capital for several years to identify any increases or decreases. This decrease could indicate a decrease in the company's ability to finance its current operations. Read about working capital and its importance in *Accounting in the News*.

The working capital at April 26, 2003, was $464,907,000; and the working capital at April 24, 2004, was $370,353,000. The decrease in working capital could indicate a decrease in the company's ability to finance its operations.

Exhibit 3.10

From the Balance Sheets of La-Z-Boy

From the Balance Sheets of La-Z-Boy
At the end of fiscal years 2004 and 2003
(in thousands)

	4/24/2004	4/26/2003
Assets		
Current assets		
Cash and equivalents	$ 33,882	$ 28,817
Receivables, net	299,801	340,467
Inventories, net	250,568	252,537
Deferred income taxes	37,969	37,734
Other current assets	31,454	19,939
Total current assets	$653,674	$679,494
Liabilities		
Current liabilities		
Short-term borrowings	$ 37,219	$ 0
Current portion of long-term debt	5,344	1,619
Accounts payable	93,298	78,931
Accrued expenses and other liabilities	147,460	134,037
Total current liabilities	$283,321	$214,587

Accounting in the NEWS

Financial Statement Analysis

Why Do Analysts Care About the Working Capital of Whole Foods Market?

It's no surprise that managers worry about what financial analysts say about their firms. When an analyst from Lehman Brothers says something positive about a firm, it could mean a jump in the firm's stock price. Of course, something positive must be going on with the firm to cause a positive report from an analyst!

In a November 2003 article about Whole Foods Market, *BusinessWeek* reported that analyst Meredith Adler gave the supermarket chain high marks for its improved productivity and working capital.

"Adler thinks the outlook is very strong, and she's pleased that Whole Foods is able to generate sufficient free cash to institute a small dividend."

On November 12, 2003, the supermarket's stock closed at $58.73 per share, and 2.2 million shares were traded that day. On November 13, 2003, the stock closed at $64.68, and 5.2 million shares traded that day. No one would attribute such a positive change to a single factor without some serious research to support it. Many factors can cause a change in a firm's stock price, but don't be surprised if you read about working capital when an analyst evaluates a firm's financial condition.

Q Why should an investor understand working capital?

A Analysts use it to evaluate a firm's financial condition, and it may affect stock price.

Sources: "Word on the Street," *Business Week Online,* November 13, 2003; wholefoods.com.

Founded in 1980 as one small store in Austin, Texas, Whole Foods Market® is now the world's leading retailer of natural and organic foods with more than 170 stores in North America and the United Kingdom. In 2005, *Fortune Magazine* named them one of the top five companies to work for.

Quick ratio

It's important that the information on the financial statements be accurate and reliable because it is used to help measure a company's ability to meet its short-term obligations. As you learned in Chapter 2, the *current ratio* is current assets divided by current liabilities. Another ratio similar to the current ratio is called the **quick ratio**, also know as the *acid-test ratio*. Instead of using all of a company's current assets in the numerator, the quick ratio uses only Cash, Short-term Investments, and Net Accounts Receivable. These three assets are the most liquid—easiest to convert to cash—so they are the most readily available for paying off current liabilities. You might see the quick ratio defined as *current assets minus inventories divided by current liabilities.* An investor or analyst will use the quick ratio as a stricter test of a company's ability to meet its short-term obligations. It measures a firm's ability to meet its short-term obligations even if the firm makes no additional sales.

Let's use the information from La-Z-Boy's balance sheet in Exhibit 3.10 to calculate both the current ratio that we studied in Chapter 2 and the quick ratio. These computations are shown in Exhibit 3.11.

> **Quick ratio:** Cash, Accounts Receivable, and Short-term Investments divided by current liabilities. This ratio measures a firm's ability to meet its current obligations.

> **In Other Words:**
> The quick ratio is sometimes called the acid-test ratio.

Can YOU do it?

Given the following information taken from the comparative balance sheets of California Pizza Kitchens, calculate the amount of working capital the company had at the end of the two years shown. Calculate the quick ratio for the same time periods. What does this information tell you?

At the end of fiscal year	2003	2004
Cash	$15,877,000	$17,719,000
Investments	18,904,000	26,415,000
Accounts receivable	2,591,000	4,548,000
Inventories	2,892,000	3,068,000
Prepaid and other current assets	3,702,000	5,089,000
Total current assets	$43,966,000	$56,839,000
Total current liabilities	$43,274,000	$45,732,000

Answer

Working capital	$692,000	$11,107,000
Quick ratio	0.86	1.06

Both the amount of working capital and the quick ratio have increased significantly between fiscal year end 2003 and fiscal year end 2004.

Exhibit 3.11

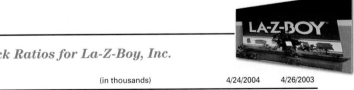

Current and Quick Ratios for La-Z-Boy, Inc.

(in thousands)	4/24/2004	4/26/2003
Current assets	$653,674	$679,494
Current liabilities	$283,321	$214,587
Current ratio	2.31	3.17
Cash and equivalents	$ 33,882	$ 28,817
Receivables, net	$299,801	$340,467
Total numerator for quick ratio	$333,683	$369,294
Current liabilities	$283,321	$214,587
Quick ratio	1.18	1.72

The current ratio declined between April 26, 2003, and April 24, 2004, by 0.86. Although the quick ratio also declined, the decline was more modest at 0.54. The decline in the ratio may be viewed as good news by the company because the firm significantly decreased its accounts receivable.

LEARNING OBJECTIVE 6

Recognize the risks and controls associated with using a traditional accounting system.

Business risk, control, & ethics

Now that you have finished learning many of the procedures associated with the traditional general ledger accounting system, let's look at the three most significant risks associated with this system:

1. Errors in recording and updating the general ledger
2. Unauthorized access to the general ledger
3. Loss of the data in the general ledger

These risks are not unique to the general ledger system. No matter how transactions are recorded, the system needs to address the risks of errors in recording the data, access to the data, and the potential loss of the data. However, we will look at these risks as they specifically apply to the general ledger.

Errors in recording and updating the general ledger

Errors in recording and posting journal entries can lead to inaccurate records and reports. These errors can be costly, both for internal decision making and external reporting. The accuracy and completeness of the recording process are crucial for a firm's success. The controls that can minimize the risk of these errors include: (1) input and processing controls, (2) reconciliation and control reports, and (3) documentation to provide supporting evidence for the recorded transactions. These controls should be present in both manual general ledger systems and computerized general ledger systems.

Companies assign codes to employees to make sure only authorized people can enter sales information.

- *Input and processing controls.* This control is designed to make sure that only authorized transactions are put into the system. For example, when a sales clerk enters a sale at a cash register, the clerk must put in an employee code before entering the data. Additional controls, such as department numbers and item numbers, help make sure that clerks enter the correct information. The computer program that controls this part of the accounting system may also have limits on the dollar amounts that can be entered. The design of the controls depends on the accounting information system and the business, but all companies should have controls to assure the accuracy of the input and processing of the data that are recorded.

- *Reconciliation and control reports.* This control is designed to catch any errors in the input and processing of the accounting data. The trial balance is an example of a control report. Computerized general ledgers are valuable because they make sure debits equal credits at every stage of the data entry. That means a trial balance *has* to balance! Equality of debits and credits with each entry is a control programmed into accounting software like Peachtree and QuickBooks. Accounting software doesn't guarantee that all the entries have been made correctly, but it does keep some errors from occurring.

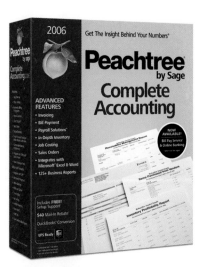
Accounting software helps accountants make sure that debits always equal credits.

- *Documentation to provide supporting evidence for the recorded transactions.* This control is designed to keep errors from occurring and also to catch errors that have occurred. The employee who puts the data into the accounting system will get that data from a document that describes the transaction. The information contained in the documentation can be compared to the data put into the accounting system. For example, when a book publishing company sends an invoice to Amazon.com for a shipment of books, it will keep a copy of this invoice to input the data into its accounting system. The publishing company may also use this invoice to verify the accuracy of the accounting entry by referring back to the original invoice.

| | GREAT BOOKS | Great Books Publishing
15 Maple Road
Lakeview
New York | | Phone: 555-555-5555
Fax: 555-555-5555
E-mail: someone@greatbooks.com | | | | | |

Invoice #:
Invoice Date:
Customer ID:

INVOICE

Bill To:
Amazon.com

Ship To:
Amazon.com

Date	Your Order #	Our Order #	Sales Rep.	FOB	Ship Via	Terms	Tax ID
June 27, 2006	12345		Jones	NJ	UPS	2/10, n/30	

Quantity	Item	Units	Description	Discount %	Taxable	Unit Price	Total
1,000	Reynolds Textbook		Ind. Filmaking ISBN 54321			60	$60.000
500	Deitmer Textbook		Music ISBN 98765			50	$25.000

REMITTANCE
Customer ID:
Date:
Amount Due:
Amount Enclosed:

Subtotal	$85.000
Tax	$ 5.100
Shipping	
Miscellaneous	
Balance Due	$90.100

COPY FOR CUSTOMER

| | GREAT BOOKS | Great Books Publishing
15 Maple Road
Lakeview
New York | | Phone: 555-555-5555
Fax: 555-555-5555
E-mail: someone@greatbooks.com | | | | | |

Invoice #:
Invoice Date:
Customer ID:

INVOICE

Bill To:
Amazon.com

Ship To:
Amazon.com

Date	Your Order #	Our Order #	Sales Rep.	FOB	Ship Via	Terms	Tax ID
June 27, 2006	12345		Jones	NJ	UPS	2/10, n/30	

Quantity	Item	Units	Description	Discount %	Taxable	Unit Price	Total
1,000	Reynolds Textbook		Ind. Filmaking ISBN 54321			60	$60.000
500	Deitmer Textbook		Music ISBN 98765			50	$25.000

REMITTANCE
Customer ID:
Date:
Amount Due:
Amount Enclosed:

COPY FOR GREAT BOOKS ACCOUNTS RECEIVABLE DEPARTMENT

Subtotal	$85.000
Tax	$ 5.100
Shipping	
Miscellaneous	
Balance Due	$90.100

Invoices are an example of an internal control. A book publisher sends an invoice to a customer and also retains a copy for its Accounts Receivable department.

Unauthorized access to the general ledger

Unauthorized access is an obvious risk for any company's accounting system. Such access would expose a company to leaks of confidential data, errors, and the cover up of theft. In manual systems, the general ledger should be locked in a secure place so that it cannot be accessed by unauthorized employees. Computerized systems have User IDs and passwords to control access to the accounting system.

Loss or destruction of general ledger data

Imagine that you are working for several hours on a report for your marketing class, and you save your work on your hard drive. You decide to step out for a coffee with friends before wrapping up. While you're gone, the computer shuts down, and you can't reboot. If you saved your work on a backup CD-ROM, you're okay. If you didn't, you have to start the report from scratch.

The general ledger contains data that are crucial parts of a company's information system, so there must be a backup and disaster recovery plan. The 2001 terrorist attack on the World Trade Center is perhaps the most vivid example of why backup and disaster recovery plans are important. Even before September 11, Fiduciary Trust International, a subsidiary of Franklin Templeton, used a method called *data shadowing*, saving data simultaneously in two separate

Can **YOU** do it?

Name three major risks a company faces with respect to its accounting system.

Answers (1) errors in recording and updating the system (2) unauthorized access (3) loss of data

Accounting in the NEWS

Risk and Control

A Disaster Recovery Plan Helps a Large Investment Firm—Franklin Templeton—Recover After 9/11

Fiduciary Trust International and its parent company Franklin Templeton Investments, a large mutual fund company based in San Mateo, California, lost 87 employees and 7 business partners at their headquarters in the South Tower of the World Trade Center (WTC) on September 11, 2001.

The company created a disaster recovery plan in the mid 1980s that consisted of a data backup system. After the 1993 bombing at the WTC, the company was forced to leave its headquarters for five weeks. At that point, the company created more disaster recovery plans. Part of those plans was a process called "data shadowing," in which data are saved simultaneously in two separate

locations. According to William Yun, the president of Fiduciary Trust International, the practice paid off on September 11. The company was able to recover all of the morning transactions that occurred before the attacks.

The key issues for the company on September 11, 2001, were employee safety and communication with the families of employees. A less important issue, but one that arose quite soon after the tragedy, was how to restart business. Having an offsite facility with a copy of the data, created at the time of the transactions, enabled the company to conduct wire transfers for cash and securities on the day after the attacks. On September 13, the company was able to increase its activities; and, when equity markets reopened on Monday, September 17, Fiduciary was ready to resume its core business.

Q How can a company protect itself from losing its data in some sort of disaster?

A It should backup its data off-site.

Data shadowing is an important part of a company's disaster recovery plan because it allows a company to retrieve data from a temporary location.

Source: Statement of William Y. Yun to the National Commission on Terrorist Attacks Upon the United States, November 19, 2003, www.9-11commission.gov.

locations. Read about it in **Accounting in the News**. Although the loss of accounting data is insignificant in comparison to the human loss suffered in that tragic event, it did bring the issue of lost and destroyed data to the attention of the companies that were affected that day.

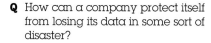

YOU make the call:

Should Cisco allow its salespeople to enter their transactions directly into the firm's accounting system?

Now that you have studied the general ledger accounting system and the controls needed to ensure accurate accounting records, you should have an opinion on this question: Should Cisco Systems allow the salespeople to record their own sales transactions? The best answer is no. Even though some efficiencies might be gained by allowing the salespeople to record their own transactions, there are several solid reasons why it would not be a good idea. First, salespeople want to record the revenue as soon as possible, maybe even a little prematurely. It takes someone knowledgeable about the accounting standards to make decisions regarding the timing of revenue recognition. Second, allowing so many people access to the firm's accounting system reflects poor control over the system. In particular, input controls could easily be compromised with a large number of people having access to the system.

Let's Take a Test Drive

Real-World Problem:
Cisco Systems

Cisco Systems is a leading manufacturer of networking equipment and technology for the Internet. Due to the large volume of transactions, you can bet that Cisco Systems does not use a manual general ledger. However, the firm does have millions of transactions to track and financial statements to prepare for its shareholders. In Exhibit 3.4, you saw that the firm's sales for the fiscal year ended July 31, 2004, totaled over $22 billion. Keeping accurate records of its transactions is clearly a challenge for Cisco Systems.

Concepts

The general ledger system shows how information from business transactions makes its way to the financial statements. The general ledger system is an accounting information system based on the relationships in the accounting equation: That is, increases to assets and expense accounts are recorded as debits (left side) and increases to liabilities, shareholders' equity, and revenue accounts are recorded as credits (right side). Every transaction affects at least two accounts, and debits must equal credits in recording any transaction. The original recording of a transaction is called a journal entry, and journal entries are recorded chronologically as the business events occur. The information is reorganized by account when the journal entries are posted to the general ledger. The general ledger is a book (or computer file) with all of a company's accounts with their monetary balances. The first three steps of the accounting cycle are:

1. Analyze and record the transactions in the journal.
2. Post the journal entries to the general ledger.
3. Prepare an unadjusted trial balance at the end of the accounting period—a list of all the accounts and their balances to confirm that debits equal credits in the accounting records. At this point, we're well on our way to preparing the financial statements.

The Mechanics

To put these concepts into practice, start with the following accounts and their balances for Cisco Systems at August 1, 2004, the beginning balances for the fiscal year ended July 31 (all of these amounts are fictional).

Account	Debit	Credit
Cash	$ 4,925	
Accounts Receivable	2,500	
Other Current Assets	2,938	
Accounts Payable		$ 340
Income Taxes Payable		175
Salaries Payable		520
Short-term Notes Payable		58
Other Current Liabilities		450
Long-term Liabilities		750
Common Stock		5,470
Retained Earnings		2,600
Total	$10,363	$10,363

Suppose Cisco Systems' transactions for the fiscal year ended July 31, 2005, could be summarized as follows (amounts in trial balance and in the transactions are in millions of dollars):

1. Paid $200 cash for cleaning services for the year.
2. Provided services to customers for $17,000. Of that total, $7,000 was collected in cash.
3. Spent $2,850 cash on research and development.
4. Paid off the beginning balance in Accounts Payable.

5. Paid off the beginning balance in Salaries Payable.
6. Purchased $300 worth of supplies on account. (None were used during the year.) Use Accounts Payable to record the liability.
7. Paid off the short-term Notes Payable plus $2 interest.
8. Collected $8,900 cash from customers on Accounts Receivable.
9. Paid off the income taxes owed at the start of the year.
10. Paid employees $4,000 for work done this year.
11. Paid $5,900 cash for Operating Expenses.
12. Paid off the Other Current Liabilities of $450.

Instructions

1. Prepare journal entries for the transactions.
2. Set up T-accounts with beginning balances and post the journal entries to T-accounts.
3. Prepare a trial balance.
4. Prepare an income statement for the year and balance sheet at year-end.

Solution 1: Journal Entries

Transaction	Debit	Credit
1. Cleaning Expense	200	
Cash		200
To record payment of cash for cleaning service		
2. Cash	7,000	
Accounts Receivable	10,000	
Service Revenue		17,000
To record service revenue earned, part cash, part on account		
3. Research and Development Expenses	2,850	
Cash		2,850
Payment of research and development costs		
4. Accounts Payable	340	
Cash		340
Payment made on accounts payable		
5. Salaries Payable	520	
Cash		520
Payment of salaries previously recorded		
6. Supplies	300	
Accounts Payable		300
Purchase of supplies on account		
7. Short-term Notes Payable	58	
Interest Expense	2	
Cash		60
Payment on short-term loan-principal and interest		
8. Cash	8,900	
Accounts Receivable		8,900
To record the collection of cash on accounts receivable		
9. Income Taxes Payable	175	
Cash		175
Payment of federal income taxes		

10. Salaries Expense	4,000	
Cash		4,000
Payment of salaries		
11. Operating Expenses	5,900	
Cash		5,900
Payment of operating expenses		
12. Other Current Liabilities	450	
Cash		450
Payment of other current liabilities		

Solution 2: T-Accounts

Note: The beginning balances are labeled **BB**. Each transaction has the number corresponding to the journal entry.

| Assets | | = | Liabilities | + | Shareholders' Equity |

Cash

BB	4,925	200	(1)
(2)	7,000	2,850	(3)
(8)	8,900	340	(4)
		520	(5)
		60	(7)
		175	(9)
		4,000	(10)
		5,900	(11)
		450	(12)
	6,330		

Accounts Receivable

BB	2,500	8,900	(8)
(2)	10,000		
	3,600		

Supplies

| (6) | 300 | |

Other Current Assets

| BB | 2,938 | |

Accounts Payable

(4)	340	340	BB
		300	(6)
		300	

Other Current Liabilities

| (12) | 450 | 450 | BB |

Salaries Payable

| (5) | 520 | 520 | BB |

Short-term Notes Payable

| (7) | 58 | 58 | BB |

Income Taxes Payable

| (9) | 175 | 175 | BB |

Long-term Liabilities

| | | 750 | BB |

Common Stock

| | | 5,470 | BB |

Retained Earnings

| | | 2,600 | BB |

Service Revenue

| | | 17,000 | (2) |

Cleaning Expense

| (1) | 200 | |

Research and Development Expenses

| (3) | 2,850 | |

Interest Expense

| (7) | 2 | |

Salaries Expense

| (10) | 4,000 | |

Operating Expenses

| (11) | 5,900 | |

Solution 3: Trial Balance at July 31, 2005 (in millions)

ACCOUNTS	Debit	Credit
Cash	$ 6,330	
Accounts Receivable	3,600	
Supplies	300	
Other Current Assets	2,938	
Accounts Payable		$ 300
Long-term Liabilities		750
Common Stock		5,470
Retained Earnings		2,600
Service Revenue		17,000
Cleaning Expense	200	
Research and Development Expenses	2,850	
Interest Expense	2	
Salary Expense	4,000	
Operating Expenses	5,900	
	$26,120	$26,120

Cisco Systems, Inc.
Income Statement
For the year ended July 31, 2005
(in millions)

Service revenue		$17,000
Expenses:		
Cleaning expense	$ 200	
R&D expenses	2,850	
Interest expense	2	
Salary expense	4,000	
Operating expenses	5,900	
Total expenses		12,952
Net income		$ 4,048

Cisco Systems, Inc.
Balance Sheet
At July 31, 2005
(in millions)

Assets	
Cash	$6,330
Accounts receivable	3,600
Supplies	300
Other current assets	2,938
Total assets	$13,168
Liabilities and Shareholders' Equity	
Accounts payable	300
Long-term liabilities	750
Common stock	5,470
Retained earnings**	6,648
Total liabilities and shareholders' equity	$13,168

**Beginning RE $2,600 + Net income $4,048, which would be shown on the statement of Retained Earnings.

Rapid Review

1. **Explain the general ledger system and use debits and credits to record balance sheet transactions.** The *general ledger* system is based on the accounting equation and is called *double-entry accounting or bookkeeping system*. This is a clever system, with checks and balances that help an accountant minimize errors and analyze the effects of transactions on the financial statements. Information is stored and organized in a way that provides the information for the four basic financial statements. Journal entries record *debits* and *credits* to the accounts affected by a business transaction chronologically. Debits and credits work with the accounting equation to record transactions in such a way that asset accounts increase with debits (left) and liability and equity accounts increase with

credits (right). The entries are then posted to the general ledger, which reorganizes them into the affected accounts.

2. **Use debits and credits to record income statement transactions.** Revenue accounts are increased with credits and expense accounts and the dividend account are increased with debits.

3. **Explain the first three steps in the accounting cycle and the purpose of each step.**

Steps	Purpose
Step 1: Analyze and record transactions in the journal.	Ensure that information is recorded accurately on a timely basis.
Step 2: Post the journal entries to thegeneral ledger.	Reorganize the data by accounts
Step 3: Prepare a trial balance, a list of all the accounts with their debit or credit balances.	Confirm that debits equal credits in the accounting records.

We'll review accounting cycle steps 4–8 in the next chapter.

4. **Post journal entries to the general ledger and prepare a trial balance.** To see if you've mastered this learning objective, you should try some of the problems at the end of the chapter that are labeled with LO 4. In accounting, practice is mandatory!

5. **Compute and explain working capital and the quick ratio.** Working capital and the quick ratio measure a company's ability to meet its short-term obligations. *Working capital* is current assets minus current liabilities.

> Current assets – current liabilities = working capital

Quick ratio is the following sum: Cash + Accounts Receivable + Short-term Investments, divided by current liabilities.

6. **Recognize the risks associated with using a traditional accounting system.** The three primary risks associated with any accounting information system, including the general ledger system, are: (1) errors in recording and updating the information, (2) unauthorized access, and (3) loss or destruction of data.

Key Terms

Accounting cycle, p. 108
Chart of accounts, p. 104
Credit (CR), p. 102
Debit (DR), p. 102

General ledger, p. 104
Journal, p. 103
Journal entry, p. 103
Posting, p. 104

Quick ratio, p. 119
T-account, p. 101
Trial balance, p. 109
Working capital, p. 117

Have You Increased Your Business IQ?

Answer these questions to find out.

1. The general ledger (system) is
   a. An accounting system no longer in use
   b. A system for keeping track of accounting information that is widely used
   c. Often called the "book of original entry" where transactions are first recorded
   d. An information system for all business data—accounting, marketing, production, and so on
2. What does ERP stand for?
   a. Enterprise resource planning
   b. Enterprise research project
   c. Excess resources planning
   d. Everyone required to plan
3. Debits and credits are
   a. Terms adopted from bankers to describe cash deposits and withdrawals
   b. Used to increase and decrease account balances
   c. Terms used by credit card companies to describe overdue accounts
   d. No longer used in accounting systems

4. Which of the following is *not* a risk faced by firms in relation to their accounting records?
   a. Errors in updating the information
   b. Too many accountants may be included
   c. Unauthorized access to the company's books
   d. Loss of financial data due to some sort of disaster or crisis
5. What type of information does the current ratio and the amount of working capital provide?
   a. Information about a firm's operating efficiency
   b. Information about the portion of debt in the firm's capital structure
   c. Information about a firm's liquidity
   d. Information about the firm's performance

Now, check your answers.

1. b   2. a   3. b   4. b   5. c

- If you answered all five questions correctly, you've increased your business IQ by studying this chapter. It doesn't mean you've mastered all of the accounting concepts in the chapter. It simply means that you understand some of the general business concepts presented in this chapter.
- If you answered 2 to 4 questions correctly, you've made some progress, but your business IQ has plenty of room to grow. You might want to skim over the chapter again.
- If you answered 0 or 1 question correctly, you can do more to improve your business IQ. Better study the chapter again.

Questions

1. What is the difference between the journal and the general ledger?
2. Why would a company use a journal rather than recording transactions directly into the general ledger?
3. What is posting and why is it a necessary procedure in accounting?
4. What is an account?
5. What is a T-account and how is it used in accounting?
6. What do the terms debit and credit mean?
7. How are the rules of debit and credit applied to the different accounts?
8. What is a trial balance and what is its purpose?
9. Explain on which side of an account (debit or credit) the normal balance will appear. Give examples to support your explanation.
10. What is working capital and what does it measure?
11. What is the quick ratio and what does it measure?
12. Explain the impact of revenues and expenses on retained earnings.
13. Explain the first three steps in the accounting cycle.
14. What are the most common risks associated with the general ledger accounting system?

Multiple Choice

1. Which of the following accounts has a normal debit balance?
   a. Rent Expense
   b. Accounts Payable
   c. Sales Revenue
   d. Retained Earnings
2. Which of the following journal entries records a cash sale?
   a. Debit Revenue, credit Sales
   b. Debit Sales, credit Cash
   c. Debit Cash, credit Sales
   d. Credit Cash, credit Sales
3. Which of the following journal entries records the payment of operating expenses?
   a. Debit Operating Expenses, credit Sales
   b. Debit Operating Expenses, credit Cash
   c. Debit Cash, credit Operating Expenses
   d. Credit Operating Expenses, credit Sales
4. Posting is the process of
   a. Recording journal entries
   b. Recording amounts from journal entries in the general ledger
   c. Making sure debits equal credits
   d. Correcting any errors made in the recording process
5. A T-account is
   a. A page from the journal
   b. A list of all the firm's accounts, each with its debit or credit balance

c. A summary of the financial statements
d. A representation of an account from the general ledger

6. A list of all of a company's accounts is called
   a. A chart of accounts
   b. An ERP system
   c. A general journal
   d. An accounting information system

7. The normal balance in an asset account is
   a. Credit
   b. Debit
   c. The same as the normal balance in a revenue account
   d. Depends on the type of asset.

8. When a firm's accounting clerk recorded the purchase of an asset—such as a building or piece of equipment—that cost $1,000, she recorded a debit to an expense account rather than a debit to an asset account. The purchase occurred on the last day of the accounting period. What effect did this error have on the firm's net income for the period?
   a. Net income was overstated by $1,000
   b. Net income was understated by $1,000
   c. The error had no effect on income
   d. The effect cannot be determined

9. Journal entries are recorded
   a. At the end of the accounting period
   b. At the end of every week
   c. As the transactions occur
   d. Whenever the accountant has the spare time to do it

10. When a firm wants to correct an error in a journal entry, the accountant will
    a. Erase the mistake and re-record the entry
    b. Record a new journal entry to correct the error
    c. Call the Securities and Exchange Commission for permission
    d. Make sure another employee witnesses the change

Short Exercises

SE3-1. Identify normal balances.
LO 1, 2

For each of the following accounts, indicate whether it has a normal debit balance or a normal credit balance and indicate what type of account it is.

a. Sales Revenue
b. Service Revenue
c. Accounts Receivable
d. Utilities Expense
e. Salaries Expense
f. Accounts Payable
g. Interest Expense

SE3-2. Record journal entries.
LO 1, 2

Redco Company pays cash expenses of $5,000. Record the journal entry. Where and when would this transaction be recorded?

SE3-3. Analyze business transactions.
LO 1, 2

The following transactions occurred during a recent accounting period. For each transaction, name the account that would be credited in the journal entry.

a. Issued stock for cash.
b. Borrowed money from bank.
c. Provided services to customers for cash.
d. Provided services to customers on account.

SE3-4. Record journal entries.
LO 2

Capboy Company earned $5,000 of cash revenues and incurred $2,950 worth of expenses on account during the period. Capboy also paid dividends of $500 to its shareholders. Give the journal entry for each transaction.

SE3-5. Record journal entries.
LO 2

UMC Company recorded the following transaction:

Accounts Receivable	500	
Sales		500

Give the transaction that resulted in this journal entry.

LO 2

SE3-6. Record journal entries.

Dante Company paid employees $1,000 for the week's work. Give the journal entry.

LO 3, 4

SE3-7. Post to T-accounts.

The balance in Cash was $5,000 at the beginning of the month. Cash sales for the month were $2,500 and sales on account were $3,000. Cash expenses totaled $1,950. Use a T-account for Cash. Post the beginning balance and the transactions to the Cash account. What is the ending Cash balance?

LO 1, 2

SE3-8. Analyze business transactions.

Give three examples of transactions that result in a debit to Cash. Give three examples of transactions that result in a credit to Cash.

LO 1, 2

SE3-9. Record journal entries.

Bovina Company was started on January 1, 2005. During its first week of business, the company paid $3,600 for insurance to be used in the future. None will be used until next year. Give the journal entry to record the purchase.

LO 1, 2

SE3-10. Identify accounts.

For each of the following accounts, indicate whether the account has a normal debit balance or a normal credit balance and indicate what type of account it is.

a. Cash	f. Salaries Payable	k. Insurance Expense
b. Accounts Receivable	g. Common Stock	l. Supplies Expense
c. Building	h. Retained Earnings	m. Utilities Expense
d. Accounts Payable	i. Sales Revenue	n. Rent Expense
e. Notes Payable	j. Interest Revenue	

LO 2

SE3-11. Record journal entries.

During February 2006, ARRP Company provided $18,000 worth of services on account. The accounting system recorded the appropriate journal entry to recognize the revenue. Give the journal entry to record ARRP's receipt of the cash in March.

LO 3, 4

SE3-12. Prepare a trial balance.

Using the accounts given, prepare a trial balance. What does this tell you?

Cash	$5,000	Accounts Payable	$3,500
Short-term Investments	7,500	Salaries Payable	2,400
Accounts Receivable	3,500	Long-term Debt	5,600
Inventory	2,460	Common Stock	12,340
Equipment	20,000	Retained Earnings	14,620

LO 5

SE3-13. Calculate working capital and the quick ratio.

Pickup Company had the following accounts and balances at year-end. Calculate the amount of working capital and the quick ratio for the year.

Cash	$5,000	Accounts Payable	$3,500
Short-term Investments	7,500	Salaries Payable	2,400
Accounts Receivable	3,500	Long-term Debt	5,600
Inventory	2,460	Common Stock	12,340
Equipment	20,000	Retained Earnings	14,620

LO 6

SE3-14. Identify risks.

Brown's Brick Company has hired you to assess its internal controls. What are the three major risks you should look for related to the company's general ledger accounting information system?

LO 6

SE3-15. Risks and controls.

What are the risks of having multiple information systems in a single company? How might a company control for or eliminate those risks?

SE3-16. Appendix: Using T-accounts to analyze problems.

Easy Company started the period with a balance of $5,000 in Accounts Receivable. During the period, the company made sales on account of $13,000. At the end of the period, the balance in Accounts Receivable was $3,900. How much cash did the company collect on its Accounts Receivable during the period?

SE3-17. Appendix: Using T-accounts to analyze problems.

CarMax started the month with $150,000 of supplies. During the period, the company used $290,000 worth of supplies. If there was $90,000 worth of supplies at the end of the month, what was the cost of the supplies CarMax must have purchased during the month?

Exercise Set A

E3-1A. Record journal entries.
LO 1, 2

The TJ Company engaged in the following transactions during July. Give the journal entry for each.

1. Paid cash of $3,500 for July rent.
2. Purchased $5,000 of supplies on account, for future use.
3. Collected $10,000 cash from customers for July service revenues earned.
4. Paid for the supplies purchased in transaction 2.
5. Purchased a new delivery van for $25,000. Paid $3,000 cash and signed a note for the remainder.

E3-2A. Record journal entries.
LO 1, 2

For each transaction for Ricco Company during April 2006, prepare the journal entry.

1. Purchased laptop computers for $35,000 from Dell Corporation on account. That means the firm bought the computers on credit rather than paying cash.
2. Paid $2,000 cash for April rent on office space.
3. Received $22,500 cash from customers who received services last month from Ricco on account.
4. Provided services to Jessup Company for $10,000 cash.
5. Paid Office Depot $3,000 cash for office supplies purchased and used in April.
6. Stockholders contributed an additional $30,000 in the business in exchange for common stock.
7. Paid Dell for the computers purchased in transaction 1.
8. Incurred advertising expense for April of $1,200 on account. (Use Accounts Payable to record the obligation.)

E3-3A. Post to T-accounts.
LO 4

Post the journal entries from E3-2A to T-accounts. Assume the company has a beginning balance of $5,000 in Cash, $22,500 in Accounts Receivable, and $27,500 in Retained Earnings. Determine the ending balance in each account.

E3-4A. Record journal entries, post to T-accounts, and prepare a trial balance.
LO 1, 2, 4

Prepare journal entries for the transactions below for Networking Services, Inc., that occurred during the month of August 2010, post them to T-accounts, determine the ending balance in each account, and then prepare a trial balance.

1. Issued stock to new owners for $100,000 in cash.
2. Purchased delivery van for $23,000 cash for use in business.
3. Purchased supplies on account for future use for $2,500.
4. Billed customers $2,600 for services performed.
5. Paid $1,300 cash as partial payment for supplies purchased in transaction 3.
6. Paid $1,200 cash for current operating expenses.
7. Received $700 cash from customers billed in transaction 4.
8. Paid dividends of $1,000 cash to stockholders.

E3-5A. Post journal entries to T-accounts and prepare a trial balance.
LO 3, 4

Below are selected transactions from the journal of Foto88, Inc., during its first month of business. Post these transactions to T-accounts and then prepare a trial balance.

Date	Transactions	Debit	Credit
May 1	Cash	12,600	
	Common Stock		12,600
7	Cash	2,100	
	Service Revenue		2,100
15	Office Equipment	20,000	
	Cash		8,000
	Notes Payable		12,000

26	Accounts Receivable	3,250	
	Service Revenue		3,250
30	Cash	1,925	
	Accounts Receivable		1,925

LO 1, 2   **E3-6A. Analyze business transactions from journal entries.**
Refer to the journal entries in E3-5A. Give the business transaction that resulted in each entry.

LO 3, 4   **E3-7A. Calculate missing amounts; prepare trial balance and financial statements.**
Given the following accounts and balances at June 30, calculate the value for Accounts Payable. Reorganize the trial balance by listing balance sheet accounts first, followed by the income statement accounts. Then, prepare the income statement and the statement of changes in shareholders' equity for the month and the balance sheet at June 30. Note: The balance in Common Stock was from a prior month.

Accounts Payable		?
Accounts Receivable	$20,469	
Cash	15,660	
Common Stock		$40,000
Delivery Equipment	52,000	
Dividends	2,300	
Supplies Expense	758	
Insurance Expense	523	
Notes Payable, Short-term		20,000
Prepaid Insurance	2,600	
Repair Expense	1,200	
Retained Earnings		8,560
Salaries Expense	4,428	
Salaries Payable		1,200
Service Revenue		15,610

LO 1, 2, 3, 4   **E3-8A. Analyze business transactions from T-accounts.**
The following T-accounts show some posted transactions for a brand new company. Explain the transaction that resulted in each entry.

Cash		Accounts Receivable		Inventory	
a. 6,000	b. 980	c. 4,000		d. 5,000	

Accounts Payable		Salaries Payable		Common Stock	
	d. 5,000		e. 2,000		a. 6,000

Sales Revenue		Operating Expenses		Salaries Expense	
	c. 4,000	b. 980		e. 2,000	

LO 1, 2   **E3-9A. Prepare journal entries and analyze timing of revenue recognition.**
For each of the following transactions, give the journal entry. Then, tell whether or not the transaction is one that results in the recognition of revenue or expenses.

1. On January 31, Dell, Inc., paid its computer service technicians $80,000 in salaries for services provided during the month.
2. Shell Oil used $5,000 worth of electricity in its headquarters building during March. Shell received the bill, but will not pay it until sometime in April.
3. Jamie's Inn earned $22,000 in rental revenue. Assume rental revenues were earned on account.
4. The Home Depot collected $59,000 in investment revenue earned during the year.

E3-10A. Prepare journal entries and post to T-accounts.   LO 1, 2, 3, 4

For each of the following transactions, prepare the journal entry and then post the journal entries to T-accounts.

1. Received contributions of $40,000 cash by new shareholders in return for company stock.
2. Borrowed $12,000 from bank.
3. Purchased land for $9,500.
4. Loaned $3,250 to an employee who signed a short-term note.
5. Purchased $3,000 worth of office equipment for cash.

E3-11A. Prepare financial statements.   LO 3, 4

Using the given trial balance, prepare the income statement and the statement of changes in shareholders' equity for June, and the balance sheet at June 30. Note: The balance in Common Stock was from a prior month.

Gardner Plant Corporation
Trial Balance
June 30, 2005

Account	DR	CR
Cash	$ 6,094	
Accounts Receivable	5,800	
Supplies	10,340	
Other Current Assets	3,700	
Accounts Payable		$ 3,000
Income Taxes Payable		875
Salaries Payable		795
Short-term Notes Payable		150
Other Current Liabilities		380
Long-term Notes Payable		600
Common Stock		5,200
Retained Earnings		7,750
Sales Revenue		18,850
Interest Revenue		2,140
Rent Expense	9,280	
Interest Expense	1,030	
Other Operating Expenses	3,496	
Total	$39,740	$39,740

E3-12A. Analyze business transactions from journal entries.   LO 2

Analyze the following journal entries for Seashore Yacht Club and give the general explanation that would be required for each entry.

Description	Debit	Credit
a. Cash	10,000	
Common Stock		10,000
b. Land	7,000	
Cash		7,000
c. Building	55,000	
Cash		55,000
d. Cash	10,000	
Notes Payable		10,000
e. Supplies	400	
Cash		400
f. Prepaid Insurance	1,650	
Cash		1,650

g.	Cash	25,000	
	Service Revenue		25,000
h.	Rent Expense	9,240	
	Cash		9,240

LO 1, 2, 3

E3-13A. Analyze accounting errors.

Premier Company pays its employees every week. The total payroll amounts to $50,000 each week. Suppose the accountant made the journal entry for $60,000 instead of $50,000. How would Premier's accountant correct this error? Why?

LO 5

E3-14A. Calculate working capital and the quick ratio.

DBG Company had the following accounts and balances at year-end. Calculate the amount of working capital and the quick ratio for the year.

Cash	$25,000	Accounts Payable	$12,000
Accounts Receivable	6,750	Salaries Payable	8,550
Short-term Investments	9,825	Interest Payable	1,215
Inventory	6,590	Short-term Notes Payable	11,250
Supplies	3,620	Long-term Notes Payable	9,200
Prepaid Insurance	5,600	Common Stock	13,420
Equipment, net	55,000	Retained Earnings	56,750

E3-15A. Appendix: Using T-accounts to analyze problems.

Jeffery Company started the period with a balance of $15,000 in Accounts Payable. During the period, the company purchased additional inventory on account for $17,000. At the end of the period, the balance in Accounts Payable was $12,500. How much cash did the company pay on Accounts Payable during the period?

E3-16A. Appendix: Using T-accounts to analyze problems.

Cat Woman Enterprises started the period with a balance of $130,000 in the Land account. During the period, the company purchased additional land of $75,000. At the end of the period, the balance in the Land account was $145,000. How much land did the company sell during the period?

Exercise Set B

> Your professor may ask you to complete selected "Group B" exercises and problems using Prentice Hall Grade Assist (**PHGA**). PHGA is an online tool that can help you master the chapter's topics by providing multiple variations of exercises and problems. You can rework these exercises and problems—each time with new data—as many times as you need, with immediate feedback and grading.

LO 1, 2

E3-1B. Record journal entries.

The Mister Hsieh Fencing Company engaged in the following transactions during April. Give the journal entry for each. (Explanations are not necessary.)

1. Paid cash of $2,750 for April insurance.
2. Purchased $2,500 of supplies on account for future use.
3. Earned $8,500 for services performed for customers during April on account.
4. Paid for the supplies purchased in transaction 2.
5. Purchased a new computer for $16,250. Paid $3,250 cash and signed a note for the remainder.

LO 1, 2

E3-2B. Record journal entries.

Prepare the journal entry for each transaction of Mike's Pressure Cleaning Services, Inc., for May 2009.

1. Purchased a pressure-cleaning machine for $18,500 on account, which means purchased the machine on credit rather than with cash.
2. Paid $3,500 cash for other operating expenses.

3. Paid $5,725 cash to the employees for salaries owed from prior month.
4. Provided services to the Glenn Hawk Community for $16,500 on account.
5. Paid travel expenses of $1,630 cash for the month.
6. Stockholders contributed an additional $17,800 in the business in exchange for common stock.
7. Received $7,500 cash from customers who received services last month from Mike's on account.
8. Incurred cash advertising expenses of $1,682 for May.

E3-3B. Post to T-accounts.   LO 4
Post the journal entries from E3-2B to T-accounts. Assume the company has a beginning balance of $9,225 in Cash, $14,050 in Accounts Receivable, $5,725 in Salaries Payable, and $17,550 in Common Stock. Determine the ending balance in each account.

E3-4B. Record journal entries, post to T-accounts, and   LO 2, 4
prepare a trial balance.
Prepare the journal entries for the transactions below for Investing-In-You Consultants, Inc., that occurred during the month of September 2008, post them to T-accounts, determine the ending balance in each account, and then prepare a trial balance.

1. Issued common stock to new owners for contributions of $25,000 in cash.
2. Purchased a computer for $1,850 cash for use in business.
3. Purchased supplies, for future use, on account for $1,875.
4. Billed customers $2,050 for services performed.
5. Made a partial payment of $1,375 cash for supplies purchased in transaction 3.
6. Paid $1,500 cash for September's insurance expense.
7. Received $620 cash from customers billed in transaction 4.
8. Paid operating expenses of $75 to have the computer serviced.

E3-5B. Post journal entries to T-accounts and prepare a   LO 3, 4
trial balance.
Below are selected transactions from the journal of Pictures, Frames and More, Inc., during its first month of business. Post them to T-accounts and then prepare a trial balance.

Date	Account Titles	Debit	Credit
July 1	Cash	18,550	
	Common Stock		18,550
7	Photo Equipment	17,500	
	Cash		4,000
	Notes Payable		13,500
15	Cash	5,250	
	Service Revenue		5,250
26	Accounts Receivable	11,825	
	Service Revenue		11,825
30	Cash	1,650	
	Accounts Receivable		1,650

E3-6B. Analyze business transactions from journal   LO 2
entries.
Refer to the journal entries in E3-5B. Give the business transaction that resulted in each entry.

E3-7B. Calculate missing amounts; prepare trial balance   LO 1, 2, 3, 4
and financial statements.
Given the following accounts and balances at December 31, calculate the value for Accounts Receivable. Reorganize the trial balance by listing balance sheet accounts first, followed by the income statement accounts. Then, prepare the income

statement and the statement of changes in shareholders' equity for December, and the balance sheet at December 31. Note: The balance in Common Stock was from a prior month.

Accounts Payable		$18,325
Accounts Receivable	?	
Cash	$17,295	
Common Stock		25,500
Production Equipment	35,000	
Dividends	2,115	
Rent Expense	674	
Travel Expenses	775	
Notes Payable, Short-term		10,500
Prepaid Rent	2,022	
Other Operating Expenses	1,685	
Retained Earnings		9,750
Salaries Expense	3,750	
Salaries Payable		1,050
Service Revenue		25,320

LO 1, 2, 3, 4   **E3-8B.** **Analyze business transactions from T-accounts.**
The following T-accounts show some transactions that were posted for a brand new company. Explain the transaction that resulted in each entry.

Cash		Interest Receivable		Supplies	
a. 8,450	b. 2,000	c. 1,125		d. 3,125	

Accounts Payable		Notes Payable		Common Stock	
	d. 3,125		e. 1,525		a. 8,450

Interest Income		Computer		Salaries Expense	
	c. 1,125	e. 1,525		b. 2,000	

LO 1, 2   **E3-9B.** **Prepare journal entries and analyze timing of revenue recognition.**
Give the journal entry for each of the following transactions. Then, tell whether or not the transaction is one that results in the recognition of revenues or expenses.

   a. On April 15, Mike's Pressure Cleaning Services, Inc., paid employees $3,000 in salaries for services provided during the first two weeks of April.
   b. Mister Hsieh Fencing Company used $1,000 worth of radio advertising during April. Mister received the bill, but will not pay it until sometime in May.
   c. During 2006, Tootie's Pet Training School, Inc., earned $125,000 in service revenues. Assume all services were performed on account.
   d. Susan's Investment Company collected $130,000 cash in investment revenue earned during 2004.

LO 1, 2, 3, 4   **E3-10B.** **Prepare journal entries and post to T-accounts.**
For each of the following transactions, prepare the journal entry and then post the journal entries to T-accounts.

   1. Received contributions of $15,500 cash from new owners in exchange for company stock.
   2. Purchased laptop computers for the staff for $22,500 by signing a note at First Bank.
   3. Paid $1,500 for the current months' rent.
   4. Earned service revenue and received cash payment from the customer in the amount of $17,825.
   5. Distributed cash dividends of $750 to owners.

LO 3, 4   **E3-11B.** **Prepare financial statements.**
Using the given trial balance, prepare the income statement and the statement of changes in shareholders' equity for December, and the balance sheet at December 31, 2006. Note: The balance in Common Stock was from a prior month.

Green Tree Flower Corporation
Trial Balance
December 31, 2006

Account	DR	CR
Cash	$ 7,150	
Accounts Receivable	6,750	
Gardening Supplies	15,850	
Other Current Assets	4,250	
Accounts Payable		$ 2,500
Interest Payable		85
Salaries Payable		650
Short-term Notes Payable		375
Other Current Liabilities		280
Long-term Notes Payable		695
Common Stock		8,500
Retained Earnings		6,000
Service Revenue		23,386
Interest Revenue		2,500
Insurance Expense	8,621	
Utilities Expense	500	
Other Operating Expenses	1,850	
Totals	$44,971	$44,971

E3-12B. Analyze business transactions from journal entries.   LO 1, 2

Analyze the following journal entries for Manuel's Gourmet Cooking Classes, Inc., and give the explanation that would be required for each entry.

Description	Debit	Credit
a. Cash	26,250	
Common Stock		26,250
b. Teaching Supplies	1,115	
Cash		1,115
c. Laptop Computer	2,285	
Notes Payable		2,285
d. Cash	15,000	
Service Revenue		15,000
e. Travel Expenses	315	
Cash		315
f. Prepaid Rent	1,725	
Cash		1,725
g. Accounts Receivable	12,500	
Service Revenue		12,500
h. Insurance Expense	8,135	
Cash		8,135
i. Salaries Expense	375	
Cash		375

E3-13B. Analyze accounting errors.   LO 1, 2, 3

Seven Moon Atlas Company pays its rent every month. The rent amounts to $75,000 each month. Suppose the accountant made the journal entry for $90,000 instead of $75,000. How would Seven's accountant correct this error? Why?

LO 5   **E3-14B. Calculate working capital and the quick ratio.**
Winter Equipment Supply Company had the following accounts and balances at year-end. Calculate the amount of working capital and the quick ratio.

Cash	$20,000	Accounts Payable	$10,820
Accounts Receivable	6,125	Salaries Payable	7,555
Short-term Investments	8,671	Interest Payable	725
Inventory	8,295	Short-term Note Payable	1,005
Supplies	15,325	Long-term Notes Payable	4,710
Prepaid Rent	2,750	Common Stock	24,415
Machine, net	32,850	Retained Earnings	44,786

E3-15B. Appendix: Using T-accounts to analyze problems.
Nicole's Crystal Corporation started the period with a balance of $20,000 in Accounts Payable. During the period, the company purchased additional supplies on account of $22,000. At the end of the period, the balance in Accounts Payable was $12,500. How much cash did the company pay on Accounts Payable during the period?

E3-16B. Appendix: Using T-accounts to analyze problems.
Steven Dachshund Breeders, Inc., started the period with a balance of $135,000 in the Land account. During the period, the company purchased additional land for $80,000. At the end of the period, the balance in the Land account was $125,000. How much land did the company sell during the period?

Problem Set A

LO 1, 2, 3, 4   **P3-1A. Record journal entries; post to T-accounts; and prepare a trial balance.**
Sharp Electronics Repair Service, Inc., was started on July 1. The following selected events and transactions took place during July.

1. Stockholders contributed $125,000 cash to the business in exchange for common stock.
2. Purchased equipment costing $70,000 by signing a long-term note.
3. Purchased advertising in local newspaper for $3,000 cash.
4. Purchased supplies for $42,000 on account.
5. Paid salaries of $2,500 to employees.
6. Paid $1,000 for a one-year insurance policy.
7. Paid $600 cash dividends.
8. Earned service revenues of $38,500 on account.
9. Paid $25,000 on accounts payable.

Required

a. Prepare journal entries for the given transactions.
b. Set up T-accounts and post the journal entries to the accounts.
c. Prepare Sharp's trial balance at July 31.

LO 1, 2, 3, 4   **P3-2A. Record journal entries; post to T-accounts; and prepare a trial balance and financial statements.**
The following transactions occurred during the fiscal year ended December 31, 2006, for Shelby Dog Grooming Corporation, a specialty pet groomer. This was the firm's first year of business.

1. Formed the business as a corporation, issuing $60,000 in common stock to local investors in exchange for cash.
2. Purchased grooming supplies for $20,000 on account.
3. Paid operating expense in the amount of $12,000.
4. Earned service revenues of $60,000, all on account.
5. Paid utilities expense for the year of $15,000.
6. Paid employees $17,500 for work done.
7. Paid vendors $17,000 on purchases made in transaction 2.
8. Collected $25,000 cash on sales made in transaction 4.
9. The Shelby Dog Grooming Corporation celebrated a successful first year by paying a dividend to shareholders of $5,000.

Required

a. Record the journal entry for each transaction, including explanations.
b. Set up T-accounts and post the journal entries to the accounts.
c. Prepare a trial balance.
d. Prepare the four basic financial statements. [Note to instructor: These will be unadjusted financial statements.]

P3-3A. Analyze business transactions from T-accounts; prepare a trial balance and the financial statements; and calculate the working capital and quick ratio.

LO 3, 4, 5

The following T-accounts show beginning balances (labeled **BB**) and posted journal entries for Aerobics for Life, Inc., during the fiscal year ended June 30, 2008.

Cash					Supplies			Accounts Payable		
BB	25,000	14,400	(5)	**BB**	3,200				3,500	**BB**
(1)	4,000	1,945	(7)	(2)	16,200				16,200	(2)
(4)	8,250	20,000	(8)							

Accounts Receivable					Office Equipment			Long-term Notes Payable		
BB	5,675	4,000	(1)	(6)	5,095				2,000	**BB**
(3)	19,000								5,095	(6)

Land					Rent Expense			Common Stock		
BB	46,700			(5)	14,400				32,500	**BB**
(8)	20,000									

Service Revenue					Operating Expenses			Retained Earnings		
		19,000	(3)	(7)	1,945				42,575	**BB**
		8,250	(4)							

Required

a. For each posted journal entry, describe the transaction that resulted in the entry.
b. Compute the balances in the accounts and prepare a trial balance.
c. Prepare the four financial statements. [Note to instructor: These will be unadjusted financial statements.]
d. Calculate the working capital and quick ratio and explain what each measures.

P3-4A. Post to T-accounts and prepare a trial balance.

LO 1, 2, 3, 4

CNN started its fiscal year with the accounts and balances shown. Then, the company engaged in the following transactions.

Retained Earnings	$ 9,000
Prepaid Insurance	2,000
Equipment	3,000
Common Stock	5,000
Accounts Receivable	5,000
Accounts Payable	2,000
Cash	1,000
Supplies	5,000

Transactions during CNN's fiscal year were:

1. Issued additional stock for $45,500.
2. Collected $10,000 cash from customers for service revenues earned during the year.
3. Paid cash for $3,500 of operating expenses incurred.
4. Purchased supplies for $23,900 on account.
5. Purchased equipment for $12,340 by signing a short-term note payable.
6. Paid $20,000 on accounts payable.
7. Earned service revenue of $7,000 on account.
8. Paid cash for $2,100 of operating expenses incurred.

Required

a. Prepare a beginning trial balance from the accounts and balances listed above.
b. Set up T-accounts and insert the beginning balances and label them **BB**. Then, post the transactions to the T-accounts.
c. Prepare an ending trial balance.

LO 1, 2, 3, 4, 5 **P3-5A. Record journal entries; post to T-accounts; prepare a trial balance and financial statements; and calculate working capital and quick ratio.**

The balance sheet for Senior Services at June 30 is shown below, followed by the transactions for July.

Senior Services
Balance Sheet
At June 30

Assets

Cash	$15,940
Accounts receivable	13,350
Supplies	2,000
Equipment	40,600
	$71,890

Liabilities and Shareholders' Equity

Accounts payable	$20,675
Short-term notes payable	10,935
Common stock	20,000
Retained earnings	20,280
	$71,890

These transactions took place during July:

July	5	Received $5,430 in cash on June 30 for accounts receivable.
	10	Paid employee salaries of $6,240.
	15	Received $5,850 cash for services provided.
	18	Paid $10,250 on accounts payable.
	21	Paid rent for July, $2,000.
	25	Provided services to customers on account, $12,900.
	29	Paid $4,200 for employee salaries, $1,100 for utilities, and $675 in other expenses.
	31	Paid $2,205 cash dividends.

Required

a. Set up T-accounts with beginning balances taken from the June 30 balance sheet. Use **BB** to indicate the beginning balances.
b. Journalize and post the July transactions to the T-accounts.
c. Prepare a trial balance.
d. Prepare the four basic financial statements. [Note to instructor: These will be unadjusted financial statements.]
e. Calculate the working capital and quick ratio and explain what each measures.

LO 2, 3, 4 **P3-6A. Record journal entries; post to T-accounts; and prepare a trial balance and financial statements.**

Given the following transactions for Chancellor Repair Industries, Inc., for 2007:

1. The owners started the business by contributing $50,000 cash in exchange for common stock.
2. The company purchased office equipment for $9,000 cash.
3. The company purchased land for $35,000 by signing a long-term note payable.
4. The company earned $52,000 of service revenue of which $36,000 was collected in cash.
5. The company purchased $1,550 worth of parts and supplies on account (Other Payables).
6. The company paid $6,000 in cash for operating expenses.
7. The company paid $3,000 on the long-term note (principal) and paid $350 interest expense.
8. The company collected $10,000 on Accounts Receivable (from transaction 4).
9. The company paid $1,000 of Other Payables (from transaction 5).

Required

a. Prepare journal entries for the transactions.
b. Set up T-accounts and post the journal entries.

c. Prepare a trial balance at December 31, 2007.
d. Prepare the four financial statements. [Note to instructor: These will be unadjusted financial statements.]

P3-7A. Analyze business transactions from journal entries; post to T-accounts; and analyze cash flows.   LO 2, 3, 4

Bartlett's Auto Service Center recorded the following journal entries during the first week in July. Assume Bartlett's ended June with a balance of $75,000 in Cash and Retained Earnings.

1	Supplies	14,000	
	Accounts Payable		14,000
2	Cash	70,000	
	Common Stock		70,000
3	Equipment	124,000	
	Cash		124,000
4	Operating Expenses	15,000	
	Cash		15,000
5	Cash	23,000	
	Equipment		23,000
6	Dividends	2,400	
	Cash		2,400

Required

a. For each journal entry, describe the transaction.
b. Post the journal entries to T-accounts and prepare a trial balance at July 31.
c. For each cash flow, tell whether it is an operating, investing, or financing cash flow.

P3-8A. Appendix: Using T-accounts to analyze problems.

The balances shown for the accounts below for Universal Parts Corporation are beginning and ending balances for its most recent fiscal year.

	Beginning Balance	Ending Balance
Accounts Receivable	$4,000	$3,200
Accounts Payable	2,200	3,100
Salaries Payable	2,160	3,160
Interest Receivable	475	900

The company has provided the following information:

a. All sales are made on account. During the year, $20,000 of sales were made.
b. All purchases are made on account. Universal paid vendors $5,000 cash during the year.
c. All salaries are recorded with a debit to Salaries Expense and a credit to Salaries Payable on the last day of the month. The cash is actually paid to employees on the fifth of the subsequent month. During the year, $42,000 in salaries expense was incurred, that is, earned by employees.
d. The company has several investments that earn interest. All interest revenue is recorded when the investment company sends the monthly statement to Universal on the last day of the month. The cash is usually received during the first week of the subsequent month. Interest revenue earned and recorded this year totaled $1,200.

Required

Use T-account analysis to find the following amounts for the year.

a. Cash collected from customers (on accounts receivable)
b. Purchases of inventory made (all on account)
c. Cash paid to employees
d. Cash collected for interest

Problem Set B

> Your professor may ask you to complete selected "Group B" exercises and problems using Prentice Hall Grade Assist **(PHGA)**. PHGA is an online tool that can help you master the chapter's topics by providing multiple variations of exercises and problems. You can rework these exercises and problems—each time with new data—as many times as you need, with immediate feedback and grading.

LO 1, 2, 3, 4

P3-1B. Record journal entries, post to T-accounts, and prepare a trial balance.
Flexsteel Cleaning Corporation was started on March 1. The following events and transactions took place during March.

1. Stockholders contributed $345,600 cash to the business in exchange for common stock.
2. Purchased land costing $170,000 with $70,000 cash and a long-term note for $100,000.
3. Paid for advertising for March on Google's web site, $1,500 cash.
4. Purchased supplies for $62,000 on account.
5. Paid salaries of $5,500 to employees for work done.
6. Paid $1,000 for insurance for future use.
7. Paid $2,000 cash dividends.
8. Earned service revenues of $120,350 on account.
9. Paid $60,000 on accounts payable.

Required

a. Prepare journal entries for the given transactions.
b. Set up T-accounts and post the journal entries to the accounts.
c. Prepare Flexsteel Cleaning Corporation's trial balance at March 31.

LO 1, 2, 3, 4

P3-2B. Record journal entries, post to T-accounts, and prepare a trial balance and financial statements.
The following transactions occurred during the fiscal year ended September 30, 2005, for Toy Box Learning Center, a children's tutoring service. This was the firm's first year of business.

1. Formed the business as a corporation, issuing $100,000 in common stock to local investors.
2. Purchased supplies for $35,000 on account.
3. Paid rent expense for the year in the amount of $6,000.
4. Paid insurance expense for the year in the amount of $750.
5. Earned service revenue of $52,000. Half was collected in cash, the remainder was on account.
6. Paid other operating expenses of $31,500.
7. Paid employees $11,200 for work done.
8. Paid vendors $30,000 on purchases made in transaction 2.
9. Collected $18,000 cash on sales made in transaction 5.
10. Purchased a small building for $250,000 to move the store from the rental space starting January 2006. Paid cash of $30,000 and signed a long-term note for the remainder.

Required

a. Record the journal entry for each transaction, including explanations.
b. Set up T-accounts and post the journal entries to them.
c. Prepare a trial balance.
d. Prepare the four basic financial statements. [Note to instructor: These will be unadjusted financial statements.]

LO 1, 2, 3, 4

P3-3B. Analyze business transactions from T-accounts, prepare a trial balance and financial statements, and calculate the working capital and quick ratio.
The following T-accounts show beginning balances (labeled **BB**) and posted journal entries for Student Credit Consultation Company during the fiscal year ended June 30, 2011.

Cash				Supplies			Accounts Payable		
BB	20,573	500	(4)	**BB**	4,600		(8)	2,500	3,596	**BB**
(1)	10,000	4,000	(7)	(4)	500				350	(5)
(3)	30,000	2,500	(8)							
		7,320	(9)							

Accounts Receivable				Office Equipment			Notes Payable		
BB	20,598			(7)	4,000			22,500	**BB**
(2)	12,340	30,000	(3)					3,000	(6)

Land			Rent Expense			Common Stock		
BB	36,900		(5)	350			21,000	**BB**
(6)	3,000						10,000	(1)

Service Revenue			Operating Expenses			Retained Earnings		
	12,340	(2)	(9)	7,320			35,575	**BB**

Required

a. For each posted journal entry, describe the transaction that resulted in the entry.

b. Compute the balances in the accounts and prepare a trial balance.

c. Prepare the four financial statements. [Note to instructor: These will be unadjusted financial statements.]

d. Calculate the working capital and quick ratio and explain what each measures.

P3-4B. Post to T-accounts and prepare a trial balance.   LO 1, 2, 3, 4

Meyer Service Corporation started its fiscal year with the accounts and balances shown. Then, the company engaged in the following transactions.

Retained Earnings	$ 11,000
Prepaid Rent	3,000
Land	3,000
Common Stock	7,000
Accounts Receivable	6,000
Accounts Payable	3,500
Cash	5,000
Supplies	4,500

Transactions during Meyer Service Corporation's fiscal year were:

1. Issued additional stock for $20,000.
2. Purchased supplies for $15,000 on account.
3. Earned service revenues of $14,500 on account.
4. Paid cash for $8,650 of operating expenses incurred.
5. Borrowed $5,600 from a local bank to be repaid next year.
6. Collected $15,500 on accounts receivable.
7. Paid $10,000 on accounts payable.

Required

a. Prepare a beginning trial balance from the accounts and balances listed previously.

b. Set up T-accounts and insert the beginning balances. (Use BB to indicate beginning balances.) Then, post the transactions to the T-accounts.

c. Prepare an ending trial balance.

P3-5B. Record journal entries, post to T-accounts, prepare a trial balance and financial statements, and calculate working capital and quick ratio.   LO 1, 2, 3, 4, 5

The balance sheet for Prison Services at May 31 is shown below, followed by the transactions for June.

Prison Services
Balance Sheet
At May 31, 2007

Assets

Cash	$ 75,870
Accounts receivable	46,760
Short-term notes receivable	50,000
Equipment	120,000
	$292,630

Liabilities and Equity

Accounts payable	$52,700
Short-term notes payable	25,780
Common stock	73,560
Retained earnings	140,590
	$292,630

These transactions took place during June:

June	1	Collected $40,000 in cash on May 31 accounts receivable.
	6	Paid employee salaries of $24,500.
	10	Received $54,900 in cash for services provided.
	14	Paid $50,000 on accounts payable.
	18	Paid rent for June, $3,200.
	24	Provided services to customers on account, $32,750.
	27	Paid $14,200 for employee salaries, $4,100 for utilities, and $2,675 in other expenses.
	30	Paid $2,000 cash dividends.

Required

a. Set up T-accounts with beginning balances taken from the May 31 balance sheet. (Use **BB** to indicate beginning balances.)
b. Journalize and post the June transactions to the T-accounts.
c. Prepare a trial balance at June 30.
d. Prepare the four basic financial statements. [Note to instructor: These will be unadjusted financial statements.]
e. Calculate the working capital and quick ratio and explain what each measures.

LO 1, 2, 3, 4

P3-6B. Record journal entries, post to T-accounts, and prepare trial balance and financial statements.

Given the following transactions for Jennings Corporation for 2005:

1. The owners started the business as a corporation by contributing $150,000 cash.
2. The company purchased land for $75,000 cash.
3. The company purchased office equipment for $35,000 by signing a long-term note payable.
4. The company earned $150,000 of service revenue of which $100,000 was collected in cash.
5. The company paid $7,000 cash for cleaning services.
6. The company paid $6,000 in cash for utilities.
7. The company paid $500 on the long-term note (principal) and paid $60 interest expense.
8. The company collected $40,000 on Accounts Receivable (from transaction 4).
9. The company paid $1,000 cash dividends to shareholders.

Required

a. Prepare journal entries for the transactions.
b. Set up T-accounts and post the journal entries.
c. Prepare a trial balance at December 31, 2005.
d. Prepare the four financial statements. [Note to instructor: These will be unadjusted financial statements.]

LO 1, 2, 3, 4

P3-7B. Analyze business transactions from journal entries, post to T-accounts, and analyze cash flows.

Bijou's Boutique recorded the following journal entries during the first week in April. Assume Bijou's ended March with a balance of $325,000 in Cash, $25,000 in Common Stock, and $300,000 in Retained Earnings.

1	Prepaid Rent	6,000	
	Cash		6,000
2	Cash	10,000	
	Common Stock		10,000
3	Equipment	22,500	
	Notes Payable		22,500
4	Land	150,000	
	Cash		150,000
5	Building	160,000	
	Cash		160,000
6	Prepaid Insurance	480	
	Cash		480

Required

a. For each journal entry, describe the transaction.
b. Post the journal entries to T-accounts and prepare a trial balance at April 30.
c. For each cash flow, tell whether it is an operating, investing, or financing cash flow.

P3-8B. Appendix: Using T-accounts to analyze problems.

The balances shown for the accounts below for Delphi Desk Company are the beginning and ending balances for its most recent fiscal year.

	Beginning Balance	Ending Balance
Accounts Receivable	$5,000	$6,200
Accounts Payable	4,200	3,000
Salaries Payable	4,168	2,168
Interest Receivable	1,475	500

The company has provided the following information:

a. All sales are made on account. During the year, Delphi made $10,000 of sales.
b. All purchases are made on account. Delphi paid vendors $8,000 cash during the year.
c. All salaries are recorded with a debit to Salaries Expense and a credit to Salaries Payable on the last day of the month. The cash is actually paid to employees on the fifth of the subsequent month. During the year, $30,000 in salaries expense was incurred, that is, earned by employees.
d. The company has several investments that earn interest. All interest revenue is recorded when the investment company sends the monthly statement to Delphi on the last day of the month. The cash is usually received during the first week of the subsequent month. Interest revenue earned and recorded this year totaled $3,000.

Required

Use T-account analysis to find the following amounts for the year:

a. Cash collected from customers (on Accounts Receivable)
b. Purchases of inventory made (all on account)
c. Cash paid to employees
d. Cash collected for interest

Financial Statement Analysis

LO 1, 4, 5

FSA3-1. Use the 10-K from Target Corporation in Appendix B at the back of the book, to answer these questions:
  a. Does Target use a general ledger system? How can you tell?
  b. Look at the notes to the financial statements for any mention of risks related to the accounting information system. Also, can you find any controls for these risks that Target has in place?

c. Calculate the amount of working capital for the two most recent fiscal years. What information does this provide?

d. Calculate the quick ratio for the two most recent fiscal years. What information does this ratio provide?

LO 1.5   **FSA3-2.** Use Bed Bath & Beyond's balance sheet shown below to answer these questions.

> **Bed Bath & Beyond**
> **Balance Sheet**
> **At February 28, 2008**
> (in thousands)

Assets
Current assets:

Cash and cash equivalents	$ 825,015
Short term investment securities	41,580
Merchandise inventory	1,012,334
Other current assets	90,357
Total current assets	1,969,286
Long term investment securities	210,788
Property and equipment, net	516,164
Other assets	168,785
Total assets	$2,865,023

Liabilities and Shareholders' Equity
Current liabilities:

Accounts payable	$ 398,650
Accrued expenses and other current liabilities	337,039
Income taxes payable	33,845
Total current liabilities	769,534
Deferred rent and other liabilities	104,669
Total liabilities	874,203
Shareholders' Equity	
Preferred stock	
Common stock	3,003
Additional paid-in capital	433,404
Retained earnings	1,554,413
Total shareholders' equity	1,990,820
Total liabilities and shareholders' equity	$2,865,023

a. In Bed Bath & Beyond's accounting information system, is Cash and Cash Equivalents one account or the sum of many accounts? Explain.

b. If the company purchased merchandise inventory on account, what journal entry would the company make? Is there any evidence that the company does purchase inventory on account?

c. Does Other Current Assets have a debit or credit balance in the company's records? Why?

d. Calculate Bed Bath & Beyond's working capital at the balance sheet date. What does this mean?

e. Calculate Bed Bath & Beyond's quick ratio at the balance sheet date. What does this mean?

LO 1.5.6   **FSA3-3.** Use Time Warner's balance sheet shown below to answer the following questions.

a. Cash and equivalents increased between December 31, 2002 and December 31, 2003. Suppose the total cash collected during the year was $5,500 million. How much cash was disbursed?

b. The liabilities section shows that Accounts Payable decreased during the year. Suppose total inventory purchases (debit Inventory, credit Accounts Payable) were $3,000 million during 2003. How much cash was paid to vendors during the year?

Time Warner
Consolidated Balance Sheet
(in millions)

| | At December 31 | |
	2003	2002
Assets		
Current assets		
Cash and equivalents	$ 3,040	$ 1,730
Receivables, less allowances of $2.379 and $2.085 billion .	4,908	4,846
Inventories	1,390	1,376
Prepaid expenses and other current assets	2,930	2,883
Total current assets	12,268	10,835
Non-current inventories and film costs	4,465	3,739
Investments	3,657	5,094
Property, plant and equipment	12,559	11,534
Intangible assets	43,885	40,544
Goodwill	39,459	36,986
Other assets	5,490	6,786
Total assets	$121,783	$115,518
Liabilities and Shareholders' Equity		
Current liabilities		
Accounts payable	$ 1,629	$ 2,244
Other payables	2,733	2,289
Deferred revenue	1,175	1,159
Debt due within one year	2,287	155
Other current liabilities	7,694	7,617
Total current liabilities	15,518	13,464
Long-term debt	23,458	27,354
Deferred income taxes	13,291	9,803
Deferred revenue	1,793	1,839
Other liabilities	11,685	10,241
Shareholders' equity		
Series LMCN-V Common Stock	2	2
Time Warner Common Stock	44	43
Paid-in capital	155,578	155,134
Accumulated other comprehensive income (loss), net	(291)	(428)
Retained earnings (deficit)	(99,295)	(101,934)
Total shareholders' equity	56,038	52,817
Total liabilities and shareholders' equity	$121,783	$115,518

c. From the information on the balance sheet, where in the company's accounting system do you believe there is the most risk? Why?

d. Calculate the amount of working capital and the quick ratio at the end of each of the two years shown. What information does this provide?

Critical Thinking Problems

Risk and Control
Use the annual report from Wal-Mart in Appendix A at the back of the book to answer these questions.

1. When you look at the financial statements for Wal-Mart, can you tell if the company uses a general ledger system? Explain.

2. Find at least four pieces of quantitative information included in the annual report (but *not* in the notes to the financial statements) that would not be recorded in a general ledger system.

3. In the notes to the financial statements, find two examples of quantitative information that you believe would not be found in the general ledger.

Ethics

DVD-Online, Inc., is in its second year of business. The company is totally Web-based, offering DVD rentals to online customers for a fixed monthly fee. For $30 per month, a customer receives three DVDs each month, one at a time as the previous one is returned. No matter how many DVDs a customer uses (up to three), the fee is fixed at $30 per month. Customers sign a contract for a year; so DVD-Online recognizes $360 sales revenue each time a customer signs up for the service. The owner of DVD-Online, John Richards, has heard about GAAP, but he doesn't see any reason to follow these accounting principles. Although DVD-Online is not publicly traded, John puts the company's financial statements on the Web page for customers to see.

   a. Explain how DVD-Online would account for its revenue if it followed GAAP.
   b. Explain to John Richards why he should use GAAP, and describe why his financial statements may now be misleading.
   c. Do you see this as an ethical issue? Explain.

Group Assignment

Some of the new accounting information systems do not have a running total for Accounts Receivable. Instead, the system keeps track of all credit sales made and all cash collected from credit sales. Then, if the amount of outstanding Accounts Receivable is needed, it can be computed by finding the difference between credit sales and cash collected from credit sales. In groups, discuss the benefits of this way of keeping data. See if you can think of some other financial statement amounts that could be derived from other amounts rather than being kept in the accounting records directly.

Internet Exercise: Intuit, Inc.

The accounting cycle illustrated in this chapter may be simplified with the aid of a computerized general ledger system. Intuit, Inc., is a leader in e-finance and develops and supports Quicken, the leading personal finance software; TurboTax, the best-selling tax preparation software; and QuickBooks, the most popular small business accounting software. For this exercise, go to http://.finance. yahoo.com.

IE3-1. Enter the symbol INTU in the "Enter Symbol" space. Then, click on GO. Review the information provided and comment on one item of interest.

IE3-2. In the left-hand column, scroll down to Financials. For the most recent year, list the amounts reported for Cash, Common Stock, Total Revenues, and Interest Expense. Note that these amounts are reported in thousands.
   a. Which financial statement reports each of these amounts?
   b. What was the beginning balance for each of these accounts?
   c. Which of these accounts has a normal debit balance?
   d. Which of these accounts has a normal credit balance?

IE3-3. What are the advantages of a computerized general ledger system such as QuickBooks developed by Intuit? Is it important to understand the accounting cycle even though computerized general ledger systems are available? Explain why or why not.

Additional Study Material

Visit www.prenhall.com/reimers for self-study quizzes, spreadsheet templates to use to complete homework assignments, and an accounting cycle tutorial.

CONTINUING CASE STUDY

Building your Excel skills with The MP3 Store

In this exercise the information provided in the MP3 case will be used to create an Excel worksheet and financial statements. During the month of March, The MP3 Store engaged in the following transactions:

March 5   Billed customers $1,500 for MP3 repairs performed on account. The cost of the repairs was $600 which was paid in cash.

March 15   Paid the $200 balance in Accounts Payable.

March 20   Collected $1,000 in cash from customers billed on March 5th.

March 25   Completed an additional $3,200 in repairs. Of the repairs, $600 were paid in cash. The rest were on account.

The cost of the completed repairs was $1,800. Cash of $1,100 was paid. The balance was on account.

March 26   Paid $350 for advertising to promote the opening of the new store. The advertising campaign will run the month of April. (*Hint:* Record as a prepaid asset, since the service won't be provided until next month.)

March 29   Purchased a computer system for $1,500 on account.

March 30   Paid cash for the following office furniture and fixtures in preparation of the April 1st opening

- Display cases—$4,000
- Office furniture (desks & chairs)—$3,000

March 31   Borrowed $5,000 on a one-year note payable. The interest rate is 7%.

Instructions

1. Open a new Excel worksheet.
2. Create T-accounts for the following Accounts:

    - Assets—Cash, Accounts Receivable, Prepaid Rent, Prepaid Insurance, Prepaid Advertising, Supplies, Computer System, Office Furniture & Fixtures
    - Liabilities—Accounts Payable and Notes Payable
    - Shareholder Equity accounts— Contributed Capital, Retained Earnings, Repair Revenue, Repair Expense

    Put all the asset accounts in Columns B and C and the liability and shareholder equity accounts in Columns F and G. Use the **Merge and Center** button for your account titles and **Format, Cells, Border** to create your T's. Click Column Headings A and E then the **Align Right** button to align your references. Repeat the process with Columns D and H, but this time use the **Align Left** button. (*Hint:* Once you have created one or two of the T-accounts, copy and edit them to create the rest.)

3. Input the beginning balances from the end of February in the appropriate T-accounts.
4. Beginning in Cell J1, create the following bold column headings: Ref., Date, Journal Entry, DR and CR. Input your journal entries starting in Cell J2. Remember what you learned in Chapter 2 about formulas and copying text and numbers. The account titles on the T-accounts should be copied to the journal entries and each journal entry amount should be entered once as a debit and copied to the credit column. Use the **Increase Indent** button to indent the credit side of each entry.
5. Using the same copy techniques, post your journal entries to the T-accounts. Include the Ref.
6. Once all entries have been posted, the T-accounts need to be totaled or footed. To enhance the appearance and show the totals, underlines and double underlines are used. Instead of formatting cells, you may use the **Underline U** and **Double Underline D** buttons. The **Underline** should already appear on your toolbar, but the **Double Underline** will

most likely need to be added. To add the button, click the down arrow at the end of the toolbar. Click **Add or Remove Buttons** and **Customize**. When the dialog box appears select **Format** under Categories. Scroll down the Commands until you find the **Double Underline** button. Click and drag it to the toolbar.

7. Total and foot your T-accounts using appropriate formulas and **Auto Sum.** The ending balance for each account should be double underlined. When an account has both debit and credit entries, reduce the font size on the intermediate totals to 8.

8. Prepare a Trial Balance using the account titles and balances from your footed T-Accounts. Place the Trial Balance below your T–Accounts (beginning in Cell A46). Copy the titles from the T-Accounts. If they are not properly aligned highlight them and click the **Align Left** ![align left icon] button.

Copy your debit balances to Column C and your credit balances to Column D. After all balances are copied total your debits and credits. If you are not in balance, go back and check your entries and postings. If you are in balance save your file to disk by clicking the **Save** ![save icon] button. Name your file MP33.

9. It is now time to prepare the financial statements using the techniques you learned in Chapter 2. Because the worksheet is so large, it is best to prepare the statements on Sheet 2. Fortunately within Excel you may copy between sheets just as you copy between cells. Start by renaming Sheets 1 and 2. Point your cursor at Sheet Tab 1 and right click. Select **Rename** and type "Chapter 3 Trial Balance." Repeat with Sheet Tab 2 and rename it "Chapter 3 Statements." Copy the account titles and dollar amounts from the Trial Balance to the Statements by clicking between the two sheets. Fill in additional information and headings as required. Analyze the cash account to prepare the Statement of Cash Flows, using appropriate formulas.

10. Print your worksheets by highlighting selected sections: T-Accounts; Journal Entries; Trial Balance; Financial Statements—print based on how you set up your worksheet—one or two statements per page. Once you have highlighted your choice, choose **File Print** and **Selection** from the menu.

11. Save your file to disk by clicking the **Save** ![save icon] button and exit Excel.

Using T-accounts to Analyze Problems

In Chapter 3, you learned that accountants use T-accounts to represent the general ledger. There's another way you can use T-accounts—one that can be an excellent tool for solving accounting problems. Let's start with an example.

Suppose a company started the year with a balance in Accounts Receivable of $500. That means the year started with last year's customers owing the company $500. During the year, the company made sales on account of $1,250. At the end of the year, the company had an Accounts Receivable balance of $350. That means the year has ended with customers owing the company $350. If all sales are recorded with a debit to Accounts Receivable and a credit to Sales Revenue—that is, sales are made on account, how much cash did the company collect from customers during the year?

You can use a T-account to arrive at the solution.

1. Insert the $500 beginning balance in Accounts Receivable.

2. Insert the sales of $1,250 as a debit to Accounts Receivable. (The credit, not shown, would be to Sales Revenue.)

3. Insert the unknown amount of cash collected as a credit, here denoted with an x. (The debit, not shown here, will be to Cash.) The x is the number we are trying to find.

4. Insert the ending balance of $350 on the debit side of the Accounts Receivable account.

Accounts Receivable

500	
1,250	x
350	

Beginning balance + sales on account – collections on accounts receivable = Ending balance
$500 + 1,250 - x = 350$
Solve for x. You'll find that $x = 1,400$.

How did you find this solution? You started with $500 of Accounts Receivable and added $1,250 more with sales on account. If there is only $350 remaining in Accounts Receivable, you must have collected the other $1,400.

Another way to think about the problem is to take the equation and add **X** to both sides. In Algebra, some people think of this as, "moving **X** to the other side of the equation by changing its sign."

Start with the equation: $500 + 1,250 - x = 350$.
Now add x to both sides and the result is: $500 + 1,250 = x + 350$

Take a good look at this equation and how it corresponds to the T-account. Notice that the beginning balance plus debits must equal the ending balance plus any credits.

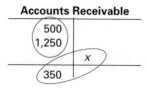

Accounts Receivable

The total circled in red must equal the total circled in blue:

$$500 + 1{,}250 = x + 350$$
$$1{,}750 = x + 350$$
$$1{,}750 - 350 = x$$
$$1{,}400 = x$$

For the Accounts Receivable account, the transactions during the period can be summarized as total credit sales and total cash collected on Accounts Receivable. There may actually be dozens of individual transactions, but they can be summarized with these two amounts: amount of credit sales and amount of cash collected from customers.

As you saw in the example, Accounts Receivable may have a beginning balance and an ending balance. That means that there are four numbers in the T-account: beginning balance, credit sales, cash collections, and ending balance. *If you have any three of these numbers, you can calculate the fourth number.*

Let's try another example, this time with an account that has a normal credit balance. We'll use Accounts Payable. The beginning balance is the amount the company owes its vendors at the beginning of the accounting period. Any credits to the account are increases, indicating additional amounts owed to vendors as a result of purchases made on account. Any debits to the account are decreases, indicating amounts that have been paid to vendors. When we use T-accounts for finding unknown amounts, we assume that there are no unusual debits or credits made to the accounts unless they are specifically mentioned. Our working assumption is that any account has only its normal transactions. For Accounts Payable, those are making purchases from the vendor on account and making payments to the vendor.

Here's a T-account for Accounts Payable. Suppose the beginning balance equals $2,350. During the year, the company purchased $12,600 of inventory on account and paid vendors a total of $14,000. How much does the company owe its vendors at year end? Look at the T-account for Accounts Payable:

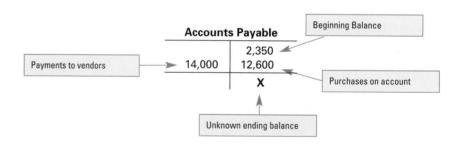

Remember the second approach we took with the Accounts Receivable account? Let's try that with Accounts Payable. Because Accounts Payable has a normal credit balance, the beginning balance plus all credits equals the ending balance plus all debits. In most problems we analyze with T-accounts, there will be only one debit and one credit to summarize the additions to and deductions from the account during the period.

Accounts Payable

	2,350
14,000	12,600
	x

As shown by the circles, 14,000 + **X** = 2,350 + 12,600.
Solving for **X**, you find that **X** = $950.

In the most general terms, you might say this: In any T-account, the beginning balance plus any additions must equal the deductions plus the ending balance. In other words, a number that goes into a T-account has to either go out or be left in the ending balance.

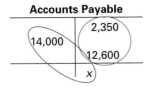

Can YOU do it?

Suppose your company had $10,000 in Accounts Receivable at the beginning of April. During the month, the company had credit sales of $54,690 and ended the month with Accounts Receivable of $8,700. How much cash did the company collect from its credit customers during April?

Answer Set up a T-account for Accounts Receivable. The beginning balance is $10,000 (a debit balance for an asset) and credit sales of $54,690 are added to that as a debit to Accounts Receivable (and a credit to Sales Revenue, not shown here). Either these receivables were collected, meaning customers paid for them, or they were not. So the total credits (cash collected from customers) plus the ending balance must equal $10,000 + $54,690. If the ending balance is $8,700, the cash collected must be $64,690 – $8,700 = $55,990.

Accounts Receivable

10,000	
54,690	*x*
8,700	

Alternatively: 10,000 + 54,690 = 8,700 + *x*.
Solving for *x*: *x* = $55,990

chapter 4

Accrual Accounting Concepts and the Accounting Cycle

Here's where you've been . . .

- You learned about the general ledger accounting system.

- You learned about the steps in the accounting cycle.

- You learned how to analyze transactions and record them using debits and credits.

- You learned how to prepare the financial statements.

Here's where you're going . . .

- You'll learn to record transactions when the exchange of the cash for goods and services and the delivery of the goods and services happen at different times.

- You'll learn to define accruals and deferrals.

- You'll learn to make adjusting entries and prepare the financial statements.

- You'll learn to complete the accounting cycle with closing entries.

YOU make the call:

How should Bed Bath & Beyond account for a customer's payment in advance?

When a new school year starts, you might have a new dorm room or a new apartment to set up. You'll need towels, shower curtains, and kitchen gadgets.

Have you ever been to a store like Bed Bath & Beyond or Linens 'n Things? These specialty home retailers have expanded quickly, especially Bed Bath & Beyond. Between 1992 and 2004, the chain grew from 34 stores to 575 stores.

Suppose Bed Bath & Beyond enters into a contract with Marriott Hotels to decorate the bathrooms in one of its hotels. Marriott Hotels agrees to pay Bed Bath & Beyond $50,000 in advance for merchandise and services to be performed in the next year. Coincidentally, suppose Bed Bath & Beyond needs approximately $50,000 more sales revenue to meet analysts' expectations for current earnings. By recording Marriott's advance payment as revenue upon receipt, Bed Bath & Beyond would be able to meet analysts' expectations for current earnings. However, would this accounting treatment be acceptable? Should Bed Bath & Beyond recognize the $50,000 payment as revenue? *You make the call.*

Learning Objectives

When you are finished studying this chapter, you should be able to:

1. Define accrual accounting and explain how income is measured.
2. Explain accruals and deferrals and how they affect the financial statements.
3. Make adjusting entries and prepare the four financial statements.
4. Explain closing the books, and why it is done.
5. Compute and explain the debt-to-total-assets ratio.
6. Identify controls that help a firm reduce the risk of failing to record a transaction.

LEARNING OBJECTIVE 1

Define accrual accounting and explain how income is measured.

Measuring Income—Recording Revenues and Expenses

Bed Bath & Beyond, like all companies, is concerned about its net income. As you have learned, net income is the difference between all the revenue the company earned during the accounting period and all the costs related to earning that revenue. Accountants use accrual-basis accounting for the financial statements, which means they recognize revenue—record revenue in the general ledger—when it is earned, and they recognize expenses when they are incurred to generate that revenue. Revenues are earned when the company delivers a product or performs a service for customers. Expenses are incurred when the company uses resources or services to help generate the revenue that has been recorded. Cash-basis accounting, in contrast to accrual-basis accounting, involves recording revenues and expenses only when cash is collected and disbursed. Managers, shareholders, creditors, and the government are interested in accrual-basis net income and the resulting earnings per share, which companies report to the public quarterly through the news media and to the SEC. These interested parties use the accrual-basis net income to determine whether or not the company is making a profit.

Accountants evaluate business activities for specific periods of time—months, quarters, or years. This method of using specific time periods is called the *time-period assumption*. The way we divide the revenues and expenses among those time periods is a crucial part of accounting: If revenue is *earned*—but not necessarily *collected*—in a certain time period, accountants must include that revenue on the income statement for that period—not the period before or after. For example, if a company has performed a service for a customer, then the income statement for that period must include the revenue earned, even if it has *not* yet been collected. This method of recording revenue is the foundation of accrual-basis accounting, a fundamental part of GAAP.

The income statement will usually appear as the first of the four required statements in a company's annual report. Exhibit 4.1 shows the income statement for Bed Bath & Beyond for the year ended February 28, 2004. When you see net sales of $4.48 billion for the year, you know that all the sales made in that fiscal year are included in that amount, even if the company hasn't collected some of the cash from its customers by February 28, 2004. Similarly, the operating expenses listed—$3.84 billion—are only the expenses incurred in that fiscal year, whether or not the company paid for those expenses by February 28, 2004.

Exhibit 4.1

Income Statement for Bed Bath & Beyond

Bed Bath & Beyond

From the Consolidated Statement of Earnings
Bed Bath & Beyond Inc. and Subsidiaries
For fiscal year ended Februrary 28, 2004

(in thousands except per share data)

Net sales	$4,477,981
Operating expenses	3,838,638
Operating profit	639,343
Interest income	10,202
Earnings before income taxes	649,545
Provision for income taxes	250,075
Net earnings	$ 399,470
Earnings per share	$ 1.35

Net sales at Bed Bath & Beyond were $4.48 billion for the fiscal year ended February 28, 2004. This amount includes all sales made in that fiscal year, even if the company had not collected some of the cash from its customers by February 28, 2004. Similarly, the operating expenses of $3.84 billion are the expenses incurred in that fiscal year, whether or not the company paid for those expenses by February 28, 2004.

Timing Differences

When a company collects cash for a product or service at the time it provides it to the customer, the transaction is easy to record. Unfortunately, financial transactions are often complex because of *timing differences*. Here are examples of two timing differences:

- A customer uses Bed Bath & Beyond's credit card to pay for candles. The company has provided the customer with a product, but it won't collect cash for several weeks. There's a time difference between when the company earns revenue by providing a product or service to customers and the time it *collects* the cash from the customers.
- Bed Bath & Beyond needs new lighting in one of its stores. An electrician requires payment in advance for installing the lighting. When the company sends the electrician the check in advance, no expense is recorded. The company will recognize the expense after the work is performed. There's a time difference between when the company *pays* for the expense and when it actually *incurs* the expense.

Exhibit 4.2 shows how accountants deal with timing differences. Read the caption under the exhibit carefully to see the full range of possible timing differences.

You can think of the timing problem in accounting in two simple ways:

1. Action before dollars are paid or collected
2. Dollars paid or collected before action

An example of action before dollars is when a sale is made *on account*. A customer buys on credit and agrees to pay later. The act of selling the product or performing the service takes place before dollars are exchanged for payment. This type of transaction is called an **accrual**.

An example of dollars before action is when a firm buys insurance. Insurance must be purchased in advance of the time period to which it applies. The dollars are exchanged first, and the insurance is used later. Buying supplies like paper, folders, and toner cartridges is another example of

LEARNING OBJECTIVE 2

Explain accruals and deferrals and how they affect the financial statements.

Study Tip

Timing differences arise in two situations: (1) when a company earns revenue in one accounting period and collects it in another and (2) when a company incurs expenses in one accounting period and pays for them in another.

Accrual: A transaction in which the revenue has been earned or the expense has been incurred, but no cash has been exchanged.

Exhibit 4.2

Timing Differences in Accounting Transactions

	Accounting period–1	**Accounting period 0**	**Accounting period+1**
	The accounting period *before* the substance of the transaction takes place	The accounting period in which the substance of the transaction takes place	The accounting period *after* the substance of the transaction has taken place
When does the customer pay?	Customer pays in the period *before* the company provides the product or service. PAYS BEFORE THE SERVICE	Customer pays in the same period the company provides the product or service. PAYS AT THE TIME OF SERVICE	Customer pays in the period *after* the company provides the product or service. PAYS AFTER THE SERVICE
Example of the Transaction	Fire insurance policy	$20.50	Credit Card Statement
When is revenue earned or expenses incurred?	Defer—postpone—the recognition of revenue and expense until Period 0.	Recognize the revenue and expenses THIS PERIOD!	Revenue or expense was accrued in Period 0. Now the cash is simply collected.

- If a customer pays for a product or service before the company provides it, cash receipt is recorded in Period –1, but the company must wait until Period 0 to recognize the revenue.

- If a customer pays for a product or service when the company provides it, there is no timing difference. Revenue is recognized at the time payment is received.

- If a customer pays for a product or service after the company provides it, the company records the revenue in Period 0, the previous period, but does not record the payment until Period +1.

Deferral: A transaction in which the cash is exchanged before the revenue is earned or the expense is incurred.

a deferral: Dollars are exchanged first, and the action of using the supplies occurs later. Recognizing the revenue or expense is put off until the action of earning the revenue or using the item occurs. This type of transaction is called a **deferral**.

Study Tip

Here's a good way to help you remember the difference between an accrual and a deferral:

<u>A</u>ccrual = <u>A</u>ction before Dollars
<u>D</u>eferral = <u>D</u>ollars before Action

Back to the accounting cycle

Recall the accounting cycle you learned about in the last chapter. Exhibit 4.3 shows the eight steps of the accounting cycle:

1. Analyze and record transactions in the journal.
2. Post the journal entries to the general ledger.
3. Prepare an unadjusted trial balance at the end of the accounting period.
4. Prepare adjusting journal entries and post them to the general ledger.
5. Prepare an adjusted trial balance.

Exhibit 4.3

The Accounting Cycle

The accounting cycle consists of 8 steps. We covered steps 1, 2, and 3 in Chapter 3. Now we'll cover steps 4–8.

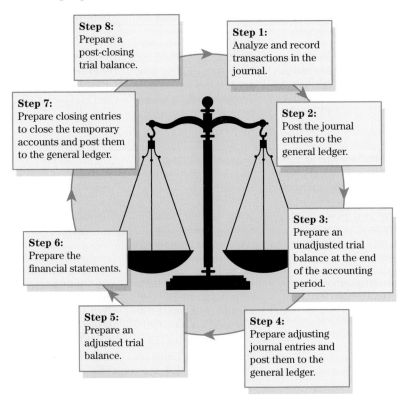

6. Prepare the financial statements.
7. Prepare closing entries and post them to the general ledger.
8. Prepare a post-closing trial balance.

During the day-to-day operations of a firm, routine journal entries are made and regularly posted to the general ledger. Then, just before the firm prepares its financial statements for the period, the firm's accountants identify accounts with balances that are not up-to-date and make adjustments to these accounts. The adjustments are called *adjusting journal entries*. Making the adjustments is step 4 in the accounting cycle. Let's examine the various situations that call for an adjusting entry. Exhibit 4.4 summarizes the types of adjusting entries.

Accrual transactions

If a company has earned revenue, the income statement must include that revenue. If a company incurred an expense to earn that revenue, the income statement must also include that expense. Accruals can pertain to both revenues and expenses. **Accrued revenue** is revenue earned but not yet received in cash or previously recorded. **Accrued expenses** are expenses incurred but not yet paid in cash or previously recorded.

Let's look at three common examples of accruals:

- Interest revenue and interest expense
- Receivables with interest
- Other revenue and expense

Accrued revenue: Revenue earned but not yet received in cash or previously recorded.

Accrued expenses: Expenses incurred but not yet paid in cash or previously recorded.

Exhibit 4.4

Adjusting Entries and Accruals and Deferrals

	Accrued Revenues	Accrued Expenses	Deferred Revenues	Deferred Expenses
Action or Dollars first?	ACTION first, DOLLARS will follow.	ACTION first, DOLLARS will follow.	DOLLARS first, ACTION will follow.	DOLLARS first, ACTION will follow.
Description	The company earned some revenue, but the company has not received the cash.	The company has incurred an expense by using up resources to earn revenue, but the resources have not been paid for by the end of the period.	The company has received payment for a service to be performed in the future or for goods to be delivered in the future.	The company has paid in advance for goods or services that have not yet been used to earn revenue. The company has incurred the cost, but it is not yet an expense.
Examples	Interest revenue earned from bank accounts. Goods delivered, but customer has not been billed yet.	Employees have worked, but the company will not pay them until the first of the next month. The company owes interest for the previous month on a loan, but it has not paid the interest yet.	Customer has paid in advance for next month's services. Customers have paid in advance for magazine subscriptions to be delivered next year.	The company has purchased supplies to be used next year. The company has paid rent in advance.
The Adjusting Entry	An adjusting entry will record: Accrued Revenue.	An adjusting entry will record: Accrued Expense.	The original entry recorded the receipt of the cash and a liability representing the customers' claims to the cash until it is earned by the company. The adjusting entry will record any revenue that has been earned by the date of the financial statements and is no longer considered Deferred Revenue.	The original entry recorded the expenditure as an asset. The adjusting entry will record any portion of that amount that has been used at the date of the financial statements. The entry will make sure the remaining amount is the correct amount of Deferred Expense.

Adjusting entries are needed for four types of transactions: (1) accrued revenues, (2) accrued expenses, (3) deferred revenues, and (4) deferred expenses. Accrued revenues and expenses are amounts that have not been recorded in the normal course of business. Deferred revenues and expenses were recorded when the cash was exchanged. Although the transactions were recorded correctly at the time, the amounts of revenues earned or expenses actually used may have changed by the time the financial statements are prepared. For deferrals, the entries are made to "adjust" the numbers in the accounting records so that they will be correct for the financial statements.

Accruals for Interest Expense and Interest Revenue A common timing difference that you're probably familiar with relates to borrowing or lending money. When you borrow money, you pay interest for the use of that money. If you're a small business owner and you borrow $5,000 from a bank on January 1, 2006, and agree to repay it with 4% interest on January 1, 2007, you will have to pay back a total of $5,200. You'll see how to calculate that soon. On January 1, 2006, when you borrow the money, you get the $5,000 cash, an asset, and you increase your liabilities.

On the pages that follow, we'll concentrate on the journal entry for each transaction and adjustment for the $5,000 bank loan. You'll see the journal entry and the transaction's effect on the accounting equation so that you can see the relationship between the two.

The journal entry is:

Date	Transaction	Debit	Credit
1/1/06	Cash	5,000	
	Notes Payable		5,000
	To record the loan from the bank		

The accounting equation is:

Assets	=	Liabilities	+	Shareholders' Equity	
				Contributed Capital +	**Retained Earnings**
Cash		Notes Payable			
5,000		5,000			

When you get ready to prepare the financial statements for the year ending December 31, 2006, Notes Payable will be shown as a liability on the balance sheet. That's because on December 31, 2006, you still owe the bank the full amount of the loan. What about the $5,000 cash you received? You may still have it, but it is more likely you spent it during the year to keep your business running.

What about the cost of borrowing the money? On December 31, 2006, one full year has passed since you borrowed the money. The passing of time means that you have incurred interest expense.

- Interest expense is the cost of using someone else's money.
- Time passing is the action related to interest expense.

Although the action of using someone else's money during the year has taken place, the dollars for interest have not been exchanged because you have not made the interest payment for using that money. To make the December 31, 2006, financial statements correct, you must show the interest expense of $200. Here is the formula for calculating interest:

$$\text{Interest} = \text{Principal} \times \text{Rate} \times \text{Time}$$
$$I = P \times R \times T$$

Interest rates, like the 4% annual interest, always pertain to a year. As of December 31, 2006, the interest payable on the note would be $5,000 \times 0.04 \times 12/12$ or $200.

Principal	x	Annual Interest Rate	x	Time (fraction of a year)	=	Interest
$5,000	x	4%	x	12/12	=	$200

The last part of the formula gives the time as a portion of a year, or the number of months out of 12. Whenever you have to accrue interest, you must be careful to count the months that apply. That will help you make sure you put the right amount of interest expense on the income statement for exactly the period of time you had use of the borrowed money. Also, you must show the obligation called *Interest Payable* on the balance sheet. Interest Payable is a liability, indicating the bank's claim to the $200 as of December 31, 2006. The liability section of the balance sheet will show both the $5,000 loan and the $200 interest.

To record interest expense, the following adjusting entry is used:

Date	Transaction	Debit	Credit
12/31/06	Interest Expense	200	
	Interest Payable		200
	To accrue interest expense for 2006 on bank loan		

Study Tip

Suppose you borrow $1,000 for two years at 8%. The interest expense for one year is $80. That's $1,000 \times 0.08 \times 12/12$. Now suppose you borrow $1,000 for 10 years at 8%. The interest expense for one year is $80. That's $1,000 \times 0.08 \times 12/12$. Notice that the life of the loan does not affect the year's interest expense.

The accounting equation is:

Assets	=	Liabilities	+	Shareholders' Equity		
					Contributed Capital	+	Retained Earnings
		Interest Payable				Interest Expense
		200				−200

The adjusting journal entry increases Interest Payable, a liability, and increases the balance in Interest Expense. Making this adjustment is called accruing interest expense, and the expense itself is called an accrual or an accrued expense. Interest Expense will be on the income statement for the period even though it has not been paid by the end of the period. The liability for an expense incurred but not yet paid is often called an **accrued liability**.

> **Accrued liability:** The liability for an expense incurred but not yet paid.

Study Tip

A company often puts many liabilities like interest payable and salaries payable into a single amount on the balance sheet. These accrued liabilities are also called accrued expenses. It may seem odd to have a balance sheet item that contains the word "expense," but it's the word "accrued" that makes "accrued expenses" a liability.

Receivables with Interest In most of our examples, a company borrows money. Sometimes, however, a company lends money to another company or to an employee. If a company lends money, it accrues interest revenue during the time the loan is outstanding. The amount of interest revenue recorded at the time an income statement is prepared is calculated with the same formula used to calculate interest expense, $I = P \times R \times T$. The amount of interest revenue will increase Interest Receivable, an asset, and will increase Interest Revenue, which increases shareholders' equity.

Suppose a company loaned $200 to an employee on October 1, 2005, at 10% interest, to be repaid on January 1, 2006. The transaction on October 1 decreases Cash and increases Other Receivables, as shown in the following journal entry. Because we use Accounts Receivable to describe amounts customers owe the company, we call the amounts owed by anyone who is not a customer Other Receivables.

The journal entry for this transaction looks like this:

Date	Transaction	Debit	Credit
Oct. 1, 2005	Other Receivables	200	
	Cash		200
	To record amount loaned to employee		

The accounting equation is:

Assets		=	Liabilities	+	Shareholders' Equity		
					Contributed Capital	+	Retained Earnings
Cash	Other Receivables						
−200	200						

On December 31, the company will record interest revenue. Why? Because some time has passed, and interest revenue has been earned during the period. The company wants the revenue on the period's income statement. Interest revenue has accrued during the time the loan has been outstanding. With interest, the action is the passage of time, so the action has taken place, even though the cash won't change hands until the following January 1. The company's accountant would record Interest Revenue of $5 (= $200 × 0.10 × 3/12). The accountant would also record Interest Receivable of $5. By doing all of this, the financial statements would accurately reflect the following situation on December 31:

- The company has earned $5 of interest revenue as of December 31.
- Interest revenue has not been received on December 31.

The journal entry for this transaction looks like this:

Date	Transaction	Debit	Credit
Dec. 31, 2006	Interest Receivable	5	
	Interest Revenue		5
	To record interest earned in 2006 on employee loan		

The accounting equation is:

Assets	=	Liabilities	+	Shareholders' Equity	
				Contributed Capital +	Retained Earnings
Interest Receivable					Interest Revenue
5					5

When the company actually receives the cash for the interest on January 1, along with the repayment of the $200 principal, the company will not record interest revenue. Instead, the total $205 cash is recorded as an increase in Cash and a decrease in Other Receivables by $200 and Interest Receivable by $5. The timing difference resulted in recording the interest revenue in one period and the cash collection in another.

This is what the journal entry looks like:

Date	Transaction	Debit	Credit
Jan. 1, 2006	Cash	205	
	Other Receivables		200
	Interest Receivable		5
	To record receipt of loan collection and interest from employee		

The accounting equation is:

Assets			= Liabilities +	Shareholders' Equity	
				Contributed Capital +	Retained Earnings
Cash	Other Receivables	Interest Receivable			
205	−200	−5			

Can **YOU** do it?

1. If you borrowed $1,000 at 7%, how much interest would you pay for having that money for only six months? Interest rates are always assumed to be per year.

2. If you have an outstanding loan and you record interest expense before you actually make the cash payment for the interest, is this an accrual or a deferral? Explain your answer.

3. Why would a company record interest expense or interest revenue before any cash is exchanged?

Answers (1) $1,000 × .07 x 6/12 = $35 (2) An accrual. The action of using the money has occurred before the exchange of cash. (3) To be sure interest expense or interest revenue gets on the correct income statement—when it is earned (revenue) or incurred (expense).

Accruals for Other Revenues and Expenses There are other types of revenues and expenses, besides interest, that must be accrued at the end of the period so that the financial statements will accurately reflect the business transactions for the period. For example, if a company provides services for a customer during 2007, the company has to record the revenue on the 2007 income statement, whether or not the customer paid the bill in 2007. Why? Because the company provided the services in 2007. The company cannot record any cash received for this action in 2007 because no cash was received in 2007 as a result of services rendered. This timing difference means that the revenue is recorded as an Accounts Receivable rather than as Cash.

Revenue and receivables are often paired together in accruals. An increase in Accounts Receivable and an increase in Revenue will balance the accounting equation. Then, when the cash is actually collected, sometimes called *realized*, it is not recognized as revenue because it was already recognized in a previous period. That is, receipt of the cash in the following year is not recognized as revenue because the revenue was already recognized in the prior year.

In addition to revenue for services provided, expenses may also need to be accrued. When the firm gets to the end of an accounting period and is ready to prepare financial statements, the accountant must examine the firm's records and business transactions to find any expenses incurred but not recorded. These are the expenses the firm hasn't paid for yet. If the firm paid for them, the accountant would have recorded the expenses when the cash was paid. When a firm receives a bill for expenses like utilities, it will record the expense and a related payable. If the firm has done that, it won't have to accrue the expense at the end of the period.

However, there are some typical expenses that companies do not record until the end of the period. These expenses have to be accrued. On Bed Bath

Study Tip

To realize means the cash is collected. Sometimes revenue is recognized before it is realized. Recall that to recognize means to record revenue on the income statement.

Can **YOU** do it?

Suppose a firm earns $100 revenue on March 1, but does not collect the cash from the customer until April 1. Use this example to explain how accountants use the terms *recognize* and *realize*.

Answer Yes. To recognize revenue means to record it so that it is included on the income statement for the period. In this example, revenue is recognized in March. To realize cash means to collect it, and the cash in this example is realized in April.

Exhibit 4.5

─────────────────────────────────── **Bed Bath & Beyond**

Balance Sheet for Bed Bath & Beyond

The liabilities section of this balance sheet shows Accrued expenses and other current liabilities in the amount of $337,039,000. This amount represents expenses that have been recognized, which means they appear on the income statement for the current period or the income statement of a prior period, but the cash has not been paid to the creditors yet.

```
                    Balance Sheet
                  Bed Bath & Beyond
                 At February 28, 2004
                     (in thousands)
```

Assets

Current assets

Cash and cash equivalents	$ 825,015
Short term investment securities	41,580
Merchandise inventory	1,012,334
Other current assets	90,357
Total current assets	1,969,286
Long term investment securities	210,788
Property and equipment, net	516,164
Other assets	168,785
Total assets	$2,865,023

Liabilities and Shareholders' Equity

Current liabilities:

Accounts payable	$ 398,650
Accrued expenses and other current liabilities	337,039
Income taxes payable	33,845
Total current liabilities	769,534
Deferred rent and other liabilities	104,669
Total liabilities	874,203

Shareholders' Equity

Common stock	3,003
Additional paid-in capital	433,404
Retained earnings	1,554,413
Total shareholders' equity	1,990,820
Total liabilities and shareholders' equity	$2,865,023

> *Expense* is an unusual word to see on the balance sheet. However, *expense* is here because of the word accrued. *Accrued* means that money hasn't been paid yet, but the expense has been included on the income statement.

& Beyond s balance sheet in Exhibit 4.5, look in the liabilities section. There is an amount called Accrued expenses and other current liabilities in the amount of $337,039,000. This amount represents expenses that have been recognized—shown on the income statement for the current period or the income statement of a prior period, but the cash has not been paid to the creditors yet.

One of the most common accruals is a company's payroll expense. A company ordinarily records salaries expense when it pays its employees. In the accounting equation, that transaction would reduce Cash and reduce Retained Earnings by increasing Salaries Expense. The journal entry would be a debit to Salaries Expense and a credit to Cash. What do you do if the end of an accounting period does not coincide with payday? You need to record the salaries expense for the work that your employees have done during this accounting period even though you have not yet paid them. The amount you've already paid them would have been recorded as salaries expense at the time of the payment. To report the correct amount of salaries expense for the period, unpaid salaries also need to be recorded.

Suppose your company's fiscal year end is December 31. If you last paid your employees on December 29, at year-end you will owe them $3,000 for two days' work. You will need to accrue this expense so that it is included in this year's salaries expense. In other words, this accrual will increase Salaries Payable and increase Salaries Expense. This is the journal entry:

Date	Transaction	Debit	Credit
Dec. 31	Salaries expense	3,000	
	Salaries payable		3,000
	To accrue salaries expense at year end		

The employees have already performed the work, but the cash will not be exchanged until the next payday in the next accounting period.

Deferral transactions

The word *defer* means to put off or postpone. In accounting, a deferral refers to a transaction in which the dollars have been exchanged before the economic substance of the transaction—the action—has taken place. Deferral can refer to both revenues and expenses. As you read and study the examples of deferrals that follow, remember that you are taking the point of view of the business rather than the consumer. There are two types of deferrals:

1. Deferrals of revenue
2. Deferrals of expenses

Deferrals of Revenue When a customer pays in advance for Internet service to providers such as AOL and Earthlink, the transaction is an example of a deferred revenue. The company receives the cash *before* it provides the service to the customer. **Deferred revenue** is a liability resulting from the receipt of cash before the recognition of revenue.

> **Deferred revenue:** A liability resulting from the receipt of cash before the recognition of revenue.

You or your friends have probably shopped online for music CDs, DVDs, and books on Amazon.com or eBay. Suppose a company decides to start selling products on the Internet. The company owner is a conservative guy who isn't too sure about this new way of doing business, so he decides to delay shipping products until he has received a customer's check and it has cleared the bank. When the company receives a check for $80 for an order, the owner must defer recognition of the revenue until he ships the products. Even though the owner will immediately deposit the check, the company does not have claim to the cash until the products sold to the customers are shipped. Because the claim to the cash remains with the customer at the time the company receives and deposits the check, the company must record a liability for the customer's claim. The customer's claim is usually recorded in an account called **Unearned Revenue**. Unearned Revenue is a common account name for deferred revenue.

> **Unearned revenue:** A liability that represents the amount of goods or services that a company owes its customers. The cash has been collected, but the action of earning the revenue has not taken place.

Here's how this cash receipt is recorded:

> **In Other Words:**
> Unearned revenue is often called deferred revenue.

Transaction	Debit	Credit
Cash	80	
Unearned Revenue		80
To record receipt of cash in advance of sale		

Date	Transaction	Debit	Credit
Dec. 31, 2006	Rent Expense	6,000	
	Prepaid Rent		6,000
	To record rent expense for November and December		

This is the accounting equation:

Assets	=	Liabilities	+	Shareholders' Equity	
				Contributed Capital +	**Retained Earnings**
Prepaid Rent					Rent Expense
–6,000					–6,000

The journal entry puts two months' rent expense in an income statement account, Rent Expense. That leaves one month of rent, $3,000, on the balance sheet as Prepaid Rent. The rent expense for November and December—$6,000—will be shown on the income statement for the year ended December 31.

 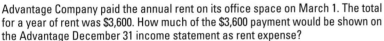

Can **YOU** do it?

> Advantage Company paid the annual rent on its office space on March 1. The total for a year of rent was $3,600. How much of the $3,600 payment would be shown on the Advantage December 31 income statement as rent expense?
>
> *Answer* $3,600/12 = $300
> $300 × 10 months = $3,000

Supplies Most companies purchase supplies in advance. A company buying supplies is exchanging one asset, cash, for another asset, supplies. The accountant does not treat supplies as an expense until the company uses the supplies. Suppose a company had no supplies on hand on March 1 and purchased $500 worth of supplies on March 3. Here's how the purchase is recorded:

Date	Transaction	Debit	Credit
March 3	Supplies	500	
	Cash		500
	To record purchase of supplies		

This is the accounting equation:

Assets		=	Liabilities	+	Shareholders' Equity	
					Contributed Capital +	**Retained Earnings**
Cash	Supplies					
–500	500					

If monthly financial statements are prepared, the company will count and show the amount of unused supplies on March 31 as an asset on the March 31 balance sheet. Only the amount of unused supplies will be an asset on that date. The difference between the amount available to use during March and the amount remaining on March 31 must be the amount of supplies used. This amount, representing supplies used, will be an expense on the income statement.

Suppose the company counts the supplies on March 31 and finds that there are $150 worth of supplies left. How many dollars of supplies were used? $500 minus $150 = $350. After supplies have been counted, the company must make an adjustment to record the correct amounts for the financial statements. Here's how the Supplies Account would look.

	Supplies		
BB	0		
Purchases	500	X	Used
EB	150		

The beginning balance (BB) is zero. The company purchased $500 of supplies, and the ending balance (EB) is $150. What's the dollar amount of supplies used? If the company had $500 worth of supplies during the period and has $150 left at the end of the period, then the expense (supplies used) must have been $350, shown as X on the credit side of the account.

This journal entry shows the necessary adjustment:

Date	Transaction	Debit	Credit
March 31	Supplies Expense	350	
	Supplies		350
	To record use of supplies during March		

This is the accounting equation:

Assets	=	Liabilities	+	Shareholders' Equity	
				Contributed Capital +	**Retained Earnings**
Supplies					Supplies Expense
−350					−350

The $350 expense must be subtracted from the $500 balance in the Supplies account. That will leave $150 for the amount of supplies to be shown on the March 31 balance sheet. The income statement for the month of March will show $350 in Supplies Expense.

Then, suppose that on April 4 the company purchases an additional $500 worth of supplies. Exhibit 4.8 shows this as transaction (3) in the T-accounts. On April 30, as the company is preparing financial statements for April, the remaining supplies are counted. If $200 worth of supplies are on hand on April 30, what adjustment should the company make to its accounts? Recall that at the end of March, there were $150 worth of supplies on hand. That means that April started with those supplies. Then the company purchased an additional $500 worth of supplies. That means the company had $650 of supplies available to use during April. What dollar amount of supplies did the company actually use? Because $200 worth of supplies remain, the company used $450 of supplies during April. The adjustment at the end of April would reduce Supplies, an asset, by $450 and would record $450 as Supplies Expense. Exhibit 4.8 shows this adjustment as entry (4) in the T-accounts.

If you are still having trouble understanding how a company accounts for the purchase and use of supplies, check out the example in Exhibit 4.9.

Exhibit 4.8

T-Accounts for Supplies Transactions

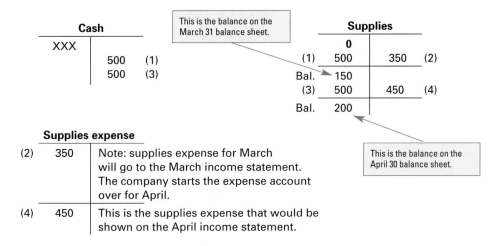

Exhibit 4.9

Deferred Expenses—Supplies

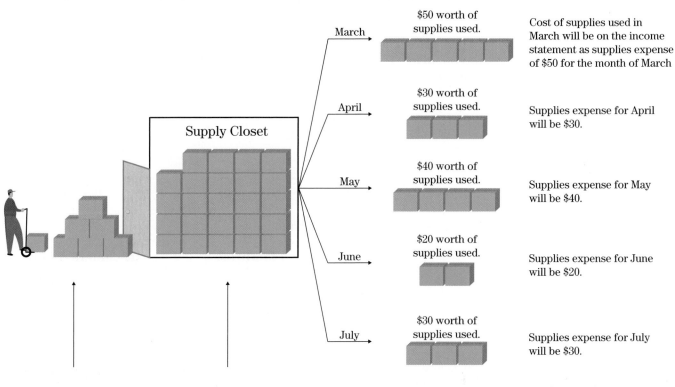

This exhibit shows how an asset like Supplies becomes an expense as the supplies are used.

Equipment and Depreciation When a company purchases an asset that will be used for more than one accounting period, the cost of the asset is *not* recognized as an expense when the asset is purchased. When a company buys an asset—like a computer or office furniture—the accountant records the purchase. The purchase is an asset exchange because the company is exchanging one asset, cash, for another asset, equipment. After the purchase, the income statement will show a portion of that equipment's cost in each accounting period in which the equipment is used to generate revenue.

The cost of equipment is spread over several periods because of the matching principle, which states that expenses and the revenues they help generate need to be on the same income statement. For example, suppose Bed Bath & Beyond purchases a new computer for its office for $5,000 at the beginning of its fiscal year, March 1, 2006. When the purchase is made, the company will record the acquisition of the new asset and the cash payment, as shown in this journal entry:

Date	Transaction	Debit	Credit
March 1, 2006	Office Equipment	5,000	
	Cash		5,000
	To record purchase of computer		

This is the accounting equation:

Assets		=	Liabilities	+	Shareholders' Equity	
					Contributed Capital	+	**Retained Earnings**
Cash	Office Equipment					
−5,000	5,000					

If Bed Bath & Beyond were to classify the purchase of the computer as an expense in 2006, it would be doing a poor job of matching revenues and expenses. The company wants to recognize the expense of the computer during the several years in which it uses the computer to help generate revenue.

The expense of using the computer is called **Depreciation Expense**. Don't confuse depreciation in this accounting context with depreciation commonly used to mean decline in market value. *Depreciating* an asset means to recognize the cost of the asset as an expense over more than one period. **Depreciation** is the process of allocating the cost of an asset to the accounting periods in which

Depreciation expense: A single period's reduction to the cost of the asset, shown on the income statement; also the name of the account in which the expense is recorded.

Depreciation: The process of allocating the cost of an asset to the accounting periods in which it is used.

the asset is used. Depreciation is an allocation process, not a way to determine the market value of the asset.

As the asset is used and the company wants to reduce the asset's amount on its balance sheet, the company's accountant doesn't subtract the amount of the expense directly from the asset's purchase price, like it does with Prepaid Insurance or Supplies. Instead, the balance sheet shows the subtractions separately. In terms of debits and credits, recording depreciation expense does not involve a credit to the Equipment account itself. Instead, the credits are put in a separate account called **Accumulated Depreciation**. Accumulated Depreciation is an example of a **contra-asset**, an account that offsets—reduces—the amount of the asset. The balance in Accumulated Depreciation will be deducted, on the balance sheet, from the asset account to which it relates. The Equipment account will have its own Accumulated Depreciation account. As the equipment is used in the company's operation, the Accumulated Depreciation account is used to record the credits that reflect the decrease in the amount reported as Equipment on the firm's balance sheet. Keeping the credits in a separate account allows a financial statement user to estimate the age of the assets by comparing the original cost of the assets with the amount of accumulated depreciation. Studying a simple example should help you understand this concept.

Let's return to Bed Bath & Beyond's purchase of a computer for $5,000 on March 1, 2006. When the company prepares its year-end financial statements at February 28, 2007, depreciation expense must be recognized. In the accounting records, the amount shown for the computer needs to be reduced to show its use for one year. Depreciation expense reduces net income and, consequently, the shareholders' claims to the company assets. Suppose Bed Bath & Beyond has estimated the annual depreciation to be $1,000. (You'll learn how to calculate depreciation expense in Chapter 8.)

The total reduction in the dollar amount of equipment, at any particular point in time, will be the balance in the Accumulated Depreciation account. Each year, the balance in the Accumulated Depreciation account increases. Accumulated Depreciation is not the same as Depreciation Expense. The Accumulated Depreciation account balance is all the depreciation taken over the entire life of the asset to the date of the financial statements, and the Depreciation Expense account balance is the amount of depreciation for a single year.

On the balance sheet, the original cost of the equipment is shown along with the deduction for accumulated depreciation, the total amount of depreciation that has been recorded during the time the asset has been owned.[1] The resulting amount is called the **book value** of the equipment. The book value is the cost minus the accumulated depreciation related to the asset. You might think of it as the "unused" portion of the equipment. Book value is the net amount that is included when the total assets are added up on the balance sheet.

Here is the year-end adjustment to record depreciation of the asset after its first year of use. Using straight-line depreciation, the same amount will be added to Accumulated Depreciation and recorded as the current year's depreciation expense. Only in the first year will the balance in Accumulated Depreciation equal the annual depreciation expense. Recall that this company's fiscal year ends February 28.

Date	Transaction	Debit	Credit
Feb. 28, 2007	Depreciation Expense	1,000	
	Accumulated Depreciation, Office Equipment		1,000
	To record one year's depreciation on office equipment		

[1] The requirement is that a financial statement user be able to calculate the cost of the assets and the total accumulated depreciation.

Accumulated depreciation: The total amount of depreciation that has been recorded during an asset's use. A company deducts accumulated depreciation from the cost of the asset on the balance sheet.

Contra-asset: A type of account that offsets an asset. It is deducted from the asset on the balance sheet.

Study Tip

A contra account has three characteristics: (1) On a financial statement it is immediately subtracted from the associated account, (the account it's contra to), (2) It has the opposite type of balance (debit or credit) than its associated account, and (3) The name of the account will give you a hint as to what account it is contra to. For example, Accumulated Depreciation indicates the account has something to do with depreciating assets.

Book value: The cost of an asset minus the total accumulated depreciation recorded for the asset.

In Other Words: Carrying value is another expression for book value.

This is the accounting equation:

Assets	=	Liabilities	+	Shareholders' Equity		
				Contributed Capital	+	Retained Earnings
Accumulated Depreciation – Office Equipment						Depreciation Expense
−1,000						−1,000

Accumulated Depreciation is shown on the balance sheet as a *deduction* from the cost of the equipment. The Depreciation Expense is shown on the income statement. The book value of the asset is $4,000 (cost minus accumulated depreciation) at the end of the first year.

After the second year of use, the company would record the same adjusting entry: a debit of $1,000 to Depreciation Expense and a credit of $1,000 to Accumulated Depreciation. The amount in the Accumulated Depreciation account will then be $2,000. The Depreciation Expense for the year is $1,000 because it represents the cost of using the equipment for a single year. The balance in the Accumulated Depreciation account equals all the depreciation expense that has been recognized for the life of the asset through the year of the financial statement. The book value of the computer at the end of the second year is $3,000. The book value of the computer is calculated by subtracting the balance in Accumulated Depreciation through the second year—$2,000—from the $5,000 cost of the equipment.

Exhibit 4.10 shows how Bed Bath & Beyond might depreciate the computer over several years. The company records the purchase of the computer as an asset, and spreads the expense of using the computer over the years it is used.

Exhibit 4.10

The cost of the computer will be spread over the income statements of the time periods it is used as depreciation expense. Part of the expense is being deferred, that is put off, until the computer is actually used.

Computer was purchased on March 1, 2006, for $5,000. It will be depreciated by $1,000 per year.

Year ended February 28	2007	2008	2009	2010	2011
Depreciation Expense (income statement)	$1,000	$1,000	$1,000	$1,000	$1,000
Accumulated Depreciation (balance sheet)	$1,000	$2,000	$3,000	$4,000	$5,000
Book value	$4,000	$3,000	$2,000	$1,000	–0–

Can YOU do it?

Tango Company purchased a computer on January 1, 2007, for $5,500. The company plans to depreciate the asset by $1,100 per year. What is the book value of the machine at the end of 2007?

Answer The book value at the end of 2007, after one year of use, will be $4,400. That's $5,500 minus $1,100 depreciation for 2007.

Making Adjusting Entries and Preparing the Financial Statements

LEARNING OBJECTIVE 3

Make adjusting entries and prepare the four financial statements.

Now that you know how to adjust the accounting records for accruals and deferrals, let's work through the first six steps of the accounting cycle with a comprehensive example. Exhibit 4.11 shows a trial balance taken from the accounting records of Sam's Service Company at the beginning of its fiscal year, January 1, 2006.

During 2006, Sam's Service Company engaged in the following transactions:

1. Paid $45,000 in advance for rent for convention space for 2007.
2. Provided services to customers for $80,000 on account.
3. Purchased and paid cash of $1,500 for a three-year insurance policy that began on January 1, 2006.
4. Purchased $2,000 worth of supplies for cash.
5. Collected $130,000 from customers who had purchased services on credit.
6. Received $3,000 payment in advance for services to be performed for customers in early 2007.
7. Paid $40,000 on accounts payable.

Exhibit 4.11

Trial Balance for Sam's Service Company at January 1, 2006

	DR	CR
Account		
Cash	$140,200	
Accounts Receivable	70,000	
Supplies	10,000	
Equipment*	60,000	
Accumulated Depreciation		$ 12,000
Accounts Payable		50,000
Salaries Payable		2,000
Long-term Notes Payable**		25,200
Common Stock		124,000
Retained Earnings		67,000
	$280,200	$280,200

*Equipment is depreciated by $12,000 each year.
**This is a four-year note signed on December 31, 2005. The interest rate is 10%, and interest is to be paid annually on January 1, beginning in 2007. The principal is to be repaid January 1, 2010.

8. Paid the $2,000 owed to employees from prior year (see trial balance) plus an additional $37,500 for salaries earned by employees in the current year, for a total payment of $39,500.

9. Paid cash for $15,000 worth of miscellaneous operating expenses.

10. Paid cash dividends of $5,000 to shareholders.

The first step in the accounting cycle is to record the routine transactions chronologically as they occur. Exhibit 4.12 on page 179 shows how Sam's Service records the journal entry for each transaction. The *second step in the accounting cycle* is to post the journal entries to the general ledger. Exhibit 4.13 on page 180 shows this second step. The empty T-accounts will be used later when we post the adjusting entries.

The third step in the accounting cycle is preparing an unadjusted trial balance. This is shown in Exhibit 4.14 on page 181. The trial balance confirms that the entries have been posted in such a way that debits equal credits.

Then, review the trial balance to identify the accounts that might need to be adjusted. *The fourth step in the accounting cycle is to make the adjusting entries and post them.*

When the accountant is getting ready to adjust the accounts in anticipation of preparing the financial statements, more information is often needed. Here are some additional facts that Sam's accountant uncovered:

1. Although not anticipated, the company actually provided $500 worth of services to the customer from transaction 6 before the end of 2006.

2. At year-end, employees had worked for two days for which they had not been paid. The next pay day is January 3. The total salaries expense for those two days was $750.

3. Sam's had $8,000 worth of supplies left at year-end.

In addition to making an adjusting entry for each of these three facts, Sam's accountant will also have to make adjustments for (1) expired insurance, (2) depreciation, and (3) interest on the note payable. The adjusting journal entries are shown in Exhibit 4.15 on page 181, and the T-accounts are shown again in Exhibit 4.16 on page 182 with the adjusting entries posted. They are:

Adjustment 1 (A-1): Recognize $500 that has been earned from the advance payment.

Adjustment 2 (A-2): Accrue salaries expense of $750.

Adjustment 3 (A-3): Book the supplies expense of $4,000 ($12,000 minus $8,000 remaining).

Adjustment 4 (A-4): Record one year's insurance expense of $500. (The insurance was $1,500 for 3 years, which is $500 per year.)

Adjustment 5 (A-5): Record one year's depreciation expense of $12,000.

Adjustment 6 (A-6): Accrue one year's interest expense of $2,520 on the note (10% × $25,200 × 12/12).

The fifth step in the accounting cycle is to prepare an adjusted trial balance. This shows all of the accounts with the balances that will appear on the financial statements. Exhibit 4.17 on page 183 shows the adjusted trial balance for Sam's Service Company.

The sixth step of the accounting cycle is preparing the financial statements. The statements are easily prepared from an adjusted trial balance. Start with the income statement accounts to prepare the income statement. Then, transfer the net income amount to the statement of changes in shareholders' equity. Use the amounts from the statement of changes in shareholders' equity in the equity section of the balance sheet. The amounts for assets and liabilities are taken from the adjusted trial balance. Finally, the statement of cash flows is prepared from reviewing every transaction posted to the Cash account and classifying it as a cash flow from operating activities, investing activities, or financing activities.

Study Tip

You'll find that it's very easy to make mistakes in this process. Don't get discouraged. You'll get better with lots of practice!

Exhibit 4.12

Journal Entries for Sam's Service Company

Reference Number (Ref.)	Transaction	Debit	Credit
1	Prepaid Rent	45,000	
	Cash		45,000
	To record payment of rent in advance		
2	Accounts Receivable	80,000	
	Service Revenue		80,000
	To record revenue earned		
3	Prepaid Insurance	1,500	
	Cash		1,500
	To record purchase of a three-year insurance policy		
4	Supplies	2,000	
	Cash		2,000
	To record the purchase of supplies		
5	Cash	130,000	
	Accounts Receivable		130,000
	To record collection on accounts receivable		
6	Cash	3,000	
	Unearned Revenue		3,000
	To record collection in advance from customers		
7	Accounts Payable	40,000	
	Cash		40,000
	To record payment to vendors		
8	Salaries Payable	2,000	
	Salaries Expense	37,500	
	Cash		39,500
	To record payment of salaries to employees		
9	Miscellaneous Operating Expenses	15,000	
	Cash		15,000
	To record operating expenses		
10	Dividends*	5,000	
	Cash		5,000
	To record payment of dividends to shareholders		

*A company may debit Retained Earnings directly when paying dividends, or it may use a special Dividends account.

Exhibit 4.13

T-Accounts for Sam's Service Company (before adjustments)

Assets = **Liabilities** + **Shareholders' Equity**

| | | **Contributed Capital** | = | **Retained Earnings** |

Cash

BB	140,200	45,000	(1)
(5)	130,000	1,500	(3)
(6)	3,000	2,000	(4)
		40,000	(7)
		39,500	(8)
		15,000	(9)
		5,000	(10)
125,200			

Accounts Receivable

BB	70,000	130,000	(5)
(2)	80,000		
20,000			

Supplies

BB	10,000	
(4)	2,000	
12,000		

Prepaid Insurance

(3)	1,500	

Prepaid Rent

(1)	45,000	

Equipment

BB	60,000	

Accumulated Depreciation (equipment)

	12,000	BB

Accounts Payable

(7)	40,000	50,000	BB
		10,000	

Salaries Payable

(8)	2,000	2,000	BB
		0	

Interest Payable

Unearned Revenue

	3,000	(6)

Long-term Notes Payable

	25,200	BB

Common Stock

	124,000	BB

Retained Earnings

	67,000	BB

Dividends

(10)	5,000	

Service Revenue

	80,000	(2)

Salaries Expense

(8)	37,500	

Miscellaneous Operating Expenses

(9)	15,000	

Depreciation Expense

Insurance Expense

Interest Expense

Supplies Expense

Step 2 of the accounting cycle: post the journal entries to the general ledger. Beginning account balances are noted with **BB**. Numbers in parentheses can help you trace the amounts back to the journal entries in Exhibit 4.12.

Exhibit 4.14

Unadjusted Trial Balance

Step 3 of the accounting cycle: prepare an unadjusted trial balance. These balances come from the T-accounts in Exhibit 4.13.

	Debit	Credit
Cash	$125,200	
Accounts Receivable	20,000	
Supplies	12,000	
Prepaid Insurance	1,500	
Prepaid Rent	45,000	
Equipment	60,000	
Accumulated Depreciation		$12,000
Accounts Payable		10,000
Salaries Payable		—
Unearned Revenue		3,000
Long-term Notes Payable		25,200
Common Stock		124,000
Retained Earnings		67,000
Dividends	5,000	
Service Revenue		80,000
Salaries Expense	37,500	
Miscellaneous Operating Expenses	15,000	
	$321,200	$321,200

Exhibit 4.15

Adjusting Journal Entries

Reference Number (Ref.)	Journal Entry	Debit	Credit
A-1	Unearned Revenue	500	
	Revenue		500
	To recognize earned portion of advance payment		
A-2	Salaries Expense	750	
	Salaries Payable		750
	To record accrual for unpaid salaries		
A-3	Supplies Expense	4,000	
	Supplies		4,000
	To record supplies used during the period		
A-4	Insurance Expense	500	
	Prepaid Insurance		500
	To record the use (expiration) of insurance		
A-5	Depreciation Expense	12,000	
	Accumulated Depreciation		12,000
	To record one year's depreciation expense		
A-6	Interest Expense	2,520	
	Interest Payable		2,520
	To record interest expense on note payable		

Exhibit 4.16

T-Accounts with Adjusting Entries

	Assets	=	Liabilities	+	Shareholders' Equity		
					Contributed Capital	+	Retained Earnings

Cash

BB	140,200	45,000	(1)
(5)	130,000	1,500	(3)
(6)	3,000	2,000	(4)
		40,000	(7)
		39,500	(8)
		15,000	(9)
		5,000	(10)
125,200			

Accounts Receivable

BB	70,000	130,000	(5)
(2)	80,000		
20,000			

Supplies

BB	10,000	4,000	(A-3)
(4)	2,000		
8,000			

Prepaid Insurance

(3)	1,500	500	(A-4)
1,000			

Prepaid Rent

(1)	45,000	

Equipment

BB	60,000	

Accumulated Depreciation (Equipment)

		12,000	BB
		12,000	(A-5)
		24,000	

Accounts Payable

(7)	40,000	50,000	BB
		10,000	

Salaries Payable

(8)	2,000	2,000	BB
		750	(A-2)
		750	

Interest Payable

		2,520	(A-6)

Unearned Revenue

(A-1)	500	3,000	(6)
		2,500	

Long-term Notes Payable

		25,200	BB

Common Stock

		124,000	BB

Retained Earnings

		67,000	BB

Dividends

(10)	5,000	

Service Revenue

		80,000	(2)
		500	(A-1)
		80,500	

Salaries Expense

(8)	37,500	
(A-2)	750	
38,250		

Miscellaneous Operating Expenses

(9)	15,000	

Depreciation Expense

(A-5)	12,000	

Insurance Expense

(A-4)	500	

Interest Expense

(A-6)	2,520	

Supplies Expense

(A-3)	4,000	

Adjusting entries are highlighted in blue.

Exhibit 4.17

These account balances come from the T-accounts in Exhibit 4.16.

Adjusted Trial Balance

	Debits	Credits
Cash	$125,200	
Accounts Receivable	20,000	
Supplies	8,000	
Prepaid Insurance	1,000	
Prepaid Rent	45,000	
Equipment	60,000	
Accumulated Depreciation		$ 24,000
Accounts Payable		10,000
Salaries Payable		750
Unearned Revenue		2,500
Interest Payable		2,520
Long-term Notes Payable		25,200
Common Stock		124,000
Retained Earnings		67,000
Dividends	5,000	
Service Revenue		80,500
Salaries Expense	38,250	
Miscellaneous Operating Expenses	15,000	
Depreciation Expense	12,000	
Insurance Expense	500	
Interest Expense	2,520	
Supplies Expense	4,000	
	$336,470	$336,470

Exhibit 4.18 on page 184 shows the four financial statements. Compare them to the adjusted trial balance as you study the statements. Take your time and trace each amount from Exhibit 4.17 to make sure that you can see how the amount is reported on the four financial statements.

Closing the Revenue and Expense Accounts

LEARNING OBJECTIVE 4
Explain closing the books and why it is done.

The seventh step in the accounting cycle is closing the temporary accounts. Revenue accounts and expense accounts are **temporary accounts**. The balances in these accounts at the end of a period represent the accumulations of each revenue and expense amount for that particular period only. Through the process of closing the books, the balance in each revenue and expense account is transferred to the Retained Earnings account. This process will update the Retained Earnings account by including the effect of the period's net income and reduce all revenue and expense accounts to zero. Thus, all revenue and expense accounts will start each new accounting period with a zero balance so that they will include only the activities of the new accounting period.

The balance sheet will balance only when the revenue and expense amounts are incorporated into the Retained Earnings balance. Net income is added to Retained Earnings when we prepare the statement of changes in shareholders' equity, but the amounts from the revenue and expense accounts have not, at this point, been formally transferred to the Retained Earnings account in the general ledger.

Temporary accounts: Accounts with balances that are brought to zero at the end of the accounting period. This includes all revenue and expense accounts and the dividends account.

In Other Words:
Temporary accounts are sometimes called nominal accounts.

Exhibit 4.18

Financial Statements for Sam's Service Company

1. Prepare the Income Statement first. Then, transfer the net income to the Statement of Changes in Shareholders' Equity.

Sam's Service Company
Income Statement
For the fiscal year ended December 31, 2006

Revenues		
Sales		$ 80,500
Expenses		
Salaries expenses	$ 38,250	
Miscellaneous operating expenses	15,000	
Depreciation expenses	12,000	
Insurance expense	500	
Interest expense	2,520	
Supplies expense.............	4,000	72,270
Net income		$ 8,230

Sam's Service Company
Statement of Changes in Shareholders' Equity
For the fiscal year ended December 31, 2006

Common stock	
Beginning balance	$ 124,000
Contributions during the month	0
Ending balance	124,000
Retained Earnings	
Beginning balance	$ 67,000
Net income	8,230
Dividends	(5,000)
Ending balance	70,230
Total shareholders' equity................	$ 194,230

2. The net income is added to the beginning balance in Retained Earnings

4. The Statement of Cash Flows explains how Cash changed from its beginning balance of $100,000 to its ending balance of $150,000.

Sam's Service Company
Statement of Cash Flows
For the fiscal year ended December 31, 2006

Cash from operating activities		
Cash received from customers	$ 133,000	
Cash paid to vendors	(40,000)	
Cash paid for rent.............	(45,000)	
Cash paid to employees	(39,500)	
Cash paid for misc.		
operating expenses	(15,000)	
Cash paid for insurance	(1,500)	
Cash paid for supplies	(2,000)	
Cash from (used by) operations		$(10,000)
Cash from investing activities		0
Cash from financing activities		
Dividends paid	(5,000)	
Decrease in cash during the month	(15,000)	
Add beginning cash	140,200	
Cash balance at January 31		$ 125,200

Sam's Service Company
Balance Sheet
At December 31, 2006

Assets		
Cash		$125,200
Accounts receivable		20,000
Supplies		8,000
Prepaid rent		45,000
Prepaid insurance		1,000
Total current assets		199,200
Equipment	$60,000	
Less accumulated depreciation	(24,000)	36,000
Total assets		$235,200
Liabilities and Shareholders Equity		
Liabilities		
Accounts payable		$ 10,000
Salaries payable		750
Unearned revenue		2,500
Interest payable		2,520
Total current liabilities		15,770
Long-term notes payable		25,200
Shareholders' equity		
Common stock		124,000
Retained earnings		70,230
Total liabilities and shareholders' equity		$235,200

3. The new Retained Earnings balance goes on the new Balance Sheet.

To prepare the four financial statements for Sam's Service Company, we must first calculate net income. The red arrow shows that net income from the income statement then goes to the statement of changes in shareholders' equity. From the statement of changes in shareholders' equity, two different amounts will go to the equity section of the balance sheet: Contributed Capital and Retained Earnings. Follow these amounts with the blue arrows. That is how net income gets incorporated into Retained Earnings. Finally, the statement of cash flows explains the change in cash from one year to the next. Here, the company started with $140,200 cash and ended the period with $125,200. This Cash balance on the balance sheet is explained by the statement of cash flows. The green arrow shows the relationship between these two statements.

The mechanics of closing the books

Revenue and expense accounts are reduced to zero by preparing end-of-the-period journal entries called **closing entries**. Each temporary account having a credit balance is debited for the amount of that balance and each temporary account having a debit balance is credited for the amount of that balance. For example, a revenue account having a $300 credit balance would be closed out by debiting the account for $300. The related credit entry is made to Retained Earnings, which causes Retained Earnings to increase. Revenue increases Retained Earnings, so closing entries is the process of making revenues increase Retained Earnings in the accounting records for the period.

Closing a revenue account increases Retained Earnings, but closing an expense account *decreases* Retained Earnings. For example, an expense account with a $100 debit balance would be closed by crediting the account for $100. The related debit entry is made to Retained Earnings, which causes Retained Earnings to decrease.

Keep in mind the reason for having revenue accounts and expense accounts.

> **Closing entries:** End-of-period journal entries that formally reduce the revenue and expense accounts (and dividends account) to zero.

1. We want the revenues and expenses to eventually be recorded in Retained Earnings. For a single accounting period, usually a year, the revenues and expenses are recorded separately from Retained Earnings so that we can report them on the year's income statement. Then, we want those amounts included in Retained Earnings for the balance sheet.

2. We want the revenue and expense accounts to have a zero balance so they can start over, ready for amounts that will be recorded during the coming year. Remember, the income statement covers a single accounting period. We don't want to mix up last year's revenue with this year's revenue in our revenue accounts or last year's expenses with this year's expenses in our expense accounts.

When a company pays dividends, it often uses a temporary account, Dividends, to record the transaction. This account also needs to start each accounting period with a zero balance because it keeps track of the dividends paid for a single accounting period.

Asset accounts, liability accounts, and shareholders' equity accounts are **permanent accounts, or real accounts**. A balance in any of these accounts is carried over from the end of one period to the beginning of the next. For example, the amount of cash shown in the Cash account will never be zero, unless the company spends its last cent. The same is true about all balance sheet accounts. Think about your own personal records. If you keep track of the cash in your bank account, you will have a continuous record of your cash balance. On the date of a personal balance sheet, you would see how much cash you have on that particular date. As the next year begins, you still have that cash. It doesn't go away because a new year begins.

> **Permanent accounts or real accounts:** Accounts with balances that carry over from the end of one period to the beginning of the next; these accounts are never closed. They are the asset, liability, and shareholders' equity accounts.

In contrast to the continuous record in a permanent account, let's consider a simple example of a temporary account. Suppose you were keeping a list of your grocery expenses for the year so you can budget your money for the following year. At the end of the year, after you have reported the amount of those expenses on your annual income statement, you would start a new list for the next year. Because an income statement reports expenses for a period of time, your grocery expenses for one year would be reported on one income statement, but those expenses would not apply to the following year. You want the grocery expense account to be empty when you begin the next year. Revenue and expense amounts must apply to a specific time period for them to make sense.

Let's return to Sam's Service Company. Because the accounting period for Sam's is over, the firm's accountant will make closing entries. Exhibit 4.19 shows the closing journal entries, which are recorded after the financial statements are prepared.

The closing journal entries are recorded to bring to zero the balances in all revenue accounts, expense accounts, and the Dividends account. The first entry brings all the revenue and expense accounts to zero, and the amount that makes the journal entry balance is a credit of $8,230. Look back at the income statement in Exhibit 4.18, and you'll see that $8,230 is net income.

Exhibit 4.19

Closing Entries for Sam's Service Company

Date	Journal Entry	Debit	Credit
Dec. 31	Sales Revenue	80,500	
	Salaries Expense		38,250
	Misc. Operating Expenses		15,000
	Depreciation Expense		12,000
	Insurance Expense		500
	Interest Expense		2,520
	Supplies Expense		4,000
	Retained Earnings		8,230
	Retained Earnings	5,000	
	Dividends		5,000
	To close Dividends account		

These accounts and their balances are all found in the T-accounts at the end of the period.

This is a calculated amount to get the journal entry to balance. If you enter transactions correctly, this amount added to retained earnings will be net income.

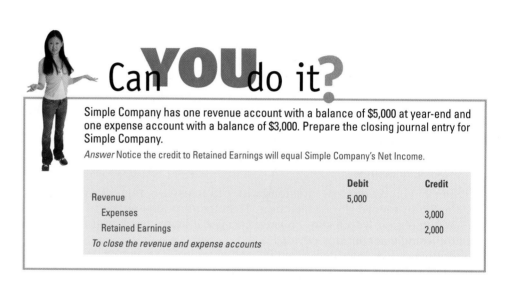

Can **YOU** do it?

Simple Company has one revenue account with a balance of $5,000 at year-end and one expense account with a balance of $3,000. Prepare the closing journal entry for Simple Company.

Answer Notice the credit to Retained Earnings will equal Simple Company's Net Income.

	Debit	Credit
Revenue	5,000	
Expenses		3,000
Retained Earnings		2,000
To close the revenue and expense accounts		

Study Tip

A post-closing trial balance is simply a list of all the accounts and their debit balances or credit balances, prepared after the temporary accounts have been closed. Only balance sheet accounts will appear on the post-closing trial balance.

The temporary general ledger accounts are not closed on December 31. The company has to finish all of the fiscal year's business before the accounts can be closed. Closing the books often takes a company weeks or even months. There are continuing efforts to decrease the time it takes to close the books, and you can read about it in ***Accounting in the News***.

The eighth and final step in the accounting cycle is to prepare a post-closing trial balance. Remember, pre means *before* and post means *after*. After the temporary accounts are closed, preparing a trial balance—a list of all the accounts with their debit or credit balances—accomplishes three things:

1. It is a final check of the equality of debits and credits in the general ledger.

2. It confirms that we are ready to start our next period with only real (permanent) accounts.

3. It gives us the beginning balances on which to build the next year's financial information.

Exhibit 4.20 shows the post-closing trial balance for Sam's Service Company.

Exhibit 4.20

Post-closing trial balance for Sam's Service Company

The final step in the accounting cycle is to prepare a post-closing trial balance that lists all the accounts with their debit or credit balances.

	DR	CR
Cash	$125,200	
Accounts Receivable	20,000	
Supplies	8,000	
Prepaid Rent	45,000	
Prepaid Insurance	1,000	
Equipment	60,000	
Accumulated Depreciation		$ 24,000
Accounts Payable		10,000
Salaries Payable		750
Unearned Revenue		2,500
Interest Payable		2,520
Long-term Notes Payable		25,200
Common Stock		124,000
Retained Earnings		70,230
	$259,200	$259,200

Accounting in the NEWS

Technology

How Can Accountants Decrease the Time It Takes to Close the Books?

At the end of a fiscal year, a company has to close its books. But there's more to do after that: Get preliminary results to management, have auditors complete their work and sign off on the numbers, and issue a press release. KPMG, one of four largest accounting firms in the world, conducted two surveys to find out how much time companies spent closing the books. In 1999, the whole process took about 34 days. In 2001, the process still took about 34 days. In 2005, many firms still took almost a month to close their books. At one time, Cisco thought it could close its books almost instantaneously—a virtual close. Janet Kersnar, the editor-in-chief of *CFO Europe*, had this to say in October 2002:

Whatever happened to the "virtual close"? Three years ago, as E-business dominated corporate agendas, it seemed that all companies would soon be able to close their books and produce financial statements in scarcely more time than it takes to click a mouse. A handful of companies, notably Cisco Systems, were lauded for showing the way.

Why does it still take so long to close the books—despite technology? According to a KPMG manager, there are two main reasons. First, executives underestimated the amount of work it takes to shorten the cycle. It requires real change in a firm's processes, and that's not easy to achieve. Second, regulators and investors are spending more time evaluating the financial information that corporations provide because of the accounting fraud perpetrated by Enron and WorldCom. According to the *Wall Street Journal*, in 2005 corporate auditors reported that the Sarbanes-Oxley Act has "improved the process of closing the books." Also helping speed up the closing process is the SEC requirement that companies file the 10-K within 60 days after the close of the fiscal year, as opposed to the previous 90 days. As technology continues to improve the way corporations manage their financial records, keep your eye on

Will technology help accountants close the books in less than 34 days?

the closing process. Someday a virtual close may be a reality.

Q. What has the SEC done to shorten the time it takes a company to close the books?

A. It has changed the deadline for filing the annual 10-K from 90 days after the end of the fiscal year to 60 days.

Sources: Judith Burns, "Corporate Accounting Controls to Get Fresh Scrutiny Wednesday," *WSJ Online*, April 12, 2005; Janet Kersnar, "Virtual Close: Not So Fast," *CFO.com*, October 15, 2002.

The accounting cycle begins with the transactions of a new accounting period. The cycle includes recording and posting the transactions, adjusting the books, preparing financial statements, and closing the temporary accounts to get ready for the next accounting period.

Debt-to-total-assets ratio: A solvency ratio defined as total liabilities divided by total assets.

Study Tip

You know that total assets = total liabilities + total shareholders' equity. So you can express the debt-to-total-assets ratio as debt-to-(debt + equity). What percentage of the firm's total financing is debt?

Financial Statement Analysis

In Chapters 2 and 3, you learned to evaluate a firm's short-term liquidity using the current and quick ratios. To evaluate a firm's long-term liquidity, we use *solvency ratios*.

The most common solvency ratio is the **debt-to-total-assets ratio**. Just as you would deduce from its name, the debt-to-total-assets ratio is computed by dividing total liabilities by total assets.

$$\text{Debt-to-total-assets ratio} = \frac{\text{Total liabilities}}{\text{Total assets}}$$

The debt-to-total-assets ratio measures the percentage of assets that is financed by creditors. If you were a bank loan officer trying to decide if you should make a large loan to a particular firm, would you like to see a high or low number for this ratio? Lower ratios look better to a creditor. However, as with all ratios, a single value has very little meaning. The bank loan officer would look at trends in the ratio and the value of the ratio for similar firms and for the firm's industry. When comparing firms of different sizes, simply looking at the amount of debt doesn't allow meaningful comparison. That's why computing a ratio is useful. Using the information from the balance sheets of Wendy's International and Steak n Shake Company, shown in Exhibit 4.21, let's calculate the debt-to-total-assets ratio for each. Notice how much more debt Wendy's has in total dollars, but Steak n Shake has a higher debt-to-total-assets ratio.

The debt-to-total-assets ratio for Wendy's is (dollars in thousands):

$$\frac{\$1,405,407}{\$3,164,013} = 0.44$$

Exhibit 4.21

Selected Financial Data from Wendy's International and Steak n Shake Company

($ in thousands)	Wendy's International, Inc.	Steak n Shake Company
Total Assets	$3,164,013	$433,463
Total Liabilities	$1,405,407	$213,748
Total Shareholders' Equity	$1,758,606	$219,715

The debt-to-total assets ratio for Steak n Shake is:

$$\frac{\$213,748}{\$433,463} = 0.49$$

Close to half of each company's financing is provided by creditors. We'll learn more ratios to help us evaluate a firm's performance in the Chapter 5.

Business risk, control, & ethics

LEARNING OBJECTIVE 6
Identify controls that help a firm reduce the risk of failing to record a transaction.

You learned how to record transactions, prepare trial balances, and prepare financial statements in this chapter, but how can you make sure every transaction is recorded in the accounting system? What kinds of controls do firms need?

One common control is the use of pre-numbered documents. As the accounting clerk is recording invoices, for example, he or she will be sure that all of the numbers in the sequence are included. If the clerk starts with invoice #119 and ends with invoice #151, the clerk has to be sure to record *all* of the invoices between 119 and 151. If one is missing, the clerk will find out what happened to it. Having pre-numbered documents, and then accounting for them, will reduce the risk of omitting a transaction from the accounting system.

Another control to reduce the risk of omitting a transaction is segregation of duties. Segregation of duties means that the same person does not authorize a transaction, record the asset, and have physical custody of the asset. It is crucial that the person who does the record-keeping for an asset does not have physical control of the asset. For example, suppose a cashier at Bed Bath & Beyond is responsible for counting the money in the cash register at the end of the day (physical custody) and then recording that amount for the accounting clerk (record-keeping). That cashier could take a couple of twenty-dollar bills and make sure the recorded amount does not include them. While ethics plays a role in whether or not a cashier would take the cash, controls are always necessary. Even ethical people can be tempted under some conditions. In practice, someone other than the cashier will count the money and report that amount to the accounting department.

Businesses such as dry cleaners use pre-numbered documents to keep track of customer transactions.

Have you ever made a purchase at a store that will give you your purchase free if the cashier fails to give you a receipt? That is one way to introduce segregation of duties without hiring an extra person. The cashier has physical custody of the assets, and you assist in the record keeping by checking your receipt for accuracy. The cashier has to put the money in the cash register and record the sale to get a receipt for the customer. The next time you purchase something from a store that promises a free purchase if you don't receive the receipt, you will recognize that this is a control put in place by the store's management to reduce the risk that a clerk will fail to record a transaction.

Every part of the business process—sales, collections, purchases, and obtaining financing—needs to have controls to manage the risks associated with the process. As you learn more about these business processes in the chapters to come, think about the risks and the controls needed to minimize risks. Even though a firm will try to hire employees with high ethical standards, controls are needed to make sure the policies and procedures of the firm are followed.

YOU make the call:

How should Bed Bath & Beyond account for a customer's payment in advance?

Now that you have studied the income statement and what is included in the calculation of net income, you should be able to answer this question: Should Bed Bath & Beyond recognize the $50,000 payment from the Marriott as revenue? The answer is no. Only the amount Bed Bath & Beyond has actually earned by providing goods or services should be included in the company's revenues for the period. The advanced payment from Marriott will be recorded as a liability—Unearned Revenue. When the company earns the $50,000 by actually doing the work to earn it, Bed Bath & Beyond will change the unearned revenue to earned revenue, and the $50,000 will be included on the income statement.

Let's Take a Test Drive

Real-World Problem:
Bed Bath & Beyond

Each year Bed Bath & Beyond has thousands of transactions. The company's net sales for the year ended February 28, 2004 were more than $4.4 billion. Imagine how many customer purchases were needed to total that amount of sales. Bed Bath & Beyond made millions of dollars of purchases from its vendors during the year. With such a large operation, accountants need to review the records to see if any adjustments need to be made for the financial statements. There may be adjustments needed for revenues and expenses for rent, insurance, supplies, depreciation, and interest. Every business will have its own particular accounts that need to be adjusted at the end of the accounting period. The accountants will make the adjustments and then prepare the financial statements. As preparation for the next fiscal year, the accountants will then prepare closing entries.

Concepts

Accountants want the income statement to reflect the revenues and expenses for the period covered by the statement—none from the period before or the period after. Accountants also want the balance sheet to show the correct amount of assets and liabilities on the date of the statement. To do that, accountants must allocate revenues and expenses to the correct periods. This allocation is done by making adjustments at the end of the accounting period.

- Sometimes a company incurs an expense but pays for it later. Sometimes a company earns revenue but collects the cash for that revenue later.

- Accountants do *not* base the recognition of revenues and expenses on the collection of cash or on the disbursement of cash. Revenue and expenses are recognized—that's when they show up on the income statement—when the economic substance of the transaction has taken place. The economic substance of a transaction is the action of earning revenue by providing goods and services to customers or incurring expenses by using resources to earn that revenue.

- When the action has been completed but the dollars have not yet changed hands, it is called an *accrual*. Action comes first, and payment for that action comes later. The company accrues—builds up or accumulates—revenue it has earned or expenses it has incurred, even though the cash has not been exchanged.

- In some situations, the payment comes first and the action for that payment comes later. Sometimes the company pays in advance for goods or services that it will use to generate revenue in a future period, and sometimes customers pay in advance for those goods or services provided in a later period. These situations are called *deferrals*. Dollars are exchanged, but the company defers recognition of the revenue or expense until the action of the transaction is complete.

See if you can apply these concepts to some of the transactions for Bed Bath & Beyond.

The Mechanics

Suppose that Bed Bath & Beyond (BB&B) had a special division just for decorating. This division, called BB&B Decorating, does not sell any merchandise. Instead, it provides decorating services for a fee. Suppose BB&B Decorating began the month of January 2007 with the following trial balance. (This is the December 31, 2006 post-closing trial balance.)

	DR	CR
Account		
Cash	$200,000	
Supplies	20,000	
Equipment*	100,000	
Accumulated Depreciation		$ 10,000
Miscellaneous Payables		40,000
Salaries Payable		4,000
Long-term Notes Payable		50,000
Common Stock		126,000
Retained Earnings		90,000
	$320,000	$320,000

*Equipment is depreciated by $10,000 each year, which is $833 per month.

The following transactions occurred during January 2007.

1. Purchased additional supplies for $12,000 on account. (Record the liability as Miscellaneous Payables.)
2. Paid salaries owed to employees at December 31, 2006.
3. Provided decorating services for $84,000 cash.
4. Paid entire balance in Miscellaneous Payables (including purchase in 1 above.)
5. Purchased $15,000 worth of supplies on account. (Record as Miscellaneous Payables.)
6. Paid six months' worth of rent on buildings for $6,000, starting in January.
7. Made a payment on the long-term loan of $5,000. Of this amount, $4,950 was principal and $50 was interest for January.

Additional information:

1. There was $5,000 worth of supplies left on hand at the end of the month.
2. The equipment is being depreciated at $833 per month.
3. At month end, the following expenses for January (to be paid in February) had not been recorded: Utilities $350 and Salaries $4,600.

Instructions

1. Set up T-accounts and post the beginning balances.
2. Prepare journal entries for each of the transactions and post them to the T-accounts. Add any accounts you need as you go along.
3. Prepare the adjusting entries needed for depreciation, supplies, rent, and accrued liabilities and post them to the T-accounts.
4. Prepare an adjusted trial balance.
5. Prepare the four basic financial statements for the month of January.
6. Prepare the closing entries.

Solution

Reference Number (Ref.)	Journal Entry	Debit	Credit
1	Supplies	12,000	
	Miscellaneous Payables		12,000
2	Salaries Payable	4,000	
	Cash		4,000
3	Cash	84,000	
	Decorating Revenue		84,000
4	Miscellaneous Payables	52,000	
	Cash		52,000
5	Supplies	15,000	
	Miscellaneous Payables		15,000
6	Prepaid Rent	6,000	
	Cash		6,000
7	Long-term Notes Payable	4,950	
	Interest Expense	50	
	Cash		5,000
Adjusting Journal Entries			
A1	Supplies Expense	42,000	
	Supplies		42,000
A2	Depreciation Expense	833	
	Accumulated Depreciation		833
A3a	Utilities Expense	350	
	Utilities Payable		350
A3b	Salaries Expense	4,600	
	Salaries Payable		4,600
A4	Rent Expense	1,000	
	Prepaid Rent		1,000

The T-accounts show all of the regular journal entries plus the adjusting entries (shaded).

Assets	=	Liabilities	+	Shareholders' Equity

Cash

BB	200,000	4,000	(2)
(3)	84,000	52,000	(4)
		6,000	(6)
		5,000	(7)
	217,000		

Supplies

BB	20,000		
(1)	12,000		
(5)	15,000	42,000	(A1)
	5,000		

Prepaid Rent

(6)	6,000	1,000	(A4)
	5,000		

Equipment

BB	100,000	
	100,000	

Accumulated Depreciation

	10,000	BB
	833	(A2)
	10,833	

Miscellaneous Payables

		40,000	BB
(4)	52,000	12,000	(1)
		15,000	(5)
		15,000	

Salaries Payable

(2)	4,000	4,000	BB
		4,600	(A3b)
		4,600	

Utilities Payable

	350	(A3a)
	350	

Long-term Notes Payable

(7)	4,950	50,000	BB
		45,050	

Common Stock

	126,000	BB
	126,000	

Retained Earnings

	90,000	BB
	90,000	

Decorating Revenue

	84,000	(3)
	84,000	

Supplies Expense

(A1)	42,000	
	42,000	

Rent Expense

(A4)	1,000	
	1,000	

Interest Expense

(7)	50	
	50	

Depreciation Expense

(A2)	833	
	833	

Utilities Expense

(A3a)	350	
	350	

Salaries Expense

(A3b)	4,600	
	4,600	

Adjusted Trial Balance at January 31

Cash	$217,000	
Supplies	5,000	
Prepaid Rent	5,000	
Equipment	100,000	
Accumulated Depreciation		$ 10,833
Misc. Payables		15,000
Salaries Payable		4,600
Utilities Payable		350
Long-term Notes Payable		45,050
Common Stock		126,000
Retained Earnings		90,000
Decorating Revenue		84,000
Supplies Expense	42,000	
Rent Expense	1,000	
Interest Expense	50	
Depreciation Expense	833	
Utilities Expense	350	
Salaries Expense	4,600	
	$375,833	$375,833

BB&B Decorating
Income Statement
For the month of January 2007

Revenues	$ 84,000
Operating expenses	48,833
Net income.............................	$ 35,167

BB&B Decorating
Statement of Retained Earnings
For the month of January 2007

Retained earnings

Beginning balance.........................	$ 90,000
Net income...............................	35,167
Ending balance	$125,167

BB&B Decorating
Statement of Cash Flows
For the month of January 2007

Cash from operating activities	
Cash from customers	$ 84,000
Cash paid for operating expenses	(62,000)
Cash paid for interest	(50)
Total cash from operations	21,950
Cash from investing activities	
Cash from financing activities	
Cash paid on loan principal	(4,950)
Total cash inflow........................	17,000
Add beginning cash balance	200,000
Cash balance at January 31	$217,000

BB&B Decorating
Balance Sheet
At January 31, 2007

Assets

Cash	$217,000
Supplies	5,000
Prepaid rent	5,000
Total current assets	227,000
Equipment (net of $10,833 accumulated depreciation)	89,167
Total assets	$316,167

Liabilities and Shareholders' Equity

Liabilities

Miscellaneous payables	$ 15,000
Salaries payable	4,600
Utilities payable	350
Total current liabilities	19,950
Long-term notes payable	45,050
Shareholders' equity	
Common stock	126,000
Retained earnings	125,167
Total liabilities and shareholders' equity	$316,167

Rapid Review

1. **Define accrual accounting and explain how income is measured.** *Accrual accounting* means that revenue is recognized when it is earned by providing goods and services to customers and expenses are recognized when they are incurred by using economic resources or services to help generate that revenue. The revenues and expenses are matched for the income statement. The cash may be received or paid before or after the economic substance of the transaction is complete.

2. **Explain accruals and deferrals and how they affect the financial statements.** *Accruals* are transactions in which the economic substance of the transaction occurs before the cash is exchanged. These transactions must be included in the calculation of net income and result in a payable or a receivable to record the expected future cash outflow or inflow. *Deferrals* are transactions in which the cash is exchanged before the substance of the transaction has occurred. The cash must be recorded,

so any revenue or expense must be *deferred*—postponed from being reported on the income statement—until the revenue is earned or the expense is incurred.

3. **Make adjusting entries and prepare all four financial statements.** At the end of the period, a company's accountant will review the accounting records to be sure that there are no accounts with balances that are not up-to-date. *Adjusting entries* are made for accrued revenues and expenses and for deferred revenues and expenses. After the accountant makes the adjusting entries, the financial statements can be prepared.

4. **Explain closing the books and why it is done.** Finally, the accountant will close the temporary accounts. That means he or she will record the journal entries that will transfer the balances of revenue and expense accounts to Retained Earnings. The revenue and expense accounts are reduced to zero balances, ready for the next accounting period. The Dividends account will also be closed to Retained Earnings.

5. **Compute and explain the debt-to-total assets ratio.** The *debt-to-total-assets ratio* is total debt divided by total assets. This ratio helps managers evaluate the firm's long-term solvency.

$$\text{Debt-to-total-assets ratio} = \frac{\text{Total liabilities}}{\text{Total assets}}$$

6. **Identify controls that help a firm reduce the risk of failing to record a transaction.** Two are: (1) using prenumbered documents and (2) segregating the duties of record-keeping from the physical control of the assets.

Key Terms

Accrual, p. 157
Accrued expenses, p. 159
Accrued liability, p. 162
Accrued revenue, p. 159
Accumulated depreciation, p. 175
Book value, p. 175

Closing entries, p. 185
Contra-asset, p. 175
Debt-to-total-assets ratio, p. 188
Deferral, p. 158
Deferred expense, p. 168
Deferred revenue, p. 166

Depreciation, p. 174
Depreciation expense, p. 174
Permanent accounts, p. 185
Real accounts, p. 185
Temporary accounts, p. 183
Unearned revenue, p. 166

Have You Increased Your Business IQ?

Answer these questions to find out.

1. According to accountants, an accrued liability is an
   a. amount owed for expenses already incurred.
   b. amount paid for expenses already incurred.
   c. amount owed to vendors for inventory purchases.
   d. estimate of amounts owed for future expenses.
2. According to accountants, a deferred revenue is
   a. A revenue earned but not yet collected from a customer.
   b. An expense incurred to earn the revenue.
   c. A revenue that has been collected in advance, but not yet earned.
   d. The estimated revenue from a new product launch.
3. Depreciation expense is
   a. The estimated reduction in market value of long-term assets.
   b. The cost of the asset.
   c. Never shown in the financial statements.
   d. The periodic expense associated with the use of a long-term asset.
4. Real accounts are ones that are
   a. Shown on the balance sheet.
   b. Shown on the income statement.
   c. Closed at the end of each fiscal year.
   d. Temporary.
5. The relationship between the income statement and the balance sheet is explained
   a. In the notes to the financial statements.
   b. By the statement of cash flows.
   c. Is an advanced topic to be learned in an advanced accounting course.
   d. By the statement of changes in shareholders' equity.

Now, check your answers.

1. a   2. c   3. d   4. a   5. d

- If you answered all five questions correctly, you've increased your business IQ by studying this chapter. It doesn't mean you've mastered all of the accounting concepts in the chapter. It simply means that you understand some of the general business concepts presented in this chapter.
- If you answered 2 to 4 questions correctly, you've made some progress, but your business IQ has plenty of room to grow. You might want to skim over the chapter again.
- If you answered 0 or 1 question correctly, you can do more to improve your business IQ. Better study the chapter again.

Questions

1. What is accrual-basis accounting?
2. What is a deferral? Give an example of a deferred expense and an example of a deferred revenue.
3. What is an accrual? Give an example of an accrued expense and an example of accrued revenue.
4. Are revenues always recognized and realized in the same accounting period? Explain your answer.
5. What is the matching principle? To which category of accounts does this principle relate?
6. What is the purpose of adjusting entries, and when are they recorded?
7. What is interest? How is interest calculated?
8. What is the relationship between liabilities and expenses? What is the relationship between assets and revenues?
9. What is depreciation?
10. What is the purpose of closing entries and when are they recorded?
11. What type of account is Dividends? Is this account closed at the end of the period?
12. What is the debt-to-total-assets ratio and what does it measure?
13. Which accounts will appear on a post-closing trial balance?
14. If a business purchases a piece of equipment to be used in the operations of the business sometime in the future but has not begun to use it yet, will the business recognize depreciation expense in the current accounting period for this asset? Explain your answer.
15. What are real accounts? What are temporary accounts? Give examples of both.
16. What does it mean to close the books?
17. Which accounts in the general ledger will not have beginning balances at the start of an accounting period? Why is this?
18. Give an example of a control to help ensure completeness in recording transactions.

Multiple Choice

1. If Errands Etc. receives a $500 payment for future services, what does the firm record?
   a. $500 increase in Cash only
   b. $500 increase in Cash and a $500 decrease in Revenue
   c. Nothing until the firm actually pays the bill
   d. $500 increase to Cash and a $500 increase in a short-term liability.
2. On January 1, 2007, Thirty Plus Company paid $2,400 for an insurance policy that covers the 2007 calendar year. How much insurance expense will the firm show on its first-quarter income statement on March 31?
   a. $400
   b. $1,200
   c. $600
   d. $2,400
3. On May 15, Hodges Design received a $350 payment from customer for services the firm provided during the prior accounting period. How will this payment affect net income for May?
   a. Net income will increase by $350
   b. Net income will increase by $175

c. Income will decrease by $350
d. There will be no effect on net income.

4. The carrying (book) value of an asset is
   a. An account with a credit balance that offsets an asset account on the balance sheet
   b. The original cost of an asset minus the accumulated depreciation
   c. The original cost of an asset
   d. Equivalent to accumulated depreciation.

5. Receiving a payment for a credit sale made in a previous accounting period will
   a. Decrease assets and decrease owner's equity
   b. Increase assets and increase liabilities
   c. Have no net effect on total assets
   d. Increase revenues and increase assets

6. When a company pays cash in June to a vendor for goods purchased in May, the company should
   a. Debit Cash and credit Inventory
   b. Debit Accounts Payable and credit Cash
   c. Credit Accounts Receivable and debit Cash
   d. Credit Accounts Payable and debit Inventory

7. Z Company's accountant forgot to make an adjusting entry at the end of the year to record depreciation expense on the equipment. What effect did this omission have on the company's financial statements?
   a. Understated assets and liabilities
   b. Overstated assets and shareholders' equity
   c. Understated liabilities and overstated shareholders' equity
   d. Overstated assets and understated shareholders' equity

8. Phillip's Camera Store had a Retained Earnings balance of $1,000 on January 1, 2008. For year 2008, sales were $10,500 and expenses were $6,500. Cash dividends of $2,500 were distributed on December 31, 2008. What was the amount of Retained Earnings on December 31, 2008?
   a. $4,000
   b. $1,500
   c. $2,500
   d. $1,500

9. When prepaid insurance has been used, the following adjusting entry will be necessary:
   a. Debit to Insurance Expense, credit to Cash
   b. Debit to Prepaid Insurance, credit to Insurance Expense
   c. Debit to Insurance Expense, debit to Prepaid Insurance
   d. Debit to Insurance Expense, credit to Prepaid Insurance

10. Closing revenue accounts will include
    a. A credit to the revenue accounts
    b. A credit to the expense accounts
    c. A debit to Retained Earnings
    d. A credit to Retained Earnings

11. Closing expense accounts will include
    a. A debit to the revenue accounts
    b. A debit to the expense accounts
    c. A debit to Retained Earnings
    d. A credit to Retained Earnings

12. Closing the Dividends account will
    a. Increase Retained Earnings
    b. Decrease Retained Earnings
    c. Increase net income
    d. Decrease net income

13. Which of the following is a temporary account?
    a. Prepaid Expenses
    b. Accrued Liabilities
    c. Accumulated Depreciation
    d. Depreciation Expense

Short Exercises

SE4-1. Analyze effect of transactions on net income.   LO 1

The following transactions occurred during a recent accounting period. For each, tell whether it (1) increases net income, (2) decreases net income, or (3) does not affect net income.

a. Issued stock for cash.
b. Borrowed money from bank.
c. Provided services to customers on credit.
d. Paid rent in advance.
e. Used some of the supplies.
f. Paid salaries to employees for work done this year.

SE4-2. Calculate net income and retained earnings.   LO 1.4

Capboy Company earned $5,000 of revenues and incurred $2,950 worth of expenses during the period. Capboy also paid dividends of $500 to its shareholders. What was net income for the period? Assuming this is the first year of operations for Capboy, what is the ending balance in Retained Earnings for the period?

LO 2

SE4-3. **Account for interest expense.**

UMC Company purchased equipment on November 1, 2008, and gave a three-month, 9% note with a face value of $10,000. How much interest expense will be recognized on the income statement for the year ending December 31, 2008? What effect does this adjustment have on the statement of cash flows for 2008? Is this adjustment an accrual or deferral?

LO 2, 3

SE4-4. **Account for supplies expense.**

MBI Corporation started the month with $600 worth of supplies on hand. During the month, the company purchased an additional $760 worth of supplies. At the end of the month, $390 worth of supplies was left on hand. What amount would MBI Corporation show as Supplies Expense on its income statement for the month? Is this adjustment an accrual or deferral?

LO 2, 3

SE4-5. **Account for insurance expense.**

Bovina Company was started on January 1, 2005. During its first week of business, the company paid $3,600 for 18 months of fire insurance with an effective date of January 1. When Bovina Company prepares its income statement for the period ending December 31, 2005, how much prepaid insurance will be shown on the balance sheet, and how much insurance expense will be shown on the income statement? Is this adjustment an accrual or deferral?

LO 2, 3

SE4-6. **Account for depreciation expense.**

Suppose a company purchases a piece of equipment for $9,000 at the beginning of the year. The equipment will be depreciated at $3,000 per year. What is the book value of the equipment at the end of the first year? What is the book value of the equipment at the end of the second year?

LO 2, 3

SE4-7. **Account for insurance expense.**

The correct amount of prepaid insurance shown on a company's December 31, 2007, balance sheet was $800. On July 1, 2008, the company paid an additional insurance premium of $400. On the December 31, 2008, balance sheet, the amount of prepaid insurance was correctly shown as $500. What amount of insurance expense should appear on the company's 2008 income statement? Is this adjustment an accrual or deferral?

LO 2, 3

SE4-8. **Account for unearned revenue.**

Able Company received $4,800 from a customer on April 1 for services to be provided in the coming year, in an equal amount for the 12 months beginning April. In the Able information system, these cash receipts are recorded as Unearned Revenue. What adjustment will Able have to make when preparing the December 31 financial statements? Prepare the journal entry for the adjustment. What is the impact on the financial statements if the necessary adjustment is not made? Is this adjustment an accrual or deferral?

LO 2, 3

SE4-9. **Account for supplies expense.**

Peter's Pizza started the month with $500 worth of cleaning supplies. During the month, Peter's Pizza purchased an additional $300 worth of supplies. At the end of the month, $175 worth of supplies remained unused. Give the amounts that would appear on the financial statements for the month for supplies expense and supplies-on-hand. Is this adjustment an accrual or deferral?

LO 2, 3, 4

SE4-10. **Identify accounts.**

From the following list of accounts: (1) identify the assets or liabilities that commonly require an adjusting entry at the end of the accounting period, (2) indicate whether it relates to a deferral or accrual, and (3) tell which accounts should be closed at year-end.

Cash	Common Stock
Accounts Receivable	Retained Earnings
Prepaid Insurance	Sales Revenue
Supplies	Interest Revenue
Building	Depreciation Expense
Accumulated Depreciation—Building	Insurance Expense
Unearned Revenue	Supplies Expense
Interest Payable	Utilities Expense
Salaries Payable	Rent Expense

SE4-11. Account for unearned revenue.
LO 1.2

On January 1, 2006, the law firm of Munns and Munns was formed. On February 1, 2006, the company was paid $18,000 in advance for services to be performed monthly during the next 18 months. During the year, the firm incurred and paid expenses of $5,000. Is the adjustment for the services related to an accrual or a deferral? Assuming that these were the only transactions completed in 2006, prepare the firm's income statement, statement of cash flows, statement of retained earnings, and balance sheet for 2006.

SE4-12. Calculate net income.
LO 1

Suppose a company had the following accounts and balances at year-end:

Service Revenue	$7,400
Interest Revenue	2,200
Unearned Revenue	3,250
Operating Expenses	5,450
Prepaid Rent	1,030

Calculate net income by preparing the income statement for the year.

SE4-13. Calculate net income and prepare closing entries.
LO 4

Suppose a company had the following accounts and balances at year-end:

Service Revenue	$5,400
Interest Revenue	1,200
Rent Expense	1,240
Other Operating Expenses	3,050
Dividends	1,000

Calculate net income by preparing the income for the year. Then, give the closing entries necessary at year-end.

SE4-14. Debt-to-total-assets ratio.
LO 5

Suppose that a firm's debt-to-total-assets ratio started the year at 0.80. At the end of the year, the ratio is 0.60. Do you think this is a positive or negative change? What could have caused the decrease?

SE4-15. Identify internal controls.
LO 6

You have been hired to assess the internal controls of Brown's Brick Company. To your dismay, the firm has a very poor system of internal controls. Write a memo to Pat Brown, the chief executive officer, explaining the types of controls the firm needs to ensure accurate and complete financial reporting.

Exercise Set A

E4-1A. Account for salaries expense.
LO 2.3

Royal Company pays all salaried employees biweekly. Overtime pay, however, is paid in the next biweekly period. Royal accrues salary expense only at its December 31 year-end. Information about salaries earned in December 2007 is as follows:

- Last payroll was paid on December 26, 2007, for the two-week period ended December 26, 2007.
- Overtime pay earned in the two-week period ended December 26, 2007 was $5,000.
- Remaining workdays in 2007 were December 29, 30, 31; no overtime was worked on these days.
- The regular biweekly salaries total $90,000.

Using a five-day workweek, what will Royal Company's balance sheet show as a salaries payable liability on December 31, 2007?

E4-2A. Account for unearned revenue.
LO 2.3

The TJ Company collects all service revenue in advance. The company showed a $12,500 liability on its December 31, 2006 balance sheet for Unearned Service Revenue. During 2007, customers paid $50,000 for future services and the income statement for the year ended December 31, 2007 reported Service Revenue of $52,700. What amount for the liability Unearned Service Revenue will appear on the balance sheet at December 31, 2007?

LO 2.3   **E4-3A. Account for interest expense.**
Sojourn Company purchased equipment on November 1, 2006, and gave a three-month, 9% note with a face value of $20,000. On maturity, the note plus interest will be paid to the bank. Fill in the blanks in the following chart:

	Interest Expense	Cash Paid for Interest
November 30, 2006	_____	_____
December 31, 2006	_____	_____
January 31, 2007	_____	_____

LO 2.3   **E4-4A. Account for insurance expense.**
Baker Company paid $3,600 on July 1, 2005, for a two-year insurance policy. It was recorded as Prepaid Insurance. Prepare the journal entry to record the necessary adjustment Baker will have to make to properly report expenses when preparing the December 31, 2005, financial statements. Show how the adjustment affects the accounting equation.

LO 2.3   **E4-5A. Account for rent expense.**
Susan rented office space for her new business on March 1, 2008. To receive a discount, she paid $3,600 for 12 months rent in advance. How will this advance payment appear on the financial statements prepared at year-end, December 31? Assume no additional rent was paid in 2009. Use the following chart for your answers:

	Rent Expense for the Year	Prepaid Rent at December 31
2008	_____	_____
2009	_____	_____

LO 2.3   **E4-6A. Account for unearned revenue.**
In November and December 2009, Uncle's Company, a newly organized magazine publisher, received $72,000 for 1,000 three-year (36-month) subscriptions to a new monthly magazine at $24 per year, starting with the first issue in March 2010. Fill in the following chart for each of the given years to show the amount of revenue to be recognized on the income statement and the related liability reported on the balance sheet. Uncle's Company's fiscal year-end is December 31.

	Revenue Recognized	Unearned Revenue at December 31
2009	_____	_____
2010	_____	_____
2011	_____	_____
2012	_____	_____

LO 2.3   **E4-7A. Account for insurance expense.**
Yodel & Company paid $3,600 on June 1, 2008 for a two-year insurance policy beginning on that date. The company recorded the entire amount as prepaid insurance. By using the following chart, calculate how much expense and prepaid insurance will be reported on the year-end financial statements. The company's fiscal year ends December 31.

	Insurance Expense	Prepaid Insurance at December 31
2008	_____	_____
2009	_____	_____
2010	_____	_____

LO 2.3   **E4-8A. Account for depreciation expense.**
Thomas Toy Company purchased a new delivery truck on January 1, 2006 for $24,000. The truck's depreciation expense is estimated to be $4,000 per year. The company's fiscal year ends on December 31.

1. How much depreciation expense will be shown on the income statement for the year ending December 31, 2008?
2. hat is the book value (also called carrying value) of the truck on the balance sheet for each of the six years beginning with December 31, 2006?

E4-9A. Analyze timing of revenue recognition.   <u>LO 1</u>

Give the journal entry for each of the following transactions. Then, tell whether or not the transaction is one that results in the recognition of revenue or expenses.

a. Dell paid its computer service technicians $80,000 in salaries for the month ended January 31.

b. Shell Oil used $5,000 worth of electricity in its headquarters building during March. Shell received the bill, but will not pay the bill until sometime in April.

c. In 2007, Chico's had $22 million in catalogue sales. Assume all sales were recorded as credit sales.

d. Home Depot collected $59 million in interest and investment revenue during 2007.

E4-10A. Account for rent expense.   <u>LO 2, 3</u>

BNP Company started the year with $3,000 of prepaid rent, $15,000 of cash, and $18,000 of common stock. During the year, BNP paid additional rent in advance amounting to $10,000. The rent expense for the year was $12,000. Give the journal entry for the rent payment and the adjusting journal entry to record the rent expense. Then, post the transactions to T-Accounts. What was the balance in Prepaid Rent on the year-end balance sheet?

E4-11A. Account for insurance expense.   <u>LO 2, 3</u>

Precore Company began the year with $6,500 of prepaid insurance. During the year, Precore pre-paid additional insurance premiums amounting to $8,000. The company's insurance expense for the year was $10,000. Set up T-accounts for Prepaid Insurance and Insurance Expense and show how this information would be reflected in those accounts. What is the balance in Prepaid Insurance at year-end?

E4-12A. Account for rent expense and prepare financial statements.   <u>LO 1, 2, 3</u>

On March 1, 2005, Quality Consulting was formed when the owners contributed $35,000 cash to the business in exchange for common stock. On April 1, 2005, the company paid $24,000 cash to rent office space for the coming year. The consulting services generated $62,000 of cash revenue during 2005. Based on this information alone, record all necessary journal entries for the year. Prepare an income statement, statement of changes in shareholders' equity, and statement of cash flows for the year ended December 31, 2005, and a balance sheet at December 31, 2005.

E4-13A. Account for depreciation expense.   <u>LO 1, 2, 3</u>

Southeast Pest Control was started when its owners invested $20,000 in the business in exchange for common stock on January 1, 2006. The cash received by the company was immediately used to purchase a $15,000 heavy-duty chemical truck, which will be depreciated by $3,000 per year. The company earned $13,000 of cash revenue during 2006. Based on this information alone, record all necessary journal entries for the year. Prepare an income statement, statement of changes in shareholders' equity and statement of cash flows for the year ended December 31, 2006, and a balance sheet at December 31, 2006.

E4-14A. Classify accounts.   <u>LO 2, 3, 4</u>

Tell whether each of the following items would appear on the income statement, statement of changes in shareholders' equity, balance sheet, or statement of cash flows. Some items may appear on more than one statement. When applicable tell whether the item is a permanent account or a temporary account.

Interest Receivable	Accounts Payable
Salary Expense	Common Stock
Notes Receivable	Dividends
Unearned Revenue	Total Assets
Cash Flow From Investing Activities	Net Income
Insurance Expense	Consulting Revenue
Retained Earnings	Depreciation Expense
Prepaid Insurance	Supplies Expense
Cash	Salaries Payable
Accumulated Depreciation	Supplies
Prepaid Rent	Cash Flow From Financing Activities
Accounts Receivable	Land
Total Shareholders' Equity	Cash Flow From Operating Activities

LO 1, 2, 3   **E4-15A. Analyze business transactions from journal entries.**

Analyze the following journal entries for Starwood Yacht Repair Corporation and explain the transaction or event that resulted in each entry.

	Description	Debit	Credit
a.	Cash	150,000	
	Common Stock		150,000
b.	Land	25,000	
	Cash		25,000
c.	Building	125,000	
	Cash		125,000
d.	Cash	100,000	
	Long-term Note Payable		100,000
e.	Supplies	500	
	Cash		500
f.	Prepaid Insurance	650	
	Cash		650
g.	Cash	15,000	
	Service Revenue		15,000
h.	Supplies Expense	375	
	Supplies		375
i.	Insurance Expense	325	
	Prepaid Insurance		325
j.	Salaries Expense	500	
	Salaries Payable		500
k.	Depreciation Expense	1,000	
	Accumulated Depreciation—Building		1,000
l.	Interest Expense	100	
	Interest Payable		100

LO 3, 4   **E4-16A. Prepare financial statements and closing entries.**

Refer to E4-15A. Assume all beginning balances are zero. Prepare the four financial statements for the period ended December 31, 2009. Then, prepare the closing entries. (*Hint:* Post the entries to T-accounts to determine the individual account balances.)

LO 6   **E4-17A. Internal controls.**

Suppose the accounting clerk for Bed Bath & Beyond was preparing invoices for the company's business customers and made an error on one of them. Rather than keep the ruined invoice, #1459, she simply threw it away and prepared a new one (#1460). What problem could this create?

Exercise Set B

Your professor may ask you to complete selected "Group B" exercises and problems using Prentice Hall Grade Assist (**PHGA**). PHGA is an online tool that can help you master the chapter's topics by providing multiple variations of exercises and problems. You can rework these exercises and problems—each time with new data—as many times as you need, with immediate feedback and grading.

E4-1B. Account for salaries expense.   LO 2, 3

Jack's Finance & Budget Consulting pays all salaried employees monthly on the first Monday following the end of the month. Overtime, however, is recorded as compensatory (comp) time for all employees. The firm allows employees to exchange all comp time not used during the year for pay on June 30 and pays it on July 15. The firm accrues salary expense only at its June 30 year-end. Information about salaries earned in June 2008 is as follows:

- Last payroll was paid on June 2, 2008, for the month ended May 31, 2008.
- Comp pay exchanged at year-end totals $150,000.
- The regular yearly salaries total $1,500,000.

Using a 12-month fiscal work year, what will Jack's Finance & Budget Consulting Inc. balance sheet show as Salaries Payable liability on June 30, 2008?

E4-2B. Account for unearned revenue.   LO 2, 3

The Joe & Einstein Cable Company collects all service revenue in advance. Joe & Einstein showed a $16,825 liability on its June 30, 2008, balance sheet for unearned service revenue. During the following fiscal year, customers paid $85,000 for future services, and the income statement for the year ended June 30, 2009, reported service revenue of $75,850 after adjustments. What amount for the liability Unearned Service Revenue will appear on the balance sheet at June 30, 2009?

E4-3B. Account for interest expense.   LO 2, 3

The Judie Voich Pet Grooming Company purchased a computer on December 30, 2007, and gave a four-month, 7% note with a face value of $6,000. On maturity, the note plus interest will be paid to the bank. Fill in the blanks in the following chart:

	Interest Expense	Cash Paid for Interest
January 31, 2008	_____	_____
February 29, 2008	_____	_____
March 31, 2008	_____	_____
April 31, 2008	_____	_____

E4-4B. Account for insurance expense.   LO 2, 3

More & Blue Painting Professionals paid $6,300 on February 1, 2006, for a three-year insurance policy. In the More & Blue information system, this was recorded as Prepaid Insurance. Prepare the journal entry to record the necessary adjustment More & Blue will have to make to properly report expenses when preparing the June 30, 2006, financial statements. Show how the adjustment affects the accounting equation.

E4-5B. Account for rent expense.   LO 2, 3

Utopia Dance Clubs rented an old warehouse for its newest club on October 1, 2006. To receive a discount, Utopia paid $2,970 for 18 months rent in advance. How will this advance payment appear on the financial statements prepared at year-end, December 31? Assume no additional rent is paid in 2007 and 2008. Use the following chart for your answers:

	Rent Expense for the Year	Prepaid Rent at December 31
2006	_____	_____
2007	_____	_____
2008	_____	_____

E4-6B. Account for unearned revenue.   LO 2, 3

In May and June 2010, Lynn Haven Gazette, a newly organized newspaper publisher, received $12,000 for 500 two-year (24-months) subscriptions to a new monthly community events newspaper at $12 per year, starting with the first issue in September 2010. Fill in the following chart for each of the given years to show the amount of revenue to be recognized on the income statement and the related liability reported on the balance sheet. Lynn Haven Gazette's fiscal year-end is June 30.

	Revenue Recognized	Unearned Revenue at June 30
2010	_____	_____
2011	_____	_____
2012	_____	_____

LO 2, 3   **E4-7B. Account for insurance expense.**

All Natural Medicine Corporation paid $2,178 on August 1, 2009, for an 18-month insurance policy beginning on that date. The company recorded the entire amount as Prepaid Insurance. By using the following chart, calculate how much expense and prepaid insurance will be reported on the year-end financial statements. The company's year-end is December 31.

	Insurance Expense	**Prepaid insurance at December 31**
2009	_____	_____
2010	_____	_____
2011	_____	_____

LO 2, 3   **E4-8B. Account for depreciation expense.**

E. Hutson Pastries purchased a new delivery van on July 1, 2007, for $35,000. The van's depreciation is estimated at $7,000 per year. The company has a fiscal year-end of June 30.

1. How much depreciation expense will be shown on the income statement for the year ending June 30, 2010?
2. What is the book value (also called carrying value) of the truck on the balance sheet for each of the five years beginning with June 30, 2008?

LO 1   **E4-9B. Analyze timing of revenue recognition.**

For each of the following transactions, give the journal entry. Then, tell whether or not the transaction is one that results in the recognition of revenue or expenses.

a. On April 15, Mike's Pressure Cleaning Services paid its employees $3,000 in salaries for services provided during the first two weeks of April.
b. Mister Hsieh Fencing Company used $1,000 worth of radio advertising during April. Mister received the bill, but it will not pay the bill until sometime in May.
c. During 2007, Tootie's Pet Training School earned $125,000 in service revenues. Assume all services were offered on account.
d. Susan's Investment Company collected $130,000 in interest and investment revenue earned during 2008.

LO 2, 3   **E4-10B. Account for rent expense.**

Florida's Number One Credit Solution Organization started the year with $1,850 of prepaid rent, $25,000 cash, and $26,850 of retained earnings. During the year, Florida paid additional rent in advance amounting to $16,275. The rent expense for the year was $16,850. Give the journal entry for the rent payment and the adjusting journal entry to record the rent expense. Then, post the transactions to T-accounts. What was the balance in Prepaid Rent on the year-end balance sheet?

LO 2, 3   **E4-11B. Account for insurance expense.**

J.B. Eriksen's Construction Company began the year with $18,500 prepaid insurance. During the year, J.B. Eriksen prepaid additional insurance premiums amounting to $96,000. The company's insurance expense for the year was $104,500. Set up T-accounts for Prepaid Insurance and Insurance Expense and show how this information would be reflected in those accounts. What is the balance in Prepaid Insurance at year-end?

LO 1, 2, 3   **E4-12B. Account for rent expense, insurance expense, and prepare financial statements.**

On February 1, 2010, Breeder's Choice Pet Trainers was formed when the owners invested $25,626 cash in the business in exchange for common stock. On March 1, 2010, the company paid $22,212 cash to rent office space for the next 18 months and paid $3,414 cash for 6 months of prepaid insurance. The training services generated $115,725 of cash revenue during the remainder of the year. Based on this information alone, record all necessary journal entries for the year. Prepare an income statement, a statement of changes in shareholders' equity, and a statement of cash flows for the year ended June 30, 2010, and a balance sheet at June 30, 2010.

LO 1, 2, 3   **E4-13B. Account for depreciation expense and prepare financial statements.**

Northeast Termite Specialists was started when its owners invested $32,685 in the business in exchange for common stock on July 1, 2010. Part of the cash received to start the company was immediately used to purchase a $17,000 high-pressure chemical sprayer, which is being depreciated at $1,700 per year. The company earned $68,315 of cash revenue during the year and had cash operating expenses of $27,205, excluding depreciation. Based on this information alone, record all necessary journal entries for the year. Prepare an income statement, a statement of changes in shareholders' equity, and a statement of cash flows for the year ended June 30, 2011, and a balance sheet at June 30, 2011.

E4-14B. Identify accounts.   LO 2, 3, 4

From the following list of accounts: (1) identify the assets or liabilities that may require an adjusting entry at the end of the accounting period, (2) indicate whether it relates to a deferral or accrual, and (3) tell which accounts are permanent accounts and which are temporary accounts.

Cash	Common Stock
Accounts Receivable	Retained Earnings
Prepaid Insurance	Sales Revenue
Prepaid Rent	Interest Revenue
Supplies	Equipment
Depreciation Expense	Accumulated Depreciation—Equipment
Insurance Expense	Unearned Revenue
Supplies Expense	Interest Payable
Utilities Expense	Salaries Payable
Rent Expense	Accounts Payable
Interest Receivable	Other Operating Expense

E4-15B. Analyze business transactions from journal entries.   LO 1, 2, 3

Analyze the following journal entries for Information Resource Services and explain the transaction or event that resulted in each entry.

Description	Debit	Credit
a. Cash	115,000	
Common Stock		115,000
b. Computer	7,500	
Cash		7,500
c. Land	105,000	
Cash		105,000
d. Cash	85,000	
Long-term Note Payable		85,000
e. Supplies	1,000	
Cash		1,000
f. Prepaid Rent	825	
Cash		825
g. Cash	13,150	
Service Revenue		13,150
h. Supplies Expense	615	
Supplies		615
i. Rent Expense	275	
Prepaid Rent		275
j. Salaries Expense	795	
Salaries Payable		795
k. Depreciation Expense	1,500	
Accumulated Depreciation—Computer		1,500
l. Interest Expense	50	
Interest Payable		50

LO 3, 4   **E4-16B. Prepare financial statements and closing entries.**
Refer to E4-15B. Assume all beginning balances are zero. Prepare the four financial
statements for the period ending June 30, 2007. Then, prepare the closing entries.
(*Hint:* Post the entries to T-accounts to determine the individual account balances.)

LO 6   **E4-17B. Analyze internal controls.**
Prism Steel Company has just started business. When the company receives an order,
usually over the phone, the sales clerk records it on a prenumbered form. What is the
purpose of using a prenumbered form for this? Explain.

Problem Set A

LO 2, 3   **P4-1A. Record adjusting entries and prepare income
statement.**
Selected amounts (at December 31, 2007) from Soul Tan, Polish & Refine's information
system appear as follows:

1. Long-term Notes Payable	$ 500,000
2. Cash	150,000
3. Common Stock	60,000
4. Equipment	840,000
5. Prepaid Insurance	30,000
6. Inventory	250,000
7. Prepaid Rent	140,000
8. Retained Earnings	130,000
9. Salaries and Wages Expense	328,000
10. Service Revenue	2,000,000

Required

a. There are five adjustments that need to be made before the financial statements
can be prepared at year-end. Give the journal entry for each.
   1. The equipment, purchased on January 1, 2007, is being depreciated at $70,000
   per year.
   2. Interest accrued on the notes payable is $1,000 as of December 31, 2007.
   3. Unexpired insurance at December 31, 2007, is $7,000.
   4. The rent payment of $140,000 covered the four months from December 1,
   2007, through March 31, 2008.
   5. Salaries and wages of $28,000 were earned by employees but unpaid at
   December 31, 2007.
b. Prepare an income statement for the year ended December 31, 2007, for Soul Tan,
Polish & Refine.

LO 2, 3   **P4-2A. Record adjusting entries and calculate net income.**
The records of RCA Company revealed the following recorded amounts at December
31, 2006, before adjustments:

Prepaid Insurance	$ 1,800
Cleaning Supplies	2,800
Unearned Service Fees	3,000
Notes Payable	5,000
Service Fees	96,000
Wages Expense	75,000
Truck Rent Expense	3,900
Truck Fuel Expense	1,100
Insurance Expense	0
Supplies Expense	0
Interest Expense	0
Interest Payable	0
Wages Payable	0
Prepaid Rent—Truck	0

Before RCA prepares the financial statements for the business, adjustments must be
made for the following items:

1. The prepaid insurance represents an 18-month policy purchased early in January.
2. A physical count on December 31 revealed $500 of cleaning supplies still on hand.
3. On December 1, a customer paid for three months of service in advance.

4. The truck rent is $300 per month in advance. January 2007 rent was paid late in December.
5. The bank loan was taken out October 1. The interest rate is 12% (1% per month) for one year.
6. On Wednesday, December 31, the company owed its employees for working three days. The normal workweek is five days with wages of $1,500 paid at the end of the week.

Required

a. Prepare the journal entries to record the adjustments for given items 1 through 6.
b. Prepare an income statement for the year ended December 31, 2006, for RCA Company.

P4-3A. Account for depreciable assets.

Charlotte & Gary Motorcycle Repair Corporation purchased a machine on January 1, 2008, for $8,000 and is depreciating it at a rate of $2,000 per year.

Required

a. Give the journal entries to record the purchase of the machine and the first year's depreciation.
b. Show how the machine will be presented in the asset section of the balance sheet at December 31, 2008, and December 31, 2009, after appropriate adjustments.
c. What amount of depreciation expense will be shown on the income statement for 2008? What amount will be shown for 2009?
d. Set up T-accounts for the machine and its accumulated depreciation account. Post the entries to the T-accounts for four years of the asset's life. What do you notice about the book value of the asset at the end of four years?

LO 2

P4-4A. Record adjusting entries.

The following is a partial list of financial statement items from the records of Marshall's Company at December 31, 2008.

Prepaid Insurance	$12,750
Prepaid Rent	18,000
Interest Receivable	0
Salaries Payable	0
Unearned Fees	30,000
Interest Income	10,000

Additional information includes the following:

1. The insurance policy indicates that on December 31, 2008, only 5 months remain on the 24-month policy that originally cost $18,000.
2. Marshall's has a note receivable with $2,500 of interest due from a customer on January 1, 2009.
3. The accounting records show that one-third of the fees paid in advance by a customer on July 1, 2008, has now been earned.
4. The company purchased $18,000 of prepaid rent for 9 months on August 1, 2008.
5. At year-end, Marshall's owed $7,000 worth of salaries to employees for work done in December 2008. The next payday is January 5, 2009.

Required

a. Prepare the adjusting entries that must be made prior to the preparation of the financial statements for the year ended December 31, 2008.
b. Open T-accounts for the relevant accounts and post the journal entries to each account.
c. For the accounts used in the problem, calculate the balances that would be shown on Marshall's financial statements for the year ended December 31, 2008.

LO 2, 3

P4-5A. Record adjusting entries.

The following is a list of financial statement items from Sugar & Spice Cookie Company as of December 31, 2007:

Prepaid Insurance	$ 6,000
Prepaid Rent Expense	10,000
Wages Expense	25,000
Unearned Subscription Fees	70,000
Interest Expense	38,000

LO 2, 3

Additional information:

1. The company paid a $7,200 premium on a three-year business insurance policy on July 1, 2006.
2. Sugar & Spice borrowed $200,000 on January 2, 2007, and must pay 11% interest on January 2, 2008, for the entire year of 2007.
3. The books show that $60,000 of the unearned subscription revenue has now been earned.
4. The company paid 10 months of rent in advance on November 1, 2007.
5. Wages for December 31 of $2,000 will be paid to employees on January 3, 2008.

Required

a. Prepare the adjusting entries that must be made prior to the preparation of the financial statements for the year ended December 31, 2007.
b. Open T-accounts for the relevant accounts and post the journal entries to each account.
c. Calculate the account balances that would appear on the financial statements.

LO 2   **P4-6A. Record adjusting entries.**

The Fruit Packing Company has the following account balances at the end of the year:

Prepaid Insurance	$8,000
Unearned Revenue	4,200
Wages Expense	6,790
Taxes Payable	4,168
Interest Revenue	2,475

The company also has the following information available at the end of the year:

1. Of the prepaid insurance, $3,000 has now expired.
2. Of the unearned revenue, $2,000 has been earned.
3. The company must accrue an additional $1,500 of wages expense.
4. The company has earned an additional $500 of interest revenue, not yet received.

Required

a. Open T-accounts for each of the accounts shown above.
b. Post the required adjustments directly to the T-accounts.
c. Calculate the balances in each account after the adjustments.
d. Indicate whether each adjustment is an accrual or deferral.

LO 2, 3, 4   **P4-7A. Record adjusting entries and prepare financial statements.**

The accounting records for Sony Snowboard Company, a snowboard repair company, contained the following balances as of December 31, 2006:

Assets		Liabilities and Equity	
Cash	$40,000	Accounts Payable	$17,000
Accounts Receivable	16,500	Common Stock	45,000
Land	20,000	Retained Earnings	14,500
Totals	$76,500		$76,500

The following accounting events apply to Sony's 2007 fiscal year:

a.	Jan. 1	The company acquired an additional $20,000 cash from the owners in exchange for common stock.
b.	Jan. 1	Sony purchased a computer that cost $15,000 for cash. The computer will be depreciated by $5,000 per year.
c.	Mar. 1	The company borrowed $10,000 by issuing a one-year note at 12%.
d.	May 1	The company paid $2,400 cash in advance for a one-year lease for office space.
e.	June 1	The company paid dividends to the owners of $4,000 cash.
f.	July 1	The company purchased land that cost $17,000 cash.
g.	Aug. 1	Cash payments on accounts payable amounted to $6,000.
h.	Aug. 1	Sony received $9,600 cash in advance for 12 months of service to be performed monthly for the next year, beginning on receipt of payment.
i.	Sept. 1	Sony sold a parcel of land for $13,000, the amount the firm originally paid for it.
j.	Oct. 1	Sony purchased $795 of supplies on account.

k. Nov. 1   Sony purchased short-term investments for $18,000. The investments pay
            a fixed rate of 6%.
l. Dec. 31 The company earned service revenue on account during the year that
            amounted to $40,000.
m. Dec. 31 Cash collections from accounts receivable amounted to $44,000.
n. Dec. 31 The company incurred other operating expenses on account during the
            year of $5,450.

The following additional information is available at December 31:

1. Salaries that had been earned by the sales staff but not yet paid amounted to $2,300.
2. Supplies worth $180 were on hand at the end of the period.

Based on the preceding transaction data, there are five additional adjustments that
need to be made before the financial statements can be prepared.

Required

a. Open T-accounts and record the account balances as of December 31, 2006.
b. Prepare the journal entries to record the transactions that occurred during
   2007 and the necessary adjusting entries at year-end. (Land is not
   depreciated.)
c. Post the journal entries to the T-accounts. (*Hint:* some new accounts must be
   opened.)
d. Prepare all four financial statements for the year ended December 31, 2007.
e. Prepare the closing entries.

P4-8A. Record adjusting entries and prepare financial statements.

LO 2, 3, 4

Here are transactions for Pops Company for 2007:

1. The owners started the business as a corporation by contributing $30,000 cash in
   exchange for common stock.
2. The company purchased office equipment for $8,000 cash and land for $15,000
   cash. Depreciation on the office equipment is estimated at $1,000 per year. (Land
   is not depreciated.)
3. The company earned total revenue of $22,000 of which $16,000 was collected in cash.
4. The company purchased $890 worth of supplies for cash.
5. The company paid $6,000 in cash for other operating expenses.
6. At the end of the year, the company owed employees $2,480 for work that the
   employees had done in 2007. The next payday, however, is not until January 4, 2008.
7. Only $175 worth of supplies was left at the end of the year.

Required

a. Prepare the journal entries to record the transactions that occurred during 2007.
b. Post the journal entries to the T-accounts.
c. Post any needed adjusting entries to the T-accounts.
d. Prepare all four financial statements for the year ended December 31, 2007.
e. Prepare the closing entries.

P4-9A. Record adjusting entries and prepare financial statements.

LO 2, 3, 4

On June 1, Joel Adams started a computer business as a corporation. Joel started the
business by contributing $25,000 in exchange for common stock. He paid two months
of rent in advance, totaling $500. On June 3, Joel purchased supplies for $600 and two
computers at a total cost of $6,500. Joel estimates depreciation for the computers will
total $2,167 per year. Joel hired an office assistant, agreeing to pay the assistant $800
per month to be paid $400 on June 15 and June 30. On June 27, Joel paid $300 for a
radio advertisement to announce the opening of the business. Joel earned revenue of
$4,200 in June of which he collected $2,800 in cash. At the end of the month, Joel had
only $130 worth of supplies on hand.

Required

a. Prepare the journal entries to record the transactions that occurred during the
   month of June and the adjusting entries that must be made prior to the
   preparation of the financial statements for the month ended June 30.
b. Post the journal entries to the T-accounts.
c. Prepare the four financial statements for Adams' company for the month ended
   June 30.
d. Prepare the closing entries.

LO 1, 2, 3, 4, 5   P4-10A. Record adjusting and closing entries and prepare financial statements.

Here is an unadjusted trial balance for Casa Bella Interiors and some additional data for the fiscal year ended May 31, 2006.

Casa Bella Interiors
Unadjusted Trial Balance
May 31, 2006

	DR	CR
Cash	$ 4,300	
Accounts Receivable	9,300	
Notes Receivable	1,000	
Interest Receivable	0	
Prepaid Rent	1,700	
Supplies	400	
Office Equipment	23,400	
Accumulated Depreciation—		
Office Equipment		$ 1,600
Accounts Payable		500
Salaries Payable		0
Interest Payable		0
Unearned Service Revenue		2,600
Long-term Notes Payable		8,400
Common Stock		5,000
Additional Paid-in Capital		2,300
Retained Earnings		5,000
Service Revenue		19,800
Salaries Expense	4,650	
Rent Expense		
Depreciation Expense		
Advertising Expense	450	
	$45,200	$45,200

Additional data:

1. Depreciation on the office equipment for the year is $500.
2. Salaries owed to employees at year-end, but not yet recorded or paid, total $750.
3. Prepaid rent that has expired at year-end amounts to $800.
4. Interest due at year-end on the notes receivable is $120.
5. Interest owed at year-end on the notes payable is $840.
6. Unearned service revenue that has actually been earned by year-end totals $1,500.

Required

a. Prepare T-accounts for Casa Bella, using the unadjusted trial balance, and post the adjusting entries to the T-accounts.
b. Then, prepare an adjusted trial balance.
c. Prepare an income statement and a balance sheet.
d. Prepare the closing entries.
e. Prepare a post-closing trial balance.

LO 1, 2, 3, 4   P4-11A. Analyze business transactions and prepare financial statements.

The accounting department for Setting Sun Vacation Rentals recorded the following journal entries for 2009, the first year of business. Setting Sun generates revenue by renting waterfront condominiums to vacationers in the area. When a reservation is made in advance, Setting Sun collects half the week's rent to hold the reservation. However, Setting Sun does not require reservations, and sometimes customers will come in to rent a unit the same day. These types of transactions require that Setting Sun's accounting department record some cash receipts as unearned revenues and others as earned revenues.

Description	Debit	Credit
a. Cash	50,000	
Common Stock		50,000
b. Office Supplies	300	
Accounts Payable		300
c. Prepaid insurance	12,000	
Cash		12,000
d. Building	225,000	
Long-term Note Payable		225,000
e. Cash	5,000	
Unearned Rent Revenue		5,000
f. Utility Expense	225	
Cash		225
g. Accounts Payable	300	
Cash		300
h. Cash	12,000	
Rent Revenue		12,000
i. Unearned Rent Revenue	3,000	
Rent Revenue		3,000
j. Supplies Expense	130	
Supplies		130
k. Insurance Expense	6,000	
Prepaid Insurance		6,000
l. Interest Expense	100	
Interest Payable		100
m. Depreciation Expense	1,500	
Accumulated Depreciation—Building		1,500
n. Dividends	5,000	
Cash		5,000
o. Salaries Expense	1,200	
Salaries Payable		1,200

Required

a. Explain the transaction or event that resulted in each journal entry.
b. Post entries *a* through *o* to T-accounts and calculate the balance in each account.
c. Did Setting Sun Vacation Rentals generate net income or net loss for the period ending December 31, 2009? How can you tell?
d. Prepare the four financial statements required at year-end.
e. Prepare the closing entries.

Problem Set B

Your professor may ask you to complete selected "Group B" exercises and problems using Prentice Hall Grade Assist (**PHGA**). PHGA is an online tool that can help you master the chapter's topics by providing multiple variations of exercises and problems. You can rework these exercises and problems—each time with new data—as many times as you need, with immediate feedback and grading.

LO 2, 3   **P4-1B. Record adjusting entries and prepare income statement.**

Selected amounts (at December 31, 2008) from Budget Planning Company's accounting records are shown below. No adjustments have been made.

1.	Long-term Notes Payable	$ 350,000
2.	Cash	250,000
3.	Common Stock	30,000
4.	Equipment	780,000
5.	Prepaid Insurance	140,000
6.	Inventory	175,000
7.	Prepaid Rent	120,000
8.	Retained Earnings	330,000
9.	Salaries and Wages Expense	428,000
10.	Service Revenue	3,000,000

Required

a. There are five adjustments that need to be made before the financial statements for the year ended December 31, 2008, can be prepared. Give the journal entry for each.
   1. The equipment (purchased on January 1, 2008) is being depreciated at a rate of $65,000 per year.
   2. Interest on the notes payable needs to be accrued for the year in the amount of $40,000.
   3. Unexpired insurance at December 31, 2008, is $40,000.
   4. The rent payment of $120,000 was made on June 1. The rent payment is for 12 months beginning on the date of payment.
   5. Salaries of $58,000 were earned but unpaid at December 31, 2008.
b. Prepare an income statement for the year ended December 31, 2008, for Budget Planning Company.

LO 2, 3   **P4-2B. Record adjusting entries and calculate net income.**

The records of Jimenez Electric Company showed the following amounts at December 31, 2007, before adjustments:

Prepaid Insurance	$ 1,500
Supplies	3,500
Unearned Service Fees	4,000
Notes Payable	30,000
Service Fees	106,000
Salaries Expense	65,000
Prepaid Rent	3,900
Insurance Expense	0
Supplies Expense	0
Rent Expense	0
Interest Expense	0
Interest Payable	0
Salaries Payable	0

Before Mr. Jimenez prepares the financial statements for his business, adjustments must be made for the following items:

1. The prepaid insurance is for a 12-month policy purchased on March 1 for cash. The policy is effective from March 1, 2007, to February 28, 2008.
2. A count of the supplies on December 31 revealed $400 worth still on hand.
3. One customer paid for 4 months of service in advance on December 1. By December 31, one month of the service had been performed.
4. The prepaid rent was for 10 months of rent for the company office building, beginning June 1.
5. The bank loan was taken out November 1. The interest rate is 12% (1% per month) for 1 year.
6. As of December 31, the company owed its employees $5,000 for work done in 2007. The next payday is not until January 2008.

Required

a. Set up T-accounts and post each of the transactions to them.
b. Prepare an income statement for the year ended December 31, 2007, for Jimenez Electric Company.

P4-3B. Account for depreciable assets.   LO 2

Super Clean Dry-cleaning purchased a new piece of office equipment on January 1, 2009, for $18,000. The company estimates the depreciation expense at $6,000 per year.

Required

a. Give the journal entries to record the purchase of the office equipment and the depreciation for the two years.
b. Prepare the asset section of the balance sheet at December 31, 2009 and December 31, 2010 after appropriate adjustments.
c. What amount of accumulated depreciation will be shown on the balance sheet at the end of 2009? What amount will be shown on the balance sheet at the end of 2010?
d. Set up T-accounts for the equipment and its Accumulated Depreciation account. Post the entries to the T-accounts for three years of the asset's life. What do you notice about the book value of the asset at the end of three years?

P4-4B. Record adjusting entries.   LO 2, 3

The following is a partial list of financial statement items from the records of Starnes Company at December 31, 2006.

Prepaid Rent	$20,000
Prepaid Insurance	12,000
Service Revenue	35,000
Wages Expense	8,000
Unearned Service Revenue	18,000
Interest Expense	5,000

Additional information includes the following:

1. The insurance policy indicates that on December 31, 2006, only 5 months remain on the 12-month policy that originally cost $12,000.
2. Starnes has a note payable with $2,500 of interest that must be paid on January 1, 2007.
3. The accounting records show that two-thirds of the service revenue paid in advance by a customer on March 1 has now been earned.
4. The company purchased $20,000 of prepaid rent for 10 months on August 1.
5. At year-end, Starnes Company owed $500 worth of salaries to employees for work done in December. The next payday is January 3, 2007.

Required

a. Prepare the adjusting entries that must be made prior to the preparation of the financial statements for the year ended December 31, 2006.
b. Open T-accounts for the relevant accounts and post the journal entries to each account. (If you need an account not listed, assume its beginning balance is zero.)
c. For the accounts used in this problem, calculate the balances that would be shown on Starnes financial statements for the year ended December 31, 2006.

P4-5B. Record adjusting entries.   LO 2, 3

The following is a list of financial statement items from Chunky Candy Company as of June 30, 2008. Chunky's fiscal year is from July 1 to June 30.

Prepaid Insurance	$ 3,600
Prepaid Rent	5,000
Wages Expense	12,000
Unearned Subscription Revenue	30,000
Interest Expense	0

Additional information:

1. The company paid a $3,600 premium on a three-year insurance policy on January 1, 2008.
2. Chunky borrowed $100,000 on July 1, 2007, with an interest rate of 11%. No interest has been paid as of June 30, 2008.
3. The books show that $10,000 of subscriptions have now been earned.
4. The company paid 10 months of rent in advance on March 1, 2008.
5. Wages for June 30 of $2,000 will be paid to employees on July 3.

Required

a. Prepare the adjusting journal entries that must be made prior to the preparation of the financial statements for the fiscal year ending June 30, 2008.
b. Open T-accounts for the relevant accounts and post the journal entries to the accounts.
c. For the accounts used in this problem, calculate the balances that would appear on the financial statements.

LO 2, 3   **P4-6B. Record adjusting entries.**

The Delphi Desk Company has the following amounts in its records at the end of the fiscal year:

Prepaid Insurance	$5,000
Unearned Rental Revenue	4,200
Wages Expense	6,790
Accounts Payable	4,168
Interest Income	2,475

The company also has the following information available at the end of the year:

1. Of the prepaid insurance, $1,000 has now expired.
2. Of the unearned rental revenue, $1,000 has been earned.
3. The company must accrue an additional $1,250 of wages expense.
4. A bill for $300 from the company that provides the desks that Delphi Desk Company sells arrived on the last day of the year. Nothing has been recorded or paid, related to this invoice.
5. The company has earned an additional $300 of interest revenue, not yet received.

Required

a. Open T-accounts for each of the accounts shown.
b. Post the required adjustments directly to the T-accounts.
c. Calculate the balances in each account after the adjustments.
d. Indicate whether each adjustment is an accrual or deferral.

LO 2, 3, 4   **P4-7B. Record adjusting entries and prepare financial statements.**

The accounting records for Beta Company contained the following balances as of December 31, 2008:

Assets		Liabilities and Shareholders' Equity	
Cash	$50,000	Accounts Payable	$17,500
Accounts Receivable	26,500		
Prepaid Rent	3,600	Common Stock	48,600
Land	10,500	Retained Earnings	24,500
Totals	$90,600		$90,600

The following accounting events apply to Beta's 2009 fiscal year:

a. Jan. 1   Beta purchased a computer that cost $18,000 for cash. Depreciation is $6,000 per year.
b. Mar. 1   The company borrowed $20,000 by issuing a two-year note at 12%.
c. May 1   The company paid $6,000 cash in advance for a six-month lease starting on July 1 for office space.
d. June 1   The company paid dividends of $2,000 to the owners.
e. July 1   The company purchased land that cost $15,000 cash.
f. Aug. 1   Cash payments on accounts payable amounted to $5,500.
g. Aug. 1   Beta received $13,200 cash in advance for 12 months of service to be performed monthly for the next year, beginning on receipt of payment.
h. Sept. 1   Beta sold a parcel of land for $13,000, the amount it originally paid for the land.
i. Oct. 1   Beta purchased $1,300 of supplies on account.
j. Nov. 1   Beta purchased short-term investments for $10,000. The investments earn 5% per year.
k. Dec. 31   The company earned service revenue on account during the year that amounted to $50,000.
l. Dec. 31   Cash collections from accounts receivable amounted to $46,000.
m. Dec. 31   The company incurred other operating expenses on account during the year that amounted to $5,850.

The following additional information is available at December 31:

1. Salaries that had been earned by the sales staff but not yet paid amounted to $2,300.
2. Supplies on hand at the end of the period totaled $200.
3. The beginning balance of $3,600 in Prepaid Rent was completely used up by the end of the year.

Based on the preceding transaction data, some additional adjustments need to be made before the financial statements can be prepared.

Required

a. Open T-accounts and record the account balances as of December 31, 2008.
b. Prepare the journal entries to record the transactions that occurred during 2009 and the necessary adjusting entries at year-end. (Land is not depreciated.)
c. Post the journal entries to the T-accounts. (*Hint:* some new accounts must be opened.)
d. Prepare all four financial statements for the year ended December 31, 2009.
e. Prepare the closing entries.

P4-8B. Record adjusting entries and prepare financial statements.

LO 2, 3, 4

Given the following transactions for Security Company for 2008:

1. The owners started the business as a corporation by contributing $50,000 cash in exchange for common stock.
2. Security Company purchased office equipment for $5,000 cash and land for $15,000 cash.
3. The company earned a total of $32,000 in revenue, of which $20,000 was collected in cash.
4. The company purchased $550 worth of supplies for cash.
5. The company paid $6,000 in cash for operating expenses.
6. At the end of the year, Security Company owed employees $3,600 for work that the employees had done in 2008. The next payday, however, is not until January 4, 2009.
7. Only $120 worth of supplies was left at the end of the year.
8. The depreciation expense on the office equipment is $1,000 per year.

Required

a. Prepare the journal entries to record the transactions that occurred during 2008.
b. Post the journal entries to the T-accounts.
c. Post any needed adjusting entries to the T-accounts.
d. Prepare all four financial statements for the year ended December 31, 2008.
e. Prepare closing entries.

P4-9B. Record adjusting entries and prepare financial statements.

LO 2, 3, 4

On September 1, 2008, Irene Shannon started Shannon Check Verification Services as a corporation. Irene started the business by contributing $37,000 in exchange for common stock. The new company paid four months of rent in advance totaling $1,200 and paid ten months of insurance in advance totaling $6,500. Both rent and insurance coverage began September 1. On September 6, the company purchased supplies for $800. Irene hired one employee to help her and agreed to pay the assistant $1,000 per month, paid on the last day of each month. Irene's company paid $200 on September 10 for a newspaper advertisement to announce the opening of the business. The company earned service revenue of $4,200 in September, of which $2,800 was cash. At the end of the month, the firm had only $100 worth of supplies on hand.

Required

a. Prepare the journal entries to record the transactions that occurred during the month of September and the adjusting entries that must be made prior to the preparation of the financial statements for the month ended September 30.
b. Post the journal entries to the T-accounts.
c. Prepare the four financial statements for Shannon Check Verification Services for the month ended September 30.

LO 1, 2, 3, 4, 5 **P4-10B. Prepare accruals, deferrals, financial statements, closing.**

Puppy Studs provides a stud service for serious dog breeders. The company's accountant prepared the following unadjusted trial balance at the end of its fiscal year, March 31:

Unadjusted Trial Balance

	DR	CR
Cash	$ 52,200	
Accounts Receivable	47,500	
Prepaid Insurance	20,000	
Prepaid Rent	1,800	
Supplies	10,350	
Equipment	137,500	
Accumulated Depreciation		$ 1,700
Accounts Payable		3,500
Unearned Service Revenue		3,000
Long-term Notes Payable		35,000
Common Stock		50,500
Additional Paid-in Capital		91,450
Retained Earnings		87,120
Dividends	5,320	
Service Revenue		226,850
Miscellaneous Operating Expenses	149,450	
Salaries Expense	75,000	
	$499,120	$499,120

Additional facts:

1. The company owes its employees $2,500 for work done in this fiscal year. The next payday is not until April.
2. $2,000 worth of the unearned service revenue has actually been earned at year-end.
3. The equipment is depreciated at the rate of $1,700 per year.
4. At year-end, $600 worth of prepaid rent and $15,000 of prepaid insurance remains unexpired.
5. Interest on the long-term note for a year at the rate of 6.5% is due on April 1.
6. Supplies on hand at the end of the year amounted to $2,100.
7. On the last day of the fiscal year, the firm earned $20,000. The customers paid $10,000 with cash and the remainder was on account. However, the accountant left early that day so the day's revenue did not get recorded in the general ledger.

Required

a. Set up T-accounts for Puppy Studs using the unadjusted trial balance. Then, record the necessary adjustments.
b. Then, prepare an adjusted trial balance.
c. Prepare an income statement and a balance sheet.
d. Prepare the closing entries.
e. Prepare a post-closing trial balance.

LO 2, 3, 4 **P4-11B. Analyze business transactions and prepare financial statements.**

The accounting department for SummerFest Promotions recorded the following journal entries for 2008. SummerFest Promotions generates revenue by selling tickets for local events such as concerts and sporting events. Sometimes tickets are sold in advance, and sometimes customers will purchase their tickets the same day as the event. These types of transactions require that the SummerFest accounting department record some cash receipts as unearned revenues and others as earned revenues.

	Description	Debit	Credit
a.	Cash	150,000	
	Common Stock		150,000
b.	Office Supplies	475	
	Accounts Payable		475

Description	Debit	Credit
c. Prepaid Rent	18,000	
Cash		18,000
d. Building	375,000	
Note Payable (long-term)		375,000
e. Cash	16,000	
Unearned Ticket Revenue		16,000
f. Utilities Expense	525	
Cash		525
g. Accounts Payable	475	
Cash		475
h. Cash	50,000	
Ticket Revenue		50,000
i. Unearned Ticket Revenue	10,000	
Ticket Revenue		10,000
j. Supplies Expense	300	
Supplies		300
k. Rent Expense	7,000	
Prepaid Rent		7,000
l. Interest Expense	225	
Interest Payable		225
m. Depreciation Expense	2,000	
Accumulated Depreciation—Building		2,000
n. Dividends	7,500	
Cash		7,500
o. Salaries Expense	5,500	
Salaries Payable		5,500

Required

1. Explain the transaction or event that resulted in each journal entry.
2. Post entries *a* through *o* to T-accounts and calculate the balance in each account.
3. Did SummerFest Promotions generate net income or net loss for the fiscal year ending June 30, 2008? How can you tell?
4. Prepare the four financial statements required at year-end.
5. Prepare the closing entries.

Financial Statement Analysis

FSA4-1. Use the 10-K report from Target in the Appendix to the book to answer these questions:

LO 2, 3, 5

  a. Does Target have any deferred expenses? What are they, and where are they shown?
  b. Does Target have accrued expenses? What are they, and where are they shown?
  c. What is the difference between a deferred expense and an accrued expense?
  d. Calculate the debt-to-total-assets ratio for the past two years. What information does this provide?

LO 2, 3   **FSA4-2.** Use Bed Bath & Beyond's balance sheet to answer these questions:

a. The current asset section does not show any prepaid expenses. Does this mean the company doesn't have any such assets? Why or why not?

b. The liabilities section shows Accounts Payable. What does this represent? Have the associated expenses been recognized?

c. The liabilities section shows Income Taxes Payable. What will Bed Bath & Beyond do to satisfy this liability?

d. Bed Bath & Beyond has an item called Deferred Rent and Other Liabilities on the balance sheet, which is not part of current liabilities. What do you think the placement of this liability indicates?

Bed Bath & Beyond
Balance Sheet
At February 28, 2004
(in thousands)

Assets
Current assets:

Cash and cash equivalents	$825,015
Short term investment securities	41,580
Merchandise inventory	1,012,334
Other current assets	90,357
Total current assets	1,969,286
Long term investment securities	210,788
Property and equipment, net	516,164
Other assets	168,785
Total assets	$2,865,023

Liabilities and Shareholders' Equity
Current liabilities:

Accounts payable	$398,650
Accrued expenses and other	
current liabilities	337,039
Income taxes payable	33,845
Total current liabilities	769,534
Deferred rent and other liabilities	104,669
Total liabilities	874,203

Shareholders' equity
Preferred stock

Common stock	3,003
Additional paid-in capital	433,404
Retained earnings	1,554,413
Total shareholders' equity	1,990,820
Total Liabilities and	
Shareholders' Equity	$2,865,023

FSA4-3. Use the balance sheet from Cisco Systems shown here as it appeared on the company's web site to (1) find three examples of amounts than might have been affected by adjusting entries, (2) find an account that provides an example of accrual accounting, and (3) find an example of a deferral. (Find different examples for each requirement.) There are lots of accounts on the balance sheet that you have not studied. Just ignore them for now.

LO 2.3

Cisco Systems
Balance Sheet
(in millions)

	Q3 FY 2004 5/1/2004
Assets	
Current assets:	
Cash and cash equivalents	$ 3,949
Short-term investments	4,912
Accounts receivable, net	1,540
Inventories	1,121
Deferred tax assets	1,905
Lease receivables, net	65
Prepaid expenses and other current assets	581
Total current assets	14,073
Investments	10,085
Property and equipment, net	3,351
Goodwill	4,198
Purchased intangible assets, net	387
Lease receivables, net	293
Other assets	2,810
Total assets	$35,197
Liabilities and Shareholders' Equity	
Current liabilities:	
Accounts payable	$ 604
Income taxes payable	848
Accrued compensation	1,432
Deferred revenue	3,420
Other accrued liabilities	1,899
Restructuring liabilities	71
Total current liabilities	8,274
Deferred revenue	937
Total liabilities	9,211
Minority interest	5
Shareholders' equity	25,981
Total Liabilities and Shareholders' Equity	$35,197

LO 2, 3   **FSA4-4.** Use the following information from Apple Computer to answer these questions: (1) If the company had Prepaid Insurance or Prepaid Rent on the balance sheet date, in what line item on the balance sheet would it be included? (2) What might be included in the Accrued Expenses? Give a couple of examples and the journal entries that might have been recorded to get these accrued expenses on the balance sheet. (3) What does the term "net" after Property, Plant and Equipment mean? Explain how you would find the cost of Apple's Property, Plant and Equipment.

Apple Computer
Selected items from the Balance Sheet
At September 27, 2003
(in millions)

Current assets:	
Cash and cash equivalents	$3,396
Short-term investments	1,170
Accounts receivable (net)	766
Inventories	56
Other current assets	499
Total current assets	5,887
Property, plant, and equipment (net)	669
Goodwill	85
Other assets	174
Total assets	$6,815
Current liabilities:	
Accounts payable	1,154
Accrued expenses	899

LO 2, 3   **FSA4-5.** Use AOL Time Warner's balance sheet shown below to answer the following questions:

AOL Time Warner
Consolidated Balance Sheet
At December 31, 2002
(in millions)

Assets	
Current assets	
Cash and equivalents	$ 1,730
Receivables, less allowances of $2.379 and $1.889 billion	5,667
Inventories	1,896
Prepaid expenses and other current assets	1,862
Total current assets	11,155
Non-current inventories and film costs	3,351
Investments	5,138
Property, plant and equipment	12,150
Intangible assets	44,206
Goodwill	36,986
Other assets	2,464
Total assets	$115,450

Liabilities and Shareholders' Equity

Current liabilities

Accounts payable	$ 2,459
Other payables	3,184
Deferred revenue	1,209
Debt due within one year	155
Other current liabilities	6,388
Total current liabilities	13,395
Long-term debt	27,354
Deferred income taxes	10,823
Deferred revenue	990
Other liabilities	10,071
Total liabilities	62,633

Shareholders' equity

Series LMCN-V Common Stock	2
AOL Time Warner Common Stock	43
Paid-in capital	155,134
Accumulated other comprehensive income (loss), net	(428)
Retained earnings (loss)	(101,934)
Total shareholders' equity	52,817
Total Liabilities and Shareholders' Equity	$115,450

a. Which current asset reflects deferred expenses? Explain what it means to defer expenses and give the adjustment to the accounting equation that was probably made to record this asset.

b. The liabilities section shows two different amounts as deferred revenue. Why would the company need to show both of these amounts? Give the journal entry that resulted in the Deferred Revenue appearing on the balance sheet.

Critical Thinking Problems

Risk and Control

Refer to the Wal-Mart annual report provided in the Appendix at the end of the book. What characteristics of Wal-Mart's business create risks for the company that would not be experienced by most retailers (unique risks)? Is there any evidence that Wal-Mart has internal controls to minimize these risks? Use the entire annual report to answer this question.

Ethics

Mary Johnson, a new accounting clerk, has just spent over six hours preparing an accounting worksheet for her company to help in the preparation of the month's financial statements. The company is applying for a loan, and the bank wants financial statements for the month prepared according to GAAP. Mary's boss, the company's CFO, told Mary that the debt-to-total-assets ratio should be no higher than 0.5. Her calculations show the value of that ratio as 0.55. Because the ratio is so close to the required 0.5, her boss has instructed her to find a way to decrease the ratio by decreasing the amount of debt or increasing the amount of assets. He tells her it's not a big deal because it does not change net income for the month.

Should Mary follow the CFO's instructions? If not, what should she say and do? Explain your answer.

Group Assignment

Go to the web sites of McDonald's and Wendy's. For each company, compute the debt-to-total-assets ratio. How do they compare to each other? If you were a banker, to which company would you prefer to lend money?

Internet Exercise: Darden

Go to www.darden.com to complete the exercises that follow.

IE4-1. If you were at a Darden property, what might you be doing? List two of the Darden chains.

IE4-2. Click on The Numbers followed by Annual Report and Financials and then select the HTML version of the most recent annual report. Find the balance sheets by clicking "next" or using the "contents" scroll bar. Does Darden use a calendar year for its fiscal year? How can you tell?

IE4-3. Refer to the asset section of the balance sheet, then answer the following:
   a. List the title of one asset account that includes accrued revenue—amounts earned but not yet received in cash.
   b. List the title of one asset account that includes amounts that have been paid for in cash but have not yet been expensed.
   c. List the title of one asset account that includes amounts that will be depreciated.
   d. For each account listed in *a* through *c*, identify the amount reported for the most recent year. Do these amounts still need adjusting? Explain why or why not.

IE4-4. List the amounts reported for total current assets and total current liabilities for the most recent year. Compute working capital. For Darden, what does the amount of working capital indicate?

IE4-5. For the two most recent years list the amounts reported for total assets, total liabilities, and total stockholders' equity. For each type of account, identify what the trend indicates. Does the accounting equation hold true both years?

Please note: Internet web sites are constantly being updated. Therefore, if the information is not found where indicated, please explore the web site further to find the information.

Additional Study Materials

Visit www.prenhall.com/reimers for self-study quizzes, spreadsheet templates to use to complete homework assignments, and an accounting cycle tutorial.

CONTINUING CASE STUDY

Building your Excel skills with The MP3 Store

The MP3 Store is ready to open for business. The company had a minor setback due to problems with a supplier and thus will not be able to begin purchasing and reselling MP3 players until May. Thus, in April, the company will continue to repair MP3 players and promote the store.

April 1	The store opens for business.
April 10	Paid the March 31st Accounts Payable balance.
April 20	Collected the A/R balance due from customers on March 31st.
April 28	By the 28th, the company had performed a total of $5,500 worth of repairs. Of the repairs, $4,000 was paid in cash and the balance was on account. The total cost of the repairs was $1,900 which was paid in cash.
April 30	Because April 30 was such a busy day, The MP3 Store didn't pay the assistant manager her $1,600 April salary. It will be paid on May 2.

This chapter is very similar to Chapter 3. You need to prepare journal entries—the monthly entries entered above and the adjusting journal entries. You must also prepare two trial balances and the financial statements.

You have a choice, start from scratch and redo what you did in Chapter 3 OR try working with a copy of the work you did in Chapter 3 and making changes as needed. If you want to try working with a copy, follow steps 1–3. If you start from scratch, start with step 4.

Instructions

1. Open your Chapter 3 file. Save it as MP34. Rename your sheet tabs to reflect that this is Chapter 4.

2. Before you begin working on Chapter 4, you need to clear out some of the Chapter 3 contents. You may do this by

selecting **Edit, Clear** and **Contents** from the menu or by using the Delete key. To clear large sections at once, highlight the area to be cleared first. Clear the contents in your journal entries and T-accounts. Leave the Trial Balance as it is for now.

3. You need to adjust the size of some of your T-accounts. Insert and increase the length of your Supplies and Prepaid accounts by two lines each. If you want to reduce the size of your worksheet, you may also reduce the length of all the other T-accounts by one or two lines each by deleting lines and moving accounts as needed. You need some new T-accounts in this chapter. Highlight 30 rows at the end of the T-accounts and select **Insert, Rows** from the menu.

4. Using your preferred copy and paste techniques, create the new T-accounts: Accumulated Depreciation, Interest Payable, Salaries Payable, Salaries Expense, Advertising Expense, Depreciation Expense, Insurance Expense, Interest Expense, Rent Expense, and Supplies Expense. To limit the number of additional rows needed, put the Accumulated Depreciation, Interest Payable, and Salaries Payable accounts under the assets and the rest of the accounts under the Repair Expense T-account.

5. Copy the ending balances from the Chapter 3 T-accounts to the beginning balances in the Chapter 4 accounts. Make sure that you pick up the correct beginning balance for Retained Earnings. (*Hint*: Look at the financial statements and copy the correct amount from them.) Input and post the journal entries given above and prepare a trial balance, following the procedures used in Chapter 3. If you are working with a copy of Chapter 3, change the title of the existing trial balance to "Unadjusted Trial Balance" and insert lines for the new accounts that have balances. After all balances are copied, total your debits and credits. If you are not in balance, go back and check your entries and postings. If you are in balance save your file to disk by clicking the **Save** button.

6. Prepare and post the necessary adjusting journal entries.

- One month of the 6 months' rent has expired as has one month of the 12-month insurance policy.

- The advertising paid for in March was used.
- There are $120 of the supplies left on hand at April 30th.
- One month of depreciation needs to be recorded for the computer system and the office furniture & fixtures. The company is using straight-line depreciation with no residual value. The assets have an expected useful life of 5 years. (*Hint:* Calculate the depreciation using a formula—divide the total asset cost by 60 and round the answer to the nearest dollar.)
- One month's interest on the 7% Notes Payable needs to be recorded. Use a formula and round to the nearest dollar.

7. Before preparing financial statements, you need to prepare an adjusted trial balance. Although you will need to input the correct cell values for the numbers, you can copy the title and the account names. For formatting purposes, put the adjusted trial balance underneath the unadjusted trial balance. Start with copying just the title and change "Unadjusted" to "Adjusted." If you used formulas to input the titles, you must do a special paste to keep the titles in your new trial balance. Highlight the titles and use your preferred copy technique. While the copy area is highlighted select **Edit** and **Paste Special** from the menu bar. When the Paste Special box appears choose Values. Move to the Paste area and hit Enter. Insert rows for the new accounts added during the adjustment process and use appropriate cell references to input the ending balances. When you are in balance, save your file.

8. Prepare financial statements following the techniques you have learned in earlier chapters. Due to the large number of expenses in April, use a three column format for the income statement. Put the expense amounts in Column C and the total in Column D. Combine the Long-Term Assets (Computer System and Office Furniture & Fixtures) together and subtract the Accumulated Depreciation putting the amounts in Column H and the total in Column I.

9. Once your financial statements are complete, print your work in sections using the technique from Chapter 3. Save your file and exit Excel.

chapter 5

Accounting for Merchandising Operations

Here's where you've been . . .

- **You learned how to complete the accounting cycle with adjusting entries and closing entries.**

Here's where you're going . . .

- **You'll learn how merchandise is acquired and sold.**

- **You'll learn how inventory purchases and sales are recorded in a firm's accounting records.**

YOU make the call:

How could Target increase its gross profit on sales?

Have you ever found a bargain at a store like Target that was so good that you wondered how the store could make a profit? Or, have you ever paid such a high price for an item that you felt the store was overcharging you? The difference between the sales price of merchandise and the cost of the merchandise to the firm is called the gross profit. Suppose that Target Corporation's accountants decided that for Target to reach its earnings goal for the year, it needed to increase its gross profit to pay for rising administrative and operating costs. How could Target increase its gross profit? *You make the call.*

Learning Objectives

When you are finished studying this chapter, you should be able to:

1. Describe the differences between service and merchandising firms.
2. Explain how merchandise is acquired and perform the related record keeping.
3. Explain how sales are made and perform the related record keeping.
4. Explain the differences between a periodic and perpetual inventory system.
5. Explain the difference between a single-step income statement and a multiple-step income statement.
6. Compute the gross profit ratio and profit margin ratio to evaluate a firm's profitability.
7. Recognize the special risks and controls related to inventory.

LEARNING OBJECTIVE 1

Describe the differences between service and merchandising firms.

Merchandising Firms

Merchandising firms can be subdivided into two categories: retail firms and wholesale firms. Target and Office Depot are *merchandising firms* because they buy merchandise to sell to their customers. These firms are also called *retailers* because they earn their revenue by selling their products directly to the final consumer. Other retail firms include The Home Depot and PetSmart. *Wholesale firms* is the second category of merchandising firms. Wholesale firms sell their products to retail firms. Have you ever heard of Ingram Micro? In 2005, this company was ranked the sixth largest firm in the category of electronics and office equipment wholesalers by *FORTUNE* Magazine and was ranked number 76 on the FORTUNE 500 list. We are most familiar with retail firms, so we'll focus on retail firms in this chapter. However, everything you learn will also apply to wholesalers.

While service firms, such as Merry Maids and Comcast Corporation, provide services to their customers, merchandising firms, such as Target, sell products. The revenue that Target and other merchandising firms earn is often called *sales revenue* or simply *sales*. The total cost of the merchandise sold during a period is called the **cost of goods sold**. The difference between sales revenue and cost of goods sold is called the **gross profit**.

Cost of goods sold: The total cost of the merchandise sold during a period.

Gross profit: The difference between sales revenue and cost of goods sold.

In Other Words:
Gross profit is often called gross margin.

An operating cycle

The *operating cycle* for a merchandising firm is a series of business activities that describes how a company takes cash and turns it into more cash. Exhibit 5.1 shows the operating cycle for a typical merchandising firm. For example, Target starts with cash, buys inventory, sells that inventory to customers often creating accounts receivable, and then collects the cash from the customers. Target's goal is to end up with more cash than it started with. For its fiscal year ended January 31, 2005, Target's net income was over $3.1 billion, and it generated over $3.8 billion of cash from operating activities. It was a very good year for Target.

Exhibit 5.1

An Operating Cycle

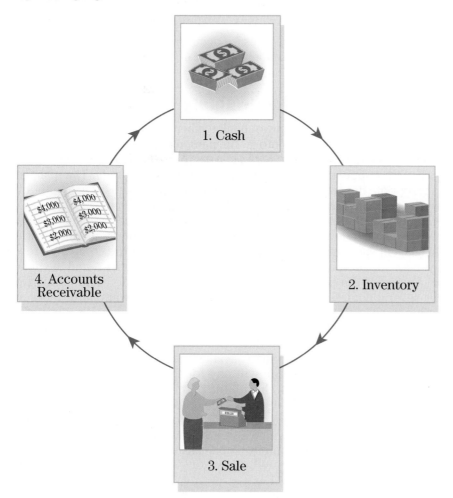

Acquiring Merchandise for Sale

Now that you know about the operating cycle of a business, we'll focus on the activity of buying the inventory. Acquiring the goods it plans to sell is an important activity for merchandising firms.

Stroll down the aisle of Staples or Office Max and imagine keeping track of all that merchandise. All goods owned and held for sale in the regular course of business are considered *merchandise inventory*. In contrast, supplies and equipment are used by most firms rather than sold by those firms, in which case they would not be considered inventory. Only the items a firm sells are considered inventory. Most large corporations have large purchasing departments dedicated exclusively to acquiring inventory. Regardless of their size, firms must keep meticulous track of their inventory purchases through their information systems. An information system refers to the way the firm records and reports its transactions, including inventory and sales.

A merchandising firm records the inventory as a current asset until it is sold. According to the matching principle, inventory should be expensed in the period in which it is sold. So when it is sold, inventory becomes an expense—Cost of Goods Sold. The sales of particular goods and the cost of those goods sold during the period are matched—put on the same income statement. You

LEARNING OBJECTIVE 2

Explain how merchandise is acquired and perform the related record keeping.

In Other Words:
Merchandise inventory is often simply called inventory.

can see that the value of the inventory affects both the balance sheet and the income statement. Why does the value of inventory matter? On its February 28, 2004, balance sheet, Best Buy had over $2.6 billion worth of inventory, making up over 30% of the company's total assets. That's a significant amount of the firm's assets.

Let's take a look at the procedures for acquiring inventory, and then focus on how to do the related record keeping.

Acquisition process for inventory

The process of acquiring inventory begins when someone in a firm decides to order merchandise for the inventory. The person requesting the purchase sends a document, called a *purchase requisition*, to the company's purchasing agent. For example, suppose that Office Depot needs to order paper. The manager of the appropriate department would submit a purchase requisition in either hard copy or electronic form to the purchasing agent. The purchasing agent selects a vendor to provide the paper, based on the vendor's prices, quality of goods or services needed, and the ability to deliver them in a timely manner. The purchasing agent specifies in a *purchase order*—a record of the company's request to a vendor for goods or services—what is needed, the prices, and the delivery time. A copy of the purchase order is sent to the vendor, and Office Depot keeps several copies for internal record keeping. An example of a purchase order is shown in Exhibit 5.2.

Office Depot's purchasing agent sends one copy of the purchase order to the receiving department and one to the accounts payable department. The receiving department will let the accounts payable department know when the goods have arrived. Accounts payable will pay for the goods when it receives an invoice from the vendor to match with the purchase order. The process can be much more complicated, but it always includes cooperation between departments so that the company pays for only the goods ordered and received.

Modern technology has provided a shorter and more efficient way to manage inventory. At Wal-Mart, for example, no one has to explicitly order merchandise

Exhibit 5.2

Purchase Order from Office Depot

Taking Care of Business	Phone: 555-555-5555
	Fax: 555-555-5555
	E-mail: someone@example.com

Office Depot

Purchase Order

Bill To:

2200 Old Germantown Road
Delray Beach
FL 33445

Ship To:

Office Depot Warehouse
2510 Depot Road
Delray Beach
FL 33445

Req By	Ship When	Ship Via	FOB	Buyer	Terms	Tax ID
Purchasing Agent	On receipt	UPS	Delray Beach, FL	Supplies Dept.	n/30	

Quantity	Item	Units	Description	Discount %	Taxable	Unit Price	Total
1,000	RP34590	20,000	Reams of HP Photo Paper			2.00	40,000

Purchse Order #:
Date:
Vendor ID: HP6501

Subtotal	
Tax	
Shipping	
Miscellaneous	
Balance Due	40,000

when it is needed. Using bar codes at the cash registers as each item is sold, the computerized inventory system is programmed to recognize when Wal-Mart should acquire more inventory, and the information goes directly to the vendor's computerized system. Even when the process is automated, the underlying transaction is the same: Inventory is acquired from a vendor to be available to sell to a firm's customers, and the firm wants to be sure it pays for only the merchandise it has received.

Recording purchases

Now that you are familiar with the procedures for purchasing inventory, you are ready to learn to account for its cost. The costs of acquiring inventory include all costs the company incurs to purchase the items and get them ready for sale. Many people in the firm need details about the cost of inventory including the person requesting the goods, the CFO, and the CEO. This inventory information is also needed for the financial statements.

There are two ways for firms to record their inventory transactions—perpetual and periodic. These two different methods describe the timing of the firm's inventory record keeping. When a company uses a **perpetual inventory system**, the accountant records every purchase of inventory directly to the Inventory account at the time of the purchase. Similarly, each time an item is sold, the accountant will remove the cost of the item—the cost of goods sold—from the Inventory account. In the example that follows, Quality Lawn Mowers, a fictitious firm, uses a perpetual inventory record-keeping system. We'll discuss a **periodic inventory** record-keeping system—one in which the Inventory account is updated only at the end of the period—later in the chapter.

Let's use Quality Lawn Mowers for an example of how to account for the costs of inventory. Keep in mind that the company uses a perpetual record-keeping system. Suppose Quality Lawn Mowers purchased 100 lawn mowers on account for $150 each from Black & Decker, a manufacturer of power tools and lawn mowers. This is the journal entry that Quality Lawn Mowers would record:

Perpetual inventory system: A method of record keeping that involves updating the accounting records at the time of every purchase, sale, and return.

Periodic inventory system: A method of record keeping that involves updating the accounting records only at the end of the accounting period.

Date	Transaction	Debit	Credit
June 1	Inventory	15,000	
	Accounts Payable		15,000
	To record the purchase of inventory on account		

This is the accounting equation:

Assets	=	Liabilities	+	Shareholders' Equity	
				Contributed Capital	+ Retained Earnings
Inventory		Accounts Payable			
15,000		15,000			

Who Pays the Freight Costs to Obtain Inventory? The cost a company records in its inventory account is not always the amount quoted by the vendor because of shipping costs. Remember that the cost of inventory includes all the costs to obtain the merchandise and get it ready to sell. When a merchandising firm pays for transportation costs for goods purchased, the freight cost is called *freight in* and is considered part of the cost of the inventory. The shipping terms are negotiated between the buyer and the vendor.

FOB (free on board) shipping point: The buying firm pays the shipping costs. The amount is called freight-in and is included in the cost of the inventory.

FOB (free on board) destination: The vendor (selling firm) pays the shipping costs, so the buyer has no freight-in cost to account for.

Study Tip

FOB shipping point and FOB destination are terms that describe whether the buyer or seller pays the freight for a purchase. Instead of the words *shipping point* and *destination*, an actual shipping document will have the name of the city from which the goods are shipped or to which the goods are going. See Exhibit 5.3 for details.

If the terms of purchase are **FOB (free on board) shipping point**, title to the goods passes to the buyer at the shipping point (the vendor's warehouse), and the buyer is responsible for the cost of the transportation from that point on. If the terms are **FOB destination**, the vendor—Black & Decker—pays for the transportation costs until the goods reach their destination, when title passes to the buyer.

When you're the vendor and you pay for goods to be delivered to your customers, the expense goes on your income statement as *Freight-out* or *Delivery Expense*. Freight-out is an operating expense, while freight-in is part of the cost of the inventory. Exhibit 5.3 shows the relationships among the FOB selling point, FOB destination, buyer, and vendor.

The details of inventory purchases, like the shipping terms, can affect the cost of the inventory. A company must pay attention to these costs because such costs can make a difference in the profitability of the company.

Suppose the shipping cost for the 100 lawn mowers purchased by Quality Lawn Mowers was $343. If the shipping terms were FOB destination, then Black & Decker paid the shipping cost; and there is no journal entry for Quality Lawn Mowers. However, suppose the terms were FOB shipping point. That means that title changes hands at the point of shipping—the vendor's warehouse. Because Quality Lawn Mowers then owns the goods while they are in transit, Quality Lawn Mowers will have to pay the shipping costs. The $343 will be included as part of the cost of the inventory. Shipping costs are usually paid to the shipping company in cash.

The journal entry would be:

Date	Transaction	Debit	Credit
June 1	Inventory	343	
	Cash		343
	To record the shipping costs of inventory		

Exhibit 5.3

Shipping Terms

Title passes here at **FOB shipping point**....or...Title passes here at **FOB destination**.

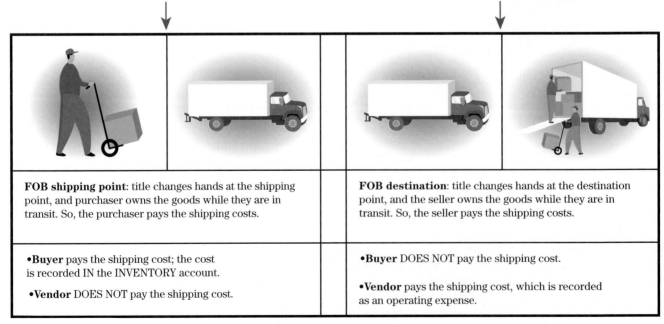

FOB shipping point: title changes hands at the shipping point, and purchaser owns the goods while they are in transit. So, the purchaser pays the shipping costs.

• **Buyer** pays the shipping cost; the cost is recorded IN the INVENTORY account.

• **Vendor** DOES NOT pay the shipping cost.

FOB destination: title changes hands at the destination point, and the seller owns the goods while they are in transit. So, the seller pays the shipping costs.

• **Buyer** DOES NOT pay the shipping cost.

• **Vendor** pays the shipping cost, which is recorded as an operating expense.

Shipping terms determine who owns the goods, and at what point the owner pays the shipping costs. The firm that owns the goods while they are in transit must include the cost of those goods in its inventory.

This is the accounting equation:

Assets		=	Liabilities	+	Shareholders' Equity	
					Contributed Capital	Retained + Earnings
Cash	Inventory					
−343	343					

Purchase Returns and Allowances Some goods may need to be returned to the vendor because the firm ordered too much inventory, ordered the wrong items, or found the goods slightly damaged. When a firm returns goods, the transaction is called a *purchase return*. In the firm's accounting system, the amount of purchase returns will be deducted from the cost of the inventory. Because the company put the cost of the items in the Inventory account, that account will be decreased when goods are returned. The details of the returns will be noted in another part of the company's information system. The firm wants to know exactly how much merchandise it is returning in any given accounting period. A firm should be sure it understands the vendor's return policy. Often, near the end of the year, a vendor will institute a very liberal return policy to make a sale. Nevertheless, the firm should buy only the amount of inventory it actually needs, not a larger amount with the idea of returning it when the next accounting period starts.

Goods damaged or defective may be kept by the purchaser with a cost reduction called a *purchase allowance*. When a company has a purchase allowance, it is like getting a discounted purchase price so the Inventory account will be reduced. A purchase allowance is different from a purchase return because the goods are kept by the purchaser in the case of a purchase allowance.

When an item is returned, Accounts Payable, which shows the amount a firm owes its vendors, will be reduced with a debit. The Inventory account will be decreased with a credit. Suppose Quality Lawn Mowers returned two of the lawn mowers because they were defective. This is the journal entry the company would record:

Date	Transaction	Debit	Credit
June 3	Accounts Payable	300	
	Inventory		300
	To record the return of goods to manufacturer (2 mowers @ $150 each)		

This is the accounting equation:

Assets		=	Liabilities	+	Shareholders' Equity	
					Contributed Capital	Retained + Earnings
Inventory			Accounts Payable			
−300			−300			

Similarly, if a vendor gives the firm a purchase allowance, the amount owed to the vendor is reduced with a debit to Accounts Payable. The credit will reduce the balance in the Inventory account. **Purchase returns and purchase allowances** are often grouped together in one expression—purchase returns and allowances.

Purchase Discounts In addition to purchase returns and allowances, purchase discounts can also cause a difference between the vendor's quoted price and the cost the purchasing company records for inventory purchases.

Purchase returns and allowances: Amounts that decrease the cost of inventory purchases due to returned or damaged merchandise.

A purchase discount is a reduction in the purchase price in return for prompt payment. For example, a vendor offering a purchase discount for prompt payment from a customer would describe it in terms like this:

> 2/10, n/30

This term is read as "two-ten, net-thirty" and means the vendor will give a 2% discount if the buyer pays for the entire purchase within 10 days of the invoice date. If not, the full amount is due within 30 days. A vendor may set any discount terms. What does 3/15, n/45 mean? The vendor will give a 3% discount if payment is made within 15 days. Otherwise, full payment must be made within 45 days. The number of days a customer has to pay an invoice starts on the day after the date of the invoice. For example, an invoice dated June 9 with the terms 2/10, n/30 gives the customer until June 19 to pay with the discount applied. The full amount is due by July 9.

A firm should take advantage of purchase discount offers from vendors because it can amount to significant savings. If a vendor offers the terms 2/10, n/30, the vendor is actually charging the firm almost 36% annual interest to use the money if the firm doesn't pay within the discount period and waits until the last day, the thirtieth day. Here's how we calculated the high interest rate of 36%. If the discount period expires, and the firm hasn't paid until the thirtieth day after the invoice date, the firm is "borrowing" the money from the vendor for an additional 20 days. Because the firm did not pay within the discount period, the vendor has earned 2% in 20 days. And, 2% interest on a "loan" over 20 days is the same as a 36% annual rate, determined with the help of a simple ratio:

> $2\% \div 20 \text{ days} = x \div 360$

Solve for x and you get $x = 36\%$ annual interest—if you consider a year as having 360 days. Some companies borrow the money from the bank (at 10% or 12% annual interest) to take advantage of sales discounts.

Suppose Black & Decker offers Quality Lawn Mowers the terms 1/10, n/30. Quality takes advantage of this discount and pays for the inventory on June 19. Recall that it purchased the inventory on June 1, so the payment is made within the discount period. Quality Lawn Mowers owes the vendor $14,700 because $300 worth of merchandise from the original purchase of $15,000 was returned. The 1% discount amounts to $147. That means that the company will pay the vendor $14,553 (= 14,700 − 147). Here is the way Quality Lawn Mowers would record the payment:

Date	Transaction	Debit	Credit
June 19	Accounts Payable	14,700	
	Cash		14,553
	Inventory		147
	To record the payment of inventory with a purchase discount		

This is the accounting equation:

Assets		=	Liabilities	+	Shareholders' Equity	
					Contributed Capital	**Retained + Earnings**
Cash	Inventory		Accounts Payable			
−14,553	−147		−14,700			

Before the payment, Quality's Accounts Payable showed $14,700 owed to the vendor. That's why the entire $14,700 must be debited out of Accounts Payable. Because only $14,553 was actually paid, this is the amount credited to the Cash account. That leaves the discount amount to balance the journal entry. The credit decreases the Inventory account because inventory purchase was recorded at $14,700, which turned out *not* to be the cost of the inventory. The credit for $147 adjusts the Inventory account balance to the actual cost of the goods purchased.[1]

If Quality Lawn Mowers did not pay within the discount period, the payment would be recorded with a debit to Accounts Payable for $14,700 and a credit to Cash for $14,700.

Summary of Purchases for Quality Lawn Mowers Let's trace the activity in the Inventory account for Quality Lawn Mowers. First, the original purchase of the 100 lawn mowers was recorded with a debit to Inventory for $15,000. In the T-account in Exhibit 5.4, this is shown as transaction (1). Then, transaction (2) shows the payment of shipping costs of $343. Next, transaction (3) shows the return of two lawn mowers—$300 worth of inventory. Finally, recall that the company took advantage of the purchase discount. That is shown in transaction (4) with a credit of $147. The balance in the Inventory account is now $14,896 for 98 lawn mowers. That's $152 per unit. This amount is called the *cost of goods available for sale*. If Quality had started the period with a beginning inventory, cost of goods available for sale would have included the amount of the beginning inventory. A simple way to think about the calculation of cost of goods available for sale is:

Beginning inventory (in this example, there is none)	0
+ Net purchases (this is total purchases less returns and allowances and discounts)15,000 – 300 – 147	14,553
+ Shipping costs (freight-in)	343
= Cost of goods available for sale	$14,896

Exhibit 5.4

T-Account for Quality Lawn Mowers's Inventory

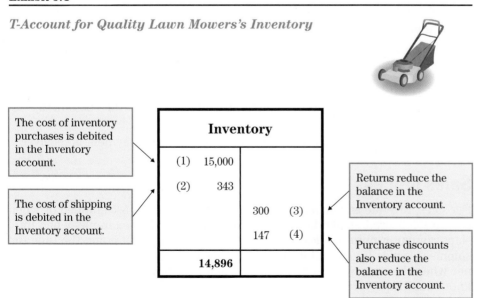

The cost of inventory purchases is debited in the Inventory account.

The cost of shipping is debited in the Inventory account.

Inventory			
(1)	15,000		
(2)	343		
		300	(3)
		147	(4)
	14,896		

Returns reduce the balance in the Inventory account.

Purchase discounts also reduce the balance in the Inventory account.

This T-account shows all the entries related to purchasing goods that affected Quality Lawn Mowers's Inventory account. (1) shows the original purchase of lawn mowers for $15,000, (2) shows the payment of shipping costs at $343, (3) shows the return of two lawn mowers at $300, and (4) shows a purchase discount of $147. The Inventory account balance is $14,896.

[1]This method of accounting for a purchase discount is called the gross method because the full amount of the purchase price is recorded at the time of the purchase. There is another way called the net method in which the purchase price is recorded as if the discount would be taken. Either way, the firm's records must eventually reflect the actual cost of the inventory. You will learn more about these methods in a more advanced accounting course.

In each separate situation, calculate the cost of the inventory purchased.

1. A Company purchased merchandise FOB destination for $10,000. Terms were 2/10, n/30 and payment was made in 8 days. Freight cost was $90.
2. B Company purchased merchandise FOB shipping point for $10,000. Terms were 2/10, n/30 and payment was made in 29 days. Freight cost was $90.
3. C Company purchased merchandise FOB shipping point for $10,000. Terms were 2/10, n/30 and payment was made in 8 days. Freight cost was $90.

Answers (1) $9,800 [$10,000 − 2% discount; vendor paid the freight] (2) $10,090 [Discount expired; buyer paid the freight] (3) $9,890 [$10,000 − 2% discount + $90 freight]

LEARNING OBJECTIVE 3

Explain how sales are made and perform the related record keeping.

Study Tip

When you are accounting for sales and purchases, be careful to keep track of whether you are the seller or the purchaser.

Selling Merchandise

You now know how a company records the transactions related to the purchase of inventory. Now, let's look at what happens when the company sells the inventory.

Sales are reported net of returns, allowances, and any discounts given to customers. What you just learned about purchasing inventory also applies to selling the inventory, but everything is reversed. Instead of purchase returns and allowances, we'll have sales returns and allowances. Instead of purchase discounts, we'll have sales discounts.

Here are the typical business activities that take place when a firm makes a sale:

1. Customer places an order.
2. Company approves the order.
3. Warehouse selects goods for shipment.
4. Company ships goods.
5. Company bills customer for goods.
6. Company receives payment for the goods.

Computers can perform some of these steps. Whether a firm performs the steps manually or with a computer, the objectives of those steps are the same:

- to assure that the firm sells its goods or services to customers who will pay.
- to assure that the goods or services delivered are what the customers ordered.
- to assure that the customers are correctly billed and payment is received.

Sales process

For sales, revenue is typically recognized when the goods are shipped or when they are delivered, depending on the shipping terms. For example, when Intel ships computer chips to IBM with the terms FOB shipping point, the time the shipment leaves Intel will be the point at which Intel recognizes the revenue, not when the order is placed and not when IBM pays for the purchase. You know that the shipment of the goods is preceded by many crucial activities such as planning, marketing, and securing orders. Yet, no revenue is recognized until it is actually earned.

Exhibit 5.5 shows part of the note that IBM has included in the financial statements about its revenue recognition. Does payment have to be received before revenue is recognized at IBM? NO! Remember, GAAP is accrual accounting.

Exhibit 5.5

How Does IBM Recognize Revenue?

IBM®

This is just a small part of IBM's description of its revenue recognition from the Notes to the Financial Statements (for the year ended December 31, 2004). When you look at a firm's financial statements, be sure to read the notes to learn about the firm's revenue recognition policy.

The company recognizes revenue when it is realized or realizable and earned. The company considers revenue realized or realizable and earned when it has persuasive evidence of an arrangement, delivery has occurred, the sales price is fixed or determinable, and collectibility is reasonably assured. Delivery does not occur until products have been shipped or services have been provided to the client, the risk of loss has transferred to the client and client acceptance has been obtained, client acceptance provisions have lapsed, or the company has objective evidence that the criteria specified in the client acceptance provisions have been satisfied. The sale price is not considered to be fixed or determinable until all contingencies related to the sale have been resolved.

Recording sales

When a sale is made, it is recorded with a credit to *Sales Revenue*, often simply called *Sales*. Continuing our example with Quality Lawn Mowers, suppose the company sold 10 lawn mowers to Sam's Yard Service for $4,000 on account. The journal entry for the sale would be:

Date	Transaction	Debit	Credit
June 20	Accounts Receivable	4,000	
	Sales Revenue		4,000
	To record the sale of 10 lawn mowers for $400 each		

This is the accounting equation:

Assets	=	Liabilities	+	Shareholders' Equity		
				Contributed Capital	+	Retained Earnings
Accounts Receivable						Sales Revenue
4,000						4,000

When a sale is made, the inventory is reduced. Because Quality Lawn Mower has sold 10 lawn mowers, the cost of those mowers will be deducted from the balance in the Inventory account. Recall that each lawn mower had a cost of $152. Removing the 10 mowers from inventory will require a credit of $1,520 (= $152 × 10). Cost of Goods Sold, an expense account, will get the corresponding debit for $1,520.

Date	Transaction	Debit	Credit
June 20	Cost of Goods Sold	1,520	
	Inventory		1,520
	To reduce the inventory for the sale of 10 lawn mowers at a cost of $152 each		

This is the accounting equation:

Assets	=	Liabilities	+	Shareholders' Equity		
				Contributed Capital	+	**Retained Earnings**
Inventory						Cost of Goods Sold
−1,520						−1,520

Sales Returns and Allowances A company's customers may return items, and the company may provide allowances on items it sells. These amounts will either be recorded as a reduction to Sales Revenue or in a separate account called **Sales Returns and Allowances**. If a separate account is used, it will have a normal debit balance. This account is an example of a **contra-revenue account**, the balance of which will be deducted from Sales Revenue for the income statement. Often, you will simply see the term *Net Sales* on the income statement. This is gross sales minus the amount of returns and allowances. When a customer returns an item to the company, the customer's Account Receivable will be reduced with a credit (or cash will be returned to the customer with a credit to the Cash account). The Sales Returns and Allowances account will be increased with a debit, and the balance in the account will eventually be deducted from Sales Revenue.

Suppose Sam's Yard Service, the company that purchased the 10 lawn mowers, discovers that one of them is dented and missing a couple of screws. Sam's Yard Service calls Quality Lawn Mowers to complain, and the salesman for Quality Lawn Mowers offers Sam's Yard Service an allowance of $100 on the damaged lawn mower. Sam's Yard Service agrees and will fix the lawn mower. Here is the journal entry that Quality Lawn Mowers will make to adjust the amount of the sale and the amount Sam's Yard Service owes Quality Lawn Mowers.

Date	Transaction	Debit	Credit
June 25	Sales Returns and Allowances	100	
	Accounts Receivable		100
	To record allowance of $100 on a damaged mower sold to Sam's Yard Service		

This is the accounting equation:

Assets	=	Liabilities	+	Shareholders' Equity		
				Contributed Capital	+	**Retained Earnings**
Accounts Receivable						Sales Returns and Allowances
−100						−100

Similarly, if a customer returns an item, the transaction will be recorded with a debit to Sales Returns and Allowances and a credit to that customer's account (Accounts Receivable). When an item is returned, it must be recorded back into the Inventory and removed from the Cost of Goods Sold.

If this were the only sales transaction Quality Lawn Mowers made during the accounting period, the Net Sales on the income statement would be $3,900 (= $4,000 − 100). Because Sales Returns and Allowances is a contra-revenue account, it is subtracted from Sales Revenue. Notice that you could have simply reduced the balance in the Sales Revenue account from $4,000 to $3,900 with a debit to achieve the same result on the income statement.

Sales returns and allowances: An account that holds amounts that reduce sales due to customer returns or allowances for damaged merchandise.

Contra-revenue: An account that is an offset to a revenue account and therefore deducted from the revenue for the financial statements.

Study Tip

A firm may simply debit the Sales account directly for returns and allowances. Even if there are no formal accounts for returns and allowances, the firm will keep track of these amounts. The information will be needed for future decisions.

Sales Discounts and Shipping Terms The terms of **sales discounts**, reductions in the sales price for prompt payment, are expressed exactly like the terms you learned for purchases. A company will offer sales discounts to its customers to motivate them to pay promptly.

Suppose Quality Lawn Mowers offers Sam's Yard Service the terms 2/10, n/30 for the sale. If Sam's Yard Service pays its account within 10 days of the invoice date, Quality Lawn Mowers will reduce the amount due by 2%. This is an offer Sam's Yard Service should not refuse. Below is the journal entry that Quality Lawn Mowers will record upon receipt of Sam's Yard Service payment of $3,822. That's 98% of the amount of the invoice of $3,900. Don't forget the earlier $100 sales allowance that reduced the amount from $4,000 to $3,900.

Just as with sales returns and allowances, the amount of a sales discount could be debited directly to the Sales Revenue account, reducing the balance by $78. Whether or not you use a separate account to keep track of sales discounts, the income statement will show the net amount of sales. In this example, the calculation for net sales is:

Sales Revenue	$4,000
– Allowance given	– 100
– Sales discounts	– 78
Net sales	$3,822

Notice in the journal entry below that the collection of cash from the customer is equal to net sales.

Date	Transaction	Debit	Credit
June 29	Cash	3,822	
	Sales Discounts	78	
	Accounts Receivable		3,900
	To record the receipt of payment in full from Sam's Yard Service		

This is the accounting equation:

Assets		= Liabilities	+	Shareholders' Equity	
				Contributed Capital +	**Retained Earnings**
Cash	Accounts Receivable				Sales Discounts
3,822	–3,900				–78

Notice two important things about the way the payment from Sam's Yard Service is recorded:

1. Sales Discounts is a contra-revenue account like Sales Returns and Allowances. The amount in the Sales Discounts account will be subtracted from Sales Revenue along with any Sales Returns and Allowances to get Net Sales for the income statement.

2. Accounts Receivable must be reduced with a credit for the full amount that shows as Sam's Yard Service's Accounts Receivable balance. Even though the cash collected is less than this balance, Sam's Yard Service account is paid in full with this payment, so the entire balance in Quality Lawn Mowers' Accounts Receivable for Sam's Yard Service must be removed.

In addition to Sales Returns and Allowances and Sales Discounts, a company will be concerned with shipping costs. You already learned about who pays for shipping depending on the shipping terms: FOB destination and FOB shipping point. When paying the shipping costs, the vendor will likely set prices high enough to cover the shipping. When the vendor pays the shipping costs, those costs are classified as operating expenses. Look back over Exhibit 5.3 on page 230. When you are working an accounting problem with shipping costs, be careful to properly identify your company as the purchaser or the vendor of the goods being shipped.

Can **YOU** do it?

For each problem, calculate net sales for the selling company. Also, tell whether or not the selling company had to pay the freight costs.

1. Toy Company sold merchandise for $10,000 with the following terms:

   FOB destination; 2/10, n/30.
   The customer paid 8 days from the invoice date.
   Freight cost was $200.

2. Apex Company sold merchandise for $2,500 with the following terms:

   FOB shipping point; 2/10, n/30.
   Customer paid after 29 days.
   Freight cost was $90.

Answers (1) $9,800 [$10,000 − 2% discount taken; Freight-out is an operating expense.] (2) $2,500 [Discount expired; freight paid by customer.]

Summary of Purchases and Sales for Quality Lawn Mowers A firm starts with beginning inventory, purchases additional inventory, and then sells the inventory. The calculation below shows what happens. Study the calculation in conjunction with Exhibit 5.6, which provides a summary of the purchase and sales transactions shown in the inventory T-account.

Beginning inventory	0
+ Purchases (net) (15,000 − 300 − 147)	14,553
+ Freight-in	343
= Cost of goods available for sale	14,896
− Cost of goods sold	1,520
= Ending inventory	$13,376

Sales Taxes In addition to collecting sales revenue, most retail firms must also collect a sales tax for the state government. A sales tax is a percentage of the sales price. Suppose that Quality Lawn Mowers sold a mower to a customer, Carrie, for $400 and the sales tax rate is 4%. Here's how Quality Lawn Mowers would record receipt of $416 cash from the customer:

Transaction	Debit	Credit
Cash	416	
Sales Revenue		400
Sales Tax Payable		16
To record cash sales with sales taxes.		

[Note: Quality Lawn Mowers would also have to record the cost of goods sold and reduction in inventory related to the sale.]

Exhibit 5.6

Inventory T-Account

This is Quality Lawn Mowers's Inventory account, showing all the purchase entries as well as the entry to record the reduction in Inventory for Cost of Goods Sold.

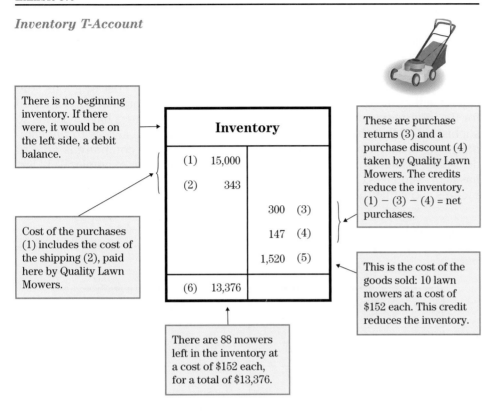

There is no beginning inventory. If there were, it would be on the left side, a debit balance.

Cost of the purchases (1) includes the cost of the shipping (2), paid here by Quality Lawn Mowers.

These are purchase returns (3) and a purchase discount (4) taken by Quality Lawn Mowers. The credits reduce the inventory. (1) − (3) − (4) = net purchases.

This is the cost of the goods sold: 10 lawn mowers at a cost of $152 each. This credit reduces the inventory.

There are 88 mowers left in the inventory at a cost of $152 each, for a total of $13,376.

This is the accounting equation:

Assets	=	Liabilities	+	Shareholders' Equity	
				Contributed Capital	+ Retained Earnings
Cash				Sales Tax Payable	Sales Revenue
416				16	400

Although Quality Lawn Mowers collects the 4% sales tax from Carrie's purchase, that money does not belong to the firm. Instead, the firm owes it to the Department of Revenue in its state. Firms usually pay sales taxes quarterly.

Recording Inventory: Perpetual Versus Periodic Record Keeping

LEARNING OBJECTIVE 4

Explain the differences between a perpetual and a periodic inventory system.

We've discussed buying and selling inventory. In our examples so far, the company used a perpetual inventory record-keeping system. With every purchase and after every sale, the inventory records were updated. As you learned earlier in the chapter, this is called a perpetual inventory system because it requires a continuous updating at the time of every purchase and sale.

The other method, mentioned briefly earlier in the chapter, is called periodic. When a firm uses a periodic inventory system, the firm's accountant waits until the end of an accounting period to adjust the balance in the Inventory account. In that case, purchases are put in a separate account called Purchases. Using the periodic method, the firm will update the inventory records at the end of each accounting period. Exhibit 5.7 compares the two inventory systems.

Because of technology advances, an increasing number of companies are using perpetual inventory systems. For example, when you go shopping at Target and take your cart to the checkout counter, the cashier scans each of your items. The record-keeping system enables Target and stores like Kroger, Safeway, and Macy's, to do the equivalent of making the cost of goods sold adjustment at the time of sale. Of course, much more information is captured for the information system at the same time. Many companies have systems so sophisticated that the supplier of specific items will have access to the company's inventory via the Internet so that the supplying company is able to deliver goods to the purchasing company automatically. For example, Wal-Mart has many suppliers that automatically deliver goods when Wal-Mart's inventory records show that the inventory has fallen to some preset level.

A *perpetual system* keeps track of the inventory with every sale. Each time a lawn mower is sold, it is recorded as cost of goods sold. In a *periodic system*, the inventory records do not change during the period. At the end of the period, the inventory is counted, and the cost of goods sold is computed as the difference between what should be in the inventory (beginning inventory plus any purchases) and what is left (ending inventory). In this example, there was no beginning inventory, and one lawn mower out of the four that were purchased remained in the ending inventory. So cost of goods sold must be the cost of three mowers.

Exhibit 5.7

Perpetual Versus Periodic Inventory

Perpetual		Periodic	
Purchased	Sold	Purchased	Sold
	Yes		
	Yes		
	Yes		
	No		
End of the Period		**End of the Period**	
Inventory records show: 1	Cost of goods sold records show: 3	Inventory records show: 4	Cost of goods sold records show: 0
		Count it: 1	Calculate it: 4 minus 1 = 3

If you want to know more about using a periodic inventory system, you can read about it in the Appendix to this chapter. Understanding the accounts and the way cost of goods sold is determined using a periodic system may increase your understanding of the way an accounting system works.

Differences between perpetual and periodic inventory systems

One of the primary advantages of a perpetual system is that inventory records are always current, and a physical count can be compared to the records to see if there is any inventory shrinkage. *Inventory shrinkage* is a reduction in the inventory by damage, loss, or theft by either employees or customers. A perpetual system allows a company to identify shrinkage. However, a perpetual system may be too cumbersome for firms that do not have up-to-date computerized support. A company may keep the physical count of its inventory current by recording each reduction in the amount of inventory sold without actually recording the cost of goods sold. That is a way to monitor the inventory for potential shrinkage without actually using a perpetual system for the accounting records. Read more about inventory shrinkage in ***Accounting in the News***.

When a company uses a periodic system, the accounting records are updated only at the end of the period. Recall from the example of Quality Lawn Mowers, the accountants must count the ending inventory and back into the amount for cost of goods sold. In other words, if the inventory is gone, it must have been sold. That means that any inventory shrinkage is not separately identified from the inventory sold. All missing inventory is considered inventory sold and its cost will be included in the firm's cost of goods sold expense for the period.

Accounting in the NEWS

Ethics

Would You Help Yourself to a Few Steaks?

Imagine you work for a large steakhouse, such as Outback Steakhouse, and you have access to the food storage area. This weekend you are having a large cookout for your friends. You have seen your coworkers take food, particularly expensive steaks, with them after their shift. Nobody seems to pay attention to how many steaks are being kept and removed from inventory. You could take several steaks for your cookout, and it is very likely that nobody will know the steaks are missing. Should you do it?

This scenario plays out every day in companies across the country. Inventory shrinkage—a reduction in inventory due to theft, damage, and/or administrative errors—is one of the most significant costs facing merchandising (retail) firms.

The extent of this problem is highlighted in a study by Ernst & Young that estimates "the U.S. retail industry loses a staggering $46 billion annually to inventory shrinkage, and that employee theft delivers the heaviest blow in terms of dollars lost." Performing a physical count of inventory and reconciling the physical count to the accounting records will indicate shrinkage. Any shrinkage results in accounting that reduces the inventory asset and increases an expense—thereby reducing net income.

In today's competitive environment managers are constantly looking for ways to reduce expenses. With improvements in point-of-sale (POS) technologies, managers are better able to track inventory and reduce shrinkage. Ultimately, however, managers need to hire ethical employees and put controls in place to minimize employee theft.

Thinking Critically

Have you ever worked for a retail company and helped yourself to some products? If you became a manager at a retail company like Target, how would you deal with an employee who you

If you work for a restaurant or other type of business, it may be tempting to take a few items for your personal use. When many employees act on this impulse, the losses to businesses and shareholders add up.

caught taking company products? What if the employee was a friend who was having financial trouble?

Q How can a firm reduce inventory shrinkage?

A Hire ethical employees and put effective controls in place.

Source: "Ernst & Young Study Estimates Retailers Lose $46 Billion Annually to Inventory Shrinkage; Employee Theft Is Biggest Problem," *Business Wire*, May 13, 2003.

Can **YOU** do it?

A company has $500 worth of inventory on March 1 and purchases $1,000 worth of merchandise with terms 2/10, n/30 during the month. The company pays within the discount period. Shipping terms are FOB shipping point, with shipping costs of $100. At the end of March, the inventory manager takes a physical count of the inventory and finds there is $250 worth remaining. Calculate the cost of goods sold for March.

Answer $1,330 [BI $500 + Purchases $980 + $100 − EI $250 = $1,330]

LEARNING OBJECTIVE 5

Explain the difference between a single-step income statement and a multiple-step income statement.

Single-step income statement: An income statement in which all revenues are presented first, and all expenses are subtracted in one step to arrive at net income.

The income statement for Target provides the details needed to calculate its gross profit, but the calculation is not done on the statement itself. This is a single-step income statement.

Multiple-step Income Statement

We've discussed the details of buying and selling inventory. Now, let's look at how inventory information is shown on the financial statements. Some merchandising firms use a simple format for their income statement called a **single-step income statement**. All revenues are presented first, and all expenses are subtracted in one step to arrive at net income. Exhibit 5.8 shows Target's single-step income statement. Notice that Target calls the statement *Consolidated* Results of Operations. The word *consolidated* is frequently in the title of each of a company's financial statements. Consolidated means that all of the smaller companies that are owned by the firm are included in the balances shown in the statement. For Target, that means the revenue and expenses from Archer Farms, a brand of products owned by Target, are part of the income statement shown.

Exhibit 5.8

Target's Income Statement

Target Corporation
Consolidated Results of Operations

(in millions, except per share data)

For years ended	Jan. 29 2005	Jan. 31 2004
Sales	$45,682	$40,928
Net credit card revenues	1,157	1,097
Total revenues	46,839	42,025
Cost of sales	31,445	28,389
Selling, general and administrative expense	9,797	8,657
Credit card expense	737	722
Depreciation and amortization	1,259	1,098
Interest expense	570	556
Earnings from continuing operations before income taxes	3,031	2,603
Provision for income taxes	1,146	984
Earnings from continuing operations	$ 1,885	$ 1,619
Earnings from discontinued operations net of $46 and $116 tax	75	190
Gain from discontinued operations, net of $761 tax	1,238	—
Net earnings	$ 3,198	$ 1,809

Target's fiscal year ends on the Saturday nearest January 31. Unless otherwise stated, references to years in the annual report relate to fiscal years rather than to calendar years. That means Target refers to the fiscal year ended January 29, 2005, as fiscal year 2004.

Exhibit 5.9

Target's Income Statement Reformatted as Multiple-Step

The income statement for Target could be presented in a multi-step format as shown here. Notice that net income (net earnings) is the same no matter how the statement is formatted. A subtotal for gross profit appears in the multiple-step income statement but not in the single-step income statement.

Target Corporation
Consolidated Results of Operations
For fiscal years ended January 29 and 31
(in millions, except per share data)

	Jan. 29 2005	Jan. 31 2004
Sales	$45,682	$40,928
Cost of sales	31,445	28,389
Gross profit	14,237	12,539
Operating Expenses		
Selling, general and administrative expense	(9,797)	(8,657)
Depreciation and amortization	(1,259)	(1,098)
Net credit card revenue	420	375
Operating income	3,601	3,159
Other income and expenses from operations		
Interest expense	(570)	(556)
Earnings from continuing operations before income taxes	3,031	2,603
Provision for income taxes	1,146	984
Earnings from continuing operations	$ 1,885	$ 1,619
Earnings from discontinued operations net of $46 and $116 tax	75	190
Gain from discontinued operations, net of $761 tax	1,238	—
Net Earnings	$ 3,198	$ 1,809

Other merchandising firms present their income statement in a multi-step format. A **multiple-step income statement** highlights the components of net income, including: (1) Gross Profit, which is Sales minus Cost of Goods Sold, (2) Operating Income, which is Gross Profit minus Operating Expenses, and (3) Other Revenues and Expenses, which are those not directly related to the firm's day-to-day operations.

Take another look at Target's income statement in Exhibit 5.8. Let's reformat the statement to be a multiple-step income statement. We'll need to rearrange some of the items and add some subtotals. Exhibit 5.9 above shows the multiple-step version of Target's Income Statement.

Exhibit 5.9 is a multiple-step income statement because it provides a Gross Profit, the subtotal of Sales minus Cost of Sales, a subtotal for Operating Income, and a category for Other Income and Expenses. When a firm uses a multiple-step format, it is easier for the financial statement user to see the gross profit and to calculate the gross profit ratio, which is gross profit as a percent of sales. Next, we'll look at the gross profit ratio and the profit margin ratio.

> **Multiple-step income statement:** An income statement that highlights the components of net income.

Financial Statement Analysis—Gross Profit Ratio and Profit Margin Ratio

LEARNING OBJECTIVE 6

Compute the gross profit ratio and profit margin ratio to evaluate a firm's profitability.

Each of the four financial statements is useful to investors and other users. For example, the balance sheet tells investors a firm's financial position and ability to meet its short-term obligations. The current ratio, quick ratio, and the amount of working capital you studied in the last two chapters are calculated from amounts on the balance sheet. In addition to analysis of a firm's financial position and ability to meet its short-term obligations, investors are very interested in a firm's performance. That information comes from the income statement. An important ratio for measuring a firm's performance is the gross profit ratio. You know that gross profit equals sales minus cost of goods sold. The **gross profit ratio** is defined as gross profit divided by sales.

> **Gross profit ratio:** Gross profit divided by sales revenue.

> **In Other Words:**
> Gross profit ratio is often called the gross margin ratio, the gross profit rate, and the gross profit percentage.

$$\text{Gross profit ratio} = \frac{\text{Gross profit}}{\text{Sales}}$$

The ratio measures the portion of sales dollars a company has left after paying for the goods sold. The remaining amount will have to cover all other operating costs, such as salary expense and insurance expense, and be large enough to have something left for profit.

In the 2004 fiscal year (which actually ended on January 29, 2005), Target's gross profit was $14,237 million. The gross profit ratio—gross profit as a percent of sales—was 31.2% for fiscal year 2004.

$$\frac{\text{Gross profit}}{\text{Sales}} = \frac{14{,}237}{45{,}682} = 31.17\%$$

This ratio is very important to a retail company. As with all ratios, it is useful to compare this ratio across several years. Look at Target's income statement, and compute the gross profit ratio for 2003. Simply divide the gross profit by sales. You should see that Target's gross margin ratio has improved. In fiscal year 2004, it was 31.2, and in 2003, it was 30.6.

$$\frac{\text{Gross profit}}{\text{Sales}} = \frac{12{,}539}{40{,}928} = 30.64\%$$

When an income statement is presented in a multiple-step format, calculating the gross profit ratio is straightforward. Look at the partial income statements of Barnes & Noble in Exhibit 5.10. Each year, the gross profit has been increasing, but sales have also been increasing. Calculating the gross profit ratio for each year helps us evaluate a firm's performance. As shown in the last row of Exhibit 5.10, the gross profit ratio appears relatively constant—although half a percent could be a big improvement for the firm.

A retail company is particularly interested in its gross profit ratio and how it compares to that of prior years or that of competitors. When businesspeople talk about a product's margins, they are talking about the gross profit. There is no specific amount that signifies an acceptable or good gross profit. For example, the margin on a grocery store item is usually smaller than that of a car dealership because a grocery store turns over its inventory more frequently than does a car dealership. When a grocery store like Kroger or Whole Foods Market buys a grocery item, like a gallon of milk, the sales price of that item is not much higher than its cost. Because a grocery store sells so many different items and a large quantity of each, the gross profit on each item does not have to be very big to accumulate into a sizable gross profit for the store. However, when a company sells larger items, such as cars, televisions, or clothing, and not so many of them, it needs to have a larger gross profit on each item. For its fiscal year ended January 29, 2005, Kroger's gross profit was 27%, while Chico's, with the same fiscal year-end, had a gross profit of 61%. Read about Dell's gross profit in *Accounting in the News*.

Exhibit 5.10

Partial Income Statements for Barnes & Noble

BARNES&NOBLE
BOOKSELLERS

The income statements for Barnes & Noble are multiple-step statements, showing a subtotal for Gross Profit.

Barnes & Noble, Inc.
Taken from the Consolidated Statements of Operations
For the fiscal year ended
(in thousands)

	Jan. 31, 2005	Jan. 31, 2004	Feb. 1, 2003
Fiscal Year	2004	2003	2002
Sales	$4,873,595	$4,372,177	$3,916,544
Cost of sales	3,386,619	3,060,462	2,731,588
Gross profit	1,486,976	1,311,715	1,184,956
Sales and administrative expenses	1,052,345	910,448	816,597
Depreciation and amortization	181,553	166,825	154,844
Pre-opening expenses	8,862	8,668	11,933
Impairment charge	—	—	25,328
Operating profit	$ 244,216	$ 225,774	$ 176,254
Gross profit ratio	30.51%	30.00%	30.26%

Accounting in the NEWS

Financial Statement Analysis

Dell's Gross Profit

When you think about financial statement analysis, you usually think about current and potential investors, and their need to evaluate the performance of a company. However, a company's managers need to perform some financial statement analysis, too. One of the most useful ratios for operating managers is the gross profit percentage, sometimes called the gross profit rate. In April 2004, Dell raised its revenue outlook for the first quarter without raising its profit forecast. When would an increase in revenue *not* result in an increase in earnings?

According to the *Wall Street Journal,* "profit gains were restrained by a late April jump in memory-chip prices. Dell

benefits from falling component prices because it keeps inventory tight and turns around its manufacturing quickly. When component prices are flat or rising, however, it loses some of its inventory cost advantage, crimping profits."

Here's what happened. . .

"Dell wasn't able to adjust to the higher component prices quickly enough, costing it about $30 million in lost profit," said James M. Schneider, CFO. Its gross profit margin, a measure of profitability after manufacturing costs, declined to 18%, the lowest level in seven quarters. "We sprinted a little with revenue to cover those cost increases. Had the memory prices not surged, the higher revenue would have added a penny to per-share results," he said.

Do margins matter? Yes, so keep your eye on Dell's revenue and the resulting earnings.

Q Why did Dell lose $30 million in profit in 2004?

Dell has a loyal following, but the rising price of memory chips caused the company's profits to tumble in 2004.

A Prices of inputs increased so fast that Dell couldn't raise its prices fast enough to keep up.

Source: "Dell Reports a 22% Increase in Net," by Gary McWilliams from the *Wall Street Journal,* May 14, 2004. Copyright 2004 by Dow Jones & Co Inc. Reproduced with permission of Dow Jones & Co Inc. in the format Textbook via Copyright Clearance Center

Profit margin ratio: Measures the percentage of each sales dollar that results in net income.

In Other Words:
Profit margin ratio is often called return on sales.

You can also learn about a firm's profitability by computing a **profit margin ratio**. Similar to the gross profit ratio, the profit margin ratio is based on a percent of sales. This ratio is defined as net income divided by sales. The size of a firm's gross profit may not translate into income. The costs subtracted from the gross profit to yield net income are important. The lower those costs, the higher the firm's net income. The profit margin ratio provides information about how well a firm is controlling all of its costs, including the cost of goods sold.

$$\text{Profit margin ratio} = \frac{\text{Net income}}{\text{Net sales}}$$

Exhibit 5.11 shows the gross profit ratio and the profit margin ratio for two years for Target, Wal-Mart, and Barnes & Noble. Target has the highest gross profit ratio and the highest profit margin ratio.

Can YOU do it?

Using the information below, calculate the gross profit ratio and the profit margin ratio for Books-A-Million for the two latest fiscal years. The company's fiscal year is the same as Barnes & Noble's; the fiscal year is 52 weeks ending on the Saturday nearest January 31. Compare these ratios to those of Barnes & Noble shown in Exhibit 5.11.

(in millions)	2005	2004
Sales	475.2	458.2
Cost of Goods Sold	339.9	330.9
Net Income	10.2	7.1

Answer

	2005	2004
Gross Profit (in millions)	$135.3	$127.3
Gross Profit Ratio	28.47%	27.78%
Profit Margin Ratio	2.15%	1.56%

Barnes & Noble has a better gross profit ratio and a better profit margin ratio than Books-A-Million, which means that Barnes & Noble is controlling costs better than Books-A-Million. However, Books-A-Million improved its ratios significantly from 2004 to 2005, while Barnes & Noble's profit margin decreased slightly.

Both the gross profit ratio and the profit margin ratio provide information for comparing the performances of different companies like Target, Wal-Mart, and Barnes & Noble. The ratio comparison indicates that Target is slightly better than Wal-Mart at controlling all of its costs, and both are doing better than Barnes & Noble.

Exhibit 5.11

Comparing Gross Profit Ratios and Profit Margin Ratios

($ in millions)	Target		Wal-Mart		Barnes & Noble	
FYE January 29; 31	2005	2004	2005	2004	2005	2004
Sales	$ 45,682	$ 40,928	$285,222	$256,329	$ 4,873	$ 4,372
Gross profit	14,237	12,539	65,429	57,582	1,487	1,312
Net income	3,198	1,809	10,267	9,054	143	152
Gross profit ratio ...	31.17%	30.64%	22.94%	22.46%	30.52%	30.01%
Profit margin ratio ..	7.00%	4.42%	3.60%	3.53%	2.93%	3.48%

Business risk, control, & ethics

LEARNING OBJECTIVE 7

Recognize the special risks and controls related to inventory.

Inventory is a very important asset and ties up a large percentage of a firm's cash. The firm must evaluate and control the risk of losing inventory. Have you ever read how much money retail companies lose from shoplifting? The *16th Annual Retail Theft Survey* reported that over $2 billion was lost from shoplifting and employee theft in just 24 U.S. retail companies in 2004. It's no surprise that retail firms like Macy's and Wal-Mart are very concerned about inventory theft. All consumers pay for that loss in higher merchandise prices, therefore, good controls on inventory are important to both the company and the consumer.

Like any of a company's assets, the inventory must be protected from damage and theft. The policies and procedures we've discussed can help reduce the risks associated with the actual purchase of the inventory—selecting a reliable vendor and making sure the items received are the ones ordered. To safeguard inventory from theft, companies can use controls like locking storage rooms and limiting access to the inventory. When you buy clothes from The Limited or the GAP, you might notice a sensor attached to the clothing that the salesclerk must remove before you leave the store. You may have experienced the unpleasant beeping of such sensors if a storeclerk forgets to remove the device. Other items like CDs and DVDs will set off a beeper if you try to leave the store without having the cashier de-sensor them.

The policies and procedures for ordering inventory and providing the inventory to the customer when it is purchased are important and should be designed with risk control in mind. Read about a company that needs to take another look at its inventory controls in *Accounting in the News*.

Segregation of duties is a control that helps companies minimize the risk of losing inventory to error or theft. The person who keeps the inventory records should not be the same person who has physical control of the inventory. This separation of record keeping and physical control of assets makes it impossible for a single individual to steal the inventory and cover it up with false record keeping. When this control is in place and functioning properly, it would take collusion—that's two or more people getting together on the plan—to lose inventory in this way.

Large retail firms like Target have extensive inventory controls. There are many places—from the receiving dock to the front door of the store—where Target must keep an eye on its inventory. When goods arrive at the receiving dock, a clerk will make a record of the type and amount of merchandise that has arrived on a copy of the original purchase order without any quantities listed. The firm wants the receiving clerk to independently check the type and amount of goods that have been received. This record will be sent to the accounts payable department, where a clerk in that department will compare the record of the goods received with the original purchase order, which was sent over earlier from the purchasing department. Do you see the controls in place to safeguard the incoming shipments of merchandise? Several different departments are keeping a record of the goods ordered and received. The receiving clerk sends the merchandise to the inventory department, where physical custody of the goods is separate from the record keeping, which we have seen is verified by several departments.

Companies lose billions of dollars each year to shoplifting. Can you identify any controls that could prevent or detect this theft?

Segregation of duties: The control of having different individuals perform related duties; when the person with physical control of an asset is not the same person who keeps the accounting records for that asset.

Accounting in the NEWS

Risk and Control

The Never-ending Battle to Control Inventory

Almost all managers are aware of the risk of inventory being stolen. However, even businesses with seemingly good controls still have thefts as this anecdote by journalist Barry Brandman shows.

From outward appearances, it was just another day at a large East Coast distribution center (DC). Dock workers appeared to be busy carrying out their responsibilities, which included selecting, loading, receiving, and storing product.

For two workers, however, that morning was anything but ordinary.

A truck driver arrived at the DC, signed in, and was told at which door to pick up his load. After backing in his truck, he approached his assigned lane and began counting the staged product. This trucker, however, was only going through the motions because he already knew exactly how many cases would be waiting for him. Two hours prior to his arrival, he had received a call on his cell phone

from the shipping lead—his accomplice—at the DC, who informed him that he had deliberately staged an extra 12 cases of inventory with the driver's order.

The trucker told a forklift operator that his order was correct. Then it was loaded.

As the driver approached the guardhouse on his way out of the complex, he wasn't concerned about getting caught. The security guard had no way of knowing how much product the driver had when he arrived, nor how much he was supposed to have when he departed. The guard peered inside the cargo area of his vehicle, then waived the trucker through the gate. The security officer had no way of knowing that he had just allowed more than $9,000 of stolen product to leave the complex.

After departing the facility, the trucker detoured off his assigned route, dropping off the hot goods to a rented storage facility. Within three days, he had negotiated to sell the stolen inventory for 30% of its actual value.

Several days later, when the trucker returned to the DC, he split the cash proceeds with the shipping lead. The two thieves had no concern about being caught. After all, they had repeated this scam more than 50

Hiring honest employees may be a company's best inventory-control method.

times over the last 16 months, causing an inventory loss of more than $1 million."

According to Brandman, the company had several controls in place including: 24-hour security guard service, an alarm system, closed-circuit cameras with video recording, inventory counts, and an inventory scanning system.

As you can see, the ultimate internal control for any company is to hire honest employees.

Q What is the best internal control a company can have?

A Honest employees.

Source: Barry Brandman, "How $1.2 Million of Inventory Vanished into Thin Air," *Transportation & Distribution* (October 2001).

YOU make the call:

How could Target increase its gross profit on sales?

Now that you have studied the relationship between sales and cost of goods sold, you should be able to answer the question we posed at the start of the chapter: How can Target increase its gross profit? There are two ways: One is to increase the sales prices of its products, and the other is to reduce the costs of those products. In this chapter, you saw that there are several ways firms can reduce the cost of inventory. They include: (1) purchasing a lower-cost product, (2) reducing shipping costs, (3) reducing sales returns and allowances by increasing the quality of the products, and (4) reducing inventory theft. You may even recall reading about how Wal-Mart has lowered its cost of goods sold, thus increasing its gross profit, by forming close relationships with its vendors.

Let's Take a Test Drive

Real-World Problem:
Target Corporation

Each year, Target buys and sells millions of dollars worth of inventory. During the fiscal year ended January 29, 2005, the company had sales of over $45 billion. The accounting work to keep track of the thousands of underlying transactions is extensive, and the company wants to keep errors to a minimum. The accounting system must keep track of purchases, purchase returns and allowances, any freight charges for inventory purchases, purchase and sales discounts, sales, sales returns, and the reduction in the Inventory account when sales are made. Target's balance sheet at January 29, 2005, reports inventory of $5,384 million.

As you see from Target's income statement in Exhibit 5.9 on page 243, the Cost of Goods Sold for the year was $31,445 million. Thousands of transactions took place to achieve these numbers.

Concepts

The main accounting concept related to the purchase and sale of merchandise inventory is that all costs necessary to purchase goods and prepare them for sale should be included in the cost of the inventory. It follows from the matching principle that the cost of the goods sold should be matched with the revenue earned from selling those goods. That is, sales and the cost of those sales will appear on the same income statement. The cost of those goods not yet sold will be included in the Inventory on the balance sheet.

The Mechanics

Suppose Target started the year with merchandise inventory that cost $5,384. During the year, Target:

1. Purchased $38,000 worth of goods from suppliers, with the terms 2/10, n/30, FOB shipping point. Freight costs were $1,420.
2. Returned $2,500 worth of those purchases to suppliers.
3. Paid suppliers for purchases within the discount period.
4. Made $72,000 sales on account to customers of inventory that cost $36,000.
5. Accepted $648 worth of sales returns from customers of goods that had an original cost to the firm of $324. (Record both the sales and the cost components of the transaction.)

Instructions

1. Assume Target uses a perpetual inventory system. Give the journal entry for each of the following transactions.
2. Post the relevant entries to the Inventory T-account.

Solution

Transaction	Debit	Credit
1a. Inventory	38,000	
Accounts Payable		38,000
1b. Inventory	1,420	
Cash		1,420
2. Accounts Payable	2,500	
Inventory		2,500

3.	Accounts Payable	35,500	
	Cash		34,790
	Inventory		710
	(Calculation: 35,500 − .02(35,500) = 34,790)		
4a.	Accounts Receivable	72,000	
	Sales Revenue		72,000
4b.	Cost of Goods Sold	36,000	
	Inventory		36,000
5a.	Sales Returns and Allowances	648	
	Accounts Receivable		648
5b.	Inventory	324	
	Cost of Goods Sold		324

Inventory

Beginning Inventory	5,384		
Purchases	38,000	2,500	Purchase Returns
Freight-in	1,420	710	Purchase Discounts
		36,000	Cost of Goods Sold
Sales Returns at Cost	324		
Ending Inventory	5,918		

Rapid Review

1. **Describe the differences between service and merchandising firms.** *Service* firms provide services to customers, while *merchandising* firms sell products to customers. There are two main types of merchandising firms: *wholesalers* and *retailers*.

2. **Explain how merchandise is acquired and do the related record keeping.** Merchandise is acquired through procedures that often include requesting the merchandise via a purchase requisition, ordering the goods via a purchase order, and receiving the goods. All of the costs of acquiring goods to resell are included in the cost of the inventory.

3. **Explain how sales are made and perform the related record keeping.** Sales are made to customers, often beginning with a sales order and ending with the collection for the sale when the customer remits payment upon receipt of an invoice from the seller. Sales Revenue on the income statement is matched with the corresponding cost of the goods, an expense called *Cost of Goods Sold*.

4. **Explain the differences between a periodic and perpetual inventory system.** When a company makes a journal entry at the time of each sale, to record the reduction of inventory and the corresponding cost of goods sold, the company is using a *perpetual inventory system*. If a company waits until the end of the accounting period to adjust the inventory balance and to record the cost of goods sold, by a physical count of the inventory, the company is using a *periodic inventory system*. Both systems should produce the same information.

5. **Explain the difference between a single-step income statement and a multiple-step income statement.** A *single-step income statement* presents revenues first, and all expenses are subtracted in one step to arrive at net income. A *multiple-step income statement* highlights three sections of the income statement: (1) Gross Profit, (2) Income from Operations, and (3) Other Revenues and Expenses.

6. **Compute the gross profit ratio and profit margin ratio to evaluate a firm's profitability.** Two common ratios, computed easily from the information in a multi-step income statement, are used to evaluate a merchandising firm's profitability.

They are the *gross profit ratio (gross margin ratio)* and the *profit margin ratio.*

$$\text{Gross profit ratio} = \frac{\text{Gross profit}}{\text{Sales}}$$

$$\text{Profit margin ratio} = \frac{\text{Net income}}{\text{Sales}}$$

7. **Recognize the special risks and controls related to inventory.** The largest risk with inventory is *inventory shrinkage*—losing inventory by events other than sales. Controls should be in place to safeguard the inventory, including separation of physical control of the inventory and the record keeping for the inventory, as well as controlled access to the inventory.

Key Terms

Contra-revenue, p. 236
Cost of goods sold, p. 226
FOB (free on board) destination, p. 230
FOB (free on board) shipping point, p. 230
Gross profit, p. 226
Gross profit ratio, p. 244

Multiple-step income statement, p. 243
Periodic inventory system, p. 229
Perpetual inventory system, p. 229
Profit margin ratio, p. 246
Purchase returns and allowances, p. 231

Sales discount, p. 237
Sales returns and allowances, p. 236
Segregation of duties, p. 247
Single-step income statement, p. 242

Have You Increased Your Business IQ?

Answer these questions to find out.

1. A multiple-step income statement will have a subtotal for
   a. assets.
   b. gross profit.
   c. operating expenses.
   d. prior year's taxes.
2. The difference between perpetual and periodic inventory systems is
   a. the timing of recording cost of goods sold.
   b. the timing of payment for inventory purchases.
   c. one is for manufacturing firms and one is for merchandising firms.
   d. perpetual can only be used for high volume items.
3. FOB shipping point and FOB destination describe
   a. how quickly a firm must pay its vendors to receive a discount.
   b. when the inventory will be shipped.
   c. when the title to the inventory changes hands.
   d. who pays the sales tax on the goods.
4. One of the risks associated with inventory is
   a. buying too much.
   b. buying too little.
   c. shrinkage.
   d. all of the above.
5. Separation of duties means that the person who has physical control of an asset should
   a. also do the record keeping for the asset.
   b. not have access to cash.
   c. not do the record keeping for the asset.
   d. not check the locks on the storage units without being accompanied by another employee.

Now, check your answers.

1. b   2. a   3. c   4. d   5. c

- If you answered all five questions correctly, you've increased your business IQ by studying this chapter. It doesn't mean you've mastered all of the accounting concepts in the chapter. It simply means that you understand some of the general business concepts presented in this chapter.

- If you answered 2 to 4 questions correctly, you've made some progress, but your business IQ has plenty of room to grow. You might want to skim over the chapter again.
- If you answered 0 or 1 question correctly, you can do more to improve your business IQ. Better study the chapter again.

Questions

1. Describe the difference between a service and a merchandising firm.
2. What is an operating cycle?
3. What is the difference between a purchase requisition and a purchase order?
4. What do the terms FOB shipping point and FOB destination mean? If your business is the buyer, which terms of purchase will increase the total cost of inventory?
5. What is the difference between freight in and freight out?
6. What is the difference between a purchase return and a purchase allowance?
7. What is the effect of purchase returns and allowances on the overall cost of inventory to the buyer?
8. What is a purchase discount? What is the effect of a purchase discount on the overall cost of inventory to the buyer?
9. What do the terms 1/10, n/45 mean?
10. What is a contra-revenue account? Give two examples of contra-revenue accounts.
11. Why would a company want to keep sales returns and allowances in a separate account rather than simply deducting them directly from Sales?
12. What is the effect of sales returns and allowances on the total sales revenue of the seller?
13. What is a sales discount? What is the effect of a sales discount on the total sales revenue of the seller?
14. What are the differences between a perpetual and a periodic record-keeping system?
15. What is inventory shrinkage?
16. What are the risks associated with inventory?
17. What is a multiple-step income statement?
18. What does the gross margin ratio measure? How is it calculated?
19. What does the profit margin ratio measure? How is it calculated?
20. What is segregation of duties? Why is this important to a merchandising firm?

Multiple Choice

1. The primary source of revenue of a merchandising firm is _____, while the most significant expense(s) is(are) _____.
   a. sales revenue, cost of goods sold
   b. service revenue, operating expenses
   c. service revenue, cost of goods sold
   d. sales revenue, operating expenses
2. When inventory is purchased, it is recorded as a(n) _____ and when sold it becomes a(n) _____.
   a. liability, withdrawal
   b. asset, expense
   c. liability, asset
   d. asset, contra asset
3. If a buyer, using a perpetual inventory system, returns merchandise purchased on account to the vendor, the buyer would
   a. debit Inventory and credit Accounts Payable
   b. debit Accounts Payable and credit Inventory

   c. debit Purchase Returns and Allowances and credit Accounts Payable
   d. debit Accounts Payable and credit Purchase Returns and Allowances
4. Rock Solid Climbing Equipment Company purchased 100 pairs of hiking boots from Love's Shoe Supply. Love's quoted a price of $2,500 for the boots. The salesperson agreed to give Rock Solid a 10% good customer discount. How will Rock Solid record the purchase of the boots? The purchase was made on account.
   a. debit Inventory for $2,500, credit Accounts Payable for $2,250, and credit Revenue for $250
   b. debit Accounts Payable for $2,250 and credit Inventory for $2,250
   c. debit Purchase Returns and Allowances for $2,250 and credit Accounts Payable for $2,250
   d. credit Accounts Payable for $2,250 and debit Inventory for $2,250

5. If the shipping terms are FOB destination and the freight bill is $200, how would the buyer record the freight payment?
   a. Debit Inventory and credit Cash for $200
   b. Debit Freight-out Expense and credit Cash for $200
   c. Debit Freight-in and credit Cash for $200
   d. No journal entry is required
6. When the seller accepts a return of merchandise from the buyer that was originally sold on account, the seller's journal entry would include a
   a. debit Sales Revenue and credit Cash
   b. debit Sales Returns and Allowances and credit Accounts Receivable
   c. debit Sales Returns and Allowances and credit Sales Revenue
   d. debit Accounts Receivable and credit Sales Revenue

Use the following information to answer questions 7 through 10.

Sales Revenue	$480,000
Cost of Goods Sold	300,000
Sales Discounts	20,000
Sales Returns and Allowances	15,000
Operating Expenses	85,000
Interest Revenue	5,000

7. What is the net sales revenue?
   a. $400,000
   b. $445,000
   c. $415,000
   d. $455,000
8. What is the gross margin?
   a. $145,000
   b. $105,000
   c. $140,000
   d. $ 90,000
9. What is the net income?
   a. $ 60,000
   b. $ 65,000
   c. $ 55,000
   d. $180,000
10. What is the profit margin ratio?
    a. 13.54%
    b. 14.61%
    c. 44.83%
    d. 21.67%

Short Exercises

SE5-1. Identification of accounts.   LO 1
For each of the following accounts, tell whether or not it would be found in the financial records of a service firm, a merchandising firm, or both.

a. Service Revenue
b. Cost of Goods Sold
c. Purchase Returns and Allowances
d. Salary Expense
e. Sales Revenue
f. Accounts Receivable
g. Inventory
h. Accounts Payable

SE5-2. Calculate cost of inventory.   LO 2
Party Decorating Resources began operations on May 1. The following transactions took place in the month of May.

a. Cash purchases of merchandise during May were $300,000.
b. Purchases of merchandise on account during May were $400,000.
c. The cost of freight to deliver the merchandise to Party was $25,000; the terms were FOB shipping point. The freight bill was paid in May.
d. Party returned $22,000 of merchandise purchased in transaction a to the supplier for a full refund.
e. The store manager's salary of $3,000 for the month was paid in cash.

Calculate the amount that Party Decorating Resources should record for the total cost of merchandise inventory purchased in May.

SE5-3. Record purchase of merchandise inventory.   LO 2, 4
Using the data from SE5-2, prepare the journal entries to record the transactions for the month of May, assuming Party Decorating Resources uses a perpetual inventory system.

LO 2   **SE5-4. Calculate cost of inventory.**

Given the following information related to the purchases of inventory during the month of February:

Inventory purchased on February 10, paid for on February 18.

Invoice Price	$5,000
Terms of Sale	2/10, n/30
Shipping Terms	FOB shipping point
Shipping Costs	$250
Salary for Inventory Stocker	$750
Electricity for Storage Area	$300

Calculate the amount that would be recorded as the total cost of inventory for the month of February.

LO 2   **SE5-5. Analyze purchase discount.**

Saint Jose's Java Haven purchased $18,750 worth of inventory from Coffee Suppliers with terms of 2/15, n/45 for its grand opening. How many days does Saint Jose's have to take advantage of the purchase discount? How many days does Saint Jose's have to pay if it does not take advantage of the purchase discount?

LO 3   **SE5-6. Analyze sales discount.**

Using data from SE5-5, how much cash will Coffee Suppliers collect assuming Saint Jose's pays within 15 days? What is the amount of the discount?

LO 2   **SE5-7. Calculate cost of inventory.**

For each of the following independent situations, calculate the amount that the purchasing company would record as the cost of each inventory purchase:

a. Invoice price of goods is $5,000. Purchase terms are 2/10, n/30, and the invoice is paid in the week of receipt. The shipping terms are FOB shipping point, and the shipping costs amount to $200.

b. Invoice price of goods is $3,000. Purchase terms are 4/10, n/30, and the invoice is paid within the week of receipt. The shipping terms are FOB destination, and the shipping costs amount to $250.

c. Invoice price of goods is $2,500. Purchase terms are 2/10, n/30, and the invoice is paid 15 days after receipt. The shipping terms are FOB shipping point, and the shipping costs amount to $250.

LO 2   **SE5-8. Analyze and record purchase discount.**

French Pastry Corporation makes a purchase of $12,000 of inventory, subject to terms of 3/10, n/45 and FOB shipping point. The freight charges were $150. French returned $500 of defective merchandise inventory prior to payment. What is the amount of the payment, assuming French pays within 10 days?

LO 3, 4   **SE5-9. Record sale of merchandise inventory.**

Rachel Edward's Fabric Corporation uses a perpetual inventory system. Record the journal entries for the following transactions:

1. On April 12, Rachel Edward's sold $500,000 of merchandise with terms 2/10, n/30. The cost of the merchandise sold was $230,000.
2. On April 16, the customer returned $100,000 of the merchandise purchased on April 12 because it was the wrong color. The cost of the merchandise returned was $46,000.
3. On April 20, the customer paid the balance due Rachel Edward's.

LO 3, 5   **SE5-10. Calculate income statement amounts.**

Rachel started the month of April with $300,000 of inventory. Using the information in SE5-9, post the transactions to T-accounts. Calculate the Net Sales Revenue, Cost of Goods Sold, and gross profit that would appear on Rachel Edward's Fabric Corporation's multiple-step income statement for the month of April.

LO 5   **SE5-11. Prepare multiple-step income statement.**

Using the following data, prepare a multiple-step income statement for International Furniture for the month ended July 31, 2006. Assume there are no other revenues or expenses for the period.

Cost of Goods Sold	$625,700
Freight-out	120,300
Net Sales Revenue	1,085,650

SE5-12. Calculate cost of goods sold and gross margin. LO 2, 5
The following amounts are from the 2007 and 2008 income statements of International Furniture. Using the given information, calculate the missing amounts. Assume there are no other revenues or expenses than those provided.

Date	Sales Revenue	Cost of Goods Sold	Gross Profit	Freight- out	Net Income
July 31, 2007	$1,175,000	x	$589,000	x	$476,488
July 31, 2008	$1,249,000	$605,000	x	x	$538,300

SE5-13. Calculate gross profit and profit margin ratios. LO 6
Kidman Corporation reported net sales of $550,000; cost of goods sold of $275,000; and net income of $60,000. Calculate the gross profit, gross profit ratio, and the profit margin ratio.

SE5-14. Analyze gross profit and profit margin ratios. LO 6
Explain the difference between what is measured by the gross profit and the profit margin ratios.

SE5-15. Risk and Control. LO 7
Henry is in charge of the inventory for a local restaurant. Because the business is small, Henry has both physical control of the inventory and responsibility for the record keeping. What control is missing that could prevent Henry from taking inventory from the restaurant for his home? Suppose the restaurant cannot hire anyone else to help Henry. What controls should the restaurant owner employ with respect to inventory?

SE5-16. Appendix: Periodic inventory system.
Green House Nursery uses a periodic inventory system. At December 31, 2009, the end of the company's fiscal year, a physical count of inventory revealed an ending inventory balance of $220,000. The following items were *not* included in the physical count:

- Inventory shipped to a customer on 12/30 FOB destination (inventory arrived at customer's location on 1/5/09)   10,000
- Inventory shipped to a customer on 12/29 FOB shipping point (inventory arrived at customer's location on 1/3/09)   5,000
- Inventory purchased from a supplier, shipped FOB destination on 12/29, in transit at year-end   4,000

What should Green report as Inventory on their December 31, 2009, balance sheet?

SE5-17. Appendix: Periodic inventory system.
Dessert Delight Company started the period with $5,000 in its Inventory account. The company purchased $3,500 of inventory, and returned $375 worth of inventory during the period. A count of the ending inventory revealed there was $2,960 worth of inventory on hand. Assume the company uses a periodic inventory system. What was Dessert's cost of goods sold for the period?

SE5-18. Appendix: Periodic inventory system.
Oriental Rug Corporation uses a periodic inventory system and had no beginning inventory. Assuming the following transactions were the only ones to occur during the month, prepare the journal entries. Prepare the journal entry needed to record the cost of goods sold at the end of April.

1. On April 1, Oriental purchased inventory in the amount of $300,000 cash.
2. On April 12, Oriental sold $500,000 of merchandise with terms 2/10, n/30. The cost of the merchandise sold was $230,000.
3. On April 16, the customer returned $100,000 of the merchandise purchased on April 12 because it was defective. The cost of the merchandise returned was $46,000.
4. On April 20, the customer paid the balance due Oriental Corporation.
5. On April 30, the physical inventory count showed ending inventory of $116,000.

Exercise Set A

LO 2

E5-1A. Record purchase of merchandise inventory.

Assume the following transactions for Home Depot took place during May. Home Depot uses a perpetual inventory system. Prepare the journal entry for each:

May 2   Purchased refrigerators from GE at a total cost of $500,000 terms 1/10, n/30.

May 9   Paid freight of $800 on refrigerators purchased from GE.

May 16   Returned refrigerators to GE because they were damaged. Received a credit of $5,000 from GE.

May 22   Sold refrigerators costing $100,000 for $180,000 to Pizzeria Number 1, terms n/30.

May 24   Gave a credit of $3,000 to Pizzeria Number 1 for the return of a refrigerator not ordered. Home Depot's cost was $1,200.

LO 2

E5-2A. Record purchase of merchandise inventory.

Gallop Industries engaged in the following transactions during August. The company uses a perpetual inventory system. Prepare the journal entry for each.

August 7   Purchased merchandise from Hecht Company for $26,000, terms 2/10, n/30.

August 10   Paid freight costs of $900 on merchandise purchased from Hecht Company.

August 24   Returned some of August 5 purchase to Hecht Company, which cost $2,800.

August 30   Paid the amount due to Hecht Company in full.

LO 2

E5-3A. Record purchase of merchandise inventory.

On July 16, John's Restaurant Supplies purchased $5,000 worth of merchandise from a supplies company with terms 2/10, n/30, FOB destination. Freight costs were $300. On July 18, John's returned $500 worth of goods that did not meet its specifications. On July 25, John's paid the supplies company in full. John's uses a perpetual inventory system. Prepare the journal entries for John's transactions.

LO 3, 5

E5-4A. Calculate net sales and gross margin.

The adjusted trial balance at June 30, 2007, for Music Bargains shows the following accounts and balances:

Sales	$700,000
Sales Returns and Allowances	20,000
Sales Discounts	24,000
Freight-out (delivery expenses)	7,000
Cost of Goods Sold	250,000
Operating Expenses	100,000

What amount should Music Bargains report as Net Sales and as Gross Margin on its income statement for the year ended June 30, 2007?

LO 5

E5-5A. Prepare multiple-step income statement.

Using the data from E5-4A, prepare Music Bargains's multiple-step income statement for the year ended June 30, 2007.

LO 6

E5-6A. Calculate gross profit ratio and profit margin ratio.

Using the data from E5-4A, what is Music Bargains's gross profit ratio and profit margin ratio for the period? What type of information does each ratio provide to users of Music's financial statement?

LO 2, 3

E5-7A. Record sale of merchandise inventory: perpetual inventory system.

The Ultimate Bike Shop had the following transactions:

April 3   Sold $5,000 of merchandise inventory (costing $2,750) to Bicycles Unlimited with terms 1/15, n/30, and FOB destination. Freight costs associated with this sale were $175.

April 5   Bicycles Unlimited returned one bike from the sale (April 3) in the amount of $475. The cost of the returned bike was $285.

April 10   Sold $3,500 of bicycles and accessories (costing $1,375) to The Great Outdoors Company with terms 4/10, n/30, and FOB shipping point. Freight costs associated with this sale were $85.

April 14   Granted an allowance of $75 to The Great Outdoors Company because
one of the bicycles arrived without the seat.
April 19   Collected the amount owed from Bicycles Unlimited.
April 20   Collected the amount owed from The Great Outdoors Company.

Prepare the journal entries recorded by The Ultimate Bike Shop for the month of April
assuming they use a perpetual inventory system.

E5-8A. Record merchandising transactions: perpetual inventory system.

LO 2, 3

The Fedora Company had a beginning inventory balance of $25,750 and engaged in the
following transactions:

June 2   Purchased $4,000 of merchandise inventory from Plumes Incorporated
with terms 2/10, n/30, and FOB destination. Freight costs associated with
this purchase were $225.
June 4   Returned $400 of damaged merchandise to Plumes Incorporated.
June 6   Sold $7,000 of merchandise to Fancy Caps, terms 1/15, n/30, and FOB
shipping point. Freight costs were $125. The cost of the inventory sold was
$3,500.
June 9   Paid the amount owed to Plumes Incorporated.
June 10   The Fedora Company granted Fancy Caps an allowance on the June 6 sale
of $300 for minor damage found on several pieces of merchandise.
June 22   Received total payment owed from Fancy Caps.
June 24   Paid sales salaries of $1,850.
June 25   Paid the rent on the showroom, $1,200.

Prepare the journal entries The Fedora Company will make to record these
transactions assuming they use a perpetual inventory system.

E5-9A. Record merchandising transactions and calculate ending inventory: perpetual inventory system.

LO 2, 3

Using the data from E5-8A, post the journal entries to T-accounts. Assume Fedora began
the year with Cash of $3,650, Inventory of $25,570 as given in E5-8A, Contributed
Capital of $25,000, and Retained Earnings of $4,220. What is the amount of Inventory
that will appear on The Fedora Company's balance sheet at June 30?

E5-10A. Prepare a multiple-step income statement.

LO 5

Using the data from E5-8A, prepare a multiple-step income statement for The Fedora
Company for the month ended June 30.

E5-11A. Calculate the gross profit and profit margin ratios.

LO 6

Using the income statement prepared in E5-10A, calculate the gross profit ratio and
the profit margin ratio for The Fedora Company.

E5-12A. Prepare multiple-step and single-step income statements.

LO 5, 6

On its income statement for the fiscal year ended on the Saturday nearest December
31, 2007, Safeway reported the following (in millions):

Rent Expense	$ 368	Operating and Administrative Expenses	$7,718
Cost of Goods Sold	22,302	Freight-out	704
Net Sales	32,399		

Assume these were all the reported amounts. Prepare a multiple-step and a single-step
income statement. Then calculate the gross profit ratio and the profit margin ratio.

E5-13A. Calculate gross profit and profit margin ratios.

LO 6

On its income statement for the fiscal year ended January 31, 2003, Lowe's Companies
showed Net Sales of $26,491 million, Cost of Sales of $18,465 million, and Net Earnings
of $1,471 million. Calculate the gross profit ratio and the profit margin ratio for the year.

E5-14A. Prepare multiple-step and single-step income statements and calculate gross profit and profit margin ratios.

LO 5, 6

On its income statement for the fiscal year ended on March 31, 2009, Wet Seal reported
the following (in thousands):

Other Operating Expenses	$104,130	Freight-out	$2,105
Cost of Goods Sold	430,971	Freight-in	1,875
Net Sales	608,509		

Prepare a multiple-step income statement. Then, calculate the gross profit ratio and the profit margin ratio. (Note: When the accountant prepared the income statement, he listed freight-in even though it had already been included in the cost of inventory.)

LO 7   E5-15A. Risk and control.
How much of a problem for retail firms is shoplifting? From your own experience, name two or three controls that stores have in place to prevent this type of inventory shrinkage.

LO 7   E5-16A. Risk and control.
Why would the receiving department's copy of a purchase order have no quantities given for the ordered goods?

E5-17A. Appendix: Periodic inventory system.
The Cooking Pie Company uses a periodic inventory system and started the period with no beginning inventory. Assuming the following transactions were the only ones to occur during the month of July, prepare the journal entries. Then, prepare the journal entry needed to record the Cost of Goods Sold at the end of July.

1. On July 10, Cooking purchased inventory in the amount of $150,000 cash.
2. On July 13, Cooking sold $250,000 of merchandise with terms 2/10, n/30. The cost of the merchandise sold was $100,000.
3. On July 17, the customer returned $25,000 of the merchandise purchased on July 13 because it was defective. The cost of the merchandise returned was $10,000.
4. On July 22, the customer paid the balance due Cooking.
5. On July 31, the physical inventory count showed ending inventory of $60,000.

E5-18A. Appendix: Periodic inventory system.
The adjusted trial balance for Hansel Company shows the following accounts and balances:

Purchases	$400,000
Purchase Returns and Allowances	34,000
Purchase Discounts	20,000

What is the amount of net purchases for Hansel Company during the period?

E5-19A. Appendix: Periodic inventory system.
The trial balance for Sports Gear Corporation on December 31, the end of its fiscal year, showed the following accounts and balances:

Merchandise Inventory (beginning)	$ 24,500
Purchases	150,000
Purchase Returns and Allowances	12,500
Freight-in	4,500
Sales Returns and Allowances	10,200
Freight-out	2,450
Purchase Discounts	1,500

A count of the merchandise inventory on December 31 showed $32,000 worth of inventory. Calculate the Cost of Goods Sold.

Exercise Set B

Your professor may ask you to complete selected "Group B" exercises and problems using Prentice Hall Grade Assist **(PHGA)**. PHGA is an online tool that can help you master the chapter's topics by providing multiple variations of exercises and problems. You can rework these exercises and problems—each time with new data—as many times as you need, with immediate feedback and grading.

LO 2   E5-1B. Record purchase of merchandise inventory.
Assume the following transactions for Nicole's Appliance & Electronic Company took place during March. Nicole's uses a perpetual inventory system. Prepare the journal entry for each.

March 3   Purchased televisions from Sanyo at a total cost of $650,000 with terms 2/10, n/25.
March 8   Paid freight of $1,000 on televisions purchased from Sanyo.

March 16   Returned televisions to Sanyo because they were damaged. Received a credit of $15,000 from Sanyo.

March 22   Sold televisions costing $125,000 for $225,000 to Joe's Sports Bar & Grille, terms n/15.

March 28   Gave a credit of $2,800 to Joe's Sports Bar & Grille for the return of a television not ordered. Nicole's cost was $1,600.

E5-2B. Record purchase of merchandise inventory.   LO 2
Lee Ann Industries engaged in the following transactions during July. The company uses a perpetual inventory system. Prepare the journal entry for each.

July 8   Purchased merchandise from Bailey Company for $28,000 with terms 1/10, n/15.

July 10   Paid freight costs of $750 on merchandise purchased from Bailey Company.

July 13   Returned $1,500 worth of July 8 purchase to Bailey Company.

July 23   Paid the amount due to Bailey Company in full.

E5-3B. Record purchase of merchandise inventory.   LO 2
On January 13, Brick & Masonry purchased $13,000 worth of merchandise from Builders Surplus with terms 4/05, n/30, FOB destination. Freight costs were $175. On January 15, Brick returned $175 worth of goods that did not meet its specifications. On January 17, Brick paid Builders Surplus in full. Brick uses a perpetual inventory system. Prepare the journal entries for Brick's transactions.

E5-4B. Calculate net sales and gross margin.   LO 3, 5
The adjusted trial balance at December 31, 2009, for Pets & Supplies Company shows the following accounts and balances:

Sales	$650,000
Sales Returns and Allowances	15,000
Sales Discounts	8,000
Freight-out (delivery expenses)	5,000
Cost of Goods Sold	210,000
Operating Expenses	200,000

What amount should Pets & Supplies Company report as Net Sales and as gross profit on its multiple-step income statement for the year ended December 31, 2009?

E5-5B. Prepare multiple-step income statement.   LO 5
Using the data from E5-4B, prepare Pets & Supplies Company's multiple-step income statement for the year ended December 31, 2009.

E5-6B. Calculate gross profit ratio and profit margin ratio.   LO 6
Using the data from E5-4B, what is Pets & Supplies Company's gross profit ratio and profit margin ratio for the period? What type of information does each ratio provide to users of Pet's financial statements?

E5-7B. Record sale of merchandise inventory: perpetual inventory system.   LO 2, 3
The Exquisite Aquarium Shop had the following transactions. Prepare the journal entries recorded by The Exquisite Aquarium Shop for the month of June assuming they use a perpetual inventory system.

June 3   Sold $15,000 of merchandise inventory (costing $8,250) to Aquariums Unlimited with terms 2/10, n/25, and FOB destination. Freight for this sale was $525.

June 6   Aquariums Unlimited returned one aquarium from the sale (June 3) in the amount of $1,425. The cost of the returned aquarium was $855.

June 10   Sold $10,500 of aquariums and accessories (costing $4,125) to The Great Fish Reef Company with terms 4/15, n/30, and FOB shipping point. Freight costs associated with this sale were $255.

June 14   Granted an allowance of $225 to The Great Fish Reef Company because one of the aquariums arrived without the stand.

June 16   Collected the amount owed from Aquariums Unlimited.

June 24   Collected the amount owed from The Great Fish Reef Company.

LO 2, 3   **E5-8B. Record merchandising transactions: perpetual inventory system.**

Discount Wines had a beginning inventory balance of $85,450 and engaged in the following transactions:

October	2	Purchased $15,000 of merchandise inventory from Joe's Winery with terms 2/10, n/30, and FOB destination. Freight costs for this purchase were $750.
October	5	Returned $100 of damaged merchandise to Joe's.
October	6	Sold $18,000 of merchandise to Tasty Catering Service, terms 2/15, n/30, and FOB shipping point. Freight costs were $155. The cost of the inventory sold was $10,500.
October	10	Paid the amount owed to Joe's.
October	10	Discount granted Tasty an allowance on the October 6 sale of $200 for some soured wine.
October	23	Received payment from Tasty.
October	29	Paid sales salaries of $1,500.
October	31	Paid the rent on the warehouse, $1,450.

Prepare the journal entries Discount Wines will make to record these transactions assuming they use a perpetual inventory system.

LO 2, 3   **E5-9B. Record merchandising transactions and calculate ending inventory: perpetual inventory system.**

Using the data from E5-8B, post the journal entries to T-accounts. Assume Discount Wines began the year with Cash of $15,000, Inventory of $85,450 as given in E5-8B, Contributed Capital of $80,000, and Retained Earnings of $20,450. What is the amount of ending inventory that will appear on the firm's balance sheet at October 31?

LO 5   **E5-10B. Prepare a multiple-step income statement.**

Using the data from E5-8B, prepare a multiple-step income statement for Discount Wines for the month ended October 31.

LO 6   **E5-11B. Calculate the gross profit and profit margin ratios.**

Using the income statement prepared in E5-10B, calculate the gross profit ratio and the profit margin ratio for Discount Wines.

LO 5, 6   **E5-12B. Prepare multiple-step and single-step income statements.**

On its income statement for the fiscal year ended on Friday, June 30, 2006, Vinyl Hyper-Drive reported the following (in thousands):

Salary Expense	$ 150	Other Operating Expenses	$8,018
Cost of Goods Sold	15,302	Freight-out	615
Net Sales	38,381		

Assume these were all the reported amounts. Prepare a multiple-step and single-step income statement. Then calculate the gross profit ratio and the profit margin ratio.

LO 6   **E5-13B. Calculate gross profit and profit margin ratios.**

On its income statement for the fiscal year ended March 31, 2008, Alien Technology showed Net Sales of $15,491 million, Cost of Sales of $12,465 million, and Net Earnings of $2,541 million. Calculate the gross profit ratio and the profit margin ratio for the year.

LO 5, 6   **E5-14B. Prepare multiple-step and single-step income statement and calculate gross profit and profit margin ratios.**

On its income statement for the fiscal year ended on December 31, 2007, Brutus & Gabby Cotton Company reported the following (in millions):

Rent Expense	$ 14	Freight-out	$185
Cost of Goods Sold	851	Freight-in	168
Net Sales	1,952		

First, prepare a single-step income statement. Then, prepare a multiple-step income statement. Then, calculate the gross profit ratio and the profit margin ratio. (Note: When the accountant prepared the income statement he listed freight-in even though it had already been included in the cost of inventory.)

E5-15B. Risk and control. LO 7

Name two or three ways that Wal-Mart protects its inventory. If you have ever worked for a retail firm, did you experience firsthand some of the controls the firm had in place to prevent employee theft? If so, name them. If not, can you think of any that a firm might have?

E5-16B. Risk and control. LO 7

In many retail firms, several people look at documents that show the amount of inventory received in any given shipment. Name two and tell why this is a good idea.

E5-17B. Appendix: Periodic inventory system.

Sandra's Aquatic Nursery uses a periodic inventory system and started the period with no beginning inventory. Assuming the following transactions were the only ones to occur during the month of May for Sandra's, prepare the journal entries. Then, prepare the journal entry needed to record the Cost of Goods Sold at the end of May.

1. On May 9, Sandra's purchased inventory in the amount of $15,000 cash.
2. On May 14, Sandra's sold $25,000 of merchandise with terms 2/10, n/30. The cost of the merchandise sold was $10,000.
3. On May 17, the customer returned $2,500 of the merchandise purchased on May 14 because it was defective. The cost of the merchandise returned was $1,000.
4. On May 22, the customer paid the balance due Sandra's.
5. On May 31, the physical inventory count showed ending inventory of $6,000.

E5-18B. Appendix: Periodic inventory system.

The adjusted trial balance for Gretchen Company shows the following accounts and balances:

Purchases	$318,000
Purchase Returns and Allowances	15,000
Purchase Discounts	8,500

What is the amount of net purchases for Gretchen Company during the period?

E5-19B. Appendix: Periodic inventory system.

The trial balance for Environmental Enhancement Corporation on June 30, the end of its fiscal year, showed the following accounts and balances:

Merchandise Inventory (beginning)	$18,250
Purchases	115,000
Purchase Returns and Allowances	10,500
Freight-in	3,250
Sales Returns and Allowances	8,470
Freight-out	2,150
Purchase Discounts	570

A count of the merchandise inventory on June 30 showed $22,750 worth of inventory. Calculate the Cost of Goods Sold.

Problem Set A

P5-1A. Analyze purchases of merchandise inventory. LO 2

The Battier Company made the following purchases in March of the current year:

March 2   Purchased $5,000 of merchandise, terms 1/10, n/30, FOB shipping point.

March 5   Purchased $2,000 of merchandise, terms 2/15, n/45, FOB shipping point.

March 10   Purchased $4,000 of merchandise, terms 3/5, n/15, FOB destination.

Required

a. For each of the purchases listed, how many days does the company have to take advantage of the purchase discount?
b. What is the amount of the cash discount allowed in each case?
c. Assume the freight charges are $350 on each purchase. What is the total amount of freight that Battier has to pay?
d. What is the total cost of inventory for Battier Company for the month of March assuming that all discounts were taken?

LO 2   **P5-2A. Analyze purchases of merchandise inventory.**

The Williams Company made the following purchases in May of the current year:

May 3	Purchased $3,000 of merchandise, terms 2/10, n/30, FOB destination.
May 12	Purchased $2,800 of merchandise, terms 2/10, n/60, FOB shipping point.
May 22	Purchased $6,000 of merchandise, terms 3/05, n/20, FOB destination.

Required

a. For each purchase, by what date is the payment due assuming the company takes advantage of the discount?
b. For each purchase, when is the payment due if the company does not take advantage of the discount?
c. In each case, what is the amount of the cash discount allowed?
d. Assume the freight charges are $400 on each purchase. For which purchase(s) is Williams Company responsible for the freight charges?
e. What is the total cost of inventory for the month of May assuming that all discounts were taken?

LO 2, 3, 5, 6   **P5-3A. Record merchandising transactions and prepare single-step and multiple-step income statement: perpetual inventory system.**

At the beginning of February, Ace Distribution Company was started with a contribution of $10,000 cash from its shareholders. The company engaged in the following transactions during the month of February:

a. February 2   Purchased merchandise on account from Enter Supply Co. for $7,100 with the terms 2/10, n/45.
b. February 5   Sold merchandise on account to Exit Company for $6,000 with the terms 2/10, n/30, and FOB destination. The cost of the merchandise sold was $4,500.
c. February 6   Paid $100 freight on the sale to Exit Company.
d. February 8   Received credit from Enter Supply Co. for merchandise returned for $500.
e. February 10   Paid Enter Supply Co. in full.
f. February 12   Received payment from Exit Company for sale made on February 5.
g. February 14   Purchased merchandise for cash $5,200.
h. February 16   Received refund from supplier for returned merchandise on February 14 cash purchase of $350.
i. February 17   Purchased merchandise on account from Inware Distributors $3,800 with the terms 1/10, n/30.
j. February 18   Paid $250 freight on February 17 purchase.
k. February 21   Sold merchandise for cash $10,350. The cost of the merchandise sold was $8,200.
l. February 24   Purchased merchandise for cash for $2,300.
m. February 25   Paid Inware Distributors for purchase on February 17.
n. February 27   Gave refund of $200 to customer from February 21. The cost of the returned merchandise was $135.
o. February 28   Sold merchandise of $3,000 on account with the terms 2/10, n/30. The merchandise cost $2,300.

Required

a. Prepare the journal entries for each transaction, assuming Ace Distribution Company uses a perpetual inventory system.
b. Post the transactions to T-accounts. Be sure to start with the opening balances in Cash and Common Stock described at the beginning of the problem.
c. Calculate the balance in the Inventory account at the end of February.
d. Prepare a single-step and multiple-step income statement for the month of February.
e. Calculate the profit margin ratio.

LO 2, 3, 5, 6   **P5-4A. Record merchandising transactions and prepare single-step and multiple-step income statement: perpetual inventory system.**

Rack-it-up Company sells clothing racks to retail shops like Talbot's and Chico's. Rack-it-up was started with a contribution of $25,000 cash from its shareholders. During the month of October, the following transactions took place:

a. October 1   Purchased 50 large racks on account from the manufacturer for $100 each. The terms were 2/10, n/30, and FOB destination.

b. October 5   Sold 10 large racks to Dress Mart on account for $120 each, with terms 1/10, n/30, and FOB destination. The cost of the racks sold was $1,000.

c. October 9   Paid the manufacturer for the October 1 purchase.

d. October 14   Received payment in full from Dress Mart.

e. October 17   Sold 20 large racks to Clothes Barn on account for $110 each, with terms 1/10, n/30, and FOB shipping point. The cost of the racks sold was $1,950.

f. October 18   Received cash refund of $392 for 4 large racks returned to the manufacturer.

g. October 20   Purchased 30 medium racks on account from the manufacturer for $70 each, with terms n/30 and FOB destination.

h. October 24   Sold 16 medium racks to Chico's for $100 each. Chico's paid cash. Shipping terms were FOB shipping point. The cost of the racks sold was $1,560.

i. October 28   Received credit of $45 for a slightly damaged rack in the October 20 shipment.

j. October 31   Paid for the purchase on October 20.

Required

a. Assume the company uses a perpetual inventory system. Give the journal entry for each transaction. Assume the freight costs for each shipment (in or out) amounted to $100.

b. Post the entries to T-accounts. Be sure to start with the opening balances in Cash and Common Stock described at the beginning of the problem.

c. Calculate the cost of goods sold for October and the ending balance in Inventory.

d. Prepare a single-step and multiple-step income statement for the month of February.

e. Calculate the profit margin ratio.

P5-5A. Record merchandising transactions and prepare multiple-step income statement: perpetual inventory system.

LO 2, 3, 5, 6

The following transactions occurred during March 2007 at the Five Oaks Tennis Club:

a. March 3   Purchased racquets and balls on credit from Spaulding Company for $700, with terms 3/05, n/30.

b. March 4   Paid freight of $50 on the March 3 purchase.

c. March 6   Sold merchandise to members on credit for $400, with terms n/30. The merchandise sold cost $300.

d. March 10   Received credit of $40 from Spaulding for a damaged racquet that was returned.

e. March 11   Purchased tennis shoes from Reebok for cash of $3,000.

f. March 13   Paid Spaulding Company in full.

g. March 14   Purchased tennis shirts and shorts from Nike Sportswear on credit for $5,000, with terms 2/10, n/45.

h. March 15   Received credit of $50 from Nike Sportswear for damaged merchandise.

i. March 18   Sold merchandise to members on account, $950, terms n/30. The cost of the merchandise sold was $500.

j. March 22   Received $650 in cash payment on account from members.

k. March 21   Paid Nike Sportswear in full.

l. March 26   Granted an allowance of $30 to members for tennis clothing that faded when washed. (Customers kept the clothes.)

m. March 30   Received $320 in cash payments on account from members.

n. March 30   Paid cash operating expenses of $300 for the month.

Required

a. Prepare the journal entries for the March transactions, assuming the company uses a perpetual inventory system.

b. Suppose the Five Oaks Tennis Club started the month with Cash of $8,000; Merchandise Inventory of $2,000; and Common Stock of $10,000. Post the journal entries to T-accounts.

c. Prepare a trial balance at March 31, 2007.

d. Prepare Five Oaks multiple-step income statement for the month ended March 31, 2007.

e. Prepare Five Oaks Tennis Club's balance sheet at March 31, 2007.

f. Calculate the gross margin and profit margin ratios for Five Oaks. Explain what each ratio measures.

LO 2, 4, 7   **P5-6A. Analyze results of physical count of inventory and calculate cost of goods sold.**

Beard Company uses a perpetual inventory system. The company's accounting records showed the following related to June 2005 transactions:

		Units	Cost
	Beginning Inventory, June 1	200	$ 600
+	Purchases during June	1,700	5,100
=	Goods Available for Sale	1,900	$5,700
−	Cost of Goods Sold	1,500	4,500
=	Ending Inventory, June 30	400	$1,200

On June 30, 2005, Beard conducted a physical count of its inventory and discovered there were only 375 units of inventory on hand.

Required

a. Using the information from the physical count, correct Beard's Cost of Goods Sold for June.

b. How would this correction change the financial statements for the year?

c. What are some possible causes of the difference between the inventory amounts in Beard's accounting records and the inventory amount from the physical count?

LO 2, 3, 5   **P5-7A. Analyze accounting methods and prepare corrected income statement.**

You are the accountant for Baldwin Company, and your assistant has prepared the following income statement for the year ended September 30, 2006.

Baldwin Company
Income Statement
For the year ended September 30, 2006

(in thousands)

Sales revenue		$850,000
Sales returns and allowances	$ 22,500	
Freight costs	14,300	(36,800)
Net Sales		813,200
Expenses		
Cost of goods sold	540,000	
Selling expenses	150,000	
Insurance expense	20,000	
Administrative expenses	40,000	
Dividends	8,000	
Total expenses		758,000
Net Income		$ 55,200

You have uncovered the following errors:

1. Sales Revenue includes $5,000 of items that have been back ordered. (The items have not been delivered to the customers, and the customers have not been billed for the items.)

2. Selling Expenses includes $250 of allowances that were given to customers who received damaged products.

3. Insurance Expense includes $100 worth of insurance that applies to 2007.

4. Administrative Expenses include a loan made to a worker who has had some serious financial trouble and needed $500 to pay a hospital bill. The worker plans to repay the money by the end of December.

Required

a. Prepare a corrected multiple-step income statement for the year. Baldwin shows sales as the net amount only on its income statement.

b. Write a memo to your assistant explaining why the income statement is incorrect and what the correct statement would show.

P5-8A. Appendix: Periodic inventory system.

Use the data on Ace Distribution in P5-3A to complete this problem.

Required

a. Assume the company uses a periodic inventory system. Prepare the journal entries for each transaction.
b. Post the transactions to T-accounts. Be sure to start with the opening balances in Cash and Common Stock described at the beginning of the problem.
c. Calculate cost of goods sold for February and the balance in Inventory at the end of February. (Note: In a real periodic system, the ending inventory would be counted and the cost of goods sold would be a calculated amount.)
d. Prepare a single-step and multiple-step income statement for the month of February.
e. Calculate the profit margin ratio.

P5-9A. Appendix: Periodic inventory system.

Use the data on Rack-it-up Company in P5-4A to complete this problem.

Required

a. Assume the company uses a periodic inventory system. Give the journal entry for each transaction. Assume the freight costs for each shipment (in or out) amounted to $100.
b. Post the entries to T-accounts. Be sure to start with the opening balances in Cash and Common Stock described at the beginning of the problem.
c. Calculate the cost of goods sold for October and the balance in Inventory at the end of October.
d. Prepare a single-step and multiple-step income statement for the month of October.
e. Calculate the profit margin ratio.

P5-10A. Appendix: Periodic inventory system.

Use the data on Five Oaks Tennis Club in P5-5A to complete this problem.

Required

a. Assume the company uses a periodic inventory system. Prepare the journal entries for the March transactions.
b. Suppose the Five Oaks Tennis Club started the month with Cash of $8,000; Merchandise Inventory of $2,000; and Common Stock of $10,000. Post the journal entries to T-accounts.
c. Prepare a trial balance at March 31.
d. Calculate the cost of goods sold for March and the balance in Inventory at the end of march.
e. Prepare Five Oaks multiple-step income statement for the month ended March 31.
f. Prepare Five Oaks Tennis Club's balance sheet at March 31.
g. Calculate the gross margin and profit margin ratios for Five Oaks. Explain what each ratio measures.

Problem Set B

> Your professor may ask you to complete selected "Group B" exercises and problems using Prentice Hall Grade Assist (**PHGA**). PHGA is an online tool that can help you master the chapter's topics by providing multiple variations of exercises and problems. You can rework these exercises and problems—each time with new data—as many times as you need, with immediate feedback and grading.

P5-1B. Analyze purchases of merchandise inventory.   LO 2

The Winning Lacrosse Company made the following purchases in April of the current year:

April 4   Purchased $6,000 of merchandise, terms 2/15, n/30, FOB shipping point.
April 9   Purchased $7,500 of merchandise, terms 3/05, n/30, FOB destination.
April 13   Purchased $8,000 of merchandise, terms 1/10, n/45, FOB shipping point.

Required

a. For each of the listed purchases, how many days does the company have to take advantage of the purchase discount?
b. What is the amount of the cash discount allowed in each case?

c. Assume the freight charges are $425 on each purchase. What is the total amount of freight that Winning Lacrosse Company has to pay?

d. What is the total cost of inventory for Winning Lacrosse Company for the month of April assuming that all discounts were taken?

LO 2   P5-2B. Analyze purchases of merchandise inventory.

Billy Bob's Baseball Barn made the following purchases in March of the current year:

March 1   Purchased $4,500 of baseball gloves, terms 3/15, n/25, FOB shipping point.

March 10   Purchased $7,200 of sports wear, terms 2/10, n/20, FOB destination.

March 15   Purchased $4,900 of softballs and baseballs, terms 1/05, n/15, FOB shipping point.

Required

a. For each purchase, by what date is the payment due assuming the company takes advantage of the discount?

b. For each purchase, when is the payment due if the company does not take advantage of the discount?

c. In each case, what is the amount of the cash discount allowed?

d. Assume the freight charges are $275 on each purchase. For which purchases is Billy Bob's Baseball Barn responsible for the freight charges?

e. What is the total amount of inventory costs for the month of March assuming that all discounts were taken?

LO 2, 3, 5, 6   P5-3B. Record merchandising transactions and prepare single-step and multiple-step income statements: perpetual inventory system.

At the beginning of April, Morgan Parts Company was started with a contribution of $20,000 cash from its shareholders. The company engaged in the following transactions during the month of April:

a. April 3   Purchased merchandise on account from Thompson Supply Co. for $5,000 with terms 1/10, n/30.

b. April 4   Sold merchandise on account to Brown Company for $3,500, terms 2/10, n/30. The cost of the merchandise sold was $1,500.

c. April 7   Paid $100 freight on the sale to Brown Company.

d. April 8   Received credit from Thompson Supply Co. for merchandise returned for $500.

e. April 10   Paid Thompson Supply Co. in full.

f. April 15   Received payment from Brown Company for sale made on April 4.

g. April 16   Purchased merchandise for cash $3,200.

h. April 17   Received refund from supplier for returned merchandise on April 16 cash purchase of $350.

i. April 19   Purchased merchandise on account from Kelsey Distributors $4,100, terms 2/10, n/30.

j. April 20   Paid $350 freight on April 19 purchase.

k. April 21   Sold merchandise for cash $12,170. The cost of the merchandise sold was $9,500.

l. April 24   Purchased merchandise for cash for $5,300.

m. April 25   Paid Kelsey Distributors for purchase on April 19.

n. April 27   Gave refund of $800 to customer from April 21. The cost of the returned merchandise was $535.

o. April 28   Sold merchandise of $2,000 on account with terms 2/10, n/30. The merchandise cost $1,200.

Required

a. Assume the company uses a perpetual inventory system. Prepare the journal entries for each transaction.

b. Post the transactions to T-accounts. Be sure to start with the opening balances in Cash and Common Stock described at the beginning of the problem.

c. Calculate the balance in the Inventory account at the end of April.

d. Prepare a single-step and multiple-step income statement for the month of April.

e. Calculate the profit margin ratio.

P5-4B. Record merchandising transactions and prepare single-step and multiple-step income statements: perpetual inventory system.

LO 2, 3, 5, 6

NCR Supplier sells plant food and spray to retail landscaping and gardening stores. At the beginning of May, NCR had a $15,000 balance in Cash and Common Stock. During the month of May, the first month of business, the following transactions took place:

a. May 3   Purchased 500 pounds of plant food on account from the manufacturer for $20 per pound, with the terms 1/05, n/30, and FOB destination. Freight costs were $90.

b. May 6   Sold 50 pounds of plant food to Center Street Garden Supply for $35 per pound on account, with terms 2/10, n/30, and FOB destination. Freight costs were $15.

c. May 10   Paid the manufacturer for the May 3 purchase.

d. May 15   Received payment in full from Center Street Garden Supply.

e. May 17   Sold 200 pounds to Perry's Plants on account for $34 each, with terms 1/10, n/30, and FOB shipping point. Freight costs were $100.

f. May 19   Returned 10 pounds of spoiled plant food to the manufacturer and received cash payment of $20 per pound.

g. May 20   Purchased 300 pounds of plant food on account from the manufacturer for $20 per pound, with the terms n/30, FOB destination. Freight costs were $50.

h. May 24   Sold 150 pounds of plant food to Sam's Pest Control for $24 each, cash. Sam's picked up the order so there were no shipping costs.

i. May 31   Paid for the purchase on May 20.

Required

a. Assume the company uses a perpetual inventory system. Give the journal entry for each transaction.

b. Post the entries to T-accounts. Be sure to start with the May beginning balance in Cash and Common Stock as stated at the beginning of the problem.

c. Calculate the cost of goods sold for May and the Inventory ending balance.

d. Prepare a single-step and multiple-step income statement for the month of May.

e. Calculate the profit margin ratio.

P5-5B. Record merchandising transactions and prepare multiple-step income statement: perpetual inventory system.

LO 2, 3, 5, 6

The following transactions occurred during April 2007 at the Winter Park Tennis Club:

a. April 2   Purchased racquets and balls on account from Penn Company for $500, with terms 2/10, n/30.

b. April 3   Paid freight of $30 on April 2 purchase.

c. April 5   Sold merchandise to members on account for $600, with the terms n/30. The merchandise sold cost $280.

d. April 10   Received credit of $50 from Penn Company for a damaged racquet that was returned.

e. April 11   Purchased tennis shoes from Nike for cash of $2,500.

f. April 13   Paid Penn Company in full.

g. April 14   Purchased tennis shirts and shorts from Tiger Sportswear on account for $3,000, with the terms 5/10, n/30.

h. April 15   Received credit of $80 from Tiger Sportswear for damaged merchandise.

i. April 18   Sold merchandise on account to members for $650, with the terms n/30. The cost of the merchandise sold was $400.

j. April 22   Received $500 in cash payment on account from members.

k. April 24   Paid Tiger Sportswear in full.

l. April 26   Granted an allowance of $30 to members for tennis shoes that had poor quality strings. The customers kept the shoes.

m. April 30   Received cash payments from members that paid all accounts in full.

Required

a. Assume the company uses a perpetual inventory system. Prepare the journal entries for the April transactions.

b. Suppose the Winter Park Tennis Club started the month with Cash of $7,000; Merchandise Inventory of $3,200; and Common Stock of $10,200. Post the journal entries to T-accounts.

c. Prepare a trial balance at April 30, 2007.

d. Prepare Winter Park Tennis Club's multiple-step income statement for the month ended April 30, 2007.

e. Prepare Winter Park Tennis Club's balance sheet at April 30, 2007.
f. Calculate the gross margin and profit margin ratios for Winter Park Tennis Club. Explain what each ratio measures.

LO 2, 4, 7   **P5-6B. Analyze results of a physical count of inventory and calculate cost of goods sold.**

Barney's Flowerpot Company uses a perpetual inventory system, so both the cost of goods sold is recorded and the inventory records are updated at the time of every sale. The company's accounting records showed the following related to May 2006 transactions:

		Units	Cost
	Beginning Inventory, May 1	300	$ 600
+	Purchases during May	4,000	8,000
=	Goods Available for Sale	4,300	8,600
−	Cost of Goods Sold	3,300	6,600
=	Ending Inventory, May 31	1,000	$2,000

On May 31, 2006, Barney's conducted a physical count of its inventory and discovered there were 900 units of inventory on hand.

Required

a. Using the information from the physical count, correct Barney's Cost of Goods Sold for May.
b. How would this correction change the financial statements for the year?
c. What are some possible causes of the difference between the inventory amounts in Barney's accounting records and the inventory amount from the physical count?

LO 2, 3, 5   **P5-7B. Analyze accounting methods and prepare corrected income statement.**

You are the accountant for Celebration Company, and your assistant has prepared the following income statement for the year ended December 31, 2006.

Celebration Company
Income Statement
For the year ended December 31, 2006
(in thousands)

Sales revenue		$650,000
Sales returns and allowances	$ 18,100	
Freight expenses	2,000	
Selling expenses	48,300	(68,400)
Net Sales		581,600
Expenses		
Cost of goods sold	350,000	
Salary expenses	82,000	
Rent expense	10,000	
Administrative expenses	23,500	
Dividends	4,000	
Total expenses		469,500
Net Income		$112,100

You have uncovered the following facts:

1. Sales revenue includes $6,000 of items that have been back ordered. (The items have not been delivered to the customers, although the customers have paid for the items.)
2. Selling Expenses includes $4,000 of allowances that were given to customers who received damaged products.
3. Rent Expense includes $400 worth of rent that applies to 2007.
4. Salary Expenses includes $10,000 loaned to one of the executives for a boat.

Required

a. Prepare a corrected multiple-step income statement for the year. Celebration shows sales as the net amount only on its income statement.
b. Regarding the errors, write a memo to your assistant explaining why each item is incorrect and what the correct accounting treatment should be.

P5-8B. Appendix: Periodic inventory system.

Use the data about Morgan Parts Company in P5-3B to complete this problem.

Required

a. Assume the company uses a periodic inventory system. Prepare the journal entries for each transaction.

b. Post the transactions to T-accounts. Be sure to start with the opening balances in Cash and Common Stock described at the beginning of the problem.

c. Calculate cost of goods sold for April and calculate the balance in the Inventory account at the end of April.

d. Prepare a single-step and a multiple-step income statement for the month of April.

e. Calculate the profit margin ratio.

P5-9B. Appendix: Periodic inventory system.

Use the data about NCR Supplier in P5-4B to complete this problem.

Required

a. Assume the company uses a periodic inventory system. Give the journal entry for each transaction.

b. Post the entries to T-accounts. Be sure to start with the beginning balance in Cash and Common Stock as stated at the beginning of the problem.

c. Calculate the cost of goods sold for May and calculate the balance in the Inventory account at the end of May.

d. Prepare a single-step and a multiple-step income statement for the month of May.

e. Calculate the profit margin ratio.

P5-10B. Appendix: Periodic inventory system.

Use the data about Winter Park Tennis Club in P5-5B to complete this problem.

Required

a. Assume the company uses a periodic inventory system. Prepare the journal entries for the April transactions.

b. Suppose the Winter Park Tennis Club started the month with Cash of $7,000; Merchandise Inventory of $3,200; and Common Stock of $10,200. Post the journal entries to T-accounts.

c. Prepare a trial balance at April 30, 2007.

d. Calculate the cost of goods sold for April and the ending balance in Inventory.

e. Prepare Winter Park Tennis Club's multiple-step income statement for the month ended April 31, 2007.

f. Prepare Winter Park Tennis Club's balance sheet at April 30, 2007.

g. Calculate the gross margin and profit margin ratios for Winter Park. Explain what each ratio measures.

Financial Statement Analysis

FSA5-1. Below are income statements from AutoZone for the fiscal years ended August 30, 2003, and August 31, 2002. For each year, calculate the gross margin, the gross margin ratio, and the profit margin ratio. How does AutoZone's most recent performance compare to the prior year?

AutoZone
Consolidated Statements of Income
(in thousands)

	For the year ended	
	Aug. 30, 2003	Aug. 31, 2002
Net Sales	$5,457,123	$5,325,510
Cost of sales	2,942,114	2,950,123
Operating, selling, and administrative expenses	1,597,212	1,604,379
Operating profit	917,797	771,008
Interest expense, net	84,790	79,860
Income before taxes	833,007	691,148
Income taxes	315,403	263,000
Net Income	$ 517,604	$ 428,148

FSA5-2. Below are the income statements for Williams-Sonoma for the fiscal years ended February 2, 2003, and February 3, 2002. Compare the company's performance for the two years. Is the company controlling its cost of goods sold? Is the company controlling its other expenses well? Be able to support your answers.

Williams-Sonoma
Consolidated Statements of Earnings
(in thousands)

	For the year ended	
	Feb. 2, 2003	Feb. 3, 2002
Net Revenues	$2,360,830	$2,086,662
Cost of goods sold	1,409,229	1,292,673
Gross margin	951,601	793,989
Selling, general, and administrative expenses	749,299	666,015
Interest expense, net	20	5,868
Income before taxes	202,282	122,106
Income taxes	77,879	47,010
Net Income	$ 124,403	$ 75,096

FSA5-3. Use the following income statements from Tiffany & Co. to evaluate the company's profitability. Calculate the gross margin ratio and the profit margin ratio for the three years shown. Comment on your findings.

Tiffany & Co.
Consolidated Statements of Earnings
For the Years Ended January 31
(in thousands)

	2004	2003	2002
Net sales	$2,000,045	$1,706,602	$1,606,535
Cost of Sales	842,663	695,154	663,058
Gross Profit	1,157,382	1,011,448	943,477
Selling, general and administrative expenses	801,863	692,251	633,580
Earnings from operations	355,519	319,197	309,897
Interest expense and financing costs	14,906	15,129	19,834
Other (income) expenses, net	(2,072)	4,431	751
Income before taxes	342,685	299,637	289,312
Provision for income taxes	127,168	109,743	115,725
Net Earnings	$ 215,517	$ 189,894	$ 173,587

Critical Thinking Problems

Risk and Control

Retail businesses face unique risks due to the inventory they must have. Due to modern technology and changing inventory procedures, some of the risks that existed just a few years ago may no longer exist for some companies, and new risks have appeared. Use what you know about Wal-Mart and its relationship to its vendors to identify the risks it faces with its inventory. Do you think a smaller company with less sophisticated inventory control would have the same risks?

Ethics

Retail stores often give employees a discount on items purchased. Suppose you worked for a retail store like Target. As a cashier, you have the authority to ring up discounts for employees who make purchases in your department. You have a friend who regularly shops in your department, and she has asked you for the employee discount. She picks out her purchases, and you set them aside until you are ready to leave work for the day. Then, you purchase the items from another salesclerk, who gives you the employee discount. You, in turn, take the purchases to your friend, who repays you for the cost of the items.

Is this behavior ethical? If you were the store owner, how would you feel about this sort of employee behavior? What controls could the store manager put in place to prevent this?

Group Assignment

Use the financial information from Amazon.com shown below to analyze the company's performance. For the most recent year, the company earned a profit. However, for the two years prior to that, the company reported huge losses. Calculate the ratios you studied in this chapter. Comment on the performance of Amazon.com for the time periods shown. Be ready to support your conclusions.

Amazon.com
Income Statement
For the Years Ended December 31
(in thousands)

	2003	2002	2001
Net sales	$5,263,699	$3,932,936	$3,122,433
Cost of sales	4,006,531	2,940,318	2,323,875
Gross profit	1,257,168	992,618	798,558
Selling, general, and administrative expenses	986,573	928,494	1,210,815
Earnings from operations	270,595	64,124	(412,257)
Non-operating expenses	234,877	209,888	114,170
Other (income) expenses, net	436	3,368	40,850
Net income (loss)	$ 35,282	$ (149,132)	$ (567,277)

Internet Exercises: SYSCO Corporation

SYSCO (Systems and Services Company) is the leading foodservice marketer and distributor in North America. Since the initial public offering in 1970, when sales were $115 million, SYSCO has grown to $29.3 billion in sales for fiscal year 2004.

Go to www.sysco.com:

IE5-1. Is SYSCO a wholesale merchandising firm or retail merchandising firm? How can you tell?

IE5-2. Click on *Investors* and select *Financial Reports* from the list and open the most current annual report.

  a. Review the income statement (consolidated results of operations). Is the income statement a multiple-step or single-step statement? How can you tell?

  b. For the three most recent years, calculate the gross profit. Is gross profit increasing or decreasing? Is this trend favorable or unfavorable? Explain your answer.

  c. Calculate the gross profit ratio and the profit margin ratio for the three most recent years. What do each of these ratios measure? Considering only these ratios, does SYSCO appear to be headed in the right direction? Explain why or why not.

  d. Refer to the Notes section of SYSCO's Summary of Accounting policies:
    1. How does SYSCO treat sales incentives such as rebates or discounts?
    2. What elements are included in cost of inventory?

IE5-3. Click on ***Customers***.

a. List three different types of products that SYSCO sells.
b. Is quality assurance important to SYSCO? Explain your answer.
c. According to their website how and why should you become a SYSCO customer?

Please note: Internet Web sites are constantly being updated. Therefore, if the information is not found where indicated, please explore the annual report further to find the information.

Additional Study Materials

Visit www.prenhall.com/reimers for self- self-study quizzes and spreadsheet templates to use to complete homework assignments.

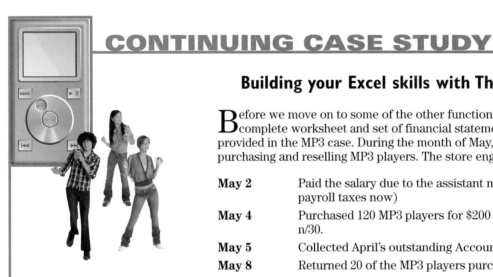

CONTINUING CASE STUDY

Building your Excel skills with The MP3 Store

Before we move on to some of the other functions in Excel, you will do one more complete worksheet and set of financial statements using the information provided in the MP3 case. During the month of May, The MP3 Store finally began purchasing and reselling MP3 players. The store engaged in the following transactions:

May 2	Paid the salary due to the assistant manager. (Don't worry about payroll taxes now)
May 4	Purchased 120 MP3 players for $200 each, on account. Terms are 2/10, n/30.
May 5	Collected April's outstanding Accounts Receivable balance.
May 8	Returned 20 of the MP3 players purchased on May 4.
May 12	Paid for the remaining 100 MP3 players. (*Hint:* Don't forget your purchase discount.)
May 20	By May 20, the company had sold 60 MP3 players for $350 each. All sales were made on account. The sales tax rate is 6%. The MP3 store uses the perpetual inventory system.
May 29	Customers paid for 40 of the MP3 players sold during the month.
May 30	Paid the assistant manager $2,000 for May work.
May 31	By the end of the month, 10 more MP3 players had been sold for $350. Customers paid cash.

Instructions

1. For this chapter you are on your own. The techniques you learned in Chapters 1–4 should enable you to complete the journal entries, prepare the T-accounts, and prepare the trial balances and financial statements. (Note: a statement of cash flows is not required for this chapter). Think about the project before you begin. Do you want to start from scratch—with a new blank worksheet *or* do you want to use the worksheets you created in Chapter 4 and edit them? The choice is yours. The solution was prepared by editing the Chapter 4 file. Don't forget your adjusting journal entries. There were no supplies left on hand at the end of May.

2. When you are finished, print and save your file to disk by clicking the **Save** button. Name your file MP35.

Recording Transactions Using Periodic Inventory

Recording Purchases of Merchandise

As you learned in this chapter, in a perpetual inventory system, all amounts affecting the inventory are debited and credited directly into the Inventory account. Purchases are debited into the Inventory account, freight costs are debited into the Inventory account, and cost of goods sold is credited out of the Inventory account at the time of each sale. Inventory is a very busy account in a perpetual system. In a periodic inventory system, by contrast, these routine transactions are not put in the Inventory account. The periodic system adjusts the Inventory account at the end of the period, hence the name *periodic*. Here's what happens when the firm purchases inventory. An account called Purchases is created as a temporary account to hold the purchases for the accounting period. Every purchase of inventory is debited into the Purchases account. The Purchases account has a normal debit balance.

If the firm returns inventory items to the vendor, the amounts are not credited to the Inventory account. Instead, the firm uses an account called Purchase Returns and Allowances. It is a contra-purchases account because it reduces the amount of the firm's purchases by using a separate account that will offset purchases when the firm does the computations at the end of the period. Purchase Returns and Allowances has a normal credit balance. Similarly, purchase discounts are also kept in a separate contra-purchases account called Purchase Discounts, which has a normal credit balance.

Freight costs to obtain inventory (inventory shipped FOB shipping point by the vendor) will be debited to their own account, usually called Freight-in. This account has a normal debit balance.

Comparing Record Keeping for Perpetual and Periodic Inventory

Let's take some simple inventory transactions and make the journal entries for both a perpetual and a periodic inventory system. In this example, the firm has no beginning inventory.

1. Yakity Yak Company purchased 100 phones on account for its inventory from Sungsong Company for $35 each, with terms 2/10, n/30.

2. Yakity Yak paid the freight company $500 because the shipping terms were FOB shipping point.
3. Yakity Yak returned 10 phones and received full credit from Sungsong.
4. Yakity Yak received a purchase discount of 2% for paying within 10 days of receiving the invoice.
5. Yakity Yak sold 50 phones for cash during the period for $95 each.

At the end of the period, a physical count of the inventory was taken. There were 40 phones remaining.

		Perpetual Inventory System			Periodic Inventory System		
1.	Purchase	Inventory	3,500		Purchases	3,500	
		Accounts Payable		3,500	Accounts Payable		3,500
2.	Freight	Inventory	500		Freight-in	500	
		Cash		500	Cash		500
3.	Return	Accounts Payable	350		Accounts Payable	350	
		Inventory		350	Purchase Returns		350
4.	Discount	Accounts Payable	3,150		Accounts Payable	3,157	
		Cash		3,087	Cash		3,087
		Inventory		63	Purchase Discount		63
		($3,150 × 2%)					
5.	Sale	Cash	4,750		Cash	4,750	
		Sales Revenue		4,750	Sales Revenue		4,750
		Cost of Goods Sold	1,993				
		Inventory		1,993			
		$39.86* × 50 = $1,993 rounded					

*($3,500 + 500 − 350 − 63) ÷ 90 phones = $39.86 each

Here's what the inventory account looks like using a perpetual system:

Inventory			
Assume no			
beginning balance			
1.	3,500		
2.	500	3.	350
		4.	63
		5.	1,993 (rounded)
Balance	1,594		

That's 40 phones (counted in the physical inventory) @ $34.86 each.

In a periodic system, all of the purchase-related accounts—Purchases, Purchase Returns and Allowances, and Purchase Discounts—are used to calculate Net Purchases. The firm will subtract Ending Inventory from Net Purchases to calculate the Cost of Goods Sold for the period. If something is not in the Ending Inventory, the firm will have to assume it was sold. There is no way to identify inventory shrinkage when using the periodic method.

Purchases	$3,500	
Less Purchase Returns	(350)	
Less Purchase Discounts	(63)	
Plus Freight-in	500	
Goods Available for Sale	3,587	($3,587 ÷ 90 = $39.855555 or 39.86 rounded)
Less Ending Inventory (counted)	1,594	($39.86 × 40)
Cost of Goods Sold	$1,993	($3,587 – 1,594)

In a periodic system, a journal entry is made at the end of the period to bring the temporary accounts related to purchases to balances of zero. The journal entry balances with a debit to Cost of Goods Sold, which was not recorded during the period, and a debit to Inventory, which puts the ending Inventory in the accounting records. In this example, recall there was no beginning inventory. So the Inventory account has no balance until this final journal entry is made:

Transaction	Debit	Credit
Inventory	1,594 (counted)	
Cost of Goods Sold	1,993 (to balance the journal entry)	
Purchase Returns and Allowances	350	
Purchase Discounts	63	
Purchases		3,500
Freight-in		500
To record the ending inventory and the cost of goods sold.		

The value for Cost of Goods Sold is a calculated amount—whatever is needed to make the journal entry balance. Now, the accounting records have both Inventory and Cost of Goods Sold balances for the period's financial statements.

No matter which method a firm uses, the cost of goods sold will be the same under both methods as long as there is no inventory shrinkage.

chapter 6

Reporting and
Analyzing Inventory

Here's where you've been . . .

- **You learned how merchandise is acquired and sold.**

- **You learned how inventory purchases and sales are recorded in the company's accounting records.**

Here's where you're going . . .

- **You'll learn the four inventory cost flow assumptions.**

- **You'll learn to calculate the cost of inventory and cost of goods sold using each assumption.**

- **You'll learn to evaluate whether a firm manages its inventory efficiently.**

YOU make the call:

Should Best Buy reduce the value of its television inventory?

If you've shopped for a television lately, you've probably noticed LCD and plasma TVs everywhere. What happened to the old, big-tube TVs? And what does a company do when it still has these old products (or old goods) in its inventory? This is a concern for a retail firm like Best Buy because inventory is a very large part of its assets. On its balance sheet at February 26, 2005, the firm had over $2.8 *billion* worth of inventory.

Suppose an inventory manager determines that the value of some old inventory of televisions is no longer worth the amount that Best Buy has recorded in its accounting records. The manager believes that, because the old televisions will likely sell for less than the company paid for them, the inventory should be written down to a smaller amount. This, of course, means that the company would have to make a journal entry that would reduce net income to lower the recorded amount of the Inventory. Should the manager suggest this journal entry to the boss? Should the value of the inventory on Best Buy's books be reduced? *You make the call.*

Learning Objectives

When you are finished studying this chapter, you should be able to:

1. Explain and apply the four cost flow assumptions for valuing inventory and cost of goods sold.
2. Explain the effects of the inventory cost flow assumption on the financial statements.
3. Explain the lower-of-cost-or-market rule for valuing inventory.
4. Evaluate a firm's inventory management using the inventory turnover ratio.
5. Recognize special risks and controls associated with inventory.

LEARNING OBJECTIVE 1

Explain and apply the four cost flow assumptions for valuing inventory and cost of goods sold.

Study Tip

Cost of goods available for sale is a dollar amount that is generally calculated as beginning inventory plus purchases made during the period.

Inventory Cost Flow Assumptions

In Chapter 5, you learned about the costs that must be included in the inventory. All costs to prepare the inventory for sale become part of the cost of the inventory and then, when the goods are sold, become part of the cost of goods sold expense. That's just the beginning of the story. Inventory costing gets more complicated when the cost of the merchandise changes with different purchases. Suppose Oakley ships 120 pairs of its new sunglasses to Sunglass Hut. The cost to Sunglass Hut is $50 per pair. Then, suppose that just a month later, Sunglass Hut needs more of the popular sunglasses and buys another 120 pairs. This time, however, Oakley charges $55 per pair. If Sunglass Hut sold 140 pairs of Oakley sunglasses during the month to its customers, which ones did it sell? The problem is how to divide the cost of the inventory between the period's cost of goods sold and the ending (unsold) inventory.

We could determine the cost of goods sold if we knew how many pairs costing $50 were sold and how many pairs costing $55 were sold. Suppose Sunglass Hut has no method of keeping track of that information. The store simply knows 140 pairs were sold for $1,400 and 100 pairs are left in inventory. There were 240 pairs available for sale at a total cost of $12,600. This amount—the total cost of the inventory that is available to sell during an accounting period—is the *cost of goods available for sale.*

(120 pairs @ $50 per pair) + (120 pairs @ $55 per pair)
= $12,600 cost of goods available for sale

How should the store allocate that amount—$12,600—between the 140 pairs sold (cost of goods sold) and the 100 pairs not sold (ending inventory) for the month?

The store's accountant will have to make an assumption about which pairs of sunglasses flowed out of inventory to customers and which pairs remain in inventory. Did the store sell all of the $50 pairs and some of the $55 pairs? Or did the store sell all of the $55 pairs and some of the $50 pairs? The assumption the accountant makes is called an *inventory cost flow assumption*, and it has to be made to calculate the Cost of Goods Sold for the income statement and the cost of ending Inventory for the balance sheet. The actual physical flow of the goods does *not* have to be consistent with the inventory cost flow assumption. The inventory manager could actually know that all of the $50 pairs could not have been sold because of the way shipments are stored below the display counter, yet the store is still allowed to use the assumption that the $50 pairs were sold first in calculating cost of goods sold. *Inventory cost flow* refers to the physical passage of goods through a business. In accounting, we are concerned with *inventory cost flow*—that is, the flow of the cost associated with the goods that pass through a company—rather than with inventory flow, which refers to the actual physical movement of goods.

Generally accepted accounting principles (GAAP) allow a company to select one of several inventory cost flow assumptions. Studying several of these methods will help you understand how accounting choices can affect the amounts on the financial statements, even when the transactions are identical. There are four basic inventory cost flow assumptions used to calculate the cost of goods sold and the cost of ending inventory:

1. Specific identification
2. Weighted average cost
3. First-in, first-out (FIFO)
4. Last-in, first-out (LIFO)

Specific identification

The **specific identification** method is one way of assigning the dollar amounts to cost of goods sold and ending inventory. Instead of assuming which inventory items are sold, a firm that uses specific identification actually keeps track of which goods were sold because the firm records the actual cost of the specific goods sold.

With the specific identification method, each item sold must be identified as coming from a specific purchase of inventory, at a specific unit cost. Specific identification can be used for determining the cost of each item of a small quantity of large, luxury items such as cars or yachts. However, this method would take too much time and money to use to determine the cost of each item of many identical items, like pairs of identical sunglasses. Companies that specialize in large, one-of-a-kind products, like Boeing's 767-300ER delivered to Ethiopian Airlines in June 2004, will definitely use specific identification. However, when you go into Foot Locker to buy a pair of Nike running shoes, the store accountant will *not* know exactly what the store paid Nike for that specific pair of shoes. The cost of goods sold will be determined by a method other than specific identification.

Let's use a simple example to show how specific identification works. Exhibit 6.1 shows how a car dealership identifies the cost of each car sold, which is the amount the dealership paid the car manufacturer. Suppose you

Study Tip

Weighted average cost, FIFO, and LIFO are assumptions about the flow of inventory costs from the balance sheet Inventory account to the income statement Cost of Goods Sold account, not the actual physical flow of the goods.

Specific identification: The inventory cost flow method in which the actual cost of the specific goods sold is recorded as cost of goods sold.

Exhibit 6.1

Inventory Cost Using Specific Identification

Each car's cost to the dealership is identified as the car is sold. The cost of goods sold will reflect the cost of each specific car sold.

$25,000
$23,000
$22,000

own a Volkswagen car dealership. You buy one Volkswagen for $22,000, a second for $23,000, and a third for $25,000. These three items for the inventory may look identical to a customer, but each car actually has its own unique VIN (vehicle identification number). You will know exactly what your dealership paid the manufacturer for each car. Suppose you sold two cars during the accounting period. What is the cost of goods sold? You will specifically identify the cars sold. If you sold the $22,000 car and the $25,000 car, then cost of goods sold would be $47,000 and ending inventory would be $23,000. However, if you sold the $23,000 car and the $25,000 car, then cost of goods sold would be $48,000 and ending inventory would be $22,000.

Weighted average cost

Weighted average cost: The inventory cost flow method in which the weighted average cost of the goods available for sale is used to calculate the cost of goods sold and the ending inventory.

In Other Words:
Weighted average cost is often called average cost.

Few firms use specific identification because it is costly to keep track of each individual item in inventory. Instead, most firms use one of the other inventory cost flow assumptions: weighted average cost, FIFO, or LIFO. A firm that uses **weighted average cost** averages the cost of the items available for sale and then uses that weighted average cost to value both cost of goods sold and the ending inventory. An average unit cost is calculated by dividing the *total cost* of goods available for sale by the *total number* of units available for sale. This average unit cost is *weighted* because the number of units at each different price is used to weight the unit costs. The calculated average unit cost is applied to all units sold to get cost of goods sold and applied to all units remaining to get a value for ending inventory. Companies like Best Buy, Intel, Starbucks, and Chico's use the weighted average cost method to calculate the cost of goods sold and the cost of ending inventory. Exhibit 6.2 shows how the weighted average cost method works for a shop that sells sunglasses.

Study Tip

You can't simply average the unit costs of $50, $60, and $68. Because there are two pairs of $50 sunglasses, the $50 gets twice as much weight as the other costs. That's why it's called the weighted-average method.

Exhibit 6.2

Weighted Average Inventory Costing

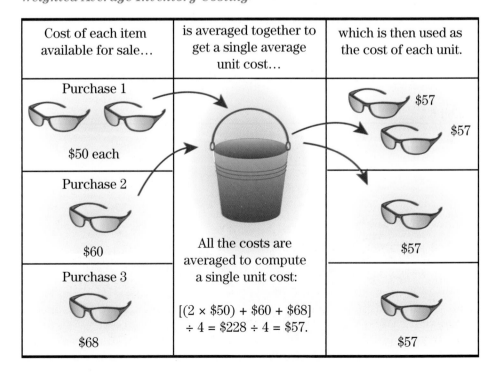

Cost of each item available for sale…	is averaged together to get a single average unit cost…	which is then used as the cost of each unit.
Purchase 1 $50 each		$57 $57
Purchase 2 $60	All the costs are averaged to compute a single unit cost: $$[(2 \times \$50) + \$60 + \$68] \div 4 = \$228 \div 4 = \$57.$$	$57
Purchase 3 $68		$57

Consider the sunglasses shown in Exhibit 6.2. The store purchased four pairs from the manufacturer. The first two pairs cost $50, the third pair cost $60, and the fourth pair cost $68. The total cost of goods available for sale is:

$$(2 \times \$50) + \$60 + \$68 = \$228$$

Averaged over four pairs, the weighted average cost per pair is $57:

$$\$228 \div 4 = \$57$$

If the store now sold three pairs to customers, the cost of goods sold would be:

$$3 \times \$57 = \$171$$

The ending inventory would be $57. Notice that the cost of goods sold of $171 plus the ending inventory of $57 add up to $228, the cost of goods available for sale.

$$
\begin{array}{ll}
\$171 & \text{Cost of goods sold} \\
\underline{+\ 57} & \text{Ending inventory} \\
\$228 & \text{Cost of goods available for sale}
\end{array}
$$

First-in, first-out method (FIFO)

The **first-in, first-out (FIFO) method** is the common assumption in inventory cost flow that the first items purchased are the first ones sold. The cost of the first goods purchased is assigned to the first goods sold. The cost of the goods on hand at the end of a period is determined from the most recent purchases. Apple Computers, Barnes & Noble, and Wendy's use FIFO.

Let's use the four pairs of sunglasses we used earlier for the weighted average method to see how FIFO works. Suppose the glasses were purchased in the order shown in Exhibit 6.3. No matter which ones were actually sold first, the costs of the oldest purchases will become cost of goods sold. If the store sold three pairs, the cost of goods sold would be:

$$\$50 + \$50 + \$60 = \$160$$

The ending inventory would be $68. Again notice that the cost of goods sold of $160 plus the ending inventory of $68 equals $228, the costs of goods available for sale:

$$
\begin{array}{ll}
\$160 & \text{Cost of goods sold} \\
\underline{+\ 68} & \text{Ending inventory} \\
\$228 & \text{Cost of goods available for sale}
\end{array}
$$

Last-in, first-out method (LIFO)

The **last-in, first-out (LIFO) method** is the inventory cost flow assumption that the most recently purchased goods are sold first. The cost of the last goods purchased is assigned to the cost of goods sold, so the cost of the ending inventory is assumed to be the cost of the goods purchased earliest. Firms from diverse industries use LIFO: Caterpillar, manufacturer of machinery and engines; Pepsico, the owner of PepsiCo Beverages North America and Frito-Lay; and McKesson Corporation, a pharmaceutical and health care company.

First-in, first-out (FIFO) method: The inventory cost flow method that assumes the first items purchased are the first items sold.

Study Tip

Using FIFO, the oldest costs go to the income statement as Cost of Goods Sold, and the most recent costs are on the balance sheet as (ending) Inventory.

Last-in, first-out (LIFO) method: The inventory cost flow method that assumes the last items purchased are the first items sold.

Study Tip

Using LIFO, the most recent costs go to the income statement as Cost of Goods Sold, and the oldest costs are on the balance sheet as ending Inventory.

Exhibit 6.3

FIFO Inventory Cost Flow Method

Cost of goods available for sale	The actual order of the items sold is not necessarily known, but the costs flow "as if" this were the flow of the goods:	
	Cost of goods sold	Ending inventory
Purchase 1 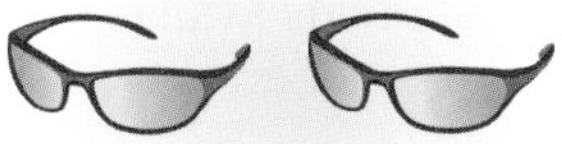 $50 each		
Purchase 2  $60		
Purchase 3  $68		
$228	**$160**	**$68**

Let's use the four pairs of sunglasses again to see how LIFO works. Suppose the glasses were purchased in the order shown in Exhibit 6.4. No matter which ones were actually sold first, the costs of the most recent purchases will become cost of goods sold. If the store sold three pairs, the cost of goods sold would be:

$$\$68 + \$60 + \$50 = \$178$$

The ending inventory would be $50. Again notice that the cost of goods sold of $178 plus the ending inventory of $50 equals $228, the cost of goods available for sale:

$178 Cost of goods sold
+ 50 Ending inventory
$228 Cost of goods available for sale

Firms that use LIFO must provide extra disclosures in their financial statements. Exhibit 6.5 shows an example of the disclosure about inventory provided by Tootsie Roll Industries. Although Tootsie Roll uses LIFO, it discloses information about the current cost of the ending inventory. Remember that LIFO inventory will be valued at the oldest costs because the more recent costs

Exhibit 6.4

LIFO Inventory Cost Flow Method

Cost of goods available for sale	The actual order of the items sold is not necessarily known, but the costs flow "as if" this were the flow of the goods:	
	Cost of goods sold	Ending inventory
Purchase 1 $50 each		
Purchase 2 $60		
Purchase 3 $68		
$228	**$178**	**$50**

have gone to the income statement as Cost of Goods Sold. The old inventory is often described as old "LIFO" layers. When a LIFO firm keeps a safety stock of inventory, never selling its entire inventory, those LIFO layers may be there for a long time. LIFO is controversial because a firm can make an extra purchase of inventory at the end of the period and change its cost of goods sold without making another sale. Whether or not it is ethical to buy extra inventory for the sole purpose of changing the period's cost of goods sold is something you

Exhibit 6.5

LIFO Disclosure in Notes to the Financial Statements

From Note 1 in Tootsie Roll Industries' 2004 Annual Report:

Inventories (dollars in millions):
Inventories are stated at cost, not to exceed market. The cost of substantially all of the company's inventories ($54,795 and $42,735 at December 31, 2004 and 2003, respectively) has been determined by the last-in, first-out (LIFO) method. The excess of current cost over LIFO cost of inventories approximates $5,868 and $6,442 at December 31, 2004 and 2003, respectively.

should think about. Even if you believe it is not ethical, you should be aware that it can be done when using LIFO.

Take a look at Exhibit 6.6 for a simple comparison of three methods for calculating the cost of goods sold and the cost of ending inventory—weighted average cost, FIFO, and LIFO.

Can **YOU** do it?

Jayne's Jewelry Store purchased three diamond and emerald bracelets during March. The price of diamonds has fluctuated wildly during the month, causing the supplying firm to change the price of the bracelets it sells to Jayne's Jewelry Store.

a. On March 5, the first bracelet cost $4,600.

b. On March 15, the second bracelet cost $5,100.

c. On March 20, the third bracelet cost $3,500.

Suppose Jayne's Jewelry Store sold two of these bracelets for $7,000 each.

1. Using FIFO, what is the cost of goods sold for these sales? What is the gross profit?

2. Using LIFO, what is the cost of goods sold for these sales? What is the gross profit?

3. Using weighted average cost, what is the cost of goods sold?

Answers (1) Cost of goods sold is $4,600 + $5,100 = $9,700 and the gross profit is $14,000 − $9,700 = $4,300. (2) Cost of goods sold is $3,500 + $5,100 = $8,600, and the gross profit is $14,000 − $8,600 = $5,400. (3) Weighted average cost of the bracelets is: $13,200/3 = $4,400. The cost of goods sold for the sale of two bracelets would be 2 × $4,400 = $8,800.

This exhibit compares three methods for calculating the cost of goods sold and the cost of ending inventory—weighted average cost, FIFO, LIFO—using the example with four pairs of sunglasses. The three pairs of sunglasses sold and the pair left in ending inventory are not identifiable here to emphasize that the actual physical flow of goods does not matter to the inventory cost flow method.

Exhibit 6.6

A Comparison of Weighted Average Cost, FIFO, and LIFO

Purchases	Cost of goods sold	Ending inventory
$50 each $60 $68		
WEIGHTED AVERAGE COST	$57 + $57 + $57 = **$171**	**$57**
FIFO	$50 + $50 + $60 = **$160**	**$68**
LIFO	$68 + $60 + $50 = **$178**	**$50**

How Inventory Cost Flow Assumptions Affect Financial Statements

LEARNING OBJECTIVE 2

Explain the effects of the inventory cost flow assumption on the financial statements.

Did you notice that the same set of facts and economic transactions in the examples you just studied resulted in *different* numbers on the financial statements for Cost of Goods Sold and for ending Inventory? In the following sections, you'll learn how the firm's choice of inventory cost flow assumptions affects the financial statements.

Differences in reported inventory and cost of goods sold under different cost flow assumptions

Exhibit 6.7 shows inventory for Katelyn's Photo Shop. The shop sells a unique type of disposable camera that is relatively inexpensive. Let's calculate the cost of goods sold and ending inventory for the month of January using weighted average cost, FIFO, and LIFO, all using periodic record keeping. If you want to see the same problem using perpetual inventory, go to Appendix A.

No matter which method a company selects, the cost of goods *available* for sale—beginning inventory plus purchases—is the same. Here is a calculation for cost of goods available for sale:

> Cost of Goods Available for Sale = Beginning Inventory + Purchases

For Katelyn's Photo Shop for January, the cost of goods available for sale is $238:

$$\$80 \quad + \quad \$60 \quad + \quad \$98 \quad = \$238$$
(8 cameras × $10 each) + (5 cameras × $12 each) + (7 cameras × $14 each)

The inventory cost flow assumption and record-keeping method determine how that dollar amount of cost of goods available for sale is divided between cost of goods sold and ending inventory.

Recall from Chapter 5 that a firm can update its accounting records with every sale—perpetual record-keeping—or at the end of the accounting period—periodic record-keeping. To keep the number of calculations to a minimum as you learn about inventory cost flow, we'll use periodic for the examples that follow. No matter which record-keeping method a firm uses, the concept of cost flow differences between FIFO, LIFO, and weighted average cost are the same. If you want to see the same problem done with a perpetual record-keeping system, study the Appendix to the chapter. Now, let's get started with weighted average cost.

Average Cost—Periodic Weighted Average Let's calculate Katelyn's cost of goods sold and ending inventory using the weighted average cost method to demonstrate this inventory cost flow assumption. When the firm chooses a periodic record-keeping system, the computations for this method of keeping track of inventory are the simplest of all methods. Katelyn adds up beginning inventory and all purchases to get the cost of goods available for

Exhibit 6.7

Inventory Records for Katelyn's Photo Shop

January 1	Beginning Inventory	8 cameras	@ $10 each
January 8	Sales	3 cameras	@ $50 each
January 16	Purchase	5 cameras	@ $12 each
January 20	Sales	8 cameras	@ $55 each
January 30	Purchase	7 cameras	@ $14 each

sale. Katelyn previously calculated that amount to be $238. Then, she divides $238 by the total number of cameras available for sale—that's the number of cameras that comprised the $238—to get a weighted average cost per camera. Katelyn had a total of 20 (= 8 + 5 + 7) cameras available for sale. Dividing $238 by 20 cameras gives $11.90 per camera. That weighted average unit cost is used to compute cost of goods sold and ending inventory:

$$
\begin{array}{ccc}
11 & \times \quad \$11.90 & = \$130.90 \text{ cost of goods sold.} \\
\text{(Number of Cameras Sold)} & \text{(Per Unit Cost)} &
\end{array}
$$

$$
\begin{array}{ccc}
9 & \times \quad \$11.90 & = \$107.10 \text{ ending inventory.} \\
\text{(Number of Cameras in Ending Inventory)} & \text{(Per Unit Cost)} &
\end{array}
$$

Cost of goods sold ($130.90) and ending inventory ($107.10) add up to $238.

FIFO Periodic At the end of the month, Katelyn's knows the total number of cameras sold in January was 11. Using FIFO, Katelyn's counts the oldest cameras in the inventory as *sold*. The first items to go in the inventory are the first to go out to the income statement as Cost of Goods Sold. So the firm counts the beginning inventory of 8 cameras at $10 each as the first part of cost of goods sold. On January 16, Katelyn's purchased 5 cameras, so the firm will include 3 of those as part of cost of goods sold, too. That makes 11 cameras sold during the month. The income statement will show $116 as expense, or cost of goods sold. Here's how you calculate that number:

8 cameras @ $10 per camera	= $ 80
3 cameras @ $12 per camera	= $ 36
Cost of Goods Sold	= **$116**

What's left in the Inventory on the balance sheet?

2 cameras @ $12 per camera	= $ 24
7 cameras @ $14 per camera	= $ 98
Ending Inventory	= **$122**

Notice that the cost of goods sold plus the ending inventory equals $238—the cost of goods available for sale during January. Exhibit 6.8 shows the FIFO inventory cost flow for Katelyn's Photo.

LIFO Periodic When you use any inventory cost flow method with periodic record keeping, you start by calculating the total number of cameras sold during the month. We know that in January, Katelyn's Photo sold 11 cameras. Using LIFO, Katelyn counts cameras from the latest purchase as those sold first. The cost of the last items put in the inventory are the first to go to the income statement as Cost of Goods Sold. For LIFO, we start at the bottom of the list of purchases in the sequence in which the cameras were purchased.

The purchase on January 30 was 7 cameras, so Katelyn's counts the cost of those as part of cost of goods sold first.

The purchase on January 16 was 5 cameras, so the firm will count 4 of them in the cost of goods sold to get the total of 11 cameras sold. The total cost of goods sold will be:

7 cameras @ $14 per camera	= $ 98
4 cameras @ $12 per camera	= $ 48
Cost of Goods Sold	= **$146**

What's left in the inventory?

1 camera @ $12 per camera	= $12
8 cameras @ $10 per camera	= $80
Ending Inventory	= **$92**

Study Tip

Notice that the specific cameras purchased on January 30 don't have to be sold to treat them "as if" they were sold. In this case, Katelyn's couldn't have sold them. A firm's inventory cost flow assumption does not have to mimic the actual physical flow of the goods.

Exhibit 6.8

FIFO *Inventory Cost Flow Assumption for Katelyn's Photo Shop*

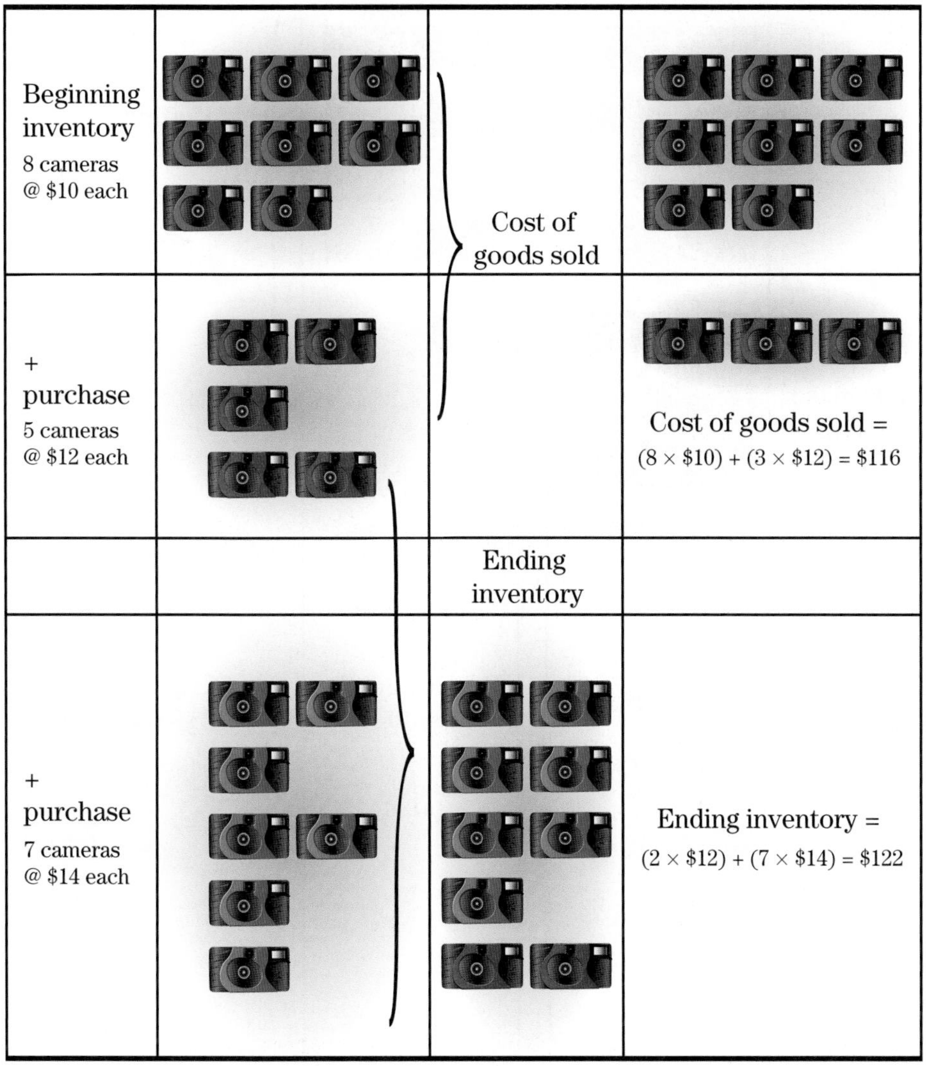

Beginning inventory 8 cameras @ \$10 each		Cost of goods sold	
+ purchase 5 cameras @ \$12 each			Cost of goods sold = $(8 \times \$10) + (3 \times \$12) = \$116$
		Ending inventory	
+ purchase 7 cameras @ \$14 each			Ending inventory = $(2 \times \$12) + (7 \times \$14) = \$122$

Even though an inventory cost flow assumption does not need to mimic the physical flow of goods, it is a useful way to visualize what is happening. In this exhibit, think of each color of camera as representing the particular cost of a camera in that purchase. The green cameras cost \$10 each; the red cameras cost \$12 each; and the blue cameras cost \$14 each. Katelyn's Photo starts with 8 cameras, purchases 5 more and then 7 more, and sells 11 cameras. That leaves 9 cameras in the ending inventory.

Notice that the cost of goods sold (\$146) plus the ending inventory (\$92) equals cost of goods available for sale (\$238). Exhibit 6.9 shows the LIFO inventory cost flow for Katelyn's Photo.

Conclusions About Inventory Cost Flow Assumptions Firms use all of the combinations of the three inventory cost flow assumptions—weighted average, FIFO, and LIFO—and two record-keeping methods you studied in Chapter 5—perpetual and periodic. Accountants and firms have modified these methods to meet the needs of specific industries. Sometimes firms keep perpetual records of inventory in units but wait until the end of the period to calculate the cost of goods sold using the periodic method. Even though there are several variations and combinations, we'll stick to periodic record keeping for our examples. For now, remain aware that the method a company selects to account for inventory can make a difference in the reported Cost of Goods Sold, Inventory, and net income.

Even though an inventory cost flow assumption does not need to mimic the physical flow of goods, it is a useful way to visualize what is happening. In this exhibit, think of each color of camera as representing the particular cost of a camera in that purchase. The green cameras cost $10 each, the red cameras cost $12 each, and the blue cameras cost $14 each. Katelyn's Photo starts with 8 cameras, purchases 5 more and then 7 more, and sells 11 cameras. That leaves 9 cameras in the ending inventory.

Exhibit 6.9

LIFO Inventory Cost Flow Assumption for Katelyn's Photo Shop

Beginning inventory 8 cameras @ $10 each			**Ending inventory** $(8 \times \$10) +$ $(1 \times \$12) =$ **$92**
+ purchase 5 cameras @ $12 each			
+ purchase 7 cameras @ $14 each		**Cost of goods sold** $(7 \times \$14) +$ $(4 \times \$12) =$ **$146**	

Can YOU do it?

Jones Saddle Company had the following transactions during August 2005:

- Purchased 30 units @ $20 per unit on August 10, 2005.
- Purchased 20 units @ $21 per unit on August 15, 2005.
- Purchased 20 units @ $23 per unit on August 21, 2005.
- Sold 35 units @ $30 per unit on August 30, 2005.

Calculate the cost of goods sold using each of these inventory cost flow assumptions: (1) FIFO, (2) LIFO, and (3) weighted average cost.

Answers (1) FIFO: $705 [(30 × $20) + (5 × $21)] (2) LIFO: $775 [(20 × $23) + (15 × $21)] (3) $21.143 (rounded) × 35 = $740

Exhibit 6.10

Summary of Katelyn's Photo Inventory Data

Inventory Cost Flow Assumption	FIFO	LIFO	Weighted Average
Cost of Goods Sold	$116	$146	$131
Ending Inventory	$122	$ 92	$107

Note: Amounts are rounded to the nearest dollar.

Income tax effects of LIFO and FIFO

You see that the inventory cost flow assumption makes a difference in the amounts reported on the income statement for Cost of Goods Sold and on the balance sheet for Inventory. What effect do you think the inventory cost flow assumption has on the statement of cash flows? Let's look at the income statement and the statement of cash flows for Katelyn's Photo for an explanation of what could make a company prefer one assumption over another. First, let's review Exhibit 6.10 above, which summarizes the calculations of sales and cost of goods sold under each method.

Sales revenue and operating expenses are the same no matter what inventory cost flow assumption is used. Earlier we learned that sales revenue amounted to $590, and operating expenses, in addition to Cost of Goods Sold, were $50 for the period. Now, look at Exhibit 6.11. Notice that we have added two new numbers: Operating Expenses, paid in cash, of $50 and the income taxes of 30%. Exhibit 6.11 shows the income statement for each inventory cost flow assumption.

Before you decide that FIFO is best because it provides a higher net income, notice that this is true only in a period of increasing inventory costs. Additionally, we really need to look at the statement of cash flows to see what effect the inventory cost flow method has on cash flows. Exhibit 6.12 shows the statements of cash flow under each inventory cost flow assumption.

If you compare Exhibits 6.11 and 6.12 you will notice that, although LIFO produces the lowest net income, it produces the largest cash flow from operations. That's due to the income tax savings that result from the lower net income. LIFO will yield the largest cash flow in a period of rising costs of inventory. If Katelyn's uses LIFO instead of FIFO, she will save $9 on income taxes and have that money to spend on advertising or hiring new workers. Think of these savings in millions. Firms often save millions of dollars by using LIFO when inventory costs are rising. The disadvantage of using LIFO is that net income will be lower than it would have been with FIFO or weighted average cost.

Exhibit 6.11

Income Statements for Katelyn's Photo Using Various Inventory Cost Flow Assumptions

Inventory Cost Flow Assumption	FIFO	LIFO	Weighted Average
Sales*	$590	$590	$590
Cost of goods sold	116	146	131
Operating expenses	50	50	50
Income before taxes	424	394	409
Income taxes (30%)	127	118	123
Net income	**$297**	**$276**	**$286**

*(3 × $50) + (8 × $55) = $590

Recall that the cost of the inventory has been rising. That means LIFO will yield a higher cost of goods sold and a lower taxable income. Cost of Goods Sold and Income taxes are highlighted because those amounts are why LIFO income is lower than FIFO income.

All inventory methods produce the same cash flows for all items except income taxes.

Exhibit 6.12

Statements of Cash Flow for Katelyn's Photo Using Various Inventory Cost Flow Assumptions

Inventory Cost Flow Assumption	FIFO	LIFO	Weighted Average
Cash collected from customers	$590	$590	$590
Cash paid for inventory	238	238	238
Cash paid for operating expenses	50	50	50
Cash inflow before income taxes	302	302	302
Cash paid for income taxes	127	118	123
Net cash from operation activities	**$175**	**$184**	**$179**

How do firms choose an inventory cost flow method?

Now, let's think about some of the factors that might influence a firm's choice of inventory cost flow assumptions:

1. *Compatibility with similar companies.* A firm will often choose a method that other firms in the same industry use. Then, a manager can easily compare inventory levels to those of the competition. Also, investors like to compare similar companies without the complication of different inventory methods. Best Buy, for example, uses weighted average cost to value its inventory. Circuit City, a similar firm and competitor of Best Buy, also uses weighted average cost.

2. *Maximize tax savings and cash flows.* A firm may want to maximize tax savings and cash flows. As you saw in our analysis of Katelyn's Photo with various inventory methods, when inventory costs are rising, cost of goods sold is larger when a company uses LIFO rather than FIFO. There's a difference because the higher costs of the more recent purchases go to the income statement as Cost of Goods Sold, and the older, lower costs are left on the balance sheet in Inventory. Higher cost of goods sold

This is just part of the inventory disclosure made by Books-A-Million in the notes to its January 29, 2005 financial statements. Notice the justification for the change in inventory methods, highlighted.

Exhibit 6.13

Disclosure of a Change in Inventory Cost Flow Methods

Inventories

Inventories are valued at the lower of cost or market, using the retail method. Market is determined based on the lower of replacement cost or estimated realizable value. Using the retail method, store and warehouse inventories are valued by applying a calculated cost to retail ratio to the retail value of inventories.

Effective February 2, 2003, the Company changed from the first-in, first-out (FIFO) method of accounting for inventories to the last-in, first-out (LIFO) method. Management believes this change was preferable in that it achieves a more appropriate matching of revenues and expenses. The impact of this accounting change was to increase "Costs of Products Sold" in the consolidated statements of operations by $0.4 million and $0.7 million for the fiscal years ended January 29, 2005 and January 31, 2004, respectively. This resulted in an after-tax decrease to net income of $0.3 million or $0.01 per diluted share for fiscal 2005 and an after-tax decrease to net income of $0.4 million or $0.02 per diluted share for fiscal 2004. The cumulative effect of a change in accounting principle from the FIFO method to LIFO method is not determinable. Accordingly, such change has been accounted for prospectively.

expense results in a lower net income. Although financial accounting and tax accounting are usually quite different, the IRS requires any company that uses LIFO for income taxes to also use LIFO for its financial statements. This is called the LIFO conformity rule. So, if a firm wants to take advantage of lower income taxes when inventory costs are rising, the firm must also be willing to report a lower net income to its shareholders. Reducing income taxes is the major reason firms select LIFO.

3. *Maximize net income.* In a period of rising prices, a higher net income will come from using FIFO. That's because older, lower costs will go to the income statement as Cost of Goods Sold. Suppose you are a CFO whose bonus depends on reaching a specific level of earnings. You may forego the tax benefits of LIFO to keep your net income higher with FIFO.

Whatever inventory cost flow method a firm uses, the method should be used consistently so that financial statements from one period can be compared to those from the previous period. A firm can change inventory cost flow methods only if the change improves the measurement of the firm's performance or financial position. Exhibit 6.13 gives an example of the type of disclosure a firm must make if it changes inventory cost flow methods.

Study Tip

If a firm uses LIFO for income taxes, then the firm must also use LIFO for its financial statements. This is called the LIFO conformity rule. In a period of rising prices, LIFO saves income taxes, but it also makes net income lower.

Complications in Valuing Inventory: Lower-of-Cost-or-Market Rule

LEARNING OBJECTIVE 3

Explain the lower-of-cost-or-market rule for valuing inventory.

Inventory is an asset on the balance sheet, recorded at cost. As you have seen, that asset can be a significant amount. To make sure that inventory is not overstated, GAAP requires companies to compare the cost of their inventory at the end of the period with the market value of that inventory, based on either individual items or total inventory. The company must use the lower of either the cost or the market value of its inventory for the financial statements. This is called the **lower-of-cost-or-market (LCM) rule**. When you study any company's annual report, the note about inventory methods will almost always mention the lower-of-cost-or-market valuation rule. In Exhibit 6.13, the first sentence in Books-A-Million's note about inventory confirms that the company has applied the required LCM rule.

Lower-of-cost-or-market (LCM) rule: Rule that requires firms to use the lower of either the cost or the market value (replacement cost) of its inventory on the date of the balance sheet.

Estimating the market value of inventory is the difficult part of the LCM rule. The market value used is **replacement cost**. That's the cost to buy similar inventory items from the supplier to replace the inventory. A company compares the cost of the inventory, as it is recorded in the accounting records, to the replacement cost at the date of the financial statements and uses the lower of the two values for the balance sheet. Although there are a few more complications in applying this rule, the concept is straightforward. Inventory must not be overstated. When the inventory value is reduced, the adjustment to reduce the inventory also reduces net income.

Replacement cost: The cost to buy similar items in inventory from the supplier to replace the inventory.

Comparing the cost of inventory to its current replacement cost is more than a simple accounting requirement. Information about the current replacement cost of inventory is important for formulating sales strategies related to various items in inventory and for inventory purchasing decisions.

It is common for the inventory of companies like T-Mobile and Sony to lose value or quickly become obsolete because of new technology. These companies cannot know the value of the inventory with certainty, so they will often estimate the reduction in inventory. Knowing how a company values its inventory is essential for analyzing a company's financial statements. Read about the estimates Best Buy makes to value its inventory in *Accounting in the News*.

Study Tip

Remember the historical cost principle from Chapter 2? With inventory, accountants are conservative and therefore feel it is so important not to overstate assets that GAAP diverges from historical cost and will reduce the value of the inventory on the balance sheet when necessary.

Accounting in the NEWS

Financial Statement Analysis

Best Buy Shows How Estimates of Inventory Reserves Can Change Net Income

Managers of merchandising companies understand that they must control inventory shrinkage and inventory value reductions due to factors such as inventory obsolescence. Therefore, managers will estimate a budget of inventory loss reserves because they cannot measure the loss precisely until a future event occurs—usually when they sell merchandise. Let's see how Best Buy discloses its inventory reserves.

First, Best Buy describes its inventory reserves:

We value our inventory at the lower of the cost of the inventory or fair market value through the establishment of markdown and inventory loss reserves.

Then, the company describes the judgments and uncertainties involved in inventory valuation:

Our markdown reserve represents the excess of the carrying value, typically cost, over the amount we expect to realize from the ultimate sale or other disposal of the inventory based on our assumptions regarding forecasted consumer demand, the promotional environment, inventory aging and technological obsolescence.

Finally, the company discloses a numerical estimate of the potential loss due to errors in the estimate of the inventory reserve:

If our estimates regarding physical inventory losses are inaccurate, we may be exposed to losses or gains that could be material. A 10% difference in actual physical inventory losses reserved for at February 26, 2005, would have affected net earnings by approximately $5 million for the fiscal year ended February 26, 2005.

If Best Buy was incorrect in estimating its inventory losses by $5 million, would you

New, faster technologies are replacing old ones every few years. That means a company like Best Buy doesn't want to get stuck with an inventory of old computer hardware.

consider it significant? Consider that Best Buy's net earnings were $984 million for the fiscal year ended February 26, 2005.

Q Why would inventory losses need to be estimated before a firm actually knows the precise amount of the loss?

A Accountants want to be sure Inventory is not overstated on the balance sheet, so Inventory must often be written down by using an estimate.

Source: Best Buy, 10-K Report for the Fiscal Year Ended February 26, 2005.

Can YOU do it?

At the end of the year, Jule Company had inventory of $345,000. If the replacement cost of the inventory is $350,000, what amount will Jule show on the year-end balance sheet? Suppose the replacement cost were $339,000. In that case, what amount would Jule show on the year-end balance sheet?

Answers $345,000 (the lower); $339,000 (the lower)

LEARNING OBJECTIVE 4

Evaluate a firm's inventory management using the inventory turnover ratio.

Financial Statement Analysis: Inventory Turnover

Merchandising companies make a profit by selling their inventory. The faster they sell their inventory, the more profit they make. Buying inventory and then selling it makes the inventory "turn over." After a company sells its inventory, it must purchase new inventory. The more often this happens, the more profit a company makes. Financial analysts and investors are very interested in how quickly a company turns over its inventory. Turnover rates vary a great deal from industry to industry. Industries with small gross margins, such as the candy industry, usually turn over their inventories more quickly than industries with large gross margins, such as the auto industry.

The **inventory turnover ratio** is defined as cost of goods sold divided by the average inventory on hand during the year. The ratio measures how quickly a firm is selling its inventory. Let's calculate the inventory turnover ratio for Best Buy for the fiscal year ended on February 28, 2005. The year's Cost of Goods Sold, found on the income statement, is $20,938 million. The average inventory can be calculated from the beginning and ending inventory amounts shown on the balance sheet. For Best Buy, the inventory was $2,607 million at February 28, 2004 and $2,851 at February 28, 2005. To get the average, we'll just add them and divide by two. The ratio calculation is:

$$\text{Inventory turnover ratio} = \frac{\text{Cost of goods sold}}{\text{Average inventory}}$$

$$\text{Inventory turnover ratio} = \frac{\$20,938}{\$2,729} = 7.7 \text{ times}$$

This ratio of 7.7 means that Best Buy turns over—sells and replaces—its inventory almost eight times each year.

Although managers want to turn over inventory rapidly, they also want enough inventory on hand to meet customer demand. Managers can monitor inventory by using the inventory turnover ratio to find out the number of days items stay in inventory. In this example, 365 (days in a year) divided by 7.7 (inventory turnover ratio) = 47.4 days. Managers closely watch both the inventory turnover ratio and **average days in inventory**.

Let's compare Best Buy to Circuit City. For Circuit City's fiscal year ended on February 29, 2005, the year's cost of goods sold, found on the income statement, is $7,903.6 million. The average inventory can be calculated from the beginning and ending inventory amounts shown on the balance sheet. For Circuit City, the average inventory is $1,517 million + $1,460 million divided by 2. The ratio calculation is:

$$\text{Inventory turnover ratio} = \frac{\text{Cost of goods sold of } \$7,903.6 \text{ million}}{\text{Average inventory of } \$1,488.5 \text{ million}} = 5.3 \text{ times}$$

This ratio of 5.3 means that Circuit City turns over—sells and replaces—its inventory slightly over five times each year. In days, this means the average number of days an item is in the inventory is 68.9 days (= 365 ÷ 5.3). The comparison shows that Best Buy is turning over its inventory faster than Circuit City.

It takes more than a single ratio to come to any conclusions about a firm's performance. We've now studied three ratios that address a firm's inventory and sales performance: gross margin ratio (Chapter 5), profit margin ratio (Chapter 5), and inventory turnover ratio (Chapter 6). Exhibit 6.14 shows these ratios for five companies in two different industries.

Inventory is such an important asset to a firm that financial analysts and investors are very concerned that it is properly reported on the financial statements. Auditing standards require auditors to make a physical count of the inventory to make it very difficult for a company to falsify the amount of inventory it has. Performing financial analysis of Inventory and Cost of Goods Sold on the financial statements can often point to potential problems for a merchandising firm. Read about the financial statement analysis tools that might help uncover fraud, in *Accounting in the News*.

Can YOU do it?

Office Depot reported Inventory of $1,336,341 and $1,305,589 on its balance sheets at December 27, 2003 and December 28, 2002, respectively. During the fiscal year ended on December 27, 2003, the company's Cost of Goods Sold was $8,484,420. (Numbers are in thousands.) What was Office Depot's inventory turnover ratio for the year? How many days, on average, did merchandise remain in the inventory?

Answers Inventory turnover ratio = 8,484,420 ÷ [(1,336,341 + 1,305,589) ÷ 2] = 6.42.
Average days in inventory = 365 ÷ 6.42 = 56.85 days

Accounting in the NEWS

Ethics

Would You Pad Inventory to Protect Your Job?

Imagine that you are working your way through college and have a good job at a merchandising company. You get paid better than your friends and you like your job, but you have a demanding boss who has fired two of your coworkers for questioning his authority. Employees receive a memo stating that the auditors will be coming in on Saturday to count inventory. Later, you see your boss and he asks you if you can work late on Friday night and you agree. On Friday night all of the employees leave for the night and only you and your boss remain. Your boss tells you that a truck is going to be coming in and you need to help unload the cartons and then wrap plastic film around groups of cartons. While wrapping the cartons you notice that the cartons contain only Styrofoam—not merchandise. Furthermore, you worked with these auditors last year on inventory and you know that they only count cartons; they do not open them.

This type of fraud is called *inventory padding or physical padding*, and is used to artificially inflate inventory and cover up inventory shrinkage. Artificial inventory inflation increases assets and decreases cost of goods sold—increasing net income. Joseph Wells, a well-known fraud examiner, suggests that the best way to determine the quantity of inven-

tory on hand is to count it—all of it. However, Wells says that several problems can still occur even with a full count:

- Management representatives follow the auditor and record the test counts. After the audit, management can add phony inventory to the items not tested. This will falsely increase the total inventory values.
- Auditors announce when and where they will conduct their test counts. For companies with multiple inventory locations, this advance warning permits management to conceal shortages at locations that auditors will not visit.
- Sometimes auditors do not take the extra step of examining packed boxes. To inflate inventory, management stacks empty boxes in the warehouse.

Frequently, a full count is too costly to be feasible. In this case, and because of the potential problems listed above, examining trends using ratio analysis are very important. Wells recommends performing analytical procedures to look for these relationships or trends:

- Inventory and sales—are increases in inventory accompanied by increases in sales?
- Inventory turnover—is it decreasing?
- Shipping costs—are they decreasing as a percentage of inventory?
- Inventory and other assets—is inventory increasing more than total assets?
- Cost of goods sold and sales—is the gross profit increasing significantly?
- Cost of goods sold—is it different on the tax returns than in the financial accounting records?

Although companies try to keep track of inventory, it's often too costly to do a full count more than once a year. This article describes several methods to spot inventory fraud that do not involve counting inventory.

No single one of these relationships means there is inventory fraud. These trends need to be considered in relation to the others, to what's happening in the industry, and to current economic conditions.

Thinking Critically

Would you tell your boss that you don't feel it is right to pad inventory? Would you go along with your boss but talk to the auditors? Is there a third approach you could take?

Q Give an example of a ratio that might help determine if inventory is overstated.

A Inventory as a percentage of sales, calculated for several years, would be useful. If it is increasing, you should investigate for a logical explanation.

Source: "Ghost Goods: How to Spot Phantom Inventory" by Joseph T. Wells from the *Journal of Accountancy.* Copyright 2001 by AM INST OF CERTIFIED PUBLIC AC. Reproduced with permission of AM INST OF CERTIFIED PUBLIC AC in the format Textbook via Copyright Clearance Center.

Exhibit 6.14

Ratios for Firms in Different Industries for the 2004 Fiscal Year

(dollars in millions)	Retail Grocery Stores			Electronic Retail Stores		
	Safeway, Inc.	Whole Foods Market, Inc.		Best Buy	Circuit City	Radio Shack
Fiscal year ended	January 1, 2005	September 30, 2004		February 26, 2005	February 28, 2005	December 31, 2004
Gross profit ratio **(Gross profit ÷ sales)**	$\frac{\$10{,}595.3}{\$35{,}822.9}$ = **29.6%**	$\frac{\$1{,}314.1}{\$3{,}865.0}$ = **34.0%**		$\frac{\$6{,}495}{\$27{,}433}$ = **23.7%**	$\frac{\$2{,}568.7}{\$10{,}472.4}$ = **24.5%**	$\frac{\$2{,}434.5}{\$4{,}841.2}$ = **50.3%**
Profit margin ratio (Net **income ÷ sales**)	$\frac{\$560.2}{\$35{,}822.9}$ = **1.56%**	$\frac{\$129.5}{\$3{,}865.0}$ = **3.35%**		$\frac{\$984}{\$27{,}433}$ = **3.59%**	$\frac{\$61.7}{\$10{,}472.4}$ = **0.59%**	$\frac{\$337.2}{\$4{,}841.2}$ = **7.0%**
Inventory turnover ratio	**9.4** times	**18.2** times		**7.7** times	**5.3** times	**2.7** times
Average days in inventory	38.8 days	20.1 days		47.4 days	68.9 days	135.2 days

This exhibit shows the three ratios accountants use to determine a firm's inventory and sales performance: gross profit ratio (Chapter 5), profit margin ratio (Chapter 5), and inventory turnover ratio (Chapter 6). For retail grocery stores, the turnover is quite fast, especially for Whole Foods Market because people buy groceries all the time. Notice also that Best Buy has the fastest inventory turnover for the electronic retail stores shown, which may indicate they are managing their inventory more efficiently than Circuit City and RadioShack.

Business risk, control, & ethics

LEARNING OBJECTIVE 5

Recognize special risks and controls associated with inventory.

In Chapter 5, we talked about protecting inventory from damage and theft. Losing inventory by theft or damage is a major risk for all firms. One of the most important aspects of internal control is safeguarding assets. Locking inventory and hiring security guards are common ways to protect these assets. Some kinds of inventory, like food, must be stored in a climate-controlled environment, and a failure of the system could result in significant losses. Firms like Darden, the parent company of Red Lobster and Olive Garden, have to prepare for inventory risks related to severe weather. An extended period without electricity could result in huge inventory losses.

Another risk with equally serious financial implications is losing inventory due to obsolescence. If you were the manager of Best Buy, you'd hate to have a warehouse full of VHS tapes when DVDs are available. If you were the manager of CompUSA, you'd hate to have an inventory full of Pentium 3 computers when Pentium 4, a much faster and more efficient model, became available.

Firms that deal with cutting-edge technologies are at most risk for having obsolete inventory. Sprint PCS or T-Mobile would not want to have a huge inventory of analog-only phones now that digital phones are the better choice. With the new Bluetooth technology, the cell phone business is at risk with its old inventories. Each year, a company's inventory is evaluated for obsolescence at the same time the lower-of-cost-or-market rule is applied. Inventory must be written off, which will increase the cost of goods sold, when it is deemed to be obsolete. For example, in the notes to its financial statements, Tweeter Home Entertainment Group, the owner of HiFi Buys, Electronic Interiors, Showcase Home Entertainment, and Sound Advice, has an extensive note about inventory obsolescence, shown in Exhibit 6.15.

Out-of-date technology doesn't sell.

Tweeter Home Entertainment Group sells cutting-edge technologies that are at most risk for having obsolete inventory. The company, therefore, has an extensive note about inventory Obsolescence.

Exhibit 6.15

Tweeter Home Entertainment Group's Note About the Risk of Inventory Obsolescence

Inventory Obsolescence

Inventory represents a significant portion of our assets (38.1%). Our profitability and viability is highly dependent on the demand for our products. An imbalance between purchasing levels and sales could cause rapid and material obsolescence, and loss of competitive price advantage and market share. We believe that our product mix has provided sufficient diversification to mitigate this risk. At the end of each reporting period, we reduce the value by our estimate of what we believe to be obsolete, and we recognize an expense of the same amount, which is included in Cost of Sales in our consolidated statement of operations.

Inventory losses have an ethical component. The obvious one is that unethical people may steal a firm's inventory. Less obvious is the opportunity that inventory provides for misstating the value of the firm's assets. Failure to write-down inventory that has lost value means that earnings will be overstated by the amount of the decline in inventory. As you know by now, managers rarely want

Accounting in the NEWS

Risk and Control

Wal-Mart Controls Inventory with RFID Tags

You are probably familiar with universal product codes (UPC) because they are used on the products you buy at the grocery store. The cashier scans the UPC to send the product's price to the cash register. Radio Frequency Identification (RFID) tags—sometimes called "smart labels"—are like universal product codes. However, RFID tags are better than UPCs because they have radio antennae that can communicate with computers. When this technology is used in a grocery store, a cashier will not have to scan products one-by-one. Instead, a computer will record what is in a grocery cart by communicating with the RFID tags.

Wal-Mart management has recognized the potential advantages for controlling inventory with RFID tags and is on the leading edge of implementing this technology. According to *CFO Magazine*:

[Wal-Mart] now operates 4,300 stores globally and maintains a fleet of 7,000 tractors and 35,000 trailers. It owns and operates 108 distribution centers in the United States alone—many of them more than a million square feet. Those distribution centers are at the heart of Wal-Mart's remarkable success. By strategically placing retail outlets near distribution centers, the company can resupply its stores directly—often on a daily basis. "We follow what the stores sell, and orders are customized for the stores," says Tom Williams, a company spokesman. "For us, tracking inventory is extremely important."

This new inventory initiative is so important that Wal-Mart wants all of its suppliers to place radio frequency identification (RFID) tags on all cases and pallets shipped to Wal-Mart distribution centers by January 1, 2006. However, Wal-Mart gave its top 100 vendors until just January 2005 to use RFID tags. According to *BusinessWeek Online*, it's fair to say most of its suppliers have lived up to the letter of the mandate, if not the spirit. While they have technically met Wal-Mart's order to tag specified bulk shipments sent to three Texas warehouses, they haven't exactly rallied to the RFID banner.

For Wal-Mart, it's all about lowering costs. The company sees this new RFID

Wal-Mart cashiers scan UPCs to help the company keep track of what's selling. The company is on the leading edge of implementing a new technology—RFID tags

tag technology for tracking inventory as a sure way to do just that by ensuring that throughout the year they have the inventory of products that will satisfy consumer demand.

Q What inventory cost flow method would Wal-Mart be able to use with RFID tags?

A Specific identification.

Sources: Sarah Lacy, "RFID: Plenty of Mixed Signals," *Business Week Online,* January 31, 2005; Esther Shein, "Radio Flier: Wal-Mart Presents Its Vendors With an Offer They Can't Refuse." *CFO Magazine,* November 1, 2003.

to recognize expenses that don't produce any revenue, and they often look for ways to boost earnings. Inventory valuation is an area where the flexibility of accounting standards can lead to manipulation of earnings. When you study a firm's financial statements, be sure to read the notes to the financial statements about the firm's policy on writing down its obsolete inventory.

To avoid having obsolete inventory, a firm needs an inventory system that moves merchandise quickly between supplier, warehouse, and retail store. Read about Wal-Mart's plan to speed up its entire inventory network, in **Accounting in the News**.

YOU make the call:

Should Best Buy reduce the value of its television inventory?

Now that you have studied the way inventory is recorded, how cost of goods sold is determined using different inventory cost flow methods, and how inventory must be valued for the balance sheet, you are ready to answer the question: Should Best Buy reduce the value of its inventory?

As you learned in this chapter, inventory must be valued at the lower of its cost or its market value at the date of the balance sheet. The manager should evaluate the replacement cost of the inventory and book a reduction in the inventory to reflect the lower of the two values—cost or market. Accountants want to be sure investors are not misled by overstated inventory values.

Let's Take a Test Drive

Real World Problem:
Best Buy

Keeping track of inventory is a serious job for a company as large as Best Buy. The company has thousands of products and has sales each year in the billions of dollars. The company turns over its inventory almost eight times each year, so the company makes many purchases in the course of a year's transactions. Best Buy's managers and accountants have decided to use weighted average cost for its inventory cost flow. Managers want to know if inventories would be significantly different if they selected FIFO or LIFO instead.

Concepts

To value its inventory and cost of goods sold, a retail firm must decide on an inventory cost flow assumption. GAAP allows a company to (1) specifically identify the cost of each of the items sold or (2) make an inventory cost flow assumption of FIFO, LIFO, or weighted average cost. The physical flow of the goods does not have to mimic the cost flow, but the inventory cost flow assumption method chosen should be the one that best measures the firm's performance.

Inventory is an important asset and must be properly valued for the financial statements. Two valuation issues are crucial: (1) inventory must be valued at the lower of cost or market (replacement cost) and (2) inventory must be evaluated for obsolescence. Any obsolete inventory must be written off.

That means the inventory must be reduced and the value of the obsolete inventory must be included as a cost of the income statement.

The Mechanics

To compare the inventory methods for Best Buy, we'll look at a single item to keep the analysis simple. Our results will apply to the other items in Best Buy's inventory as well. Suppose Best Buy started the year with an inventory of 50 plasma TVs that cost Best Buy $2,010 each, for a total inventory of $100,500. During a recent month, Best Buy:

1. Made the following purchases:
   - 200 TVs for $2,000 each
   - 150 TVs for $1,800 each
   - 100 TVs for $1,500 each
2. Sold 420 TVs for $4,000 each.
3. Incurred other operating expenses of $250,000.

Instructions

1. Calculate the cost of goods sold for the month and the inventory at the end of the month. Do these calculations using three methods: weighted average cost, FIFO, and LIFO.
2. Assume these are the only transactions for the period. Calculate net income using each of the three methods. Which provides the highest net income? What is causing this method to produce the highest net income?

Solution

1. Cost of goods sold:

	No. of Units	Unit Cost	Total Cost
Beginning inventory	50	$2,010	$100,500
Purchases	200	$2,000	$400,000
	150	$1,800	$270,000
	100	$1,500	$150,000
Goods available for sale	500		$920,500
Units sold	420		

Cost of goods sold:

Weighted average cost $ 1,841   = $920,500/500
Cost of goods sold =   420 × $1,841
Cost of goods sold = $773,220

FIFO	50	$100,500
	200	$400,000
	150	$270,000
	20	$ 30,000
Cost of goods sold =	420	$800,500

FIFO: Oldest units are sold first

LIFO	100	$150,000
	150	$270,000
	170	$340,000
Cost of goods sold =	420	$760,000

LIFO: Newest units are sold first

2. Net Income

	Weighted Average Cost	FIFO	LIFO
Sales revenue	$1,680,000	$1,680,000	$1,680,000
Cost of goods sold	773,220	800,500	760,000
Gross profit	906,780	879,500	920,000
Other operating expenses	250,000	250,000	250,000
Net income	$ 656,780	$ 629,500	$ 670,000

Net income is highest using LIFO because the cost of the inventory is going down. More often, costs go up so companies use LIFO to minimize net income. In this case, the technology advances are likely driving down the cost of plasma TVs.

Rapid Review

1. **Explain and apply the four cost flow assumptions for valuing inventory and cost of goods sold.** The four inventory cost flow assumptions are (1) *specific identification*—each item's cost is identified when sold to determine cost of goods sold; (2) *weighted average cost*—the cost of inventory items is averaged to provide a weighted average cost to calculate cost of goods sold; (3) *FIFO*—cost of first items purchased (first in) are the first costs to go to cost of goods sold (first out); and (4) *LIFO*—cost of last items purchased (last in) are the first costs to go to cost of goods sold (first out).

2. **Explain the effects of the inventory cost flow assumption on the financial statements.** The inventory cost flow assumption determines which costs go to the income statement and which costs remain as ending inventory. If inventory costs remain constant, all inventory cost flow assumptions will produce the same results. However, in a period of rising prices, LIFO will result in the lowest net income due to the larger cost of goods sold; and FIFO will result in the highest net income. Weighted average cost usually produces a cost of goods sold between that of FIFO and LIFO.

3. **Explain the lower-of-cost-or-market rule for valuing inventory.** The *lower-of-cost-or-market rule* requires a company to value its inventory at the lower of the cost of the inventory and the market (replacement) cost of the inventory. This is an example of the conservative nature of accounting. Accountants want to be sure inventory is not overstated.

4. **Evaluate a firm's inventory management using the inventory turnover ratio.** The *inventory turnover ratio* is defined as cost of goods sold divided by average inventory.

$$\text{Inventory turnover ratio} = \frac{\text{Cost of goods sold}}{\text{Average inventory}}$$

This ratio tells how many times each year a firm's inventory is turned over. The larger the turnover ratio, the more quickly a firm is selling its inventory. If the ratio is too low, inventory may not be turning over fast enough. If the ratio is too high, the firm should be sure it is not keeping its inventory too low to meet customer demand. Along with the gross margin ratio and the profit margin ratio, the inventory turnover ratio provides information about how well a firm is managing its inventory. To calculate the average number of days an item is in the inventory, divide 365 days by the inventory turnover ratio:

$$\text{Average days in inventory} = \frac{365}{\text{Inventory turnover ratio}}$$

5. **Recognize special risks and controls associated with inventory.** In addition to the risk of shrinkage due to loss and theft, inventory risk includes the possibility of obsolescence. A firm must guard against having obsolete inventory. One way to reduce this risk is to turn over the inventory as quickly as possible.

Key Terms

Have You Increased Your Business IQ?

Answer these questions to find out.

1. Most companies don't use specific identification to calculate cost of goods sold because
   a. it is not allowed under GAAP.
   b. the cost is prohibitive.
   c. it puts the firm at a tax disadvantage.
   d. it often overstates ending inventory.
2. The purpose of the lower-of-cost-or-market rule is
   a. to make sure inventory is not understated.
   b. to make sure inventory is not overstated.
   c. to enforce the historical cost principle.
   d. to make sure inventory is valued at its current selling price.
3. LIFO is often preferred to FIFO because
   a. income taxes are minimized when prices are rising.
   b. net income is larger.
   c. LIFO is easier to apply.
   d. it is the accepted method worldwide.
4. Inventory turnover ratio (sometimes called "turns") measures the
   a. appropriate level of inventory to keep on hand.
   b. percentage of inventory left at the end of the period.
   c. inventory's shrinkage.
   d. number of times the firm replaces its inventory during the period.
5. Firms that discover they have obsolete inventory must
   a. get rid of the inventory immediately.
   b. make sure that it is the next inventory sold.
   c. have made an error in the amount of inventory purchased.
   d. reduce the book value of the inventory and record a loss.

Now, check your answers.

1. b   2. b   3. a   4. d   5. d

- If you answered all five questions correctly, you've increased your business IQ by studying this chapter. It doesn't mean you've mastered all of the accounting concepts in the chapter. It simply means that you understand some of the general business concepts presented in this chapter.
- If you answered 2 to 4 questions correctly, you've made some progress, but your business IQ has plenty of room to grow. You might want to skim over the chapter again.
- If you answered 0 or 1 question correctly, you can do more to improve your business IQ. Better study the chapter again.

Questions

1. What is the difference between the physical flow of inventory and the inventory cost flow?
2. Describe the four primary inventory cost flow assumptions.
3. If inventory costs are rising, which method (FIFO, LIFO, or weighted average cost) results in the lowest net income? Explain your answer.
4. If inventory costs are rising, which method (FIFO, LIFO, or weighted average cost) results in the highest net income? Explain your answer.
5. Does LIFO or FIFO give the "best" balance sheet value for ending Inventory? Explain your answer.
6. Which inventory cost flow assumption provides the best "matching" of current costs with revenues on the income statement? Explain your answer.
7. How do income taxes affect the choice between LIFO and FIFO?
8. What is the LIFO conformity rule? What is this rule's significance?
9. Explain the lower-of-cost-or-market rule and why it is necessary.

10. What are some of the risks associated with inventory? How do managers minimize these risks?
11. What does the inventory turnover ratio measure? What does average days in inventory mean?
12. If there were an error in the ending inventory, where else would there be an error in the financial statements?

Multiple Choice

1. Crate & Co. had beginning inventory of $10,000 in 2006. During 2006, the company bought $27,000 worth of inventory for cash. The inventory was bought under terms FOB shipping point. The freight charges were $500 and were paid in cash. Later that year, Crate & Co. sold the entire inventory for $50,000 on account under terms FOB destination. The freight on the sale cost $400, and was paid in cash.

   Considering the transactions above, what amount of gross profit would be reported on Crate & Co.'s 2006 Income Statement?
   a. $22,600
   b. $22,100
   c. $23,000
   d. $22,500

Use the following information to answer the questions 2–5:

Inventory data for Merry Merchandising is provided below. Sales for the period were 2,800 units. Each unit sold for $8. The company uses a periodic inventory system.

Date		Number of Units	Unit Cost	Total Cost
January	Beginning Inventory	1,000	$3.00	$ 3,000
February	Purchases	600	$3.50	$ 2,100
March	Purchases	800	$4.00	$ 3,200
April	Purchases	1,200	$4.25	$ 5,100
Totals		3,600		$13,400

2. Determine the ending inventory assuming the company uses the FIFO cost flow method.
   a. $3,400
   b. $2,400
   c. $9,200
   d. $10,000
3. Determine the cost of goods sold assuming the company uses the FIFO cost flow method.
   a. $3,400
   b. $10,000
   c. $10,200
   d. $2,400
4. Determine the ending inventory assuming the company uses the weighted average cost flow method. (Round unit cost to 2 decimal places.)
   a. $2,300
   b. $3,300
   c. $9,800
   d. $2,976
5. Determine the gross profit assuming the company uses the LIFO cost flow method.
   a. $11,400
   b. $14,400
   c. $22,400
   d. $19,700

6. Using LIFO will produce a lower net income than using FIFO under which of the following conditions?
   a. Inventory costs are decreasing.
   b. Inventory costs are increasing.
   c. Inventory costs are not changing.
   d. Sales prices are decreasing.
7. The lower-of-cost-or-market rule keeps a firm from
   a. overstating inventory on the balance sheet.
   b. understating inventory on the balance sheet.
   c. overstating cost of goods sold on the income statement.
   d. increasing inventory turnover.
8. The inventory turnover ratio provides information about
   a. cost of the inventory.
   b. sales value of the inventory.
   c. amount of time merchandise is in the inventory.
   d. time it takes for a supplier to deliver inventory.
9. The LIFO conformity rule requires a firm to use
   a. the same inventory cost flow method for financial statements and income taxes.

b. LIFO for any international
inventory.
c. FIFO for income taxes when LIFO
is used for financial statements.
d. LIFO for financial statements when
LIFO is used for income taxes.
10. If a company has a very small gross
margin per inventory item, then
a. it will be difficult to make a profit.

b. the company relies on inventory
turning over rapidly.
c. the company is paying too much
for its inventory items.
d. the company should raise the
selling price of its products.

Short Exercises

LO 1   **SE6-1. Calculate cost of goods sold.**
The Blades Company purchased 500 electric saws for $250 each and sold them for
$450. If Blades sold half of the electric saws, what is the cost of goods sold? Explain
why no inventory cost flow assumption is needed for this calculation.

LO 1   **SE6-2. Calculate cost of goods sold.**
Stone Company acquired 3,000 transformers for $120 each and sold half of them for
$170 and the other half for $175. What is the (1) cost of goods available for sale, (2)
cost of goods sold, (3) gross profit? Why is a cost flow assumption unnecessary to
make these calculations?

LO 1   **SE6-3. Calculate cost of goods sold and ending inventory:
weighted average cost–periodic.**
Calculate the cost of goods sold and the cost of the ending inventory using the
weighted average inventory cost flow assumption:

Sales	100 units @ $15 per unit
Beginning Inventory	90 units @ $ 6 per unit
Purchases	60 units @ $ 9 per unit

LO 1   **SE6-4. Calculate cost of goods sold and ending inventory:
FIFO–periodic.**
Using the data from SE6-3, calculate the cost of goods sold and the cost of the ending
inventory using the FIFO cost flow assumption.

LO 1   **SE6-5. Calculate cost of goods sold and ending inventory:
LIFO.**
Using the data from SE6-3, calculate the cost of goods sold and the cost of the ending
inventory using the LIFO periodic cost flow assumption.

LO 2   **SE6-6. Analyze effect of inventory cost flow method on
net income.**
Given the information below, calculate the amount by which net income would differ
between FIFO and LIFO.

Beginning Inventory	3,000 units @ $100
Purchases	8,000 units @ $130
Units Sold	6,000 units @ $225

LO 2   **SE6-7. Analyze effect of inventory cost flow method on
gross margin.**
Given the information below, calculate the amount by which gross margin would differ
between FIFO and LIFO.

Beginning Inventory	1,500 units @ $55
Purchases	2,750 units @ $58
Units Sold	2,250 units @ $99

LO 3   **SE6-8. Apply the lower-of-cost-or-market rule.**
The following information pertains to item #006LL of inventory of The Roberts Company:

	Per Unit
Cost	$180
Replacement Cost	181
Selling Price	195

The physical inventory indicates 2,000 units of item #006LL on hand. What amount will be reported on The Roberts Company's balance sheet for this inventory item?

SE6-9. Apply the lower-of-cost-or-market rule.

LO 3

In each case listed below, select the correct amount for the inventory on the year-end balance sheet:

(a)	Ending inventory at cost	$24,500
	Ending inventory at replacement cost	$23,000
(b)	Ending inventory at cost	$27,000
	Ending inventory at replacement cost	$28,500

SE6-10. Apply the lower-of-cost-or-market rule.

LO 3

Daylight Company ended its fiscal year with inventory recorded at its cost of $15,679. Due to changes in the market, Daylight would be able to replace this inventory for $15,400. How much will Daylight's balance sheet show for Inventory on the year-end balance sheet?

SE6-11. Calculate the inventory turnover ratio and average days in inventory.

LO 6

Using the following information, calculate the inventory turnover ratio and average days in inventory for Barkley Company for the year ended December 31, 2012 (Round to two decimal places.):

Sales	$125,000
Cost of Goods Sold	75,000
Ending Inventory, December 31, 2011	15,275
Ending Inventory, December 31, 2012	18,750
Net Income	26,500

SE6-12. Risk and control.

LO 5

What is obsolete inventory? Name two things a firm can do to protect itself from this risk.

SE6-13. Appendix B: Inventory errors.

How would each of the following inventory errors affect net income for the year? Assume each is the only error during the year.

a. Ending Inventory is overstated by $3,000.
b. Ending Inventory is understated by $1,500.
c. Beginning Inventory is understated by $3,000.
d. Beginning Inventory is overstated by $1,550.

SE6-14. Appendix B: Inventory errors.

The Leed Company's records showed the following at the end of the fiscal year:

Beginning Inventory	$ 26,000
Ending Inventory	38,000
Cost of Goods Sold	128,000

A physical inventory was taken and showed that the inventory was actually $39,500. If the Leed Company fails to correct the error, what effect will it have on the financial statements for the year? How would Leed Company's accountant correct the error?

SE6-15. Appendix B: Inventory errors.

The Landing Company's records reported the following at the end of the fiscal year:

Beginning Inventory	$ 40,000
Ending Inventory	27,500
Cost of Goods Sold	280,000

A physical count showed that the ending inventory was actually $26,000. If the inventory amount is not corrected, what is the effect on each of the financial statements? How would Landing Company's accountant correct the error?

SE6-16. Appendix C: Estimating inventory.

Computer Games wants to estimate its inventory balance for its quarterly financial statements for the first quarter of the year. Given the following, what is your best estimate?

Beginning Inventory	$75,800
Net Sales	92,500
Net Purchases	50,500
Gross Margin Percentage	20%

Exercise Set A

LO 1 **E6-1A. Calculate cost of goods sold and ending inventory–periodic.**
Mira Company's records show inventory purchases as follows in the order given:

1. 500 units @ $5 per unit
2. 400 units @ $6 per unit
3. 300 units at $7 per unit

If Mira Company sold 1,000 units, what was the value of ending inventory (1) using FIFO, (2) using LIFO, (3) using weighted average cost? Use periodic record keeping.

LO 1 **E6-2A. Calculate cost of goods sold and ending inventory: periodic FIFO and LIFO.**
Given the following information:

Jan 1	Beginning Inventory	25 units @ $10 each
Feb 28	Purchase	60 units @ $12 each
April 30	Purchase	40 units @ $13 each
Sept 15	Purchase	50 units @ $14 each
Dec 31	Ending Inventory	40 units

a. Calculate the cost of goods sold and the cost of the ending inventory using FIFO.
b. Calculate the cost of goods sold and the cost of the ending inventory using LIFO.

LO 1 **E6-3A. Calculate cost of goods sold and ending inventory: periodic FIFO.**
Best TV Sales and Service began the month of May with two television sets in inventory, Model# TV5684; each unit cost $125. During May, five additional television sets of the same model were purchased. Best's May transactions are as follows:

May 10	purchased 2 units @ $127
May 13	sold 2 units @ $225
May 16	purchased 1 unit @ $130
May 18	sold 1 unit @ $225
May 23	sold 2 units @ $225
May 24	purchased 2 units @ $135

Assume Best uses a periodic inventory system and the FIFO cost flow method:

a. Calculate the Cost of Goods Sold that will appear on Best's income statement for the month of May.
b. Determine the Inventory that will appear on Best's balance sheet at the end of May.

LO 1 **E6-4A. Calculate cost of goods sold and ending inventory: periodic LIFO.**
Use the data in E6-3A to answer the following questions. Assume Best uses a periodic inventory system and the LIFO cost flow method.

a. Calculate the Cost of Goods Sold that will appear on Best's income statement for the month of May.
b. Determine the Inventory that will appear on Best's balance sheet at the end of May.

LO 2 **E6-5A. Calculate cost of goods sold: periodic FIFO and LIFO.**
Given the following information for March 2006, calculate the cost of goods sold for the month using (a) LIFO periodic, and then using (b) FIFO periodic. Explain why the two methods produce a different amount for cost of goods sold.

Inventory, March 1, 2006	10 units @ $ 5 each
Purchase, March 10	30 units @ $ 6 each
Sale, March 15	20 units @ $15 each
Purchase, March 20	15 units @ $ 7 each

LO 2 **E6-6A. Calculate gross margin: periodic FIFO and LIFO.**
Using the data in E6-5A, calculate the gross margin for the month using (a) LIFO periodic, and then using (b) FIFO periodic. Explain what effect the two methods have on the amount of gross margin reported on the income statement.

LO 2 **E6-7A. Calculate gross margin: periodic FIFO and LIFO.**
Given the following information, calculate the gross margin under (a) FIFO and under (b) LIFO.

Sales	200 units @ $50 per unit
Beginning Inventory	60 units @ $40 per unit
Purchases	175 units @ $45 per unit

E6-8A. Apply the lower-of-cost-or-market rule.

LO 3

In each case, indicate the correct amount to be reported for the inventory on the year-end balance sheet.

(a) Ending Inventory at cost	$125,000
Ending Inventory at market	$121,750
(b) Ending Inventory at cost	$117,500
Ending Inventory at market	$120,250

E6-9A. Apply the lower-of-cost-or-market rule.

LO 3

Use the following data to answer the following questions:

Ending Inventory at cost, December 31, 2011	$ 17,095
Ending Inventory at replacement cost, December 31, 2011	16,545
Cost of Goods Sold, balance at December 31, 2011	250,765
Sales Revenue, balance at December 31, 2011	535,780
Cash, balance at December 31, 2011	165,340

What Inventory amount will this firm report on its balance sheet at December 31, 2011?

E6-10A. Calculate the inventory turnover ratio.

LO 4

A company calculated its inventory turnover ratio for the past two years. This year the inventory turnover ratio is 6.3, and last year the inventory turnover ratio was 7.5. Use this data to answer the following questions:

a. Will this change in the inventory turnover ratio be viewed as good news or bad news? Explain your answer.
b. Does the change indicate that more or less capital has been tied up in inventory this year compared to last year?

E6-11A. Risk and control.

LO 5

Explain how the lower-of-cost-or-market rule for inventory is related to accounting for obsolete inventory. What is the overriding purpose of each?

E6-12A. Risk and control.

LO 5

Suppose an unethical manager wanted to keep his firm's net income as high as possible for a particular quarter to make sure he would get his bonus. The inventory manager has informed him that some obsolete inventory should be written off. What effect does writing down the value of the inventory have on net income? How will the manager respond to the inventory manager?

E6-13A. Appendix A: Perpetual inventory system—FIFO.

Use the data in E6-3A to answer the following questions. Assume Best uses a perpetual inventory system and the FIFO cost flow method.

a. Calculate the Cost of Goods Sold that will appear on Best's income statement for the month of May.
b. Determine the cost of Inventory that will appear on Best's balance sheet at the end of May.

E6-14A. Appendix A: Perpetual inventory system—LIFO.

Use the data in E6-3A to answer the following questions. Assume Best uses a perpetual inventory system and the LIFO cost flow method.

a. Calculate the Cost of Goods Sold that will appear on Best's income statement for the month of May.
b. Determine the cost of Inventory that will appear on Best's balance sheet at the end of May.

E6-15A. Appendix B: Inventory errors.

Sloppy Company uses a periodic inventory system. On December 31, 2006, at the end of the fiscal year, the inventory remaining on hand was miscounted. They counted $130,000 worth of inventory, but they forgot to count a stack of goods in the corner with a cost of $10,000. If this error goes undetected, how will it affect the financial statements for the year ending December 31, 2006? If their accountant discovered the error just before the financial statements were released, what journal entry would correct the error?

E6-16A. Appendix B: Inventory errors.
The Rim Company's records reported the following at the end of the fiscal year:

Beginning Inventory $ 90,000
Ending Inventory   72,000
Cost of Goods Sold   395,000

A physical inventory count showed that the ending inventory was actually $62,000. If this error is not corrected, what effect would it have on the income statement for this fiscal year and for the following fiscal year? What journal entry would correct this error?

E6-17A. Appendix B: Inventory errors.
Ian's Small Appliances reported cost of goods sold as follows:

	2005	2006
Beginning inventory	$130,000	$ 50,000
Purchases	275,000	240,000
Cost of goods available for sale	405,000	290,000
Ending inventory	50,000	40,000
Cost of goods sold	355,000	250,000

Ian's made two errors:

1. 2005 ending inventory was understated by $5,000.
2. 2006 ending inventory was overstated by $2,000.

Calculate the correct cost of goods sold for 2005 and 2006.

E6-18A. Appendix C: Estimating inventory.
The following information is available for the Rocklin Office Supply Company:

Inventory, October 1, 2006 $240,000
Net purchases for the month of October   750,000
Net sales for the month of October   950,000
Gross margin percentage (historical)   40%

Estimate the cost of goods sold for October and the ending inventory at October 31.

E6-19A. Appendix C: Estimating inventory.
The records of California Ship Products revealed the following information related to inventory destroyed in an earthquake:

Inventory, beginning of period $300,000
Purchases to date of earthquake   160,000
Net sales to date of earthquake   550,000
Gross margin percentage   20%

The company needs to file a claim for lost inventory with its insurance company. What is the estimated value of the lost inventory?

Exercise Set B

> Your professor may ask you to complete selected "Group B" exercises and problems using Prentice Hall Grade Assist (**PHGA**). PHGA is an online tool that can help you master the chapter's topics by providing multiple variations of exercises and problems. You can rework these exercises and problems—each time with new data—as many times as you need, with immediate feedback and grading.

LO 1   **E6-1B. Calculate cost of inventory—periodic.**
Office Supplies Unlimited's records show inventory of 200 units valued at $20,000 at the beginning of March. During the month, the firm made the following purchases:

March 5   100 units @ $105 per unit
March 15   250 units @ $110 per unit
March 25   150 units @ $115 per unit

At the end of the month, there were 175 units remaining in the inventory. Calculate the cost of goods sold for March using (a) FIFO, (b) LIFO, and (c) weighted average cost.

E6-2B. Calculate cost of goods sold and ending inventory: periodic FIFO and LIFO.   <u>LO 1</u>

Given the following information:

Jan 1	Beginning inventory	20 candles @ $14 each
Mar 15	Purchase	75 candles @ $13 each
June 30	Purchase	50 candles @ $12 each
Oct 10	Purchase	45 candles @ $11 each
Dec 31	Ending inventory	30 candles

a. Calculate the cost of goods sold and the cost of the ending inventory using FIFO.
b. Calculate the cost of goods sold and the cost of the ending inventory using LIFO.

E6-3B. Calculate cost of goods sold and ending inventory: periodic FIFO.   <u>LO 1</u>

Glad Radio Sales & Service began the month of April with three top-of-the-line radios in inventory, Model #RD58V6Q; each unit cost $235. During April, 9 additional radios of the same model were purchased. The following are the transactions for April:

April 9	purchased 3 units @ $230
April 11	sold 5 units @ $350
April 17	purchased 2 units @ $195
April 18	sold 1 unit @ $350
April 20	sold 2 units @ $350
April 28	purchased 4 units @ $180

Assume Glad uses a periodic inventory system and the FIFO cost flow method.

a. Calculate the cost of goods sold that will appear on Glad's income statement for the month of April.
b. Determine the cost of inventory that will appear on Glad's balance sheet at the end of April.

E6-4B. Calculate cost of goods sold and ending inventory: periodic LIFO.   <u>LO 1</u>

Use the data in E6-3B to answer the following questions. Assume Glad uses a periodic inventory system and the LIFO cost flow method.

a. Calculate the cost of goods sold that will appear on Glad's income statement for the month of April.
b. Determine the cost of inventory that will appear on Glad's balance sheet at the end of April.

E6-5B. Calculate cost of goods sold: periodic FIFO and LIFO.   <u>LO 2</u>

Given the following information for July 2006, calculate the cost of goods sold for the month using (a) LIFO periodic, and then using (b) FIFO periodic. Explain why the two methods produce a different amount for cost of goods sold.

Inventory, July 1, 2006	15 units @ $ 7 each
Purchase, July 8	20 units @ $ 6 each
Sale, July 22	25 units @ $13 each
Purchase, July 25	15 units @ $ 5 each

E6-6B. Calculate gross margin: periodic FIFO and LIFO.   <u>LO 2</u>

Using the data in E6-5B, calculate the gross margin for the month using (a) LIFO periodic and then using (b) FIFO periodic. Explain what effect the two methods have on the amount of gross margin reported on the income statement.

E6-7B. Calculate gross margin: periodic FIFO and LIFO.   <u>LO 2</u>

Given the following information, calculate the gross margin under (a) FIFO and under (b) LIFO.

Sales	225 units @ $30 per unit
Beginning inventory	105 units @ $20 per unit
Purchases	180 units @ $32 per unit

E6-8B. Apply the lower-of-cost-or-market rule.   <u>LO 3</u>

In each case, indicate the correct amount to be reported for the inventory on the year-end balance sheet.

(a) Ending Inventory at cost	$275,000
Ending Inventory at market	$271,250
(b) Ending Inventory at cost	$185,250
Ending Inventory at market	$187,550

LO 3 **E6-9B. Apply the lower-of-cost-or-market rule.**
Use the data below to answer the following questions:

Ending Inventory at cost, June 30, 2010	$ 25,180
Ending Inventory at replacement cost, June 30, 2010	25,130
Cost of Goods sold, balance at June 30, 2010	150,550
Sales Revenue, balance at June 30, 2010	275,625
Cash, balance at June 30, 2010	285,515

ASB Hardware uses a periodic inventory system and the FIFO cost flow method to account for its inventory. What Inventory amount will ASB Hardware report on its balance sheet at June 30, 2010?

LO 4 **E6-10B. Calculate the inventory turnover ratio.**
A company calculated its inventory turnover ratio for the past two years. This year the inventory turnover ratio is 7.2, and last year the inventory turnover ratio was 8.3. Use this data to answer the following questions:

a. Will analysts view this change in the inventory turnover ratio as good news or bad news? Explain your answer.
b. Does the change indicate that more or less capital has been tied up in inventory this year compared to last year?

LO 5 **E6-11B. Risk and control.**
What types of industries are at most risk for having obsolete inventory? If you were a financial analyst, how would you determine if a firm has to deal with significant amounts of obsolete inventory?

LO 5 **E6-12B. Risk and control.**
Risks associated with inventory include (1) theft, (2) damage, and (3) obsolescence. For each item, give an example of a company you believe is seriously faced with this risk and explain why.

E6-13B. Appendix A: Perpetual inventory—FIFO.
Use the data in E6-3B to answer the following questions. Assume Glad uses a perpetual inventory system and the FIFO cost flow method.

a. Calculate the cost of goods sold that will appear on Glad's income statement for the month of April.
b. Determine the cost of inventory that will appear on Glad's balance sheet at the end of April.

E6-14B. Appendix A: Perpetual inventory—LIFO.
Use the data in E6-3B to answer the following questions. Assume Glad uses a perpetual inventory system and the LIFO cost flow method.

a. Calculate the cost of goods sold that will appear on Glad's income statement for the month of April.
b. Determine the cost of inventory that will appear on Glad's balance sheet at the end of April.

E6-15B. Appendix B: Inventory errors.
Susan's Fresh Foods Company uses a periodic inventory system. On June 30, 2007, at the end of the fiscal year, the inventory remaining on hand was miscounted. They counted $140,000 worth of inventory, but they forgot to count a stack of goods in the corner with a cost of $20,000. If this error goes undetected, how will it affect the financial statements for the year ending June 30, 2007? If their accountant discovered the error just before the financial statements were released, what journal entry would correct the error?

E6-16B. Appendix B: Inventory errors.
Tire Pro Company's records reported the following at the end of the fiscal year:

Beginning Inventory	$ 80,000
Ending Inventory	85,000
Cost of Goods Sold	295,000

A physical inventory count showed that the ending inventory was actually $78,000. If this error is not corrected, what effect would it have on the income statement for this fiscal year and for the following fiscal year? What journal entry would correct this error?

E6-17B. Appendix B: Inventory errors.

Jack's Hi-Tech Electronics reported cost of goods sold as follows:

	2007	2008
Beginning inventory	$250,000	$ 40,000
Purchases	285,000	460,000
Cost of goods available for sale	535,000	500,000
Ending inventory	40,000	90,000
Cost of goods sold	$495,000	$410,000

Jack's made two errors:

1. 2007 ending inventory was understated by $8,000.
2. 2008 Ending Inventory was overstated by $12,000.

Calculate the correct cost of goods sold for 2007 and 2008.

E6-18B. Appendix C: Estimating inventory.

The following information is available for the International Computer Company:

Inventory, July 1, 2007	$180,000
Net purchases for the month of October	645,000
Net sales for the month of October	790,000
Gross margin percentage (historical)	30%

Estimate the cost of goods sold for July and the ending inventory at July 31.

E6-19B. Appendix C: Estimating inventory.

The records of Florida Tool Shop revealed the following information related to inventory destroyed in Hurricane Frances:

Inventory, beginning of period	$300,000
Purchases to date of hurricane	140,000
Net sales to date of hurricane	885,000
Gross margin percentage	55%

The company needs to file a claim for lost inventory with its insurance company. What is the estimated value of the lost inventory?

Problem Set A

P6-1A. Calculate cost of goods sold and ending inventory and analyze the effect of each method on the financial statements (periodic).

LO 1, 2

Jefferson Company had the following sales and purchases during 2006, its first year of business:

January 5	Purchase	40 units @ $100 each
February 15	Sale	15 units @ $150 each
April 10	Sale	10 units @ $150 each
June 30	Purchase	30 units @ $105 each
August 15	Sale	25 units @ $150 each
November 28	Purchase	30 units @ $110 each

Required

Calculate the ending inventory, the cost of goods sold, and the gross margin for the December 31, 2006 financial statements under each of the following assumptions:

a. FIFO periodic
b. LIFO periodic
c. Weighted average cost periodic

How will the differences between the methods affect the income statement for the year and balance sheet at year end?

LO 1, 2, 3, 4 **P6-2A. Calculate cost of goods sold and ending inventory; analyze the effects of each method on financial statements; apply lower-of-cost-or-market rule; calculate inventory turnover ratio.**

The following series of transactions occurred during 2006:

January 1	Beginning Inventory	70 units @ $10
January 15	Purchased	100 units @ $11
February 4	Sold	60 units @ $20
March 10	Purchased	50 units @ $12
April 15	Sold	70 units @ $20
June 30	Purchased	100 units @ $13
August 4	Sold	110 units @ $20
October 1	Purchased	80 units @ $14
December 5	Sold	50 units @ $21

Required

a. Calculate the value of the ending inventory and cost of goods sold assuming the company uses a periodic inventory system and the FIFO inventory cost flow assumption.

b. Calculate the value of the ending inventory and cost of goods sold assuming the company uses a periodic inventory system and the LIFO inventory cost flow assumption.

c. Calculate the value of the ending inventory and cost of goods sold assuming the company uses a periodic inventory system and the weighted average cost inventory cost flow assumption.

d. Which of the three methods will result in the highest cost of goods sold?

e. Which of the three methods will provide the most current Inventory value for the balance sheet?

f. How will the differences between the methods affect the income statement and balance sheet for the year?

g. At the end of the year, the current replacement cost of the inventory is $1,100. Indicate at what amount the company's inventory will be reported using the lower-of-cost-or-market rule for each method (FIFO, LIFO, and weighted average cost).

h. Calculate the company's inventory turnover ratio and average days in inventory for the year for each inventory cost flow method used in the problem.

LO 1 **P6-3A. Calculate cost of goods sold and ending inventory.**

The For Fish Company sells commercial fish tanks. The company began 2006 with 1,000 units of inventory on hand. These units cost $150 each. The following transactions related to the company's merchandise inventory occurred during the first quarter of 2006:

January 20	Purchase	500 units @ $160 each
February 18	Purchase	600 units @ $170 each
March 28	Purchase	400 units @ $180 each
Total Purchases		1,500 units

All unit costs include the purchase price and freight charges paid by For Fish. During the quarter ending March 31, 2006, sales in units totaled 1,700 units leaving 800 units in ending inventory. The company uses a periodic inventory system.

Required

Calculate ending inventory at March 31 and cost of goods sold for the quarter using:

a. FIFO
b. LIFO
c. Weighted average cost

LO 1, 2, 3, 4 **P6-4A. Calculate cost of goods sold and ending inventory; analyze effects of each inventory cost flow method on financial statements; apply lower-of-cost-or-market rule; calculate inventory turnover ratio.**

Given the following information for Grant's Print Shop, a small company with a December 31 year end.

At January 1, 2006:

- Cash amounted to $19,375
- Beginning Inventory was $16,000 (160 units @ $100 each)
- Contributed Capital was $15,000
- Retained Earnings was $20,375

Transactions during 2006:

- Purchase #1—150 units @ $110 cash each
- Purchase #2—190 more units @ $120 cash each
- Cash sales were 390 units @ $200 each
- Paid $11,500 cash for operating expenses
- Paid cash for income tax at a rate of 30% of net income before taxes.

Required

a. Compute the cost of goods sold for the year ended December 31, 2006, and (ending) inventory at December 31, 2006 using each of the following inventory cost flow methods:
  1. FIFO periodic
  2. LIFO periodic
  3. Weighted average cost periodic
b. For each method, prepare the balance sheet at December 31, and a multiple-step income statement, statement of cash flows, and statement of changes in shareholders' equity for Grant's Print Shop for the year ended December 31, 2006.
c. What is income before income taxes and net income after income taxes under each of the three inventory cost flow assumptions? What observations can you make about net income from the analysis of the three methods?
d. At the end of the year, the current replacement cost of the inventory is $12,750. Indicate at what amount the company's inventory will be reported using the lower-of-cost-or-market rule for each method (FIFO, LIFO, and weighted average cost).
e. For each method, calculate the inventory turnover ratio and average days in inventory for 2006.

P6-5A. Calculate cost of goods sold, ending inventory, and inventory turnover ratio.

LO 1, 4

The following merchandise inventory transactions occurred during the month of June for the Furlong Corporation:

June 1	Inventory on hand, 1,000 units @ $8.00 each.
June 7	Sold 750 units @ $10.50.
June 18	Purchased 2,000 units @ $8.80 each.
June 21	Sold 2,225 units @ $10.50.
June 27	Purchased 2,500 units @ $10.00 each.

Required

a. Assume Furlong uses a periodic inventory system, compute the cost of goods sold for the month of June and (ending) inventory at June 30 using each of the following inventory cost flow methods:
  1. FIFO
  2. LIFO
  3. Weighted average cost
b. Using the information for item *a*, calculate the inventory turnover ratio and average days in inventory for the month of June for each method.
c. *Appendix A, perpetual inventory system.* Assume Furlong uses the perpetual inventory system. Compute the cost of goods sold for the month of June and (ending) inventory at June 30 using each of the following inventory cost flow methods:
  1. FIFO
  2. LIFO

P6-6A. Calculate cost of goods sold and ending inventory— periodic FIFO.

LO 1

Cheny Company buys and then resells a single product. The product is a commodity and is subject to rather severe cost fluctuations. Below is information concerning Cheny's inventory activity during the month of June 2007:

June 1	430 units on hand, $3,010
June 4	Sold 200 units
June 6	Purchased 500 units @ $11 per unit
June 10	Purchased 200 units @ $9 per unit
June 15	Sold 300 units
June 20	Purchased 150 units @ $6 per unit
June 25	Sold 400 units
June 29	Purchased 50 units @ $8 per unit

Cheny uses a periodic inventory system.

Required

Calculate cost of goods sold (units and cost) for the month of June 2007 and ending inventory (units and cost) at June 30, 2007, using FIFO.

LO 1, 2, 4   **P6-7A. Analyze effect of inventory cost flow method on financial statements and inventory turnover ratio.**
Green Bay Cheese Company is considering changing inventory cost flow methods. Green Bay's primary objective is to maximize profits. Currently, the firm uses weighted average cost. Data for 2006 are provided below:

Beginning Inventory (10,000 units)	$ 14,500
Purchases	
60,000 units @ $1.50	90,000
50,000 units @ $1.60	80,000
70,000 units @ $1.70	119,000
Sales	
130,000 units @ $3.00	390,000

Operating expenses were $120,000 and the company's income tax rate is 30%.

Required

a. Use the information above to prepare the income statement for 2006 using each of the following methods:
   1. FIFO periodic
   2. LIFO periodic
b. Which method provides the more current balance sheet Inventory balance? Explain your answer.
c. Which method provides the more current cost of goods sold? Explain your answer.
d. Which method provides the better inventory turnover ratio for the year? Explain your answer.
e. In order to meet Green Bay's goal, what is your recommendation to Green Bay Cheese Company? Explain your answer.

LO 1, 2   **P6-8A. Analyze effect of inventory cost flow method on cost of goods sold and net income.**
Stiles Company and Wycoff Company both began their operations on January 2, 2006. Both companies had exactly the same amount of business during 2006. They purchased exactly the same number of units of merchandise inventory during the year at exactly the same cost, and they sold exactly the same number of inventory units at exactly the same selling price during the year. They also purchased exactly the same type and amount of property, plant, and equipment and paid exactly the same amount for those items. At the end of 2006, the two companies prepared income statements for the year. Stiles reported gross profit of $92,000 and Wycoff reported gross profit of $65,000.

Required

a. If both companies reported $105,350 for sales revenue, what was the cost of goods sold for each company?
b. What could have caused the reported gross profit for the two companies to be different? Be specific in your explanation.

LO 1, 2   **P6-9A. Calculate cost of goods sold and ending inventory and analyze inventory errors.**
RD Company had purchases of inventory during the month of April as follows:

Beginning Inventory	800 units @ $20 each
Date	**Purchases**
April 15	400 units @ $21 each
April 20	400 units @ $22 each

RD Company uses a periodic inventory system and counted 700 units on hand at the end of April. All units are sold for $40 each.

Required

a. Calculate units sold for the year.
b. Calculate the ending inventory (cost) and cost of goods sold using FIFO and LIFO.

c. How much difference does the inventory cost flow assumption change net income (assume no income taxes)?

d. *Appendix B, inventory errors.* Suppose that 100 units were erroneously left out of the count of the ending inventory. What effect does the error have on the cost of goods sold and net income for the month under each of the inventory cost flow assumptions in b? Support your conclusion by calculating the ending inventory and cost of goods sold using FIFO and LIFO adjusting for the 100 unit error.

P6-10A. Calculate the inventory turnover ratio.

LO 4

Use the information from the financial statements of Papa John's International below to answer the questions that follow.

For the year ended	Dec 28, 2003	Dec 29, 2002	Dec 29, 2001
(Amounts in thousands)			
Sales (domestic)	$416,049	$429,813	$445,849
Cost of sales	92,488	98,717	110,632
Inventory	17,030	16,341	12,659

Required

a. Calculate the gross profit ratio for the last two years shown.
b. Calculate the inventory turnover ratio for the last two years shown.
c. What information do these comparisons provide?

P6-11A. Appendix B: Inventory errors.

Beard Company uses a perpetual inventory system. The company's accounting records showed the following related to June 2009 transactions:

	Units	Cost
Beginning Inventory, June 1	200	$ 600
+ Purchases during June	1,700	5,100
= Cost of goods Available for Sale	1,900	5,700
− Cost of Goods Sold	1,500	4,500
= Ending Inventory, June 30	400	$1,200

On June 30, 2009, Beard conducted a physical count of its inventory and discovered there were only 375 units of inventory actually on hand.

Required

a. Prepare the adjusting entry that would correct Beard's records as shown above to reflect the results of the physical inventory count.
b. How would this correction change the financial statements for the year?
c. What are some possible causes of the difference between the inventory amounts in Beard's accounting records and the inventory amount from the physical count?

P6-12A. Appendix C: Estimating inventory.

Carter Company sells peanuts to tourists on Route 15 in Georgia. A hurricane destroyed the entire inventory in late August. To file an insurance claim, Jimmy, the owner of the company, must estimate the value of the lost inventory. Records from January 1 through the date of the hurricane in August indicated that Carter Company started the year with $4,000 worth of inventory on hand. Purchases for the year amounted to $9,000, and sales up to the date of the hurricane were $16,000. Gross margin percentage has traditionally been 30%.

Required

a. How much should Jimmy request from the insurance company?
b. Suppose that one case of peanuts was spared by the hurricane. The cost of that case was $700. How much was the inventory loss under these conditions?

Problem Set B

LO 1, 2   ## P6-1B. Calculate cost of goods sold and ending inventory and analyze the effect of each method on financial statements (periodic).

Washington Company had the following sales and purchases during 2009, its first year of business:

January 8	Purchase	125 units @ $100 each
February 20	Sale	75 units @ $150 each
April 13	Sale	35 units @ $150 each
June 28	Purchase	235 units @ $105 each
August 2	Sale	175 units @ $150 each
November 24	Purchase	140 units @ $110 each

Required

Calculate the ending inventory, the cost of goods sold, and the gross margin for the December 31, 2009 financial statements under each of the following assumptions:

a. FIFO periodic
b. LIFO periodic
c. Weighted average cost periodic

How will the differences between the methods affect the income statement and balance sheet for the year?

LO 1, 2, 3, 4   ## P6-2B. Calculate cost of goods sold and ending inventory; analyze effects of each inventory cost flow method on financial statements; apply lower-of-cost-or-market rule; calculate inventory turnover ratio.

Hillary's Diamonique buys and then resells a single product. Here is some information concerning Hillary's inventory activity during the month of August 2007:

August 2	860 units on hand, $10,320
August 6	Sold 400 units @ $14
August 8	Purchased 640 units @ $11 per unit
August 12	Purchased 425 units @ $10 per unit
August 15	Sold 600 units @ $12
August 21	Purchased 300 units @ $9 per unit
August 24	Sold 800 units @ $16
August 31	Purchased 100 units @ $8 per unit

Hillary's uses a periodic inventory system.

Required

a. Calculate the value of the ending inventory and cost of goods sold assuming the company uses a periodic inventory system and the FIFO inventory cost flow assumption.
b. Calculate the value of the ending inventory and cost of goods sold assuming the company uses a periodic inventory system and the LIFO inventory cost flow assumption.
c. Calculate the value of the ending inventory and cost of goods sold assuming the company uses a periodic inventory system and the weighted average cost inventory cost flow assumption.
d. Which of the three methods will result in the highest cost of goods sold for August?
e. Which of the three methods will provide the most current Inventory value for Hillary's balance sheet?
f. How would the differences between the methods affect Hillary's income statement for August and balance sheet at August 31?
g. At the end of the month, the current replacement cost of the inventory is $6,730. Indicate at what amount the company's inventory will be reported using the lower-of-cost-or-market rule for each method (FIFO, LIFO, and weighted average cost).
h. Calculate the company's inventory turnover ratio and average days in inventory for the month for each method in items a., b., and c.

LO 1   ## P6-3B. Calculate cost of goods sold and ending inventory— periodic.

Sandy's Clean Carpet Company sells commercial vacuums. The company's fiscal year begins July 1, 2006, and ends June 30, 2007. Sandy's began the year with 1,500 units of inventory on hand. These units cost $200 each. The following transactions related to the company's merchandise inventory occurred during the first quarter of the year:

July 15	Purchased	450 units @ $195 each
August 28	Purchased	575 units @ $190 each
September 10	Purchased	600 units @ $185 each
Total Purchases		1,625 units

All unit costs include the purchase price and freight charges paid by Sandy's Clean Carpet. During the quarter ending September 30, 2006, sales in units totaled 1,950 units. The company uses the periodic inventory system.

Required

Calculate ending inventory at September 30 and cost of goods sold for the quarter using:

a. FIFO
b. LIFO
c. Weighted average cost

P6-4B. **Calculate cost of goods sold and ending inventory; analyze effects of each inventory cash flow method on financial statements; apply lower-of-cost-or-market rule; calculate inventory turnover ratio.**   LO 1, 2, 3, 4

Given the following information for Nan's Toy Extravaganza, a firm with a June 30 year end:

At July 01, 2006:

- Cash amounted to $27,000
- Beginning Inventory was $30,000 (750 units @ $40 each)
- Contributed Capital was $12,000
- Retained Earnings was $45,000

Transactions during July 2006–June 2007:

- Purchase of 825 units @ $41 cash each
- Purchase of 375 more units @ $43 cash each
- Cash sales were 1,150 units @ $56 cash each
- Paid $8,500 cash for operating expenses
- Paid cash for income taxes at a rate of 40% of net income before taxes

Required

a. Compute the cost of goods sold for the year ended June 30, 2007, and ending inventory at June 30, 2007 using each of the following inventory cost flow methods:
   1. FIFO periodic
   2. LIFO periodic
   3. Weighted average cost periodic
b. For each method, prepare the balance sheet at June 30, 2007, and a multiple-step income statement, and statement of cash flows for Nan's for the fiscal year ended June 30, 2007.
c. What is income before income taxes and net income after income taxes under each of the three inventory cost flow assumptions? What observations can you make about net income from the analysis of the three methods?
d. At the end of the year, the current replacement cost of the inventory is $33,000. Indicate at what amount the company's inventory will be reported using the lower-of-cost-or-market rule for each method (FIFO, LIFO, and weighted average cost).
e. For each method, calculate the inventory turnover ratio and average days in inventory for the fiscal year ended June 30, 2007.

P6-5B. **Calculate cost of goods sold, ending inventory, and inventory turnover ratio.**   LO 1, 4

The following merchandise inventory transactions occurred during the month of November for Party Heaven:

November 5	Inventory on hand, 2,000 units @ $4.00 each
November 12	Sold 1,500 units @ $6.00
November 16	Purchased 4,000 units @ $4.40 each
November 23	Sold 4,300 units @ $6.00
November 29	Purchased 5,000 units @ $5.00 each

a. Assume Party Heaven uses a periodic inventory system, and compute the cost of goods sold and ending inventory at November 30 using each of the following inventory cost flow methods:
 1. FIFO
 2. LIFO
 3. Weighted average cost
b. Using the information for item *a*, calculate the inventory turnover ratio and average days in inventory for the month of November for each method.
c. *Appendix A: Perpetual inventory system.* Assume Party Heaven uses the perpetual inventory system and compute the cost of goods sold and ending inventory at November 30 using each of the following inventory cost flow methods:
 1. FIFO
 2. LIFO

LO 1

P6-6B. Calculate cost of goods sold, and ending inventory— periodic FIFO.

Ashe Company buys and then resells a single product. The following is information concerning Ashe's inventory activity during the month of May 2006:

May 1	420 units on hand, $5,040 total cost
May 3	Sold 300 units
May 7	Purchased 600 units @ $11 per unit
May 11	Purchased 200 units @ $10 per unit
May 16	Sold 500 units
May 21	Purchased 350 units @ $9 per unit
May 26	Sold 270 units
May 30	Purchased 50 units @ $8 per unit

Ashe uses a periodic inventory system.

Required

Calculate cost of goods sold (units and cost) for the month of May 2006 and ending inventory (units and cost) at May 31, 2006, using FIFO.

LO 1, 2, 4

P6-7B. Analyze effect of inventory cost flow method on financial statements and inventory turnover ratio.

Castana Company is considering changing inventory cost flow methods. Castana's primary objective is to minimize its income tax liability. Currently, the firm uses weighted average cost. Data for 2007 are provided below:

Beginning Inventory (2,000 units)	$ 10,000
Purchases	
5,000 units @ $6.00	30,000
4,000 units @ $6.50	26,000
6,000 units @ $7.00	42,000
Sales	
15,000 units @ $10 each	150,000

Operating expenses were $12,000 and the company's income tax rate is 25%.

Required

a. Use the information above to prepare the income statement for 2007 using each of the following methods:
 1. FIFO
 2. LIFO
b. Which method provides the more current Inventory balance? Explain your answer.
c. Which method provides the more current cost of goods sold? Explain your answer.
d. Which method provides the better inventory turnover ratio for the year? Explain your answer.
e. Which method will help Castana's Company meet its goal of minimizing income tax liability? Explain your answer.

LO 1, 2

P6-8B. Analyze effect of inventory cost flow method on cost of goods sold and gross margin.

Brutus Company and Gabrielle Company both began their operations on July 1, 2008. Both companies had exactly the same amount of business during the 2008–2009 fiscal year. They purchased exactly the same number of units of merchandise inventory during the year at exactly the same cost, and they sold exactly the same number of inventory units at exactly the same selling price during the year. They also purchased exactly the same type and amount of property, plant, and equipment and paid exactly the same amount for those items. For the fiscal year ended June 30, 2009, the two companies prepared income statements for the year. Brutus reported a gross profit of $84,250 and Gabrielle reported a gross profit of $75,680.

Required

a. If both companies reported $120,000 for sales revenue, what was the cost of goods sold for each company?
b. What could have caused the reported gross profit for the two companies to be different? Be specific in your explanation.

P6-9B. Calculate cost of goods sold and ending inventory and analyze inventory errors.

<u>LO 1, 2</u>

Joe's Medical Supply had purchases of inventory during the month of August as follows:

Beginning Inventory	750 units @ $30 each
Date	**Purchases**
August 12	325 units @ $28 each
August 23	275 units @ $26 each

Joe uses a periodic inventory system and counted 300 units on hand at the end of August. All units are sold for $50 each.

Required

a. Calculate units sold for the month.
b. Calculate the ending inventory (cost) and cost of goods sold using FIFO and LIFO.
c. *Appendix B, inventory errors.* Suppose that 50 units were erroneously left out of the count of the ending inventory. What effect does the error have on the cost of goods sold and net income for the month under each of the inventory cost flow assumptions in b? Support your conclusion by calculating the ending inventory and cost of goods sold using FIFO and LIFO, adjusting for the 50 unit error.

P6-10B. Calculate the inventory turnover ratio.

<u>LO 4</u>

Use the information from the financial statements of Wendy's for 2003 and 2002 to complete the problems that follow.

For year ended	Dec 28, 2003	Dec 29, 2002	Dec 30, 2001
(amounts in thousands)			
Sales	$2,534,135	$2,187,438	$1,925,319
Cost of Goods Sold	1,634,562	1,383,665	1,229,277
Inventory	54,353	47,433	45,334

Required

a. Calculate the gross margin profit for the last two years shown.
b. Calculate the inventory turnover ratio for the last two years shown.
c. What information do these comparisons provide?

P6-11B. Appendix B: Inventory errors

Barney's Flowerpot Company uses a perpetual inventory system. The company's accounting records showed the following related to September 2008 transactions:

		Units	Cost
	Beginning inventory, Sept 1	200	$ 600
+	Purchases during Sept	1,700	5,100
=	Cost of goods available for sale	1,900	$5,700
−	Cost of goods sold	1,500	4,500
=	Ending inventory, Sept 30	400	$1,200

On September 30, 2008, Barney's conducted a physical count of its inventory and discovered there were actually 425 units of inventory on hand.

Required

a. Prepare the adjusting entry that would correct Barney's records, as shown above, to reflect the results of the physical inventory count.
b. How would this correction change the financial statements for the month?
c. What are some possible causes of the difference between the inventory amounts in Barney's accounting records and the inventory amount from the physical count?

P6-12B. Appendix C: Estimating inventory.
Cynthia's Cotton Candy Company sells cotton candy to visitors at a traveling county fair. During a drought, a fire destroyed the entire inventory in late July. To file an insurance claim, Cynthia, the owner of the company, must estimate the value of the lost inventory. Records from January 1 through the date of the fire in July indicated that Cynthia's Cotton Candy Company started the year with $4,250 worth of inventory on hand. Purchases for the year amounted to $8,000, and sales up to the date of the fire were $17,500. Gross profit percentage has traditionally been 35%.

Required
   a. How much should Cynthia request from the insurance company?
   b. Suppose that one case of cotton candy mix was spared by the fire. The cost of that case was $50. How much was the inventory loss under these conditions?

Financial Statement Analysis

LO 4   **FSA6-1. Analyze inventory management.**
Use the information from Pier 1 Imports to analyze the firm's inventory management. Calculate the gross margin ratio, the profit margin ratio, and the inventory turnover ratio. How do you think Pier 1 is managing its inventory? What other information would be useful in answering this question?

<table>
<tr><td colspan="2" align="center">Pier 1 Imports
Statement of Operations
For the fiscal year ended February 28, 2004
_(in thousands)</td></tr>
</table>

Net Sales	$1,868,243
Operating costs and expenses:	
Cost of sales	1,086,623
Selling and administrative expenses	544,536
Depreciation and amortization	50,927
Operating income	186,157
Interest and investment (income)	(2,851)
Interest expense	1,692
Income before income taxes	187,316
Provision for income taxes	69,315
Net income	$ 118,001

From the balance sheet at February 28, 2004
   Inventory $373,870 (in thousands)

From the balance sheet at March 1, 2003
   Inventory $333,350 (in thousands)

LO 4   **FSA6-2. Analyze inventory management.**
Use the information below to analyze Amazon.com's inventory management.

(in thousands)	For the year ended Dec. 31, 2003	For the year ended Dec. 31, 2004
Sales	$5,263,699	$6,921,124
Cost of sales	4,006,531	5,319,127
Net income	35,282	588,451
Inventory (at year end)	293,917	479,709

Write a short report for Amazon.com's shareholders with your comments about its inventory management.

Critical Thinking Problems

Risk and Control

In this chapter, you learned that retail firms are at risk that their inventory will become obsolete. Do Wal-Mart and Target have similar problems with obsolete inventory? What can a firm like Best Buy do to minimize this risk? What types of firms are at the most risk? What types of firms are at the least risk?

Ethics

Brendan's Music Company uses LIFO for inventory, and the company's profits are quite high this year. The cost of the inventory has been steadily rising all year, and Brendan is worried about his income taxes. His accountant has suggested that the company make a large purchase of inventory to be received during the last week in December. The accountant has explained to Brendan that this would reduce his income significantly.

a. Brendan doesn't understand the logic of the accountant's suggestion. Explain how the purchase would affect taxable income.
b. Is this ethical? Brendan is uncertain about the appropriateness of this from a legal and an ethical perspective.

Group Assignment

Select a retail firm that you think might be concerned about obsolete inventory and another that you believe would not be very concerned. Then, find the financial statements and calculate the inventory turnover ratio of these two firms for the past two fiscal years. Are your results what you expected? Explain what you expected to find and your results.

Internet Exercise: GAP

Gap Inc. was founded in 1969 by Donald and Doris Fisher in San Francisco, California, with a single store and a handful of employees. Today, they are one of the world's largest specialty retailers with three of the most recognized brands in the apparel industry (*Gap, Banana Republic, and Old Navy*). Gap Inc. has more than 150,000 employees supporting about 3,000 stores in the United States, United Kingdom, Canada, France and Japan.

Go to www.gapinc.com:

IE6-1. Click on "Financials & Media" and open the most current "Annual Report to Shareholders."

a. Which inventory cost flow assumption is used to measure the cost of inventory? Does Gap Inc. value inventory at the lower-of-cost-or-market value? If so, how is market value determined? Does this policy comply with GAAP?
b. For the three most recent years, list the amounts reported for Net Sales and Total Net Earnings. Is Net Sales increasing or decreasing? Is Total Net Earnings increasing or decreasing? Are these trends favorable or unfavorable? Explain your answer.
c. Using the financial statements, calculate the inventory turnover ratio for the two most recent years. Did the inventory turnover ratio increase or decrease? What does this measure? What does Gap Inc. do to identify inventory that is slow-moving and how is this inventory treated?
d. For cost of goods sold Gap Inc. uses Cost of Goods Sold and Occupancy Expenses. What is included in this amount?

IE6-2. Click on "Social Responsibilities."

a. Does Gap Inc. do anything to ensure its garment workers are treated fairly? If so, why is this important for Gap Inc. to do?
b. Click on "How Our Clothes Are Made." List and briefly describe Gap Inc.'s five steps of their product life cycle.

Please note: Internet web sites are constantly being updated. Therefore, if the information is not found where indicated, please explore the annual report further to find the information.

Additional Study Materials

Visit www.prenhall.com/reimers for self-study quizzes and spreadsheet templates to use to complete homework assignments.

CONTINUING CASE STUDY

Building your Excel skills with The MP3 Store

During the month of June, The MP3 Store engaged in the following transactions. The company is using LIFO and the perpetual inventory system. Recall from Chapter 5 that the beginning inventory consists of 30 MP3 players purchased for $196 each.

June 2	Purchased 50 MP3 players for $210 each, on account. Terms are 2/10, n/30.*
June 5	Collected May's outstanding A/R balance.
June 13	Paid for the 50 MP3 players purchased on June 2 and purchased 40 more for $215 each. The 40 units were purchased for cash.
June 22	Purchased 75 MP3 players for $220 each and paid cash.*
June 28	Received a phone bill for $157. It is due July 15th and will not be paid until July 14.
June 29	Paid the assistant manager $2,000 for June work.
June 30	By the end of the month, the company had sold a total of 150 MP3 players for $350 each. The sales tax rate is 6%. Of the sales, 95 were for cash and 55 were on account.*
June 30	Recorded the required adjusting entries for depreciation, interest, rent, and insurance.

*Although the firm uses a perpetual inventory system, you will not be given the specific dates of the sales. That means you will have to make the sales entry at the end of the period. Simply treat it as if the firm made a single large sale at the end of the period. When purchases are made, put them in the Inventory account. When sales are recorded, record the reduction inventory and the Cost of Goods Sold. Frequently, firms do keep track of UNITS of inventory on a perpetual basis but make a single inventory adjustment at the end of the period. The sales are provided in one summary amount to simplify the inventory record keeping necessary for the continuing case.

Instructions

1. Prepare the necessary journal entries, T-accounts, trial balances, and financial statements. (Note: A Statement of Cash Flows is not required for this chapter.)

2. When you are finished print and save your file to disk by clicking the **Save** button. Name your file MP36.

Perpetual Inventory Systems

When a firm uses a perpetual inventory system, the inventory is reduced each time a sale is made. Technology makes it easy for a firm to use the perpetual system, but the calculations for the periodic system are much simpler. That's why we focused on the periodic system in the chapter. Learning the periodic system helps you learn about the differences between the inventory cost flow assumptions—weighted average, FIFO, and LIFO—even though that is not the more widely used method. In this appendix, you'll learn how the calculations are made using a perpetual system, the one that most companies use.

To learn more about the specific record keeping associated with perpetual inventory systems, read and study the examples that follow. The data is taken from the main example in the chapter, Katelyn's Photo Company, and is repeated here for reference.

January 1	Beginning Inventory	8 cameras	@ $10 each
January 8	Sales	3 cameras	@ $20 each
January 16	Purchase	5 cameras	@ $12 each
January 20	Sales	8 cameras	@ $22 each
January 30	Purchase	7 cameras	@ $14 each

Weighted Average Perpetual

If a company were to select perpetual record keeping with the weighted average inventory cost flow assumption, the accountant would have to calculate a new weighted average cost every time a purchase is made and every time a sale is made. The method is often called moving weighted average because the average changes with every transaction. A modern firm's computer system can handle this record keeping with ease. However, it can be pretty messy to use the weighted average perpetual system with only a calculator.

When Katelyn's Photo sells 3 cameras on January 8, the weighted average cost of a camera is simply the cost carried in the beginning inventory. So the cost of goods sold for the January 8 sale is $30. That leaves 5 cameras at a cost of $10 each in the inventory. On January 16, Katelyn's purchases 5 cameras at $12 each. The weighted average cost for a camera is now:

$$\frac{(5 \times \$10) + (5 \times \$12)}{10 \text{ total}} = \$11 \text{ each}$$

On January 20, Katelyn's Photo sells 8 cameras. The costs of goods sold is $88, and there are 2 cameras left in the inventory at a weighted average cost of $11 each.

When the purchase of 7 cameras at $14 each occurs on January 30, a new weighted average cost must be computed:

$$\frac{(2 \times \$11) + (7 \times \$14)}{9 \text{ total cameras}} = \$13.33 \text{ each}$$

The cost of goods sold for the period = $88 + 30 = $118.
The ending inventory for the period = $120 (9 cameras × $13.33 each, rounded).

FIFO Perpetual

When a perpetual record-keeping system is used, the cost of goods sold for each sale must be calculated and recorded *at the time of the sale.* Only the cameras from the purchases as of the date of a sale—meaning prior and up to the date of a sale—are available to become part of the cost of goods sold. Perpetual record keeping requires you to pay attention to the dates on which goods are purchased and sold. Katelyn's first sale is on January 8. Only cameras from the beginning inventory are available for Katelyn's to use to calculate the cost of goods sold for the January 8 sale. The other purchases are in the future, and Katelyn's doesn't know anything about them on January 8! The cost of goods sold for the January 8 sale is 3 cameras × $10 per camera = $30.

Next, 8 cameras were sold on January 20. Because the inventory cost flow assumption is FIFO, Katelyn's uses the cameras left in the beginning inventory as part of the cost of goods sold. So the cost of goods sold for the January 20 sale has to start with the 5 cameras remaining in the beginning inventory—that will be 5 × $10 each = $50. To get the other 3 needed to make the total of 8 sold, Katelyn's will count 3 from the January 16 purchase. That's 3 at $12 = $36. So the total cost of goods sold for the January 20 sale is $86 (= $50 + $36).

To summarize the cost of goods sold:

```
3 cameras @ $10 each = $ 30—Sale on January 8
5 cameras @ $10 each = $ 50 ⎫
                            ⎬—Sale on January 20
3 cameras @ $12 each = $ 36 ⎭
Total                   $116
```

What's left in the ending inventory?

```
2 cameras @ $12 each = $ 24
7 cameras @ $14 each = $ 98
Total                   $122
```

If you refer back to the chapter, you will notice that doing all of the work to figure out the cost of goods sold using FIFO *perpetual* gives the same amount as FIFO *periodic*, which is much easier to calculate.

Is this coincidence, or is there a predictable pattern here? Look at the particular cameras that were assumed to be sold under the two methods. You'll see that it's more than coincidence. No matter how the company does the actual record keeping, either FIFO method—perpetual or periodic—will give the same dollar amount of cost of goods sold and the same dollar amount of ending inventory for the period. Unfortunately, this is *not* true for LIFO.

LIFO Perpetual

Choosing LIFO perpetual makes life a bit more difficult for the accounting system than choosing FIFO. Each time a sale is made, the cost of goods sold is determined by using the last purchase as of the date of the sale. The amounts may differ slightly between LIFO periodic and LIFO perpetual because of timing differences between sales and purchases.

Katelyn's first sale is on January 8. Only cameras from the beginning inventory are available for Katelyn's to use to calculate the cost of goods sold for the January 8 sale. The other purchases are in the future, and Katelyn's doesn't know anything about them on January 8! The cost of goods sold for the January 8 sale is 3 cameras × $10 per camera = $30.

Next, 8 cameras were sold on January 20. Because the inventory cost flow assumption is LIFO, Katelyn uses the cameras from the most recent purchase as of January 20 to determine the cost of goods sold. So the cost of goods sold for the January 20 sale has to start with the 5 cameras from the January 16 purchase. That's 5 at $12 = $60. To get the remaining 3 cameras she needs for the total 8 sold on January 20, Katelyn will have to pick up 3 from the beginning inventory: 3 at $10 = $30. So the total cost of goods sold for the January 20 sale is $90 (= $60 + $30).

To summarize the cost of goods sold:

$$
\begin{array}{ll}
3 \text{ cameras @ \$10 each} = \$\ 30 & \text{—Sale on January 8} \\
5 \text{ cameras @ \$12 each} = \$\ 60 \\
3 \text{ cameras @ \$10 each} = \$\ 30 & \Big\} \text{—Sale on January 20} \\
\text{Total} \qquad\qquad\qquad \underline{\$120}
\end{array}
$$

What's left in the ending inventory?

$$
\begin{array}{l}
2 \text{ cameras @ \$10 each} = \$\ 20 \\
7 \text{ cameras @ \$14 each} = \underline{\$\ 98} \\
\text{Total} \qquad\qquad\qquad \underline{\$118}
\end{array}
$$

If you look back in the chapter, you will see that LIFO periodic had a slightly higher cost of goods sold, $146. That's because under periodic record keeping, Katelyn's was allowed to "pretend" to have sold the inventory purchased on January 30. That is, the inventory cost flow assumption allowed an assumed flow of goods that could not possibly have taken place.

Conclusion

In every case, notice that cost of goods sold and ending inventory together total $238, the cost of the goods available for sale. That's true for FIFO, LIFO, and weighted average using either a perpetual or a periodic system. You can read about how a firm makes this important calculation in the notes to the financial statements.

Inventory Errors

You know that the cost of the beginning inventory plus the cost of purchases equals the cost of goods available for sale. The cost of goods available for sale is then divided between the cost of goods sold and the ending inventory. That is,

Beginning inventory (BI)
+ Purchases
Cost of goods available for sale
− Ending inventory
Cost of goods sold

Because inventory directly affects cost of goods sold, a major expense, errors in the calculation of beginning inventory or ending inventory will affect net income. Tracing the effects of errors requires slow, focused deliberation. To show how inventory errors can affect income, here's a simple numerical example that shows an ending inventory error and a beginning inventory error. Read each description below and study the related examples.

Ending Inventory Errors

Suppose a firm has the correct amount for beginning inventory and the correct amount for purchases. Then, cost of goods available for sale is correct. Ending inventory is *overstated*, cost of goods sold must be *understated*. Why? It's because ending inventory and cost of goods sold are the two parts of cost of goods available for sale. Cost of goods sold is an expense. If the expense deducted from sales is too small, the result is that net income will be too large. Suppose you have correctly calculated the cost of goods available for sale (beginning inventory + purchases) to be $10. Those goods will either be sold— and become part of cost of goods sold—or they will *not* be sold—and will still be part of the inventory.

So, the cost of goods available for sale consists of two parts—cost of goods sold and ending inventory. Suppose the correct ending inventory is $2, but you erroneously give it a value of $3. If ending inventory is incorrectly valued at $3, then cost of goods sold will be valued at $7. Remember, the ending inventory and cost of goods sold must add up to $10 in this example. What is wrong with cost of goods sold? If ending inventory is actually $2, then cost of goods sold *should* be $8. See what happens? You understate cost of goods sold when you overstate the ending inventory. Anytime you understate an expense, you will overstate net income.

If ending inventory is too small—*understated*, cost of goods sold must be too large—*overstated*. The result is that net income will be *understated*. Let's use the same example, in which the cost of goods available for sale was correctly computed at $10. If ending inventory is actually $2 but you erroneously understate it as $1, then cost of goods sold will be valued as $9. It should be $8. So, an understatement in ending inventory has caused an overstatement of cost of goods sold. If you overstate an expense, then you will understate net income.

When you understate the beginning inventory by $1, you end up with cost of goods sold understated by $1. This understated expense will result in an overstatement of net income.

Exhibit 6B.1

Error in the Beginning Inventory

	Calculated Amounts	Correct Amounts
Beginning Inventory	$ 1 (understated from prior year error)	$ 2
+ Purchases	+ $15	+ $15
Cost of Goods Available for Sale	$16	$17
− Ending Inventory	$ 6	$ 6
Cost of Goods Sold	$10	$11

Beginning Inventory Errors

If ending inventory is overstated in 2006, then beginning inventory in 2007 will be overstated. After all, it's the same number. Errors in the ending inventory will, therefore, affect two consecutive years—ending inventory one year and beginning inventory the following year.

If beginning inventory is *overstated*, then the cost of goods available for sale is *overstated*. If ending inventory is counted correctly, then cost of goods sold will be *overstated*. So, net income will be *understated*. Let's continue the previous example. If you value beginning inventory at $3 (and the correct value is $2) and you *correctly* add the purchases for the second year—say, $15 worth—then, the cost of goods available for sale will be $18. Keep in mind, the correct amount is $17. At year-end, you count the ending inventory correctly at $6. The calculated cost of goods sold would be $12. Ending inventory and cost of goods sold must total $18. However, we know that the true cost of goods available for sale is $17. If the correct ending inventory is $6, then the correct cost of goods sold is $11. The calculated cost of goods sold was overstated by $1. When an expense is overstated, then net income will be understated.

If beginning inventory is *understated*, then the cost of goods available for sale is *understated*. If ending inventory is counted correctly, then cost of goods sold will be *understated*. So, net income will be *overstated*. Try thinking about the example in the format given in Exhibit 6B.1.

As you can see, when you understate the beginning inventory, you end up with cost of goods sold understated. This understated expense will result in an overstatement of net income.

Note that over a period of two years the errors will counterbalance—they will cancel each other out. However, it is important that the financial statements be correct *each* year, not every other year, so a company will correct inventory errors if they are discovered, rather than wait for the errors to cancel each other out.

 Can**YOU**do it?

Berry Corporation miscounted the ending inventory for the year ended December 31, 2005. The balance sheet reported Inventory of $360,000, but $25,000 worth of items were omitted from that amount. Berry reported net income of $742,640 for the year. What effect did this inventory error have on Berry's cost of goods sold for the year? What is the correct net income for the year ended December 31, 2005?

Answers Ending inventory was understated, so cost of goods sold was overstated. Too much expense was deducted, so net income should have been higher by $25,000 for a correct net income of $767,640.

Gross Profit Method of Estimating Ending Inventory

There are times when a company might want to *estimate* the cost of the ending inventory rather than counting the units to calculate the cost. For example, if a company prepares monthly or quarterly financial statements, GAAP allows ending inventory to be estimated for reporting on those financial statements. This saves a company the trouble of counting the inventory every quarter. Also, if the inventory is destroyed or stolen, the company will have a reliable estimate of the cost of the destroyed inventory for the insurance claim.

First, you must know the usual *gross profit percentage*—the gross margin ratio you learned about in Chapter 5—for the company. Gross profit percentage is gross profit divided by sales. You can calculate the gross profit ratio using prior years' sales and cost data. Then, you multiply that percentage by the sales for the period, which gives the estimated gross profit. You then subtract the estimated gross profit from sales to get the estimated cost of goods sold. Because you know (a) beginning inventory (from the last period's financial statements), (b) purchases (from your records), and (c) an estimate for cost of goods sold, you can estimate ending inventory.

For example, suppose Super Soap Company lost its entire inventory in a flood on April 16. Super Soap had prepared a set of financial statements on March 31, when the inventory on hand was valued at $2,500. During the first part of April, purchases amounted to $3,500. The usual gross margin percentage in this business is 40%. If Super Soap had sales of $8,200 during the first 16 days of April, how much inventory was lost?

- If sales were $8,200 and the usual gross profit percentage is 40%, then the gross profit would be $3,280.

- If sales were $8,200 and gross profit is $3,280, then cost of goods sold would be $4,920. In other words, if the gross profit percentage is 40%, then the other 60% must be the cost of goods sold. So 60% of $8,200 = cost of goods sold = $4,920.

- Beginning inventory + purchases – cost of goods sold = ending inventory $2,500 + $3,500 – $4,920 = $1,080. This is our best estimate of the lost inventory.

Can YOU do it?

Suppose Base Company began May with inventory of $2,000 and purchased $8,000 worth of inventory during the first half of May. Sales for the first half of May amounted to $12,000. Then, a fire destroyed the remaining inventory. Base Company has had a gross margin ratio of approximately 30% for the first four months of the year. Approximately how much inventory did Base Company lose in the fire?

Answer $12,000 × 0.7 = Cost of Goods Sold
$8,400 worth of inventory has been sold.
$10,000 – $8,400 = $1,600 worth of inventory must have been lost in the fire.

chapter 7

Cash, Accounts Receivable, and Bad Debts Expense

Here's where you've been . . .

- **You learned about the four inventory cost flow assumptions.**

- **You learned to calculate the cost of inventory and cost of goods sold using each assumption.**

- **You learned to evaluate how efficiently a firm manages its inventory.**

Here's where you're going . . .

- **You'll learn how a firm accounts for and reports cash and receivables.**

- **You'll learn to account for customers who do not pay their bills.**

YOU make the call:

How should Hershey Foods deal with a customer firm filing for bankruptcy?

If you loan money to a friend, you expect to get the money back in the near future. What happens, however, if your friend files for bankruptcy?

Do you expect to get your money back? Companies, regardless of size, sell products to other companies on credit and expect to be paid in the future—but they don't always get their money. On April 1, 2003, for example, Hershey received an unwelcome surprise: One of its major customers with an outstanding account of $5 million, Fleming Companies, filed for reorganization under Chapter 11 of the U.S. Bankruptcy Code. This means Fleming has requested a legal reorganization of its business affairs, including its debts.

Most business-to-business sales are made on account. The sales revenue appears on the income statement even though the firm has not collected the cash. How will Fleming's bankruptcy affect Hershey's financial statements for the fiscal year ended December 31, 2003? *You make the call.*

Learning Objectives

When you are finished studying this chapter, you should be able to:

1. Calculate bad debts expense and explain how a firm evaluates and reports accounts receivable.
2. Account for and report notes receivable.
3. Explain how a firm controls cash and prepares a bank reconciliation.
4. Describe how cash is reported on the financial statements.
5. Analyze a firm's accounts receivable with ratio analysis.
6. Identify the risks and controls associated with cash and receivables.

LEARNING OBJECTIVE 1

Calculate bad debts expense and explain how a firm evaluates and reports accounts receivable.

Accounts Receivable and Bad Debts Expense

In Chapter 6, we examined inventory, one of a merchandising firm's most important assets. In this chapter, we examine two other important assets—cash and receivables. Recall from the many balance sheets that you have seen in the previous chapters that the balance in the Cash account is the first asset listed, and the other assets follow in order of liquidity. Accounts Receivable is usually listed after Cash. Even though the order on the balance sheet is Cash, Accounts Receivable, and then Inventory, the order of these accounts in the operating cycle is the reverse. A firm acquires inventory, sells it and records the accounts receivable, and then collects the cash. We discussed inventory in the previous chapter, so we'll start this chapter with accounts receivable and then conclude with a discussion of cash. That's where all firms would like to conclude their operating cycle!

As you know, often firms sell goods and services on account, which means they extend credit to customers and collect the cash later. Let's look at why firms extend credit and how firms record transactions in Accounts Receivable.

Extending credit

Accounts receivable: A current asset that arises from sales on credit of goods and services to a customer; the total customers owe a firm.

In Other Words: Accounts Receivable is also called Trade Receivables.

When a firm makes a sale on account, the amount is recorded in **Accounts Receivable**, sometimes simply called *receivables*. Why would a firm make sales on account? To attract business. While many *retail* firms use bank credit cards to satisfy customer demand to delay payment, those firms that buy and sell from other firms simply extend credit to their customers. Most firms will deal with only vendors who allow payment to be made sometime after delivery of the goods. Transactions with firms that do business with other firms and not with the ultimate consumer are called Business-to-Business (B2B) transactions.

Exhibit 7.1 shows Hershey Foods' current asset section of its December 31, 2004, and December 31, 2003, balance sheets. Notice that the second asset listed is *Accounts receivable trade (net)*. The balance in Accounts Receivable is the total owed to the firm by its customers. Sometimes a firm will call the amounts owed by customers *Trade* Accounts Receivable to distinguish them from amounts owed by others who are not customers. When a person or firm that is not a customer owes the firm, the firm will call them *Other Receivables*. For example, Hershey may lend money to one of its subsidiaries to cover a cash shortfall. This would be an Other Receivable.

Unfortunately, a firm cannot expect to collect 100% of its Accounts Receivable balance. That is, not all customers will pay what they owe. For

The Current Asset section of the balance sheet starts with Cash and Cash Equivalents, followed by Accounts Receivable.

Exhibit 7.1

Current Asset Section of Hershey Foods Corporation Comparative Balance Sheets

Current Asset Section of Hershey Foods Corporation Comparative Balance Sheets (partial) *(in millions)*		
	At December 31, 2004	At December 31, 2003
Assets		
Current assets		
Cash and cash equivalents	$ 54,837	$ 114,793
Accounts receivable trade (net)	408,930	407,612
Inventories	557,180	492,859
Prepaid expenses and other...................	161,494	116,305
Total current assets........................	$1,182,441	$1,131,569

example, some customers are unable to pay as a result of a downturn in the economy or as a result of bankruptcy. If the amount a firm collects from credit sales as a percentage of total accounts receivable is low, the uncollected amounts will be costly to the firm. Every firm makes its own judgment about the percentage of uncollectible accounts it is comfortable with—there's no rule or specific amount. Having customers who don't pay is part of doing business, and a firm designs its credit policy to strike an acceptable balance between maximizing sales and minimizing the accounts receivable that are never paid.

Most companies offer credit to their customers, and they often have significant accounts receivable. Under GAAP, when a firm reports Accounts Receivable on its balance sheet, the amount must be what the firm expects to collect. The amount is called the *net realizable value (NRV)* of Accounts Receivable. Notice in Exhibit 7.1 that the term "net" follows the Accounts Receivable account title. Net means Hershey's has deducted the amount the firm believes is uncollectible from total Accounts Receivable. A firm generally uses the **allowance method** to calculate the uncollectible amount.

A firm using GAAP applies the matching principle by putting the expense of having nonpaying customers on the same income statement as the revenue from sales made to those customers. To make this match, Hershey's will estimate and record as an expense the amount it believes it won't collect each period. Accounts receivable that a firm cannot collect are called bad debts, and the expense to record bad debts is called **bad debts expense.**

Recording uncollectible accounts

To understand how firms account for bad debts, let's start by looking at the journal entry. Then, we'll discuss how a firm arrives at the dollar amounts. The journal entry to record bad debts expense using the allowance method is an adjusting journal entry made at the end of the accounting period. The adjusting journal entry starts with a debit to Bad Debts Expense. This adjusting entry will put the expense on the income statement for the period. What about the credit portion of the journal entry? Because the accounts that won't be collected have not been identified at year-end when the expense is estimated, the amount cannot be directly deducted from—credited out of—Accounts Receivable. Because the total in Accounts Receivable is simply the addition of all the individual customers' outstanding account balances, the firm would have to know the name of

Allowance method: A method of accounting for bad debts in which the amount of uncollectible accounts is estimated at the end of each accounting period.

Bad debts expense: The expense to record uncollectible accounts receivable.

In Other Words:
Bad debts expense is also known as uncollectible accounts expense.

Study Tip

Remember that to expense an item means to put it on the income statement as an expense.

Allowance for Uncollectible Accounts:
An account that is a contra-asset to Accounts Receivable and is used to hold the credits until the firm can identify specific accounts that are bad and write them off.

In Other Words:
Allowance for Uncollectible Accounts is often called the Allowance for Doubtful Accounts or the Reserve for Bad Debts.

the person who is not paying to make the credit directly to Accounts Receivable. The accounts that a firm estimates it will not collect—its *uncollectible accounts*— are credited to an account called the **Allowance for Uncollectible Accounts**. This account is a contra-asset and is used to hold the credits until the firm can identify specific accounts that are bad and write them off. The balance in the Allowance for Uncollectible Accounts is the amount that appears on the balance sheet as a *deduction* from Accounts Receivable. Here is the adjusting journal entry made when the firm wants to record $5,000 as bad debts expense.

Date	Transaction	Debit	Credit
12/31	Bad Debts Expense	5,000	
	Allowance for Uncollectible Accounts		5,000
	To record bad debts expense for the year		

The accounting equation is:

Assets	=	Liabilities	+	Shareholders' Equity	
				Contributed Capital	+ **Retained Earnings**
Allowance for Uncollectible Accounts					Bad Debts Expense
−5,000*					−5,000

*The Allowance for Uncollectible Accounts is actually increased in this transaction, but total assets are decreased. That's why the amount is shown as a negative.

The amount remaining when you subtract the balance in the Allowance for Uncollectible Accounts from the total amount of Accounts Receivable is the *carrying value* of Accounts Receivable. Accountants use this terminology consistently for many different amounts on the balance sheet. Do you recall the name of the remainder when Accumulated Depreciation is subtracted from the cost of equipment? It's called the *book value* or carrying value of equipment on the balance sheet. As you just learned, for Accounts Receivable, the remainder is also called the net realizable value.

In Other Words:
Carrying value is also called book value.

Methods of estimating bad debts expense

Now that you know the terminology involved in accounting for bad debts, let's look at the procedures accountants use to estimate those bad debts. Using the allowance method, you have two ways of estimating uncollectible accounts expense: The percentage of sales method and the accounts receivable method. Let's look at each one in detail.

Allowance Method—Percentage of Sales Method The *percentage of sales method* focuses on the income statement and the amount of the current period's sales for which collection will likely not be made. For the purpose of putting the most meaningful amount on the income statement, the question is: How much of the sales revenue will go uncollected? The Bad Debts Expense is recorded as a percentage of sales, and the balancing amount is credited to the Allowance for Uncollectible Accounts.

Suppose you own a firm that has credit sales of $100,000 a year. To prepare your financial statements, you need to estimate the portion of those sales for which you will not collect payment. You have to *estimate* the amount of bad debts expense based on past experience because you can't predict exactly which customers won't pay their bills.

Suppose you routinely lose about 5% of your credit sales due to nonpayment. You want to show Bad Debts Expense of $5,000 on your income statement in the same period as the $100,000 worth of sales on which that $5,000 is estimated. Why? To match the expenses with the related revenues.

The accountant makes an adjustment to record the bad debts expense for the income statement and to reduce total Accounts Receivable in the same period as the sale, long before the firm is able to identify the specific bad-debt customers. Again, this is due to the matching principle—getting the sales revenue and the related bad debts expense on the same income statement. The firm records the amount in a contra-asset account, the Allowance for Uncollectible Accounts. Here is the adjusting journal entry to recognize bad debts expense:

Study Tip

Using the percentage of sales method to estimate the allowance focuses on the income statement. The firm makes its estimate of uncollectible accounts based on credit sales or on total sales, when credit and cash sales are not easily separated.

Date	Transaction	Debit	Credit
Dec. 31	Bad Debts Expense	5,000	
	Allowance for Uncollectible Accounts		5,000
	To record bad debts expense for the year ended Dec. 31		

This is the accounting equation:

Assets	=	Liabilities	+	Shareholders' Equity	
				Contributed Capital	+ Retained Earnings
Allowance for Uncollectible Accounts					Bad Debts Expense
−5,000					−5,000

To summarize, the Allowance for Uncollectible Accounts is a contra-asset account. The contra-asset holds the credits for Accounts Receivable, representing uncollectible accounts. Those credits cannot be recorded directly in Accounts Receivable because at the time the accountant records the expense, the firm doesn't know exactly whose accounts will go unpaid.

Allowance Method—Accounts Receivable Method The second method of calculating the Allowance for Uncollectible Accounts and corresponding bad debts expense is the *accounts receivable method*. This method focuses on the balance sheet. A firm starts by estimating how much of the year-end balance of Accounts Receivable it believes it will not collect. This estimate reduces the amount of Accounts Receivable on the balance sheet so that a firm reports the amount it estimates it will collect, the net realizable value. To put the most meaningful amount on the balance sheet, the question is: How much of the total amount of Accounts Receivable will go uncollected? Most often firms use an aging schedule to estimate this amount. An **aging schedule** is a list of the individual accounts that make up the total balance in Accounts Receivable categorized by how long the payment has been outstanding. Another way to estimate the amount is to take a percentage of the total balance in Accounts Receivable. Using the accounts receivable method of estimating the balance needed in the Allowance for Uncollectible Accounts is sometimes called the *aging method* and sometimes called the *percent of accounts receivable method*. Both names are simply more specific names for the accounts receivable method. Using this method, the bad debts expense equals the amount needed to get the balance in the Allowance for Uncollectible Accounts to the amount to be subtracted from Accounts Receivable to make it equal to the net realizable value.

Hershey Foods uses the accounts receivable method (aging method) to estimate uncollectible accounts. Read how the firm describes the method in Exhibit 7.2. Notice that the firm mentions using the allowance method, assessing collectibility of accounts and using aging analysis to make its estimates.

Study Tip

As you know, a contra-asset is the opposite of an asset. It is deducted from its asset "partner" on the balance sheet. You now know about two contra assets: Accumulated Depreciation and Allowance for Uncollectible Accounts. These contra assets are sometimes called *valuation accounts* because deducting them helps companies ensure the related assets are properly valued for the balance sheet.

In Other Words:
The *accounts receivable method* is also called the *aging method* (when the firm uses an aging schedule) or the *percent of accounts receivable method* (when the firm uses a percentage of the total balance in Accounts Receivable).

Aging schedule: An analysis of the amounts owed to a firm by the length of time they have been outstanding.

Study Tip

You can think of the accounts receivable method as the balance sheet method because the bad debts estimate is made by examining Accounts Receivable, with a focus on getting the correct net realizable value of Accounts Receivable on the balance sheet.

Exhibit 7.2

Hershey Foods' Description of its Allowance for Uncollectible Accounts from Its 10-K for the Year Ended December 31, 2004

In the normal course of business, the Company extends credit to customers that satisfy pre-defined credit criteria. The Company believes that it has little concentration of credit risk due to the diversity of its customer base. Accounts Receivable–Trade, as shown on the Consolidated Balance Sheets, were net of allowances and anticipated discounts. An allowance for doubtful accounts is determined through analysis of the aging of accounts receivable at the date of the financial statements, assessments of collectibility based on historical trends and an evaluation of the impact of current and projected economic conditions. The Company monitors the collectibility of its accounts receivable on an ongoing basis by analyzing the aging of its accounts receivable, assessing the credit worthiness of its customers and evaluating the impact of reasonably likely changes in economic conditions that may impact credit risks. Estimates with regard to the collectibility of accounts receivable are reasonably likely to change in the future.

Hershey makes it clear that estimating uncollectible accounts involves a number of factors, all of which are subject to change.

Now let's see how a firm would estimate bad debts expense using the balance in Accounts Receivable as the starting point. Suppose the balance in Accounts Receivable for Good Guys Co. at December 31, 2006, before any adjustments have been made, is $42,550. In this example, we haven't even been told the amount of sales. To use the accounts receivable method, Good Guys Co. decides to prepare an aging schedule of Accounts Receivable, as shown in Exhibit 7.3. As you just learned, an aging schedule is an analysis of the amounts

Notice that the amounts owed to the firm decrease with age. That's because most of the customers who purchased items on account pay their bills on time. Also notice that the percentages used to estimate the uncollectible portion increases across time. In this example, if an account is overdue by more than 90 days, there is a 50% chance it will never be collected.

Exhibit 7.3

Aging Schedule of Accounts Receivable

Customer	Total	Current	1–30	31–60	61–90	Over 90
			Number of days past due			
J. Adams	$500	$300	$200			
K. Brown	$200	$200				
L. Cannon	$650		$300	$350		
M. Dibbs	$600				$200	$400
Other customers	$41,500	$25,000	$10,000	$3,000	$2,500	$1,000
	$43,450	$25,500	$10,500	$3,350	$2,700	$1,400
Estimated percentage uncollectible		1%	3%	8%	20%	50%
Total estimated bad debts	$2,078	$255	$315	$268	$540	$700

The amounts in this row are totals of many individual customers' accounts.

The sum of these amounts is $2,078.

owed to a firm by the length of time they have been outstanding. As accounts become more overdue, they are increasingly unlikely to be collected.

Based on the aging of Accounts Receivable, management estimates the uncollectible amount at the end of the year to be $2,078. You can see how that total is calculated in Exhibit 7.3. So the net realizable value—the amount of Accounts Receivable the firm thinks it will collect—is $40,472. That is the total $42,550 minus $2,078. That amount is what Good Guys wants the balance sheet to show—the book value—at December 31, 2006. GAAP requires the firm to disclose the total Accounts Receivable balance and its net realizable value. Some companies show the details on the balance sheet, and others include the details in the notes to the financial statements. Exhibit 7.4 shows how Good Guys might present its Accounts Receivable.

In the *first year* of using the allowance method, with a zero balance in the Allowance account, Good Guys estimated uncollectible accounts of $2,078. This is the journal entry that Good Guys will record:

Date	Transaction	Debit	Credit
Dec. 31	Bad Debts Expense	2,078	
	Allowance for Uncollectible Accounts		2,078
	To record bad debts expense for the year ended Dec. 31		

This is the accounting equation:

Assets	=	Liabilities	+	Shareholders' Equity	
				Contributed Capital	+ **Retained Earnings**
Allowance for Uncollectible Accounts					Bad Debts Expense
−2,078					−2,078

Remember that rather than deducting the $2,078 directly from Accounts Receivable, the accountant will keep that amount in a separate allowance account, a contra-asset account, and show it on the balance sheet as a deduction from Accounts Receivable. Bad Debts Expense appears on the income statement as an operating expense.

Writing off a specific account

During the following year, 2007, the firm will identify specific bad accounts and remove them from the books. That's when the firm finds out that a specific customer is not going to be able to pay his or her outstanding accounts receivable.

Study Tip

There is no net effect on assets and no bad debts expense recorded when a specific account is written off.

The details shown in this presentation may not appear on the face of all balance sheets, but the information will be disclosed in the notes. In all cases, financial statement users should be able to figure out a firm's Allowance for Uncollectible Accounts.

Exhibit 7.4

Balance Sheet Presentation of Accounts Receivable

Balance Sheet, December 31, 2006

Current Assets:

Accounts receivable	$42,550
Allowance for uncollectible accounts	(2,078)
Net accounts receivable	$40,472

When the firm eventually identifies the specific bad account and wants to remove it from the books, it will be done by deducting the amount from Accounts Receivable and also removing the amount from the Allowance for Uncollectible Accounts. Removing the amount from Accounts Receivable reduces assets. Removing the amount from the Allowance for Uncollectible Accounts *increases* assets by reducing the amount that will be deducted from Accounts Receivable on the balance sheet. That means there is no net effect on assets when the account is actually written off. There is no bad debts expense recorded when the firm actually writes off a specific customer's account using the allowance method. That's because the firm already recognized the bad debts expense when the accountant made the bad debts estimate for the adjusting journal entry at the time of the financial statements.

When the firm writes off a specific account, the accountant is simply reclassifying an *unnamed* bad debt to a *named* bad debt. This is the journal entry to write off a specific account:

Transaction	Debit	Credit
Allowance for Uncollectible Accounts	400	
Accounts Receivable (ABC Co.)		400
To record the write off of ABC Co.'s account, identified as uncollectible		

This is the accounting equation:

Assets		=	Liabilities	+	Shareholders' Equity	
					Contributed Capital	+ Retained Earnings
Accounts Receivable	Allowance for Uncollectible Accounts					
−400	400*					

*The Allowance is reduced when a specific account is written off. Because the Allowance for Uncollectible Accounts is deducted from Accounts Receivable, reducing the amount subtracted actually increases assets. That's why the amount is shown as having a positive effect on assets.

Study Tip

Using the accounts receivable (AR) method, the balance in the Allowance for Uncollectible Accounts is always considered in the calculation of Bad Debts Expense. After the desired balance in the Allowance for Uncollectible Accounts at the end of the period is calculated, it is adjusted for any amount still in the Allowance for Uncollectible Accounts to arrive at the amount of the journal entry for Bad Debts Expense.

Only when you use the allowance method *with accounts receivable as the basis for estimating bad debts expense* do you adjust your new estimate for any over- or under-estimation you made the previous accounting period.[1] If you write off more bad debts than you had estimated, you will end up with a debit balance in the Allowance for Uncollectible Accounts. However, you will adjust the balance in the Allowance for Uncollectible Accounts when you do the end-of-period adjusting entries so that it will have the desired credit balance for the end-of-period balance sheet. If you write off fewer bad debts than you had estimated, you will end up with a credit balance in the Allowance for Uncollectible Accounts. The next example will show you what to do if this happens.

Let's return to Good Guys. Recall that the firm recorded $2,078 in its Allowance for Uncollectible Accounts at December 31, 2006. This amount will be used for 2007 write-offs. Suppose the firm identifies M. Dibbs, who owes the firm $600, as an uncollectible account customer in February 2007. That means the firm's accountant or credit manager feels sure that the firm will not be able to collect his specific account. The effect on the accounting equation is a reduction in both the Allowance for Uncollectible Accounts and Accounts Receivable. There is no

[1]Adjustments to the amount of the Allowance for Uncollectible Accounts using the percent-of-sales method are done by adjusting the percentage from year-to-year if the Allowance for Uncollectible Accounts gets too large or too small.

effect on the *net* amount of Accounts Receivable. Writing off a specific account is a matter of cleaning up the firm's books. Instead of remaining an unidentified bad account, the firm can now put a name with $600 worth of bad debts. The firm already recognized the expense with the estimate it made at the end of the prior year, so no expense is recognized when a specific name is put with the uncollectible account. Here is the journal entry to write off Dibbs' account:

Study Tip

The journal entry to write off a specific person's account is the same whether the percentage-of-sales method or the accounts receivable method is used.

Date	Transaction	Debit	Credit
Feb. 2007	Allowance for Uncollectible Accounts	600	
	Accounts Receivable (Dibbs)		600
	To record a write off of a specific account identified as uncollectible		

This is the accounting equation:

Assets	=	Liabilities	+	Shareholders' Equity	
				Contributed Capital	+ **Retained Earnings**
Accounts Receivable	Allowance for Uncollectible Accounts				
−600	600				

Can you see what happens when you write off a specific account? With the allowance method, there is *no* effect on a firm's net Accounts Receivable when the firm writes off a specific account. Instead, the firm removes the account from its receivables and removes an equal amount from the allowance. This is why:

	Balances on the Year-end Balance Sheet After Adjustments	Effect of Writing Off Dibbs' Account	Balances After Writing Off Dibbs' Account
Accounts Receivable	$42,550	(600)	$41,950
Allowance for Uncollectible Accounts	(2,078)	600	(1,478)
Net Accounts Receivable	$40,472		$40,472

Suppose that, by the end of the year, Good Guys has identified and written off $1,400 of accounts in addition to Dibbs' account, for a total of $2,000 worth of specific bad accounts. This process of identifying and writing off continues throughout the year as the accounts are identified. That means last year's estimate of bad debts of $2,078 was $78 more than the total of the accounts actually identified and written off. The firm will ignore that difference and estimate the next year's bad debts expense in the same way as it did for the prior year. Good Guys will prepare another aging schedule and again make an estimate of uncollectible accounts. Follow along by looking at the T-accounts in Exhibit 7.5 on the next page. Suppose credit sales for the year amounted to $100,000 and collections totaled $90,550, leaving a balance in Accounts Receivable of $50,000. Here's a summary of the activity in Accounts Receivable for the year:

- Beginning balance was $42,550 (ending 2006 balance)
- Add credit sales of $100,000
- Deduct collections of $90,550
- Deduct the total write-offs of $2,000.

This example begins with an Accounts Receivable balance of $42,550. (1) The Allowance for Uncollectible Accounts is recorded along with Bad Debts Expense for the year ended December 31, 2006 for $2,078. During 2007, the firm has credit sales of $100,000 and collections of $90,550. Both are shown in Accounts Receivable. (2) and (3) show that during 2007, $2,000 worth of bad debts are identified and written off: Dibbs for $600 and another totaling $1,400. The journal entry to write off these accounts is a debit to the Allowance for Uncollectible Accounts and a credit to Accounts Receivable. At December 31, 2007, the balance in the Allowance for Uncollectible Accounts is $78 (credit), reflecting an amount left over from last year of $78. (4) When the estimate of bad debts of $2,500 at 12-31-07 is calculated, it is reduced by $78 because there is $78 "left over" in the Allowance for Uncollectible Accounts. The amount for the journal entry for bad debts expense is the amount needed to get the Allowance for Uncollectible Accounts to the desired balance.

Exhibit 7.5

Allowance for Uncollectible Accounts Using Accounts Receivable to Estimate Bad Debts Expense

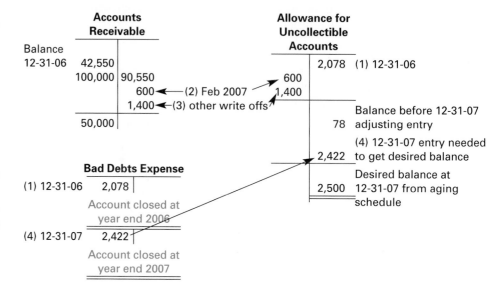

This activity leaves an ending balance of $50,000 in Accounts Receivable. Suppose an aging schedule produced an estimate of uncollectible accounts of $2,500. Good Guys wants the balance sheet to use this estimate as the reduction in Accounts Receivable, showing the book value or carrying value of Accounts Receivable as $47,500.

Now, Good Guys has to take into consideration that it has a balance in the Allowance account from last year's recording of bad debts expense. Good Guys will record bad debts expense this year of only $2,422 (= $2,500 − $78). The amount carried over from last year, $78, is still in the Allowance for Uncollectible Accounts, so the firm needs to add only $2,422 to the Allowance for Uncollectible Accounts to get the total $2,500 needed for the balance sheet. So the firm's bad debts expense in the second year would be $2,422, and the Allowance for Uncollectible Accounts balance at year-end will be the desired $2,500.

Study the summary of this example in Exhibit 7.5 to make sure you understand the procedures for estimating and recording bad debts expense and the procedures for actually writing off a specific account.

When the accounts receivable method for estimating the allowance is used, the balance in the Allowance for Uncollectible Accounts account and the Bad Debts Expense are guaranteed to be equal only in the first year. After that, they would be equal only if the estimate of bad debts for the previous year is exactly equal to the accounts identified as uncollectible and written off—and that rarely happens. Each year, the expense usually shows a little adjustment for the over- or under-estimate from the previous year's entry. Making the adjustment for the Allowance for Uncollectible Accounts is part of the adjusting entries the firm records at the end of the accounting period. The amount of the bad debts estimate affects net income. To help ensure their bonuses or good salary increases, unethical managers could manipulate bad debts estimates to inflate net income. Read about using the allowance to misstate net income in ***Accounting in the News***.

Exhibit 7.6 provides a summary of the allowance method for bad debts. Refer to the exhibit when you are trying to learn the differences between methods of calculating the amounts for the Allowance for Uncollectible Accounts and Bad Debts Expense.

Accounting in the NEWS

Ethics

American International Group Helps Clients Smooth Earnings

Assume that you are a manager of a clothing merchandising firm with significant accounts receivable. You plan on working for the firm for at least 10 years, and you understand that your accumulated bonuses over the 10 years will be higher if net income is smoothly increasing year after year rather than increasing some years and decreasing in others. You know that if you sometimes overstate bad debts expense and sometimes understate it, you will have smooth increases in net income. Over time, the overstatements and understatements of bad debts expense will average out in the financial statements. Is this practice ethical?

According to Frances Ayres, accounting professor, managers engage in "income smoothing" because they may believe the following:

- Smooth earnings are more highly valued.
- Smooth earnings minimize the risk of possible violation of agreements with lenders.
- Income smoothing can maximize management bonuses.

One of the largest and most profitable insurance companies in the world, American International Group (AIG) is in trouble with the SEC for allegedly helping its corporate clients deceive investors by backdating insurance policies to let the clients recognize losses over several accounting periods to "smooth earnings." Investigators also believe AIG executives were involved in making accounting adjustments that manipulated levels of their setting the balances in reserves. While there is no argument that reserves like the Allowance for Uncollectible Accounts requires a great deal of judgment, AIG may have made the adjustments without proper support.

Thinking Critically

If you're a manager who suspects another manager of manipulating bad debts expense, what would you do: Ignore the situation? Confront the manager? Bring the manipulation to the attention of a supervisor? Explain the rationale behind your choice of action.

Recognizing losses over several accounting periods is called "income smoothing." In 2005, managers at American International Group were charged with manipulating levels of the companies reserves by backdating insurance policies.

Q How do investors view income smoothing?

A Although the market likes smooth earnings, investors are skeptical unless the activities of both the economy and the firm are also "smooth."

Sources: Ian McDonald and Theo Francis, "AIG Probe May Find More Officials Knew of Accounting Moves," *Wall Street Journal Online*, May 10, 2005; Paula Dwyer, "AIG: Why the Feds are Playing Hardball," *Business Week Online*, October 24, 2004; Frances L. Ayres, "Perceptions of Earnings Quality: What Managers Need to Know," *Management Accounting* (March, 1994).

Can YOU do it?

Suppose at the end of the year, Pendleton Corp. records showed the following:

Allowance for Doubtful Accounts (excess from prior year)	100 credit balance
Bad Debts Expense*	-0-
Accounts Receivable	10,000

*Bad Debts Expense has a -0- balance because no adjustments have been made.

Pendleton estimated the end-of-year uncollectible accounts receivable to be $500, based on an aging schedule of current Accounts Receivable.

1. Calculate the amount of Bad Debts Expense that should be shown on the income statement for the year.
2. What will be the net Accounts Receivable on the year-end balance sheet?

Answers (1) $400 (= $500 desired balance − $100 remaining balance before adjustments)
(2) $9,500 (= $10,000 − $500)

Exhibit 7.6

Allowance Methods of Accounting for Bad Debts

Method of Estimating Bad Debts Expense	Procedure	Journal Entry	DR	CR	Effect on Income Statement	Effect on Balance Sheet

Sales method	Take a % of sales to record as bad debts expense.	Bad Debts Expense
		  Allowance for
		  Uncollectible
		  Accounts
		($$ is the % of sales)
			$$	$$	Reduces income with Bad Debts Expense.	Reduces assets with a credit to the Allowance for Uncollectible Accounts (a contra-asset).

Accounts Receivable method	Prepare an aging schedule or use a single percentage of the total balance in Accounts Receivable to estimate the balance needed in the Allowance for Uncollectible Accounts	Bad Debts Expense
		  Allowance for
		  Uncollectible
		  Accounts
		($$ is the *adjustment* to the Allowance for Uncollectible Accounts to get the balance needed)
			$$	$$	Reduces income with Bad Debts Expense	Reduces assets with a credit to the Allowance for Uncollectible Accounts (a contra-asset).

For both methods:
Writing off a specific account under both methods:
		Allowance for
		Uncollectible
		Accounts
		  Accounts
		  Receivable
		(specific person's account)
			$$	$$	No effect on income statement	No net effect on the balance sheet.

The direct write-off method

Direct write-off method: A method of accounting for bad debts in which they are written off—booked as Bad Debts Expense—in the period in which they are identified as uncollectible.

As you have learned, when a firm reports Accounts Receivable on its balance sheet, the amount must be what the firm expects to collect—that amount is the real asset. Most publicly traded firms use the allowance method because GAAP requires it when a firm has a significant amount of bad debts. There is another option called the **direct write-off method**. Using this method, a firm does not make any estimates of bad debts. The bad debts expense is recorded only when a specific account is identified as uncollectible. A firm uses the direct write-off method only when it has so few bad debts that almost all accounts receivable will be collected. Otherwise, the firm would be violating GAAP because it would not be matching the bad debts expense with the appropriate sales revenue.

The accountant removes the "bad" account from the accounting records by crediting it out of Accounts Receivable. The Bad Debts Expense account is debited. Using the direct write-off method, a firm reports total Accounts Receivable on the balance sheet. Here is the journal entry, made when the firm discovers that Jane Doe, who owes the firm $200, will not pay.

Transaction	Debit	Credit
Bad Debts Expense	200	
Accounts receivable, J. Doe		200
To record write off of a specific account identified as uncollectible using the direct write-off method		

This is the accounting equation:

Assets	=	Liabilities	+	Shareholders' Equity	
				Contributed Capital +	Retained Earnings
Accounts Receivable (J. Doe)					Bad Debts Expense
−200					−200

Remember that the direct write-off method is not considered GAAP. Very few firms that extend credit to customers use this method if they follow GAAP because specific bad debts are written off in the period they are discovered rather than in the earlier period of the sale, which violates the matching principle.

Notes Receivable

You've learned about the most significant receivables a firm has—accounts receivable. Another common receivable is a **promissory note**, which is a written promise to pay a specified amount of money at a specified time. The person or firm making the promise to pay is called the **maker**, and the person or firm receiving the money is called the **payee**. A promissory note is also called a notes receivable. The main differences between accounts receivable and notes receivable related to accounting are time and interest.

First, notes receivable usually have a collection period longer than accounts receivable. For example, with accounts receivable, a firm usually expects a customer to pay his account within 30 days of the invoice date. Recall that many companies offer their customers terms like 2/10, n/30, where 30 designates the maximum length of time a customer may take to pay. If a customer is late with a payment, the firm often imposes a late charge. A note receivable usually has a time period longer than a month associated with it, and the customer or firm who owes will have to pay interest along with the principal repayment. Frequently, a firm will renegotiate an overdue account by allowing the customer to sign a promissory note giving the customer more time to pay and charging interest on the loan.

Second, accounts receivable generally have no interest charges, while a note receivable always has interest charges. The firm calculates the interest on a note receivable in the same way it calculates interest on any debt:

$$\text{Interest} = \text{Principal} \times \text{Rate} \times \text{Time}$$

If the note is a short-term note, which the firm will classify as a current asset, the length of the note is less than a year. When calculating interest on a short-term note, be sure to keep the interest rate and the time period in the same units. Interest rates are always recorded on a note as annual rates, so the time period must be expressed as a portion of a year. A simple example will demonstrate the procedure for calculating the interest on a note.

Suppose Procter and Gamble allowed Pop's Grocery Store to renegotiate an overdue account with a promissory note, dated May 1. The amount of the note is $5,000, due in 90 days, at an interest rate of 8%. Procter and Gamble would record the note with the following journal entry:

LEARNING OBJECTIVE 2

Account for and report notes receivable.

Promissory note: A written promise to pay a specific amount of money at a particular time.

Maker: The person or firm making the promise to pay a promissory note.

Payee: The person or firm receiving the payment from a promissory note.

Date	Transaction	Debit	Credit
May 1	Notes Receivable (NR)	5,000	
	Accounts Receivable (AR)		5,000
	To record a note receivable in settlement of an accounts receivable		

This is the accounting equation:

Assets		=	Liabilities	+	Shareholders' Equity	
					Contributed Capital	+ Retained Earnings
Accounts Receivable	Notes Receivable					
–5,000	5,000					

When Pop's repays the note, it will also pay 90 days' worth of interest. The interest is calculated as follows:

$I = P \times R \times T$
$I = \$5,000 \times 0.08 \times 90/365$ [Time is 90 out of 365 days in a year.] *
$I = \$98.63$

*Portion of a year can be expressed in months; eg. 3/12

The journal entry that Procter and Gamble will make when Pop's repays the note with interest will be:

Date	Transaction	Debit	Credit
July 30	Cash	5,098.63	
	Notes Receivable (NR)		5,000.00
	Interest Revenue		98.63
	To record collection of note plus interest		

This is the accounting equation:

Assets		=	Liabilities	+	Shareholders' Equity	
					Contributed Capital	+ Retained Earnings
Cash	Notes Receivable					Interest Revenue
5,098.63	–5,000.00					98.63

If a note is outstanding when a firm is ready to prepare financial statements, any interest that the firm has earned but not recorded must be accrued. The firm will calculate interest for the time that has passed and record interest revenue and interest receivable.

Can **YOU** do it?

Dell Products allowed a customer to give a note receivable in payment of a delinquent accounts receivable. The note was a six-month note for $3,000, and the interest rate was 8%. If the note was issued on September 1, how would the note and any related interest be reported on Dell's December 31 balance sheet?

Answer

Current assets:		
	Notes Receivable	$3,000
	Interest Receivable	$ 80 [3,000 × 0.08 × 4/12]

Controlling Cash

LEARNING OBJECTIVE 3

Explain how a firm controls cash and prepares a bank reconciliation.

Now that you've learned about accounts receivable and notes receivable, let's turn to the asset we want the receivables to become: Cash. At the end of 2004, Hershey Foods had over $54 million in cash and cash equivalents. That is a lot of money, and Hershey's management wants to make sure it is safe. Because cash is often the target of misappropriation, firms have to keep tight control of this asset.

Assignment of responsibilities for cash

A key control you learned about in Chapter 5 is segregation of duties. For cash, segregation of duties means the person who has the physical custody of cash—anyone who has actual physical access to cash at any time and who can write checks and make deposits—cannot be the same person who does the record keeping for cash. If the same person had responsibility for both, it would be easy for that person to keep some of the cash and alter the records to hide the theft.

Simply having two people involved in the same task can help protect a firm from fraud. For example, if the firm typically receives cash and checks in the mail from its customers, having two people open the envelopes together is a common practice. Stealing money would require collusion—that's when two or more people have to work together to commit fraud. At banks, you will often see two people counting cash together. Having people share this responsibility decreases both errors and fraud.

Bank reconciliations

Almost all companies use banks to help them keep track of and safeguard their cash. The bank assists its customers by providing a bank statement. A **bank statement** is a summary of the activity in a bank account—deposits, checks, debit card transactions—sent monthly to the account owner.

Someone in the firm will perform a bank reconciliation, which involves comparing the general ledger Cash balance and the bank statement cash balance for that month. A **bank reconciliation** is more than simply part of the record keeping for cash. The bank reconciliation is a crucial part of controlling cash.

As we all know, the bottom line in our checkbook or ATM spending records seldom agrees with the bottom line on our monthly bank statement. That's true for a business, too: The Cash balance in a firm's records seldom agrees with the Cash balance on its monthly bank statement. The two cash balances don't agree because there are transactions that are recorded in one place but not recorded in the other place due to timing differences. Sometimes the bank knows about a transaction that the firm hasn't recorded on its books, and sometimes the firm knows about a transaction that the bank hasn't recorded on its books. For example, a firm may make a deposit on the last day of June, but the deposit may not appear on the June statement due to the bank's delay in recording the deposit. Even more often, the checks a firm has written may not have reached the bank for payment—that is, the checks have not *cleared* the bank at the date of the statement. In other words, the bank doesn't know about those transactions on the date of the statement. The monthly bank statement, which contains all of the deposits, checks, ATM transactions, and other miscellaneous items, has to be reconciled to the general ledger Cash account. See Exhibit 7.7 for an example of a bank statement.

Bank statement: A summary of the activity in a bank account sent each month to the account owner.

Bank reconciliation: A comparison between the general ledger Cash balance and the bank statement's Cash balance to identify the reasons for any differences.

In Other Words:
A bank reconciliation is often called a cash reconciliation.

Study Tip

Even though it may be called a "bank" reconciliation, it is done by the firm to get the correct Cash balance for the firm's books.

Steps in the Reconciliation Reconciling the monthly bank statement to the general ledger Cash account is an important element of internal control and requires two major steps:

1. Start with the balance on the monthly bank statement, called the *balance per bank*, and make adjustments for all the transactions that have been

Exhibit 7.7

Bank Statement

AB Andover Bank
Andover, MA 01844

	Statement Date
	June 30, 2006

Account Statement

Jessica's Chocolate Shop
15 Main Street
Andover, MA 01844

356814
ACCOUNT NUMBER

Balance Last Statement	Deposits and Credits		Checks and Debits		Balance This Statement
	No.	Total Amount	No.	Total Amount	
19,817.02	13	20,579.05	12	12,509.93	27,886.14

DEPOSITS AND CREDITS		CHECKS AND DEBITS			DAILY BALANCE	
Date	Amount	Date	No.	Amount	Date	Amount
6-2	733.30	6-2	235	560.50	6-2	19,989.82
6-3	689.50	6-3	236	1,450.00	6-3	19,229.32
6-6	3,000.00	6-4	237	1,090.50	6-4	18,138.82
6-7	4,000.00	6-5	238	1,500.48	6-5	16,638.34
6-8	999.28	6-6	239	890.60	6-7	21,246.87
6-9 CM	1,070.00	6-7	240	1,500.87	6-8	21,777.25
6-11	1,500.72	6-8	241	468.90	6-9	22,847.25
6-12	750.25	6-11	242	2,220.85	6-11	22,127.12
6-13	1,205.50	6-12	243	1,300.08	6-12	21,577.29
6-27	1,200.00	6-29	NSF	225.65	6-27	23,982.79
6-29	3,450.80	6-29	452	875.85	6-29	26,332.09
6-30	1,979.70	6-30	DM	50.00	6-30	27,886.14
		6-30	461	375.65		

Symbols: **ATM** Automatic Teller Machine   **CM** Credit Memo   **EC** Error Correction   Reconcile Your
NSF Not Sufficient Funds   **DM** Debit Memo   **INT** Interest Earned   **SC** Service Charge   Account Promptly

recorded in the firm's books but not recorded in the bank's books because the bank did not get the transaction recorded as of the date of the bank statement.

2. Start with the general ledger Cash balance, called the *balance per books*, and make adjustments for all the transactions that the bank has recorded but have not been recorded on the firm's books.

After the above steps are complete, each section of the bank reconciliation should show the same reconciled Cash balance. That balance will be the actual amount of cash the firm had on the date of the bank statement. The actual amount is called the *true cash balance*. A firm reconciling a bank statement divides a schedule into two parts, as shown in Exhibit 7.8.

Exhibit 7.8

Format for Bank Reconciliation

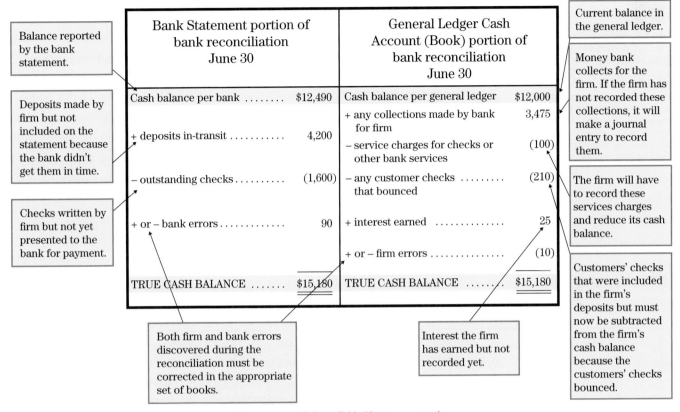

To prepare a bank reconciliation, an accountant would create a worksheet divided into two parts: the Bank Statement (on the left) and the General Ledger Cash Account (on the right). Focus on the types of adjustments. We'll use the example dollar amounts later in Exhibits 7.9 and 7.10.

Reconciling Items The right side of Exhibit 7.8 shows items that will need journal entries to adjust the firm's books. Adjustments will *never* be required for transactions already recorded in the general ledger. The left part of Exhibit 7.8 shows deposits in-transit and outstanding checks. These items will not need adjusting journal entries because they have already been recorded in the general ledger, and the bank will eventually receive and record those transactions in its records.

Performing a bank reconciliation enables a firm to:

1. Locate any errors, whether made by the bank or by the firm.
2. Make adjustments to the Cash account in the firm's books for transactions the bank has recorded but the firm has not yet recorded in its Cash account.

The bank reconciliation begins with the *balance per bank* and the *balance per books* as of the bank statement date. Each of these balances is then adjusted to arrive at the true cash balance. A bank reconciliation has eight common adjustments. Three common adjustments may be needed to make the bank statement balance with information from the general ledger:

1. **Outstanding checks** are deducted from the balance per bank.
2. **Deposits in transit** are added to the balance per bank.
3. Errors made by the bank may require additions or deductions.

Outstanding checks: Checks written by a firm that have not yet cleared the bank. That is, the checks have not been presented to the bank for payment.

Deposits in transit: Bank deposits made but not included on the month's bank statement because the deposit did not reach the bank's record-keeping department in time to be included on the current bank statement.

Study Tip

One part of the worksheet starts with the Cash balance from the bank statement. The general ledger provides information for adjustments that will be made to find the firm's true cash balance. The other part of the worksheet starts with the firm's Cash balance from the general ledger. The bank statement provides information for adjustments that will be made to calculate the firm's true cash balance.

Five common adjustments[2] are made to the general ledger balance with information from the bank statement:

1. Collections made by the bank on behalf of the firm are added to the balance per books.

2. Service charges by the bank appear on the bank statement and are deducted from the balance per books.

3. A customer's non-sufficient-funds (NSF) check is deducted from the balance per books.

4. Interest earned on a checking account is added to the balance per books.

5. Errors made by the firm may require additions or deductions.

Exhibit 7.9 shows how each item on the bank side is treated in the bank reconciliation, and Exhibit 7.10 shows how each item on the books side is treated in the reconciliation. The dollar amounts come from the example in Exhibit 7.8. Remember that a bank reconciliation is not part of the formal records of the firm. It is just a worksheet, and any changes that the firm needs to make to its records must be done with journal entries.

Exhibit 7.9

Items Used on the Bank Side of a Bank Reconciliation

Item	What happens to the item during the bank reconciliation?	What happens to the item in the firm's books?
1. Outstanding checks–checks the firm has written, but they haven't cleared the bank at the time of the bank statement.	Adjustment is needed to deduct the total amount of the outstanding checks, ($1,600), from the balance per bank, $12,490.	No adjustment is needed because the cash was already deducted when the checks were written.
2. Deposits in transit—deposits the firm made too late for the bank to include them on the bank statement.	Adjustment is needed to add the total amount of the deposits, $4,200, to the balance per bank.	No adjustment is needed because the cash was already added when the deposits were made.
3. Any errors the bank has made.	Suppose the bank should have recorded a deposit as $980 but instead recorded it as $890. In this case, add $90 to the bank's balance.	No adjustment is needed because the bank's records are wrong. The firm had the deposit recorded correctly.

[2]There are actually an unlimited number of adjustments that may need to be made, but these are the five most common.

Exhibit 7.10

Items Used on the Book Side of a Bank Reconciliation

Item	What happens to the item during the bank reconciliation?	What happens to the item in the firm's books?
1. Amounts collected by the bank on behalf of the firm; in this example, a Notes receivable	Add $3,475 to the balance per books.	Journal entry: Cash 3,475 Notes receivable 3,475 [Note: Often part of the collection is interest.]
2. Service charges—amounts the bank charges for its services	Deduct $100 from the balance per books.	Journal entry: Bank expense 100 Cash 100
3. Non-sufficient-funds (NSF) checks—checks the firm received from customers and deposited that bounced!	Deduct $210 from the balance per books.	Journal entry: Accounts receivable 210 (specific account) Cash 210
4. Interest earned on the bank account balance	Add $25 to the balance per books.	Journal entry: Cash 25 Interest revenue 25
5. Any errors the firm has made in its records.	Suppose the firm recorded a check it wrote to a vendor for $480 when the check was actually $490. In this case, deduct $10 from the balance per books.	Journal entry: Accounts payable 10 Cash 10

Exhibit 7.10 shows the information already included in the calculation of the bank's balance at the date of the bank statement but unknown to the firm until the bank statement is received.

An Example of a Bank Reconciliation and the Adjustments Let's take the relevant information below on ABC Light Company and prepare the bank reconciliation. Make sure you can identify where each amount is included in the reconciliation.

ABC Light Company	
Information from the bank statement:	
Balance per bank statement, June 30, 2006	$4,890
Note Receivable and interest collected by bank for ABC Light Co.	1,030
Bank service charges	10
Customer check returned and marked "NSF"	100
Information from ABC's general ledger:	
Company's books Cash balance, June 30, 2006	1,774
Checks outstanding on 6/30/06: No. 298	1,300
304	456
306	2,358
Deposit made after bank hours by ABC Light Co. on 6/30/06	1,750

Keep these two additional facts in mind as you prepare the bank reconciliation.

1. The bank statement showed the bank had mistakenly charged ABC Light Company for a $150 check that was written by the ABC *Chemical* Company.
2. During June, ABC Light Company's bookkeeper recorded payment of an account payable incorrectly as $346. The check was paid by the bank in the correct amount of $364.

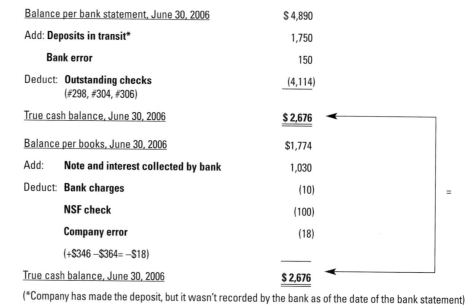

ABC Light Company
Bank Reconciliation
June 30, 2006

Balance per bank statement, June 30, 2006	$ 4,890
Add: **Deposits in transit***	1,750
Bank error	150
Deduct: **Outstanding checks**	(4,114)
(#298, #304, #306)	
True cash balance, June 30, 2006	**$ 2,676**
Balance per books, June 30, 2006	$1,774
Add: **Note and interest collected by bank**	1,030
Deduct: **Bank charges**	(10)
NSF check	(100)
Company error	(18)
(+$346 −$364= −$18)	
True cash balance, June 30, 2006	**$ 2,676**

(*Company has made the deposit, but it wasn't recorded by the bank as of the date of the bank statement)

As you learned earlier in the chapter, a bank reconciliation is simply a work-sheet—it is not a formal part of the firm's accounting system. Nothing included on the worksheet actually corrects the accounting records. The accounting records will need to be adjusted with journal entries to account for every item on the "Balance per books" part of the reconciliation. Here are the journal entries that ABC Light Company would make to bring its accounting records up-to-date following the bank reconciliation:

Transaction	Debit	Credit
Cash	1,030	
Notes Receivable		1,000
Interest Revenue		30
To record collection of notes receivable		

This is the accounting equation:

Assets		=	Liabilities	+	Shareholders' Equity	
					Contributed Capital	**Retained** + **Earnings**
Cash	Notes Receivable					Interest Revenue
1,030	−1,000					30

Transaction	Debit	Credit
Bank Fees Expense	10	
Cash		10
To record bank charges		

This is the accounting equation:

Assets	=	Liabilities	+	Shareholders' Equity	
				Contributed Capital +	**Retained Earnings**
Cash					Bank Fees Expense
−10					−10

Transaction	Debit	Credit
Accounts Receivable (specific person's account)	100	
Cash		100
To record NSF check from customer		

This is the accounting equation:

Assets		=	Liabilities	+	Shareholders' Equity	
					Contributed Capital	Retained + Earnings
Cash	Accounts Receivable					
−100	100					

Transaction	Debit	Credit
Accounts Payable	18	
Cash		18
To correct an error in recording a check to a vendor		

This is the accounting equation:

Assets	=	Liabilities	+	Shareholders' Equity	
				Contributed Capital	Retained + Earnings
Cash		Accounts Payable			
−18		−18			

The Bank's Terminology When you open a bank account, you make a deposit by giving the bank some of your money. It doesn't really belong to the bank, so the bank will record it as a liability. The bank will debit Cash and credit your account, which is like an Accounts Payable to the bank. So when the bank says it *credits* your account, it is literally making a journal entry with a credit to your account. In the past few years, debit cards have become very popular. When you spend money using your debit card, the bank deducts the amount from your account. Because your account is a liability to the bank,

Can YOU do it?

ABC Light Company's unadjusted book balance amounted to $2,400. The company's bank statement included a debit memo for bank service charges of $100. There were two credit memos in the bank statement. One was for $300, which represented a collection that the bank made for ABC. The second credit memo was for $100, which represented the amount of interest that ABC had earned during the accounting period. Outstanding checks amounted to $250, and there were no deposits in transit. Based on this information, what is ABC's true cash balance?

Answer To find the solution, you need to know the following information:

Balance per books = $2,400

Deduct service charges = 100

Add collection = 300

Add interest = 100

Given this information, the solution is $2,700

Outstanding checks are ignored because we are working with only the "balance per books" side of the reconciliation.

when you use your debit card, the bank literally *debits* your account. That debit reduces your balance.

Often a firm's bank statement will have debit memos and credit memos. The debit memos are charges to the account, reducing the balance in the firm's account. The credit memos are additions to the account, increasing its balance. The bank statement might include a debit memo for new checks that were ordered. In contrast, the bank would include a credit memo for any interest the account has earned. When you hear the terms *debit* and *credit* used in business, you can be sure that the meaning is derived from the accounting meanings of those terms and used from the viewpoint of that business.

Reporting Cash

LEARNING OBJECTIVE 4

Describe how cash is reported on the financial statements.

Cash is an asset you will find on two financial statements: the balance sheet and the statement of cash flows. On the balance sheet, the amount of cash a firm has on the date of the balance sheet is reported. A firm often has a number of cash accounts—checking accounts and savings accounts in various banks. For example, a firm will often have a special bank account for its payroll. All of the firm's cash accounts will be combined for presentation on the balance sheet. Let's see how Hershey Foods reports cash on its balance sheet. Refer back to Exhibit 7.1 on page 331.

Cash equivalents

On the balance sheet of Hershey Foods, the first asset is *Cash and Cash Equivalents*. It is the first asset listed on almost all balance sheets. **Cash equivalents** are highly liquid investments with a maturity of three months or less that a firm can easily convert into a known amount of cash. U.S. Treasury Notes are a common cash equivalent. The notes to the financial statements disclose how a firm defines its cash equivalents. Exhibit 7.11 shows the note defining cash equivalents from the financial statements of Hershey Foods.

Although it is infrequent, a negative balance in Cash should be listed as a current liability. This balance would indicate that a firm has checks outstanding in excess of its available cash. As you might guess, a firm does not want to have a negative Cash balance.

Cash equivalents: Highly liquid investments with a maturity of three months or less that a firm can easily convert into a known amount of cash.

The statement of cash flows

In addition to its prominent place on the balance sheet, cash has its very own statement. As you learned in previous chapters, the statement of cash flows describes all of the cash flows for the period, which explains the change in Cash from one balance sheet to the next. The amount of cash shown on the

Exhibit 7.11

Disclosure About Cash and Cash Equivalents

This note to the financial statements of Hershey Foods Corporation defines "cash equivalents" as it is used by the firm.

From the notes to the financial statements of Hershey Foods Corporation:

CASH EQUIVALENTS. Cash equivalents consist of highly liquid debt instruments, time deposits, and money market funds with original maturities of three months or less. The fair value of cash and cash equivalents approximates the carrying amount.

latest balance sheet will be the bottom line in the statement of cash flows. The statement of cash flows is an important financial statement because a business cannot survive if it doesn't have enough cash to pay its employees, vendors, rent, and other expenses.

LEARNING OBJECTIVE 5

Analyze a firm's accounts receivable with ratio analysis.

Analyzing Accounts Receivable with Ratio Analysis

Keeping control of cash through the bank reconciliation process helps ensure the correct numbers are getting to the financial statements. It's important that the numbers about sales and accounts receivable are accurate because managers and others use those numbers to measure the firm's ability to meet its short-term obligations. When the *current ratio* is computed—that is, *Current Assets divided by Current Liabilities*—the numerator includes accounts receivable, because it is a current asset. Another ratio similar to the current ratio that you learned about in Chapter 3 is called the *quick ratio*, also know as the *acid-test ratio*. Instead of using all of a firm's current assets in the numerator, the quick ratio uses only cash, short-term investments, and net accounts receivable. These three assets are the most liquid—easiest to convert to cash—so they are the most available for paying off current liabilities. An investor or analyst will use the quick ratio as a stricter test of a firm's ability to meet its short-term obligations.

Another important ratio that involves accounts receivable is the **accounts receivable turnover ratio (AR turnover ratio)**. This ratio—net credit sales divided by average net accounts receivable—measures a firm's ability to collect the cash from its credit customers. The ratio tells how many times, on average, the process of selling on account and collecting the receivables is repeated during the period. Exhibit 7.12 shows the three ratios managers can use to evaluate liquidity and receivables.

Exhibit 7.13 shows information from two years' worth of financial statements for Hershey Foods and the calculation of the AR turnover ratio. The denominator of this ratio is the average of the beginning balance and ending balance of net accounts receivable. This particular ratio is useful for a firm to track over time to make sure receivables are being collected promptly.

> **Accounts receivable turnover ratio:** Net credit sales divided by average net accounts receivable; measures a firm's ability to collect the cash from its credit customers.

Exhibit 7.12

Three Liquidity Ratios Involving Accounts Receivable

Ratio	Description	Equation	When to Use
Current Ratio	Measure of liquidity	$\dfrac{\text{Total Current Assets}}{\text{Total Current Liabilities}}$	To evaluate a firm's ability to meet its short-term obligations
Quick Ratio or Acid-test Ratio	Strict measure of liquidity	$\dfrac{\text{Cash} + \text{Short-term Investments} + \text{Net Current Receivables}}{\text{Total Current Liabilities}}$	To evaluate quite conservatively a firm's ability to meet its short-term obligations
Accounts Receivable Turnover Ratio	Measure of rate of accounts receivable collections, another measure of liquidity	$\dfrac{\text{Net Credit Sales}}{\text{Average Net Accounts Receivable}}$	To measure how quickly a firm is collecting its receivables. Another indication of a firm's ability to meet its short-term obligations

Exhibit 7.13

Hershey Foods Corporation: Accounts Receivable Turnover Ratio

(in thousands)	December 31, 2004*	December 31, 2003	December 31, 2002
Receivables (net)	$408,930	$407,612	$370,976
Sales	$4,429,248	$4,172,551	
AR Turnover Ratio	10.85 times	10.72 times	

* Balance sheet amounts are as of the date shown, and sales are for the fiscal year ended on the date shown.

The accounts receivable (AR) turnover ratio equals credit sales divided by average net accounts receivable. Often, however, financial statements do not provide separate amounts for cash and credit sales, so we use total sales for the numerator. It's very important to be consistent in the calculation of ratios that are compared over time and from company to company. For example, if you use total sales to compute the AR turnover ratio at the end of this year, then you must also use total sales next year to have a basis for comparison.

Here's how we calculated the AR turnover ratio to be 10.85 times:

$$\frac{\$4,429,248}{(\$408,930 + \$407,612) \div 2} = \frac{\$4,429,248}{\$408,271} = 10.85 \text{ times}$$

If the average turnover of accounts receivable is 10.85 times, we can calculate how long it takes for Hershey Foods, on average, to collect its receivables. If we divide 365—the number of days in a year—by the AR turnover ratio, we will get the number of days it takes, on average, to collect its receivables. For the fiscal year ending (FYE) December 31, 2003, we will divide 365 days by 10.72 times = 34.05 days. That means that it takes a little over a month for Hershey Foods to collect its accounts receivable. For FYE 2004, we divided 365 by 10.85 = 33.64 days. Hershey Foods has slightly decreased its average number of days to collect its sales revenues, which is an improvement. Notice that the higher the AR turnover ratio (10.85 times vs. 10.72 times), the faster the firm is collecting its accounts receivable.

If we calculate the AR turnover ratio for a retail firm, the turnover ratio will be higher and the average number of days to collect for a sale will be lower than our calculations for a wholesale firm like Hershey Foods. That's because a wholesale firm extends credit to almost all customers and, therefore, does not have as many cash sales as a retail firm. When we use total sales as our numerator in the ratio, which include cash sales, we are slightly underestimating the time it takes to collect an account. For example, look at the information in Exhibit 7.14 for Books-A-Million, a retail firm.

The AR turnover ratio is:

$$\frac{\$460,159}{(\$7,271 + \$7,799) \div 2} = 61.07 \text{ times}$$

A retail firm will turn over its receivables very quickly. Remember that the total sales dollars includes cash sales.

Exhibit 7.14

Books-A-Million: Accounts Receivable and Sales

(Dollars in thousands)	AR at 1/31/04	AR at 2/1/03	Sales for FYE 1/31/04
	$7,271	$7,799	$460,159

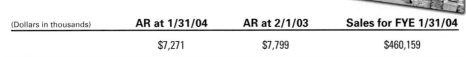

To get the average number of days to collect for a sale, we divide 365 days by 61.07, which is 5.98 days. That is significantly shorter than the average 33 days Hershey Foods takes to collect its credit sales! Most of the sales for Books-A-Million are cash, and the amount of credit sales is not disclosed separately. Using a sales amount that includes cash sales makes the AR turnover ratio much higher because it artificially inflates the numerator. Internally, managers will use only credit sales in the calculation of the AR turnover ratio. For external users, that information may not be available. Different industries and even different firms in the same industry may have very different AR turnover ratios. As you have learned, you must use ratio analysis carefully.

Identify the risks and controls associated with cash and receivables.

Business risk, control, & ethics

You've learned about two of the most important assets a firm has—cash and receivables. Now we're ready to resume our discussion about the way a firm makes sure the risks related to these assets are minimized. Remember that an important purpose of internal controls is to be sure a firm's assets are safeguarded and that the related financial records are accurate and reliable.

Earlier in the chapter, you learned about one of the most important controls a firm can have: segregation of duties. This control means that the person who is responsible for the record keeping related to an asset does not have physical custody or access to the asset.

In addition to segregation of duties, there are three more key controls that help a firm safeguard its assets and enhance the accuracy and reliability of its financial records: (1) clear assignment of responsibility for physical control of the assets, (2) specific procedures for documentation related to the assets, and (3) independent internal verification of the data. Let's look at each of these more closely as they relate to cash and accounts receivable.

Exhibit 7.15

Clear Assignment of Responsibility

Clear assignment of responsibility

The responsibility for safeguarding cash can be assigned to a variety of people in the firm. For example, in some retail stores, each cashier is responsible for safeguarding the cash in his register. At the end of the cashier's shift, the money is counted and the amount compared to the register's recorded sales. If the cashier is short by $10, it will be that cashier's responsibility to make up the $10 shortage. As shown in Exhibit 7.15, when a new cashier comes on duty, she will have her own cash drawer for which she is responsible.

Exhibit 7.16

Documentation Procedures

Specific procedures for documentation related to the assets

Documentation procedures are another critical control for cash and accounts receivable. Have you ever returned an item to a department store? You may have been asked to fill out a form with your name, address, and the reason for the return. One reason for this procedure, shown in Exhibit 7.16, is to provide documentation for the refund. Either a cash refund or a credit to your account, if your purchase was on account, must be accompanied by supporting documentation to help ensure that refunds are granted only for legitimate returns.

Independent internal verification of the data

Have you ever purchased something from a store that has a sign by the cash register that reads: IF YOU DO NOT GET A RECEIPT, YOUR PURCHASE IS FREE? That sign is a control to be sure that the cashier is properly recording all sales. The cashier will not be able to take your cash and put it in his pocket without ringing it up on the cash register to produce a receipt. Why? Because if he were to do that, you would ASK for a receipt and get your purchase free as well! You are helping the owners make sure they get their cash and that the sale is properly documented. Exhibit 7.17 gives an example of this type of control.

Control of cash is crucial for all firms. Exhibit 7.18 summarizes clues of potential cash-related fraud. Read about the special control issues related to cash in *Accounting in the News*.

Exhibit 7.17

Independent Internal Verification of Data

Exhibit 7.18

Red Flags for Cash-Related Fraud

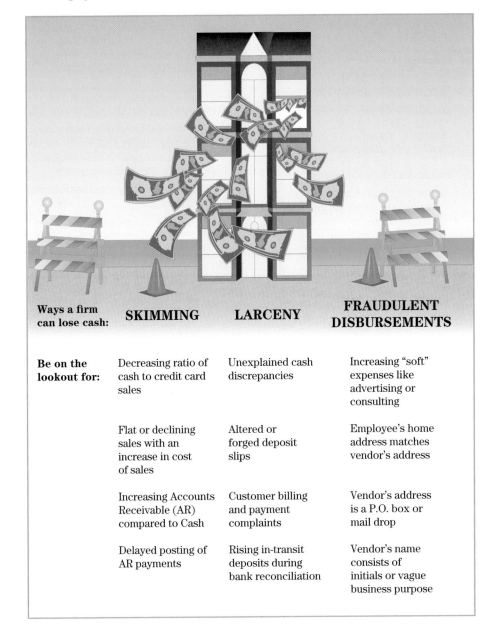

Ways a firm can lose cash:	SKIMMING	LARCENY	FRAUDULENT DISBURSEMENTS
Be on the lookout for:	Decreasing ratio of cash to credit card sales	Unexplained cash discrepancies	Increasing "soft" expenses like advertising or consulting
	Flat or declining sales with an increase in cost of sales	Altered or forged deposit slips	Employee's home address matches vendor's address
	Increasing Accounts Receivable (AR) compared to Cash	Customer billing and payment complaints	Vendor's address is a P.O. box or mail drop
	Delayed posting of AR payments	Rising in-transit deposits during bank reconciliation	Vendor's name consists of initials or vague business purpose

Accounting in the NEWS

Risk and Control

Association of Certified Fraud Examiners Report Cash Is Easy to Steal

The Association of Certified Fraud Examiners (ACFE), in its *2004 Report to the Nation on Occupational Fraud and Abuse*, reported that the majority of asset misappropriation involved cash. The reason is obvious—cash is easy to conceal and transport, and it has an immediate and known value. There are three main types of cash embezzlement: skimming, larceny, and fraudulent disbursements. Out of 508 cases in the study, 87% involved cash. According to Joseph T. Wells, the founder of the ACFE, the three main ways cash is misappropriated are:

1. Skimming: "the removal of cash prior to its entry into the accounting system."
2. Larceny: "the removal of cash from the organization after it has been entered into the accounting records."
3. Fraudulent disbursements: "can be subdivided into at least six specific types: check tampering, false

register disbursements, billing schemes, payroll schemes, expense reimbursement schemes and other fraudulent disbursements."

To protect itself from embezzlement, Wells suggests a firm watch for the following:

Skimming

- A decreasing ratio of cash to credit card sales.
- Flat or declining sales with increasing cost of sales.
- Increasing Accounts Receivable compared with Cash.
- Delayed posting of accounts-receivable payments.

Larceny

- Unexplained cash discrepancies.
- Altered or forged deposit slips.
- Customer billing and payment complaints.
- Rising "in transit" deposits during bank reconciliations.

Fraudulent disbursements

- Increasing "soft" expenses such as consulting or advertising.
- Employee home address matching a vendor's address.
- Vendor address is a post office box or mail drop.

Cash is an easy asset to steal. This article lists several ways for a company to identify theft.

- Vendor name consisting of initials or having a vague business purpose. (Employees often use their own initials when setting up dummy companies; for example, "JTW Enterprises").
- Excessive voided, missing, or destroyed checks.

Q What are the three main types of cash embezzlement? Give an example of each based on news stories you have read or heard about.

A Skimming, larceny, and fraudulent disbursements.

Sources: Association of Certified Fraud Examiners, *2004 Report to the Nation on Occupational Fraud and Abuse,* www.cfenet.com/resources/rttn.asp; Joseph T. Wells, "Enemies Within," *Journal of Accountancy* (December, 2001).

YOU make the call:

How will the bankruptcy of a major customer affect Hershey Foods' financial statements?

If you read the notes to the financial statements, you would find that Hershey Foods added an additional $5 million to its Allowance for Uncollectible Accounts at December 31, 2003, to cover the possible losses from the bankrupt customer, Fleming Company. This addition means that Hershey Foods' Net Income for 2003 was lower by $5 million due to the client's bankruptcy. What about actually writing off the account? By the end of 2004, the bankruptcy was settled. In 2004, when it wrote off any loss related to Fleming Company, Hershey did not have any expense. Fleming's account was written off against the Allowance for Uncollectible Accounts. We don't know the details of the settlement, but we do know that Hershey made sure the Allowance for Uncollectible Accounts did not have anything left for the Fleming account at December 31, 2004. Here's what the company said in its notes to the financial statements at December 31, 2004:

> Receivables, as shown on the Consolidated Balance Sheets, were net of allowances and anticipated discounts of $21.1 million and $16.5 million as of December 31, 2003, and 2002, respectively. The higher amount as of December 31, 2003 was principally related to an increase of $5.0 million to cover estimated exposure to the bankruptcy of Fleming Company, Inc., announced on April 3, 2003.

Let's Take a Test Drive

Real World Problem:
Hershey Foods Corporation

Suppose Hershey Foods Corporation has acquired several new customers during the fiscal year ended December 31, 2007. The firm's accountant has to review the year's transactions, make sure they have been properly recorded, and then decide on an adequate allowance for uncollectible accounts. Because receivables are a significant asset, companies like Hershey Foods are careful to record all amounts due from their customers and to make estimates of uncollectible accounts that are as accurate as possible.

Concepts

The most important concept related to accounts receivable is that Hershey Foods must record its receivables at their net realizable value (NRV). Recall that the expression *to realize* means to actually get the money. The NRV of accounts receivable is the amount Hershey Foods actually expects to receive. Why doesn't the firm expect to collect all of its receivables? A firm like Hershey sets its credit policies in such a way that there are almost always a few customers who don't pay. If the firm were to set a credit policy to eliminate any bad debts, it would be so restrictive that the firm would lose a significant number of sales. Having bad debts is part of doing business, and a firm designs its credit policy to strike an acceptable balance between maximizing sales and minimizing bad debts.

Extending credit

As Hershey Foods adjusts its accounting records to get ready for the preparation of financial statements, the firm's accounting department will study the firm's credit sales and patterns of payment by its credit customers. With this information, the firm will record its estimated bad debts for the period so that the Bad Debts Expense will match the Sales on the income statement for the year.

To summarize, the most important points about accounts receivable are: (1) the value on the balance sheet at fiscal year-end will be the net realizable value (NRV) of accounts receivable, and (2) the firm will estimate bad debts for the period to match them with the period's sales and to book the reduction in Accounts Receivable to reduce it to its NRV. The journal entry is a debit to Bad Debts Expense and a credit to the contra-asset called the Allowance for Uncollectible Accounts.

Mechanics

Suppose the transactions that follow reflect the activities of Hershey Foods Corporation during its fiscal year ended December 31, 2007.

1. Sold $900,000 of merchandise with the terms 2/10, n/30.

2. Collected payment for 80% of the sales within the discount period.

3. Accepted a three-month note from Nature's Grocery Store Chain for $8,000 on October 1, 2007 (due on January 1, 2008), with an interest rate of 6%, in payment of its $8,000 outstanding balance in Accounts Receivable.

4. Had $100,000 of credit card sales. (These were made using American Express—AMEX— business accounts, and Hershey Foods paid a 2% service charge to AMEX for these transactions.)

5. Wrote off a bad account for $4,000 after the bankruptcy court approved a reorganization plan for one of its struggling customers.

6. Incurred operating expenses, including cost of goods sold, of $375,000, paid in cash. (*Note:* Because the focus is on Accounts Receivable in this problem, simply record this transaction as a debit to Operating Expenses and a credit to Cash. How the firm actually records this depends on its choice of periodic or perpetual inventory, which is not addressed in this problem.)

Instructions

1. Post each of the transactions to T-accounts. The firm started the year with a balance of $150,000 in Accounts Receivable and a balance of $4,500 in the Allowance for Uncollectible Accounts.

2. Make the adjusting entry to book bad debts expense. Hershey Foods uses the allowance method of accounting for uncollectible accounts, based on a percentage of the ending balance in Accounts Receivable. (Use the same percentage—3%—the firm used to calculate the bad debts expense for 2006. Also, be sure to accrue interest receivable on the note in transaction 3 above.)

3. Prepare an income statement for the year ended December 31, 2007.

Solution

The journal entries are labeled with the transaction number from the given information. The entries labeled "Adj." are the two adjusting entries: one to record the period's bad debts expense and the other to accrue interest on the note receivable.

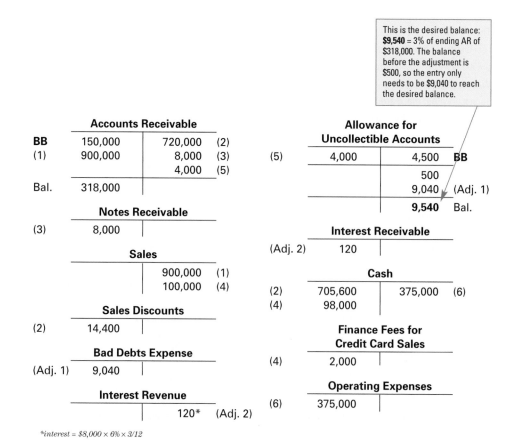

This is the desired balance: **$9,540** = 3% of ending AR of $318,000. The balance before the adjustment is $500, so the entry only needs to be $9,040 to reach the desired balance.

interest = $8,000 × 6% × 3/12

Hershey Foods Corporation
Income Statement (fictitious)
For the Year Ended December 31, 2007

Sales revenue	$1,000,000
Less sales discounts	(14,400)
Net sales	985,600
Operating expenses	(386,040)
Other income (expenses)	120
Net income	$599,680

Operating expenses include: $375,000 from the operating expenses account, $9,040 bad debts expense, and $2,000 credit card fees.

Rapid Review

1. **Calculate bad debts expense and explain how a firm evaluates and reports accounts receivable.** If a firm has significant uncollectible accounts, the firm must estimate the amount of those bad debts in the same period the sales are recognized. The estimated Bad Debts Expense is recorded and Accounts Receivable is reduced with the use of a contra-asset called the *Allowance for Uncollectible Accounts*. The amount of bad debts expense may be estimated using either credit sales for the period or the balance in Accounts Receivable at the end of the period. Only if uncollectible accounts are insignificant can a firm use an alternative method called the *direct write-off method*. Using this method, bad accounts are written off as they are identified. No estimate is made in advance.

2. **Account for and report notes receivable.** Notes receivable are recorded as either short or long-term assets, depending on how soon the notes will be collected. Notes receivable involve interest, which must be accrued at the end of the accounting period if the interest has not been collected.

3. **Explain how a firm controls cash and prepares a bank reconciliation.** Cash is controlled by restricting access to the asset and enforcing segregation of duties between record keeping and physical control of the cash. A significant control is the bank reconciliation. Preparing a *bank reconciliation* requires taking the firm's general ledger Cash account and reconciling it with the monthly bank statement.

4. **Describe how cash is reported on the financial statements.** Cash is almost always the first asset listed on the balance sheet and includes very liquid, short-term investments called *cash equivalents*. The statement of cash flows is the financial statement devoted to explaining the change in the Cash account from one balance sheet date to the next.

5. **Analyze a firm's accounts receivable with ratio analysis.** The most usual ratio used to analyze accounts receivable is the *accounts receivable (AR) turnover ratio*. This ratio, defined as Sales divided by average Accounts Receivable, measures how quickly a firm collects the money for its credit sales.

$$\text{Accounts Receivable turnover ratio} = \frac{\text{Net Credit Sales}}{\text{Average Net Accounts Receivable}}$$

6. **Identify the risks and controls associated with cash and receivables.** Cash and receivables are controlled by segregation of duties, clear assignment of responsibility for the asset, proper documentation, and periodic review and independent verification of the data.

Key Terms

Accounts receivable, p. 330
Accounts receivable
  turnover ratio, p. 352
Aging schedule, p. 333
Allowance for uncollectible
  accounts, p. 332

Allowance method, p. 331
Bad debts expense, p. 331
Bank reconciliation, p. 343
Bank statement, p. 343
Cash equivalents, p. 351
Deposits in transit, p. 345

Direct write-off method,
  p. 340
Maker, p. 341
Outstanding checks, p. 345
Payee, p. 341
Promissory note, p. 341

Have You Increased Your Business IQ?

Answer these questions to find out.

1. Using the allowance method for estimating bad debts expense is an example of
   a. historical cost.
   b. matching.
   c. going concern.
   d. a new requirement of Sarbanes-Oxley.
2. An aging schedule shows a firm's
   a. receivables categorized by size.
   b. receivables categorized by interest rate.
   c. fixed assets arranged by age.
   d. receivables categorized by age.
3. The person who makes the bank deposits should
   a. also do the bank reconciliation.
   b. not work for the firm.
   c. not update the firm's cash records when making the deposit.
   d. be paid extra for the risk involved.
4. Cash equivalents are
   a. current accounts receivable.
   b. highly liquid investments.
   c. current assets like inventory that can be quickly turned into cash.
   d. All of these answers are correct.
5. When a firm uses the allowance method for estimating bad debts expense, what happens to net Accounts Receivable when a specific customer's account is written off?
   a. Nothing
   b. It increases
   c. It decreases
   d. Cannot be determined

Now, check your answers.

1. b   2. d   3. c   4. b   5. a

- If you answered all five questions correctly, you've increased your business IQ by studying this chapter. It doesn't mean you've mastered all of the accounting concepts in the chapter. It simply means that you understand some of the general business concepts presented in this chapter.
- If you answered 2 to 4 questions correctly, you've made some progress but your business IQ has plenty of room to grow. You might want to skim over the chapter again.
- If you answered 0 or 1 question correctly, you can do more to improve your business IQ. Better study the chapter again.

Questions

1. Describe how accounts receivable arise. What does the balance in Accounts Receivable represent?
2. How do trade receivables differ from other receivables?
3. Define net realizable value, book value, and carrying value as they relate to Accounts Receivable.
4. Explain the difference between the direct write-off method and the allowance method. Which method is preferred and why?
5. If a company uses the allowance method, what effect does writing off a specific account have on income?

6. Describe the two allowance methods used to estimate the amount of Bad Debts Expense that appears on the income statement.
7. Which method of calculating the allowance focuses on the income statement? Explain.
8. Which method of calculating the allowance focuses on the balance sheet? Explain.
9. What is the difference between accounts receivable and notes receivable?
10. Explain how the segregation of duties serves a major control for safeguarding cash.
11. What is a bank reconciliation and what does it determine?
12. What are two common adjustments made to the balance per bank statement?
13. Describe two common adjustments made to the balance per books.
14. Once the bank reconciliation is complete, which adjustments are recorded in the accounting records?
15. What does true cash balance refer to?
16. Identify and explain the financial statements on which cash is reported.
17. Explain why it is important to have physical control of cash.
18. What is the formula to calculate the accounts receivable turnover ratio, and what does the formula measure?
19. How does a firm use its accounts receivable turnover ratio to determine the average number of days it takes to collect its accounts receivables?

Multiple Choice

Use the following information to answer multiple-choice questions 1 and 2: At the end of the year, before any adjustments are made, the accounting records for Sutton Company show a balance of $100,000 in Accounts Receivable. The Allowance for Uncollectible Accounts has a credit balance of $2,000. (This means last year's estimate was too large by $2,000.) The company uses accounts receivable to estimate bad debts expense. An analysis of accounts receivable results in an estimate of $27,000 of uncollectible accounts.

1. The Bad Debts Expense on the income statement for the year would be
   a. $27,000
   b. $25,000
   c. $23,000
   d. $29,000
2. Net realizable value of the receivables on the year-end balance sheet would be
   a. $100,000
   b. $75,000
   c. $73,000
   d. $77,000
3. Suppose a firm uses the percentage of sales method for estimating bad debts expense. The firm has credit sales for the year of $200,000 and a balance of $80,000 in Accounts Receivable. The firm estimates that 2% of its credit sales will never be collected. What is the bad debts expense for the year?
   a. $1,600
   b. $2,000
   c. $4,000
   d. $3,600

Use the following information for the next four questions. Fred's Supply Store just received its monthly bank statement from Local Street Bank. The bank gives a balance of $45,000. Fred's accounting clerk has calculated that outstanding checks amount to $20,000. Fred's Supply Store made a deposit of $5,000 on the last day of the month, and it was not included on the bank statement. Bank service fees, not yet recorded on the store's books, were shown on the statement as $35. The bank statement also included an NSF check returned from a new customer in the amount of $250.

4. What is the store's true cash balance at the end of the month?
   a. $25,000
   b. $30,000
   c. $29,715
   d. $29,750
5. How should outstanding checks be treated on the bank reconciliation?
   a. They should be deducted from the balance per books.
   b. They should be added to the balance per books.
   c. They should be deducted from the balance per bank.
   d. They should be added to the balance per bank.
6. Which items would need to be recorded in a journal entry for Fred's Supply Store's accounting records?
   a. Outstanding checks and the deposit in transit.
   b. NSF check.
   c. Bank service fee.
   d. Both NSF check and bank service fee.

7. What was the Cash balance in the general ledger before Fred's Supply Store began the bank reconciliation?
   a. $30,285
   b. $30,250
   c. $45,250
   d. $25,285

8. Scott Company uses the allowance method of accounting for bad debts. During May, the company found out that one of its largest customers filed for bankruptcy. If Scott Company decides to write off the customer's account, what effect will doing that have on Scott Company's net income for the period?
   a. Bad debts expense will decrease income.
   b. Writing off the receivable will decrease income.
   c. Both a. and b. will happen.
   d. There is no effect on net income.

Use the following information for the next two questions. Troutwig Company uses the allowance method to account for bad debts expense. The firm routinely estimates that 5% of its ending balance in Accounts Receivable will be uncollectible. At year-end, when Troutwig's accountant is ready to make the adjusting entry to book the year's bad debts expense, the balance in Accounts Receivable is $500,000 (debit balance) and the balance in the Allowance for Uncollectible Accounts is $1,000 (credit balance).

9. How much bad debts expense should Troutwig's accountant record?
   a. $25,000
   b. $26,000
   c. $24,000
   d. $5,000

10. What is the net realizable value of Accounts Receivable on the year-end balance sheet?
    a. $475,000
    b. $476,000
    c. $474,000
    d. $500,000

Short Exercises

LO 1

SE7-1. Determine bad debts expense; direct write-off method.

Quality Autoparts Company sells merchandise to auto repair shops and car dealerships. Quality has always used the direct write-off method of accounting for bad debts because of very tight credit policies and predominately cash sales. During 2006, credit sales were $520,450 and the year-end balance in Accounts Receivable was $173,500. Quality estimates that about half of one percent of the accounts receivable will not be collected. Unfortunately, just prior to the end of 2006, one of Quality's best customers filed for bankruptcy and has informed Quality that it will not be able to pay its outstanding balance of $23,000. That amount, however, is included in Quality's $173,500 Accounts Receivable balance. How should Quality record the $23,000 in its accounting records? That is, what amount of Bad Debts Expense will Quality recognize on the income statement for 2006?

LO 1

SE7-2. Determine bad debts expense; percentage of sales method.

Beret and Sons Furniture has a liberal credit policy and has been experiencing a high rate of uncollectible accounts. The company estimates that 5% of credit sales become bad debts. Due to the significance of this amount, the company uses the allowance method for accounting for bad debts. During 2006, credit sales amounted to $430,000. The year-end Accounts Receivable balance was $192,000. What was the Bad Debts Expense for the year?

LO 1

SE7-3. Determine bad debts expense; percentage of sales method.

The 2005 year-end unadjusted trial balance shows:

Accounts Receivable (AR)	$50,000
Allowance for Uncollectible Accounts	$1,000 credit
Net Sales	$200,000

Using the percentage of sales method, the company estimates 2% of sales will become uncollectible. What is the bad debts expense for 2005? What will be the net realizable value of Accounts Receivable on the year-end balance sheet?

SE7-4. Determine bad debts expense; accounts receivable method.   LO 1

On January 1, 2007, a company's Accounts Receivable balance was $8,900 and the Allowance for Uncollectible Accounts balance was $600 (credit). This information came from the December 31, 2006 balance sheet. During 2007, the company reported $77,000 of credit sales and wrote off $400 of specific receivables as uncollectible. Cash collections of receivable were $69,000 for the year. The company estimates that 3% of the year-end accounts receivable will be uncollectible. What is bad debts expense for the year ended December 31, 2007?

SE7-5. Determine bad debts expense; accounts receivable method.   LO 1

At the end of the year, before any adjustments are made, the accounting records for Briggs Company show a balance of $200,000 in Accounts Receivable. The Allowance for Uncollectible Accounts has a credit balance of $2,000. The company uses accounts receivable to estimate bad debts expense. An analysis of accounts receivable accounts results in an estimate of $30,000 of uncollectible accounts. What is Bad Debts Expense for the year? What is the net realizable value of Accounts Receivable on the year-end balance sheet?

SE7-6. Determine bad debts expense; percentage of accounts receivable method.   LO 1

Bett Company had the following balances at year-end prior to recording any adjustments:

Credit Sales	$160,000
Accounts Receivable	$30,000
Allowance for Uncollectible Accounts	$100 debit balance

Following completion of an aging analysis, the accountant for Bett Company estimated that $1,100 of the receivables would be uncollectible. What amount of Bad Debts Expense would Bett show on the year's income statement? What information would be disclosed on the balance sheet?

SE7-7. Determine bad debts expense; accounts receivable method.   LO 1

The 2006 year-end unadjusted trial balance shows:

Accounts Receivable (AR)	$50,000
Allowance for Uncollectible Accounts	$500 credit (excess from last year's estimate)
Net Sales	$400,000

Using the accounts receivable method, the company estimates $4,000 of ending accounts receivable will be uncollectible. What is the bad debts expense for 2006? What will be the net realizable value of Accounts Receivable on the year-end balance sheet?

SE7-8. Write off uncollectible accounts.   LO 1

Chastain's Upholstery has determined that Global Builders' Accounts Receivable balance of $5,500 is uncollectible. Prepare the journal entry to write off the account using (a) the direct write-off method and (b) the allowance method.

SE7-9. Analyze notes receivable.   LO 2

On May 1, 2005, Bob's Music renegotiated its overdue accounts balance of $2,500 with Spectrum Electronics by signing a 60-day promissory note at an interest rate of 9%. What is the principal amount of the note? What is the due date of the note? How much will Bob's Music repay on the due date of the note?

SE7-10. Analyze bank reconciliation items.   LO 3

For each item below, indicate whether or not the balance per books should be adjusted. For each item that affects the balance per books, indicate whether the item should be added to (+) or subtracted from (−) the balance per books.

Item	Balance per Books Adjusted?	+/−
Outstanding checks	*No*	*n/a*
Service charge by bank		
NSF check from customer		
Deposits in transit		
Error made by the bank		
Note receivable collected by the bank		

LO 3   **SE7-11. Analyze cash reconciliation items.**
For each item below, indicate whether or not the balance per bank should be adjusted. For each item that affects the balance per bank, indicate whether the item should be added to (+) or subtracted from (−) the balance per bank.

Item	Balance per Bank Adjusted?	+/−
Outstanding checks	*Yes*	—
Service charge by bank		
NSF check from customer		
Deposits in transit		
Error made by the bank		
Note receivable collected by the bank		

LO 3   **SE7-12. Calculate the true cash balance.**
At March 31 OAS Company has this information available about its cash account:

Cash balance per bank	$6,000
Outstanding checks	$1,500
Deposits in transit	$1,200
Bank service charge	$100

Determine the true Cash balance per bank at March 31.

LO 3   **SE7-13. Calculate the true cash balance.**
On the September bank statement, the ending balance as of September 30 was $9,550.48. The Cash balance in the general ledger was $10,053.57. Consider the following information:

Outstanding checks	$1,876.67
Interest earned on the account	$32.18
NSF check from G. Murphy	$391.55
Deposits in transit	$2,020.39

What is the company's true cash balance at September 30?

LO 3   **SE7-14. Analyze errors in a bank reconciliation.**
Datatech's accountant wrote a check to a supplier for $1,050, but erroneously recorded it on the company's books as $1,500. She discovered this when she saw the monthly bank statement and noticed that the check had cleared the bank for $1,050. How would this be handled in bank reconciliation? Would Datatech need to make any adjustments to its accounting records?

LO 5   **SE7-15. Calculate accounts receivable turnover ratio.**
Candid Company had the following balances:

	December 31, 2007	December 31, 2006
Receivables, net	$ 325,000	$ 285,000
Sales (all credit)	$1,757,000	$1,248,700

Calculate the accounts receivable turnover ratio for 2007. On average, how many days does it take Candid Company to collect its accounts receivable?

Exercise Set A

LO 1   **E7-1A. Determine bad debts expense; percentage of sales method.**
The Beautiful Bow Company uses the allowance method to account for bad debts. During 2006, the company recorded $800,000 in credit sales. At the end of 2006, account balances were: Accounts Receivable, $120,000; Allowance for Uncollectible Accounts, $3,000 (credit).

If bad debts expense is estimated to be 3% of credit sales, how much bad debts expense will be on the year-end income statement?

E7-2A. Analyze effects of accounts receivable transactions: percentage of sales method. LO 1

At the beginning of 2008, Darcy's Floor Coverings had the following account balances: Accounts Receivable, $325,000 and Allowance for Uncollectible Accounts, $7,500 (credit). During the year, credit sales were $825,000, sales returns and allowances were $31,750, and $10,000 of specific customer accounts were written off. Collections on accounts receivable were $622,000. At year-end, Darcy's Floor Coverings estimated that 5% of net credit sales were uncollectible.

a. Record the necessary journal entries for 2008.
b. What is the net realizable value of Accounts Receivable at year-end?
c. What amount of bad debts expense will appear on the income statement for 2008?

E7-3A. Determine bad debts expense; accounts receivable method. LO 1

A company started the year with Accounts Receivable of $20,000 and an Allowance for Uncollectible Accounts of $2,500 (credit). During the year, sales (all on account) were $80,000 and cash collections for sales amounted to $77,000. Also, $2,400 worth of uncollectible accounts were specifically identified and written off. Then, at year-end, the company estimated that 5% of ending Accounts Receivable would be uncollectible. Answer the questions below.

a. What is the journal entry to record bad debts expense?
b. What amount will be shown on the year-end income statement for bad debts expense?
c. What is the balance in the Allowance for Uncollectible Accounts after all the adjustments have been made?

E7-4A. Determine bad debts expense; accounts receivable method. LO 1

Havana Honda uses the allowance method for bad debts and adjusts the allowance for uncollectible accounts to a desired amount based on an aging of accounts receivable. At the beginning of 2007, the Allowance for Uncollectible Accounts had a credit balance of $18,000. During 2007, credit sales totaled $480,000 and receivables of $14,000 were written off. The year-end aging indicated that a $21,000 allowance for uncollectible accounts was required. What is the bad debts expense for 2007? What information will be disclosed on the balance sheet at year-end? What information does this provide someone who is evaluating Havana Honda's annual performance?

E7-5A. Analyze effects of accounts receivable transactions: accounts receivable method. LO 1

Western Wear Corporation began 2006 with Accounts Receivable of $1,240,000 and a balance in the Allowance for Uncollectible Accounts of $36,000. During 2006, credit sales totaled $5,190,000 and cash collected from customers totaled $5,380,000. Actual write offs of specific accounts receivable in 2006 were $33,000. At year-end, an accounts receivable aging schedule indicated a desired allowance of $32,300.

a. Enter the amounts described in the Accounts Receivable T-account for 2006.
b. What is the net realizable value of Accounts Receivable at year-end?
c. What is the Bad Debts Expense for the year 2006?

E7-6A. Analyze and record notes receivable. LO 2

On October 1, 2009, ACME Athletic Equipment Company purchased athletic equipment on account for $10,500 from Sporting Goods Unlimited with terms 2/10, net 30. (ACME uses perpetual inventory so it will record the purchase directly to its Inventory account. Sporting Goods Unlimited uses periodic inventory, so cost of goods sold will not be recorded until the firm's year end.) On November 1, ACME renegotiated its account by signing a 90-day promissory note, at an interest rate of 10%. Prepare the journal entries that would be recorded on October 1 and November 1 for both companies. Determine the due date of the note and prepare the journal entry to record the collection of the note on the books of both companies. (Assume both firms have a June 30 year end, so no interest has been accrued by either company.)

LO 3

E7-7A. Prepare a bank reconciliation.

The bank statement for David's Landscaping had an ending balance as of February 28 of $38,334.96. Also listed on the statement was a service charge for $16. Check No. 1248 that David's wrote to pay for equipment purchased February 25 had not cleared the bank yet—the amount was $7,250. Deposits in transit were $4,115.73. David's bank collected a $1,100 note for the firm in February. After reviewing the bank statement and cancelled checks, David's discovered that the bank mistakenly deducted $297.15 from its account on a check that was written by David's Lighting.

Calculate the true cash balance as of February 28.

LO 3 **E7-8A. Prepare a bank reconciliation.**

The advertising firm, Carolyn & Co., had the following information available concerning its Cash account for the month of July:

Balance per Carolyn & Co. books, July 31	$18,280.54
Outstanding checks	6,440.29
NSF check from customer	2,800.00
Note collected by bank	3,000.00
Deposits in transit	5,860.50
Miscellaneous fees:	
Charge for collection of note	25.00
Charge for checks	62.50
Interest earned on bank account	421.38

Calculate the true cash balance as of July 31.

LO 3 **E7-9A. Prepare a bank reconciliation.**

Prepare a bank reconciliation for Jay Gordon's Brake Shop for the month of November using the following information:

Balance per First National Bank statement at Nov. 30	$14,003.90
Outstanding checks	5,765.44
NSF checks from customers	366.71
Deposits in transit	3,542.26
Interest earned on account	184.56
Service charge	30.00
Cash balance per Jay Gordon's records (at Nov. 30)	11,992.87

Give the journal entries to record any needed adjustments to the general ledger's Cash balance. What is the net effect on net income? Will net income be increased or decreased? By what amount?

LO 3 **E7-10A. Prepare a bank reconciliation.**

Prepare a bank reconciliation for Cheri's Bakery using the following information:

Company's cash account balance, March 31	$5,599.20
Bank statement ending balance, March 31	3,904.37
Deposits in transit	2,504.57
Outstanding checks:	
No. 3941	633.15
No. 3956	194.59

Cheri found an error in the books: Check No. 3928 for $142.60 was correctly deducted from the bank account, but was mistakenly recorded in the books as $124.60.

LO 3 **E7-11A. Identify and correct errors in a bank reconciliation.**

Jane Johnson is having trouble with the bank reconciliation at March 31. Her reconciliation is shown below:

Cash balance per books	$4,015
Less: Deposits in transit	(590)
Add: Outstanding checks	730
Adjusted balance per books	$4,245
Cash balance per bank	$3,700
Add: NSF check	430
Less: Bank service charge	(25)
Adjusted balance per bank	$4,105

a. Identify the errors Jane made in the preparation of the bank reconciliation.
b. What is the correct cash balance?
c. Prepare the adjusting journal entries needed to update the general ledger's Cash account.

E7-12A. Calculate the accounts receivable turnover ratio.   LO 5

Using the data from E7-2A, calculate the accounts receivable turnover ratio for 2008. On average, how many days does it take Darcy's Floor Coverings to collect its accounts receivable?

E7-13A. Risk and control.   LO 6

Why would a firm offer customers a free purchase if the customer is not offered a receipt?

E7-14A. Risk and control.   LO 6

Give two examples of physical controls of cash in a retail store like Target.

Exercise Set B

> Your professor may ask you to complete selected "Group B" exercises and problems using Prentice Hall Grade Assist (**PHGA**). PHGA is an online tool that can help you master the chapter's topics by providing multiple variations of exercises and problems. You can rework these exercises and problems—each time with new data—as many times as you need, with immediate feedback and grading.

E7-1B. Determine bad debts expense; percentage of sales method.   LO 1

Extreme Sport uses the allowance method to account for bad debts. During 2007, the company recorded $650,000 in credit sales. At the end of 2007, account balances were: Accounts Receivable, $185,000; Allowance for Uncollectible Accounts, $5,000 (credit). If bad debts expense is estimated to be 4% of credit sales, how much Bad Debts Expense will be on the year-end income statement?

E7-2B. Analyze effects of accounts receivable transactions: percentage of sales method.   LO 1

At the beginning of 2009, Runnels' Bicycle Shop had the following account balances: Accounts Receivable, $285,000 and Allowance for Uncollectible Accounts, $8,250 (credit). During the year, credit sales were $965,000, sales returns and allowances were $18,250, and $5,750 of specific customer accounts were written off. Cash collections on accounts receivable amounted to $819,000. At year-end, Darcy's estimated that 6% of net credit sales were uncollectible.

a. Record the necessary journal entries for 2009.
b. What is the net realizable value of Accounts Receivable at year-end?
c. What amount of Bad Debts Expense will appear on the income statement for 2009?

E7-3B. Determine bad debts expense; accounts receivable method.   LO 1

A company started the year with Accounts Receivable of $15,000 and an Allowance for Uncollectible Accounts of $3,500. During the year, sales (all on account) were $110,000 and cash collections for sales amounted to $105,000. Also, $2,000 worth of uncollectible accounts were specifically identified and written off. Then, at year-end, the company estimates that 15% of ending accounts receivable will be uncollectible. Answer the questions below:

a. What is the journal entry to record bad debts expense?
b. What amount will be shown on the year-end income statement for Bad Debts Expense?
c. What is the balance in the Allowance for Uncollectible Accounts after all adjustments have been made?

E7-4B. Determine bad debts expense; accounts receivable method.   LO 1

Panama City Toyota uses the allowance method for bad debts and adjusts the Allowance for Uncollectible Accounts to a desired amount based on an aging of accounts receivable. At the beginning of 2009, the Allowance for Uncollectible Accounts had a credit balance of $15,000. During 2009, credit sales totaled $530,000 and receivables of $12,000 were written off. The year-end aging indicated that a $19,000 allowance for uncollectible accounts was required. What is the bad debts expense for 2009? What information will be disclosed on the balance sheet at year-end? What information does this provide someone who is evaluating Panama City Toyota's annual performance?

LO 1   **E7-5B. Analyze effects of accounts receivable transactions: accounts receivable method.**

Designer Jean Industries began 2008 with Accounts Receivable of $1,650,000 and a balance in the Allowance for Uncollectible Accounts of $26,000. During 2008, credit sales totaled $7,290,000 and cash collected from customers totaled $8,280,000. Actual write offs of specific accounts receivable in 2008 were $23,000. At end of the year, an accounts receivable aging schedule indicated a required allowance of $27,500. No accounts receivable previously written off were collected.

a. Enter the amounts described in the Accounts Receivable T-account for 2008.
b. What is the net realizable value of accounts receivable at year-end?
c. What is the bad debts expense for the year 2008?

LO 2   **E7-6B. Analyze and record notes receivable.**

On April 1, 2008, Tropical Aquatics purchased aquariums and equipment on account, for $25,000 from Tanks In All Shapes & Sizes with terms 3/15, net 30. On May 1, Tropical Aquatics renegotiated its accounts by signing a 60-day promissory note, at an interest rate of 8%. Prepare the journal entries that would be recorded on April 1 and May 1 for both companies. Assume Tropical Aquatics uses a perpetual inventory system, so the firm will record the purchase directly to its Inventory account. Tanks, in contrast, uses a periodic inventory system, so no adjustments will be made to cost of goods sold or to inventory until the end of the year. Determine the due date of the note and prepare the journal entry to record the collection of the note on the books of both companies.

LO 3   **E7-7B. Prepare a bank reconciliation.**

The bank statement for Rodney's Lawn Maintenance had an ending balance as of March 31 of $25,450.85. Also listed on the statement was a service charge for $21. Check No. 1825 that Rodney's wrote to pay for equipment purchased March 30 had not cleared the bank yet—the amount was $5,415. Deposits in transit were $7,850.25. Rodney's bank collected a $1,275 note for the firm in March. After reviewing the bank statement and cancelled checks, Rodney's discovered that the bank mistakenly deducted $1,875.93 from the firm's account on a check that was written by Rogers's Lawn Maintenance.

Calculate the true cash balance as of March 31.

LO 3   **E7-8B. Prepare a bank reconciliation.**

The marketing firm Razzle & Dazzle had the following information available concerning its Cash account for the month of May:

Balance per Razzle & Dazzle books, May 31	$15,375.21
Outstanding checks	8,720.85
NSF check from customer	1,650.00
Note and interest collected by bank	4,650.00
Deposits in transit	8,215.50
Miscellaneous fees:	
Charge for collection of note	75.00
Charge for checks	32.50
Interest earned on bank account	84.62

Calculate the true cash balance as of May 31.

LO 3   **E7-9B. Prepare a bank reconciliation.**

Prepare a bank reconciliation for Bobbi's Burger Barn for the month of June 30 using the following information:

Balance per USA National Bank statement at June 30	$15,023.05
Outstanding checks	4,215.83
NSF checks from customer	250.68
Deposits in transit	2,452.87
Interest revenue	251.32
Service charge	15.00
Cash balance per Bobbi's records at June 30	13,274.45

Give the journal entries to record any needed adjustments to the general ledger's cash balance. What is the net effect on net income? Will net income be increased or decreased? By what amount?

E7-10B. Prepare a bank reconciliation.   LO 3
Prepare a bank reconciliation for Randy's Toy Box using the following information:

Company's cash account balance, August 31	$6,500.00
Bank statement ending balance, August 31	5,100.44
Deposits in transit	2,504.57
Outstanding checks:	
No. 4051	1,052.15
No. 4056	25.59

Error found in Randy's books—Check No. 4052 for $825.69 was correctly deducted from the bank account but was mistakenly recorded in the books as $852.96.

E7-11B. Identify and correct errors in a bank reconciliation.   LO 3
Brettina Aguilera is having trouble with the bank reconciliation at March 31. Her reconciliation is shown below:

Cash balance per bank	$7,578.65
Add: NSF check	305.00
Less: Bank service charge	31.00
Adjusted balance per bank	$8,824.25
Cash balance per books	$9,362.65
Less: Deposits in transit	1,875.00
Add: Outstanding checks	427.00
Adjusted balance per books	$7,959.65

a. Identify the errors Brettina made in the preparation of the bank reconciliation.
b. What is the correct Cash balance?
c. Prepare the adjusting journal entries needed to update the general ledger Cash account.

E7-12B. Calculate the accounts receivable turnover ratio.   LO 5
Using the data from E7-2B, calculate the accounts receivable turnover ratio for 2009. On average, how many days does it take Runnels' Bicycle Shop to collect its accounts receivable?

E7-13B. Risk and control.   LO 3, 6
Name three ways a firm can lose cash. How could these frauds be detected?

E7-14B. Risk and control.   LO 3, 6
Explain why it is so crucial for a firm to have good controls over its cash.

Problem Set A

P7-1A. Analyze effects of accounts receivable transactions: percentage of sales method.   LO 1, 5
Evaluate the following scenarios, assuming both companies use the percentage of sales method for estimating bad debts expense:

1. At year end, Nash Company has Accounts Receivable of $84,000. The Allowance for Uncollectible Accounts has a credit balance prior to adjustment of $300. Net credit sales for the year were $250,000 and 3% is estimated to be uncollectible.
2. At year end, Bridges Company has Accounts Receivable of $83,000. The Allowance for Uncollectible Accounts has a debit balance prior to adjustment of $400. Net credit sales for the year were $250,000 and 3% is estimated to be uncollectible.

Required

For each situation described above, compute the following:

a. The bad debts expense for the year.
b. The balance in the Allowance for Uncollectible Accounts account at year end.
c. The net realizable value of Accounts Receivable at year end.
d. Assuming Nash Company had a net Accounts Receivable balance of $76,000 at the beginning of the year, what is Nash's accounts receivable turnover ratio?
e. Assuming Bridges Company had a net Accounts Receivable balance of $85,000 at the beginning of the year, what is Bridges' accounts receivable turnover ratio?

LO 1   **P7-2A. Determine bad debts expense; accounts receivable method.**

Evaluate the following scenarios, assuming both companies use the accounts receivable method of estimating bad debts expense:

1. At year-end, Vio Company has Accounts Receivable of $14,000. The Allowance for Uncollectible Accounts has a credit balance prior to adjustment of $300. An aging schedule prepared on December 31 indicates that $1,100 of Vio's accounts receivable is uncollectible. Net credit sales were $125,000 for the year.
2. At year-end, Demato Company has Accounts Receivable of $25,700. The Allowance for Uncollectible Accounts has a debit balance prior to adjustment of $400. An aging schedule prepared on December 31 indicates that $2,300 of Demato's accounts receivable is uncollectible. Net credit sales were $240,000 for the year.

Required

For each situation described above, compute the following:

a. The Bad Debts Expense for the year.
b. The balance in the Allowance for Uncollectible Accounts at year end.
c. The net realizable value of Accounts Receivable at year end.
d. Based solely on the data provided above, how many days it takes each company to collect its receivables, and which company is doing a better job of collecting its receivables. Explain your answer. (Use ending A/R balances rather than the average balance since the beginning balances are not given.)

LO 1, 2   **P7-3A. Account for accounts receivable and notes receivable transactions.**

Baby Trails Toys had the following transactions occur during the first half of 2009:

Jan 2   Sold merchandise on account to Thumbelina & Company, $14,000 with terms 1/10, net 30. The cost of the merchandise sold was $8,000.

Feb 4   Sold merchandise on account to Teddy Bears Incorporated, $12,500, with terms 2/10, net 45. The cost of the merchandise sold was $7,500.

Feb 9   Received $1,000 of the amount due from Teddy Bears Incorporated from the Feb 4 sale. (No discount is applied unless the amount is paid in full.)

Feb 13   Accepted a 90-day, 10% note for $14,000 from Thumbelina & Company on account from the Jan 2 sale.

Mar 22   Accepted a 60-day, 8% note for the remaining balance on Teddy Bears Incorporated account from the Feb 4 sale.

Mar 25   Sold merchandise on account to Tots R Us, $12,000 with terms 2/10, net 30. The cost of the merchandise sold was $6,250.

Mar 31   Baby Trails began accepting MasterCard on March 1 with deposits submitted monthly. The deposits for the month totaled $24,000. MasterCard charges a 3% fee. The cost of the merchandise sold was $13,000.

Apr 30   Wrote off the Tots R Us account as uncollectible after receiving news that the company declared bankruptcy. Baby Trails Toys uses the allowance method for accounting for uncollectible accounts.

Apr 30   April's MasterCard sales totaled $30,000. Cost of goods sold was $16,000.

May 4   Received payment in full from Thumbelina & Company.

May 21   Received payment in full from Teddy Bears Incorporated.

May 31   May's MasterCard sales totaled $45,000. Cost of goods sold was $18,000.

June 5   Sold merchandise on account to Thumbelina & Company, $12,000 with terms 1/10, net 30. The cost of the merchandise was $6,850.

June 10   Sold merchandise on account to Teddy Bears Incorporated, $15,000, with terms 2/10, net 45. The cost of the merchandise sold was $9,000.

June 12   Collected the amount due from Thumbelina & Company for the June 5 sale.

June 22   Collected the amount due from Teddy Bears Incorporated for the June 10 sale.

June 30   June's MasterCard sales totaled $40,000. Cost of goods sold was $25,000.

June 30   In addition to those listed above, the firm had other transactions during the period, such that Baby Trails Toys had, on June 30, $250,000 in Accounts Receivable and an Allowance account with a debit balance of $1,500. The net credit sales for the first six months of the year were $890,000. Assume that Baby Trails Toys uses the percentage of sales method of accounting for uncollectible accounts. The firm's historical data indicates that approximately 3% of net credit sales are uncollectible.

Required

Prepare the necessary journal entries to record the above transactions. Round to the nearest dollar. (Assume the firm uses a perpetual inventory record keeping system.)

P7-4A. Calculate the beginning bank balance.   LO 3

Consider the following about Computer Tech's cash account for the month of April.

1. Cash per Computer Tech's records was $85,834.99 at April 30.
2. Customer payments of $16,008.13 were received April 30, but not deposited until May 1.
3. Checks totaling $22,461.87 were issued in April, but had not cleared the bank as of the statement date (April 30).
4. According to the bank statement, service charges for April were $54.50, and the bank collected a $4,900 note, including interest, on April 19.

Required

Given the above information, determine the April 30 balance that appears on Computer Tech's bank statement. (Hint: compute the true cash balance first.)

P7-5A. Prepare a bank reconciliation.   LO 3

Central Copy Center's ending Cash balance for October was $9,110.45. The owner deposited $773.14 on October 31 that did not appear on the bank statement. The bank collected a note of $500, of which $20 was interest, for Central Copy Center and charged them $25 for the service. The ending balance on the bank statement for October was $9,022.39. After comparing the company's records with the bank statement, checks totaling $503.65 were found to be outstanding. Besides the collection fee, there were $30 in other service charges. Also, the statement showed that Central Copy Center earned $180 in interest revenue on the account and that checks amounting to $380.57 turned out to be NSF. Finally, an error in recording was discovered: Check No. 4320 for $318.04 was paid to one of Central Copy Center's vendors. The bank incorrectly deducted $381.04 from Central Copy Center's account referencing Check No. 4320.

Required

a. Using the above information about Central Copy Center's Cash account, prepare a bank reconciliation for the month of October.
b. Prepare the necessary journal entries to update the general ledger accounts.

P7-6A. Prepare a bank reconciliation.   LO 3

On June 30, 2007, Roddick Company had a Cash balance in its general ledger of $11,595. The company's bank statement from Chase Bank showed a June 30 balance of $12,540. The following facts have come to your attention:

1. Roddick's June 30 deposit of $2,500 was not included on the bank statement because it was dropped in the night depository after bank hours on June 30.
2. The bank's general service charge for the month was $40.
3. The bank collected a note receivable of $2,000 for Roddick Company along with an additional $58 for interest. The bank deducted a $10 fee for this service. Roddick Company had not accrued any interest on the note.
4. Roddick's bookkeeper erroneously recorded a payment to Federer Company for $892 as $829. The check cleared the bank for the correct amount of $892.
5. Roddick's outstanding checks at June 30 totaled $1,500.

Required

a. Prepare a bank reconciliation as of June 30.
b. Prepare the journal entries needed to update the general ledger accounts.

P7-7A. Identify and correct errors in a bank reconciliation.   LO 3

Analyze the following errors that appeared on General Electronics' bank statement and in the accounting records:

1. The bank recorded a deposit of $200 as $2,000.
2. The company's bookkeeper mistakenly recorded a deposit of $530 as $350.
3. The company's bookkeeper mistakenly recorded a payment of $250 received from a customer as $25 on the bank deposit slip. The bank caught the error and made the deposit for the correct amount.
4. The bank statement shows that a deposit for $2,300 was erroneously recorded by the bank as $2,330. General Electronics will call to let the bank know so the bank can correct its mistake.
5. The bookkeeper wrote a check for $369 but erroneously wrote down $396 as the cash disbursement in the company's records.

Required

For each error, describe how the correction would be shown on the company's bank reconciliation.

LO 5 **P7-8A. Calculate current, quick, and accounts receivable turnover ratios.**

Information from Mystic Corporation's balance sheet at December 31, 2008 and income statement for the year ended December 31, 2008 is as follows:

Cash	$ 35,000
Cost of Goods Sold	550,000
Unearned Revenue	15,000
Rent Expense	12,000
Accounts Receivable, net	73,000
Accounts Payable	10,000
Equipment, net	225,000
Interest Payable	1,350
Net Income	65,000
Inventory	350,000
Salaries Payable	15,000
Short-term Investments	15,000
Office Supplies	5,000
Prepaid Insurance	12,000
Land	75,000
Long-term Notes Payable	110,000
Sales Revenue	775,000
Interest Expense	1,500
Insurance Expense	5,000

Required

a. Calculate Mystic Corporation's current and quick ratios. (Round to two decimal places.) Explain what each ratio measures.
b. Calculate the corporation's accounts receivable turnover ratio. The Accounts Receivable balance at December 31, 2007 was $87,000. (Round to two decimal places.) Explain what the accounts receivable turnover ratio measures.
c. On average, how many days does it take Mystic to collect its receivables?

Problem Set B

Your professor may ask you to complete selected "Group B" exercises and problems using Prentice Hall Grade Assist **(PHGA)**. PHGA is an online tool that can help you master the chapter's topics by providing multiple variations of exercises and problems. You can rework these exercises and problems— each time with new data—as many times as you need, with immediate feedback and grading.

LO 1,5 **P7-1B. Analyze effects of accounts receivable transactions: percentage of sales method.**

Evaluate the following scenarios, assuming both companies use the percentage of sales method for estimating bad debts expense:

1. At year end, Bonnie Company has Accounts Receivable of $112,000. The Allowance for Uncollectible Accounts has a credit balance prior to adjustment of $400. Net credit sales for the year were $315,000 and 3% is estimated to be uncollectible.
2. At year end, Clyde Company has Accounts Receivable of $220,000. The Allowance for Uncollectible Accounts has a debit balance prior to adjustment of $200. Net credit sales for the year were $175,000 and 3% is estimated to be uncollectible.

Required

For each situation described above, compute the following:

a. The Bad Debts Expense for the year.
b. The balance in the Allowance for Uncollectible Accounts account at year end.

c. The net realizable value of Accounts Receivable at year end.

d. Assuming Bonnie Company had a net Accounts Receivable balance of $105,000 at the beginning of the year, what is the firm's accounts receivable turnover ratio?

e. Assuming Clyde Company had a net Accounts Receivable balance of $226,000 at the beginning of the year, what is the firm's accounts receivable turnover ratio?

P7-2B. **Determine bad debts expense; accounts receivable method.**   LO 1

Evaluate the following scenarios, assuming both companies use the accounts receivable method of estimating bad debts expense:

1. At year end, Tate Company has Accounts Receivable of $89,000. The Allowance for Uncollectible Accounts has a credit balance prior to adjustment of $750. An aging schedule prepared on December 31 indicates that $2,100 of Tate's accounts receivable is uncollectible. Net credit sales were $325,000 for the year.

2. At year end, Bradley Company has Accounts Receivable of $75,250. The Allowance for Uncollectible Accounts has a debit balance prior to adjustment of $625. An aging schedule prepared on December 31 indicates that $3,200 of Bradley's accounts receivable is uncollectible accounts. Net credit sales were $452,000 for the year.

Required

For each situation described above, compute the following:

a. The bad debts expense for the year.

b. The balance in the Allowance for Uncollectible Accounts at year end.

c. The net realizable value of Accounts Receivable at year end.

d. Based solely on the data provided above, how many days it takes each company to collect its receivables, and which company is doing a better job of collecting its receivables. Explain your answer. (Use the ending balance in net A/R to compute the ratio.)

P7-3B. **Account for accounts receivable and notes receivable.**   LO 1, 2

Storkville Baby Boutique had the following transactions occur during the first half of 2006:

Jan 2	Sold merchandise on account to Tiny Tots Toys, $24,000 with terms 1/10, net 30. The cost of the merchandise sold was $18,000.
Feb 3	Accepted a 90-day, 10% note for $24,000 from Tiny Tots Toys on account from the Jan 2 sale.
Feb 4	Sold merchandise on account to Stuffed Animals Unlimited, $22,500, with terms 2/10, net 45. The cost of the merchandise sold was $17,250.
Feb 9	Received $10,000 of the amount due from Stuffed Animals Unlimited from the Feb 4 sale. (No sales discount is applied because the total invoice amount was not paid.)
Mar 22	Accepted a 60-day, 10% note for the remaining balance on Stuffed Animals Unlimited account from the Feb 4 sale.
Mar 25	Sold merchandise on account to Little Angels Boutique, $22,000 with terms 2/10, net 30. The cost of the merchandise sold was $16,500.
Mar 31	Storkville began accepting Visa on March 1 with deposits submitted monthly. The deposits for the month totaled $44,000. (Cost of merchandise sold was $25,000.) Visa charges a 2% fee.
Apr 30	Wrote off the Little Angels Boutique account as uncollectible after receiving news that the company declared bankruptcy. Storkville Baby Boutique uses the allowance method for accounting for uncollectible accounts.
Apr 30	April's Visa sales totaled $52,000. Cost of goods sold was $27,000.
May 4	Received payments in full from Tiny Tots Toys.
May 21	Received payment in full from Stuffed Animals Unlimited.
May 31	May's Visa sales totaled $65,000. Cost of goods sold was $34,000.
June 5	Sold merchandise on account to Tiny Tots Toys, $22,000 with terms 1/10, n/30. The cost of the merchandise was $16,850.
June 10	Sold merchandise on account to Stuffed Animals Unlimited, $35,000, with terms 2/10, net 45. The cost of the merchandise sold was $29,000.
June 15	Collected the amount due from Tiny Tots Toys for the June 5 sale.

June 22   Collected the amount due from Stuffed Animals Unlimited for the June 10 sale.

June 30   June's Visa sales totaled $28,000. Cost of goods sold was $18,000.

June 30   In addition to those given, the firm had other transactions during the period such that, at June 30, Storkville Baby Boutique had $156,000 in Accounts Receivable and an Allowance for Uncollectible Accounts with a debit balance of $700. The net credit sales for the first six months of the year were $650,000. Assume that Storkville Baby Boutique uses the percentage of sales method of accounting for uncollectible accounts. The firm's historical data indicates that approximately 2.5% of net credit sales are uncollectible.

Required

Prepare the necessary journal entries to record the above transactions. Round to the nearest dollar. Assume the firm uses a perpetual inventory record keeping system.

LO 3

P7-4B. Calculate the beginning book balance.

Consider the following information about Martin Office Furniture for the month of June.

1. Deposits in transit as of June 30, $3,785.15.
2. Interest revenue earned, $1,300.
3. Bank service charges amounted to $48.
4. Error discovered: Bank deducted from Martin Office Furniture's account a check for $161.03 that was written by Morton Office Supply.
5. The following checks were still outstanding as of the bank statement date:

16012	$10,460.60
16006	200.58
16017	532.27

6. The Martin Office Furniture accountant recorded a deposit of $332 as $223.
7. The bank returned a check from a customer as NSF, $1,059.17.
8. Balance per the bank June 30, $45,020.59.

Required

Given the above information, determine the June 30 balance that appears on Martin Office Furniture's books prior to the bank reconciliation. (Hint: compute the true cash balance first.)

LO 3

P7-5B. Prepare a bank reconciliation.

Country's Copies ending Cash balance for April was $8,877.12. The owner deposited $757.24 on April 30 that did not appear on the bank statement. The bank collected a note of $2,500 for Country's Copies, of which $125 was interest, and charged them $20 for the service. The ending balance on the bank statement for April was $10,917.60. After comparing the company's records with the bank statement, checks totaling $550.98 were found to be outstanding. Besides the collection fee, there was $25 in other service charges. Also, the statement showed that Country's Copies earned $225 in interest revenue on the account and that checks amounting to $415.26 turned out to be NSF. Finally, an error in recording was discovered: Check No. 5624 for $813.40 was paid to one of Country's Copies' vendors. The bank incorrectly deducted $831.40 from Country's Copies' account referencing Check No. 5624.

Required

a. Using the above information about Country's Copies Cash account, prepare a bank reconciliation for the month of April.
b. Prepare the necessary journal entries to update the general ledger accounts.

LO 3

P7-6B. Prepare a bank reconciliation.

On May 31, 2006, Sharp Company had a Cash balance in its general ledger of $6,675. The company's bank statement from National Bank showed a May 31 balance of $8,240. The following facts have come to your attention:

1. Sharp's May 31 deposit of $1,000 was not included on the bank statement because it was dropped in the night depository after bank hours on May 31.
2. The bank's general service charge for the month was $100.

3. The bank collected a note receivable of $1,500 for Sharp Company along with an additional $58 for interest. The bank deducted a $30 fee for this service. Sharp Company had not accrued any interest on the note.
4. Sharp's bookkeeper erroneously recorded a payment to Williams Company for $192 as $129. The check cleared the bank for the correct amount of $192.
5. Sharp's outstanding checks at May 31 totaled $1,200.

Required

a. Prepare a bank reconciliation as of May 31.
b. Prepare the journal entries needed to update the general ledger accounts.

P7-7B. Identify and correct errors in a bank reconciliation.   LO 3

Analyze the following errors that appeared on White Electric's bank statement and in the accounting records:

1. The bank recorded a deposit of $300 as $30.
2. The company's bookkeeper mistakenly recorded a deposit of $240 as $420.
3. The company's bookkeeper mistakenly recorded a payment of $450 received from a customer as $45 on the bank deposit slip. The bank caught the error and made the deposit for the correct amount.
4. The bank statement shows that a check that was written by the company for $392 was erroneously paid (cleared the account) as $329.
5. The bookkeeper wrote a check for $275 but erroneously wrote down $257 as the cash disbursement in the company's records.

Required

For each error, describe how the correction would be shown on the company's bank reconciliation.

P7-8B. Calculate current, quick, and accounts receivable   LO 5
turnover ratios.

Information from River Corporation's balance sheet at December 31, 2008, and income statement for the year ended December 31, 2008, is as follows:

Cash	$ 15,000
Cost of Goods Sold	515,000
Unearned Revenue	25,000
Rent Expense	24,000
Accounts Receivable, net	115,000
Accounts Payable	13,000
Equipment, net	165,000
Interest Payable	1,780
Net Income	48,000
Inventory	212,000
Salaries Payable	12,000
Short-term Investments	8,000
Office Supplies	1,250
Prepaid Insurance	6,000
Land	35,000
Long-term Notes Payable	60,000
Sales Revenue	1,825,000
Interest Expense	1,350
Insurance Expense	800

Required

a. Calculate River Corporation's current and quick ratios. (Round to two decimal places.) Explain what each ratio measures.
b. Calculate the corporation's accounts receivable turnover ratio. The Accounts Receivable balance at December 31, 2007, was $122,000. (Round to two decimal places.) Explain what the accounts receivable turnover ratio measures.
c. On average, how many days does it take River to collect its receivables?

Financial Statement Analysis

LO 1.5   **FSA7-1. Analyze accounts receivable and calculate accounts receivable turnover ratio.**

Use the following information from the financial statements of Winnebago to answer the questions below:

From Current Assets (amounts in thousands)	August 30, 2003	August 28, 2004
Cash and cash equivalents	$99,381	$75,545
Receivables, less Allowance for doubtful accounts ($134 and $161, respectively)	30,885	46,112

a. Does Winnebago have significant credit sales? If so, what evidence supports your opinion?

b. Sales for the fiscal year ended on August 28, 2004, were $1,114,154 (in thousands). Compute the accounts receivable turnover ratio and comment on what it tells you about Winnebago's credit and collection policies. What would make the ratio more useful for this assessment?

c. Can you tell what Bad Debts Expense was for the fiscal year ended August 28, 2004? Explain.

LO 1   **FSA7-2. Analyze accounts receivable.**

An examination of the balance sheet of Family Dollar Stores shows no allowance for bad debts.

a. Under what conditions would a company be allowed to omit this account from the balance sheet? Does this make sense for Family Dollar Stores?

b. Look up the company on the Internet and find the most recent financial statements. Is there any information on how the firm accounts for its bad debts in the notes to the statements?

LO 1.5   **FSA7-3. Analyze accounts receivable and calculate accounts receivable turnover ratio.**

The following information has been adapted from the annual financial statements of The General Mills.

From the balance sheet:		

(in millions)	May 25, 2003	May 26, 2002
ASSETS		
Current Assets		
Cash and cash equivalents	$703	$975
Trade accounts receivable, less allowance of $28 and $21, in 2003 and 2002 respectively	980	1,010
Inventories	1,082	1,055
Prepaid expenses, deferred income taxes and other current assets	414	397
Total Current Assets	3,179	3,437
Property, plant and equipment, net	2,980	2,764
Goodwill and intangible assets, net.....................	10,272	8,563
Other assets	1,796	1,776
Total Assets	$18,227	$16,540

From the income statement:		

(in millions)	Fiscal years ended	May 25, 2003	May 26, 2002
Net revenues		$10,506	$7,949
Cost of sales		6,109	4,662
Gross Profit		$ 4,397	$3,287

Required

a. What are the total amounts of accounts receivable for each of the two years given *before* considering the possible uncollectible accounts? That is, what are gross accounts receivable?

b. Do you think the company has a significant amount of bad debts? Why or why not?

c. Shortly after the financial statements were released, the company was notified that a major customer, who owes the company over $10,000, had filed for bankruptcy. If the company had received that information before the financial statements were released, what amounts might have been changed to reflect the accounting for the account receivable of the bankrupt customer? Explain.

d. Calculate the accounts receivable turnover ratio for 2003 and 2002. (Net accounts receivable at the end of 2001 was $1,000 million.) Also, calculate the number of days it takes, on average, to collect for a sale. Explain this information to the company's management.

Critical Thinking Problems

Risk and Control

1. Suppose one person opens the cash receipts (checks received in the mail), makes the bank deposits, and keeps the accounts receivable records. What potential problems could arise from the lack of separation of duties?

2. Why would a store offer a free purchase to a customer who does not receive a receipt?

Ethics

You work in the billing and collections department of a small corporation. The firm's sales terms are 2/10, n/30, and most of the customers pay within the discount period. Over the years you've been there, you have become quite friendly with the finance manager of one of the customers. One day, he calls you and asks you to change the date on your last invoice to his company to give him an extra week to pay and still be within the discount period. He offers to take you to dinner at the city's finest restaurant in exchange for this little favor.

It would be a simple change in the records, and no one would ever know. It would, you think, also create some goodwill with the customer. Would you make the change? Why or why not?

Group Assignment

The information below has been taken from Sears' balance sheet at the end of two recent fiscal years. In groups, discuss the potential reasons for the changes in the Current Assets from 2002 to 2003. Then, search the Internet for information to help you explain the changes. (The fiscal year ends on the Saturday nearest December 31.)

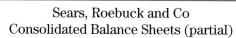

Sears, Roebuck and Co Consolidated Balance Sheets (partial) (in millions)		
	At December 27, 2003	December 28, 2002
Assets		
Current assets		
Cash and cash equivalents	$9,057	$1,962
Credit card receivables	1,998	32,563
Less allowance for uncollectible accounts	42	1,832
Net credit card receivables	1,956	30,731
Other receivables	733	891
Merchandise inventories, net	5,335	5,115
Prepaid expenses and deferred charges	407	535
Deferred income taxes	708	749
Total current assets	$18,196	$39,983

Internet Exercise: Intel Corporation

Intel, by far the world's number-one maker of semiconductor chips, commands more than 80% of the PC microprocessor market. Compaq and Dell are Intel's largest customers. Go to www.intel.com and complete the following steps.

IE7-1. Under "Quotes and Research" enter the company symbol INTC, the stock symbol of the Intel Corp., and then choose Financials. Find the Annual Income Statement to answer the following questions.

  a. Identify the amounts reported for Total (Net Sales) Revenue for the three most recent years.

  b. In general, who are Intel's customers? Who are Intel's two largest customers? Do you think Intel primarily has credit sales or cash sales? Why? Does Intel extend credit to its customers or do Intel's customers use credit cards to pay the amounts owed?

IE7-2. Find the Annual Balance Sheet to answer the following questions.

  a. Identify the amounts reported for Trade Accounts Receivable, net, for the three most recent year ends. Does this represent amounts owed by customers or amounts that the company estimates it will actually collect from customers?

  b. Does Intel use the allowance method or the direct write-off method to record uncollectible accounts? How can you tell?

IE7-3. Refer to the Balance Sheet to answer the following questions.

  a. Compute the accounts receivable turnover ratio for the two most recent years. In which year did the company collect receivables the quickest? How can you tell?

  b. For the most recent year, how long does it take on average for Intel to collect for a sale? Do you think the credit terms might be net/45 or net/60? Explain why.

Additional Study Materials

Visit www.prenhall.com/reimers for self-study quizzes and spreadsheet templates to use to complete homework assignments.

CONTINUING CASE STUDY

Buiding your Excel skills with The MP3 Store

During the month of July, The MP3 Store engaged in the following transactions. The company is using LIFO and the perpetual inventory system. Recall from Chapter 5 that the beginning inventory consists of 40 MP3 players purchased for $220 and 5 MP3 players purchased for $196 each.

July 2	Purchased 120 MP3 players for $225 each for cash.
July 5	Collected 3/4 of June's outstanding accounts receivable balance.
July 13	Paid the telephone bill that was due and the sales tax payable from May and June sales.
July 23	Received and paid a $175 telephone bill.
July 29	Paid the assistant manager $2,000 for June work.
July 30	In July, the company sold a total of 155 MP3 players for $350 each. The sales tax rate is 6%. Of the 155 units sold, 80 were for cash and 75 were on account.
July 30	Due to the success of the business, the company decided to buy a small piece of land so that it can eventually build its own store. The land cost of $25,000 was paid in cash.

July 30   The company's accountant explains that the company needs to start estimating bad debts and decides that it would be appropriate to record 5% of the total outstanding accounts receivable to be uncollectible.

July 31   Received notice that a customer who owes $250 from previous purchases has filed for bankruptcy. The debt will not be paid.

July 31   The owners decide to pay off the notes payable and interest that is due.

July 31   Recorded the required adjusting entries for depreciation, rent, and insurance.

Instructions

1. Prepare the necessary journal entries, T-accounts, trial balances, and financial statements. (Note: A statement of cash flows is required for this chapter.)

2. When you are finished, print and save your file to disk by clicking the **Save** button. Name your file MP37.

chapter 8

Reporting and Interpreting Long-Term Operational Assets

Here's where you've been . . .

- **You learned to account for cash and accounts receivable.**

- **You learned why it's important to control cash.**

- **You learned how a company accounts for bad debts.**

Here's where you're going . . .

- **You'll learn to account for the purchase and use of buildings, manufacturing plants, equipment, natural resources, and intangible assets.**

- **You'll learn how transactions related to long-term assets are presented on the financial statements.**

YOU make the call:

How should Staples account for the purchase of a local office supply store?

Started in 1986, Staples has become one of the largest office supply firms in the world with sales of over $14 billion in 2004. Suppose that Staples has decided to purchase George Stuart Office Supply, a local Orlando office supply store. Staples hires an appraiser to evaluate the market price of the individual assets and liabilities of George Stuart Office Supply. Although the appraiser values the net assets of George Stuart Office Supply at $2 million, Staples offers the owners $3 million for its store building, furniture, and inventory of office machines and supplies. Why

would Staples pay more for the assets than their fair market value? Staples' CFO has no problem with the purchase price of George Stuart Office Supply and asks a new accounting clerk to record the transaction. The clerk wants to record the purchased assets at a value of $3 million because that is what the company is paying for them. Is this the correct way to record the purchase according to GAAP? How should Staples account for the purchase of a local office supply store? *You make the call.*

Learning Objectives

When you are finished studying this chapter, you should be able to:

1. Explain how long-term assets are classified, how their cost is computed, and how they are reported.
2. Explain and compute how tangible assets are written off over their useful lives and reported on the financial statements.
3. Explain and compute how intangible assets are written off over their useful lives and reported on the financial statements.
4. Explain how decreases in value, repairs, changes in productive capacity, and changes in estimates of useful life and salvage value of assets are reported on the financial statements.
5. Record the disposal of a long-term asset and explain how it appears in the financial statements.
6. Describe how long-term assets are reported on the financial statements.
7. Use return-on-assets (ROA) and the asset turnover ratio to help evaluate the firm's performance.
8. Recognize the risks associated with long-term assets and the controls that can minimize those risks.

LEARNING OBJECTIVE 1

Explain how long-term assets are classified, how their cost is computed, and how they are reported.

In Other Words:
Long-term assets, fixed assets, long-lived assets, capital assets, and *operating assets* are used to describe assets that will be used for more than one accounting period.

Acquiring Plant Assets

So far, you've studied the accounting cycle and know how transactions make their way to the financial statements. In this chapter, we'll look at the purchase of long-term assets that are used in the operation of a business.[1]

All businesses purchase long-term assets such as computers, copy machines, and furniture and short-term assets such as folders, paper, and pens. Acquiring long-term assets, often called *fixed assets*, is usually more complicated than acquiring short-term assets. Purchasing long-term assets is complex for several reasons. With long-term assets, a firm must put a great deal of care in selecting the vendor because the relationship could last for a significant amount of time. The monetary investment in long-term assets is typically much greater than the investment in short-term assets, and it is more difficult to dispose of long-term assets if the company makes a bad decision. For example, a new computer system for tracking inventory would cost a firm like Staples thousands of dollars more than the purchase of a new telephone for the employee lounge. If Staples' manager didn't like the kind of phone that was purchased, it would be simple to give it away or donate it to the local Goodwill and buy another. What happens if the manager decides the wrong computerized inventory system was purchased? It's significantly harder to get rid of the long-term asset, and it could reflect poorly on the manager who made the decision to purchase the system in the first place.

Before a firm purchases a long-term asset, it must determine how much revenue that asset will generate and how much the asset will cost. The revenue must exceed the cost, or the asset shouldn't be purchased. The cost of a long-term asset must include all of the costs to get the asset ready for use. Long-term assets often require extensive setup and preparation before they become operational, and employees need to be trained to use them. A firm must consider all of these costs in the process of acquiring a long-term asset. If Staples purchases

---

[1]A company may purchase long-term assets strictly for investment purposes rather than use, like shares of stock in another firm. We'll talk about these in Chapter 12. In this chapter, long-term assets refer to those used in the operation of the business. They are sometimes called *operational* assets.

a new computerized inventory system, it may require new hardware and software, and employees will need to be trained to use the new system. All of these costs will be recorded as part of the cost of the asset.

What assets to buy and how to pay for them are decisions that do not affect the income statement *at the time of the purchase*. Recording the purchase of a long-term asset affects the balance sheet and potentially the statement of cash flows. As you saw in Chapter 4, a business defers recognizing the expense of a long-term asset until the asset is actually used in the business. When the asset is used and the expense is recognized, the expense is called depreciation expense. This deferral is an example of a timing difference. We've purchased a long-term asset at one point in time in the past, and we'll use that asset over a subsequent period of time.

Types of long-lived assets: tangible and intangible

There are two categories of fixed assets: **tangible assets** and **intangible assets**. Exhibit 8.1 shows the long-term asset section of Staples' balance sheet, where you will see both types of fixed assets.

Common tangible assets are property, plant, and equipment (PPE). Common intangible assets are trademarks, patents, and copyrights. We'll discuss these in detail later in the chapter.

Tangible assets: Assets with physical substance—they can be seen and touched.

Intangible assets: Rights, privileges, or benefits that result from owning long-lived assets that do not have physical substance.

Acquisition costs

Consider the purchase of a long-term asset. The *historical cost principle* requires a company to record an asset at the amount paid for the asset—its cost. The cost for property, plant, and equipment includes all expenditures that are reasonable and necessary to get an asset in place and ready for use. The reason for recording all of these costs on the balance sheet, as part of the cost of the asset, is to defer recognition of the expense until the asset is actually used to generate

You won't know the meaning of some terms Staples has used, but you will learn about them in this chapter.

Exhibit 8.1

From the Balance Sheet of Staples

From the Balance Sheet of Staples, Inc.
(in thousands)

	January 29, 2005	January 31, 2004
Property and equipment:		
Land and buildings	$ 649,175	$ 601,063
Leasehold improvements	762,946	692,837
Equipment	1,140,234	1,045,605
Furniture and fixtures	597,293	533,104
Total property and equipment	3,149,648	2,872,609
Less accumulated depreciation and amortization	1,548,774	1,367,308
Net property and equipment	1,600,874	1,505,301
Lease acquisition costs, net of accumulated amortization	38,400	44,227
Intangible assets, net of accumulated amortization	222,520	209,541
Goodwill	1,321,464	1,202,007
Other assets	106,578	63,066
Total long-term assets	$3,289,836	$3,024,142

These are *tangible* assets: (Land and buildings, Leasehold improvements, Equipment, Furniture and fixtures, Total property and equipment)

These are *intangible* assets: (Lease acquisition costs, net of accumulated amortization, Intangible assets, net of accumulated amortization, Goodwill)

revenue. This is, as you know, the matching principle, which provides the foundation for accrual-basis accounting. The assets are put on the balance sheet and then written off as expenses over the accounting periods in which they are used to generate revenue. Here are some common components of the cost of property, plant, and equipment:

1. When a firm purchases land to use as the location of a building or factory, the acquisition cost includes:
   a. Price paid for the land
   b. Real estate commissions
   c. Attorneys' fees
   d. Costs of preparing the land for use, such as clearing or draining
   e. Costs of tearing down existing structures

   In general, the cost of land does not become an expense over time. Because land typically retains its usefulness and is not consumed to produce revenue, its cost remains on the balance sheet as a long-term asset. Even if the land's value increases, financial statements will show the land at cost.

2. Acquisition cost of plant, which includes:
   a. Purchase cost of buildings or factories
   b. Costs to update or remodel the facilities
   c. Any other costs to get the plant operational

3. Acquisition cost of equipment, which includes:
   a. Purchase cost
   b. Freight-in—cost to have the equipment delivered
   c. Insurance while in transit
   d. Installation costs, including test runs

4. Acquisition cost of a building, which may include:
   a. Architects' or contractors' fees
   b. Construction costs
   c. Cost of renovating or repairing the building

In contrast to the accounting treatment of land, even if a firm expects a building to increase in value, the asset will still be depreciated. In practice, most assets used in a business to generate revenues will decrease in value as they are used. Remember that depreciation is not meant to value an asset at its market value. Rather, it is the systematic allocation of the cost of an asset to the periods in which the asset is used by the firm to generate revenue.

Can YOU do it?

For each of the following costs, tell whether it should be recorded as an asset or recorded as an expense at the time of the transaction:

1. Payment for employee salaries
2. Purchase of a new delivery truck
3. Rent paid in advance
4. Rent paid in arrears (after the use of the building)

Answers (1) expense; (2) asset; (3) asset; (4) expense

Basket purchase allocation

Figuring out the acquisition cost of certain assets can be difficult. Buying a building with the land it occupies is an example of a "basket purchase" because we are acquiring two assets for a single price. For our accounting records, we need to calculate a separate cost for each asset. Why? The company will depreciate the building but it will not depreciate the land. The firm divides the purchase price between the building and land by using the **relative fair market value method**. Suppose a company purchased a building and its land together for one price of $100,000. The company would obtain a market price, usually in the form of an appraisal, for each item separately. Then, the company uses the relative amounts of the individual appraisals to divide the purchase price of $100,000 between the two assets. Suppose the building appraised at $90,000 and the land appraised at $30,000. The total appraised value is $120,000 (= $90,000 + $30,000).

> **Relative fair market value method:**
> A way to allocate the total cost for several assets purchased together to each of the individual assets. This method is based on the assets' individual market values.

The building accounts for three-quarters of the total appraised value:

$$\$90,000 \div \$120,000 = 3/4$$

So, the accountant records the building at 3/4 of the total cost of the basket purchase:

$$3/4 \times \$100,000 = \$75,000$$

The cost assigned to the land will be the remaining $25,000:

$$\$100,000 - \$75,000 = \$25,000$$

Or if you want to calculate it,

$$1/4 \times \$100,000 = \$25,000$$

This same method—using the fractions of the total appraised value—can be used for any number of assets purchased together for a single price.

 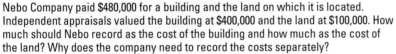 Can **YOU** do it?

Nebo Company paid $480,000 for a building and the land on which it is located. Independent appraisals valued the building at $400,000 and the land at $100,000. How much should Nebo record as the cost of the building and how much as the cost of the land? Why does the company need to record the costs separately?

Answers 4/5 of the costs (400,000/500,000 × $480,000) = $384,000 should be recorded as the cost of the building, and 1/5 of the cost (100,000/500,000 × $480,000) = $96,000 should be recorded as the cost of the land. These two costs need to be separated because Nebo will depreciate the building but not the land.

Using Long-Term Tangible Assets: Depreciation and Depletion

LEARNING OBJECTIVE 2

Explain and compute how tangible assets are written off over their useful lives and reported on the financial statements.

Now that you are familiar with the types of assets a firm may have and the costs associated with their acquisition, we are ready to talk about using the assets. Until property, plant, and equipment are put into use, their costs remain as

Capitalizing: To record a cost as an asset rather than recording it as an expense.

Study Tip

Expensing a cost is the opposite of capitalizing a cost. Expensing means to put a cost on the income statement as an expense.

Depreciation: A systematic and rational allocation process to recognize the expense of long-term assets over the periods in which the assets are used.

In Other Words:
Property, plant, and equipment (PPE) is an expression that is often used for fixed assets.

Amortization: To write off the cost of a long-term asset over more than one accounting period.

Depletion: The amortization of a natural resource.

assets on the balance sheet. As soon as the firm uses the asset to help generate revenue, the financial statements will show that use with some amount of expense on the income statement. Recording a cost as an asset, rather than recording it as an expense, is called **capitalizing** the cost. That cost will be recognized as an expense during the periods in which the asset is used. Recall from Chapter 4 that **depreciation** is a systematic and rational allocation process to recognize the expense of long-term assets over the periods in which the assets are used. Depreciation is an example of the matching principle—matching the cost of an asset with the revenue it helps generate. For each year a company plans to use an asset, the company will plan to recognize depreciation expense on the income statement.

If you hear or read, "The asset is worth $10,000 on our books," that does not mean the asset is really worth that amount if it were sold. Instead, it means that $10,000 is the *carrying value* or *book value* of the asset in the accounting records—it is the amount not yet depreciated. It's called the carrying value because that is the amount we add to our assets on the balance sheet. The amount not yet depreciated is also known as the book value because it is the value of the asset on the accounting records. As you read about the specific methods of depreciating assets, refer to the vocabulary of depreciation in Exhibit 8.2.

Accountants primarily use three terms to describe how a cost is written off over several accounting periods. **Amortization** is the most general expression for writing off the cost of a long-term asset. *Depreciation* is the specific word that describes the amortization of certain kinds of property, plant, or equipment. **Depletion** is the specific term that describes the amortization of a natural resource. There is no specific term for writing off intangible assets, so accountants use the general term *amortization* to describe writing off the cost of intangible assets.

All of these terms—depreciation, depletion, and amortization—refer to allocating the cost of an asset to more than one accounting period.

Accountants use several methods of depreciation for the financial statements. We'll discuss three of the most common:[2]

1. Straight-line depreciation
2. Activity (units of production) depreciation
3. Declining balance depreciation

Let's look at each one in detail.

Can **YOU** do it?

For each of the following kinds of long-term assets, give the term for writing-off the asset.

1. Equipment
2. Franchise
3. Oil well
4. Building

Answers (1) depreciation; (2) amortization; (3) depletion; (4) depreciation

---

[2]Firms use a fourth method of depreciation called *Modified Accelerated Cost Recovery System (MACRS)* for preparing taxes. The firm prepares the financial statements for shareholders and must follow GAAP. The firm prepares the income tax return for the IRS and must follow the tax code. Our focus in this chapter is how to report depreciation on the financial statements, although you can learn about MACRS depreciation in the appendix to this chapter.

Declining balance depreciation

You've learned about the straight-line depreciation method and the activity depreciation method. The third method is **declining balance** depreciation. This method is considered an **accelerated depreciation** method, one that allows more depreciation in the early years of an asset's life and less in the later years. The higher depreciation charges will occur in the early, more productive years when the equipment is generating more revenue. Depreciating more of the asset in the first few years also helps even out the total expenses related to an asset. In later years, the depreciation expense is lower but repair expenses are likely to be increasing.

The declining-balance method speeds up an asset's depreciation by applying a constant rate to the declining book value of an asset. Frequently, a firm uses a version of the declining-balance method called double-declining balance. The firm takes 200% of the straight-line rate to use as the annual depreciation rate. For example, if the useful life of an asset were five years, the straight-line rate would be 1/5, or 20%. That's because 20% of the asset would be depreciated each year for five years using straight-line depreciation. The rate used for *double-declining balance* depreciation would be 40%, which is 200%, or twice, the straight-line rate. Here's how this method works and why it is called double-declining balance. Every year, the accountant depreciates the carrying value, or book value, of the asset by an amount equal to *two divided by the useful life in years*.

> Book Value × (2/Estimated Useful Life in Years) = Yearly Expense

An example will demonstrate an easy way to calculate twice the straight-line rate. Suppose the useful life of an asset is four years. The double-declining rate would be:

$$2 \div 4 \text{ years} = 1/2.$$

Alternatively, you could calculate the straight-line rate and then double it:

$$100\% \div 4 \text{ years} = 25\% \text{ per year} = \text{Straight-line rate}$$
$$\text{Double it: } 50\% = \text{Double-declining balance rate}$$

Using this depreciation method for Holiday Hotel's orange juice machine, the book value at the beginning of the first year is $12,500—its acquisition cost. Notice that the calculation of the annual depreciation expense ignores any salvage value because book value equals cost minus accumulated depreciation. Recall that the useful life of the juice machine is six years. So the depreciation rate is:

$$2 \div 6 \text{ years} = 1/3$$

and the depreciation expense for the first year is:

$$1/3 \times \$12,500 = \$4,167$$

The book value on the balance sheet at December 31, 2006, will be:

$$\$12,500 - \$4,167 = \$8,333$$

For the second year, the accountant again calculates the amount of depreciation as 1/3 of the *book value* (*not* the cost). For the second year, the depreciation expense is:

$$1/3 \times \$8,333 = \$2,778 \text{ (rounded)}$$

Declining balance: An accelerated depreciation method based on the declining book value of an asset over its useful life.

Accelerated depreciation: Methods in which larger amounts of the cost of an asset are written off early in the life of an asset and smaller amounts are written off later in the life of the asset.

The accumulated depreciation at the end of the second year is:

$$\$4,167 + \$2,778 = \$6,945$$

The book value on the December 31, 2007, balance sheet is:

$$\$12,500 - \$6,945 = \$5,555$$

Although salvage value is ignored in the calculation of each year's expense, you must always keep the salvage value in mind so that the book value of the asset is never lower than its salvage value. Exhibit 8.6 shows how Holiday Hotel's orange juice machine would be depreciated using double-declining balance depreciation.

Sometimes depreciation expense for the last year of the asset's useful life is more than the amount calculated by multiplying the book value by the double-declining rate, and sometimes it is less. When the asset has a large salvage

Exhibit 8.6

Double-declining Balance Depreciation

Year	Depreciation Rate = 1/3 or 33.333%	Book Value Before Depreciating the Asset for the Year	Depreciation Expense for the Year	Accumulated Depreciation (At the End of the Year)	Book Value at the End of the Year: $12,500 – Accumulated Depreciation
2006	.33333	$12,500	$4,167	$ 4,167	$8,333
2007	.33333	$ 8,333	$2,778	$ 6,945	$5,555
2008	.33333	$ 5,555	$1,852	$ 8,797	$3,703
2009	.33333	$ 3,703	$1,234	$10,031	$2,469
2010	.33333	$ 2,469	$ 823	$10,854	$1,646
2011	.33333	$ 1,646	$1,146*	$12,000	$ 500**

*The calculation of (0.33333 × $1,646) indicates depreciation expense of $549. Because this is the last year of its useful life and the book value after this year's depreciation should be $500, the depreciation expense must be $1,146 to bring the total accumulated depreciation to $12,000.

**The depreciation expense for Year 6 must be calculated to make this the book value at the end of the useful life—because the book value should be the estimated salvage value.

With double-declining depreciation, depreciation expense is larger in the early years of the asset's life and smaller in the later years. The book value is decreasing at a decreasing rate. Still, the balance in Accumulated Depreciation is working its way up until it reaches the cost minus salvage value. A firm always wants the book value of the asset to be equal to the estimated salvage value at the end of its useful life.

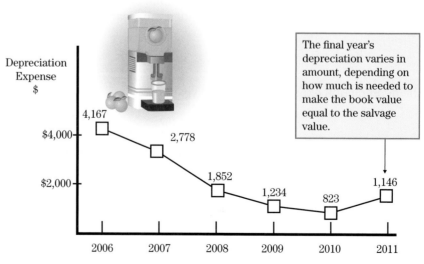

The final year's depreciation varies in amount, depending on how much is needed to make the book value equal to the salvage value.

Exhibit 8.7

Depreciation Methods

Method	Formula for Depreciation Expense
Straight-line	$\dfrac{\text{Acquisition Cost} - \text{Salvage Value}}{\text{Estimated Useful Life in Years}}$ = Yearly Depreciation Expense
Activity	$\dfrac{\text{Acquisition Cost} - \text{Salvage Value}}{\text{Estimated Useful Life in Activity Units}}$ = Unit Depreciation Rate Rate × Actual Activity Level for the Year = Yearly Depreciation Expense
Double-declining balance	Beginning-of-the-year Book Value × (2/Estimated Useful Life in Years) = Yearly Depreciation Expense

value, the depreciation expense in the last year will have to be less than the amount calculated using the double-declining depreciation rate and the carrying value. When the asset has no salvage value, the depreciation expense in the last year will have to be more than the calculated amount. The last year's depreciation expense will be the amount needed to get the book value of the asset equal to the salvage value.

Exhibit 8.7 above summarizes the calculation for the three depreciation methods.

Over the useful life of the asset, the same total depreciation will be recognized no matter which method is used. Exhibit 8.8 compares the depreciation expense of the orange juice machine with the three different depreciation methods.

 Can **YOU** do it?

An asset costs $50,000, has an estimated salvage value of $5,000, and a useful life of five years. Calculate the amount of depreciation expense for the second year using the double-declining balance method.

Answers $50,000 × 2/5 = $20,000 for the first year
New book value = $50,000 − $20,000 = $30,000
$30,000 × 2/5 = $12,000 for the second year

Exhibit 8.8

Comparison of Depreciation Expense by Year over the Life of the Orange Juice Machine for Holiday Hotels

Year	Straight-line	Activity	Double-declining Balance
2006	$ 2,000	$ 1,800	$ 4,167
2007	$ 2,000	$ 2,050	$ 2,778
2008	$ 2,000	$ 1,950	$ 1,852
2009	$ 2,000	$ 2,300	$ 1,234
2010	$ 2,000	$ 2,150	$ 823
2011	$ 2,000	$ 1,750	$ 1,146
Total Depreciation Expense During the Life of the Asset	$12,000	$12,000	$12,000

Exhibit 8.9

Fixed Assets from Cleveland-Cliffs Balance Sheet at December 31, 2004

Cleveland-Cliffs
From the Balance Sheet
December 31, 2004

(in millions)

Properties	
Plant and equipment	$ 416.5
Minerals	20.9
	437.4
Allowances* for depreciation and depletion	(153.5)
Total Properties	$283.9

This is another way of expressing "accumulated" depreciation and depletion amounts.

Depletion

Now that you know how equipment and similar kinds of fixed assets are written off using various depreciation methods, let's turn our attention to the way natural resources are written off. When a company uses a natural resource to obtain benefits for the operation of its business, the write-off of the asset is called *depletion*. For example, Cleveland-Cliffs, the largest producer of iron ore pellets in North America, uses depletion to expense iron ore. The company shows depreciation and depletion together on the balance sheet. Exhibit 8.9 above shows the fixed assets portion of the firm's balance sheet. Often, all amounts of depreciation, depletion, and amortization are captured in a single total on the balance sheet.

Depletion is similar to the activity depreciation method, but it applies only to writing off the cost of natural resources. Examples of such natural resources are land being used for oil wells and mines. A depletion cost per unit is calculated by dividing the cost of the natural resource less any salvage value by the estimated units of activity or output available from that natural resource. The depletion cost per unit is then multiplied by the units pumped, mined, or cut per period to determine the total depletion related to the activity during the period.

Suppose a company purchases the rights to an oil well in Texas for $100,000, estimating the well will produce 200,000 barrels of oil during its life. The depletion rate per barrel is:

$100,000 ÷ 200,000 barrels = $0.50 per barrel

If 50,000 barrels are produced in the year 2005, then the depletion related to the 50,000 barrels produced in 2005 will be:

$0.50 per barrel × 50,000 barrels = $25,000

On the December 31, 2005, balance sheet, the book value of the oil rights will be:

$100,000 − $25,000 = $75,000

LEARNING OBJECTIVE 3

Explain and compute how intangible assets are written off over their useful lives and reported on the financial statements.

Using Intangible Assets: Amortization

In addition to tangible assets, most firms have intangible assets, which are rights, privileges, or benefits that result from owning long-lived assets. Intangible assets have long-term value to the firm, but they are not visible or touchable. Their value resides in the rights and privileges given to the owners of the asset. These rights are often represented by contracts. Like tangible assets, they are recorded at cost, which includes all of the costs a firm incurs to obtain the asset.

If an intangible asset has an indefinite useful life, like goodwill or trademarks, the assets are not amortized. However, the firm will periodically evaluate them for any permanent decline in value and then write them down if necessary. The idea here is that the balance sheet should include any asset that has future value to produce revenue for the firm, but the asset should never be valued at more than it will be able to generate for the firm. Writing down an asset because of a permanent decline in value means reducing the amount of the asset and recording an expense that will go to the income statement.

Intangible assets that have a limited life are written off over their useful life or legal life, whichever is shorter, using straight-line amortization. That means an equal amount is expensed each year. Firms use an Accumulated Amortization account for each intangible asset because the accumulated amortization must be reported. Accumulated depreciation and accumulated amortization are often added together for the balance sheet presentation. Firms often have one or more of the intangible assets described next.

Copyrights

Copyright is a form of legal protection for authors of "original works of authorship," provided by U.S. law. When you hear the term copyright, you probably think of written works like books and magazine articles. Copyright protection extends beyond written works to musical and artistic works and is available to both published and unpublished works. According to the 1976 Copyright Act, the owner of the copyright can:

- copy the work.
- use the work to prepare related material.
- distribute copies of the work to the public by sale, rental, or lending.
- perform the work publicly, in the case of literary, musical, dramatic, and choreographic works.
- in the case of sound recordings, perform the work publicly by means of a digital audio transmission.

Read about Google's plans to digitize books in *Accounting in the News* on page 398. Do you think this plan will violate any copyright laws?

All costs to obtain and defend copyrights are part of the cost of the asset. Copyrights are amortized using straight-line amortization over their legal life or their useful life, whichever is shorter.

> **Copyright:** A form of legal protection for authors of "original works of authorship," provided by U.S. law.

Patents

A **patent** is a property right that the U.S. government grants to an inventor "to exclude others from making, using, offering for sale, or selling the invention throughout the United States or importing the invention into the United States for a specified period of time in exchange for public disclosure of the invention when the patent is granted." For example, Micron Technology filed for a patent for a computer memory device in February 2004. IBM obtained a patent for a vibration-driven wireless network in April 2000. Did you know that universities apply for hundreds of patents each year for their inventions? In 2004, the University of California applied for 424 patents—more patents than any other university.

As with copyrights, costs to defend patents are capitalized as part of the cost of the asset. Patents are amortized using straight-line amortization over their useful life or legal life, whichever is shorter. For example, most patents have a legal life of 20 years. However, a company may believe the useful life of a patent is less than that. If the company believes the patent will provide value for only 10 years, the company should use the shorter time period for amortizing the asset.

> **Patent:** A property right that the U.S. government grants to an inventor "to exclude others from making, using, offering for sale, or selling the invention throughout the United States or importing the invention into the United States" for a specified period of time.

Accounting in the NEWS

Technology

Google This: "Copyright Law"

Google can search an astonishing 8 billion Web pages. That's not much compared with the knowledge stored in the world's libraries. It's little wonder, then, that many scholars and readers were thrilled when Google (GOOG) announced in December 2004 that it planned to scan the complete texts of millions of books from major libraries around the globe and make them searchable online.

Google's library project would make digital versions of whatever libraries hand over—including copyrighted books—regardless of whether authors or publishers agree. Already, five major libraries—Harvard, Stanford, Oxford, Michigan, and the New York Public Library—are sending books for Google to digitize. The goal is to gather as much of the world's knowledge as

possible and make it accessible on Google. For public domain books, users will be able to see full text. For copyrighted books, viewing will be "only a few sentences," says Google. When Google gets up to speed, its scanning machines will be able to process 5,000 books a day. At the time this book is going to press, Google has postponed its plan. It has given publishers until November 2005 to opt out of the program. In late 2005, a group of major book publishers announced the filing of a lawsuit against Google over its plans to digitally copy and distribute copyrighted works without permission of the copyright owners. The suit is being coordinated and funded by the Association of American Publishers (AAP). See if you can get the latest news on Google's plan.

Do you think Google's project violates the current copyright laws? Many attorneys believe it does, and you can be sure that authors and publishers are concerned about the protection of their books. What does copyright law have to do with accounting?

Imagine having millions of volumes of books in one vast index that you can access from your computer. Is this a good idea, or is Google freeloading on the work of authors and publishers?

Q How many web pages can Google search?

A 8 billion

Source: Burt Helm and Hardy Green, "Google This: Copyright Law," *Business Week Online—News and Commentary,* June 5, 2005. Reprinted from the June 5, 2005 issue of *BusinessWeek Online—News Commentary.* Copyright © 2005 by The McGraw-Hill Companies. Reprinted by permission. "Publishers Sue Google Over Plans to Digitize Books," Association of American Publishers, Inc., October 19, 2005.

Trademarks

Trademark: A symbol, word, phrase, or logo that legally distinguishes one company's product from any others.

A **trademark** is a symbol, word, phrase, or logo that legally distinguishes one company's product from any others. One of the most well-recognized trademarks is Nike's swoosh symbol. In many cases, trademarks are not amortized because their useful lives are indefinite. Registering a trademark with the U.S. Patent and Trademark Office provides 10 years of protection, renewable as long as the trademark is in use.

Franchises

Franchise: An agreement that authorizes someone to sell or distribute a company's goods or services in a certain area.

A **franchise** is an agreement that authorizes someone to sell or distribute a company's goods or services in a certain area. The initial cost of buying a franchise is the franchise fee, and this is the intangible asset that is capitalized. It is amortized over the life of the franchise if there is a definite life. If the life of the franchise is indefinite, it will not be amortized. In addition to the initial fee, franchise owners pay an ongoing fee to the company that is usually a percentage of sales. You might be surprised at some of the top franchises for 2005. They include Subway, Curves, and Quiznos.

Goodwill

Goodwill: The excess of cost over market value of the net assets when one company purchases another company.

Goodwill is the excess of cost over market value of the net assets when one company purchases another company. When the term *goodwill* is used in everyday conversation, it refers to favorable qualities. However, when you see

Goodwill on a company's balance sheet, you know that it is a result of purchasing another company for more than the fair market value of its net assets. Goodwill is an advanced topic for intermediate or advanced accounting courses. However, you should have a general understanding of goodwill because it appears on the balance sheet of many firms.

Suppose that The Home Depot purchased Pop's Hardware store for $950,000. The inventory and building—all of Pop's assets—were appraised at $750,000; and the small hardware store had no debt. Why would The Home Depot pay more than the market value for the assets of Pop's Hardware? Pop's Hardware store had been in business for many years, and the store had a terrific location and a loyal customer base. All of this is goodwill that Pop's had developed over years of business. GAAP does not allow a company to recognize its internally developed goodwill, so Pop's financial statements do not include goodwill. Now that The Home Depot has decided to purchase Pop's Hardware, however, the goodwill will be recorded. Here's the journal entry that The Home Depot would make (assuming it is a cash purchase):

Transaction	Debit	Credit
Various Assets	750,000	
Goodwill	200,000	
Cash		950,000
To record the purchase of Pop's Hardware		

This is the accounting equation.

	Assets		= Liabilities +	Shareholders' Equity	
				Contributed Capital +	Retained Earnings
Cash	Various Assets	Goodwill			
−950,000	750,000	200,000			

What happens to the intangible asset *goodwill*? Goodwill is not amortized because it is assumed to have an indefinite life. Even though goodwill is not amortized, companies must evaluate goodwill to make sure it is not overvalued on the balance sheet. Goodwill that has lost some of its value must be written down—that is, the asset is reduced and a loss is recorded. You can read about a firm's goodwill in the notes to the financial statements.

Research and development costs

Research and development (R&D) costs have benefits to the firm—at least that is the goal of R&D. However, R&D costs are expensed and are *not* capitalized as part of the cost of an asset because it is not clear that these costs represent something of value. Software development costs are considered research costs until they result in a product that is technologically feasible, so these costs must also be expensed as they are incurred. However, once the software is considered technologically feasible, the costs incurred from that point on are capitalized as part of the cost of the software. Deciding when a piece of software is technologically feasible is another example of how firms need to use judgment when making accounting decisions. The firm's developers and computer experts would make this judgment.

LEARNING OBJECTIVE 4

Explain how decreases in value, repairs, changes in productive capacity, and changes in estimates of useful life and salvage value of assets are reported on the financial statements.

Changes After the Purchase of the Asset

We started the chapter with a discussion of the types and costs of long-term assets. Then, we discussed how the accounting records show the firm's use of those assets. Now we discuss how to adjust financial statements to record three things that take place after an asset has been in use. First, the asset may lose value due to circumstances outside the firm's control. Second, the firm may make expenditures to maintain or improve the asset during its useful life. And third, the firm may need to revise its prior estimates of an asset's estimated life and salvage value. Let's look briefly at each of these circumstances.

Asset impairment

Impairment: A permanent decline in the market value of an asset such that its book value exceeds the market value.

By now you know that accountants want to avoid overstating assets on the balance sheet or revenue on the income statement. That's why a firm that is getting ready to prepare its financial statements must evaluate its long-term assets, including goodwill and other intangible assets, for **impairment**—a permanent reduction in the market value of an asset below its book value—if certain changes have occurred. Such changes include:

1. A downturn in the economy that causes a significant decrease in the market value of a long-lived asset.
2. A change in how the company uses an asset.
3. A change in the business climate that could affect the asset's value.

An asset is considered impaired when the book value of the asset or group of assets is greater than its market value. Impairment is not easy to measure, but you will read about it in the notes to almost every set of financial statements. Evaluating an asset for impairment is similar to valuing inventory at the lower-of-cost-or-market, which you learned about in Chapter 6. Because testing an asset for impairment can be quite difficult, it is a topic reserved for more advanced courses. However, you should be familiar with the terminology because you will see it in almost every annual report.

Exhibit 8.10 shows a portion of the disclosure made by Staples regarding its reported asset impairment of $156.3 million. A company must disclose in the notes to the financial statements a description of the impaired asset and the facts and circumstances leading to the impairment.

Asset impairment is a relatively new concept, so different firms' disclosures may vary and should be read carefully to see how each firm evaluates impairment. Staples' asset impairment was $156.3 million in 2000 for goodwill and fixed assets. In 2004, the notes to Staples' financial statements continue to mention the 2000 write off.

Exhibit 8.10

Disclosure About Asset Impairment in Staples' Notes to the Financial Statements

From NOTE C Asset Impairment and Other Charges

During the fourth quarter of fiscal year 2000, Staples recognized impairment losses of $205.8 million. Staples identified certain negative conditions at Staples Communications as indicators of asset impairment. In accordance with Company policy at that time, management assessed the recoverability of the long-lived assets of Staples Communications by using expected future undiscounted cash flows to value the assets' carrying value. Based on this assessment, Staples recognized impairment losses of $156.3 million related to the goodwill and fixed assets of Staples Communications. Also included in this charge is the write-down of investment values in various e-commerce companies of $49.5 million due to a decline in fair value that is other than temporary. These write-downs were a result of significant reductions in valuations for Internet stocks, discontinued operations at certain companies and significant devaluation of certain companies due to cash constraints and failed business models.

Expenditures to improve an asset or extend its useful life

Another change in the value of an asset may be the result of the firm spending money to improve its assets. Any expenditure that will benefit more than one accounting period is called a **capital expenditure**. A capital expenditure is recorded as an asset when it is incurred, and it is expensed or amortized over the accounting periods in which it is used.

Just the opposite of a capital expenditure is an expenditure that does not extend the useful life or improve the asset. Any expenditure that will benefit only the current accounting period is expensed in the period in which it is incurred.

Many companies establish policies that categorize purchased items as capital expenditures or revenue expenditures, often based on dollar amounts. The accounting constraint of *materiality* applies here so that small dollar amounts can simply be expensed.

Remodeling and improvement projects are capital expenditures because they will offer firms benefits over a number of years:

- **Remodeling**, such as a new wiring system to increase the efficiency of the electrical system of a building.
- **Improvements**, such as a more energy-efficient air-conditioning system.

Ordinary repairs are recognized as current expenses because they are routine and do not increase the useful life of the asset or its efficiency.

- Ordinary repairs, such as painting, tune-ups for vehicles, or cleaning and lubrication of equipment are expenditures that are necessary to maintain an asset in good operating condition.

Suppose the computer terminals at Staples' corporate offices need a monthly tune-up and cleaning. The cost of this maintenance would be an expense—recognized in the period the work was done. But suppose Staples upgraded its computer hardware to expand its capability or its useful life. This cost would be considered a capital expenditure and capitalized—recorded as part of the cost of the asset and depreciated along with the asset over its remaining useful life.

> **Capital expenditure:** A cost that will be recorded as an asset, not an expense, at the time it is incurred. Recall that this is called capitalizing a cost.

> **In Other Words:**
> Capital expenditures to improve an asset are sometimes referred to as betterments.

> **In Other Words:**
> An expenditure on a fixed asset that is recorded as an expense in the accounting period in which it is incurred is sometimes called a revenue expenditure.

Revising estimates of useful life and salvage value

Sometimes managers have used an asset and determined that they need to revise their estimates of its useful life or the salvage value of the asset. Evaluating estimates related to fixed assets is an ongoing part of accounting for those assets. In accounting for long-term assets, revising an estimate is not treated like an error—you don't go back and correct any previous records or financial statements. Those amounts were correct *at the time*—because the best estimates *at that time* were used for the calculation. Suppose managers believe that a smoothly running machine will offer a useful life beyond the original estimate. The undepreciated balance less the estimated salvage value would be spread over the new estimated remaining useful life. Similarly, if managers come to believe that the salvage value of the machine will be greater than their earlier estimate, the depreciation will be recalculated with the new salvage value. This approach is similar to treating the undepreciated balance like the *cost* at the time of the revised estimate and using the new estimates of useful life and salvage value to calculate the depreciation expense for the remaining years of the asset's life.

Suppose Staples purchased a copy machine that cost $50,000, with an estimated useful life of four years and an estimated salvage value of $2,000. Using straight-line depreciation, a single year's depreciation is:

$$\frac{\$50,000 - \$2,000}{4 \text{ years}} = \frac{\$48,000}{4 \text{ years}} = \$12,000 \text{ per year}$$

Suppose that we have depreciated the machine for two years. That would make the book value $26,000:

$$\underset{\text{Cost}}{\$50,000} - \underset{\substack{\text{Depreciation}\\ \text{Year 1}}}{\$12,000} - \underset{\substack{\text{Depreciation}\\ \text{Year 2}}}{\$12,000} = \$26,000$$

As we begin the third year of the asset's life, we realize that we will be able to use it for three *more* years—rather than two more years as we originally estimated—but we now believe the salvage value at the end of that time will be $1,000—not $2,000 as originally estimated.

The depreciation expense for the first two years will not be changed. The motto here is: *the past is past.* For the next three years, however, the depreciation expense will be different than it was for the first two years. The acquisition cost of $50,000 less $24,000 of accumulated depreciation gives us the undepreciated balance of $26,000. This amount is treated as if it were now the cost of the asset. The estimated salvage value is $1,000, and the estimated remaining useful life is three years. Here's the calculation:

$$\frac{\$26,000 - \$1,000}{3 \text{ years}} = \frac{\$25,000}{3 \text{ years}} = \$8,333 \text{ per year}$$

The asset will now be depreciated for three years at $8,333 per year. At the end of that time the book value of the asset will be $1,000 (= $26,000 − ($8,333 per year × 3 years)).

At the beginning of 2005, White Company hired a mechanic to perform a major overhaul of its main piece of equipment at a cost of $2,400. The equipment originally cost $10,000 at the beginning of 2001, and the book value of the equipment on the December 31, 2004, balance sheet was $6,000. At the time of the purchase, White Company estimated that the equipment would have a useful life of ten years and no salvage value. The overhaul at the beginning of 2005 extended the useful life of the equipment. White Company's new estimate is that the equipment will now last until the end of 2012—eight years from the date of the overhaul. White uses straight-line depreciation for all of its assets. Calculate the depreciation expense for White's income statement for the year ended December 31, 2006.

Answer $6,000 + $2,400 = $8,400 new depreciable amount
$8,400 / 8 years remaining life = $1,050 per year

You may recall from Chapter 4 that a firm could manipulate its income by its decision to capitalize or expense a cost. Another potential for manipulation comes from the estimates of useful lives and salvage values of long-term assets. Read about it in *Accounting in the News* and test your ethics on this issue.

LEARNING OBJECTIVE 5

Record the disposal of a long-term asset and explain how it appears in the financial statements.

Selling Long-Term Assets

We've bought the long-term asset and used it—depreciating, depleting, or amortizing it over its useful life. Now, let's deal with getting rid of an asset. Disposing of an asset means to sell it, trade it in,[3] or simply toss it in the trash. When would a company sell an asset? Sometimes an asset is sold because it is

---

[3]The accounting for a transaction in which an asset is traded in for a similar asset is a topic covered in a more advanced accounting course.

Accounting in the NEWS

"Managing" Depreciation and Amortization

Imagine that you are a manager of a manufacturing company. All of your competitors estimate the useful life of their machinery and equipment as five years. However, you have decided to estimate the useful life of your company's machinery and equipment as ten years. By spreading the depreciation expense over more years, you know that net income will increase. Is this practice ethical?

According to an article from Knowledge@Wharton:

Greed, fear, and the relatively low chances of getting caught are the primary drivers behind corporate misreporting, suggests Howard Schilit, the founder of the Center for Financial Research & Analysis in Rockville,

MD. "Public companies are run by competitive, successful leaders who are not used to losing," he says. "So if Wall Street expects a particular quarter's earnings to be $1 a share, and a customer suddenly defers an order worth three cents a share, a CEO may have the mindset to exploit accounting's flexibility to make the numbers anyway."

A firm may modify its depreciation and amortization schedules to decrease these expenses when the firm needs a bit more net income, or a firm may increase these expenses if it is clear the firm will not make its numbers for the accounting period. These changes are usually easy to make and can often be justified to the auditors—at least the first time.

Thinking Critically

Would you change your estimates of the useful life or salvage value of an asset to reach your earnings target for one year? How about for two years?

Q How can extending the useful life of an asset increase net income?

Engineers and mechanics are often in the best position to help accountants estimate the useful life and salvage value of the firm's equipment.

A The depreciation expense is reduced by spreading the remaining cost of the asset over more years, which increases income.

Source: "Accounting Games Companies Play (Especially with Revenues and Costs)," *Knowledge@Wharton* (June 30–July 13, 2004), http://knowledge.wharton.upenn.edu accessed on July 8, 2004.

---

no longer useful to the company. Other times an asset is replaced with a newer model, even though there is remaining productive capacity in the current asset. You calculate the gain or loss on the disposal of an asset by comparing the cash received for the sale of the asset—also known as *cash proceeds*—and the asset's book value at the time of disposal. One of three situations will exist:

1. Cash proceeds are greater than the book value. There will be a *gain*.
2. Cash proceeds are less than the book value of the asset. There will be a *loss*.
3. Cash proceeds are equal to the book value. If cash proceeds equal book value, there is no gain or loss.

Suppose you decide to sell an asset that was purchased seven years ago. At the time of the purchase, you estimated it would last ten years. The asset cost $25,000, and you used straight-line depreciation with estimated salvage value of zero. So the depreciation expense each year was $2,500:

$$\frac{\$25,000 - \$0}{10 \text{ years}} = \$2,500 \text{ per year}$$

Now, seven years later, you sell the asset for $8,000. Is there a gain or loss on the sale? First, calculate the book value at the date you sold the asset.

Book Value = Cost − Accumulated Depreciation
Book Value = $25,000 − (7 years × $2,500 per year)
Book Value = $25,000 − $17,500 = $7,500

Then, subtract the book value from the cash proceeds to calculate the gain or loss on the sale.

$$\$8,000 - \$7,500 = \$500$$

Because the proceeds of $8,000 are larger than the book value of $7,500, there is a gain on the sale. A gain is a special kind of revenue that is shown on the income statement. A gain is special because it is not a normal part of business operations. You are not in business to buy and sell the equipment you use in your business, so the income from such a transaction is given a special name—*gain*.

Another way to calculate the gain or loss on the sale of an asset is to record the three amounts you know:

1. Record the cash proceeds with a debit to Cash.
2. Remove the cost of the asset from the asset's account—equipment, for example—account with a credit to that account.
3. Remove the amount of accumulated depreciation related to the asset with a debit to the Accumulated Depreciation account.

The number needed to balance the journal entry will be a gain if the journal entry needs a credit to balance. The number will be a loss if the journal entry needs a debit to balance. You can see from the incomplete journal entry below that a credit will balance the journal entry.

Transaction	Debit	Credit
Cash	8,000	
Accumulated Depreciation	17,500	
Equipment		25,000
Needed Credit		**500**

Without the needed credit, the debit side is $500 larger than the credit side of the journal entry, so an additional credit of $500 is needed. That would be a gain, and the full journal entry would look like this:

Transaction	Debit	Credit
Cash	8,000	
Accumulated Depreciation—Equipment	17,500	
Equipment		25,000
Gain on Sale of Equipment		500

This is the accounting equation.

	Assets		=	Liabilities	+	Shareholders' Equity	
						Contributed Capital	+ Retained Earnings
Cash	Equipment	Accumulated Depreciation— Equipment					Gain on the sale of equipment
8,000	−25,000	17,500					500

Now suppose, instead, you sell the asset after seven years for $5,000 rather than $8,000. Is there a gain or loss on the sale? You already know the book value is $7,500 at the date of the sale.

Subtract the book value from the cash proceeds.

$$\$5{,}000 - \$7{,}500 = -\$2{,}500$$

Because the proceeds are less than the book value, there is a loss on the sale. A loss is a special kind of expense, and it is shown on the income statement. You are not in business to buy and sell equipment, so the reduction in income from this transaction is given a special name—*loss*.

Suppose you sold the asset for exactly the book value, $7,500. There would be no gain or loss on the sale. Look at the journal entry below to see the effect of selling an asset for its book value.

Transaction	Debit	Credit
Cash	7,500	
Accumulated Depreciation—Equipment	17,500	
Equipment		25,000

This is the accounting equation.

Assets			=	Liabilities	+	Shareholders' Equity	
						Contributed Capital	Retained + Earnings
Cash	Equipment	Accumulated Depreciation— Equipment					
7,500	−25,000	17,500					

There is no gain or loss. Selling an asset for its book value, therefore, does not affect the income statement.

Can YOU do it?

Perry Plants Company owned an asset that originally cost $24,000. The company sold the asset on January 1, 2005, for $8,000 cash. Accumulated depreciation on the day of sale was $18,000. Determine whether Perry should recognize a gain or a loss on the sale. If so, how much?

Answers Proceeds = $8,000
Book value = $6,000
GAIN on sale = $2,000 ($8,000 − $6,000)

Presentation of Long-Term Assets on the Financial Statements

LEARNING OBJECTIVE 6

Describe how long-term assets are reported on the financial statements.

In this chapter you have seen that both tangible and intangible long-term assets are recorded at the amount the firm paid for them. The assets are shown on the balance sheet in the last half of the asset section, after current assets. Because the carrying value of property, plant, and equipment (PPE) is the difference between the cost of the asset and its accumulated depreciation, accountants say that PPE is valued at its *amortized cost* or its depreciated cost. The notes to the financial statements are a good place to learn the types of assets, approximate age of the assets, and depreciation method(s) used.

The use of long-term assets is shown on the income statement with Depreciation and Amortization Expense. Often, the amount is included in the sum of several accounts for presentation on the income statement.

The statement of cash flows will indicate any cash expenditures for PPE as cash used for investing activities. Any cash received from the sale of long-term assets will be shown as an inflow in the same section—cash from investing activities—of the statement. Don't forget that the gain or loss on the sale of an asset, reported on the income statement, is not the cash related to the sale. Only the cash collected from the sale will appear on the statement of cash flows.

Financial Statement Analysis—Return on Assets and Asset Turnover Ratio

You know how a firm records the purchase of long-term assets and how it accounts for the use of the assets. Now we will look at how you can use the information about long-term assets to help evaluate the performance of the firm.

Return on assets

A company purchases assets to help generate future revenue. Remember the definition of an asset—something of value used by a business to generate revenue. A ratio that measures how well a company is using its assets to generate revenue is **return on assets (ROA)**. ROA is an overall measure of a company's profitability. Like much of the terminology in accounting, the name of this ratio is descriptive. A company's *return* is what the company is getting back. We want to measure that return as a percentage of assets. So return on assets is literally *return*—net income—divided by *assets*.

$$\text{Return on Assets} = \frac{\text{Net Income} + \text{Interest Expense}}{\text{Average Total Assets}}$$

This ratio measures a company's success in using its assets to earn income for the people financing the business—both owners and creditors. Since interest expense is part of what has been earned to pay creditors, it is added back to the numerator. Net income is the return to the owners, and interest expense is the return to the creditors. So you add interest expense back to net income for the numerator. The denominator is average total assets.

Using a ratio like ROA gives financial statement users a way to standardize net income across companies. Exhibit 8.11 provides an example. In 2004, Ethan Allen Interiors had a Net Income Plus Interest Expense of $80,119,000. La-Z-Boy Incorporated had a Net Income Plus Interest Expense of $5,457,000. Clearly, Ethan Allen is outperforming La-Z-Boy in total net income plus interest expense. But that comparison doesn't tell us how well each company is using its assets to make that net income. If we divide net income plus interest expense by average total assets, we'll get the return on assets for the year.

Exhibit 8.11

A Comparison of Ethan Allen and La-Z-Boy

Ethan Allen —

Asset turnover ratio: Measures how efficiently a company is using its assets.

	Ethan Allen	**La-Z-Boy**
For fiscal year ended	June 30, 2004	April 24, 2004
Net income* + interest expense	$80,119,000	$5,457,000
Beginning assets	$735,008,000	$1,123,066,000
Ending assets	$658,367,000	$1,047,496,000
Average assets	$696,687,500	$1,085,281,000
Return on assets	11.5%	0.5%

Before the effect of a change in accounting principle for La-Z-Boy.

It is clear in this comparison that Ethan Allen is earning a much better return with its total assets than La-Z-Boy is earning with its assets. The industry average for return on assets is 6.6%. Ethan Allen's return on assets is 11.5%, while La-Z-Boy's return on assets is only 0.5%.

Asset turnover ratio

The **asset turnover ratio** indicates how efficiently a company is using its assets. The ratio is defined as *net sales divided by average total assets*. The ratio answers the question: How many dollars of sales are generated by each dollar invested in assets?

$$\text{Asset Turnover Ratio} = \frac{\text{Net Sales}}{\text{Average Total Assets}}$$

Let's look at Ethan Allen and La-Z-Boy again. Sales for Ethan Allen for a recent fiscal year totaled $955,107,000, while sales for La-Z-Boy totaled $1,998,876,000. The asset turnover ratio for each is:

	Ethan Allen	**La-Z-Boy**
Sales	$955,107,000	$1,998,876,000
Average Assets	$696,687,500	$1,085,281,000
Asset Turnover Ratio	1.37	1.84

Asset turnover ratios vary significantly from industry to industry, so it is important to compare firms only in the same industry. Although La-Z-Boy is not earning a good return on its assets, you can see that it is generating a good amount of sales with its assets.

Remember that all ratios have this in common: To be meaningful, ratios must be compared to the ratios from other years with the same company or with other companies. Industry standards are also often available for common ratios to help investors and analysts evaluate a company's performance using ratio analysis.

Can YOU do it?

Given the following information for Office Depot and Staples, calculate the return on assets and the asset turnover ratio for each. Which company appears to be using its assets more effectively?

	Office Depot	**Staples**
For the fiscal year ended	**Dec. 27, 2003**	**Jan. 31, 2004**
Sales	$12,358,566,000	$13,181,222,000
Net Income plus Interest Expense	$ 331,100,000	$ 522,811,000
Beginning Assets	$ 4,765,812,000	$ 5,721,388,000
Ending Assets	$ 6,145,242,000	$ 6,503,046,000

Answers

	Office Depot	Staples
Average Assets	$5,455,527,000	$6,112,217,000
Return on Assets	6.07%	8.55%
Asset Turnover Ratio	2.27	2.16

The ratios give conflicting information. Staples has a higher return on assets but Office Depot has a higher asset turnover ratio.

LEARNING OBJECTIVE 8

Recognize the risks associated with long-term assets and the controls that can minimize those risks.

Business risk, control, & ethics

A firm risks losing long-term assets because of theft. This risk is not a problem with some large assets, such as a factory, but it is a very serious problem with smaller, mobile, fixed assets, such as cars, computers, and furniture and fix-

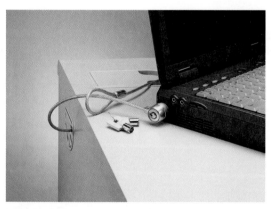

tures. Even large assets, like buildings and factories, are at risk for damage due to vandalism, hurricanes, or terrorist activities. One of the major functions of any company's internal control system is to safeguard all assets from theft and damage—whether intentional or unintentional. The cost of safeguarding assets can be tremendous, as can the cost of replacing them if they are destroyed. The damage done to long-term assets by Hurricane Katrina in August 2005 to the Gulf Coast will amount to billions of dollars.

Physical controls to safeguard assets may be as simple as a lock on a warehouse door, a video camera in a retail store, or a security guard who remains in an office complex overnight. Even when assets are protected in a secure facility with guards, fences, or alarms, the company must be sure that only the appropriate people have access to the assets.

Laptop computers are easy prey for thieves. By using a security lock, workers can protect their computers and, more importantly, the information stored on those computers.

Complete and reliable record keeping for the assets is also part of safeguarding assets. As with assets like cash and inventory, the people who are responsible for the record keeping for long-term assets should be different than the people who have physical custody of the assets.

Monitoring is another control to safeguard assets. This means that someone needs to make sure the other controls—physical controls, separation of duties, and any other policies and procedures related to protecting assets—are operating properly. Often, firms have internal auditors—their own employees—who perform this function as part of their job responsibilities. You may recall that it was an internal auditor who first blew the whistle on the Enron fraud.

Accounting in the NEWS

Risk and Control

Do You Download Sony Music?

Copyright laws have become a topic of national conversation. When you download music from the Internet, are you violating any copyright laws? When you copy an article from a website for a class presentation, are you violating any copyright laws? When you download a trial version of computer software and never switch to the paid version, are you violating any copyright laws? Now, think of all of these questions from the firm's point of view. Sony Records wants you to buy its latest CD, and Time Magazine wants you to buy the latest issue. After all, firms are in business to make money, and they can only do that when they find paying customers.

The framers of the U.S. Constitution gave Congress the power to regulate the ownership of intellectual property. They recognized that "intellectual property was important and too easy to steal. By limiting the term of exclusive ownership and permitting intellectual property to pass into the public domain after a set term of years, they hoped to reduce the temptation to steal it." Unfortunately, the last 215 years have seen the legal issues of intellectual property become a "legislative muddle" with hundreds of exceptions and exclusions cluttering the copyright statutes. This, in turn, creates significant risks and potential costs to the firms that depend on their ownership of these intangible assets for their survival and success.

When you see a significant amount of intangible assets like trademarks and copyrights on a firm's balance sheet, dig a little deeper into the risks the firm may be facing with these assets. As technology continues to change the copyright landscape, be sure to consider the firm's point of view as well as your view as an individual consumer.

Record labels like Sony want customers to purchase music CDs rather than download music from the Internet.

Source: "Go Go Google: Copyright law needs drastic change to keep up with technology," by Thomas G. Donlan. *Barrons's Online,* August 22, 2005.

Intangible assets present special risks to a firm. As you learned earlier in the chapter, Google's attempt to digitize all the books in the libraries of several major universities has brought new concerns over copyright laws. The value of these intangible assets—trademarks and copyrights—on a firm's balance sheet and the potential costs of defending these rights can amount to significant sums of money. Technology and ethics have collided, resulting in many questions about the legal and ethical dimensions of current copyright laws. Read about some of the relevant issues in *Accounting in the News*.

YOU make the call:

How should Staples account for the purchase of a local office supply store?

Staples is purchasing a local office supply store for $3 million. The net assets of the local store have a market value of $2 million. Why would Staples pay more than the market value of the assets? Due to intangible benefits like location and customer loyalty, the purchase price of a company is often more than the market value of its net assets.

The clerk wants to record the purchased assets described above at a value of $3 million because that is what the company is paying for them. Is this the correct way to record the purchase according to GAAP? How should Staples account for the purchase of a local office supply store? You learned in this chapter that there is an intangible asset called goodwill, which is defined as the excess of the purchase price over the market value of the tangible assets.

Staples will record the tangible assets at their market value and will record the remaining $1 million as goodwill. Can you see why recording the assets for the total cost is different than recording the assets at market value with separate goodwill recorded? If the assets were recorded at the full $3 million, that amount would be depreciated over the useful life of the assets. On the other hand, goodwill is not written off each year. It must be evaluated each year for impairment. If the value of the goodwill is estimated to be less than the recorded amount, the difference will be written off against net income.

- -

Let's Take a Test Drive

Real World Problem:
Staples

Staples opened 77 new stores in North America in 2004. The company also grew through acquisitions, including the acquisition of a 59-store chain in the United Kingdom. It's clear that Staples engages in many transactions involving property, plant, and equipment each year. The company must record these assets, depreciate or amortize them, and make sure nothing has happened to indicate impairment. Staples also has intangible assets, including goodwill. Again, Staples has to record the intangible assets at cost, amortize some of them, and evaluate goodwill for impairment.

Concepts

The matching concept is the primary concept underlying the way accountants record a company's long-term assets used in operations. All the costs of an asset are capitalized, booked as assets on the balance sheet, and written off over the useful life of the asset. Property and equipment are depreciated using one of several methods: straight-line, activity method, or an accelerated method. Intangible assets, like copyrights and franchises, are amortized over their useful life or legal life, whichever is shorter.

The other underlying concept is that of conservatism. In an effort to be sure that assets are not overstated, accountants write down assets that are impaired. Read the notes to the financial statements for additional information about how a firm accounts for its long-term operating assets.

The Mechanics

Suppose Staples started the fiscal year (ended January 31, 2007) with the following accounts and balances:

Account	DR	CR
Cash	$390,000	
Accounts Receivable	136,000	
Inventory	106,350	
Prepaid Insurance	3,000	
Equipment	261,000	
Accumulated Depreciation—Equipment		$ 75,800
Accounts Payable		26,700
Salaries Payable		13,500
Unearned Revenue		35,000
Long-term Note Payable		130,000
Other Long-term Liabilities		85,000
Common Stock		250,000
Retained Earnings		280,350
	$896,350	$896,350

Suppose the company engaged in the following transactions during its fiscal year ended January 31, 2007:

1. The company purchased some new equipment at the beginning of the fiscal year. The invoice price was $158,500, but the manufacturer of the equipment gave Staples a 3% discount for paying cash for the equipment on delivery. Delivery terms were FOB shipping point, and shipping costs amounted to $1,500, and Staples paid $700 for a special insurance policy to cover the equipment while in transit. Installation cost was $3,000, and Staples spent $6,000 training the employees to use the new equipment. Additionally, Staples hired a new supervisor at an annual salary of $75,000 to be responsible for the printing services area where the new equipment will be used. All payments were made in cash as the costs were incurred.

2. Sold some old equipment with an original cost of $12,300 and related accumulated depreciation of $11,100. Proceeds from sale amounted to $1,500.

3. Collected cash of $134,200 on accounts receivable.

4. Purchased $365,500 worth of inventory during the year. Paid cash of $200,000, with the remainder purchased on account. (Assume perpetual inventory system.)

5. Paid insurance premium of $12,000.

6. Paid $170,000 on accounts payable.

7. Paid employees total cash for salaries of $72,250. (This includes the amount owed at the beginning of the year.)

8. Sales to customers: $354,570. Collected $200,000 in cash, and the remainder was on account. (Inventory sold cost $110,000. Cost of goods sold was recorded at the time of the sale—perpetual record keeping.) The company uses only one revenue account: Sales and Service Revenue.

9. Paid $50,000 to reduce principal of the long-term note, and paid interest of $10,400.

10. Operating expenses of $30,000 were paid in cash.

Other information:

a. Salaries of $10,250 were owed to employees at year end (earned but not paid).

b. Insurance left unused at year end amounted to $2,000.

c. The company estimates that the new equipment will last for 20 years and have a salvage value of $2,945 at the end of its useful life.

d. Previously purchased fixed assets are being depreciated at a rate of 10% per year.

e. Unearned revenue of $21,000 has been earned at year end. This is service revenue.

Instructions

Prepare T-accounts for the company. Then, post the beginning balances and the transactions for the year. Prepare an unadjusted trial balance at year end, make adjusting entries, and prepare single-step income statement, statement of changes in shareholders' equity, the statement of cash flows for the fiscal year, and the balance sheet at January 31, 2007.

Solution

Cash			
BB 390,000	164,945	(1)	
(2)	1,500	200,000	(4)
(3) 134,200		12,000	(5)
(8) 200,000		170,000	(6)
		72,250	(7)
		60,400	(9)
		30,000	(10)

Accounts Receivable	
BB 136,000	134,200 (3)
(8) 154,570	

Inventory	
BB 106,350	110,000 (8)
(4) 365,500	

Prepaid Insurance	
BB 3,000	13,000 (b)
(5) 12,000	

Equipment	
BB 261,000	
(1) 164,945	12,300 (2)

Accumulated Depreciation— Equipment	
(2) 11,100	75,800 **BB**
	32,970 (c&d)

Accounts Payable	
(6) 170,000	26,700 **BB**
	165,500 (4)

Salaries Payable	
(7) 13,500	13,500 **BB**
	10,250 (a)

Unearned Revenue	
(e) 21,000	35,000 **BB**

Long-term Notes Payable	
(9) 50,000	130,000 **BB**

Other Long-term Liabilities	
	85,000 **BB**

Common Stock	
	250,000 **BB**

Sales and Service Revenue		Cost of Goods Sold		Retained Earnings	
	354,570 (8)	(8) 110,000			280,350 **BB**
	21,000 (e)				

Insurance Expense		Salaries Expense		Operating Expenses	
(b) 13,000		(7) 58,750		(10) 30,000	
		(a) 10,250			

Interest Expense		Depreciation Expense		Gain on Sale of Equipment	
(9) 10,400		(c&d) 34,200			300 (2)

1. The cost of the equipment includes shipping, installation, and insurance.

Cost of new	
equipment	$158,500
3% discount	4,755
Net invoice amount	$153,745
Shipping	1,500
Insurance	700
Training	6,000
Installation	3,000
Total Cost to Record	**$164,945**

Journal entry to record the purchase of equipment is:

Equipment	164,945	
Cash		164,945

2. Journal entry to record the sale is:

Accumulated Depreciation—Equipment	11,100	
Cash	1,500	
Equipment		12,300
Gain on Sale of Equipment		300

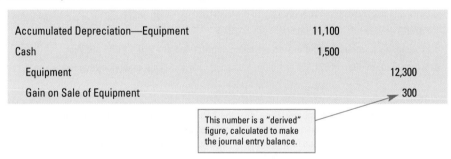

This number is a "derived" figure, calculated to make the journal entry balance.

3. Journal entry to record receipt of cash for Accounts Receivable is:

Cash	134,200	
Accounts Receivable		134,200

4. Journal entry to record purchase of inventory is:

Inventory	365,500	
Cash		200,000
Accounts Payable		165,500

5. Journal entry to record purchase of insurance is:

Prepaid Insurance	12,000	
Cash		12,000

6. Journal entry to record payment on Accounts Payable is:

Accounts Payable	170,000	
Cash		170,000

7. Journal entry to record payment of salaries (payable and expense) is:

Salaries Expense	58,750	
Salaries Payable	13,500	
Cash		72,250

8. Journal entries to record sales and cost of goods sold are:

Cash	200,000	
Accounts Receivable	154,570	
Sales and Service Revenue		354,570
Cost of Goods Sold	110,000	
Inventory		110,000

9. Journal entry to record payment of principal and interest is:

Long-term Notes Payable	50,000	
Interest Expense	10,400	
Cash		60,400

10. Journal entry to record operating expenses is:

Operating Expenses	30,000	
Cash		30,000

Adjusting entries:

a.	Salaries Expense	10,250	
	Salaries Payable		10,250

b.	Insurance Expense	13,000	
	Prepaid Insurance		13,000

c. and d.

NEW ASSET

$164,945	Cost
−2,945	Salvage value
162,000	Depreciable base
÷ 20 years	Useful life
= $8,100	Annual Depreciation Expense

OLD ASSETS
10% per year depreciation
10% of $248,700 = $24,870 Annual Depreciation Expense

Journal entry to record annual depreciation expense is:

Depreciation Expense	32,970	
Accumulated Depreciation—Equipment		32,970

Note: In the actual accounts, there would be an Accumulated Depreciation account for each group of assets.

e. Journal entry to record portion of unearned revenue that has been earned at year end is:

Unearned Service Revenue	21,000	
Sales and Service Revenue		21,000

After the journal entries are posted, a trial balance can be prepared from the balances in the T-accounts.

Adjusted Trial Balance

Account	Debit	Credit
Cash	$ 16,105	
Accounts Receivable	156,370	
Inventory	361,850	
Prepaid Insurance	2,000	
Equipment	413,645	
Accumulated Depreciation—Equipment		$ 97,670
Accounts Payable		22,200
Salaries Payable		10,250
Unearned Revenue		14,000
Long-term Note Payable		80,000
Other Long-term Liabilities		85,000
Common Stock		250,000
Retained Earnings		280,350
Sales and Service Revenue		375,570
Cost of Goods Sold	110,000	
Insurance Expense	13,000	
Salaries Expense	69,000	
Operating Expenses	30,000	
Interest Expense	10,400	
Depreciation Expense	32,970	
Gain on Sale of Equipment		300
	$1,215,340	$1,215,340

Staples, Inc. Income Statement For the year ended January 31, 2007		
Revenues:		
Sales and service revenue		$375,570
Gain on sale of equipment		300
Total revenue		$375,870
Expenses:		
Cost of goods sold	$110,000	
Insurance expense	13,000	
Salaries expense	69,000	
Operating expenses	30,000	
Interest expense	10,400	
Depreciation expense	32,970	(265,370)
Net Income		$110,500

Staples, Inc. Statement of Changes in Shareholders' Equity For the year ended January 31, 2007	
Contributed capital:	
Common stock, beginning	$250,000
Additions during the year	—
Ending contributed capital	$250,000
Retained earnings:	
Beginning balance.......................	$280,350
+Net income	110,500
−Dividends	—
Ending balance	$390,850
Total shareholders' equity	$640,850

Staples, Inc.
Statement of Cash Flows
For the year ended January 31, 2007

Cash from operations:		
Cash from customers	$334,200	
Cash paid to vendors	(370,000)	
Cash paid for insurance	(12,000)	
Cash paid for other operating...	(30,000)	
expenses		
Cash paid to employees........	(72,250)	
Cash paid for interest..........	(10,400)	$(160,450)
Cash from investing activities:		
Proceeds from sale of asset	$ 1,500	
Purchase of new assets	(164,945)	(163,445)
Cash from financing activities:		
Payment on long-term note.....	(50,000)	
Net increase (decrease) in cash		$(373,895)
Beginning cash balance........		390,000
Ending cash balance..........		$ 16,105

Staples, Inc.
Balance Sheet
January 31, 2007

Assets:	
Cash	$ 16,105
Accounts receivable	156,370
Prepaid insurance	2,000
Inventory	361,850
Total current assets	536,325
Equipment (net of accumulated depreciation of $97,670)	315,975
Total assets	$852,300
Liabilities and Shareholders' Equity	
Liabilities:	
Accounts payable	$ 22,200
Unearned revenue	14,000
Salaries payable	10,250
Total current liabilities	46,450
Long-term note payable	80,000
Other long-term liabilities	85,000
Shareholders' Equity:	
Common stock	250,000
Retained earnings	390,850
Total liabilities and shareholders' equity	$852,300

Rapid Review

1. **Explain how long-term assets are classified, how their cost is computed, and how they are reported.** Long-term assets are classified as non-current on the balance sheet. Their cost consists of all expenditures to purchase the asset and get it up and running. The costs—invoice, delivery, set-up, and employee training, for example—are capitalized and then written off over their useful lives.

2. **Explain and compute how tangible assets are written off over their useful lives and reported on the financial statements.** Assets are written off in one of several ways. For plant and equipment, an asset may be written off using either *straight-line depreciation, activity method depreciation*, or the *double-declining balance methods*.

3. **Explain and compute how intangible assets are written off over their useful lives and reported on the financial statements.** Some intangible assets are amortized over their useful lives (straight-line), but others, most prominently *goodwill*, is not written off unless it is deemed to be impaired.

4. **Explain how decreases in value, repairs, changes in productive capacity, and changes in estimates of useful life and salvage value of assets are reported on the financial statements.** Assets may need to be evaluated for impairment. If the book value of an asset exceeds its market value, it is considered *impaired* and must be written down to market value. Repairs and maintenance costs that simply keep an asset functioning normally are expensed in the period they are incurred. Any expenditures that extend the useful life or expand the productivity of an asset will be capitalized with the asset and written off over the periods in which the asset is used. A firm may need to revise the estimated life or salvage value of an asset during its useful life.

5. **Record the disposal of a long-term asset and explain how it appears in the financial statements.** When an asset is sold or otherwise disposed of, the original cost will be credited out of the asset account, the accumulated depreciation pertaining to that asset will be debited out of the Accumulated Depreciation account,

and the cash proceeds (if any) are debited to Cash. The journal entry is balanced with a debit or credit. If a debit is needed, it is a loss on the disposal of the asset. If a credit is needed, it is a gain on the disposal of the asset. The gain or loss will be shown on the income statement.

6. **Describe how long-term assets are reported on the financial statements.** Long-term assets are reported at cost minus accumulated depreciation, known as *amortized cost*. The annual depreciation or amortization is shown on the income statement as an expense. Any gains or losses from the sale of long-term assets are also included on the income statement. The cash used to pay for long-term assets and the cash proceeds from the sale of long-term assets are shown as Cash Flows from Investing Activities on the statement of cash flows. The notes to the financial statements contain a great deal of information about the firm's assets and methods of amortization.

7. **Use return-on-assets (ROA) and the asset turnover ratio to help evaluate the firm's performance.** These two ratios are used to evaluate how well a company is using its assets.

$$\text{ROA} = \frac{\text{Net Income} + \text{Interest Expense}}{\text{Average Total Assets}}$$

$$\frac{\text{Asset Turnover}}{\text{Ratio}} = \frac{\text{Net Sales}}{\text{Average Total Assets}}$$

8. **Recognize the risks associated with long-term assets and the controls that can minimize those risks.** A serious risk associated with many long-term assets is that someone will steal or damage the assets. Safeguarding assets can be addressed with physical controls such as locks, other security devices, and accurate record keeping. Intangible assets present special risks to a firm and are gaining prominence.

Key Terms

Accelerated depreciation, p. 393
Activity method, p. 391
Amortization, p. 386
Asset turnover ratio, p. 407
Capital expenditure, p. 401
Capitalizing, p. 386

Copyright, p. 397
Declining balance, p. 393
Depletion, p. 386
Depreciation, p. 386
Franchise, p. 398
Goodwill, p. 398
Impairment, p. 400
Intangible assets, p. 383
Patent, p. 397

Relative fair market value method, p. 385
Return on assets (ROA), p. 406
Salvage value, p. 387
Straight-line depreciation, p. 387
Tangible assets, p. 383
Trademark, p. 398

Have You Increased Your Business IQ?

Answer these questions to find out.

1. In accounting, depreciation indicates:
   a. an asset's decline in market value.
   b. the amount of cash used to get the asset up and running.
   c. a systematic allocation of the cost of the asset to the periods in which the asset is used.
   d. an increase in value for land, which is assumed to appreciate rather than depreciate.

2. Goodwill is seen on almost every balance sheet of very large corporations. What does it represent?
   a. The value of the customer base the corporation has established.
   b. The excess of the purchase price over the market value of the net assets of another company the corporation has purchased.
   c. The amount of potential revenue resulting from the reputation of the firm.
   d. Intangible assets like patents and trademarks that cannot be seen or touched.

3. A loss is
   a. an expense related to depreciation.
   b. shown separately on the balance sheet.
   c. a deduction from income similar to an expense, but related to a nonoperating event.
   d. an indication that a firm paid too much for an asset.
4. A capital expenditure is
   a. one for which a new issue of stock will be required.
   b. recorded as a revenue expenditure.
   c. the costs of acquiring capital (money) for the firm.
   d. recorded as an asset.
5. Depreciation and depletion are special terms for
   a. amortizing specific types of assets.
   b. manufacturing firms.
   c. current assets.
   d. intangible assets.

Now, check your answers.

1. c   2. b   3. c   4. d   5. a

- If you answered all five questions correctly, you've increased your business IQ by studying this chapter. It doesn't mean you've mastered all of the accounting concepts in the chapter. It simply means that you understand some of the general business concepts presented in this chapter.
- If you answered 2 to 4 questions correctly, you've made some progress but your business IQ has plenty of room to grow. You might want to skim over the chapter again.
- If you answered 0 or 1 question correctly, you can do more to improve your business IQ. Better study the chapter again.

Questions

1. Describe the difference between tangible and intangible assets.
2. What is the difference between capitalizing and expensing a cost?
3. What is depreciation?
4. What does amortization mean?
5. Explain the difference between depreciation and depletion.
6. How do firms determine the cost of property, plant, and equipment?
7. What is a basket purchase? What accounting problem does this type of purchase create, and how do firms remedy the accounting problem?
8. What is the carrying value, or book value, of an asset? Do either of these values relate to the market value of the asset? Explain your answer.
9. What is the residual value, or salvage value, of an asset?
10. What is the difference between depreciation expense and accumulated depreciation? On which financial statement(s) do these items appear?
11. How does depreciation apply the matching principle?
12. Explain the difference between the three depreciation methods allowed by GAAP.
13. What is a copyright and how is it accounted for?
14. What is a patent and how is it accounted for?
15. What does it mean for an asset to be impaired?
16. What types of costs related to long-term operational assets are capitalized and what types are expensed?
17. How is a gain or loss on the disposal of an asset calculated? On which financial statement(s) would the gain or loss appear?
18. How does goodwill arise?
19. How is the return on assets (ROA) ratio calculated and what does this ratio measure?
20. How is the asset turnover ratio calculated and what does this ratio measure?
21. List two types of controls that safeguard assets. Why is safeguarding assets important?

Multiple Choice

1. Which of the following is an intangible asset?
   a. Franchise
   b. Oil reserves
   c. Land
   d. Repairs
2. Depreciation is the systematic allocation of the cost of an asset
   a. Over the periods during which the asset is paid for
   b. Over the periods during which the market value of the asset decreases
   c. Over the periods during which the company uses the asset
   d. Over the life of the company
3. Writing off a cost means
   a. Putting the cost on the balance sheet as an asset
   b. Evaluating the useful life of the asset
   c. To record the cost as an expense
   d. Deferring the expense
4. Suppose a firm purchases a new building for $500,000 and spends an additional $50,000 making alterations to it before it can be used. How much will the firm record as the cost of the asset?
   a. $500,000
   b. $550,000
   c. $450,000
   d. It depends on who performed the alterations.
5. Suppose a firm buys a piece of land with a building for $100,000. The firm's accountant wants to divide the cost between the land and building for the firm's financial records. Why?
   a. Land is always more expensive than buildings
   b. Land will not be depreciated but the building will be depreciated, so the accountant needs two different amounts
   c. Land will appreciate and its recorded cost will have to increase over time, while the building will be depreciated
   d. To separate Depreciation Expense from Accumulated Depreciation after the first year
6. When an expenditure to repair an existing asset extends the useful life of the asset, the cost should be
   a. Classified as a revenue expenditure because it will result in increased revenue
   b. Capitalized and written off over the remaining life of the asset
   c. Expensed in the period of the repair

   d. Added to accumulated depreciation
7. When goodwill is determined to be impaired, a firm will
   a. Increase its book value to market value.
   b. Sell it immediately.
   c. Reduce the value of the goodwill with a charge against income.
   d. Reduce the value of the goodwill with a charge to paid-in capital.
8. When a company's balance sheet shows the asset Goodwill for $300,000, it means
   a. The company has developed a strong reputation valued at $300,000 if the company were to be sold.
   b. The company is worth $300,000 more than the balance sheet indicates.
   c. The company purchased another company and paid $300,000 more than the fair market value of the company's net assets.
   d. The company has invested $300,000 in new equipment during the period.
9. Suppose a firm purchased an asset for $100,000 and estimated its useful life as 10 years with no salvage value on the date of the purchase. The firm uses straight-line depreciation. After using the asset for five full years, the firm changes its estimate of the useful life to four remaining years (a total of nine rather than the original ten). How much depreciation expense will the firm recognize in the sixth year of the asset's life?
   a. $12,500
   b. $10,000
   c. $11,111
   d. $31,111
10. Suppose a firm purchased an asset for $50,000 and depreciated it using straight-line depreciation for its 10-year useful life, no salvage value. At the end of the seventh year of use, the firm decided to sell the asset. Proceeds from the sale were $17,500. What was the gain or loss from the sale of the asset? How did the sale affect the statement of cash flows?
   a. $2,500 loss; $2,500 cash outflow from investing activities.
   b. $2,500 gain; $17,500 cash inflow from investing activities.
   c. $32,500 loss; $17,500 cash inflow from investing activities.
   d. $17,500 gain; $17,500 cash inflow from investing activities.

Short Exercises

SE8-1. Calculate the cost of an asset.   LO 1
Gruber Window Fashions bought a new wood-cutting machine as a part of its venture into manufacturing interior shutters. The invoice price of the machine was $90,000. Gruber also had the following expenses associated with purchasing this machine.

Delivery Charge	$2,850
Installation	2,500
Power to Run the Machine for the First Year	450

What amount should Gruber record on the books for this equipment?

SE8-2. Calculate the cost of an asset.   LO 1
Settler Company was quickly outgrowing its rented office space. The company decided that it could raise enough capital to buy land and build a new office building. The building was completed on September 15. Consider the following costs incurred for the new building:

Building Materials	$110,000
Labor Costs (including Architect's Fees)	205,000
Rental of Equipment Used in the Construction	9,000
Maintenance on the Building from Sept. 15–Dec. 31	14,000

What amount should Settler Company record on the books for its new building?

SE8-3. Account for basket purchase.   LO 1
Tylo Corporation obtained a building, its surrounding land, and a delivery truck in a lump-sum purchase for $230,000. An appraisal set the value of land at $180,000, the building at $145,000, and the truck at $25,000. At what amount should Tylo record each new asset on its books?

SE8-4. Account for basket purchase.   LO 1
Villa Corporation purchased three buildings at a total cost of $960,000. The appraised values of the individual buildings were as follows:

Building 1	$600,000
Building 2	400,000
Building 3	200,000

What amounts should be recorded as the cost for each of the buildings in Villa Corporation's accounts?

SE8-5. Calculate depreciation expense: straight-line.   LO 2
Calculate the annual straight-line depreciation expense for an asset that cost $12,000, has a useful life of five years, and has an estimated salvage value of $2,000.

SE8-6. Calculate depreciation expense: activity method.   LO 2
Using the activity method, calculate the first two years of depreciation expense for a copy machine that cost $14,000, has an estimated useful life of five years or 50,000 copies, and has an estimated salvage value of $4,000. The number of copies produced each year is as follows:

	Number of Copies Produced
Year 1	12,000
Year 2	10,500
Year 3	9,700
Year 4	9,100
Year 5	8,700

SE8-7. Calculate depreciation expense: double-declining balance.   LO 2
Using the double-declining balance method, calculate the annual depreciation expense that will be recorded each year for an asset that cost $12,000, has a useful life of five years, and has an estimated salvage value of $2,000. Explain what accounting issue arises, if any, in the fourth and fifth years.

SE8-8. Determine the cost of an asset.   LO 2
If an asset with no salvage value is being depreciated at a rate of $1,000 per year using the straight-line method over a useful life of six years, how much did the asset cost?

LO 2   **SE8-9. Calculate depreciation expense: straight-line.**
A machine is purchased on January 2, 2006, for $50,000, and it has an expected life of four years and no estimated salvage value. If the machine is still in use five years later, what amount of depreciation expense will be reported for the fifth year?

LO 2   **SE8-10. Determine the useful life of an asset.**
Suppose an asset cost $20,000 and has an estimated salvage value of $2,000. At the end of three years, the carrying value of the asset is $11,000. What is the useful life of the asset? Assume straight-line depreciation.

LO 2   **SE8-11. Calculate depletion expense.**
CNA Enterprises purchases an oil field and expects it to produce 1,000,000 barrels of oil. The oil field, acquired in January 2006, cost CNA $1.5 million. In 2006, 280,000 barrels were produced. In 2007, the oil field produced 350,000 barrels. Prepare the journal entries to record the depletion for each of these years.

LO 2   **SE8-12. Calculate depletion expense.**
Earthlink Mining purchased a copper mine for $12,000,000. The company expects the mine to produce 6,000,000 tons of copper over its five-year useful life. During the first year of operations, the company extracts 750,000 tons of copper. How much depletion should Earthlink Mining record for the first year?

LO 3   **SE8-13. Intangible assets.**
Edgewood Company obtained a patent for a new invention. The costs associated with the patent totaled $35,000. With the rapid development of new technology, Edgewood's engineers have estimated the invention will not have any value after 10 years. The patent has a legal life of 20 years. How will Edgewood amortize the cost of the patent?

LO 3   **SE8-14. Amortization of intangible assets.**
Barclay Company purchased a patent for $50,000 on January 1, 2007. The estimated useful life is 10 years. Legal life is greater than 10 years. What is the amortization expense for the fiscal year ended December 31, 2007?

LO 4   **SE8-15. Analyze revenue and capital expenditures.**
For each of the following, tell whether it should be classified as (a) a revenue expenditure (expensed), (b) a capital expenditure (capitalized), or (c) neither.

a. Paid $2,000 for routine repairs.
b. Paid cash dividends to shareholders.
c. Paid $6,000 for repairs that will extend the asset's useful life.
d. Purchased a patent for $5,000 cash.
e. Purchased a machine for $10,000 and gave a two-year note.
f. Paid $50,000 for an addition to a building.
g. Paid $1,000 for routine maintenance on a machine.

LO 4   **SE8-16. Analyze revenue and capital expenditures.**
Categorize each of the following as a capital expenditure or a revenue expenditure for Dalton & Sons and explain why.

a. In accordance with the long-term maintenance plan, paid for a newly reshingled roof. The new shingles replaced similar old shingles.
b. Built an annex to the building for the executive offices.
c. Improved the ventilation system to increase energy efficiency in the building.
d. Replaced parts in major equipment as needed.

LO 4   **SE8-17. Calculate depreciation expense with change in estimate of salvage value.**
On January 1, 2007, the Lance Corporation purchased a machine at a cost of $55,000. The machine was expected to have a useful life of 10 years and no salvage value. The straight-line depreciation method was used. In January 2009, the estimate of salvage value was revised from $0 to $6,000. How much depreciation should Lance Company record for 2009?

LO 4   **SE8-18. Asset impairment.**
Delta Airlines has determined that several of its planes are impaired. The book value of the planes is $10 million, but the market value of the planes is $9 million. How should Delta treat this decline?

SE8-19. Account for disposal of an asset.   LO 5
A machine is purchased on January 2, 2005, for $100,000. It has an expected useful life of 10 years and no salvage value. After 9 years, the machine is sold for $3,000 cash. Will there be a gain or loss on the sale? How much?

SE8-20. Account for disposal of an asset.   LO 5
The Topspin Company sold some old equipment for $65,000. The equipment originally cost $100,000, had an estimated useful life of 10 years, and had no estimated salvage value. It was depreciated for 5 years using the straight-line method. In the year of the sale, what amount of gain or loss, if any, should Topspin Company report on its income statement?

SE8-21. Financial statement presentation.   LO 6
At what value are fixed assets like property, plant, and equipment shown on the balance sheet? How is that amount calculated?

SE8-22. Ratio analysis.   LO 7
Financial ratios are often used to evaluate a company's performance. What ratio would provide information about how efficiently a company is using its assets? Using the financial statements provided at the end of the chapter for Staples (in the "Let's Take a Test Drive" problem), calculate that ratio for 2007 for Staples, and explain what information it provides.

SE8-23. Risks and controls.   LO 8
Write a paragraph describing a specific risk associated with long-term assets and some possible controls that might minimize the risk.

SE8-24. Risks and controls.   LO 8
Give an example of an industry with a particular interest in copyright laws. What risks do firms in that industry face?

Exercise Set A

E8-1A. Account for basket purchase.   LO 1
Coca-Cola purchases a building and land for $180,000. An independent appraiser provides the following market values: building—$150,000; land—$50,000.

a. How much of the purchase price should Coca-Cola allocate to each of the assets?
b. If the building has a useful life of 10 years and an estimated salvage value of $35,000, how much depreciation expense should Coca-Cola record each year using the straight-line method?
c. Using the double-declining balance method, what would the book value of the building be at the end of 3 years?

E8-2A. Calculate the cost of an asset and depreciation expense.   LO 1, 2
Corona Company purchased land for $75,000 cash and a building for $300,000 cash. The company paid real estate closing costs of $8,000, and allocated that cost to the building and the land based on the purchase price. Renovation costs on the building were $35,000.

a. Give the journal entry to record the purchase of the property, including all related expenditures. Assume that all transactions were for cash and that all purchases occurred at the beginning of the year.
b. Compute the annual straight-line depreciation, assuming a 20-year estimated useful life and a $10,000 estimated salvage value for the building. Prepare the journal entry to record the first year of depreciation.
c. What would be the book value of the building at the end of the second year?
d. What would be the book value of the land at the end of the second year?

E8-3A. Calculate depreciation expense: straight-line and activity methods.   LO 2
Best-Goods Company purchased a delivery truck for $35,000 on January 1, 2006. The truck had an estimated useful life of 7 years or 210,000 miles. Best-Goods estimated the truck's salvage value to be $5,000. The truck was driven 21,000 miles in 2006 and 31,500 miles in 2007.

a. Compute the depreciation expense for 2006 and 2007, first using the straight-line method, then the activity method.
b. Prepare the journal entries to record depreciation expense for each of these years, first using the straight-line method, then the activity method.
c. Which method portrays more accurately the actual use of this asset? Explain your answer.

LO 2   **E8-4A.** **Calculate depreciation expense: straight-line and double-declining balance methods.**
On January 1, 2006, Norris Company purchased equipment for $42,000. Norris also paid $1,200 for shipping and installation. The equipment is expected to have a useful life of 10 years and a salvage value of $3,200.

a. Compute the depreciation expense for the years 2006 through 2008, using the straight-line method.
b. Compute the depreciation expense for the years 2006 through 2008, using the double-declining balance method.
c. What is the book value of the equipment at the end of 2008 under each method?

LO 2   **E8-5A.** **Calculate depreciation under alternative methods.**
Avery Corporation bought a new piece of equipment at the beginning of the year at a cost of $15,400. The estimated useful life of the machine is five years, and its estimated productivity is 75,000 units. Its salvage value is estimated to be $400. Yearly production was Year 1—15,000 units; Year 2—18,750 units; Year 3—11,250 units; Year 4—22,500 units; and Year 5—7,500. Complete a separate depreciation schedule for each of the methods given below for all five years. (Round your answers to the nearest dollar.)

a. Straight-line
b. Activity
c. Double-declining balance

LO 2   **E8-6A.** **Calculate depreciation under alternative methods.**
Using the information from E8-5A, suppose the production in Year 5 was actually 9,000 rather than 7,500 units. How would this difference in production change the amount of depreciation for Year 5 under each method? Explain.

LO 2   **E8-7A.** **Calculate depreciation under alternative methods.**
Propel Company bought a machine for $65,000 cash at the beginning of 2004. The estimated useful life is five years and the estimated salvage value is $5,000. The estimated productivity is 150,000 units. Units actually produced were 49,500 in 2004 and 36,000 in 2005. Calculate the depreciation expense for 2004 and 2005 under each of the methods given below. (Round your answers to the nearest dollar.)

a. Straight-line
b. Activity
c. Double-declining balance

LO 3   **E8-8A.** **Calculate and record depletion.**
On January 1, 2008, American Oil Company purchased the rights to an offshore oil well for $45,000,000. The company expects the oil well to produce 9,000,000 barrels of oil during its life. During 2008, American Oil removed 315,000 barrels of oil.

a. Prepare the journal entry to record the purchase on January 1, 2008.
b. How much depletion should American Oil Company record for 2008?
c. What is the book value of the oil rights at December 31, 2008, the end of the fiscal year?

LO 3   **E8-9A.** **Amortization of intangible assets.**
Becker and Associates registered a trademark with the U.S. Patent and Trademark Office. The total cost of obtaining the patent was $165,000. Although the patent has a legal life of 20 years, the firm believes it will be useful for only 10 years. What will Becker and Associates record for its annual amortization expense? Show the journal entry.

LO 3   **E8-10A.** **Valuing goodwill.**
Carpenter Tools decides to acquire a small local tool company called Local Tools. Local Tools has net assets with a market value of $230,000 but Carpenter pays $250,000. Why? Give the journal entry to record the purchase.

E8-11A. Evaluate asset impairment.

During its most recent fiscal year, Bargain Airlines had to ground 10 of its 747s due to a potential problem with the wing flaps. Although the planes had been repaired by the end of the fiscal year, the company believed the problems indicated the need for an evaluation of potential impairment of these planes. The results of the analysis indicated that the planes had permanently declined in value by $120 million below their book value. What effect would this decline in value have on Bargain Airlines' net income for the year?

E8-12A. Distinguish between capital and revenue expenditures.

Classify the following items as either a capital expenditure or a revenue expenditure (an expense).

a. Oil change for the delivery truck.
b. Replaced the engine in the delivery truck.
c. Sales tax paid on the new delivery truck.
d. Installed a new, similar roof on the office building.
e. Freight and installation charges for a new computer system.
f. Repainted the administrative offices.
g. Purchased and installed a new toner cartridge in the laser printer.
h. Replaced several missing shingles on the roof.
i. The cost of employee training prior to using the new computer system.
j. Replaced the brake pads on the delivery truck.

E8-13A. Evaluate and account for capital and revenue expenditures and calculate depreciation expense.

Yester Mfg. Co. has had a piece of equipment for six years. At the beginning of the seventh year, the equipment wasn't performing as well as expected. First, Yester re-lubricated the equipment, which cost $150. Then, the company replaced some worn-out parts, which cost $520. Finally, at the beginning of the seventh year, the company completed a major overhaul of the equipment that not only fixed the machine but also added new functionality and extended its useful life by three years (to a total of ten years) with no salvage value. The overhaul cost $10,000. (Originally, the machine cost $60,000, had a salvage value of $4,000, and an estimated useful life of seven years.)

a. Which of these costs are capital expenditures? How would these amounts appear on the financial statements?
b. Which are revenue expenditures? How would these amounts appear on the financial statements?
c. Assuming Yester Mfg. uses the straight-line method of depreciation, how much depreciation expense will be reported on the income statements for years 7 through 10?

E8-14A. Evaluate and account for capital and revenue expenditures and calculate depreciation expense.

Sharper Company operates a small repair facility for its products. At the beginning of 2006, the accounting records for the company showed the following balances for its only piece of equipment, purchased at the beginning of 2004:

Equipment	$115,000
Accumulated Depreciation	20,000

During 2006, the following costs were incurred for repairs and maintenance on the equipment:

Routine Maintenance and Repairs	$ 650
Major Overhaul of the Equipment that Improved Efficiency	22,000

The company uses straight-line basis, and it now estimates the equipment will last for a total of 11 years with a $5,000 estimated salvage value. The company's fiscal year ends on December 31.

a. Give the adjusting entry that was made at the end of 2005 for depreciation on the equipment.
b. After the overhaul at the beginning of 2006, what is the remaining estimated life of the equipment?
c. Give the journal entries to record the two expenditures for repairs and maintenance during 2006.
d. What is the amount of depreciation expense the company will record for 2006?

LO 5   **E8-15A.** **Account for disposal of an asset.**

Zellwiger Plumbing bought a van for $60,000. The van is expected to have a 10-year useful life and a salvage value of $4,000.

   a. If Zellwiger sells the van after 3 years for $20,000, would the company realize a gain or loss? How much? (Assume straight-line depreciation.)

   b. What would be the gain or loss if the company sold the van for $30,000 after 6 years?

LO 5   **E8-16A.** **Account for disposal of an asset.**

Troy Wilson Athletic Gear purchased a packaging machine four years ago for $18,000. The machinery was expected to have a salvage value of $2,000 after an eight-year useful life. Assuming straight-line depreciation is used, calculate the gain or loss realized if after four years the machinery was sold for:

   a. $11,400

   b. $ 7,800

LO 5   **E8-17A.** **Account for disposal of an asset.**

Dave's Delivery disposed of a delivery truck after using it four years. The records of the company provide the following information:

Delivery truck	$38,000
Accumulated Depreciation	23,000

Calculate the gain or loss on the disposal of the truck for each of the following independent situations:

   a. Dave's Delivery sold the truck to Papa John's Pizza for $12,000.

   b. Dave's Delivery sold the truck to Cornerstone Grocery for $15,000.

   c. Dave's Delivery sold the truck to John's Plumbing for $16,000.

   d. The truck was stolen out of Dave's parking lot, and the company had no insurance.

LO 5   **E8-18A.** **Account for disposal of an asset.**

Sweet Tooth Bakery disposed of an oven after using it for four years. The oven originally cost $40,000 and had associated accumulated depreciation of $29,000. Calculate the gain or loss on the disposal of the oven for each of the following situations:

   a. The company sold the oven to a homeless shelter for $8,000.

   b. The company sold the oven to a local restaurant for $10,000.

   c. The company gave the oven to a hauling company in return for hauling the oven to the local dump. The oven was totally worthless.

   d. Prepare the journal entry for a. b. and c. to record the disposal of the oven.

LO 5, 6   **E8-19A.** **Gain or loss and cash flow.**

Arco Incorporated sold assets with an original cost of $15,000 and accumulated depreciation of $9,000. If the cash proceeds from the sale were $7,000, what was the gain or loss on the sale? On which financial statement would that amount be shown? How much would be shown on the statement of cash flows and in which section?

LO 6   **E8-20A.** **Financial statement of presentation.**

For each of the following, give the financial statement on which it would appear:

   a. Book value of fixed assets of $56,900

   b. Proceeds from sale of fixed assets of $20,000

   c. Loss on sale of fixed assets of $12,500

   d. Accumulated depreciation on equipment of $10,000

   e. Depreciation expense on equipment of $2,000

   f. Impairment write-down on assets of $45,000

LO 7   **E8-21A.** **Calculate return on assets and asset turnover ratios.**

Using the Wal-Mart annual report in the Appendix at the back of the book, calculate the following ratios for the most recent fiscal year and explain what each ratio measures:

   a. Return on assets (ROA)

   b. Asset turnover ratio

E8-22A. Risk and control.
Look at Wal-Mart's annual report in the Appendix at the back of the book. What types of fixed assets does the firm have? What risks do you think Wal-Mart faces with respect to these assets, and how is Wal-Mart controlling those risks?

Exercise Set B

> Your professor may ask you to complete selected "Group B" exercises and problems using Prentice Hall Grade Assist (**PHGA**). PHGA is an online tool that can help you master the chapter's topics by providing multiple variations of exercises and problems. You can rework these exercises and problems—each time with new data—as many times as you need, with immediate feedback and grading.

E8-1B. Account for basket purchase.
Premium Bottling Company purchases a building and land for a total cash price of $200,000. An independent appraiser provides the following market values: building—$175,000; land—$75,000.

a. How much of the purchase price should the company allocate to each of the assets?
b. If the building has a useful life of 10 years and an estimated salvage value of $40,000, how much depreciation expense should Premium record each year using the straight-line method?
c. Using the double-declining balance method, what would the book value of the building be at the end of 3 years?

E8-2B. Calculate the cost of an asset and depreciation expense.
Wilson, Smith & Knight Beer Brewers purchased a building for $125,000 cash and the land for $275,000 cash. The company paid real estate closing costs of $6,000, and allocated that cost to the building and the land based on the purchase price. Renovation costs on the building were $45,000.

a. Give the journal entry to record the purchase of the property, including all related expenditures. Assume that all transactions were for cash and that all purchases occurred at the beginning of the year.
b. Compute the annual straight-line depreciation, assuming a 20-year estimated useful life and an $11,875 estimated salvage value for the building. Prepare the journal entry to record the first year of depreciation.
c. What would be the book value of the building at the end of the fifth year?
d. What would the book value of the land be at the end of the tenth year?

E8-3B. Calculate depreciation expense: straight-line and activity methods.
Walt's Water Pressure Company purchased a van for $45,000 on July 1, 2008. The van had an estimated useful life of 6 years or 250,000 miles. Walt's estimated the van's salvage value to be $3,000. The van was driven 25,000 miles in the year ended June 30, 2009, and 30,000 miles in the year ended June 30, 2010.

a. Compute the depreciation expense for 2009 and 2010, first using the straight-line method, then the activity method.
b. Prepare the journal entries to record depreciation expense for each of these years, first using the straight-line method, then the activity method.
c. Which method portrays more accurately the actual use of this asset? Explain your answer.

E8-4B. Calculate depreciation expense: straight-line and double-declining balance methods.
On January 1, 2008, Hsieh & Wen's Gourmet Taste of Asia purchased kitchen equipment for $51,500. Hsieh & Wen's was also charged $1,650 for shipping and installation. The equipment is expected to have a useful life of 8 years and a salvage value of $3,150.

a. Compute the depreciation expense for the years 2008 through 2010, using the straight-line method.
b. Compute the depreciation expense for the years 2008 through 2010, using the double-declining balance method. Round your answers to the nearest dollar.
c. What is the book value of the equipment at the end of 2008 under each method?

LO 2   **E8-5B. Calculate depreciation under alternative methods.**
Designer Jeans bought a new piece of equipment at the beginning of the year at a cost of $24,500. The estimated useful life of the machine is four years, and its estimated productivity is 85,000 units. Its salvage value is estimated to be $500. Yearly production for Year 1 was 34,000 units; Year 2 was 25,500 units; Year 3 was 19,125 units; and Year 4 was 6,375 units. Complete a separate depreciation schedule for each of the methods given below for all four years. (Round your answers to the nearest dollar.)

    a. Straight-line
    b. Activity
    c. Double-declining balance

LO 2   **E8-6B. Calculate depreciation under alternative methods.**
Using the information from E8-5B, suppose the production in Year 4 was actually 8,500 rather than 6,375 units. How would this change the amount of depreciation for Year 4 under each method? Explain.

LO 2   **E8-7B. Calculate depreciation under alternative methods.**
Brother's Helper Manufacturing bought a machine for $172,000 cash at the beginning of 2007. The estimated useful life is eight years and the estimated salvage value is $4,000. The estimated productivity is 265,000 units. Units actually produced were 92,750 in 2007 and 55,650 in 2008. Calculate the depreciation expense for 2007 and 2008 under each of the methods given below. (Round your answers to the nearest dollar.)

    a. Straight-line
    b. Activity
    c. Double-declining balance

LO 2   **E8-8B. Calculate and record depletion.**
On January 1, 2007, West Mountain Mining Company purchased the rights to a coal mine for $15,000,000. The company expects the coal mine to produce 10,000,000 pounds of coal. During 2007, West Mountain Mining removed 550,000 pounds of coal.

    a. Prepare the journal entry to record the purchase on January 1, 2007.
    b. How much depletion should West Mountain Mining Company record for 2007?
    c. What is the book value of the coal rights at December 31, 2007, the end of the fiscal year?

LO 3   **E8-9B. Amortization of intangible assets.**
Microtech registered a trademark with the U.S. Patent and Trademark Office. The total cost of obtaining the trademark was $55,000. Although the trademark has a legal life of 20 years, the firm believes it will be renewed indefinitely. What will Microtech record for its annual amortization expense?

LO 3   **E8-10B. Valuing goodwill.**
Evans has decided to acquire a competitor firm. The competitor firm has assets with a market value of $430,000 and liabilities with a market value of $210,000, and Evans pays $250,000. Why? Give the journal entry to record the purchase.

LO 4   **E8-11B. Evaluate asset impairment.**
During its fiscal year ended June 30, Super Shippers Delivery Service had to decommission 1,500 delivery trucks due to a potential problem with the fuel tank. Although the trucks had been repaired by the end of the fiscal year, the company determined the problems required an evaluation of potential impairment of these trucks. The results of the analysis indicated that the trucks had permanently declined in value by $7.5 million below their book value. What effect would this decline have on Super Shippers' net income for the year?

LO 1, 4   **E8-12B. Distinguish between capital and revenue expenditures.**
Classify the following items as either a capital expenditure or a revenue expenditure (expense).

    a. Filter change for the moving van.
    b. Painting the moving van.
    c. Sales tax paid on the new moving van.
    d. Installed a new energy-efficient air-conditioning system for the office building.
    e. Cleaning and lubrication of sewing equipment.

f. Routine yearly maintenance on copy machine.
g. Purchased and installed a new set of energy efficient deep-fryers.
h. Replaced several cracked tiles in company bathroom floor.
i. The cost of employee training prior to using the new energy efficient deep-fryers.
j. Replaced the tires on the moving van.

E8-13B. Evaluate and account for capital and revenue expenditures and calculate depreciation expense.

<u>LO 2, 4</u>

Shiny & New Auto Mechanic Shop has had a piece of equipment for five years. At the beginning of the sixth year, it wasn't performing as well as it should have been. First, Shiny & New had the equipment serviced, which cost $175. Then, the company tried replacing some worn-out parts, which cost $480. Finally, at the beginning of the sixth year, it completed a major overhaul of the equipment that not only fixed the machine, but also added new functionality to it and extended the useful life by four years (to a total of ten years with five remaining) with no salvage value. The overhaul cost $20,000. (Originally, the machine cost $65,000, had a salvage value of $5,000, and an estimated useful life of six years.)

a. Which of these costs are capital expenditures? How would these amounts appear on the financial statements?
b. Which are revenue expenditures? How would these amounts appear on the financial statements?
c. Assuming Shiny & New uses the straight-line method of depreciation, how much depreciation expense will be reported on the income statements for years six through ten?

E8-14B. Evaluate and account for capital and revenue expenditures and calculate depreciation expense.

<u>LO 2, 4</u>

Global Electronics operates a manufacturing plant for production of its products. At the beginning of 2008, the accounting records for the company showed the following balances for its only piece of equipment, purchased at the beginning of 2005:

Equipment	$94,000
Accumulated Depreciation	54,000

During 2008, the following cash costs were incurred for repairs and maintenance on the equipment:

Routine maintenance and repairs	$ 575
Major overhaul of the equipment that improved efficiency	30,000

The company uses straight-line depreciation, and estimates the equipment will last for five years beginning in 2008 with a $4,000 estimated salvage value. The company's fiscal year ends on December 31.

a. Give the adjusting entry that was made at the end of 2007 for depreciation on the equipment.
b. After the overhaul, at the beginning of 2008, what is the remaining estimated life?
c. Give the journal entries to record the two expenditures for repairs and maintenance during 2008.
d. What is the amount of depreciation expense the company will record for 2008?

E8-15B. Account for disposal of an asset.

<u>LO 5</u>

Renee & Chesney Flower Shop purchased a delivery van for $51,000. The company expects the van to have an eight-year useful life and a salvage value of $3,000.

a. If Renee & Chesney sells the van after two years for $40,500, would it realize a gain or loss? How much? (Assume straight-line depreciation.)
b. What would be the gain or loss if the van were sold for $18,250 after five years?

E8-16B. Account for disposal of an asset.

<u>LO 5</u>

Brenda Sue's Stitch & Sew purchased a sewing machine four years ago for $29,000. The company expects the machine to have a salvage value of $4,000 after a ten-year useful life. Assuming the company uses straight-line depreciation, calculate the gain or loss realized if the company sells the machine after four years for:

a. $ 14,250
b. $ 18,600

LO 5   **E8-17B.** **Account for disposal of an asset.**

Kat & Jen's Solar Tan disposed of a high-pressure tanning bed that had been used in the business for three years. The records of the company provide the following information:

High-pressure Tanning Bed	$39,000
Accumulated Depreciation	18,000

Calculate the gain or loss on the disposal of the tanning bed for each of the following independent situations:

a. Kat & Jen's sold the tanning bed to Dark Bodies for $21,000.
b. Kat & Jen's sold the tanning bed to a customer for $22,550.
c. Kat & Jen's sold the tanning bed to Angela's Fitness Center for $18,000.
d. The tanning salon was broken into and the tanning bed was stolen; Kat & Jen's had no insurance.

LO 5   **E8-18B.** **Account for disposal of an asset.**

Crystal Clean Steamers disposed of an industrial wet/dry vacuum that had been used in the business for five years. The vacuum originally cost $51,000 and had associated accumulated depreciation of $32,500. Calculate the gain or loss on the disposal of the vacuum for each of the following situations:

a. The company sold the vacuum to a local church for $16,250.
b. The company sold the vacuum to a competitor for $21,475.
c. The company called the city trash collectors to pick up the vacuum because it was totally worthless.
d. Prepare the journal entry for a. b. and c. to record the disposal of the vacuum.

LO 4, 5   **E8-19B.** **Gain or loss and cash flow.**

Safin Incorporated sold assets with an original cost of $37,000 and accumulated depreciation of $30,000. If the cash proceeds from the sale were $4,000, what was the gain or loss on the sale? On which financial statement would that amount be shown? How much would be shown on the statement of cash flows and in which section?

LO 6   **E8-20B.** **Financial statement presentation.**

For each of the following, give the financial statement on which it would appear:

a. Book value of fixed assets of $56,900
b. Proceeds from sale of fixed assets of $20,000
c. Loss on sale of fixed assets of $12,500
d. Accumulated depreciation on equipment of $10,000
e. Depreciation expense on equipment of $2,000
f. Impairment write-down on assets of $45,000

LO 7   **E8-21B.** **Calculate return on assets and asset turnover ratios.**

Using the Target 10-K report in the Appendix at the back of the book, calculate the following ratios for the most recent fiscal year and explain what each measures:

a. Return on assets (ROA)
b. Asset turnover ratio

LO 8   **E8-22B.** **Risk and control.**

Firms with large fixed assets like land and factories often think that their assets are safe because they are too large to be stolen. What risks do you think exist for these firms with respect to such assets, and how might they be controlled?

Problem Set A

LO 1, 2   **P8-1A.** **Calculate capitalized cost and depreciation expense.**

Acme Print Shop purchased a new printing press in 2006. The invoice price was $158,500, but the manufacturer of the press gave Acme a 2% discount for paying cash for the machine on delivery. Delivery costs amounted to $1,500, and Acme paid $500 for a special insurance policy to cover the press while in transit. Installation cost was $1,350, and Acme spent $3,000 training the employees to use the new press. Additionally, Acme hired a new supervisor at an annual salary of $65,000 to be responsible for keeping the press on-line during business hours.

Required

a. What amount should be capitalized for this new asset?
b. To calculate the depreciation expense for 2006, what other information do you need? Do you think the company should gather this information before purchasing the asset? Why or why not?

P8-2A. Calculate and analyze depreciation under alternative methods.

LO 2

On January 1, 2007, the Oviedo Manufacturing Company purchased equipment for $170,000. The estimated useful life of the equipment is four years, and the estimated salvage value is $10,000. The company expects the equipment to produce 480,000 units during its service life. Actual units produced were:

Year	Units
2007	100,800
2008	130,080
2009	139,200
2010	109,920

Required

a. Calculate the depreciation expense for each year of the four-year life of the equipment using
   1. Straight-line method
   2. Double-declining balance method
   3. Activity method (Round your answers to the nearest dollar.)
b. How does the choice of depreciation methods affect net income in each of the years? How does the choice of depreciation methods affect the balance sheet in each of the years?

P8-3A. Calculate and analyze depreciation under alternative methods.

LO 2

Federal Express purchased a new truck on January 1, 2007, at a cost of $100,000. The estimated useful life is five years with a salvage value of $10,000.

Required

a. Prepare two different depreciation schedules for the equipment—one using the straight-line method, and the other using the double-declining balance method. (Round to the nearest dollar.)
b. Determine which method would result in the greatest net income for the year 2007.
c. How would taxes affect management's choice between these two methods for the financial statements?

P8-4A. Calculate and analyze depreciation under alternative methods.

LO 2

Peps Co. purchased a new machine at the beginning of 2006 for $6,400. The company expects the machine to last for five years and have a salvage value of $400. The estimated productive life of the machine is 100,000 units. Yearly production: in 2006—28,000 units; in 2007—22,000 units; in 2008—16,000 units; in 2009—14,000 units; in 2010—20,000 units.

Required

a. Calculate the depreciation for each year using each of these depreciation methods:
   1. Straight-line
   2. Activity based on units
   3. Double-declining balance (Round to the nearest dollar.)
b. For each method, give the amount of accumulated depreciation that would be shown on the balance sheet at the end of each year.
c. Calculate the book value of the machine at the end of each year for each method.

P8-5A. Intangible assets.

LO 3

LB had the following balances in its intangible assets accounts at the beginning of the year. The patents have a remaining useful life of ten years, and the copyright has a remaining useful life of seven years. The transactions for the year related to these assets are also shown below.

Patents	$35,000
Copyright	21,000
Goodwill	40,000

Transactions during the year:

1. At the beginning of the year, LB filed for a new patent. The costs totaled $20,000. Its useful life is estimated at ten years.
2. LB incurred research and development costs of $60,000, related to new product development. No new products have been identified.
3. LB evaluated the goodwill for impairment and reduces its book value by $2,000.
4. LB successfully defended one of its patents in court. Fees totaled $24,000.

Required

Prepare the necessary journal entries for each of the transactions, including the adjusting entries. Then, prepare the intangible assets section of the balance sheet at year end.

LO 1, 2, 3, 4   **P8-6A. Analyze and correct accounting errors related to long-term assets.**

Due to an umpire strike early in 2006, Umpire's Empire had some trouble with its information processing and some errors were made in accounting for certain transactions. Evaluate the following independent situations that occurred during the year:

1. At the beginning of 2006, a building and land were purchased together for $100,000. Even though the appraisers determined that 90% of the price should be allocated to the building, Umpire's decided to allocate the entire purchase price to the building. The building is being depreciated straight-line over 40 years, with an estimated salvage value of $10,000.
2. During the year, Umpire did some research and development on a new gadget to keep track of balls and strikes. The R&D cost $20,000, and Umpire capitalized it. The company intends to write it off over 5 years, using straight-line depreciation with no salvage value.
3. Near the beginning of the year, Umpire spent $10,000 on routine maintenance for its equipment, and the accountant decided to capitalize these costs as part of the equipment. (Equipment is depreciated over 5 years with no salvage value.)
4. Umpire spent $5,000 to extend the useful life of some of its equipment. The accountant capitalized the cost.

Required

a. For each, describe the error made, and list the effect, if any, that the error would have on the following items for Umpire's 2006 Financial Statements: income, long-term assets, and retained earnings if it were *not* corrected. If there is no error, simply write N/A next to the item.
b. Give the journal entry that would need to be made to correct the company's accounting records and make the 2006 financial statements accurate. If there is no error, write N/A next to the item.

LO 4   **P8-7A. Change in estimates for depreciation.**

In January 2004, Harvey's Hoola Hoop Company purchased a computer system that cost $37,000. Harvey's estimates that the system will last for five years and will have a salvage value of $2,000 at the end of 2008, and the company uses the straight-line method of depreciation. Analyze each of the following independent scenarios.

1. Before the depreciation expense is recorded for the year 2006, computer experts tell Harvey's that the system can be used until the end of 2008 as planned but that it will be worth only $500.
2. Before depreciation expense is recorded for the year 2006, Harvey's decides that the computer system will only last until the end of 2007. The company anticipates the value of the system at that time will still be $2,000.
3. Before depreciation expense is recorded for the year 2006, Harvey's decides that the computer system will last until the end of 2008, but that it will be worth only $1,000 at that time.

4. Before the depreciation expense is recorded for the year 2006, computer experts tell Harvey's that the system can be used until the end of 2012 if he spends $4,000 on upgrades. However, the estimated salvage value at that time would be $0. Harvey's decides to follow the experts' advice and upgrade the computer system.

Required

Calculate the amount of depreciation expense related to the computer system Harvey's Hoola Hoop Company will report on its income statement for the year ended December 31, 2006.

P8-8A. Account for disposal of an asset.

LO 5

Analyze each of the following independent scenarios.

1. A truck that cost $25,000, had an estimated useful life of 5 years with no salvage value, was being depreciated using the straight-line method. After 4 years, the company sold the truck for $6,000.
2. A machine that cost $50,000, had an estimated useful life of 12 years and a salvage value of $2,000, was being depreciated using the straight-line method. After 10 years, the machine was completely worn out and sold for $400 as scrap.
3. An asset that cost $40,000, had a salvage value of $2,000, and an estimated useful life of 4 years, was being depreciated using the double-declining balance method. After 3 years, the company sold the asset for $11,000.
4. A machine that cost $15,000, with an estimated useful life of 5 years and no salvage value, was being depreciated using the straight-line method. After 4 years, the company deemed the asset worthless and hauled it to the dump.

Required

For each scenario, calculate the gain or loss, if any, that would result upon disposal.

P8-9A. Calculate depreciation under alternative methods and account for disposal of an asset.

LO 2, 5

Bella Interiors purchased a new sewing machine on January 2, 2007, for $48,000. The company expects the machine to have a useful life of five years and a salvage value of $3,000. The company's fiscal year ends on December 31.

Required

a. Calculate the depreciation expense for the fiscal years 2007 and 2008 using each of the following methods:
1. Straight-line
2. Double-declining balance
b. Assume that Bella Interiors decided to use the straight-line method and that the sewing machine was sold at the end of December 2009, for $27,000. What was the gain or loss on the sale? On which financial statement would the gain or loss appear? What information does this accounting calculation provide for future decisions?

P8-10A. Calculate and analyze depreciation under alternative methods and account for disposal of an asset.

LO 2, 5

Perfect Heating and Air purchased a truck three years ago for $50,000. The company expects the truck to have a useful life of five years with no salvage value. The company has taken three full years of depreciation expense.

Required

a. Assume that the company uses straight-line depreciation. If the truck is sold for $25,000, will there be a gain or loss on the sale? If so, how much? How will the sale affect the financial statements for the year? Prepare the journal entry to record the sale of the truck.
b. Assume that the company uses double-declining balance depreciation. If the truck is sold for $15,000, will there be a gain or loss on the sale? If so, how much? How will the sale affect the financial statements for the year? Prepare the journal entry to record the sale of the truck.
c. Assume the company uses straight-line depreciation and sells the truck for $20,000. Would there be a gain or loss on the sale? How would that change if the company had been using double-declining balance depreciation?

Problem Set B

> Your professor may ask you to complete selected "Group B" exercises and problems using Prentice Hall Grade Assist (**PHGA**). PHGA is an online tool that can help you master the chapter's topics by providing multiple variations of exercises and problems. You can rework these exercises and problems—each time with new data—as many times as you need, with immediate feedback and grading.

LO 1, 2   **P8-1B. Calculate capitalized cost and depreciation expense.**

The executives for Sea World decided to buy a piece of property adjacent to the park with an old, run-down motel. The cost of the land with the old motel was $1,500,000. Real estate commissions and fees including the title search were $317,850. Sea World paid its attorney $15,000 to review the contract and complete the purchase of the land on July 1, 2008. The resort paid $25,750 for the old motel to be demolished and an additional $17,850 for sugar white sand to be hauled in to prepare the land for use. The company paid $80,000 for some palm trees for the new area. Sea World hired three new employees at a salary of $35,000 a year each to maintain the landscaping for the new area.

Required

a. What amount should be capitalized for this new asset?
b. Would there be any depreciation expense for land at the end of 2008? Explain your answer.

LO 2   **P8-2B. Calculate and analyze depreciation under alternative methods.**

WTA Tennis Academy purchased a new ball machine at a cost of $18,000 at the beginning of January 2005. The machine was estimated to have a salvage value of $2,000 at the end of its useful life of four years. A machine like this is supposed to deliver 160,000 hours of service. The actual number of hours that the machine was used per year was:

Year	Hours
2005	40,000
2006	60,800
2007	39,200
2008	20,000

Required

a. Calculate the depreciation expense for each year of the four-year life of the ball machine using:
   1. Straight-line method
   2. Activity method
   3. Double-declining method
b. How does the choice of depreciation methods affect income in each of the years?
c. How does the choice of depreciation methods affect the balance sheet in each of the years?

LO 2   **P8-3B. Calculate and analyze depreciation under alternative methods.**

Sugar's Candy Company purchased an automated display rack on January 1, 2008, at a cost of $35,000. The company estimates the display rack has a useful life of five years with a salvage value of $5,000.

Required

a. Prepare two different depreciation schedules for the equipment—one using the straight-line method, and the other using the double-declining balance method. (Round to the nearest dollar.)
b. Determine which method would result in the greatest net income for the year 2010.
c. How would taxes affect management's choice between these two methods for the financial statements?

P8-4B. Calculate and analyze depreciation under alternative methods.

LO 2

Clean Water Co. purchased a new water filter at the beginning of 2010 for $200,000. It is expected to last for eight years and have a salvage value of $32,000. The estimated productive life of the machine is 200,000 units. Yearly production: in 2010—45,000 units; in 2011—29,000 units; in 2012—41,000 units; in 2013—22,000 units; in 2014—25,000 units; in 2015—15,000 units; in 2016—16,000 units; and in 2017—7,000 units.

Required

a. Calculate the depreciation for each year using each of these depreciation methods:
   1. Straight-line
   2. Activity based on units
   3. Double-declining balance (Round to the nearest dollar)
b. For each method, give the amount of accumulated depreciation that would be shown on the balance sheet at the end of each year.
c. Calculate the book value of the machine at the end of each year for each method.

P8-5B. Intangible assets.

LO 3

Larkin had the following balances in its intangible asset accounts at the beginning of the year. The trademarks have a remaining useful life of five years, and the copyright has a remaining useful life of ten years. The transactions for the year related to these assets are also shown below.

Trademarks	$85,000
Copyright	50,000
Goodwill	80,000

Transactions during the year:

1. At the beginning of the year, Larkin filed for a new trademark. The costs totaled $40,000. Its useful life is estimated at five years.
2. Larkin incurred research and development costs of $30,000, related to new product development. No new products have been identified.
3. Larkin evaluated the goodwill for impairment and reduces its book value by $20,000.
4. Larkin successfully defended its copyrights in court. Fees totaled $10,000.

Required

Prepare the necessary journal entries for each of the transactions including adjusting entries. Then, prepare the intangible assets section of the balance sheet at year end.

P8-6B. Analyze and correct accounting errors related to long-term assets.

LO 1, 2, 4

During 2007, Jule's Gym had some trouble with its information processing due to several hurricanes, and some errors were made in accounting for certain transactions. The firm uses straight-line depreciation for all of its long-term assets. Evaluate the following independent situations that occurred during the year:

1. At the beginning of the year, a basket purchase of a building and land was made for $350,000. The appraisers indicated that the market value of the land was $135,000, and the market value of the building was $250,000. So, Jule's Gym allocated $135,000 of the purchase price to the land and the remainder of the purchase price to the building. The building has an estimated useful life of 20 years and an estimated salvage value of $25,000.
2. The plumber spent a great deal of time repairing broken toilets in one of the gym's buildings this year. Total cost, which Jule's Gym capitalized, was $5,000. Jule's Gym decided it was best to leave it on the books as an asset and not write it off, since the toilets will be used for quite a few more years. (Use 20 years as the estimated remaining useful life of the toilets.)
3. Jule's Gym purchased a new van. It cost $20,000 and is expected to last three years. It has a salvage value of $2,000. To properly equip it for transporting gym equipment between locations, the inside was customized at a cost of $6,000. The cost of the van was capitalized, and the cost of the customization was expensed.
4. Jule's Gym spent $5,500 on routine maintenance of its exercise equipment. The cost was expensed.

Required

a. For each, describe the error made, and list the effect, if any, that the error would have on the following items for Jule's Gym's 2007 Financial Statements: Net Income, Long-term Assets, and Retained Earnings if it were not corrected. If there is no error, simply write N/A next to the item.
b. Give the journal entry that would be needed to correct the company's accounting records and make the 2007 financial statements accurate. If there is no error, write N/A next to the problem.

LO 4   **P8-7B. Change in estimates for depreciation.**

In July 2006, Hallmark Company purchased a computer system that cost $7,000. The company estimates that the system will last for five years and will have a salvage value of $2,000. The company uses the straight-line method of depreciation and has a June 30 fiscal year-end. Analyze each of the following independent scenarios.

1. Before depreciation expense is recorded for the year ended June 30, 2009, the company decides that the computer system will last until the end of June 2011, but that it will be worth only $800 at that time.
2. Before the depreciation expense is recorded for the fiscal year ended June 30, 2009, Hallmark decides that that the computer system will only last until the end of 2010. The company anticipates the value of the system at that time will still be $2,000.
3. Before depreciation expense is recorded for the fiscal year ended June 30, 2009, Hallmark decides that the computer system will last until the end of 2011, but will be worth only $1,500 at that time.
4. Before the depreciation expense is recorded for the fiscal year ended June 30, 2009, the company's computer experts decide that the system can be used until the end of June 2013 if the company spends $1,000 on upgrades. However, the estimated salvage value at that time would be 0. Hallmark decides to follow the experts' advice and upgrade the computer system.

Required

Calculate the amount of depreciation expense related to the computer system Hallmark will report on its income statement for the fiscal year ended June 30, 2009.

LO 5   **P8-8B. Account for disposal of an asset.**

Analyze each of the following independent scenarios.

1. A company van cost $32,000, had an estimated useful life of eight years with no salvage value, and was being depreciated using the straight-line method. After six years, the company sold it for $12,000.
2. A copy machine that cost $35,000, had a salvage value of $5,000, and an estimated useful life of five years, was being depreciated using the double-declining balance method. After two years, it was sold for $10,000.
3. A company truck that cost $48,000, had an estimated useful life of seven years and a salvage value of $6,000, was being depreciated using the straight-line method. After five years of many miles of driving on tough terrain, the truck was completely worn out and sold for $850, for spare parts.
4. A state-of-the-art computer that cost $29,000, had a salvage value of $2,000, and an estimated useful life of four years, was being depreciated using the double-declining balance method. After three years, it was sold for $6,000.

Required

For each scenario, calculate the gain or loss, if any, that would result upon disposal.

LO 2, 5   **P8-9B. Calculate depreciation under alternative methods and account for disposal of an asset.**

A&W Root Beer Company bought new brewery equipment on January 1, 2008, for $64,000. The company expects the equipment to have a useful life of eight years and a salvage value of $8,000. The company's fiscal year ends on December 31.

Required

a. Calculate the depreciation expense for the fiscal years 2008 and 2009 using each of the following methods:
   1. Straight-line
   2. Double-declining balance

b. Assume that the company decided to use the double-declining method and that the brewery equipment was sold at the end of December 2009, for $42,000. What was the gain or loss on the sale? On which financial statement would the gain or loss appear? What information does this accounting calculation provide for future decisions?

P8-10B. Calculate and analyze depreciation under alternative methods and account for disposal of an asset.

LO 2, 5

The Queen Grande View Hotel purchased a van three years ago for $62,000. The company expects the van to have a useful life of four years and a $10,000 salvage value. Queen Grande View has taken three full years of depreciation expense.

Required

a. Assume that Queen Grande View uses straight-line depreciation. If the van is sold for $20,000, will there be a gain or loss on the sale? If so, how much? How will it affect Queen Grande View's financial statements for the year? Prepare the journal entry to record the sale of the van.

b. Assume that Queen Grande View uses double-declining balance depreciation. If the van is sold for $9,750, will there be a gain or loss on the sale? If so, how much? How will it affect Queen Grande View's financial statements for the year? Prepare the journal entry to record the sale of the van.

c. Assume Queen Grande View uses double-declining depreciation and sells the van for $23,000. Would there be a gain or loss on the sale? How would that change if Queen Grande View had been using straight-line balance depreciation?

Financial Statement Analysis

FSA8-1. Analyze long-term assets on the balance sheet.

LO 6

Use the following information from The Home Depot Annual Report to answer the questions below:

(numbers in millions)	January 30, 2005	February 1, 2004
Property and Equipment, at cost:		
Land	$6,932	$6,397
Building	12,325	10,920
Furniture, Fixtures and Equipment	6,195	5,163
Leasehold Improvements	1,191	942
Construction in Progress	1,404	820
Capital Leases	390	352
	28,437	24,594
Less Accumulated Depreciation and Amortization	5,711	4,531
Net Property and Equipment	$22,726	$20,063

Note on Depreciation and Amortization

The Company's Buildings, Furniture, Fixtures and Equipment are depreciated using the straight-line method over the estimated useful lives of the assets. Leasehold improvements are amortized using the straight-line method over the life of the lease or the useful life of the improvement, whichever is shorter. The Company's Property and Equipment is depreciated using the following estimated useful lives

	Life
Buildings	10–45 years
Furniture, Fixtures and Equipment	3–20 years
Leasehold Improvements	5–30 years

Required

a. Can you tell how much The Home Depot paid for the buildings it owns? If so, how do you know?

b. Can you tell how much the buildings are worth (the market value)?

c. With your knowledge of fixed assets, speculate about what Leasehold Improvements might be. Suppose The Home Depot leased a large warehouse for a new store. What would the firm need to do to get the building ready for use?

d. The Home Depot says it is modernizing its stores and building many new stores (175 in 2004). Is this supported by any of the information on the portion of The Home Depot's balance sheet shown above?

LO 1, 2, 4, 6   **FSA8-2. Analyze long-term assets on the balance sheet.**
Use the information from the 2004 Sony Annual Report to answer the questions below:

Dollars in millions	**March 31, 2004**
Property, plant and equipment (Note 8):	
Land	$ 1,825
Buildings	8,952
Machinery and equipment	19,741
Construction in progress	947
	31,465
Less—Accumulated depreciation	18,340
	13,125
Other Assets:	
Intangibles, net (Notes 9 and 14)	2,385
Goodwill (Note 9)	2,672

Property, Plant and Equipment and Depreciation

Property, plant, and equipment are stated at cost. Depreciation of property, plant, and equipment is computed on the declining-balance method for Sony Corporation and Japanese subsidiaries and on the straight-line method for foreign subsidiary companies at rates based on estimated useful lives of the assets, principally, ranging from 15 years up to 50 years for buildings and from 2 years up to 10 years for machinery and equipment. Significant renewals and additions are capitalized at cost. Maintenance and repairs, and minor renewals and betterments are charged to income as incurred.

Goodwill and Other Intangible Assets

Goodwill and certain other intangible assets that are determined to have an indefinite life are not amortized and are tested for impairment on an annual basis and between annual tests if an event occurs or circumstances change that would more likely than not reduce the fair value below its carrying amount. Fair value for those assets is generally determined using a cash flow analysis.

Intangible assets that are determined not to have an indefinite life mainly consist of artist contracts, music catalogs, acquired patent rights and software to be sold, leased or otherwise marketed. Artist contracts and music catalogs are amortized on a straight-line basis principally over a period of up to 40 years. Acquired patent rights and software to be sold, leased or otherwise marketed are amortized on a straight-line basis over 3 to 10 years.

Required

a. What is Sony's primary method for depreciating its assets?
b. How much did Sony pay for the machinery and equipment it owns?
c. Are any of the assets listed as Property, plant, and equipment not being depreciated?
d. Can you tell how much depreciation expense Sony had for the fiscal year ended March 31, 2004?
e. Explain what the $18,340 million of Accumulated Depreciation represents.
f. Can you find a sentence in the notes that summarizes the accounting treatment for major overhaul or additions to assets discussed in the chapter?
g. Describe how Sony evaluates Goodwill for impairment.

LO 2, 3, 5, 6   **FSA8-3. Analyze long-term assets on the balance sheet.**
Use the Target 10-K report from the Appendix at the back of the book to help you answer the following questions:

a. What type of depreciable assets does Target have? What methods does the company use to depreciate these assets?
b. Does Target have any intangible assets? What are they and how are they being written off?
c. What can you tell about the age and/or condition of Target's long-term assets? Is the company continuing to invest in property, plant, and equipment?
d. Is the company making good use of its assets? How can you evaluate this?

Critical Thinking Problems

Risk and Control

What kinds of risks does Target face with respect to safeguarding its assets? What types of controls do you think it has to minimize these risks? Are any specific controls mentioned in the 10-K report provided in the Appendix at the back of the book?

Ethics

Rachel works in a real estate office that is equipped with up-to-date copiers, scanners, and printers. She is frequently the only employee working in the office in the evenings and often has spare time to do personal work. She has begun to use the office equipment for her children's school reports and for her husband's business. Do you think Rachel's use of the office equipment is harmless, or is she behaving unethically? Why? If you believe her behavior is unethical, what controls could be in place to prevent it? Have you ever used office resources for personal tasks? Under what conditions could such use of office resources be justified?

Group Assignment

Select one of the three depreciation methods presented in the chapter. Discuss reasons why the method should be used and reasons why the method is not a good choice. Determine the method you think is most consistent with the objectives of financial reporting.

Internet Exercise: Best Buy

Best Buy is the number-one specialty retailer of consumer electronics, personal computers, entertainment software, and appliances. Ahead of rival Circuit City in sales but not store count, Best Buy has about 420 stores in 41 states, with heavy concentrations in the Midwest, Texas, California, and Florida. Best Buy's Musicland Stores subsidiary operates 1,300 music and video retail stores under the Sam Goody, Suncoast, On Cue, and Media Play names.

IE8-1. Select Best Buy's most recent annual report in the HTML format. Use the consolidated balance sheets to answer the following questions. At the most recent year-end, examine Property and Equipment.

a. What is the acquisition cost of these assets?
b. What is the book value (carrying value)?
c. What amount of the acquisition cost has already been expensed?
d. Are any of the assets listed not being depreciated?

IE8-2. Use the notes to financial statements to answer the following questions (usually the information can be found in note 1):

a. Find the heading Property and Equipment. What depreciation method does Best Buy use for property and equipment? What is the range of useful lives for buildings and for fixtures and equipment? Do these useful lives make sense?
b. Find the heading Goodwill. What type of an asset is goodwill? Does Best Buy expense this asset? Explain what the company does.

IE8-3. Under "Excel Spreadsheets" select the 10-Year Summary.

a. Identify the amount reported for total assets at the four most recent year ends. In which year did Best Buy acquire Musicland? How can you tell? Comment on the change in assets between the year of the Musicland acquisition and the previous year.
b. Identify the amount reported for Revenues and Net Earnings (net income) for the three most recent years.
c. Compute the asset turnover ratio for the two most recent fiscal years. In which fiscal year did the company make best use of its assets? How can you tell?

Additional Study Materials

Visit www.prenhall.com/reimers for self-study quizzes and spreadsheet templates to use to complete homework assignments.

CONTINUING CASE STUDY

Building your Excel skills with The MP3 Store

During the month of August, The MP3 Store engaged in the following transactions. The company is using LIFO and the perpetual inventory system. Recall from Chapter 7 that the beginning inventory consists of 10 MP3 players purchased for $196 each.

August 1	Purchased an electronic cash register for $1,400 cash. The cash register has an estimated useful life of 5 years and an estimated residual (salvage) value of $200.
August 2	Purchased 175 MP3 players for $227 each on account.
August 3	Paid the sales tax payable from July sales.
August 10	Collected $30,000 of July's outstanding A/R balance.
August 15	Due to a store remodeling, the owners decide to sell some display cases that originally cost $1,200. The cases sold for $1,000. (*Hint:* Don't forget to record depreciation for 1/2 month before recording the sale.)
August 16	Received and paid a $150 telephone bill.
August 18	Collected $10,000 of the outstanding accounts receivable balance.
August 20	Paid all of the accounts payable balance.
August 29	Paid the assistant manager $2,000 for August work.
August 30	By the end of the month, the company had sold a total of 130 MP3 players for $350 each. The sales tax rate is 6%. Of the sales, 25 were for cash and 105 were on account.
August 31	Recorded the required adjusting entries for depreciation, rent, insurance, and bad debts (5% of the outstanding Accounts Receivable). Use double declining balance depreciation for the new cash register and record 1/12 of the first year's depreciation for the month of August.

Requirements:

1. Prepare the necessary journal entries, T-accounts, trial balances, and financial statements. (Note: A Statement of Cash Flows is required for this chapter.)

2. When you are finished print and save your file to disk by clicking the **Save** button. Name your file MP38.

Depreciation and Taxes

The accounting information a company presents on its financial statements is not the same information the company reports to the IRS on its federal income tax return. The company follows GAAP reporting standards when preparing financial statements because those statements are provided to shareholders, who are the owners of the company. The information for taxes is determined by the legal rules of the Internal Revenue Code. GAAP and the IRS require different information to be reported, so companies will use an information system that can produce two sets of data.

For depreciating fixed assets, corporations use a method called the **Modified Accelerated Cost Recovery System (MACRS)** to calculate the deduction for their tax returns. MACRS is allowed for tax purposes but not GAAP. The goal of MACRS is to give companies incentive to invest in new property, plant, and equipment. If an asset can be written off quickly—large depreciation deductions over a small number of years—the tax benefit from the depreciation deductions leaves the company more cash to invest in new assets.

How does more depreciation expense result in lower taxes? Suppose a company's income before depreciation and before taxes is $10,000. If depreciation expense for taxes is $2,000, then the company has taxable income of $8,000. Suppose the company's tax rate is 25%. Then, the company must pay $2,000 (= $8,000 × 0.25) in taxes. (Net income will be $6,000.)

Now, suppose the company can depreciate the assets using a more accelerated depreciation method that results in $4,000 worth of depreciation expense. Income before depreciation and taxes is $10,000, so income before taxes will be $6,000 (= $10,000 − $4,000). With a tax rate of 25%, the company will have to pay $1,500 in taxes. (Net income will be $4,500).

When depreciation expense is larger, the amount of taxes a company must pay is smaller. A smaller tax bill means less cash has to be paid to the IRS, so the company's net cash flow for the year will be greater. However, as we have seen from comparing straight-line depreciation and double-declining balance depreciation, *over the life of an asset*, the total depreciation expense is the same no matter what method the company uses. The difference between the methods is reflected in the way the total depreciation is allocated to the years the asset is used. The reason a company wants to use an accelerated method like MACRS for tax purposes is so that the largest deductions are taken as soon as possible. Saving tax dollars *this* year is preferred to saving them *next* year because it is cash the company can use to buy assets that can increase production and therefore profits.

Modified Accelerated Cost Recovery System (MACRS): The common accelerated depreciation method used for taxes. It is not acceptable for GAAP.

Reporting and Understanding Liabilities

Here's where you've been . . .

- **You learned how firms account for the purchase of long-term operational assets.**

- **You learned how firms account for the use of long-term operational assets.**

- **You learned how firms account for the disposal of long-term operational assets.**

Here's where you're going . . .

- **You'll learn how firms account for current liabilities.**

- **You'll learn how firms account for long-term liabilities.**

YOU make the call:

How should Hewlett-Packard account for warranty expense?

Hewlett-Packard, with annual revenue of $79.9 billion for its fiscal year ended October 31, 2004, is a leading provider of technology products and services. The company is the number-one seller in the world of inkjet and laser printers.

Hewlett-Packard provides a basic warranty on all its products. Let's suppose that a typical service warranty is for two years and is provided with each sale at no additional charge. Suppose also that Hewlett-Packard estimates that the cost of honoring these particular warranties over the next two years will be approximately $2 million. Because the company will spend this money over the next two years, the new accounting manager decides to expense $1 million each year. One employee believes that the entire amount should be expensed this year. Another employee tells the manager that $980,000 has actually been disbursed to pay for warranty expenses during the year and that this amount should be recorded as warranty expense. Which of these choices do you think is correct? How much expense should Hewlett-Packard show on its current income statement related to warranties? *You make the call.*

Learning Objectives

When you are finished studying this chapter, you should be able to:

1. Define a definitely determinable liability and explain how payroll is recorded.
2. Define an estimated liability and explain how to account for warranties.
3. Explain how long-term notes and mortgages work.
4. Record the issue of bonds and payment of interest to bondholders.
5. Explain capital structure and compute the debt-to-equity and the times-interest-earned ratios.
6. Identify the major risk associated with long-term debt and the related controls.

LEARNING OBJECTIVE 1

Define a definitely determinable liability and explain how payroll is recorded.

Study Tip

Notice in Exhibit 9.1 that Hewlett-Packard has Employee Compensation and Benefits as one of its current liabilities. This liability is just another way to express the liability resulting from employees' work. Every company has its own way of naming accounts. Some names are very standard—like Accounts Receivable and Accounts Payable. Others can be different for various companies. Hewlett-Packard has Taxes on Earnings, which some companies will call Taxes Payable.

Definitely determinable liabilities: Obligations that can be measured exactly, like the amount of a note payable.

Definitely Determinable Liabilities

You've learned how a firm acquires and accounts for many of its assets—inventory, property and equipment, and operating items such as insurance and supplies. Now we'll see that a firm pays for those assets with current liabilities and long-term liabilities. Liabilities, as you know, represent amounts a company owes its creditors. Creditors are the people and other firms that sold something to the company or have loaned money to the company and expect to be repaid.

A liability is recognized—recorded in the accounting records so that it will appear on the balance sheet—when an obligation is incurred. When Hewlett-Packard receives processors from Intel, Hewlett-Packard records the asset in Inventory and the liability in Accounts Payable. Liabilities are based on past transactions and are generally recognized when incurred. Exhibit 9.1 shows the liability section of Hewlett-Packard's balance sheet. As we discuss various types of liabilities, you may want to refer back to this exhibit.

Definitely determinable liabilities are liabilities that can be measured exactly. When Walgreens purchases drugs from pharmaceutical supplier McKesson Corporation, Walgreens knows the cost of the drugs and will record the liability at its exact amount. The company also knows the amount of the obligation and records it with an increase in Inventory and an increase in Accounts Payable. Examples of liability accounts are Accounts Payable, Bank Loans or Lines of Credit, and Notes Payable. In Exhibit 9.1, Hewlett-Packard's balance sheet for the year ended October 31, 2004, shows Accounts Payable of $9,377 million. That is the amount Hewlett-Packard owes its suppliers, and it is a definitely determinable liability. When Office Depot buys paper from International Paper Company on account, Office Depot's accountant will debit the Inventory account, increasing an asset, and will credit the Accounts Payable account, increasing a liability. Some accrued liabilities, such as Salaries Payable and Unearned Revenue, are often definitely determinable.

Accounting for payroll

Payroll is an example of a common business expense that results in a definitely determinable, current liability. The government requires firms to supply them with the amounts of federal, state, and Social Security taxes each worker pays, so firms have to record more information about payroll than other accounts on the balance sheet. Accounting for payroll can take significant company resources, so frequently a company will hire another company like Automatic Data Processing (ADP) to manage its payroll.

Exhibit 9.1

Adapted from Hewlett-Packard's Consolidated Statements of Financial Position

Hewlett-Packard's balance sheet has a typical liability section. In 2004, Hewlett-Packard had total liabilities of **$38,574** million. You'll learn more about each type of liability in this chapter.

Hewlett-Packard, Inc. (HP)
From the Consolidated
Statement of Financial Position
(in millions)

	At October 31, 2004	At October 31, 2003
Liabilities		
Current Liabilities		
Notes payable and short-term borrowings	$ 2,511	$1,080
Accounts payable	9,377	9,285
Employee compensation and benefits	2,208	1,755
Taxes on earnings	1,709	1,599
Deferred revenue	2,958	2,496
Other accrued liabilities	9,825	9,254
Total current liabilities	28,588	25,469
Long-term debt	4,623	6,494
Other liabilities	5,363	5,007
Total liabilities	$38,574	$36,970

These are amounts that the company plans to settle in the coming fiscal year.

Deferred revenue is HP's *Unearned Revenue*—HP has collected the cash but still owes products or services to customers.

Learning a little about payroll will help you understand your next check from your employer and will help you see how liabilities are recorded. Suppose Hewlett-Packard hires a former police officer to guard the company's headquarters building for a salary of $500 per week. That amount is the employee's *gross pay*. As you may know from your work experience, gross pay is not the amount the employee takes home. Exhibit 9.2 shows where each piece of a paycheck goes.

From the gross pay amount, the company makes several deductions. First, the company withholds income taxes. To withhold taxes means that the

Exhibit 9.2

Where Does Your Paycheck Go?

Everybody wants a piece of the payroll pie. The amounts that are withheld in this example don't include health insurance premiums, state income taxes, or retirement contributions. Most people take home even less than 72% of their gross pay.

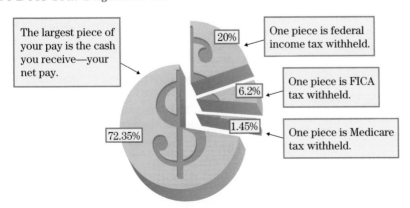

The largest piece of your pay is the cash you receive—your net pay.

One piece is federal income tax withheld. 20%

One piece is FICA tax withheld. 6.2%

One piece is Medicare tax withheld. 1.45%

72.35%

In Other Words:
Social Security taxes are called FICA taxes because they became law with the passage of the Federal Insurance Contributions Act of 1935.

employer, Hewlett-Packard, deducts money from the employee's pay and sends it to the U.S. government. And in doing so, Hewlett-Packard is acting as an *agent* for the government.

Second, the U.S. government requires the company to deduct Social Security taxes at the current legal rate (6.2% as this book was going to press) and Medicare taxes at the current legal rate (1.45% as this book was going to press). These two amounts must be "matched" by the employer. That means in addition to being an agent for the government, the company must also make its own payment. The company's payment is classified as payroll tax expense. Because the Social Security program is the subject of so much debate, you might want to read about some university students' opinions on the topic in ***Accounting in the News***.

Let's calculate the various amounts that Hewlett-Packard must withhold from the $500 gross pay of the security guard. Assuming 20% is withheld for federal income taxes (FIT), Hewlett-Packard would deduct $100. We'll use Social Security taxes at 6.2%, which amounts to $31.00, and Medicare taxes at 1.45%, which amounts to $7.25. So the amount Hewlett-Packard will pay the employee is:

$$\$500.00 - \$100.00 - \$31.00 - \$7.25 = \$361.75$$
$$\text{Gross Pay} - \text{FIT} - \text{FICA} - \text{Medicare Taxes} = \text{Net Pay}$$

The $361.75 Hewelett-Packard pays the employee is called net pay or net wages. The withheld amounts are payable to the various governmental agencies

Accounting in the NEWS

Ethics

Drop It—University Students Voice an Opinion on Bush's Plan for Social Security Reform

If you are currently working, the money you contribute to Social Security is *not* going into a savings account or trust fund in your name. Instead, your money goes to people who are retired—your elderly neighbors or family members. You've probably heard the expression "baby boomer." This term refers to people born between 1945 and 1964. Birth rates declined in the late 1960s, which means that when baby boomers retire in the next 10 to 20 years, there won't be enough younger workers to pay all of them the Social Security benefits they have earned.

President Bush's plan to allow workers to contribute to private accounts was not widely supported in 2005 among retirees, baby boomers—or even university students.

A coalition of student-body presidents from across the U.S. is opposing the president's plan for Social Security with a petition calling for the White House and Congress to protect the 70-year-old program, Andrea Jones wrote in the Atlanta Journal-Constitution. "The perspective of young people has been mostly overlooked," University of Georgia student president Adam Sparks said. "I want to make sure I'm paying into something that will still be solvent," said Mark Kresowik, president of the student government at the University of Iowa. The statement from the student leaders said the best ways to address Social Security's shortfalls are "to examine the levels at which workers pay into the system, ensure that benefits remain at the current levels for the neediest recipients, and reassess the payout to others."

Thinking Critically

Do you think all people are equally equipped to manage their own retirement funds? What are the ethical issues involved in the government's decisions about Social Security?

A certain portion of your paycheck goes to current retirees who collect Social Security. The baby boom generation and falling birth rates are putting pressure on the Social Security system.

Q How are current Social Security payments funded?

A From contributions from current workers and their employees.

Source: "Drop It" by Jennifer Johnson from the *Wall Street Journal Online,* May 20, 2005. Copyright 2005 by Dow Jones & Co Inc. Reproduced with permission of Dow Jones & Co Inc. in the format Textbook via Copyright Clearance Center.

designated. Here's how the company's accountant would record the disbursement to the employee:

Transaction	Debit	Credit
Salaries Expense	500.00	
Cash		361.75
Federal Income Taxes Payable (FIT)		100.00
FICA Payable (Social Security)		31.00
Medicare Taxes Payable		7.25
To record salaries expense		

This is the accounting equation:

Assets	=	Liabilities			+	Shareholders' Equity		
						Contributed Capital	+	**Retained Earnings**
Cash		FIT Payable	FICA Payable	Medicare Taxes Payable				Salary Expense
−361.75		100.00	31.00	7.25				−500.00

When Hewlett-Packard makes a payment to the government for Social Security and Medicare, the company will "match" those amounts. Often, these payments are made through the firm's bank. A company "deposits" its payroll taxes, which actually means the bank forwards the payment to the government for the company. Here's how Hewlett-Packard would record the payment to the government, including the company's portion:

Transaction	Debit	Credit
Federal Income Taxes Payable	100.00	
FICA Payable (Social Security)	31.00	
Medicare Taxes Payable	7.25	
Employer's Payroll Tax Expense (31.00 + 7.25)	38.25	
Cash		176.50
To record payments to governmental agencies from payroll		

This is the accounting equation:

Assets	=	Liabilities			+	Shareholders' Equity		
						Contributed Capital	+	**Retained Earnings**
Cash		FIT Payable	FICA Payable	Medicare Taxes Payable				Payroll Tax Expense
−176.50		−100.00	−31.00	−7.25				−38.25

There are other taxes the employer must pay to state and federal agencies, such as state and federal unemployment taxes. These are part of the employer's payroll expense.

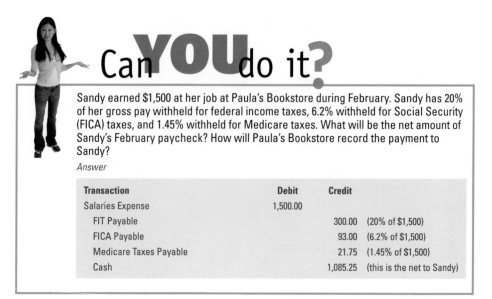

Can **YOU** do it?

Sandy earned $1,500 at her job at Paula's Bookstore during February. Sandy has 20% of her gross pay withheld for federal income taxes, 6.2% withheld for Social Security (FICA) taxes, and 1.45% withheld for Medicare taxes. What will be the net amount of Sandy's February paycheck? How will Paula's Bookstore record the payment to Sandy?

Answer

Transaction	Debit	Credit	
Salaries Expense	1,500.00		
FIT Payable		300.00	(20% of $1,500)
FICA Payable		93.00	(6.2% of $1,500)
Medicare Taxes Payable		21.75	(1.45% of $1,500)
Cash		1,085.25	(this is the net to Sandy)

LEARNING OBJECTIVE 2

Define an estimated liability and explain how to account for warranties.

Estimated liabilities: Obligations with some uncertainty in the amount, like the cost involved in honoring a warranty.

Estimated Liabilities

Estimated liabilities are obligations whose amounts are not certain. At the time of a sale, amounts a company will spend to honor product warranties are an example of estimated liabilities. Warranty Liability is the estimated future costs for repair and replacement to honor a product's warranty. When Hewlett-Packard provides warranties on the computers it sells, the firm's accountant will record an estimate of the cost of providing the warranty at the time of a sale or at the end of an accounting period—*before* the firm has spent any money to honor the warranty. That means the amount will have to be estimated. Why? The matching principle is the reason that firms estimate liabilities *before* the exact amounts can be determined. The firm wants to *match* the warranty expense with the sale to which it relates. Accounting for warranties is similar to accounting for bad debts. To follow the matching principle, firms will estimate the expenses so they can be matched to the appropriate revenues.

Accounting for warranties

Why would a company provide a warranty on a product or service? Whether or not to provide a warranty is a sales and marketing decision a company must make. Suppose Circuit City provides a two-year warranty with each television it sells, but Best Buy provides a three-year warranty with its televisions. If a television at both stores is the same price and quality, wouldn't you prefer to buy your television from Best Buy? Because the company does not spend the cash to fix or replace the item *at the time of the sale*, a liability is recorded along with the warranty expense. The liability is an adjustment made either at the time of the sale or when it's time to prepare financial statements. Liabilities are increased by the same amount as Warranty Expense.

Suppose Bil Jac Dog Food Supplies guarantees its food to be fresh for up to one year after the date of sale. Bil Jac ships 1,000 cases to Pet Supermarket at $100 per case. At that time, Bil Jac estimates that it will cost about 2% of sales to honor its freshness guarantee. That is, about 2% of the sales will be returned and replaced with fresh food. The cost to replace a case is approximately $70, the cost of the inventory. Here's how Bil Jac will calculate the warranty expense for this sale:

$$1,000 \text{ cases} \times 2\% \times \$70 = 20 \times \$70 = \$1,400.$$

The journal entry to record the warranty expense will be:

Transaction	Debit	Credit
Warranty Expense	1,400	
Warranty Payable		1,400
To record warranty expense for sale to Pet Supermarket		

This is the accounting equation:

Assets	=	Liabilities	+	Shareholders' Equity	
				Contributed Capital +	**Retained Earnings**
		Warranty Payable			Warranty Expense
		1,400			−1,400

What happens when a company actually pays the cash to repair a product with a warranty? No expense is recorded. Instead, the liability previously set up—recorded—is reduced. Accountants call this *writing off the cost against the liability*. Actual expenditures result in a reduction to Cash or some other asset—like supplies used to fix the item—and an equal reduction in the amount of the liability. If Discount Pet Supermarket returns a case of dog food to Bil Jac because it was not fresh, Bil Jac makes the following journal entry when the new case is shipped to the customer:

Transaction	Debit	Credit
Warranty Payable	70	
Inventory		70
To record replacement under warranty		

Assets	=	Liabilities	+	Shareholders' Equity	
				Contributed Capital +	**Retained Earnings**
Inventory		Warranty Payable			
−70		−70			

Let's look at one more example to help clarify what happens to the warranty liability as warranted products are repaired. Suppose Brooke's Bike Company sells 100 bicycles during June and provides a one-year warranty with each bike. The accountant estimates future repairs and replacement related to the June sales to be approximately $30 per bicycle. No expenditures are made related to the warranties during the month of June. What amount of warranty expense would appear on Brooke's June income statement? Brooke's Bike Company would show the entire amount, $3,000, as an expense for the month. What is the amount of the June 30 liability (Warranty Payable or Estimated Warranty Liability)? The total $3,000 would be shown as a liability on the balance sheet. The journal entry to record the estimated warranty expense is:

Transaction	Debit	Credit
Warranty Expense	3,000	
Warranty Payable		3,000
To record estimated future warranty costs		

Assets	=	Liabilities	+	Shareholders' Equity	
				Contributed Capital +	**Retained Earnings**
		Warranty Payable			Warranty Expense
		3,000			−3,000

Now suppose July is a slow month, and Brooke's Bike Company doesn't sell any bicycles. However, there are several bicycles from sales in June that are repaired in July. The repairs cost Brooke's $250, which we will assume are made with cash. What amount of Warranty Expense would appear on Brooke's July income statement? None. Brooke's Bike Company recognized the expense when the sale was made, so no expense is recognized when the repairs are made. The amount is written off against the liability. So the amount of the July 31 liability (Warranty Payable or Estimated Warranty Liability) is $3,000 − $250 = $2,750. Here's the journal entry, followed by the accounting equation, and then by the transactions shown in the Warranty Payable T-account:

Transaction	Debit	Credit
Warranties Payable	250	
Cash		250
To record the cost of fulfilling warranties		

Assets	=	Liabilities	+	Shareholders' Equity	
				Contributed Capital +	**Retained Earnings**
Cash		Warranty Payable			
−250		−250			

Here, we've assumed the credit is made to Cash, which would happen if the shop paid someone in cash to repair the bike. Here's what has happened in the Warranty Payable account in both July and August:

	Warranty Payable	
		3,000 (June 30)
(during July) 250		
		2,750 (July 31 balance)
(during Aug) 500		
		2,250 (Aug 31 balance)

See if you understand how Hewlett-Packard accounts for warranties. Exhibit 9.3 shows the detailed information from the firm's financial statements.

Exhibit 9.3

Note About Warranties from Hewlett-Packard's Notes to the Financial Statements at October 31

Every company that offers a product warranty will describe the terms of the warranty and how the company accounts for warranty expense in its notes to the financial statements. Accruals for Warranties Issued is the amount credited to the liability account for current year's sales, and Settlements Made are the actual expenditures. Because the amounts set aside for warranties are estimates, the company often makes adjustments. Here you can see that Hewlett-Packard reduced the liability with a small adjustment each year.

From Hewlett-Packard's Notes to the Financial Statements
(in millions)

	2004	2003
Information regarding the changes in HP's aggregate product warranty liabilities is as follows at October 31:		
Product warranty liability at beginning of year	$1,987	$2,157
Accruals for warranties issued	2,504	2,233
Adjustments related to pre-existing warranties (including changes in estimates)	(86)	(17)
Settlements made (in cash or in kind)	(2,365)	(2,386)
Product warranty liability at end of year	$2,040	$1,987

Can YOU do it?
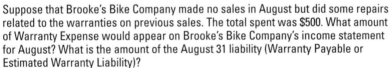

Suppose that Brooke's Bike Company made no sales in August but did some repairs related to the warranties on previous sales. The total spent was $500. What amount of Warranty Expense would appear on Brooke's Bike Company's income statement for August? What is the amount of the August 31 liability (Warranty Payable or Estimated Warranty Liability)?

Answers No expense would appear on the August income statement. The liability for the June sales was set up in June, and the expenditures are written off against the liability. In July, $250 was spent to honor warranties, and now $500 is spent. The total is $750. The original liability was set up for $3,000. The balance at August 31 is $2,250 (= $3,000 − $750).

Long-Term Notes Payable and Mortgages

LEARNING OBEJCTIVE 3
Explain how long-term notes and mortgages work.

You've learned how companies record current liabilities. In this section, we learn how companies record long-term liabilities. When a company borrows money for longer than one year, that obligation is usually called a *long-term note payable*. Long-term notes differ from short-term notes in several ways. Recall from Chapter 2 that short-term notes are debt obligations that a company will repay in one year or sooner. A company may repay long-term notes in a lump sum at the note's maturity or with a series of equal payments over the life of the note. A car loan is an example of a loan with payments made over the life of the loan. The monthly payments are a combination of interest and principal. With each monthly payment, the borrower is paying that month's interest on the loan as well as paying back a small part of the principal balance due. Each month when the bank calculates the interest on the outstanding principal balance, the interest amount becomes a smaller portion of the payment. Why? Because the total amount of each payment stays the same, but the principal decreases. A larger part of each monthly payment is, therefore, available to reduce the outstanding principal. Exhibit 9.4 shows why the interest amount on a loan becomes smaller for a loan of $100,000, with a

Exhibit 9.4

Payments Comprised of Interest and Principal

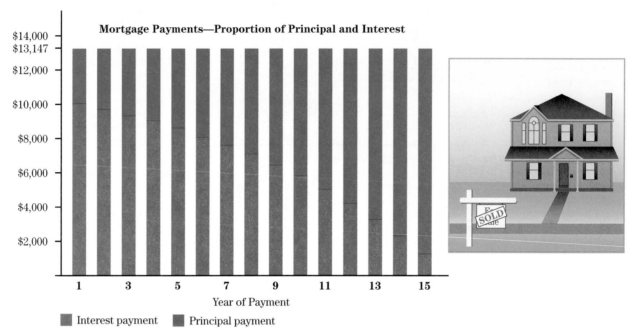

This graph shows the payment schedule for a $100,000 loan for 15 years at 10% annual interest. There will be 15 annual payments of approximately $13,147 each. With each payment, the principal balance is reduced, so there is less interest expense each year. Because the payment stays the same, more of the payment goes toward reducing the principal each year. The graph shows how the proportion of interest in each payment decreases over time, while the proportion of principal in each payment increases over time.

15-year term, and an interest rate of 10% per year. The annual payment is the same every year, but the portion of the payment that is interest expense decreases, while the portion of the payment that reduces the outstanding principal balance increases.

A mortgage loan is a note payable that gives the lender a claim against that property if the borrower does not make payments. Like most long-term notes, mortgage loans are debt obligations commonly repaid in periodic installments—each payment is part principal and part interest.

Suppose you sign, on January 1, a $100,000, three-year mortgage with SunTrust with an 8% annual interest rate to buy a piece of land. Payments are to be made annually on December 31 of each year in the amount of $38,803.35. How did SunTrust figure out that annual payment for the $100,000 loan for three years at 8% annual interest?

The amount of the annual payment is based on a concept called the time value of money. "Time value of money" means there is value in having money for a period of time. That value is the interest the money can earn if invested. The bank gives you $100,000 today, so you must repay that amount plus interest for the time you have that amount or any part of it. The bank calculates what it would receive if it invested the $100,000 for 3 years at an interest rate of 8%. That is the amount the bank expects to receive from you. The value today of the sum of those three payments in the future—a $38,803.35 payment at the end of each of the next three years—is called the **present value (PV)** of those three payments Each payment is discounted to an amount equivalent to having the money today. When an amount of money earns interest, then that interest will itself earn interest during the time it is invested. Interest computed on both the principal and any interest earned but not paid or received is called compound interest.

Present value (PV): The value today of a given amount to be invested or received in the future assuming compound interest. (That means that both the principal and any interest not paid or received are earning interest.)

Discounting the cash flows strips the amounts of the interest built-in for the passage of time, bringing them back to equivalent dollars today. In this example, the dollars today amount to $100,000. The interest rate used in the calculation of present value amounts is also called the **discount rate**. In this example the discount rate is 8%.

In our mortgage example, $100,000 is the present value. SunTrust has calculated the three annual payments to be $38,803.35. The present value of those three payments, discounted at the interest rate of 8% per year, equals $100,000. Payments are annual, and the first payment will be made at the end of the first year of the loan. After the three payments, both the principal and the interest will be repaid. You can read about how to calculate present value in Appendix A at the end of this chapter. As you read how to make the computations, refer to Exhibit 9.5, which shows how each payment reduces the outstanding principal. This is called an amortization schedule for this loan.

How much of the first payment is interest expense and how much goes toward paying back the principal? Remember, *interest* is the cost of using someone else's money. The interest is based on the amount of the principal, the interest rate, and the amount of time for which the money is borrowed:

> Interest = Principal × Rate × Time

The bank lends you $100,000 on Day 1 of the note. On Day 365, you make a $38,803.35 payment to the bank. The interest on the $100,000 for the year that has just passed is:

> $100,000 principal × 0.08 annual interest rate × 1 year = $8,000
> $100,000 × 0.08/year × 1 year = $8,000

You borrowed the entire $100,000 for a full year, so you multiply the principal by the annual rate and by the one-year duration to get the interest expense for the year. Of the $38,803.35 payment, $8,000 is interest, so the remaining portion of the payment—$30,803.35—is repayment of principal. Here's how the first payment would be recorded:

Transaction	Debit	Credit
Interest Expense	8,000.00	
Mortgage Payable	30,803.35	
Cash		38,803.35
To record the first mortgage payment		

Discounting: Computing the present value of future cash flows.

Discount rate: The interest rate used to compute the present value of future cash flows.

Study Tip

With respect to a mortgage, to amortize means to reduce the amount of the debt in installments over the life of the liability. A mortgage amortization schedule shows how the payments reduce the principal over the life of the loan.

Exhibit 9.5

Amortization Schedule for a Mortgage

Mortgage Balance		Annual Payment	Interest portion of payment (8% × mortgage balance)	Amount of mortgage reduction (annual payment – interest portion)
Beginning balance $100,000.00	1st	$38,803.35	$8,000.00	$30,803.35
After 1st payment $ 69,196.65	2nd	$38,803.35	$5,535.73	$33,267.62
After 2nd payment $ 35,929.03	3rd	$38,803.35	$2,874.32	$35,929.03
After 3rd payment -0-				

This is the accounting equation:

Assets	=	Liabilities	+	Shareholders' Equity	
				Contributed Capital +	Retained Earnings
−38,803.35		−30,803.35			−8,000
Cash		Mortgage Payable			Interest Expense

The principal of the mortgage has been reduced. In other words, the outstanding balance is lower—meaning you have less of the bank's money at the end of the first year. Therefore, the interest owed the bank for the *second* year will be smaller than the interest paid for the first year. That's because the interest rate will be applied to a smaller principal—that is, a smaller outstanding balance. Again, we use the interest formula to calculate the portion of the payment that is interest for the second year, and then subtract the interest from the total payment to calculate the amount of the payment that reduces the principal.

- Outstanding balance due at the start of the second year: $69,196.65 (= $100,000 original principal − $30,803.35 reduction in principal from the first payment).
- Interest expense for Year 2: $69,196.65 principal for Year 2 × .08 annual interest rate × 1 year = $5,535.73.

The amount of interest you owe the bank is smaller each year because the outstanding balance of the note is smaller each year. At the end of Year 2, the bank receives the second payment of $38,803.35. As the preceding calculation shows, $5,535.73 of that payment is interest expense. The rest of the payment—$33,267.62 (= $38,803.35 − $5,535.73)—reduces the outstanding balance. After the second payment, the outstanding balance is $35,929.03. For the third payment of $38,803.35:

- New principal = $35,929.03
- Interest expense for Year 3 = $35,929.03 × 0.08/year × 1 year = $2,874.32

When you subtract the interest of $2,874.32 from the third payment of $38,803.35, the remaining $35,929.03 reduces the principal—in this case, to zero. Is it just coincidence that the remaining outstanding balance is exactly that amount? No, the bank did the present value calculations with the principal, interest rate, and length of the loan so that it would come out to exactly that amount at the end of the third year.

Study Tip

Our mortgage example required annual payments, but many loans have monthly payments. When you are working with a loan with monthly payments, you need to divide the annual interest rate by 12 to make it a monthly interest rate. The time period and the interest rate time have to match.

Can YOU do it?

Tompkins Corporation purchased a building on January 1 by signing a long-term $600,000 mortgage with monthly payments of $5,500. The mortgage carries an interest rate of 9% per year. How much of the first payment is interest and how much is principal?

Answers Interest = $600,000 × 9% × 1/12 = $4,500 interest.
The total payment is $5,500, so the principal reduction is the remaining $1,000.

Long-Term Liabilities: Raising Money by Issuing Bonds

LEARNING OBJECTIVE 4

Record the issue of bonds and payment of interest to bondholders.

Long-term notes and mortgages are one way to borrow money with repayment over an extended period of time. Often, companies want to raise large amounts of money to build new stores or warehouses. One way to borrow this money is to issue bonds to the general public.

What is a bond?

A **bond** is an interest-bearing, long-term note payable issued by corporations, universities, and governmental agencies. Issuing bonds means a company is borrowing money from individual investors as well as other companies that want to invest. A *bond certificate* is a written agreement that specifies the company's responsibility to pay interest and repay the principal to the bondholders at the end of the term of the bond. The bond certificate will show the interest rate, the face amount of the bond, and the term of the bond. Exhibit 9.6 shows an actual bond certificate.

Bond: An interest-bearing, long-term note payable issued by corporations, universities, and governmental agencies.

Exhibit 9.6

Bond Certificate

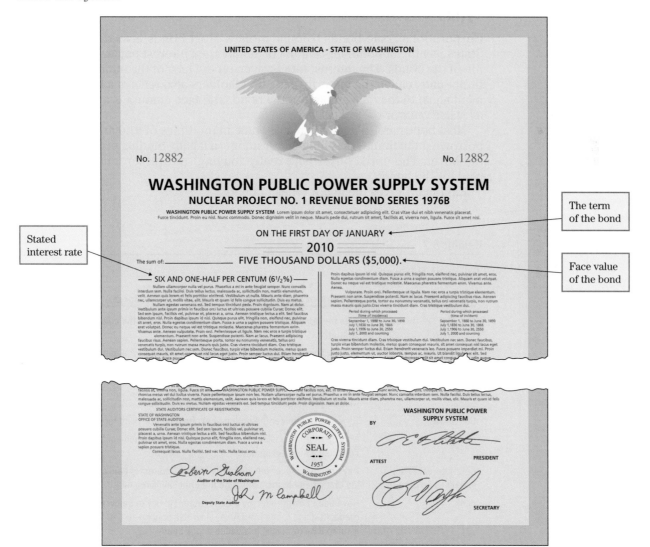

There are three main reasons why a company would borrow money by issuing bonds rather than going to a bank for a loan:

1. Firms can borrow more money from issuing bonds than a bank may be willing to loan.

2. Bondholders are typically willing to loan money for a longer time. Many bonds are 15-, 20-, or 30-year bonds. Some banks won't loan businesses money for such long periods of time. Bondholders are willing to lend money for a long time because they can convert bonds into cash at any time by selling the bond to another investor in the bond market.

3. The rate of interest on a bond—that's the rate the borrower has to pay the bondholder—is commonly lower than the rate on loans charged by banks. Banks pay one rate of interest to people who deposit their money in saving accounts—that's the savings rate of interest—but charge a higher interest rate to loan money—that's the borrowing rate of interest.

A disadvantage to a firm of borrowing money by issuing bonds is that the firm may be restricted from borrowing additional money from other sources, or the firm may be required to maintain a certain debt-to-equity ratio—the ratio of liabilities to shareholders' equity. These restrictions, called bond covenants, are specified in the bond agreement to protect the interests of the bondholders. Recall that creditors, including bondholders, have priority over the claims of owners.

Types of bonds

Corporations issue bonds to raise money. Most bonds issued in the United States pay the bondholders annual or semiannual interest payments during the life of the bonds. The interest rate is given on the face of the bond. At a specific future date, called the maturity date, bondholders also receive a lump sum payment equal to the face amount of the bond. The face amount is also referred to as *stated value* or the *par value* of the bond.

Most bonds are issued with a face value in multiples of $1,000. The company borrowing the money is selling—or issuing—a legally binding promise to repay the buyer. The initial buyer isn't really "buying" but rather lending the price paid for the bond.

Exhibit 9.7 gives the major types of bonds.

In Other Words:
Face value, par value, and *stated value* of a bond are all synonyms.

Exhibit 9.7

Types of Bonds

Type of Bond	Feature of the Bond or Description of the Bond
Secured	Give the bondholders a claim to a specific asset of the company in case of default
Unsecured (also known as debenture)	Are not linked to specific assets and are issued on the general credit of the company
Term	All mature on the same date
Serial	Mature periodically over a period of several years
Convertible	Give the bondholder the option of exchanging the bond for common stock
Callable	May be retired—called—prior to maturity at the option of the issuer for a specified amount of money
Zero-interest (also known as zero-coupon)	Pay no interest over the life of the bonds. (Interest is paid at the end of the life of the bond at the same time the principal is repaid.)
Junk	Have been downgraded by a bond rating agency to below investment grade. (Ratings range from AAA—low risk bonds—to C or D. When a bond is rated BB– or below, it is called a junk bond.)

Accounting in the NEWS

General Motors and Ford Motor Go to the Junk Yard

Bond ratings indicate the probability that the issuing company will default, based on an analysis of the issuer's financial condition and profit potential. Standard & Poor's (S&P) bond ratings go from AAA (low risk) to D (in default). When a bond's rating falls below BB (high risk), it is considered a junk bond.

On May 5, 2005, Standard & Poor's Ratings Services lowered its long- and short-term corporate credit ratings on two of the Big Three U.S. auto makers—General Motors (**GM**) and Ford Motor (**F**)—below investment grade. Long-term ratings on GM, its General Motors Acceptance Corp. unit, and all related entities were lowered to BB from BBB–. Ford, its Ford Motor Credit subsidiaries, and all related entities—except those of

Hertz—were reduced to BB+ from BBB–. The rating outlook for both Ford and GM is negative.

GM and Ford will find it much more difficult to raise money now that their bonds have been lowered to junk status. Junk bonds are riskier, so the issuer must pay a higher return to investors. Junk bonds typically pay 3% or 4% more than investment grade bonds. Here's how *The Motley Fool* summarized GM's problems:

> GM is laying out huge sums of cash to pay its unionized workforce's salaries, to shoulder the medical benefits, and to finance the pensions. And with its market share declining, it's simply not making enough cash to pay for all this. With its new "junk" status, the situation will only get worse. Institutions that are forbidden to invest in junk bonds will have to sell off their portfolios. They won't be able to buy new GM bonds when the company needs to refinance. And, of the institutions that *can* buy GM's junk, they'll be charging GM higher interest rates. In other words, the downgrade is going to increase GM's cost of doing busi-

Ford would like more business on its showroom floors. Ford's sales and bond rating plummeted in 2005.

ness—a cost it already can barely afford.

When you invest in a corporation like General Motors by buying one of its bonds, there is a risk that the bonds will be downgraded to junk status. This will cause their market price to drop significantly.

Q Why would anyone invest in junk bonds?

A The bonds pay a higher return because of their high risk.

Sources: "GM and Ford Go to the Junk Yard," *Business Week Online,* May 5, 2005; Rich Smith, "Auto-pocalypse Now," *The Motley Fool,* May 6, 2005.

Read about General Motors and Ford having their bonds downgraded to junk bond status in *Accounting in the News*.

Issuing bonds payable: getting the money

First, let's discuss how the market sets the price for a bond. Then, we'll look at the details of a bond issued at various prices.

Suppose Muzby Minerals issued a $1,000, zero-interest bond due in six years. That means the bondholder will lend the company some amount of money—which we have not calculated yet—for a payment of $1,000 six years from now. Zero interest means that no interest will be paid during the life of the bond. How much would you pay for this bond? Clearly, you would pay something less than $1,000. That's because $1,000 cash today is worth more than $1,000 cash in six years. You would invest the $1,000 today and have more than $1,000 in six years because you could earn interest on the money. You can read about the time value of money in the appendix to the chapter.

The amount you would pay for this $1,000, six-year, zero-interest bond is the amount you would have to invest today to have it grow to $1,000 in six years. Remember from our discussion of mortgages that this amount is its *present value*, and finding the present value of a future cash flow is called *discounting* the future amount. You would pay the present value for the bond to receive $1,000 in six years. To calculate the bond's price, you need to know the **market rate of interest**. That is the interest rate investors demand for lending money to the firm. The market rate of interest for a particular bond is considered the interest rate that an investor could earn in an equally risky investment. If the market rate of interest was 4%, how much would you pay for the $1,000, six-year, zero-interest

Market rate of interest: The interest rate investors demand for lending money to the firm.

Study Tip

Bond prices are set by the market so that issuing firms will always have to pay the market rate of interest and investors will always earn the market rate of interest—no matter what the bond's stated rate of interest is.

Exhibit 9.8

Cash Flows Defined by a Six-year, $1,000, 5% Bond

Year	0	1	2	3	4	5	6
Cash flow to bondholder		$50	$50	$50	$50	$50	$50 $1,000

Each cash flow is discounted back to today's value.

It may be helpful to think of a bond as a series of cash payments. When a firm issues a bond, it is selling the bondholder a series of future payments. How much the bondholder will pay for those cash payments depends on the market rate of interest at the time the bonds are issued.

bond? You'd pay the present value of $1,000 discounted back six years using 4%. That value is $790.31.[1] You would lend Muzby Minerals $790.31, and the firm would pay you $1,000 at the end of six years. If you could find a bank to pay you 4% annually on your deposit of $790.31, it would grow to be $1,000 in six years.

Most bonds are not zero-interest but instead have interest payments made to the bondholders over the life of the bond. Suppose Muzby Minerals issued a $1,000 bond for six years with a stated interest rate of 5%. Exhibit 9.8 shows the cash flows associated with this bond.

If the market rate of interest and the stated rate of interest are the same, investors will pay exactly the face value for the bonds. However, if the market rate were *more* than 5%, investors would pay less for the bond because it would not take an amount as high as $1,000 today to cover the future 5% interest payments and the principal payment at the end of the life of the bonds. The present value of the cash flows would be less than $1,000, so the bonds would sell at less than par. That is called *issuing bonds at a discount.*

If, on the other hand, the market rate of interest were *less* than 5%, investors would have to pay more for the bond because it would take more than $1,000 today to cover the future 5% interest payments and the principal payment at the end of the life of the bonds. The present value of the cash flows would be greater than $1,000, so the bonds would sell for more than par value. That is called *issuing bonds at a premium.*

Read Appendix A to learn more about discounting the cash flows to calculate the issue price of the bonds. Read Appendix B to learn how to calculate the proceeds from a bond issue by discounting the future cash flows associated with the bonds.

Fortunately, the bond market is quite efficient at pricing bonds, and the market provides the bond's selling price to investors. When a bond is issued, the price of a bond is stated in terms of a percentage of its face value. If a $1,000 face bond is stated as selling for 98 3/8, that means it is selling for 98 3/8 % of $1,000 ($1,000 × 0.98375), or $983.75. Bonds will be issued one of three ways:

1. A bond selling at 100 is selling at par—100% of its face value.
2. A bond selling below 100 is selling at a discount—less than 100% of its face value.
3. A bond selling above 100 is selling at a premium—more than 100% of its face value.

Let's look at an example of bonds issued at par, at less than the par value, and at more than the par value and see how the transactions are recorded.

[1]The mathematics of discounting cash flows to calculate the issue price of a bond can be done using (1) Present Value tables, (2) financial calculators, and (3) Excel spreadsheet formulas. To learn more about how to discount cash flows, study Appendices A and B at the end of this chapter.

Can **YOU** do it?

Echo Company issued $100,000 worth of 8% bonds at 101. What were the proceeds of the bond issue? Was the market rate of interest higher or lower than 8% when the bonds were issued?

Answers The proceeds were $100,000 × 1.01 = $101,000. The market interest rate must have been lower than the stated rate because the company received a premium from the bondholders.

Bonds Sold at Par Value Suppose Hewlett-Packard issues a single $1,000, 4.5% per year, five-year bond on January 1, 2006. The market rate at the time of issue is 4.5%. That means other investments with the same amount of risk are paying an annual return of 4.5%. When the bond's interest rate and the market rate of interest are the same, the bond will be issued at par. Cash is increased by $1,000. Remember, when a company issues bonds, it is borrowing money. The cash receipt is recorded, and a liability is recorded. The $1,000 increase in Cash is balanced with a $1,000 increase in Bonds Payable shown in the following journal entry:

Date	Transaction	Debit	Credit
January 1, 2006	Cash	1,000	
	Bonds Payable		1,000
	To record the issue of a $1,000 bond at par		

This is the accounting equation:

Assets	=	Liabilities	+	Shareholders' Equity		
				Contributed Capital	+	**Retained Earnings**
Cash		Bonds Payable				
1,000		1,000				

It is easy to understand how a company reports bonds issued at par. However, it's not possible for a company to issue bonds on the exact day when the interest for the bond is specified. There is a time delay because the bond certificates have to be printed, and the company has to file the bond issue along with prospective financial statements with state regulators and the SEC *before* it can issue the bonds. Very often the market interest rates will change between the time a stated interest rate is selected and printed on the bonds and the time the bonds are issued. Exhibit 9.9 shows the relationship between the market interest rate and bonds' stated interest rates.

Bonds Sold at a Discount Suppose Hewlett-Packard is offering a $1,000 bond with a stated rate of 4.5% when the market rate of interest is 5%. That means that other opportunities exist—with the same risk—that would earn 5%. Would you be willing to buy a $1,000, 4.5% bond if you could invest that same $1,000 in an equivalent investment that pays 5%? Probably not. The company issuing the bond will pay $45 in annual interest, while there are other investments willing to pay $50 in annual interest. Because the issuing company went to a lot of expense to print the bonds and prepare them for issue, it's not possible to simply change the rate of interest. The company is stuck with what is

Whether a bond is issued at par, at a discount, or at a premium depends on the relationship between the market rate of interest and the stated rate on the face of the bond.

Exhibit 9.9

Bonds Issued at Par, at a Discount, or at a Premium

Bonds Issued at	Interest Rates	Bonds Will Sell for
Par	Stated rate of interest = market rate of interest	Face amount
Discount	Stated rate of interest < market rate of interest	Less than the face amount
Premium	Stated rate of interest > market rate of interest	More than the face amount

stated on the bonds—4.5% annual interest payments, that's $45 annually, and the face value of $1,000 to be paid out at maturity.

To make up for the difference between the stated rate of 4.5% and the market rate of 5%, the company issuing the bonds has to be willing to sell the bonds for *less* than $1,000—that is, at a discount. The amount investors will be willing to pay for the bond is equal to the present value of the future cash flows the bondholder will receive. Bonds sold at less than the face value are sold at a *discount*.

A $1,000, five-year, 4.5% bond issued when the market interest rate is 5% would be issued at approximately 98 (98% of face value).[2] The journal entry to record the issue of the bond is:

Transaction	Debit	Credit
Cash	980	
Discount on Bonds Payable	20	
Bonds Payable		1,000
To record issue of $1,000 bond at 98		

This is the accounting equation:

Assets	=	Liabilities		+	Shareholders' Equity	
					Contributed Capital +	Retained Earnings
Cash		Bonds Payable	Discount on Bonds Payable			
980		1,000	−20			

Discount on Bonds Payable is a contra-liability account and its balance is deducted from Bonds Payable on the balance sheet. It is the difference between the face value of the bond and its selling price, when the selling price is less than the face value. Discount on Bonds Payable works like other contra-accounts—

Discount on bonds payable: A contra-liability that is deducted from Bonds Payable on the balance sheet; it is the difference between the face value of the bond and its selling price, when the selling price is less than the face value.

[2]The present value of the future cash flows of $45 annually for 5 years and the lump sum principal payment at the end of 5 years of $1,000, when the market rate of interest is 5%, is equal to $978.35. To make the calculations simple, we'll round off to $980, which is 98% of the face value, for this example. Refer to Appendix B for details on calculating the issue price of the bond.

Accumulated Depreciation and Allowance for Uncollectible Accounts. You learned about contra-accounts in Chapter 4. Every contra-account has a partner account. For example, the contra-account Accumulated Depreciation is partnered with a fixed asset account like Equipment. Discount on Bonds Payable is shown on the balance sheet with its partner account Bonds Payable, and it is a deduction from the balance in Bonds Payable. Contra-accounts are considered valuation accounts. They are used to value the associated asset or liability.

In the long-term liabilities portion of the balance sheet, the bond would be reported net of the balance in its Discount account. The net value of Bonds Payable is also called the **carrying value** of the bonds.

> **Carrying value (of a bond):** The amount that the balance sheet will show as the net value of the bond, similar meaning to the *carrying value* of a fixed asset.

Bonds Payable	$1,000
Less Discount on Bonds Payable	20
Net Bonds Payable	$ 980

Bonds Sold at a Premium Suppose Hewlett-Packard is offering a $1,000 bond with a stated rate of 4.5% when the market rate of interest is 4%. That means that other opportunities with the same risk would earn 4%. Would you be willing to buy a $1,000, 4.5% bond if you could invest that same $1,000 in an equivalent investment that pays 4%? You probably would. If the market rate of return for an investment of equivalent risk were less than the stated bond rate, people would flock to buy the bonds, *if* the bonds were issued at the $1,000 face value. However, that won't happen because the market for bonds operates on supply and demand, so the market will respond by bidding up the price of that bond. In other words, the demand for the bond causes the price of the bond to increase.

Investors should be willing to pay more than $1,000 for the Hewlett-Packard face value bond because the bond will pay $45 in annual interest when other similar investments pay only $40 for the same $1,000 invested. The extra amount the bondholder is willing to pay for that bond is called a *premium*. Hewlett-Packard would issue the bond for approximately $1,020. That amount is the present value of the future cash flows associated with the bond, using the market rate of interest: $45 each year for 5 years and $1,000 at the end of 5 years.[3] The journal entry to record the issue of a single bond would be:

Transaction	Debit	Credit
Cash	1,020	
Bonds Payable		1,000
Premium on Bonds Payable		20
To record the issue of $1,000 bond at 102		

This is the accounting equation:

Assets	=	Liabilities	+	Shareholders' Equity	
				Contributed Capital +	**Retained Earnings**
Cash		Bonds Payable	Premium on Bonds Payable		
1,020		1,000	20		

The amount of the face value of the bond (Bonds Payable at $1,000) and the **Premium on Bonds Payable** (at $20) are both liabilities. They appear next to each other on Hewlett-Packard's balance sheet. Premium on Bonds Payable is called

> **Premium on bonds payable:** An adjunct liability account that is added to Bonds Payable on the balance sheet; it is the difference between the face value of the bond and its selling price when the selling price is more than the face value.

[3]See Appendix B to learn how this calculation is made.

an *adjunct liability*. Adjunct means an add-on and describes the relationship between Bonds Payable and Premium on Bonds Payable. The Premium on Bonds Payable is a partner of the Bonds Payable liability it is paired with, and they are added together on the balance sheet. This is how this bond would be shown on the balance sheet—its carrying value—on its issue date:

Bonds Payable	$1,000
Premium on Bonds Payable	20
Net Bonds Payable	$1,020

 Can**YOU**do it**?**

If Silverstone Company issues a $1,000 bond with a stated interest rate of 9% when the market rate is 8%, will the bond sell for a discount or a premium? How much will the bondholders receive each year from Silverstone Company?

Answer Bonds will be issued at a premium because the stated rate is higher than the market rate. Payments are $90 per year (9% × $1,000) interest plus $1,000 at maturity.

Paying interest to the bondholders: amortizing bond discounts and premiums

The annual interest payment to the bondholders is calculated with the interest formula:

$$\text{Interest} = \text{Principal} \times \text{Interest Rate} \times \text{Time}$$

In the example of Hewlett-Packard issuing a $1,000, 4.5%, five-year bond, each interest payment will be $45.

Interest = $1,000 principal × 0.045 annual interest rate × 1 year = $45.

On December 31, the transaction of paying the interest will be recorded as follows:

Date	Transaction	Debit	Credit
Dec. 31	Interest Expense	45	
	Cash		45
	To record interest payment on bonds issued at par		

This is the accounting equation:

Assets	=	Liabilities	+	Shareholders' Equity	
				Contributed Capital +	**Retained Earnings**
Cash					Interest Expense
−45					−45

Each interest payment will be identical. Remember, the company has to pay the bondholders according to the terms printed on the face of the bond. The cash to be paid at each interest date is determined before the company goes to the market to sell the bond. *Whether the bond is issued at par, at a discount, or at a premium, the cash paid to the bondholder is determined by the terms on the face of the bond.* For any bond, the principal amount to be repaid at the end of the term of the bond is stated on the face of the bond and is used to calculate the interest payments. Notice that the firm's Interest Expense—which will be on the income statement—is equal to the cash payment to the bondholders. This is true only when the bond's stated interest rate and the market interest rate are the same at issue—when bonds are issued at par.

When bonds are issued at a discount or premium, the amount of that bond discount or a bond premium must be written off over the life of the bond. Because the firm will pay the bondholder the face amount of the bond at maturity, the carrying value of the bond must be equal to the face amount of the bond at maturity. Making this happen by getting the balance in the Discount on Bonds Payable or Premium on Bonds Payable to zero is called amortizing the discount or premium. The result of amortizing the discount or premium is that interest expense will not equal the interest payment to the bondholders. You can see the effect of amortizing a bond premium or discount by using a method called *straight-line amortization*, which involves dividing the premium or discount equally over the number of interest payment periods. Let's see how straight-line amortization works.

Study Tip

A bond's cash flows to the bondholder—the interest payments and the principal payment at maturity—are set by what is printed on the face of the bond. This amount is determined before the market rate of interest has been determined at the time of the issue. The cash payments are always the same, no matter if the bond is issued at par, at a discount, or at a premium.

Interest Payment and Interest Expense for Bonds Issued at a Discount

Let's continue the example of Hewlett-Packard issuing a $1,000, 4.5% bond when the market rate of interest is 5%. The difference between the $1,000 face of the bond and the issue price of $980 is an additional cost of borrowing the money—the interest—to the company. Hewlett-Packard borrows $980 but has to pay the bondholders $1,000 at the end of the life of the bond. That $1,000 is in addition to the $45 annual interest payments. So each time Hewlett-Packard makes an interest payment to the bondholders, the company will recognize a little of the $20 discount as interest expense. The matching principle applies here: The extra $20 interest expense will be spread over the life of the bonds. Exhibit 9.10 shows the amortization schedule.

Here is an example of the journal entry the company would make when it pays the annual interest to its bondholders. The $20 Discount account (debit balance) will be credited by $4 each of the five times the company pays interest to the bondholders. At that time, the balance in Discount on Bonds Payable will be zero (at maturity).

Study Tip

When a bond is issued at a premium or at a discount, the interest payments to bondholders will not be equal to the firm's interest expense.

Transaction	Debit	Credit
Interest Expense	49	
Cash		45
Discount on Bonds Payable		4
To record interest payment on bonds with a discount		

This is the accounting equation:

Assets	=	Liabilities	+	Shareholders' Equity	
				Contributed Capital +	Retained Earnings
Cash		Discount on Bonds Payable			Interest Expense
−45		4*			−49

*Even though the discount is being reduced, this amount is positive because the net value of the liability, Bonds Payable, will increase as a result of this entry.

Notice that the carrying value of the bond—issue amount less unamortized discount—is gradually increasing over the life of the bond until it is equal to the face value. Also notice that interest payment and interest expense are *not* equal.

Exhibit 9.10

Straight-line Amortization Schedule for a Bond Issued at a Discount

Period	Carrying Value at Beginning of Period	Cash Interest Payment to Bondholders	Amortization of Discount ($20 ÷ 5 years)	Interest Expense	Unamortized Bond Discount	Carrying Value at Year-end
0						$ 980
1	$980	$45	$4	$49	$16	$ 984
2	$984	$45	$4	$49	$12	$ 988
3	$988	$45	$4	$49	$ 8	$ 992
4	$992	$45	$4	$49	$ 4	$ 996
5	$996	$45	$4	$49	$ 0	$1,000

The extra cost of borrowing the money increases Interest Expense by $4 each year, and the balance in Discount on Bonds Payable goes down by $4 each year. That means the amount subtracted from Bonds Payable declines each year, so the carrying value of Bonds Payable increases each year. At the maturity date of the bond, the carrying value of the bonds will equal the face value, and the Discount on Bonds Payable balance will be zero.

Amortizing a Premium on Bonds Payable Amortization of a bond premium is similar to the amortization of a bond discount. In the case of a bond premium, however, the company borrows more than it has to repay. In our example, Hewlett-Packard issued the $1,000 face bonds for $1,020 when the market rate of interest was less than the stated rate of 4.5%. The company will only have to repay the bondholders $1,000 at maturity, so the extra $20 the company received reduces the total cost of borrowing. Over the life of the bonds, the Premium on Bonds Payable account will be reduced to zero. Using straight-line amortization, the company will debit the Premium on Bonds Payable account (which has a credit balance) $4 each of the five times the company makes an interest payment to the bondholders. Here is an example of a journal entry the company would make to record an interest payment:

Transaction	Debit	Credit
Interest Expense	41	
Premium on Bonds Payable	4	
Cash		45
To record interest payment on bonds with a premium		

This is the accounting equation:

Assets	=	Liabilities	+	Shareholders' Equity	
				Contributed Capital +	Retained Earnings
Cash		Premium on Bonds Payable			Interest Expense
−45		−4			−41

Exhibit 9.11

Straight-line Amortization Schedule for a Bond Issued at a Premium

Period	Carrying Value at Beginning of Period	Cash Interest Payment to Bondholders	Amortization of Premium ($20 ÷ 5 years)	Interest Expense	Unamortized Bond Premium	Carrying Value at Year-end
0						$1,020
1	$1,020	$45	$4	$41	$16	$1,016
2	$1,016	$45	$4	$41	$12	$1,012
3	$1,012	$45	$4	$41	$ 8	$1,008
4	$1,008	$45	$4	$41	$ 4	$1,004
5	$1,004	$45	$4	$41	$ 0	$1,000

Notice that the carrying value of the bond—issue amount plus unamortized premium—is gradually decreasing over the life of the bond until it is equal to the face value. Also notice that interest payment and interest expense are *not* equal.

Amortization of the Premium *decreases* the interest expense by $4, and the balance in the Premium account is now $16. Each time the company makes an interest payment, the interest expense will be a little lower than the interest payment to the bondholders. The Premium on Bonds Payable is reduced, which reduces the carrying value of Bonds Payable. At the maturity date of the bond, the Premium on Bonds Payable balance will be zero, and the carrying value of the bonds will equal the face value. Exhibit 9.11 shows the amortization schedule.

The demand from the bond market will set the price of the bond to earn exactly the market rate of return. It's not a good or bad thing to issue bonds at a premium or a discount. Bonds are always issued so that the company will pay the going rate of interest to borrow money.

In some cases, firms use the *effective interest method* to compute the amortization amounts for bond discounts and premiums. The effective interest method is required by GAAP unless the difference between that method and the straight-line method is not material. The effective interest method is similar to the way we accounted for mortgages. You can learn more about this method in Appendix C.

Market for trading bonds

After they are issued, bonds are bought and sold in a secondary market. Just like stock, after the corporation completes the original issue, buyers and sellers get together via the bond market to trade bonds. These trades have no effect on the firm's financial records or financial statements. Just like there is a New York Stock Exchange, there is also a New York Bond Exchange. Learn how to read a bond table in *Accounting in the News*.

The price of a bond on the secondary market may be different from the original bond price, depending on whether interest rates have increased or decreased since the date of the original bond issue. Bond prices have an inverse relationship with interest rates: When interest rates increase, bond prices decrease, and vice versa. Because interest payments on a bond are fixed, when the market rate of interest goes down, those fixed rates look better. For example, suppose a $1,000 bond pays 9% per year. If the market rate of interest is 9%, the bond would sell for $1,000. If the market rate of interest goes up to 10%, this $1,000, 9% bond is not as attractive as other investments. So, the price of this bond will go down. That's the inverse relationship: If the market interest rate goes up, the bond price goes down. If the market rate of interest goes down to 8%, then the $1,000, 9% bond is a very attractive investment, and the price of the bond will go up.

Accounting in the NEWS

Financial Statement Analysis

How to Read a Bond Quote

Newspapers and financial web sites typically report data about corporate bonds. Below are some data for an IBM bond.

This IBM bond has a stated interest rate of 8 3/8%, and it will mature in 2019. Bonds usually have a face value of $1,000. The closing price for this bond is 126.25, which means $1,262.50. Since this bond is selling for more than its face value, it is selling at a premium. Similarly, when bonds sell for less than face value they sell at a discount.

Unlike stocks that have volume reported in number of shares, bond volume *does not* indicate the number of bonds sold. Rather, it is the dollar volume in thousands of dollars. For IBM, the volume was $3,000. The net change shows that the bond was selling for $1.75 more in the prior trading session. The rating of A is from S&P's rating codes and gives investors a measure of the risk associated with the bond. The higher the rating, the less the associated risk. Under S&P's ratings, only AA and AAA are less risky than A.

The final attribute listed below is whether a bond is callable. If a bond is callable, the corporation can "call" the bond, that is, pay off the debt. Corporations will sometimes call the bond if interest rates drop, because they can

You can check out the bond values of your favorite companies in newspapers like *The Wall Street Journal* and various financial web sites.

redeem the bonds and issue new ones at a lower interest rate.

Q Why do bond prices change every day?

A Interest rates change daily, and they have the most significant influences on bond prices.

Corporate Bond	Current Yield	Volume	Closing Price	Net Change	Rating	Callable
IBM 8 3/8 19	6.6	3	126.25	−1.75	A	No

Source: "Bond Investing," *SmartMoney.com*, May 21, 2005. Reprinted by permission of SmarttMoney.com.

LEARNING OBJECTIVE 5

Explain capital structure and compute the debt-to-equity and the times-interest-earned ratios.

Capital structure: The combination of debt and equity that a company chooses.

Financial Statement Analysis—Financial Leverage and Debt Ratios

You know that the two ways to finance a business are debt and equity. The combination of debt and equity that a company chooses is called its **capital structure**. That's because debt and equity are the two sources of capital, and every company can choose the proportion of each that makes up its total capital.

When should a company borrow money? A very simplistic cost/benefit analysis would suggest that when the benefit of borrowing the money—what it can earn for the business—exceeds the cost of borrowing the money—interest expense—then borrowing money is a good idea.

Look back at Hewlett-Packard's balance sheet in Exhibit 9.1 on page 443. Hewlett-Packard's total debt is $38,574 million. That is 51% of its financing (debt + equity = $76,138 million at October 31, 2004). How does the company's percentage of total debt compare with other firms in related industries? At December 31, 2004, IBM had total liabilities of $79,436 million and total debt plus equity of $109,183 million. Debt is almost 73% of IBM's capital structure. At December 31, 2004, Gateway had liabilities of $1,527 million and total debt and equity of $1,772 million. Debt is 86% of Gateway's capital structure. However, another well-known firm in the industry has an extremely low percentage of debt. At June 30, 2004, Microsoft had liabilities of $16,820 million and $81,732 million in total debt and equity. Debt is only 21% of its capital structure. Microsoft is known for its extremely low level of debt. There is no rule about how much debt a firm should have. If you take a finance course, you'll study the topic of optimal capital structure and find there is no simple answer.

Closely related is the concept of **financial leverage**, which means using borrowed funds to increase earnings. If a company earns more with the money it borrows than it has to pay to borrow that money, it is called *positive financial leverage*. Suppose Anna Chase has invested $50,000 in her new business and has no debt. If the business earns $5,000 net income during the year, then she has earned a return on her investment of 10%. Suppose Anna wants to expand her business. She might earn an additional $5,000 the next year if she borrows an additional $50,000. If the after-tax cost of borrowing the money is 8%, then Anna would be taking advantage of financial leverage if she borrows the money. That's because earnings could increase by more than the cost of borrowing the money. The new total income for the second year—$5,000 + $5,000 – $4,000 interest—would be $6,000. Anna's return on equity for the second year is $6,000 ÷ $50,000 = 12%.

Two financial ratios measure a company's debt position and its ability to meet its interest payments. The first is the **debt-to-equity ratio**:

> **Financial leverage:** Using borrowed money to increase earnings.

$$\text{Debt-to-equity ratio} = \frac{\text{Total Liabilities}}{\text{Total Shareholders' Equity}}$$

> **Debt-to-equity ratio:** Total liabilities divided by total stockholders' equity. The ratio compares the value of claims of creditors with the value of claims of owners.

This ratio compares the amount of creditors' claims to the assets of the firm with owners' claims to the assets of the firm. A firm with a high debt-to-equity ratio is often referred to as a highly leveraged firm. A debt-to-equity ratio around 100% (half debt and half equity) is quite common. Exhibit 9.12 shows the debt-to-equity ratios for McDonald's and Wendy's.

The second ratio related to long-term debt is called the **times-interest-earned ratio**. This ratio measures a company's ability to meet its interest obligations:

> **Times-interest-earned ratio:** Ratio that measures a company's ability to make the interest payments on its debt.

$$\text{Times-interest-earned ratio} = \frac{\text{Income from Operations}}{\text{Interest Expense}}$$

It is important to make sure you've excluded the company's interest expense from the numerator. Sometimes the numerator of the ratio is defined as net income + interest expense. The ratio measures the number of times operating income can cover interest expense. The more interest expense a company has, the smaller the ratio will be. If a company has any trouble covering its interest expense, that company clearly has too much debt.

Let's look at the times-interest-earned ratio for McDonald's and Wendy's, each with a capital structure of about half debt and half equity. Exhibit 9.13 shows the income from operations, the interest expense, and the times-interest earned ratio for both firms. Both firms appear to have no trouble meeting their interest payments.

Exhibit 9.12

Debt, Equity, and Debt-to-equity Ratios for Wendy's and McDonald's

McDonald's – Wendy's

> The debt-to-equity ratios show that creditors have financed a greater percentage of McDonald's business than Wendy's business. How much debt should a company have? Unfortunately, there is no easy answer.

(in millions)	McDonald's	Wendy's
Total Liabilities	$13,636.0	$1,481.9
Total Equity	$14,210.5	$1,715.7
Debt-to-equity Ratio	96%	86%

Even though Wendy's has a lower debt-to-equity ratio, its interest coverage is not as good as McDonald's.

Exhibit 9.13

McDonald's

Times-interest-earned for McDonald's and Wendy's

(in millions)	McDonald's	Wendy's
Income from operations	$3,540.5	$226.6
Interest expense	$ 358.4	$50.0
Times-interest-earned ratio......	9.88 times	4.53 times

The details of a company's long-term debt are often found in the notes to the financial statements, rather than on the face of the balance sheet, so it's important to study these notes. For example, the liabilities section of Sherwin Williams' balance sheet, shown in Exhibit 9.14, shows only the basic amounts of long-term obligations, while the notes give the details.

The top part of this exhibit shows the numbers taken from the year-end balance sheet. The detailed breakdown of the long-term debt amounts is taken from Sherwin Williams' Notes to the Financial Statements.

Exhibit 9.14

SHERWIN WILLIAMS

Details of Long-term Debt from the Financial Statements of Sherwin Williams

From the Financial Statements
of Sherwin Williams
(thousands of dollars)

From Liabilities and Shareholders' Equity Section

	At December 31,		
	2004	2003	2002
Total current liabilities	$1,520,137	$1,154,170	$1,083,496
Long-term debt	**488,239**	**502,992**	**506,682**
Postretirement benefits other than pensions	221,975	216,853	213,749
Other long-term liabilities	392,849	349,736	286,495
Minority interest	3,705		
Shareholders' equity:			
Total shareholders' equity	1,647,246	1,458,857	1,341,890
Total Liabilities and Shareholders' equity	$4,274,151	$3,682,608	$3,432,312

From the Notes to the Financial Statements:

Note 7 — Long-Term Debt

	Due Date	Amount Outstanding		
		2004	2003	2002
6.85% Notes	2007	$ 198,143	$ 203,173	$ 204,202
7.375% Debentures	2027	139,929	149,921	149,917
7.45% Debentures	2097	146,942	147,932	149,420
5% to 8.5% Promissory notes .... through 2007		1,725	1,285	1,643
9.875% Debentures	2016	1,500	1,500	1,500
Long-term debt before SFAS No. 133 adjustments		488,239	503,811	506,682
Fair value adjustments to 6.85% Notes in			(819)	
accordance with SFAS No. 133		$488,239	$502,992	$506,682

Can YOU do it?

Calculate the debt-to-equity ratio for Sherwin Williams for each of the years shown in Exhibit 9.14. What trend do you see, and how might an investor interpret it?

Answers 2004: 2,626,905 (total liabilities) ÷ 1,647,246 (total equity) = 1.59%.
2003: 2,223,751 (total liabilities) ÷ 1,458,857 (total equity) = 1.52%.
2002: 2,090,422 (total liabilities) ÷ 1,715,940 (total equity) = 1.22%.
The company has more debt than equity, and 2004 is a three-year high in the debt-to-equity ratio. This doesn't appear to be good news, but we would need some industry comparisons for meaningful analysis.

Business risk, control, & ethics

The primary risk for a company associated with long-term debt is the risk of not being able to make the debt payments. The more debt a business has, the more risk there is that the company won't be able to pay the debt as it becomes due. That would result in serious financial trouble, possibly even bankruptcy. For Hewlett-Packard, this does not seem to be a problem. As you just read, the firm's debt is approximately half of its capital structure, a much lower percentage than similar firms. The inability of a firm to pay its debt is a significant risk for the creditors and investors, too. If a company has trouble making its debt payments, you would not like to be one of its creditors or an investor.

There are two things a company can do to minimize the risk associated with long-term debt.

1. Be sure a thorough business analysis accompanies any decision to borrow money. This is where the concept of positive financial leverage comes in. The company must make sure there is a high probability of earning a higher return with the borrowed funds than the interest costs associated with borrowing the funds. How high should the probability be is an individual business decision. The more money involved, the higher the probability should be.

2. Study the characteristics of various types of debt—terms, interest rates, ease of obtaining the money—and evaluate their attractiveness in your specific circumstances, given the purpose of the loan and the financial situation of the company. For example, bonds are more flexible than a bank loan because the terms and cash flows can be varied, but a bank loan can be arranged more quickly than a company can issue bonds.

As you know, debt shows up on a firm's balance sheet. When a firm structures a transaction to keep debt off of its balance sheet, it is called *off-balance-sheet financing*.[4] The topic is a bit complicated for an introductory course, but you should be familiar with the expression and its general meaning. Off-balance-sheet financing is not always illegal or a violation of GAAP, but there are well-known cases where GAAP was violated to keep debt off a firm's balance sheet. This was the major fraud at Enron. The firm used creative bookkeeping to kept debt off the balance sheet that actually should have been shown there. This example shows that ethics touches every aspect of accounting, even how debt is recorded.

LEARNING OBJECTIVE 6

Identify the major risk associated with long-term debt and the related controls.

Both small business owners and large corporations can minimize their risk of defaulting on loans by conducting business analyses and evaluating the characteristics of various types of debt before borrowing.

[4]Appendix D discusses capital vs. operating leases. Operating leases are an example of off-balance-sheet financing because the future lease payments are not shown as liabilities on a firm's balance sheet.

Can**YOU**do it?

What is the major risk associated with having long-term debt on the balance sheet?

Answer There is a risk that the company will not be able to make its debt payments.

YOU make the call:

How should Hewlett-Packard account for its warranty expense?

Now that you have studied how a company accounts for warranties, you should be able to help Hewlett-Packard's accountant record the estimated cost of the company's two-year warranty. Even though the warranty is for two years, all of the estimated costs would be recognized as expense in the year of the sale. This will match the expense to the related sales, which means putting them on the same income statement. The journal entry should be a debit to Warranty Expense and a credit to Warranty Payable. Then, when expenditures are actually made, they would be written off against—debited to—the liability. Hewlett-Packard would record the $980,000 when spent as a debit to the Warranty Payable and a credit to Cash. That way all of the expense is recorded with the sale, and no expense is recognized when the warranties are actually honored.

Let's Take a Test Drive

Real World Problem:
Hewlett-Packard

Accounting for liabilities is an important part of Hewlett-Packard's operations. Look back at Exhibit 9.1 to see the variety of liabilities reported on Hewlett-Packard's recent balance sheet. In addition to the straightforward liabilities, like Accounts Payable, Hewlett-Packard has to estimate its warranty liability each period, make sure all expenses are appropriately accrued, and record any transactions related to its long-term debt.

Concepts

Liabilities recorded in the accounting records can be classified as definitely determinable or estimated. Hewlett-Packard has both types. The amounts Hewlett-Packard owes its vendors and many of its accrued expenses are definitely determinable. That is, the amounts are certain. The most significant estimated liability for Hewlett-Packard is its warranty costs. Each period, Hewlett-Packard estimates its future expenditures to honor product warranties. This amount is then booked as Warranty Expense and Warranty Payable. When the costs to actually repair merchandise are disbursed, the liability is debited (and Cash is credited). This treatment allows Warranty Expense to match the Sales Revenue from the products that have the warranty.

The two major ways to borrow large amounts of money for longer than a year are bank loans and bonds. Look back at Hewlett-Packard's balance sheet in Exhibit 9.1. The balance sheet shows long-term debt, but you would need to read the notes to find out the details of types of debt and maturities.

The Mechanics

To test your knowledge of how Hewlett-Packard would account for some of the common transactions related to liabilities, consider each of the following fictitious transactions:

1. On February 1, the first day of the fiscal year, Hewlett-Packard issued $5,000,000 worth of 10-year, 8% bonds at 98. Interest is payable annually on February 1. The discount will be amortized by $10,000 with each interest payment.

2. Hewlett-Packard borrowed $10,000,000. The loan is for 20 years at 6.5% with quarterly payments of $202,998. Hewlett-Packard borrowed the money on the last day of the third quarter of the fiscal year, and made the first payment on the last day of the fiscal year.

3. Hewlett-Packard spent $55,780 to honor warranties on products sold previously.

4. Hewlett-Packard purchased $675,000 worth of inventory on account. The firm uses a perpetual record keeping inventory system.

5. Hewlett-Packard paid vendors $563,000.

6. Of the beginning amount of Unearned Revenue, Hewlett-Packard earned $57,000 during the year.

7. Hewlett-Packard received $25,990 in advance from customers for products to be delivered next year.

8. Hewlett-Packard estimated it will spend $50,000 in the next two years honoring warranties related to this year's sales. (Two-year warranties on all products.)

Suppose Hewlett-Packard started the year with the following liability accounts and balances:

Accounts Payable	$75,500
Unearned Revenue	$57,960
Warranty Payable*	$68,950

Note: In Exhibit 9.1, HP included its warranty liability in "Other Accrued Liabilities" on its balance sheet.

Instructions

1. For each transaction, give the journal entry.
2. Give the adjusting entries that Hewlett-Packard needs to make as the result of these transactions.
3. Prepare the liability section of Hewlett-Packard's balance sheet at the end of the fiscal year.

Solution

1. Here are the journal entries:

   1. On February 1, the first day of the fiscal year, Hewlett-Packard issued $5,000,000 worth of 8%, 10-year bonds at 98. Interest is payable annually on the first of February. The discount will be amortized by $10,000 with each interest payment.

      Proceeds are 98% of the face, $4,900,000. Bonds Payable is always recorded at face value, $5,000,000. That leaves $100,000 to balance the journal entry as Discount on Bonds Payable.

Transaction	Debit	Credit
Cash	4,900,000	
Discount on Bonds Payable	100,000	
Bonds Payable		5,000,000

   2. Hewlett-Packard borrowed $10,000,000. The loan is for 20 years at 6.5% with quarterly payments of $202,998. Hewlett-Packard borrowed the money on the last day of the third quarter of the fiscal year, and made the first payment on the last day of the fiscal year.

      Recording the loan is a straight-forward entry. Proceeds are debited to Cash, and the liability, Notes Payable, is recorded.

Transaction	Debit	Credit
Cash	10,000,000	
Notes Payable		10,000,000

The first payment consists of interest for one-quarter on the full loan amount of $10,000,000. This calculation shows interest expense of $162,500. $10,000,000 × .065 × 3/12 = $162,500. The remainder of the payment ($202,998 − $162,500 = $40,498) is a reduction in the loan principal.

Transaction	Debit	Credit
Notes Payable	40,498	
Interest Expense	162,500	
Cash		202,998

3. Hewlett-Packard spent $55,780 to honor warranties on products sold previously. Amounts expended to honor warranties do not result in an expense. Remember, the expense for warranties is booked in the year of the sale. Then, the expenditures to honor the warranties are written off against the liability.

Transaction	Debit	Credit
Warranty Payable	55,780	
Miscellaneous Accounts*		55,780

*Cash, Salaries Payable, Inventory, or whatever was used to honor the warranties.

4. Hewlett-Packard purchased $675,000 worth of inventory on account. This is a straightforward entry to record Inventory and Accounts Payable.

Transaction	Debit	Credit
Inventory	675,000	
Accounts Payable		675,000

5. Hewlett-Packard paid vendors $563,000. This is a straightforward entry to record a reduction in Accounts Payable.

Transaction	Debit	Credit
Accounts Payable	563,000	
Cash		563,000

6. Of the beginning amount of Unearned Revenue, Hewlett-Packard earned $57,000 during the year The entry reduces the amount of Unearned Revenue and "moves" it to Revenue that will go on the income statement.

Transaction	Debit	Credit
Unearned Revenue	57,000	
Revenue		57,000

7. Hewlett-Packard received $25,990 in advance from customers for products to be delivered next year. Cash received but not yet earned must be booked as a liability, Unearned Revenue, until it is earned.

Transaction	Debit	Credit
Cash	25,990	
Unearned Revenue		25,990

8. Hewlett-Packard estimated it will spend $50,000 in the next two years honoring warranties related to this year's sales. (Two-year warranties on all products.)

The entire amount of the estimated warranty costs are recorded in the year of the sale (due to the matching principal). The expense shows up on the income statement, and the liability will be in the current liabilities section of the balance sheet.

Transaction	Debit	Credit
Warranty Expense	50,000	
Warranty Payable		50,000

2. The last journal entry needed is an accrual to record the interest on the Bonds Payable. The bonds were issued on the first day of the fiscal year, so an entire year's interest expense has been incurred. The Interest Expense needs to be on the income statement for the year. The obligation, Interest Payable, will be shown in the current liabilities section of the balance sheet.

Transaction	Debit	Credit
Interest Expense	410,000	
Discount on Bonds Payable		10,000
Interest Payable		400,000

3. The T-accounts with posted journal entries for three of the existing liabilities are shown below. See if you can trace each addition and deduction back to the relevant journal entry.

Accounts Payable			Unearned Revenue			Warranty Payable	
563,000	75,500 **BB**		57,000	57,960 **BB**		55,780	68,950 **BB**
	675,000			25,990			50,000
	187,500			26,950			63,170

Here is the liabilities section of the year-end balance sheet:

Current Liabilities:	
Accounts payable	$187,500
Interest payable	400,000
Unearned revenue	26,950
Warranty liability	63,170
**Current portion of long-term debt	168,681
Total current liabilities	846,301
Long-term Liabilities	
**Notes payable	9,790,821
Bonds payable (net of a discount of $90,000)	4,910,000
Total liabilities	$15,547,122

** A partial amortization schedule for long-term loan with quarterly payments is shown below. In the next fiscal year, four of those payments will be due. Only the principal portion is recorded as a current liability because the interest has not yet been incurred at the end of the year. The total current portion is the sum of the highlighted values in the "Principal reduction" column. The remaining amount of the note payable, highlighted in the "Principal" column, is shown as a long-term liability.

Principal	Payment	Interest per Quarter	Principal Reduction	
$10,000,000	$202,998	$162,500	$40,498	
9,959,502	202,998	161,842	41,156	
9,918,346	202,998	161,173	41,825	
9,876,521	202,998	160,493	42,505	$168,681
9,834,016	202,998	159,803	43,195	
9,790,821	202,998	159,101	43,897	
9,746,924	202,998	158,388	44,610	

Rapid Review

1. **Define a definitely determinable liability and explain how payroll is recorded.** A *definitely determinable liability* is one whose amount is known, and it is recorded when incurred. A typical example is payroll. The firm knows how much to record for Salary Expense. The firm serves as an agent for the government to collect Social Security, Medicare, and income taxes from the employee.

2. **Define an estimated liability and explain how to account for warranties.** An *estimated liability* is one whose amount is not certain, but it has been incurred and must be recorded to get the expense on the income statement. The other side of recording that expense is the liability. Warranties are a typical example. At the time of the sale, a firm does not know exactly how much the warranty will cost. When the cost of providing warranties is significant, a company will record Warranty Expense in the same period as the sale and book a liability for the future warranty costs. Then, when the cost to honor the warranties is actually incurred, it will be written off against Warranty Liability.

3. **Explain how long-term notes and mortgages work.** Long-term mortgages usually have payments that include both principal and interest. To calculate the portion of the payment that is interest expense, multiply the interest rate by the outstanding principal balance just before the payment. Then, subtract that amount of interest from the payment to find the amount of principal reduction.

4. **Record the issue of bonds and payment of interest to bondholders.** Bonds are issued at par, at a discount, or at a premium. The bonds are shown on the balance sheet—the carrying value—at a "net" amount: any applicable discount (premium) is deducted from (added to) the face value of the bonds.

5. **Explain capital structure and compute the debt-to-equity and the times-interest-earned ratios.** Capital structure refers to the proportion of debt and equity a firm has. *Debt to equity* is, as it sounds, the firm's total debt divided by the firm's equity. *Times interest earned* is defined as operating income (or net income + interest expense) divided by interest expense. It tells investors and creditors how easy or difficult it was for the firm to meet the current period's interest obligation.

$$\text{Debt-to-equity ratio} = \frac{\text{Total Liabilities}}{\text{Total Shareholders' Equity}}$$

$$\text{Times-interest-earned ratio} = \frac{\text{Income from Operations}}{\text{Interest Expense}}$$

6. **Identify the major risk associated with long-term debt and the related controls.** The major risk for the firm is that it will not be able to make its debt payments. The best control for this risk is sound financial planning and the profitable operation of the firm.

Key Terms

Bond, p. 453
Capital structure, p. 464
Carrying value, p. 459
Debt-to-equity ratio, p. 465
Definitely determinable liabilities, p. 442

Discount on bonds payable, p. 458
Discount rate, p. 451
Discounting, p. 451
Estimated liabilities, p. 446
Financial leverage, p. 465

Market rate of interest, p. 455
Premium on bonds payable, p. 459
Present value, p. 450
Times-interest-earned ratio, p. 465

Have You Increased Your Business IQ?

Answer these questions to find out.

1. A definitely determinable liability is one that
   a. has been paid.
   b. accrues interest to the debt holder.
   c. can be measured exactly.
   d. is the estimated amount owed for future expenses.
2. Capital structure refers to a firm's
   a. amount of property, plant, and equipment.
   b. relative amounts of debt and equity.
   c. ability to meet its long-term obligations.
   d. interest rate on its long-term debt.
3. An amortization schedule for a typical mortgage shows the
   a. increase in principal over the life of the mortgage.
   b. cost of the asset reduced by its estimated residual value.
   c. increase in interest expense over the life of the mortgage.
   d. reduction in the principal over the life of the mortgage.
4. Warranty expense is recognized
   a. in the same period as the sale to which it pertains.
   b. when the warranty is honored.
   c. when the costs related to the warranty are actually paid.
   d. as an interest expense on the income statement.
5. A bond will be sold at a premium or discount when
   a. the market rate of interest is equal to the interest on the face of the bond.
   b. the maturity is shorter than 30 years.
   c. the market rate of interest and the rate stated on the face of the bond are different.
   d. the market rate of interest is greater than 15%.

Now, check your answers.

1. c   2. b   3. d   4. a   5. c

- If you answered all five questions correctly, you've increased your business IQ by studying this chapter. It doesn't mean you've mastered all of the accounting concepts in the chapter. It simply means that you understand some of the general business concepts presented in this chapter.
- If you answered 2 to 4 questions correctly, you've made some progress, but your business IQ has plenty of room to grow. You might want to skim over the chapter again.
- If you answered 0 or 1 question correctly, you can do more to improve your business IQ. Better study the chapter again.

Questions

1. What are the two main sources of financing for a business?
2. What is the difference between a definitely determinable liability and an estimated liability? Give examples of both.
3. When is the expense related to warranties recognized? How is the cost of repairing a product under warranty accounted for?
4. What is a mortgage?
5. When installment loan payments on a mortgage are made, the amount paid reduces cash. What other two items on the financial statement are affected?
6. What is the difference between how bonds are repaid compared to other forms of financing that require installment payments?
7. What advantage is there to obtaining financing using bonds compared to getting a loan from a bank?
8. What does the expression time value of money mean?
9. How are the interest payments associated with a bond calculated?
10. Explain the difference between the stated rate and the market rate of interest on a bond.
11. What is another name for the face value of a bond?

12. When is a bond issued at a discount? When is a bond issued at a premium?
13. How is the carrying value of a bond computed? At maturity, what is the carrying value of a bond that was issued at a premium?
14. What is the difference between a convertible bond and a callable bond?
15. What are zero coupon bonds and how do they differ from bonds with a stated rate?
16. How is the debt-to-equity ratio calculated, and what does this ratio measure?
17. How is the times-interest-earned ratio calculated, and what does this ratio measure?
18. To what does the term capital structure refer?
19. Explain financial leverage.

Multiple Choice

1. On January 1, 2006, Sonata Company issued 10-year bonds with a face value of $400,000 and a stated rate of 10%. The cash proceeds from the bond issue amounted to $354,120. Sonata Company will pay interest to the bondholders annually. How much cash will Sonata pay the bondholders on the first payment date?
   a. $40,000
   b. $48,000
   c. $35,412
   d. $42,494
2. Refer to the information in question 1. How did the market interest rate compare to the stated rate on the date the bonds were issued?
   a. The market rate is higher than the stated rate.
   b. The market rate is lower than the stated rate
   c. Both rates are the same
   d. Cannot be determined
3. Partco estimated that its warranty costs would be $900 for items sold during the current year. During the year, Partco paid $750 to repair merchandise that was returned by customers. What is the amount of warranty expense for the current year?
   a. $750
   b. $900
   c. $150
   d. Cannot be determined
4. Which of the following is a long-term liability?
   a. Salaries Payable
   b. Mortgage Payable
   c. Unearned Revenue
   d. Accounts Payable
5. The amount a company owes its employees for current work done is
   a. Shown on the balance sheet as Pension Liability

   b. Shown as a current liability
   c. Called Post-retirement Benefits on the balance sheet
   d. Not shown on the balance sheet
6. Liabilities are often estimated because
   a. The related expense needs to be recorded to match the appropriate revenues
   b. It gives managers a way to manage assets
   c. They are usually not disclosed until they are settled
   d. The related assets are already recorded
7. Bonds issued at an interest rate that is higher than the prevailing market rate are issued at
   a. A premium
   b. A discount
   c. Par
   d. Cannot be determined
8. A $1,000 bond with a stated rate of 8% is issued when the market rate is 10%. How much interest will the bondholders receive each year?
   a. $100
   b. $80
   c. $20
   d. $800
9. The carrying value of a bond is the
   a. Face value
   b. Face value minus any discount or plus any premium
   c. Face value minus any interest paid
   d. Amount of principal and interest owed to the bondholders
10. Positive financial leverage means that a company
   a. Has more debt than equity
   b. Earns more with borrowed money than the cost of borrowing it
   c. Has the correct amount of debt
   d. Has more equity than debt

Short Exercises

LO 1, 2 **SE9-1. Classify liabilities.**
Tell whether each of the following liabilities is definitely determinable or an estimate: Accounts Payable, Unearned Revenue, and Warranty Payable.

SE9-2. Classify liabilities.   LO 1

Taylor Company has the following obligations at December 31: (a) a note payable for $10,000 due in six months, (b) unearned revenue of $12,500, (c) interest payable of $15,000, (d) accounts payable of $60,000, and (e) note payable due in two years. For each obligation, indicate whether it should be classified as a current or a non-current liability.

SE9-3. Account for payroll.   LO 1

Jimmy Paycheck earned $1,500 per month as the manager of a recording studio. Jimmy has 25% of his earnings withheld for federal income taxes. There are no other amounts withheld except for those required by the federal government. What are the other amounts that must be deducted from Jimmy's earnings? Calculate the net amount Jimmy will receive on his next paycheck.

SE9-4. Account for payroll.   LO 1

Use the data from SE9-3 to (a) prepare the journal entry to record the Salary Expense that would be recorded on the books of the recording studio and (b) prepare the journal entry to record the required payment to the federal government by the studio.

SE9-5. Account for warranties.   LO 2

Key Company offers a three-year warranty on its premium door locks. During the year, the company had sales of $100,000. Related to the sales, warranty costs should be approximately $3,000 per year. How much Warranty Expense related to these sales will Key Company's income statement show in the year of the sales? How much Warranty Expense related to these sales will Key Company have in the two years after the sales?

SE9-6. Account for warranties.   LO 2

Coughlin Rug Co. started 2005 with a $5,000 balance in its Warranty Payable account. The firm had sales of $100,000 in 2005. The company expects to incur future warranty expenses related to these sales that will amount to 6% of sales. There was $4,000 of warranty obligations paid in cash during 2005 related to the 2005 sales. How much Warranty Expense would Coughlin Rug Co. show on the income statement for the 2005 fiscal year? What is the amount of Warranty Payable on the balance sheet at the end of 2005?

SE9-7. Account for warranties.   LO 2

Nunez Company began the year with $30,000 in its Warranty Payable account. During the year, the firm spent $20,000 to honor past warranties. Will $20,000 be the Warranty Expense for the year? Why or why not?

SE9-8. Account for long-term liabilities.   LO 3

Fastrac Corporation is considering borrowing some money and is evaluating the different options for financing. As the chief financial officer, write a memo to the corporation's board of directors explaining the difference between how a mortgage and a bond is repaid.

SE9-9. Account for long-term liabilities.   LO 3

J-Gas Company has arranged to borrow $25,000 for five years at an interest rate of 8%. The annual payments will be $6,261.41. When J-Gas makes its first payment at the end of the first year of the loan, how much of the payment will be interest?

SE9-10. Account for long-term liabilities.   LO 3

Feathers and Furs borrowed $75,000 to buy a new faux fur storage facility. The company borrowed the money for 10 years at 12%, and the monthly payment is $1,076.03. When the company makes the first monthly payment, by how much will the payment reduce the principal of the loan?

SE9-11. Account for long-term liabilities.   LO 3

Curtain Company borrowed $10,000 at 9% for seven years. The loan requires annual payments of $1,986.01. When Curtain Company makes the first annual payment, how much of the payment will be interest and how much will reduce the principal of the loan?

SE9-12. Account for long-term liabilities.   LO 3

On July 1, 2006, Maxine's Equipment Company signed a long-term note with the local bank for $50,000. The term of the note was 10 years, at an annual interest rate of 8%. If Maxine's makes annual payments of $7,451.47, beginning on June 30, 2007, how much of the first payment will be interest?

LO 4   **SE9-13. Account for bonds.**

If a $1,000 bond is selling at 95, how much cash will the issuing company receive? If a $1,000 bond is selling at par, how much cash will the issuing company receive? If a $1,000 bond is selling at 101, how much cash will the issuing company receive?

LO 4   **SE9-14. Account for bonds.**

If $100,000 of 8% bonds are issued (sold) for $95,000, was the market rate of interest at the time of issue higher or lower than 8%? What is the amount of the annual interest payments to be received by the bondholders?

LO 4   **SE9-15. Account for bonds.**

For each of the following situations, tell whether the bond described will be issued at a premium, at a discount, or at par.

   a. Colson Company issued $200,000 worth of bonds with a stated interest rate of 10%. At the time of issue, the market rate of interest for similar investments was 9%.

   b. Dean Company issued $100,000 worth of callable bonds with a stated rate of 12%. At the time of issue, the market rate of interest for similar investments was 9%.

   c. Liddy Company issued $200,000 worth of bonds with a stated rate of 8%. At the time of issue, the market rate of interest for similar investments was 9%.

LO 4   **SE9-16. Account for bonds.**

For each of the following, compute the proceeds from the bond issue.

   a. Haldeman Hair Systems issued $20,000 worth of bonds at 106.

   b. Erlichman Egg Company issued $100,000 worth of bonds at 99.

   c. Carl's Cutlery Company issued $500,000 worth of bonds at 96 1/2.

LO 4   **SE9-17. Account for bonds.**

Altoona Company was able to issue (sell) $200,000 of 9% bonds for $220,000 because its credit rating is excellent and market interest rates have fallen. How much interest will be paid in cash during the first year? Will the interest expense be higher or lower than the interest payment?

LO 5   **SE9-18. Calculate the debt-to-equity ratio.**

Suppose that for fiscal year 2006 GM's current assets totaled $57,855 (in millions), total assets totaled $449,999 (in millions), current liabilities totaled $71,264 (in millions), and total liabilities totaled $424,424 (in millions). Calculate the debt-to-equity ratio for GM at the end of fiscal 2006.

LO 5   **SE9-19. Calculate the times-interest-earned ratio.**

Suppose that for fiscal year 2006, GM's total revenues were $185,524 (in millions), cost of goods sold was $152,071 (in millions), interest expense was $9,464 (in millions), income from operations was $2,981 (in millions), and net income was $1,822 (in millions). Calculate the times-interest-earned ratio for GM for 2006.

LO 6   **SE9-20. Risk and Controls.**

GuGa's Shirt Company wants to borrow $35,000. What should the company consider before proceeding?

Exercise Set A

LO 1   **E9-1A. Classify liabilities.**

For each item in the list below, tell whether it is a definitely determinable liability, an estimated liability, or neither.

   a. Amount owed to vendor for purchase of inventory

   b. Potential loss from pending lawsuit

   c. Amount of warranty obligations

   d. Amount of loan payment due next year

   e. Amount of vacation pay to accrue for employees for next year

LO 1   **E9-2A. Account for payroll.**

If a company has gross payroll of $20,000, federal income tax withheld of $4,000, and FICA (Social Security) taxes withheld of $1,240, and Medicare taxes of $290.

   a. How much will the balance sheet show for Salaries Payable (to employees)?

   b. How much will the income statement show for Salaries Expense?

   c. What type of liability is Salaries Payable?

E9-3A. Account for payroll.   LO 1

During February, Winter Company's employees earned salaries of $50,000. Social Security (FICA) withheld was $3,100. Medicare taxes withheld were $725; federal income taxes withheld were $10,000; and employees' contributions to United Way withheld totaled $500. Prepare the journal entry to record Salaries Expense and Salaries Payable at the end of February. Winter Company will pay employees their February salaries during the first week in March.

E9-4A. Account for warranties.   LO 2

When Park Avenue Pet Shop sells a puppy, it provides a health warranty. If a puppy becomes ill in the first two years after the sale, Park Avenue Pet Shop will pay the vet bill up to $300. Because this is normally a significant expense for the shop, the accountant insists that Park Avenue Pet Shop record an Estimated Warranty Liability at the end of every year before the financial statements are prepared. The shop estimates that 10% of puppies sold become ill under the terms of the warranty. The average vet bill is $100. On December 31, 2006, the accountant made the appropriate entry to record that liability based on sales for the year of 1,500 puppies. On March 30, 2007, the store received a $50 vet bill from one of its customers, who had bought a puppy in 2006. Park Avenue Pet Shop wrote a check for $50 to reimburse the puppy's owner.

a. Prepare the journal entry to record Estimated Warranty Liability at December 31, 2006.
b. Prepare the journal entry to record the payment of the vet bill on March 30, 2007.
c. What effect did this payment have on the 2007 financial statements of Park Avenue Pet Shop?

E9-5A. Account for long-term liabilities.   LO 3

Stephen's Storage Company needed some long-term financing and arranged for a $100,000, 20-year mortgage loan on December 31, 2005. The interest rate is 9% per year, with $11,000 payments made at the end of each year.

a. What is the amount of interest expense related to this loan for 2006?
b. What amount of liability should appear on the December 31, 2006 balance sheet?
c. What is the amount of interest expense related to this loan for 2007?
d. What amount of liability should appear on the December 31, 2007 balance sheet?

E9-6A. Account for long-term liabilities.   LO 3

Grace's Gems purchased some property on December 31, 2004, for $100,000, paying $20,000 in cash and obtaining a mortgage loan for the remaining $80,000. The interest rate is 8% per year, with $2,925 payments made at the end of March, June, September, and December.

a. What amounts should appear as Interest Expense on the quarterly income statements and as liabilities on the quarterly balance sheets during 2005?
b. What amount of Interest Expense should appear on the year 2005 income statement?

E9-7A. Account for long-term liabilities.   LO 3

Suppose Dell Corporation signed a $500,000, 10-year, 8% note payable to finance the expansion of its business on January 1. The terms provide for semiannual payments of $36,791 on June 30 and December 31. Prepare the journal entries to record Dell's receipt of the proceeds and the first two semi-annual payments.

E9-8A. Account for long-term liabilities.   LO 3

On April 1, Mark Hamm borrowed $15,000 on an 8-month, 6% note from State Bank of New York to open a business, Gymnastics World. The debt was in the company's name. The note and interest will be repaid on November 30.

a. Prepare the journal entry to record the receipt of the funds.
b. Suppose Gymnastics World wants to prepare an income statement for the month of April. Prepare the entry needed to accrue interest for the month.
c. Assume that Gymnastics World accrues the interest expense related to this note at the end of each month. What is the balance in the Interest Payable account September 30?
d. Prepare the entry required on November 30, when the loan is repaid with the interest. (Assume all necessary interest accruals were made at the appropriate time.)

LO 4   **E9-9A.** **Account for bonds.**
On December 31, 2006, Bert's Batteries issued $10,000 worth of 10% bonds at 94. These are 10-year bonds with interest paid annually on December 31.

  a. What are the interest payments for the first two years?
  b. Was the market interest rate higher or lower than 10% at the date of issue?
  c. Will the interest expense be higher or lower than the interest payment?

LO 4   **E9-10A.** **Account for bonds.**
On December 31, 2005, Carl's Cartons issued $100,000 worth of 9% bonds at 104. The interest on these bonds is paid annually on December 31.

  a. What are the interest payments for the first two years?
  b. Was the market interest rate higher or lower than 9% at the date of issue?
  c. Will the interest expense be higher or lower than the interest payment?

LO 4   **E9-11A.** **Account for bonds.**
On January 1 Amico Company issued $200,000, 10%, five-year bonds at face value. Interest is payable on January 1. Prepare the journal entries to record the following:

  a. The bond issue
  b. The accrual of interest on December 31
  c. The payment of interest on January 1

LO 4   **E9-12A.** **Account for bonds.**
On December 31, 2006, Dave's Delivery Service issued $10,000 worth of 10% bonds at approximately 89. These are 10-year bonds with interest paid semiannually on June 30 and December 31.

  a. What are the interest payments for the first two years?
  b. Was the market interest rate higher or lower than 10% at the date of issue?
  c. Will the interest expense be higher or lower than the interest payment?

LO 4   **E9-13A.** **Account for bonds.**
On June 30, 2005, Ellie's Electronics issued $20,000 face value of 10% bonds at 105. They were 10-year bonds with interest paid semiannually, on December 31 and June 30.

  a. What are the interest payments for the first two years?
  b. Was the market interest rate higher or lower than 10% at the date of issue?
  c. Will the interest expense be higher or lower than the interest payment?

LO 4   **E9-14A.** **Account for bonds.**
On June 30, 2006, Fred's Fudge Co. issued $50,000 worth of 10% bonds for $50,000. The interest is paid annually on June 30.

  a. What are the interest payments for the first two years?
  b. Was the market interest rate higher or lower than 10% at the date of issue?
  c. Will the interest expense be higher or lower than the interest payment?

Use the following financial data for eBay to answer E9-15A and E9-16A:

eBay
Consolidated Balance Sheet (adapted)

(in thousands, except per share amounts)

	December 31,	
	2003	**2004**
Assets		
Total current assets	2,145,882	2,911,149
Total assets	$5,820,134	$7,991,051
Liabilities and Stockholders' Equity		
Total current liabilities	$ 647,276	$1,084,870
Total liabilities	923,892	1,262,710
Total stockholders' equity	4,896,242	6,728,341
	$5,820,134	$7,991,051

eBay
Consolidated Statement of Income (adapted)

(in thousands, except per share amounts)

| | Year Ended December 31, | | |
	2002	2003	2004
Net revenues	$1,214,100	$2,165,096	$3,271,309
Cost of net revenues	213,876	416,058	614,415
Gross profit	1,000,224	1,749,038	2,656,894
Total operating expenses	646,027	1,119,797	1,597,652
Income from operations	354,197	629,241	1,059,242
Interest and other income, net	49,209	37,803	77,867
Interest expense	(1,492)	(4,314)	(8,879)
Impairment of certain equity investments	(3,781)	(1,230)	—
Income before cumulative effect of accounting change, income taxes and minority interests	398,133	661,500	1,128,230
Provision for income taxes	(145,946)	(206,738)	(343,885)
Minority interests	(2,296)	(7,578)	(6,122)
Income before cumulative effect of accounting change	249,891	447,184	778,223
Cumulative effect of accounting change, net of tax	—	(5,413)	—
Net income	$ 249,891	$ 441,771	$ 778,223

E9-15A. Calculate the debt-to-equity ratio.   LO 5
Using the information provided above for eBay, calculate the debt-to-equity ratio for
2003 and 2004. Provide an explanation of what this ratio measures and whether the
ratio has improved from 2003 to 2004.

E9-16A. Calculate the times-interest-earned ratio.   LO 5
Using the information provided above for eBay, calculate the times-interest-earned
ratio for 2003 and 2004. Provide an explanation of what this ratio measures and
whether the ratio has improved from 2003 to 2004.

E9-17A. Risk and control.   LO 6
You've probably heard people brag that they are debt-free. Do you think it's a good
idea for a corporation to be debt free? Explain.

E9-18A. Appendix A: Calculate payments using time value of money concepts.
For each of the following, calculate the payment each loan would require. Assume the
payments are made at the end of the period in each case. Interest rates are annual
rates.

a. principal = $30,000; interest rate = 5%; term = 5 years; payments = annual
b. principal = $30,000; interest rate = 8%; term = 5 years; payments = annual
c. principal = $30,000; interest rate = 8%; term = 10 years; payments = annual
d. principal = $30,000; interest rate = 8%; term = 10 years; payments = semiannual
e. principal = $30,000; interest rate = 12%; term = 5 years; payments = monthly

E9-19A. Appendices B and C: Calculate bond amounts using time value of money concepts.
Jamison Corporation issued $100,000, 8%, 10-year bonds on January 1, 2005, when
the market rate of interest was 10%. Proceeds were $87,711. Interest is payable
annually on January 1. Jamison uses the effective-interest method to amortize bond
premiums and discounts. Prepare the journal entries to record (round to the
nearest dollar):

a. The issuance of the bonds
b. The accrual of interest and the discount amortization on December 31,
2005
c. The payment of interest on January 1, 2006

E9-20A. Appendices B and C: Calculate bond amounts using time value of money concepts.

Benedon Company issued $180,000, 11%, 10-year bonds on January 1, 2006, when the market rate of interest was 10%. The proceeds were $191,060. Interest is payable annually on January 1. Benedon uses the effective-interest method to amortize bond premiums and discounts.

Prepare the journal entries (rounded to the nearest dollar) to record the following:

a. The issuance of the bonds
b. The accrual of interest and the premium amortization on December 31, 2006
c. The payment of interest on January 1, 2007

Exercise Set B

> Your professor may ask you to complete selected "Group B" exercises and problems using Prentice Hall Grade Assist (**PHGA**). PHGA is an online tool that can help you master the chapter's topics by providing multiple variations of exercises and problems. You can rework these exercises and problems—each time with new data—as many times as you need, with immediate feedback and grading.

LO 1, 2

E9-1B. Classify liabilities.

For each item in the list below, tell whether it is a definitely determinable liability, an estimated liability, or neither.

a. Amount of cash revenue received from customer that is unearned
b. Corporate income tax for the year
c. Coupons unredeemed at the end of the year
d. Amount of salaries payable to accrue at the end of the year
e. Account payable owed to vendor for purchase on credit

LO 1

E9-2B. Account for payroll.

If a company has gross payroll of $30,000, federal income tax withheld of $6,000, and FICA (Social Security) taxes withheld of $1,860, and Medicare taxes of $435:

a. How much will the balance sheet show for Salaries Payable (to employees)?
b. How much will the income statement show for Salaries Expense?
c. What type of liability is Salaries Payable?

LO 1

E9-3B. Account for payroll.

During March, The Wessue Coffee Emporium's employees earned salaries of $18,000. Social Security (FICA) withheld was $1,116; Medicare taxes of $261; federal income taxes withheld were $3,600; and employees' contributions to the American Red Cross withheld totaled $175. Prepare the journal entry to record Salaries Expense and Salaries Payable at the end of March. Wessue will pay employees their March salaries during the first week in April.

LO 2

E9-4B. Account for warranties.

When M, K, & Boyd Pools Plus installs a pool, it provides a three-year warranty (from the date of the sale) for repairs needed that are not considered general maintenance. If a pool should need to be repaired in the first three years after the sale, M, K, & Boyd will repair the pool for a cost of up to $1,000. Because this is normally a significant expense, the accountant insists that M, K, & Boyd record an Estimated Warranty Liability at the end of every year before the financial statements are prepared. The firm estimates that 15% of the pools will need warranty-related repairs, and the average cost of a repair is $800. For the year ended June 30, 2008, the accountant made the appropriate entry to record that liability based on sales and installations for the year of 360 pools. On January 1, 2009, M, K, & Boyd paid $750 to an independent contractor to repair a pool for one of its customers, who had purchased the pool on March 15, 2008.

a. Prepare the journal entry to record Estimated Warranty Liability at June 30, 2008.
b. Prepare the journal entry to record the payment of the repair bill on January 1, 2009.
c. For the year ended June 30, 2009, what effect did this payment have on the financial statements of M, K, & Boyd Pools Plus?

E9-5B. Account for long-term liabilities.

LO 3

Don & Brenda's Gourmet Bread Shop needed some long-term financing and arranged for a $250,000, 15-year mortgage loan on December 31, 2007. The interest rate is 5.5% per year, with $24,906 payments made at the end of each year.

a. What is the amount of Interest Expense related to this loan for 2008?
b. What amount of liability should appear on the December 31, 2008 balance sheet?
c. What is the amount of Interest Expense related to this loan for 2009?
d. What amount of liability should appear on the December 31, 2009 balance sheet?

E9-6B. Account for long-term liabilities.

LO 3

Molly Merry's Accounting Firm purchased some property on December 31, 2006, for $150,000, paying $30,000 in cash and obtaining a mortgage loan for the remaining $120,000. The interest rate is 12% per year, with $8,065 payments made at the end of March, June, September, and December. (The loan is amortized quarterly.)

a. What amounts should appear as Interest Expense on the quarterly income statements and as liabilities on the quarterly balance sheets during 2007?
b. What amount of Interest Expense should appear on the income statement for the year ended December 31, 2007?

E9-7B. Account for long-term liabilities.

LO 3

Suppose Cindy & Owen Cold Desserts signed a $185,000, nine-year, 6% note payable to finance the expansion of its business on January 1. The terms provide for semiannual payments of $13,451 on June 30 and December 31. Prepare the journal entries to record Cindy & Owen's receipt of the loan proceeds and the first two payments.

E9-8B. Account for long-term liabilities.

LO 3

On March 1, Delvis Cromartie borrowed $7,500 on a five-month, 8% note from Florida First Bank & Trust to open a business, Orchids & Such Nursery. The debt was in the company's name. The note and interest will be repaid on July 31.

a. Prepare the journal entry to record the receipt of the funds.
b. Suppose Orchids & Such Nursery wants to prepare an income statement for the month of March. Prepare the entry needed to accrue interest for the month.
c. Assume that Orchids & Such Nursery accrues the Interest Expense related to this note at the end of each month. What is the balance in the Interest Payable account May 31?
d. Prepare the entry required on July 31, when the loan is repaid with the interest. (Assume all necessary interest accruals were made at the appropriate time.)

E9-9B. Account for bonds.

LO 4

On June 30, 2007, Jamie's Suitcases & Travel issued $25,000 worth of 8% bonds at 106. These are five-year bonds with interest paid annually on June 30.

a. What are the interest payments for the first two years?
b. Was the market interest rate higher or lower than 8% at the date of issue?
c. Prepare the journal entry to record the Interest Expense and payment for June 30, 2008. Use straight-line amortization.

E9-10B. Account for bonds.

LO 4

On February 28, 2009, Newman & Spears Enterprises issued $150,000 worth of 7% bonds at 92. The interest on these bonds is paid annually on February 28.

a. What are the interest payments for the first two years?
b. Was the market interest rate higher or lower than 7% at the date of issue?
c. Will the interest expense be higher or lower than the interest payment?

E9-11B. Account for bonds.

LO 4

On January 1, A&A Construction issued $300,000, 8%, 10-year bonds at face value. Interest is payable on January 1. Prepare the journal entries to record the following:

a. The bond issue
b. The accrual of interest on December 31
c. The payment of interest on January 1

E9-12B. Account for bonds.

LO 4

On June 30, 2008, McCorvey's Lawn Service issued $7,500 worth of 6% bonds at approximately 102. These are five-year bonds with interest paid semiannually on

December 31 and June 30. The firm uses straight-line amortization for bond discounts and premiums.

a. What are the interest payments for the first two years?
b. Was the market interest rate higher or lower than 6% at the date of issue?
c. Will the interest expense be higher or lower than the interest payment?

LO 4   **E9-13B. Account for bonds.**
On December 31, 2007, State of the Art Electronics issued $40,000 face value of 12% bonds at 96. They were eight-year bonds with interest paid semiannually, on June 30 and December 31. The firm uses straight-line amortization for bond discounts and premiums.

a. What are the interest payments for each six months of the first two years?
b. Was the market interest rate higher or lower than 12% at the date of issue?
c. Prepare the journal entry to record the Interest Expense and payment for June 30 and December 31, 2008.

LO 4   **E9-14B. Account for bonds.**
On June 30, 2008, Nikki C. Records issued $35,000 worth of 8% bonds for $35,000. The interest is paid annually on June 30.

a. What are the interest payments for the first two years?
b. Was the market interest rate higher or lower than 8% at the date of issue?
c. Will the interest expense be higher or lower than the interest payment?

Use the following financial data for Netflix to answer E9-15B and E9-16B:

Netflix
Consolidated Balance Sheet (adapted)
(in thousands, except per share amounts)

	December 31, 2003	December 31, 2004
Assets		
Total current assets	138,946	187,346
Total assets	$176,012	$251,793
Liabilities and Stockholders' Equity		
Total current liabilities	$ 63,019	$ 94,910
Total liabilities	$ 63,304	$ 95,510
Total stockholders' equity	112,708	156,283
	$176,012	$251,793

Netflix
Consolidated Statement of Income (adapted)
(in thousands, except per share amounts)

	2002	2003	2004
Net revenues	$152,806	$272,243	$506,228
Cost of net revenues	78,136	148,360	276,458
Gross profit	74,670	123,883	229,770
Total operating expenses	85,343	119,411	210,416
Income from operations	(10,673)	4,472	19,354
Interest and other income, net	1,697	2,457	2,592
Interest expense	(11,972)	(417)	(170)
Income before income taxes	(20,948)	6,512	21,776
Provision for income taxes	—	—	(181)
Net income	$(20,948)	$ 6,512	$ 21,595

LO 5   **E9-15B. Calculate the debt-to-equity ratio.**
Using the information provided above for Netflix, calculate the debt-to-equity ratio for 2003 and 2004. Provide an explanation of what this ratio measures and whether the ratio has improved from 2003 to 2004.

E9-16B. Calculate the times-interest-earned ratio.   LO 5

Using the information provided above for Netflix, calculate the times-interest-earned ratio for 2003 and 2004. Provide an explanation of what this ratio measures and whether the ratio has improved from 2003 to 2004.

E9-17B. Risk and control.   LO 6

What risks do firms face when borrowing money? How does this affect investors?

E9-18B. Appendix A: Calculate payments using time value of money concepts.

For each of the following, calculate the payment each loan would require. Assume the payments are made at the end of the period in each case. Interest rates are annual rates.

a. principal = $25,000; interest rate = 6%; term = 5 years; payments = annual
b. principal = $25,000; interest rate = 9%; term = 5 years; payments = annual
c. principal = $35,000; interest rate = 7%; term = 8 years; payments = annual
d. principal = $35,000; interest rate = 7%; term = 8 years; payments = semi-annual
e. principal = $40,000; interest rate = 12%; term = 3 years; payments = monthly

E9-19B. Appendices B and C: Calculate bond amounts using time value of money concepts.

Designer Clothes issued $200,000, 10%, 10-year bonds on July 1, 2007, when the market rate of interest was 8%. Proceeds were $226,840. Interest is payable annually on July 1. Designer uses the effective-interest method to amortize bond premiums and discounts. Prepare the journal entries to record (round to the nearest dollar):

a. The issuance of the bonds
b. The accrual of interest and the premium amortization on June 30, 2008
c. The payment of interest on July 1, 2008

E9-20B. Appendices B and C: Calculate bond amounts using time value of money concepts.

Panama City Tan Solutions issued $75,000, 7%, 15-year bonds on July 1, 2008, when the market rate of interest was 9%. The proceeds were $62,909. Interest is payable annually on July 1. Panama City Tan uses the effective-interest method to amortize bond premiums and discounts.

Prepare the journal entries (rounded to the nearest dollar) to record the following:

a. The issuance of the bonds
b. The accrual of interest and the discount amortization on June 30, 2009
c. The payment of interest on July 1, 2009

Problem Set A

P9-1A. Account for current liabilities.   LO 1

On March 1, 2007, the accounting records of Stein Company showed the following liability accounts and balances.

Accounts Payable	$21,600
Short-term Notes Payable	10,000
Interest Payable	800
Unearned Service Revenue	12,500

1. On March 1, Stein Company signed a three-month note for $12,000 at 7.5%.
2. During March, Stein Company paid off the $10,000 short-term note and Interest Payable shown on the March 1 balance sheet.
3. Stein paid off the beginning Accounts Payable.
4. During the month, Stein purchased $25,000 of merchandise on account. (Use perpetual inventory system.)

Required

a. Prepare journal entries for the transactions described.
b. Prepare adjusting entries.
c. Prepare the Current Liabilities section of the balance sheet at March 31, 2007.

P9-2A. Account for warranties.   LO 2

In June, Hopps had sales of $3,500 of its pogo sticks. The company gives a six-month warranty with the purchase of a pogo stick. When Hopps recorded the sales in June, the company also estimated that it would spend $350 to honor those warranties. When the company prepared its June financial statements, no sticks had been brought in for repair. In July, however, five people brought in their broken pogo sticks, and Hopps spent a total of $50 repairing them (at no charge to the customers, since the sticks were under warranty). Assume that there was no beginning balance (June 1) in the Warranty Payable account and that no additional sales were made in July (no new warranties were given in July).

Required

a. How much Warranty Expense would Hopps show on its income statement for the month of June?
b. Would Hopps have Warranty Payable on the balance sheet at June 30? If so, how much?
c. How much Warranty Expense would Hopps show on its income statement for the month of July?
d. Would Hopps have Warranty Payable on the balance sheet at July 31? If so, how much?

LO 2   P9-3A. Account for warranties.

The following took place during the month of May at Mega TV Shop:

1. Mega sold $50,000 worth of their own brand of television. Each is guaranteed for 12 months. Any defective television will be repaired or replaced free of charge during that period.
2. The company has estimated that it will cost $5,000 during the next year to honor the warranties on the May sales.
3. During June, Mega TV Shop spent $1,050 to honor warranties related to May sales.

Mega TV Shop prepares monthly financial statements. The May 1 balance in the Warranty Payable account was zero.

Required

a. What amount of Warranty Expense would be shown on the May income statement?
b. What amount of Warranty Payable would be shown on the May balance sheet?
c. What effect does recording Warranty Expense have on Shareholders' Equity?
d. What effect did spending the $1,050 in June have on Shareholders' Equity?

LO 3   P9-4A. Account for notes payable with periodic payments of principal and interest.

The SD Company engaged in the following transactions related to long-term liabilities during 2006:

1. On March 1, borrowed $25,000 for a machine. The loan is to be repaid in equal annual payments of $6,344 at the end of each of the next five years (beginning February 28, 2007); and the interest rate SD Company is paying for this loan is 8.5%.
2. On October 1, borrowed $120,000 from Suwannee Local Bank at an interest rate of 7.25%. The loan is for 10 years, and SD Company will make annual payments of $17,283 on September 30 of each year.

Required

a. For each loan described, prepare an amortization schedule for the first four payments. Be sure to show the reduction in principal and the interest expense for each payment.
b. What total interest expense related to these two loans would SD Company show on its income statement for the year ended December 31, 2006?
c. How much Interest Payable would be shown on SD's balance sheet at December 31, 2006?

LO 3   P9-5A. Account for notes payable with periodic payments of principal and interest.

Joe Brinks is making plans to finance a series of projects. Below is a list of projects he is considering.

1. Purchase a truck for $30,000 to be repaid in equal monthly payments of $601 over the next five years. The bank has quoted an interest rate of 7.5%.
2. Purchase a piece of land, whose owner is offering to sell it to Joe for $25,000. The seller would accept five annual payments of $6,595 at 10%.
3. Purchase land and building for $50,000, with a down payment of $5,000, and semi-annual payment of $3,095 for the next ten years at an interest rate of 6.5%.

Required

For each independent scenario described above, record the journal entries for the first two payments.

P9-6A. Account for bonds payable.

LO 4

Julie's Jewels issued $20,000 worth of 5-year bonds at 102 1/2. The bonds have a stated rate of 8%.

Required

a. Was the market interest rate at the time of issue higher or lower than 8%? How do you know?
b. What were the proceeds from the bond issue?
c. Will the interest expense each period be higher or lower than the interest payment?
d. Will the book value of the bonds be higher or lower than $20,000 after five years?

P9-7A. Account for bonds payable.

LO 4

Matrix Construction issued $1 million of its 10% bonds on July 1, 2006, at 98. The bonds mature on June 30, 2011. Interest is payable semi-annually on June 30 and December 31.

Required

a. What were the proceeds from the bond issue?
b. Was the market interest rate at the time of issue higher or lower than 10%?
c. Will interest expense be higher or lower than the interest payment?
d. What will the book value of the bonds be at maturity?

P9-8A. Appendices B and C: Account for bonds using time value of money concepts.

Newman Corporation issued $100,000 of bonds on January 1, 2006. The bonds mature on January 1, 2016. Interest is payable annually on December 31. The stated rate of interest is 8%, and the market rate of interest was 10% at the time of issue.

Required

a. Calculate the proceeds for the bond issue. How would issuing the bonds affect the financial statements for Newman (on the date of issue)?
b. Prepare an amortization schedule for the first three years of the life of the bonds, showing the interest expense and the carrying value at the end of each interest period. Newman uses the effective interest method for amortizing discounts and premiums.
c. How much Interest Expense related to these bonds would Newman show on its income statement for the year ended December 31, 2007? (Assume effective interest method.)
d. Calculate Interest Expense for the year ended December 31, 2007, using the straight-line method of amortization. Then, compare that amount to the amount calculated using the effective interest method. Which method do you think Newman should use and why?

Problem Set B

Your professor may ask you to complete selected "Group B" exercises and problems using Prentice Hall Grade Assist (**PHGA**). PHGA is an online tool that can help you master the chapter's topics by providing multiple variations of exercises and problems. You can rework these exercises and problems—each time with new data—as many times as you need, with immediate feedback and grading.

P9-1B. Account for current liabilities.

LO 1

On May 1, 2006, the accounting records of Sea Salt Company showed the following liability accounts and balances.

Accounts Payable	$35,600
Short-term Notes Payable	15,000
Interest Payable	950
Unearned Service Revenue	6,000

1. On May 1, Sea Salt Company signed a six-month note for $20,000 at 6%.
2. During May, Sea Salt Company paid off the $15,000 short-term note and the Interest Payable shown on the May 1 balance sheet.
3. The company also paid off the beginning balance in Accounts Payable.
4. During the month, Sea Salt purchased $40,000 of merchandise on account. (Use a perpetual inventory system.)

Required

a. Prepare journal entries for the transactions described.
b. Prepare adjusting entries.
c. Prepare the Current Liabilities section of the balance sheet at May 31, 2006.

LO 2   **P9-2B. Account for warranties.**

In 2005, Best Buy had sales of $70,000 for its new video recorders. The company gives a two-year warranty with the purchase of each video recorder. When Best Buy recorded the sales, the company also estimated that it would spend $6,000 to honor those warranties. When the company prepared its annual financial statements, no video recorders had been brought in for repair. In January 2006, however, 20 people brought in their broken video recorders, and Best Buy spent a total of $450 repairing them (at no charge to the customers, since the video recorders were under warranty). At the beginning of 2005, the balance in the Warranty Payable account was zero. Assume no additional sales were made in January 2006 (no new warranties were given in January).

Required

a. How much Warranty Expense related to the sales of video recorders would Best Buy show on an income statement for the year 2005?
b. Would Best Buy have a Warranty Liability on the balance sheet at the end of 2005? If so, how much?
c. How much Warranty Expense would Best Buy show on an income statement for the month of January 2006 related to these video recorders?
d. Would Best Buy have a Warranty Liability on the balance sheet at January 31, 2006? If so, how much?

LO 2   **P9-3B. Account for warranties.**

Holly's Hoops prepares monthly financial statements. The following took place during the month of July at Holly's Hoops. At the beginning of July, the balance in the Warranty Payable account was zero.

1. $5,000 worth of hoops was sold. Each is guaranteed for 12 months. Any defective hoop will be repaired or replaced free of charge during that period.
2. Holly estimated that it would cost $600 during the next year to honor the warranties on the July sales.
3. During August, Holly spent $250 to honor warranties related to July sales.

Required

a. What amount of Warranty Expense would be shown on the July income statement?
b. What amount of Warranty Liability would be shown on the July balance sheet?
c. What effect did recording the Warranty Expense have on Shareholders' Equity?
d. What effect did spending the $250 in August have on Shareholders' Equity?

LO 3   **P9-4B. Account for notes payable with periodic payments of principal and interest.**

The McIntyre Company engaged in the following transactions related to long-term liabilities during 2006.

1. On July 1, borrowed $50,000 for a new piece of office equipment. The loan is to be repaid in equal annual payments of $8,701 at the end of each of the next eight years (beginning June 30, 2007); and the interest rate McIntyre is paying for this loan is 8%.
2. On October 1, borrowed $200,000 from Shell Point Local Bank at an interest rate of 9.5%. The loan is for ten years, and McIntyre will make annual payments of $31,853 on September 30 of each year.

Required

a. For each loan described, prepare an amortization schedule for the first four payments. Be sure to show the reduction in principal and the interest expense for each payment.
b. What total Interest Expense related to these two loans would McIntyre Company show on its income statement for the year ended December 31, 2006?
c. How much Interest Payable would be shown on McIntyre's balance sheet at December 31, 2006?

P9-5B. Account for notes payable with periodic payments of principal and interest.   LO 3

Don Black is making plans for a series of projects. Below is a list of transactions he is considering.

1. Purchase a boat for $50,000 to be repaid in equal monthly payments of $977.51 over the next six years. The bank has quoted an interest rate of 12%.
2. Purchase a property for $125,000. The seller would accept 10 semiannual payments of $15,411.37 at 8%.
3. Sell some old equipment for $8,000. Don is willing to accept quarterly payments of $1,092 for the next two years at an interest rate of 8%.
4. Purchase land and building for $250,000, with a down payment of $50,000, and semiannual payments of $16,048.52 for the next ten years at an interest rate of 10%.

Required

For each situation described, prepare the journal entries for the first two payments.

P9-6B. Account for bonds payable.   LO 4

Glassworks issued $150,000 worth of six-year bonds with a stated interest rate of 7.5% and interest payable annually on December 31. The bonds were issued at 98. The bonds were issued on January 1, 2007. The fiscal year-end for Glassworks is December 31.

Required

a. Was the market interest rate at the time of issue higher or lower than 7.5%? Explain.
b. Will the interest payment be more or less than the interest expense each year?
c. Will the carrying value be more or less than $150,000 after three years? After four years? At maturity?

P9-7B. Account for bonds payable.   LO 4

Venus Rug Company issued $80,000 worth of 10-year bonds at 103. The bonds have a stated rate of 9%.

Required

a. What were the proceeds from the bond issue?
b. Describe the change in carrying value of the bonds over the 10-year life.
c. Will interest expense be larger or smaller than the interest payment each year?

P9-8B. Appendices B and C: Account for bonds using time value of money concepts.

Morgan Corporation issued $1,000,000 of bonds on January 1, 2004. The bonds mature on January 1, 2012. Interest is payable annually each December 31. The stated rate of interest is 11%, and the market rate of interest was 10% at the time of issue.

Required

a. Calculate the proceeds for the bond issue. How would issuing the bonds affect the financial statements for Morgan (on the date of issue)?
b. Prepare an amortization schedule for the first three years of the life of the bonds, showing the interest expense and the carrying value at the end of each interest period. Morgan uses the effective interest method for amortizing discounts and premiums.
c. How much Interest Expense related to these bonds would Morgan show on its income statement for the year ended December 31, 2005? (Assume effective interest method.)

    d. Calculate the Interest Expense for the year ended December 31, 2005, using the straight-line method of amortization. Then, compare that amount to the amount calculated using the effective interest method. Which method do you think Morgan should use and why?

Financial Statement Analysis

LO 5, 6

FSA9-1. Calculate debt-to-equity ratio and analyze financial data.

The following information comes from annual report of The Limited.

<table>
<tr><td colspan="3" align="center">The Limited
From the Consolidated Balance Sheet
_(in millions)</td></tr>
</table>

	At January 31, 2004	At February 1, 2003
Liabilities and Shareholders' Equity		
Current liabilities		
Accounts payable	$ 453	$ 456
Accrued expenses and other	660	607
Income taxes	279	196
Total current liabilities	$1,392	$1,259
Deferred income taxes	134	125
Long-term debt	648	547
Other long-term liabilities	433	455
Commitments and contingencies		
(see Note 7)		
Shareholders' equity		
Common stock	262	261
Paid-in capital	1,674	1,693
Retained earnings	3,417	2,906
Less: treasury stock, at average cost	(87)	—
Total shareholders' equity	5,266	4,860
Total Liabilities and Shareholders' Equity	$7,873	$7,246

Required

1. Calculate the debt-to-equity ratio for the years shown.
2. Who would be interested in this information and why?
3. Suppose you were considering investing in some stock. What do you think of the change in this ratio from 2003 to 2004?
4. If The Limited has bonds payable, where do you think they might be included on the balance sheet?
5. What risks are associated with the long-term debt on The Limited's balance sheet?

LO 5, 6

FSA9-2. Calculate debt-to-equity ratio and analyze financial data.

The following information (next page) comes from annual report of La-Z-Boy Company.

Required

1. Calculate the debt-to-equity ratio for the years ended April 24, 2004 and April 26, 2003.
2. Who would be interested in this information and why?
3. Suppose you were considering investing in some La-Z-Boy stock. What do you think of the change in this ratio from 2003 to 2004?
4. If La-Z-Boy has bonds payable, where do you think they might be included on the balance sheet?
5. What risks are associated with the long-term debt on La-Z-Boy's balance sheet?

La-Z-Boy Company
Consolidated Balance Sheet
(in thousands, except par value)

	As of	
	4/24/04	4/26/03
Assets [not shown]	$1,047,496	$1,123,066
Liabilities and Shareholders' Equity		
Current liabilities		
Short-term borrowings	$37,219	$—
Current portion of long-term debt and capital leases	5,344	1,619
Accounts payable	93,298	78,931
Accrued expenses and other current liabilities	147,460	134,037
Total current liabilities	283,321	214,587
Long-term debt	180,988	221,099
Capital leases	819	1,272
Deferred income taxes	20,219	36,928
Other long-term liabilities	39,821	39,241
Total liabilities	525,168	513,127
Shareholders' equity		
Preferred shares—5,000 authorized; none issued	----	----
Common shares, $1 par value—150,000 authorized;		
52,031 outstanding in 2004 and 55,027		
outstanding in 2003	52,031	55,027
Capital in excess of par value	216,156	216,081
Retained earnings................................	253,012	342,628
Accumulated other comprehensive income (Loss) ...	1,129	(3,797)
Total shareholders' equity	522,328	609,939
Total Liabilities and Shareholders' Equity	$1,047,496	$1,123,066

FSA9-3. Calculate the debt-to-equity and times-interest-earned ratios and analyze financial data.

LO 5, 6

Use Target's financial statements in the appendix at the back of the book to answer the following questions:

1. What types of debt does Target have? Where did you find this information?
2. Compute the times-interest-earned ratio and the debt-to-equity ratio for at least two consecutive years. What information do these ratios provide?

Critical Thinking Problems

Risk and Control

One of the risks of borrowing money is changing interest rates. For example, if a company issues bonds when the market rate is 7%, what happens if the market rate goes down while the bonds are outstanding? Name some actions a company could take to control for this risk. For several companies that have outstanding long-term debt, read the notes to the financial statements that address this interest rate risk.

Ethics

Lucy Shafer wants to borrow $100,000 to expand her dog-breeding business. She is preparing a set of financial statements to take to the local bank with her loan application. She currently has an outstanding loan from her uncle for $50,000. Lucy's uncle is letting her borrow the money at a very low interest rate, and she does not have to make any principal payments for five years. Due to the favorable terms of the loan from her uncle, Lucy has decided that it is not significant enough to disclose on her financial statements. Instead, Lucy has classified the $50,000 as Contributed Capital, and the interest payments are included in Miscellaneous Expenses on Lucy's income statement.

1. What are the effects of Lucy's classifications on the financial statements?
2. Are there any ratios that might be of interest to the local bank that will be misstated by Lucy's actions?
3. Do you think Lucy's actions are unethical? Suppose Lucy's uncle agrees to be a partner in the company until Lucy can afford to buy his share by repaying the $50,000 with interest. Does that change your opinion?

Group Assignment

With the class divided into groups, assign one of the following companies to each group:

Alaska Airlines
Delta Airlines
Northwest Airlines
Southwest Airlines
United Airlines

For your company, analyze the liability section of the balance sheet. For each liability, write a short description. Use information from the notes to help you. Then, calculate the debt-to-equity ratio for the years with available information. What tentative conclusions can you draw about the debt position of your airline?

Internet Exercise: General Motors and Starbucks

General Motors remains the world's number one maker of cars and trucks, including brands such as Buick, Cadillac, Chevrolet, GMC, Pontiac, Saab, and Saturn. Go to the following website: http://finance.yahoo.com.

IE9-1. In the symbol box at the top of the page, enter the company symbol GM, the stock symbol of General Motors, and then choose Financials from the menu on the left. Find the Annual Balance Sheet.

a. Identify amounts reported for total long-term debt at the three most recent year-ends. For the most recent year-end how much of the debt does GM have to pay back? Do these amounts indicate the future value of the debt? Explain why or why not.
b. Identify amounts reported for Interest Expense for the three most recent years. Did Interest Expense increase or decrease? What might cause this change? Is this the amount of interest paid during the year? Which financial statement reports this information?
c. Identify amounts reported for Total Liabilities and Total Stockholders' Equity at the three most recent year-ends. Calculate the debt-to-equity ratio (total liabilities to total equity) for each year-end. Is General Motors primarily financing assets with liabilities or equities? How can you tell? Is the ratio increasing or decreasing? Is this trend favorable or unfavorable? Explain why.

IE9-2. Starbucks is the number-one specialty coffee retailer, operating more than 8,300 coffee shops. The company also sells coffee beans to restaurants, businesses, airlines, and hotels, and offers mail-order and online shopping.

a. In the symbol box, enter the company symbol SBUX, the stock symbol of Starbucks, and then choose Financials. Find the Annual Balance Sheet. Identify amounts reported for Total Liabilities and Total Stockholders' Equity at the three most recent year-ends.
b. Calculate the debt-to-equity ratio (total liabilities to total stockholders' equity) for each year-end.
c. Do owners or creditors have more claims on Starbucks' assets? How can you tell?

IE9-3. Review the information you recorded for General Motors and Starbucks. Which corporation has a higher level of financial risk? Explain why.

Additional Study Materials

Visit www.prenhall.com/reimers for self-study quizzes and spreadsheet templates to use to complete homework assignments.

CONTINUING CASE STUDY

Building your Excel skills with The MP3 Store

During the month of September, The MP3 Store engaged in the following transactions. The company is using LIFO and the perpetual inventory system. Recall from Chapter 8 that the beginning inventory consists of 45 MP3 players purchased for $227 and 10 MP3 players purchased for $196 each.

September 4	Purchased 105 MP3 players for $230 each on account.
September 6	Paid the sales tax payable from August sales.
September 10	Collected $28,500 of August's outstanding A/R balance.
September 13	Wrote off a $900 accounts receivable as uncollectible.
September 17	Received and paid a $150 telephone bill.
September 21	Collected $11,300 of the outstanding accounts receivable balance.
September 23	Paid all of the accounts payable balance.
September 28	Paid the assistant manager $2,000 for September work, recording the appropriate payroll taxes. In addition to Social Security and Medicare, the FIT withheld was $200.
September 29	The payroll taxes due were paid and submitted.
September 29	By the end of the month, the company had sold a total of 143 MP3 players for $350 each. The sales tax rate is 6%. Of the sales, 26 were for cash and 117 were on account. The company is now offering an unconditional one year warranty and estimates that 4% of the sales will be returned under warranty.
September 30	Two MP3 players were returned under warranty and replaced with new units from inventory.
September 30	Recorded the required adjusting entries for depreciation, rent, insurance and bad debts (5% of outstanding Accounts Receivable). The company also submitted the payroll taxes due to the government.

Instructions

1. Prepare the necessary journal entries, T-accounts, trial balances, and financial statements. (Note: A Statement of Cash Flows is not required for this chapter.)

2. When you are finished print and save your file to disk by clicking the **Save** button. Name your file MP39.

Time Value of Money and Present Values

The Time Value of Money

If you ever used a credit card or borrowed money for longer than one year, you have experience with the *time value of money*. The term means that money has value over time. That's because money that you invest can earn interest. A person would prefer to receive a dollar today rather than receive a dollar a year from now because the dollar received today can earn interest during the year. Then, it will be worth *more* than a dollar a year from now.

Simple Versus Compound Interest

We calculated the interest on the principal of a loan in several chapters, including Chapter 9. When interest is computed on the principal only, it is called *simple interest*. Simple interest usually applies to short-term loans, which are loans with terms of one year or less.

When interest is computed on the principal of a loan *plus* any interest that has been earned but not collected or paid, it is called *compound interest*. The interest earned during a year is added to the original principal, and that new larger amount is used to calculate the interest earned during the next year. Each year, the interest is calculated on a larger amount. The larger amount comes from adding each successive year's earned interest to the prior year's interest plus the initial principal.

Exhibit 9A.1 shows what happens to $1,000 if you invest it today and watch it grow over 10 years. You can easily see that compound interest makes your money grow much faster than simple interest.

You can use the concept of compound interest to do the following:

1. Calculate the amount of money you need to deposit today—the *present value* of an amount—to grow to a specific amount by some future date.
2. Take future amounts of money and convert them to today's dollars.

Let's work through an example.

How much money will you have in 10 years if you deposit $1,000 today and it earns 10% interest per year?

- If the money earns simple interest, you'll have $2,000 at the end of 10 years. Each year, the principal of $1,000 will earn $100.
- If the money earns compound interest, you'll have $2,594 at the end of 10 years. Each year, the principal *plus the previously earned interest* will earn interest.

Exhibit 9A.1

Simple Versus Compound Interest

Deposit today at 10% annual interest	You'll have this much at the end of **Year 1**	...at the end of **Year 2**	...at the end of **Year 3**	...at the end of **Year 4**	...at the end of **Year 5**	...at the end of **Year 6**	...at the end of **Year 7**	...at the end of **Year 8**	...at the end of **Year 9**	You'll have this much at the end of **Year 10**
Simple interest										
$1,000	$1,100	$1,200	$1,300	$1,400	$1,500	$1,600	$1,700	$1,800	$1,900	$2,000
Compound interest										
$1,000	$1,100	$1,210	$1,331	$1,464	$1,611	$1,772	$1,949	$2,144	$2,358	$2,594

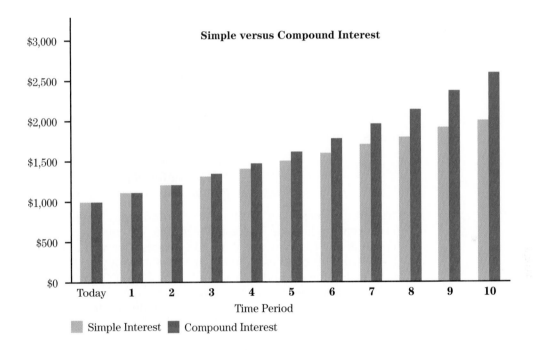

Present Value

Sometimes we want to know how much a future amount is worth today. For example, when we calculate the issue price of a bond, we are taking those future cash flows and calculating what they are worth today. That is, we want to know the present value of the future cash flows.

Present value of a single amount

The present value of a sum of money to be received in the future is the value in *today's dollars*. If you are promised a payment of $100 one year from today, how much is this worth today? In other words, how much would you have to deposit today to have it grow to be $100 in a year? That's what happens when you make a deposit at a bank today and the amount grows to a larger future value. Here's the formula for calculating future value:

$$FV_n = PV(1 + i)^n$$

where n = the number of years
i = the interest rate
PV = the present value of the future sum of money
FV_n = the future value of the investment at the end of n years

If we solve the equation for PV, we get

$$PV = FV_n \left(\frac{1}{(1 + i)^n} \right)$$

Let's figure out the present value of $100 one year from now at an annual interest rate of 10%.

$$PV = \$100 \ (1/(1+ 0.10)^1)$$
$$PV = \$100 \ (0.90909)$$
$$PV = \$90.91$$

This calculation shows that having $90.91 today is equivalent to having $100 in one year, when the annual interest rate is 10%. We can check it out logically: If we deposit $90.91 today and it earns 10% interest per year, at the end of the year we will have $99.9999—which is very close to $100.

Let's figure out the present value of $100 two years from now at an annual interest rate of 10%:

$$PV = \$100 \ (1/(1+ 0.10)^2)$$
$$PV = \$100 \ (0.82644628)$$
$$PV = \$82.6446$$

This calculation shows that having $82.6446 today is equivalent to having $100 in two years, when the interest rate is 10%. We can check it out logically: If we deposit $82.6446 today and earn 10% interest, we will have $90.909 [= 82.6446 (1 + 0.10)] after one year. Then, our $90.909 has a year to earn 10% interest, so at the end of the second year we will have $99.9999—which rounds to $100.

Fortunately, we do not have to use the formula to calculate the present value of a future amount. We can use a present value table, a financial calculator, or Excel. Let's look at a present value table first.

The present value table is based on $1. Find the factor from the table in Exhibit 9A.2 and multiply the factor by the dollars in our problem. Find the 10% column and the 2-year row. The factor from the table is 0.82645. Multiply that factor by $100, and the present value is $82.645.

Compute present value on your financial calculator (some calculators may differ slightly):

- Enter $100 for the future value (**FV** key).
- Enter 10 for the interest rate (**i%** key, sometimes the I/Y key).

Exhibit 9A.2

From the Present Value of $1 Table

(n) periods	8%	9%	10%	11%
1	0.92593	0.91743	0.90909	0.90090
2	0.85734	0.84168	**0.82645**	0.81162
3	0.79383	0.77218	0.75131	0.73119
4	0.73503	0.70843	0.68301	0.65873

- Enter 2 for the number of periods (**n** key).
- Press **CPT** and then **PV** to compute the present value.

You should see $82.645 in the display.

As you learned in the chapter, finding the present value of a future amount is called discounting the cash flow, and when discounting a cash flow, the interest rate is called the discount rate.

Can **YOU** do it?

John wants to have $5,000 in five years. How much should he deposit today to have $5,000 in five years if the annual interest rate is 10%? In other words, what is the present value of $5,000 in five years? Try using the formula, the present value table, and your financial calculator (if you have one).

Answer 5000 × 0.62092 = $3,104.60

Present value of an annuity

In addition to discounting a single amount—often referred to as a lump sum—we may need to calculate the present value of a *series* of payments. A stream of deposits or payments that are the same and made periodically over equally spaced intervals is called an **annuity**. Its name comes from the idea of *annual* payments, because most annuities are annual. The present value of an annuity has many practical applications. Most present value problems involving annuities have payments at the end of the period, and they are called **ordinary annuities**. First, let's look at a simple example to see how the formulas work. Then, we'll look at some examples that should be familiar to you—buying a motorcycle or a car by borrowing money and making payments to repay the loan.

> **Annuity:** A series of equal cash receipts or cash payments over equally spaced intervals of time.

> **Ordinary annuity:** An annuity whose payments are made at the end of each interval or period.

Suppose you are selling your old motorcycle and a friend offers you a series of four payments of $500 each at the end of each of the next four years. How much is your friend actually offering for your motorcycle? It's *not* simply 4 × $500, or $2,000, because of the time value of money. Getting $500 a year from now is *not* the same as getting $500 today. To find out how much a series of four payments of $500 over the next four years is worth today, you need to use an appropriate interest rate and discount the payments to get the present value of each payment. Suppose the interest rate is 5% per year.

The first payment, made at the end of one year, will be discounted back one year. The second payment, made at the end of two years, will be discounted back two years. And so on, for the third and fourth payments. The present value of the series of payments will be the sum of the individual present value amounts. Here's how it looks in the formula:

$$PV = FV_n \left(\frac{1}{(1+i)^n} \right)$$

$$PV = \$500(1/(1+.05)^1) = 500(0.95238) = \$\ 476.19$$

$$PV = \$500(1/(1+.05)^2) = 500(0.90703) = \$\ 453.51$$

$$PV = \$500(1/(1+.05)^3) = 500(0.86384) = \$\ 431.92$$

$$PV = \$500(1/(1+.05)^4) = 500(0.82270) = \$\ 411.35$$

$$\text{Total } PV = \underline{\$1,772.97}$$

Exhibit 9A.3

Present Value of an Annuity Table

(n) periods	4%	5%	6%	7%
3	2.77509	2.72325	2.67301	2.62432
4	3.62990	**3.54595**	3.46511	3.38721
5	4.45182	4.32948	4.21236	4.10020
6	5.24214	5.07569	4.91732	4.76654

This calculation shows that, if you could deposit $1,772.97 today to earn 5%, you would be indifferent between receiving $1,772.97 today and receiving four payments of $500 each at the end of each of the next four years. Another way to express the same idea is that your friend is paying you $1,772.97 for your motorcycle by offering you the four $500 annual payments. The difference between the total payments of $2,000 and the $1,772.97 price of the motorcycle is interest.

The present value of an annuity table, shown in Exhibit 9A.3, compiles the individual factors from the present value of $1 table in Exhibit 9A.2. Use the present value of an annuity table to solve the same problem. Find the column for 5% and the row for 4 (periods), and you'll see the factor of 3.54595. If you multiply the payment of $500 by the factor 3.54595 you'll get **$1,772.98**. (It's off a cent due to rounding the factors above.)

Compute present value on your financial calculator.

- Enter $500 as the payment (**PMT** key);
- Enter 4 as the number of periods (**n** key);
- Enter 5 as the interest rate (**i%** or the I/Y key); then
- Press the *CPT* key, followed by the *PV* key.

You'll see $1,772.98 in the display. That's the present value of the series of payments.

Let's look at buying a car as an example. Suppose you find a car that you want to buy for $23,000. You have $1,000 for a down payment, and you'll have to borrow $22,000. If you borrow the money for three years at an annual interest rate of 6%, how much will be your monthly payments? Pay special attention to the timing of the payments in this situation. Rather than making annual payments, you'll be making monthly payments. To accommodate this payment plan, you'll need to make sure your time periods, n, and your interest rate, $i\%$, are both expressed with the same time frame. If the period is a month, the annual interest rate must be changed to a monthly interest rate. You are borrowing money for 36 periods (= 3 years × 12 months per year) at a rate of 1/2% (= 0.50% or .005) per month (that's an annual rate of 6%).

In this case, you have the present value—that's the amount you are borrowing for the car. Calculate the *series of payments* using the present value of an annuity table, shown in Exhibit 9A.4, and then try it with a financial calculator.

Exhibit 9A.4

Present Value of an Annuity Table

(n) periods	0.50%	1%	2%	3%
35	32.03537	29.40858	24.99862	21.48722
36	**32.87102**	30.10751	25.48884	21.83225
37	33.70250	30.79951	25.96945	22.16724
38	34.52985	31.48466	26.44064	22.49246

Exhibit 9A.5

Present Value of a $1 Table

The Present Value of a Single Amount ($1)

$$PV = \frac{1}{(1+r)^n}$$

Periods	0.50%	1%	2%	3%	4%	5%	6%	7%	8%	9%	10%	11%	12%	13%	14%	15%
1	0.99502	0.99010	0.98039	0.97087	0.96154	0.95238	0.94340	0.93458	0.92593	0.91743	0.90909	0.90090	0.89286	0.88496	0.87719	0.86957
2	0.99007	0.98030	0.96117	0.94260	0.92456	0.90703	0.89000	0.87344	0.85734	0.84168	0.82645	0.81162	0.79719	0.78315	0.76947	0.75614
3	0.98515	0.97059	0.94232	0.91514	0.88900	0.86384	0.83962	0.81630	0.79383	0.77218	0.75131	0.73119	0.71178	0.69305	0.67497	0.65752
4	0.98025	0.96098	0.92385	0.88849	0.85480	0.82270	0.79209	0.76290	0.73503	0.70842	0.68301	0.65873	0.63552	0.61332	0.59208	0.57175
5	0.97537	0.95147	0.90573	0.86261	0.82193	0.78353	0.74726	0.71299	0.68058	0.64993	0.62092	0.59345	0.56743	0.54276	0.51937	0.49718
6	0.97052	0.94205	0.88797	0.83748	0.79031	0.74622	0.70496	0.66634	0.63017	0.59627	0.56447	0.53464	0.50663	0.48032	0.45559	0.43233
7	0.96569	0.93272	0.87056	0.81309	0.75992	0.71068	0.66506	0.62275	0.58349	0.54703	0.51316	0.48166	0.45235	0.42506	0.39964	0.37594
8	0.96089	0.92348	0.85349	0.78941	0.73069	0.67684	0.62741	0.58201	0.54027	0.50187	0.46651	0.43393	0.40388	0.37616	0.35056	0.32690
9	0.95610	0.91434	0.83676	0.76642	0.70259	0.64461	0.59190	0.54393	0.50025	0.46043	0.42410	0.39092	0.36061	0.33288	0.30751	0.28426
10	0.95135	0.90529	0.82035	0.74409	0.67556	0.61391	0.55839	0.50835	0.46319	0.42241	0.38554	0.35218	0.32197	0.29459	0.26974	0.24718
11	0.94661	0.89632	0.80426	0.72242	0.64958	0.58468	0.52679	0.47509	0.42888	0.38753	0.35049	0.31728	0.28748	0.26070	0.23662	0.21494
12	0.94191	0.88745	0.78849	0.70138	0.62460	0.55684	0.49697	0.44401	0.39711	0.35553	0.31863	0.28584	0.25668	0.23071	0.20756	0.18691
13	0.93722	0.87866	0.77303	0.68095	0.60057	0.53032	0.46884	0.41496	0.36770	0.32618	0.28966	0.25751	0.22917	0.20416	0.18207	0.16253
14	0.93256	0.86996	0.75788	0.66112	0.57748	0.50507	0.44230	0.38782	0.34046	0.29925	0.26333	0.23199	0.20462	0.18068	0.15971	0.14133
15	0.92792	0.86135	0.74301	0.64186	0.55526	0.48102	0.41727	0.36245	0.31524	0.27454	0.23939	0.20900	0.18270	0.15989	0.14010	0.12289
16	0.92330	0.85282	0.72845	0.62317	0.53391	0.45811	0.39365	0.33873	0.29189	0.25187	0.21763	0.18829	0.16312	0.14150	0.12289	0.10686
17	0.91874	0.84438	0.71416	0.60502	0.51337	0.43630	0.37136	0.31657	0.27027	0.23107	0.19784	0.16963	0.14564	0.12522	0.10780	0.09293
18	0.91414	0.83602	0.70016	0.58739	0.49363	0.41552	0.35034	0.29586	0.25025	0.21199	0.17986	0.15282	0.13004	0.11081	0.09456	0.08081
19	0.90959	0.82774	0.68643	0.57029	0.47464	0.39573	0.33051	0.27651	0.23171	0.19449	0.16351	0.13768	0.11611	0.09806	0.08295	0.07027
20	0.90506	0.81954	0.67297	0.55368	0.45639	0.37689	0.31180	0.25842	0.21455	0.17843	0.14864	0.12403	0.10367	0.08678	0.07276	0.06110
21	0.90056	0.81143	0.65978	0.53755	0.43883	0.35894	0.29416	0.24151	0.19866	0.16370	0.13513	0.11174	0.09256	0.07680	0.06383	0.05313
22	0.89608	0.80340	0.64684	0.52189	0.42196	0.34185	0.27751	0.22571	0.18394	0.15018	0.12285	0.10067	0.08264	0.06796	0.05599	0.04620
23	0.89162	0.79544	0.63416	0.50669	0.40573	0.32557	0.26180	0.21095	0.17032	0.13778	0.11168	0.09069	0.07379	0.06014	0.04911	0.04017
24	0.88719	0.78757	0.62172	0.49193	0.39012	0.31007	0.24698	0.19715	0.15770	0.12640	0.10153	0.08170	0.06588	0.05323	0.04308	0.03493
25	0.88277	0.77977	0.60953	0.47761	0.37512	0.29530	0.23300	0.18425	0.14602	0.11597	0.09230	0.07361	0.05882	0.04710	0.03779	0.03038
30	0.86103	0.74192	0.55207	0.41199	0.30832	0.23138	0.17411	0.13137	0.09938	0.07537	0.05731	0.04368	0.03338	0.02557	0.01963	0.01510
35	0.83982	0.70591	0.50003	0.35538	0.25342	0.18129	0.13011	0.09366	0.06763	0.04899	0.03558	0.02592	0.01894	0.01388	0.01019	0.00751
40	0.81914	0.67165	0.45289	0.30656	0.20829	0.14205	0.09722	0.06678	0.04603	0.03184	0.01109	0.01538	0.01075	0.00753	0.00529	0.00373

(*PV* = present value, *r* = interest rate per period in decimal form, *n* = number of periods)

Exhibit 9A.6

Present Value of an Annuity Table

The Present Value of Annuity $1.00 in Arrears*

$$PV_a = \frac{1}{r}\left(1 - \frac{1}{(1+r)^n}\right)$$

Periods	0.50%	1%	2%	3%	4%	5%	6%	7%	8%	9%	10%	11%	12%	13%	14%	15%
1	0.99502	0.99010	0.98039	0.97087	0.96154	0.95328	0.94340	0.93458	0.92593	0.91743	0.90909	0.90090	0.89286	0.88496	0.87719	0.86957
2	1.98510	1.97040	1.94156	1.91347	1.86609	1.85941	1.83339	1.80802	1.78326	1.75911	1.73554	1.71252	1.69005	1.66810	1.64666	1.62571
3	2.97025	2.94099	2.88388	2.82861	2.77509	2.72325	2.67301	2.62432	2.57710	2.53129	2.48685	2.44371	2.40183	2.36115	2.32163	2.28323
4	3.95050	3.90197	3.80773	3.71710	3.62990	3.54595	3.46511	3.38721	3.31213	3.23972	3.16987	3.10245	3.03735	2.97447	2.91371	2.85498
5	4.92587	4.85343	4.71346	4.57971	4.45182	4.32948	4.21236	4.10020	3.99271	3.88965	3.79079	3.69590	3.60478	3.51723	3.43308	3.35216
6	5.89638	5.79548	5.60143	5.41719	5.24214	5.07569	4.91732	4.76654	4.62288	4.48592	4.35526	4.23054	4.11141	3.99755	3.88867	3.78448
7	6.86207	6.78219	6.47199	6.23028	6.00205	5.78637	5.58238	5.38929	5.26037	5.03295	4.86842	4.71220	4.56376	4.42261	4.28830	4.16042
8	7.82296	7.65168	7.32548	7.01969	6.73274	6.46321	6.20979	5.97130	5.74664	5.53482	5.33493	5.14612	4.96764	4.79877	4.63886	4.48732
9	8.77906	8.56602	8.16224	7.78611	7.43533	7.10782	6.80169	6.51523	6.24689	5.99525	5.75902	5.53705	5.32825	5.13166	4.94637	4.77158
10	9.73041	9.47130	8.98259	8.53020	8.11090	7.72173	7.36009	7.02358	6.71008	6.41766	6.14457	5.88923	5.65022	5.42624	5.21612	5.01877
11	10.67703	10.36763	9.78685	9.25262	8.76048	8.30641	7.88687	7.49867	7.13896	6.80519	6.49506	6.20652	5.93770	5.68694	5.45273	5.23371
12	11.61893	11.25508	10.57534	9.95400	9.38507	8.86325	8.38384	7.94269	7.53608	7.16073	6.81369	6.49236	6.19437	5.91765	5.66029	5.42062
13	12.55615	12.13374	11.34837	10.63496	9.98565	9.39357	8.85268	8.35765	7.90378	7.48690	7.10336	6.74987	6.42355	6.12181	5.84236	5.58315
14	13.48871	13.00370	12.10625	11.29607	10.56312	9.89864	9.29498	8.74547	8.24424	7.78615	7.36669	6.98187	6.62817	6.30249	6.00207	5.72448
15	14.41662	13.86505	12.84926	11.93794	11.11839	10.37966	9.71225	9.10791	8.55948	8.06069	7.60608	7.19087	6.81086	6.46238	6.14217	5.84737
16	15.33993	14.71787	13.57771	12.56110	11.65230	10.83777	10.10590	9.44665	8.85137	8.31256	7.82371	7.37916	6.97399	6.60388	6.26506	5.95423
17	16.25863	15.56225	14.29187	13.16612	12.16567	11.27407	10.47726	9.73622	9.12164	8.54363	8.02155	7.54879	7.11963	6.72909	6.37286	6.04716
18	17.17277	16.39827	14.99203	13.75351	12.65930	11.68959	10.82760	10.05909	9.37189	8.75563	8.20141	7.70162	7.24967	6.83991	6.46742	6.12797
19	18.08236	17.22601	15.67846	14.32380	13.13394	12.08532	11.15812	10.33560	9.60360	8.95011	8.36492	7.83929	7.36578	6.91797	6.55037	6.19823
20	18.98742	18.04555	16.35143	14.87747	13.59033	12.46221	11.46992	10.59401	9.81815	9.12855	8.51356	7.96333	7.46944	7.02475	6.62313	6.25933
21	19.88798	18.85698	17.01121	15.41502	14.02916	12.82115	11.76408	10.83553	10.01680	9.29224	8.64869	8.07507	7.56200	7.10155	6.68696	6.31246
22	20.78406	19.66038	17.65805	15.93692	14.45112	13.16300	12.04158	11.06124	10.20074	9.44243	8.77154	8.17574	7.64465	7.16951	6.74294	6.35866
23	21.67568	20.45582	18.29220	16.44361	14.85684	13.48857	12.30338	11.27219	10.37106	9.58021	8.88322	8.26643	7.71843	7.22966	6.79206	6.39844
24	22.56287	21.24339	18.91393	16.93554	15.24696	13.79864	12.55036	11.46933	10.52876	9.70661	8.98474	8.34814	7.78432	7.28288	6.83514	6.43377
25	23.44564	22.02316	19.52346	17.41315	15.62208	14.09394	12.78336	11.65358	10.67478	9.82258	9.07704	8.42174	7.84314	7.32998	6.87293	6.46415
30	27.79405	25.80771	22.39646	19.60044	17.29203	15.37245	13.76483	12.40904	11.25778	10.27365	9.42691	8.69379	8.05518	7.49565	7.00266	6.56598
35	32.03537	29.40858	24.99862	21.48722	18.66461	16.37419	14.49825	12.94767	11.65457	10.56682	9.64416	8.85524	8.17550	7.58557	7.07005	6.61661
40	36.17223	32.83469	27.35548	23.11477	19.79277	17.15909	15.04620	13.33171	11.92461	10.75736	9.77908	8.95105	8.24378	7.63438	7.10504	6.64178

*Payments (or receipts) at the end of each period.

(PV_a = present value of an annuity, r = interest rate per period in decimal form, n = number of periods in which a payment is made or received)

$$PV(A) = PMT \,(\text{factor for 36 periods, 0.50\%})$$

where $PV(A)$ = the present value of an annuity

PMT = the amount of each payment in the series of payments and the factor for 36 periods, 0.50% per period, where period means month, comes from the present value of an annuity table, like the one shown in Exhibit 9A.4.

Instead of knowing the payment and calculating the present value, we know the present value and need to compute the amount of the payment.

$$\$22{,}000 = PMT\,(32.87102)$$

Solving for PMT, we get $669.28. So, your monthly car payment will be **$669.28**.

Compute the payment on your financial calculator.

- Enter $22,000 as the present value (**PV** key);
- Enter 36 as the number of periods (**n** key);
- Enter .5 as the interest rate (**i%** or I/Y key); then
- Press the **CPT** key, followed by the **PMT** key.

You'll see **$669.28** in the display.

Can YOU do it?

Suppose you want to borrow $50,000 from your rich uncle, and he is willing to let you repay him over the next 10 years, with a payment every year. He has determined that 6% is a fair (annual) interest rate. How much will your payments be? Use the present value of an annuity table, and then check your answer by using your financial calculator if you have one.

Answer Factor(10yrs., 6%) PMT = 50,000 (the PV)
7.36009 PMT = 50,000
PMT = 50,000 ÷ 7.36009 = $6,793.40 (rounded)

Calculating the Proceeds from a Bond Issued at a Premium or a Discount

As you learned in Chapter 9, when the stated interest rate on the face of a bond and the market interest rate at the time of issue are equal, the proceeds from the bond issue will be the face or par value of the bond. When those two interest rates are not equal, the bond will be issued at a discount or premium. Let's look closer at each.

Bonds Issued at a Premium: Stated Rate on Bonds Is Greater Than the Market Rate of Interest

Study Tip

As discussed in Appendix A, tables have been devised and financial calculators have been programmed using interest-compounding formulas to help do this calculation.

Suppose Hewlett-Packard issues a $1,000 face value, 10-year, 11.5% bond, with interest payable annually. At the time of issue, the market interest rate is 10%. How much money will Hewlett-Packard get for the bond?

- First, calculate the bond's annual interest payments of $115 (= $1,000 × 0.115 per year × 1 year). There will be 10 of these payments (one each year for 10 years).

- Next, calculate the present value of an annuity of $115 for 10 years at an annual rate of 10%—the market rate of interest. What we need to determine is the equivalent amount of all those interest payments in today's dollars.

This process, called *discounting a series of cash flows*, involves calculating the present value of future cash flows. Using the present value of an annuity table, the relevant factor is 6.14457, so the present value of the 10 annual interest payments over 10 years is:

$$\$115 \times 6.14457 = \$706.63$$

Or you could use your financial calculator to discount the cash flows:

- *PMT* = 115
- *i%* or I/Y = 10%
- *n* = 10 periods
- Press *CPT* and then *PV*
- The display will show $706.63 (rounded to nearest cent)

This calculation means $706.63 today is equivalent to getting 10 payments of $115 over the next 10 years, if the market interest rate is 10% per year.

- Now, determine the present value of the principal repayment. It will be a single payment of $1,000, 10 years from now. At the current market rate of interest, how much would you have to invest today to have it grow to be

$1,000 in 10 years? To calculate today's value of this $1,000 future payment, use the factor from the present value of $1 table (a single payment rather than a series of payments)—for 10 years at 10 percent. The factor is 0.38554 so the present value of the $1,000 principal is

$$\$1,000 \times 0.38554 = \$385.54$$

- Or using your financial calculator:
  - $FV = \$1,000$
  - $i\%$ or $I/Y = 10\%$
  - $n = 10$ periods
  - Press CPT, then PV
  - The display will show $385.54
- Today's value—the present value—of the total of the future cash flows is $1,092.17 (= $706.63 + $385.54), even though the face amount of the bond is only $1,000. This bond would be selling for around 109 2/8 today, according to the convention of pricing bonds. Here's how Hewlett-Packard would record this bond issue:

Cash	1,092.17	
Bonds Payable		1,000.00
Premium on Bonds Payable		92.17

This is the accounting equation:

Assets	=	Liabilities		+	Shareholders' Equity	
					Contributed Capital	Retained + Earnings
Cash		Bonds Payable	Premium on Bonds Payable			
1,092.17		1,000.00	92.17			

The amount of the face of the bond (Bonds Payable at $1,000) and the Premium on Bonds Payable ($92.17) are both liabilities. They appear next to each other on the balance sheet. Premium on Bonds Payable is called an adjunct liability, which means an add-on. Adjunct liability describes the relationship between Bonds Payable and Premium on Bonds Payable. Premium on Bonds Payable is a partner of the Bonds Payable liability it is matched with, and they are added together on the balance sheet.

Bonds Issued at a Discount: Stated Rate on Bonds Is Less Than the Market Rate of Interest

Now, suppose Hewlett-Packard is issuing a $1,000, 10-year, 11.5% bond at a time when the market interest rate is 12%. Who would be interested in buying this bond? Nobody—no one would want to pay $1,000 for the series of payments at the stated 11.5% annual interest rate. Hewlett-Packard would have to offer the bond at a discount. What should be the price of the bond to attract buyers?

- First calculate the annual interest payments of $115 (= $1,000 × 0.115 × 1). There will be 10 of these payments.

- Use the factor from the present value of an annuity table to calculate the present value of the interest payments over 10 years at 12% per year. The relevant factor is 5.65022, so the value of the interest payments is:

$$5.65022 \times \$115 = \$649.78$$

- Now find the value of the principal repayment. How much is needed today to grow to $1,000 in 10 years at 12% per year? The present value is calculated with the present value factor of one for 10 periods and 12% per period. The PV of $1 gives us a factor of 0.32197, so the present value is:

$$\$1,000 \times 0.32197 = \$321.97$$

- Hewlett-Packard can sell the bond for a total of $971.75 (= $649.78 + $321.97) even though its face value is $1,000. The bond market would quote a price of approximately 97 1/8 or 97.125 according to the usual way of expressing bond prices.

This bond is being sold at a discount. This is the journal entry Hewlett-Packard uses to record the bond's issue:

Cash	971.75	
Discount on Bonds Payable	28.25	
Bonds Payable		1,000.00

This is the accounting equation:

Assets	=	Liabilities		+	Shareholders' Equity	
					Contributed Capital	+ **Retained Earnings**
Cash		Bonds Payable	Discount on Bonds Payable			
971.75		1,000.00	−28.25			

Discount on Bonds Payable is a contra-liability and is deducted from Bonds Payable on the balance sheet. It works like the other contra-accounts—Accumulated Depreciation and Allowance for Uncollectible Accounts—we have studied in prior chapters. Discount on Bonds Payable is shown on the balance sheet with its partner account, and it is a deduction from the balance in its partner account.

appendix

Amortizing Bond Discounts and Premiums: The Effective Interest Method

As you learned in the chapter, bond discounts and bond premiums are written off over the life of the bonds. That means the amount of the discount or premium is reduced until it reaches zero. We used the straight-line method of amortization in the chapter. However, the effective interest method is required under GAAP.

Actual Interest Expense on the Outstanding Principal Balance

To show how a discount is written off using the effective interest method, let's continue the example of a bond issued at a discount—$1,000 bond issued for $971.75. The stated rate on the bond is 11.5%, and the market rate of interest is 12%. When the bonds are issued, the value of the net liability—*bonds payable* minus the discount—is $971.75 (= $1,000 minus $28.25). Each time interest is paid to the bondholders, a portion of the discount is written off. The amount of the amortization is the difference between the **interest expense** and the **interest payment** to the bondholders.

Suppose the bond is issued on January 1. The first interest payment to the bondholders, on December 31, will be $115 (= $1,000 × 0.115 × 1 year). The Interest Expense—shown on the income statement—is *not equal* to the interest payment to the bondholders. The *Interest Expense* is calculated using the usual interest rate formula— $I = P \times R \times T$. In this case, the principal amount borrowed during the year from January 1 through December 31 is $971.75. That's the amount the bondholders actually loaned the company on the date of the bond issue. The interest rate is 12%, which is the market rate at the date of issue, and the time period is one year.

$$\text{Interest Expense} = \$971.75 \times 0.12 \times 1 = \$116.61$$

The difference between the interest payment of $115.00 and the interest expense of $116.61 is the amount that reduces the discount. After the payment is made, the discount is reduced by $1.61 (= $115 minus 116.61). The discount that began with $28.25 at issue is now reduced to $26.64. The amount of the discount is reduced each time the company makes an interest payment. Doing this is called writing off or amortizing the discount, and this method of calculating the amount of the write-off is called the effective interest method of amortization.

The value of the bonds payable minus the *un*amortized discount is called the carrying value or book value of the bonds.

Interest expense: Is calculated by multiplying the carrying value of a bond by the market rate of interest at the date of the bond's issue.

Interest payment: Is calculated by using the rate stated on the face of the bond.

Study Tip

Remember, a bond's book value is the net amount added into the total liabilities on the balance sheet.

503

Over the life of the bonds, the discount is amortized, so that the *carrying value of the bonds at the date of maturity is exactly the face value.* In other words, the amount of the discount is reduced—a portion at each interest payment date—to zero over the life of the bonds. Getting the discount to zero will make the face value equal to the carrying value. After all, the face value is exactly the amount that must be paid to the bondholders at the maturity date of the bonds.

- Amortizing a bond discount will *decrease* the unamortized bond discount and *increase* the carrying value of the bond.
- Amortizing a bond premium will *decrease* the unamortized bond premium and *decrease* the carrying value of the bond.

The amortization of bond premiums or discounts is a natural result of calculating the correct interest expense for the period when the company makes an interest payment to the bondholder. Remember, the amount of the cash payments to the bondholders is established before the bond is issued. Consequently, the calculation of the payments to the bondholders is independent of the market interest rate at the date of the bond's issue. But, the market rate of interest does determine the amount of money the bondholders are willing to pay for the bonds to get the fixed payments at specified times in the future.

The demand from the bond market will set the price of the bond so that it will earn exactly the market rate of return. A company must estimate the proceeds when making the business decision to issue bonds.

Let's take a closer look at bonds issued at a discount to see how the interest payments to the bondholder and the interest expense to the issuer are different.

Payment of interest to bondholders and amortization of a discount

Organizing the information about a bond issue in a table like the one shown in Exhibit 9C.1 emphasizes the pattern in the calculation of the interest expense related to a bond issued at a discount. The bond is a 10-year, annual interest bond. Notice how cash proceeds amount to $971.75, even though its face value is $1,000. Why wouldn't bondholders pay the full $1,000 for the bond? No one will pay $1,000 because the market rate of interest is 12% and this bond has a stated rate of only 11.5%.

How much interest does the firm that issued the bond owe the bondholder on the first interest date? The bondholder actually loaned the firm $971.75 at the market rate of interest, 12%. For the first year of the life of the bond, the

Exhibit 9C.1

Format for the Amortization Schedule for a Bond Issued at a Discount

Period	Carrying Value at Beginning of Period	Annual Interest Expense	Interest Payment (Cash)	Amortization of Discount	Unamortized Discount	Carrying Value
0	At issue . . .				$28.25	$971.75
1	$971.75		$115.00			
			$115.00 etc.			

entire balance of $971.75 was outstanding. So, the calculation of the interest expense for the first year is:

$$\$971.75 \times 0.12 \times 1 = \$116.61$$

Although the interest expense is $116.61, the firm is only going to pay the bond-holder $115.00—that's the amount predetermined by the stated rate of interest and face amount of the bond. The firm actually owes the bondholder an additional $1.61. Because the payment to the bondholder is fixed, the extra $1.61 will be added to the outstanding principal balance of $971.75. Now, after the first interest payment, the new principal balance is $973.36 (= $971.75 + 1.61). The $1.61—the difference between the interest expense and the interest payment—is amortization of the discount.

Here's how the payment to the bondholder of $115.00 and the discount amortization affect the accounting equation:

Study Tip

Remember that the Discount is a contra-liability. That is, the balance in the Discount is subtracted from the balance in Bonds Payable. As it is amortized, less and less is subtracted, until zero is subtracted from Bonds Payable. So, a reduction in the discount is actually an increase (hence the +) in total liabilities.

Assets	=	Liabilities	+	Sharholders' Equity
−115.00 Cash		1.61 Discount on Bonds Payable		−116.61 Interest Expense

Without getting too technical, let's analyze why issuing a bond at a discount results in interest expense *greater* than the actual cash payment to the bondholder. Because the interest rate in the market is higher than the interest rate the bond is paying, the difference between the $1,000 face amount to be repaid and the $971.75 issue price might be thought of as some extra interest—in addition to the periodic payments—that the bond issuer has to pay to borrow the $971.75.

Each time an interest payment is made to the bondholder, a small portion of the discount is written off as interest expense. At the maturity date of the bond, the discount will be zero.

See if you can fill in the table in Exhibit 9C.2 for the first two interest dates. We just calculated the interest expense for the first year of $116.61. Because the bond always pays $115.00, the amount of $1.61 was added to the amount owed to the bondholder. And because a discount is used to reduce the face to the amount actually owed, the discount must get smaller. What's the goal? You want the discount to be zero at maturity. A discount of zero means the bond's book value equals the bond's face value.

When you are sure you understand the calculations needed to get the figures for the second interest payment, fill in the numbers for the third and fourth interest payments.

Exhibit 9C.2

Continuation of the Amortization Schedule for a Bond Issued at a Discount

Period	Carrying Value at Beginning of Period	Annual Interest Expense (0.12 × carrying value)	Interest Payment (Cash)	Amortization of Discount (Expense minus cash paid)	Unamortized Bond Discount	Carrying Value ($1,000 − unamortized discount)
0	At issue . . .				$28.25	$971.75
1	$971.75	$116.61	$115.00	$1.61	$26.64	$973.36
2	$973.36	$116.80	$115.00	$1.80	$24.84	$975.16
3			$115.00			
4			$115.00			

See if you can figure out how the numbers for the second interest payment in Exhibit 9C.2 have been calculated.

Answers Interest expense = $973.36 × 0.12
Interest expense = $116.80
Interest payment = $115.00
Difference is discount amortization = $1.80

Payment of interest to bondholders and amortization of a premium

Let's use the same bond but assume it was issued at a premium. Recall, the market rate of interest of 10% is lower than the bond's stated rate of 11.5%, so the bondholder will pay a premium for the bond's series of payments. The format for the amortization schedule is shown in Exhibit 9C.3.

In this example, the bondholder pays $1,092.17 for the bond. The interest expense incurred is calculated using the market rate interest. For the first year, the interest expense is:

$$\$1,092.17 \times 0.10 \times 1 = \$109.22$$

When the bond issuer makes the cash payment of $115, that amount pays the bondholder the interest for the six months plus a small amount of the principal. The amount of principal paid off is the difference between the interest payment and the interest expense:

$$\$115.00 - \$109.22 = \$5.78$$

This $5.78 is amortization of the premium. The premium of $92.17 will be reduced a little bit each time the bond issuer makes an interest payment to the bondholder, until the premium is zero at maturity. At maturity, the bond issuer pays the bondholder the $1,000 face amount.

Here's how the interest payment to the bondholder affects the accounting equation:

Assets	=	Liabilities	+	Shareholders' Equity
−115.00 Cash		−5.78 Premium on Bonds Payable		−109.22 Interest Expense

Exhibit 9C.3

Format for the Amortization Schedule for a Bond Issued at a Premium

Period	Carrying Value at Beginning of Period	Annual Interest Expense	Interest Payment (Cash!)	Amortization of Bond Premium	Unamortized Bond Premium	Carrying Value
0	At issue:				$92.17	$1,092.17
1	$1,092.17		$115.00			
			$115.00			
			Etc.			

Exhibit 9C.4

Continuation of the Amortization Schedule for a Bond Issued at a Premium

Period	Carrying Value at Beginning of Period	Annual Interest Expense	Interest Payment (Cash!)	Amortization of Bond Premium	Unamortized Bond Premium	Carrying Value
0	At issue:				$92.17	$1,092.17
1	$1,092.17	$109.22	$115.00	$5.78	$86.39	$1,086.39
2	$1,089.39	$108.64	$115.00	$6.36	$80.03	$1,080.03
			Etc.			

And here's why issuing a bond at a premium results in interest expense to the bond issuer that is less than the actual cash payment to the bondholder: The 10% interest rate in the market is lower than the 11.5% interest rate specified on the bond. Therefore, we can think of the premium the bondholder paid as a payment in advance to the bond issuer to help meet the 11.5% payment due the bondholder, a sort of refund of future interest.

Each time a cash payment for interest is made to the bondholder, a small portion of the premium is written off. How much? The difference between the interest payment and the interest expense will be the amount of the premium amortization. At maturity, the premium will be zero.

Can **YOU** do it?

See if you can fill in the table in Exhibit 9C.3 for the first two interest rate dates.

Answers First payment:
  Interest expense = $1,092.17 × 0.10 = $109.22
  Interest payment = $115.00
  Difference is premium amortization = $5.78
Second payment:
  Interest expense = ($1,092.17 – $5.78) × 0.10 = $108.64
  Interest payment = $115.00
  Difference is premium amortization = $6.36

As calculated above, the interest expense for the first year is $109.22. Because the cash paid as interest to the bondholder each time it is due is $115.00, there is a difference of $5.78 that will be deducted from the premium. Because the original premium increases the amount owed to an amount *larger* than the face of the bond, the premium must be made smaller over the life of the bond.

The goal of the issuer is to reduce the premium to zero at maturity, so that the bond will have a book value equal to its face value. When you understand the calculations needed to get the figures for the second interest payment, fill in the numbers for the third and fourth interest payments.

Straight-line Versus Effective Interest Methods of Amortization

Even though GAAP requires the effective interest method of amortization for bond discounts and premiums, the straight-line method can be used if the amounts are not significantly different. So many firms actually do use the straight-line method. Also, it is a simple way to demonstrate the concept of the discount, or premium, increasing or decreasing interest expense while the payment remains the same.

To use the straight-line method of amortization, you don't have to know the interest rate to calculate the interest expense. Each period the interest expense is the same; the amortization is the same; and, of course, the payment is the same. You can see how that makes the calculations easy. The numbers in this example are small, and the difference doesn't seem to be very significant. When a company has hundreds of thousands, or even millions, of dollars of bonds outstanding, the two methods can produce significantly different amounts of interest expense. In that case, the company would have to use the effective interest method.

Leases and Pensions

In addition to warranties and bonds, there are two other long-term liabilities that you will see on almost every balance sheet—leases and pension liabilities. Although the topics are complicated and covered in depth in more advanced accounting courses, you should recognize what these liabilities are and what they mean to a company.

Capital Leases

For accounting purposes, there are two types of leases: operating leases and capital leases. Operating leases are recorded in the accounting records only when a lease payment is made. It is just like renting a car or an apartment: You pay someone else to use their assets. The notes to the financial statements will show the estimated future payments of these types of leases, but there is nothing recorded on the balance sheet.

In contrast, a capital lease is a lease in form only; in substance it is a purchase.[5] Even though they are called "leased" assets, they are recorded on the books as if they were purchased. When the lessee company—the company leasing the assets—records the assets, the company records a corresponding liability. Companies lease a range of capital including equipment, buildings, furniture, and warehouses. The asset will be depreciated just like the other assets owned by the firm, and you will often see Capital Leases listed in the notes as one of the firm's assets. On the other side of the balance sheet, the amount of the liability represents the future lease payments the company will have to make, excluding the interest. The liability is often called Obligations Under Capital Leases. The notes to the financial statements will include the details of the future payments a company will make.

GAAP provides detailed guidance on when a lease can be classified as an operating lease and when it must be classified as a capital lease. The lease will have to be recorded as a capital lease if the lessee is going to either pay for the asset over the course of the lease, have the asset for almost all its useful life, or take ownership of the asset at the end of the lease for a very low cost. Classifying a lease as a *capital* lease, rather than as an *operating* lease, adds debt to a company's balance sheet. Be sure to check out the notes to the financial statements to see if the company has operating leases. That's a way to keep the debt off the balance sheet. When firms structure transactions to do this, it's called off-balance-sheet financing.

Pensions

The topic of pension liabilities could fill a book, and the related accounting issues are complicated. However, because you will see pension liabilities on many firms' balance sheets and you will hear and read a lot about pension

---

[5]There are legal differences between a capital lease and a purchase, which is why firms lease assets rather than making an outright purchase.

plans in the news, you should understand the basic concept behind the liability (or asset) on the balance sheet.

When a firm has a defined benefit retirement plan, it will have an obligation to pay a specific retirement benefit to the employees covered by the plan. For example, many states have defined benefit plans. The state makes regular contributions to a pension fund, and retired employees will collect a pension from this fund and its earnings. When a company calculates the amount of its pension obligation for a certain accounting period according to GAAP, it must record that obligation. The annual cash contribution to the pension fund may be more or less than its annual obligation. Most often the company funds less than the obligation, resulting in a pension liability. Suppose a company has evaluated its pension obligation as $100,000 for the period. The company decides to contribute $75,000 to its pension fund, so that leaves a $25,000 difference. Here's what the journal entry would look like:

Transaction	Debit	Credit
Pension Expense	100,000	
Cash		75,000
Accrued Pension Liability		25,000

Accounting in the NEWS

Risk and Control

Employee Benefits: Trouble on the Horizon

In the good old days of corporate America, companies promised generous retirement and health care benefits to employees. At the time of the promises, it would be difficult for managers to foresee how life expectancies would rise and how employee benefit costs would follow to a point where companies promised more than they could deliver. When companies cannot make good on their promised benefits, a federal government agency—the Pension Benefit Guaranty Corporation (PBGC)—steps in. However, currently, the PBGC is technically insolvent. According to a *BusinessWeek* cover story:

The cost of honoring PBGC's commitments could be higher than anyone is expecting. The government bailout fund has relied on having enough healthy companies to pony up premiums to cover plans that fail. But in a scenario of rising plan terminations, healthy companies with strong plans still in the PBGC system would be asked to pay more. For corporations already fretting that pensions have become a competitive liability and a turnoff to investors, this could be the tipping point. Faced with higher insurance costs, they could opt out, rapidly accelerating the system's decline as the remaining healthy participants become overwhelmed by the needy. In the end, the problem would land with Congress, which could be forced to undertake a savings-and-loan-type bailout. It's almost too painful to think about, and so no one does. But when the bill comes due, it will almost certainly be addressed to taxpayers.

Most worrisome is the record number of pension plans in danger of going under. According to the PBGC, as of September 2003, there was at least $86 billion in pension obligations promised by companies deemed financially weak. That's up from $35 billion the year before. And it's on top of a record number of companies that managed to dump their troubled pension plans on the PBGC last year: 152. In 2003, a record 206,000 people became PBGC pensioners, including 95,000 from its biggest takeover ever, Bethlehem Steel Corp.

If necessary, the federal government will likely rescue the PBGC. Neverthe-

Times have changed, and many retirees may not receive the generous pensions they expected.

less, if and when that happens, you, as a taxpayer, will ultimately pay a price for the unfilled promises made years ago.

Q. If the PBGC fails, who or what will have to take on the costs?

A The federal government, meaning the taxpayers.

Source: Nanette Byrnes with David Welch, "The Benefits Trap: Old-line Companies Have Pledged a Trillion Dollars to Retirees. Now They're Struggling to Compete with New Rivals, and Many Can't Pay the Bill." Reprinted from the July 29, 2004 issue of *BusinessWeek Online.* Copyright © 2004 by The McGraw-Hill Companies. Reprinted by permission.

This is the accounting equation:

Assets	=	Liabilities	+	Shareholders' Equity		
				Contributed Capital	+	Retained Earnings
Cash		Accrued Pension Liability				Pension Expense
−75,000		25,000				−100,000

The FASB requires the disclosure of a great deal of information about a firm's pension plan and its funding. Most investors are concerned about pension under-funding. That is, are the obligations of the firm to retirees greater than the fair value of the pension fund's assets?

A related area of concern is postretirement benefits. These benefits are a firm's promise to pay costs other than pensions to its retirees. For example, a firm often pays a portion of a retiree's health insurance. Until recently, these costs were expensed as they were incurred. Now the FASB has adopted rules to make the accounting for postretirement benefits the same as the accounting for pensions. The expense should be accrued in the period in which the employee helps the firm generate revenue. This is another example of the matching principle.

There are FASB rules and laws passed by Congress that address how a company funds its pension plan. Although these rules and laws are quite complicated, you should recognize the common liability related to pensions on the balance sheet and look in the notes to the financial statements for additional information about a firm's pension costs and pension funding. As the baby boomers reach retirement age, meeting its pension obligations will become a serious problem for many large corporations. Read about the problem in *Accounting in the News*.

chapter 10

Reporting and Understanding Shareholders' Equity

Here's where you've been . . .

- **You learned how a firm accounts for and reports current and long-term liabilities.**

Here's where you're going . . .

- **You'll learn how a company accounts for and reports contributions from owners, payment of dividends, and retained earnings.**

YOU make the call:

How does a Papa John's shareholder earn a return on an investment in the company's stock?

The first company-owned Papa John's restaurant opened in 1985, and the first franchised restaurant opened in 1986. By July 24, 2005, there were 2,883 Papa John's restaurants in operation, consisting of 571 company-owned and 2,312 franchised restaurants. You've probably had a pizza or two from a Papa John's in your neighborhood, but have you ever considered investing in the stock of Papa John's?

There are two ways for the shareholders to make money from an investment in the stock of Papa John's, or any other company. One is by appreciation in the price of the stock. The second is from dividends paid by the company. If you decide to invest in Papa John's, how do you earn a return on your investment? *You make the call.*

Learning Objectives

When you are finished studying this chapter, you should be able to:

1. Explain how a company finances its business with equity.
2. Account for the payment of cash dividends and calculate the allocation of dividends between common and preferred shareholders.
3. Define treasury stock, explain why a company would purchase treasury stock, and account for its purchase.
4. Explain stock dividends and stock splits.
5. Define retained earnings and account for its increases and decreases.
6. Compute return on equity and earnings per share, and explain what these ratios mean.
7. Recognize the business risks associated with equity and the related controls.

LEARNING OBJECTIVE 1

Explain how a company finances its business with equity.

Components of Shareholders' Equity in a Corporation—Contributed Capital

Every business has owners. There are three general forms of business organization:

1. Sole proprietorships
2. Partnerships
3. Corporations

No matter which form a business takes, it needs money—contributions—from the owners to operate.

With sole proprietorships and partnerships, individual owners use their own money or borrow money from family, friends, or banks. Corporations have access to more money because they sell stocks to investors. In this chapter, we'll focus on how the firm acquires and accounts for money from owners.

The claims of the owners to the assets of the firm are called shareholders' equity or stockholders' equity. Recall there are two major parts to stockholders' equity—Contributed Capital and Retained Earnings. Each part is recorded and reported on the balance sheet as a separate amount. *Contributed Capital* is the amount owners have invested in the corporation. Contributed capital is subdivided into two parts: *Capital Stock* and *Additional Paid-in Capital.*

In Other Words:
Paid-in capital is another name for contributed capital.

Study Tip

The form of capital contributions is usually cash, but contributions of other assets are possible.

Authorized shares: Maximum number of shares of stock a firm is authorized to offer to the public as specified in the corporate charter.

Issued shares: Shares of stock that have been offered and sold to shareholders.

Stock—authorized, issued, and outstanding

In return for their contributions, the owners receive shares of stock, representing ownership equal to the fair value of those contributions. The form of capital contributions is usually cash, but contributions of other assets are possible. When a corporation is formed, the state in which the firm incorporates requires an agreement that specifies characteristics of the firm. For example, the charter sets a maximum number of **authorized shares** of stock it can issue. **Issued shares** are shares offered and sold to shareholders—in batches, during times when a company needs capital.

Exhibit 10.1 shows the Shareholders' Equity section of Papa John's International Balance Sheet at December 26, 2004, and December 28, 2003.

Exhibit 10.1

Shareholders' Equity from Papa John's International Balance Sheet

As you read about the different parts of shareholders' equity, refer to this information from the balance sheet of Papa John's Pizza.

Shareholders' Equity Section from
Papa John's International Balance Sheet
(in thousands)

	At Dec 26, 2004	Dec 28, 2003
Shareholders' equity		
Preferred stock ($0.01 par value per share; authorized 5,000,000; no shares issued)		
Common stock ($0.01 par value per share; authorized 50,000,000 shares; issued 32,483,243 shares in 2004 and 31,716,105 shares in 2003)	$ 325	$ 317
Additional paid-in capital	242,656	219,584
Accumulated other comprehensive income/(loss)	(555)	(3,116)
Retained earnings	317,142	293,921
Treasury stock (15,753,410 shares in 2004, and 13,603,587 in 2003 at cost)	(420,345)	(351,434)
Total shareholders' equity	$139,223	$159,272

Notice the number of shares of common stock authorized is 50 million and the number of shares issued is 32.48 million at December 26, 2004.

An issued share of stock does not have to remain outstanding. **Outstanding shares** are owned by stockholders rather than by the corporation.

When a company buys back its stock, those shares of stock are called **treasury stock**. Any stock that has been *issued* by a company may be either *outstanding*, which is owned by investors, or *treasury stock*, which is held in the company's treasury. Notice in Exhibit 10.1 that Papa John's has a significant amount of Treasury Stock (over 15 million shares at December 26, 2004), shown at the end of the equity section where it is subtracted from total equity.

Exhibit 10.2 shows the relationships among authorized shares, issued shares, outstanding shares, and treasury shares.

> **Outstanding shares:** Shares of stock that are owned by shareholders rather than by the corporation; *issued* shares minus *treasury* shares.

> **Treasury stock:** Shares of stock that a firm has bought back. Treasury stock is issued but not outstanding.

Exhibit 10.2

Authorized, Issued, and Outstanding Stock

In this example, 1,000,000 shares are *authorized*, but only 300,000 are *issued*. Of the issued shares, 290,000 are *outstanding*, and 10,000 are *treasury shares*.

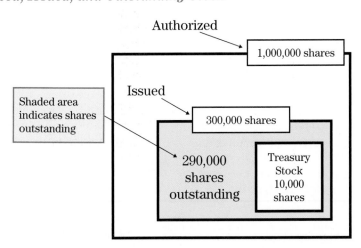

Common stock

Common stock: The most widespread form of ownership in a corporation; common stockholders have a vote in the election of the firm's board of directors.

Common stock, as the name suggests, is the most common type of capital stock representing ownership of a corporation. All corporations must have common stock. The owners of common stock have the right to:

1. Vote for members of the board of directors.
2. Share in the corporation's profits.
3. Share in any assets left if the corporation has to dissolve (for example, if the company has to go out of business due to bankruptcy).
4. Acquire more shares when the corporation issues new stock, often referred to as a pre-emptive right.[1]

In 2004, Google offered its stock to the public for the first time. This event is called an initial public offering (IPO). Google has two types of common stock. Read about them in *Accounting in the News*.

Par value: Value assigned to a share of stock in the corporate charter.

The corporate charter determines a fixed per-share amount called the **par value** of the stock.[2] Par value is an arbitrary amount and has no real meaning in today's business environment, and most states do not require a par value. The corporation must maintain a specific amount of capital, as determined by the state or contained in the corporate charter. That amount could be the total par value of the outstanding stock. Frequently, however, other means are used to determine legal capital to protect creditors. Exhibit 10.1 shows that Papa John's common stock has a par value of $0.01 per share.

If you know the par value per share of the common stock and you know the dollar amount in the Common Stock account, you can calculate the number of shares that have been issued. Let's use Papa John's balance sheet in Exhibit

Accounting in the NEWS

Risk and Control

Who Runs the Show at Google?

When Google made its initial public offering in 2004, founders Larry Page and Sergey Brin wanted to maintain control of their company. Offering shares of Google to the public could have been risky to Page and Brin because stockholders own and run, via election of the board of directors, the company. How did Page and Brin keep control? They formed their public corporation with two classes of common stock. Here's how it works:

Prospective Google shareholders awaiting the much anticipated $2.7 billion initial public offering found that the company is wrapping itself in a takeover defense that keeps cofounders Larry Page and Sergey Brin firmly in control. A two-tier voting structure gives Class B stockholders—Page and Brin, for the most part—10 votes for each share, with 1 vote for each of the Class A shares being offered. "In the transition to public ownership, we have set up a corporate structure that will make it harder for outside parties to take over or influence Google," its Securities and Exchange Commission filing explained. That "will also make it easier for our management team to follow the long-term, innovative approach" that the company favors.

Q How did the founders of Google make sure they kept control of the company?

A They issued two different types of common stock. The type they

In late October 2005, Google's shares reached a new high of $346.43 on the Nasdaq Stock Market. Page and Brin, both 32, each held Google stakes worth $12 billion.

personally kept has 10 votes for each share, compared to the normal investors' one vote per share.

Source: Lori Calabro, "Letting Down Your Guard," *CFO Magazine*, June 3, 2004. "Blockbuster 3Q profits for Internet search site," Associated Press, Friday October 21, 2005.

[1]Many corporate charters have removed this right due to the difficulty it creates in raising new capital.
[2]Some stocks don't have a par value. The firm may establish a "stated" value when the stock is issued.

10.1 on page 515 to see how that can be done. At December 26, 2004, the Common Stock account has a balance of $325,000, and the par value of the stock is $0.01 per share. To calculate the number of shares issued, divide the Common Stock balance by the par value per share to see how many shares are represented by the balance in the Common Stock account:

$$\frac{\$325{,}000}{\$0.01} = 32{,}500{,}000 \text{ shares}$$

Because the Common Stock account balance was rounded to $325,000, the number of shares from the calculation will also be rounded. The actual number of shares issued is 32,483,243. Our rounded calculation shows 32,500,000 shares.

Stock is usually sold for more than its par value. In some states, it is a legal requirement that stock sell for at least par value. Suppose the par value of a company's stock is $2 per share, the market price of the stock on the date the stock is issued is $10 per share, and the company issues 100 shares. Here's how to calculate the dollar amount that will be recorded as Common Stock.

$2 par per share × 100 shares = $200

The amount of $200 will be shown on the balance sheet in an account separate from any contributions in excess of the par value. The remaining $8 per share will be credited to another paid-in capital account.

$8 excess over par (per share) × 100 shares = $800

The total par value amount—$200—is called common or capital stock, and the excess contributions amount—$800—is called *additional paid-in capital*. Both amounts are reported on the balance sheet. Exhibit 10.3 shows how the amount of cash from the issue of stock is divided between the two paid-in capital accounts. Remember that *paid-in capital* designates both *capital stock* and *additional paid-in capital*. All amounts of contributed capital are called paid-in capital.

Suppose the corporate charter of Papa John's International authorizes 50 million shares of common stock at par value $0.01 per share. Suppose the company issues 300,000 shares at $15 per share. Here's how Papa John's would record the transaction:

In Other Words:
Additional paid-in capital is also called paid-in capital in excess of par.

Study Tip

The excess of the issue price over the par value is shown on the balance sheet as a separate amount called Additional Paid-in Capital. Only the par value per share times the number of shares issued will be recorded as Common Stock.

Transaction	Debit	Credit	
Cash	4,500,000		(300,000 shares × $15 per share)
Common Stock		3,000	(300,000 shares × $0.01 par value)
Additional Paid-in Capital		4,497,000	(300,000 shares × $14.99 per share)
To record the issue of stock			

This is the accounting equation:

Assets	=	Liabilities	+	Shareholders' Equity		
				Contributed Capital		Retained Earnings
				Common Stock	Additional Paid-in Capital	
Cash						
4,500,000				3,000	4,497,000	

One hundred shares of stock are issued for $10 each. Par value is $2 per share. The proceeds from the stock issue, $1,000, is divided between two accounts: Common Stock and Additional Paid-in Capital.

Exhibit 10.3

Recording the Issue of Stock

Cash ($10 per share)	Common Stock at par ($2 per share)	Additional Paid-in Capital ($8 per share)
Company receives cash from issuing stock 	The amount, $10, is divided between two accounts: Common Stock and Additional Paid-in Capital	
Stock Value: 100 × $10 per share = $1,000	Common Stock: 100 × $2 per share = $200 + Additional Paid-in Capital: 100 × ($10 − $2) per share = $800	

How would this transaction be shown on Papa John's financial statements? Suppose the company is issuing the stock for the first time. The Shareholders' Equity section of the balance sheet would show this information in the part of the statement that shows Contributed Capital.

Contributed capital	
Common stock (par value $0.01 per share; 50 million shares authorized; 300,000 shares issued and outstanding)	$ 3,000
Additional paid-in capital	4,497,000

Preferred stock

In addition to common stock, corporations may have a second type of capital stock—**preferred stock**. Owners of preferred stock must receive their dividends before the common shareholders and also have a preferred claim on assets. If a firm goes out of business, the preferred shareholders receive assets that remain after the creditors have been paid. The common shareholders then get any remaining assets. However, the owners of preferred stock usually do not have voting rights.

Investors don't just buy stock and become owners in a corporation—they also sell stock. As you may know from reading the business news, it is illegal to buy or sell stock on the basis of inside information. Test your ethics in *Accounting in the News*.

Preferred stock: A special type of ownership in a corporation; preferred stockholders don't get to vote for the board of directors, but they do get their dividends before the common shareholders.

Accounting in the NEWS

Insider Trading at Interstate Bakeries

You've read about Martha Stewart and her untimely sale of ImClone stock. Her friend, Sam Waksal, was convicted of insider trading—buying or selling stock using information you are not allowed to use to trade stocks—and is serving a 10-year prison sentence. This isn't an isolated case. Here's an excerpt from a *Wall Street Journal* article that shows how a casual conversation between a father and son resulted in charges of insider trading.

Arriving in Las Vegas for a board meeting of Interstate Bakeries, E. Garrett Bewkes Jr., a director, called his son, Robert, a broker at UBS, at his home in Darien, Conn. The two men talked almost every day, swapping bits of family and market gossip, and this day, in February 2003, was no exception.

Mr. Bewkes, who had been given an internal report documenting the company's deteriorating financial condition, complained to his son that "business was lousy," according to regulatory filings. Mr.

Bewkes, a former Paine Webber director, added that if his son owned any of the stock in Interstate, which makes Wonder bread and Hostess cakes, he should get rid of it. . . .

Ten minutes later, Robert Bewkes, a broker at UBS for 12 years, sold $230,000 worth of Interstate Bakeries stock for himself, his family and a few select clients, filings show. For the Bewkeses, what had begun as a father-and-son chat suddenly became something much more ominous, according to regulators: trading on inside information.

When Interstate issued a statement about a major earnings decline, its stock price dropped 25% in one day. An investigation by the New York Stock Exchange uncovered the Interstate Bakeries price drop. It didn't take long for the investigators to find Robert Bewkes's timely sale of 16,000 shares and file charges of insider trading.

Thinking Critically

Suppose your college roommate's mother was on the board of directors at a company in which your parents had a large investment. Your friend mentions that his mother's firm was losing a lot of money to new competitors. Would you call your parents to warn them to sell their stock?

Martha Stewart reads a statement after sentencing at Manhattan federal court, Friday, July 16, 2004, in New York. Stewart served five months in prison and five months of home confinement for lying to investigators about a stock sale. At right is her attorney Robert G. Morvillo.

Q Was it illegal for Mr. Bewkes to tell his son the company was in trouble?

A Probably not, but it certainly was illegal for his son to trade on the information.

Source: "Psst. Why Insider Trading Keeps Going" by Landon Thomas, Jr. from *The New York Times*, May 16, 2004, Section 3, p. 1. Copyright 2004 by Dow Jones & Co Inc. Reproduced with permission of Dow Jones & Co Inc. in the format Textbook via copyright Clearance Center.

Can YOU do it?

Suppose General Mills issued 10,000 shares of $1 par per share common stock for $20 per share. How would the company record this transaction?

Answer

Cash	200,000	
Common Stock ($1 par per share)		10,000
Additional Paid-in Capital		190,000

Cash Dividends

LEARNING OBJECTIVE 2

Account for the payment of cash dividends and calculate the allocation of dividends between common and preferred shareholders.

People buy stock in a corporation because they hope the value of the corporation will increase. Selling stock for more than its cost is one way the shareholder can make money on the investment. The other way is by receiving distributions from the firm.

Dividends: Distributions of a corporation's earnings to the shareholders.

The distributions shareholders receive from the earnings of the corporation are called **dividends**. The board of directors decides the amount of dividends to be paid and when they will be paid to the shareholders. The directors are also free not to pay dividends at any time they believe it is in the best interest of the corporation. The board of directors may want to reinvest the available cash in the business by buying more equipment or inventory. Microsoft Corporation, for example, was started in 1975 and did not pay a dividend until 2003. Some firms traditionally pay a dividend, and others have never paid a dividend. Exhibit 10.4 shows excerpts from the notes to the financial statements of General Electric and Papa John's that explain the dividend policy. Notice that General Electric pays a dividend and Papa John's does not. Often new companies don't pay any dividends because they want to reinvest all of their earnings in the business. Established companies often don't have the growth potential of new firms and can attract investors with regular dividend payments.

When the board of directors decides that a cash dividend will be paid, there are three important dates: the declaration date, the date of record, and the payment date.

Important dates related to dividends

Dividend declaration date: The date on which the board of directors decides a dividend will be paid and announces it to the shareholders.

Declaration Date   The **dividend declaration date** is the date on which the board of directors decides a dividend will be paid and announces it to shareholders. On this date, a legal liability called *Dividends Payable* is created. The amount of this liability is balanced in the accounting equation with a reduction to a temporary account called Dividends or directly to Retained Earnings. If a firm uses a Dividends account, it will be closed to Retained Earnings at the end of the accounting period. Dividends are not deducted from Contributed Capital because they are a distribution of *earnings*, not a distribution of an owner's original paid-in capital. The journal entry to record the declaration of $50,000 dividends to be divided among the shareholders is:

Transaction	Debit	Credit
Dividends or Retained Earnings	50,000	
Dividends Payable		50,000
To record declaration of dividends by the board of directors		

Some firms, like General Electric, consistently pay a dividend. Other firms, like Papa John's, do not pay dividends. Compare the note to the financial statement for General Electric (left) and Papa John's (right).

Exhibit 10.4

Notes to General Electric and Papa John's Financial Statements

General Electric	Papa John's
WE DECLARED $8.6 BILLION IN DIVIDENDS IN 2004. *Per-share dividends of $0.82 were up 6% from 2003, following a 5% increase from the preceding year. In December 2004, our Board of Directors raised our quarterly dividend 10% to $0.22 per share. We have rewarded our shareowners with over 100 consecutive years of dividends, with 29 consecutive years of dividend growth, and our dividend growth for the past five years has significantly outpaced that of companies in the Standard & Poor's 500 stock index.*	*Since our initial public offering of common stock in 1993, we have not paid dividends on our common stock, and have no current plans to do so.*

This is the accounting equation:

Assets	=	Liabilities	+	Shareholders' Equity	
				Contributed Capital	Retained + Earnings
		Dividends Payable			Dividends or Retained Earnings
		50,000			–50,000

Remember, dividends are not included as an expense on the income statement because they are not related to generating revenue. Rather than a *deduction* from a company's earnings, dividends are considered a *distribution* of a company's earnings to owners in proportion to their share of ownership.

Date of Record The date of record is used to determine exactly who will receive the dividends. Anyone owning the stock on this date is entitled to the dividend. After a corporation originally sells stock to investors, they are free to trade—sell and buy—shares of stock with other people. Whoever owns the stock on the *date of record* will receive the dividend. A stockholder may own the stock for only one day and receive the full dividend amount. After this date, stock is said to be ex-dividend. That is, if it is traded after the date of record, the new owner will not get the dividend. The firm does not make a journal entry on the date of record.

Payment Date The payment date is when the cash is actually paid to the shareholders. This payment has the same effect on the accounting equation as the payment of any liability: assets (Cash) are reduced and liabilities (Dividends Payable) are reduced:

Transaction	Debit	Credit
Dividends Payable	50,000	
Cash		50,000
To record payment of dividends previously declared		

This is the accounting equation:

Assets	=	Liabilities	+	Shareholders' Equity	
				Contributed Capital	Retained + Earnings
Cash		Dividends Payable			
–50,000		–50,000			

Distribution of dividends between common and preferred shareholders

The corporation must give holders of preferred stock a certain amount of dividends before common stockholders can receive any dividends. Dividends on preferred stock are usually fixed at a percentage of the par value of the stock.

For example, preferred stock characterized as *10% preferred ($100 par)* will receive a dividend of $10 in any year the corporation's board of directors declares a dividend. The preferred shareholders must get their $10 per preferred share before the common shareholders receive any dividends. The board of directors has discretion about whether or not to pay dividends to the preferred shareholders, but the board doesn't decide on the amount of the dividend for the preferred shareholders. The dividend for preferred shareholders is typically shown on the face of the preferred stock certificate. There are two types of preferred stock—cumulative and noncumulative:

> **Cumulative preferred stock:** Stock whose holders must receive any past, unpaid dividends before a company can pay any current dividends to any shareholders.

> **Noncumulative preferred stock:** Stock whose holders do not necessarily receive past, unpaid dividends; past dividends do not accumulate.

> **Dividends in arrears:** Dividends owed to holders of cumulative preferred stock but not yet declared.

- **Cumulative preferred stock** means the fixed dividend amount accumulates from year to year, and the entire amount of all past unpaid dividends must be paid to the preferred shareholders before any dividends can be paid to the common shareholders. Most preferred stock is cumulative preferred stock.
- With **noncumulative preferred stock**, the board determines whether or not to make up any missed dividends to the preferred shareholders.

Any dividends owed to holders of cumulative preferred stock from past years but undeclared and unpaid are called **dividends in arrears**. The corporation does not consider such dividends liabilities but does disclose them in the notes to the financial statements. Only after a dividend is actually declared is it considered a liability.

An example of dividend payment

Suppose JG Company has the following stock outstanding:

- 1,000 shares of 9%, $100 par, cumulative preferred stock, and
- 50,000 shares of $0.50 per share par common stock.

The company last paid dividends in December 2005. With the 2005 payment, JG paid all dividends through December 31, 2005. There were no dividends in arrears prior to 2006. No dividends were paid in 2006. On October 1, 2007, the board of directors declares a total of $30,000 in dividends for its shareholders to be paid on December 15 to all shareholders of record on November 1. How much of the dividend will go to the preferred shareholders, and how much will go to the common shareholders?

First, calculate the annual dividend for the preferred shareholders:

$$1,000 \text{ shares} \times \$100 \text{ par value} \times 0.09 = \$9,000$$

Because the preferred stock is cumulative and no dividends were paid to the preferred shareholders in 2006, JG must first pay the 2006 dividend of $9,000 to the preferred shareholders. Then, JG must pay the current year's (2007) $9,000 dividend to the preferred shareholders. The company pays a total of $18,000 to the preferred shareholders, and the remaining $12,000 to the common shareholders.

On the date of declaration, October 1, the company incurs the legal liability for the dividend payment. Here's how the company records the transaction:

Transaction	Debit	Credit
Dividends or Retained Earnings	30,000	
Dividends Payable, Preferred Shareholders		18,000
Dividends Payable, Common Shareholders		12,000
To record declaration of dividends		

This is the accounting equation:

Assets	=	Liabilities		+	Shareholders' Equity	
					Contributed Capital +	Retained Earnings
		Dividends Payable, Preferred Shareholders	Dividends Payable, Common Shareholders			Dividends or Retained Earnings
		18,000	12,000			−30,000

On the declaration date, the company records the liability. If JG were to prepare its balance sheet, it would show a current liability called Dividends Payable. This liability is a debt owed to the shareholders for dividends. A corporation may list the liability to common shareholders separately from the liability to preferred shareholders, as shown in the preceding example, or the corporation may combine the preferred and common dividends into one amount for total Dividends Payable.

On December 15, when JG actually pays the cash to the shareholders to fulfill the obligation, cash is reduced and the liability—Dividends Payable—is removed from the records. Here's how the company records the transaction:

Transaction	Debit	Credit
Dividends Payable, Preferred Shareholders	18,000	
Dividends Payable, Common Shareholders	12,000	
Cash		30,000
To record payment of dividends previously declared		

This is the accounting equation:

Assets	=	Liabilities		+	Shareholders' Equity	
					Contributed Capital +	Retained Earnings
		Dividends Payable, Preferred Shareholders	Dividends Payable, Common Shareholders			
Cash						
−30,000		−18,000	−12,000			

Suppose the preferred stock was noncumulative. Then, JG would have to pay only the current year's dividend of $9,000 to the preferred shareholders, and the remaining $21,000 would go to the common shareholders.

Can YOU do it?

A corporation has 10,000 shares of 8% cumulative preferred stock and 20,000 shares of common stock outstanding. Par value for each is $100. No dividends were paid last year, but this year $200,000 in dividends is paid to stockholders. How much of this $200,000 goes to the holders of preferred stock?

Answers (100 × 10,000 × 0.08) = $80,000 for last year and $80,000 for this year for a total of *$160,000* to the preferred shareholders. The remaining $40,000 goes to the common shareholders.

LEARNING OBJECTIVE 3

Define treasury stock, explain why a company would purchase treasury stock, and account for its purchase.

Treasury Stock

Companies can trade—buy and sell—their own stock on the open market.[3] *Treasury stock* refers to common stock that has been issued and subsequently purchased by the company that issued it. Once it is purchased by the company, the stock is considered treasury stock until it is resold or retired—taken completely out of circulation.

Why do firms buy their own stocks?

There are five main reasons why companies purchase shares of their own stock:

1. *To have stock to distribute to employees for compensation plans.* When a firm wants to give employees or corporate executives shares of stock, the firm will use treasury shares. Issuing new shares is a costly and time-consuming project, with many requirements set by the SEC, so firms typically issue new shares only to raise a significant amount of money.

2. *To return cash to the shareholders using a way that is more flexible for both the firm and the shareholder than paying cash dividends.* Firms that have a great deal of cash will often buy their own stock as a way to get the cash to the shareholders. The firm has complete flexibility over when to buy the stock and how much to buy, and the individual shareholders have complete flexibility over whether or not they sell their shares back to the company. This flexibility benefits the firm and the shareholder. The firm can control the mix of debt and equity in its capital structure. For example, it can reduce equity by buying back stock. The shareholders can decide when to take cash out of their investment in the firm by deciding whether or not to sell back their stock.

3. *To increase the company's earnings per share.* When a firm decreases the number of shares outstanding, earnings per share will increase with no change in net income due to the mathematics of the EPS calculation. However, a firm must consider that the cash used to buy back the stock would have earned some return—at least interest revenue—which would increase the numerator by some amount.

4. *To reduce the cash needed to pay future dividends.* When a firm reduces the number of shares outstanding, the total cash needed for dividends decreases. Treasury shares do not receive dividends.

5. *To reduce chances of a hostile takeover.* Top management or the board of directors may help their firm resist a takeover by making sure the treasury stock is distributed or sold to the right people—those who would resist the takeover. Buying stock also reduces cash reserves, which are a popular attraction for takeover attempts.

Boards of directors decide if and when a firm will pursue a strategy to buy back their shares. It has become quite common, and you can read about it in the firm's notes to the financial statements. Exhibit 10.5 shows an excerpt from the notes to the financial statements of PetsMart for the fiscal year ended January 30, 2005. Notice that PetsMart has a very active stock repurchase program. Over half of the firms that trade on the New York Stock Exchange regularly purchase their own stock.

---

[3]The Securities and Exchange Commission has strict rules about when a company may trade in their own stock. This topic is beyond the scope of introductory financial accounting and may be studied in finance or in advanced accounting courses.

Exhibit 10.5

PetsMart Purchases Its Own Common Stock

Common Stock Purchase Program
In April 2000, the Board of Directors approved a plan to purchase our common stock. In March 2003, the Board of Directors extended the term of the purchase of our common stock for an additional three years through March 2006 and increased the authorized amount of annual purchases to $35.0 million. In September 2004, the Board of Directors approved a program authorizing the purchase of up to $150.0 million of our common stock through fiscal year 2005. This program replaces the March 2003 program. During fiscal 2004, we purchased 2,680,778 shares of our common stock for approximately $80.0 million, or an average price of $29.84 per share, under the March 2003 and September 2004 programs. At January 30, 2005, approximately $105.0 million remained available for purchase under these programs.

Accounting for the purchase

Here are some important facts about treasury stock:

- The purchase of treasury stock reduces a company's assets (Cash) and reduces shareholders' equity. Suppose Papa John's decided to buy back some of the stock it issued in our earlier example. Treasury Stock is most often recorded at cost. Here is the journal entry the company will record if it buys back 100 shares at $16 per share:

Transaction	Debit	Credit
Treasury Stock	1,600	
Cash		1,600
To record purchase of treasury stock		

This is the accounting equation:

Assets	=	Liabilities	+	Shareholders' Equity	
				Contributed Capital	+ Retained Earnings
Cash				Treasury Stock	
−1,600				−1,600	

The par value and how much the stock was previously issued for do not matter. Using the cost method, treasury stock is simply recorded at the amount the firm pays to repurchase it.

- Treasury stock holdings for the company are shown as a reduction in the total of shareholders' equity on the balance sheet. Therefore, Treasury Stock is a type of shareholders' equity. Unlike other equity accounts, however, the cost of Treasury Stock reduces shareholders' equity. Due to its presence in the shareholders' equity section of the balance sheet and its negative effect on total equity, Treasury Stock is called a **contra-equity account** and is subtracted from total shareholders' equity.

- No gains or losses are recorded in the company's financial records when a company purchases treasury stock or later resells it. Even if a company acquired one of its own shares for $4 and later sold it for $6, the company would not show a gain of $2. Instead, the company had more money come in from the sale of stock—which is Contributed Capital.

Study Tip

Transactions between a firm and its shareholders never result in a gain or loss. These transactions affect a firm's contributed capital, not its earned capital.

Contra-equity account: An account that is a reduction to total shareholders' equity.

Suppose a company originally issued 100,000 shares of $1 par common stock for $15 per share. Several years later, the company decides to buy back 1,000 shares of common stock. The stock is selling for $50 per share at the time of the stock repurchase. (a) What is the journal entry to record the stock repurchase? (b) After the transaction, how many shares are issued and how many shares are outstanding?

Answers

| (a) Treasury Stock | 50,000 | | (1,000 shares × $50 per share) |
| Cash | | 50,000 | |

(b) 100,000 shares are issued and 99,000 shares are outstanding.

Selling treasury stock

If treasury stock is sold, the shares sold will be removed from Treasury Stock at the price the firm paid for the stock when it was repurchased. If the treasury stock is sold at a price higher than its cost, the excess will be classified as Paid-in Capital from Treasury Stock.

Suppose a firm purchased 1,000 treasury shares at $50 per share. A year later, the firm sells half of the shares for $60 each. Removing 500 shares of treasury stock at $50 cost will increase Total Shareholders' Equity by reducing Treasury Stock, a contra stockholders' equity account. Here is how the firm would record selling 500 shares of stock that cost $50 per share for $60 per share:

Transaction	Debit	Credit
Cash	30,000	
Treasury Stock		25,000
Paid-in Capital from Treasury Stock		5,000
To record sale of treasury stock		

This is the accounting equation:

Assets	=	Liabilities	+	Shareholders' Equity		
				Contributed Capital	+	**Retained Earnings**
Cash				Paid-in Capital from Treasury Stock	Treasury Stock	
30,000				5,000	25,000	

There would be 500 shares remaining in Treasury Stock, each at a cost of $50.

Suppose the firm sold those shares for $48 per share. As in the previous example, the treasury stock must be removed from the total amount of treasury stock at its cost. In this example, instead of having additional paid-in capital, the firm would reduce a Paid-in Capital account to balance the accounting equation. The difference between the cost and the reissue price—$2 per share × 500 shares = $1,000—would be deducted from Paid-in Capital from Treasury Stock. Here is how a firm would record selling 500 treasury shares—that originally cost the company $50 per share—for a reissue price of $48:

Transaction	Debit	Credit
Cash	24,000	
Paid-in Capital from Treasury Stock	1,000	
Treasury Stock		25,000
To record sale of treasury stock		

This is the accounting equation:

Assets	=	Liabilities	+	Shareholders' Equity	
				Contributed Capital +	**Retained Earnings**
Cash				Paid-in Capital from Treasury Stock	Treasury Stock
24,000				−1,000	25,000

If the amount in the account Paid-in Capital from Treasury Stock were insufficient to cover the $2 decrease in stock price, then Retained Earnings would be reduced—debited—by the amount needed to balance the accounting equation.

Reporting treasury stock

Treasury Stock is most often reported as a deduction from shareholders' equity on the balance sheet. Exhibit 10.6 shows how the shares The Limited has repurchased are reported on its balance sheet. You'll see that Treasury Stock, a contra-equity account, is deducted from total shareholders' equity.

Always remember, there are never any gains or losses from treasury stock transactions. Exchanges between a company and its owners—issue of stock, payment of dividends, purchase or sale of treasury stock—do not affect the income statement.

Exhibit 10.6

Treasury Stock on The Limited's Balance Sheets

From ***The Limited's*** Balance Sheet
(in millions)

Shareholders' equity	January 29, 2005	January 31, 2004
Common stock	$ 262	$ 262
Paid-in capital	1,649	1,674
Retained earnings	3,392	3,417
Less: treasury stock, at average cost	(2,968)	(87)
Total shareholders' equity	$2,335	$5,266

The Limited's Board of Directors (BOD) is committed to a significant stock repurchasing program. In February 2005, the BOD authorized the repurchase of an additional $100 million of the Company's common stock. Through March 23, 2005, 1.1 million shares had been repurchased under this program for $26.8 million, at an average price of $24.33 per share. According to the firm, this is part of a strategy to increase shareholder value.

LEARNING OBJECTIVE 4

Explain stock dividends and stock splits.

Stock Dividends and Stock Splits

You've learned about issuing stock and buying back stock. There are two other transactions that a company may have with stock: a stock dividend and a stock split.

Stock dividends

Stock dividend: A company's distribution of new shares of stock to the company's current shareholders.

A corporation may want to pay a dividend to shareholders but not have sufficient cash on hand. Instead of giving the shareholders cash, the corporation gives the shareholders additional shares of stock in the company. This is called a **stock dividend**. Recording the stock dividend simply reclassifies amounts in the shareholders' equity accounts. The corporation that issues a stock dividend converts retained earnings to contributed capital, thereby giving the stockholders a more direct claim to that portion of equity. A stock dividend is not income to the shareholder.

GAAP distinguishes between a small stock dividend—usually considered less than 25% of a company's outstanding stock—and a large stock dividend—greater than 25% of a company's outstanding stock. For a small stock dividend, the company uses the market value of the stock for the journal entry because a small stock dividend has a negligible effect on a stock's market price. For a large stock dividend, the company uses the par value of the stock for the journal entry because a large stock dividend puts so much new stock in the market that the market price per share adjusts to the increased number of shares.

Suppose a company declares and issues a 10% stock dividend to its current shareholders. The stock has a par value of $1 per share, and the current market price is $18 per share. The company will record the stock dividend at its market value. Before the stock dividend, the company has 150,000 shares outstanding. Therefore, the company will issue 15,000 new shares (150,000 × 10%) to shareholders. Here's how this company will record the stock dividend:

Transaction	Debit	Credit
Dividends or Retained Earnings	270,000	
(15,000 shares × $18 per share)		
Common Stock		15,000
Additional Paid-in Capital		255,000
To record the declaration of a small stock dividend		

This is the accounting equation:

Assets	=	Liabilities	+	Shareholders' Equity			
				Contributed Capital		+	**Retained Earnings**
				Common Stock	Additional Paid-in Capital		Dividends or Retained Earnings
				15,000	255,000		–270,000

This is sometimes called *capitalizing* retained earnings. Exhibit 10.7 shows how the equity section of the balance sheet is affected by a stock dividend.

When considering stock dividends, remember that stock dividends do not increase any shareholder's percentage of ownership in the company. If you owned 5% of the company before the stock dividend, you own 5% of the company after the stock dividend. After the dividend, your 5% includes more shares—but every shareholder's portion of ownership remains the same.

Stock splits

Stock splits occur when a corporation increases the number of shares and proportionately decreases the par value. It's different than a stock dividend. The outstanding shares are "split" into two or more shares with a corresponding division of the par value. Sometimes a firm will call in all the old shares and reissue new shares. Other times, the firm will issue additional split shares with a notice to the shareholders of a change in par value of all shares. Suppose you own 100 shares of Albertson's stock. It has a par value of $1 a share and a market value of $24 a share. Suppose Albertson's Board of Directors votes to split the stock 2 for 1. After the split, instead of having 100 shares with a par value of $1 a share, you have 200 shares with a par value of $0.50 each.

Theoretically, a stock split should not affect the stock price beyond splitting the price in the same proportions as the stock split. For example, if a share was trading for $24 before a 2-for-1 split, a new share should trade for $12.

> **Stock split:** The division of the current shares of stock by a specific number to increase the number of shares.

Exhibit 10.7

Shareholders' Equity Before and After a Stock Dividend

> A stock dividend does not change total shareholders' equity. It simply takes a small portion of Retained Earnings and reclassifies it as paid-in capital.

Shareholders' Equity

	Before Stock Dividend	After Stock Dividend
Shareholders' Equity		
Common stock, $1 par	$ 150,000	$165,000
Additional paid-in capital	600,000	855,000
Total paid-in capital	750,000	1,020,000
Retained earnings	950,000	680,000
Total shareholders' equity	$1,700,000	$1,700,000

However, a stock split almost always results in a small increase in the price of the stock beyond its proportionate share of the original price. The price of the share in this example would trade for something greater than $12. Some finance experts believe that the stock is now easier to trade at the lower price, which equates to increased demand, which, in turn, results in an increased stock price.

Companies record the details of the stock split parenthetically in the shareholders' equity part of the financial statements. There are no journal entries.

Can YOU do it?

1. Compare a stock split and a stock dividend.

2. Suppose you own 1,500 shares, which is 3%, of ABC Company's outstanding stock. If ABC declares a 2-for-1 stock split, how many shares will you own? What percentage ownership will your shares now represent?

Answers (1) A stock split is a division of the par value of the stock and an increase in the number of shares owned by each shareholder, proportionate to the pre-split ownership distribution. A stock dividend is a distribution of stock to the current shareholders as a dividend, similarly maintaining the pre-dividend distribution of ownership. (2) You'll own 3,000 shares, which will still be 3% of the outstanding stock.

LEARNING OBJECTIVE 5

Define retained earnings and account for its increases and decreases.

Retained earnings: The total amount of net income (minus net losses) minus all dividends paid or distributed since the company began.

In Other Words:
Retained earnings is sometimes called *earned capital*.

Study Tip

Retained earnings is *not* cash.

Retained Earnings

Retained earnings is the amount of all the earnings of the firm—since its beginning—that have not been distributed to the stockholders. Retained earnings may also be called *earned capital*.

Retained earnings includes:

1. Net incomes since the day the company began, minus
2. Any net losses since the day the company began, minus
3. Any dividends paid or distributed to shareholders since the company began.

Because Retained Earnings is a part of shareholders' equity, the change in Retained Earnings during the period is contained in the financial statements. Sometimes the part of the shareholders' equity statement that provides the details of the changes in retained earnings is shown separately and called a statement of retained earnings.

Can YOU do it?

Suppose B&B Company started the year with Retained Earnings of $84,500. During the year, B&B had net income of $25,600 and declared cash dividends of $12,200. What was the ending balance in Retained Earnings?

Answer $84,500 + $25,600 − $12,200 = $97,900

Financial Statement Analysis

LEARNING OBJECTIVE 6

Compute return on equity and earnings per share and explain what these ratios mean.

The shareholders' equity of a firm can provide information useful for financial statement analysis. There are two ratios that help us evaluate the return to shareholders:

1. Return on equity
2. Earnings per share

Return on equity

Return on equity (ROE) measures the amount of income earned with each dollar of common shareholders' investment in the firm.

Return on equity (ROE): A measure of income the firm earns for each dollar of investment from the common shareholders.

$$\text{Return on Equity} = \frac{\text{Net Income} - \text{Preferred Dividends}}{\text{Average Common Shareholders' Equity}}$$

To calculate ROE, we need the amount of common shareholders' equity at the beginning and at the end of the accounting period. Common shareholders' equity is all the equity *except* the preferred shareholders' equity. The ratio uses common shareholders' equity because common shareholders are considered to be the *true* owners of the firm. Then, we use the net income, reduced by the amount of preferred dividends paid each year, for the numerator. The reason for deducting preferred dividends from net income is that we are calculating the return to the *common* shareholder. The ratio takes preferred shareholders out of both the numerator and denominator. Recall that common shareholders are entitled to the earnings of the firm only after preferred dividends are paid. Return on equity tells us how well the company is using the common shareholders' contributions and earnings retained in the business.

Exhibit 10.8 shows the information needed to calculate Papa John's return on equity for two consecutive years. The size of the return needs to be compared to other similar companies or to industry standards for a meaningful analysis of a firm's performance. Notice that Papa John's ROE has decreased quite significantly—from about 23.9% to about 15.6%. Any analyst would want to get more information about such a significant decline.

Papa John's annual report would show that the company's return on equity for 2004 was 15.6% and 23.9% for 2003. Remember that when we calculate the ratios, we use a straight average of beginning and ending common shareholders' equity for the denominator.

Exhibit 10.8

Return on Equity for Papa John's International

(in millions)	For the year ended December 26, 2004	For the year ended December 28, 2003
Net income	$23,221	$33,563
Average common equity	$(139,223 + 159,272)/2 = $149,248	$(159,272 + 121,947)/2 = $140,610
Return on equity	15.6%	23.9%

Earnings per share

Earnings per share (EPS): The most well-known accounting number because financial analysts use it to evaluate a company's performance. EPS is a company's net income on a per-share basis.

Earnings per share (EPS) is perhaps the most well-known and used ratio because analysts and investors use current earnings to predict future dividends and stock prices. This ratio is the per-share portion of net income of each common shareholder.

$$\text{Earnings Per Share} = \frac{\text{Net Income} - \text{Preferred Dividends}}{\text{Weighted Average Number of Common Shares Outstanding}}$$

The "earnings" in the numerator of this ratio begins with net income. Because EPS is designated as the earnings for the *common* shareholders, preferred dividends must be deducted from net income.

An investor who saw the corporation's net income increase year after year, might be fooled into thinking that he was doing better each year. The investor might be worse off, however, if the amount of common stock outstanding has been increasing because those increases could dilute the investor's portion of the earnings. Even though net income went up, it has to be shared among many more owners. EPS helps an investor predict stock prices which is why it is a popular ratio.

All financial statements provide EPS because it is required by GAAP. EPS is the most common indicator of a company's overall performance. EPS are forecast by financial analysts, anticipated by investors, managed by business executives, and announced with great anticipation by major corporations. Some people believe that too much emphasis is put on EPS. Read about it in *Accounting in the News*.

Papa John's International's income statement in Exhibit 10.9 shows two amounts for earnings per share. The first is called *basic earnings per share*. This

Accounting in the NEWS

Financial Statement Analysis

Bristol-Myers Squibb's Earnings Per Share

Be careful not to put too much reliance on a firm's EPS because it's just one number of many that an investor should consider when evaluating a firm's performance. EPS has been considered *the* number to watch, so firms go to great lengths to meet analysts' expectations. This is what one large company, Bristol-Myers Squibb, did to increase earnings so that its EPS would reach or exceed analysts' expectations.

Bristol-Myers Squibb (NYSE: BMY) committed the classic example of a practice called "channel stuffing" to artificially inflate its quarterly and annual earnings... Distributors were enticed to purchase products in an amount sufficient to meet quarterly sales projections from senior manage-

ment at Bristol-Myers, but at quantities in excess of sales for the wholesalers. In other words, Bristol-Myers was stuffing its distribution channel.

In April 2002, the company disclosed the practice, and the price per share was cut in half. As a result of inappropriate revenue recognition, Bristol-Myers was forced to restate four years of earnings.

Could you have seen beyond the firm's quarterly earnings reports? According to The Motley Fool, "a diligent investor could have noticed some troubling trends." Analysis of the firm's accounts receivable and revenue by quarter would have aroused suspicion. The fourth quarter's increase in accounts receivable compared to revenue was much larger than any of the other quarters. The accounts receivable were not being collected, and the amounts were significant.

The lesson is simple: Don't rely on any single number. The relationships between the amounts on the financial statements reveal important information. Financial statement analysis is an

Bristol-Myers Squibb is a global pharmaceutical company. After disclosing an accounting practice that artificially inflated its earnings, the company was forced to restate four years of earnings.

important tool when evaluating a firm's earnings.

Q What accounting amounts are affected by channel stuffing?

A Sales are overstated, and the balance in Accounts Receivable is overstated.

Source: J. Graham, "Earnings Madness," *The Motley Fool,* June 8, 2004, www.fool.com. Copyright © 1995–2005 The Motley Fool, Inc. Reprinted by permission.

The income statement shows earnings per share after the calculation of net income. Often, a firm presents both basic and diluted EPS as shown here on the income statement for Papa John's.

Exhibit 10.9

Adapted from the Income Statement for Papa John's

Better Ingredients.
Better Pizza.

Adapted from the Income Statement for Papa John's International, Inc. For the year ended December 26, 2004 (in thousands, except per share amounts)	
Total revenues	$942,426
Cost and expenses	
Cost of sales	409,489
Salaries and benefits	159,100
All other expenses	350,616
Net income (loss)	$ 23,221
Weighted-average number of shares—basic	17,207
Weighted-average number of shares—diluted	17,405
Earnings (loss) per share—basic	$ 1.35
Earnings (loss) per share—diluted	$ 1.33

is a straight forward calculation of earnings divided by the weighted average number of common shares outstanding. The second is called *diluted earnings per share*. This is a "what-if" calculation: *What if* all of the potential securities that could have been converted into common stock actually had been converted to common stock at year-end? Those securities could be securities like convertible bonds or exercised stock options, both of which could be exchanged for shares of common stock. If you were a shareholder, you might want to know the worst-case scenario for your EPS. That's referred to as the diluted EPS. Calculations for diluted EPS can be complicated and are done by a company's accountant when the annual financial statements are prepared.

Business risk, control, & ethics

LEARNING OBJECTIVE 7

Recognize the business risks associated with equity and the related controls.

Generally, we have been looking at the risks faced by the firm. Let's start by looking at the risks associated with equity from the owner's point of view.

Risks faced by owners

Anyone who purchases a share of stock in a company risks losing that money. In addition to the risk, however, is the potential of earning a corresponding significant return.

In the first few months of 2000, technology stocks were booming. It was called the dot-com boom because so many of the new firms were Internet based. In March 2000, the NASDAQ (National Association of Securities Dealers Automated Quotation System), the U.S. technology stock price index, closed at a peak of 5,048.62, more than double its value just 14 months before. Many investors reaped the reward of the stock price increases. Then, prices began to fall. One day after reaching its peak, the NASDAQ lost almost 3% of its value. By October 2002, it had dropped to 1,114.11, a loss of 78% of its peak value. The dot-com boom had become the dot-com bust.

Many investors made money in the dot-com boom, and some technology firms did not lose their value. For example, if you bought a share of stock in eBay in July

Pets.com is one of several companies that could not get people to visit and buy products on its Web site. Investors in these types of Internet businesses lost much of their money. The dot-com bust of 2000 sends a clear message that investors need to diversify.

2002, you paid approximately $14 for that share of stock. You could have sold it in January of 2005 for over $57. This is the reward side of the risk associated with equity ownership for an individual investor.

How can the risk of stock ownership be controlled? The best way to minimize the risks of stock ownership is to diversify your investments. If you own stock in many different types of firms, the stock prices of some should go up when others are going down. For example, if you own stock in a firm in the retail grocery business, like Kroger, it might be wise to balance that investment with stock in a restaurant like Darden, the parent company of Olive Garden and Red Lobster. Then, if the popular trend is to eat at home, the grocery store stock might increase in value. If eating out becomes more popular, then the restaurant stock might become more valuable. This example is quite simplistic, and finance experts have a much more complicated concept of diversification. The bottom line, however, is quite straightforward. Don't put all your eggs in one basket.

Other risks of stock ownership result from the problems associated with the separation of ownership and management that is common in today's corporation. Considering the potential damage that can result from the actions of unethical management, investors considering ownership in a large corporation must take this risk seriously. Controls that monitor the behavior and decisions of management—such as boards of directors and independent audits—will help minimize these risks. Many of these risks are addressed by the Sarbanes-Oxley Act of 2002, which you can read more about in Chapter 13.

Public or private?

Since the passage of the Sarbanes-Oxley (SOX) Act of 2002, firms are rethinking the costs and benefits of being a publicly-traded company. There are advantages of the corporate form of business organization, particularly when the corporation's stock is available for widespread ownership via the capital markets. It is easier for a firm to raise funds, and stock provides an excellent source of bonuses for managers.

Fewer firms are going public because the legal requirements have increased. Read about it in **Accounting in the News**. According to estimates of AMR Research, a marketing research firm, companies spent over $6.1 *billion* in 2004 on SOX compliance. According to *The Wall Street Journal*, estimates of the cost per company range from $1.6 million to $4.4 million—each year. We'll talk more about the requirements in Chapter 13.

YOU make the call:

How does a Papa John's shareholder earn a return on an investment in the company's stock?

If you read the chapter carefully, you noticed that Papa John's has never paid a dividend. Look back at the statement in Exhibit 10.4: "Since our initial public offering of common stock in 1993, we have not paid dividends on our common stock, and have no current plans to do so." The way a shareholder earns a return from an investment in Papa John's must be from appreciation in the value of the stock. If you were to look at Papa John's Statement of Shareholders' Equity, you would find that no dividends are shown on the statement. However, if you bought a share of Papa John's stock in September 2000, you would have paid approximately $25 for the stock. At the beginning of September 2005, that share of stock was worth $47.

Accounting in the NEWS

Risk and Control

Vermont Teddy Bear Company Says No Thanks to SOX

The Vermont Teddy Bear Company makes and sells "BearGrams"— stuffed bears dressed in costumes as gifts for special occasions. Elisabeth Robert transformed Vermont from a money-losing small company into a much bigger, profitable company with $55.8 million in sales in 2004. When The Vermont Teddy Bear Company announced that it would go private on May 16, 2005, there was no secret about the motivation. In its own press release, the Company said:

As a private company, Vermont Teddy Bear will no longer face the challenges of a small company trying to comply with increasingly complex and costly public company requirements. We will have more time and resources to devote to growing our business.

In 2000, more than a thousand private companies filed an application with the SEC to make an initial public offering of stock. By 2003, the number had declined by over 60% to only four hundred. Why are companies unwilling to take the risks associated with being a publicly traded firm? According to *Business Week Online*, one of the reasons for the decline in the number of small firms that want to go public is the increasing cost of regulation, particularly the requirements of Sarbanes-Oxley.

Just when investors and bankers are counting on Google to bring the good times back to the market for initial public offerings, a slew of small fry have decided that being a public company isn't really worth it. Bankers expect a record number of U.S. companies to go private this year, topping last year's 86. Three years ago, only 53 did. Some outfits aren't even bothering to go public in the first place. Says Mark A. Filippell, a senior managing director in investment banking at Cleveland-based KeyCorp (KEY): "Many entrepreneurs no longer dream of going public because they see the hassle outweighing the potential benefit."

Q Who or what has contributed to the new hesitance to go public?

Founded in 1981 by John Sortino, who sold handcrafted teddy bears in an open-air market in Burlington, Vermont, the Vermont Teddy Bear Company became the creative alternative to flowers.

A Lawmakers and standards-setters have added a significant new cost with going public: the requirements of the Sarbanes-Oxley Act.

Sources: Scott Kirsner, "Four Leaders You Need to Know," *Fast Company* February. 2005, page 71; The Vermont Teddy Bear Company, press release, May 16, 2005, http://ir. vtbearcompany.com/index.php?id=185; and Emily Thornton, "Why Small Companies Want a Little Privacy," *Business Week Online*, May 24, 2004, www.Businessweek.com.

Let's Take a Test Drive

Real World Problem:
Papa John's International

Papa John's, like most major corporations, engages in equity transactions during the year. The shareholders' equity section of the balance sheet in Exhibit 10.1 shows that the company engaged in the following transactions during the fiscal year ended December 28, 2004:

- Issued new stock for more than the par value.
- Earned a net income.
- Purchased some of its own stock (treasury stock).

You can tell that Papa John's engaged in these transactions by observing the changes in the account balances in Exhibit 10.1. For each of these transactions, Papa John's had to record and report the results.

Concepts

Publicly traded corporations issue stock to raise money. Proceeds from issuing common stock are recorded in two parts of shareholders' equity: Common Stock and Additional Paid-in Capital. The Common Stock account is credited with the dollar value of the number of shares issued multiplied by the par value per share of the stock. The remaining proceeds—the amount of the issue price above par value—is credited to Additional Paid-in Capital. These two accounts are the primary contributed capital accounts. The other part of the shareholders' equity is Retained Earnings. After a company is started with contributions from owners, the company will earn revenue and incur expenses. Retained Earnings is equal to all the net incomes minus any net losses minus any dividends paid or distributed during the life of the company.

The Mechanics

Now suppose that Papa John's engaged in the following transactions in the fiscal year ended December 28, 2007 (fictitous):

1. Issued 100,000 shares of common stock, par value of $0.01 per share, for $24 per share.
2. Earned a net income of $50,680,000.
3. Declared cash dividends of $300,000.
4. Repurchased 25,000 shares of its own stock (treasury stock) for an average cost of $22 per share.

Instructions

Give the journal entry for each of the transactions. Then, update the shareholders' equity section of Papa John's balance sheet given below by filling in the shaded areas.

Papa John's
Shareholder's Equity Section of the Balance Sheet
(in thousands)

Shareholders' Equity:	At 12/28/07	12/28/06
Preferred stock ($0.01 par value per share; authorized 5,000,000 shares; no shares issued		
Common stock ($0.01 par value per share; authorized 50,000,000 shares; xxxxxx shares issued in 2007 and 31,716,105 shares in 2006)		$ 317
Additional paid-in capital—common stock		219,584
Accumulated other comprehensive income/(loss)	(3,116)	(3,116)
Retained earnings		293,921
Treasury stock (xxxxxx) shares in 2007, and 13,603,587 shares in 2006 at cost)		(351,434)
Total Shareholders' Equity		$159,272

Solution

1.	Cash	2,400,000	
	Common Stock		1,000
	Additional Paid-in Capital		2,399,000
2.	*Revenue and expense accounts	50,680,000	
	Dividends or Retained Earnings		50,680,000

*Revenue accounts would be closed with debits and expense accounts would be closed with credits. The net amount will increase Retained Earnings.

3.	Dividends or Retained Earnings	300,000	
	Dividends Payable		300,000
4.	Treasury Stock	550,000	
	Cash		550,000

Remember that dollars in the journal entries are in actual units, while the dollars in the balance sheet are in thousands. Number of shares are the actual numbers as shown.

Shareholders' Equity (dollars in thousands):	At 12/28/07	12/28/06
Preferred stock ($0.01 par value per share; authorized 5,000,000 shares; no shares issued		
Common stock ($0.01 par value per share; authorized 50,000,000 shares; 31,816,105 shares issued in 2007 and 31,716,105 shares in 2006)	$ 318	$ 317
Additional paid-in capital	221,983	219,584
Accumulated other comprehensive income/(loss)	(3,116)	(3,116)
Retained earnings	344,301	293,921
Treasury stock (13,628,587 shares in 2007, and 13,603,587 shares in 2006 at cost)	(351,984)	(351,434)
Total Shareholders' Equity	$211,502	$159,272

Rapid Review

1. **Explain how a company finances its business with equity.** Corporations raise money by issuing preferred stock and common stock. The number of shares of stock can be classified as authorized, issued, and outstanding.

2. **Account for the payment of cash dividends and calculate the allocation of dividends between common and preferred shareholders.** Preferred shareholders get their dividends before the common shareholders. The amount of the dividend is fixed by the par value and the percentage given on the stock certificate. The remaining dividends, out of the total declared by the board of directors, go to the common shareholders. Remember, a firm does not have to pay dividends. Some, like Papa John's, have never paid a cash dividend.

3. **Define treasury stock, explain why a company would purchase treasury stock, and account for its purchase.** *Treasury stock* is stock a firm has issued and later repurchased on the open market. A firm might buy its own stock to have shares available for employees and managers as part of compensation packages.

4. **Explain stock dividends and stock splits.** A *stock dividend* is a dividend consisting of shares of stock rather than cash. Each shareholder receives an amount of stock that will maintain the pre-dividend proportion of ownership. A *stock split* is when the company reduces the par value and increases the number of shares proportionately. For example, if you own five shares of

$3 par stock and the company enacts a 3-for-1 split, the new par value of the stock is $1 and you will now own 15 shares. This reduces the market price of the stock. (No journal entries are required for stock splits.)

5. **Define retained earnings and account for its increases and decreases.** The balance in Retained Earnings is the sum of all the net incomes minus any net losses and minus any dividends declared over the entire life of the company. It is the company's earnings that have been kept in the company.

6. **Compute return on equity and earnings per share, and explain what these ratios mean.** *Return on equity* is defined as net income for the common shareholders divided by average common shareholders' equity. It measures a company's profitability. Earnings per share is defined as net income divided by the average number of shares outstanding (again, common shareholders only). This measures each common shareholder's proportionate share of net income.

7. **Recognize the business risks associated with equity and the related controls.** As an owner, your biggest risk related to stock ownership is the potential for a decrease in the value of your stock. Because owners and managers are often different, the owners may have a problem monitoring the decisions of the managers. For firms, the risk of being publicly traded relates to the complicated requirements set forth by the SEC and the Sarbanes-Oxley Act.

Key Terms

Authorized shares, p. 514
Common stock, p. 516
Contra-equity account,
  p. 525
Cumulative preferred
  stock, p. 522
Dividend declaration date,
  p. 520

Dividends, p. 520
Dividends in arrears, p. 522
Earnings per share (EPS),
  p. 532
Issued shares, p. 514
Noncumulative preferred
  stock, p. 522
Outstanding shares, p. 515

Par value, p. 516
Preferred stock, p. 518
Retained earnings, p. 530
Return on equity (ROE),
  p. 531
Stock dividend, p. 528
Stock split, p. 529
Treasury stock, p. 515

Have You Increased Your Business IQ?

Answer these questions to find out.

1. The number of shares outstanding equals
   a. the number of shares authorized minus the number of shares issued.
   b. the number of shares issued minus the number of shares of treasury stock.
   c. the number of shares issued plus the number of shares of treasury stock.
   d. the number of shares authorized minus the number of shares of treasury stock.
2. Contributed capital equals
   a. paid-in capital plus retained earnings.
   b. common stock plus additional paid-in capital.
   c. retained earnings minus treasury stock.
   d. paid-in capital minus treasury stock.
3. A stock split will
   a. increase the number of shares outstanding.
   b. decrease the price of a share of stock.
   c. change the stock's par value.
   d. all of the above.
4. Dividends are declared by
   a. the firm's board of directors.
   b. the firm's CEO.
   c. the firm's preferred shareholders.
   d. the firm's common shareholders.
5. Earnings per share is
   a. shown on the face of the balance sheet.
   b. always calculated before taxes and interest.
   c. net income for the common shareholder on a per share basis.
   d. a financing cash flow.

Now, check your answers.

1. b   2. b   3. d   4. a   5. c

- If you answered all five questions correctly, you've increased your business IQ by studying this chapter. It doesn't mean you've mastered all of the accounting concepts in the chapter. It simply means that you understand some of the general business concepts presented in this chapter.
- If you answered 2 to 4 questions correctly, you've made some progress, but your business IQ has plenty of room to grow. You might want to skim over the chapter again.
- If you answered 0 or 1 question correctly, you can do more to improve your business IQ. Better study the chapter again.

Questions

1. What are the two primary ways for a company to finance its business?
2. What is the difference between common stock and preferred stock?
3. Explain how par value affects the issuance of common stock and preferred stock.
4. What is the difference between Paid-in Capital and Additional Paid-in Capital on the balance sheet?

5. What are the two ways that shareholders can make money on an investment in a corporation's stock?
6. Are dividends expenses of a corporation? Explain why or why not.
7. What are the three dates corporations consider when issuing a dividend?
8. What is the difference between cumulative and noncumulative preferred stock?
9. What are dividends in arrears?
10. What is treasury stock and why might a company acquire it?
11. What effect does the purchase of treasury stock have on a company's financial statements?
12. Would treasury stock be considered authorized, issued, and/or outstanding? Explain your answer.
13. Explain the difference between stock dividends and cash dividends.
14. What is the effect of a stock dividend on a company's financial statements?
15. What is a stock split and what effect does it have on a company's shareholders' equity?
16. What are the two sections of the shareholders' equity section of the balance sheet? Explain what each section reports.
17. How is return on equity calculated? What does this ratio measure?
18. Explain how earnings per share (EPS) is calculated. What does this ratio measure?
19. Of all the financial ratios you have studied, which is the only one that is reported in the financial statements? On which financial statement will it appear?

Multiple Choice

1. Suppose a firm begins the year with a Retained Earnings balance of $70,000. During the year, the firm earns net income of $31,000, declares and pays a cash dividend of $4,000, and declares and issues a small stock dividend of 10,000 shares when the market price of the stock is $2 per share. What is the year-end balance in Retained Earnings?
   a. $101,000.
   b. $15,000.
   c. $77,000.
   d. $35,000.

2. Feder Company's board of directors has declared $50,000 of dividends. The company has 5,000 shares of $100 par, 4%, noncumulative preferred stock and 10,000 shares of common stock issued and outstanding. Feder Company did not pay dividends last year. How much of the $50,000 will go to the common shareholders?
   a. $50,000.
   b. $20,000.
   c. $10,000.
   d. $30,000.

3. Pierce and Sons purchased 100 shares of its own $2 par common stock for $30 per share. The stock was originally issued by Pierce and Sons for $20 per share. What effect will this treasury stock purchase have on the firm's income statement?
   a. No effect.
   b. The income statement will show a gain of $10 per share, or $1,000.
   c. The income statement will show an expense of $3,000, the cost of the shares.

d. The income statement will show an expense of $200, the par value of the shares.

4. If a firm's total amount of paid-in capital is $200,000 and the Common Stock account has a balance of $5,000, then the balance in Additional Paid-in Capital must be
   a. $205,000.
   b. $200,000 minus the balance in Retained Earnings.
   c. $195,000.
   d. $5,000.

5. Suppose treasury stock that cost $10,000 is sold for $12,000. What is the effect of the sale on the firm's financial statements?
   a. Increase assets by $12,000 and stockholders' equity by $10,000.
   b. Increase income by a gain of $2,000.
   c. Increase assets by $12,000 cash, decrease assets by $10,000 of treasury stock, and increase a paid-in capital account by $2,000.
   d. Increase assets by $12,000 and increase stockholders' equity by $12,000.

6. If a company purchased 50 shares of its own stock for $6 per share and later sold it for $8 per share, how would the company record the sale?
   a. Record a gain of $2 per share.
   b. Record an increase to a paid-in capital account of $100.
   c. Reduce Cash by $100.
   d. Increase Cash by $100.

7. The number of shares of stock designated as *issued* on the year-end balance sheet are those shares that
   a. Were issued during the year.
   b. Have been issued during the
      firm's life.
   c. Are authorized to be issued.
   d. Are those that have been
      repurchased during the year.
8. If a firm has basic EPS of $1, then its
diluted EPS will generally be
   a. Greater than $1.
   b. Equal to $1.
   c. Less than $1.
   d. Unrelated to basic EPS, so it
      may be either greater or less than
      $1.
9. A firm issues 500 shares of common
stock with a par value of $1 per share

for $20 per share. Which of the fol-
lowing is true?
   a. The firm will record an increase to
      Common Stock of $10,000.
   b. The firm will record an increase to
      Additional Paid-in Capital of $9,500.
   c. The firm will record an increase
      to Retained Earnings of $9,500.
   d. The firm will record an increase to
      Additional Paid-in Capital of $500.
10. Dividends of $50,000, previously
declared, are paid to shareholders.
The firm will record
   a. An expense of $50,000.
   b. A reduction in paid-in capital of
      $50,000.
   c. A reduction in Retained Earnings
      of $50,000.
   d. A decrease in Cash of $50,000.

Short Exercises

LO 1 **SE10-1. Classify stock.**
Delta Corporation's corporate charter authorizes the company to sell 450,000,000
shares of $1.50 par common stock. As of December 31, 2006, the company had issued
180,915,000 shares for an average price of $4 each. Delta has 57,000,000 shares of
treasury stock. How many shares of common stock will be disclosed as authorized,
issued, and outstanding on the December 31, 2006, balance sheet?

LO 1 **SE10-2. Classify stock.**
Sunshine Corporation began operations on July 1, 2005. When Sunshine's first fiscal
year ended on June 30, 2006, the balance sheet showed 200,000 shares of common
stock issued and 195,000 shares of common stock outstanding. During the second
year, Sunshine repurchased 10,000 shares for the treasury. No new shares were issued
in the second year. On the balance sheet at June 30, 2007, how many shares would be
classified as issued? How many shares are outstanding?

LO 1 **SE10-3. Record issuance of common stock.**
Vest Corporation sells and issues 100 shares of its $10 par value common stock at $11
per share. Give the journal entry for this transaction.

LO 1 **SE10-4. Analyze effect of issuance of common stock on
financial statements.**
Ice Video Corporation issued 5,000 shares of $0.01 par value common stock for $32.50
per share. How much cash did Ice Corporation receive from the stock issue? How will
the transaction be shown in the shareholders' equity section of the balance sheet?

LO 1 **SE10-5. Analyze effect of issuance of common stock on
financial statements.**
If a company issues 10,000 shares of $1 par common stock for $8.50 per share, what is
the effect on total paid-in capital? What is the effect on Additional Paid-in Capital?

LO 1 **SE10-6. Analyze effect of issuance of common stock on
financial statements.**
Stockton Company reported total stockholders' equity of $58,000 on its December 31,
2006, balance sheet. During 2006, it reported net income of $4,000, declared and paid a
cash dividend of $2,000, and issued additional common stock of $20,000. What was
total stockholders' equity at the beginning of the year, on January 1, 2006?

LO 2 **SE10-7. Analyze effect of dividends on financial
statements.**
On December 15, 2005, the board of directors of Seat Corporation declared a cash
dividend, payable January 8, 2006, of $1.50 per share on the 100,000 common shares
outstanding. The accounting period ends December 31. How will this be reflected on
the balance sheet at December 31, 2005?

SE10-8. Distribute dividend between preferred and common shareholders.

LO 2

In 2006, the board of directors of Tasty Bakery Corporation declared total dividends of $40,000. The company has 2,000 shares of 6%, $100 par, preferred stock outstanding. There are no dividends in arrears. How much of the $40,000 will be paid to the preferred shareholders? How much will be paid to the common shareholders?

SE10-9. Calculate number of outstanding shares of preferred stock.

LO 2

Taxi Company paid $30,000 to its preferred shareholders in 2007. The company has issued 6%, $100 par, preferred stock and there were no dividends in arrears. How many shares of preferred stock were outstanding (on the date of record)?

SE10-10. Distribute dividend between preferred and common shareholders.

LO 2

Bates Corporation has 7,000 shares of 5%, $100 par, cumulative preferred stock outstanding and 50,000 shares of $1 par common stock outstanding. If the board of directors declares $80,000 of total dividends and the company did not pay dividends the previous year, how much will the preferred and common shareholders receive?

SE10-11. Analyze effect of treasury stock on financial statements.

LO 3

Fitness and Fashion Corporation decided to buy back some of its own stock to have on hand for end-of-year bonuses. If there were 30,000 shares issued and outstanding before the stock repurchase and the company bought 590 shares, how many shares were classified as issued and how many as outstanding after the treasury stock purchase?

SE10-12. Record purchase of treasury stock.

LO 3

If Fitness and Fashion Corporation paid $10 per share for 590 shares of its own stock, what is the journal entry to record the transaction? How would the transaction be reflected in the shareholders' equity section of the balance sheet?

SE10-13. Record sale of treasury stock.

LO 3

Suppose Fitness and Fashion Corporation paid $10 per share for 590 shares of its own common stock on August 30, 2005, and then resold those treasury shares for $11.50 per share on September 25, 2005. Give the journal entry for the transaction on September 25, 2005. What effect does this transaction have on the shareholders' equity section of the balance sheet?

SE10-14. Analyze effect of stock dividend on financial statements.

LO 4

Zorro Company declared and issued a 10% stock dividend on June 1, 2006. Before this dividend was declared and issued, there were 220,000 shares of $0.10 par common stock outstanding. After the stock dividend, how many shares are outstanding? What is the par value of each share?

SE10-15. Analyze effect of stock split on financial statements.

LO 4

Romax Company announced a 2-for-1 stock split on its common stock. Before the announcement, there were 120,000 shares of $1 par common stock outstanding. Determine how many shares of common stock will be outstanding after the stock split. What will be the par value of each share? What effect does the stock split have on total shareholders' equity?

SE10-16. Calculate retained earnings balance.

LO 5

On January 1, 2007, Harrison Corporation started the year with a $422,000 balance in Retained Earnings. During 2007, the company earned net income of $130,000 and declared and paid dividends of $20,000. Also, the company received cash of $450,000 from a new issue of common stock. What is the balance in Retained Earnings on December 31, 2007?

SE10-17. Calculate return on equity.

LO 6

Use the following data to calculate the return on equity for General Motors (GM). For 2003, GM's current assets totaled $57,855 (in millions), total assets totaled $449,999 (in millions), total liabilities totaled $424,424 (in millions), net income was $3,822 (in millions). At the end of 2002, the current assets were $62,397 (in millions), total assets were $369,053 (in millions), and total liabilities were $361,960 (in millions). General

Motors has no preferred stock. Calculate the return on equity (ROE) for GM for 2003. Make sure you use *average* shareholders' equity in your calculation.

LO 6   **SE10-18.** **Calculate net income amount using return on equity ratio.**

Octevo Corporation had a return on shareholders' equity (ROE) of 12% in 2006. If total average shareholders' equity for Octevo Corporation was $500,000 and the company has no preferred stock, what was net income for 2006?

LO 6   **SE10-19.** **Calculate earnings per share.**

Spikes started and ended the year with 400,000 shares of common stock issued and outstanding. Net income was $35,000. Calculate earnings per share (EPS) for the year.

LO 7   **SE10-20.** **Risk and control.**

What is the major risk of stock ownership and what can be done to minimize the risk?

Exercise Set A

LO 1.5   **E10-1A.** **Analyze equity section of balance sheet.**

PetsMart reported the following information on the financial statements included with its 2004 annual report. Were any new shares of common stock issued between February 1, 2004 and January 30, 2005? Did the company report a net income for the year ended January 30, 2005? Explain how you know.

(dollars in thousands)	Jan. 30, 2005	Feb. 1, 2004
Common Stock, par value $0.0001		
Authorized: 250,000,000 shares;		
Issued and outstanding		
149,517,000 shares at Jan. 30, 2005	$ 15	$ 14
144,813,000 shares at Feb. 1, 2004		
Paid-in capital	792,400	705,265
Retained earnings	286,380	132,544

LO 1.5   **E10-2A.** **Classify stock and prepare shareholders' equity section of balance sheet.**

Redmon Company's corporate charter allows it to sell 200,000 shares of $1 per share par value common stock. To date, the company has issued 50,000 shares for a total of $125,000. Last month, Redmon repurchased 1,000 shares for $3 per share.

a. If Redmon were to prepare a balance sheet, how many shares would it show as authorized, issued, and outstanding?
b. In addition to the shareholders' equity described above, Redmon Company also has $350,000 in Retained Earnings. Using this information, prepare the shareholders' equity section of Redmon Company's balance sheet.

LO 1.3   **E10-3A.** **Record stock transactions.**

Give the journal entry for each of the following transactions:

April 1	Issued 50,000 shares of $0.01 par value common stock for cash of $300,000.
June 1	Issued 1,000 shares of $100 par value preferred stock for cash at $120 per share.
June 30	Purchased 2,000 shares of treasury stock (common) for $6 per share. That is, the company bought its own common stock in the stock market.

LO 1.3   **E10-4A.** **Analyze effects of stock transactions on financial statements.**

Refer to the information in E10-3A. How many shares of common stock will be classified as issued at June 30? How many shares will be classified as outstanding?

LO 2   **E10-5A.** **Analyze effects of dividends on financial statements.**

Glenco Company had a net income of $250,000 for the year ended December 31, 2006. On January 15, 2007, the board of directors met and declared a dividend of $0.50 per share for each of the 300,000 outstanding shares of common stock. The board voted to make the actual distribution on March 1 to all shareholders of record as of February 1. What is (a) the date of declaration, (b) the date of record, and (c) the date of payment? If Glenco Company were to prepare a balance sheet on January 31, how would it report the dividends (if at all)?

E10-6A. Distribute dividend between preferred and common shareholders.

Framer Company has 4,000 shares of 9%, $100 par, cumulative preferred stock outstanding, and 10,000 shares of $1 par value common stock outstanding. The company began operations on January 1, 2005, and all of the stock was issued when the company was started. The cash dividends declared and paid during each of the first three years of Framer's operations are shown below. Calculate the amounts that went to the preferred and the common shareholders each year.

Year	Total Dividends Paid	Dividends to Preferred Shareholders	Dividends to Common Shareholders
2005	$120,000		
2006	60,000		
2007	80,000		

E10-7A. Analyze equity section of balance sheet.

Jazz Company had the following shareholders' equity section on the December 31, 2007 balance sheet:

Preferred stock, 8%, $100 par, cumulative	$1,250,000
Common stock, $2 par value	800,000
Additional paid-in capital, common stock	3,500,000
Retained earnings	3,467,000
Total shareholders' equity	$9,017,000

a. How many shares of common stock are classified as issued?
b. How many shares of common stock are outstanding?
c. How many shares of preferred stock are outstanding?
d. What was the average selling price of a share of common stock?
e. If $150,000 of dividends was declared, and there were no dividends in arrears, how much of the dividend would go to the common shareholders?

E10-8A. Record stock transactions.

Quicksilver Corporation is authorized to issue both preferred and common stock. Quicksilver's preferred stock is $200 par, 5% preferred stock. During the first month of operations, the company engaged in the following transactions related to its stock. Give the journal entry for each of the following transactions.

Jan. 1   Issued 30,000 shares of $1 par value common stock for cash at $51 per share.
Jan. 10   Issued 1,000 shares of preferred stock at par.
Jan. 15   Purchased 2,000 shares of common stock to be held in the treasury for $53 per share.
Jan. 20   Issued 40,000 shares of $1 par value common stock for cash at $56 per share.
Jan. 21   Sold 1,500 shares of the treasury stock purchased on January 15 for $56 per share.
Jan. 31   Declared a $25,000 dividend.

E10-9A. Prepare equity section of the balance sheet.

Use the data from E10-8A to prepare the shareholders' equity section of the balance sheet at January 31. The balance in Retained Earnings at month end is $125,000.

E10-10A. Analyze equity accounts.

The following balances were shown on the year-end balance sheets for 2006 and 2007 for Columbia Company. For each item, give the most likely reason for the change from one year to the next.

	12/31/06	12/31/07	Explanation?
Common stock	$45,000	$50,000	
Additional paid-in capital	200,000	230,000	
Retained earnings	182,500	200,000	
Treasury stock	(3,450)	(5,450)	

E10-11A. Analyze equity section of balance sheet.

Answer the following questions using the shareholders' equity section of Camp Corporation's balance sheet at December 31 given on the next page.

Shareholders' Equity

Preferred stock, cumulative, 10,000 shares authorized, 3,000 shares issued and outstanding	$ 300,000
Additional paid-in capital, preferred stock	30,000
Common stock, $0.10 par, 750,000 shares authorized, 600,000 shares issued	60,000
Additional paid-in capital, common stock	234,000
Retained earnings	975,000
	1,599,000
Less: Treasury stock (8,000 common shares)	(85,200)
Total shareholders' equity	$1,513,800

a. How many shares of common stock are outstanding?
b. On average, what was the issue price of the common shares issued?
c. What is the par value of the preferred stock?
d. If the total annual dividend on preferred stock is $24,000, what is the dividend rate on preferred stock?
e. On average, how much per share did the company pay for the treasury stock?

LO 1, 2, 3, 4

E10-12A. Record stock transactions.
On the first day of the fiscal year, Zenith Corporation had 190,000 shares of $1 par (per share) common stock issued and outstanding. The stock was issued for $10 per share and the Retained Earnings balance was $350,000. Prepare the journal entry for each of the following transactions that occurred during the year:

a. Issued 10,000 additional shares of common stock for $15 per share.
b. Declared and distributed a 10% small stock dividend when the stock was trading for $15 per share.
c. Issued 5,000 additional shares of common stock for $14 per share.
d. Declared a cash dividend on outstanding shares of $1.20 per share.
e. Paid the dividend declared in item *d*.
f. Purchased 500 shares of treasury stock for $15 per share.
g. Sold 200 shares of treasury stock for $17 per share.
h. Sold 250 shares of treasury stock for $14 per share.
i. Declared a 2-for-1 stock split.

LO 1, 2, 3, 4

E10-13A. Prepare equity section of the balance sheet.
Use the data from E10-12A to prepare the shareholders' equity section of the balance sheet at year-end. Net income for the year was $400,000. (Split the treasury shares in 1., but remember that treasury stock does not get dividends of any kind.)

LO 1, 3, 5

E10-14A. Prepare equity section of the balance sheet.
The following account balances can be found in the general ledger of Abco Corporation at year-end. Prepare the shareholders' equity section of the balance sheet.

Retained Earnings	$ 870,000
Treasury Stock (8,000 common shares at cost)	64,000
Common Stock ($1 par, 600,000 shares authorized, 200,000 shares issued)	200,000
Additional Paid-in Capital, Common Stock	1,500,000
Preferred Stock ($10 par value, 9%, 80,000 shares authorized, 15,000 shares issued)	150,000
Additional Paid-in Capital, Preferred Stock	45,000

LO 6

E10-15A. Calculate return on equity and earnings per share.
The following financial information is available for Cable Corporation at the end of its two most recent fiscal years. The company has no preferred stock. Calculate (1) return on equity for 2006 and (2) earnings per share for 2005 and 2006. What do the ratios indicate about the company's performance during the year?

(amounts in thousands)	**2006**	**2005**
Average common stockholders' equity	$1,328	$1,150
Dividends declared for common stockholders	500	485
Net income	2,015	1,422
Average number of common shares outstanding during the year	2,186	1,950

E10-16A. **Analyze effects of equity transactions on financial statements.**

LO 1, 2, 3, 4, 5

Analyze the following transactions and indicate the dollar increase (+) or decrease (−) each has on the balance sheet. If there is an overall change in shareholders' equity, also indicate whether Contributed Capital, Retained Earnings, or Treasury Stock is affected. If the transaction has no effect on the balance sheet, enter NA for that item. The first row is filled in for you as an example.

	Assets	Liabilities	Shareholders' Equity	Equity Section Affected
Issued 1,000 shares of $1 par common stock at par.	+ 1,000		+ 1,000	Contributed Capital
Issued 1,500 shares of $1 par common stock for $14 per share.				
Declared a cash dividend of $0.25 per share.				
Paid the $0.25 cash dividend.				
Purchased 200 shares of treasury stock for $17 per share.				
Sold 100 shares of treasury stock for $17 per share.				
Declared and distributed a 10% common stock dividend when the stock was selling for $15 per share.				
Announced a 2-for-1 stock split.				
Issued 2,000 shares of $100 par, 4% noncumulative preferred stock, for $110 per share.				

E10-17A. **Risk and Control.**

LO 7

Explain what it means to diversify stock ownership. Why would an investor diversify?

Exercise Set B

Your professor may ask you to complete selected "Group B" exercises and problems using Prentice Hall Grade Assist (**PHGA**). PHGA is an online tool that can help you master the chapter's topics by providing multiple variations of exercises and problems. You can rework these exercises and problems—each time with new data—as many times as you need, with immediate feedback and grading.

E10-1B. **Analyze equity section of balance sheet.**

LO 1, 5

Best Buy reported the following information on the financial statements included with its 2005 Annual Report. Were any new shares of common stock issued between February 28, 2004 and February 26, 2005? Did the company report a net income for the year ending February 26, 2005? Explain how you know.

(dollars in millions)	Feb. 26, 2005	Feb. 28, 2004
Common Stock, par value $0.10. Authorized: 1,000,000,000 shares; Issued and outstanding 328,342,000 shares at Feb. 26, 2005 324,648,000 shares at Feb. 28, 2004	$ 33	$ 32
Paid-in Capital	952	836
Retained Earnings	3,315	2,468

LO 1, 5   **E10-2B. Classify stock and prepare shareholders' equity section of balance sheet.**
Womack Grove Entertainment's corporate charter allows it to sell 300,000 shares of $2 par value common stock. To date, the company has issued 100,000 shares for a total of $275,000. Last month, Womack Grove repurchased 500 shares for $3.75 per share.

    a. If Womack Grove was to prepare a balance sheet, how many shares would it show as authorized, issued, and outstanding?
    b. In addition to the shareholders' equity described above, Womack Grove also has $415,000 in Retained Earnings. Using this information, prepare the shareholders' equity section of Womack Grove Entertainment's balance sheet.

LO 1, 3   **E10-3B. Record stock transactions.**
Give the journal entry for each of the following transactions:

October 1	Issued 75,000 shares of $0.10 par value common stock for cash of $187,500.
December 1	Issued 1,500 shares of $125 par value preferred stock for cash at $150 per share.
December 31	Purchased 10,000 shares of treasury stock (common) (the company bought its own common stock in the stock market) for $2.50 per share.

LO 1, 3   **E10-4B. Analyze effects of stock transactions on financial statements.**
Refer to the information in E10-3B. How many shares of common stock will be classified as issued at December 31? How many shares will be classified as outstanding?

LO 2   **E10-5B. Analyze effects of dividends on financial statements.**
Rich Land had a net income of $315,000 for the year ended June 30, 2008. On July 15, 2008, the board of directors met and declared a dividend of $0.25 per share for each of the 500,000 outstanding shares of common stock. The board voted to make the actual distribution on September 1 to all shareholders of record as of August 1. What is (a) the date of declaration, (b) the date of record, and (c) the date of payment? If Rich Land were to prepare a balance sheet on July 31, how would it report the dividends (if at all)?

LO 2   **E10-6B. Distribute dividends between preferred and common shareholders.**
Lawver Electronics has 8,000 shares of $150 par, 12% cumulative preferred stock outstanding, and 15,000 shares of $2 per share par value common stock outstanding. The company began operations on January 1, 2007. All stock was issued at the begininng of 2007. The cash dividends declared and paid during each of the first three years of Lawver's operations are shown below. Calculate the amounts that went to the preferred shareholders and the common shareholders (SHs) each year.

Year	Total Dividends Paid	Dividends to Preferred Shareholders	Dividends to Common Shareholders
2007	$150,000		
2008	125,000		
2009	176,000		

LO 1, 2   **E10-7B. Analyze equity section of balance sheet.**
Market Street Music Corporation had the following stockholders' equity section on the December 31, 2007, balance sheet:

Preferred stock, $150 par, 6% cumulative	$2,250,000
Common stock, $1 par value	400,000
Additional paid-in capital, common stock	1,020,000
Retained earnings	5,325,000
Total	$8,995,000

    a. How many shares of common stock are classified as issued?
    b. How many shares of common stock are outstanding?
    c. How many shares of preferred stock are outstanding?
    d. What was the average selling price of a share of common stock?
    e. If $175,000 of dividends was declared, and there were $35,000 dividends in arrears, how much of the dividend would go to the common shareholders?

E10-8B. Record stock transactions.   LO 1, 2, 3

Dark Knight Comics is authorized to issue both preferred and common stock. Dark Knight's preferred stock is $175 par, 8% preferred stock. During the first month of operations, the company engaged in the following transactions related to its stock. Give the journal entry for each of the following transactions.

July 1	Issued 40,000 shares of $0.50 per share par value common stock for cash at $42 per share.
July 8	Issued 1,500 shares of preferred stock at par.
July 14	Purchased 2,750 shares of common stock to be held in the treasury for $43 per share.
July 22	Issued 35,000 shares of $0.50 per share par value common stock for cash at $47 per share.
July 26	Sold 1,750 shares of the treasury stock purchased on July 14 for $47 per share.
July 31	Declared a $22,500 dividend.

E10-9B. Prepare equity section of the balance sheet.   LO 1, 2, 3

Use the data from E10-8B to prepare the shareholders' equity section of the balance sheet at July 31. Retained Earnings at month end are $125,000.

E10-10B. Analyze equity accounts.   LO 1, 2, 3, 4, 5

The following balances were shown on the year-end balance sheets for 2007 and 2008 for High Note Publishing Company. For each item, give the most likely reason for the change from one year to the next.

	12/31/07	12/31/08	Explanation?
Common Stock	$35,000	$43,000	
Additional paid-in Capital	115,000	155,000	
Retained Earnings	142,000	160,500	
Treasury Stock	(2,125)	(2,625)	

E10-11B. Analyze equity section of balance sheet.   LO 1, 2, 3

Answer the following questions using the shareholders' equity section of Fantasy Films Corporation's balance sheet at June 30 given below:

Shareholders' Equity

Preferred stock, cumulative, 15,000 shares authorized, 4,000 shares issued and outstanding	$ 420,000
Additional paid-in capital, preferred stock	40,000
Common stock, $0.05 par, 500,000 shares authorized, 250,000 shares issued	12,500
Additional paid-in capital, common stock	675,000
Retained earnings	1,005,000
	2,152,500
Less: Treasury stock (4,000 common shares at cost)	(13,000)
Total shareholders' equity	$2,139,500

a. How many shares of common stock are outstanding?
b. On average, what was the issue price of the common shares issued?
c. What is the par value of the preferred stock?
d. If the total annual dividend on preferred stock is $25,200, what is the dividend rate on preferred stock?
e. On average, how much per share did the company pay for the treasury stock?

E10-12B. Record stock transactions.   LO 1, 2, 3, 4, 5

On the first day of the fiscal year, JKB Construction had 185,000 shares of $0.50 per share par value common stock issued at $13.50 per share and outstanding. The Retained Earnings balance was $165,000. Prepare the journal entry for each of the following transactions that occurred during the year:

a. Issued 15,000 additional shares of common stock for $16 per share.
b. Declared and distributed a 20% stock dividend.
c. Issued 10,000 additional shares of common stock for $15 per share.
d. Declared a cash dividend on outstanding shares of $1.10 per share.
e. Paid the dividend declared in item *d*.
f. Purchased 1,000 shares of treasury stock for $16 per share.
g. Sold 250 shares of treasury stock for $18 per share.

h. Sold 200 shares of treasury stock for $15 per share.
i. Declared a 2-for-1 stock split.

LO 1, 2, 3, 4, 5   **E10-13B. Prepare equity section of the balance sheet.**
Use the data from E10-12B to prepare the shareholders' equity section of the balance sheet at year-end. Net income for the year was $320,000. Split the treasury shares (i.), but remember that treasury shares do not get any dividends.

LO 1, 3, 5   **E10-14B. Prepare equity section of the balance sheet.**
The following account balances can be found in the general ledger of Athletics Supply Corporation at year-end. Prepare the shareholders' equity section of the balance sheet.

Retained Earnings	$ 450,000
Treasury Stock (4,000 common shares at cost)	36,000
Common Stock ($2 par, 500,000 shares authorized, 175,000 shares issued)	350,000
Additional Paid-in Capital, Common Stock	2,712,500
Preferred Stock ($8 par value, 8%, 90,000 shares authorized, 20,000 shares issued)	160,000
Additional Paid-in Capital, Preferred Stock	50,000

LO 6   **E10-15B. Calculate return on equity and earnings per share.**
The following financial information is available for Sugar Treats Corporation at the end of its two most recent fiscal years. The company has no preferred stock. Calculate (1) return on equity for 2006 and (2) earnings per share for 2005 and 2006. What do the ratios indicate about the company's performance during the year?

(amounts in thousands)	2006	2005
Average common stockholders' equity	$1,560	$1,235
Dividends declared for common stockholders	$ 300	$ 265
Net income	$3,010	$1,565
Average number of common shares outstanding during the year	2,050	1,635

LO 1, 2, 3, 4, 5   **E10-16B. Analyze effects of equity transactions on financial statements.**
Analyze the following transactions and indicate the dollar increase (+) or decrease (−) each has on the balance sheet. If there is an overall change in shareholders' equity, also indicate whether Contributed Capital, Retained Earnings, or Treasury Stock is affected. If the transaction has no effect on the balance sheet, enter NA for that item. The first row is filled in for you as an example.

	Assets	Liabilities	Shareholders' Equity	Equity Section Affected
Issued 1,000 shares of $0.50 par common stock at par.	+500		+ 500	Contributed Capital
Issued 2,500 shares of $0.50 par common stock for $6.50 per share.				
Declared a cash dividend of $0.50 per share.				
Paid the $0.50 cash dividend.				
Purchased 175 shares of treasury stock for $9 per share.				
Sold 65 shares of treasury stock for $9 per share.				
Declared and distributed a 5% common stock dividend when the stock was selling for $8 per share.				
Announced a 2-for-1 stock split.				
Issued 5,000 shares of $75 per share par value, 6% noncumulative preferred stock at par.				

E10-17B. Risk and Control.

LO 7

Explain the risks associated with the separation of ownership and management. Can you think of a way to minimize those risks?

Problem Set A

P10-1A. Account for stock transactions.

LO 1

Restoration Corporation was started on January 1, 2007. The company is authorized to issue 30,000 shares of 6%, $100 par value preferred stock and 800,000 shares common stock with a par value of $1 per share. The following stock transactions took place during 2007.

Jan. 3	Issued 10,000 shares of common stock for cash at $4 per share.
April 1	Issued 5,000 shares of preferred stock for cash at $105 per share.
June 1	Issued 40,000 shares of common stock for cash at $4.50 per share.
Sept. 1	Issued 1,000 shares of preferred stock for cash at $102 per share.
Dec. 1	Issued 15,000 shares of common stock for cash at $5 per share.

Required

a. Prepare journal entries for the transactions.
b. Post to the shareholders' equity accounts. (Use T-accounts.)
c. Prepare the contributed capital portion of the shareholders' equity section of the balance sheet at December 31, 2007.

P10-2A. Analyze and record stock dividend transactions.

LO 4

As of December 31, 2007, Chips Company had 100,000 shares of $10 par value common stock issued and outstanding. The Retained Earnings balance was $125,000. On January 15, 2008, Chips Company declared and issued a 5% stock dividend to its common shareholders. At the time of the dividend, the market value of the stock was $15 per share.

Required

a. Prepare the journal entry for the stock dividend.
b. How many shares of stock are outstanding after the stock dividend?
c. If you owned 3% of the outstanding common stock of Chips Company before the stock dividend, what is your percentage ownership after the stock dividend?

P10-3A. Analyze and record stock transactions and prepare equity section of balance sheet.

LO 1, 2, 3, 4, 5

The following information pertains to the equity accounts of Fragrant Soap Company.

1. Contributed capital on January 1, 2007 was comprised of 70,000 issued and outstanding shares of common stock with par value of $0.50; Additional Paid-in Capital of $350,000; and Retained Earnings of $500,000.
2. During the first quarter of 2007, Fragrant Soap Company issued an additional 10,000 shares of common stock for $6 per share.
3. On June 15, the company declared a 2-for-1 stock split.
4. On September 30, the company declared and distributed a 10% stock dividend. The market price of the stock on that date was $5 per share.
5. On October 1, the company declared a dividend of $0.25 per share to be paid on October 31.
6. Near the end of the year, the company's CEO decided the company should buy 1,000 shares of its own stock. At that time, the stock was trading for $6 per share in the stock market.
7. Net income for 2007 was $49,500.

Required

a. Prepare all the necessary journal entries for the transactions including the entry to close net income to Retained Earnings.
b. Enter the beginning balances in T-accounts and post the journal entries to them.
c. Prepare the shareholders' equity section of the balance sheet at December 31, 2007.

LO 1, 2, 3, 5, 6 **P10-4A. Record stock transactions, prepare equity section of balance sheet, and calculate ratios.**

On January 1, 2007, the Expedite Corporation shareholders' equity account balances were as follows:

Preferred stock (6%, $100 par noncumulative, 25,000 shares authorized)	$ 500,000
Common stock ($5 par value, 8,000,000 shares authorized)	4,500,000
Additional paid-in capital, Preferred stock	20,000
Additional paid-in capital, Common stock	6,300,000
Retained earnings	20,380,000
Treasury stock—Common (5,000 shares, at cost)	70,000

During 2007, Expedite Corporation engaged in the following transactions:

Jan. 5	Issued 10,000 shares of common stock for $15 per share.
Feb. 9	Purchased 2,000 additional shares of common treasury stock at $13 per share.
June 1	Declared the annual cash dividend on preferred stock, payable June 30.
Dec. 1	Declared a $0.25 per share cash dividend to common shareholders, payable December 31, 2007.

Net income for the year was $2,330,000.

Required

a. Prepare all the necessary journal entries for the transactions including the entry to close net income to Retained Earnings.
b. Enter the beginning balances in T-accounts and post the journal entries to them.
c. Prepare the shareholders' equity section of the balance sheet at December 31, 2007.
d. Calculate earnings per share and return on common shareholders' equity.

LO 1, 2, 5 **P10-5A. Prepare equity section of balance sheet.**

On October 1, 2007, Marble Company had 400,000 shares of $2 par common stock issued and outstanding. The shareholders' equity accounts at October 1, 2007 had the following balances:

Common stock	$ 800,000
Additional paid-in capital	2,400,000
Retained earnings	9,800,000

The following transactions occurred during fiscal year ended September 30, 2008:

1. On October 30, issued 30,000 shares of 9%, $100 par, cumulative preferred stock at $102.
2. On November 30, reacquired 8,000 shares of its common stock for $8.50 per share.
3. Net income for the year ended September 30, 2008 was $3,875,000.

Required

Prepare the shareholders' equity section of Marble's balance sheet at September 30, 2008.

LO 1, 2, 3, 5 **P10-6A. Analyze equity section of balance sheet.**

The following information is from the shareholders' equity sections from comparative balance sheets for Wildwood Company:

	December 31, 2007	December 31, 2006
Common stock ($10 par)	$420,000	$400,000
Additional paid-in capital	326,000	306,000
Retained earnings	55,000	51,000
Total shareholders' equity	$801,000	$757,000

Net income for the year ended December 31, 2007 was $70,000.

Required

a. How many new shares of common stock were issued during 2007?
b. What was the average issue price of the stock issued during 2007?
c. What was the amount of dividends declared during 2007?
d. Did the company have any treasury shares at the end of 2007?

P10-7A. Analyze equity section of balance sheet.

LO 1, 2, 5

At December 31, 2006, Plasma Company reported the following on its comparative balance sheets (amounts in thousands):

	December 31	
	2006	**2005**
Common stock		
Authorized: 1,200 shares		
Issued: 950 shares at 2006	$ 475	
900 shares at 2005		$ 450
Additional paid-in capital	19,000	17,550
Retained Earnings	45,500	31,300

Required

a. What is the par value of the company's common stock?
b. Did the company issue any new shares during the year ended December 31, 2006?
c. What was the approximate (average) issue price of the stock issued during the year?
d. Did Plasma Company earn net income (loss) during the year? Assuming no dividends were paid, how much was net income (loss)?

P10-8A. Analyze equity section of balance sheet.

LO 1, 2, 3, 4, 5

The following information is from the shareholders' equity section of the comparative balance sheets of Aloha Cruises:

(amounts in thousands, except share data)

Shareholders' Equity:	June 30, 2006	June 30, 2005
Common stock, $0.10 par value;	$ 25.0	$ 22.0
250,000 shares issued and _____		
shares outstanding at June 30, 2006;		
and 220,000 shares issued and		
_____ shares outstanding at June		
30, 2005.		
Additional paid-in capital	3,580.0	3,014.0
Retained earnings	8,237.0	7,450.0
Treasury stock, at cost, 14,200 shares at	213.0	171.6
June 30, 2006 and 12,000 shares at		
June 30, 2005		

Required

a. What was the average issue price per share of the 250,000 shares classified as "issued" at June 30, 2006? (Round the answer to the nearest cent.)
b. What was the average issue price of the 30,000 shares of common stock issued during the fiscal year ended June 30, 2006?
c. How many shares were outstanding at June 30, 2006? How many shares were outstanding at June 30, 2005?
d. How many shares did the company buy back during the year? What was the average cost of a share of the treasury shares purchased during the year?
e. If no dividends were paid, what was net income for the year ended June 30, 2006?

Problem Set B

Your professor may ask you to complete selected "Group B" exercises and problems using Prentice Hall Grade Assist (**PHGA**). PHGA is an online tool that can help you master the chapter's topics by providing multiple variations of exercises and problems. You can rework these exercises and problems— each time with new data—as many times as you need, with immediate feedback and grading.

P10-1B. Account for stock transactions.

LO 1

Simba Corporation was started on July 1, 2007. The company is authorized to issue 100,000 shares of 5%, $100 par value preferred stock and 1,800,000 shares common stock with a par value of $2 per share. The following stock transactions took place during the fiscal year ended June 30, 2008.

1. Issued 40,000 shares of common stock for cash at $23.50 per share.
2. Issued 10,000 shares of preferred stock for cash at $101 per share.
3. Issued 40,000 shares of common stock for cash at $24.80 per share.
4. Issued 7,000 shares of preferred stock for cash at $102 per share.
5. Issued 25,000 shares of common stock for cash at $25 per share.

Required

a. Prepare journal entries for the transactions.
b. Post to the shareholders' equity T-accounts.
c. Prepare the contributed capital portion of the shareholders' equity section at June 30, 2008.

LO 4   **P10-2B. Analyze and record stock dividend transactions.**
At December 31, 2007, Robby's Shoe Company had 200,000 shares of $5 par common stock issued and outstanding. The Retained Earnings balance was $165,000. On January 15, 2008, Robby's declared and issued a 3% stock dividend to its common shareholders. At the time of the dividend, the market value of the stock was $20 per share.

Required

a. Prepare the journal entry for the stock dividend.
b. How many shares of stock are outstanding after the stock dividend?
c. If you owned 5% of the outstanding common stock of Robby's Shoe Company before the stock dividend, what is your percentage ownership after the stock dividend?

LO 1, 2, 3, 4, 5   **P10-3B. Analyze and record stock transactions and prepare equity section of balance sheet.**
The following information pertains to All Batteries Company.

1. Contributed capital on October 1, 2007 was comprised of 50,000 issued and outstanding shares of common stock with par value of $1; Additional paid-in Capital of $250,000; and Retained Earnings of $400,000.
2. During the first quarter of the fiscal year, All Batteries Company issued an additional 20,000 shares of common stock for $8 per share.
3. On March 15, the company declared a 2-for-1 stock split.
4. On June 30, the company declared and distributed a 5% stock dividend. The market price of the stock on that date was $6 per share.
5. On July 1, the company declared a dividend of $0.50 per share to be paid on July 31.
6. During September 2008, All Batteries Company's CEO decided the company should buy 6,000 shares of its own stock. At that time, the stock was trading for $7 per share.
7. Net income for the year ended September 30, 2008, was $87,500.

Required

a. Prepare all the necessary journal entries for the transactions including the entry to close net income to Retained Earnings.
b. Enter the beginning balances in T-accounts and post the journal entries to them.
c. Prepare the equity section of the balance sheet at September 30, 2008.

LO 1, 2, 3, 5, 6   **P10-4B. Record stock transactions, prepare equity section of balance sheet and calculate ratios.**
On January 1, 2008, the Premier Corporation equity account balances were as follows:

Preferred Stock (8%, $100 par noncumulative, 15,000 shares authorized)	$ 400,000
Common Stock ($1 par value, 5,000,000 shares authorized)	1,000,000
Additional Paid-in Capital, Preferred Stock	20,000
Additional Paid-in Capital, Common Stock	21,500,000
Retained Earnings	50,450,000
Treasury Stock–Common (10,000 shares, at cost)	230,000

During 2008, Premier Corporation engaged in the following transactions:

Jan. 7	Issued 5,000 shares of common stock for $25 per share.
Feb. 8	Purchased 1,000 additional shares of common treasury stock at $24 per share.
June 1	Declared the annual cash dividend on preferred stock, payable June 30.
Dec. 1	Declared a $0.30 per share cash dividend to common shareholders payable December 31, 2008.

Net income for the year was $1,980,000.

Required

a. Prepare all the necessary journal entries for the transactions including the entry to close net income to Retained Earnings.
b. Enter the beginning balances in T-accounts and post the journal entries to them.
c. Prepare the shareholders' equity section of the balance sheet at December 31, 2008.
d. Compute earnings per share and return on common shareholders' equity.

LO 1, 2, 5

P10-5B. Prepare equity section of balance sheet.
On July 1, 2006, Philbrick Company had 500,000 shares of $1 par common stock issued and outstanding. The stockholders' equity accounts at July 1, 2006 had the following balances:

Common Stock	$ 500,000
Additional Paid-in Capital	36,500,000
Retained Earnings	22,700,000

The following transactions occurred during fiscal year ended June 30, 2007:

1. On July 30, issued 50,000 shares of $100 par value, 6% cumulative preferred stock at $103.
2. On October 1, reacquired 20,000 shares of its common stock for $76 per share.
3. Declared annual dividends for preferred shareholders on June 29, 2007.
4. Net income for the year ended June 30, 2007 was $5,150,000.

Required

Prepare the shareholders' equity section of Philbrick's balance sheet at June 30, 2007.

LO 1, 2, 3, 5

P10-6B. Analyze equity section of balance sheet.
The following information was shown on the recent comparative balance sheets for Jule's Dot-Com Company:

	December 31, 2006	December 31, 2005
Common stock ($1 par)	$520,000	$400,000
Additional paid-in capital	326,000	296,000
Retained earnings	65,000	50,000
Total shareholders' equity	$911,000	$746,000

Net income for the year ended December 31, 2006 was $75,000.

Required

a. How many shares of common stock were issued to new shareholders during 2006?
b. What was the average issue price of the stock issued during 2006?
c. What was the amount of dividends declared during 2006?
d. Did the company have any treasury shares at the end of 2006?

LO 1, 2, 5

P10-7B. Analyze equity section of balance sheet.
At June 30, 2007, High Quality Mining Company reported the following on its comparative balance sheet, which included 2006 amounts for comparison (amounts in millions):

	June 30	
	2007	**2006**
Common stock		
Authorized: 2,500 shares		
Issued: 1,450 shares in 2007	$ 14,500	
1,400 shares in 2006		$ 14,000
Additional paid-in Capital	4,350	2,890
Retained Earnings	15,500	14,300

Required

a. What is the par value of the company's common stock?
b. Did the company issue any new shares during the fiscal year ended June 30, 2007?
c. What was the approximate (average) issue price of the stock issued during the year?
d. Did High Quality Mining Company earn net income (loss) during the year? Assuming no dividends were paid this year, what was net income (loss)?

<u>LO 1, 2, 3, 4</u>   **P10-8B. Analyze equity section of balance sheet.**
This information is from the equity section of the comparative balance sheets of
Tick Tock.

(in thousands, except share data)

Shareholders' Equity	September 30, 2005	September 30, 2004
Common stock, $0.10 par value; 450,000 shares issued and _____ shares outstanding at September 30, 2005; and 425,000 shares issued and _____ shares outstanding at September 30, 2004.	$ 45.0	$ 42.5
Additional paid-in capital	9,475.0	8,925.0
Retained earnings	25,237.0	21,450.0
Treasury stock at cost, 21,340 shares at Sept. 30, 2005 and 17,148 shares at Sept. 30, 2004	(448.1)	(343.0)

Required

a. What was the average issue price per share of the 450,000 shares classified as "issued" at September 30, 2005? (Round the answer to the nearest cent.)
b. What was the average issue price of the 25,000 shares of common stock issued during the fiscal year ended September 30, 2005?
c. How many shares were outstanding at September 30, 2005? How many shares were outstanding at September 30, 2004?
d. How many shares did the company buy back during the year? What was the average cost of a share of the treasury shares purchased during the year?
e. If no dividends were paid, what was net income for the year ended September 30, 2005?

Financial Statement Analysis

<u>LO 1, 2, 5</u>   **FSA10-1. Analyze equity section of balance sheet.**
The Coca-Cola Company reported the following information on its comparative
balance sheet at December 31(amounts in millions):

	December 31	
	2004	**2003**
Common stock, par value _____ Authorized: 5,600 shares Issued: 3,500.5 shares in 2004 3,494.8 shares in 2003	$ 875	$ 874
Capital Surplus	4,928	4,395
Reinvested Earnings	29,105	26,687

Required

a. Explain what Capital Surplus and Reinvested Earnings each represent.
b. What is the approximate par value of Coca-Cola's common stock?
c. How many new shares of common stock did the company issue during the fiscal year ended December 31, 2004?
d. What was the approximate (average) issue price of the stock issued during the year?
e. Did Coca-Cola earn a net income during the year?
f. If Coca-Cola paid dividends of $0.50 per share, what would you estimate net income for the year to be?

<u>LO 1, 3</u>   **FSA10-2. Analyze equity section of balance sheet.**
The following information (next page) is from the comparative balance sheets of
Linens 'n Things:

Adapted from Linens 'n Things & Subsidiaries
Consolidated Balance Sheets

(in thousands, except share amounts)

Shareholders' Equity:	January 1, 2005	January 3, 2004
Preferred stock, *$0.01 par value,* *1,000,000 shares authorized;* *none issued and outstanding.*		
Common stock, *$0.01 par value;* *135,000,000 shares authorized;* *45,460,467 shares issued and* _____ *shares outstanding at* *January 1, 2005; and 45,052,255* *shares issued and* _____ *shares* *outstanding at January 3, 2004.*	$ 455	$ 450
Additional paid-in capital	372,627	362,483
Retained earnings	440,914	380,393
Other comprehensive gain	2,619	1,391
Treasury stock, *at cost, 259,571* *shares at January 1, 2005 and* *258,636 shares at January 3, 2004.*	(7,262)	(7,340)
Total shareholders' equity	$809,353	$737,377

Required

a. How many shares of common stock were outstanding at January 1, 2005?

b. How many shares of common stock were outstanding at January 3, 2004?

c. What was the average issue price per share of the 45,460,467 shares classified as "issued" at January 1, 2005? (Round the answer to the nearest cent.)

d. How many shares of treasury stock did the company purchase during the fiscal year ended January 1, 2005?

e. What was the average price per share paid for the treasury shares purchased during the fiscal year ended January 1, 2005?

f. What was the average issue price of the shares of common stock issued during the fiscal year ended January 1, 2005?

FSA10-3. **Analyze equity section of balance sheet.**

LO 3, 6

Use the annual report of Wal-Mart in Appendix A at the back of the book to answer the following:

In addition to selling treasury stock, a company may use treasury stock when stock options are exercised or when debt is converted to stock. Did Wal-Mart use some of its treasury shares to do this during the most recent fiscal year? Where, in the financial statements, is this disclosed? Describe how the dollar amount of Treasury Shares on the comparative balance sheets decreased while, at the same time, the statement of cash flows shows a cash outflow for the purchase of treasury shares.

Compute the return-on-equity ratio for the two most recent consecutive years. What information do these ratios provide?

Critical Thinking

Risk and Control

What kinds of risks do the owners of Wal-Mart face? Would you prefer to be a creditor or an owner of Wal-Mart? Explain why.

Ethics

AVX Electronics is very close to bringing a revolutionary new computer chip to the market. The company fears that it could soon be the target of a takeover by a giant telecommunications company if this news were to leak before the product is introduced. The current AVX management intends to redistribute the company's stock holdings so its managers will have a larger share of ownership. So, management has decided to buy back 20% of the company's common stock while the price is still quite

low and distribute it to the managers—including themselves—as part of the company's bonus plan. Are the actions of AVX management ethical? Explain why this strategy would reduce the risk of a hostile takeover. Was any group hurt by this strategy?

Group Assignment

In groups, select two companies that you would invest in if you had the money. Find their financial statements on the Internet and examine the shareholders' equity section of their balance sheets. What does your analysis tell you about the firm? Is this a good investment? Explain your findings and conclusion.

Internet Exercise: Hershey Foods Corporation

Hershey is the market leader, ahead of Mars in the U.S. candy business. The company makes such well-known chocolate and candy brands as Hershey's Kisses, Reese's Peanut Butter Cups, Twizzlers, Jolly Rancher, Mounds, Super Bubble Gum, and Kit Kat (licensed from Nestlé). Its products are sold throughout North America and exported to over 90 countries.

Go to www.hersheys.com.

IE10-1. Explore "Investor's Relations." In what city is the Hershey factory located? The current stock quote (market price) of Hershey's stock is how much per share? Is this market price reflected on the Hershey balance sheet? If it is, where is it found?

Access the most recent annual report and find the consolidated balance sheets to answer the following questions. (Note: These financial statements are read with an Acrobat Reader, which may be downloaded free by clicking on Get Acrobat Reader.)

IE10-2. How many types of stock have been authorized and issued? For the most recent year, how many shares are issued and are outstanding?

IE10-3. For the most recent year end, identify total stockholders' equity. Of this total, how much was contributed by shareholders for issued shares? On average, how much did shareholders pay per issued share? Is the average issue price more or less than the current market price? Give an explanation for this difference.

IE10-4. For the most recent year end, what amount of stockholders' equity is retained earnings? What is the name of the Retained Earnings account? Did the balance increase or decrease during the year? What might cause this change?

IE10-5. Has the company reacquired any of its common stock? How you can tell? What is reacquired stock called? When a company reacquires stock does total stockholders' equity increase or decrease? Why might a company want to reacquire issued shares?

IE10-6. (Optional) For a study break visit Hershey's Kidztown at www.kidztown.com and go to "Fun and Games" to play. (Hope you have fun.)

Additional Study Materials

Visit www.prenhall.com/reimers for self-study quizzes and spreadsheet templates to use to complete homework assignments.

CONTINUING CASE STUDY

Building your Excel skills with The MP3 Store

During the month of October, the owners of The MP3 Store finally received their stock certificates. Each of the four owners has 1,000 shares of $10 par value common stock. The company is authorized to sell a total of 10,000 shares. During the month, the company engaged in the following transactions. The company is using LIFO and the perpetual inventory system. Recall from Chapter 9 that the beginning inventory consists of 5 MP3 players purchased for $227 and 10 MP3 players purchased for $196 each.

October 1   Paid the $600 monthly rent.

October 3   Declared a $15.00 per share dividend on common stock to be paid on October 29th.

October 4   Purchased 80 MP3 players for $232 each and paid cash.

October 6   Paid the sales tax payable from September sales.

October 10 Collected $30,150 of the outstanding A/R balance.

October 17 Received and paid a $165 telephone bill.

October 26 The owners sold 500 shares of common stock to another investor for $6,500 cash.

October 28 Paid the assistant manager $2,000 for October work, recording the appropriate payroll taxes. In addition to Social Security and Medicare, the FIT withheld was $200.

October 29 The dividend declared on October 3rd was paid to the owners.

October 30 Sales for the month were as follows (all units sold for $350 each): 48 units for cash and 39 units on account. The sales tax rate is 6%. The company estimates that 4% of the sales will be returned under warranty.

October 31 Recorded the required adjusting entries for depreciation, insurance, bad debts (5% of outstanding Accounts Receivable) and payroll tax expense.

Instructions

1. Prepare the necessary journal entries, T-accounts, trial balances, and financial statements. (Note: A Classified Balance Sheet and Statement of Cash Flows is required for this chapter.)

2. When you are finished print and save your file to disk by clicking the **Save** button. Name your file MP310.

Preparing and Analyzing the Statement of Cash Flows

Here's where you've been . . .

- **You learned how a company accounts for and reports contributions from owners, payment of dividends, and retained earnings.**

Here's where you're going . . .

- **You'll learn to prepare a statement of cash flows from an income statement and comparative balance sheets.**

YOU make the call:

Does The Home Depot's statement of cash flows indicate that the company is in good financial shape?

Although the popular press focuses on earnings, investors can learn a great deal about a company by analyzing the statement of cash flows. It's important for a company to have sufficient cash to meet its obligations, and generally that cash should come from operations. If we analyze the statement of cash flows for the years leading up to serious financial difficulties for a firm, we could probably find the early signs of the coming difficulty.

The Home Depot employs over 300,000 people and has approximately 1,695 stores in 50 states, the District of Columbia, Puerto Rico, eight Canadian provinces, and Mexico. There's probably a Home Depot store near your school or home. For the fiscal year ended January 30, 2005, The Home Depot spent $3.9 billion to build 175 new stores and remodel existing stores. Given the company's expansion, do you think it's worthwhile to invest in this company? An important question for a potential investor to ask is this: "Does The Home Depot's statement of cash flows indicate that the company is in sound financial condition?" *You make the call.*

Learning Objectives

When you are finished studying this chapter, you should be able to:

1. Categorize cash flows as operating, investing, or financing cash flows.
2. Explain the difference between accrual-basis and cash-basis accounting.
3. Explain the difference between the two methods of preparing and presenting the statement of cash flows.
4. Compute cash from operating activities using the indirect method.
5. Compute cash from operating activities using the direct method.
6. Compute cash from investing activities and cash from financing activities.
7. Prepare a complete statement of cash flows and know the required supplemental disclosures.
8. Use the statement of cash flows to help evaluate a firm's past and future performance.
9. Identify the risk of investing in a given firm by using the statement of cash flows and the related controls.

LEARNING OBJECTIVE 1

Categorize cash flows as operating, investing, or financing cash flows.

Cash from operating activities: All cash receipts and cash disbursements that result from transactions involving revenues and expenses.

Cash from investing activities: All cash receipts and cash disbursements from transactions involving long-term assets and investments in other firms.

Cash from financing activities: All cash receipts and all cash disbursements from issuing debt, receiving contributions from owners, and paying dividends to owners.

Categories of Cash Flows

Now that you have worked through the balance sheet, you are ready to take a closer look at the statement of cash flows. In many cases, analysts and investors consider this the most important of the four basic financial statements. The purpose of the statement of cash flows is to provide information about a firm's cash inflows and outflows. Where did the firm's cash come from and where did it go? There is no doubt that cash and the control of cash are vital to a company. Read about the fraud associated with cash in *Accounting in the News*.

As you learned, the statement of cash flows is divided into three categories of cash flows: **Cash from operating activities**, **cash from investing activities**, and **cash from financing activities**. Transactions that result in operating cash flows

Can**YOU**do it

Give the three categories of cash flows and an example of a cash inflow and a cash outflow in each category.

Answer

Category of Cash Flow	Examples
(1) Cash from operating activities—inflow	Cash collected from customers
Cash from operating activities—outflow	Cash paid to vendors
(2) Cash from investing activities—inflow	Cash proceeds from sale of land
Cash from investing activities—outflow	Cash paid for equipment
(3) Cash from financing activities—inflow	Proceeds from loan
Cash from financial activities—outflow	Dividends paid

Accounting in the NEWS

Would You Help Yourself to the Company's Cash?

One of the ways employees steal from their companies is by taking cash. According to the Association of Certified Fraud Examiners in its 2004 *Report to the Nation on Occupational Fraud and Abuse,* the asset that was most frequently targeted for fraud was cash. Approximately 93% of the asset misappropriation cases in the study involved the theft of an organization's cash.

The report breaks down the cash schemes into three categories:

- *Fraudulent disbursements* involve an employee causing his or her organization to disburse funds through some trick or device. Common examples include submitting false invoices or false timecards.
  - *Skimming* involves an employee stealing cash from an organization before the cash is recorded on the organization's books and records.
- *Cash larceny* involves an employee stealing cash from an organization after it has been recorded on the organization's books and records.

Among these three categories, fraudulent disbursements were reported most frequently and had a median loss of $125,000 per occurrence.

Thinking Critically

Would you submit a false invoice or a false travel reimbursement request to collect a little extra cash? Suppose no one would ever know.

We've all been told that it's wrong to steal. In an office setting, employees may be tempted to steal from the company by taking office supplies, taking cash, or padding their expense report.

Q What is the most common way employees steal cash from a firm?

A Fraudulent disbursements.

Source: "2004 Report to the Nation on Occupational Fraud and Abuse," Association of Certified Fraud Examiners. Reprinted with permission.

Exhibit 11.1

The Statement of Cash Flows

	Operating	**Investing**	**Financing**
Types of transactions	Cash related to the day-to-day activities of running the business—revenue and expense transactions	Cash related to buying and selling assets that the firm plans to use for longer than one year	Cash receipts and disbursements related to loans (principal only); cash contributions from and distributions to owners
Examples			
Inflows	Cash collections from customers	Cash proceeds from the sale of land or building	Cash proceeds from a new stock issue
Outflows	Cash paid to vendors for inventory	Cash paid for new land or building	Cash dividends paid to shareholders
Cash flows are generally related to these balance sheet accounts	Current assets and current liabilities	Long-term assets	Long-term liabilities and shareholders' equity

A firm's statement of cash flows will include every cash inflow and outflow. The cash flows are divided into three categories: operating, investing, and financing.

come from the activities reported on the income statement. From a balance sheet perspective,

- cash transactions that   the firm's current assets and current liabilities are generally classified as operating transactions.
- cash transactions that affect the firm's long-term assets are classified as investing transactions.
- cash transactions that affect the firm's long-term debt and equity accounts are classified as financing transactions.

Exhibit 11.1 on page 561 provides a review of the three parts of the statement of cash flows and the typical transactions that result in each category.

Accrual-Basis Accounting Versus Cash-Basis Accounting

LEARNING OBJECTIVE 2

Explain the difference between accrual-basis and cash-basis accounting.

Companies that follow GAAP maintain their accounting records using accrual-basis accounting. You learned about accrual accounting in Chapter 2. Preparing the statement of cash flows is the process of converting the records of the business from accrual to cash basis. Accrual-basis accounting and cash-basis accounting are not generally the same for at least two reasons. First, a company will record a sale and recognize the revenue on the income statement when the merchandise is delivered, even though the company does not receive cash upon delivery. So, the amount of revenue earned from sales for an accounting period may not be the same as the amount of cash collected during the period. At the end of the accounting period, when the company is preparing its financial statements, there may be outstanding accounts receivable because customers may still owe the company money. Second, the company may have collected cash during the period from sales made during the prior accounting period—accounts receivable from the prior year may have been paid off. To calculate the cash collected from customers for the statement of cash flows, the company has to make an adjustment for the change in accounts receivable.

Suppose a company began 2006 with Accounts Receivable of $500. These accounts receivable were recorded when the revenue from the sales was recognized. During 2006, the company had sales, all on account, of $3,000. At the end of 2006, the balance in Accounts Receivable was $600. How much cash was collected from customers during 2006? Because Accounts Receivable started with a balance of $500 and ended with a balance of $600, there is an increase that represents sales that have not been collected from the customers. So, while sales amounted to $3,000, only $2,900 worth of those sales must have been collected in cash. The T-account for Accounts Receivable below shows these transactions. The three amounts on the debit side are given. The beginning and ending balances come from two consecutive balance sheets, and credit sales come from the income statement.[1]

Accounts Receivable			
Beginning balance	500		
Credit sales	3,000	?	Cash collected
Ending balance	600		

---

[1]For simplicity, we'll assume all sales are on account.

This T-account will balance when the amount of cash collected is $2,900. Here is the equation used to find the amount of cash collected:

$500	+	$3,000	−	?	=	$600
Beginning		Sales on		Cash		Ending
Balance		Account		Collected		Balance

Solving for Cash Collected: $500 + $3,000 − $600 = Cash Collected
Cash Collected = $2,900

Another way to think about the cash collected from customers is to suppose that customers paid off their old accounts of $500. If total sales were $3,000 and there is an ending Accounts Receivable balance of $600, then $2,400 of the current sales must have been collected. The beginning balance in Accounts Receivable of $500 and current sales of $2,400 were collected—making the total cash collected from customers during the period $2,900. Here's how that would look in the Accounts Receivable account. As you can see, the amount needed to balance the T-account below in the blank next to "Remaining cash collected" is $2,400. So the total cash collected from customers is $500 + $2,400 = $2,900.

Accounts Receivable

Beginning balance	500	500	Cash collected from last period's customers
Credit sales	3,000	?	Remaining cash collected
Ending balance	600		

The number for every item on the income statement is potentially different from the cash related to it. For example, sales is potentially different from cash collected from customers. Cost of goods sold is potentially different from cash paid for inventory. Insurance expense is potentially different from the cash paid for insurance—and so on.

Changes in a current asset or a current liability occur because of differences between the accrual-based income statement amount and the cash amount. Consider an expense on the income statement. Suppose Salary expense is shown on the year's income statement as $75,000. For the statement of cash flows, we want "cash paid to employees" as an operating cash outflow. What could make the amount of salaries expense different from cash paid to employees? First, we could have paid some employees cash that we owed them from last year. The cash payment would reduce the liability Salaries Payable. If we did pay some salaries we owed at the beginning of the year, that cash paid would be in addition to any current year's salaries paid to employees. What else could make cash paid to employees different from salaries expense? We could have incurred salaries expense that will not be paid until next year. In other words, we recognized some salaries expense that did not get paid to the employees. We must have recorded it as Salaries Payable. In both cases, the difference between Salaries Expense and cash paid to employees shows up as a change in Salaries Payable from the beginning of the year to the end of the year. *We apply this type of reasoning to each current asset and each current liability on the balance sheet to prepare the statement of cash flows.*

As you read this example, follow along in the T-account for Salaries Payable. Suppose we started the year with Salaries Payable of $690. Let's say our Salaries Expense for the year, as shown on the income statement, is $75,000. If the balance in Salaries Payable is $500 at year-end, how much cash was actually paid to employees? First, we must have paid off the amount we owed at the beginning of the year—$690. Then, since the ending balance in Salaries Payable is $500, we must have paid only $74,500 of the current salaries expense.

$75,000	–	$500	=	$74,500
Salaries		Amount		Cash Paid
Expense		Unpaid		to Employees
Current		at Year-end		for Current Period's Work

$690	+	$74,500	=	$75,190
Cash		Cash		Total Cash Paid
Paid for Last		Paid for This		
Period's Work		Period's Work		

Salaries Payable

		690	Beginning balance
Cash paid to employees	690		
Remaining cash paid to employees	?	75,000	Salaries expense
		500	Ending balance

Another way to interpret what happened is to say that we paid the full $75,000 of this year's expense in cash *and* we paid down our Salaries Payable by $190 ($690 down to $500). That makes the total cash paid to employees equal to $75,190 (= $75,000 + $190).

Can YOU do it?

Robo Company began the year with $25,000 in Accounts Receivable. During the year, Robo's sales totaled $50,000. At the year-end, Robo had an Accounts Receivable balance of $15,000. How much cash did Robo collect from customers during the year? How is that amount of cash classified on the statement of cash flows?

Answer $60,000 cash collected from operating activities ($25,000 + $50,000 – $15,000 = $60,000)

You've learned how the amounts on the income statement differ from cash flows and how to convert many individual line items on the income statement to cash amounts. Now we're going to apply what you just learned to the actual preparation of a statement of cash flows. Even if you never have to prepare this statement in your future career, learning how it's done will help you understand all the financial statements and business transactions.

LEARNING OBJECTIVE 3

Explain the difference between the two methods of preparing and presenting the statement of cash flows.

Direct method: Way of preparing the statement of cash flows that shows every cash inflow and every cash outflow, identified by analyzing every item on the income statement.

Indirect method: Way of preparing the statement of cash flows that starts with net income and makes adjustments for all the items that do not affect cash and adjustments for changes in current assets and current liabilities to arrive at cash from operating activities.

Overview of the Two Methods of Preparing and Presenting the Statement of Cash Flows[2]

Generally Accepted Accounting Principles (GAAP) describe two ways of preparing the statement of cash flows: the **direct method** and the **indirect method**. These two methods are named for the way in which the operating section of the statement of cash flows—cash from operating activities—is prepared:

1. Directly, by converting every number on the income statement to its cash amount, or
2. Indirectly, by starting with net income and adjusting it until you have the cash from operating activities.

For the other two sections of the statement of cash flows, investing and financing, there is only one way to compute the cash flows: the transactions are directly identified. So, in any discussion about different methods of preparing a

[2]Note to the instructor: This section can be omitted without any loss of continuity.

statement of cash flows, the difference between the direct method and the indirect method applies to only *cash from operating activities*.

Let's look at a simple example of the difference between these methods of preparing the statement of cash flows. We'll start with the first month of business for a small company, with the following transactions:

1. Purchase of inventory for $250: Paid $200 cash to vendor and put $50 on account (accounts payable).
2. Sales of $600: $500 for cash and $100 on account (accounts receivable). The cost of goods sold for the sale is $250 (the entire inventory was sold).
3. Paid $30 for supplies and used $20 worth of them: $10 worth of supplies remain for next month.

Here's how you calculate the amount of cash the company collected and disbursed, resulting in cash from operating activities:

Cash Paid for Inventory	$(200)
Cash Collected from Customers	500
Cash Paid for Supplies	(30)
Net Cash Flow	$270

Here's how you calculate net income:

Sales	$ 600
Cost of Goods Sold	(250)
Supplies Expense	(20)
Net Income	$ 330

Exhibit 11.2 shows how cash from operating activities section of the statement of cash flows would be presented using the direct and indirect methods.

This change from accrual numbers to cash numbers can be done in the two ways shown in Exhibit 11.2—direct or indirect. The direct method examines each item on the income statement, one by one. The indirect method is more mechanical: Net income is adjusted for all noncash items on the income statement and all of the changes in the current assets and current liabilities that relate to the items on the income statement.

Study Tip

The difference between the direct and indirect methods of preparing the statement of cash flows is the way cash from operations is computed. Despite this difference, both methods produce the same amount of cash from operations.

Exhibit 11.2

Comparison of the Direct and Indirect Methods for the Statement of Cash Flows

Statement of Cash Flows

(cash from operating activities only)

Direct Method		Indirect Method	
Cash from operating activities:		Cash from operating activities:	
Cash collected from customers	$500	Net income	$330
Cash paid for supplies	(30)	– increase in accounts receivable	(100)
Cash paid to vendors for inventory	(200)	– increase in supplies	(10)
Net operating cash flow	$270	+ increase in accounts payable	50
		Net operating cash flow	$270

Statement of Cash Flows—Indirect Method[3]

More than 90% of companies—including The Home Depot—use the indirect method for preparing the statement of cash flows because it is easier to use than the direct method. For example, if a company uses the direct method, it would have to prepare a reconciliation of net income and net cash from operating activities in addition to preparing the statement of cash flows.[4]

We'll need comparative balance sheets and the income statement for the time period between the two balance sheet dates to prepare the statement of cash flows. Let's start with net income for Yurman for the year ended December 31, 2007. Exhibits 11.3 and 11.4 provide most of the information we need to prepare the statement of cash flows. Our focus is on an analysis of the current assets and current liabilities sections of the balance sheet. As you know, these are the balance sheet accounts affected by operations.

Using two steps, let's prepare the cash from operating activities section of the statement of cash flows using the indirect method for Yurman for the year ended December 31, 2007.

Steps in calculating cash from operations— indirect method

Step 1: Start with Net Income and Adjust It for Any Noncash Items To prepare the operating section of the statement of cash flows using the indirect method, start with net income and add back any noncash expenses like depreciation. For Yurman, we add back to net income the $75 depreciation expense. When the firm calculated the net income of $9,225, it subtracted $75 for depreciation expense, but it was *not* a cash outflow. So we add $75 back to net income to change net income to a cash number. There are no other noncash items on Yurman's income statement. However, other common noncash items are gains or losses on the sale of long-term assets. Gains are added to arrive at net income, so we would subtract them from net income to undo their noncash

Study Tip

Don't get the idea that depreciation increases cash flows. It doesn't. Depreciation is added back to net income when calculating cash from operations because it had been subtracted to get net income.

Exhibit 11.3

Income Statement for Yurman

Yurman, Inc.
Income Statement
For the year ended December 31, 2007

Sales		$20,000
Cost of goods sold		6,000
Gross profit		14,000
Other expenses		
Rent expense	$ 1,000	
Salaries expense	3,000	
Insurance expense	500	
Interest expense	200	
Depreciation expense	75	4,775
Net income		$ 9,225

[3]Note to the instructor: This section can be omitted without any loss of continuity.
[4]As this book goes to press, the FASB is considering revisiting the cash flow presentation method. Don't be surprised if the FASB decides to make the direct method mandatory.

Exhibit 11.4

Comparative Balance Sheets for Yurman

Yurman, Inc.
Comparative Balance Sheets

	At December 31, 2006	At December 31, 2007
Assets		
Cash	$ 6,695	$18,275
Accounts receivable	150	250
Inventory	100	1,300
Prepaid insurance	125	75
Prepaid rent...................................	200	400
Total current assets	7,270	20,300
Equipment (net of $150 and $225 accumulated depreciation)	3,850	4,775
Total assets	$11,120	$25,075
Liabilities and Shareholders' Equity		
Accounts payable	$ 800	$ 500
Salaries payable	50	150
Interest payable	150	80
Total current liabilities	1,000	730
Long-term notes payable	0	2,000
Shareholders' Equity		
Common stock and additional paid-in capital	5,000	8,000
Retained earnings	5,120	14,345
Total liabilities and shareholders' equity	$11,120	$25,075

effect on income. Losses, like those from selling assets at less than their book value, are deducted to arrive at net income, so we would add them back. So the first step in this example is to add back $75 Depreciation Expense.

Step 2: Adjust for Changes in Current Assets and Current Liabilities Next, we examine each current asset account and each current liability account for changes during the month. Start with current assets from the comparative balance sheets in Exhibit 11.4 above.

Accounts Receivable Accounts Receivable increased by $100 during the year. That increase represents sales for which the company has not yet collected any cash. So we need to subtract $100 from net income to convert net income into a cash number. Remember, the $100 was included in the Sales amount on the income statement. Because we didn't collect the $100, it is subtracted from net income to help get net income converted to net cash from operating activities. So part of step 2 in this example is to subtract the $100 increase in Accounts Receivable.

Inventory The next change in a current asset is the increase in Inventory of $1,200. This $1,200 represents purchases made that have not yet shown up as expenses on the income statement because the items have not been sold. Since we did purchase them, the amount needs to be deducted from net income because it was a cash outflow that didn't get subtracted in the calculation of net income. So part of step 2 in this example is to deduct the $1,200 increase in Inventory.

Prepaid Insurance Prepaid Insurance decreased from $125 to $75, which means that, of the $500 deducted as Insurance Expense on the income statement, $50 was not purchased this period. That means $50 was not a cash outflow this period. This $50 will have to be added back to net income because $500 was subtracted, but only $450 was actually paid in cash for insurance. So part of step 2 in this example is to add the $50 decrease in Prepaid Insurance.

Prepaid Rent Prepaid Rent is the next item on the balance sheet because we are looking at all current assets and current liabilities as part of step 2. Prepaid Rent started with a balance of $200 and ended with a balance of $400, indicating that all the Rent Expense of $1,000 for this period *plus* the $200 increase in Prepaid Rent had to be paid. Only $1,000 was deducted in the calculation of net income, so now we must deduct the additional $200—the increase in Prepaid Rent—from net income. So part of step 2 is to deduct the $200 increase in Prepaid Rent.

Accounts Payable Now, we are ready to look at the current liabilities. The first current liability is Accounts Payable, which began with a balance of $800 and ended with a balance of $500. That means the company paid down its Accounts Payable by $300 in addition to the cash paid for current period purchases. We'll have to subtract the decrease of $300 in Accounts Payable from net income as we convert net income from accrual to cash. So part of step 2 is to deduct the decrease of $300 in Accounts Payable.

Salaries Payable The next current liability is Salaries Payable, which began the period with a balance of $50 and ended with a balance of $150. The increase in Salaries Payable means that some of the Salaries Expense on the income statement wasn't paid but instead was booked to Salaries Payable. The increase of $100 will be added because the total expense of $3,000 was deducted to arrive at net income, but only $2,900 was actually paid in cash to employees. So part of step 2 in this example is to add the $100 increase in Salaries Payable.

Interest Payable The last current liability on the balance sheet is Interest Payable, which started with a balance of $150 and ends with a balance of $80. The decrease means that the company paid down the amount of interest it owes by $70. That's in addition to the interest expense of $200 that was deducted in the calculation of net income. We'll have to subtract the $70 decrease in Interest Payable from net income. So part of step 2 in this example is to deduct the $70 decrease in Interest Payable.

Summary of Steps in Preparing Cash from Operations—Indirect Method Exhibit 11.5 summarizes the procedures for adjusting net income for noncash items and for increases and decreases to current asset and current liability accounts. You may need to refer to this exhibit when you are learning how to prepare the statement of cash flows.

Exhibit 11.5

Indirect Method: Changing Net Income to Cash from Operations

What to Do	Example
Start with net income	Net Income
Add any noncash expenses	+ depreciation expense
Subtract any gains	− gain on the sale of equipment
Add back any losses	+ loss on the sale of equipment
Deduct an increase in a current asset	− increase in Accounts Receivable
	− increase in Prepaid Rent
Add a decrease in a current asset	+ decrease in Inventory
	+ decrease in Prepaid Insurance
Add an increase in a current liability	+ increase in Accounts Payable
	+ increase in Salaries Payable
Deduct a decrease in a current liability	− decrease in Income Taxes Payable
	− decrease in Accrued Liabilities

Exhibit 11.6

Statement of Cash Flows—Indirect Method

Yurman, Inc.
Partial Statement of Cash Flows
For the year ended December 31, 2007
(Indirect Method)

Net income	$9,225
+Depreciation expense	75
–Increase in accounts receivable	(100)
–Increase in inventory	(1,200)
+Decrease in prepaid insurance	50
–Increase in prepaid rent	(200)
–Decrease in accounts payable	(300)
+Increase in salaries payable	100
–Decrease in interest payable	(70)
Net cash from operating activities	$7,580

For our example, Exhibit 11.6 shows all the additions and subtractions used to prepare the cash from operating activities section of the statement of cash flows. The statement starts with net income and makes all the adjustments we discussed.

The net cash flow from operations is the same whether we prepare the statement by examining every cash transaction, as we did in previous chapters, or by using the *indirect method* shown in Exhibit 11.6.

 Can **YOU** do it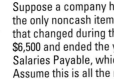

Suppose a company had net income of $50,000 for the year. Depreciation Expense, the only noncash item on the income statement, was $7,000. The only current asset that changed during the year was Accounts Receivable, which began the year at $6,500 and ended the year at $8,500. The only current liability that changed was Salaries Payable, which began the year at $2,500 and ended the year at $3,000. Assume this is all the relevant information. Calculate net cash from operating activities.

Answer Begin with net income and add back Depreciation Expense: $50,000 + $7,000 = $57,000. Then, subtract the $2,000 increase in Accounts Receivable. Sales on account were included in net income but should be deducted if the cash has not been collected. Next, add the $500 increase in Salaries Payable. Some of the salaries expense, which was deducted on the income statement, was not paid at the balance sheet date.

$50,000 + $7,000 – $2,000 + $500 = $55,500 Net Cash from Operating Activities

Cash Flows from Operating Activities— Direct Method[5]

LEARNING OBJECTIVE 5

Compute cash from operating activities using the direct method.

Let's examine the direct method for computing the cash from the operations section of the statement of cash flows. Although few companies prepare and present a statement of cash flows using the direct method, learning the method will help you understand how and why accrual-basis and cash-basis accounting differ.

[5]Note to instructor: This section can be omitted without any loss of continuity.

The direct method of computing cash flows from operations begins with an analysis of each amount on the income statement. Item by item, analyze every amount on the statement to determine how much cash was disbursed or collected related to that item. Look at the balance sheet at the beginning of the period and the balance sheet at the end of the period to find the information needed to change revenues into cash collected from customers and expenses into cash paid for expenses. Let's use a simple example to see how this works. We start at the beginning of the income statement, as shown in Exhibit 11.7, for the year and analyze each amount to change it from accrual to cash. We'll need to use the comparative balance sheets shown in Exhibit 11.8 to help.[6]

Changing revenues from accrual-basis to cash-basis

The only revenue account for Yurman is Sales. Sales on the income statement for the year ended December 31, 2007, amounted to $20,000. We need to know how much cash was collected from customers during the year. Generally, Accounts Receivable is the only balance sheet account we need to analyze to change the accrual amount for Sales on the income statement to the amount of cash sales for the statement of cash flows.

Accounts Receivable Start by observing how Accounts Receivable changed during the year. Yurman started the year with $150 in Accounts Receivable and ended the year with a $250 balance in Accounts Receivable. By comparing the balance sheet at the beginning of the year with the balance sheet at the end of the year, both shown in Exhibit 11.8, you can see Accounts Receivable increased by $100. The increase came from current sales that the customers purchased on account, and Yurman has not yet collected the cash.

Exhibit 11.7

Income Statement for Yurman

Yurman, Inc.
Income Statement
For the year ended December 31, 2007

Sales		$20,000
Cost of goods sold		6,000
Gross profit		14,000
Other expenses		
Rent expense	$ 1,000	
Salaries expense	3,000	
Insurance expense	500	
Interest expense	200	
Depreciation expense	75	4,775
Net income		$ 9,225

[6]Exhibits 7 and 8 are Exhibits 3 and 4 repeated here for easy reference. Also, your instructor may have asked you to omit the section on the indirect method of preparing a statement of cash flows, which contained those exhibits.

Exhibit 11.8

Comparative Balance Sheets for Yurman

Yurman, Inc.
Comparative Balance Sheets

	At December 31, 2006	At December 31, 2007
Assets		
Cash	$ 6,695	$18,275
Accounts receivable	150	250
Inventory	100	1,300
Prepaid insurance	125	75
Prepaid rent	200	400
Total current assets	7,270	20,300
Equipment (net of $150 and $225 accumulated depreciation)	3,850	4,775
Total assets	$11,120	$25,075
Liabilities and Shareholders' Equity		
Accounts payable	$ 800	$ 500
Salaries payable	50	150
Interest payable	150	80
Total current liabilities	1,000	730
Long-term notes payable	0	2,000
Shareholders' Equity		
Common stock and additional paid-in capital	5,000	8,000
Retained earnings	5,120	14,345
Total liabilities and shareholders' equity	$11,120	$25,075

You can use T-accounts to see how Accounts Receivable changed:

Accounts Receivable

Beginning balance	150		
Credit sales	20,000	?	Cash collected
Ending balance	250		

To balance the T-account, solve for the blank next to Cash collected:

$$\$150 + \$20,000 - \$250 = \$19,900$$

Here's the reasoning: the beginning balance in Accounts Receivable was $150. During the year, credit sales of $20,000 were made. That amount is from Sales on the income statement. The ending balance in Accounts Receivable is $250. So, the cash collected from customers must have been $19,900 (= $20,000 − $100 increase in Accounts Receivable).

Changing expenses from accrual basis to cash basis

Most firms have only one or two revenue accounts on their income statements, but they often have many expense accounts. Each one needs to be examined to determine how much of the amount shown is actually a cash outflow.

Cost of Goods Sold The next amount on the income statement is Cost of Goods Sold during the year of $6,000. How does that amount compare to the amount of cash paid to vendors during the year? Did the company sell anything it bought the previous month from the beginning inventory? Or, did the company buy more goods in 2007 than it actually sold in 2007? To answer these questions, we need to look at what happened in the Inventory account during the year. The beginning Inventory balance was $100. The ending Inventory balance was $1,300. That means Yurman bought enough merchandise to sell $6,000 worth *and* build up the Inventory balance by $1,200. So purchases must have been $7,200.

Now that we know how much inventory Yurman purchased during the year, we need to know if the company paid cash for it. To see how the purchase of $7,200 worth of inventory compares to the cash paid to vendors, look at the change in Accounts Payable (to vendors). The beginning balance in Accounts Payable was $800, and the ending balance was $500. That means the company must have paid $7,200 to vendors for the year's purchases *and* the $300 to reduce the balance in Accounts Payable. So the total paid to vendors was $7,500.

Here are the T-account entries for this computation. Start with Inventory and then move to Accounts Payable.

First, calculate the amount of purchases:

Inventory			
Beginning balance	100		
Purchases	?	6,000	Cost of goods sold
Ending balance	1,300		

Solve for the blank next to Purchases:
$100 + Purchases − $1,300 = $6,000
Purchases   = $7,200

Then, take the value for purchases ($7,200) and use it in the Accounts Payable account to find the amount paid to vendors. Here's the T-account for Accounts Payable:

Accounts Payable			
		800	Beginning balance
Cash paid to vendors	?		
		7,200	Purchases
		500	Ending balance

Solve for the blank next to Cash paid to vendors:
Cash paid to vendors = 800 + 7,200 − 500
Cash paid to vendors = 7,500

As you see, to translate Cost of Goods Sold on the income statement to cash paid to vendors on the statement of cash flows, you must analyze two accounts: Inventory and Accounts Payable.

Rent Expense The next expense on the income statement is $1,000 Rent Expense. How much cash was actually paid for rent? Follow along in the T-account shown on the next page. When a company pays in advance for rent, the payment is generally recorded as Prepaid Rent. Examining the change in Prepaid Rent will help us figure out how much cash was paid for rent during the month. Prepaid Rent started with a balance of $200 and ended with a balance of $400. The increase means that the company paid all of the current rent expense *and* must have paid an additional $200 to increase the balance in Prepaid Rent. That means the company paid a total of $1,200 cash for rent.

Study Tip

If there were any Rent Payable, we'd have to add the analysis of that account to our calculation of Cash Paid for Rent.

Prepaid Rent

Beginning balance	200		
Cash paid for rent	**A**	1,000	Rent expense
Ending balance	400		

A = Cash paid for rent = $1,200

Salaries Expense The next expense on the income statement is $3,000 Salaries Expense. The balance sheet account that we must analyze to find the cash paid to employees is Salaries Payable. The beginning balance in Salaries Payable was $50, and the ending balance was $150. You can think of that increase in Salaries Payable as the amount of current salaries expense that was not paid to employees during the period and that the company owes. So the cash paid to employees was $2,900.

Salaries Payable

Cash paid to employees **C**		50	Beginning balance
		3,000	Salaries expense
		150	Ending balance

C = Cash paid to employees = $2,900

Insurance Expense The next expense on the income statement is $500 Insurance Expense. The calculation of cash paid for insurance is like the calculation we just completed for Cash Paid for Rent. We look at the change in Prepaid Insurance. During the year, Prepaid Insurance started at $125 and ended at $75. That means the company used $50 worth of the Prepaid Insurance it started with—that's insurance expense that the company didn't have to pay for during this period. So, of the Insurance Expense, the company must have paid cash of $450.

Prepaid Insurance

Beginning balance	125		
Cash paid for insurance	**B**	500	Insurance expense
Ending balance	75		

B = Cash paid for insurance = $450

Interest Expense The next item on the income statement is $200 of Interest Expense. We analyze Interest Payable to determine how much interest the company paid. The amount the company owed for interest at the beginning of the year was $150 and only $80 at the end of the year. That means the company must have paid all of the current expense—$200—plus $70 to reduce the amount in Interest Payable. So, the total cash paid for interest was $270.

Interest Payable

Cash paid for interest **D**		150	Beginning balance
		200	Interest expense
		80	Ending balance

D = Cash paid for interest = $270

The last expense on the income statement is Depreciation Expense. Depreciation expense is a noncash expense, which means we don't have any cash outflow when we record depreciation expense. Any cash we might spend to buy equipment is considered an investing cash flow and does not affect Depreciation Expense. *Depreciation is one expense we can skip when we are preparing the cash flow from operations using the direct method.*

Suppose AJ Company's Inventory increased during the year by $5,000 and Accounts Payable decreased by $2,000. Cost of Goods Sold for the year was $37,600. How much cash was paid to vendors during the year?

Answer Purchases of Inventory were $37,600 + $5,000 = $42,600
All of them must have been paid for plus another $2,000 was paid to reduce Accounts Payable.
Total paid to vendors: $42,600 + $2,000 = $44,600

LEARNING OBJECTIVE 6
Compute cash from investing activities and cash from financing activities.

Cash from Investing and Financing Activities

When you've mastered the cash from operating activities section of the statement of cash flows, you've mastered the most difficult part of the statement of cash flows. Now let's turn our attention to the other two sections: cash from investing activities and cash from financing activities. No matter which method you use to prepare the statement of cash flows, the cash from investing activities and cash from financing activities sections are prepared the same way—by reviewing noncurrent balance sheet accounts. The primary amounts on the balance sheet to review for investing activities are Property, Plant, and Equipment and Other Long-term Assets. The accounts to review for financing activities are Long-term Notes Payable, Bonds Payable, Common Stock, and Retained Earnings (for the dividends).

Investing cash flows

Let's start with investing cash flows. In Exhibit 11.8, Yurman's balance sheet showed only one long-term asset: Equipment. The T-accounts below will help us analyze what happened in the Equipment account.

Equipment			Accumulated Depreciation	
Beginning balance	4,000	Disposal would have been here	150	Beginning balance
+ Equipment purchase	x		75	Depreciation expense
Ending balance	5,000		225	Ending balance

Separating the Equipment account from its Accumulated Depreciation account allows us to figure out if any equipment was sold. If any equipment had been sold, the Accumulated Depreciation account would not balance without a debit. However, in this case, the Accumulated Depreciation account balanced with only the year's Depreciation Expense, which came from the income statement, so no debits are needed to balance the Equipment account. We can solve for x in the Equipment T-account: The Equipment account started with $4,000 and ended the period with $5,000. The increase indicates that $x = \$1,000$. This is the company's only investing activity: the cash outflow of $1,000 for the purchase of new equipment.

Financing cash flows

For the financing section of the statement of cash flows, we need to include any principal payments on loans, any new capital contributions, such as newly issued stock, or dividends paid to the stockholders. Yurman has only one long-term liability, Long-term Notes Payable, and it increased by $2,000. This amount is a cash inflow because Yurman borrowed cash with a long-term note. In the shareholders' equity section, Common Stock and Additional Paid-in Capital (listed here as one amount for simplicity) increased by $3,000. That increase would have come from newly issued stock.

The last account to consider is Retained Earnings, which is where you find out if the company paid dividends this year. Let's look at the T-account for Retained Earnings:

Retained Earnings

This is where dividends would be if they had been declared.	5,120 Beginning balance
	9,225 Net income
	14,345 Ending balance

We know that the company did not declare any dividends because net income—$9,225—explained the entire change in Retained Earnings. That is, the account balances without a debit for Dividends.

Having done an analysis of long-term assets, long-term liabilities, and shareholders' equity, we are ready to prepare the complete statement of cash flows.

Can **YOU** do it?

Suppose Evans Company showed a gain of $500 on its income statement related to the sale of fixed assets. If the book value of the assets sold was $3,500, what was the cash inflow from the sale of the assets? Where would the cash inflow be shown on the statement of cash flows?

Answers Cash proceeds from the sale were $3,500 + $500 gain = $4,000. This amount will be shown as a cash inflow in the investing activities section of the statement of cash flows.

Putting It All Together to Prepare the Statement of Cash Flows

LEARNING OBJECTIVE 7

Prepare a complete statement of cash flows and know the required supplemental disclosures.

We've discussed how to prepare the three sections of the statement of cash flows. Now we are ready to prepare the complete statement.

Cash from operating, investing, and financing activities

To compute cash from operating activities using the indirect method, begin with net income. Adjust net income for any noncash items, and then adjust net income for any changes in current assets and current liabilities. To compute cash from operating activities with the direct method, examine each item on the income statement and convert it to a cash amount by referring to changes in the appropriate current assets and current liabilities.

To prepare the investing activities section, analyze the changes in long-term asset accounts like the Property, Plant, and Equipment accounts and their related Accumulated Depreciation accounts.

To prepare the financing activities section, analyze the changes in long-term debt and equity accounts. Although net income has been accounted for in the operating section, you will have to analyze changes in Retained Earnings to see if the company paid dividends. Dividend payment is a financing activity.

Exhibit 11.9 shows the complete statement of cash flows for Yurman for the year ended December 31, 2007. Notice that it explains exactly how the firm went from its beginning Cash balance of $6,695 to its ending Cash balance of $18,275. The panel on the right shows the statement of cash flows using the indirect method, and the panel on the left shows the statement using the direct method. Refer to the method you have used in class to prepare the statement.

Exhibit 11.9

Statements of Cash Flows

Yurman, Inc.
Statement of Cash Flows
(Direct Method)
For the year ended December 31, 2007

Cash from operating activities:

Cash collected from customers	$19,900
Cash paid to vendors	(7,500)
Cash paid to employees	(2,900)
Cash paid for rent	(1,200)
Cash paid for insurance	(450)
Cash paid for interest	(270)
Net cash from operating activities	$ 7,580

Cash from investing activities:

Purchase of equipment	(1,000)

Cash from financing activities

Proceeds from loan	2,000
Proceeds from issue of new stock	3,000
Net cash provided by financing activities	5,000

Net increase in cash	11,580
Add beginning cash balance	6,695
Ending cash balance	$18,275

Yurman, Inc.
Statement of Cash Flows
(Indirect Method)
For the year ended December 31, 2007

Cash from operating activities:

Net income	$ 9,225
+ Depreciation expense	75
− Increase in accounts receivable	(100)
− Increase in inventory	(1,200)
+ Decrease in prepaid insurance	50
− Increase in prepaid rent	(200)
− Decrease in accounts payable	(300)
+ Increase in salaries payable	100
− Decrease in interest payable	(70)
Net cash from operating activities	$ 7,580

Cash from investing activities:

Purchase of equipment	(1,000)

Cash from financing activities

Proceeds from loan	2,000
Proceeds from issue of new stock	3,000
Net cash provided by financing activities	5,000

Net increase in cash	11,580
Add beginning cash balance	6,695
Ending cash balance	$18,275

Only the cash from operating activities differs between the direct and indirect methods. The shaded portions are identical.

Study Tip

Cash related to interest—either an inflow or outflow—is categorized as cash from operating activities.

Supplementary disclosures

In addition to the main statement, there are three pieces of information that accompany a statement of cash flows: (1) noncash financing and investing activities, (2) cash paid for interest, and (3) cash paid for income taxes.

Suppose Yurman had purchased a piece of equipment with a note payable. No cash flows would be recorded in the company's records. The transaction would be a debit to the Equipment account and a credit to Notes Payable. Whenever a company engages in a significant financing or investing activity that skips the cash inflow and cash outflow steps, it must be disclosed on the statement of cash flows—even though the company never actually received or paid out any cash. The cash is considered *implicit* in the transaction. It's *as if* Yurman borrowed the cash with a notes payable and then spent the cash to buy the equipment. So you should see significant investing and financing transactions disclosed even though they are not included in the statement itself.

We can't see the specific amounts a firm pays for in interest and income taxes because those amounts are often part of subtotals and totals on the financial statements. When a firm uses the indirect method, these amounts must be disclosed separately on the statement of cash flows because the amounts are important to investors and financial analysts.

Wrapping up the statement of cash flows

Frequently, we get lost in calculations and lose sight of the big picture. The statement of cash flows explains what happened in the Cash account during the accounting period. It provides information about the cash that is being generated or used by operations, the cash being generated or used from investing activities, and the cash being generated or used from financing activities. Because the calculation of net income involves many more choices by managers, the statement of cash flows is more objective and subject to less manipulation than income. To complete the statement of cash flows, we add the beginning Cash balance from the balance sheet to the change in Cash. That gives us the ending Cash balance. So, the statement of cash flows explains the change in Cash from one balance sheet date to the next.

Look at The Home Depot's Statement of Cash Flows shown in Exhibit 11.10. First, notice the organization of the statement. The statement has the three

Exhibit 11.10

Adapted from the Consolidated Statements of Cash Flows

For the year ended January 30, 2005, the net decrease in Cash, $630 million, can be traced back to the comparative balance sheets for The Home Depot. At the beginning of the year, the Cash balance was $1,103 million. At the end of the year, the Cash balance was $506 million. The purpose of the statement of cash flows is to describe in detail this change in the Cash balance. Notice the supplementary disclosures provided after the statement.

> ### The Home Depot, Inc. and Subsidiaries
> ### Statement of Cash Flows (adapted)
> ### For the year ended January 30, 2005
> (in millions)

CASH FLOWS FROM OPERATING ACTIVITIES:	
Net Earnings	$5,001
Reconciliation of Net Earnings to Net Cash Provided by Operations:	
Depreciation and Amortization	1,319
Increase in Receivables	(266)
Increase in Merchandise Inventories	(849)
Increase in Accounts Payable and Accrued Liabilities	917
Increase in Deferred Revenue	263
Increase in Income Taxes Payable	2
Increase in Other Long-Term Liabilities	119
Other	398
Net Cash Provided by Operations	6,904
CASH FLOWS FROM INVESTING ACTIVITIES:	
Capital Expenditures, net of $38 of non-cash capital expenditures	(3,948)
Payments for Businesses Acquired, net	(727)
Proceeds from Sales of Property and Equipment	96
Purchases of Investments	(25,890)
Proceeds from Maturities of Investments	25,990
Net Cash Used in Investing Activities	(4,479)
CASH FLOWS FROM FINANCING ACTIVITIES:	
Proceeds from Long-Term Borrowings, net of discount	995
Repayments of Long-Term Debt	(510)
Repurchase of Common Stock	(3,106)
Proceeds from Sale of Common Stock, net	285
Cash Dividends Paid to Stockholders	(719)
Net Cash (Used in) Provided by Financing Activities	(3,055)
(Decrease) Increase in Cash and Cash Equivalents	(630)
*Effect of Exchange Rate Changes on Cash and Cash Equivalents	33
Cash and Cash Equivalents at Beginning of Year	1,103
Cash and Cash Equivalents at End of Year	$ 506
SUPPLEMENTAL DISCLOSURE OF CASH PAYMENTS MADE FOR:	
Interest, net of interest capitalized	78
Income taxes	$2,793

*This is something you have not covered in this text. You should have an idea about the meaning of everything else on this statement.

In Other Words:
Net Earnings is another expression for Net Income.

required parts: (1) cash provided by operating activities, (2) cash flows from investing activities, and (3) cash flows from financing activities. Second, notice the first section—cash provided by operating activities—is prepared using the indirect method. The statement starts with the amount for Net Earnings.

Then, there are several adjustments to that amount. Look at the adjustments in Exhibit 11.10 and see if you understand what information they provide. For example, Depreciation and Amortization are added back to net income to work toward cash from operating activities because the amount for depreciation and the amount for amortization were *subtracted* in the original computation of net income even though they were not *cash* expenditures. That subtraction is *undone* by adding the amounts back to net income. Investors are looking for a positive cash flow from operations because it is crucial for the continuing success of any business.

The cash flows from investing activities section of the statement shows capital expenditures as the first entry. Capital expenditure refers to the purchase of items like property, plant, and equipment. These are costs that have been capitalized by The Home Depot. Other entries in the cash flows from investing activities section include cash inflows and outflows related to the purchase and sale of assets *not* related to the normal operations of The Home Depot. The cash flows from investing activities section of the statement of cash flows gives information about the company's plans for the future. Investments in property, plant, and equipment may indicate an expansion or, at the very least, a concern about keeping the company's infrastructure up to date. Over time, a company's failure to invest in the infrastructure may lead to a problem with aging equipment and other long-term assets.

The cash flows from financing activities section of the statement of cash flows shows the cash flows related to the way the company is financed. You should recognize some of the items—proceeds from sale of stock and dividends paid. Other items are beyond the scope of an introductory course; however, all of them relate to The Home Depot's financing. This information on stock and dividends, when combined with the information on the balance sheet, gives the financial statement user a complete picture of the way the company is financing the business.

Accounting in the NEWS

Risk and Control

Financial Fitness—Better Get in Shape

Starting a new business requires a good product or service and a sound marketing plan. But many entrepreneurs don't pay enough attention to the financial aspects of their business, according to Bradley Feld, the managing director of a company that provides capital to start-up firms. And what is the first item on Feld's financial-fitness checklist? You guessed it—CASH.

Cash is king: No matter what, don't run out of money. Nothing else in this article matters if you run out of money. This means know your burn

rate (the net cash that is flowing out of your business each month) and be aware that your low cash point for any given month may not be at the end of the month. In other words, don't get caught making plans based on full-month figures only to find that you don't have enough money to pay your most important vendor on the 15th because customers won't be paying until the 30th.

Want to start a business? Show me the money—and make it cash!

Q What is a firm's "burn rate"?

A The amount of cash outflow each month.

Source: Bradley Feld, "The Entrepreneur's Financial-Fitness Checklist," *BusinessWeek Online*, March 24, 2004. Reprinted from the March 24 2004 issue of *BusinessWeek Online*, Copyright © 2004 by The McGraw-Hill Companies. Reprinted by permission.

Entrepreneurs spend years nurturing and building their businesses. Those that stay in business know how to control cash.

Following the calculation of the net change in cash for the year, Exhibit 11.10 shows the reconciliation from the year's beginning Cash balance to the year's ending Cash balance. Second, there is supplementary information disclosed on the cash paid for interest and the cash paid for taxes during the year, as required by GAAP.

No matter what form the statement of cash flows takes, the most important thing to remember is that a firm needs cash to survive. Why is cash important for new businesses? Read about it in *Accounting in the News*.

Financial Statement Analysis—Using Cash Flows to Evaluate Performance

LEARNING OBJECTIVE 8

Use the statement of cash flows to help evaluate a firm's past and future performance.

The statement of cash flows is a crucial part of the financial reporting for any company. Often, creditors and investors will look at this statement first when they are analyzing the financial condition of a firm. For managers of the firm, however, the statement of cash flows is important because it shows the firm's actual sources and uses of cash, which can be compared to the budgeted amounts.

Free cash flow

From the statement of cash flows, managers and analysts often calculate an amount called **free cash flow**. Free cash flow is defined as net cash flow from operations minus dividends and minus capital expenditures. This calculation gives a measure of a firm's ability to engage in long-term investment opportunities and a firm's financial flexibility. How important is free cash flow? Read about it in *Accounting in the News*.

> **Free cash flow:** Measures a firm's ability to engage in long-term investment opportunities; calculated as net cash flow from operations minus dividends and minus capital expenditures.
> Free Cash Flow = Net Cash from Operating Activities – Dividends – Capital Expenditures

Accounting in the NEWS

Financial Statement Analysis

Free Cash—We All Want Some

According to The Motley Fool,

Free cash flow is the lifeblood of a company, so it's surprising that analysts don't talk about it much more often.

"Free cash flow." That has the ring of something everyone should want. Break it down into its parts.

Free. Who can argue with free?

Cash. Ah, crisp new cash—a printed ticket to opportunity.

Flow: a consistent happening. Put it all together and what do you have?

A flow of free cash.

Great! Where do I sign up?

We celebrate free cash flow (FCF) all across The Motley Fool because it is the most important thing that a public company can accomplish. Lacking free cash flow, it's difficult for a business to pursue new opportunities, acquire other businesses, or pay dividends. When achieving free cash flow, a company is much more capable of those things plus paying down debt, saving cash for a rainy year, and building shareholders' equity.

There are a number of ways that analysts define free cash flows. The most common is the definition we studied in the chapter:

Free Cash Flow = Net Cash from Operating Activities – Cash Dividends – Capital Expenditures

Analysts and investors don't give the statement of cash flows the attention it deserves, according to *The Motley Fool*. By scrutinizing the elements of net cash from operations, a knowledgeable investor may be able to make adjustments that can make the calculation of free cash flow even more useful, like

Whether a business is new or well established, it needs to work hard to attract customers to buy its products and keep the business running.

removing unusual or nonrecurring amounts. When you get ready to invest, don't forget free cash flow. After all, who doesn't love cash?

Q Why does a company need a positive free cash flow?

A To take advantage of available opportunities.

Source: Jeff Fischer, "Joy of Free Cash Flow," *The Motley Fool*, February 28, 2002. From Permissions Dept: Copyright © 1995–2005 The Motley Fool, Inc. Reprinted by permission.

Exhibit 11.11

Calculation of Free Cash Flows for Home Depot

(in millions)	For the Year ended January 30, 2005
Net cash provided by operations (1)	$6,904
Net cash for capital expenditures (2)	(3,948)
Net cash for dividends (3)	(719)
Free cash flow (1) – (2) – (3)	$2,237

The statement of cash flows in Exhibit 11.10 on page 577 shows the amounts we need to calculate the free cash flow for The Home Depot for the fiscal year ended January 30, 2005. We will subtract cash for capital expenditures and cash for dividends from the net cash provided by operations. Exhibit 11.11 shows the calculation. The Home Depot's free cash flow of $2,237 million indicates that the firm has plenty of cash to pursue new opportunities. As with ratios, a number like free cash flow means more when you are able to compare it to that of other periods or other firms.

Although many ratios you've learned about up to this point have well-accepted definitions, ratio analysis is a flexible tool. Analysts make up ratios to gain insights into a company's past and future performance. There are several ratios from the statement of cash flows that provide information to help managers, lenders, and investors. We'll talk about two of them, but keep in mind that there are many more.

Cash flow adequacy ratio

Cash flow adequacy ratio: Measures the firm's ability to generate enough cash from operating activities to pay for its capital expenditures.

The **cash flow adequacy ratio** is defined as net cash from operating activities divided by net cash required for investing activities. The cash required for investing activities is the cash paid for capital expenditures and acquisitions minus the cash proceeds from the disposal of capital assets. As you can tell from its components, this ratio measures a firm's ability to generate the cash it needs for investing activities from its operations. Unlike the calculation for free cash flow, this ratio takes into account that a firm may generate significant cash from the sale of long-term assets. Using the data from The Home Depot's statement of cash flows in Exhibit 11.10, let's calculate the firm's cash flow adequacy ratio. The required amounts are shown in Exhibit 11.12. In the case of The Home Depot, the ratio doesn't provide much more information than the

Exhibit 11.12

Calculation of Cash Flow Adequacy Ratio for Home Depot

(dollars in millions)	For the Year ended January 30, 2005
Net cash provided by operations (1)	$6,904
Net cash for capital expenditures (2)	3,948
Net cash proceeds from sale of capital assets (3) . . .	(96)
Net cash required for investing activities (2 – 3)	$3,852
Cash flow adequacy ratio (1) ÷ (2 – 3)	1.79

measure of free cash flow because the firm did not generate a significant amount of cash from selling capital assets.

$$\text{Cash Flow Adequacy Ratio} = \frac{\text{Net Cash from Operating Activities}}{\text{Cash Outflow for Capital Expenditures} - \text{Cash Proceeds from Sale of Capital Assets}}$$

Cash needed to pay current liabilities

The **current cash debt coverage ratio** measures a firm's ability to generate the cash it needs in the short-run.

$$\text{Current Cash Debt Coverage Ratio} = \frac{\text{Net Cash Provided by Operations}}{\text{Average Current Liabilities}}$$

Current cash debt coverage ratio: A ratio that measures a firm's ability to generate the cash it needs in the short-run; calculated as net cash provided by operations divided by average current liabilities.

This ratio helps managers and analysts evaluate a firm's liquidity. Recall other measures of a firm's liquidity that you learned in earlier chapters—current ratio, quick ratio, and amount of working capital. The current cash debt coverage ratio also measures a firm's liquidity but in a very direct way. The cash a company can generate from its day-to-day operations is the cash available to meet its current obligations. Again using The Home Depot's statement of cash flows shown in Exhibit 11.10 plus the value for current liabilities from The Home Depot's annual balance sheets (not shown), we'll calculate the current cash debt coverage ratio for the fiscal year ended January 30, 2005. It is shown in Exhibit 11.13. For The Home Depot, this ratio is quite low. Logically, you would think that, like the current ratio,[7] the cash debt coverage ratio should be greater than one. After all, the information from the ratio is whether or not the firm generates enough cash from operations to pay the liabilities from operations (current liabilities).

Now that we have calculated The Home Depot's free cash flows and a ratio that helps determine the firm's ability to meet its current debt, how do you think The Home Depot is doing? The firm's free cash flow looks good, and the cash flow adequacy ratio is greater than one. However, the current cash debt coverage ratio may suggest a problem. The value of this ratio is less than one

Exhibit 11.13

Calculation of Current Cash Debt Coverage Ratio for Home Depot

(dollars in millions)	For the Year ended January 30, 2005
Net cash provided by operations (1)	$6,904
*Beginning current liabilities (2)	9,554
*Ending current liabilities (3)	10,529
Average current liabilities [(2)+(3)] ÷ 2 = (4)	$10,041.5
Net cash flow from operating activities divided by average current liabilities (1)÷(4)	**0.69**

*Values taken from The Home Depot's balance sheets

---

[7]You don't have The Home Depot's balance sheet, so you can't calculate the current ratio. It is 1.35, indicating that Home Depot will be able to meet its current obligations with current assets. If you were to look at The Home Depot's balance sheet, you would find that over 70% of the firm's current assets are in merchandise inventory.

for the most recent year, leaving open the possibility that Home Depot is not generating enough cash from operations to meet its current obligations. However, because The Home Depot generates so much cash on a daily basis, cash debt coverage ratio of less than 1 is probably quite adequate.

As you have learned by now, no single ratio allows you to come to any definite conclusions. For a conclusion you need to look at many ratios and several years of financial statements, as well as gather information about the firm's industry and business practices. You must always apply caution when interpreting ratios because financial statement analysis can be a complicated and difficult task.

Can **YOU** do it?

DRP Company reported net cash from operating activities of $45,600. Suppose the firm purchased $25,000 worth of new long-term assets and did not pay any dividends during the year. The firm's average current liabilities for the year were $40,000. What was the firm's free cash flow during the year?

Answer Free Cash Flow = Net Cash from Operations − Purchase of Long-term Assets − Dividends = $45,600 − $25,000 = $20,600

LEARNING OBJECTIVE 9

Identify the risk of investing in a given firm by using the statement of cash flows and the related controls.

Business risk, control, & ethics

In Chapter 7, you learned about the controls a company should have to minimize the risks associated with cash. Now let's talk about investors' risks associated with the statement of cash flows. A thorough analysis of the statement of cash flows is extremely important. Read about it in *Accounting in the News*.

The misleading financial statements that have been at the heart of such failures as Enron and WorldCom are the income statement and the balance sheet. Managers can rarely falsify cash inflows and outflows, so few people think of this statement as a place where the ethics of a firm's management could be tested. However, managers can manipulate the classification of the cash flows.

Because analysts are often looking for positive net cash flows from operations, especially in established companies, a firm's managers may feel some pressure to make sure that this part of the statement of cash flows is positive. There's an opportunity to engage in the same type of manipulation as WorldCom did when it classified

People of all ages need to be aware of the risks they face when investing in a company. Seniors need to be particularly cautious because they may not have enough working years left to recoup losses. Learning how to read an annual report helps investors track the health of a company.

expenses that belonged on the income statement as long-term assets on the balance sheet. Someone could misclassify cash outflows for operations as investing cash outflows. This changes the whole nature of such expenditures. Operating expenses are the costs of doing business, so investors want to see a low number. Investing cash outflows are often interpreted as a positive signal for future growth of the firm, so investors want to see a high number. There is a great deal of information in the statement of cash flows, and it deserves careful consideration when you are analyzing a firm's financial statements. As with the information provided by the other financial statements, the statement of cash flows provides reliable information only when the firm's management is ethical.

Accounting in the NEWS

Risk and Control

Look Out for Cash Burners

Look for cash burners . . . to find out if a firm may be going up in smoke. Investing in a firm that uses more cash than it makes may be a risk you don't want to take.

The statement of cash flows provides a great deal of information for financial analysis and could help you spot a cash burner. That's a firm that is using more cash than it is making. According to Harry Domash's WinningInvesting.com, cash flows analysis can help you spot companies that are candidates for bankruptcy. Here's an example of such a company: Consolidated Freightways Corporation. Before filing for Chapter 11 bankruptcy protection in 2002, the firm was the nation's third largest long-distance freight hauler. Founded in Portland, Oregon, in 1929, Consolidated Freightways shipped goods to more than 80 countries from the United States.

In July 2004, the firm filed a liquidation plan with the SEC.

Consolidated Freightways made headlines in 2002 when it filed for bankruptcy and ceased operations. According to news reports, Consolidated's shareholders were likely to lose their entire investment. We've heard a lot recently about investors being duped by accounting fraud. But Consolidated simply ran out of cash to pay its bills. Any investor with access to the Internet could have used its cash flow statements to determine that Consolidated was a risky business long before the firm filed for bankruptcy protection.

Consolidated was a cash burner in its last few years, meaning that it used more cash than it made. Because of the way accounting is done, it's possible for firms to appear profitable, but lose money on a cash basis. That is why many investors pay more attention to cash flows than to reported earnings.

When you are evaluating a firm as a potential investment, don't forget to do a thorough analysis of the statement of

In September 2002, Consolidated Freightways, a long-distance freight hauler, filed for Chapter 11 bankruptcy protection and laid off more than 15,000 workers.

cash flows. You want to keep your cash away from firms that are burning it!

Q Why is there an emphasis on cash flows?

A A firm can show a positive net income but be spending more cash than it is collecting. This is important information for investors.

Source: Winning Investing.com www.winninginvesting.com/ detecting_cash_burners, August 22, 2004. Reprinted by permission of Harry Domash. www.winninginvesting.com.

YOU make the call:

Does The Home Depot's statement of cash flows indicate that the company is in good financial shape?

Now that we've completed the analysis of The Home Depot's statement of cash flows, we have insight into the firm's financial condition. The firm's free cash flow is significant and is almost a billion dollars larger on the most recent statement of cash flows than it was just a year before, and the cash flow adequacy ratio is greater than one. The cash flow from operations does not cover the current liabilities, which could be a problem. It has, however, improved since last year.

By now, you know that you really can't come to a firm conclusion about the financial condition of The Home Depot or any other company by analyzing a single statement. That's why GAAP requires *four* statements. If you want to learn more about The Home Depot's financial condition, take a look at its income statement and balance sheet, available on the company's web site.

Let's Take a Test Drive

Real World Problem
The Home Depot

All companies must prepare a statement of cash flows as part of their annual financial statements, which means they must have accurate records with a lot of detailed information. The other financial statements do not provide the complete information that investors need to make evaluations of the company's past performance and future performance.

Concepts

The statement of cash flows has three parts: cash from operating activities, cash from investing activities, and cash from financing activities. Each provides information about a different activity of the firm. The first section, cash from operating activities, gives information about the ability of the firm to generate cash from its normal, day-to-day operations. You learned that many companies go bankrupt because they run out of cash. Young companies may not produce positive net cash flows from operations as they are getting established. However, after a company has operated for a few years, investors look for a positive net cash flow from operating activities.

Cash from investing activities is important because it indicates a firm's investment in the future. Young firms have net cash outflows from investing activities as they are getting their businesses established. Mature companies will not spend as much on long-term assets.

Cash from financing activities shows us the sources of a firm's financing. You can learn a great deal from examining how a firm obtains funding. In conjunction with the balance sheet, you can observe the extent of a firm's debt and equity financing and trends in the way a company is financed.

The Mechanics

Suppose The Home Depot provided you with the following comparative balance sheets and the related income statement. (Notice the most recent year is in the right column.) Assume The Home Depot did not purchase any PP&E during the year.

The Home Depot Comparative Balance Sheets (in millions)		
At	January 30, 2008	January 29, 2009
Assets		
Cash	$ 23,000	$ 39,200
Accounts receivable	12,000	23,450
Merchandise inventory	25,200	28,100
Prepaid rent	6,000	5,500
Property, plant, and equipment (PP&E)	79,500	70,000
Accumulated depreciation	(24,000)	(29,000)
Total assets	$121,700	$137,250
Liabilities and Shareholders' Equity		
Accounts payable	$ 12,300	$ 26,200
Income taxes payable	10,000	8,100
Long-term notes payable	39,700	25,800
Common stock and additional paid-in capital	18,500	20,000
Retained earnings	41,200	57,150
Total liabilities and shareholders' equity	$121,700	$137,250

Home Depot
Income Statement
For the year ended January 29, 2009
(in millions)

Sales		$234,900
Cost of goods sold		178,850
Gross margin		56,050
Selling expenses	$24,000	
General expense*	8,500	32,500
Income from operations		23,550
Interest expense		1,200
Income before income taxes		22,350
Income tax expense		3,400
Net income		$18,950

* includes rent expense of $2,000 and depreciation expense of $6,000

Instructions

Prepare a statement of cash flows. Your instructor will tell you whether to use the indirect method or the direct method. Solutions for each are provided. All amounts are in millions.

Solution

Direct Method

To prepare the operating section using the direct method, we'll go down the income statement and convert the accrual amounts to cash amounts by referring to the related current asset or current liability account.

1. Convert Sales to Cash collected from customers:

   Sales = $234,900

   Increase in Accounts Receivable (AR) from $12,000 to $23,450 = $11,450

   The increase in AR is the amount of sales Home Depot did NOT collect in cash, so the **cash collected from customers** is $234,900 − $11,450 = **$223,450**

   Accounts Receivable

Beginning balance	12,000		
Credit sales	234,900	223,450	Cash collected
Ending balance	23,450		

2. Convert cost of goods sold to cash paid to vendors: This takes two steps. First, convert cost of goods sold to total purchases:

   Cost of goods sold = $178,850

   Increase in inventory from $25,200 to $28,100 = $2,900 of additional purchases

   The increase in inventory is added to the cost of goods sold to get total purchases = $178,850 + $2,900 = $181,750 for total purchases.

   Then, convert total purchases to cash paid to vendors:

   Total purchases = $181,750

   Increase in Accounts Payable of $12,300 to $26,200 = $13,900 represent purchases that did not get paid for, so **cash paid to vendors** = $181,750 − $13,900 = **$167,850**

   In the T-account, solve for purchases:

   Inventory

Beginning balance	25,200		
Purchases	181,750	178,850	Cost of goods sold
Ending balance	28,100		

   Then, take the value for purchases (181,750) and use it in the Accounts Payable account to find the amount of cash paid to vendors:

   Accounts Payable

		12,300	Beginning balance
Cash paid to vendors	167,850	181,750	Purchases
		26,200	Ending balance

3. Convert Selling Expenses to Cash: Because there are no current assets or current liabilities related to Selling Expenses (like Accrued Selling Expenses), Home Depot must have paid cash for this entire amount. So **cash paid for selling expenses = $24,000.**

4. Convert General Expenses to cash:

General Expenses = $8,500. This includes $2,000 Rent Expense and $6,000 Depreciation. So we could break down the General Expenses as follows:

Rent Expense	$2,000
Depreciation Expenses	$6,000
Other Expenses	$ 500

First, Rent Expense is related to Prepaid Rent on the balance sheet. Prepaid Rent decreased from $6,000 to $5,500. This means the company used rent it had already (last year) paid for, so the decrease in Prepaid Rent reduces the Rent Expense by $500 to get **cash paid for rent =** $2,000 − 500 = **$1,500**

Prepaid Rent

Beginning balance	6,000		
Cash paid for rent	1,500	2,000	Rent expense
Ending balance	5,500		

Depreciation Expense is a noncash expense, so there is no cash flow associated with it. Other expenses of $500 must have been all cash because there are no associated current assets or current liabilities on the balance sheet.

So the total **cash paid for General Expenses** = $1,500 + $500 = **$2,000.**

5. Change Interest Expense to cash paid for interest:

Interest Expense = $1,200

This must have been all cash because there were no current assets or current liabilities associated with it.

Cash paid for interest = $1,200

6. Change Income Tax Expense to cash paid for taxes:

Income Tax Expense = $3,400

Decrease in Income Taxes Payable from $10,000 to 8,100 = 1,900, which represents additional taxes the company paid beyond the Income Tax Expense on the income statement.

Cash paid for income taxes = $3,400 + $1,900 = **$5,300**

Income Taxes Payable

		10,000	Beginning balance
Cash paid for income taxes	5,300	3,400	Income tax expense
		8,100	Ending balance

We have now converted all the income statement items to cash inflows and outflows and are ready to prepare the first part of the statement of cash flows.

Cash from Operating Activities (in millions)	
Cash collected from customers	$223,450
Cash paid to vendors	(167,850)
Cash paid for selling expenses	(24,000)
Cash paid for general expenses	(2,000)
Cash paid for interest	(1,200)
Cash paid for income taxes	(5,300)
Net cash provided by operations	**$ 23,100**

7. Next, calculate cash from investing activities. An analysis of long-term assets shows that Property, Plant, and Equipment decreased by $9,500. A decrease is caused by disposing of assets. Because the income statement showed no gain or loss from disposal of long-term assets, the assets must have been sold for book value. The Property, Plant, and Equipment account decreased by $9,500 (the cost of the PPE sold) and the Accumulated Depreciation account increased by $5,000. Recall from the income statement that Depreciation Expense for the year was $6,000. If Accumulated Depreciation only increased by $5,000, then $1,000 must have been subtracted. That means the PPE sold had a book value of $8,500 (= $9,500 – $1,000). Because there was no gain or loss on the disposal, the company must have received proceeds equal to the book value. So proceeds from **disposal of PPE was an investing cash inflow of $8,500.**

Property, Plant, and Equipment (PPE)

Beginning balance	79,500		
No PPE purchases		9,500	Cost of PPE sold
Ending balance	70,000		

Accumulated Depreciation

		24,000	Beginning balance
Sale of PPE	1,000	6,000	Depreciation expense
		29,000	Ending balance

To calculate the cash flows from financing activities, we analyze what happened in the long-term liability accounts and the shareholders' equity accounts. Long-term Notes Payable decreased from $39,700 to $25,800. That must have been a **cash outflow of $13,900.** Common Stock and Additional Paid-in Capital increased by $1,500. That must have been **a cash inflow from the issue of stock of $1,500.** Lastly, we need to see if the company paid any dividends during the year. Retained Earnings increased from $41,200 to $57,150 = $15,950. How does that compare to net income? Net income was $18,950 but Retained Earnings only increased by $15,950, so **$3,000 must have been paid as dividends.**

We are now ready to put the whole statement together using the direct method:

The Home Depot
Statement of Cash Flows—Direct method
For the year ended January 29, 2009
(in millions)

Cash from operating activities		
Cash collected from customers	$223,450	
Cash paid to vendors	(167,850)	
Cash paid for selling expenses	(24,000)	
Cash paid for general expenses	(2,000)	
Cash paid for interest	(1,200)	
Cash paid for income taxes	(5,300)	
Net cash provided by operations		$23,100
Cash from investing activities		
Cash proceeds from sale of asset		8,500
Cash from financing activities		
Cash paid on loan principal	$(13,900)	
Cash proceeds from stock issue	1,500	
Cash paid for dividends	(3,000)	
Net cash used for financing activities		(15,400)
Increase in cash during the year		$16,200
Cash balance, beginning of the year		23,000
Ending cash balance		$39,200

Indirect Method

To prepare the statement using the indirect method, we start with net income. We must adjust it for any noncash expenses and the change in every current asset and every current liability. The other two sections—cash from investing activities and cash from financing activities—are the same as we prepared for the direct method.

The Home Depot
Statement for Cash Flows—Indirect method
For the year ended January 29, 2009
(in millions)

Cash from operating activities		
Net income	$ 18,950	
Add back depreciation expense	6,000	
Deduct the increase in AR	(11,450)	
Deduct the increase in inventory	(2,900)	
Add decrease in prepaid rent	500	
Add increase in accounts payable	13,900	
Deduct decrease in income taxes payable	(1,900)	
Cash provided by operatimg activities		$23,100
Cash from investing activities		
Cash proceeds from asset disposal		8,500
Cash from financing activities		
Cash paid on loan principal	$(13,900)	
Cash proceeds from stock issue	1,500	
Cash paid for dividends	(3,000)	
Net cash used for financing activities		(15,400)
Net increase in cash during the year		$16,200
Cash balance, beginning of the year		23,000
Ending cash balance		$39,200

Rapid Review

1. **Categorize cash flows as operating, investing, or financing cash flows.** *Operating cash flows* are cash firms spend on everyday operations such as sales, cash paid for inventory, and cash paid for other operating expenses. *Investing cash flows* are cash that firms spend on long-term assets. *Financing cash flows* are the firm's sources of capital—debt and equity—and the payment made to creditors and owners. Interest is always considered an operating cash flow.

2. **Explain the difference between accrual-basis and cash-basis accounting.** Accrual amounts from the income statement are not necessarily cash. They can be converted to cash by examining the current asset or current liability account(s) related to the income statement item. For example, to convert Sales to cash collected from customers, you must examine the change in Accounts Receivable.

3. **Explain the difference between the two methods of preparing and presenting the statement of cash flows.** Using the *direct method*, each cash flow from operating activities is calculated individually by converting each income statement amount to its cash amount. Using the indirect method, cash from operating activities is calculated by starting with net income and making adjustments to convert it to cash from operating activities.

4. **Compute cash from operating activities using the indirect method.** To use the *indirect method*, start with net income and adjust it for noncash items like gains, losses, and depreciation expense. Then, make adjustments for all of the changes in current assets and current liabilities that occurred during the year (except Dividends Payable, which would be related to a financing cash flow). Here is a summary of the adjustments for current assets and current liabilities that must be made when using the indirect method (from Exhibit 11.5):

Increase in a current asset	– from Net Income
Decrease in a current asset	+ to Net Income
Increase in a current liability	+ to Net Income
Decrease in a current liability	– from Net Income

5. **Compute cash from operating activities using the direct method.** To use the direct method, convert every number on the income statement to a cash amount. Make sure all the changes in current assets and current liabilities have been accounted for.

6. **Compute cash from investing activities and cash from financing activities.** Compute cash from investing activities by examining changes in long-term asset accounts, and compute cash from financing activities by examining long-term liability accounts and equity accounts.

7. **Prepare a complete statement of cash flows and know the supplemental disclosures.** After you compute the net cash flows from operating activities, investing activities, and financing activities, preparing the statement is easy!

8. **Use the statement of cash flows to help evaluate a firm's past and future performance.** The following are examples of cash flow amounts that provide insight into a firm's financial condition: *free cash flow, cash flow adequacy ratio,* and the *current cash debt coverage ratio.*

> Cash Flow Adequacy Ratio =
> $$\frac{\text{Net Cash from Operating Activities}}{\substack{\text{Cash Outflow for Capital Expenditures} - \\ \text{Cash Proceeds from Sale} \\ \text{of Long-Term Capital Assets}}}$$

> Current Cash Debt Coverage Ratio =
> $$\frac{\text{Net Cash Provided by Operations}}{\text{Average Current Liabilities}}$$

9. **Identify the risk of investing in a given firm by using the statement of cash flows and the related controls.** Before you invest in a firm, look at its statement of cash flows. A growing or established firm should be generating positive cash flows from operations. Investing cash flows may provide insights into the firm's plans for the future. Be sure to look at the firm's cash situation over several years and also compare the firm's sources and uses of cash to those of the competitors.

> Free Cash Flow = Net Cash from Operating Activities – Dividends – Capital Expenditures

Key Terms

Cash flow adequacy ratio, p. 580

Cash from financing activities, p. 560

Cash from investing activities, p. 560

Cash from operating activities, p. 560

Current cash debt coverage ratio, p. 581

Direct method, p. 564

Free cash flow, p. 579

Indirect method, p. 564

Have You Increased Your Business IQ?

Answer these questions to find out.

1. The statement of cash flows has three sections, which are
   a. current, long-term, and permanent.
   b. assets, liabilities, and equity.
   c. operating activities, investing activities, and financing activities.
   d. operations, earnings before interest and taxes, net income.

2. Depreciation is included on the statement of cash flows using the indirect method because
   a. it was subtracted in the calculation of net income so it is added back to nullify the effect on cash flows.
   b. the purchase of the asset is reflected in depreciation, so a portion is included in the statement of cash flows each year the asset is used.
   c. it is a cash expense.
   d. it must be an error and should not be on the statement.

3. Dividends are considered a cash flow from
   a. operating activities.
   b. assets.
   c. financing activities.
   d. investing activities.

4. Cash from the sale of long-term assets would appear in which section of the statement of cash flows?
   a. Operating
   b. Financing
   c. Investing
   d. It would not be on this financial statement
5. Which method of preparing the statement of cash flows is most often used?
   a. Direct method
   b. Indirect method
   c. Specific tracing of each cash transaction
   d. All are used by about the same number of firms

Now, check your answers.

1. c   2. a   3. c   4. c   5. b

- If you answered all five questions correctly, you've increased your business IQ by studying this chapter. It doesn't mean you've mastered all of the accounting concepts in the chapter. It simply means that you understand some of the general business concepts presented in this chapter.
- If you answered 2 to 4 questions correctly, you've made some progress but your business IQ has plenty of room to grow. You might want to skim over the chapter again.
- If you answered 0 or 1 question correctly, you can do more to improve your business IQ. Better study the chapter again.

Questions

1. What is the purpose of the statement of cash flows?
2. Which two financial statements are required to prepare the statement of cash flows?
3. Describe the three categories of cash flows that explain the total change in cash for the year.
4. Why is the statement of cash flows so important?
5. Can you think of a way that modern technology could make it easy to prepare a statement of cash flows?
6. What are the two traditional approaches for preparing and presenting the statement of cash flows? What is the difference between these two approaches?
7. Which types of business transactions would result in cash from operating activities? Give three examples of transactions that would be classified as cash flows from operations.
8. Which types of business transactions would result in cash flows from investing activities? Give three examples of transactions that would be classified as cash flows from investing activities.
9. Which types of business transactions would result in cash flows from financing activities? Give three examples of transactions that would be classified as cash flows from financing activities.
10. How is depreciation expense treated when using the direct method of preparing the statement of cash flows? When using the indirect method?
11. Which general ledger account(s) must be analyzed to determine the cash collected from customers? How is this cash flow classified?
12. Which general ledger account(s) must be analyzed to determine the proceeds from the sale of a building? How is this cash flow classified?
13. Which general ledger account(s) must be analyzed to determine the cash paid to vendors? How is this cash flow classified?
14. Which general ledger account(s) must be analyzed to determine the cash paid for dividends? How is this cash flow classified?
15. How is interest collected or interest paid classified on the statement of cash flows?
16. Define free cash flow and explain what this amount indicates about a firm.
17. Define the cash flow adequacy ratio and explain what this ratio measures.
18. How might a firm misstate the statement of cash flows to give investors a better impression of the firm's operations?

Multiple Choice

Use the following information to answer Questions 1–3.

Quality Products engaged in the following cash transactions during May:

Cash paid for inventory	$ 5,000
Cash proceeds from loan	7,000
Cash paid for interest	400
Cash collected from customers	26,500
Cash proceeds from new stock issued	25,000
Salaries paid to employees	4,600
Purchase of new delivery van	20,000

1. How much is total cash from financing activities?
   a. $7,000
   b. $25,000
   c. $31,600
   d. $32,000
2. How much is total cash from investing activities?
   a. $(20,000) (outflow)
   b. $(25,000) (outflow)
   c. $25,000
   d. $32,000
3. How much is total cash from operating activities?
   a. $26,500
   b. $(3,500) (outflow)
   c. $16,500
   d. $16,900
4. Cash from the sale of treasury stock
   a. Would not be included in the statement of cash flows.
   b. Would be classified as a contra-equity cash flow.
   c. Would be classified as an investing cash flow.
   d. Would be classified as a financing cash flow.
5. The cash proceeds from the sale of a building will be
   a. The cost of the building.
   b. The book value of the building.
   c. The book value plus any gain or minus any loss.
   d. Shown on the financing portion of the appropriate financial statement.
6. If a firm has investing cash inflows of $5,000, financing cash inflows of $24,000, and a net cash inflow for the year of $12,000, how much is cash from operating activities?
   a. Net cash inflow of $17,000
   b. Net cash inflow of $29,000
   c. Net cash outflow of $17,000
   d. Net cash outflow of $19,000

7. Depreciation for the year was $50,000 and net income was $139,500. If the company used cash for all transactions except those related to long-term assets, how much was cash from operating activities?
   a. $139,500
   b. $189,500
   c. $89,500
   d. Cannot be determined from the given information

Use the following information to answer Questions 8–10.

The income statement and additional data for Frances Company for the year ended December 31, 2006 follows.

Sales Revenue	$400,000
Cost of Goods Sold	$165,000
Salary Expense	$ 70,000
Depreciation Expense	$ 55,000
Insurance Expense	$ 20,000
Interest Expense	$ 10,000
Income Tax Expense	$ 18,000
Net Income	$ 62,000

Accounts Receivable decreased by $12,000. Inventories increased by $6,000 and Accounts Payable decreased by $2,000. Salaries Payable increased by $8,000. Prepaid Insurance increased by $4,000. Interest Expense and Income Tax Expense equal their cash amounts. Frances Company uses the direct method for its statement of cash flows.

8. How much cash did Frances Company collect from customers during 2006?
   a. $400,000
   b. $412,000
   c. $406,000
   d. $388,000
9. How much cash did Frances Company pay its suppliers during 2006?
   a. $173,000
   b. $165,000
   c. $167,000
   d. $163,000
10. How much cash did Frances Company pay for insurance during the year?
    a. $20,000
    b. $24,000
    c. $16,000
    d. $48,000

Short Exercises

LO 1   **SE11-1. Identify cash flows.**
Given the following cash transactions, classify each as a cash flow from: (a) operating activities, (b) investing activities, or (c) financing activities:

    a. payment to employees for work done
    b. dividends paid to shareholders
    c. payment for new equipment
    d. payment to supplier for inventory
    e. interest payment to the bank related to a loan

LO 1   **SE11-2. Identify cash flows.**
Given the following cash transactions, classify each as a cash flow from: (a) operating activities, (b) investing activities, or (c) financing activities:

    a. Principal payment to the bank for a loan
    b. Collection from customers to whom sales were previously made on account
    c. Collection from customers for cash sales
    d. Collection for sale of land that had been purchased as a possible factory site
    e. Petty cash used to pay for doughnuts for staff

LO 2   **SE11-3. Calculate and identify cash flows.**
College Television Company had Supplies on its balance sheet at December 31, 2006 of $20,000. The income statement for 2007 showed Supplies Expense of $50,000. The balance sheet at December 31, 2007 showed Supplies of $25,000. If no supplies were purchased on account (all were cash purchases), how much cash did College Television Company spend on supplies during 2007? How would that cash outflow be classified on the statement of cash flows? Show the transactions in the Supplies T-account.

LO 2   **SE11-4. Calculate and identify cash flows.**
Jill Corporation reported credit sales of $950,000 for 2006. Jill's accounts receivable from sales were $40,000 at the beginning of 2006 and $50,000 at the end of 2006. What was the amount of cash from sales collected in 2006? How would the cash from this transaction show up on the statement of cash flows? Use the Accounts Receivable T-account to find the answer.

LO 4   **SE11-5. Evaluate adjustments to net income using indirect method.**
The income statement for Lilly's Company for the year ended June 30, 2008 showed Sales of $50,000. During the year, the balance in Accounts Receivable increased by $7,500. What adjustment to net income would be shown in the operating section of the statement of cash flows prepared using the indirect method related to this information? How much cash was collected from customers during the fiscal year ended June 30, 2008?

LO 4   **SE11-6. Evaluate adjustments to net income using indirect method.**
The income statement for Sharp Company for the month of May showed Insurance Expense of $250. The beginning and ending balance sheets for the month showed an increase of $50 in Prepaid Insurance. There were no payables related to insurance on the balance sheet. What adjustment to net income would be shown in the operating section of the statement of cash flows prepared using the indirect method related to this information? How much cash was paid for insurance during the month?

LO 4   **SE11-7. Evaluate adjustments to net income using indirect method.**
During 2005, Cable Direct incurred Salary Expense of $37,500, as shown on the income statement. The January 1, 2005 balance sheet showed Salaries Payable of $10,450; and the December 31, 2005 balance sheet showed Salaries Payable of $15,200. What adjustment to net income would be shown in the operating section of the statement of cash flows prepared using the indirect method related to this information? How much cash was paid to employees (for salary) during 2005?

SE11-8. **Evaluate adjustments to net income using indirect method.**   LO 4

Havelen's Road Paving Company had Depreciation Expense of $43,000 on the income statement for the year. How would this expense be shown on the statement of cash flows prepared using the indirect method? Why?

SE11-9. **Calculate and identify cash flows using indirect method.**   LO 4

Beta Company spent $40,000 for a new delivery truck during the year. Depreciation Expense of $2,000 related to the truck was shown on the income statement. How are the purchase of the truck and the related depreciation reflected on the statement of cash flows prepared using the indirect method?

SE11-10. **Evaluate adjustments to net income under indirect method.**   LO 4

B&W reported Net Income of $1.2 million in 2006. Depreciation for the year was $120,000, Accounts Receivable increased $728,000, and Accounts Payable decreased $420,000. Compute net cash provided by operating activities using the indirect approach.

SE11-11. **Evaluate adjustments to net income under indirect method.**   LO 4

In 2007, Jewels Company had net income of $350,000. The depreciation on plant assets during 2007 was $73,000, and the company incurred a loss on the sale of plant assets of $20,000. Compute net cash provided by operating activities under the indirect method.

SE11-12. **Evaluate adjustments to net income under indirect method.**   LO 4

The comparative balance sheets for JayCee Company showed the following changes in current asset accounts: Accounts Receivable decreased by $50,000, Prepaid Expenses decreased by $23,000, and Merchandise Inventory increased by $17,000. These were all the changes in the current assets and current liability accounts (except Cash). Net income for the year was $275,500. Compute net cash provided by operating activities using the indirect method.

SE11-13. **Calculate and identify cash flows using direct method.**   LO 5

Sales for 2005 were $50,000; Cost of Goods Sold was $35,000. If Accounts Receivable increased by $2,000, Inventory decreased by $1,300, Accounts Payable decreased by $2,000, and Other Accrued Liabilities decreased by $1,000, how much cash was paid to vendors/suppliers during the year? How would the cash from this transaction show up on the statement of cash flows?

SE11-14. **Calculate and identify cash flows using direct method.**   LO 5

During 2007, Cameron Company had $300,000 in cash sales and $3,500,000 in credit sales. The Accounts Receivable balances were $450,000 and $530,000 at December 31, 2006 and 2007, respectively. What was the total cash collected from all customers during 2007? How would the cash from this transaction show up on the statement of cash flows? Use the Accounts Receivable T-account to find the answer.

SE11-15. **Calculate and identify cash flows.**   LO 6

C & S Supply had $125,000 of Retained Earnings at the beginning of the year and a balance of $150,000 at the end of the year. Net income for the year was $80,000. What transaction occurred to cause the decrease in Retained Earnings? How would this decrease be shown on the statement of cash flows?

SE11-16. **Calculate and identify cash flows.**   LO 6

A building cost $55,000 and had accumulated depreciation of $15,000 when it was sold for a gain of $5,000. It was a cash sale. How would the cash from this transaction show up on the statement of cash flows? Show the transaction in the T-accounts for Building and Accumulated Depreciation.

LO 8. 9 **SE11-17. Use statement of cash flows for decision-making.**
If you were interested in investing in a company, what item(s) on the statement of cash flows would be of most interest to you? Why?

LO 8. 9 **SE11-18. Risk and control.**
If you were an investor, why would you look at the statement of cash flows? Which amounts would provide information about the risk to an investor?

LO 9 **SE11-19. Risk and control.**
If you believe there is a risk that a firm is not taking advantage of long-term investment opportunities, how would the statement of cash flows help you confirm or disconfirm this belief?

Exercise Set A

LO 1 **E11-1A. Identify cash flows.**
For each of the following items, tell whether it is a cash inflow or cash outflow and the section of the statement of cash flows in which the item would appear.

Item	Inflow or Outflow	Section of the Statement
a. Cash collected from customers		
b. Proceeds from issue of stock		
c. Interest payment on loan		
d. Principal repayment on loan		
e. Cash paid for advertising		
f. Proceeds from sale of treasury stock		
g. Money borrowed from the local bank		
h. Cash paid to employees (salaries)		
i. Purchase of equipment		
j. Cash paid to vendors for inventory		
k. Taxes paid		

LO 1. 5 **E11-2A. Identify cash flows.**
For each transaction, indicate the amount of the cash flow, give the section of the statement in which each cash flow would appear, indicate whether each results in an inflow or outflow of cash. Assume the statement of cash flows is prepared using the direct method.

Amount	Inflow or Outflow	Section of the Statement
a. Issued 100 shares of $2 par common stock for $12 per share.		
b. Borrowed $5,000 from a local bank to expand the business.		
c. Purchased $700 of supplies for $400 cash and the balance on account.		
d. Hired a carpenter to build some bookcases for the office for $500 cash.		
e. Earned revenue of $9,000 receiving $7,000 cash and the balance on account.		
f. Hired a student to do some typing and paid him $300 cash.		
g. Repaid $1,000 of the bank loan along with $150 interest.		
h. Paid dividends of $400.		

LO 5 **E11-3A. Prepare operating section of statement of cash flows using the direct method.**
Use the income statement for Clark Corporation for last year and the information from the comparative balance sheets shown for the beginning and the end of the year to prepare the operating section of the statement of cash flows using the direct method.

Sales		$100,000
Cost of goods sold		35,000
Gross margin		65,000
Operating expenses		
Wages	$2,500	
Rent	1,200	
Utilities	980	
Insurance	320	5,000
Net Income		$ 60,000

Account	Beginning of the Year	End of the Year
Accounts receivable	$10,000	$12,000
Inventory	21,000	18,500
Prepaid insurance	575	400
Accounts payable	9,000	10,400
Wages payable	850	600
Utilities payable	150	-0-
Prepaid Rent	-0-	-0-

E11-4A. Prepare operating section of statement of cash flows using the indirect method.   LO 4

Use the information from E11-3A to prepare the operating section of the statement of cash flows using the indirect method. Then, compare it with the statement you prepared for E11-3A. What are the similarities? What are the differences? Which statement do you find most informative?

E11-5A. Calculate change in cash.   LO 1, 5

Given the following information, calculate the change in cash for the year.

Cash received from sale of equipment	$ 20,000
Cash paid for salaries	8,250
Depreciation expense for the year	12,450
Cash received from issue of stock	150,000
Cash collected from customers	87,900
Cash received from sale of land	14,500
Cash paid for operating expenses	2,000
Cash paid to vendor for inventory	32,480

E11-6A. Calculate operating cash flows.   LO 2, 5

Use T-accounts and the information given for Sharp Company to calculate:

a. Cash paid for salaries
b. Cash paid for income taxes
c. Cash paid for inventory items
d. Cash collected from customers

From the financial statements for Sharp Company:	Income Statement Amount for the Year	Beginning of the Year	End of the Year
Sales revenue	$95,600		
Accounts receivable		$8,700	$10,000
Salaries expense	31,400		
Salaries payable		2,300	2,100
Cost of goods sold	24,300		
Inventory		4,800	9,000
Accounts payable		2,500	3,000
Income tax expense	28,500		
Income taxes payable		7,400	8,200

E11-7A. Prepare operating section of statement of cash flows and determine the method used.   LO 2, 5

Use the information from E11-6A to calculate the cash flow from operations for Sharp Company. Based on the information provided, which method of preparing the statement of cash flows does Sharp use?

LO 1, 6   **E11-8A. Calculate cash flows from investing and financing activities.**

The following events occurred at Gadgets during 2006:

January 15	Issued bonds for $250,000.
March 8	Purchased new machinery for $80,000.
May 10	Sold old machinery for $30,000, resulting in a $10,000 loss.
July 14	Paid interest of $20,000 on the bonds.
September 25	Borrowed $5,000 from a local bank.
October 30	Purchased a new computer for $3,000.
December 31	Paid cash dividends of $4,600.

Compute Gadgets' net cash flow from (1) investing activities and from (2) financing activities for 2006.

LO 1, 5   **E11-9A. Calculate operating cash flows using the direct method.**

The following information applies to Computer Company:
Income Statement for the year ended December 31, 2007

Sales	$ 20,000
Cost of goods sold	(15,200)
Gross profit	4,800
Rent expense	(1,000)
Net income	$ 3,800

1. Accounts Receivable started the year with a balance of $1,000 and ended the year with a balance of $3,300.
2. The beginning balance in Accounts Payable (to vendors) was $2,000, and the ending balance was zero. Inventory at the end of the year was the same as it was at the beginning of the year.
3. The company started the year with $5,000 of Prepaid Rent, and ended the year with $4,000 of Prepaid Rent.

Use T-accounts to determine the following cash flows:

a. Cash collected from customers for sales during the year
b. Cash paid to vendors for inventory during the year
c. Cash paid for rent during the year

LO 4   **E11-10A. Calculate operating cash flows using the indirect method.**

Brass Company reported net income of $290,000 for 2007. The company also reported Depreciation Expense of $70,000 and a gain of $3,000 on the sale of equipment. The comparative balance sheet shows a decrease in Accounts Receivable of $8,000 for the year, a $5,000 decrease in Accounts Payable, and a $1,700 increase in Prepaid Insurance. Prepare the cash from operating activities section of the statement of cash flows for 2007 using the indirect method.

LO 4   **E11-11A. Calculate operating cash flows using the indirect method.**

The following information has been taken from Tram's balance sheets at December 31, 2005, and 2006. Prepare the net cash from operating activities section of the company's statement of cash flows for the year ended December 31, 2006, using the indirect method.

	At December 31,	
	2006	**2005**
Current assets		
Cash	$103,000	$ 99,000
Accounts receivable	90,000	79,000
Inventory	150,000	142,000
Prepaid expenses	47,000	50,000
Total current assets	$390,000	$370,000
Current liabilities		
Accrued expenses	$ 17,000	$ 15,000
Accounts payable	60,000	92,000
Total current liabilities	$ 77,000	$107,000

Net Income for the year ended December 31, 2006 was $185,000. Depreciation
Expense was $25,000.

E11-12A. Calculate operating cash flows using the direct LO 5
method.
Compton Company completed its first year of operations on December 31, 2006. The
firm's income statement for the year showed Revenues of $175,000 and Operating
Expenses of $84,000. The balance in Accounts Receivable was $54,000 at year-end and
payables related to operating expense were $21,000. Compute net cash from operating
activities using the direct method.

E11-13A. Calculate operating cash flows using the direct LO 1, 5
method.
During the fiscal year ended September 30, 2006, Napster Company engaged in
the following transactions. Using the relevant transactions, prepare the cash from
operating activities section of the statement of cash flows using the direct
method.

  a. Paid interest of $7,000.
  b. Collected $175,000 on accounts receivable.
  c. Made cash sales of $128,000.
  d. Paid salaries of $52,000.
  e. Recorded depreciation expense of $27,000.
  f. Paid income taxes of $32,000.
  g. Sold equipment for cash of $152,000.
  h. Purchased new equipment for cash of $41,000.
  i. Made payments to vendors of $62,700.
  j. Paid dividends of $20,000.
  k. Purchased land for cash of $174,000.
  l. Paid operating expenses of $32,500.

E11-14A. Prepare the statement of cash flows using the LO 2, 4
indirect method.
Use the following information for Just Nuts Company to prepare a statement of cash
flows using the indirect method:

Just Nuts Company
Balance Sheet

	At June 30,	
	2007	**2006**
Assets		
Cash	$193,000	$120,500
Accounts receivable	64,000	60,000
Inventories	120,000	175,000
Land	95,000	120,000
Equipment	250,000	180,000
Accumulated depreciation	(75,000)	(45,000)
Total assets	$647,000	$610,500
Liabilities and Shareholders' Equity		
Accounts payable	$ 42,000	$ 50,000
Bonds payable	160,000	220,000
Common stock and additional paid-in capital	200,000	180,000
Retained earnings	245,000	160,500
Total liabilities and shareholders' equity	$647,000	$610,500

Additional information:

  a. Net income for the fiscal year ended June 30, 2007 was $95,000.
  b. Cash dividends were declared and paid.
  c. Bonds payable amounting to $60,000 were redeemed for cash of $60,000. There
      was no gain or loss on the redemption
  d. Common stock was issued for $20,000 cash.
  e. No equipment was sold during the period.
  f. Land was sold for its book value of $25,000. No land was purchased.

LO 8   **E11-15A. Analyze statement of cash flows.**

The information below has been taken from the most recent statement of cash flows of Expansion Company:

Net cash provided by operating activities	$ 932,000
Net cash used by investing activities	$(1,180,500)
Net cash provided by financing activities	$ 2,107,000

a. What information do these subtotals from the statement of cash flows tell you about Expansion Company?
b. What additional information would you want to see before you analyze Expansion Company's ability to generate positive operating cash flows in the future?

LO 8   **E11-16A. Compute free cash flow.**

Use the Pier 1 Imports consolidated statement of cash flows presented below to compute the company's free cash flow for 2003 and 2004. What does the free cash flow tell you about Pier 1?

Pier 1 Imports, Inc.
Consolidated Statements of Cash Flows
(in thousands)

	For the Year Ended		
	Feb. 28, 2004	Mar. 1, 2003	Mar. 2, 2002
CASH FLOW FROM OPERATING ACTIVITIES			
Net income	$118,001	$129,386	$100,209
Adjustments to reconcile net income to net cash provided by continuing operating activities:			
Depreciation and amortization	64,606	57,934	51,504
Loss on disposal of fixed assets	143	980	247
Deferred compensation	8,264	5,043	5,059
Lease termination expense	3,258	395	——
Deferred income taxes	184	18,748	(2,238)
Tax benefit from options exercised by employees	4,897	6,867	628
Other	4,935	949	(2,564)
Changes in cash from:			
Inventories	(40,520)	(57,917)	34,804
Other accounts receivable and other current assets	(16,927)	(14,362)	(8,213)
Accounts payable and accrued expenses	32,678	33,364	43,468
Accrued income taxes payable	184	(3,940)	21,952
Other noncurrent assets	(2,027)	(759)	(32)
Net cash provided by operating activities	177,676	176,688	244,824
CASH FLOW FROM INVESTING ACTIVITIES:			
Capital expenditures	(121,190)	(99,042)	(57,925)
Proceeds from disposition of properties	34,450	6,330	16,682
Net change in restricted cash	(8,752)	(500)	(500)
Beneficial interest in securitized receivables	(5,143)	4,082	30,783
Net cash used in investing activities	(100,635)	(89,130)	(10,960)
CASH FLOW FROM FINANCING ACTIVITIES:			
Cash dividends	(26,780)	(19,520)	(15,134)
Purchases of treasury stock	(76,009)	(78,474)	(44,137)
Proceeds from stock options exercised Stock purchase plan and other net	15,125	17,305	13,463
Borrowing under long-term debt	—	—	712
Repayment of long-term debt and notes payable	(6,390)	(364)	——
Net cash used in financing activities	(94,054)	(81,053)	(45,096)
Change in cash and cash equivalents	(17,013)	6,505	188,768
Cash and cash equivalents at beginning of year	242,114	235,609	46,841
Cash and cash equivalents at end of year	$225,101	$242,114	$235,609

Source: Pier 1 Imports, *Fiscal Year 2004 Annual Report,* www.pier1.com/investorrelations/annualreports.asp.

E11-17A. Compute cash flow adequacy ratio.   <u>LO 8</u>

Use the Pier 1 Imports consolidated statement of cash flows from E11-16A to compute the company's cash flow adequacy ratio and for 2003 and 2004.

E11-18A. Compute the cash flow needed to pay current liabilities.   <u>LO 8</u>

Use the Pier 1 Imports consolidated statement of cash flows from E11-16A to compute the current cash debt coverage ratio for 2004. The current liabilities at February 28, 2004 were $279,888 (in thousands) and at February 28, 2003, they were $243,589 (in thousands).

E11-19A. Risk and control.   <u>LO 9</u>

Using the Pier 1 statement of cash flows from E11-16A, determine whether or not the firm appears to be taking advantage of new investment opportunities. Is the firm in a growth stage or a more mature stage of its business life? What evidence supports your opinion?

Exercise Set B

> Your professor may ask you to complete selected "Group B" exercises and problems using Prentice Hall Grade Assist **(PHGA)**. PHGA is an online tool that can help you master the chapter's topics by providing multiple variations of exercises and problems. You can rework these exercises and problems—each time with new data—as many times as you need, with immediate feedback and grading.

E11-1B. Identify cash flows.   <u>LO 1</u>

For each of the following items, tell whether it is a cash inflow or cash outflow and the section of the statement of cash flows in which the item would appear.

Item	Inflow or Outflow	Section of the Statement
a. Cash paid to vendor for supplies		
b. Purchase of treasury stock		
c. Principal repayment on bonds		
d. Interest payment on bonds		
e. Cash paid for salaries		
f. Cash from issuance of common stock		
g. Cash dividends paid		
h. Cash paid for rent and utilities		
i. Purchase of computer		
j. Cash paid for company vehicle		
k. Income taxes paid		

E11-2B. Identify cash flows.   <u>LO 1, 5</u>

For each transaction, indicate the amount of the cash flow, give the section of the statement in which each cash flow would appear, and indicate whether each results in an inflow or outflow of cash. Assume the statement of cash flows is prepared using the direct method.

Amount	Inflow or Outflow	Section of the Statement
a. Issued 150 shares of $3 par common stock for $15 per share.		
b. Sold $4,500 of inventory. Received $3,500 in cash and remaining $1,000 on account.		
c. Purchased a $1,500 computer by paying cash of $1,000 and signing a short-term note for the other $500.		
d. Paid $500 for routine maid service to clean office.		
e. Paid rent and utility expenses totaling $1,250.		

	Amount	Inflow or Outflow	Section of the Statement

f. Hired a runner to carry correspondences between offices and paid her $250.

g. Repaid the $500 short-term note along with $100 interest.

h. Purchased $1,500 of treasury stock.

LO 5   **E11-3B. Prepare operating section of statement of cash flows using the direct method.**

Use the income statement for Kristen Harrison's Cosmetics for last year and the information from the comparative balance sheets shown for the beginning and the ending of the year to prepare the operating section of the statement of cash flows using the direct method.

Sales		$150,000
Cost of goods sold		55,000
Gross profit		95,000
Operating expenses		
Wages	$3,750	
Rent	1,600	
Utilities	850	
Insurance	175	6,375
Net income		$ 88,625

Account	Beginning of the Year	End of the Year
Accounts receivable	$12,000	$10,000
Inventory	18,200	19,700
Prepaid insurance	100	200
Accounts payable	8,000	7,400
Wages payable	725	850
Utilities payable	-0-	275
Prepaid rent	-0-	-0-

LO 4   **E11-4B. Prepare operating section of statement of cash flows using the indirect method.**

Use the information from E11-3B to prepare the operating section of the statement of cash flows using the indirect method. Then, compare it with the statement you prepared for E11-3. What are the similarities? What are the differences? Which statement do you find most informative?

LO 1, 5   **E11-5B. Calculate change in cash.**

Given the following information, calculate the net change in cash during the year.

Cash received from sale of company van	$15,000
Cash paid for utilities and rent	5,150
Interest expense paid during the year	10,650
Cash paid for purchase of treasury stock	25,000
Cash collected from customers	68,250
Cash received from issuance of bonds	114,500
Cash paid for salaries	12,000
Cash paid to do a major repair of equipment to prolong its useful life for five more years	32,480

LO 2, 5   **E11-6B. Calculate operating cash flows.**

Use T-accounts and the information given for Carpet & Tile Company to calculate:

a. Cash paid for utilities
b. Cash paid for interest
c. Cash paid for inventory items
d. Cash collected from customers

From the financial statements for Carpet & Tile Company:	Income Statement Amount for the Year	Balance Sheet Beginning of the Year	End of the Year
Sales revenue	$105,750		
Accounts receivable		$6,500	$1,200
Utilities expense	20,300		
Utilities payable		2,500	2,700
Cost of goods sold	25,600		
Inventory		7,800	6,000
Accounts payable		1,500	3,000
Interest expense	15,750		
Interest payable		6,400	5,300

E11-7B. Prepare operating section of statement of cash flows and determine the method used.
LO 2, 5

Use the information from E11-6B to calculate the cash flow from operations for Carpet & Tile Company. Based on the information provided, which method of preparing the statement of cash flows does Carpet & Tile use?

E11-8B. Calculate cash flows from investing and financing activities.
LO 1, 6

The following events occurred at Garden & Home Store during 2009:

January 25	Issued common stock for $175,000.
February 8	Purchased a delivery truck for $65,000.
April 15	Sold old delivery truck for $28,500, resulting in a $3,500 gain.
July 24	Borrowed $7,500 from a local bank.
September 20	Purchased new machinery for $18,000.
December 15	Paid interest of $150 on the loan.
December 31	Paid cash dividends of $1,750.

Compute Garden & Home Store's net cash flows from (1) investing activities and from (2) financing activities for the year ended December 31, 2009.

E11-9B. Calculate operating cash flows using the direct method.
LO 5

The following information applies to Electronics Plus:

Income Statement for the year ended June 30, 2010

Sales	$ 35,000
Cost of goods sold	(20,600)
Gross profit	14,400
Rent expense	(1,400)
Net income	$13,000

1. Accounts Receivable started the year with a balance of $1,500 and ended the year with a balance of $500.
2. The beginning balance in Accounts Payable (to vendors) was $1,650, and the ending balance was $550. Inventory at the end of the year was the same as it was at the beginning of the year.
3. The company started the year with $3,000 of Prepaid Rent, and ended the year with $1,600 of Prepaid Rent.

Use T-accounts to determine the following cash flows:

a. Cash collected from customers for sales during the year
b. Cash paid to vendors for inventory during the year
c. Cash paid for rent during the year

E11-10B. Calculate operating cash flows using the indirect method.
LO 4

St. Augustine Steel reported net income of $320,000 for 2008. The company also reported Depreciation Expense of $65,000 and a loss of $5,000 on the sale of equipment. The comparative balance sheet shows a decrease in Accounts Receivable of $6,500 for the year, a $3,500 increase in Accounts Payable, and a $1,450 decrease in

Prepaid Rent. Prepare the cash from operating activities section of the statement of cash flows for 2008 using the indirect method.

LO 4 **E11-11B. Calculate operating cash flows using the indirect method.**
The following information has been taken from Fix-It Company's balance sheets at June 30, 2007, and 2008. Prepare the net cash from operating activities section of the company's statement of cash flows for the year ended June 30, 2008, using the indirect method.

	At June 30,	
	2008	**2007**
Current assets		
Cash	$105,000	$ 95,000
Accounts receivable	80,000	89,000
Inventory	210,000	188,000
Prepaid expenses	53,000	45,000
Total current assets	$448,000	$417,000
Current liabilities		
Accrued expenses payable	$ 18,000	$ 22,000
Accounts payable	85,000	63,000
Total current liabilities	$103,000	$ 85,000

Net income for the year ended June 30, 2008 was $215,000. Depreciation Expense was $30,500.

LO 5 **E11-12B. Calculate operating cash flows using the direct method.**
Capital Appliances completed its first year of operations on June 30, 2007. The firm's income statement for the year showed Revenues of $180,000 and Operating Expenses of $62,000. The balance in Accounts Receivable was $30,000 at year-end and payables related to operating expense were $18,500. Compute net cash from operating activities using the direct method.

LO 1,5 **E11-13B. Calculate operating cash flows using the direct method.**
During the fiscal year ended March 31, 2008, Radio Technology engaged in the following transactions. Using the relevant transactions, prepare the cash from operating activities section of the statement of cash flows using the direct method.

a. Paid $130,000 on accounts payable related to operating expenses.
b. Collected $185,000 on accounts receivable.
c. Made cash sales of $315,000.
d. Paid salaries of $40,000.
e. Recorded amortization expense of $15,000.
f. Declared a 2-for-1 stock split.
g. Paid interest on loan in the amount of $21,500.
h. Repaid principal of loan for $275,000.
i. Sold equipment for $295,000.
j. Paid dividends of $15,000.
k. Purchased a new building for cash of $215,000.
l. Paid operating expenses of $65,500.

LO 2,4 **E11-14B. Prepare the statement of cash flows using the indirect method.**
Use the following information for LAW Office Products and Supplies to prepare a statement of cash flows for the year ended December 31, 2007, using the indirect method:

LAW Office Products and Supplies, Inc.
Balance Sheet

	At December 31, 2007	2006
Assets		
Cash	$ 55,000	$ 23,500
Accounts receivable	78,000	64,000
Inventories	180,000	169,000
Land	135,000	105,000
Equipment	350,000	260,000
Accumulated depreciation	(90,000)	(60,000)
Total assets	$708,000	$561,500
Liabilities and Shareholders' Equity		
Accounts payable	$ 35,000	$ 40,000
Bonds payable	185,000	215,000
Common stock and additional paid-in capital	225,000	175,000
Retained earnings	263,000	131,500
Total liabilities and shareholders' equity	$708,000	$561,500

Additional information:

a. Net income for the fiscal year ended December 31, 2007 was $145,000.
b. Cash dividends were declared and paid.
c. Bonds payable amounting to $30,000 were redeemed for cash of $30,000.
d. Common stock was issued for $50,000 cash.
e. No equipment or land was sold during the year.

E11-15B. Analyze statement of cash flows.　　　　　　　　　　LO 8

The information below has been taken from the most recent statement of cash flows of Innovative Electronics Company:

Net cash provided by operating activities	$ 845,000
Net cash used by investing activities	(530,000)
Net cash provided by financing activities	1,675,000

a. What information do these subtotals from the statement of cash flows tell you about Innovative Electronics Company?
b. What additional information would you want to see before you analyze Innovative Electronics Company's ability to generate positive operating cash flows in the future?

E11-16B. Compute free cash flow.　　　　　　　　　　　　　LO 8

Use the Best Buy consolidated statement of cash flows presented below to compute the company's free cash flow for 2004 and 2005. What does the free cash flow tell you about Best Buy?

Best Buy
Consolidated Statements of Cash Flows
(in millions)

For the Fiscal Years Ended	February 26, 2005	February 28, 2004	March 1, 2003
Operating Activities			
Net earnings	$984	$ 705	$ 99
(Gain) loss from and disposal of discontinued operations, net of tax	(50)	95	441
Cumulative effect of change in accounting principles, net of tax			82
Earnings from continuing operations	934	800	622

Adjustments to reconcile earnings from continuing operations to total cash provided by operating activities from continuing operations:			
Depreciation	459	385	310
Asset impairment charges	22	22	11
Deferred income taxes	(28)	(14)	(37)
Other	23	16	15
Changes in operating assets and liabilities, net of acquired assets and liabilities:			
Receivables	(30)	(27)	(89)
Merchandise inventories	(240)	(507)	(256)
Other assets	(190)	(25)	(21)
Accounts payable	347	272	(5)
Other liabilities	243	250	117
Accrued income taxes	301	197	111
Total cash provided by operating activities from continuing operations	1,841	1,369	778
Investing Activities			
Additions to property and equipment	(502)	(545)	(725)
Purchases of available-for-sale securities	(7,789)	(2,989)	(1,844)
Sales of available-for-sale securities	7,118	2,175	1,610
Other, net	7	1	49
Total cash used in investing activities from continuing operations	(1,166)	(1,358)	(910)
Financing Activities			
Long-term debt payments	(371)	(17)	(13)
Issuance of common stock under employee stock purchase plan and for the exercise of stock options	256	114	40
Repurchase of common stock	(200)	(100)	—
Dividends paid	(137)	(130)	—
Net proceeds from issuance of long-term debt	—	—	18
Other, net	(7)	46	(15)
Total cash (used in) provided by financing activities from continuing operations	(459)	(87)	30
Effect of Exchange Rate Changes on Cash	9	1	—
Net Cash Used in Discontinued Operations		(53)	(79)
Increase (Decrease) in Cash and Cash Equivalents	225	(128)	(181)
Cash and Cash Equivalents at the Beginning of the Year	245	373	554
Cash and Cash Equivalents at End of Year	$470	$ 245	$ 373
Supplemental Disclosure of Cash Flow Information			
Income tax paid	$241	$ 306	$ 283
Interest paid	35	22	24
Capital and financing lease obligations incurred	117	26	—

LO 8   **E11-17B. Compute cash flow adequacy ratio.**
Use the Best Buy consolidated statement of cash flows presented above to compute the company's cash flow adequacy ratio for 2004 and 2005.

LO 8   **E11-18B. Compute the cash flow needed to pay current liabilities.**
Use the Best Buy consolidated statement of cash flows presented above to compute the current cash debt coverage ratio for 2005. The current liabilities at February 26, 2005 were $4,959 (in millions) and at February 28, 2004 were $4,501 (in millions).

LO 9   **E11-19B. Risk and control.**
Use the Best Buy consolidated statement of cash flows presented above to determine whether or not the firm appears to be taking advantage of new investment opportunities.

Is the firm in a growth stage or a more mature stage of its business life? What evidence supports your opinion?

Problem Set A

P11-1A. Prepare the statement of cash flows (direct or indirect method).

LO 4, 5

The income statement for the year ending December 31, 2007, and the balance sheets at December 31, 2006, and December 31, 2007, for Samsula Service Company are presented below.

Samsula Service Company
Income Statement
For the Year Ended December 31, 2007
(in thousands, except earnings per share)

Service revenue.		$92,000
Expenses:		
Wages and salaries	$60,000	
Advertising.	10,000	
Rent.	4,800	
Depreciation	3,600	
Miscellaneous	5,200	
Total expenses		83,600
Income before taxes		8,400
Income taxes.		2,940
Net income.		$ 5,460
Earnings per share.		$ 0.55

Samsula Service Company
Comparative Balance Sheets
At December 31
(in thousands)

	2007		2006	
Assets:				
Current assets:				
Cash		$ 6,910		$ 3,500
Accounts receivable		12,000		14,000
Supplies.		200		370
Prepaid advertising		800		660
Total current assets		$19,910		$18,530
Property, plant, & equipment				
Equipment	$44,000		$40,000	
Less: Accumulated depreciation	(21,600)		(18,000)	
Total property, plant, & equipment		22,400		22,000
Total assets.		$42,310		$40,530
Liabilities and Shareholders' Equity:				
Current liabilities				
Wages & salaries payable		$ 2,700		$ 3,300
Taxes payable		1,900		1,780
Total current liabilities		4,600		5,080
Shareholders' equity:				
Common stock	$30,000		$30,000	
Retained earnings	7,710		5,450	
		37,710		35,450
Total liabilities and shareholders' equity.		$42,310		$40,530

Required

a. Prepare a statement of cash flows for the year ending December 31, 2007, using (a) the direct method and (b) the indirect method. Assume no sales of PPE during the year.

b. Why is the statement of cash flows important to the company and to parties external to the company?

c. As a user, which format would you prefer—direct or indirect—and why?

d. Evaluate the way in which the company spent its cash during the year. Do you think the company is in a sound cash position?

LO 8   **P11-2A. Calculate free cash flow and cash flow ratios.**
Use the statement of cash flows prepared in P11-1A and the financial statements presented to complete the following requirements.

Required

Calculate the following for Samsula for 2007:

a. Free cash flow
b. Cash flow adequacy ratio
c. Current cash debt coverage ratio

LO 4   **P11-3A. Calculate operating cash flows using the indirect method.**
The information shown below is from the comparative balance sheets of Reba's Record Company at December 31, 2006, and 2005:

(in thousands)	At December 31, 2006	2005
Current assets:		
Cash	$3,500	$2,990
Accounts receivable	1,825	2,200
Inventory	2,150	1,380
Prepaid rent	320	270
Total current assets	$7,795	$6,840
Current liabilities:		
Accounts payable	$1,890	$1,050
Salaries payable	2,500	3,800
Total current liabilities	$4,390	$4,850

Net income for 2006 was $356,000. Depreciation Expense of $135,000 was included in the operating expenses for the year

Required

Use the indirect method to prepare the cash from operations section of the statement of cash flows for Reba's Record Company for the year ended December 31, 2006.

LO 4   **P11-4A. Calculate operating cash flows using the indirect method.**
The information shown on the following page comes from the balance sheets of TCB Company at June 30, 2008 and 2007.

Net income for the year ended June 30, 2008, was $86,900. Included in the operating expenses for the year was Depreciation Expense of $102,000.

Required

Using the indirect method, prepare the cash from operating activities section of TCB Company's statement of cash flows for the year ended June 30, 2008.

TCB Company
Balance Sheets (Adapted)
June 30, 2008, and June 30, 2007
(in thousands)

	2008	2007
Current assets:		
Cash	$2,110	$2,650
Accounts receivable	1,254	977
Inventory	730	856
Prepaid insurance	127	114
Total current assets	$4,221	$4,597
Current liabilities:		
Accounts payable	$1,054	$1,330
Wages payable	2,100	1,750
Total current liabilities	$3,154	$3,080

P11-5A. Calculate operating cash flows using the indirect method. LO 4

Ridge Oak Land Corporation had the following information available for 2007:

	January 1	December 31
Accounts Receivable	$78,000	$71,000
Prepaid Insurance	48,000	36,000
Inventory	56,000	75,000

Ridge Oak Land Corporation reported net income of $270,000 for the year. Depreciation Expense, included on the income statement, was $24,200.

Required

Assume this is all the information relevant to the statement of cash flows. Use the indirect method to prepare the cash flow from operating activities section of Ridge Oak Land Corporation's statement of cash flows.

P11-6A. Calculate investing and financing cash flows. LO 6

To prepare its statement of cash flows for the year ended December 31, 2006, Myers Company gathered the following information:

Loss on sale of machinery	$8,000
Proceeds from sale of machinery	50,000
Proceeds from bond issue (face value $100,000)	80,000
Amortization of bond discount	1,000
Dividends declared	25,000
Dividends paid	15,000
Purchase of treasury stock	30,000

Required

a. Prepare the cash from investing activities section of the statement of cash flows.
b. Prepare the cash from financing activities section of the statement of cash flows.

P11-7A. Calculate investing and financing cash flows. LO 6

To prepare its statement of cash flows for the year ended December 31, 2005, Martin Company gathered the following information:

Gain on sale of equipment	$4,000
Proceeds from sale of equipment	10,000
Purchase of equipment	80,000
Dividends declared	5,000
Dividends paid	2,000
Proceeds from sale of treasury stock	90,000
Repayment of loan principal	21,000
Payment of interest on loan	210

Required

a. Prepare the cash from investing activities section of the statement of cash flows.
b. Prepare the cash from financing activities section of the statement of cash flows.

LO 6   **P11-8A. Calculate investing and financing cash flows.**
To prepare its statement of cash flows for the year ended December 31, 2006, Repass
Company gathered the following information:

Dividends paid	$ 18,500
Purchase of treasury stock	50,000
Proceeds from bank loan	150,000
Gain on sale of equipment	7,000
Proceeds from sale of equipment	20,000
Proceeds from sale of common stock	260,000

Required

a. Prepare the cash from investing section of the statement of cash flows.
b. Prepare the cash from financing section of the statement of cash flows.

LO 8   **P11-9A. Analyze statement of cash flows.**
Use the statement of cash flows for the Matlock Company to answer the questions below:

Matlock Company
Statement of Cash Flows
For the Year Ended December 31, 2006

(in thousands)

Cash flows from operating activities:		
Net income		$1,500
Depreciation expense	$ 210	
Decrease in accounts receivable	320	
Increase in inventory	(70)	
Increase in prepaid rent	(10)	
Increase in accounts payable	150	600
Net cash provided by operating activities		$2,100
Cash flows from investing activities:		
Purchase of equipment	$(1,000)	
Proceeds from sale of old equipment	200	
Net cash used by investing activities		(800)
Cash flows from financing activities:		
Repayment of long-term mortgage	$(1,350)	
Proceeds from sale of common stock	500	
Payment of cash dividends	(200)	
Net cash used by financing activities		(1,050)
Net increase in cash during 2006		$ 250
Cash balance, January 1, 2006		346
Cash balance, December 31, 2006		$ 596

Required

a. How did Matlock Company use the majority of its cash during 2006?
b. What information does this give you about Matlock Company?
c. What was Matlock Company's major source of cash during 2006?
d. Is this an appropriate source of cash for the long run? Explain.
e. Calculate Matlock's free cash flow and cash flow adequacy ratio for 2006.

Problem Set B

Your professor may ask you to complete selected "Group B" exercises and problems using Prentice
Hall Grade Assist (**PHGA**). PHGA is an online tool that can help you master the chapter's topics by
providing multiple variations of exercises and problems. You can rework these exercises and problems—each time with new data—as many times as you need, with immediate feedback and grading.

P11-1B. Prepare the statement of cash flows (direct or indirect method).

LO 3, 5

Below are the income statements for Oviedo Oil Company for the year ended December 31, 2007, and the balance sheets at December 31, 2006, and December 31, 2007:

Oviedo Oil Company
Income Statement
For the Year Ended December 31, 2007

Sales revenue.		$150,000
Cost of goods sold		63,000
Gross profit		87,000
Other expenses:		
Wages & salaries	$32,000	
Depreciation	4,500	
Miscellaneous	12,400	
Total other expenses		48,900
Income before taxes		$ 38,100
Income taxes		(8,200)
Net income.		$ 29,900

Oviedo Oil Company
Comparative Balance Sheets
At December 31
(in thousands)

	2007		2006	
Assets:				
Current assets:				
Cash.		$ -0-		$ 6,400
Accounts receivable		2,900		2,700
Inventory		60,000		42,000
Total current assets		$ 62,900		$51,100
Property, plant, & equipment				
Equipment	$ 82,300		$39,000	
Less: Accumulated depreciation	(20,100)		(15,600)	
Total property, plant, & equipment		62,200		23,400
Total assets		$125,100		$74,500
Liabilities and Shareholders' Equity:				
Current liabilities:				
Accounts payable.	$ 6,400		$ 5,700	
Salaries payable	1,500		1,300	
Taxes payable	1,900		2,100	
Total current liabilities	$ 9,800		$ 9,100	
Notes payable	30,000		10,000	
Total liabilities		$ 39,800		$19,100
Shareholders' equity				
Common stock	$ 40,000		$40,000	
Retained earnings	45,300		15,400	
		85,300		55,400
Total liabilities and shareholders' equity.		$125,100		$74,500

Required

  a. Prepare a statement of cash flows for the year ended December 31, 2007 using (a) the direct method and (b) the indirect method. Assume no sale of equipment during the year.

  b. Why is the statement of cash flows important to the company and to parties external to the company?

  c. As a user, which format—direct or indirect—would you prefer and why?

  d. Evaluate the way in which the company spent its cash during the year. Do you think the company is in a sound cash position?

LO 8   **P11-2B. Calculate free cash flow and cash flow ratios.**
Use the statement of cash flows prepared in P11-1B and the financial statements presented to complete the following requirements.

Required

Calculate the following for Oviedo for 2007:

  a. Free cash flow

  b. Cash flow adequacy ratio

  c. Cash flow from operating activities divided by average current liabilities

LO 3, 4   **P11-3B. Calculate operating cash flows using the indirect method.**
The information shown below is from the comparative balance sheets of Faith's Music Company at December 31, 2008, and 2007:

Faith's Music Company
Balance Sheets
At December 31
(in thousands)

	2008	2007
Current assets:		
Cash	$2,500	$2,990
Accounts receivable	3,725	2,080
Inventory	1,050	1,300
Prepaid insurance	520	470
Total current assets	$7,795	$6,840
Current liabilities:		
Accounts payable	$2,890	$1,650
Salaries payable	1,500	3,200
Total current liabilities	$4,390	$4,850

Net income for the year ended December 31, 2008 was $206,000. Depreciation Expense of $85,000 was included in the operating expenses for the year.

Required

Use the indirect method to prepare the cash from operations section of the statement of cash flows for Faith's Music Company for the year ended December 31, 2008.

LO 4   **P11-4B. Calculate operating cash flows using the indirect method.**
The information on the next page comes from the balance sheets of Walker Corporation at September 30, 2008, and 2007.

    Net income for the year ended September 30, 2008 was $146,000. Included in the operating expenses for the year was Depreciation Expense of $112,000.

Required

Use the indirect method to prepare the cash from operating activities section of Walker Corporation's statement of cash flows for the year ended September 30, 2008.

Walker Corporation
Balance Sheets (Adapted)
September 30, 2008, and September 30, 2007
(in thousands)

	2008	2007
Current assets:		
Cash	$2,110	$1,650
Accounts receivable	1,254	1,977
Inventory	700	656
Prepaid insurance	157	314
Total current assets	$4,221	$4,597
Current liabilities:		
Accounts payable	$2,000	$2,330
Wages payable	1,154	750
Total current liabilities	$3,154	$3,080

P11-5B. Calculate operating cash flows using the indirect method.   LO 4

Treasures Corporation had the following information available for 2006:

	January 1	December 31
Accounts Receivable	$70,000	$76,000
Prepaid Insurance	58,000	36,000
Inventory	86,000	65,000

Treasures Corporation reported net income of $130,000 for the year. Depreciation Expense, included on the income statement, was $20,800.

Required
Assume this is all the information relevant to the statement of cash flows. Use the indirect method to prepare the cash flow from operating activities section of Treasures Corporation's statement of cash flows.

P11-6B. Calculate investing and financing cash flows.   LO 6
To prepare its statement of cash flows for the year ended December 31, 2005, Wright's Company gathered the following information:

1. Proceeds from bond issue (face value $100,000)	$120,000
2. Amortization of bond premium	1,000
3. Dividends declared	15,000
4. Dividends paid	12,000
5. Purchase of treasury stock	50,000
6. Loss on sale of machinery	18,000
7. Proceeds from sale of machinery	30,000

Required
  a. Prepare the cash from investing activities section of the statement of cash flows
  b. Prepare the cash from financing activities section of the statement of cash flows.

P11-7B. Calculate investing and financing cash flows.   LO 6
To prepare its statement of cash flows for the year ended December 31, 2005, Bowden Company gathered the following information:

Dividends declared	$15,000
Dividends paid	12,000
Proceeds from sale of treasury stock	70,000
Repayment of loan principal	32,000

Payment of interest on loan	320
Gain on sale of equipment	3,500
Proceeds from sale of equipment	11,000
Purchase of equipment	75,000

Required

a. Prepare the cash from investing activities section of the statement of cash flows.
b. Prepare the cash from financing activities section of the statement of cash flows.

LO 6   **P11-8B. Calculate investing and financing cash flows.**
To prepare its statement of cash flows for the year ended December 31, 2007, Mango Company gathered the following information:

Proceeds from bank loan	$257,000
Gain on sale of equipment	17,500
Proceeds from sale of equipment	45,000
Proceeds from sale of common stock	160,000
Dividends paid	15,400
Purchase of treasury stock	75,000

Required

a. Prepare the cash from investing activities section of the statement of cash flows.
b. Prepare the cash from financing activities section of the statement of cash flows.

LO 4, 7, 8   **P11-9B. Analyze statement of cash flows.**
Use the statement of cash flows for the SS&P Company to answer the questions below:

SS&P Company
Statement of Cash Flows
For the Year Ended December 31, 2007
(in thousands)

Cash flows from operating activities:			
Net income			$ 2,500
Depreciation expense		$ 510	
Decrease in accounts receivable		720	
Increase in inventory		(90)	
Increase in prepaid rent		(20)	
Decrease in accounts payable		(150)	970
Net cash provided by operating activities			3,470
Cash flows from investing activities:			
Purchase of equipment		$ (3,000)	
Proceeds from sale of old equipment		900	
Net cash used by investing activities			(2,100)
Cash flows from financing activities:			
Repayment of long-term mortgage		$ (7,500)	
Proceeds from sale of common stock		2,100	
Payment of cash dividends		(1,200)	
Net cash used by financing activities			(6,600)
Net decrease in cash during 2007			$ (5,230)
Cash balance, January 1, 2007			10,580
Cash balance, December 31, 2007			$ 5,350

Required

a. How did SS&P Company use the majority of its cash during 2007?
b. What information does this give you about SS&P Company?

c. How did SS&P Company obtain the majority of its cash during 2007?
d. Is this an appropriate source of cash for the long run? Explain.
e. Calculate SS&P's free cash flow and cash flow adequacy ratio for 2007.

Financial Statement Analysis

FSA11-1. Analyze statement of cash flows.

LO 8

Use Target's financial statements in Appendix B in the back of the book to answer the following questions:

a. What were the major sources and uses of cash during the most recent fiscal year? What does this indicate about Target's cash position?
b. What evidence, if any, is there that Target is expanding?

FSA11-2. Analyze statement of cash flows.

LO 8

The statements of cash flows shown below are from Maytag[8] Corporation's 10-K.

Maytag
Consolidated Statements of Cash Flows
Year Ended
(in thousands)

	1-Jan 2005	3-Jan 2004	28-Dec 2003
Operating activities:			
Net income (loss)	$(9,006)	$120,133	$188,794
Adjustments to reconcile net income to net cash provided by continuing operating activities:			
Net (gain) loss from discontinued operations	(339)	(5,755)	2,607
Minority interests	—	—	3,732
Depreciation	168,205	164,680	162,600
Amortization	1,577	1,105	1,108
Deferred income taxes	2,636	56,660	88,643
Restructuring charges, net of cash paid	36,859	45,939	62,483
Asset impairment	—	11,217	—
Loss on investments	—	7,185	—
Goodwill impairment—Commercial Products	9,600	—	—
Front-load washer litigation, net of cash paid	23,092	—	—
Gain on sale; property disposition	(9,711)	—	—
Adverse judgment on pre-aquisitions dist. lawsuit	10,505	—	—
Changes in working capital items exclusive of business acquisitions:			
Accounts receivable	(29,207)	1,403	35,211
Inventories	(46,836)	5,801	(21,985)
Other current assets	14,444	27,422	(74,905)
Trade payables	75,095	103,095	47,589
Other current liabilities	15,711	(10,804)	(792)
Pension expense	63,024	64,779	52,561
Pension contributions	(94,324)	(268,119)	(193,108)
Postretirement benefit liability	(6,110)	20,595	12,255
Other	45,740	9,046	(2,076)
Net cash provided by continuing operating activities	$270,955	$354,382	$364,717

[8]As this book is going to press, Whirlpool is making a bid to take over Maytag. If that happens, you will not be able to find financial statements for Maytag after the takeover because the information will be combined with Whirlpool's information and be presented as Whirlpool's consolidated financial statements.

Required

Answer the following questions:

a. Did Maytag use the direct method or the indirect method for preparing the statement of cash flows?

b. Did Accounts Receivable increase or decrease from fiscal year-end (FYE) January 3, 2004, to January 1, 2005?

c. Why is Depreciation, a noncash expense, included on the statement of cash flows?

d. On the most recent statement of cash flows, Inventory is shown as a negative number (subtracted). However, the prior year's statement shows a positive number (added). Describe what happened to the balance in the Inventory account during each of those years.

e. Trade Payables are the same as Accounts Payable. Did the balance in Trade Payables increase or decrease during the year? Explain.

f. Over the three-year period, Maytag's net income has decreased to the point of being a loss in the most recent year shown. Yet net cash from operating activities is larger than net income and positive for all three years. How would you explain this to a friend who wants to invest in Maytag's stock?

LO 8, 9   **FSA11-3. Analyze statement of cash flows.**

On the next page, you will find the statement of cash flows for Chico's for the years ended January 29, 2005, and January 31, 2004.

Required

Answer the following questions:

a. Does Chico's use the direct method or the indirect method for preparing the statement of cash flows?

b. Did Receivables increase or decrease during the most recent fiscal year?

c. Why is Depreciation, a noncash expense, included on the statement of cash flows?

d. On both years' statements, Inventory is shown as a negative number (subtracted). Describe what happened to the balance in the Inventory account during each of those years.

e. Did the balance in Accounts Payable increase or decrease during the most recent fiscal year? Explain.

f. Do you think Chico's is expanding? Find some numbers to support your answer.

g. Calculate Chico's free cash flow for both years. What do these values indicate?

h. Do you see any particular risks indicated by Chico's cash flow patterns?

Chico's Fashion, Inc.
Consolidated Statement of Cash Flows
(in thousands)

	For the fiscal year ended	
	January 29, 2005	January 31, 2004
CASH FLOWS FROM OPERATING ACTIVITIES:		
Net income	$141,206	$100,230
Adjustments to reconcile net income to net cash provided by operating activities		
Depreciation and amortization, cost of goods sold	3,605	1,970
Depreciation and amortization, other	32,481	21,130
Deferred tax benefit	(2,986)	1,336
Tax benefit of options exercised	27,297	15,126
Deferred rent expense, net	6,450	1,874
Loss from disposal of property and equipment	311	3,746
(Increase) decrease in assets		
Receivables, net	1,069	(1,953)
Inventories	(18,280)	(4,658)
Prepaid expenses and other	(2,734)	(1,281)
Increase in liabilities		
Accounts payable	8,929	(3,175)
Accrued liabilities	26,272	11,035
Total adjustments	82,414	45,150
Net cash provided by operating activities	223,620	145,380
CASH FLOWS FROM INVESTING ACTIVITIES:		
Purchases of marketable securities	(404,211)	(166,855)
Proceeds from sale of marketable securities	257,299	153,447
Acquisition of The White House, Inc. net of cash acquired	—	(87,636)
Acquisition of franchise store	(1,307)	—
Purchases of property and equipment	(93,065)	(52,300)
Net cash used in investing activities	129,248	5,444
CASH FLOWS FROM FINANCING ACTIVITIES:		
Proceeds from issuance of common stock	22,684	15,231
Repurchase of common stock..........................	(4,992)	—
Payments on capital leases	(1,278)	(344)
Principal payments on debt	—	—
Deferred finance costs		
Net cash provided by financing activities	16,414	14,887
Net (decrease) increase in cash and cash equivalents ..	(1,250)	6,923
CASH AND CASH EQUIVALENTS		
Beginning of period	15,676	8,753
CASH AND CASH EQUIVALENTS		
End of period..	$ 14,426	$ 15,676
SUPPLEMENTAL DISCLOSURES OF CASH FLOW INFORMATION		
Cash paid for interest	$ 107	$ 142
Cash paid for income taxes	$ 56,489	$ 47,855

Critical Thinking Problems

Risk and Controls

To be successful, a company must anticipate its cash flows. What evidence can you find in the Wal-Mart annual report in Appendix A, in the back of the book, that this company does adequate cash planning? Is there any information not available in the annual report that would help you make this evaluation?

Ethics

After two years of business, the Lucky Ladder Company decided to apply for a bank loan to finance a new store. Although the company had been very successful, it had never prepared a cash budget. The owner of Lucky Ladder Company used the information from the first two years of business to reconstruct cash forecasts, and he presented them with his financial statements as though they had been prepared as part of the company's planning. Do you think this behavior was ethical? What would you do in similar circumstances? Why?

Group Assignment

To prepare the class for a debate about the format of the statement of cash flows, assign the direct method to half of the groups in the class and the indirect method to the other half of the groups. Have each group prepare arguments about the superiority of their assigned method of presenting the operating section of the statement of cash flows. Think about both theoretical and practical aspects of the decision.

Internet Exercise: Carnival Corp.

Carnival Corp. prides itself on being "The Most Popular Cruise Line in the World®"—a distinction achieved by offering a wide array of quality cruise vacations.

IE11-1. Go to www.carnival.com, select "About Us."

a. Select "World's Leading Cruise Lines" and list three of the seven cruise lines operated by the Carnival Corp. Close the "World's Leading Cruise Lines" window.
b. Select "News," "Virtual Press Kit" and then "Carnival Cruise Lines' Fleet Information." Within the past five years, how many new ships has Carnival put into service?
c. Are the payments for ships considered capital expenditures or revenue expenditures? On the statement of cash flows, which business activity category will report these payments?

IE11-2. Go to www.carnival.com, select "About Us" and find "Investor Relations." You'll find a link to the annual report (PDF file). Find the annual cash flow statement (page 7 of the 2004 annual report) to answer the following questions.

a. Does Carnival use the direct method or the indirect method to prepare the statement of cash flows? How can you tell? Which activity section is affected by this choice of method?
b. For the most recent year, list the amount of net cash inflow or outflow from each of the three major types of activities reported on the statement of cash flows. Which type of activity is providing the most cash? Is this considered favorable or unfavorable?
c. For the most recent year, what amount is reported for net income and net cash from operating activities? Are these amounts the same? Explain why or why not.
d. For the most recent year, did Carnival report cash inflows or outflows for capital expenditures? Is this considered favorable or unfavorable? Explain why. What do you think these capital expenditures were for? What was the net amount of the capital expenditure? Which activity section reports this information?
e. For the most recent year, what amount of cash dividends did Carnival pay out? For the most recent year, did Carnival issue or retire more common stock? What was the net amount issued or retired? For the most recent year, did Carnival issue

or retire more debt? What was the net amount issued or retired? Which activity section reports this information?

f. Does this statement of cash flows indicate a strong or weak position? Explain why.

Please note: Internet web sites are constantly being updated. Therefore, if the information is not found where indicated, please explore the web site further to find the information.

Additional Study Materials

Visit www.prenhall.com/reimers for self-study quizzes and spreadsheet templates to use to complete homework assignments.

chapter 12

Using Financial Statement Analysis to Evaluate Firm Performance

Here's where you've been . . .

- **You learned to construct a statement of cash flows from an income statement and comparative balance sheets.**

Here's where you're going . . .

- **You'll learn to use vertical analysis, horizontal analysis, and ratio analysis.**

YOU make the call:

Should you invest in Wal-Mart or Target?

Do you have any money invested in the stock market? Just a few decades ago, only a very small percentage of people owned stocks. Today, however, a majority of Americans own stock because they participate in retirement plans at work. In these plans, the employee makes contributions to a fund and has some control over how the funds are invested. When investors are trying to decide which company's stock to purchase, they do a great deal of financial statement analysis. This analysis involves determining if a company has a good return on investment, has enough liquid assets to pay its bills, and has good prospects for the future.

Suppose that you and a friend each have $1,000 to invest in either Wal-Mart or Target. One of you will invest in Wal-Mart and the other one will invest in Target to see which stock does better. You flip a coin to see who gets to pick a company, and you are the winner. You must choose between Wal-Mart and Target, and your friend will have to invest in the other company. Which company would you choose? *You make the call.*

Learning Objectives

When you are finished studying this chapter, you should be able to:

1. Recognize and explain the components of net income.
2. Perform and interpret a horizontal analysis and a vertical analysis of financial statement information.
3. Perform a basic ratio analysis of a set of financial statements and explain what the ratios mean.
4. Recognize the risks of investing in stock and explain how to control those risks.

LEARNING OBJECTIVE 1

Recognize and explain the components of net income.

A Closer Look at the Income Statement

You've learned a great deal about the basic financial statements and how accountants record, summarize, and report transactions. There is information you can easily see in the financial statement, but there is also information that is difficult to see. It's important to look beyond the size and source of the numbers to see what the numbers *mean*. We've been examining the individual parts of the financial statements. Now we'll examine all the parts of the four financial statements together to answer the following questions: What information do financial statements provide? What does the information mean? How can we use it?

Before beginning the detailed analysis of the financial statements, we need to take a closer look at some of the characteristics of the income statement. Because earnings—that is, net income—is the focus of financial reporting, companies worry about how current and potential investors will interpret the announcement of earnings each quarter. It's not uncommon for companies to be accused of manipulating their earnings to appear more profitable than they actually are. In an effort to make the components of earnings clear and to represent exactly what they should to financial statement users, the Financial Accounting Standards Board (FASB) requires that two items be separated from the regular earnings of a company. The major reason for segregating these items is that they should not be considered as part of the ongoing earnings of the firm. Reported earnings is an amount used to predict future earnings, but these two items are not expected to be repeated in the future.

1. Discontinued operations
2. Extraordinary items

Exhibit 12.1 shows the components of net income.

Discontinued operations

If you pay attention to the financial news, you're bound to hear about a company selling off a division. In 2004, Motorola, one of the largest communications firms in the world, discontinued operating its semiconductor business segment so that the segment could form its own firm, Freescale Semiconductor. The gains or losses from these kinds of transactions are shown on the income statement. Firms are always evaluating the contribution that the various divisions make to the profits of the firm. If a division isn't profitable or no longer fits the strategy of the firm, a firm may sell it to remain profitable or change the firm's focus. Parts of a company's operations that are eliminated are called **discontinued operations**.

Discontinued operations: Those parts of the firm that a company has eliminated by selling a division.

Exhibit 12.1

Components of Net Income

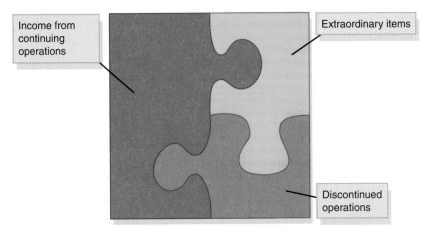

Income from continuing operations

Extraordinary items

Discontinued operations

When a firm eliminates a division, the financial implications are shown separately from the regular operations of the firm. Why would this separation be useful? Earnings is an important number because it is used to evaluate the performance of a firm and to predict its future performance. To make these evaluations and predictions more meaningful, it is important that one-time transactions be separated from recurring transactions. This separation allows investors to see one-time transactions as exceptions to the normal operations of the firm. In addition to the gain or loss from the sale, the earnings or loss for the accounting period for the discontinued operations must also be shown separately. Let's look at an example of a firm with discontinued operations. In 2007, Muzby Manufacturing sold off a major business segment—the crate-production division, because the firm wanted to focus its operations on its core business, which did not include the crate division. Both the current year's income or loss from the crate-production division and the gain or loss from the sale of those operations are shown separately on the income statement. Suppose:

Study Tip

The related gain or loss from discontinued operations is shown net of taxes after income from continuing operations.

1. Muzby Manufacturing's income from continuing operations before taxes was $395,600.
2. Taxes related to that income were $155,000.
3. The discontinued segment contributed income of $12,000 during the year.
4. Taxes related to that contributed income were $1,900.
5. The discontinued segment was sold for a gain of $63,000.
6. The taxes related to the profit from that gain were $28,000.

Exhibit 12.2 shows how this information would be presented on the income statement for Muzby Manufacturing.

Extraordinary items

You've learned that discontinued operations are the first item that accountants disclose separately on the income statement. The second item is the financial effect of any event that is *unusual* in nature and *infrequent* in occurrence. The financial effects of such events are called **extraordinary items**. To qualify as extraordinary, the events must be abnormal and must *not* be reasonably expected to occur again in the foreseeable future. There is a great deal of judgment required to decide if an event should be considered *extraordinary*.

Extraordinary items: Events that are unusual in nature and infrequent in occurrence.

The highlighted portion of the income statement shows how amounts related to discontinued operations are presented.

Exhibit 12.2

Showing Discontinued Operations on the Income Statement

> **Muzby Manufacturing**
> **Income Statement**
> **For the year ended December 31, 2007**

Income from continuing operations before income taxes		$395,600
Income tax expense		155,000
Income from continuing operations		240,600
Discontinued operations		
Income from discontinued (net of taxes of $1,900)	$10,100	
Gain on disposal of crate-production segment (net of taxes of $28,000)	35,000	45,100
Net income		$285,700

Examples of occurrences that have been considered extraordinary include eruptions of a volcano, a takeover of foreign operations by the foreign government, and the effects of new laws or regulations that result in a one-time cost to comply. Each situation is unique and must be considered in light of the environment in which the business operates.

Suppose Muzby Manufacturing has a factory in China, and the Chinese government decides to take possession of all American businesses in the country. The value of the lost factory is $200,000. U.S. tax law allows companies to write off this type of extraordinary loss, which means the company receives a tax savings. Suppose the applicable tax savings is $67,000. Exhibit 12.3 shows how Muzby Manufacturing would present the information on its income statement for the year.

Reporting taxes

In general, firms report total revenues and expenses and then subtract the associated taxes. However, the financial effects of discontinued operations and extraordinary items are shown net of tax.

Exhibit 12.3

Showing Extraordinary Items on the Income Statement

> **Muzby Manufacturing**
> **Income Statement**
> **For the year ended December 31, 2007**

Income from continuing operations before income taxes		$395,600
Income tax expense		155,000
Income from continuing operations		240,600
Discontinued operations		
Income from discontinued crate-production segment (net of taxes of $1,900)	$10,100	
Gain on disposal of crate-production segment (net of taxes of $28,000)	35,000	45,100
Income before extraordinary item		$285,700
Loss on extraordinary item		
Expropriation of foreign operation (net of taxes of $67,000)		(133,000)
Net income		$152,700

Can**YOU**do it**?**

What does it mean for a company to show discontinued operations and extraordinary items *net of tax*? What's the alternative?

Answer Those items must be shown after the tax consequences have been subtracted because this method of reporting the items net of taxes keeps the tax implications of these items separate from the company's regular tax expense. The alternative is to show the items before the tax implications, and then include the tax savings or tax increases in the company's regular tax expense.

Horizontal and Vertical Analysis of Financial Information

LEARNING OBJECTIVE 2
Perform and interpret a horizontal analysis and a vertical analysis of financial statement information.

Now that you are prepared to recognize extraordinary items and discontinued operations that may appear on the income statement, you are ready to analyze an entire statement or set of statements.

There are three primary ways to analyze financial information: horizontal analysis, vertical analysis, and ratio analysis.

Horizontal analysis

Horizontal analysis is a technique for evaluating a financial statement amount over a period of time. The purpose of a horizontal analysis is to express the change in a financial statement item in percentages rather than in dollars. Financial statement users can spot trends more easily with horizontal analysis than by simply looking at the raw numbers. Consider the cash flows for Wal-Mart below. According to its last six statements of cash flows, Wal-Mart made the following cash expenditures for property, plant, and equipment.

Horizontal analysis: A technique for evaluating financial statement amounts across time.

In Other Words:
Horizontal analysis is also called *trend analysis*.

Wal-Mart Capital Expenditures
For fiscal years ended on January 31, 2000–2005
(in millions of dollars)

2005	2004	2003	2002	2001	2000
12,893	10,308	9,245	8,285	8,042	6,183

Often, the analyst selects one of the years as the reference point. It's called the base year, and the amounts reported for the other years are expressed as a percentage of the chosen base year. That means the difference between the amount of the financial statement item each year and the base year is expressed as a percentage of the base year. Suppose we choose 2000 as the base year. Then, we subtract the 2000 capital expenditures ($6,183) from 2001 capital expenditures ($8,042) and divide by the base year number ($6,183):

$$\frac{8,042 - 6,183}{6,183} = \frac{1,859}{6,183} = 30.1\%$$

Our calculation shows that during the fiscal year ended January 31, 2001, Wal-Mart increased capital expenditures by over 30% of the base year's capital expenditures. The calculation is done the same way for each year. The percentage change from the base year to 2002 is calculated as follows:

$$\frac{8,285 - 6,183}{6,183} = \frac{2,102}{6,183} = 34.0\%$$

This is only one way to do a horizontal analysis. Frequently, the analysis is done by comparing one year with the next, rather than using a fixed base year.

Wal-Mart
Capital Expenditures Comparison—Base year 2000

(in millions)

	2005	2004	2003	2002	2001	2000
Capital expenditures (in million of dollars)	$12,893	10,308	9,245	8,285	8,042	6,183
Percentage change in capital expenditures		108.5%	66.7%	49.5%	34.0%	30.1%	100%

It's usually difficult to understand the significance of a single item like capital expenditures when viewing the raw numbers. To make trends more apparent, it may be useful to express the changes in spending in percentage form. A horizontal analysis makes it clear that Wal-Mart continues to make a significant investment in its property, plant, and equipment.

Vertical analysis

Vertical analysis is similar to horizontal analysis, but the analysis involves items on a single year's financial statement. Each item on a financial statement is expressed as a percentage of a selected base amount. For example, a vertical analysis of an income statement almost always uses sales as the base amount because almost all of a firm's expenditures depend on the level of sales. Each amount on the statement is expressed as a percentage of sales. This type of analysis can point out areas in which the costs might be too large or growing without an obvious cause. For example, if managers at Wal-Mart see that employee salaries, as a percentage of sales, are increasing, they can investigate the increase and, if necessary, take action to reduce the firm's salaries expense. Vertical analysis also allows the meaningful comparison of companies of different sizes. Exhibit 12.4 shows a vertical analysis for Wal-Mart's income statements for the years ended January 31, 2005, and January 31, 2004.

 Can **YOU** do it?

Use the information from Wal-Mart to do a horizontal analysis with 2001 as the base year. What do the amounts mean?

Wal-Mart's Capital Expenditures

(in millions of dollars)

2005	2004	2003	2002	2001
12,893	10,308	9,245	8,285	8,042

Answers

	2005	2004	2003	2002	2001
Capital expenditures	12,893	10,308	9,245	8,285	8,042
Percentage change	60.3%	28.2%	15%	3%	100%

The percentage given for each year is the percentage increase over the base year.

Exhibit 12.4

Vertical Analysis

| | Wal-Mart Stores, Inc.
Consolidated Statements of Income
For the fiscal years ended
(in millions) | | | |

	January 31, 2005		January 31, 2004	
Net sales	$285,222	100.00%	$256,329	100.00%
Other income, net	2,767	0.97%	2,352	0.92%
	287,989		258,681	
Costs and expenses:				
Cost of sales	219,793	77.06%	198,747	77.54%
Selling, general, and adm. expenses	51,105	17.92%	44,909	17.52%
Operating profit	17,091	5.99%	15,025	5.86%
Interest expense (net)	986	0.35%	832	0.32%
Income from continuing operations before income taxes and minority interest	16,105	5.65%	14,193	5.54%
Provision for taxes (current and deferred)	5,589	1.96%	5,118	2.00%
Income from continuing operations before minority interest	10,516	3.69%	9,075	3.54%
Minority interest	(249)	0.09%	(214)	(0.08%)
Income from continuing operations	10,267	3.69%	8,861	3.46%
Income from discontinued operations, net of tax	—		193	0.08%
Net income	$ 10,267	3.60%	$ 9,054	3.54%

The analysis for a single year provides some information, but the comparison of two years reveals more about what's going on with Wal-Mart. The ratios look very consistent across these two years. What item(s) stands out in the analysis? There is a slight increase in profitability measures which is favorable. The notes to the financial statements are the first place to look for additional information whenever an analysis reveals something interesting or suspicious.

Ratio Analysis

Throughout this book, you've learned that ratio analysis uses information in the financial statements to formulate specific values that determine some measure of a company's financial position. Let's review all the ratios you've learned and then look at an additional category of ratios.

A review of all ratios

There are four general categories of ratios, named for what they attempt to measure:

- **Liquidity ratios:** These ratios measure a company's ability to pay its current bills and operating costs—obligations coming due in the next fiscal year.
- **Solvency ratios:** These ratios measure a company's ability to meet its long-term obligations, such as its long-term debt (like bank loans), and to survive over a long period of time.
- **Profitability ratios:** These ratios measure the operating or income performance of a company. Remember the goal of a business is to make a profit, so this type of ratio examines how well a company is meeting that goal.
- **Market indicators:** These ratios relate the current market price of the company's stock to earnings or dividends.

LEARNING OBJECTIVE 3

Perform a basic ratio analysis of a set of financial statements and explain what the ratios mean.

Liquidity ratios: Measure the company's ability to pay its current bills and operating costs.

Solvency ratios: Measure the company's ability to meet its long-term obligations and to survive over a long period of time.

Profitability ratios: Measure the operating or income performance of a company.

Market indicators: Ratios that relate the current market price of the company's stock to earnings or dividends.

The first part of Exhibit 12.5 reviews the three types of ratios you learned about in earlier chapters. One of the ratios you studied earlier is return on equity (ROE). Read about how analysts use the ROE ratio to provide insights beyond the number itself in *Accounting in the News* on page 628.

Exhibit 12.5

Common Ratios

Ratio	Definition	How to use the ratio	Chapter where you studied the ratio
LIQUIDITY			
Current ratio	$\dfrac{\text{Total current assets}}{\text{Total current liabilities}}$	To measure a company's ability to pay current liabilities with current assets. This ratio helps creditors determine if a company can meet its short-term obligations.	2
Quick ratio (also known as the acid-test ratio)	$\dfrac{\text{Cash + short-term + net accounts investment receivable}}{\text{Total current liabilities}}$	To measure a company's ability to meet its short-term obligations. This ratio is similar to the current ratio. However, by limiting the numerator to very liquid current assets, it is a stricter test.	3
Working capital	Current assets – current liabilities	To measure a company's ability to meet its short-term obligations. Although technically not a ratio, working capital is often measured as part of financial statement analysis.	3
Inventory turnover ratio*	$\dfrac{\text{Cost of goods sold}}{\text{Average inventory}}$	To measure how quickly a company is selling its inventory.	6
Accounts receivable turnover* ratio	$\dfrac{\text{Net credit sales}}{\text{Average net accounts receivable}}$	To measure a company's ability to collect the cash from its credit customers.	7
Current cash debt coverage ratio	$\dfrac{\text{Net cash from operating activities}}{\text{Average current liabilities}}$	To measure a firm's ability to generate the cash it needs to pay its current liabilities from its operations.	11
SOLVENCY			
Debt to equity ratio	$\dfrac{\text{Total liabilities}}{\text{Total shareholders' equity}}$	To compare the amount of debt a company has with the amount the owners have invested in the company.	9
Times interest earned ratio	$\dfrac{\text{Income from operations}}{\text{Interest expense}}$	To compare the amount of income that has been earned in an accounting period (before interest) to the interest obligation for the same period. If net income is used in the numerator, be sure to add back interest expense and taxes.	9
Cash flow adequacy ratio	$\dfrac{\text{Net cash from operating activities}}{\text{Net cash required for investing activities}}$	To measure a firm's ability to generate the cash it needs for investing from its operations.	11

Turnover ratios are often considered efficiency ratios.

Exhibit 12.5

(continued)

PROFITABILITY			
Return on assets	$$\dfrac{\text{Net income + interest expense}}{\text{Average total assets}}$$	To measure a company's success in using its assets to earn income for owners and creditors, those who are financing the business. Because interest is part of what has been earned to pay creditors, it is often added back to the numerator. Net income is the return to the owners and interest expense is the return to the creditors. Average total assets are the average of beginning assets and ending assets for the year.	8
Asset turnover ratio	$$\dfrac{\text{Net sales}}{\text{Average total assets}}$$	To measure how efficiently a company uses its assets.	8
Return on equity	$$\dfrac{\text{Net income – preferred dividends}}{\text{Average common shareholders' equity}}$$	To measure how much income is earned with the common shareholders' investment in the company.	10
Gross profit ratio	$$\dfrac{\text{Gross profit}}{\text{Net sales}}$$	To measure a company's profitability. It is one of the most carefully watched ratios by management because it describes the percentage of the sales price that is gross profit. A small shift usually indicates a big change in the profitability of the company's sales.	5
Profit margin ratio	$$\dfrac{\text{Net income}}{\text{Net sales}}$$	To measure the percentage of each sales dollar that results in net income.	5
Earnings per share	$$\dfrac{\text{Net income – preferred dividends}}{\text{Weighted average number of shares of common stock outstanding}}$$	To calculate net income per share of common stock.	10
MARKET INDICATORS			
Price–earnings ratio	$$\dfrac{\text{Market price per common share}}{\text{Earnings per share}}$$	To calculate the market price for $1 of earnings.	12
Dividend yield ratio	$$\dfrac{\text{Dividend per share}}{\text{Market price per share}}$$	To calculate the percentage return on the investment in a share of stock via dividends.	12

Can YOU do it?

Suppose Wal-Mart pays off a current liability with cash. What effect would this have on the company's current ratio? What effect would the payoff have on the company's working capital?

Answers This payoff would increase the current ratio. We can use a simple numerical example to illustrate why: Suppose current assets were $500 million and current liabilities were $250 million. The current ratio would be 2. Now suppose $50 million worth of current liabilities were paid off with current assets. Then, current assets would be $450 million, and current liabilities would be $200 million. The current ratio is now 2.25. When both the numerator and the denominator of a fraction are reduced by the same amount, the value of the fraction will increase. Working capital will remain unchanged. It started at $500 million minus $250 million in the example. After $50 million worth of liabilities is paid off with cash, the current assets will be $450 million and the current liabilities will be $200 million. The difference is still $250 million.

Accounting in the NEWS

Financial Statement Analysis

DuPont—more than a FORTUNE 500 Chemical Company

When you hear the name DuPont, you probably think of the big chemical company that, since its beginning in 1802 as an explosives company, has brought us products like Teflon® for our frying pans and Corian® for our countertops. To financial analysts, DuPont can have another meaning. There is a financial analysis called DuPont analysis.

In 1914, F. Donaldson Brown, an electrical engineer, joined the giant chemical company's treasury department. He developed what became known as the DuPont model of financial analysis. Here's how it works:

Analysts often break ROE into two parts to get more information about a firm's performance.

$$\text{ROE} = \text{ROA} \times \text{Financial Leverage}$$
$$\text{ROE} = \frac{\text{Net income}}{\text{Assets}} \times \frac{\text{Assets}}{\text{Equity}}$$

Here's what a writer for *The Motley Fool* had to say about DuPont analysis:

Have you ever wondered why two similar companies can have vastly different prospects and returns? You could look at earnings per share, but knowing if a company is underperforming is less important than figuring out why. Breaking apart return on equity can determine that a company's operations are improving before the market notices.

Analyzing the parts of ROE in this way, called DuPont analysis, helps investors judge the quality of a firm's ROE. Suppose two firms had the same ROE, but one had a much higher financial leverage value than the other. To many analysts, this would indicate a small potential for growth in ROE compared to a firm that has less debt and may be able to borrow more money for new opportunities.

Q If two firms have the same ROE, can you conclude they have the same potential for growth?

A No, the components of ROE using DuPont analysis can provide information that may differentiate between the two companies based on their financial leverage.

If you cook, you probably own a pan made by DuPont. Operating in more than 70 countries, DuPont offers a wide range of innovative products and services for markets including nutrition, apparel, electronics, and communications. DuPont also contributed to the accounting field. DuPont engineer F. Donaldson Brown developed the DuPont model of financial analysis.

Source: Bill Mann, "Selecting Stocks Using ROE," *The Motley Fool*, April 28, 2004.

Can YOU do it?

Company A has a gross profit ratio of 30%, and Company B has a gross profit ratio of 60%. Can you tell which company is more profitable? Why or why not?

Answers No, gross profit ratio does not tell which company is more profitable because one company may have higher sales than the other. For example, 30% of a large number is better than 60% of a small number. Also, the amount of costs the companies must cover beyond the cost of goods sold is unknown. The gross profit ratio is most useful for comparing companies in the same industry or evaluating performance of a single company across time.

Market indicator ratios

Price–earnings (P/E) ratio: The market price of a share of stock divided by that stock's earnings per share.

The market price of a share of stock is what an investor is willing to pay for the stock. There are two ratios that use the current market price of a share of stock to help potential investors predict what they might earn by purchasing that stock. One ratio is the **price–earnings (P/E) ratio**. This ratio is defined by its name: It's the price of a share of stock divided by the company's current earnings per share.

$$\text{P/E Ratio} = \frac{\text{Market Price Per Share}}{\text{Earnings Per Share}}$$

Investors and financial analysts believe the P/E ratio indicates future earnings potential. A high P/E ratio indicates that the company has the potential for significant growth. When a new firm has no earnings, the P/E ratio has no meaning because the denominator is zero. For the first several years of business, Amazon.com had no earnings but a rising stock price. Analysts have varying opinions about the information contained in the P/E ratio. Read about it in *Accounting in the News*.

The other market indicator ratio is the **dividend yield ratio**. This ratio is the dividend per share divided by the market price per share. You may find that the values for the dividend yield ratio are quite low compared to the return an investor would expect on an investment. Investors are willing to accept a low dividend yield when they anticipate an increase in the price of the stock.

> **Dividend yield ratio:** Dividend per share divided by the current market price per share.

Accounting in the NEWS

Technology

Do P/E Ratios Help Identify Good Stocks to Buy?

Soon after Amazon.com debuted in 1994, Jeff Bezos and his handful of employees spent late summer nights packing books in a tiny warehouse, scrambling to ship a growing gush of orders.

Today, the man who has grown accustomed to being hailed the king of Internet commerce runs a global powerhouse that did nearly $7 billion in sales last year, dealing in everything from banjo cases to wild boar baby back ribs.

That's what CTV (a Canadian broadcast communications company, www.ctv.ca) had to say about Amazon.com on July 5, 2005. A share of stock in Amazon.com sold for $1.35 ten years ago and was selling for around $45 ten years later. Do you wish you'd purchased some Amazon.com stock ten years ago and still had it today? How could you have known what a great buy the stock was in 1995? Let's look at one of the measures an analyst might use.

Analysts spend a great deal of their time determining whether a stock is undervalued or overvalued. In 1996, Yale economist Robert J. Shiller called the P/E ratio the "simplest and most widely used ratio used to predict the market." A high P/E ratio indicated either a growth stock or perhaps a stock that was overvalued. A low P/E ratio indicated a stock could be undervalued. During the late 1990s, the proliferation of dot-com companies with no earnings were selling at high prices. That made the P/E ratio worthless as an indicator (no E in P/E!). From 1996 until the end of 2003, Amazon.com did not have a P/E ratio. Historical charts note an *N/A* (not applicable) in the column for Amazon.com's P/E ratio for those years. At the end of its 2003 fiscal year, Amazon.com's P/E ratio was 498.10. At the end of its 2004 fiscal year, its P/E ratio was 32.70.

Here's what Investopedia.com has to say about the P/E ratio:

Although a simple indicator to calculate, the P/E is actually quite difficult to interpret. It can be extremely informative in some situations, while at other times it is next to meaningless. As a result, investors often misuse this term and place more value in the P/E than is warranted.

Jeff Bezos founded Amazon.com in 1994 to make book buying an easy and fast shopping experience. He expanded into other products and by 2000 had 20 million customers in 160 countries.

Q What happens to the P/E ratio when a firm has to lower its earnings in a restatement?

A The P/E ratio goes up.

Sources: "Amazon.com Nears 10-year Anniversary," *CTV.ca* www.ctv.ca/servlet/ArticleNews/print/CTVNews/11205686682 09_12/?hub=SciTech&subhub=PrintStory, July 5, 2005; "Understanding the P/E Ratio," *Investopedia.com* www.investopedia.com/university/peratio/, June 2005; Daniel Altman, "Is the P/E Ratio Becoming Irrelevant?" *The New York Times*, July 21, 2002.

Exhibit 12.6

Price/Earnings and Dividend Yield Ratios

For fiscal years ended	American Greetings January 1, 2005	General Mills May 30, 2004
Earnings per share	$ 0.95	$2.82
Dividends per share	$ 0.12	$1.10
Ending market price per share	$25.35	$46.00
Price/earnings ratio	26.68	16.31
Dividend yield ratio	0.47%	2.4%

Stocks with low growth potential, however, may need to offer a higher dividend yield to attract investors.

$$\text{Dividend-yield Ratio} = \frac{\text{Dividend Per Share}}{\text{Market Price Per Share}}$$

Exhibit 12.6 above shows the earnings per share, the dividends per share, and the market price per share for American Greetings Corporation and for General Mills. Which stock would be a better buy for long-run growth? Which would be best if you needed regular dividend income?

The types of stock that will appeal to an investor depend on the investors' preferences for income and growth. A young investor, for example, will not need dividends from retirement funds invested in stocks. These long-term investors would prefer to invest in companies with high growth potential, no matter what the dividend yield. American Greetings might be more attractive, with its high P/E ratio of 26.68, than General Mills, with its lower P/E ratio of 16.31. A retiree who needs a dividend income for living expenses will be more concerned with the size of the dividend yield of an investment and less concerned with the investment's long-term growth. General Mills would be better than American Greetings for dividends.

These two market-related ratios are very important to management and to investors because analysts and investors use them in evaluating stocks. If you examine a company's annual report, you are likely to see these ratios reported, usually for the most recent two or three years. On page 715 in the Wal-Mart Annual Report in Appendix A in the back of the book, you'll see the dividend yield ratio for the past three years. Although Wal-Mart does not directly report its P/E ratio, the annual report provides both components—earnings per share on the income statement and the quarterly high and low market price of it stock. With that information, you can compute Wal-Mart's P/E ratio.

Understanding ratios

A ratio by itself does not give much information. To be useful a ratio must be compared to the same ratios from previous periods, ratios of other companies in the industry, or industry averages. Keep in mind that, with the exception of earnings per share, the calculations to arrive at a specific ratio may vary from company to company. There are no standard or required formulas to calculate a ratio. One company may calculate a debt ratio as *debt* to *equity*, while another company may calculate a debt ratio as *debt* to *debt plus equity*. When interpreting and using any company's ratios, be sure you know how those ratios have been computed. When you are computing ratios, be sure to be consistent in your calculations so you can make meaningful comparisons among them.

Even though the only ratio that must be calculated and presented as part of the financial statements is EPS, managers typically include in their company's annual report many of the ratios we've discussed in this chapter. When these ratios are not shown as part of the financial statements, they may be included in other parts of the annual report, often in graphs depicting ratio trends over several years.

Any valuable financial statement analysis requires more than a cursory review of ratios. The analyst must look at trends, components of the values that are part of the ratios, and other information about the company that may not even be contained in the financial statements.

Using ratio analysis

Let's compute some of the ratios shown in Exhibit 12.5 for J&J Snack Foods Corp. using the company's 2004 annual report. Exhibit 12.7 shows the income statements for three years, and Exhibit 12.8 shows the balance sheets for two years.

Other information needed for the analysis:

- Market price per share at the close of fiscal year: approximately $42 per share at September 25, 2004 and $40 per share at September 27, 2003.

- No dividends were paid by J&J Snack Foods Corp. during the fiscal years ended September 25, 2004 and September 27, 2003.

Exhibit 12.7

Income Statements for J&J Snack Foods Corp.

J&J Snack Foods Corporation Consolidated Statement of Earnings (in thousands, except per share data)			
Fiscal year ended	September 25, 2004 (52 weeks)	September 27, 2003 (52 weeks)	September 28, 2002 (52 weeks)
Net sales	$416,588	$364,567	$353,187
Cost of goods sold	276,379	239,722	233,730
Gross profit	140,209	124,845	119,457
Selling, general and administrative expenses	105,017	93,998	91,191
Operating profit	35,192	30,847	28,266
Investment income	566	362	268
Interest expense and other	(113)	(113)	(521)
Earnings before taxes	35,645	31,096	28,013
Income taxes	12,935	11,194	9,900
Net earnings	$ 22,710	$ 19,902	$ 18,113
Weighted average number of basic shares	8,909	8,800	8,770
Earnings per basic share	$ 2.55	$ 2.26	$ 2.07
Weighted average number of diluted shares	9,143	9,051	9,093
Earnings per diluted share	$ 2.48	$ 2.20	$ 1.99

The accompanying notes are an integral part of these statements.

Exhibit 12.8

Balance Sheets of J&J Snack Foods Corp.

> ### J&J Snack Foods Corporation
> ### Consolidated Balance Sheets
> (in thousands, except share amounts)

	At September 25, 2004	September 27, 2003
Assets		
Current assets		
Cash and equivalents	$ 56,100	$ 37,694
Receivables, Trade, less allowances of $1,104 and $991, respectively	47,753	37,645
Other receivables	233	516
Inventories	29,587	23,202
Prepaid expenses and other	4,739	4,143
Total current assets	138,412	103,200
Property, plant, and equipment, at cost	314,880	298,609
Less: accumulated depreciation	(225,406)	(211,494)
Property, plant, and equipment, net	89,474	87,115
Other assets		
Goodwill	46,477	45,850
Other intangible assets, net	1,804	1,231
Long-term investment securities held to maturity	—	275
Other receivables	1,257	1,807
	49,538	49,163
Total assets	$277,424	$239,478
Liabilities and Shareholders' equity		
Total current liabilities	$ 47,646	$ 40,058
Long-term liabilities	19,682	16,856
Shareholders' equity		
Preferred stock, $1 par value—5,000,000 shares authorized; none issued	—	—
Common stock, no par value—25,000,000 shares authorized;		
Issued and outstanding, 9,006,000 shares and 8,757,000 shares respectively	33,069	28,143
Retained earnings	179,088	156,378
Accumulated other comprehensive loss	(2,061)	(1,957)
Total shareholders' equity	210,096	182,564
Total liabilities and shareholders' equity	$277,424	$239,478

The accompanying notes are an integral part of these statements.

All the ratios shown in Exhibit 12.9 are calculated for J&J Snacks Corp. for the fiscal years ended September 25, 2004, and September 27, 2003. Even though two years of ratios do not give us enough information for making decisions, use this as an opportunity to practice how to calculate the ratios. Exhibit 12.9 shows the computations.

Exhibit 12.9

Ratio Analysis for J&J Snack Foods Corp.

Ratio	Definition	Computation	Computation	Interpretation
LIQUIDITY		For FYE September 25, 2004	For FYE September 27, 2003	
Current ratio	$\dfrac{\text{Total current assets}}{\text{Total current liabilities}}$	$\dfrac{138,412}{47,646} = 2.91$	$\dfrac{103,200}{40,058} = 2.58$	This is quite high. Industry average for processed and packaged goods industry is 1.9.
Acid-test ratio (also known as the quick ratio)	$\dfrac{\text{Cash + short-term + net accounts}}{\text{investments \quad receivable}}$ $\overline{\text{Total current liabilities}}$	$\dfrac{56,100 + 47,753}{47,646} = 2.18$	$\dfrac{37,694 + 37,645}{40,058} = 1.88$	This is a very high acid-test ratio. Industry average is 0.8.
Working capital (technically not a ratio, but still a measure of liquidity)	Total current assets − Total current liabilities	$138,412,000 - 47,646,000 =$ $\$90,766,000$	$103,200,000 - 40,058,000 =$ $\$63,142,000$	This amount supports the strong liquidity of the firm.
Inventory turnover ratio	$\dfrac{\text{Cost of goods sold}}{\text{Average inventory}}$	$\dfrac{276,379}{(29,587 + 23,202)/2} = 10.47$	$\dfrac{239,722}{(23,202 + 22,199*)/2} = 10.56$ *From the 2002 balance sheet, not shown here.	The inventory is turning over 10 times each year. Industry average is 10.6.
Accounts receivable turnover ratio	$\dfrac{\text{Net credit sales}}{\text{Average net accounts receivable}}$	$\dfrac{416,588}{(47,753 + 37,645)/2} = 9.76$	$\dfrac{364,567}{(37,645 + 36,922*)/2} = 9.78$ *From the 2002 balance sheet, not shown here.	The company is turning over its receivables more than 9 times each year. If you divide 365 days by 9.76, you'll see that it takes the company about 37 days to collect its receivables. The industry average is 34 days.
SOLVENCY				
Debt to equity	$\dfrac{\text{Total liabilities}}{\text{Total shareholders' equity}}$	$\dfrac{47,646 + 19,682}{210,096} = 0.32$	$\dfrac{40,058 + 16,856}{182,564} = 0.31$	The company does not have excessive debt. The industry average is 0.51.

As you evaluate the ratios, keep in mind that even two years' worth of ratios is rarely enough information to come to any conclusions. Most annual reports provide the data for ten years' worth of ratios. For J&J Snack Foods Corp., almost all of the ratios appear to be moving in the right direction. Often, ratio analysis is useful for showing potential problem areas. None is obvious for J&J Snack Foods Corp. from this analysis.

Exhibit 12.9

(continued)

Times interest earned ratio	$\dfrac{\text{Income from operations}}{\text{Interest expense}}$	$\dfrac{35,192}{113} = 311$	$\dfrac{30,847}{113} = 273$	This company has no problem meeting its interest obligation. The industry average is 6.4.
PROFITABILITY				
Return on assets	$\dfrac{\text{Net income + interest expense}}{\text{Average total assets}}$	$\dfrac{22,710 + 113}{(277,424 + 239,478)/2} = 8.83\%$	$\dfrac{19,902 + 113}{(239,478 + 220,036^*)/2} = 8.71\%$ *From the 2002 balance sheet, not shown here.	This is a good return on assets. The industry average is 4.6%.
Return on equity	$\dfrac{\text{Net income} - \text{preferred dividends}}{\text{Average common shareholders' equity}}$	$\dfrac{22,710 - 0}{(210,096 + 182,564)/2} = 11.57\%$	$\dfrac{19,902 - 0}{(182,564 + 168,709)/2} = 11.33\%$	Most investors would be happy to earn an 11% return on their investment. The industry average is 10%.
Gross profit percentage	$\dfrac{\text{Gross profit}}{\text{Net sales}}$	$\dfrac{140,209}{416,588} = 33.66\%$	$\dfrac{124,845}{364,567} = 34.24\%$	The gross profit % shows that for each dollar of product the company earns in sales, approximately $0.66 is the cost of the item to J&J Snack Foods. The industry average gross profit percentage is 36.8%.
Earnings per share	$\dfrac{\text{Net income} - \text{preferred dividends}}{\text{Weighted average number of shares of common stock outstanding}}$	$\dfrac{22,710 - 0}{8,909^*} = \$2.55$ *Disclosed on the income statement.	$\dfrac{19,902 - 0}{8,800^*} = \$2.26$ *Disclosed on the income statement.	A two-year trend in EPS is not very informative. However, for the two years shown, the ratio is certainly moving in the right direction.
MARKET INDICATORS				
Price–earnings ratio	$\dfrac{\text{Market price per common share}}{\text{Earnings per share}}$	$\dfrac{\$42}{\$2.55} = 16.47$	$\dfrac{\$40}{\$2.26} = 17.70$	This P/E ratio is a bit lower than the industry average of 19.8.
Dividend yield ratio	$\dfrac{\text{Dividend per share}}{\text{Market price per share}}$	$\dfrac{0}{\$42}$ N/A	$\dfrac{0}{\$40}$ N/A	Recall that this firm did not pay dividends.

Financial Statement Analysis— It's More than Numbers

You've probably noticed the following sentence at the end of every actual financial statement you've ever seen, "The accompanying notes are an integral part of these financial statements." Some analysts believe there is more real information about the financial health of a company in the notes than in the statements themselves. Go to the appendices in the back of the book where you'll find Wal-Mart's annual statement and Target's 10-K. Look at the detailed and extensive notes that accompany the statements. The more you learn about analyzing and evaluating a company's performance, whether in subsequent courses or in actual business experience, the more you will understand the information in the notes to the financial statements. When you are comparing two or more firms, you need to know the accounting choices those firms have made—like depreciation and inventory methods—to make valid comparisons. Often, analysts compute new amounts using a different method than the one the firm used so that amounts can be meaningfully compared to those of another firm. For example, if one company uses LIFO and another uses FIFO, an analyst would convert the LIFO values to FIFO values using the disclosures required to be in the notes of firms that use LIFO.

To better appreciate the role of accounting information in business, look at a business plan. A business plan is a detailed analysis of what it would take to start and maintain the operation of a successful business. Anyone writing a business plan includes a sales forecast, expense estimates, and prospective financial statements. These are "what-if" financial statements, forecasts that are part of the business plan. Banks often require these statements before they will lend money to a new firm.

Because accounting is such an integral part of business, accounting principles will continue to change as business changes. Each year, the FASB and the SEC add and change the rules for valuing items on the financial statements. FASB is also concerned with the continued usefulness and reliability of the accounting data from electronic transactions, e-business, and real-time access to financial data. As competition takes on new dimensions, particularly due to new technology, the scrutiny of a firm's financial information will increase. Together with the influence of the financial scandals of the early 2000s, the financial information needed for good decision making will continue to grow in importance.

Business risk, control, & ethics

LEARNING OBJECTIVE 4

Recognize the risks of investing in stock and explain how to control those risks.

We already discussed, in Chapter 1, the risks associated with starting a business. Now let's take the perspective of an investor. After all, you are very likely to buy stock in a publicly traded company sometime in your life. Many working people have money in retirement funds that are invested in the stock of publicly traded companies. Additionally, the movement of the stock market affects a large number of firms and individual investors. How should you, as an investor, minimize the risks associated with stock ownership? That risk, of course, is losing your money!

First, you should be diligent about finding a financial advisor or financial analyst to help you, or you should become an expert from your own study and analysis of available stocks. You also need to know and understand some financial accounting and financial statement analysis, which you've been exposed to

We've all heard the expression, "Don't put all your eggs in one basket." Some investors learned this lesson the hard way. The dot.com bust of early 2000 eroded millions of dollars because people were too heavily invested in technology stocks.

In Other Words:
A set of investments is called a portfolio. So a diversified set of investments is often called a diversified portfolio.

in this course. However, being knowledgeable or consulting an expert does not give an investor complete protection against losses.

That leads to the second and most effective way to minimize the risks associated with stock ownership: Diversify. In everyday usage, to diversify means to vary or expand. In the language of investment, diversify means to vary the investments you make—to expand beyond a narrow set of investments. Diversification means not putting all of your eggs in one basket. A diversified set of investments allows an investor to earn a higher rate of return for a given amount of risk.

There is no way to eliminate all of the risks of stock ownership, but having many different types of investments will help you minimize your risk or, equivalently, increase your return for a given amount of risk. According to Bank One, "A diversified portfolio does not concentrate in one or two investment categories. Instead, it includes some investments whose returns zig while the returns of other investments zag."

Accounting in the News gives an example of what happens when an investor fails to diversify a portfolio. In this case, however, it is a group of paid investment managers, and the portfolio belongs to thousands of current and future retirees of United Airlines. This is a case of bad investment decisions and may also be a case of bad ethics.

Accounting in the NEWS

Risk and Control

How Wall Street Wrecked United Airline's Pension

On July 31, 2005, that was the headline of a New York Times article about United Airline's pension plan. The federal agency that guarantees pensions, the Pension Benefit Guaranty Corporation, faced one of its worst losses ever in the failure of United's pension plan. What happened to United's pension plan?

While government analysts and pension fund experts focus on United's contributions to its pension plan, Doug Wilsman, a retired pilot, is focused on the investments made by the plan's paid investment managers. In 1987, Mr. Wilsman was a pilots' representative to United's pension fund. When he discovered that the plan's managers were putting most of the assets into the

stock market, he filed a grievance with his union. He worried that the plan would not be able to come up with the money it needed to pay retirees if and when the bottom was to fall out of the stock market. He wanted the managers to diversify the pension plan's investments to include bonds that matured as pensions became due.

According to *The New York Times* article, "money managers and other professionals who ran United's pension plan walked away from the wreck unscathed—indeed, they collected about $125 million in fees over the last five years alone." As United retirees take huge cuts in their pensions, they wonder about the ethics of the outside firms that managed their pension funds. While there are dozens of rules related to pensions to make sure workers are treated fairly and that firms contribute to their pension funds, there is no rule limiting the aggressive investment strategies of pension fund managers.

In 2005, United Airlines, operating in bankruptcy protection, received court permission to terminate employee pension plans. The cause of the default? Aggressive investment by the fund managers. The federal agency that guarantees pensions, the Pension Benefit guaranty Corporation, subject to bankruptcy court approval, will assume $1.4 billion in pension payments.

Source: Mary Williams Walsh, "How Wall Street Wrecked United's Pension," *The New York Times*, July 31, 2005, section 3, p. 1.

Let's Take a Test Drive

Real World Problem:
Wal-Mart or Target

In previous chapters, the conclusion to "You Make the Call" appeared before the "Let's Take a Test Drive" problem. In this chapter, however, you need to work out this problem before you can really make the call about whether to invest your money in Target or Wal-Mart. Your task is to use ratio analysis to help evaluate the past year's performance for both Target and Wal-Mart. Analyses of several years would be even better, so don't stop with a single year if you have time to analyze more.

Concepts

An important concept underlying financial statement analysis is that comparisons provide information and insights. And to make valid comparisons, we have to compare similar things—apples to apples, not apples to oranges. When you analyze a set of financial statements, compare your results to other years of the same company, to other companies in the same industry, and to industry standards. Don't rely on a single financial statement, a single piece of information, or a single ratio when evaluating a company's past, present, and future.

The Mechanics

To decide where to invest your $1,000, you will need to use the financial statements for the two most recent years for Wal-Mart and Target provided in Appendix A and Appendix B in the back of the book.

Instructions

Calculate the ratios we calculated for J &J Snack Foods Corporation, shown in Exhibit 12.9 for the most recent year for both Target and Wal-Mart. Then, make your choice and provide supporting evidence from your analysis. What else would you like to know about these companies?

Solution

(Amounts from the financial statements are in millions, except the market-indicator ratios.)

Ratio	Definition	Target	Wal-Mart	Interpretation
LIQUIDITY				
Current ratio	Total current assets / Total current liabilities	$\dfrac{13,922}{8,220} = 1.69$	$\dfrac{38,491}{42,888} = 0.90$	All three of these ratios indicate that Target is in a better position than Wal-Mart to meet its short-term obligations. According to MSN-Money (www.msn.com), the average current ratio for the industry is 1.1.
Acid-test ratio (also known as the quick ratio)	Cash + short-term + net accounts investments receivable / Total current liabilities	$\dfrac{2,245 + 5,069}{8,220} = 0.89$	$\dfrac{5,488 + 1,715}{42,888} = 0.17$	
Working capital (technically not a ratio, but still a measure of liquidity)	Total current assets – Total current liabilities	$13,922 - 8,220 = 5,702$	$38,491 - 42,888 = (4,397)$	

Ratio	Definition	Target	Wal-Mart	Interpretation
Inventory turnover ratio	$\dfrac{\text{Cost of goods sold}}{\text{Average inventory}}$	$\dfrac{31{,}445}{(5{,}384 + 4{,}531)/2} = 6.34$	$\dfrac{219{,}793}{(29{,}447 + 26{,}612)/2} = 7.84$	Both companies have an inventory turnover ratio that is close to the industry average of 7.3.
Accounts receivable turnover ratio	$\dfrac{\text{Net credit* sales}}{\text{Average net accounts receivable}}$ *Most firms do not disclose amounts for cash and credit sales, so we have to use total sales in the numerator.	$\dfrac{45{,}682}{(5{,}069 + 4{,}621)/2} = 9.43$	$\dfrac{285{,}222}{(1{,}715 + 1{,}254)/2} = 192.07$	Target has significantly more accounts receivable because the company offers its own credit to customers. Wal-Mart does not. Many of Wal-Mart's sales are for cash (checks and bank cards), which inflates the numerator and the resulting ratio.
SOLVENCY				
Debt to equity ratio	$\dfrac{\text{Total liabilities}}{\text{Total shareholders' equity}}$	$\dfrac{19{,}264}{13{,}029} = 1.48$	$\dfrac{70{,}827}{49{,}396} = 1.43$	We've used total liabilities in the numerator. You'll notice that some sources use only long-term debt in the numerator.
Times interest earned ratio	$\dfrac{\text{Income from operations}}{\text{Interest expense}}$	$\dfrac{3{,}601}{570} = 6.32$	$\dfrac{17{,}091}{986} = 17.33$	Both companies appear to have their interest payments well-covered.
PROFITABILITY				
Return on assets	$\dfrac{\text{Net income + interest expense}}{\text{Average total assets}}$	$\dfrac{3{,}198 + 570}{(32{,}293 + 31{,}416)/2} = 11.83\%$	$\dfrac{10{,}267 + 986}{(120{,}223 + 105{,}405)/2} = 9.97\%$	Both companies have an ROA near the industry average of 8.75. The average ROA for the S&P 500 is only 2.5.%
Return on equity	$\dfrac{\text{Net income − preferred dividends}}{\text{Average common shareholders' equity}}$	$\dfrac{3{,}198 - 0}{(13{,}029 + 11{,}132)/2} = 26.47\%$	$\dfrac{10{,}267 - 0}{(49{,}396 + 43{,}623)/2} = 22.07\%$	Target wins this one. However, both are well above the industry average of 20.9%. The S&P 500 has an average ROE of 14.7%.

Gross profit ratio	$\dfrac{\text{Gross profit}}{\text{Net sales}}$	$\dfrac{14,237}{45,682} = 31.17\%$	$\dfrac{65,429}{285,222} = 22.94\%$	Target wins this one. The industry average is 24.9%.
Earnings per share	$\dfrac{\text{Net income} - \text{preferred dividends}}{\text{Weighted average number of shares of common stock outstanding}}$	$\dfrac{3,198 - 0}{903.8*} = \$3.54$ *Provided on income statement.	$\dfrac{10,267 - 0}{4,259*} = \$2.41$ *Provided on income statement.	This is the basic EPS. Check out the firms' income statements for diluted EPS.
MARKET INDICATORS				
Price–earnings ratio	$\dfrac{\text{Market price per common share}}{\text{Earnings per share}}$	$\dfrac{\$50.47}{\$3.54} = 14.26$	$\dfrac{\$55.00}{\$2.41} = 22.82$	This ratio fluctuates with market prices, so it could change at any moment.
Dividend yield ratio	$\dfrac{\text{Dividend per share}}{\text{Market price per share}}$	$\dfrac{\$0.31}{\$50.47} = 0.61\%$	$\dfrac{\$0.52}{\$55.00} = 0.95\%$	Both companies pay dividends.

YOU make the call:

Should you invest in Wal-Mart or Target?

Now it's time for you to make the call. Do you want to invest in Wal-Mart or in Target? This time there is no right answer. Think about all the additional information you would want to have if you actually had some money to invest. Just for fun, pick one of these companies based on the financial ratios you calculated. Follow the market for the next few months to see if you are happy with your decision.

Rapid Review

1. **Recognize and explain the components of net income.** There are two items that, if they exist, must be segregated on the income statement from income from operations. They are (1) discontinued operations smf, and (2) extraordinary items. They are reported net of tax.

2. **Perform and interpret a horizontal analysis and a vertical analysis of financial statement information.** A horizontal analysis compares a specific financial statement item across time, often with reference to a chosen base year. A vertical analysis, also known as common size statements, shows every item on a single year's financial statements as a percentage of one of the other financial

statement items. For example, a vertical analysis of an income statement calculates all income statement items as a percentage of sales. The vertical analysis of the balance sheet usually shows all items as a percentage of total assets.

3. **Perform a basic ratio analysis of a set of financial statements and explain what the ratios mean.** *Ratio analysis* is a tool used by anyone who wants to evaluate a firm's financial statements. Remember that a ratio is meaningful only when it is compared to another ratio.

4. **Recognize the risks of investing in stock and explain how to control those risks.**

Key Terms

Discontinued operations, p. 620

Dividend yield ratio, p. 629

Extraordinary items, p. 621

Horizontal analysis, p. 623

Liquidity ratios, p. 625

Market indicators, p. 625

Price–earnings ratio, p. 628

Profitability ratios, p. 625

Solvency ratios, p. 625

Vertical analysis, p. 624

Have You Increased Your Business IQ?

Answer these questions to find out.

1. Why is a gain or loss from discontinued operations shown separately on the income statement after income from continuing operations?
   a. The information is usually obtained just before the financial statements are released and cannot be easily integrated.
   b. Accountants and their clients compromise with this solution because they disagree on exactly how the information should be presented.
   c. The financial effects are non-recurring, so these effects need to be separated so that investors can easily see that.
   d. Because all gains and losses must be shown separately.
2. What does it mean to common-size an income statement?
   a. To compute every amount on the statement as a percentage of the industry averages.
   b. Isolate the amounts that are common between two sets of financial statements.
   c. Express each value on the statement as a percentage change from a base year.
   d. Express each value on the statement as a percentage of a selected amount, usually sales.
3. A high inventory turnover ratio indicates that
   a. Inventory is selling rapidly.
   b. Inventory is not moving quickly.
   c. The company is ordering too much inventory.
   d. The company is selling its inventory faster than the industry average.
4. Which ratio is meaningless in a start-up company that has not yet earned a profit?
   a. Price/Earnings ratio
   b. Gross profit ratio
   c. Inventory turnover ratio
   d. Current ratio
5. Which ratio is always shown on the face of the income statement?
   a. Gross margin
   b. Earnings per share
   c. Dividend yield
   d. Return on assets

Now, check your answers.

1. c   2. d   3. a   4. a   5. b

- If you answered all five questions correctly, you've increased your business IQ by studying this chapter. It doesn't mean you've mastered all of the accounting concepts in the chapter. It simply means that you understand some of the general business concepts presented in this chapter.
- If you answered 2 to 4 questions correctly, you've made some progress but your business IQ has plenty of room to grow. You might want to skim over the chapter again.
- If you answered 0 or 1 question correctly, you can do more to improve your business IQ. Better study the chapter again

Questions

1. Define the items that the Financial Accounting Standards Board requires a firm to report separately on the income statement. Why is this separation useful?
2. What criteria must be met for an event to be considered extraordinary? Give examples of events that would be considered to be extraordinary.

3. What does it mean to show an item net of tax?
4. What is horizontal analysis? What is the purpose of this method of analysis?
5. What is vertical analysis? What is the purpose of this method of analysis?
6. What is liquidity? Which ratios are useful for measuring liquidity and what does each measure?
7. What is solvency? Which ratios are useful for measuring solvency and what does each measure?
8. What is profitability? Which ratios are useful for measuring profitability and what does each measure?
9. What are market indicators? Which ratios are market indicators and what does each measure?
10. How are financial ratios used to determine how successfully a company is operating?

Multiple Choice

1. Suppose a firm had an extraordinary loss of $300,000 on the disposal of a division. If the firm's tax rate is 35%, how will the loss be shown in the financial statements?
   a. On the income statement, below income from operations, net of tax savings, for a net loss of $195,000
   b. On the income statement as part of the calculation of income from operations, before taxes, for a loss of $300,000
   c. As supplementary information in the notes to the financial statements
   d. As a cash outflow from financing on the statement of cash flows

2. Current assets for Kearney Company are $120,000 and total assets are $600,000. Current liabilities are $80,000 and total liabilities are $300,000. What is the current ratio?
   a. 2.00
   b. 2.50
   c. 1.90
   d. 1.50

3. Ritchie Company sold some fixed assets for a gain of $100,000. The firm's tax rate is 25%. How would Ritchie Company report this transaction on its financial statements?
   a. On the income statement as part of the calculation of income from continuing operations, net of tax, in the amount of $75,000
   b. As an extraordinary item, net of tax, in the amount of $75,000
   c. As discontinued operations, net of tax, in the amount of $75,000
   d. On the income statement as part of the calculation of income from continuing operations at the before tax amount of $100,000

4. Gerard Company reported Sales of $300,000 for 2006, $330,000 for 2007, and $360,000 for 2008. If the company uses 2006 as the base year, what were the percentage increases for 2007 and 2008 compared to the base year?
   a. 10% for 2007 and 10% for 2008
   b. 120% for 2007 and 120% for 2008
   c. 110% for 2007 and 110% for 2008
   d. 10% for 2007 and 20% for 2008

5. On June 30, Star Radio reported total current assets of $45,000, total assets of $200,000, total current liabilities of $42,000, and total liabilities of $80,000. How much working capital did Star Radio have on this date?
   a. $87,000
   b. $200,000
   c. $3,000
   d. $123,000

6. Talking Puppet Company reported a P/E ratio of $50 on the last day of the fiscal year. If the company reported earnings of $2.50 per share, how much was a share of the company's stock trading for at that time?
   a. $20 per share
   b. $125 per share
   c. $50 per share
   d. $47.50 per share

7. Singleton Company had sales of $2,000,000, cost of sales of $1,200,000, and average inventory of $400,000. What was the company's inventory turnover ratio for the period?
   a. 3.00
   b. 4.00
   c. 5.00
   d. 0.33

8. Suppose a firm had an inventory turnover ratio of 20. Suppose the firm considers a year to be 360 days. How many days, on average, does an item remain in the inventory?
   a. 5.56 days
   b. 18 days
   c. 20 days
   d. 360 days

9. Suppose a new company is trying to decide whether to use LIFO or FIFO in a period of rising inventory costs. The CFO suggests using LIFO because it will give a higher inventory turnover ratio. Is he correct?
   a. Yes, the average inventory will be lower (the ratio's denominator) and the cost of goods sold (the ratio's numerator) will be higher than if FIFO were used
   b. No, the average inventory would be the same because purchases are the same no matter which inventory method is chosen
   c. The inventory method has no effect on the inventory turnover ratio
   d. Without specific inventory amounts, it is not possible to predict the effect of the inventory method

10. If a firm has $100,000 debt and $100,000 equity, then
   a. The return on equity ratio is 1
   b. The debt-to-equity ratio is 1
   c. The return on assets ratio is 0.5
   d. The firm has too much debt

Short Exercises

LO 1   **SE12-1. Discontinued operations.**
In 2006, Earthscope Company decided to sell its satellite sales division, even though the division had been profitable during the year. During 2006, the satellite division earned $54,000 and the taxes on that income were $12,500. The division was sold for a gain of $750,000, and the taxes on the gain amounted to $36,700. How would these amounts be reported on the income statement for the year ended December 31, 2006?

LO 1   **SE12-2. Discontinued operations.**
In 2007, Office Products decided to sell its furniture division because it had been losing money for several years. During 2007, the furniture division lost $140,000. The tax savings related to the loss amounted to $25,000. The division was sold at a loss of $350,000, and the tax savings related to the loss on the sale was $50,000. How would these amounts be reported on the income statement for the year ended December 31, 2007?

LO 1   **SE12-3. Discontinued operations.**
After the terrorist attacks on the World Trade Center in 2001, Congress passed a law requiring new security devices in airports. One airport security firm had to get rid of an entire segment of the business that produced the old devices, and they suffered a significant loss on the disposal of the segment. The loss amounted to $320,000, with a related tax benefit of 10% of the loss. How would this be reported on the firm's income statement?

LO 1   **SE12-4. Extraordinary item.**
Sew and Save Company suffered an extraordinary loss of $30,000 last year. The related tax savings amounted to $5,600. How would this tax savings be reported on the income statement?

LO 2   **SE12-5. Horizontal analysis.**
Olin Copy Corporation reported the following amounts on its 2007 comparative income statement:

(in thousands)	2007	2006	2005
Revenues	$6,400	$4,575	$3,850
Cost of sales	3,900	2,650	2,050

Perform a horizontal analysis of revenues and cost of sales in both dollar amounts and in percentages for 2007 and 2006, using 2005 as the base year.

LO 2   **SE12-6. Horizontal analysis.**
Use the following information about the capital expenditures of Andes Company to perform a horizontal analysis, with 2004 as the base year. What information does this provide about Andes Company?

(in millions)	2007	2006	2005	2004
Capital expenditures	$41,400	$45,575	$43,850	$50,600

SE12-7. Vertical analysis.

Bessie's Quilting Company reported the following amounts on its balance sheet at December 31, 2007:

Cash	$ 5,000
Accounts receivable, net	40,000
Inventory	35,000
Equipment, net	120,000
Total assets	$200,000

Perform a vertical analysis of the assets of Bessie's Quilting Company. Use total assets as the base. What information does the analysis provide?

SE12-8. Vertical analysis.

Perform a vertical analysis on the following income statement, with sales as the base amount. What other information would you need to make this analysis meaningful?

Sales	$35,000
Cost of goods sold	14,000
Gross margin	21,000
Other expenses	7,000
Net income	$14,000

SE12-9. Ratio analysis.

Fireworks reported current assets of $720,000 and a current ratio of 1.2. What were current liabilities? What was working capital?

SE12-10. Ratio analysis.

A five-year comparative analysis of Low Light Company's current ratio and quick ratio follows:

	2004	2005	2006	2007	2008
Current ratio	1.19	1.85	2.50	3.40	4.02
Acid-test ratio	1.15	1.02	0.98	0.72	0.50

a. What has been happening to the liquidity of Low Light Company over the five years presented?
b. Considering both ratios, what does the trend indicate about what has happened to the makeup of Low Light's current assets over the five-year period?

SE12-11. Ratio analysis.

A company's debt to equity ratio has been increasing for the past four years. Give at least two company actions that might have caused this increase.

SE12-12. Ratio analysis.

The following is a five-year comparative analysis of Accent Company's return on assets and return on equity:

	2005	2006	2007	2008	2009
Return on assets	8%	7.5%	7.12%	6.54%	6%
Return on equity	20%	21%	21.8%	22.2%	23%

a. What does this analysis tell you about the overall profitability of Accent Company over the five-year period?
b. What does this analysis tell you about what has happened to Accent's amount of debt over the past five years?

SE12-13. Ratio analysis.

Earnings for Archibold Company have been fairly constant over the past six months, but the P/E ratio has been climbing steadily. How do you account for this climb? What does it tell you about the market's view of the company's future?

SE12-14. Risk and control.

Suppose you are the financial advisor to AHA Company, a local software development company. The CFO suggests the firm invest all of its extra cash in technology stocks.

He thinks that will demonstrate the company's confidence in that sector of the market. What advice would you give him and why?

SE12-15. Appendix A: Comprehensive income.
Give an example of a gain or loss that would be excluded from the income statement and shown directly on the balance sheet as part of accumulated other comprehensive income.

SE12-16. Appendix B: Investments.
Convey Company had some extra cash and purchased the stock of various companies with the objective of making a profit in the short run. The cost of Convey's portfolio was $79,450 at December 31, 2008. On that date, the market value of the portfolio was $85,200. How would this increase in value be reflected in Convey's financial statements for the year ended December 31, 2008?

Exercise Set A

LO 1   ### E12-1A. Discontinued operations.
Use the following information to construct a partial income statement beginning with income from continuing operations:

Income from continuing operations	$230,000
Loss during the year from operating discontinued operations	50,000
Tax benefit of loss	8,500
Loss from sale of discontinued operations	138,500
Tax savings from loss on the sale	41,000

LO 1   ### E12-2A. Extraordinary item and change in accounting principle.
Devon's Central Processing Agency suffered a $560,000 loss due to a disaster that qualifies as an extraordinary item for financial statement purposes. The tax benefit of the loss amounts to $123,000. If income from continuing operations (net of tax) amounted to $1,300,500, what is net income?

LO 2   ### E12-3A. Horizontal analysis.
Jones Furniture reported the following amounts for its sales during the past five years. Using 2004 as the base year, perform a horizontal analysis. What information does the analysis provide that was not apparent from the raw numbers?

2008	2007	2006	2005	2004
$30,000	$28,400	$26,300	$24,200	$25,400

LO 2   ### E12-4A. Vertical analysis.
Use the income statement from Color Copy to perform a vertical analysis with sales as the base.

Color Copy, Inc.

Income Statement

For the year ended September 30, 2006

Sales revenue		$10,228
Cost of goods sold		5,751
Gross profit		$ 4,477
Operating expenses:		
Depreciation—buildings and equipment	$ 100	
Other selling and administrative	2,500	
Total expenses		2,600
Income before interest and taxes		$ 1,877
Interest expense		350
Income before taxes		$ 1,527
Income taxes		150
Net income		$ 1,377

E12-5A. Current ratio and working capital.   LO 3

Calculate the current ratio and the amount of working capital for Albert's Hotels
for the years given in the following comparative balance sheets. Although two
years is not much of a trend, what is your opinion of the direction of these
ratios?

Albert's Hotels, Inc.
Balance Sheet
At December 31, 2006 and 2005

	2006	**2005**
Current assets:		
Cash	$ 98,000	$ 90,000
Accounts receivable, net	110,000	116,000
Inventory	170,000	160,000
Prepaid expenses	18,000	16,000
Total current assets	396,000	382,000
Equipment, net	184,000	160,000
Total assets	$580,000	$542,000
Total current liabilities	$206,000	$223,000
Long-term liabilities	119,000	117,000
Total liabilities	325,000	340,000
Common stockholders' equity	90,000	90,000
Retained earnings	165,000	112,000
Total liabilities and stockholders' equity	$580,000	$542,000

E12-6A. Debt to equity ratio.   LO 3

Use the balance sheets from Albert's Hotels in E12-5A to compute the debt to equity
ratio for 2006 and 2005. Suppose you calculated a debt ratio using debt plus equity as
the denominator. Which ratio—debt to equity or debt to debt plus equity—seems
easiest to interpret? As an investor, do you view the "trend" in the debt to equity ratio
as favorable or unfavorable? Why?

E12-7A. Ratio analysis.   LO 3

Zap Electronics reported the following for the fiscal years ended January 31, 2006, and
January 31, 2005:

January 31	**2006**	**2005**
(in thousands)		
Accounts receivable	$ 36,184	$ 24,306
Inventory	106,754	113,875
Current assets	174,369	124,369
Current liabilities	71,616	68,001
Long-term liabilities	12,316	35,200
Shareholders' equity	121,851	198,935
Sales	712,855	580,223
Cost of goods sold	483,463	400,126
Interest expense	335	709
Net income	11,953	4,706

Assume all sales are on credit, and the firm has no preferred stock outstanding.
Calculate the following ratios:

a. Current ratio (for both years)
b. Accounts receivable turnover ratio (for 2006)
c. Inventory turnover ratio (for 2006)
d. Debt to equity ratio (for both years)
e. Return on equity ratio (for 2006)

Do any of these ratios suggest problems for the company?

LO 3   **E12-8A. Ratio analysis.**

Evans Family Grocers reported the following for the two most recent fiscal years:

December 31	2007	2006
Cash	$ 25,000	$ 20,000
Receivables (net)	60,000	70,000
Merchandise inventory	55,000	30,000
Plant assets	280,000	260,000
Total assets	$420,000	$380,000
Accounts payable	45,000	62,000
Long-term notes payable	75,000	100,000
Common stock	135,000	122,000
Retained earnings	165,000	96,000
Total Liabilities and Shareholders' Equity	$420,000	$380,000
Net income for the year ended 12/31/07	$ 75,000	
Sales (all sales were on account)	450,000	
Cost of goods sold	210,000	
Interest expense	1,500	

Calculate the following for the year ended December 31, 2007:

  a. Current ratio

  b. Working capital

  c. Accounts receivable turnover ratio

  d. Inventory turnover ratio

  e. Return on assets

  f. Return on equity

LO 3   **E12-9A. Ratio analysis.**

Furniture Showcase reported the following for its fiscal year ended June 30, 2006:

Sales	$530,000
Cost of sales	300,000
Gross margin	230,000
Expenses*	113,000
Net income	$117,000

*Included in the expenses was
$12,000 of interest expense Assume
no income tax expense.

At the beginning of the year, the company had 50,000 shares of common stock outstanding. At the end of the year, there were 40,000 shares outstanding. The market price of the company's stock at year-end was $20 per share. The company declared and paid $80,000 of dividends near year-end.

    Calculate earnings per share, the price–earnings ratio, and times-interest-earned ratio for Furniture Showcase.

    Use the balance sheet and income statement for General Motors Corporation for E12-10A through E12-13A.

General Motors Corporation
Consolidated Balance Sheets
At December 31,

(in millions)

	2003	2002
ASSETS		
Automotive and Other Operations		
Cash and cash equivalents (Note 1)	$ 14,424	$ 12,162
Marketable securities (Note 6)	9,067	2,174
Total cash and marketable securities	23,491	14,336
Accounts and notes receivable (less allowances)	5,380	4,735
Inventories (less allowances) (Note 9)	10,960	9,737
Assets of discontinued operations	—	18,653
Net equipment on operating leases (less accumulated depreciation) (Note 10)	7,173	5,305
Deferred income taxes and other current assets (Note 11)	10,851	9,631
Total current assets	57,855	62,397
Equity in net assets of nonconsolidated affiliates	6,032	5,097
Property—net (Note 12)	36,071	34,135
Intangible assets—net (Notes 1 and 13)	1,479	7,453
Deferred income taxes (Note 11)	18,086	31,431
Other assets (Note 14)	42,262	1,461
Total Automotive and Other Operations assets	161,785	141,974
Financing and Insurance Operations		
Cash and cash equivalents (Note 1)	18,130	8,158
Investments in securities (Note 6)	13,148	14,651
Finance receivables—net (Note 8)	173,137	134,643
Loans held for sale	19,609	15,720
Net equipment on operating leases (less accumulated depreciation) (Note 10)	27,210	25,721
Other assets (Note 14)	35,488	28,186
Net receivable from Automotive and Other Operations (Note 1)	1,492	1,089
Total Financing and Insurance Operations assets	288,214	228,168
Total assets	$449,999	$370,142
LIABILITIES AND STOCKHOLDERS' EQUITY		
Automotive and Other Operations		
Accounts payable (principally trade)	$ 21,542	$ 17,919
Loans payable (Note 16)	2,813	1,994
Liabilities of discontinued operations	—	7,956
Accrued expenses (Note 15)	45,417	39,113
Net payable to Financing and Insurance Operations (Note 1)	1,492	1,089
Total current liabilities	71,264	68,071
Long-term debt (Note 16)	29,593	14,261
Postretirement benefits other than pensions (Note 17)	32,285	34,244
Pensions (Note 17)	7,952	22,633
Other liabilities and deferred income taxes (Notes 11 and 15)	15,567	13,734
Total Automotive and Other Operations liabilities	156,661	152,943
Financing and Insurance Operations		
Accounts payable	3,880	3,219
Debt (Note 16)	239,350	183,913
Other liabilities and deferred income taxes (Note 11 and 15)	24,533	22,974
Total Financing and Insurance Operations liabilities	267,763	210,106
Total liabilities	424,424	363,049
Minority interests	307	279
Total stockholders' equity	25,268	6,814
Total liabilities and stockholders' equity	$449,999	$370,142

General Motors Corporation
Consolidated Statements of Income
For the years ended December 31,

(in millions)

	2003	2002	2001
Total net sales and revenues (Notes 1 and 24)	$185,524	$177,324	$169,051
Cost of sales and other expenses (Note 5)	152,071	146,793	138,847
Selling, general, and administrative expenses	21,008	20,690	19,433
Interest expense (Note 16)	9,464	7,503	8,317
Total costs and expenses	182,543	174,986	166,597
Income from continuing operations before income taxes, equity income and minority interests	2,981	2,338	2,454
Income tax expense (Note 11)	731	644	1,094
Equity income (loss) and minority interests	612	281	(138)
Income from continuing operations	2,862	1,975	1,222
(Loss) from discontinued operations (Note 2)	(219)	(239)	(621)
Gain on sale of discontinued operations	1,179	—	—
Net income	$ 3,822	$ 1,736	$ 601

Source: www.gm.com/company/investor_information/docs/fin_data/gm03ar/download/gm03arfinancials.pdf

LO 2

E12-10A. Horizontal analysis.

Use the statement of income for General Motors Corporation provided above to perform a horizontal analysis for each item reported for the year from December 31, 2002 to December 31, 2003. What does your analysis tell you about the operations of General Motors for the year?

LO 2

E12-11A. Vertical analysis.

Use the statement of income for General Motors Corporation provided above to perform a vertical analysis for each item reported for 2003 and 2002 using Total Net Sales and Revenues as the base. What does your analysis tell you about the operations of General Motors for the years reported?

LO 3

E12-12A. Liquidity ratios.

Use the financial statements for General Motors Corporation provided above to calculate the following liquidity ratios for 2003 for the firm as a whole. What information does this provide about the firm's liquidity? (Perform your analysis using the amounts from Automotive and Other Operations.)

a. Current ratio
b. Acid-test ratio
c. Working capital
d. Inventory turnover ratio
e. Accounts receivable turnover ratio

LO 3

E12-13A. Solvency and profitability ratios.

Use the financial statements for General Motors Corporation provided above to calculate the following solvency and profitability ratios for 2003 for the firm as a whole. What information does this provide about the firm's solvency and profitability?

a. Debt to equity
b. Times interest earned ratio
c. Return on assets
d. Return on equity (assume no preferred stock)
e. Gross margin percentage

E12-14A. Risk and Control.

LO 4   Often a firm will contribute its own shares of stock to its pension fund rather than cash. What problem could this cause? How could it be avoided? Have you heard of any firm that did this and the result was a disaster?

E12-15A. Appendix B: Investments.

Omicron Corporation invested $125,000 of its extra cash in securities. Under each of the following independent scenarios, (a) calculate the amount at which the investments would be valued for the year-end balance sheet, and (b) indicate how the effect of these scenarios should be reported on the other financial statements, if at all.

1. All the securities were debt securities, with a maturity date in two years. Omicron will hold the securities until they mature. The market value of the securities at year-end was $123,000.
2. Omicron purchased the securities for trading, hoping to make a quick profit. At year-end the market value of the securities was $120,000.
3. Omicron is uncertain about how long it will hold the securities. At year-end the market value of the securities is $126,000.

E12-16A. Appendix B: Investments.

During 2007, Nike has invested $200,000 of extra cash in securities. Of the total amount invested, $75,000 was invested in bonds that Nike plans to hold until maturity (the bonds were issued at par value); $65,000 was invested in various equity securities that Nike plans to hold for an indefinite period of time; and $60,000 was invested in the stock of various companies that Nike intends to trade to make a short-term profit. At the end of the year, the market value of the held-to-maturity securities was $80,000; the market value of the trading securities was $75,000; and the market value of the available-for-sale securities was $55,000. Record all adjustments required at year-end and indicate how the effects of each group of securities will be reported on the financial statements.

Exercise Set B

Your professor may ask you to complete selected "Group B" exercises and problems using Prentice Hall Grade Assist (PHGA). PHGA is an online tool that can help you master the chapter's topics by providing multiple variations of exercises and problems. You can rework these exercises and problems—each time with new data—as many times as you need, with immediate feedback and grading.

E12-1B. Discontinued operations.   LO 1

Use the following information to construct a partial income statement beginning with income from continuing operations:

Income from continuing operations	$310,000
Loss during the year from operation of discontinued operations	75,000
Tax benefit of loss	19,400
Loss from sale of discontinued operations	105,750
Tax savings from loss on the sale	32,000

E12-2B. Extraordinary items and change in accounting   LO 1
principle.

Tropical Vacations suffered a $1,070,000 loss due to a tsunami, which qualifies as an extraordinary item for financial statement purposes. The tax benefit of the loss amounts to $155,000. If income from continuing operations (net of tax) amounted to $1,861,250, what is net income?

E12-3B. Horizontal analysis.   LO 2

Making Every Day Sunny Umbrellas reported the following amounts for Sales during the past five years. Using 2006 as the base year, perform a horizontal analysis. What information does the analysis provide that was not apparent from the raw numbers?

2010	2009	2008	2007	2006
$27,925	$30,400	$33,525	$26,250	$30,300

E12-4B. Vertical analysis.   LO 2

Use the income statement from Designers Discount, Inc. to perform a vertical analysis with sales as the base.

Designers Discount, Inc.
Income Statement
For the year ended March 28, 2008

Sales revenue		$16,374
Cost of goods sold		7,985
Gross profit on sales		$8,389
Operating expenses:		
Depreciation—buildings and equipment	$ 265	
Other selling and administrative	3,750	
Total expenses		4,015
Income before interest and taxes		$4,374
Interest expense		254
Income before taxes		$4,120
Income taxes		1,236
Net income		$2,884

LO 3   **E12-5B. Current ratio and working capital.**

Calculate the current ratio and the amount of working capital for Mike & Kat Racing Company for the years given in the following comparative balance sheets. Although two years will not show a significant trend, what is your opinion of the direction of these ratios?

Mike & Kat Racing Company
Balance Sheet
At December 31, 2008 and 2007

	2008	**2007**
Current assets:		
Cash	$186,000	$192,000
Accounts receivable, net	94,000	85,000
Inventory	185,000	170,500
Prepaid expenses	17,000	14,000
Total current assets	482,000	461,500
Equipment, net	215,000	195,000
Total assets	$697,000	$656,500
Total current liabilities	$267,000	$269,000
Long-term liabilities	185,000	190,000
Total liabilities	452,000	459,000
Shareholders' equity	163,750	148,250
Retained Earnings	81,250	49,250
Total liabilities and shareholders' equity	$697,000	$656,500

LO 3   **E12-6B. Debt to equity ratio.**

Use the balance sheets from Mike & Kat Racing Company in E12-5B to compute a debt to equity ratio for 2008 and 2007. Suppose you calculated a debt ratio using debt plus equity as the denominator. Which ratio—debt to equity or debt to debt plus equity—seems easiest to interpret? As an investor, do you view the "trend" in the debt to equity ratio as favorable or unfavorable? Why?

LO 3   **E12-7B. Ratio analysis.**

Crystal Cromartie's Frozen Foods reported the following for the fiscal years ended September 30, 2008, and September 30, 2007:

September 30	2008	2007
(in millions)		
Accounts receivable	$ 21,265	$ 13,802
Inventory	45,692	47,682
Current assets	185,716	155,716
Current liabilities	80,954	72,263
Long-term liabilities	15,251	17,852
Shareholders' equity	21,871	58,035
Sales	88,455	70,223
Cost of goods sold	60,463	52,750
Interest expense	21.5	43.2
Net income	1,842	1,006

Assume there is no outstanding preferred stock and all sales are credit sales. Calculate the following ratios:

a. Current ratio (for both years)
b. Accounts receivable turnover ratio (for 2008)
c. Inventory turnover ratio (for 2008)
d. Debt to equity ratio (for both years)
e. Return on equity (for 2008)

Do any of these ratios suggest problems for the company?

E12-8B. Ratio analysis.

LO 3

Hutson Coffee Shops reported the following for the two most recent fiscal years:

December 31	2010	2009
Cash	$ 34,000	$ 17,000
Receivables (net)	85,000	80,000
Merchandise inventory	74,000	48,000
Fixed assets	365,000	324,000
Total assets	$558,000	$469,000
Accounts payable	65,000	83,000
Long-term notes payable	82,000	112,000
Common stock	176,000	144,000
Retained earnings	235,000	130,000
Total liabilities and		
shareholders' equity	$558,000	$469,000
Net income for the year ended 12/31/10	$115,000	
Sales (all sales were on account)	620,000	
Cost of goods sold	284,000	
Interest expense	3,000	

Calculate the following for the year ended December 31, 2010:

a. Current ratio
b. Working capital
c. Accounts receivable turnover ratio
d. Inventory turnover ratio
e. Return on assets
f. Return on equity

E12-9B. Ratio analysis.

LO 3

International Imports Corporation reported the following for its fiscal year ended June 30, 2007:

Sales	$640,000
Cost of sales	470,000
Gross margin	170,000
Expenses*	94,000
Net income	$ 76,000

*Included in the expenses were $9,000 of interest expense and $14,000 of income tax expense.

At the beginning of the year, the company had 40,000 shares of common stock outstanding and no preferred stock. At the end of the year, there were 25,000 common shares outstanding and no preferred stock. The market price of the company's stock at year-end was $15 per share. The company declared and paid $46,000 of dividends near year end.

Calculate earnings per share, the price–earnings ratio, and times-interest-earned for International Imports.

Use the balance sheet and income statement for ChevronTexaco Corporation for E12-10B through E12-13B.

Chevron Texaco Corporation
Consolidated Balance Sheet
At December 31

(in millions except per-share amounts)

	2004	2003
ASSETS		
Cash and cash equivalents	$ 9,291	$ 4,266
Marketable securities	1,451	1,001
Accounts and notes receivable (less allowance: 2004—$174; 2003—$179)	12,429	9,722
Inventories:		
Crude oil and petroleum products	2,324	2,003
Chemicals	173	173
Materials, supplies and other	486	472
	2,983	2,648
Prepaid expenses and other current assets	2,349	1,789
TOTAL CURRENT ASSETS	28,503	19,426
Long-term receivables, net	1,419	1,493
Investments and advances	14,389	12,319
Properties, plant, and equipment, at cost	103,954	100,556
Less: Accumulated depreciation, depletion and amortization	59,496	56,018
	44,458	44,538
Deferred charges and other assets	4,277	2,594
Assets held for sale	162	1,100
TOTAL ASSETS	$ 93,208	$ 81,470
LIABILITIES AND STOCKHOLDERS' EQUITY		
Short-term debt	$ 816	$ 1,703
Accounts payable	10,747	8,675
Accrued liabilities	3,410	3,172
Federal and other taxes on income	2,502	1,392
Other taxes payable	1,320	1,169
TOTAL CURRENT LIABILITIES	18,795	16,111
Long-term debt	10,217	10,651
Capital lease obligations	239	243
Deferred credits and other noncurrent obligations	7,942	7,758
Noncurrent deferred income taxes	7,268	6,417
Reserves for employee benefit plans	3,345	3,727
Minority interests	172	268
TOTAL LIABILITIES	47,978	45,175
Preferred stock (authorized 100,000,000 shares, $1.00 par value; none Issued)	—	—
Common stock (authorized 4,000,000,000 shares, $0.75 par value; 2,274,032,014 and 2,274,042,114 shares issued at December 31, 2004 and 2003, respectively*)	1,706	1,706
Capital in excess of par value*	4,160	4,002
Retained earnings	45,414	35,315
Accumulated other comprehensive loss	(319)	(809)
Deferred compensation and benefit plan trust	(607)	(602)
Treasury stock, at cost (2004—166,911,890 shares; 2003—135,746,674 shares*)	(5,124)	(3,317)
TOTAL STOCKHOLDERS' EQUITY	45,230	36,295
TOTAL LIABILITIES AND STOCKHOLDERS' EQUITY	$ 93,208	$ 81,470

*2003 restated to reflect a two-for-one stock split effected as a 100 percent stock dividend in September 2004.

See accompanying Notes to the Consolidated Financial Statements.

Chevron Texaco Corporation
Consolidated Statement of Income
For the year ended December 31,

(in millions except per-share amounts)

	Year ended December 31,		
	2004	**2003**	**2002**
REVENUES AND OTHER INCOME			
Sales and other operating revenues	$150,865	$119,575	$98,340
Income (loss) from equity affiliates	2,582	1,029	(25)
Other income	1,853	308	222
Gain from exchange of Dynegy, preferred stock	—	365	—
TOTAL REVENUES AND OTHER INCOME	155,300	121,277	98,537
COSTS AND OTHER DEDUCTIONS			
Purchased crude oil and products	94,419	71,310	57,051
Operating expenses	9,832	8,500	7,795
Selling, general and administrative expenses	4,557	4,440	4,155
Exploration expenses	697	570	591
Depreciation, depletion and amortization	4,935	5,326	5,169
Taxes other than on income	19,818	17,901	16,682
Interest and debt expense	406	474	565
Minority interests	85	80	57
Write-down of investments in Dynegy, Inc.	—	—	1,796
Merger-related expenses			576
TOTAL COSTS AND OTHER DEDUCTIONS	134,749	108,601	94,437
INCOME FROM CONTINUING OPERATIONS BEFORE INCOME TAX EXPENSE	20,551	12,676	4,100
INCOME TAX EXPENSE	7,517	5,294	2,998
INCOME FROM CONTINUING OPERATIONS	13,034	7,382	1,102
INCOME FROM DISCONTINUED OPERATIONS	294	44	30
***INCOME BEFORE CUMULATIVE EFFECT OF CHANGES IN ACCOUNTING PRINCIPLES**	$ 13,328	$ 7,426	$ 1,132
Cumulative effect of changes in accounting principles	—	(196)	—
NET INCOME	$ 13,328	$ 7,230	$ 1,132

*As of May 2005, this adjustment will not be shown on the income statement. It will be recorded directly to Retained Earnings.

Source: www.chevron.com/investor/annual/2004/pdfs/cvx_2004ar_financials.pdf.

E12-10B. Horizontal analysis.
LO 2

Use the statement of income for ChevronTexaco Corporation provided above to perform a horizontal analysis for each item reported for the year from December 31, 2003 to December 31, 2004. What does your analysis tell you about the operations of ChevronTexaco for the years reported?

E12-11B. Vertical analysis.
LO 2

Use the statement of income for ChevronTexaco Corporation provided above to perform a vertical analysis for each item reported for 2004 and 2003 using sales and other operating revenues as the base. What does your analysis tell you about the operations of ChevronTexaco for the years reported?

E12-12B. Liquidity ratios.
LO 3

Use the financial statements for ChevronTexaco Corporation provided above to calculate the following liquidity ratios for 2004. What do these ratios tell about the firm?

a. Current ratio
b. Acid-test ratio
c. Working capital

LO 3 **E12-13B. Solvency and profitability ratios.**
Use the financial statements for ChevronTexaco Corporation provided on pages 652–653 to calculate the following solvency ratios and profitability for 2004 and provide the interpretation for each ratio as it relates to ChevronTexaco. (Note: Use sales and other operating revenue less purchased crude oil and products to get gross margin.)

a. Debt to equity
b. Times interest earned ratio
c. Return on assets
d. Return on equity
e. Gross margin percentage

LO 4 **E12-14B. Risk and control.**
Describe the risks of investing your money in the stock market. How can you reduce those risks? Why are you willing to take risks like these?

E12-15B. Appendix B: Investments.
Kinsey Scales invested $164,000 of its extra cash in securities. Under each of the following independent scenarios, (a) calculate the amount at which the investments would be valued for the year-end balance sheet, and (b) indicate how these scenarios should be reported on the other financial statements, if at all.

1. All the securities were debt securities, with a maturity date in two years. Kinsey will hold the securities until they mature. The market value of the securities at year-end was $158,000.
2. Kinsey purchased the securities for trading, hoping to make a quick profit. At year-end the market value of the securities was $162,000.
3. Kinsey is uncertain about how long it will hold the securities. At year-end the market value of the securities is $167,000.

E12-16B. Appendix B: Investments.
During 2009, Arctic Fans & Blowers has invested $245,000 of extra cash in securities. Of the total amount invested, $115,000 was invested in bonds that Arctic plans to hold until maturity (the bonds were issued at par); $55,000 was invested in various equity securities that Arctic plans to hold for an indefinite period of time; and $75,000 was invested in the stock of various companies that Arctic intends to trade to make a short-term profit. At the end of the year, the market value of the held-to-maturity securities was $108,000, the market value of the trading securities was $52,000, and the market value of the available-for-sale securities was $85,000. Record all adjustments required at year-end and indicate how the effects of each group of securities will be reported on the financial statements.

Problem Set A

LO 1 **P12-1A. Discontinued operations and extraordinary item.**
Each of the following items was found on the financial statements for Hartsfield Company for the year ended December 31, 2007:

Net income from continuing operations	$136,500
Gain on the sale of a discontinued segment, net of taxes of $42,000	140,000
Loss from operation of discontinued segment, net of taxes of $24,000	(80,000)
Gain on sale of land	65,000
Extraordinary loss, net of taxes of $6,000	(20,000)

Required

a. For the items listed above, indicate the financial statement and appropriate section, where applicable, on which each would appear.
b. Provide a description of each item and give as many details of each item's financial statement presentation as possible.
c. Based on the data provided, what is Hartsfield Company's tax rate?

P12-2A. Prepare an income statement.   LO 1

The Pops Corporation had the following for the year ended December 31, 2008:

Sales	$575,000
Cost of goods sold	230,000
Interest income	10,000
Gain on sale of equipment	8,000
Selling and administrative expenses	12,000
Interest expense	5,000
Extraordinary gain	15,000
Loss from discontinued segment operations	(10,500)
Gain on disposal of discontinued segment	28,000

Required

Assume the corporation is subject to a 30% tax rate. Prepare an income statement for the year ended December 31, 2008.

P12-3A. Prepare an income statement.   LO 1

The following balances appeared in the general ledger for Hacky Sak Corporation at fiscal year end September 30, 2006:

Selling and Administrative Expenses	$ 25,000
Other Revenues and Gains	50,000
Operating Expenses	75,000
Cost of Goods Sold	135,000
Net Sales	375,000
Other Expenses and Losses	15,000

In addition, the following occurred throughout the year:

1. On April 10, a tornado destroyed one of the company's manufacturing plants resulting in an extraordinary loss of $55,000.
2. On July 31, the company discontinued one of its unprofitable segments. The loss from operations was $25,000. The assets of the segment were sold at a gain of $15,000.

Required

a. Assume Hacky Sak's income tax rate is 40%; prepare the income statement for the year ended September 30, 2006.
b. Calculate the earnings per share the company would report on the income statement assuming Hacky Sak had a weighted average of 200,000 shares of common stock outstanding during the year and paid preferred dividends of $5,000.

P12-4A. Prepare horizontal and vertical analysis.   LO 2

Given the following income statements:

Year ended December 31,

(in thousands)

	2009	2008	2007
Net sales	$5,003,837	$4,934,430	$4,881,103
Cost of goods sold	2,755,323	2,804,459	2,784,392
Gross profit	2,248,514	2,129,971	2,096,711
Selling, general and administrative expenses	1,673,449	1,598,333	1,573,510
Operating income	575,065	531,638	523,201
Interest expense	61,168	71,971	80,837
Interest and net investment expense (income)	(5,761)	(6,482)	(8,278)
Other expense—net	29,540	26,046	23,365
Income before income taxes	490,118	440,103	427,277
Income taxes	186,258	167,239	166,663
Net income	$ 303,860	$ 272,864	$ 260,614

Required

a. For each of the years shown, prepare a vertical analysis, using sales as the base. Write a paragraph explaining what the analysis shows.
b. Using 2007 as the base year, prepare a horizontal analysis for sales and cost of goods sold. What information does this analysis give you?

LO 3   **P12-5A. Calculate and analyze financial ratios.**

Given the information below from a firm's financial statement:

Year ended December 31,

(in thousands)

	2009	2008	2007
Net sales (all on account)	$5,003,837	$4,934,430	
Cost of goods sold	2,755,323	2,804,459	
Gross profit	2,248,514	2,129,971	
Interest expense	61,168	71,971	
Income taxes	186,258	167,239	
Net income	$ 303,860	$ 272,864	
Cash and cash equivalents	$ 18,623	$ 19,133	$ 3,530
Accounts receivable, less allowance	606,046	604,516	546,314
Total current assets	1,597,377	1,547,290	1,532,253
Total assets	4,052,090	4,065,462	4,035,801
Total current liabilities	1,189,862	1,111,973	44,539
Long-term liabilities	1,163,696	1,237,549	
Total shareholders' equity*	1,698,532	1,715,940	1,592,180

*The firm has no preferred stock.

Required

a. Calculate the following ratios for 2009 and 2008:
   1. Current ratio
   2. Acid-test ratio (assume no short-term investments)
   3. Working capital
   4. Accounts receivable turnover ratio
   5. Debt to equity ratio
   6. Times interest earned
   7. Return on equity
   8. Gross profit percentage

b. Suppose the changes from 2008 to 2009 in each of these ratios were consistent with the direction and size of the change for the past several years. For each ratio, explain what the trend in the ratio would indicate about the company.

LO 3   **P12-6A. Calculate and analyze financial ratios.**

The following information was taken from the 2006 annual report of Presentations.

At December 31,

(in thousands)

	2006	2005
ASSETS		
Current assets		
Cash	$ 1,617	$ 1,220
Accounts receivable	1,925	3,112
Merchandise inventory	2,070	966
Prepaid expenses	188	149
Total current assets	5,800	5,447
Plant and equipment:		
Buildings, net	4,457	2,992
Equipment, net	1,293	1,045
Total plant and equipment	5,750	4,037
Total assets	$11,550	$ 9,484
LIABILITIES		
Current liabilities		
Accounts payable	$ 1,817	$ 1,685
Notes payable	900	1,100
Total current liabilities	2,717	2,785
Long-term liabilities	3,500	2,000
Total liabilities	6,217	4,785

At December 31,

(in thousands)

	2006	2005
STOCKHOLDERS' EQUITY		
Common stock, no par value	3,390	3,042
Retained earnings	1,943	1,657
Total stockholders' equity	5,333	4,699
Total liabilities and stockholders' equity	$11,550	$ 9,484
Sales revenue	$12,228	
Cost of goods sold	8,751	
Gross profit on sales	3,477	
Operating expenses:		
Depreciation—buildings and equipment	102	
Other selling and administrative	2,667	
Total expenses	2,769	
Income before interest and taxes	708	
Interest expense	168	
Income before taxes	540	
Income taxes	114	
Net income	$ 426	

Required

a. Calculate the following ratios for 2005 and 2006:
1. Debt to equity
2. Gross margin percentage
3. Current ratio
4. Acid test ratio
5. Times interest earned ratio
b. What do the ratios indicate about the success of Presentations? What additional information would help you analyze the overall performance of this company?

P12-7A. **Calculate and analyze financial ratios.**   LO 3

The financial statements of For the Kitchen include the following items:

	At June 30, 2007	June 30, 2006	June 30, 2005
Balance sheet:			
Cash	$ 17,000	$ 12,000	$ 14,000
Investments (in trading securities)	10,000	16,000	20,000
Accounts receivable (net)	54,000	50,000	48,000
Inventory	75,000	70,000	73,000
Prepaid expenses	16,000	12,000	10,000
Total current assets	172,000	160,000	165,000
Total current liabilities	$140,000	$ 90,000	$ 75,000

	June 30, 2007:	June 30 2006:
Income statement for the year ended		
Net credit sales	$420,000	$380,000
Cost of goods sold	250,000	225,000

Required

a. Compute the following ratios for the years ended June 30, 2007, and whenever possible for the year ended June 30, 2006. For each, indicate if the direction is favorable or unfavorable for the company.
1. Current ratio
2. Accounts receivable turnover
3. Inventory turnover ratio
4. Gross profit percentage
b. Suppose the industry average for similar retail stores for the current ratio is 1.7. Does this information help you evaluate For the Kitchen's liquidity?

LO 3   **P12-8A. Calculate and analyze financial ratios.**

You are interested in investing in Reese Company, and you have obtained the balance sheets for the company for the past two years.

Reese Company
Balance Sheet
At June 30, 2007 and 2006

	2007	2006
Current assets:		
Cash	$198,000	$ 90,000
Accounts receivable, net	210,000	116,000
Inventory	270,000	160,000
Prepaid rent	15,000	16,000
Total current assets	693,000	382,000
Equipment, net	280,000	260,000
Total assets	$973,000	$642,000
Total current liabilities	$306,000	$223,000
Long-term liabilities	219,000	117,000
Total liabilities	525,000	340,000
Common stockholders' equity	150,000	90,000
Retained earnings	298,000	212,000
Total liabilities and stockholders' equity	$973,000	$642,000

The following amounts were reported on the income statement for the year ended June 30, 2007:

Sales	$450,000
Cost of goods sold	215,000
Interest expense	7,500
Net income	80,000

Required

a. Compute as many of the financial statement ratios you've studied as possible with the information provided above for Reese Company. Some ratios can be computed for both years and others can be computed for only one year.
b. Would you invest in Reese Company? Why or why not? What additional information would be helpful in making this decision?

Problem Set B

Your professor may ask you to complete selected "Group B" exercises and problems using Prentice Hall Grade Assist **(PHGA)**. PHGA is an online tool that can help you master the chapter's topics by providing multiple variations of exercises and problems. You can rework these exercises and problems—each time with new data—as many times as you need, with immediate feedback and grading.

LO 1   **P12-1B. Discontinued operations and extraordinary item.**

Each of the following items was found on the financial statements for Logan Company for the year ended December 31, 2008:

Net income from continuing operations	85,000
Gain on the sale of discontinued segment, net of taxes $9,000	30,000
Loss from operation of discontinued segment, net of taxes of $9,750	(32,500)
Gain on sale of equipment	12,000
Extraordinary loss from earthquake, net of taxes $45,000	(150,000)

Required

a. For each item listed above, indicate the financial statement and appropriate section, if applicable, on which each would appear.
b. Provide a description of each item and give as many details of each item's financial statement presentation as possible.
c. Based on the data provided, what is Logan Company's tax rate?

P12-2B. Prepare an income statement.   <u>LO 1</u>

The Blues Corporation had the following for the year ended December 31, 2007:

Sales	$425,000
Cost of goods sold	185,000
Interest income	8,000
Gain on sale of equipment	4,000
Selling and administrative expenses	18,000
Interest expense	3,000
Extraordinary gain	25,000
Loss from discontinued segment operations	(9,500)
Gain on disposal of discontinued segment	36,000

Required

Assume the corporation is subject to a 40% tax rate. Prepare an income statement for the year ended December 31, 2007.

P12-3B. Prepare an income statement.   <u>LO 1</u>

The following balances appeared in the general ledger for Ski Daddle Corporation at fiscal year end December 31, 2007:

Selling and administrative expenses	$ 45,000
Other revenues and gains	80,000
Operating expenses	110,000
Cost of goods sold	185,000
Net sales	325,000
Other expenses and losses	8,000

In addition, the following occurred throughout the year:

1. On August 20, a fire destroyed one of the company's warehouses resulting in an extraordinary loss of $35,000.
2. On October 31, the company discontinued one of its unprofitable segments. The loss from operations was $35,000. The assets of the segment were sold at a gain of $19,000.

Required

a. Assume Ski Daddle Corporation's income tax rate is 30%; prepare the income statement for the year ended December 31, 2007.
b. Calculate the earnings per share the company would report on the income statement assuming Ski Daddle had 100,000 shares of common stock outstanding during the year and paid preferred dividends of $15,000.

P12-4B. Perform horizontal and vertical analysis.   <u>LO 2</u>

Here are the income statements from a firm's recent annual report:

Year ended December 31,

(in millions)

	2008	2007	2006
Net revenue	$26,971	$25,112	$23,512
Cost of sales	12,379	11,497	10,750
Selling, general and administrative expenses	9,460	8,958	8,574
Amortization of intangible assets	145	138	165
Other expenses	204	224	356
Operating profit	4,783	4,295	3,667
Income from investments	323	280	160
Interest expense	(163)	(178)	(219)
Interest income	51	36	67
Income before income taxes	4,994	4,433	3,675
Income taxes	1,424	1,433	1,244
Net income	$ 3,570	$ 3,000	$ 2,431

Required

a. For each of the years shown, perform a vertical analysis, using sales as the base. Write a paragraph explaining what the analysis shows.
b. Using 2006 as the base year, perform a horizontal analysis for Net revenue and Cost of sales. What information does this analysis give you?

LO 3   **P12-5B. Calculate and analyze financial ratios.**
The following information was taken from Disney's financial statements. Even though there are several items on the statements that you did not study in this course, you should recognize most of the financial statement items given.

The Walt Disney Company and Subsidiaries
Consolidated Balance Sheets
At September 30

(in millions, except per share data)

	2004	2003
Assets		
Current assets		
Cash and cash equivalents	$ 2,042	$ 1,583
Receivables	4,558	4,238
Inventories	775	703
Television costs	484	568
Deferred income taxes	772	674
Other current assets	738	548
Total current assets	9,369	8,314
Film and television costs	5,938	6,205
Investments	1,292	1,849
Parts, resorts and other property, at cost		
Attractions, buildings and equipment	25,168	19,499
Accumulated depreciation	(11,665)	(8,794)
	13,503	10,705
Projects in progress	1,852	1,076
Land	1,127	897
	16,482	12,678
Intangible assets, net	2,815	2,786
Goodwill	16,966	16,966
Other assets	1,040	1,190
Total assets	$53,902	$49,988
Liabilities and Shareholders' Equity		
Current liabilities		
Accounts payable and other accrued liabilities	$ 5,623	$ 5,044
Current portion of borrowings	4,093	2,457
Unearned royalties and other advances	1,343	1,168
Total current liabilities	11,059	8,669
Borrowings	9,395	10,643
Deferred income taxes	2,950	2,712
Other long-term liabilities	3,619	3,745
Minority interests	798	428
Commitments and contingencies (Note 13)	—	—
Shareholders' equity	—	—
Preferred stock, $.01 par value		
Authorized—100 million shares, Issued—none		
Common stock		
Common stock—Disney, $.01 par value		
Authorized—3.6 billion shares,		
Issued—2.1 billion shares	12,447	12,154
Common stock—Internet Group, $.01 par value	—	
Authorized—1.0 billion shares, Issued—none		
Retained earnings	15,732	13,817
Treasury stock	(1,862)	(1,527)
Other	(236)	(653)
Total liabilities and shareholders' equity	$53,902	$49,988

The Walt Disney Company and Subsidiaries
Consolidated Statements of Income
For the year ended September 30

(in millions)

	2004	2003	2002
Revenues	$30,752	$27,061	$25,329
Costs and expenses	(26,704)	(24,348)	(22,945)
Gain on sale of business	—	16	34
Net interest expense	(617)	(793)	(453)
Equity in the income of investees	372	334	225
Restructuring and impairment charges	(64)	(16)	—
Income before income taxes, minority interests and the cumulative effect of accounting	3,739	2,254	2,190
Income taxes	(1,197)	(789)	(853)
Minority interests	(197)	(127)	(101)
Income before the cumulative effect of accounting change	2,345	1,338	1,236
Cumulative effect of accounting change	—	(71)	—
Net income	$2,345	$1,267	$1,236
Earnings per share before the cumulative effect of accounting change:			
Diluted	$ 1.12	$ 0.65	$ 0.60
Basic	$ 1.14	$ 0.65	$ 0.61
Cumulative effect of accounting change per share	$ —	($ 0.03)	$ —
Earnings per share:			
Diluted	$ 1.12	$ 0.62	$ 0.60
Basic	$ 1.14	$ 0.62	$ 0.61
Average number of common and common equivalent shares outstanding:			
Diluted	2,106	2,067	2,044
Basic	2,049	2,043	2,040

Required

a. Calculate the following ratios for 2004:
  1. Current ratio
  2. Acid-test ratio
  3. Working capital
  4. Accounts receivable turnover ratio
  5. Debt to equity ratio
  6. Times interest earned
  7. Return on equity

<u>LO 3</u>   **P12-6B. Calculate and analyze financial ratios.**
The following information was taken from the annual report of ROM.

	At December 31,
	(in thousands)
	2005

ASSETS:	
Current assets:	
Cash	$ 1,220
Accounts receivable	3,112
Merchandise inventory	966
Prepaid expenses	149
Total current assets	5,447
Plant and equipment:	
Buildings, net	2,992
Equipment, net	1,045
Total plant and equipment	4,037
Total assets	$ 9,484
LIABILITIES:	
Current liabilities:	
Accounts payable	$ 1,685
Notes payable	1,100
Total current liabilities	2,785
Long-term liabilities	2,000
Total liabilities	4,785
STOCKHOLDERS' EQUITY:	
Common stock, no par value	3,042
Retained earnings	1,657
Total stockholders' equity	4,699
Total liabilities and stockholders' equity	$ 9,484
Sales for the year	$10,200
Cost of goods sold	6,750
Total assets at Dec. 31, 2004	8,980
Total liabilities at Dec. 31, 2004	4,535
Total stockholders' equity at Dec. 31, 2004	4,445

Required

a. Calculate the following ratios for 2005:
1. Debt to equity
2. Gross profit percentage
3. Current ratio
4. Acid test ratio
b. What do the ratios indicate about the success of ROM? What additional information would be useful to help you analyze the overall performance of this company?

<u>LO 3</u>   **P12-7B. Calculate and analyze financial ratios.**
The financial statements of Builder Bob's include the following items:

At	**Sept. 30, 2008**	**Sept. 30, 2007**
Balance sheet:		
Cash	$ 27,000	$ 22,000
Investments (short-term)	15,000	12,000
Accounts receivable (net)	44,000	40,000
Inventory	85,000	75,000
Prepaid rent	6,000	2,000
Total current assets	177,000	151,000
Total current liabilities	120,000	80,000

Income statement for the year ended September 30, 2008:

Net credit sales	$320,000
Cost of goods sold	150,000

Required

a. Compute the following ratios for the year ended September 30, 2008, and September 30, 2007. For each, indicate if the direction is favorable or unfavorable for the company.
  1. Current ratio
  2. Quick ratio
  3. Accounts receivable turnover (2008 only)
  4. Inventory turnover ratio (2008 only)
  5. Gross margin percentage (2008 only)
b. Which financial statement users would be most interested in these ratios?
c. Suppose the industry average for similar retail stores for the current ratio is 1.2. Does this information help you evaluate Builder Bob's liquidity?

P12-8B. Calculate and analyze financial ratios.   LO 5

You are interested in investing in Apples and Nuts Company, and you have obtained the balance sheets for the company for the past two years.

Apples and Nuts Company
Balance Sheet
At December 31, 2006 and 2005

	2006	**2005**
Current assets		
Cash	$ 98,000	$ 90,000
Accounts receivable, net	310,000	216,000
Inventory	275,000	170,000
Prepaid rent	10,000	6,000
Total current assets	693,000	482,000
Equipment, net	180,000	258,000
Total assets	$873,000	$740,000
Total current liabilities	$206,000	$223,000
Long-term liabilities	219,000	217,000
Total liabilities	425,000	440,000
Common stockholders' equity	250,000	190,000
Retained earnings	198,000	110,000
Total liabilities and stockholders' equity	$873,000	$740,000

Net Income for the year ended December 31, 2006 was $100,000.

Required

a. Compute as many of the financial statement ratios you've studied as possible with the information from Apples and Nuts Company. (Compute 2006 ratios.)
b. Would you invest in this company? Why or why not? What additional information would be helpful in making this decision?

Critical Thinking Problems

Risk and Control

Think about the risks of investing in a company and about the information provided by the financial ratios you studied in this chapter. Which financial ratios do you believe might give you information about the risk of investing in a company? Comment on those ratios from Wal-Mart and Target, which you calculated at the end of the chapter in the "Let's Take a Test Drive" section.

Ethics

Atlantis Company sells computer components and plans on borrowing some money to expand. After reading a lot about earnings management, Andy, the owner of Atlantis, has decided he should try to accelerate some sales to improve his financial statement ratios. He has called his best customers and asked them to make their usual January purchases by December 31. Andy told the customers he would allow them until the

end of February to pay for the purchases, just as if they had made their purchases in January.

    a. What do you think are the ethical implications of Andy's actions?

    b. Which ratios will be improved by accelerating these sales?

Group Assignment

In groups, try to identify the type of company that is most likely indicated by the ratios shown below. The four types of companies represented are: retail grocery, heavy machinery, restaurant, and drug manufacturer. Make notes on the arguments to support your position so that you can share them in a class discussion.

	Gross Margin Ratio	(Long-term) Debt to Equity	Accounts Receivable Turnover Ratio	Inventory Turnover Ratio	Return on Equity
1	82.9%	25%	5.5 times	1.5 times	22.9%
2	33.7%	134%	49.3 times	11.2 times	3.6%
3	25.3%	147%	2.3 times	5.0 times	5.0%
4	37.4%	62%	34.9 times	32.9 times	15.7%

Internet Exercise: Papa John's International

Papa John's has surpassed Little Caesars to become the number-three pizza chain, behind only number-one Pizza Hut and number-two Domino's Pizza. Papa John's 2,800 restaurants (about 75% are franchised) are scattered across the United States and 10 other countries. Let's examine how Papa John's compares with its competition:

IE12-1. Go to www.papajohns.com and explore "Papa John's Story" and "Our Pizza Story." What differentiates Papa John's from its competition?

IE12-2. Go to http://moneycentral.msn.com and get the stock quote for PZZA, Papa John's stock symbol. Identify the current price-to-earnings ratio and dividend yield ratio. What do these market indicators mean for Papa John's?

IE12-3. Select "Financial Results" and then "Key Ratios."

    a. Select "Financial Condition." Calculate the current ratio and quick (acid-test) ratio for Papa John's and the industry. Who would find these ratios of primary interest? Identify the debt-to-equity ratio and interest coverage ratio (another name for times interest earned ratio) for Papa John's and the industry. Is Papa John's primarily financed by debt or equity? How can you tell? Does Papa John's have the ability to pay its interest obligations? Explain why or why not.

    b. Select "Investment Returns." Identify return on equity and return on assets for Papa John's and the industry. What do these ratios measure?

    c. Select "Ten-Year Summary." Review the information provided for return on equity and return on assets. What additional information is revealed about Papa John's financial position? Is this information helpful?

IE12-4. Review the information recorded earlier. Does Papa John's compare favorably with industry averages? Support your judgment with at least two observations.

    Please note: Internet web sites are constantly being updated. Therefore, if the information is not found where indicated, please explore the web site further to find information.

Additional Study Materials

Visit www.prenhall.com/reimers for self-study quizzes and spreadsheet templates to use to complete homework assignments.

Comprehensive Income

In the chapter, you learned that the Financial Accounting Standards Board (FASB) has defined two items that companies need to separate from regular earnings on financial statements: discontinued operations smf, extraordinary items. There is a third item—**comprehensive income**.

Even though most transactions that affect shareholders' equity are found on the income statement—revenues and expenses—there are a small number of transactions that affect shareholders' equity that are excluded from the calculation of net income. We already know about two of them:

1. Owners making contributions (paid-in capital)
2. Owners receiving dividends

In addition to these two, there are several other transactions that affect equity without going through the income statement. The most common examples of these transactions are (1) unrealized gains and losses from foreign currency translations and (2) unrealized gains and losses on certain investments. Rather than including either of these kinds of gains and losses on the income statement, they are reported as a direct adjustment to equity. The reason is that these items don't really reflect a firm's performance, so firms have lobbied to have them kept out of the calculation of earnings. To keep these transactions from getting lost among all the financial statement numbers, the FASB requires the reporting of net income plus these other transactions that affect shareholders' equity in an amount called comprehensive income. Comprehensive income includes all changes in shareholders' equity during a period except those changes in equity resulting from contributions by shareholders and distributions to shareholders. There are two parts of comprehensive income: net income and *other comprehensive income*. We know what types of transactions are included in net income—revenues, expenses, discontinued operations, and extraordinary items. Items included in other comprehensive income include unrealized gains and losses from foreign currency translation and unrealized gains and losses on certain types of investments. Exhibit 12A.1 shows all of the items that affect shareholders' equity.

Both the FASB and the International Accounting Standards Board (IASB) agree that users of financial statements need to pay attention to comprehensive income because the reported items could make a significant difference in the firm's financial health. Read about it in *Accounting in the News*.

> **Comprehensive income:** The total of all items that affect shareholders' equity except transactions with the owners; comprehensive income has two parts: net income and other comprehensive income.

 Can **YOU** do it?

What is the purpose of having a statement of comprehensive income rather than a simple income statement?

Answer The FASB wants to make the changes to shareholders' equity that do not affect net income more apparent to financial statement users.

Accounting in the NEWS

International

United States and International Accounting Standards Find Common Ground

GAAP and international standards are often at odds with each other. That should come as no surprise. According to a *Wall Street Journal* article:

The U.S. and countries overseas can't even agree on what set of measurements to use in the kitchen. So how will they ever "harmonize" international standards on accounting?

However, the FASB and the International Accounting Standards Board (IASB) do agree that comprehensive income needs special attention on financial statements:

Among the next wave of projects that the boards plan to tackle: con-

current efforts to overhaul the income statement. Both boards have agreed they want to see "comprehensive income" on the income statement. Comprehensive income would include certain items that affect shareholders' equity but that aren't currently run through the income statement, such as unrealized gains and losses on certain securities. Still, there are differences between the two boards. The IASB, for instance, wants to remove net income from the income statement, while the FASB hasn't yet reached a conclusion on the matter.

Be sure to look for changes in the financial statements as the U.S. and international standards-setters come to agreement on just what items should be included and how they should be valued.

Q Where do both the IASB and the FASB want to place comprehensive income?

A On the income statement.

It's difficult for those setting U.S. Accounting Standards and those setting International Accounting Standards to agree. Recently, however, the FASB modified GAAP's treatment of a change in accounting principle to be more consistent with international standards.

Source: "Accounting's Global Rule Book" by Cassell Bryan-Low from *The Wall Street Journal Online*, Nov. 27, 2003. Copyright 2003 by Dow Jones & Co. Inc. Reproduced with permission of Dow Jones & Co. Inc. in the format Textbook via Copyright Clearance Center.

The items in the left column appear on the financial statements in the equity classifications shown in the right column.

Exhibit 12A.1

Comprehensive Income

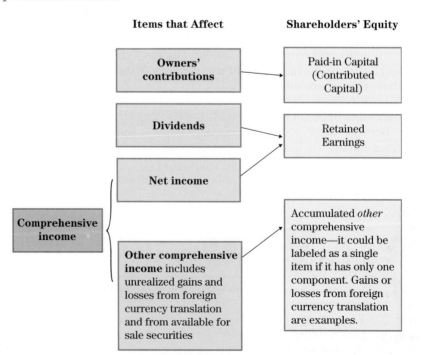

Investments in Securities

You've learned that certain gains and losses related to investments may be included in other comprehensive income. Let's take a closer look at how a firm accounts for its investments in the securities of another firm. You'll see how gains and losses on some of these investments are reported as part of comprehensive income.

When interest rates are low, a company's extra cash—meaning cash not immediately needed—may earn more in the stock market or bond market than it would in a bank savings account or certificate of deposit. That's when a company buys stocks and bonds of other companies with its extra cash. For entities like banks and insurance companies, investing cash in other companies is a crucial part of managing their assets. As you learned in previous chapters, stocks are equity securities and bonds are debt securities. Both may be purchased with a company's extra cash. When a company buys another company's debt securities or less than 20% of its equity securities, the accounting rules require firms to classify their investments in securities into one of three categories: *held to maturity, trading,* and *available for sale.*

Held-to-maturity Securities

Sometimes a company purchases debt securities and intends to keep them until they mature. Recall that all bonds have a maturity date, but equity securities do not. If a company has the intention of keeping the securities until maturity and their financial condition indicates that they should be able to do this, the securities will be classified as **held-to-maturity securities**. Such investments are recorded at cost, and they are reported at that same amount on the balance sheet—plus or minus any unamortized discount or premium. No matter how much held-to-maturity investments are worth on the market, a company will always report them at amortized cost when preparing its balance sheet.

Held-to-maturity securities: Investments in debt securities that the company plans to hold until they mature.

Trading Securities

If a company buys the securities solely to trade them and make a short-term profit, the company will classify them as **trading securities**. The balance sheet shows trading securities at their market value. A company obtains the current value of the investments from the *The Wall Street Journal* or a similar source of market prices. Those values are then shown on the balance sheet. Recording the securities at their market value is called *marking-to-market.* If the securities' cost is lower than market value, then the company will record the difference as an unrealized gain. If the securities' cost is higher than market value, then the company will record the difference as an unrealized loss. Remember, *realizing* means actually getting something. Any gain or loss on an investment the company is holding (holding means *not* selling) is something the company doesn't get (a gain) or doesn't give up (a loss) until the company sells the securities.

Trading securities: Investments in debt and equity securities that the company has purchased to make a short-term profit.

Unrealized gain or loss: An increase or decrease in the market value of a company's investments in securities is recognized either on the income statement—for trading securities—or in Other Comprehensive Income in the equity section of the balance sheet—for available-for-sale securities—when the financial statements are prepared, even though the securities have *not* been sold.

In Other Words:
An unrealized gain or loss is often called a holding gain or loss.

Unrealized gains or losses a investments in debt and equity securities that the company has purchased to make short-term profit. Such a gain or loss may also be called a *holding gain* or *loss*. The unrealized gains and losses from trading securities are reported on the income statement.

For example, suppose Avia Company has invested $130,000 of its extra cash in securities—stocks and bonds traded on the stock and bond markets. At the end of the year, the securities that cost Avia $130,000 have a market value of $125,000. On the income statement for the year, Avia will show an unrealized loss of $5,000. The loss is recorded in an adjustment made before the financial statements are prepared. Here's the journal entry:

Transaction	Debit	Credit
Unrealized Loss on Trading Securities	5,000	
*Investment in Trading Securities		5,000
*Investment in Trading Securities is shown as a current asset on the balance sheet. Unrealized Loss on Trading Securities will be shown on the income statement.		

The securities' new value of $125,000 (originally 130,000 minus loss of $5,000) has replaced their original cost. Now, $125,000 will be the "cost" and will be compared to the market value on the date of the next balance sheet. Remember, the company purchased these trading securities as investments to trade in the short run, so the firm's investment portfolio is likely to look very different at the next balance sheet date.

Available-for-Sale Securities

Available-for-sale securities:
Investments the company may hold or sell; the company's intention is not clear enough to use one of the other categories—*held-to-maturity* or *trading*.

Sometimes a company is not sure how long it will keep the debt or equity securities it has purchased. If the company does not intend to sell the securities in the short term for a quick profit or does not intend to hold them until maturity, the company will classify the securities as **available for sale**. Every year, when it is time to prepare the annual balance sheet, the cost of this group of securities is compared to the market value at the balance sheet date. The book value of the securities is then adjusted to market value, and the corresponding gain or loss is reported in shareholders' equity. Such a gain or loss is called an *unrealized* or *holding* gain or loss, just as it is called for trading securities. But

Can **YOU** do it?

A corporation has invested $50,000 in the securities of other companies. At the end of the year, that corporation's portfolio has a market value of $52,000. Describe where these securities would be shown on the annual financial statements and at what amount under each of the conditions described below:

1. The investment is classified as trading securities.

2. The investment is classified as available-for-sale.

3. The investment is classified as held-to-maturity.

Answers (1) The securities will be shown in the current asset section of the balance sheet at a value of $52,000. The write-up will be balanced with a $2,000 unrealized gain on the income statement. (2) The securities will be shown in either the current asset or the long-term asset (depending on firm's intent) section of the balance sheet at a value of $52,000. The write-up will be balanced with a $2,000 unrealized gain that will go directly to equity, as part of Accumulated Other Comprehensive Income. (3) The securities will be shown at their cost of $50,000 in the long-term asset section of the balance sheet (unless the debt securities are maturing in the coming year, in which case they would be current assets).

these gains and losses don't go on the income statement. Instead, they are included as part of Accumulated Other Comprehensive Income in the shareholders' equity section of the balance sheet.

Suppose Avia Company classified its portfolio of securities that cost $130,000 as *available for sale*. If the market value of the securities is $125,000 at the date of the balance sheet, the securities must be shown on the balance sheet at the lower amount. In this case, the unrealized loss will *not* be shown on the income statement. Instead of going through net income to Retained Earnings, the loss will go through Comprehensive Income to Accumulated Other Comprehensive Income in the shareholders' equity section of the balance sheet. The loss will be shown after Retained Earnings, either alone—and labeled as an Unrealized Loss from Investments in Securities—or combined with other non-income statement gains and losses—and labeled as Accumulated Other Comprehensive Income.

Selling the Securities

When a firm sells any of these securities—trading, available-for-sale, and held-to-maturity—the gain or loss on the sale is calculated like other accounting gains and losses. The book value of the security at the time of the sale is compared to the selling price. The selling price is often called the proceeds from the sale. If the book value is greater than the proceeds, the firm will record a loss on the sale. If the book value is less than the proceeds, the firm will record a gain on the sale. Gains and losses from the actual sale of the securities are both *realized*—the sale has actually happened—and *recognized*—the relevant amounts are shown on the income statement.

chapter 13

Quality of Earnings and Corporate Governance

Here's where you've been . . .

- **You learned to analyze a set of financial statements using vertical analysis, horizontal analysis, and ratio analysis.**

Here's where you're going . . .

- **You'll learn how to explain quality of earnings.**

- **You'll learn to identify the characteristics of high-quality earnings.**

- **You'll learn about the current issues related to corporate governance.**

YOU make the call:

WorldCom's $11 billion fraud—how did everyone miss the signs?

In 1996, Betty Vinson, pictured here, joined the accounting department of a small long-distance company that would later become WorldCom. In 2003,

Vinson faced 15 years in federal prison for her part in World-Com's $11 billion fraud: Asked by her bosses to make false accounting entries, Vinson balked—and then caved. At the end of 18 months, she had helped falsify at least $3.7 billion in profits.

When Vinson and some colleagues threatened to quit," CFO Scott Sullivan told them to "Think of [the company] as an aircraft carrier, . . . We have planes in the air. Let's get the planes landed. Once they are landed, if you still want to leave, then leave." Vinson cooperated with authorities during WorldCom's trial and in August of 2005 was sentenced to five months of jail and five months of house arrest.

Did investors, board members, and analysts all miss the signs of WorldCom's fraud? What requirements of Sarbanes-Oxley might have prevented this fraud? *You make the call.*

Sources: Susan Pulliam, "Ordered to Commit Fraud, A Staffer Balked, then Caved," *Wall Street Journal Online*, June 23, 2003. Shawn Young and Dionne Searcey, "Former Executive at WorldCom Gets 5-Month Jail Term," *Wall Street Journal*, August 5, 2005.

Learning Objectives

When you are finished studying this chapter, you should be able to:

1. Explain Wall Street's emphasis on earnings and the potential problems that result from this emphasis.
2. Define quality of earnings and explain how it is measured.
3. Recognize the common ways that firms can manipulate earnings.
4. Describe the corporate accounting failures of the early 2000s.
5. Explain the requirements of the Sarbanes-Oxley Act of 2002.
6. Evaluate a firm's corporate governance.

LEARNING OBJECTIVE 1

Explain Wall Street's emphasis on earnings and the potential problems that result from this emphasis.

Why Are Earnings Important?

You've learned about the four basic financial statements and the notes to the financial statements. To wrap up your introduction to financial accounting, we are going to step back and look at the big picture. What do investors focus on when they evaluate a firm's financial statements? How accurate is the information? Who, or what, stands behind the information to assure investors that it is truthful and reliable? These are just a few questions we will consider in this chapter. We start with the market's focus on earnings, which appear on the income statement.

How often have you read or heard about a firm's earnings? Managers estimate earnings and disclose those estimates to the public. Financial analysts study managements' earnings estimates and announce their own expected earnings for the firm. Among the hundreds of measurements shareholders consider—gross domestic product (GDP), housing starts, interest rates, unemployment figures, and budget deficits, to name a few—there is one number that Wall Street simply calls "the number." A firm's stock price moves up when earnings exceed analysts' forecasts and down when reported earnings do not meet the forecasts. According to Alex Berenson, a financial reporter for the *New York Times* and author of *The Number: How the Drive for Quarterly Earnings Corrupted Wall Street and Corporate America*, "Earnings per share is the number for which all other numbers are sacrificed. It is the distilled truth of a company's health. Earnings per share is the number that counts. Too bad it's a lie." Accountants define **earnings per share** as net income divided by the weighted average number of outstanding shares of (common) stock.

As Berenson points out, earnings alone cannot assess accurately the state of a firm's financial health. A narrow focus on a single number can result in serious miscommunication between the firm and its investors. However, reported earnings have a real effect on a firm's stock price. Read an interesting example of what can happen when there is too much emphasis on earnings in **Accounting in the News**. The example will remind you that there are honest CEOs out there.

Earnings per share (EPS): Net income divided by the weighted average number of outstanding shares of (common) stock.

Can **YOU** do it?

Describe why earnings is such an important number.

Answer Earnings are used by investors to evaluate a firm's performance. The price of a firm's stock often goes up if the firm meets expectations and goes down if the firm doesn't meet expectations.

Accounting in the NEWS

Ethics

Hardee's Focus: Ethics not Earnings

CKE Restaurants, the owner of Hardee's fast food chain, was delighted with the reports analyst C. Clive Munro published about Hardee's. As you know, positive analysts' reports can translate into higher stock prices. The CEO of CKE Restaurants, Andrew Puzder, was surprised to get an email from Munro offering to be hired as a paid consultant for the company. Puzder thought Munro was joking, so he ignored the email.

What followed was a year of bizarre communication between the analyst and CKE Restaurants. Munro began publishing negative reports about CKE and tried to get the company to pay him to stop. As CKE's revenue was rising and same-store sales were increasing, the stock price was falling. One email from Munro to Puzder read:

Hi, Andy. If you were smart, you would hire me at $25K per month (for half my time) and take me out of the game. . . . So far this year, this would have saved you $16 million in lost market value.

Rather than give in to this extortion, Puzder called the FBI. A tape-recorded phone call resulted in Munro's arrest. In February 2005, Munro pleaded guilty to one count of extortion. In July 2005, he was sentenced to a year and nine months in prison. This is a great example of ethics trumping earnings. When you read so much about fraud, don't forget that CEOs like Puzder are in the majority.

Thinking Critically

Suppose you are an analyst and have a close friend whose business is struggling due to foreign competition. You feel fairly confident that the business could become more competitive if it had more money from investors. Would you write a favorable report for one quarter? How about two quarters?

CKE Restaurants, Inc. (CKE), operates Hardee's, a fast food restaurant popular throughout the Midwestern and Southeastern United States. The CEO of CKE, Andrew Puzder, has a law degree from Washington University and worked as a trial lawyer and corporate lawyer.

Q What situation enticed Munro to try to extort money from CKE Restaurants?

A The market's focus on earnings along with Munro's position as an analyst set up a situation in which he could perpetrate the crime.

Sources: Steven Gray, "How an Analyst Got Nabbed For Extortion," *Wall Street Journal*, April 18, 2005, p. C1. "Stock Analyst's Threats Result in Prison," Associated Press, July 27, 2005. Martha K. Baker, *The Legal Advantage*, "Alumnus Andrew F. Puzder presides over the parent company of Hardee's and Carl's Jr.," March 12, 2004, page 30.

The Quality of Earnings

As you've learned, investors typically use earnings per share to evaluate a firm's performance. How accurate and reliable is this number? **Quality of earnings** is a term accountants use to describe how well a reported earnings number communicates the firm's true performance. The quality of earnings is a subjective concept, and few people agree on the definition. Bernstein and Wild, two accounting authors,[1] identify three ways to evaluate the quality of earnings:

LEARNING OBJECTIVE 2

Define quality of earnings and explain how it is measured.

Quality of earnings: Refers to how well a reported earnings number communicates the firm's true performance.

1. Firms that make more conservative choices of accounting principles often have higher quality of earnings.
2. Firms that face fewer internal and external risks that threaten their survival and profitability often have a higher quality of earnings.
3. Firms that recognize revenue early or postpone recognition of expenses often have lower quality earnings.

Sometimes the accounting choices managers make are classified as conservative or aggressive. Conservative choices are those that reduce net income and assets or increase liabilities. Aggressive choices are those that increase net income and assets or decrease liabilities. Potentially understating income or assets is more conservative than potentially overstating income or assets. Can you see why this is true? If a firm overstates earnings, shareholders may sue the

[1]Leopold Bernstein and John Wild, *2000 Analysis of Financial Statements* (New York: McGraw-Hill).

firm and its auditors; but if a firm understates earnings, shareholders are less likely to be disappointed. Higher quality earnings are associated with more conservative accounting choices. Here are some examples.

Recall that a firm has to estimate the useful life and salvage value of depreciable assets, make inventory cost flow assumptions like LIFO or FIFO, and estimate bad debts expense. Each of these choices will affect the quality of the firm's reported earnings. Consider a capital-intensive company like those in the manufacturing sector. Firms like General Motors and Dow Chemical have huge investments in property, plant, and equipment. The income statements for these firms will have a significant amount of depreciation expense for manufacturing facilities and equipment. The amount of that expense will depend on how management estimates the useful lives of the assets. What kind of choices would make earnings appear larger? The longer the estimated useful lives of property, plant, and equipment, the smaller the annual depreciation expense. The smaller the depreciation expense, the larger the reported earnings. In cases like depreciation, the more discretion that management has, the more potential there is for lower quality of the related earnings. Having more depreciable assets means more estimates and potentially lower quality of earnings because managers can make choices that increase or decrease earnings.

In other cases, a manager views a particular choice as producing higher quality earnings than another. Consider inventory methods. When a company chooses FIFO, the older inventory costs are matched with the sales revenue on the income statement. When a company chooses LIFO, however, the more recent costs are shown on the income statement. Which method produces a higher quality earnings number? Analysts generally believe that LIFO produces a better income statement number because the costs used are more current, and, therefore, produces a higher quality earnings number than FIFO produces.

Next, we'll discuss three common ways that firms can manipulate earnings, reducing the quality of their earnings. Then, we'll turn to the Sarbanes-Oxley Act, the goal of which is to increase the quality of earnings and make financial reporting more transparent.

Can YOU do it?

What makes one firm's earnings higher in quality than another's?

Answer The choices that managers make in reporting their earnings. Some choices—such as LIFO for inventory in a period of rising prices—lead to higher quality earnings than others.

LEARNING OBJECTIVE 3

Recognize the common ways that firms can manipulate earnings.

Common Ways to Manipulate Earnings

You've learned that investors are concerned about the quality of firms' earnings. *BusinessWeek's* cover on October 4, 2004, showed a magician's hat with the title "Fuzzy Numbers." Here's how the article described how difficult it is to understand a firm's financial statements: "The problem with today's fuzzy earnings numbers is not accrual accounting itself. It's that investors, analysts, and money managers are having an increasingly hard time figuring out what judgments companies make to come up with those accruals, or estimates." To help you increase your understanding of the fuzzy numbers on the financial statements, let's look at three specific accounting procedures that often reduce the quality of earnings. Unfortunately, firms often use these procedures to "cook the books." **Cooking the books** is a slang term that means to manipulate or falsify the accounting records to make the company's financial performance look better than it actually is. Although there are numerous activities used to manage earnings, many of which can be very complicated, the Securities and Exchange Commission identifies three activities that deserve special attention when you are evaluating a company's financial performance:

1. Big bath charges
2. Cookie jar reserves
3. Revenue recognition

> **Cooking the books:** A slang expression that means to manipulate or falsify the firm's accounting records to make the firm's financial performance or position look better than it actually is.

Big bath charges

The expression "big bath charges" was made famous among accountants in a 1998 speech by then chairman of the SEC, Arthur Levitt, to the New York University Center for Law and Business. According to the big bath theory of corporate financial reporting, one way to manage earnings is to maximize a current loss to get rid of expenses that belong on future income statements. When a firm is not going to meet its earnings expectations, the firm's managers "clean up" the balance sheet by writing off any expense that looks like it may need to be written off in the next few years. The reasoning goes something like this: As long as our firm is going to be punished by Wall Street for missing our earnings number, we might as well go ahead and miss it big. That will help us in the future by moving as many expenses as we can from future periods into the current period.

Accounting researchers have found evidence to support this practice by studying firms that either exceed or miss the analysts' forecasts. There are a significant number of firms that just make their earnings forecast by a very small margin. However, when a firm misses its earnings forecast, the amount by which it misses is larger, on average, than the margin for firms that make their forecasts. This is consistent with the idea of taking a *big* bath as long as you are getting in the tub.

How can you identify the big bath type of accounting practice? Read the following material:

- Several years of financial statements rather than just a single year, and look for unusual expenses and write-offs that appear out of step with previous years.
- The notes to the financial statements.
- Management's discussion and analysis about the company's performance in newspaper and business magazines.

Cookie jar reserves

Another way to manage earnings is to use reserve accounts to record expenses early and make future earnings look good. Using reserve accounts is a way to stash away amounts that can help the firm increase earnings in the future if, and when, the earnings are needed to meet earnings forecasts. In Chapter 7, you learned about the allowance method for estimating bad debts. A firm with a significant amount of uncollectible accounts must estimate future bad debts related to current sales so that the bad debts expense can be recorded in the same period as the sales to which it relates. Because bad debts expense is an estimate, and the corresponding amount is recorded in a reserve called the Allowance for Uncollectible Accounts, this accounting rule creates an opportunity for a firm to "manage" one of its expenses and, consequently, manipulate earnings.

Suppose a firm had credit sales of $1,000,000 in Year 1 and estimated that related bad debts would be 5% of sales, or $50,000. The firm would record the following journal entry:

Transaction	Debit	Credit
Bad Debts Expense	50,000	
Allowance for Uncollectible Accounts		50,000
To set up the Allowance for Uncollectible Accounts at year end		

This is the accounting equation:

Assets	=	Liabilities	+	Shareholders' Equity	
				Contributed Capital	Retained Earnings
				+	
Allowance for Uncollectible Accounts					Bad Debts Expense
–50,000					–50,000

This journal entry would reduce income by $50,000 in Year 1. During Year 2, as the actual customers who will not pay are identified and written off, no bad debts expense is recorded. Instead, the accounts are written off against the Allowance for Uncollectible Accounts. Suppose that during Year 2, $48,000 worth of accounts are written off, leaving a balance of $2,000 in the Allowance for Uncollectible Accounts. Now, at the end of Year 2, the firm must estimate its future bad debts from credit sales in Year 2. Whatever the estimate, the bad debts expense recorded for Year 2 will be $2,000 less than the estimate because the reserve—the Allowance for Uncollectible Accounts—still has $2,000 left-over from Year 1. (This example assumes the firm uses the accounts receivable method of estimating bad debts expense.)

Now let's go back to Year 1 and suppose that the firm is having a very poor year, and it will definitely miss the analysts' earnings forecasts for the year. When the firm's accountant is recording the bad debts expense for the year, there may be a temptation to record an amount that exceeds the actual estimate. Why? As long as Year 1 is a bad year, the firm might as well take as many expenses as possible to help the future. Suppose the firm recorded $60,000 worth of bad debts expense. The same amount will be recorded in the Allowance for Uncollectible Accounts. Now if $48,000 worth of bad debts are actually written off in Year 2, the balance in the Allowance for Uncollectible Accounts will be $12,000 rather than $2,000—if the Allowance for Uncollectible Accounts had been recorded at the real estimate of $50,000. The firm now has a cushion of $12,000 to reduce Year 2's bad debts expense if it needs it to increase earnings in Year 2. Using a reserve like the Allowance for Uncollectible Accounts to manipulate or to smooth earnings is a common way to use cookie jar reserves.

Cookie jar reserves and big bath charges are both ways for firms to allocate expenses to accounting periods to provide the most benefit. Sometimes a firm has a goal of smoothing earnings, and other times a firm wants to shift expenses from the future to the present to improve future earnings.

How can you tell if a firm is using cookie jar reserves? Watch for trends in the reported amounts for these reserves. Often, the specific amounts are not shown in the statements but are given in the detailed notes to the financial statements. Analyzing changes in ratios related to the reserves may also be helpful.

Revenue recognition

A third way to manage earnings is to use improper revenue recognition techniques. In the first few chapters, you learned that GAAP allows a firm to recognize revenue when (1) the firm has earned it and (2) collection is reasonably assured. This accounting principle leaves a lot of room for interpretation and judgment. A firm might violate this principle by recognizing revenue prematurely, or by creating totally fictitious revenue. These two possibilities represent two ends of a continuum—a continuum that is a "slippery slope." Improperly recognizing revenue can help a firm meet analysts' earnings forecasts and keep the firm's stock price rising. There are cases of executives making millions of dollars by selling their stock in the firm when the stock price was inflated due to fraudulent earnings.

Here are some examples of how firms have improperly recognized revenue. Firms have:

- Recorded sales of merchandise at the end of the quarter, but the goods were not delivered to the customer until the beginning of the following quarter.
- Routinely kept their books open at the end of the accounting period to continue recording sales until the sales goals for the period were met.
- Recorded sales of merchandise shipped to customers who had not placed orders for the merchandise.
- Shipped goods to salespeople in the field and recorded the sales even though the salespeople had not delivered the goods to customers.
- Shipped goods offsite to locations they controlled and recorded those shipments as sales revenue.
- Created fictitious documents for both the purchase of goods and the subsequent sale of those goods to fictitious customers.

When you analyze a firm's financial statements, how can you identify these types of revenue recognition problems? First, firms disclose their revenue recognition policies in the first note of the notes to the financial statements. If a firm has recently changed its revenue recognition policy, you should study the reasons and review the prior years' revenue patterns. Analyzing the relationship between sales and accounts receivable is quite useful in identifying early or fictitious revenue recognition. If Accounts Receivable as a percentage of Sales is increasing, you should be concerned. Every industry or business sector has its own type of revenue recognition problem. You need to understand the way revenue is recognized in your company's accounting system to know the potential for problems with early or late revenue recognition.

What We Learned from the Business Scandals of the Early 2000s

LEARNING OBJECTIVE 4

Describe the corporate accounting failures of the early 2000s.

Even with the concern over quality of earnings and managers' potential to manipulate earnings with a big bath, cookie jar reserves, or improper revenue recognition, Congress has rarely interfered with accounting standards. Until recently, the 1933 and 1934 Securities Acts were the governing laws for publicly traded firms and their auditors. However, the scandals and financial failures of the early 2000s, summarized in Exhibit 13.1, prompted Congress to pass the Sarbanes-Oxley Act of 2002. Sponsored by Senator Paul Sarbanes of Maryland, now retired, and Congressman Michael Oxley of Ohio, the Act brought the topic of corporate governance into the headlines.

Exhibit 13.1

Examples of Business Failures, 2001–2005

Company	What happened?	The Outcome of the Trials
Enron, an energy company.	Filed for bankruptcy protection in December 2001. At the time, Enron was the seventh largest company in the United States based on revenue.	Guilty: Andrew Fastow, the former CFO, was sentenced to 10 years in prison in 2004 after pleading guilty to securities and wire fraud. Kenneth Lay (pictured here), former CEO, is scheduled to go on trial for fraud in 2006.
Adelphia, a cable company.	Filed for bankruptcy protection in June 2002. At the time, Adelphia was the sixth largest cable company in the United States. John Rigas, founder and CEO, charged with conspiracy, bank fraud, and securities fraud in July 2004.	Guilty: John Rigas, founder, and Timothy Rigas, the former CFO, were found guilty in July 2004 of taking more than $2 billion from the company for their own personal use and lying to the public about Adelphia's financial condition. John Rigas was sentenced to 15 years and Timothy Rigas was sentenced to 20 years in prison.
Arthur Andersen, an accounting firm.	One of the five largest accounting firms in the world, Andersen surrendered its state licenses in August 2002 to practice before the SEC. Andersen served as the auditors of Enron and WorldCom.	Guilty Verdict Overturned: Andersen was initially found guilty in 2004 of obstructing justice in the Enron case. This marked the end of one of the five largest accounting firms in the world, which had been founded in 1914 and employed nearly 28,000 people at the time of its demise. In 2005, the Supreme Court overturned Andersen's conviction. Although the ruling came too late to save Andersen, it restored some respect for the accounting firm that was once considered the best in the world.
WorldCom, a telecommunications company.	Filed for bankruptcy protection July 2002 after disclosing it overstated profits by $3.8 billion.	Guilty: CEO Bernard Ebbers (left), a former milkman who became the CEO of WorldCom, was convicted in March 2005 on all nine counts for his role in an $11 billion accounting scandal—the largest in U.S. history. Ebbers sentenced to 25 years in prison in July 2005.
Tyco, a developer of electronics, fire and security products, healthcare products, and plastic and engineering products.	Executives Dennis Kozlowski and Mark Swartz indicted in September 2002 for allegedly stealing more than $600 million from the firm.	Guilty: Kozlowski and Swartz were convicted in June 2005, and each was sentenced to 25 years in prison.
Computer Associates, a computer company.	Former chief executive Sanjay Kumar indicted in April 2004 for fraudulent accounting of over $2 billion and obstruction of justice.	Kumar pleaded not guilty to all charges, and no trial date had been set at the time of this writing.

Corporate governance has many definitions. Simply stated, it is the way a firm governs itself, as executed by the board of directors. **Corporate governance** has been defined as a process carried out by the board of directors to provide direction and oversight on behalf of all the company's stakeholders—owners, suppliers, and customers. The term has also been defined as a set of relationships between the board of directors, management, shareholders, auditors, and any others with a stake in the company. Corporate governance is not a new concept—corporations have been governing themselves for years. However, recent scandals have brought the topic to the attention of the media, government officials, and general public.

Accounting scandals and the resulting business failures are not a modern-day phenomenon. One of the biggest business failures in history occurred in 1931, when Insull Utility Investment collapsed under the weight of a complex corporate structure held together by creative accounting. At the time, the press dubbed Insull the biggest business failure in the history of the world. Fast forward to 2001—the collapse of one of the world's largest energy companies, Enron—and to 2002—the bankruptcy of WorldCom. These failures are huge and have had an enormous impact on our economy and the employees of the companies, but failures are not new. However, there are lessons to be learned from them.

See if you can find a recent update on the scandals shown in Exhibit 13.1. One of the best ways you can be an intelligent investor, manager, or employee is to stay up to date. Read current financial publications and keep up with news events. One of the positive things to come out of these business failures and scandals is the increased attention the news media gives business issues.

What have we learned from the business failures of the last decade? Here's just a sampling.

> **Corporate governance:** The way a firm governs itself, as executed by the board of directors. Corporate governance is also described as the set of relationships between the board of directors, management, shareholders, auditors, and any others with a stake in the company.

1. Some corporate executives will do almost anything to meet earnings expectations and keep the firm's stock price stable or rising. Often, the goal is one of personal enrichment through the executives' exercise of options and the sale of company stock.

2. The ethical climate in a firm is set by top management. Chief executive officers and chief financial officers must establish and demand the integrity of the firm's disclosures—both financial and nonfinancial.

3. Auditors and their clients can get too close. An auditor's independence is a necessary condition for a meaningful audit, and auditing firms need to take a close look at the relationship(s) between a firm and its external auditors.

4. Application of GAAP is subject to significant management discretion, and firms must make their earnings more transparent.

5. No matter how good or how effective the accounting principles are, there is no way for accounting standards to stop fraud. Auditors and the SEC, however, may be able to make some progress in reducing fraud.

6. Financial statements are only part of the information investors need to evaluate a company's past, present, and future. Over-reliance on a single amount—earnings per share—can be a disaster.

As they did in the 1930s with the passage of the Securities Acts of 1933 and 1934, Congress responded to the corporate failures that came to light in the early 2000s with a new law—The Sarbanes-Oxley Act of 2002. As you read about the law, think about the problems it is meant to address. As business becomes increasingly global, the corporate governance of all countries will be important to investors. Read about it in *Accounting in the News*.

Accounting in the NEWS

International

Corporate Governance Around the World

The emphasis on corporate governance is not simply an American reaction to the Enron and World-Com scandals. In 1999, the Organisation for Economic Co-operation and Development (OECD), with over 30 member countries, issued their first set of international corporate governance principles. Since then, the OECD Principles have become a generally accepted standard in the international arena. Why are international standards important? According to the OECD:

The degree to which corporations observe basic principles of good corporate governance is an increasingly important factor for investment deci-sions. Of particular relevance is the relation between corporate governance practices and the increasingly international character of investment. International flows of capital enable companies to access financing from a much larger pool of investors. If countries are to reap the full benefits of the global capital market, and if they are to attract long-term capital, corporate governance arrangements must be credible, well understood across borders, and adhere to internationally accepted principles.

In 2004, the OECD revised the Principles to reflect the developments between 1999 and 2004. You can download a free copy at www.oecd.org.

Q Why is corporate governance an international issue?

A In some ways, the world has become a global market with international flows of capital.

To compete in today's global economy, companies can attract investors by following corporate governance practices.

Source: OECD Principles of Corporate Governance, 2004, www.oecd.org.

Can YOU do it?

What do you think auditors have learned from the recent financial failures?

Answer There are several possible answers to this question. Two important ones are: (1) independence, both actual and perceived, is crucial to doing an effective and credible job and (2) high ethical values and personal integrity are essential—in auditing and in life.

LEARNING OBJECTIVE 5

Explain the requirements of the Sarbanes-Oxley Act of 2002.

The Sarbanes-Oxley Act of 2002

No one will be able to navigate successfully in the business world without some knowledge of the Sarbanes-Oxley Act of 2002. All publicly traded companies and any international companies that trade on the U.S. stock exchanges must comply with this law. Exhibit 13.2 summarizes the key provisions of the law. We'll look at the major groups affected by the Sarbanes-Oxley and discuss how the law affects them. First, read *Accounting in the News* on page 680 to learn about Michael Oxley, whose name, along with that of Paul Sarbanes, is now recognized all over the world.

Exhibit 13.2

Key Provisions of the Sarbanes-Oxley Act of 2002

Group	Area		Description
Management	**Reporting**		Management must assess and report on the effectiveness of the company's internal control structure and procedures over financial reporting. This is part of section 404 of SOX.
	Insider Accountability		New rules require a code of ethics and a report on it in the annual 10-K.
	Penalties		New penalties exist for management if the financial statements are inaccurate or incomplete. A misrepresentation in connection with the certification can result in a fine of up to $1 million and imprisonment of up to ten years. A willful misrepresentation is punishable by a fine of up to $5 million and imprisonment of up to 20 years.
Board of Directors	**Strengthening the Board**		New rules for the composition of the boards of directors, requiring some directors to be independent of management, will strengthen the boards and the audit committees of the boards.
The External Auditors	**Strengthening Auditor Independence**		New rules for auditors include stronger rules regarding auditor independence.
The Public Company Accounting Oversight Board (PCAOB)	**Enforcement**		The new Public Company Accounting Oversight Board has the power to regulate auditing firms.

Accounting in the NEWS

Ethics

You probably read or heard about the Sarbanes-Oxley Act of 2002 before you learned about it in this book. Until the law was passed, you probably didn't know the name Michael Oxley, one of the sponsors of the bill, unless you live in Ohio. Oxley, a congressman from Ohio, has this to say about the law that bears his name, along with the name of retired senator Paul Sarbanes.

Sarbanes-Oxley is an example of American economic resilience, the ability of our system to reform, move forward, solve problems, and become more efficient. No economic system in the history of the world could with-stand the body blows we have taken in the past few years—9/11, the corporate scandals, the bursting of the tech bubble—and emerge stronger for it. I can assure you that my committee will continue to focus on investor protection, whether on the mutual fund issue or other matters, so Americans feel confident that there is a fair playing field on Wall Street.

Thinking Critically

Do you think the Sarbanes-Oxley Act has restored investor confidence? Has the law established a "fair playing field" on Wall Street?

Q What three "body blows" did the U.S. economic system suffer in the early 2000's?

A 9/11 terrorist attack, stock market bubble bursting (dot.com failures), and the corporate scandals are three

Senator Paul Sarbanes of Marlyland (right), now retired, and Congressman Michael Oxley of Ohio (left) developed the Sarbanes-Oxley Act, a sweeping corporate accountability bill signed into law by President Bush on July 30, 2002.

key "body blows" our economy has taken, according to Mike Oxley.

Source: mikeoxley.org

Key players in corporate governance

The Sarbanes-Oxley (SOX) Act has significant implications for four groups:

1. Management
   - The CEO and CFO are responsible for the firm's internal controls. The SOX Act requires the company to include, with its annual report, a separate report on the effectiveness of the company's internal controls. The firm's external auditors must attest to the accuracy of the internal control report.
   - Management has the ultimate responsibility for the accuracy of financial statements and the accompanying notes. In most firms, that responsibility is delegated to lower-level managers, but top management cannot escape ultimate legal responsibility. SOX requires the CEO and the CFO to certify the annual financial statements—they will swear that they have reviewed the statements and that, based on their knowledge, the report does not contain any false statements and does not omit any significant facts.
   - Firms must provide a mechanism for anonymous reporting of fraudulent activities in the company, including a hotline for the reporting. Whistle-blower protection is extended to company employees who lawfully disclose information that the employee reasonably believes constitutes a violation of securities laws or any law that deals with fraud against shareholders. According to SOX, no officer or agent of the company may "discharge, demote, suspend, threaten, harass, or in any other manner discriminate against an employee in the terms and conditions of employment because of any lawful act done by the employee." That means that the company cannot punish a person in any way for blowing the whistle—disclosing suspected fraud in the company. Read more about whistle blowing in *Accounting in the News*.

Study Tip

You read about internal control in Chapter 1. Formerly defined, an internal control is a process designed to provide reasonable assurance regarding the achievement of the firm's objectives in these areas:

1. reliability of financial reporting,
2. the effectiveness and efficiency of operations, and
3. compliance with applicable laws and regulations.

Accounting in the NEWS

Ethics

Would You Blow the Whistle on Fraud?

It's past midnight when a lone informant steps from the parking garage shadows and stamps out a lipstick-stained Marlboro Light. The top brass, she whispers, has looted the company, defrauded shareholders and covered up a toxic dump responsible for dozens of deaths. She hands over a stack of documents. Then a car screeches and she dashes away.

Whistle-blowing has long provided grist for Hollywood thrillers. But in these post-Enron scandal days, real-life whistle-blowers are in the spotlight—and for good reason.

The Sarbanes-Oxley Act of 2002 requires that firms have a hotline to make it easier for whistle-blowers to anonymously report any suspicious actions or behavior going on in the company, particularly as it pertains to financial information. Having such a hotline has provided unintended benefits to many companies, including Fisher Communications.

Fisher Communications is a Seattle-based broadcaster with radio and TV stations in Washington, Oregon, Idaho,

and Montana. The company started using EthicsPoint, a firm that provides hotline services, this spring to check on a laundry list of potential problems: accounting, conflict of interest, discrimination, embezzlement, falsification of contracts, reports or records, sabotage or vandalism, securities violations, substance abuse, theft, violence, and threats. The broad scope helps keep executives in touch with problems throughout a company so they can stop problems before they harm employees or stockholders.

As firms work to implement the requirements of Sarbanes-Oxley, we may see new industries popping up and old ones flourishing. Take a look at the web sites of some of the firms that provide hotline services for reporting fraud and abuse.

EthicsPoint: www.ethicspoint.com
Global Compliance Services: www.globalcomplianceservices.com
Integrity Interactive: www.integrity-interactive.com
The Network: www.tnwinc.com

Thinking Critically

Suppose you suspected your boss of taking home a significant amount of company supplies? Would you blow the whistle? What if your boss was stealing money?

Q How can an employee hotline help a company in which there is no suspicion of financial fraud?

Sherron Watkins (far right in the photo) testified before the U.S. Congress and Senate at the beginning of 2002 and was selected as one of three "People of the Year 2002" by TIME magazine. The two whistleblowers who joined her as "People of the Year" were Cynthia Cooper of WorldCom and Coleen Rowley of the FBI.

A The hotline can help identify all types of problems and potential problems that are unrelated to the financial statements, such as discrimination or operating inefficiencies.

Source: Alwyn Scott, "Sniffing Out Fraud Is Growth Industry in Post-Enron Era," *Seattle Times*, October 3, 2004. Copyright 2004, Seattle Times Company. Used with permission.

2. The board of directors (BOD)
   - These are the people who are elected by stockholders to establish general corporate policies and make decisions on major company issues, such as dividend policies. Members of the board are elected by the shareholders to represent the interests of shareholders.
   - The part of the board of directors responsible for overseeing the financial matters of the firm is the audit committee. Members of this committee are concerned with the firm's controls over financial reporting and with overseeing the external auditors.
   - SOX requires the audit committee to be made up of independent directors from the board of directors. Company managers cannot be on the committee. The audit committee is responsible for hiring, compensating, and overseeing the work of any public accounting firm hired by the company.

3. External auditors
   - These are accountants specifically trained to examine the firm's financial statements and financial controls and report on the statements

to the shareholders. External auditors give an opinion on whether or not the firm's financial statements fairly present the financial position and the results of operations in accordance with GAAP. As you know, the SEC requires all publicly traded firms to have an annual audit of the financial statements by external auditors.

- SOX requires that auditors remain independent of their clients to ensure objectivity. The SEC has always had rules about auditor independence, but the new law strengthens these rules. For example, auditors can no longer provide information processing consulting services to its audit clients.
- SOX also requires that the auditor report to the client's audit committee, which is part of the board of directors, rather than to the client's management team.

4. Public Company Accounting Oversight Board (PCAOB)

- This regulatory group was established by the SOX Act. Members are appointed by the SEC in consultation with the Chairman of the Board of Governors of the Federal Reserve System and the Secretary of the Treasury.
- The purpose of the PCAOB is to regulate the auditing profession.
- All accounting firms that audit publicly traded companies must register with the PCAOB and follow its rules.
- The SEC must approve any rules set by the PCAOB.

The purpose of the Sarbanes-Oxley Act is to strengthen financial reporting and the corporate governance of publicly traded companies. However, there are some potential disadvantages of the new requirements. Read about them in *Accounting in the News*.

Outlook for the future

We are living in a time where the way companies do business is changing. The importance of accounting and financial reporting is unquestionable. All business managers—marketing managers, production managers, human resource managers, operations managers—must be able to understand financial information and the way it is gathered and reported. All business managers must identify risks for their specific areas and create internal controls to manage those risks. For example, a marketing manager must be aware of how the accounting is done for sales commissions so that he or she can evaluate the risks associated with a salesperson's weekly sales report. Perhaps the accounting department pays the sales people their commissions each Monday for sales submitted by noon on the previous Friday. There is a risk that the salesperson will include sales that are scheduled to be completed by the end of the day on Friday so that the Friday afternoon sales will be included in Monday's payment. A control for this would be to match the salesperson's report to the shipping department's weekly shipments. Recall that, in general, revenue is not recognized until the goods are shipped. Commissions to the sales people should be paid on amounts of revenue the firm has actually earned.

Firms spend a tremendous amount of money to comply with the Sarbanes-Oxley Act's rules and regulations. According to a March 2005 survey reported in *CFO Magazine* (May 2005), nearly half of the 106 large-company CEOs surveyed said complying with Sarbanes-Oxley would cost in excess of $10 million annually. A Financial Executives Institute survey the same month of 217 public companies with average revenues of $5 billion pegged the average 404-compliance cost—the cost of reporting on internal controls—at $4.36 million. Total compliance costs for all publicly traded companies have been estimated at $7 billion per year.[2] Recent

---

[2]This was reported by Jo Lynne Koehn and Stephen Del Vecchio, "Ripple Effects of the Sarbanes-Oxley Act," *The CPA Journal*, February 2004.

Accounting in the NEWS

Risk and Control

Are There Downsides to Sarbanes-Oxley?

The reaction to the Sarbanes-Oxley Act has not been uniformly positive. The Business Higher Education Forum, a group of business leaders and business professors, has published a report suggesting that new laws cannot address the true cause of the problems. They believe the root of the problem is one of ethics. However, many companies' primary concern with the Sarbanes-Oxley Act is the high cost of implementing the new law's provisions, particularly the requirements related to internal controls set forth in Section 404. There are, however, a few other parts of the new law that could create problems. According to the April 25, 2005 *BusinessWeek* article, the shrinking role of the CEO is not all positive.

The new vigilance will almost certainly provide some desperately needed clarity in corporate governance and cut down on the old abuses. But as is often the case, the new rules may initially go too far and create their own distinctive set of problems. Directors, auditors, and lawyers are all going to command higher fees in the future. And the quality of their advice may well decline. Why? When really tough issues arise—involving risky deals, aggressive regulators, or gray-area accounting—CEOs have always been able to turn to board members and professionals for advice. Now piety reigns supreme, and candid conversations are virtually taboo.

And in addition to all of the virtues of independence, shifting power away from the CEO does have some downsides. It makes it harder for them to put together boards that can compensate for their weaknesses. And while boards need to exercise oversight, chief executives, with their deeper understanding of their company's strengths and weaknesses, are often in a better position to make critical strategic decisions.

Thinking Critically

As you read about the pros and cons of the Sarbanes-Oxley Act, think critically about how it might affect the number of potential CEOs and CFOs. Would you be willing to take the responsibilities of a CEO or CFO in the post-Enron era?

Do you buy products from eBay? Do you want rules and regulations to slow down how CEO Meg Whitman makes decisions and grows the company?

Q What is one possible disadvantage of having independent directors, that is, those with no relationship to the firm?

A They may lack the strengths needed to compensate for weaknesses of the CEO.

Sources: Edward Soule, *Embedding Ethics in Business and Higher Education*, Business Higher Education Forum, June 2005. (Free copies available by e-mailing info@bhef.com). David Henry, Mike France, and Louis Lavell, "The Boss on the Sidelines," *Business Week*, April 25, 2005. Reprinted from the April 25, 2005 issue of *Business Week*. Copyright © 2005 by The McGraw-Hill Companies. Reprinted with permission.

---

reports indicate that it is very difficult for a firm to calculate the total costs of implementing SOX.[3] Recognizing the high cost of compliance for smaller firms, current SEC chairman, Christopher Cox, announced (as this book goes to press) his support for a one-year delay for certain small firms to comply with the internal control provisions of SOX.

The new climate and new laws have resulted in a surge in employment opportunities for accounting and auditing firms. According to federal Bureau

Can YOU do it?

Explain why internal controls are so important to firms and their auditors.

Answer Managers must report on the firm's internal controls and their effectiveness. Some firms may need new ways to gather information about the effectiveness of the firm's controls. The auditors must attest to management's report, which means that the auditors must gather sufficient evidence to give their opinion on the truthfulness of management's report. These are added responsibilities for the firm's managers and the firm's auditors.

---

[3]From Carl Bialik, "How Much Is It Really Costing to Comply with Sarbanes-Oxley?", *Wall Street Journal*, June 16, 2005.

of Labor Statistics, the number of accounting jobs is expected to increase by as much as 20 percent by 2012. Currently, business schools are straining to attract and graduate enough accountants to meet the demand. The American Institute of Certified Public Accountants projects double-digit growth in hiring by most of its member firms for the next three years. Filling those jobs won't be easy, due to a shortage of accounting majors.[4]

LEARNING OBJECTIVE 6

Evaluate a firm's corporate governance.

Evaluating Corporate Governance

The Sarbanes-Oxley Act of 2002 changed the way corporations govern themselves in the United States. In 2004, a study[5] of the corporate governance in the top 100 firms in the FORTUNE 500 revealed that many companies are voluntarily *exceeding* new requirements. For example, in 81 of the top 100 companies, 75% or more of the boards are made up of independent directors, while the NYSE and NASDAQ require only a simple majority of 51%. Although boards of directors are not generally meeting more frequently, the audit committees, compensation committees, and the nominating committees met, on average, more often in 2003 than they did in 2002. These are just a few examples of changes in corporate governance in the wake of Sarbanes-Oxley. As firms evaluate the changes they must make and also decide on voluntary changes in their corporate governance, every CEO, CFO, member of a board of directors, and investor would like to know the answer to this important question: What is *good* corporate governance?

Defining and measuring good corporate governance

Most experts—managers, the SEC, and academic researchers—agree that the most important factor in good corporate governance is an ethical climate, which top management sets. Steven Baum, chairman, president, and CEO of Sempra Energy (SRE), a San Diego-based natural gas and energy supplier with 2004 revenues of over $9 billion, gives the following as the top five most important elements for strong and effective corporate governance[6]:

1. Boards of directors [should be] independent from the executive management team and composed of highly qualified directors with diverse backgrounds.

2. The CEO must encourage board involvement for the review of major management and financial decisions.

3. Financial information for shareholders should be transparent—easily understandable, simple, and straightforward.

4. Incentive-based compensation plans should offer rewards to management for performance that creates increased shareholder value.

5. Auditors should be strong and independent from the firm.

Little research exists to confirm that these, or any other, elements of corporate governance actually prevent fraud. But even if you agree that these are desirable elements, can you see how difficult it might be to measure some of these elements?

Neither lack of supporting research nor measurement difficulty has stopped the development of corporate governance rating systems. Although not yet

[4]From "Who's Counting?" *CFO Magazine*, May 1, 2005.
[5]Shearman & Sterling LLP, *Corporate Governance Practices of the 100 Largest Public Companies*, 2004. Copies are available on the firm's web site: http://shearman.com/corporategovernance/cg_publications.html.
[6]From "Ask the CEO," *Business Week Online*, May 6, 2003.

widespread, these rating systems are gaining exposure and popularity among investors. Some of those companies involved in developing rating systems for corporate governance are Institutional Shareholder Services, Governance-Metrics International, and Moody's.

How can we evaluate a firm's corporate governance?

There are two key ways to find out about a firm's corporate governance:

1. Web sites
2. Annual reports or 10-Ks

Many large firms post their corporate governance policies on their web sites, where you can find menus for corporate governance guidelines, code of ethics, and various committees of the board of directors. On some web sites, you will find information about each member of the board and of the audit, compensation, and nominating committees. For example, on the MCI— the company that was formerly WorldCom—web site, under "About MCI," there is a menu that includes "Corporate Governance" that leads you to the following information: Articles of Incorporation, Board of Directors, By-Laws, Committees and Charters, Governance Guidelines, Officers, Restoring Trust, Shareholder Recommendations, MCI Code of Ethics, and Company Values. After all that MCI has been through, it's not surprising that "Restoring Trust" is a prominent part of the corporate governance materials. The screens below show the corporate governance sections of MCI, Starbucks, and Apple web sites.

Another useful input to evaluate a firm's corporate governance is management's report on internal controls. As this book is going to press, the first reports are being released. An example of an early report is shown in Exhibit 13.3. Notice that SunTrust mentions a material weakness in its internal control system. Recall that the word *material* means significant in accounting language. The firm also mentions that remedial actions have been taken. When a firm has to report a material weakness in its internal control system, the firm can minimize the adverse effects by informing investors that it has fixed the problem.

You read earlier in the chapter that one of the requirements of the Sarbanes-Oxley Act is that management must report on the effectiveness of the company's system of internal controls. Also, the external auditors must attest to and issue a report on management's assessment of internal controls.

Just like the financial statements alone are insufficient to come to a conclusion about the value of a company, the corporate governance information provided by a company is not sufficient to draw any definite conclusions about the

Major corporations like MCI, Starbucks, and Apple post their corporate governance guidelines on their web sites.

Exhibit 13.3

SunTrust

Firm Report on Internal Control Weaknesses as Required by Section 404 of Sarbanes-Oxley.

SunTrust's Report on Internal Control Weaknesses as required by Section 404 of Sarbanes-Oxley

(Filed with the SEC in January 2005)

SunTrust Banks — Superregional bank.	Jan. 20	MATERIAL WEAKNESS IDENTIFIED — The Company disclosed in its Form 10-Q for the 2004 third quarter that there was a material weakness in the Company's internal controls over financial reporting relating to the process of establishing the allowance for loan and lease losses and that the Company would likely not be able to fully remediate the weakness in internal controls by December 31, 2004. Although significant remedial actions have been taken, SunTrust was not able to fully remediate the material weakness in internal controls as of December 31, 2004. As a result, management will disclose this material weakness in internal controls in its report in the Company's Form 10-K and indicate that the Company's internal controls over financial reporting were not effective at such date. In addition, the Company expects that the material weakness will result in an adverse opinion by the Company's independent auditors on the effectiveness of the Company's internal controls.
2003 Sales: $7.0billion Auditor: PwC		

integrity and honesty of the company and its management. However, as information about how a company's corporate governance policies are working becomes more readily available, it will be easier to evaluate this area of the company.

Can **YOU** do it?

Name two characteristics of good corporate governance.

Answer Here are a few: (1) a board of directors (BOD) with a majority of independent directors; (2) a BOD with a chairman who is not the firm's CEO, (3) a reputable and reliable internal audit function, (4) independent external auditors, (5) a strong code of ethics, with the top management setting the tone, (6) a compensation system that does not place too much reliance on the stock price but does reward increasing the firm's underlying value.

The daily newspaper is just one source of information you need to stay abreast of current business events. Weekly magazines and online magazines and papers are also available.

Staying up to date: it's up to you

As you finish your study of financial accounting, look back and see how far you've come. When you started Chapter 1, you probably didn't know a balance sheet from an income statement. Now you know the elements of the four basic financial statements and the principles that accountants use to prepare these statements. You've learned that the statements alone do not provide sufficient information for investors. The accompanying notes that you often see referenced at the bottom of each statement are an integral part of the financial statements. You've learned that companies can "cook the books," but also remember that the vast majority of accountants, managers, and business executives are honest people who are doing their best, often in difficult situations.

YOU make the call:

WorldCom's $11 billion fraud—how did everyone miss the signs?

Even after studying corporate governance, we can't say whether or not the Sarbanes-Oxley Act could have prevented the MCI-WorldCom fraud. One part of the new law that might have helped Betty Vinson is the requirement for firms to provide a way for employees to anonymously report potential fraud or abuse. Vinson's repeated doubts and concerns about what she was asked to do may have motivated her to blow the whistle.

Let's Take a Test Drive

Real-World Problem:
WorldCom

When WorldCom filed for bankruptcy in 2002, it was one of the largest financial failures in history, and regulators and investors wanted to know why this happened. Where were the members of the board of directors? Where were the auditors? It was more than a financial crisis, it was a crisis that went to the very core of the company—or perhaps we should say it went to the very top of the company. When emerging from bankruptcy protection, the company, now known as MCI, had to do more than produce positive earnings. MCI had the task of rebuilding its reputation—a task outlined in a document called "Restoring Trust."

Concepts

In this chapter, we've discussed the requirements of the Sarbanes-Oxley Act, and we've reviewed the elements of good corporate governance. Here are some of the requirements that would have made the WorldCom failure much less likely:

- A board of directors with (1) a chairman who is not the CEO; (2) some independent directors; and (3) audit, compensation, and nominating committees.
- Independent auditors who (1) are hired by and report to the audit committee of the board of directors and (2) do not perform internal audit function or accounting consulting for the client firm.
- A code of ethics and a mechanism for employees to anonymously report any suspected violation and any suspected financial irregularity.
- A system of internal controls that are understood and enforced by management.
- Managers who prepare a report on the controls, and auditors who attest to management's report.
- Financial statements that have been approved and signed by the CEO and the CFO.

Instructions

Considering these elements, what do you think MCI has done to improve its corporate governance, or, as the company calls it, restore trust. How can MCI measure its success? Read the suggested solution to see what MCI actually did.

Solution

The following is taken directly from MCI's web site. You can find more information at www.mci.com, *About us, Corporate Governance.*

The steps taken by MCI to address the problems from its WorldCom days, as suggested by the report of the court-appointed bankruptcy examiner, Dick Thornburgh, include the following:

- Recruited a new CEO who was not at the Company during the events at issue, and who brought a reputation for integrity and forthrightness in his leadership skills.
- Recruited a new CFO, General Counsel, and director of internal controls, all of whom came from outside the Company.
- Replaced its entire board of directors who were present at the time the fraud was discovered, thereby removing 100% of directors who were participants in governance under the regime of the prior CEO Bernard J. Ebbers.
- After the fraud was discovered, appointed three highly respected individuals to its Board of Directors: Nicholas Katzenbach, former U.S. Attorney General and former Under Secretary of State; Dennis Beresford, Professor of Accounting at the Terry College of Business at the University of Georgia and a former chairman of the Financial Accounting Standards Board; and C.B. Rogers, Jr., former CEO and chairman of Equifax. In addition, five highly capable individuals have joined the Board of Directors of MCI. They are former Touche Ross Chairman W. Grant Gregory; retired Bell Atlantic executive Judith Haberkorn; Patton Boggs Partner Laurence Harris; former U.S. Deputy Attorney General Eric Holder, and Cerberus Capital Management LPC Chief Operating Officer and General Counsel Mark Neporent.
- Separated the roles of Chairman and Chief Executive Officer with Nicholas Katzenbach being elected non-executive Chairman.
- Relocated the Company's finance and accounting department from its former Clinton, Mississippi, headquarters, where most of the fraud occurred, to MCI's new headquarters in Ashburn, Virginia.
- Hired more than 400 new finance and accounting personnel.
- Retained a new outside auditor, and completed a restatement of 1999–2002 earnings reports.
- Evaluated all corporate assets for value impairment, wrote off all goodwill, and wrote down asset carrying values for property, plant and equipment to achieve a realistic balance sheet.
- Terminated dozens of employees, including a number of senior officers, who either participated in inappropriate activities, who appeared to look the other way in the face of indications of suspicious activity, or who otherwise acted in a manner inconsistent with necessary standards of conduct.
- Agreed to abolish use of stock options in favor of restricted stock with full expensing of the value of equity grants on the Company's profit and loss statement.
- Initiated a thorough review of internal controls to strengthen the Company's systems and procedures for capturing and reporting financial data, and a widespread program to correct deficiencies and create a much stronger system.
- Established a new Ethics Office.
- Put in place a new Ethics Pledge program pursuant to which senior officers including the CEO pledge to pursue ethics and integrity, compliance programs and transparency and candor in financial reporting well beyond SEC requirements.
- Implemented a training program for employees on their responsibilities under the federal securities laws, accounting issues that may signal inappropriate behavior or fraud, corporate governance issues, and ethical issues.
- Entered into a financial settlement with the SEC under which $500 million in cash and $250 million in stock was paid into a trust for victims. The settlement was approved by both the U.S. District Court and the Bankruptcy Court.
- The Board of Directors has commenced using a portion of their fees (25%) to purchase stock in the corporation.
- Revised and implemented new Articles of Incorporation; By-Laws; Charters for the Audit, Compensation, Nominating and Governance, and Risk Committees; and Corporate Governance Guidelines.

Rapid Review

1. **Explain Wall Street's emphasis on earnings and the potential problems that result from this emphasis.** A firm's earnings, often expressed as *earnings per share (EPS)*, is the number analysts and investors use to evaluate a firm's performance. If analysts or firm managers predict achieving certain earnings per share, it will raise expectations if the predicted EPS is an increase over current EPS. If the firm doesn't hit the predicted number, its stock price is likely to drop. If the firm hits or exceeds the predicted number, its stock price will likely increase. If an executive is given stock options as part of his or her compensation package, that execu-

tive will have a vested interest in keeping the stock price high. That translates into pressure to make the number—whatever it takes.

2. **Define quality of earnings and explain how it is measured.** *Quality of earnings* refers to how well a particular earnings number communicates the firm's true performance. Quality of earnings is difficult to measure. Influencing factors include the firm's accounting choices and the level of risk the business faces.

3. **Recognize the common ways that firms can manipulate earnings.** Being aware of the common ways that firms manipulate earnings will help you spot them as you analyze financial statements and other company information. There are three main ways firms manipulate earnings:

   (1) Recognize revenue too soon.

   (2) Use cookie jar reserves: Use reserves to increase or decrease earnings as desired.

   (3) Use big bath charges: Write off as much as possible in a bad year to minimize expenses in future years.

4. **Describe the corporate accounting failures of the early 2000s.** The accounting scandals such as Enron and WorldCom were a result of financial statement fraud. This fraud brought attention to the role of management, boards of directors, and auditors in preventing and discovering financial statement fraud. One of the most important results was the passage of the *Sarbanes-Oxley Act of 2002*, a law sponsored by then Senator Paul Sarbanes of Maryland and Congressman Mike Oxley of Ohio.

5. **Explain the requirements of the Sarbanes-Oxley Act of 2002.** The goal of Sarbanes-Oxley, sometimes called SOX, is to improve corporate governance of publicly traded firms in an effort to prevent future financial statement frauds. The requirements include new responsibilities for management and the board of directors. Additionally, a new organization, the Public Company Accounting Oversight Board (PCAOB), has been established to monitor and regulate external auditing firms.

6. **Evaluate a firm's corporate governance.** Currently, there are a number of initiatives to measure the quality of a firm's corporate governance. Many of the qualities of good corporate governance relate to the composition and duties of the board of directors. Agencies that rate a firm's corporate governance are becoming more numerous and should play an important role in helping investors in the next decade.

Key Terms

Cooking the books, p. 675
Corporate governance, p. 679

Earnings per share, p. 672
Quality of earnings, p. 673

Questions

1. What determines the quality of earnings?
2. Why are earnings so important?
3. What events motivated Congress to pass the Sarbanes-Oxley Act of 2002?
4. What is the role of the newly created Public Company Accounting Oversight Board (PCAOB)?
5. Who is responsible for establishing auditing standards for audits of public companies? Who is responsible for establishing accounting standards for public companies? Explain these two sets of standards.
6. What provisions of Sarbanes-Oxley should increase auditor independence? Explain how.
7. What changes does Sarbanes-Oxley require for a company's board of directors?
8. What are internal controls and who is responsible for their effectiveness?
9. What is the responsibility of the audit committee of the board of directors?
10. Who is responsible for certifying the financial statements filed with the SEC?
11. What is a "cookie jar reserve," and how is it used?
12. What is the big bath theory?
13. When should a company recognize revenue?

Multiple Choice

1. Which of the following is a problem resulting from the emphasis on earnings?
   a. Managers may ignore sales forecasts.
   b. Internal controls may deteriorate.
   c. Quality of earnings may suffer.
   d. Responsibilities of lower level managers may increase.
2. A publicly traded firm must have
   a. A functioning board of directors
   b. A CFO with significant accounting experience
   c. A specific time each week to meet with employees regarding potential fraud
   d. An ethics committee
3. The audit committee is
   a. Part of the internal audit function
   b. A subset of directors who must be independent
   c. No longer part of corporate governance
   d. Chaired by a CPA
4. Who is responsible for selecting, hiring, and compensating the external auditors?
   a. CEO
   b. CFO
   c. Audit committee of the BOD
   d. All of the above.
5. High quality earnings are those that
   a. Fluctuate widely between periods
   b. Provide accurate and reliable information about a firm's earnings
   c. Exceed $1 per share
   d. Are found in the equity section of the balance sheet

Short Exercises

LO 1   **SE13-1.** What is the most important number a firm reports in the opinion of Wall Street analysts? What problems has this created?

LO 2   **SE13-2.** How do you think analysts evaluate the quality of a firm's earnings? Do you think higher quality earnings translate into higher stock prices?

LO 3   **SE13-3.** Describe the big bath theory and give some examples of items that could be written off early.

LO 3   **SE13-4.** What types of companies might have problems with revenue recognition? How can investors learn about the revenue recognition policies of a company?

LO 4   **SE13-5.** Some of the scandals of the early 2000s were the result of misapplying accounting principles and others were the result of questionable accounting principles. Which do you think describes the WorldCom failure? Why? Do you think good accounting principles can eliminate financial failures like Enron and WorldCom? Explain.

LO 5   **SE13-6.** Discuss the costs and benefits of requiring managers to report on the company's internal controls. Do you think it is necessary for the external auditor to attest to management's report? Why or why not?

LO 5   **SE13-7.** One of the requirements of the new law is that the lead auditor or coordinating partner and the reviewing partner must rotate off the audit every five years. In your opinion, what is the purpose of this requirement? Do you think it will be achieved?

LO 5, 6   **SE13-8.** What is the advantage of having a financial expert on the board of directors? Are there any drawbacks?

LO 5, 6   **SE13-9.** Discuss the advantages and disadvantages of having the audit committee deal directly with the external auditors.

LO 5, 6   **SE13-10.** Read the list of actions taken by MCI to restore trust in the solution to the *Let's Take a Test Drive* review problem on page 689. Which actions were not explicitly required by Sarbanes-Oxley? What was MCI's motivation?

LO 6   **SE13-11.** Do you think that good corporate governance can be measured? Would you use it in a decision to invest in a specific company?

Internet Exercises

IE13-1. Go to Google and type in "corporate governance." How many hits did you get? Check out a few of the links to see what type of information is available on the topic of corporate governance.

LO 6

IE13-2. Go to the PCAOB web site at www.pcaobus.org. According to its web site, what is the mission of the PCAOB? So far, do you believe it is accomplishing this mission? Why or why not?

LO 5, 6

IE13-3. Go to the Pixar web site at www.pixar.com. Follow the link to Investor Relations and then to Corporate Governance. What information is available about the company's corporate governance? See if you can find out how many times the audit committee must meet each year. Do you think that is a sufficient number of meetings? Why or why not?

LO 5, 6

IE13-4. Select a pair of companies in the same industry—such as Wal-Mart and Target, Hershey Foods and Tootsie Roll, The Home Depot and Lowe's. For the two companies you select, go to their web sites and locate the information about corporate governance. Summarize the information you found. How does the information for the two companies compare? Did you find any surprising similarities or differences? Do you think investors are interested in this information?

LO 5, 6

IE13-5. Go to www.enron.com and see if you can find the annual report for 2000. See if you can locate *Management's Responsibility for Financial Reporting*. What does it say? Do you think that the new requirements of Sarbanes-Oxley will stop frauds like those that caused the Enron collapse? Why or why not?

LO 5

IE13-6. Prior to 2003, The Walt Disney Company was severely criticized for its corporate governance practices. Go to http://corporate.disney.go.com and read about the firm's corporate governance. Check out the members of the board of directors. Are the roles of CEO and chairman of the board held by the same person? How would you evaluate Disney's corporate governance?

LO 5, 6

Wal-Mart Annual Report
(excerpted)

11-Year Financial Summary

WAL-MART

(Dollar amounts in millions except per share data)

Fiscal Years Ending January 31,	2005	2004	2003
Net Sales	**$285,222**	$256,329	$229,616
Net sales increase	**11.3%**	11.6%	12.6%
Comparative store sales increase in the United States [1]	**3%**	4%	5%
Cost of sales	**$219,793**	$198,747	$178,299
Operating, selling, general and administrative expenses	**51,105**	44,909	39,983
Interest expense, net	**986**	832	927
Effective tax rate	**34.7%**	36.1%	35.2%
Income from continuing operations	**$ 10,267**	$ 8,861	$ 7,818
Net income	**10,267**	9,054	7,955
Per share of common stock:			
Income from continuing operations, diluted	**$ 2.41**	$ 2.03	$ 1.76
Net income, diluted	**2.41**	2.07	1.79
Dividends	**0.52**	0.36	0.30
Financial Position			
Current assets of continuing operations	**$ 38,491**	$ 34,421	$ 29,543
Inventories	**29,447**	26,612	24,401
Property, equipment and capital lease assets, net	**68,567**	59,023	51,374
Total assets of continuing operations	**120,223**	105,405	92,900
Current liabilities of continuing operations	**42,888**	37,840	32,225
Long-term debt	**20,087**	17,102	16,597
Long-term obligations under capital leases	**3,582**	2,997	3,000
Shareholders' equity	**49,396**	43,623	39,461
Financial Ratios			
Current ratio	**0.9**	0.9	0.9
Return on assets [2]	**9.3%**	9.2%	9.2%
Return on shareholders' equity [3]	**22.1%**	21.3%	20.9%
Other Year-End Data			
Discount Stores in the United States	**1,353**	1,478	1,568
Supercenters in the United States	**1,713**	1,471	1,258
SAM'S CLUBs in the United States	**551**	538	525
Neighborhood Markets in the United States	**85**	64	49
Units outside the United States	**1,587**	1,355	1,272
Shareholders of record	**331,000**	335,000	330,000

(1) Comparative store sales are considered to be sales at stores that were open as of February 1 of the prior fiscal year and have not been expanded or relocated since that date.

(2) Income from continuing operations before minority interest divided by average assets.

(3) Income from continuing operations divided by average shareholders' equity.

Financial information for all years has been restated to reflect the sale of McLane Company, Inc. ("McLane") that occurred in fiscal 2004. McLane is presented as a discontinued operation. All years have been restated for the adoption of the expense recognition provisions of Financial Accounting Standards Board Statement No. 123, "Accounting and Disclosure of Stock-Based Compensation." Fiscal 1995 was not affected by the adoption.

In fiscal 2003, the company adopted Financial Accounting Standards Board Statement No. 142, "Goodwill and Other Intangible Assets." In years prior to adoption, the company recorded amortization expense related to goodwill.

2002	2001	2000	1999	1998	1997	1996	1995
$204,011	$180,787	$156,249	$130,522	$112,005	$99,627	$89,051	$78,338
12.8%	15.7%	19.7%	16.5%	12.4%	11.9%	13.7%	23.6%
6%	5%	8%	9%	6%	5%	4%	7%
$159,097	$140,720	$121,825	$102,490	$ 88,163	$78,897	$70,485	$61,929
35,147	30,822	26,025	21,778	18,831	16,437	14,547	12,434
1,183	1,196	840	598	716	807	863	669
36.2%	36.5%	36.8%	37.4%	37.0%	36.8%	36.8%	37.2%
$ 6,448	$ 6,087	$ 5,394	$ 4,240	$ 3,424	$ 2,978	$ 2,689	$ 2,643
6,592	6,235	5,324	4,397	3,504	3,042	2,737	2,681
$ 1.44	$ 1.36	$ 1.21	$ 0.95	$ 0.76	$ 0.65	$ 0.58	$ 0.58
1.47	1.39	1.19	0.98	0.77	0.66	0.59	0.59
0.28	0.24	0.20	0.16	0.14	0.11	0.10	0.09
$ 26,615	$ 25,344	$ 23,478	$ 20,064	$ 18,589	$17,385	$16,779	$14,827
22,053	20,987	19,296	16,361	16,005	15,556	15,667	13,726
45,248	40,461	35,533	25,600	23,237	19,935	18,554	15,561
81,549	76,231	68,983	48,513	44,221	38,571	36,621	31,959
26,795	28,366	25,525	16,155	13,930	10,432	10,944	9,449
15,676	12,489	13,653	6,887	7,169	7,685	8,483	7,844
3,044	3,152	3,000	2,697	2,480	2,304	2,089	1,834
35,192	31,407	25,878	21,141	18,519	17,151	14,757	12,726
1.0	0.9	0.9	1.2	1.3	1.7	1.5	1.6
8.4%	8.6%	9.8%	9.5%	8.5%	8.0%	7.9%	9.2%
19.4%	21.3%	22.9%	21.4%	19.2%	18.7%	19.6%	22.5%
1,647	1,736	1,801	1,869	1,921	1,960	1,995	1,985
1,066	888	721	564	441	344	239	147
500	475	463	451	443	436	433	426
31	19	7	4	-	-	-	-
1,154	1,054	991	703	589	314	276	226
324,000	317,000	307,000	261,000	246,000	257,000	244,000	259,000

The acquisition of the ASDA Group PLC and the company's related debt issuance had a significant impact on the fiscal 2000 amounts in this summary.

Years prior to 1998 have not been restated for the effects of the change in accounting method for SAM'S CLUB membership revenue recognition as the effects of this change would not have a material impact on this summary. The cumulative effect for this accounting change recorded in fiscal 2000 amounted to $198 million net of tax.

Certain reclassifications have been made to prior periods to conform to current presentations.

Management's Discussion and Analysis of Results of Operations and Financial Condition

WAL-MART

Overview

Wal-Mart Stores, Inc. ("Wal-Mart" or the "company") is a global retailer committed to growing by improving the standard of living for our customers throughout the world. We earn the trust of our customers every day by providing a broad assortment of quality merchandise and services at everyday low prices ("EDLP") while fostering a culture that rewards and embraces mutual respect, integrity and diversity. EDLP is our pricing philosophy under which we price items at a low price every day so that our customers trust that our prices will not change erratically under frequent promotional activity. SAM'S CLUB is in business for small businesses. Our focus for SAM'S CLUB is to provide exceptional value on brand-name merchandise at "Members Only" prices for both business and personal use. Internationally, we operate with similar philosophies.

We intend for this discussion to provide the reader with information that will assist in understanding our financial statements, the changes in certain key items in those financial statements from year to year, and the primary factors that accounted for those changes, as well as how certain accounting principles affect our financial statements. The discussion also provides information about the financial results of the various segments of our business to provide a better understanding of how those segments and their results affect the financial condition and results of operations of the company as a whole. This discussion should be read in conjunction with our financial statements and accompanying notes as of January 31, 2005, and the year then ended.

Throughout this Management's Discussion and Analysis of Results of Operations and Financial Condition, we discuss segment operating income and comparative store sales. Segment operating income refers to income from continuing operations before net interest expense, income taxes and minority interest. Segment operating income does not include unallocated corporate overhead. Comparative store sales is a measure which indicates the performance of our existing stores by measuring the growth in sales for such stores for a particular period over the corresponding period in the prior year. We consider comparative store sales to be sales at stores that were open as of February 1st of the prior fiscal year and have not been expanded or relocated since that date. Stores that were expanded or relocated during that period are not included in the calculation. Comparative store sales is also referred to as "same-store" sales by others within the retail industry. The method of calculating comparative store sales varies across the retail industry. As a result, our calculation of comparative store sales is not necessarily comparable to similarly titled measures reported by other companies.

On May 2, 2003, we announced that we had entered into an agreement to sell McLane Company, Inc. ("McLane"), one of our wholly-owned subsidiaries, for $1.5 billion. On May 23, 2003, the transaction was completed. As a result of this sale, we have classified McLane as a discontinued operation in the financial statements and these discussions and comparisons of the current and prior fiscal years. McLane's external sales prior to the divestiture were $4.3 billion in fiscal 2004 and $14.9 billion for fiscal 2003. McLane continues to be a supplier to the company.

Operations

Our operations are comprised of three business segments: Wal-Mart Stores, SAM'S CLUB and International.

Our Wal-Mart Stores segment is the largest segment of our business, accounting for approximately 67.3% of our fiscal 2005 sales. This segment consists of three different retail formats, all of which are located in the United States, including:

- Supercenters, which average approximately 187,000 square feet in size and offer a wide assortment of general merchandise and a full-line supermarket;
- Discount Stores, which average approximately 100,000 square feet in size and offer a wide assortment of general merchandise and a limited assortment of food products; and
- Neighborhood Markets, which average approximately 43,000 square feet in size and offer a full-line supermarket and a limited assortment of general merchandise.

Our SAM'S CLUB segment consists of membership warehouse clubs in the United States and accounts for approximately 13.0% of our fiscal 2005 sales. Our SAM'S CLUBs in the United States average approximately 128,000 square feet in size.

Our International operations are located in eight countries and Puerto Rico. Internationally, we generated approximately 19.7% of our fiscal 2005 sales. Outside the United States, we operate several different formats of retail stores and restaurants, including Supercenters, Discount Stores and SAM'S CLUBs. Additionally, we own an unconsolidated 37% minority interest in The Seiyu, Ltd. ("Seiyu"), a retailer in Japan.

The Retail Industry

We operate in the highly competitive retail industry in both the United States and abroad. We face strong sales competition from other general merchandise, food and specialty retailers. Additionally, we compete with a number of companies for prime retail site locations, as well as in attracting and retaining quality employees ("associates"). We, along with other retail companies, are influenced by a number of factors including, but not limited to: cost of goods, consumer debt levels, economic conditions, customer preferences, employment, labor costs, inflation, currency exchange fluctuations, fuel prices, weather patterns, insurance costs and accident costs.

Key Items in Fiscal 2005

Significant financial items during fiscal 2005 include:

- Net sales increased 11.3% from fiscal 2004 to $285.2 billion in fiscal 2005, and income from continuing operations increased 15.9% to $10.3 billion. Foreign currency exchange rates favorably impacted sales by $3.2 billion in fiscal 2005.
- Net operating cash provided by operating activities was $15.0 billion for fiscal 2005. During fiscal 2005 we repurchased $4.5 billion of our common stock under our share repurchase program and paid dividends of $2.2 billion. Additionally during fiscal 2005, we issued $5.8 billion in long-term debt securities and repaid $2.1 billion of long-term debt.

- Total assets increased 14.1%, to $120.2 billion at January 31, 2005, when compared to January 31, 2004. During fiscal 2005, we made $12.9 billion of capital expenditures which was an increase of 25.1% over capital expenditures of $10.3 billion in fiscal 2004.
- Our International segment had an operating income increase of 26.1% and a sales increase of 18.3% compared to fiscal 2004. The largest contributors to the strong international performance were our operations in Mexico and the United Kingdom. Fiscal 2005 operating income for the International segment includes a favorable impact of $150 million from changes in foreign currency exchange rates.
- SAM'S CLUB's continued focus on our business members helped drive a 13.7% increase in operating income on a 7.5% increase in sales when comparing fiscal 2005 with fiscal 2004.
- When compared to fiscal 2004, our Wal-Mart Stores segment experienced a 9.7% increase in operating profit and a 10.1% increase in sales in fiscal 2005.

Company Performance Measures

Management uses a number of metrics to assess its performance. The following are the more frequently discussed metrics:

- Comparative store sales is a measure which indicates whether our existing stores continue to gain market share by measuring the growth in sales for such stores for a particular period over the corresponding period in the prior year. Our Wal-Mart Stores segment's comparative store sales were 2.9% for fiscal 2005 versus 3.9% for fiscal 2004. The lower comparative store sales growth in fiscal 2005 is generally reflective of the softer economy in fiscal 2005, including the impact of higher fuel and utility costs on our customers. Our SAM'S CLUB segment's comparative club sales were 5.8% in fiscal 2005 compared to 5.3% in fiscal 2004. The more favorable growth in fiscal 2005 resulted from our continued focus on the business member.
- Operating income growth greater than net sales growth has long been a measure of success for us. For fiscal 2005 our operating income increased by 13.8% when compared to fiscal 2004, while net sales increased by 11.3% over the same period. Both International and SAM'S CLUB segments met this target; however, the Wal-Mart Stores segment fell slightly short.
- Inventory growth at a rate less than half of sales growth is a key measure of our efficiency. Total inventories at January 31, 2005, were up 10.7% over levels at January 31, 2004, and sales were up 11.3% when comparing fiscal 2005 with fiscal 2004. This ratio was affected in fiscal 2005 by sales which were weaker than anticipated, as well as by increased levels of imported merchandise, which carries a longer lead time.
- With an asset base as large as ours, we are focused on continuing to make certain our assets are productive. It is important for us to sustain our return on assets at its current level. Return on assets is defined as income from continuing operations before minority interest divided by average total assets. Return on assets for fiscal 2005, 2004 and 2003 was 9.3%, 9.2% and 9.2%, respectively.

Results of Operations

The company and each of its operating segments had net sales (in millions), as follows:

Fiscal year ended January 31,	2005			2004			2003	
	Net sales	Percent of total	Percent increase	Net sales	Percent of total	Percent increase	Net sales	Percent of total
Wal-Mart Stores	$191,826	67.3%	10.1%	$174,220	68.0%	10.9%	$157,120	68.4%
SAM'S CLUB	37,119	13.0%	7.5%	34,537	13.5%	8.9%	31,702	13.8%
International	56,277	19.7%	18.3%	47,572	18.5%	16.6%	40,794	17.8%
Total net sales	$285,222	100.0%	11.3%	$256,329	100.0%	11.6%	$229,616	100.0%

Our total net sales increased by 11.3% and 11.6% in fiscal 2005 and 2004 when compared to the previous fiscal year. Those increases resulted from our expansion programs and comparative store sales increases in the United States. Comparative store sales increased 3.3% in fiscal 2005 and 4.1% in fiscal 2004. As we continue to add new stores in the United States, we do so with an understanding that additional stores may take sales away from existing units. We estimate that comparative store sales in fiscal 2005, 2004 and 2003 were negatively impacted by the opening of new stores by approximately 1%. We expect that this effect of opening new stores on comparable store sales will continue during fiscal 2006 at a similar rate.

During fiscal 2005 and 2004, foreign currency exchange rates had a $3.2 billion and $2.0 billion favorable impact, respectively, on the International segment's net sales causing an increase in the International segment's net sales as a percentage of total net sales relative to the Wal-Mart Stores and SAM'S CLUB segments. Additionally, the decrease in the SAM'S CLUB segment's net sales as a percent of total company sales in fiscal 2005 and 2004 when compared to fiscal 2003 resulted from the more rapid development of new stores in the International and Wal-Mart Stores segments than the SAM'S CLUB segment.

Management's Discussion and Analysis of Results of Operations and Financial Condition

WAL-MART

Our total gross profit as a percentage of net sales (our "gross margin") was 22.9%, 22.5% and 22.3% in fiscal 2005, 2004 and 2003, respectively. Our Wal-Mart Stores and International segment sales yield higher gross margins than our SAM'S CLUB segment. Accordingly, the greater increases in net sales for the Wal-Mart Stores and International segments in fiscal 2005 and 2004 had a favorable impact on the company's total gross margin.

Operating, selling, general and administrative expenses ("operating expenses") as a percentage of net sales were 17.9%, 17.5% and 17.4% for fiscal 2005, 2004 and 2003, respectively. The increase in operating expenses as a percentage of total net sales was primarily due to a faster rate of growth in operating expenses in our Wal-Mart Stores and International segments, which have higher operating expenses as a percentage of segment net sales than our SAM'S CLUB segment. Operating expenses in fiscal 2005 were impacted by the Wal-Mart Stores and SAM'S CLUB segments' implementation of a new job classification and pay structure for hourly field associates in the United States. The job classification and pay structure, which was implemented in the second quarter of fiscal 2005, was designed to help maintain internal equity and external competitiveness.

Operating expenses in fiscal 2004 were impacted by the adoption of Emerging Issues Task Force Issue No. 02-16, "Accounting by a Reseller for Cash Consideration Received from a Vendor" ("EITF 02-16"). The adoption of EITF 02-16 resulted in an after-tax reduction in fiscal 2004 net income of approximately $140 million.

Interest, net, as a percentage of net sales increased slightly in fiscal 2005 when compared with fiscal 2004 due to higher borrowing levels and higher interest rates during fiscal 2005. For fiscal 2004, interest, net, as a percentage of net sales decreased 0.1% when compared to fiscal 2003, primarily from lower average interest rates on our outstanding debt and the positive impact of our fixed-to-variable interest rate-swap program.

Our effective income tax rates for fiscal 2005, 2004 and 2003 were 34.7%, 36.1% and 35.2%, respectively. The reduction in our effective tax rate from fiscal 2004 to fiscal 2005 is due to the passage of the Working Families Tax-Relief Act of 2004 in October 2004, which retroactively extended the work opportunity tax credit for fiscal 2005. Additionally, our fiscal 2004 effective tax rate was impacted by an increase to our valuation allowance. As a result of tax legislation in Germany in January 2004, we re-evaluated the recoverability of our deferred tax asset in Germany. This re-evaluation resulted in a $150 million charge to increase our valuation allowance in fiscal 2004. This increase in our valuation allowance caused our effective tax rate to rise to 36.1% in fiscal 2004.

In fiscal 2005, we earned income from continuing operations of $10.3 billion, a 15.9% increase over fiscal 2004. Net income in fiscal 2005 increased 13.4% from fiscal 2004 largely as a result of the increase in income from continuing operations described above, net of the $193 million previously provided in fiscal 2004 by McLane, which was disposed in the first half of fiscal 2004 and accounted for as a discontinued operation in that period. During fiscal 2004, we earned income from continuing operations of $8.9 billion, a 13.3% increase over fiscal 2003. Our net income increased 13.8% over the same period largely as a result of the increase in income from continuing operations described above and the $151 million after-tax gain on the sale of McLane recognized in fiscal 2004.

Wal-Mart Stores Segment

Fiscal Year	Segment Net Sales Increase from Prior Fiscal Year	Segment Operating Income (in millions)	Segment Operating Income Increase from Prior Fiscal Year	Operating Income as a Percentage of Segment Sales
2005	**10.1%**	**$14,163**	**9.7%**	**7.4%**
2004	10.9%	12,916	9.1%	7.4%
2003	12.9%	11,840	16.2%	7.5%

The segment net sales increases in fiscal 2005 and fiscal 2004 from the prior fiscal years resulted from comparative store sales increases of 2.9% in fiscal 2005 and 3.9% in fiscal 2004, in addition to our expansion program in the Wal-Mart Stores segment. We believe that comparative store sales in 2005 increased at a slower rate than 2004 due to a softer economy and because our customers have been impacted by higher fuel and utility costs. Our expansion programs consist of opening new units, converting Discount Stores to Supercenters, relocations that result in more square footage, as well as expansions of existing stores. Segment expansion during fiscal 2005 included the opening of 36 Discount Stores, 21 Neighborhood Markets and 242 Supercenters (including the conversion and/or relocation of 159 existing Discount Stores into Supercenters). Two Discount Stores closed in fiscal 2005. During fiscal 2005, our total expansion program added approximately 36 million of store square footage, an 8.6% increase. Segment expansion during fiscal 2004 included the opening of 41 Discount Stores, 15 Neighborhood Markets and 213 Supercenters (including the conversion and/or relocation of 130 existing Discount Stores into Supercenters). One Discount Store closed in fiscal 2004. During fiscal 2004, our total expansion program added approximately 34 million, or 8.8%, of store square footage.

While our fiscal 2005 segment operating income as a percentage of segment net sales was unchanged from fiscal 2004, segment gross margin and operating expenses as a percent of sales were each up 0.4% for the year. Our gross margin improvement can be primarily attributed to our global sourcing effort and reductions in markdowns and shrinkage as a percentage of segment net sales for fiscal 2005 when compared to fiscal 2004. The segment's operating expenses in fiscal 2005 as a percentage of segment net sales were higher than fiscal 2004 primarily due to expense pressures from associate wages and accident costs. Wages primarily increased due to our new job classification and pay structure, which was implemented in the second quarter of fiscal 2005.

The fiscal 2004 decrease in segment operating income as a percentage of segment net sales compared with fiscal 2003 resulted from a 0.4% increase in segment operating expenses, which was partially offset by a 0.3% increase in gross margin for the segment when compared with fiscal 2003. The gross margin improvement was driven primarily by a favorable shift in the mix of products sold and our global sourcing efforts, despite increased apparel markdowns in the second half of the year. Segment operating expenses in fiscal 2004 as a percentage of segment net sales were higher than fiscal 2003 primarily due to increased insurance and advertising costs.

SAM'S CLUB Segment

Fiscal Year	Segment Net Sales Increase from Prior Fiscal Year	Segment Operating Income (in millions)	Segment Operating Income Increase from Prior Fiscal Year	Operating Income as a Percentage of Segment Sales
2005	**7.5%**	**$1,280**	**13.7%**	**3.4%**
2004	8.9%	1,126	10.1%	3.3%
2003	7.8%	1,023	0.0%	3.2%

Growth in net sales for the SAM'S CLUB segment in fiscal 2005 and fiscal 2004 resulted from comparative club sales increases of 5.8% in fiscal 2005 and 5.3% in fiscal 2004, along with our expansion program. Comparative club sales in 2005 increased at a higher rate than in 2004 primarily as the result of continued focus on small business members, along with improved sales in fresh and specialty categories, including fuel. Segment expansion consisted of the opening of 13 new clubs in both fiscal 2005 and fiscal 2004. Our total expansion program added approximately 3 million of additional club square footage, or 3.7%, in fiscal 2005 and approximately 2 million, or 3.6%, of additional club square footage in fiscal 2004.

Segment operating income as a percentage of segment net sales increased slightly in fiscal 2005 when compared to fiscal 2004. The increase is due to an improvement in gross margin, partially offset by an increase in operating expenses as a percentage of segment net sales and the impact of the adoption of EITF 02-16 in fiscal 2004. The improvement in gross margin is primarily a result of strong sales in higher margin categories. Operating expenses as a percentage of segment net sales increased due primarily to higher wage costs resulting from our new job classification and pay structure, which was implemented in the second quarter of fiscal 2005. The adoption of EITF 02-16 resulted in a decrease to the segment's operating income in fiscal 2004 of $44 million.

Segment operating income as a percentage of segment net sales increased slightly in fiscal 2004 when compared to fiscal 2003, due to a reduction in operating expenses resulting from working more closely with the Wal-Mart Stores segment.

International Segment

Fiscal Year	Segment Net Sales Increase from Prior Fiscal Year	Segment Operating Income (in millions)	Segment Operating Income Increase from Prior Fiscal Year	Operating Income as a Percentage of Segment Sales
2005	**18.3%**	**$ 2,988**	**26.1%**	**5.3%**
2004	16.6%	2,370	18.6%	5.0%
2003	15.0%	1,998	57.2%	4.9%

Our International segment is comprised of wholly owned operations in Argentina, Canada, Germany, South Korea, Puerto Rico and the United Kingdom, the operations of joint ventures in China and operations of majority-owned subsidiaries in Brazil and Mexico.

The fiscal 2005 increase in the International segment's net sales primarily resulted from improved operating results, our international expansion program and the impact of foreign currency exchange rate changes. In fiscal 2005, the International segment opened 232 units, net of relocations and closings, which added 18 million, or 15.6%, of additional unit square footage. This includes the acquisition of Bompreço S.A. Supermercados do Nordeste ("Bompreço") in Brazil, which added 118 stores and 7.5 million square feet in February 2004. Additionally, the impact of changes in foreign currency exchange rates favorably affected the translation of International segment sales into U.S. dollars by an aggregate of $3.2 billion in fiscal 2005.

The fiscal 2004 increase in International net sales primarily resulted from both improved operating results and our international expansion program. In fiscal 2004, the International segment opened 83 units, net of relocations and closings, which added 9 million, or 8.5%, of additional unit square footage. Additionally, the impact of changes in foreign currency exchange rates favorably affected the translation of International segment sales into U.S. dollars by an aggregate of approximately $2.0 billion in fiscal 2004.

Management's Discussion and Analysis of Results of Operations and Financial Condition

WAL-MART

Fiscal 2005 sales at our United Kingdom subsidiary, ASDA, were 46.2% of the International segment net sales. Sales for ASDA included in our consolidated income statement during fiscal 2005, 2004, and 2003 were $26.0 billion, $21.7 billion, and $18.1 billion, respectively.

The fiscal 2005 increase in segment operating income as a percentage of segment sales compared with fiscal 2004 resulted primarily from a 0.3% improvement in gross margin. The improvement in gross margin was due to a favorable shift in the mix of products sold toward general merchandise categories which carry a higher margin. Fiscal 2005 operating income includes a favorable impact of $150 million from changes in foreign currency exchange rates.

The fiscal 2004 increase in segment operating income as a percentage of segment net sales compared with fiscal 2003 resulted from a 0.4% improvement in gross margin offset by increases in operating expenses primarily due to the adoption of EITF 02-16. The improvement in gross margin was due to an overall increase as a percentage of the segment's net sales in general merchandise sales which carry a higher margin. The International segment's operating income in fiscal 2004 included a favorable impact of $81 million from changes in foreign currency exchange rates.

Our financial results from our foreign operations could be affected by factors such as changes in foreign currency exchange rates, weak economic conditions, changes in tax law and government regulations in the foreign markets in which we operate. We minimize exposure to the risk of devaluation of foreign currencies by operating in local currencies.

Liquidity and Capital Resources

Overview

Cash flows provided by operating activities of continuing operations provide us with a significant source of liquidity. Our cash flows from operating activities of continuing operations were $15.0 billion in fiscal 2005, compared with $15.9 billion in fiscal 2004. The decrease in cash flows provided by operating activities of continuing operations is primarily attributable to differences in the timing of payroll, income and other taxes, supplier payments and the timing of the collection of receivables in fiscal 2005 compared with fiscal 2004.

Operating cash flows provided by continuing operations increased during fiscal 2004 compared with fiscal 2003 primarily due to improved operations and inventory management, accounts payable growing at a faster rate than inventories and the timing of payroll and the collection of receivables.

In fiscal 2005, we paid dividends of $2.2 billion, made $12.9 billion in capital expenditures, paid $4.5 billion to repurchase shares of our common stock, received $5.8 billion from the issuance of long-term debt and repaid $2.1 billion of long-term debt.

Working Capital

Current liabilities exceeded current assets at January 31, 2005, by $4.4 billion, an increase of $978 million from January 31, 2004. Our ratio of current assets to current liabilities was 0.9 to 1 at January 31, 2005 and 2004. At January 31, 2005, we had total assets of $120.2 billion compared with total assets of $105.4 billion at January 31, 2004.

Company Share Repurchase Program

In September 2004, our Board of Directors approved a new $10.0 billion share repurchase program, separate from and replacing the previous $7.0 billion program authorized in January 2004. Through January 31, 2005, we have repurchased $337 million of shares under the $10.0 billion share repurchase program. At January 31, 2005, approximately $9.7 billion of additional shares may be repurchased under the current authorization. There is no expiration date governing the period over which we can make our share repurchases. Under our share repurchase programs, repurchased shares are constructively retired and returned to unissued status.

Total fiscal 2005 share repurchases under our share repurchase programs were $4.5 billion. During fiscal 2004, we repurchased $5.0 billion of shares.

We consider several factors in determining when to make share repurchases, including among other things, our current cash needs, our cost of borrowing, and the market price of the stock. The increased authorization approved in September 2004, in part, contemplates possible repurchases of our shares that may become available for purchase as a result of the Standard & Poor's ("S&P") Index float adjustment implemented in March and September of 2005. Under the float adjustment, share counts used to determine the S&P indices will reflect only those shares that are available to investors, not all outstanding shares. The float adjustment will exclude shares closely held by control groups. As a result our relative weight in the S&P indices will decline as the S&P indices are adjusted in March and September of 2005. We expect that such adjustments in the S&P indices will cause investment funds that base their portfolio allocations on S&P indices to sell a portion of the shares of the company they hold in order to rebalance their funds based on the new S&P index weightings.

Common Stock Dividends

We paid dividends totaling approximately $1.6 billion or $0.36 per share in fiscal 2004. In March 2004, our Board of Directors authorized a 44% increase in our annual dividend to $0.52 per share. As a result, we paid $2.2 billion in dividends in fiscal 2005. We have increased our dividend every year since the first dividend was declared in March 1974.

On March 3, 2005, the company's Board of Directors approved an increase in annual dividends to $0.60 per share. The annual dividend will be paid in four quarterly installments on April 4, 2005, June 6, 2005, September 6, 2005, and January 3, 2006 to holders of record on March 18, May 20, August 19 and December 16, 2005, respectively.

Contractual Obligations and Other Commercial Commitments

The following table sets forth certain information concerning our obligations and commitments to make contractual future payments, such as debt and lease agreements, and contingent commitments:

(in millions)	Total	2006	2007-2008	2009-2010	Thereafter
			Payments due during fiscal years ending January 31,		
Recorded Contractual Obligations					
Long-term debt	$23,846	$3,759	$ 4,972	$ 5,811	$ 9,304
Commercial paper	3,812	3,812	–	–	–
Capital lease obligations	5,720	521	1,019	958	3,222
Unrecorded Contractual Obligations:					
Non-cancelable operating leases	9,072	730	1,326	1,108	5,908
Interest on long-term debt	10,701	1,107	1,912	1,653	6,029
Undrawn lines of credit	4,696	1,946	–	2,750	–
Trade letters of credit	2,613	2,613	–	–	–
Standby letters of credit	2,026	2,002	24	–	–
Purchase obligations	28,472	12,461	13,717	2,280	14
Total commercial commitments	$90,958	$28,951	$22,970	$14,560	$24,477

Purchase obligations include all legally binding contracts such as firm commitments for inventory purchases, utility purchases, as well as capital expenditures, software acquisition/license commitments and legally binding service contracts. Purchase orders for the purchase of inventory and other services are not included in the table above. Purchase orders represent authorizations to purchase rather than binding agreements. For the purposes of this table, contractual obligations for purchase of goods or services are defined as agreements that are enforceable and legally binding and that specify all significant terms, including: fixed or minimum quantities to be purchased; fixed, minimum or variable price provisions; and the approximate timing of the transaction. Our purchase orders are based on our current inventory needs and are fulfilled by our suppliers within short time periods. We also enter into contracts for outsourced services; however, the obligations under these contracts are not significant and the contracts generally contain clauses allowing for cancellation without significant penalty.

The expected timing for payment of the obligations discussed above is estimated based on current information. Timing of payments and actual amounts paid may be different depending on the timing of receipt of goods or services or changes to agreed-upon amounts for some obligations.

In addition to the amounts discussed and presented above, the company has made certain guarantees as discussed below for which the timing of payment, if any, is unknown.

In connection with the expansion of our distribution network in Canada, we have guaranteed specific obligations of a third-party logistics provider. In the unlikely event this provider fails to perform its financial obligations regarding certain Wal-Mart-related projects, we would be obligated to pay an amount of up to $118 million. These agreements cover periods of up to 10 years.

In connection with certain debt financing, we could be liable for early termination payments if certain unlikely events were to occur. At January 31, 2005, the aggregate termination payment was $113 million. These arrangements expire in fiscal 2011 and fiscal 2019.

In connection with the development of our grocery distribution network in the United States, we have agreements with third parties which would require us to purchase or assume the leases on certain unique equipment in the event the agreements are terminated. These agreements, which can be terminated by either party at will, cover up to a five-year period and obligate the company to pay up to approximately $163 million upon termination of some or all of these agreements.

There are no recourse provisions which would enable us to recover from third parties any amounts paid under the above guarantees. No liability for these guarantees has been recorded in our financial statements.

The company has entered into lease commitments for land and buildings for 46 future locations. These lease commitments with real estate developers provide for minimum rentals ranging from 5-30 years, which, if consummated based on current cost estimates, will approximate $30 million annually over the lease terms.

Capital Resources

During fiscal 2005, we sold $5.8 billion of notes. The proceeds from the sale of these notes were used to repay commercial paper and for other general corporate purposes.

Management's Discussion and Analysis of Results of Operations and Financial Condition

WAL-MART

At January 31, 2005 and 2004, the ratio of our debt to our total capitalization was 39% and 38%, respectively. Our objective is to maintain a debt to total capitalization ratio averaging approximately 40%.

Management believes that cash flows from operations and proceeds from the sale of commercial paper will be sufficient to finance any seasonal buildups in merchandise inventories and meet other cash requirements. If our operating cash flows are not sufficient to pay dividends and to fund our capital expenditures, we anticipate funding any shortfall in these expenditures with a combination of commercial paper and long-term debt. We plan to refinance existing long-term debt as it matures and may desire to obtain additional long-term financing for other corporate purposes. We anticipate no difficulty in obtaining long-term financing in view of our credit rating and favorable experiences in the debt market in the recent past. At January 31, 2005, S&P, Moody's Investors Services, Inc. and Fitch Ratings rated our commercial paper A-1+, P-1 and F1+ and our long-term debt AA, Aa2 and AA, respectively.

Future Expansion

Capital expenditures for fiscal 2006 are expected to be approximately $14 billion, including additions of capital leases. These fiscal 2006 expenditures will include the construction of 40 to 45 new Discount Stores, 240 to 250 new Supercenters (with relocations or expansions accounting for approximately 160 of those Supercenters), 25 to 30 new Neighborhood Markets, 30 to 40 new SAM'S CLUBs and 155 to 165 new units in our International segment (with relocations or expansions accounting for approximately 30 of these units). We plan to finance this expansion primarily out of cash flows from operations and with the issuance of commercial paper and long-term debt.

Market Risk

In addition to the risks inherent in our operations, we are exposed to certain market risks, including changes in interest rates and changes in foreign exchange rates. In prior years, we presented our market risk information in tabular format. We have changed the presentation of this information to disclose a sensitivity analysis, because we believe it provides a more meaningful representation of our market risks.

The analysis presented for each of our market risk sensitive instruments is based on a 10% change in interest or foreign currency exchange rates. These changes are hypothetical scenarios used to calibrate potential risk and do not represent our view of future market changes. As the hypothetical figures indicate, changes in fair value based on the assumed change in rates generally cannot be extrapolated because the relationship of the change in assumption to the change in fair value may not be linear. The effect of a variation in a particular assumption is calculated without changing any other assumption. In reality, changes in one factor may result in changes in another, which may magnify or counteract the sensitivities.

At January 31, 2005 and 2004, we had $23.8 billion and $20.0 billion, respectively, of long-term debt outstanding. Our weighted average effective interest rate on long-term debt,

after considering the effect of interest rate swaps, was 4.08% and 3.97% at January 31, 2005 and 2004, respectively. A hypothetical 10% increase in interest rates in effect at January 31, 2005 and 2004, would have increased annual interest expense on borrowings outstanding at those dates by $25 million and $10 million, respectively.

We enter into interest rate swaps to minimize the risks and costs associated with financing activities, as well as to maintain an appropriate mix of fixed- and floating-rate debt. Our preference is to maintain approximately 50% of our debt portfolio, including interest rate swaps, in floating-rate debt. The swap agreements are contracts to exchange fixed- or variable-rates for variable- or fixed-interest rate payments periodically over the life of the instruments. The aggregate fair value of these swaps was a gain of approximately $471 million and $681 million at January 31, 2005 and 2004, respectively. A hypothetical increase (or decrease) of 10% in interest rates from the level in effect at January 31, 2005, would result in a (loss) or gain in value of the swaps of ($123 million) or $126 million, respectively. A hypothetical increase (or decrease) of 10% in interest rates from the level in effect at January 31, 2004, would result in a (loss) or gain in value of the swaps of ($75 million) or $81 million, respectively.

We hold currency swaps to hedge the foreign currency exchange component of our net investments in the United Kingdom and Japan. In addition, we hold a cross-currency swap which hedges the foreign currency risk of debt denominated in currencies other than the local currency. The aggregate fair value of these swaps at January 31, 2005 and 2004, was a loss of $169 million and $71 million, respectively. A hypothetical 10% increase (or decrease) in the foreign currency exchange rates underlying these swaps from the market rate would result in a (loss) or gain in the value of the swaps of ($90 million) and $71 million at January 31, 2005, and ($83 million) and $65 million at January 31, 2004. A hypothetical 10% change in interest rates underlying these swaps from the market rates in effect at January 31, 2005 and 2004, would have an insignificant impact on the value of the swaps.

We have designated debt of approximately £2.0 billion and £1.0 billion as of January 31, 2005 and 2004, respectively, as a hedge of our net investment in the United Kingdom. At January 31, 2005, a hypothetical 10% increase (or decrease) in value of the U.S. Dollar relative to the British Pound would result in a gain (or loss) in the value of the debt of $380 million. At January 31, 2004, a hypothetical 10% increase (or decrease) in value of the U.S. Dollar relative to the British Pound would result in a gain (or loss) in the value of the debt of $183 million.

Summary of Critical Accounting Policies

Management strives to report the financial results of the company in a clear and understandable manner, even though in some cases accounting and disclosure rules are complex and require us to use technical terminology. In preparing our consolidated financial statements, we follow accounting principles generally accepted in the United States. These principles require us to make certain estimates and apply judgments that affect our financial position and results of operations as reflected in our financial statements. These judgments and estimates are based on past events and expectations of future outcomes. Actual results may differ from our estimates.

Management continually reviews its accounting policies, how they are applied and how they are reported and disclosed in our financial statements. Following is a summary of our more significant accounting policies and how they are applied in preparation of the financial statements.

Inventories

We value our inventories at the lower of cost or market as determined primarily by the retail method of accounting, using the last-in, first-out ("LIFO") method for substantially all merchandise inventories in the United States, except SAM'S CLUB merchandise, which is based on average cost using the LIFO method. Inventories for international operations are primarily valued by the retail method of accounting and are stated using the first-in, first-out ("FIFO") method.

Under the retail method, inventory is stated at cost, which is determined by applying a cost-to-retail ratio to each merchandise grouping's retail value. The cost-to-retail ratio is based on the fiscal-year purchase activity for each store location. The retail method requires Management to make certain judgments and estimates that may significantly impact the ending inventory valuation at cost as well as the amount of gross margin recognized. Judgments made include the recording of markdowns used to sell through inventory and shrinkage. Markdowns designated for clearance activity are recorded at the time of the decision rather than at the point of sale, when Management determines the salability of inventory has diminished. Factors considered in the determination of markdowns include current and anticipated demand, customer preferences, age of merchandise, as well as seasonal and fashion trends. Changes in weather patterns and customer preferences related to fashion trends could cause material changes in the amount and timing of markdowns from year to year.

When necessary, the company records a LIFO provision each quarter for the estimated annual effect of inflation, and these estimates are adjusted to actual results determined at year-end. Our LIFO provision is calculated based on inventory levels, markup rates and internally generated retail price indices except for grocery items, for which we use a consumer price index. At January 31, 2005 and 2004, our inventories valued at LIFO approximate those inventories if they were valued at FIFO.

The company provides for estimated inventory losses ("shrinkage") between physical inventory counts on the basis of a percentage of sales. The provision is adjusted annually to reflect the historical trend of the actual physical inventory count results. Historically, shrinkage has not been volatile.

Impairment of Assets

We evaluate long-lived assets other than goodwill for indicators of impairment whenever events or changes in circumstances indicate their carrying value may not be recoverable. Management's judgments regarding the existence of impairment indicators are based on market conditions and our operational performance, such as operating income and cash flows. The variability of these factors depends on a number of conditions, including uncertainty about future events, and thus our accounting estimates may change from period to period. These factors could cause Management to conclude that impairment indicators exist and require that impairment tests be performed, which could result in Management determining that the value of long-lived assets is impaired, resulting in a write-down of the long-lived assets.

Goodwill is evaluated for impairment annually or whenever events or changes in circumstances indicate that the value of certain goodwill may be impaired. This evaluation requires Management to make judgments relating to future cash flows, growth rates, economic and market conditions. These evaluations are based on discounted cash flows that incorporate the impact of existing company businesses. Historically, the company has generated sufficient returns to recover the cost of goodwill and other intangible assets. Because of the nature of the factors used in these tests, if different conditions occur in future periods, future operating results could be materially impacted.

Income Taxes

The determination of our provision for income taxes requires significant judgment, the use of estimates, and the interpretation and application of complex tax laws. Significant judgment is required in assessing the timing and amounts of deductible and taxable items. We establish reserves when, despite our belief that our tax return positions are fully supportable, we believe that certain positions may be successfully challenged. When facts and circumstances change, we adjust these reserves through our provision for income taxes.

Self-Insurance

We use a combination of insurance, self-insured retention and self-insurance for a number of risks including workers' compensation, general liability, vehicle liability and the company's portion of employee-related health care benefits. Liabilities associated with the risks that we retain are estimated in part by considering historical claims experience, including frequency, severity, demographic factors, and other assumptions. In calculating our liability, we analyze our historical trends, including loss development, and apply appropriate loss-development factors to the incurred costs associated with the claims made against our self-insured program. The estimated accruals for these liabilities could be significantly affected if future occurrences or loss development differ from these assumptions. For example, for workers' compensation and liability, a 1% increase or decrease to the assumptions for claims costs and loss development factors would increase or decrease our self-insurance accrual by $21 million and $53 million, respectively. A 1% increase or decrease in employee-related health care costs would increase or decrease our self-insured employee health care expense by $16 million.

Management's Discussion and Analysis of Results of Operations and Financial Condition
WAL-MART

For a listing of our significant accounting policies, please see Note 1 to our consolidated financial statements that appear after this discussion.

New Accounting Pronouncement

On February 1, 2003, the company adopted the expense recognition provisions of Statement of Financial Accounting Standards No. 123, "Accounting and Disclosure of Stock-Based Compensation" ("SFAS 123"). Under SFAS 123, compensation expense is recognized based on the fair value of stock options granted. Upon the adoption of SFAS 123, we retroactively restated the results of our operations for the accounting change. Following the provisions of SFAS 123, the consolidated statements of income for fiscal 2005, 2004 and 2003 include $122 million, $102 million and $84 million, respectively, of after-tax stock option expense, which is approximately $0.03 per share in fiscal year 2005 and $0.02 per share for fiscal years 2004 and 2003. In December, 2004, the Financial Accounting Standards Board issued a revision of SFAS 123 ("SFAS 123(R)"). We adopted the provisions of SFAS 123(R) upon its release. Prior to the adoption of SFAS 123(R), we used the Black-Scholes-Merton formula to estimate the value of stock options granted to associates. We continue to use this acceptable option valuation model following our adoption of SFAS 123(R). SFAS 123(R) requires that the benefits of tax deductions in excess of recognized compensation cost be reported as a financing cash flow, rather than as an operating cash flow as required under previously effective accounting principles generally accepted in the United States. The adoption of SFAS 123(R) did not have a material impact on our results of operations, financial position or cash flows.

Forward-Looking Statements

This Annual Report contains statements that Wal-Mart believes are "forward-looking statements" within the meaning of the Private Securities Litigation Reform Act of 1995, which statements are intended to enjoy the protection of the safe harbor for forward-looking statements provided by that Act. These forward-looking statements include statements under the caption "Liquidity and Capital Resources" in Management's Discussion and Analysis of Financial Condition and Results of Operations with respect to our capital expenditures, our ability to fund certain cash flow shortfalls by the sale of commercial paper and long-term debt securities, our ability to sell our long-term securities and our anticipated reasons for repurchasing shares of our common stock. These statements are identified by the use of the words "anticipate," "contemplate,"

"expect" and "plan," and other, similar words or phrases. Similarly, descriptions of our objectives, strategies, plans, goals or targets are also forward-looking statements. These statements discuss, among other things, expected growth, future revenues, future cash flows, future capital expenditures, future performance and the anticipation and expectations of Wal-Mart and its Management as to future occurrences and trends. These forward-looking statements are subject to certain factors, in the United States and internationally, that could affect our financial performance, business strategy, plans, goals and objectives. Those factors include the cost of goods, labor costs, the cost of fuel and electricity, the cost of healthcare, competitive pressures, inflation, accident-related costs, consumer buying patterns and debt levels, weather patterns, currency exchange fluctuations, trade restrictions, changes in tariff and freight rates, changes in tax law, the outcome of legal proceedings to which we are a party, unemployment levels, interest rate fluctuations, changes in employment legislation and other capital market, economic and geo-political conditions. Moreover, we typically earn a disproportionate part of our annual operating income in the fourth quarter as a result of the seasonal buying patterns. Those buying patterns are difficult to forecast with certainty. The foregoing list of factors that may affect our performance is not exclusive. Other factors and unanticipated events could adversely affect our business operations and financial performance. We discuss certain of these matters more fully, as well as certain risk factors that may affect our business operations, financial condition and results of operations, in other of our filings with the SEC, including our Annual Report on Form 10-K. We filed our Annual Report on Form 10-K for the year ended January 31, 2005, with the SEC on or about March 31, 2005. Actual results may materially differ from anticipated results described or implied in these forward-looking statements as a result of changes in facts, assumptions not being realized or other circumstances. You are urged to consider all of these risks, uncertainties and other factors carefully in evaluating the forward-looking statements. The forward-looking statements included in this Annual Report are made only as of the date of this report, and we undertake no obligation to update these forward-looking statements to reflect subsequent events or circumstances.

Consolidated Statements of Income

WAL-MART

(Amounts in millions except per share data)

Fiscal years ended January 31,	2005	2004	2003
Revenues:			
Net sales	$285,222	$256,329	$229,616
Other income, net	2,767	2,352	1,961
	287,989	258,681	231,577
Costs and expenses:			
Cost of sales	219,793	198,747	178,299
Operating, selling, general and administrative expenses	51,105	44,909	39,983
Operating income	17,091	15,025	13,295
Interest:			
Debt	934	729	799
Capital leases	253	267	260
Interest income	(201)	(164)	(132)
Interest, net	986	832	927
Income from continuing operations before income taxes and minority interest	16,105	14,193	12,368
Provision for income taxes:			
Current	5,326	4,941	3,883
Deferred	263	177	474
	5,589	5,118	4,357
Income from continuing operations before minority interest	10,516	9,075	8,011
Minority interest	(249)	(214)	(193)
Income from continuing operations	10,267	8,861	7,818
Income from discontinued operation, net of tax	–	193	137
Net income	$ 10,267	$ 9,054	$ 7,955
Basic net income per common share:			
Income from continuing operations	$ 2.41	$ 2.03	$ 1.77
Income from discontinued operation	–	0.05	0.03
Basic net income per common share	$ 2.41	$ 2.08	$ 1.80
Diluted net income per common share:			
Income from continuing operations	$ 2.41	$ 2.03	$ 1.76
Income from discontinued operation	–	0.04	0.03
Diluted net income per common share	$ 2.41	$ 2.07	$ 1.79
Weighted-average number of common shares:			
Basic	4,259	4,363	4,430
Diluted	4,266	4,373	4,446
Dividends per common share	$ 0.52	$ 0.36	$ 0.30

See accompanying notes.

Consolidated Balance Sheets

WAL-MART

(Amounts in millions except per share data)

January 31,	2005	2004
Assets		
Current assets:		
Cash and cash equivalents	$ 5,488	$ 5,199
Receivables	1,715	1,254
Inventories	29,447	26,612
Prepaid expenses and other	1,841	1,356
Total current assets	38,491	34,421
Property and equipment, at cost:		
Land	14,472	12,699
Buildings and improvements	46,582	40,192
Fixtures and equipment	21,461	17,934
Transportation equipment	1,530	1,269
Property and equipment, at cost	84,045	72,094
Less accumulated depreciation	18,637	15,684
Property and equipment, net	65,408	56,410
Property under capital lease:		
Property under capital lease	4,997	4,286
Less accumulated amortization	1,838	1,673
Property under capital lease, net	3,159	2,613
Goodwill	10,803	9,882
Other assets and deferred charges	2,362	2,079
Total assets	**$120,223**	**$105,405**
Liabilities and shareholders' equity		
Current liabilities:		
Commercial paper	$ 3,812	$ 3,267
Accounts payable	21,671	19,425
Accrued liabilities	12,155	10,671
Accrued income taxes	1,281	1,377
Long-term debt due within one year	3,759	2,904
Obligations under capital leases due within one year	210	196
Total current liabilities	42,888	37,840
Long-term debt	20,087	17,102
Long-term obligations under capital leases	3,582	2,997
Deferred income taxes and other	2,947	2,359
Minority interest	1,323	1,484
Commitments and contingencies		
Shareholders' equity:		
Preferred stock ($0.10 par value; 100 shares authorized, none issued)	–	–
Common stock ($0.10 par value; 11,000 shares authorized, 4,234 and 4,311 issued and outstanding in 2005 and 2004, respectively)	423	431
Capital in excess of par value	2,425	2,135
Other accumulated comprehensive income	2,694	851
Retained earnings	43,854	40,206
Total shareholders' equity	49,396	43,623
Total liabilities and shareholders' equity	**$120,223**	**$105,405**

See accompanying notes.

Consolidated Statements of Shareholders' Equity

WAL-MART

(Amounts in millions except per share data)	Number of Shares	Common Stock	Capital in Excess of Par Value	Other Accumulated Comprehensive Income	Retained Earnings	Total
Balance – January 31, 2002	4,453	$ 445	$ 1,838	$ (1,268)	$ 34,177	$ 35,192
Comprehensive income:						
Net income from continuing operations					7,818	7,818
Net income from discontinued operation					137	137
Other accumulated comprehensive income:						
Foreign currency translation				1,113		1,113
Net unrealized depreciation of derivatives				(148)		(148)
Minimum pension liability				(206)		(206)
Total comprehensive income						8,714
Cash dividends ($0.30 per share)					(1,328)	(1,328)
Purchase of company stock	(63)	(5)	(150)		(3,228)	(3,383)
Stock options exercised and other	5		266			266
Balance – January 31, 2003	4,395	440	1,954	(509)	37,576	39,461
Comprehensive income:						
Net income from continuing operations					8,861	8,861
Net income from discontinued operation					193	193
Other accumulated comprehensive income:						
Foreign currency translation				1,685		1,685
Net unrealized depreciation of derivatives				(341)		(341)
Minimum pension liability				16		16
Total comprehensive income						10,414
Cash dividends ($0.36 per share)					(1,569)	(1,569)
Purchase of company stock	(92)	(9)	(182)		(4,855)	(5,046)
Stock options exercised and other	8		363			363
Balance – January 31, 2004	4,311	431	2,135	851	40,206	43,623
Comprehensive income:						
Net income from continuing operations					10,267	10,267
Other accumulated comprehensive income:						
Foreign currency translation				2,130		2,130
Net unrealized depreciation of derivatives				(194)		(194)
Minimum pension liability				(93)		(93)
Total comprehensive income						12,110
Cash dividends ($0.52 per share)					(2,214)	(2,214)
Purchase of company stock	(81)	(8)	(136)		(4,405)	(4,549)
Stock options exercised and other	4		426			426
Balance – January 31, 2005	4,234	$423	$2,425	$2,694	$43,854	$49,396

See accompanying notes.

Consolidated Statements of Cash Flows
WAL-MART

(Amounts in millions)

Fiscal years ended January 31,	2005	2004	2003
Cash flows from operating activities			
Income from continuing operations	$ 10,267	$ 8,861	$ 7,818
Adjustments to reconcile net income to net cash provided by operating activities:			
Depreciation and amortization	4,405	3,852	3,364
Deferred income taxes	263	177	474
Other operating activities	378	173	685
Changes in certain assets and liabilities, net of effects of acquisitions:			
Decrease (increase) in accounts receivable	(304)	373	(159)
Increase in inventories	(2,635)	(1,973)	(2,219)
Increase in accounts payable	1,694	2,587	1,748
Increase in accrued liabilities	976	1,896	1,212
Net cash provided by operating activities of continuing operations	15,044	15,946	12,923
Net cash provided by operating activities of discontinued operation	–	50	82
Net cash provided by operating activities	15,044	15,996	13,005
Cash flows from investing activities			
Payments for property and equipment	(12,893)	(10,308)	(9,245)
Investment in international operations	(315)	(38)	(749)
Proceeds from the disposal of fixed assets	953	481	311
Proceeds from the sale of McLane	–	1,500	–
Other investing activities	(96)	78	(73)
Net cash used in investing activities of continuing operations	(12,351)	(8,287)	(9,756)
Net cash used in investing activities of discontinued operation	–	(25)	(83)
Net cash used in investing activities	(12,351)	(8,312)	(9,839)
Cash flows from financing activities			
Increase in commercial paper	544	688	1,836
Proceeds from issuance of long-term debt	5,832	4,099	2,044
Purchase of company stock	(4,549)	(5,046)	(3,383)
Dividends paid	(2,214)	(1,569)	(1,328)
Payment of long-term debt	(2,131)	(3,541)	(1,261)
Payment of capital lease obligations	(204)	(305)	(216)
Other financing activities	113	111	(62)
Net cash used in financing activities	(2,609)	(5,563)	(2,370)
Effect of exchange rate changes on cash	205	320	(199)
Net increase in cash and cash equivalents	289	2,441	597
Cash and cash equivalents at beginning of year [1]	5,199	2,758	2,161
Cash and cash equivalents at end of year	$ 5,488	$ 5,199	$ 2,758
Supplemental disclosure of cash flow information			
Income tax paid	$ 5,593	$ 4,358	$ 4,539
Interest paid	1,163	1,024	1,085
Capital lease obligations incurred	377	252	381

(1) Includes cash and cash equivalents of discontinued operation of $22 million for 2003.

See accompanying notes.

Notes to Consolidated Financial Statements

WAL-MART

1 Summary of Significant Accounting Policies

Consolidation

The consolidated financial statements include the accounts of Wal-Mart Stores, Inc. and its subsidiaries ("Wal-Mart" or the "company"). Significant intercompany transactions have been eliminated in consolidation. Investments in which the company has a 20 percent to 50 percent voting interest and where the company exercises significant influence over the investee are accounted for using the equity method.

The company's operations in Argentina, Brazil, China, Germany, Mexico, South Korea and the United Kingdom are consolidated using a December 31 fiscal year-end, generally due to statutory reporting requirements. There were no significant intervening events which materially affected the financial statements. The company's operations in Canada and Puerto Rico are consolidated using a January 31 fiscal year-end.

Cash and Cash Equivalents

The company considers investments with a maturity of three months or less when purchased to be cash equivalents. The majority of payments due from banks for third-party credit card, debit card and electronic benefit transactions ("EBT") process within 24-48 hours, except for transactions occurring on a Friday, which are generally processed the following Monday. All credit card, debit card and EBT transactions that process in less than seven days are classified as cash and cash equivalents. Amounts due from banks for these transactions classified as cash totaled $549 million and $866 million at January 31, 2005 and 2004, respectively.

Receivables

Accounts receivable consist primarily of receivables from insurance companies resulting from our pharmacy sales, receivables from suppliers for marketing or incentive programs and receivables from real estate transactions. Additionally, amounts due from banks for customer credit card, debit card and EBT transactions that take in excess of seven days to process are classified as accounts receivable.

Inventories

The company values inventories at the lower of cost or market as determined primarily by the retail method of accounting, using the last-in, first-out ("LIFO") method for substantially all merchandise inventories in the United States, except SAM'S CLUB merchandise, which is based on average cost using the LIFO method. Inventories of foreign operations are primarily valued by the retail method of accounting, using the first-in, first-out ("FIFO") method. At January 31, 2005 and 2004, our inventories valued at LIFO approximate those inventories if they were valued at FIFO.

Financial Instruments

The company uses derivative financial instruments for purposes other than trading to manage its exposure to interest and foreign exchange rates, as well as to maintain an appropriate mix of fixed- and floating-rate debt. Contract terms of a hedge instrument closely mirror those of the hedged item, providing a high degree of risk reduction and correlation. Contracts that are effective at

meeting the risk reduction and correlation criteria are recorded using hedge accounting. If a derivative instrument is a hedge, depending on the nature of the hedge, changes in the fair value of the instrument will either be offset against the change in fair value of the hedged assets, liabilities or firm commitments through earnings or recognized in other comprehensive income until the hedged item is recognized in earnings. The ineffective portion of an instrument's change in fair value will be immediately recognized in earnings. Instruments that do not meet the criteria for hedge accounting or contracts for which the company has not elected hedge accounting, are marked to fair value with unrealized gains or losses reported in earnings.

Capitalized Interest

Interest costs capitalized on construction projects were $120 million, $144 million, and $124 million in fiscal 2005, 2004, and 2003, respectively.

Long-lived Assets

Management reviews long-lived assets for indicators of impairment whenever events or changes in circumstances indicate that the carrying value may not be recoverable. The evaluation is done at the lowest level of cash flows, which is typically at the individual store level. Cash flows expected to be generated by the related assets are estimated over the asset's useful life based on updated projections. If the evaluation indicates that the carrying amount of the asset may not be recoverable, the potential impairment is measured based on a projected discounted cash flow method using a discount rate that is considered to be commensurate with the risk inherent in the company's current business model.

Goodwill and Other Acquired Intangible Assets

Goodwill is not amortized, rather it is evaluated for impairment annually or whenever events or changes in circumstances indicate that the value of certain goodwill may be impaired. Other acquired intangible assets are amortized on a straight-line basis over the periods that expected economic benefits will be provided. These evaluations are based on discounted cash flows and incorporate the impact of existing company businesses. The analyses require significant Management judgment to evaluate the capacity of an acquired business to perform within projections. Historically, the company has generated sufficient returns to recover the cost of the goodwill and other intangible assets.

Goodwill is recorded on the balance sheet in the operating segments as follows (in millions):

	January 31, 2005	January 31, 2004
International	**$ 10,498**	$ 9,577
SAM'S CLUB	**305**	305
Total goodwill	**$ 10,803**	$ 9,882

The change in the International segment's goodwill is primarily the result of foreign currency exchange rate fluctuations. The fiscal 2005 acquisition of Bompreço S.A. Supermercados do Nordeste also resulted in an increase to goodwill.

Notes to Consolidated Financial Statements
WAL-MART

Leases
The company estimates the expected term of a lease by assuming the exercise of renewal options where an economic penalty exists that would preclude the abandonment of the lease at the end of the initial non-cancelable term and the exercise of such renewal is at the sole discretion of the company. This expected term is used in the determination of whether a store lease is capital or operating and in the calculation of straight-line rent expense. Additionally, the useful life of leasehold improvements is limited by the expected lease term. If significant expenditures are made for leasehold improvements late in the expected term of a lease, judgment is applied to determine if a change in estimate has occurred, or if the leasehold improvements may have a useful life that is bound by the end of the original expected lease term.

Rent abatements and escalations are considered in the calculation of minimum lease payments in the company's capital lease tests and in determining straight-line rent expense for operating leases.

Foreign Currency Translation
The assets and liabilities of all foreign subsidiaries are translated using exchange rates at the balance sheet date. The income statements of foreign subsidiaries are translated using average exchange rates. Related translation adjustments are recorded as a component of other accumulated comprehensive income.

Revenue Recognition
The company recognizes sales revenue net of estimated sales returns at the time it sells merchandise to the customer, except for layaway transactions. The company recognizes layaway transactions when the customer satisfies all payment obligations and takes possession of the merchandise. Customer purchases of Wal-Mart and SAM'S CLUB shopping cards are not recognized until the card is redeemed and the customer purchases merchandise by using the shopping card.

SAM'S CLUB Membership Fee Revenue Recognition
The company recognizes SAM'S CLUB membership fee revenues both in the United States and internationally over the term of the membership, which is 12 months. The following table details unearned revenues, membership fees received from members and the amount of revenues recognized in earnings for each of the fiscal years 2005, 2004 and 2003 (in millions):

Year ended January 31,	2005	2004	2003
Deferred membership fee revenue, beginning of year	$ 449	$ 437	$ 387
Membership fees received	890	840	834
Membership fee revenue recognized	(881)	(828)	(784)
Deferred membership fee revenue, end of year	$ 458	$ 449	$ 437

SAM'S CLUB membership revenue is included in other income, net in the revenues section of the Consolidated Statements of Income.

The company's deferred membership fee revenue is included in accrued liabilities in the Consolidated Balance Sheets. The company's analysis of historical membership fee refunds indicates that such refunds have been nominal. Accordingly, no reserve exists for membership fee refunds at January 31, 2005 and 2004.

Cost of Sales
Cost of sales includes actual product cost, change in inventory, the cost of transportation to the company's warehouses from suppliers, the cost of transportation from the company's warehouses to the stores and Clubs and the cost of warehousing for our SAM'S CLUB segment.

Payments from Suppliers
Wal-Mart receives money from suppliers for various programs, primarily volume incentives, warehouse allowances and reimbursements for specific programs such as markdowns, margin protection and advertising. Substantially all allowances are accounted for as a reduction of purchases and recognized in our Consolidated Statements of Income when the related inventory is sold.

Operating, Selling, General and Administrative Expenses
Operating, selling, general and administrative expenses include all operating costs of the company that are not related to the transportation of products from the supplier to the warehouse or from the warehouse to the store. Additionally, the cost of warehousing and occupancy for our Wal-Mart Stores segment distribution facilities are included in operating, selling, general and administrative expenses. Because we do not include the cost of our Wal-Mart Stores segment distribution facilities in cost of sales, our gross profit and gross margin may not be comparable to those of other retailers that may include all costs related to their distribution facilities in costs of sales and in the calculation of gross profit and gross margin.

Advertising Costs
Advertising costs are expensed as incurred and were $1.4 billion, $966 million and $676 million in fiscal 2005, 2004 and 2003, respectively. Advertising costs consist primarily of print and television advertisements. The increase in advertising costs in 2005 and 2004 compared with 2003 is attributable to the adoption of Emerging Issues Task Force Consensus No. 02-16, "Accounting by a Reseller for Cash Consideration Received from a Vendor" ("EITF 02-16"). Upon adoption of EITF 02-16, the company began recognizing substantially all funds received from vendors as a reduction of inventory costs. Prior to the adoption of EITF 02-16, the company recorded a portion of consideration received from vendors as a reduction of expenses, such as advertising.

Pre-opening Costs
The costs of start-up activities, including organization costs and new store openings, are expensed as incurred.

Stock-based Compensation

The company recognizes expense for its stock-based compensation based on the fair value of the awards that are granted. The fair value of stock options is estimated at the date of grant using the Black-Scholes-Merton option valuation model which was developed for use in estimating the fair value of exchange traded options that have no vesting restrictions and are fully transferable. Option valuation methods require the input of highly subjective assumptions, including the expected stock price volatility. Measured compensation cost is recognized ratably over the vesting period of the related stock-based compensation award.

The fair value of the company's stock options was estimated at the date of the grant using the following assumptions:

	2005	2004	2003
Dividend yield	**1.1%**	1.0%	0.7%
Volatility	**23.2%**	32.3%	32.1%
Risk-free interest rate	**3.3%**	2.8%	3.2%
Expected life in years	**5.4**	4.5	4.6
Weighted-average fair value of options at grant date	**$11.39**	$15.83	$15.67

Insurance/Self-Insurance

The company uses a combination of insurance, self-insured retention and self-insurance for a number of risks, including workers' compensation, general liability, vehicle liability and the company-funded portion of employee-related health care benefits. Liabilities associated with these risks are estimated in part by considering historical claims experience, demographic factors, severity factors and other actuarial assumptions.

Depreciation and Amortization

Depreciation and amortization for financial statement purposes are provided on the straight-line method over the estimated useful lives of the various assets. Depreciation expense, including amortization of property under capital leases for the years 2005, 2004 and 2003 was $4.3 billion, $3.7 billion and $3.2 billion, respectively. For income tax purposes, accelerated methods of depreciation are used with recognition of deferred income taxes for the resulting temporary differences. Leasehold improvements are depreciated over the shorter of the estimated useful life of the asset or the remaining lease term. Estimated useful lives for financial statement purposes are as follows:

Buildings and improvements	5 – 50 years
Fixtures and equipment	5 – 12 years
Transportation equipment	3 – 15 years
Internally developed software	3 years

Income Taxes

Income taxes are accounted for under the asset and liability method. Deferred tax assets and liabilities are recognized for the estimated future tax consequences attributable to differences between the financial statement carrying amounts of existing assets and liabilities and their respective tax bases. Deferred tax assets and liabilities are measured using enacted tax rates in effect for the year in which those temporary differences are expected to be recovered or settled. The effect on deferred tax assets and liabilities of a change in tax rate is recognized in income in the period that includes the enactment date. Valuation allowances are established when necessary to reduce deferred tax assets to the amounts more likely than not to be realized.

In determining the quarterly provision for income taxes, the company uses an annual effective tax rate based on expected annual income and statutory tax rates. The effective tax rate also reflects the company's assessment of the ultimate outcome of tax audits. Significant or unusual items are recognized in the quarter in which they occur.

The determination of the company's provision for income taxes requires significant judgment, the use of estimates, and the interpretation and application of complex tax laws. Significant judgment is required in assessing the timing and amounts of deductible and taxable items. Reserves are established when, despite management's belief that the company's tax return positions are fully supportable, management believes that certain positions may be successfully challenged. When facts and circumstances change, these reserves are adjusted through the provision for income taxes.

Net Income Per Common Share

Basic net income per common share is based on the weighted-average outstanding common shares. Diluted net income per common share is based on the weighted-average outstanding shares adjusted for the dilutive effect of stock options and restricted stock grants. The diluted effect of stock options and restricted stock was 7 million, 10 million and 16 million shares in fiscal 2005, 2004 and 2003, respectively. The company had approximately 59 million, 50 million and 41 million option shares outstanding at January 31, 2005, 2004 and 2003, respectively, which were not included in the diluted net income per share calculation because their effect would be antidilutive as the underlying option price exceeded the average market price of the stock for the period.

Estimates and Assumptions

The preparation of consolidated financial statements in conformity with generally accepted accounting principles requires Management to make estimates and assumptions. These estimates and assumptions affect the reported amounts of assets and liabilities. They also affect the disclosure of contingent assets and liabilities at the date of the consolidated financial statements and the reported amounts of revenues and expenses during the reporting period. Actual results may differ from those estimates.

Reclassifications

Certain reclassifications have been made to prior periods to conform to current presentations.

New Accounting Pronouncements

As is more fully discussed in Note 7, the company has various stock option compensation plans for its associates. On February 1, 2003, the company adopted the expense recognition provisions of Statement of Financial Accounting Standards No. 123, "Accounting and Disclosure of Stock-Based Compensation" ("SFAS 123"). Under SFAS 123, compensation expense is recognized based on the fair value of stock options granted. Upon the adoption of SFAS 123, we retroactively restated the results of our operations for the accounting change. Following the provisions of SFAS 123, the consolidated statements of income for fiscal 2005, 2004 and 2003 include $122 million, $102 million and $84 million, respectively, of after-tax stock option expense, which is approximately $0.03 per share in fiscal year 2005 and $0.02 per share for fiscal years 2004 and 2003. In December 2004, the Financial Accounting Standards Board issued a revision of SFAS 123 ("SFAS 123(R)"). We adopted

Notes to Consolidated Financial Statements
WAL-MART

the provisions of SFAS 123(R) upon its release. Prior to the adoption of SFAS 123(R), we used the Black-Scholes-Merton formula to estimate the value of stock options granted to associates. We continue to use this acceptable option valuation model following our adoption of SFAS 123(R). SFAS 123(R) requires that the benefits of tax deductions in excess of recognized compensation cost be reported as a financing cash flow, rather than as an operating cash flow as required under previously effective accounting principles generally accepted in the United States. The adoption of SFAS 123(R) did not have a material impact on our results of operations, financial position or cash flows.

2 Commercial Paper and Long-term Debt

Information on short-term borrowings and interest rates is as follows (dollars in millions):

Fiscal year	2005	2004	2003
Maximum amount outstanding at any month-end	$7,782	$4,957	$4,226
Average daily short-term borrowings	$4,823	$1,498	$1,549
Weighted-average interest rate	1.6%	1.1%	1.7%

At January 31, 2005 and 2004, short-term borrowings consisted of $3.8 billion and $3.3 billion, respectively, of commercial paper. At January 31, 2005, the company had committed lines of $4.5 billion with 53 firms and banks, which were used to support commercial paper, and committed and informal lines of credit with various banks totaling an additional $159 million.

Long-term debt at January 31, consists of (in millions):

Interest Rate	Due by Fiscal Year	2005	2004
4.000 – 6.875%	Notes due 2010	$ 4,500	$ 3,500
2.792 – 8.000%, LIBOR less 0.140%	Notes due 2007	3,164	2,130
4.550% – 7.250%	Notes due 2014	2,883	2,854
4.150 – 5.875% LIBOR less 0.0425%	Notes due 2006	2,597	2,597
4.125%	Notes due 2012	2,000	–
5.750% – 7.550%	Notes due 2031	1,941	1,912
5.250%	Notes due 2036	1,883	–
4.375%	Notes due 2008	1,500	1,500
3.375%	Notes due 2009	1,000	1,000
5.006%	Notes due 2019[1]	500	500
6.200%	Notes due 2011[1]	500	500
6.750%	Notes due 2024	250	250
6.550% – 7.500%	Notes due 2005	–	1,750
8.500%	Notes due 2025	–	250
	Other [2]	1,128	1,263
		$23,846	$20,006

(1) Includes put option.
(2) Includes adjustments to debt hedged by derivatives.

The company has two separate issuances of $500 million debt with embedded put options. For the first issuance, beginning June 2001, and each year thereafter, the holders of $500 million of the debt may require the company to repurchase the debt at face value, in addition to accrued and unpaid interest. The holders of the other $500 million issuance may put the debt back to the company at par plus accrued interest at any time. Both of these issuances have been classified as a current liability in the Consolidated Balance Sheets.

Under the company's most significant borrowing arrangements, the company is not required to observe financial covenants. However, under certain lines of credit totaling $4.5 billion which were undrawn as of January 31, 2005, the company has agreed to observe certain covenants, the most restrictive of which relates to minimum net worth levels and amounts of additional secured debt and long-term leases. The company was not in violation of these covenants at January 31, 2005.

Long-term debt is unsecured except for $68 million, which is collateralized by property with an aggregate carrying value of approximately $171 million. Annual maturities of long-term debt during the next five years and thereafter are (in millions):

Fiscal Year Ended January 31,	Annual Maturity
2006	$ 3,759
2007	3,400
2008	1,572
2009	1,037
2010	4,774
Thereafter	9,304
Total	$ 23,846

The company has entered into sale/leaseback transactions involving buildings while retaining title to the underlying land. These transactions were accounted for as financings and are included in long-term debt and the annual maturities schedule above. The resulting obligations are amortized over the lease terms. Future minimum lease payments during the next five years and thereafter are (in millions):

Fiscal Year Ended January 31,	Minimum Payments
2006	$ 20
2007	18
2008	17
2009	11
2010	11
Thereafter	43
Total	$ 120

At January 31, 2005 and 2004, the company had trade letters of credit outstanding totaling $2.6 billion and $2.0 billion, respectively. These letters of credit were issued primarily for the purchase of inventory. At January 31, 2005 and 2004, the company had standby letters of credit outstanding totaling $2.0 billion and $1.4 billion, respectively.

3 Financial Instruments

The company uses derivative financial instruments for hedging and non-trading purposes to manage its exposure to interest and foreign exchange rates. Use of derivative financial instruments in hedging programs subjects the company to certain risks, such as market and credit risks. Market risk represents the possibility that the value of the derivative instrument will change. In a hedging relationship, the change in the value of the derivative is offset to a great extent by the change in the value of the underlying hedged item. Credit risk related to derivatives represents the possibility that the counterparty will not fulfill the terms of the contract. The notional, or contractual, amount of the company's derivative financial instruments is used to measure interest to be paid or received and does not represent the company's exposure due to credit risk. Credit risk is monitored through established approval procedures, including setting concentration limits by counterparty, reviewing credit ratings and requiring collateral (generally cash) when appropriate. The majority of the company's transactions are with counterparties rated "AA-" or better by nationally recognized credit rating agencies.

Fair Value Instruments

The company enters into interest rate swaps to minimize the risks and costs associated with its financing activities. Under the swap agreements, the company pays variable-rate interest and receives fixed-rate interest payments periodically over the life of the instruments. The notional amounts are used to measure interest to be paid or received and do not represent the exposure due to credit loss. All of the company's interest rate swaps that receive fixed interest rate payments and pay variable interest rate payments are designated as fair value hedges. As the specific terms and notional amounts of the derivative instruments exactly match those of the instruments being hedged, the derivative instruments were assumed to be perfect hedges and all changes in fair value of the hedges were recorded on the balance sheet with no net impact on the income statement.

Net Investment Instruments

At January 31, 2005, the company is party to cross-currency interest rate swaps that hedge its net investments in the United Kingdom and Japan. The agreements are contracts to exchange fixed-rate payments in one currency for fixed-rate payments in another currency. The company also has outstanding approximately £2.0 billion of debt that is designated as a hedge of the company's net investment in the United Kingdom. All changes in the fair value of these instruments are recorded in other comprehensive income, offsetting the foreign currency translation adjustment that is also recorded in other comprehensive income.

Cash Flow Instruments

The company is party to a cross-currency interest rate swap to hedge the foreign currency risk of certain foreign-denominated debt. The swap is designated as a cash flow hedge of foreign currency exchange risk. The agreement is a contract to exchange fixed-rate payments in one currency for fixed-rate payments in another currency. Changes in the foreign currency spot exchange rate result in reclassification of amounts from other accumulated comprehensive income to earnings to offset transaction gains or losses on foreign-denominated debt. The instrument matures in fiscal 2007.

The company expects that the amount of gain or loss existing in other accumulated comprehensive income to be reclassified into earnings within the next 12 months will not be significant.

Fair Value of Financial Instruments

Instrument Fiscal Year Ended January 31, (in millions)	Notional Amount		Fair Value	
	2005	2004	**2005**	2004
Derivative financial instruments designated for hedging:				
Receive fixed-rate, pay floating rate interest rate swaps designated as fair value hedges	**$ 8,042**	$ 8,292	**$ 477**	$ 697
Receive fixed-rate, pay fixed-rate cross-currency interest rate swaps designated as net investment hedges (Cross-currency notional amount: GBP 795 at 1/31/2005 and 1/31/2004)	**1,250**	1,250	**(14)**	29
Receive fixed-rate, pay fixed-rate cross-currency interest rate swap designated as a cash flow hedge (Cross-currency notional amount: CAD 503 at 1/31/2005 and 1/31/2004)	**325**	325	**(87)**	(54)
Receive fixed-rate, pay fixed-rate cross-currency interest rate swap designated as a net investment hedge (Cross-currency notional amount: ¥52,056 at 1/31/2005 and 1/31/2004)	**432**	432	**(68)**	(46)
Receive floating rate, pay fixed-rate interest rate swap designated as a cash flow hedge	**1,500**	1,500	**(5)**	(16)
	$11,549	$11,799	**$ 303**	$ 610
Non-derivative financial instruments:				
Long-term debt	**$23,846**	$20,006	**$25,016**	$21,349

Notes to Consolidated Financial Statements
WAL-MART

Hedging instruments with a favorable fair value are recorded on the Consolidated Balance Sheets as other current assets or other assets and deferred charges, based on maturity date. Those instruments with an unfavorable fair value are recorded in accrued liabilities or deferred income taxes and other, based on maturity date.

Cash and cash equivalents: The carrying amount approximates fair value due to the short maturity of these instruments.

Long-term debt: Fair value is based on the company's current incremental borrowing rate for similar types of borrowing arrangements.

Interest rate instruments and net investment instruments: The fair values are estimated amounts the company would receive or pay to terminate the agreements as of the reporting dates.

4 Other Accumulated Comprehensive Income

Comprehensive income is net income plus certain other items that are recorded directly to shareholders' equity. Amounts included in other accumulated comprehensive income for the company's derivative instruments and minimum pension liability are recorded net of the related income tax effects. The following table gives further detail regarding changes in the composition of other accumulated comprehensive income during fiscal 2005, 2004 and 2003 (in millions):

	Foreign Currency Translation	Derivative Instruments	Minimum Pension Liability	Total
Balance at January 31, 2002	$(2,238)	$ 970	$ –	$(1,268)
Foreign currency translation adjustment	1,113			1,113
Change in fair value of hedge instruments		(164)		(164)
Reclassification to earnings		16		16
Subsidiary minimum pension liability			(206)	(206)
Balance at January 31, 2003	(1,125)	822	(206)	(509)
Foreign currency translation adjustment	1,685			1,685
Change in fair value of hedge instruments		(444)		(444)
Reclassification to earnings		103		103
Subsidiary minimum pension liability			16	16
Balance at January 31, 2004	560	481	(190)	851
Foreign currency translation adjustment	**2,130**			**2,130**
Change in fair value of hedge instruments		**(235)**		**(235)**
Reclassification to earnings		**41**		**41**
Subsidiary minimum pension liability			**(93)**	**(93)**
Balance at January 31, 2005	**$2,690**	**$287**	**$(283)**	**$2,694**

5 Income Taxes

The income tax provision consists of the following (in millions):

Fiscal years ended January 31,	**2005**	2004	2003
Current:			
Federal	**$4,116**	$4,039	$3,299
State and local	**640**	333	229
International	**570**	569	355
Total current tax provision	**5,326**	4,941	3,883
Deferred:			
Federal	**311**	31	305
State and local	**(71)**	2	26
International	**23**	144	143
Total deferred tax provision	**263**	177	474
Total provision for income taxes	**$5,589**	$5,118	$4,357

Income from continuing operations before income taxes and minority interest is as follows (in millions):

Fiscal years ended January 31,	**2005**	2004	2003
United States	**$13,599**	$12,075	$10,490
Outside the United States	**2,506**	2,118	1,878
Total income from continuing operations before income taxes and minority interest	**$16,105**	$14,193	$12,368

Items that give rise to significant portions of the deferred tax accounts are as follows (in millions):

January 31,	2005	2004
Deferred tax liabilities		
Property and equipment	**$2,045**	$1,581
International, principally asset basis difference	**1,054**	1,087
Inventory	**187**	419
Capital leases	**165**	92
Other	**230**	146
Total deferred tax liabilities	**$3,681**	$3,325
Deferred tax assets		
Amounts accrued for financial reporting purposes not yet deductible for tax purposes	**$1,361**	$1,280
International loss carryforwards	**1,460**	1,186
Deferred revenue	**15**	140
Other	**506**	298
Total deferred tax assets	**3,342**	2,904
Valuation allowance	**(526)**	(344)
Total deferred tax assets, net of valuation allowance	**$2,816**	$2,560
Net deferred tax liabilities	**$ 865**	$ 765

A reconciliation of the significant differences between the effective income tax rate and the federal statutory rate on pretax income is as follows:

Fiscal years ended January 31,	2005	2004	2003
Statutory tax rate	**35.00%**	35.00%	35.00%
State income taxes, net of federal income tax benefit	**2.30%**	1.53%	1.36%
Income taxes outside the United States	**(1.81%)**	(0.20%)	(1.29%)
Other	**(0.79%)**	(0.27%)	0.16%
Effective income tax rate	**34.70%**	36.06%	35.23%

Federal and state income taxes have not been provided on accumulated but undistributed earnings of foreign subsidiaries aggregating approximately $5.3 billion at January 31, 2005 and $4.0 billion at January 31, 2004, as such earnings have been permanently reinvested in the business. The determination of the amount of the unrecognized deferred tax liability related to the undistributed earnings is not practicable. The American Jobs Creation Act, which was signed into law on October 22, 2004, created a special one-time tax deduction relating to the repatriation of certain foreign earnings. The company has not completed its evaluation of the likelihood of repatriation of our foreign earnings and the resulting effect of the one-time tax deduction.

A valuation allowance has been established to reduce certain foreign subsidiaries' deferred tax assets relating primarily to net operating loss carryforwards. During the fourth quarter of fiscal 2004, as the result of new tax legislation in Germany, we re-evaluated the recoverability of the deferred tax asset related to our German operations. Based on the results of our review, we recorded a valuation allowance resulting in a charge of $150 million.

6 Acquisitions and Disposal

Acquisitions

In February 2004, the company completed its purchase of Bompreço S.A. Supermercados do Nordeste ("Bompreço"), a supermarket chain in northern Brazil with 118 hypermarkets, supermarkets and mini-markets. The purchase price was approximately $315 million, net of cash acquired. The results of operations for Bompreço, which were not material to the company, have been included in the company's consolidated financial statements since the date of acquisition.

During May 2002, the company acquired its initial 6.1% stake in The Seiyu, Ltd. ("Seiyu"), a Japanese retail chain, for approximately $51 million. In December 2002, the company exercised in full the first in the series of warrants granted allowing us to acquire 192.8 million new shares in Seiyu for approximately $432 million. Following this exercise and our purchase of 29.3 million additional Seiyu shares in other Seiyu securities offerings, our ownership percentage in Seiyu increased to approximately 37%. Through a series of warrants exercisable through 2007, the company can contribute approximately ¥235 billion, or $2.3 billion at a January 31, 2005, exchange rate of 103.68 yen per dollar, for additional shares of Seiyu stock. If all the warrants are exercised, we will own approximately 70% of the stock of Seiyu by the end of December 2007. If the next tranche of warrants is exercised in December 2005, the company will own more than 50% of Seiyu.

Also, in December 2002, the company completed its purchase of Supermercados Amigo, Inc. ("Amigo"), a supermarket chain located in Puerto Rico with 37 supermarkets, six of which were subsequently sold. The purchase price of approximately $242 million was financed by commercial paper. The transaction resulted in approximately $197 million of goodwill. The results of operations, which were not material, are included in the consolidated company results since the date of acquisition.

Disposal

On May 23, 2003, the company completed the sale of McLane Company, Inc. ("McLane"). The company received $1.5 billion in cash for the sale. The accompanying consolidated financial statements and notes reflect the gain on the sale and the operations of McLane as a discontinued operation.

Following is summarized financial information for McLane (in millions):

Fiscal years ended January 31,	2004	2003
Net sales	$4,328	$14,907
Income from discontinued operation	$ 67	$ 221
Income tax expense	25	84
Net operating income from discontinued operation	$ 42	$ 137
Gain on sale of McLane, net of $147 income tax expense	151	–
Income from discontinued operation, net of tax	$ 193	$ 137

Notes to Consolidated Financial Statements
WAL-MART

The effective tax rate on the gain from the sale of McLane was 49% as a result of the non-deductibility of $99 million of goodwill recorded in the original McLane acquisition.

7 Stock-Based Compensation Plans

On February 1, 2003, the company adopted the expense recognition provisions of SFAS 123. Under SFAS 123, compensation expense is recognized based on the fair value of stock options granted. As a result, all prior periods presented have been restated to reflect the compensation cost that would have been recognized had the recognition provisions of SFAS 123 been applied to all awards granted to employees since February 1, 1995. Following the provisions of SFAS 123, fiscal 2005, 2004 and 2003 include $122 million, $102 million and $84 million, respectively, of after-tax stock option expense, which is approximately $0.03 per share in fiscal year 2005 and $0.02 per share for fiscal years 2004 and 2003.

In the United States and certain other countries, options granted under the stock option plans generally expire 10 years from the date of grant. Options granted prior to November 17, 1995, vest over nine years. Generally, options granted on or after November 17, 1995 and before fiscal 2001 vest over seven years. Options granted after fiscal 2001 vest over five years. Shares issued upon the exercise of options are newly issued.

The company's United Kingdom subsidiary, ASDA, offers two different stock option plans to associates. The first plan, The ASDA Colleague Share Ownership Plan 1999 ("CSOP") grants options to certain associates. Options granted under the CSOP Plan generally expire six years from the date of grant, with half vesting on the third anniversary of the date of grant and the other half on the sixth anniversary of the date of grant. The second plan, The ASDA Sharesave Plan 2000 ("Sharesave"), grants options to certain associates at 80% of market value on date of grant. Sharesave options become exercisable after either a three-year or five-year period and generally lapse six months after becoming exercisable.

At January 31, 2005, total unrecognized compensation cost for unvested stock option awards was $478 million, with a weighted-average remaining vesting period of 3.6 years.

At January 31, 2005, the aggregate intrinsic value of stock options outstanding and exercisable was $490 million and $361 million, respectively.

The following table summarizes additional information about stock options outstanding as of January 31, 2005:

Range of Exercise Prices	Number of Outstanding Options	Weighted-Average Remaining Life in Years	Weighted-Average Exercise Price of Outstanding Options	Number of Options Exercisable	Weighted-Average Remaining Life in Years	Weighted-Average Exercise Price of Exercisable Options
$ 4.24 to 11.19	700,000	1.1	$11.12	689,000	1.1	$11.12
11.75 to 13.63	3,085,000	1.5	11.84	3,067,000	1.5	11.84
17.53 to 23.33	3,819,000	3.0	19.35	3,764,000	3.0	19.35
25.00 to 38.72	2,233,000	5.6	35.23	462,000	5.3	26.86
39.86 to 45.69	5,624,000	5.6	40.34	2,648,000	4.0	40.15
46.00 to 54.98	54,889,000	8.3	50.76	12,770,000	6.7	49.57
55.25 to 60.90	10,041,000	7.2	56.51	4,303,000	7.0	56.43
$ 4.24 to 60.90	80,391,000	7.3	$47.03	27,703,000	5.2	$40.12

Further information concerning the options is as follows:

	Shares	Option Price Per Share	Weighted-Average Per Share	Total
January 31, 2002 (16,823,000 shares exercisable)	53,470,000	$ 4.24 – 63.44	$ 32.25	$ 1,724,537,000
Options granted	15,267,000	48.41 – 57.80	54.32	829,244,000
Options canceled	(3,037,000)	4.24 – 63.44	42.07	(127,752,000)
Options exercised	(6,595,000)	4.24 – 55.94	23.90	(157,588,000)
January 31, 2003 (20,053,000 shares exercisable)	59,105,000	$ 4.24 – 60.90	$ 38.38	$ 2,268,441,000
Options granted	26,136,000	47.02 – 59.92	49.65	1,297,604,000
Options canceled	(4,006,000)	4.24 – 60.90	45.09	(180,666,000)
Options exercised	(7,488,000)	4.24 – 56.80	22.89	(171,389,000)
January 31, 2004 (23,763,000 shares exercisable)	73,747,000	$ 4.24 – 60.90	$ 43.58	$ 3,213,990,000
Options granted	**18,575,000**	**44.60 – 60.46**	**52.37**	**972,825,000**
Options canceled	**(3,563,000)**	**4.24 – 58.10**	**48.01**	**(171,026,000)**
Options exercised	**(8,368,000)**	**4.24 – 56.80**	**28.08**	**(234,986,000)**
January 31, 2005 (27,703,000 shares exercisable)	**80,391,000**	**$ 4.24 – 60.90**	**$47.03**	**$3,780,803,000**

At January 31, 2005 and 2004, there were 87.5 million and 102.5 million shares, respectively, available for grant under the company's stock option plans.

The total intrinsic value of options exercised in fiscal 2005, 2004 and 2003 was $236 million, $251 million and $252 million, respectively. The income tax benefit resulting from the tax deductions triggered by employee exercise of stock options amounted to $78 million, $83 million and $84 million in fiscal 2005, 2004 and 2003, respectively.

The company issues restricted (non-vested) stock to certain associates which vests based on passage of time. Restricted stock awards are not included in the preceding tables. Restricted stock awards generally vest 25 percent after three years, 25 percent after five years and 50 percent at age 65. At January 31, 2005, 3 million restricted stock shares with vesting based on the passage of time were outstanding, with a weighted-average grant date value of $46.63.

The company issues stock-based awards for which vesting is tied to the achievement of performance criteria. These awards accrue to the associate based on the extent to which revenue growth and return on investment goals are attained or exceeded over a three-year period. Based on the extent to which the targets are achieved, vested shares may range from 0% to 150% of the original award amount. At January 31, 2005, awards representing 1.7 million shares were outstanding with a weighted-average grant date value of $53.15 per share. These awards are not included in the preceding table.

8 Litigation

The company is involved in a number of legal proceedings, which include consumer, employment, tort and other litigation. The lawsuits discussed below, if decided adversely to or settled by the company, may result in liability material to the company's financial condition or results of operations. The company may enter into discussions regarding settlement of these and other lawsuits, and may enter into settlement agreements, if it believes settlement is in the best interests of the company's shareholders. In accordance with Statement of Financial Accounting Standards No. 5, "Accounting for Contingencies," the company has made accruals with respect to these lawsuits, where appropriate, which are reflected in the company's consolidated financial statements.

The company is a defendant in numerous cases containing class-action allegations in which the plaintiffs have brought claims under the Fair Labor Standards Act ("FLSA"), corresponding state statutes, or other laws. The plaintiffs in these lawsuits are current and former hourly associates who allege, among other things, that the company forced them to work "off the clock" and failed to provide work breaks. The complaints generally seek unspecified monetary damages, injunctive relief, or both. Class certification has yet to be addressed in a majority of the cases. Class certification has been denied or overturned in Arizona, Arkansas, Florida, Georgia, Indiana, Louisiana, Maryland, Michigan, North Carolina, Ohio, Texas (state court), West Virginia, and Wisconsin. Some or all of the requested classes have been certified in California, Colorado, Massachusetts, Minnesota, Oregon, and Washington. Conditional certifications for notice purposes under the FLSA have been allowed in Georgia, Michigan, and Texas (federal court).

A putative class action is pending in California challenging the methodology of payments made under various associate incentive bonus plans, and a second putative class action in California asserts that the company has omitted to include bonus payments in calculating associates' regular rate of pay for purposes of determining overtime.

The company is currently a defendant in four putative class actions brought on behalf of assistant store managers who challenge their exempt status under the FLSA, which are pending in federal courts in Michigan, New Mexico, and Tennessee. A similar putative class action challenging the exempt status of Wal-Mart assistant store managers under California law has been filed in Los Angeles County Superior Court. No determination has been made as to class certification in any of these cases.

The company is a defendant in *Dukes v. Wal-Mart Stores, Inc.*, a class-action lawsuit commenced in June 2001 and pending in the United States District Court for the Northern District of California. The case was brought on behalf of all past and present female employees in all of the company's retail stores and wholesale clubs in the United States. The complaint alleges that the company has engaged in a pattern and practice of discriminating against women in promotions, pay, training and job assignments. The complaint seeks, among other things, injunctive relief, front pay, back pay, punitive damages, and attorneys' fees. Following a hearing on class certification on September 24, 2003, on June 21, 2004, the District Court issued an order granting in part and denying in part the plaintiffs' motion for class certification. The class, which was certified by the District Court for purposes of liability, injunctive and declaratory relief, punitive damages, and lost pay, subject to certain exceptions, includes all women employed at any Wal-Mart domestic retail store at any time since December 26, 1998, who have been or may be subjected to the pay and management track promotions policies and practices challenged by the plaintiffs. The class as certified currently includes approximately 1.6 million present and former female associates.

The company believes that the District Court's ruling is incorrect. The United States Court of Appeals for the Ninth Circuit has granted the company's petition for discretionary review of the ruling. If the company is not successful in its appeal of class certification, or an appellate court issues a ruling that allows for the certification of a class or classes with a different size or scope, and if there is a subsequent adverse verdict on the merits from which there is no successful appeal, or in the event of a negotiated settlement of the litigation, the resulting liability could be material to the company. The plaintiffs also seek punitive damages which, if awarded, could result in the payment of additional amounts material to the company. However, because of the uncertainty of the outcome of the appeal from the District Court's certification decision, because of the uncertainty of the balance of the proceedings contemplated by the District Court, and because the company's liability, if any, arising from the litigation, including the size of any damages award if plaintiffs are successful in the litigation or any negotiated settlement, could vary widely, the company cannot reasonably estimate the possible loss or range of loss which may arise from the litigation.

Notes to Consolidated Financial Statements
WAL-MART

The company is a defendant in four putative class-action lawsuits, three of which are pending in Texas, and one in Oklahoma. In each lawsuit, the plaintiffs seek a declaratory judgment that Wal-Mart and the other defendants who purchased Corporate-Owned Life Insurance ("COLI") policies lacked an insurable interest in the lives of the employees who were insured under the policies, and seek to recover the proceeds of the policies under theories of unjust enrichment and constructive trust. In some of the suits, the plaintiffs assert other causes of action, and seek punitive damages. In January 2004, the parties to the first-filed Texas lawsuit signed a settlement agreement, which received final approval from the court on October 28, 2004. The settlement will include all Texas COLI claimants who do not opt out of the settlement class. The amount to be paid by Wal-Mart under the settlement will not have a material impact on the company's financial condition or results of operations. In the Oklahoma litigation, the court has deferred ruling on plaintiffs' request to add 11 additional states to the litigation, pending a ruling on the company's motion for summary judgment.

The company is a defendant in *Mauldin v. Wal-Mart Stores, Inc.,* a class-action lawsuit that was filed on October 16, 2001, in the United States District Court for the Northern District of Georgia, Atlanta Division. The class was certified on August 23, 2002. On September 30, 2003, the court denied the company's motion to reconsider that ruling. The class is composed of female Wal-Mart associates who were participants in the associates Health and Welfare Plan at any time from March 8, 2001, to the present and who were using prescription contraceptives. The class seeks amendment of the Plan to include coverage for prescription contraceptives, back pay for all members in the form of reimbursement of the cost of prescription contraceptives, pre-judgment interest, and attorneys' fees. The complaint alleges that the company's Health Plan violates Title VII's prohibition against gender discrimination in that the Health Plan's Reproductive Systems provision does not provide coverage for prescription contraceptives.

The company is a defendant in a lawsuit that was filed on August 24, 2001, in the United States District Court for the Eastern District of Kentucky. *EEOC (Janice Smith) v. Wal-Mart Stores, Inc.* is an action brought by the EEOC on behalf of Janice Smith and all other females who made application or transfer requests at the London, Kentucky, Distribution Center from 1995 to the present, and who were not hired or transferred into the warehouse positions for which they applied. The class seeks back pay for those females not selected for hire or transfer during the relevant time period. The class also seeks injunctive and prospective affirmative relief. The complaint alleges that the company based hiring decisions on gender in violation of Title VII of the 1964 Civil Rights Act as amended. The EEOC can maintain this action as a class without certification.

9 Commitments

The company and certain of its subsidiaries have long-term leases for stores and equipment. Rentals (including, for certain leases, amounts applicable to taxes, insurance, maintenance, other operating expenses and contingent rentals) under operating leases and other short-term rental arrangements were $1.2 billion, $1.1 billion, and $1.1 billion in 2005, 2004, and 2003, respectively. Aggregate minimum annual rentals at January 31, 2005, under non-cancelable leases are as follows (in millions):

Fiscal year	Operating Leases	Capital Leases
2006	$ 730	$ 521
2007	700	514
2008	626	505
2009	578	490
2010	530	468
Thereafter	5,908	3,222
Total minimum rentals	$9,072	5,720
Less estimated executory costs		42
Net minimum lease payments		5,678
Less imputed interest at rates ranging from 4.2% to 14.0%		1,886
Present value of minimum lease payments		$3,792

The company has entered into sale/leaseback transactions involving buildings and the underlying land that were accounted for as capital and operating leases. Included in the annual maturities schedule above are $308 million of capital leases and $32 million of operating leases.

Certain of the company's leases provide for the payment of contingent rentals based on a percentage of sales. Such contingent rentals amounted to $42 million, $46 million and $51 million in 2005, 2004 and 2003, respectively. Substantially all of the company's store leases have renewal options, some of which may trigger an escalation in rentals.

In connection with the expansion of our distribution network in Canada, we have guaranteed specific obligations of a third-party logistics provider. In the unlikely event this provider fails to perform its financial obligations regarding certain Wal-Mart related projects, we would be obligated to pay an amount of up to $118 million. These agreements cover periods of up to 10 years.

In connection with certain debt financing, we could be liable for early termination payments if certain unlikely events were to occur. At January 31, 2005, the aggregate termination payment was $113 million. These arrangements expire in fiscal 2011 and fiscal 2019.

In connection with the development of our grocery distribution network in the United States, we have agreements with third parties which would require us to purchase or assume the leases on certain unique equipment in the event the agreements are terminated. These agreements, which can be terminated by either party at will, cover up to a five-year period and obligate the company to pay up to approximately $163 million upon termination of some or all of these agreements.

There are no recourse provisions which would enable us to recover from third parties any amounts paid under the above guarantees. No liability for these guarantees has been recorded in our financial statements.

The company has entered into lease commitments for land and buildings for 46 future locations. These lease commitments with real estate developers provide for minimum rentals ranging from 5-30 years, which if consummated based on current cost estimates, will approximate $30 million annually over the lease terms.

10 Retirement-Related Benefits

In the United States, the company maintains a Profit Sharing and 401(k) Retirement Savings Plan under which most full-time and many part-time associates become participants following one year of employment. The Profit Sharing component of the plan is entirely funded by the company, with an additional contribution made by the company to the associates' 401(k) component of the plan. In addition to the company contributions to the 401(k) Retirement Savings component of the plan, associates may elect to contribute a percentage of their earnings. During fiscal 2005, participants could contribute up to 25% of their pretax earnings, but not more than statutory limits.

Associates may choose from among 13 different investment options for the 401(k) Retirement Savings component of the plan. For associates who did not make an election, their 401(k) balance in the plan is placed in a balanced fund. Associates are immediately vested in their 401(k) funds and may change their investment options at any time. Additionally, fully vested associates have the same 13 investment options for the Profit Sharing component of the plan. Associates are fully vested in the Profit Sharing component of the plan after seven years of service.

Annual contributions made by the company to the United States and Puerto Rico Profit Sharing and 401(k) Retirement Savings Plans are made at the sole discretion of the company, and were $756 million, $662 million and $574 million in fiscal 2005, 2004, and 2003, respectively.

Employees in foreign countries who are not U.S. citizens are covered by various postemployment benefit arrangements. These plans are administered based upon the legislative and tax requirements in the country in which they are established. Annual contributions to foreign retirement savings and profit sharing plans are made at the discretion of the company, and were $199 million, $123 million and $132 million in fiscal 2005, 2004 and 2003, respectively.

The company's United Kingdom subsidiary, ASDA, has a defined benefit pension plan. The plan was underfunded by $419 million and $328 million at January 31, 2005 and 2004, respectively.

11 Segments

The company and its subsidiaries are principally engaged in the operation of retail stores located in all 50 states, Argentina, Canada, Germany, South Korea, Puerto Rico and the United Kingdom, through joint ventures in China, and through majority-owned subsidiaries in Brazil and Mexico. The company identifies segments based on management responsibility within the United States and in total for international units.

The Wal-Mart Stores segment includes the company's Supercenters, Discount Stores and Neighborhood Markets in the United States as well as Walmart.com. The SAM'S CLUB segment includes the warehouse membership clubs in the United States as well as samsclub.com. The International segment consists of the company's operations in Argentina, Brazil, China, Germany, Mexico, South Korea and the United Kingdom, which are consolidated using a December 31 fiscal year-end, generally due to statutory reporting requirements. There were no significant intervening events which materially affected the financial statements. The company's operations in Canada and Puerto Rico are consolidated using a January 31 fiscal year-end. The amounts under the caption "Other" in the following table are unallocated corporate overhead, including our real estate operations in the United States. The company's portion of the results of our unconsolidated minority interest in Seiyu, is also included under the caption "Other."

Notes to Consolidated Financial Statements
WAL-MART

The company measures the profit of its segments as "segment operating income," which is defined as income from continuing operations before net interest expense, income taxes and minority interest. Information on segments and the reconciliation to income from continuing operations before income taxes and minority interest are as follows (in millions):

Fiscal Year Ended January 31, 2005	Wal-Mart Stores	SAM'S CLUB	International	Other	Consolidated
Revenues from external customers	$191,826	$37,119	$56,277	$ –	$285,222
Intercompany real estate charge (income)	2,754	513	–	(3,267)	–
Depreciation and amortization	1,702	274	919	1,510	4,405
Operating income (loss)	14,163	1,280	2,988	(1,340)	17,091
Interest expense, net					(986)
Income from continuing operations before income taxes and minority interest					$ 16,105
Total assets of continuing operations	$ 29,489	$ 5,685	$40,981	$44,068	$120,223

Fiscal Year Ended January 31, 2004	Wal-Mart Stores	SAM'S CLUB	International	Other	Consolidated
Revenues from external customers	$ 174,220	$ 34,537	$ 47,572	$ –	$ 256,329
Intercompany real estate charge (income)	2,468	484	–	(2,952)	–
Depreciation and amortization	1,482	249	810	1,311	3,852
Operating income (loss)	12,916	1,126	2,370	(1,387)	15,025
Interest expense, net					(832)
Income from continuing operations before income taxes and minority interest					$ 14,193
Total assets of continuing operations	$ 27,028	$ 4,751	$ 35,230	$ 38,396	$ 105,405

Fiscal Year Ended January 31, 2003	Wal-Mart Stores	SAM'S CLUB	International	Other	Consolidated
Revenues from external customers	$ 157,120	$ 31,702	$ 40,794	$ –	$ 229,616
Intercompany real estate charge (income)	2,228	453	–	(2,681)	–
Depreciation and amortization	1,287	216	639	1,222	3,364
Operating income (loss)	11,840	1,023	1,998	(1,566)	13,295
Interest expense, net					(927)
Income from continuing operations before income taxes and minority interest					$ 12,368
Total assets of continuing operations	$ 24,868	$ 4,404	$ 30,709	$ 32,919	$ 92,900

Certain information for fiscal years 2004 and 2003 has been reclassified to conform to current-year presentation.

In the United States, long-lived assets, net, excluding goodwill were $48.9 billion and $42.7 billion January 31, 2005 and 2004, respectively. In the United States, additions to long-lived assets were $9.8 billion, $8.1 billion and $7.4 billion at January 31, 2005, 2004 and 2003, respectively. Outside of the United States, long-lived assets, net, excluding goodwill were $19.7 billion and $16.4 billion in fiscal 2005 and 2004, respectively. Outside of the United States, additions to long-lived assets were $3.1 billion, $2.2 billion and $1.8 billion in fiscal 2005, 2004 and 2003, respectively. The International segment includes all real estate outside the United States. The operations of the company's ASDA subsidiary are significant in comparison to the total operations of the International segment. ASDA sales during fiscal 2005, 2004 and 2003 were $26.0 billion, $21.7 billion and $18.1 billion, respectively. At January 31, 2005 and 2004, ASDA long-lived assets, consisting primarily of property and equipment, net, and goodwill, net, totaled $18.9 billion and $16.3 billion, respectively.

12 Quarterly Financial Data (Unaudited)

Amounts in millions except per share information	April 30,	July 31,	October 31,	January 31,
		Quarters ended		
2005				
Net sales	$64,763	$69,722	$68,520	$82,216
Cost of sales	49,969	53,533	52,567	63,723
Income from continuing operations	2,166	2,651	2,286	3,164
Net income	$ 2,166	$ 2,651	$ 2,286	$ 3,164
Basic and diluted net income per common share	$ 0.50	$ 0.62	$ 0.54	$ 0.75
2004				
Net sales	$56,718	$62,637	$62,480	$74,494
Cost of sales	43,918	48,298	48,292	58,239
Income from continuing operations	1,830	2,283	2,028	2,722
Income from discontinued operation	31	161	–	–
Net income	$ 1,861	$ 2,444	$ 2,028	$ 2,722
Basic net income per common share:				
Income from continuing operations	$ 0.41	$ 0.52	$ 0.46	$ 0.63
Income from discontinued operation	0.01	0.04	–	–
Basic net income per common share	$ 0.42	$ 0.56	$ 0.46	$ 0.63
Diluted net income per common share:				
Income from continuing operations	$ 0.41	$ 0.52	$ 0.46	$ 0.63
Income from discontinued operation	0.01	0.04	–	–
Diluted net income per common share	$ 0.42	$ 0.56	$ 0.46	$ 0.63

The sum of quarterly financial data will not agree to annual amounts due to rounding.

13 Subsequent Event

On March 3, 2005, the company's Board of Directors approved an annual dividend of $0.60 per share. The annual dividend will be paid in four quarterly installments on April 4, 2005, June 6, 2005, September 6, 2005, and January 3, 2006 to holders of record on March 18, May 20, August 19 and December 16, 2005, respectively.

Report of Independent Registered Public Accounting Firm
WAL-MART

**The Board of Directors and Shareholders,
Wal-Mart Stores, Inc.**

We have audited the accompanying consolidated balance sheets of Wal-Mart Stores, Inc. as of January 31, 2005 and 2004, and the related consolidated statements of income, shareholders' equity and cash flows for each of the three years in the period ended January 31, 2005. These financial statements are the responsibility of the company's management. Our responsibility is to express an opinion on these financial statements based on our audits.

We conducted our audits in accordance with the standards of the Public Company Accounting Oversight Board (United States). Those standards require that we plan and perform the audit to obtain reasonable assurance about whether the financial statements are free of material misstatement. An audit includes examining, on a test basis, evidence supporting the amounts and disclosures in the financial statements. An audit also includes assessing the accounting principles used and significant estimates made by management, as well as evaluating the overall financial statement presentation. We believe that our audits provide a reasonable basis for our opinion.

In our opinion, the financial statements referred to above present fairly, in all material respects, the consolidated financial position of Wal-Mart Stores, Inc. at January 31, 2005 and 2004, and the consolidated results of its operations and its cash flows for each of the three years in the period ended January 31, 2005, in conformity with U.S. generally accepted accounting principles.

We also have audited, in accordance with the standards of the Public Company Accounting Oversight Board (United States), the effectiveness of Wal-Mart Stores, Inc.'s internal control over financial reporting as of January 31, 2005, based on criteria established in *Internal Control – Integrated Framework* issued by the Committee of Sponsoring Organizations of the Treadway Commission and our report dated March 25, 2005 expressed an unqualified opinion thereon.

Ernst & Young LLP

Rogers, Arkansas
March 25, 2005

Report of Independent Registered Public Accounting Firm on Internal Control Over Financial Reporting

WAL-MART

**The Board of Directors and Shareholders,
Wal-Mart Stores, Inc.**

We have audited management's assessment, included in the accompanying Management's Report to Our Shareholders under the caption "Report on Internal Control Over Financial Reporting," that Wal-Mart Stores, Inc. maintained effective internal control over financial reporting as of January 31, 2005, based on criteria established in *Internal Control – Integrated Framework* issued by the Committee of Sponsoring Organizations of the Treadway Commission (the COSO criteria). Wal-Mart Stores, Inc.'s management is responsible for maintaining effective internal control over financial reporting and for its assessment of the effectiveness of internal control over financial reporting. Our responsibility is to express an opinion on management's assessment and an opinion on the effectiveness of the company's internal control over financial reporting based on our audit.

We conducted our audit in accordance with the standards of the Public Company Accounting Oversight Board (United States). Those standards require that we plan and perform the audit to obtain reasonable assurance about whether effective internal control over financial reporting was maintained in all material respects. Our audit included obtaining an understanding of internal control over financial reporting, evaluating management's assessment, testing and evaluating the design and operating effectiveness of internal control, and performing such other procedures as we considered necessary in the circumstances. We believe that our audit provides a reasonable basis for our opinion.

A company's internal control over financial reporting is a process designed to provide reasonable assurance regarding the reliability of financial reporting and the preparation of financial statements for external purposes in accordance with generally accepted accounting principles. A company's internal control over financial reporting includes those policies and procedures that (1) pertain to the maintenance of records that, in reasonable detail, accurately and fairly reflect the transactions and dispositions of the assets of the company; (2) provide reasonable assurance that transactions are recorded as necessary to permit preparation of financial statements

in accordance with generally accepted accounting principles, and that receipts and expenditures of the company are being made only in accordance with authorizations of management and directors of the company; and (3) provide reasonable assurance regarding prevention or timely detection of unauthorized acquisition, use, or disposition of the company's assets that could have a material effect on the financial statements.

Because of its inherent limitations, internal control over financial reporting may not prevent or detect misstatements. Also, projections of any evaluation of effectiveness to future periods are subject to the risk that controls may become inadequate because of changes in conditions, or that the degree of compliance with the policies or procedures may deteriorate.

In our opinion, management's assessment that Wal-Mart Stores, Inc. maintained effective internal control over financial reporting as of January 31, 2005, is fairly stated, in all material respects, based on the COSO criteria. Also, in our opinion, Wal-Mart Stores, Inc., maintained, in all material respects, effective internal control over financial reporting as of January 31, 2005, based on the COSO criteria.

We also have audited, in accordance with the standards of the Public Company Accounting Oversight Board (United States), the consolidated balance sheets of Wal-Mart Stores, Inc. as of January 31, 2005 and 2004, and the related consolidated statements of income, shareholders' equity and cash flows for each of the three years in the period ended January 31, 2005 and our report dated March 25, 2005 expressed an unqualified opinion thereon.

Ernst + Young LLP

Rogers, Arkansas
March 25, 2005

Management's Report to Our Shareholders
WAL-MART

Management of Wal-Mart Stores, Inc. ("Wal-Mart") is responsible for the preparation, integrity and objectivity of Wal-Mart's consolidated financial statements and other financial information contained in this Annual Report to Shareholders. Those consolidated financial statements were prepared in conformity with accounting principles generally accepted in the United States. In preparing those consolidated financial statements, Management was required to make certain estimates and judgments, which are based upon currently available information and Management's view of current conditions and circumstances.

The Audit Committee of the Board of Directors, which consists solely of independent directors, oversees our process of reporting financial information and the audit of our consolidated financial statements. The Audit Committee stays informed of the financial condition of Wal-Mart and regularly reviews Management's financial policies and procedures, the independence of our independent auditors, our internal control and the objectivity of our financial reporting. Both the independent auditors and the internal auditors have free access to the Audit Committee and meet with the Audit Committee periodically, both with and without Management present.

We have retained Ernst & Young LLP, an independent registered public accounting firm, to audit our consolidated financial statements found in this annual report. We have made available to Ernst & Young LLP all of our financial records and related data in connection with their audit of our consolidated financial statements.

We have filed with the Securities and Exchange Commission the required certifications related to our consolidated financial statements as of and for the year ended January 31, 2005. These certifications are attached as exhibits to our Annual Report on Form 10-K for the year ended January 31, 2005. Additionally, we have also provided to the New York Stock Exchange the required annual certification of our Chief Executive Officer regarding our compliance with the New York Stock Exchange's corporate governance listing standards.

Report on Internal Control Over Financial Reporting.
Management has responsibility for establishing and maintaining adequate internal control over financial reporting. Internal control over financial reporting is a process designed to provide reasonable assurance regarding the reliability of financial reporting and the preparation of financial statements for external reporting purposes in accordance with accounting principles generally accepted in the United States. Because of its inherent limitations, internal control over financial reporting may not prevent or detect misstatements. Management has assessed the effectiveness of the company's internal control over financial reporting as of January 31, 2005. In making its assessment, Management has utilized the criteria set forth by the Committee of Sponsoring Organizations ("COSO") of the Treadway Commission in *Internal Control – Integrated Framework*. Management concluded that based on its assessment, Wal-Mart's internal control over financial reporting was effective as of January 31, 2005. Management's assessment of the effectiveness of the company's internal control over financial reporting as of January 31, 2005 has been audited by Ernst & Young LLP, an independent registered public accounting firm, as stated in their report which appears in this Annual Report to Shareholders.

Evaluation of Disclosure Controls and Procedures.
We maintain disclosure controls and procedures designed to provide reasonable assurance that information, which is required to be timely disclosed, is accumulated and communicated to Management in a timely fashion. Management has assessed the effectiveness of these disclosure controls and procedures as of January 31, 2005 and determined they were effective as of that date to provide reasonable assurance that information required to be disclosed by us in the reports we file or submit under the Securities Exchange Act of 1934, as amended, is accumulated and communicated to Management, as appropriate, to allow timely decisions regarding required disclosure and are effective to provide reasonable assurance that such information is recorded, processed, summarized and reported within the time periods specified by the SEC's rules and forms.

Report on Ethical Standards.
Our company was founded on the belief that open communications and the highest standard of ethics are necessary to be successful. Our long-standing "Open Door" communication policy helps Management be aware of and address issues in a timely and effective manner. Through the open door policy all associates are encouraged to inform Management at the appropriate level when they are concerned about any matter pertaining to Wal-Mart.

Wal-Mart has adopted a Statement of Ethics to guide our associates in the continued observance of high ethical standards such as honesty, integrity and compliance with the law in the conduct of Wal-Mart's business. Familiarity and compliance with the Statement of Ethics is required of all associates who are part of Management. The company also maintains a separate Code of Ethics for our senior financial officers. Wal-Mart also has in place a Related-Party Transaction Policy. This policy applies to all of Wal-Mart's Officers and Directors and requires material related-party transactions to be reviewed by the Audit Committee. The Officers and Directors are required to report material related-party transactions to Wal-Mart. We maintain an ethics office which oversees and administers an ethics hotline. The ethics hotline provides a channel for associates to make confidential and anonymous complaints regarding potential violations of our statements of ethics, including violations related to financial or accounting matters.

H. Lee Scott
President and Chief Executive Officer

Thomas M. Schoewe
Executive Vice President and Chief Financial Officer

Fiscal 2005 End-of-Year Store Count

WAL-MART

State	Discount Stores	Supercenters	SAM'S CLUBS	Neighborhood Markets
Alabama	18	71	11	2
Alaska	7	0	3	0
Arizona	18	33	11	5
Arkansas	26	54	5	6
California	149	3	33	0
Colorado	15	40	15	0
Connecticut	28	4	3	0
Delaware	3	4	1	0
Florida	53	116	38	6
Georgia	23	88	21	0
Hawaii	7	0	2	0
Idaho	3	14	1	0
Illinois	78	45	28	0
Indiana	31	56	15	4
Iowa	20	33	7	0
Kansas	19	34	6	3
Kentucky	26	52	5	2
Louisiana	26	56	12	1
Maine	11	11	3	0
Maryland	33	6	13	0
Massachusetts	42	2	3	0
Michigan	41	30	24	0
Minnesota	33	16	13	0
Mississippi	14	51	6	1
Missouri	46	70	14	0
Montana	4	7	1	0
Nebraska	8	16	3	0
Nevada	9	12	5	4
New Hampshire	19	7	4	0
New Jersey	38	0	9	0
New Mexico	3	24	5	0
New York	53	27	18	0
North Carolina	41	65	19	0
North Dakota	8	0	2	0
Ohio	69	45	27	0
Oklahoma	33	49	8	14
Oregon	20	7	0	0
Pennsylvania	49	60	21	0
Rhode Island	7	1	1	0
South Carolina	16	45	9	0
South Dakota	5	5	2	0
Tennessee	21	75	15	4
Texas	80	219	69	28
Utah	4	24	7	5
Vermont	4	0	0	0
Virginia	22	56	13	0
Washington	24	13	3	0
West Virginia	6	23	4	0
Wisconsin	38	37	11	0
Wyoming	2	7	2	0
U.S. Totals	**1,353**	**1,713**	**551**	**85**

International/Worldwide

Country	Discount Stores	Supercenters	SAM'S CLUBS	Neighborhood Markets
Argentina	0	11	0	0
Brazil	118*	17	12	2*
Canada	256	0	6	0
China	0	38	3	2
Germany	0	91	0	0
South Korea	0	16	0	0
Mexico	529†	89	61	0
Puerto Rico	9	4	9	32**
United Kingdom	263§	19	0	0
International Totals	**1,175**	**285**	**91**	**36**
Grand Totals	**2,528**	**1,998**	**642**	**121**

* Brazil includes 2 Todo Dias, 118 Bompreço.

† Mexico includes 162 Bodegas, 50 Suburbias, 48 Superamas, 269 Vips and does not include Vips franchises.

** Puerto Rico includes 32 Amigos.

§ United Kingdom includes 256 ASDA Stores, 6 George Stores and 1 ASDA Living.

Senior Officers
WAL-MART

Eduardo Castro-Wright
Executive Vice President and Chief Operating
Officer, Wal-Mart Stores Division

M. Susan Chambers
Executive Vice President, Risk Management,
Insurance and Benefits Administration

Robert F. Connolly
Executive Vice President, Marketing
and Consumer Communications,
Wal-Mart Stores Division

Douglas J. Degn
Executive Vice President, Food, Consumables
and Hardlines Merchandising, Wal-Mart
Stores Division

David J. Dible
Executive Vice President, Specialty Group,
Wal-Mart Stores Division

Linda M. Dillman
Executive Vice President and
Chief Information Officer

Michael T. Duke
Executive Vice President, President
and Chief Executive Officer, Wal-Mart
Stores Division

Joseph J. Fitzsimmons
Senior Vice President, Finance and Treasurer

Rollin L. Ford
Executive Vice President, Logistics and
Supply Chain

David D. Glass
Chairman of the Executive Committee
of the Board of Directors

Craig R. Herkert
Executive Vice President, President and
Chief Executive Officer, The Americas,
Wal-Mart International

Charles M. Holley, Jr.
Senior Vice President and Controller

Thomas D. Hyde
Executive Vice President and
Corporate Secretary

Lawrence V. Jackson
Executive Vice President, People Division

C. Douglas McMillon
Executive Vice President, Merchandising
and Replenishment, SAM'S CLUB

John B. Menzer
Executive Vice President, President and
Chief Executive Officer,
Wal-Mart International

Thomas M. Schoewe
Executive Vice President and
Chief Financial Officer

H. Lee Scott, Jr.
President and Chief Executive Officer

Gregory E. Spragg
Executive Vice President, Operations,
SAM'S CLUB

B. Kevin Turner
Executive Vice President, President and
Chief Executive Officer, SAM'S CLUB

S. Robson Walton
Chairman of the Board of Directors

Claire A. Watts
Executive Vice President,
Product Development, Apparel and
Home Merchandising,
Wal-Mart Stores Division

Board of Directors
WAL-MART

James W. Breyer

Mr. Breyer is the Managing Partner of Accel Partners, a venture capital firm.

M. Michele Burns

Ms. Burns is the Chief Financial Officer of the Mirant Corporation.

Douglas N. Daft

Mr. Daft is the retired Chief Executive Officer and Chairman of the Board of Directors of The Coca-Cola Company.

David D. Glass

David D. Glass is Chairman of the Executive Committee of the Board of Directors of Wal-Mart.

Roland A. Hernandez

Mr. Hernandez is the retired Chief Executive Officer and Chairman of the Board of Directors of Telemundo Group, Inc., a Spanish-language television station company.

John D. Opie

Mr. Opie is the retired Vice Chairman of the Board of Directors and Executive Officer of the General Electric Co., a diversified technology, services, and products company.

J. Paul Reason

Mr. Reason is the President and Chief Operating Officer of Metro Machine Corporation, an employee-owned ship repair company.

H. Lee Scott, Jr.

H. Lee Scott, Jr. is the President and Chief Executive Officer of Wal-Mart.

Jack C. Shewmaker

Mr. Shewmaker is the President of J-COM, Inc., a consulting company, a retired Wal-Mart executive and a rancher.

Jose H. Villarreal

Mr. Villarreal is a partner in the law firm Akin, Gump, Strauss, Hauer & Feld, L.L.P.

John T. Walton

Mr. Walton is the Chairman of True North Partners, L.L.C., which holds investments in technology companies.

S. Robson Walton

S. Robson Walton is Chairman of the Board of Wal-Mart.

Christopher J. Williams

Mr. Williams is the Chairman of the Board and Chief Executive Officer of The Williams Capital Group, L.P., an investment bank.

Stock Information

WAL-MART

Market Price of Common Stock

Fiscal year ended January 31,

	2004		2005	
	High	Low	**High**	**Low**
1st Quarter	$56.58	$46.74	**$61.05**	**$54.69**
2nd Quarter	$57.32	$52.00	**$57.68**	**$51.76**
3rd Quarter	$60.08	$55.27	**$54.97**	**$51.33**
4th Quarter	$59.04	$50.74	**$57.70**	**$52.02**

Fiscal year ended January 31,

	2006	
	High	Low
1st Quarter*	$53.51	$50.65

Through March 30, 2005

Certifications

The company's Chief Executive Officer and Chief Financial Officer have filed their certifications as required by the Securities and Exchange Commission (the "SEC") regarding the quality of the company's public disclosure for each of the periods ended during the company's fiscal year ended January 31, 2005 and the effectiveness of internal control over financial reporting as of January 31, 2005. Further, the company's Chief Executive Officer has certified to the New York Stock Exchange ("NYSE") that he is not aware of any violation by the company of the NYSE corporate governance listing standards, as required by Section 303A.12(a) of the NYSE listing standards.

Shareholders

As of March 30, 2005, there were 328,620 holders of record of Wal-Mart's Common Stock.

Dividends Paid Per Share

Fiscal year ended January 31, 2004

April 7, 2003	$0.090
July 7, 2003	$0.090
October 14, 2003	$0.090
January 5, 2004	$0.090

Dividends Paid Per Share

Fiscal year ended January 31, 2005

April 5, 2004	$0.130
June 7, 2004	$0.130
September 7, 2004	$0.130
January 3, 2005	$0.130

Dividends Payable Per Share

Fiscal year ended January 31, 2006

April 4, 2005	$0.150
June 6, 2005	$0.150
September 6, 2005	$0.150
January 3, 2006	$0.150

Target 10-K
(excerpted)

CONSOLIDATED RESULTS OF OPERATIONS

(millions, except per share data)	2004	2003	2002
Sales	$ **45,682**	$ 40,928	$ 36,519
Net credit card revenues	**1,157**	1,097	891
Total revenues	**46,839**	42,025	37,410
Cost of sales	**31,445**	28,389	25,498
Selling, general and administrative expense	**9,797**	8,657	7,505
Credit card expense	**737**	722	629
Depreciation and amortization	**1,259**	1,098	967
Earnings from continuing operations before interest expense and income taxes	**3,601**	3,159	2,811
Net interest expense	**570**	556	584
Earnings from continuing operations before income taxes	**3,031**	2,603	2,227
Provision for income taxes	**1,146**	984	851
Earnings from continuing operations	$ **1,885**	$ 1,619	$ 1,376
Earnings from discontinued operations, net of $46, $116 and $152 tax	$ **75**	$ 190	$ 247
Gain on disposal of discontinued operations, net of $761 tax	$ **1,238**	$ —	$ —
Net earnings	$ **3,198**	$ 1,809	$ 1,623
Basic earnings per share			
Continuing operations	$ **2.09**	$ 1.78	$ 1.52
Discontinued operations	$ **0.08**	$ 0.21	$ 0.27
Gain from discontinued operations	$ **1.37**	$ —	$ —
Basic earnings per share	$ **3.54**	$ 1.99	$ 1.79
Diluted earnings per share			
Continuing operations	$ **2.07**	$ 1.76	$ 1.51
Discontinued operations	$ **0.08**	$ 0.21	$ 0.27
Gain from discontinued operations	$ **1.36**	$ —	$ —
Diluted earnings per share	$ **3.51**	$ 1.97	$ 1.78
Weighted average common shares outstanding:			
Basic	**903.8**	911.0	908.0
Diluted	**912.1**	919.2	914.3

See Notes to Consolidated Financial Statements throughout pages 738–752.

CONSOLIDATED STATEMENTS OF FINANCIAL POSITION

(millions)	January 29, 2005	January 31, 2004
Assets		
Cash and cash equivalents	$ 2,245	$ 708
Accounts receivable, net	5,069	4,621
Inventory	5,384	4,531
Other current assets	1,224	1,000
Current assets of discontinued operations	—	2,092
Total current assets	13,922	12,952
Property and equipment		
Land	3,804	3,312
Buildings and improvements	12,518	11,022
Fixtures and equipment	4,988	4,577
Construction-in-progress	962	969
Accumulated depreciation	(5,412)	(4,727)
Property and equipment, net	16,860	15,153
Other non-current assets	1,511	1,377
Non-current assets of discontinued operations	—	1,934
Total assets	$ 32,293	$ 31,416
Liabilities and shareholders investment		
Accounts payable	$ 5,779	$ 4,956
Accrued liabilities	1,633	1,288
Income taxes payable	304	382
Current portion of long-term debt and notes payable	504	863
Current liabilities of discontinued operations	—	825
Total current liabilities	8,220	8,314
Long-term debt	9,034	10,155
Deferred income taxes	973	632
Other non-current liabilities	1,037	917
Non-current liabilities of discontinued operations	—	266
Shareholders' investment		
Common stock*	74	76
Additional paid-in-capital	1,810	1,530
Retained earnings	11,148	9,523
Accumulated other comprehensive income	(3)	3
Total shareholders' investment	13,029	11,132
Total liabilities and shareholders' investment	$ 32,293	$ 31,416

*   **Common Stock** *Authorized 6,000,000,000 shares, $.0833 par value; 890,643,966 shares issued and outstanding at January 29, 2005; 911,808,051 shares issued and outstanding at January 31, 2004.*

Preferred Stock *Authorized 5,000,000 shares, $.01 par value; no shares were issued or outstanding at January 29, 2005 or January 31, 2004*

See Notes to Consolidated Financial Statements throughout pages 738–752.

CONSOLIDATED STATEMENTS OF CASH FLOWS

(millions)	2004	2003	2002
Operating activities			
Net earnings	$ **3,198**	$ 1,809	$ 1,623
Earnings from and gain on disposal of discontinued operations, net of tax	**1,313**	190	247
Earnings from continuing operations	**1,885**	1,619	1,376
Reconciliation to cash flow:			
Depreciation and amortization	**1,259**	1,098	967
Deferred tax provision	**233**	208	208
Bad debt provision	**451**	476	391
Loss on disposal of fixed assets, net	**59**	41	54
Other non-cash items affecting earnings	**133**	67	179
Changes in operating accounts providing/(requiring) cash:			
Accounts receivable originated at Target	**(209)**	(279)	(454)
Inventory	**(853)**	(579)	(370)
Other current assets	**(37)**	(196)	13
Other non-current assets	**(147)**	(166)	(136)
Accounts payable	**823**	721	545
Accrued liabilities	**319**	85	3
Income taxes payable	**(78)**	99	(80)
Other	**(17)**	19	29
Cash flow provided by operations	**3,821**	3,213	2,725
Investing activities			
Expenditures for property and equipment	**(3,068)**	(2,738)	(3,040)
Proceeds from disposals of fixed assets	**56**	67	32
Change in accounts receivable originated at third parties	**(690)**	(538)	(1,768)
Proceeds from sale of discontinued operations	**4,881**	—	—
Cash flow provided by/(required for) investing activities	**1,179**	(3,209)	(4,776)
Financing activities			
Decrease in notes payable, net	**—**	(100)	—
Additions to long-term debt	**10**	1,200	3,116
Reductions of long-term debt	**(1,487)**	(1,179)	(1,098)
Dividends paid	**(272)**	(237)	(218)
Repurchase of stock	**(1,290)**	(48)	(3)
Stock option exercises	**146**	36	27
Other	**56**	(10)	(20)
Cash flow (required for)/provided by financing activities	**(2,837)**	(338)	1,804
Net cash (required)/provided by discontinued operations	**(626)**	292	508
Net increase/(decrease) in cash and cash equivalents	**1,537**	(42)	261
Cash and cash equivalents at beginning of year	**708**	750	489
Cash and cash equivalents at end of year	$ **2,245**	$ 708	$ 750

Amounts presented herein are on a cash basis and therefore may differ from those shown in other sections of this Annual Report. Consistent with the provisions of SFAS No. 95, "Statement of Cash Flows," cash flows related to accounts receivable are classified as either Provided by Operations or From Investing Activities, depending on their origin.

Cash paid for income taxes was $1,742 million, $781 million and $853 million during 2004, 2003 and 2002, respectively. Cash paid for interest (including interest capitalized) was $498 million, $550 million and $526 million during 2004, 2003 and 2002, respectively.

See Notes to Consolidated Financial Statements throughout pages 738–752.

CONSOLIDATED STATEMENTS OF SHAREHOLDERS' INVESTMENT

(millions, except footnotes)	Common Stock Shares	Stock Par Value	Additional Paid-in Capital	Retained Earnings	Accumulated Other Comprehensive Income	Total
February 2, 2002	905.2	$ 75	$ 1,193	$ 6,628	$ —	$ 7,896
Consolidated net earnings	—	—	—	1,623	—	1,623
Other comprehensive income	—	—	—	—	4	4
Total comprehensive income						1,627
Dividends declared	—	—	—	(218)	—	(218)
Repurchase of stock	(.5)	—	—	(16)	—	(16)
Issuance of stock for ESOP	3.0	1	105	—	—	106
Stock options and awards	2.1	—	102	—	—	102
February 1, 2003	909.8	76	1,400	8,017	4	9,497
Consolidated net earnings	—	—	—	1,809	—	1,809
Other comprehensive income	—	—	—	—	(1)	(1)
Total comprehensive income						1,808
Dividends declared	—	—	—	(246)	—	(246)
Repurchase of stock	(1.5)	—	—	(57)	—	(57)
Issuance of stock for ESOP	0.6	—	17	—	—	17
Stock options and awards	2.9	—	113	—	—	113
January 31, 2004	911.8	76	1,530	9,523	3	11,132
Consolidated net earnings	—	—	—	3,198	—	3,198
Other comprehensive income	—	—	—	—	(6)	(6)
Total comprehensive income						3,192
Dividends declared	—	—	—	(280)	—	(280)
Repurchase of stock	(28.9)	(3)	—	(1,293)	—	(1,296)
Issuance of stock for ESOP	—	—	—	—	—	—
Stock options and awards	7.7	1	280	—	—	281
January 29, 2005	**890.6**	**$ 74**	**$ 1,810**	**$ 11,148**	**$ (3)**	**$ 13,029**

Common Stock *Authorized 6,000,000,000 shares, $.0833 par value; 890,643,966 shares issued and outstanding at January 29, 2005; 911,808,051 shares issued and outstanding at January 31, 2004; 909,801,560 shares issued and outstanding at February 1, 2003.*

In June of 2004, our Board of Directors authorized the repurchase of $3 billion of our common stock. The repurchase of our common stock is expected to be made primarily in open market transactions, subject to market conditions, and is expected to be completed over two to three years. This authorization replaced our previous repurchase programs that were authorized by our Board of Directors in January 1999 and March 2000. In 2004, we repurchased a total of 29 million shares of our common stock at a total cost of approximately $1,290 million ($44.68 per share)

Preferred Stock *Authorized 5,000,000 shares, $.01 par value; no shares were issued or outstanding at January 29, 2005, January 31, 2004 or February 1, 2003.*

Junior Preferred Stock Rights *In 2001, we declared a distribution of preferred share purchase rights. Terms of the plan provide for a distribution of one preferred share purchase right for each outstanding share of our common stock. Each right will entitle shareholders to buy one twelve-hundredth of a share of a new series of junior participating preferred stock at an exercise price of $125.00, subject to adjustment. The rights will be exercisable only if a person or group acquires ownership of 20 percent or more of our common stock or announces a tender offer to acquire 30 percent or more of our common stock.*

Dividends *Dividends declared per share were $0.31, $0.27 and $0.24 in 2004, 2003 and 2002, respectively.*

See Notes to Consolidated Financial Statements throughout pages 738–752.

NOTES TO CONSOLIDATED FINANCIAL STATEMENTS

Summary of Accounting Policies

Organization Target Corporation operates large-format general merchandise discount stores in the United States and a much smaller, rapidly growing on-line business. Additionally, our credit card operations represent an integral component of our retail business.

Consolidation The financial statements include the balances of the Corporation and its subsidiaries after elimination of material intercompany balances and transactions. All material subsidiaries are wholly owned.

Use of Estimates The preparation of our financial statements, in conformity with accounting principles generally accepted in the United States (GAAP), requires management to make estimates and assumptions that affect the reported amounts in the financial statements and accompanying notes. Actual results may differ from those estimates.

Fiscal Year Our fiscal year ends on the Saturday nearest January 31. Unless otherwise stated, references to years in this report relate to fiscal years rather than to calendar years. Fiscal years 2004, 2003 and 2002 each consisted of 52 weeks.

Reclassifications Certain prior year amounts have been reclassified to conform to the current year presentation.

Stock-based Compensation In December 2004, the Financial Accounting Standards Board finalized Statement of Financial Accounting Standards No. 123R, "Share-Based Payment" (SFAS No. 123R). SFAS No. 123R eliminates accounting for share-based compensation transactions using the intrinsic value method prescribed in APB Opinion No. 25, "Accounting for Stock Issued to Employees," and requires instead that such transactions be accounted for using a fair-value-based method. We adopted SFAS No. 123, "Accounting for Stock-Based Compensation," in accordance with the prospective transition method prescribed in SFAS No. 148, "Accounting for Stock-Based Compensation –Transition and Disclosure" in the first quarter of 2003. Therefore, the fair value based method has been applied prospectively to awards granted subsequent to February 1, 2003 (the last day of our 2002 fiscal year). We have elected to adopt the provisions of SFAS No. 123R in 2004 under the modified retrospective transition method. All prior period financial statements have been restated to recognize compensation cost in the amounts previously reported in the Notes to Consolidated Financial Statements under the provisions of SFAS No. 123. Information related to outstanding stock options and performance shares is disclosed on pages 33-34.

Revenues

The contribution to revenue from sales is recognized when the sales occur and are net of expected returns. Revenue from gift card sales is recognized upon redemption of the gift card. Commissions earned on sales generated by leased departments are included within sales and were $46 million in 2004, $32 million in 2003 and $19 million in 2002. Net credit card revenues are comprised of finance charges and late fees from credit card holders, as well as third-party merchant fees earned from the use of our Target Visa credit card. Net credit card revenues are recognized according to the contractual provisions of each applicable credit card agreement. If an account is written-off, any uncollected finance charges or late fees are recorded as a reduction of credit card revenue. The amount of our retail sales charged to our credit cards was $3,269 million, $3,006 million and $2,980 million in 2004, 2003 and 2002, respectively.

Consideration Received from Vendors

We receive income for a variety of vendor-sponsored programs such as volume rebates, markdown allowances, promotions and advertising, and for our compliance programs. Promotional and advertising allowances are intended to offset our costs of promoting and selling the vendor's merchandise in our stores and are recognized when we incur the cost or complete the promotion. Under our compliance programs, vendors are charged for merchandise shipments that do not meet our requirements, such as late or incomplete shipments, and we record these allowances when the violation occurs. Vendor income either reduces our inventory costs or our operating expenses based on the requirements of Emerging Issues Task Force (EITF) Issue No. 02-16, "Accounting by a Customer (Including a Reseller) for Certain Consideration Received from a Vendor" as discussed below.

In the first quarter of 2003, we adopted EITF No. 02-16 which resulted in the reclassification of certain vendor income items from operating expenses to inventory purchases and recognized into income as the vendors' merchandise is sold. The guidance was applied on a prospective basis only as required by EITF No. 02-16. This guidance had no material impact on sales, cash flows or financial position for any period.

In the fourth quarter of 2003, we adopted EITF No. 03-10, "Application of Issue 02-16 by Resellers to Sales Incentives Offered to Consumers by Manufacturers," which amends EITF No. 02-16. In accordance with EITF No. 03-10, if certain criteria are met, consideration received from a vendor for honoring the vendor's sales incentives offered directly to consumers (i.e. manufacturer's coupons) should not be recorded as a reduction of the cost of the reseller's purchases from the vendor. The adoption of EITF No. 03-10 did not have a material impact on net earnings, cash flows or financial position.

Buying, Occupancy and Distribution Expenses

Buying expenses primarily consist of salaries and expenses incurred by our merchandising operations, while occupancy expenses primarily consist of rent, property taxes and other operating costs of our retail, distribution and headquarters facilities. Buying and occupancy expenses classified in selling, general and administrative expenses were $1,421 million, $1,213 million and $1,063 million in 2004, 2003 and 2002, respectively. In addition, we recorded $1,035 million, $910 million and $789 million of depreciation expense for our retail, distribution and headquarters facilities in 2004, 2003 and 2002, respectively.

Advertising Costs

Advertising costs, included in selling, general and administrative expense, are expensed at first showing of the advertisement and were $888 million, $872 million and $666 million for 2004, 2003 and 2002, respectively. Advertising vendor income used to reduce advertising expenses was approximately $72 million, $58 million and $173 million for 2004, 2003 and 2002, respectively. Television and radio broadcast and newspaper circulars make up the majority of our advertising costs in all three years.

Discontinued Operations

On March 10, 2004, we began a review of strategic alternatives for our Marshall Field's and Mervyn's businesses, which included but was not limited to the possible sale of one or both as ongoing businesses to existing retailers or other qualified buyers.

On June 9, 2004, we agreed to sell Marshall Field's and the Mervyn's stores located in Minnesota to The May Department Store Company (May). We completed the sale of Marshall Field's on July 31, 2004 and the sale of the Minnesota Mervyn's stores on August 24, 2004. May acquired total assets and liabilities with a net carrying value of $1,563 million in exchange for $3,240 million cash consideration, resulting in a gain on the sale of $1,677 million or $1.14 per share.

On July 29, 2004, we agreed to sell the remaining Mervyn's retail stores and distribution centers to an investment consortium including Sun Capital Partners, Inc., Cerberus Capital Management, L.P., and Lubert-Adler/Klaff and Partners, L.P. and to sell Mervyn's credit card receivables to GE Consumer Finance, a unit of General Electric Company, for total cash consideration of $1,641 million. This sale transaction was completed as of August 28, 2004, resulting in a gain of $322 million or $.22 per share.

In accordance with SFAS No. 144, "Accounting for the Impairment or Disposal of Long-Lived Assets," the financial results of Marshall Field's and Mervyn's are reported as discontinued operations for all periods presented.

In connection with the sale of Marshall Field's, May is purchasing transition support services from us until the end of first quarter 2005. We are providing transition services to the buyer of Mervyn's for a fee until the earlier of August 2007 or the date on which an alternative long-term solution for providing these services is in place. The fees received for providing these services exceed our marginal costs, but when an allocable share of our fixed costs is included, the consideration received is essentially equal to our total costs.

The financial results included in discontinued operations were as follows:

(millions)	January 29, 2005	January 31, 2004	February 1, 2003
Revenue	$ 3,095	$ 6,138	$ 6,507
Earnings from discontinued operations before income taxes	121	306	399
Earnings from discontinued operations, net of $46, $116 and $152 tax, respectively	75	190	247
Gain on sale of discontinued operations, net of $761 tax	1,238	—	—
Total income from discontinued operations, net of tax	$ 1,313	$ 190	$ 247

There were no assets or liabilities of Marshall Field's or Mervyn's included in our Consolidated Statements of Financial Position at January 29, 2005. The major classes of assets and liabilities of discontinued operations in the Consolidated Statements of Financial Position on January 31, 2004 were as follows:

(millions)	January 31, 2004
Cash and cash equivalents	$ 8
Accounts receivable, net	1,155
Inventory	812
Other	117
Current assets of discontinued operations	$ 2,092
Property and equipment, net	$ 1,816
Other	118
Non-current assets of discontinued operations	$ 1,934
Accounts payable	$ 492
Accrued liabilities	330
Current portion of long-term debt and notes payable	3
Current liabilities of discontinued operations	$ 825
Long-term debt	$ 62
Deferred income taxes	—
Other	204
Non-current liabilities of discontinued operations	$ 266

Earnings per Share

Basic earnings per share (EPS) is net earnings divided by the average number of common shares outstanding during the period. Diluted EPS includes the incremental shares that are assumed to be issued on the exercise of stock options.

(millions, except per share data)	Basic EPS			Diluted EPS		
	2004	2003	2002	2004	2003	2002
Net earnings	$ 3,198	$ 1,809	$ 1,623	$ 3,198	$ 1,809	$ 1,623
Basic weighted average common shares outstanding	903.8	911.0	908.0	903.8	911.0	908.0
Stock options	—	—	—	8.3	8.2	6.3
Weighted average common shares outstanding	903.8	911.0	908.0	912.1	919.2	914.3
Earnings per share	$ 3.54	$ 1.99	$ 1.79	$ 3.51	$ 1.97	$ 1.78

The shares related to stock options shown above do not include shares issuable upon exercise of approximately 4.5 million and 13.2 million at January 31, 2004 and February 1, 2003, respectively, because the effect would have been antidilutive. There were no antidilutive shares issuable upon exercise at January 29, 2005.

Other Comprehensive Income

Other comprehensive income includes revenues, expenses, gains and losses that are excluded from net earnings under GAAP. In 2004 and 2003, other comprehensive income primarily included gains and losses on certain hedge transactions and the change in our minimum pension liability, net of related taxes.

Cash Equivalents

Cash equivalents represent short-term investments with a maturity of three months or less from the time of purchase and were $1,732 million, $244 million and $357 million in 2004, 2003 and 2002, respectively. The increase of $1,488 in 2004 compared to 2003 is primarily due to investment of the remaining proceeds at year end from the divestitures of Marshall Field's and Mervyn's.

Accounts Receivable

Accounts receivable are recorded net of an allowance for expected losses. The allowance, recognized in an amount equal to the anticipated future write-offs based on delinquencies, risk scores, aging trends, industry risk trends and our historical experience, was $387 million at January 29, 2005 and $352 million at January 31, 2004.

Through our special purpose subsidiary, Target Receivables Corporation (TRC), we transfer, on an ongoing basis, substantially all of our receivables to the Target Credit Card Master Trust (the Trust) in return for certificates representing undivided interests in the Trust's assets. TRC owns the undivided interest in the Trust's assets, other than the Trust's assets securing the financing transactions entered into by the Trust and the 2 percent of Trust assets held by Target National Bank (TNB). TNB is a wholly owned subsidiary of the Corporation that also services receivables. SFAS No. 140 "Accounting for Transfers and Servicing of Financial Assets and Extinguishments of Liabilities (a replacement of SFAS No. 125)" is the accounting guidance applicable to such transactions. SFAS No. 140 requires that we include the receivables within the Trust and any debt securities issued by the Trust in our Consolidated Statement of Financial Position. Notwithstanding this accounting treatment, the receivables within the Trust are owned by our wholly-owned, bankruptcy remote subsidiary, TRC, and thus are not available to general creditors of Target.

Inventory

Substantially all of our inventory and the related cost of sales are accounted for under the retail inventory accounting method using the last-in, first-out (LIFO) basis. Inventory is stated at the lower of LIFO cost or market. Inventory also includes a LIFO provision that is calculated based on inventory levels, markup rates and internally generated retail price indices. Our only accumulated LIFO reserve relates to Target Commercial Interiors and is immaterial to our consolidated financial statements. Because we have experienced price deflation recently, we have not recorded a LIFO provision for Target Stores.

Other Current Assets

Other current assets as of January 29, 2005 and January 31, 2004 consist of the following:

	2004	2003
Vendor income and other receivables	$ 428	$ 391
Deferred taxes	344	236
Other	452	373
Total	$ 1,224	$ 1,000

In addition to vendor income, other receivables relate primarily to pharmacy receivables and merchandise sourcing services provided to third parties.

Property and Equipment

Property and equipment are recorded at cost, less accumulated depreciation. Depreciation is computed using the straight-line method over estimated useful lives. Depreciation expense for the years 2004, 2003 and 2002 was $1,232 million, $1,068 million and $942 million, respectively. Accelerated depreciation methods are generally used for income tax purposes. Repair and maintenance costs were $453 million, $393 million and $355 million in 2004, 2003 and 2002, respectively.

Estimated useful lives by major asset category are as follows:

Asset	Life (in years)
Buildings and improvements	8-39
Fixtures and equipment	4-15
Computer hardware and software	4

In accordance with SFAS No. 144, "Accounting for the Impairment or Disposal of Long-Lived Assets," all long-lived assets are reviewed when events or changes in circumstances indicate that the carrying value of the asset may not be recoverable. We review assets at the lowest level for which there are identifiable cash flows, which is usually at the store level. The carrying amount of the store assets is compared to the expected undiscounted future cash flows to be generated by those assets over the estimated remaining useful life of the store. Cash flows are projected for each store based upon historical results and expectations. In cases where the expected future cash flows and fair value are less than the carrying amount of the assets, those stores are considered impaired and the assets are written down to fair value. Fair value is based on appraisals or other reasonable methods to estimate fair value. Impairment losses are included in depreciation expense for assets held and in use and included within selling, general and administrative expense on assets classified as held for sale. No impairments were recorded in 2004 or 2003 as a result of the tests performed.

Other Non-current Assets

Other non-current assets as of January 29, 2005 and January 31, 2004 consist of the following:

	2004	2003
Prepaid pension expense	$ 711	$ 580
Cash value of life insurance	439	363
Goodwill and intangible assets	206	229
Other	155	205
Total	$ 1,511	$ 1,377

Goodwill and Intangible Assets

Goodwill and intangible assets are recorded within other non-current assets at cost less accumulated amortization. Amortization is computed on intangible assets with definite useful lives using the straight-line method over estimated useful lives that range from three to fifteen years. Amortization expense for the years 2004, 2003 and 2002 was $27 million, $30 million and $25 million, respectively. At January 29, 2005 and January 31, 2004, goodwill and intangible assets by major classes were as follows:

(millions)	Goodwill		Leasehold Acquisition Costs		Other		Total	
	2004	2003	2004	2003	2004	2003	2004	2003
Gross asset	$ 80	$ 80	$ 185	$ 182	$ 201	$ 200	$ 466	$ 462
Accumulated amortization	(20)	(20)	(52)	(34)	(188)	(179)	(260)	(233)
Net goodwill and intangible assets	$ 60	$ 60	$ 133	$ 148	$ 13	$ 21	$ 206	$ 229

As required, we adopted SFAS No. 142, "Goodwill and Other Intangible Assets," during the first quarter of 2002. In 2004, 2003 and 2002, the adoption of this statement reduced annual amortization expense of certain intangible assets by approximately $5 million (less than $.01 per share). The estimated aggregate amortization expense of our definite-lived intangible assets for each of the five succeeding fiscal years, 2005 to 2009, is expected to be $24 million, $22 million, $20 million, $19 million and $19 million, respectively. During 2004, goodwill with an approximate carrying value of $63 million was sold as part of the Marshall Field's transaction. There was no goodwill included in the Mervyn's sale transaction that also occurred in 2004.

Discounted cash flow models were used in determining fair value for the purposes of the required annual goodwill impairment analysis. No impairments were recorded in 2004, 2003 and 2002 as a result of the tests performed.

Accounts Payable

Our accounting policy is to reduce accounts payable when checks to vendors clear the bank from which they were drawn. Outstanding checks included in accounts payable were $992 million and $966 million at year-end 2004 and 2003, respectively.

Accrued Liabilities

Accrued liabilities as of January 29, 2005 and January 31, 2004 consist of the following:

	2004	2003
Wages and benefits	$ 412	$ 369
Taxes payable	287	245
Gift card liability	214	169
Other	720	505
Total	$ 1,633	$ 1,288

Taxes payable consist of real estate, employee withholdings and sales tax liabilities. Gift card liability represents the amount of gift cards that have been issued but have not been presented for redemption.

Commitments and Contingencies

At January 29, 2005, our obligations included notes and debentures of $9,447 million (discussed in detail under Notes Payable and Long-term Debt below), the present value of capital lease obligations of $91 million and total future payments of operating leases with total contractual lease payments of $3,049 million, including certain options to extend the lease term that are expected to be exercised in the amount of $1,415 million (discussed in detail under Leases on page 32). In addition, commitments for the purchase, construction, lease or remodeling of real estate, facilities and equipment were approximately $544 million at year-end 2004. Merchandise royalty commitments of approximately $102 million are due during the five-year period ending in 2009. Throughout the year, we enter into various commitments to purchase inventory. In addition to the accounts payable reflected in our Consolidated Statements of Financial Position on page 25, we had commitments with various vendors for the purchase of inventory as of January 29, 2005. These purchase commitments are cancelable by their terms.

We expect to receive a share of the proceeds from the $3 billion Visa/MasterCard antitrust litigation settlement, as we are a member of the class action lawsuit. However, the amount and timing of the payment are not certain at this time.

We are exposed to claims and litigation arising out of the ordinary course of business and use various methods to resolve these matters in a manner that we believe serves the best interest of our shareholders and other constituents. Our policy is to disclose pending lawsuits and other known claims that we expect may have a material impact on our results of operations, cash flows or financial condition. Other than the matter discussed above, we do not believe any of the currently identified claims and litigated matters meet this criterion, either individually or in the aggregate.

Notes Payable and Long-term Debt

At January 29, 2005, no notes payable were outstanding. The average amount of notes payable outstanding during 2004 was $55 million at a weighted average interest rate of 1.3 percent. In 2004, notes payable balances fluctuated significantly during the year due to seasonal financing needs, proceeds from sale of Marshall Field's and Mervyn's and other factors. On July 28, 2004, our short-term borrowing reached $1,422 million, its highest level for the year.

At January 31, 2004, no notes payable were outstanding. The average amount of notes payable outstanding during 2003 was $377 million at a weighted average interest rate of 1.2 percent. On October 31, 2003, our short-term borrowing reached $1,409 million, its highest level for the year.

At January 29, 2005, two committed credit agreements totaling $1,600 million were in place through a group of 25 banks at specified rates. Of these credit lines, an $800 million credit facility expires in June 2005 and includes a one-year term-out option to June 2006. The remaining $800 million credit facility expires in June 2008. There were no balances outstanding at any time during 2004 or 2003 under these agreements.

In 2004, we issued no long-term debt. We called or repurchased $542 million of long-term debt with an average remaining life of 24 years and a weighted average interest rate of 7.0 percent, resulting in a pre-tax loss of $89 million (approximately $.06 per share), reflected in interest expense.

In 2003, we issued $500 million of long-term debt maturing in 2008 at 3.38 percent, $200 million of long-term debt maturing in 2018 at 4.88 percent and $500 million of long-term debt maturing in 2013 at 4.00 percent. We also called or repurchased $297 million of long-term debt with an average remaining life of 20 years and a weighted average interest rate of 7.8 percent, resulting in a pre-tax loss of $15 million (approximately $.01 per share), reflected in interest expense.

The portion of long-term debt secured by credit card receivables was $750 million at January 29, 2005. On January 31, 2004, we had $1,500 million of long-term debt secured by credit card receivables, $750 million of which was classified as current portion of long-term debt.

At year-end, our debt portfolio, including adjustments related to swap transactions discussed in the following derivatives section, was as follows:

Notes Payable and Long-term Debt

(millions)	January 29, 2005		January 31, 2004	
	Rate *	Balance	Rate *	Balance
Notes payable	—% $ —		—% $ —	
Notes and debentures:				
Due 2004-2008	4.0	4,045	3.1	4,953
Due 2009-2013	5.9	3,726	5.8	3,795
Due 2014-2018	3.3	234	2.3	227
Due 2019-2023	9.3	213	9.3	214
Due 2024-2028	6.7	325	6.7	400
Due 2029-2033	6.6	904	6.7	1,300
Total notes payable, notes and debentures **	5.2% $	9,447	4.7% $	10,889
Capital lease obligations		91		129
Less: current portion		(504)		(863)
Notes payable and long-term debt	$	9,034	$	10,155

---

*   *Reflects the weighted average stated interest rate as of year-end, including the impact of interest rate swaps.*

**   *The estimated fair value of total notes payable, notes and debentures, using a discounted cash flow analysis based on our incremental interest rates for similar types of financial instruments, was $10,171 million at January 29, 2005 and $11,681 million at January 31, 2004.*

Required principal payments on long-term debt over the next five years, excluding capital lease obligations, are $501 million in 2005, $751 million in 2006, $1,321 million in 2007, $1,451 million in 2008 and $751 million in 2009.

Derivatives

Our derivative instruments are primarily interest rate swaps which hedge the fair value of certain debt by effectively converting interest from a fixed rate to a variable rate. We also hold derivative instruments to manage our exposure to risks associated with the effect of equity market returns on our non-qualified defined contribution plans as discussed on page 34.

At January 29, 2005 and January 31, 2004, interest rate swaps were outstanding in notional amounts totaling $2,850 million and $2,150 million, respectively. The change in market value of an interest rate swap as well as the offsetting change in market value of the hedged debt is recognized into earnings in the current period. Ineffectiveness would result when changes in the market value of the hedged debt are not completely offset by changes in the market value of the interest rate swap. There was no ineffectiveness recognized in 2004 or 2003 related to these instruments. The fair value of outstanding interest rate swaps and net unamortized gains from terminated interest rate swaps was $45 million at January 29, 2005 and $97 million at January 31, 2004.

During 2004, we entered into two interest rate swaps with notional amounts of $200 million and two interest rate swaps with notional amounts of $250 million. We also terminated an interest rate swap with a notional amount of $200 million, resulting in a loss of $16 million that will be amortized into expense over the remaining life of the hedged debt. During 2003, we entered into interest rate swaps with notional amounts of $200 million, $500 million and $400 million. We also terminated an interest rate swap with a notional amount of $400 million, resulting in a gain of $24 million that will be amortized into income over the remaining life of the hedged debt. In 2004 and 2003, the gains and losses amortized into income for terminated swaps were not material to our results of operations.

Interest Rate Swaps Outstanding at Year-end

(millions)

	January 29, 2005			January 31, 2004		
Notional Amount	Receive Fixed	Pay Floating *	Notional Amount		Receive Fixed	Pay Floating *
$ 500	7.5%	2.4%	$	500	7.5%	1.2%
200	5.8	3.3		—	—	—
550	4.6	3.3		550	4.6	1.3
500	4.4	3.2		500	4.4	1.2
400	4.4	3.3		400	4.4	1.4
200	3.9	2.4		—	—	—
250	3.8	2.5		—	—	—
250	3.8	2.4		—	—	—
—	—	—		200	4.9	1.1
$ 2,850			$	2,150		

Reflects floating interest rate accrued at the end of the year.

The weighted average life of the interest rate swaps was approximately 3 years at January 29, 2005.

Leases

Assets held under capital leases are included in property and equipment and are charged to depreciation and interest over the life of the lease. Operating leases are not capitalized and lease rentals are expensed on a straight-line basis over the life of the lease. Rent expense on buildings, classified in selling, general and administrative expense, includes percentage rents that are based on a percentage of retail sales over contractual levels. Total rent expense was $240 million in 2004, $150 million in 2003 and $150 million in 2002. Most of the long-term leases include options to renew, with terms varying from one to 50 years. Certain leases also include options to purchase the property.

Future minimum lease payments required under noncancelable lease agreements existing at January 29, 2005, were:

Future Minimum Lease Payments

(millions)	Operating Leases	Capital Leases
2005	$ 146	$ 12
2006	142	12
2007	137	13
2008	117	13
2009	102	12
After 2009	2,405	127
Total future minimum lease payments	$ 3,049***	$ 189
Less: Interest *		(98)
Present value of minimum capital lease payments		$ 91**

*   *Calculated using the interest rate at inception for each lease.*
**   *Includes current portion of $3 million.*
*** *Total contractual lease payments include certain options to extend lease terms, in the amount of $1,415, that are expected to be exercised because the investment in leasehold improvement is significant.*

Income Taxes

Reconciliation of tax rates is as follows:

Tax Rate Reconciliation

	2004	2003	2002
Federal statutory rate	35.0%	35.0%	35.0%
State income taxes, net of federal tax benefit	3.3	3.3	3.4
Dividends on ESOP stock	(0.2)	(0.2)	(0.2)
Work opportunity tax credits	(0.2)	(0.2)	(0.2)
Other	(0.1)	(0.1)	0.2
Effective tax rate	37.8%	37.8%	38.2%

The components of the provision for income taxes were:

Income Tax Provision: Expense

(millions)	2004	2003	2002
Current:			
Federal	$ 908	$ 669	$ 550
State	144	107	93
	1,052	776	643
Deferred:			
Federal	83	184	185
State	11	24	23
	94	208	208
Total	$ 1,146	$ 984	$ 851

The components of the net deferred tax asset/(liability) were:

Net Deferred Tax Asset/(Liability)

(millions)	January 29, 2005	January 31, 2004
Gross deferred tax assets:		
Deferred compensation	$ 332	$ 297
Self-insured benefits	179	143
Accounts receivable valuation allowance	147	133
Inventory	47	44
Postretirement health care obligation	38	42
Other	128	53
	871	712
Gross deferred tax liabilities:		
Property and equipment	(1,136)	(806)
Pension	(268)	(218)
Other	(96)	(84)
	(1,500)	(1,108)
Total	$ (629)	$ (396)

In the Consolidated Statement of Financial Position, the current deferred tax asset balance is the net of all current deferred tax assets and current deferred tax liabilities. The non-current deferred tax liability is the net of all non-current deferred tax assets and non-current deferred tax liabilities.

Approximately $566 million of the proceeds attributable to the real properties sold in the Marshall Field's and Mervyn's dispositions were used to acquire replacement properties which will be used in our business. Approximately $371 million of the gain related to the sold real properties was deferred for income tax purposes as required by Section 1031 of the Internal Revenue Code until such time as the replacement properties are disposed.

Other Non-current Liabilities

Other non-current liabilities as of January 29, 2005 and January 31, 2004 consist of the following:

	2004	2003
Deferred compensation	$ 528	$ 464
Worker's compensation and general liability	317	286
Other	192	167
Total	$ 1,037	$ 917

Share Repurchase

In June 2004, our Board of Directors authorized the repurchase of $3 billion of our common stock, which we expect to complete over two to three years. This authorization replaced our previous repurchase programs that were authorized by our Board of Directors in January 1999 and March 2000. We repurchased 29 million shares at an average price per share of $44.68 during 2004, at a total cost of $1,290 million.

Stock-based Compensation

We maintain a long-term incentive plan for key employees and non-employee members of our Board of Directors. Our long-term incentive plan allows for the grant of equity-based compensation awards, including stock options, performance share awards, restricted stock awards, or a combination of awards. A majority of the awards are non-qualified stock options that vest annually in equal amounts over a four-year period. Therefore, in accordance with SFAS No. 23R, we recognize compensation expense for these awards on a straight-line basis over the four-year vesting period. These options generally expire no later than ten years after the date of the grant. Options granted to the non-employee members of our Board of Directors vest after one year and have a ten-year term. Performance share awards represent shares issuable in the future based upon attainment of specified levels of future financial performance. We use a three or four year performance measurement period for performance share awards. The number of unissued common shares reserved for future grants under the stock-based compensation plans was 51,560,249 at January 29, 2005 and 19,279,658 at January 31, 2004.

Options and Performance Share Awards Outstanding

	Options						Performance Shares
	Total Outstanding			Currently Exercisable			
(options and shares in thousands)	Number of Options	Average Price *	Average Life **	Number of Options	Average Price *	Average Life **	Potentially Issuable
February 2, 2002	31,315 $ 24.07		5.7	17,629 $ 17.04		5.7	—
Granted	6,096	30.60					552
Canceled	(561)	35.55					
Exercised	(2,063)	12.22					
February 1, 2003	34,787 $ 25.73		5.5	21,931 $ 20.89		5.4	552
Granted	4,638	38.34					573
Canceled	(407)	34.77					
Exercised	(2,859)	12.58					
January 31, 2004	36,159 $ 28.28		6.2	23,689 $ 24.48		5.2	1,125
Granted	4,072	49.12					629
Canceled/forfeited	(513)	35.32					(73)
Exercised/earned	(7,727)	20.95					(73)
January 29, 2005	**31,991 $ 32.59**		**5.8**	**22,102 $ 28.79**		**5.3**	**1,608**

* *Weighted average exercise price.*
** *Weighted average contractual life remaining in years.*

Total compensation expense related to stock-based compensation, which is the total fair value of shares vested was $60 million, $57 million and $49 million, during 2004, 2003 and 2002, respectively. The weighted-average grant date fair value of options granted during 2004, 2003 and 2002 was $13.10, $11.04 and $10.07, respectively. The total intrinsic value of options (the amount by which the stock price exceeded the strike price of the option on the date of exercise) that were exercised during 2004, 2003 and 2002 was $201 million, $72 million and $66 million, respectively.

Nonvested Options and Performance Share Awards

(options and shares in thousands)	Weighted Average Stock Options	Fair Value at Grant Date	Weighted Average Performance Shares	Fair Value at Grant Date
Nonvested at February 1, 2004	12,470	$ 11.07	1,125	$ 34.33
Granted	4,072	13.10	419	49.43
Vested/earned	(6,237)	11.25	(73)	34.44
Forfeited/cancelled	(416)	11.00	(73)	34.44
Nonvested at January 29, 2005	**9,889**	**$ 11.83**	**1,398**	**$ 38.84**

As of January 29, 2005, there was $104 million of total unrecognized compensation expense related to nonvested share-based compensation arrangements granted under our plans. That cost is expected to be recognized over a weighted-average period of 1.5 years.

We have elected to adopt the provisions of SFAS No. 123R in 2004 under the modified retrospective transition method. The beginning balances of deferred taxes, paid-in capital and retained earnings for 2003 have been restated by $54 million, $143 million and $90 million, respectively, to recognize compensation cost for fiscal years 1996 through 2002 in the amounts previously reported in the Notes to Consolidated Financial Statements under the provisions of SFAS No. 123. The requirements of SFAS No. 123R are discussed on page 23.

The Black-Scholes model was used to estimate the fair value of the options at grant date based on the following assumptions:

	2004	2003	2002
Dividend yield	.7%	.8%	.8%
Volatility	22%	29%	35%
Risk-free interest rate	3.8%	3.0%	3.0%
Expected life in years	5.5	5.0	5.0

Defined Contribution Plans

Employees who meet certain eligibility requirements can participate in a defined contribution 401(k) plan by investing up to 80 percent of their compensation. Highly compensated employees, however, are further limited by federal law and related regulation. Subject to these limits, we match 100 percent of each employee's contribution up to 5 percent of total compensation. Our contribution to the plan is initially invested in Target Corporation common stock but once vested after a period of three years the amounts are free to be diversified. Benefits expense related to these matching contributions was $118 million, $117 million and $111 million in 2004, 2003 and 2002, respectively.

In addition, we maintain other non-qualified, unfunded plans that allow participants who are otherwise limited by qualified plan statutes or regulations. They can defer compensation including remaining company match amounts, and earn returns tied to the results of either our 401(k) plan investment choices, including Target stock, or in the case of a frozen plan, market levels of interest rates, plus an additional return determined by the terms of each plan. We recognized benefits expense for these non-qualified plans of $63 million and $86 million in 2004 and 2003, respectively, and income of $20 million in 2002. We manage the risk of offering these retirement savings plans through a variety of activities, which include investing in vehicles that offset a substantial portion of our exposure to these returns. Including the impact of these related investments, net benefits expense from these plans was $23 million, $28 million, and $16 million in 2004, 2003, and 2002, respectively. We adjusted our position in some of the investment vehicles resulting in the repurchase of 0.8 million, 1.5 million and 0.5 million shares of our common stock in 2004, 2003 and 2002, respectively.

In 2004 and 2003, certain retired executives accepted our offer to exchange our obligation to them under our frozen non-qualified plan for cash or deferrals in our current non-qualified plans, which resulted in expense of $17 million in both years. Additionally, during 2002, certain non-qualified pension and survivor benefits owed to current executives were exchanged for deferrals in our current non-qualified plans and certain retired executives accepted our offer to exchange our obligation to them in our frozen non-qualified plan for deferrals in our current plans. These exchanges resulted in expense of $33 million. We expect lower future expenses as a result of these transactions because they were designed to be economically neutral or slightly favorable to us.

Participants in our non-qualified plans deferred compensation of $33 million, $42 million and $35 million in 2004, 2003 and 2002, respectively.

Pension and Postretirement Health Care Benefits

We have a qualified defined benefit pension plan that covers all U.S. employees who meet certain age, length of service and hours worked per year requirements. We also have unfunded non-qualified pension plans for employees who have qualified plan compensation restrictions. Benefits are provided based upon years of service and the employee's compensation. Retired employees also become eligible for certain health care benefits if they meet minimum age and service requirements and agree to contribute a portion of the cost. Prior to the end of 2004, but after the measurement date, we merged our three qualified U.S. pension plans into one plan. The expected impact of this merger on future accounting results is immaterial.

The Medicare Prescription Drug, Improvements and Modernization Act of 2003 (the Act) was signed into law in December 2003. As a result of the Act we recorded a reduction in our accumulated post-retirement benefit obligation of $7 million in 2004. In addition, the expense amounts shown in the table below reflect a $1 million reduction due to the amortization of the actuarial gain and reduction in interest cost due to the effects of the Act.

Obligations and Funded Status at October31, 2004

(millions)	Pension Benefits				Postretirement Health Care Benefits	
	Qualified Plans		Non-qualified Plans			
	2004	2003	2004	2003	2004	2003
Change in Benefit Obligation						
Benefit obligation at beginning of measurement period	$ 1,333	$ 1,078	$ 29	$ 23	$ 123	$ 116
Service cost	78	73	1	1	3	2
Interest cost	82	74	2	2	7	8
Actuarial loss	68	164	4	6	(6)	7
Benefits paid	(65)	(56)	(3)	(3)	(13)	(10)
Plan amendments	19	—	1	—	(7)	—
Settlement	—	—	—	—	—	—
Benefit obligation at end of measurement period	$ 1,515	$ 1,333	$ 34	$ 29	$ 107	$ 123
Change in Plan Assets						
Fair value of plan assets at beginning of measurement period	$ 1,405	$ 1,058	$ —	$ —	$ —	$ —
Actual return on plan assets	157	203	—	—	—	—
Employer contribution	201	200	3	3	13	10
Benefits paid	(65)	(56)	(3)	(3)	(13)	(10)
Fair value of plan assets at end of measurement period	$ 1,698	$ 1,405	$ —	$ —	$ —	$ —
Funded status	$ 183	$ 72	$ (34)	$ (29)	$ (107)	$ (123)
Unrecognized actuarial loss	584	587	15	12	6	12
Unrecognized prior service cost	(39)	(65)	2	3	—	1
Net amount recognized	$ 728	$ 594	$ (17)	$ (14)	$ (101)	$ (110)

Amounts recognized in the Statements of Financial Position consist of:

(millions)	Pension Benefits				Postretirement Health Care Benefits	
	Qualified Plans		Non-qualified Plans			
	2004	2003	2004	2003	2004	2003
Prepaid benefit cost	$ 733	$ 600	$ —	$ —	$ —	$ —
Accrued benefit cost	(11)	(6)	(24)	(20)	(101)	(110)
Intangible assets	—	—	2	3	n/a	n/a
Accumulated OCI	6	—	5	3	n/a	n/a
Net amount recognized	$ 728	$ 594	$ (17)	$ (14)	$ (101)	$ (110)

The accumulated benefit obligation for all defined benefit pension plans was $1,501 million and $1,237 million at October 31, 2004 and 2003, respectively. The projected benefit obligation, accumulated benefit obligation and fair value of plan assets for the pension plans with an accumulated benefit obligation in excess of plan assets were $49 million, $45 million and $5 million, respectively, as of October 31, 2004 and $34 million, $30 million and $1 million, respectively, as of October 31, 2003.

Net Pension and Postretirement Health Care Benefits Expense

(millions)	Pension Benefits			Postretirement Health Care Benefits		
	2004	2003	2002	2004	2003	2002
Service cost benefits earned during the period	$ 79	$ 74	$ 58	$ 3	$ 2	$ 2
Interest cost on projected benefit obligation	84	75	75	7	8	8
Expected return on assets	(122)	(114)	(108)	—	—	—
Recognized losses	36	18	10	1	1	1
Recognized prior service cost	(7)	(7)	1	—	—	—
Settlement/curtailment charges	1	—	(12)	(7)	—	—
Total	$ 71	$ 46	$ 24	$ 4	$ 11	$ 11

The amortization of any prior service cost is determined using a straight-line amortization of the cost over the average remaining service period of employees expected to receive benefits under the plan. Curtailment gains recorded in 2004 were a result of the sale of Marshall Field's and Mervyn's. These curtailment gains are included in the gain on disposal of discontinued operations as a result of freezing the benefits for Marshall Field's and Mervyn's employees and retaining the related assets and obligations of the plans.

Assumptions

Weighted average assumptions used to determine benefit obligations at October 31:

	Pension Benefits		Postretirement Health Care Benefits	
	2004	2003	2004	2003
Discount rate	5.75%	6.25%	5.75%	6.25%
Average assumed rate of compensation increase	2.75%	3.25%	n/a	n/a

Weighted average assumptions used to determine net periodic benefit cost for years ended October 31:

	Pension Benefits		Postretirement Health Care Benefits	
	2004	2003	2004	2003
Discount rate	6.25%	7.00%	6.25%	7.00%
Expected long-term rate of return on plan assets	8.00%	8.50%	n/a	n/a
Average assumed rate of compensation increase	3.25%	4.00%	n/a	n/a

Our rate of return on qualified plans' assets has averaged 4.9 percent and 10.2 percent per year over the 5-year and 10-year periods, respectively, ending October 31, 2004 (our measurement date).

An increase in the cost of covered health care benefits of 6 percent was assumed for 2004. The rate is assumed to be 10 percent in 2005 and is reduced by 1 percent annually to 5 percent in 2010 and thereafter. The health care cost trend rate assumption may have a significant effect on the amounts reported.

A one percent change in assumed health care cost trend rates would have the following effects:

	1% Increase	1% Decrease
Effect on total of service and interest cost components of net periodic postretirement health care benefit cost	$ —	$ —
Effect on the health care component of the postretirement benefit obligation	$ 4	$ (4)

Additional Information

Our pension plan weighted average asset allocations at October 31, 2004 and 2003 by asset category are as follows:

Asset Category

	2004	2003
Equity securities	**58%**	56%
Debt securities	**26**	26
Other	**16**	18
Total	**100%**	100%

Our asset allocation strategy for 2005 targets 55 percent in equity securities, 25 percent in debt securities and 20 percent in other assets. Equity securities include our common stock in amounts substantially less than 1 percent of total plan assets at October 31, 2004 and 2003. Other assets include private equity, mezzanine and distressed debt and timber and less than a 5 percent allocation to real estate. Our expected long-term rate of return assumptions as of October 31, 2004 are 8.5 percent, 5 percent and 10 percent for equity securities, debt securities and other assets, respectively.

Contributions

Given the qualified pension plans' funded position, we are not required to make any contributions in 2005. In similar situations in the past, we have chosen to make discretionary contributions for various purposes, including minimizing Pension Benefit Guaranty Corporation premium payments and maintaining the fully-funded status of the plans. In 2005, such discretionary contributions could range from $0 to $50 million. We expect to make contributions in the range of $5 million to $15 million to our other postretirement benefit plans in 2005.

Estimated Future Benefit Payments

The following benefit payments, which reflect expected future service, as appropriate, are expected to be paid:

(millions)	Pension Benefits	Postretirement Health Care Benefits
2005	$ 59	$ 8
2006	62	8
2007	66	8
2008	70	9
2009	75	9
2010–2014	$ 476	$ 53

Quarterly Results (Unaudited)

Due to the seasonal nature of our business, fourth quarter operating results typically represent a substantially larger share of total year revenues and earnings due to the inclusion of the holiday shopping season. The same accounting policies are followed in preparing quarterly financial data as are followed in preparing annual data. The table below summarizes results by quarter for 2004 and 2003:

(millions, except per share data)	First Quarter		Second Quarter		Third Quarter		Fourth Quarter		Total Year	
	2004	2003	2004	2003	2004	2003	2004	2003	2004	2003
Total revenues	$ 10,180	$ 8,928	$ 10,556	$ 9,594	$ 10,909	$ 9,827	$ 15,194	$ 13,676	$ 46,839	$ 42,025
Gross margin	$ 3,140	$ 2,706	$ 3,268	$ 2,874	$ 3,300	$ 2,909	$ 4,529	$ 4,050	$ 14,237	$ 12,539
Earnings from continuing operations	$ 392	$ 313	$ 360	$ 322	$ 324	$ 262	$ 809	$ 722	$ 1,885	$ 1,619
Earnings from discontinued operations, net of $25, $18, $19, $18, $2, $18, $62, $46 and $116 tax	$ 40	$ 29	$ 31	$ 29	$ 4	$ 31	$ —	$ 101	$ 75	$ 190
Gain/(loss) on disposal of discontinued operations, net of $650, $132, $(21), and $761 tax (c)	$ —	$ —	$ 1,019	$ —	$ 203	$ —	$ 16	$ —	$ 1,238	$ —
Net earnings (a) (b)	$ 432	$ 342	$ 1,410	$ 351	$ 531	$ 293	$ 825	$ 823	$ 3,198	$ 1,809
Basic earnings per share (d)										
Continuing operations	$ 0.43	$ 0.34	$ 0.40	$ 0.35	$ 0.36	$ 0.29	$ 0.91	$ 0.79	$ 2.09	$ 1.78
Discontinued operations	$ 0.04	$ 0.03	$ 0.03	$ 0.03	$ —	$ 0.03	$ —	$ 0.11	$ 0.08	$ 0.21
Gain from discontinued operations	$ —	$ —	$ 1.12	$ —	$ 0.23	$ —	$ 0.01	$ —	$ 1.37	$ —
Basic earnings per share (a) (b)	$ 0.47	$ 0.37	$ 1.55	$ 0.38	$ 0.59	$ 0.32	$ 0.92	$ 0.90	$ 3.54	$ 1.99
Diluted earnings per share (d)										
Continuing operations	$ 0.43	$ 0.34	$ 0.39	$ 0.35	$ 0.36	$ 0.29	$ 0.90	$ 0.79	$ 2.07	$ 1.76
Discontinued operations	$ 0.04	$ 0.03	$ 0.03	$ 0.03	$ —	$ 0.03	$ —	$ 0.11	$ 0.08	$ 0.21
Gain from discontinued operations	$ —	$ —	$ 1.11	$ —	$ 0.23	$ —	$ 0.01	$ —	$ 1.36	$ —
Diluted earnings per share (a) (b)	$ 0.47	$ 0.37	$ 1.53	$ 0.38	$ 0.59	$ 0.32	$ 0.91	$ 0.90	$ 3.51	$ 1.97
Dividends declared per share (d)	$ .070	$ .060	$ .080	$ .070	$ .080	$ .070	$ .080	$ .070	$ .310	$ .270
Closing common stock price (e)										
High	$ 45.63	$ 33.44	$ 46.43	$ 39.82	$ 50.02	$ 41.54	$ 52.43	$ 40.15	$ 52.43	$ 41.54
Low	$ 38.59	$ 26.06	$ 40.80	$ 33.06	$ 40.42	$ 37.55	$ 48.50	$ 37.05	$ 38.59	$ 26.06

(a) *Net earnings for first, second and third quarter of 2004 and all four quarters of 2003 has been adjusted to reflect the impact of the SFAS No. 123R restatement for those periods. The amount of the restatement was $6 million for each of the three quarters in 2004 and $8 million for each of the four quarters in 2003. The restatement impact on per share amounts for each respective quarter was all less than $0.01 per share.*

(b) *Target adjusted its method of accounting for leases related to a specific category of owned store locations on leased land which resulted in a non-cash adjustment, primarily attributable to an increase in the straight-line rent accrual, of $65 million ($0.04 per share) in the fourth quarter of 2004.*

(c) *Minor tax adjustments related to the dispositions of Marshall Field's and Mervyn's were recorded in fourth quarter 2004.*

(d) *Per share amounts are computed independently for each of the quarters presented. The sum of the quarters may not equal the total year amount due to the impact of changes in average quarterly shares outstanding.*

(e) *Our common stock is listed on the New York Stock Exchange and Pacific Exchange. At March 21, 2005, there were 18,030 registered shareholders and the closing common stock price was $50.28 per share.*

**Report of Independent Registered Public Accounting Firm
on Consolidated Financial Statements**

**The Board of Directors and Shareholders
Target Corporation**

We have audited the accompanying consolidated statements of financial position of Target Corporation and subsidiaries as of January 29, 2005, and January 31, 2004, and the related consolidated results of operations, cash flows and shareholders' investment for each of the three years in the period ended January 29, 2005. These financial statements are the responsibility of the Corporation's management. Our responsibility is to express an opinion on these financial statements based on our audits.

We conducted our audits in accordance with the standards of the Public Company Accounting Oversight Board (PCAOB) (United States). Those standards require that we plan and perform the audit to obtain reasonable assurance about whether the financial statements are free of material misstatement. An audit includes examining, on a test basis, evidence supporting the amounts and disclosures in the financial statements. An audit also includes assessing the accounting principles used and significant estimates made by management, as well as evaluating the overall financial statement presentation. We believe that our audits provide a reasonable basis for our opinion.

In our opinion, the financial statements referred to above present fairly, in all material respects, the consolidated financial position of Target Corporation and subsidiaries at January 29, 2005, and January 31, 2004, and the consolidated results of their operations and their cash flows for each of the three years in the period ended January 29, 2005, in conformity with U.S. generally accepted accounting principles.

We also have audited, in accordance with the standards of the PCAOB (United States), the effectiveness of the Corporation's internal control over financial reporting as of January 29, 2005, based on criteria established in Internal Control – Integrated Framework issued by the Committee of Sponsoring Organizations of the Treadway Commission, and our report dated March 25, 2005, expressed an unqualified opinion thereon.

As discussed in the Stock-based Compensation note to the financial statements, effective February 1, 2004, the Corporation adopted Statement of Financial Accounting Standards No. 123 (revised 2004), "Share-Based Payment" using the modified retrospective transition method.

Minneapolis, Minnesota   /s/ Ernst & Young LLP
March 25, 2005

Report of Management on Internal Control

Our management is responsible for establishing and maintaining adequate internal control over financial reporting, as such term is defined in Exchange Act Rules 13a-15(f). Under the supervision and with the participation of our management, including our chief executive officer and chief financial officer, we assessed the effectiveness of our internal control over financial reporting as of January 29, 2005 based on the framework in Internal Control – Integrated Framework issued by the Committee of Sponsoring Organizations of the Treadway Commission. Based on our assessment we conclude that the Corporation's internal control over financial reporting is effective based on those criteria.

Our management's assessment of the effectiveness of our internal control over financial reporting as of January 29, 2005 has been audited by Ernst & Young LLP, an independent registered public accounting firm, as stated in their report which is included herein.

/s/ Robert J.   /s/ Douglas A.
Ulrich   Scovanner
Robert J. Ulrich   Douglas A. Scovanner
Chairman of the Board and   Executive Vice President and
Chief Executive Officer   Chief Financial Officer
March 25, 2005

**Report of Independent Registered Public Accounting Firm
on Internal Control over Financial Reporting
The Board of Directors and Shareholders
Target Corporation**

We have audited management's assessment, included in the accompanying Report of Management on Internal Control, that Target Corporation and subsidiaries maintained effective internal control over financial reporting as of January 29, 2005, based on criteria established in Internal Control – Integrated Framework issued by the Committee of Sponsoring Organizations of the Treadway Commission (the COSO criteria). The Corporation's management is responsible for maintaining effective internal control over financial reporting and for its assessment of the effectiveness of internal control over financial reporting. Our responsibility is to express an opinion on management's assessment and an opinion on the effectiveness of the Corporation's internal control over financial reporting based on our audit.

We conducted our audit in accordance with the standards of the Public Company Accounting Oversight Board (PCAOB) (United States). Those standards require that we plan and perform the audit to obtain reasonable assurance about whether effective internal control over financial reporting was maintained in all material respects. Our audit included obtaining an understanding of internal control over financial reporting, evaluating management's assessment, testing and evaluating the design and operating effectiveness of internal control, and performing such other procedures as we considered necessary in the circumstances. We believe that our audit provides a reasonable basis for our opinion.

A company's internal control over financial reporting is a process designed to provide reasonable assurance regarding the reliability of financial reporting and the preparation of financial statements for external purposes in accordance with generally accepted accounting principles. A company's internal control over financial reporting includes those policies and procedures that (1) pertain to the maintenance of records that, in reasonable detail, accurately and fairly reflect the transactions and dispositions of the assets of the company; (2) provide reasonable assurance that transactions are recorded as necessary to permit preparation of financial statements in accordance with generally accepted accounting principles, and that receipts and expenditures of the company are being made only in accordance with authorizations of management and directors of the company; and (3) provide reasonable assurance regarding prevention or timely detection of unauthorized acquisition, use, or disposition of the company's assets that could have a material effect on the financial statements.

Because of its inherent limitations, internal control over financial reporting may not prevent or detect misstatements. Also, projections of any evaluation of effectiveness to future periods are subject to the risk that controls may become inadequate because of changes in conditions, or that the degree of compliance with the policies or procedures may deteriorate.

In our opinion, management's assessment that Target Corporation and subsidiaries maintained effective internal control over financial reporting as of January 29, 2005, is fairly stated, in all material respects, based on the COSO criteria. Also, in our opinion, the Corporation maintained, in all material respects, effective internal control over financial reporting as of January 29, 2005, based on the COSO criteria.

We also have audited, in accordance with the standards of the PCAOB (United States), the consolidated statements of financial position of Target Corporation and subsidiaries as of January 29, 2005, and January 31, 2004, and the related consolidated results of operations, cash flows, and shareholders' investment for each of the three years in the period ended January 29, 2005, of Target Corporation and subsidiaries, and our report dated March 25, 2005, expressed an unqualified opinion thereon.

Minneapolis, Minnesota   /s/ Ernst & Young LLP
March 25, 2005

10-K: A comprehensive summary of a company's performance firms are required to submit to the SEC within 60 days of the end of the company's fiscal year.

A

Accelerated depreciation: Methods in which larger amounts of the cost of an asset are written-off early in the life of an asset and smaller amounts are written-off later in the life of the asset.

Accounting: The process of identifying, measuring, and communicating financial business information to various users.

Accounting cycle: The steps an accountant follows to analyze and record business transactions, prepare the financial statements, and get ready for the next accounting period.

Accounting equation: Assets = Liabilities + Owners' Equity

Accounts receivable turnover ratio: Net credit sales divided by average net accounts receivable; measures a firm's ability to collect the cash from its credit customers.

Accounts receivable: A current asset that arises from sales on credit of goods and services to a customer; the total customers owe to a firm.

Accrual: A transaction in which the revenue has been earned or the expense has been incurred, but no cash has been exchanged.

Accrual-basis accounting: Means that accountants recognize revenue when it is earned and expenses when they are incurred to earn that revenue—no matter when the cash is received or paid.

Accrued expenses: Expenses incurred but not yet paid in cash or previously recorded.

Accrued liability: The liability for an expense incurred but not yet paid.

Accrued revenue: Revenue earned but not yet received in cash or previously recorded.

Accumulated depreciation: The total amount of depreciation that has been recorded during an asset's use. A company deducts accumulated depreciation from the cost of the asset on the balance sheet.

Activity method depreciation: The method of depreciation in which useful life is expressed in terms of the total units of activity or production expected from the asset, and the asset is written off in proportion to its activity during the accounting period.

Aging schedule: An analysis of the amounts owed to a firm by the length of time they have been outstanding.

Allowance for Uncollectible Accounts: An account that is a contra-asset to Accounts Receivable and is used to hold the credits until the firm can identify specific accounts that are bad and write them off.

Allowance method: A method of accounting for bad debts in which the amount of uncollectible accounts is estimated at the end of each accounting period.

Amortization: To write off the cost of a long-term asset over more than one accounting period.

Annuity: A series of equal cash receipts or cash payments over equally spaced intervals of time.

Asset turnover ratio: Measures how efficiently a company is using its assets.

Assets: Economic resources owned by a business as a result of past transactions that will be used in the future to generate benefits for the business.

Audit: An examination of a company's financial statements by certified public accountants to provide evidence that the financial position and the financial performance of the company are fairly stated.

Authorized shares: Maximum number of shares of stock a firm is authorized to offer to the public as specified in the corporate charter.

Available-for-sale securities: Investments the company may hold or sell; the company's intention is not clear enough to use one of the other categories—*held-to-maturity* or *trading*.

Average days in inventory: The average number of days an item is held in inventory; equal to 365 divided by the inventory turnover ratio.

B

Bad debts expense: The expense to record uncollectible accounts receivable.

Balance sheet: One of the four basic financial statements that shows the financial position of the firm at a specific point in time.

Bank reconciliation: A comparison between the general ledger Cash balance and the bank statement's Cash balance to identify the reasons for any differences.

Bank statement: A summary of the activity in a bank account sent each month to the account owner.

Bond: An interest-bearing, long-term note payable issued by corporations, universities, and governmental agencies.

Book value: The cost of an asset minus the total accumulated depreciation recorded for the asset.

C

Capital expenditure: A cost that will be recorded as an asset, not an expense, at the time it is incurred. Recall that this is called capitalizing a cost.

Capital structure: The combination of debt and equity that a company chooses.

Capitalizing: To record a cost on the balance sheet as an asset rather than recording it as an expense.

Carrying value (of a bond): The amount that the balance sheet will show as the net value of the bond, similar meaning to the carrying value of a fixed asset.

Cash equivalents: Highly liquid investments with a maturity of three months or less that a firm can easily convert into a known amount of cash.

Cash flow adequacy ratio: Measures the firm's ability to generate enough cash from operating activities to pay for its capital expenditures.

Cash from financing activities: All cash receipts and all cash disbursements from issuing debt, receiving contributions from owners, and paying dividends to owners.

Cash from investing activities: All cash receipts and cash disbursements from transactions involving long-term assets and investments in other firms.

Cash from operating activities: All cash receipts and cash disbursements that result from transactions involving revenues and expenses.

Certified public accountant (CPA): Someone who has met specific education and exam requirements that are set up by the states to make sure only individuals with the appropriate accounting knowledge and other qualifications can perform financial statement audits of corporations.

Chart of accounts: A list of all of the accounts in a firm's accounting records along with account numbers to assist in maintaining accurate accounting records.

Classified balance sheet: A balance sheet that shows a subtotal for many items including current assets and current liabilities.

Closing entries: End-of-period journal entries that formally reduce the revenue and expense accounts (and dividends account) to zero.

Common stock: A share of ownership in a corporation; the amount owners paid to get the stock is part of contributed capital on the balance sheet. The most widespread form of ownership in a corporation; common stockholders have a vote in the election of the firm's board of directors.

Comparability: Describes information that can be compared across firms because they use the same accounting principles.

Comprehensive income: The total of all items that affect shareholders' equity except transactions with the owners; comprehensive income has two parts: net income and other comprehensive income.

Consistency: The use of the same accounting methods from period to period.

Contra-asset: A type of account that offsets an asset. It is deducted from the asset on the balance sheet.

Contra-revenue: An account that is an offset to a revenue account and therefore deducted from the revenue for the financial statements.

Contra equity account: An account that is a reduction to total stockholders' equity.

Contributed capital: Equity resulting from the contributions of owners, also known as Paid-in capital.

Cooking the books: A slang expression that means to manipulate or falsify the firm's accounting records to make the firm's financial performance or position look better than it actually is.

Copyright: A form of legal protection for authors of "original works of authorship," provided by U.S. law.

Corporate governance: The way a firm governs itself, as executed by the board of directors. Corporate governance is also described as the set of relationships between the board of directors, management, shareholders, auditors, and any others with a stake in the company.

Cost of goods sold: The total cost of the merchandise sold during a period.

Credit (abbreviated as CR): The right side of an account.

Cumulative preferred stock: Stock whose holders must receive any past, unpaid dividends before a company can pay any current dividends to any shareholders.

Current assets: The assets the company plans to turn into cash or use to generate revenue in the next fiscal year.

Current cash debt coverage ratio: A ratio that measures a firm's ability to generate the cash it needs in the short-run;

calculated as net cash provided by operations divided by average current liabilities.

Current liabilities: Obligations the company will settle with current assets.

Current ratio: A liquidity ratio that measures a firm's ability to meet its short-term obligations.

D

Debit (abbreviated as DR): The left side of an account.

Debt-to-equity ratio: Total liabilities divided by total stockholders' equity. The ratio compares the value of claims of creditors with the value of claims of owners.

Debt-to-total-assets ratio: A solvency ratio defined as total liabilities divided by total assets.

Declining balance: An accelerated depreciation method based on the declining book value of an asset over its useful life.

Deferral: A transaction in which the cash is exchanged before the revenue is earned or the expense is incurred.

Deferred expense: An asset resulting from the payment of cash before the expense is incurred by using resources.

Deferred revenue: A liability resulting from the receipt of cash before the recognition of revenue.

Definitely determinable liabilities: Obligations that can be measured exactly, like the amount of a note payable.

Depletion: The amortization of a natural resource.

Deposits in-transit: Bank deposits made but not included on the month's bank statement because the deposit did not reach the bank's record-keeping department in time to be included.

Depreciation: A systematic, rational allocation process to recognize the expense of long-term assets over the periods in which the assets are used.

Depreciation expense: A single period's reduction to the cost of the asset, shown on the income statement; also the name of the account in which the expense is recorded.

Direct method: Way of preparing the statement of cash flows that shows every cash inflow and every cash outflow, identified by analyzing every item on the income statement.

Direct write-off method: A method of accounting for bad debts in which they are written off—booked as Bad Debts Expense—in the period in which they are identified as uncollectible.

Discontinued operations: Those parts of the firm that a company has eliminated by selling a division.

Discount on bonds payable: A contra-liability that is deducted from Bonds Payable on the balance sheet; the difference between the face value of the bonds and its selling price, when the selling price is less than the face value.

Discount rate: The interest rate used to compute the present value of future cash flows.

Discounting: Computing the present value of future cash flows.

Dividend declaration date: The date on which the board of directors decides a dividend will be paid and announces it to the shareholders.

Dividends: Distributions of a corporation's earnings to the shareholders.

Dividends in arrears: Dividends owed to holders of cumulative preferred stock but not yet declared.

Dividend yield ratio: Dividend per share divided by the current market price per share.

E

Earnings per share (EPS): Net income divided by the weighted average number of outstanding shares of (common) stock. The most well-known accounting number because financial analysts use it to evaluate a company's performance. EPS is a company's net income on a per share basis.

Estimated liabilities: Obligations with some uncertainty in the amount, like the cost involved in honoring a warranty.

Expenses: Costs incurred to earn revenue during an accounting period.

Extraordinary items: Events that are unusual in nature and infrequent in occurrence.

F

Financial Accounting Standards Board (FASB): A group of professional business people, accountants, and accounting scholars in the private sector (not government employees) who are responsible for setting current accounting standards.

Financial leverage: Using borrowed money to increase earnings.

Financing activities: Cash transactions involving a company's long-term creditors or owners—the firm's sources of capital.

First-in, first-out (FIFO) method: The inventory cost flow method that assumes the first items purchased are the first items sold.

FOB (free on board) destination: The vendor (selling firm) pays the shipping costs, so the buyer has no freight-in cost to account for.

FOB (free on board) shipping point: The buying firm pays the shipping costs. The amount is called freight-in and is included in the cost of the inventory.

Franchise: An agreement that authorizes someone to sell or distribute a company's goods or services in a certain area.

Free Cash Flow: Measures a firm's ability to engage in long-term investment opportunities; calculated as net cash flow from operations minus dividends and minus capital expenditures. Free Cash Flow = Net Cash from Operating Activities – Dividends – Capital Expenditures

Full-disclosure principle: The principle that requires companies to disclose any circumstances and events that would make a difference to the users of the statements.

G

(GAAP) Generally accepted accounting principles: A broad set of accounting guidelines that a firm must follow when preparing its financial statements.

General ledger: The primary record of a company's financial information. The general ledger contains all of the accounts maintained by the company—asset, liability, shareholders' equity, revenue, and expense accounts.

Going-concern assumption: The assumption that a company will continue operating in the foreseeable future.

Goodwill: The excess of cost over market value of the net assets when one company purchases another company.

Gross profit: The difference between sales revenue and cost of goods sold.

Gross profit ratio: Gross profit divided by sales revenue.

H

Held-to-maturity securities: Investments in debt securities that the company plans to hold until they mature.

Historical-cost principle: Measuring assets at their cost at the time of the purchase.

Horizontal analysis: A technique for evaluating financial statement amounts across time.

I

Impairment: A permanent decline in the market value of an asset such that its book value exceeds the market value.

Income statement: The financial statement that describes the financial performance of a company during an accounting period.

Indirect method: Way of preparing the statement of cash flows that starts with net income and makes adjustments for all the items that do not affect cash and adjustments for changes in current assets and current liabilities to arrive at cash from operating activities.

Intangible assets: Rights, privileges, or benefits that result from owning long-lived assets that do not have physical substance.

Interest: The cost of using someone else's money for some period of time.

Interest expense: Is calculated by multiplying the carrying value of a bond by the market rate of interest at the date of the bond's issue.

Interest payment: Is calculated by using the rate stated on the face of the bond.

Inventory turnover ratio: Cost of goods sold divided by average inventory cost. This ratio measures how quickly a firm is selling its inventory.

Inventory: Goods purchased by a firm to be sold to its customers or used to make products to be sold to its customers.

Investing activities: Cash transactions related to the purchase and sale of assets that last longer than a year.

Issued shares: Shares of stock that have been offered and sold to shareholders.

J

Journal: A record in which transactions are initially recorded in chronological order.

Journal entry: The record of a transaction using debits and credits.

L

Last-in, first-out (LIFO) method: The inventory cost flow method that assumes the last items purchased are the first items sold.

Liabilities: Amounts the business owes to creditors; the company's debts.

Liquidity ratios: Measure the company's ability to pay its current bills and operating costs.

Lower-of-cost-or-market (LCM) rule: Rule that requires firms to use the lower of either the cost or the market value (replacement cost) of its inventory on the date of the balance sheet.

M

Maker: The person or firm making the promise to pay a promissory note.

Market indicators: Ratios that relate the current market price of the company's stock to earnings or dividends.

Market interest rate: The interest rate investors demand for lending money to the firm.

Matching principle: Expenses are recognized—shown on the income statement—in the same period as the revenue they helped generate.

Modified Accelerated Cost Recovery System (MACRS): The common accelerated depreciation method used for taxes. It is not acceptable for GAAP.

Monetary unit assumption: An assumption that only information that can be expressed in monetary units (dollars in the United States) will be included in the financial statements.

Multiple-step income statement: An income statement that highlights the components of net income.

N

Net income: The difference between revenues and expenses when revenues exceed expenses for a specific period of time.

Net loss: The negative amount that results when expenses are greater than revenues.

Noncumulative preferred stock: Stock whose holders do not necessarily receive past, unpaid dividends; past dividends do not accumulate.

Notes to the financial statements: Information that describes the company's major accounting policies and provides other disclosures to help external users better understand the financial statements.

O

Operating activities: Those cash transactions that pertain to the day-to-day, general running of the business.

Operating cycle: The sequence of business activities starting with getting cash, using cash to purchase inputs, changing those inputs into products or services, and providing the product or service to customers, eventually getting cash back.

Ordinary annuity: An annuity whose payments are made at the end of each interval or period.

Outstanding checks: Checks written by a firm that have not yet cleared the bank. That is, the checks have not been presented to the bank for payment.

Outstanding shares: Shares of stock that are owned by shareholders rather than by the corporation; issued shares minus treasury shares.

Owners' equity: Claims of the owner to the firm's assets.

P

Par value: Value assigned to a share of stock in the corporate charter.

Patent: A property right that the U.S. government grants to an inventor "to exclude others from making, using, offering for sale, or selling the invention throughout the United States or importing the invention into the United States" for a specified period of time.

Payee: The person or firm receiving the payment from a promissory note.

Periodic inventory system: A method of record keeping that involves updating the accounting records only at the end of the accounting period.

Permanent accounts or real accounts: Accounts with balances that carry over from the end of one period to the beginning of the next; these accounts are never closed. They are the asset, liability, and shareholders' equity accounts.

Perpetual inventory system: A method of record keeping that involves updating the accounting records at the time of every purchase, sale, and return.

Posting: The process of transferring the amounts from the journal to the general ledger.

Preferred stock: A special type of ownership in a corporation; preferred stockholders don't get to vote for the board of directors, but they do get their dividends before the common shareholders.

Premium on bonds payable: An adjunct liability account that is added to Bonds Payable on the balance sheet; the difference between the face value of the bond and its selling price when the selling price is more than the face value.

Price–earnings (P/E) ratio: The market price of a share of stock divided by that stock's earnings per share.

Profit: The difference between revenue and the costs of earning that revenue.

Profitability ratios: Measure the operating or income performance of a company.

Profit margin ratio: Measures the percentage of each sales dollar that results in net income:

Promissory note: A written promise to pay a specific amount of money on demand or at a particular time.

Public Company Accounting Oversight Board (PCAOB): A private-sector, non-profit corporation created to oversee the auditors of public companies.

Purchase returns and allowances: Amounts that decrease the cost of inventory purchases due to returned or damaged merchandise.

Q

Quality of earnings: Refers to how well a reported earnings number communicates the firm's true performance.

Quick ratio: Cash, Accounts Receivable, and Short-Term Investments divided by current liabilities. This ratio measures a firm's ability to meet its current obligations.

R

Ratio: An expression of a mathematical relationship between one quantity and another.

Ratio analysis: Using ratios to analyze a firm's past performance and forecast its future performance.

Real accounts or permanent accounts: Accounts with balances that carry over from the end of one period to the beginning of the next; these accounts are never closed. They are the asset, liability, and shareholders' equity accounts.

Relative fair market value method: A way to allocate the total cost for several assets purchased together to each of the individual assets. This method is based on the assets' individual market values.

Relevant: Describes information that is important and timely, with the potential to influence decisions.

Reliable: Describes information that is verifiable and a faithful representation of a firm's financial performance.

Replacement cost: The cost to buy similar items in inventory from the supplier to replace the inventory.

Retained earnings: Equity that results from doing business and is kept in the company rather than paid out to stockholders.

Return on assets (ROA): A ratio that measures how well a company is using its assets to generate revenue.

Return on equity (ROE): A measure of income the firm earns for each dollar of investment from the common shareholders.

Revenue: The amount a business earns for the goods it sells or the services it provides.

Revenue-recognition principle: The principle that revenue should be recognized when it is earned and its collection is reasonably assured.

S

Sales discount: A reduction in the sales price of a product offered to customers for prompt payment.

Sales returns and allowances: An account that holds amounts that reduce sales due to customer returns or allowances for damaged merchandise.

Salvage value: The amount the firm believes an asset will be worth when the firm is finished using it.

Sarbanes-Oxley (SOX) Act of 2002: A law passed by Congress that sets new regulations for the ways corporations govern themselves, including requirements to make a corporation's internal controls more effective and procedures for increasing the understandability of financial reporting.

Securities and Exchange Commission (SEC): A governmental agency created by Congress to regulate the stock market and establish and enforce reporting standards for publicly traded corporations.

Segregation of duties: The control of having different individuals perform related duties; when the person with physical control of an asset is not the same person who keeps the accounting records for that asset.

Separate entity assumption: Assumption that the financial statements of a business do not include any personal financial information about owners or any other entity.

Shareholders' equity (stockholders' equity): Owners' equity of a corporation.

Single-step income statement: An income statement in which all revenues are presented first, and all expenses are subtracted in one step to arrive at net income.

Solvency ratios: Measure the company's ability to meet its long-term obligations and to survive over a long period of time.

Specific identification: The inventory cost flow method in which the actual cost of the specific goods sold is recorded as cost of goods sold.

Statement of cash flows: The financial statement that summarizes all the cash that has come into a business—its cash receipts—and all the cash that has gone out of the business—its cash payments—during an accounting period.

Statement of retained earnings: The portion of the statement of changes in shareholders' equity that describes the changes to Retained Earnings—increased by Net income and decreased by Dividends.

Stock dividend: A company's distribution of new shares of stock to the company's current shareholders.

Stock split: The division of the current shares of stock by a specific number to increase the number of shares.

Straight-line depreciation: The method of depreciation in which equal amounts of the cost of an asset are written off each year.

T

T-account: A diagram resembling the letter T that represents the place you will keep track of additions and subtractions from an account as you learn about the general ledger system.

Tangible assets: Assets with physical substance—they can be seen and touched.

Temporary accounts: Accounts with balances that are brought to zero at the end of the accounting period. This includes all revenue and expense accounts and the dividends account.

Time-period assumption: The assumption that the life of a business can be divided into meaningful time periods for financial reporting.

Times-interest-earned ratio: Ratio that measures a company's ability to make the interest payments on its debt.

Trademark: A symbol, word, phrase, or logo that legally distinguishes one company's product from any others.

Trading securities: Investments in debt and equity securities that the company has purchased to make a short-term profit.

Transaction: A business activity such as buying or selling a good or service that results in an economic exchange with another business or individual.

Treasury stock: Shares of stock that a firm has bought back. Treasury stock is issued but not outstanding.

Trial balance: A list of all of the accounts in the general ledger with their respective debit or credit balances at a given point in time. The trial balance ensures that debits = credits in the accounting records.

U

Unearned revenue: A liability that represents the amount of goods or services that a company owes its customers. The cash has been collected, but the action of earning the revenue has not taken place.

Unrealized gain or loss: An increase or decrease in the market value of a company's investments in securities is recognized either on the income statement—for trading securities—or in Other Comprehensive Income in the equity section of the balance sheet—for available-for-sale securities—when the financial statements are prepared, even though the securities have *not* been sold.

V

Vertical analysis: A technique for comparing items on a financial statement in which all items are expressed as a percent of a common amount.

W

Weighted average cost: The inventory cost flow method in which the weighted average cost of the goods available for sale is used to calculate the cost of goods sold and the ending inventory.

Working capital: Current assets minus current liabilities.

Introduction

I6 GM de Mexico 1995 used with permission of GM Media Archives; **I7** Photo Edit, Inc.; **I8** Getty Images, Inc.; **I9** J Carrier/Bloomberg News/Landov; **I10** Susan Van Etten/Photo Edit, Inc.; **I10** Federico Gambarini/dpa/Landov; **I11** AP Photo/US Senate; **I13** AP/Wide World Photos

Chapter 1

5 (top) Anthony Edwards/Getty Images, Inc.; **5 (bottom)** Scott Olson/Images Inc.; **20** David Kelly Crow/Photo Edit Inc.; **21 (top)** Mark Wilson/Getty Images, Inc.

Chapter 2

43 Tim Boyle/Getty Images, Inc.; **44, 49, 55, 56, 57 (logo)** Courtesy of Southwest Airlines; **54** © MedioImages/Super Stock; **67** Daniel Acker/Bloomberg News/ Landov; **68** © Myrleen Ferguson Cate/Photo Edit

Chapter 3

99 Dan Krauss/Newsmakers/Getty Images, Inc.; **101** © Tom Wagner/Corbis; **118** Mike Mergen/Bloomberg News/Landov

Chapter 4

155 Malcolm Linton/Bloomberg News/Landov; **168 (logo)** Reprinted with permission of Time Warner

Chapter 5

245 (logo) Reprinted with permission of Barnes and Noble; **245** Jennifer Burrell/Masterfile

Chapter 6

277 AP/Wide World Photos; **283 (logo)** Reprinted by permission of Tootsie Roll Inc.

Chapter 7

356 David Urbina/Photo Edit

Chapter 8

381 Neal Hamburg/Bloomberg News/ Landov; **398** © Mike Segar/Reuters/ Corbis; **403** © Michael Newman/Photo Edit; **407 (logo)** Reprinted with permission of Ethan Allen

Chapter 9

441 AP/Wide World Photos; **455** Mike Theiler/Getty Images, Inc.; **465, 466 (logo)** Used with permission from McDonald's Corporation; **466 (logo)** Reprinted by permission of Sherwin Williams; **467** Tim Boyle/Getty Images, Inc.

Chapter 10

513 Copyright © Michael Newman/ Photo Edit; **515, 520, 533 (logo)** Reprinted with permission of Papa John's; **520 (logo)** Reprinted with permission of General Electric; **525 (logo)** Reprinted with permission of PetsMart; **532** Christopher Barth/Bloomberg News/Landov

Chapter 11

577, 580, 581 (logo) THE HOME DEPOT ® is a registered trademark of Homer TLC, Inc. and is used with permission. These products and services are not endorsed by Homer TLC, Inc., The Home Depot, Inc. or Home Depot U.S.A., Inc., **578** Copyright © David Young-Wolff/Photo Edit; **582** Greg Wood/Agence/France Presse/Getty Image

Chapter 12

628 Mike Powell/Getty Images, Inc.; **630 (logo)** Reproduced by permission. Trademark/logo owned by American Greetings Corporation © AGC, Inc.; **630 (logo)** This logo is a registered trademark of General Mills and is used with permission; **631, 632, 633 (logo)** Reprinted with permission of J&J Snack Foods Corp.; **636 (bottom)** Paul Young/Reuters/Landov; **666** www.comstock.com

Chapter 13

671 Emile Wamsteker/Bloomberg News/Landov; **673** © Jacksonville Journal-Courier/The Image Works; **678 (top)** Getty Images, Inc.; **678 (3rd from top)** Sion Tonhig/Getty Images, Inc.; **680** Olney Vasan/Getty Images, Inc.; **685** Getty Images, Inc.; **687 (left screen)** MCI, Inc.; **687 (middle screen)** Starbucks Corp.; **687 (right screen)** Apple Computers, Inc.; **688** Jules Frazier/Getty Images, Inc.